ALSO BY PIERS BRENDON

The Dark Valley: A Panorama of the 1930s

The Windsors: A Dynasty Revealed

The Motoring Century

Our Own Dear Queen

Ike: His Life and Times

Winston Churchill: A Biography

The Life and Death of Press Barons

Eminent Edwardians: Four Figures Who Defined Their Age: Northcliffe, Balfour, Parkhurst, Baden-Powell

Hawker of Morwenstow: Portrait of a Victorian Eccentric

Hurrell Froude and the Oxford Movement

THE
DECLINE AND FALL
OF THE
BRITISH EMPIRE

1781–1997

THE
DECLINE AND FALL
OF THE
BRITISH EMPIRE

1781–1997

PIERS BRENDON

ALFRED A KNOPF   NEW YORK   2008

THIS IS A BORZOI BOOK
PUBLISHED BY ALFRED A. KNOPF

Library of Congress Cataloging-in-Publication Data
Brendon, Piers.
The decline and fall of the British Empire, 1781–1997 / by
Piers Brendon. — 1st American ed.
p.   cm.
"Originally published in Great Britain by Jonathan Cape,
London"—T.p. verso.
"This is a Borzoi book"—T.p. verso.
Includes bibliographical references and index.
ISBN 978-0-307-26829-7
1. Great Britain—Colonies—History.   2. Commonwealth
countries—History.   3. Commonwealth (Organization)—History.
4. Imperialism—History.   5. Great Britain—Civilization.   I. Title.
DA16.B675 2008
909.0971241—dc22   2008014192

Manufactured in the United States of America
First American Edition

To

Vyvyen

With love and thanks

CONTENTS

     The Route to Independence   379

14   That Is the End of the British Empire
     Singapore and Burma   421

15   The Aim of Labour Is to Save the Empire
     Ceylon and Malaya   444

16   A Golden Bowl Full of Scorpions
     The Holy Land   466

17   The Destruction of National Will
     Suez Invasion and Aden Evacuation   487

18   Renascent Africa
     The Gold Coast and Nigeria   516

19   *Uhuru*—Freedom
     Kenya and the Mau Mau   551

20   Kith and Kin
     Rhodesia and the Central African Federation   575

21   Rocks and Islands
     The West Indies and Cyprus   605

22   All Our Pomp of Yesterday
     The Falklands and Hong Kong   633

     Abbreviations   663
     Notes   665
     Sources   751
     Index   761

ILLUSTRATIONS

Section One

1 Missionary with Tahitian converts (Corbis); **2** Wedgwood anti-slavery medallion (Wilberforce House, Hull City Museums and Art Galleries/ Bridgeman Art Library); **3** Imperial interior, 1890 (Getty); **4** Lord and Lady Curzon hunt in Hyderabad, 1902 (AKG-London); **5** Hyderabad's army polo team (Corbis); **6** Sir James Grigg enters Simla, 1938 (Corbis); **7** Hong Kong Harbour seen from Victoria Park (John Hillelson Collection); **8** The CPR's Iron Horse (Vancouver Public Library, Special Collections); **9** Indian Railway engraving by Indian School (Private Collection/Bridgeman); **10** Teatime in Ceylon (Corbis); **11** Ceylon tea harvest (Corbis); **12** King Thibaw and Queen Supayalat of Burma (Corbis); **13** Christmas day in Burma, 1885 (Corbis); **14** Scottish troops beside the Sphinx, 1882 (Corbis); **15** Tourists on the Great Pyramid, 1938 (Corbis); **16** Imperial stamps (Private Collection)

Section Two

17 Sikh officers and men, 1858 (National Army Museum, London/Bridgeman); **18** Lucknow after the Mutiny (Corbis); **19** British camp in Afghanistan (Corbis); **20** Afghan riflemen on the Khyber Pass (Corbis); **21** Irish peasants in the 1880s (Corbis); **22** Dublin's General Post Office after the Easter Rising (Corbis); **23** The Rhodes Colossus (Getty); **24** Isandhlwana after the battle, 1879 (National Army Museum/Bridgeman); **25** Gold miners in De Kaap, South Africa (Corbis); **26** Boers at Spion Kop, 1900 (Corbis); **27** A meal during the siege of Ladysmith (Popperfoto); **28** Anzac Cove, Gallipoli, 1915 (Corbis); **29** Indian military hospital, Brighton Pavilion (Corbis); **30** The Japanese march on Rangoon, 1942 (Corbis); **31** Nigerian sergeant in Burma, 1944 (Imperial War Museum, London, neg. no. IND3098); **32** Trade follows the flag, ephemera (Robert Opie Collection)

Section Three

33 The Imperial appeal, ephemera (Robert Opie Collection); **34** Gandhi's Salt March, 1930 (Corbis); **35** Nehru and Jinnah, 1946 (Corbis); **36** The last Viceroy and Vicereine of India (Corbis); **37** The refugees of Partition, 1947 (Corbis); **38** Jewish refugees arrive at Haifa, 1946 (Corbis); **39** The exodus of Palestinian refugees to Gaza (Corbis); **40** British troops confront Cypriots,

Nicosia, 1955 (Corbis); **41** The troopship *Empire Ken* at Port Said, November 1956 (Getty); **42** Detaining Mau Mau suspects in Kenya, 1952 (Corbis); **43** Jomo Kenyatta is hailed as Prime Minister, 1963 (Corbis); **44** Queen Elizabeth II on her tour of Nigeria, 1956 (Corbis); **45** Kwame Nkrumah leads Ghana to Independence, 1957 (Corbis); **46** The Union Jack is lowered in Hong Kong, 1997 (Onasia)

Front endpaper

Imperial Federation map of the world showing the extent of the British Empire in 1886 © Royal Geographical Society, London

Back endpaper

World map showing shipping routes and the extent of the British Empire in 1927 © Royal Geographical Society, London

ACKNOWLEDGEMENTS

This book ranges across five continents and more than two centuries, so the debts I have incurred during the six years it took to write are correspondingly extensive.

I must first thank friends and colleagues at Churchill College, Cambridge, who have helped me in countless ways. I am especially grateful to Allen Packwood, Director of the Churchill Archives Centre, and to past and present members of his outstanding team, notably Natalie Adams, Louise King, Andrew Riley and Katharine Thomson. Dr. Dick Whittaker provided me with indispensable guidance on the Roman Empire. Hywel George gave me a unique insight into the workings of the post-war British Empire. Dr. Alan and Judy Findlay arranged an illuminating tour of the Foreign and Commonwealth Office, courtesy of their son Matthew. Lady Julia Boyd recalled experiencing the end of the British Empire in person: after the handover in Hong Kong on 30 June 1997, she witnessed the royal yacht *Britannia*, with the last Governor, the Prince of Wales and other dignitaries on board, sailing into the darkness on her final voyage.

Most of my work was done at the Cambridge University Library, an incomparable resource for the historian, and I owe thanks especially to Rachel Rowe, Godfrey Waller and Peter Meadows, the Bible Society Librarian. Elsewhere librarians and archivists went out of their way to lighten my task. I am under particular obligation to Dr. Gareth Griffith, Director of the British Empire and Commonwealth Museum, who put a room at my disposal in Bristol, where I was also able to draw on the expertise of Jo Duffy. Roderick Suddaby gave assistance at the Imperial War Museum. So did Kevin Greenbank at the Cambridge Centre for South Asian Studies. Further afield, Dr. Saroja Wettasinghe, Director of the National Archives of Sri Lanka, eased my path into her collections. Suzanne Mallon took immense trouble to introduce me to manuscript material at the Mitchell Library in Sydney.

In the course of my research I visited a number of ex-colonial clubs—the Tollygunge in Calcutta, the Bangalore Club, the Hong Kong Club and so on—where I was most courteously received. I am particularly grateful to Allan Oakley, Secretary of the High Range Club at Munnar in Kerala, and to Stanley Gooneratne, Secretary of the Hill Club in Nuwara Eliya, who was kind enough to open his records for me.

I have benefited from the aid and counsel of many individuals, among them Dan Burt, Professor Martin Daunton, Dr. Richard Duncan-Jones, Bill Kirkman, Gamini Mendis, Professor James Muller, Manus Nunan, Anthony Pemberton, Harold Rosenbaum, and Dr. Calder Walton. Sir Christopher Hum generously shared his diplomatic memories of the Sino-British negotiations over Hong Kong. Sydney Bolt reminisced with characteristic wit about Britain's war-time Raj in India as well as commenting on parts of my typescript. Michael Murphy performed the same office for my Irish sections, decorating the text with sprightly marginalia. Rex Bloomstein devoted time he could ill afford to perusing my chapter on Palestine. Richard Ingrams not only unearthed a fascinating vignette of colonial Cyprus penned by Paul Foot soon after he left the school where we all three served time, but he also sent me relevant books to review for *The Oldie*. So, with his unerring literary eye, did Jeremy Lewis. Other friends contributed in different ways: Professor Christopher Andrew, my late and much-lamented literary agent Andrew Best, Professor Vic and Pam Gatrell, Tim Jeal, Sharon Maurice, Professor Richard Overy and John Tyler. Professor James Mayall allowed me to pick his brains over long lunches.

I also enjoyed imperial lunches with Dr. Ronald Hyam, the leading British authority on the end of Empire, to whom I owe more than I can say. He supervised me when I was an undergraduate at Magdalene College, advised me subsequently and, despite seeing his own book through the press, scrutinised every word of mine. His criticisms, corrections and suggestions were of inestimable value. Needless to say, despite all this extraneous help, I alone bear the responsibility for any mistakes that remain.

I acknowledge permission to quote copyright material from manuscript sources identified at the end of this book. My thanks are especially due to the Syndics of Cambridge University Library, to Matheson & Co. Ltd., to Curtis Brown Ltd., London, on behalf of the Estate of Sir Winston Churchill (copyright Winston S. Churchill), and to the Master and Fellows of Churchill College, Cambridge. Future editions will be corrected if any copyright has been inadvertently unacknowledged.

As ever, I am grateful to my publisher Dan Franklin, who commissioned this book, waited for it with exemplary patience and welcomed it with heart-warming enthusiasm. He provided a team that made the publication process both smooth and agreeable. It consisted of Ellah Allfrey, an accomplished editor; Richard Collins, a meticulous copy editor; Lily Richards, an imaginative and indefatigable picture researcher; and Anna Crone, who did a splendid job designing the cover of the British edition. I have equal cause for gratitude to the superlative team at Knopf, who masterminded the

American edition: my editor Andrew Miller, his assistant Sara Sherbill, the jacket designer Megan Wilson, and the production editor Kevin Bourke.

Two other people played key roles in the enterprise. My friend, former publisher and literary guru, Tom Rosenthal, gave me constant encouragement and moral support. Despite being preoccupied with her own book, *Children of the Raj,* my wife Vyvyen devoted endless attention to mine, acting more as collaborator than assistant. She was vital to the genesis of this volume and, with love and gratitude, I dedicate it to her.

The title of this book, with its echoes of *The History of the Decline and Fall of the Roman Empire*, needs an explanation—if not an apology. It was chosen not because I am setting up as a rival to Edward Gibbon but because his work has a profound and hitherto unexplored relevance to my subject. No historian in his senses would invite comparison with Gibbon. His masterpiece, sustained by a prodigious intellect and an incomparable style, has no competitors. It filled the imagination of readers for two centuries and it performed a unique function as a towering piece of literary architecture. As Carlyle and others have observed, the book acts as a kind of bridge between the ancient and modern worlds, and "how gorgeously does it swing across the gloomy and multitudinous chasm of those barbarous centuries."[1] It satisfied a general desire, as its author said in his autobiography, to increase the scope of human comprehension. Our lives are short. So we

> stretch forwards beyond death with such hopes as Religion and Philosophy will suggest, and we fill up the silent vacancy that precedes our birth by associating ourselves with the authors of our existence. We seem to have lived in the persons of our forefathers.[2]

However, Gibbon's work exercised a peculiar fascination on his compatriots. If everyone looks back to seek a way forward, the British looked back especially to Rome. Their rulers were educated in the classics. Many of their elite had toured the scenes of antiquity. They lived in the light of the Renaissance. Steeped in Gibbon's tremendous drama (but ignoring his admonition about the danger of comparing epochs remote from one another), they perceived striking analogies between the two powers that dominated their respective worlds. The *Decline and Fall* became the essential guide for Britons anxious to plot their own imperial trajectory. They found the key to understanding the British Empire in the ruins of Rome.

Thus part of my purpose in this book is to assess the implications of that colossal wreck. It was construed in countless ways. British imperialists exhumed a huge miscellany of signs and portents from layer upon layer of archaeological remains. The Eternal City was a universal city, cosmic in amplitude and Delphic in utterance. It embraced a galaxy of worlds, some contrasting, others coinciding. There was republican Rome, pure, virtuous, heroic, the matrix of Macaulay's Horatius and Kipling's Regulus. Allied to it was the Stoic Rome of noble Brutus and righteous Marcus Aurelius, whose *Meditations* accompanied Cecil Rhodes on his treks across the veldt. Then there was imperial Rome, an armed despotism bent on conquest and eventually used to justify the "authoritarian politics"[3] of imperial Britain—Thomas De Quincey praised virile Caesar for deflowering Roman liberty. There was the Rome of the Antonines, who presided over a golden age of civilisation and whose Pax Romana plainly anticipated the Pax Britannica. There was pagan Rome, whose muses shed immortal lustre over the culture of the West. There was Catholic Rome, which Gibbon pilloried for combining superstition, fanaticism and corruption. He also confirmed some of the prejudices of Britain's Protestant Empire, remarking that the rapist Pope John XII deterred "female pilgrims from visiting the tomb of St. Peter, lest, in the devout act, they should be violated by his successor."[4] There was monumental Rome, imitated wherever British imperialists wished to enshrine power in stone. Finally, though this by no means exhausts the catalogue, there was decadent Rome. While aesthetes such as Swinburne and Wilde might celebrate its romantic degeneracy, stern custodians of Greater Britain, whose goal was "a physically A1 nation,"[5] saw it as an augury of racial deterioration and imperial decay.

Sigmund Freud was so impressed by all these separate but overlapping identities that he visualised Rome as a model of the mind. He imagined a city where everything was preserved, like thoughts in the unconscious, and new structures coexisted with old.

> In the place occupied by the Palazzo Caffarelli would once more stand—without the Palazzo having been removed—the Temple of Jupiter Capitolinus; and this not only in its latest shape, as the Romans of the Empire saw it, but also in its earliest one, when it still showed Etruscan forms and was ornamented with terracotta antefixes. Where the Coliseum now stands we could at the same time admire Nero's vanished Golden House. On the piazza of the Pantheon we should not only find the Pantheon of to-day, as it was bequeathed to us by Hadrian, but, on the same site, the original edifice erected by Agrippa; indeed, the same piece of ground would be supporting the Church of Santa Maria sopra Minerva and the ancient temple over which it was built.[6]

Freud checked himself, saying that he could not properly represent mental life in pictorial terms. Yet his vision of Rome as a psychic entity is marvellously suggestive. It points to the way in which the Roman past infuses the present and it shows how this multiple metropolis can be all things to all men. Rome was a vast palimpsest of human experience, barely legible, hard to decipher, inveterately oracular. The ambiguity of its messages was a positive advantage to those who were chiefly interested in the lessons that they could adduce from history. Needless to say, Britons were not alone in validating their national mythology by reference to Rome. Tsar (the Russian form of Caesar) Ivan the Great claimed Moscow as the Third Rome. Napoleon crowned himself Emperor with a laurel wreath of gold in a ceremony based on the coronation of Charlemagne—it included the attendance of twelve virgin maids, not easy to find in post-revolutionary Paris. Both Hitler and Mussolini drew on the Roman model, the Nazis claiming that England was "the modern Carthage."[7] Yet it was the British, masters of an Empire far larger than Trajan's, who seemed to have the best claim to be the "spiritual heirs of Rome."[8]

They constantly identified themselves with their imperial precursors. J. A. Froude opened his biography of Julius Caesar with the statement that "the English and the Romans essentially resemble one another."[9] Lord Bryce said that the men who won the Roman Empire and the British Raj "triumphed through force of character."[10] In his comparative study of Greater Rome and Greater Britain, Sir Charles Lucas asserted that both peoples possessed "an innate capacity for ruling."[11] Such avowals were usually made to boost the confidence of British imperialists. Indeed, the modern Empire was most often depicted as an advance on the ancient, especially in matters of liberty, probity and science—Gibbon mocked the Emperor Heliogabalus's attempt to discover the number of the inhabitants of Rome from "the quantity of spiders' webs."[12] Yet, as appears below, the contrasts were not all in Britain's favour. Lord Cromer acknowledged that Rome, whose rulers frequently came from provinces outside Italy, was far more advanced than any current power in assimilating subject peoples. Despite endorsing the kind of racial discrimination that was deeply corrosive to the British Empire, he went so far as to admit that his countrymen were "somewhat unduly exclusive."[13]

Rome warned as well as taught. Indian civil servants nervous about the North-West Frontier discussed the lessons of Roman provincial policy with W. D. Arnold, an Oxford don "haunted lest the tragedy of the Roman Empire, whose extremities grew at the expense of its heart, should repeat itself."[14] In an article about Roman ruins, a Victorian contributor to the *Edinburgh Review* tried to imagine "how much of the topography of London will be recovered from the fragments of our own literature which may be in existence a thousand years hence."[15]

To avert the decline and fall of their own Empire some Britons contemplated inveigling the United States into an Anglo-Saxon federation. John

West, the mordant historian of Tasmania, even proposed for membership the European ghost of Rome. "The American and British empires are seated on all waters," he wrote in 1852. "The lands conquered by Caesar, those discovered by Columbus, and those explored by Cook, are now joined together in one destiny."[16] Together they could dominate the world. But Gibbon, though he could be interpreted optimistically, suggested a less auspicious fate. When his first volume appeared (in 1776) the American colonies were already in revolt and the British Empire was suffering from some of the ills that destroyed the Roman Empire, notably luxury, corruption and overextension. Despite its revival and expansion over the next 150 years, Britons continued to find in Gibbon (whose Byzantine conclusion covered a millennium) intimations of their own imperial doom. After it was accomplished, classical echoes were sometimes still heard. When Harold Macmillan visited India in 1958 his fellow student of Gibbon, Prime Minister Nehru, said to him: "I wonder if the Romans ever went back to visit Britain."[17] Such reflections, which appear in protean form throughout this book, provide a counterpoint to its central theme—the decline and fall of the British Empire between 1781 and 1997.

Despite Gibbon's long goodbye to the Roman Empire, it may seem paradoxical, even perverse, to trace the collapse of the British Empire back to the revolt of the thirteen colonies. True, Washington's victory at Yorktown was a signal calamity for the mother country, foreshadowing future setbacks and anticipating the rise of an almighty American empire. But Britain's recovery was dramatic and its sustained triumph in the East evidently compensated for the debacle in the West. And there is no denying the spectacular growth of the Empire, which expanded willy-nilly throughout the Victorian age and reached its territorial apogee between the two world wars. Nevertheless, as Fernand Braudel says, the rise and fall of great powers can only be understood over an immense timescale. Without succumbing to the teleological fallacy and reading their subject backwards, historians have already detected mortal stresses inside the British Empire as early as the 1820s. Yet the evidence suggests—and the American rebels proved—that it was physically weak from the start. Furthermore, the Empire carried within it from birth an ideological bacillus that would prove fatal. This was Edmund Burke's paternalistic doctrine that colonial government was a trust. It was to be so exercised for the benefit of subject people that they would eventually attain their birthright—freedom.

The British Empire had a small human and geographical base, remote from its overseas possessions. In the late eighteenth century it gained fortuitous industrial, commercial and naval advantages that rivals were bound to erode. Having such a limited capacity to coerce, it sought accord and found local collaborators. But imperial domination, by its very nature, sapped their loyalty. Gibbon made the point with the first sentence he ever published, in his *Essay on the Study of Literature,* whereby, as he put it, he lost his "literary maidenhead."[18] "The history of empires," he wrote, "is the history of human misery." This is because the initial subjugation is invariably savage and the subsequent occupation is usually repressive. Imperial powers lack legitimacy and govern irresponsibly, relying on arms, diplomacy and propaganda. But no vindication can eradicate the instinctive hostility to alien control. Gibbon, himself wedded to liberty, went to the heart of the matter: "A more unjust and absurd constitution cannot be devised than that which condemns the natives of a country to perpetual servitude, under the arbitrary dominion of strangers."[19] Resistance to such dominion provoked vicious reprisals, such as the British inflicted after the Indian Mutiny, thus embedding ineradicable antagonism. Yet Britain's Empire, much better than any other, as even George Orwell acknowledged, was a liberal empire. Its functionaries claimed that a commitment to freedom was fundamental to their civilising mission. In this respect, Lloyd George told the Imperial Conference in 1921, their Empire was unique: "Liberty is its binding principle."[20] To people under the imperial yoke such affirmations must have seemed brazen instances of British hypocrisy. But this was, at least, the tribute that vice pays to virtue. And in the twentieth century, facing adverse circumstances almost everywhere, the British grudgingly put their principles into practice. They fulfilled their duty as trustees, giving their brown and black colonies the independence (mostly within the Commonwealth) long enjoyed by the white dominions. The British Empire thus realised its long-cherished ideal of becoming what *The Times* called in 1942 "a self-liquidating concern."[21]

Long before this Victorians had hoped that "some future Gibbon" would write "the history of the British Empire."[22] Failing that, modern historians may at least draw inspiration from his achievement and instruction from his method. Gibbon teaches, first of all, that chronology is the logic of history. This is not to say that he felt anything but contempt for mere chroniclers. He did, though, favour a narrative that relies on "the order of time, that infallible touchstone of truth."[23] Then, he is a model of irony and scepticism. Gibbon shunned universal systems. He regarded philosophical history much as he regarded rational theology, "a strange centaur!"[24] He offered lofty moral and political explanations for the disintegration of the Roman Empire, not all of them consistent. But his abstractions, including the abstract quality of his prose, reflected a sublime understanding of the concrete. Gibbon's great tapestry is distinguished by its threads. It is a theatrical representation of the past, full of character and action, both tragic and comic, set against a richly embroidered background. But the daemon was in the detail. Where Voltaire damned details as the vermin that kill masterpieces, Gibbon saw the universe in a grain of sand and captured the macrocosm in the microcosm. His history is a constellation of brilliant particulars. Often they complicated his story but he criticised simple-minded historians "who in avoiding details have avoided difficulties."[25] Walter Bagehot joked that Gibbon could never write about Asia Minor because he always wrote in a major key. On the contrary, he rejoiced in minutiae and advocated the preservation of trivia. The *Decline and Fall* includes recondite information about everything from silk to marble, from canals to windmills, from Russian sturgeon to Bologna sausage, "said to be made of ass flesh."[26] Above all, it captures the spirit of places, notably Rome in its state of eloquent ruin, through sharp circumstantial description. Thus Gibbon vividly conveys the colour, tone and texture of human life during the long span of years he covers.

This is my aim, for a shorter period, in the following pages. I endeavour to give the big picture vitality through abundance of detail, telling the imperial story in terms of people, places and events; through brief lives, significant vistas and key episodes. My stage is thronged with the British *dramatis personae* of the Empire, from the Iron Duke to the Iron Lady. There are politicians, proconsuls, officials, soldiers, traders, writers, explorers, adventurers, entrepreneurs, prospectors, missionaries, heroes and villains. But the cast list is not exhausted by the likes of Palmerston, Salisbury, Joseph Chamberlain, Churchill, Curzon, Kitchener, T. E. Lawrence, Livingstone and Rhodes. For the Empire is seen from the viewpoint of colonies as well as colonialists. So suitable parts are allotted to statesmen from the dominions (such as Laurier and Hughes), Irish leaders (such as Parnell and de Valera), white minority Prime Ministers (such as Welensky and Ian Smith), and a host of indigenous nationalists, among them Kruger, Zaghlul, Nasser, Gandhi, Nehru, Jinnah, Bandaranaike, Ba Maw, Aung San, Tunku Abdul Rahman, Makarios, Nkrumah, Azikiwe, Kenyatta and Mugabe. The characters appear against the backcloth of their circumstances, small as well as great. I trace the warp and weft of imperial existence. And some strands come under particularly close scrutiny: the food and drink empire-builders consumed, the clothes they wore, the homes they built, the clubs they joined, the struggles they endured, the loot they acquired, the jubilees, durbars and exhibitions they attended. Also observed are their trimmed moustaches and clipped foreskins, their addiction to games and work, their low-brow ideas and high-minded attitudes, their curious blend of honesty and hypocrisy, their preoccupation with protocol and prestige, their racial prejudices and the extent to which they lived in symbiosis with their charges.

Imperial settings provide a crucial dimension to this book. It surveys the vegetable Eden of the West Indies, horribly scarred by slavery. It inspects the pristine, topsy-turvy world of Australia and the idyllic wilderness of New Zealand, apparently a once and future Britain in the southern hemisphere. It visits the jungles of Asia and Africa, which became a breathing presence in so much imperial life and literature. It gauges the impact of nature on man and vice versa. And it considers especially the collision between topography and technology: the passage of steam-driven, screw-powered, iron leviathans through the Suez Canal; the railroad, stretching across prairies, mountains, forests and plains, that bound together land masses the size of Canada and India; the Maxim gun by which "civilisation" subdued "savagery." The book also explores imperial cities—London, Dublin, Jerusalem, Ottawa, Kingston, Lagos, Nairobi, Cairo, Delhi, Rangoon, Singapore and Hong Kong. It contrasts white palaces and coloured slums. It decodes the messages conveyed by imperial architecture. These were often mixed. Government House in Melbourne was modelled on Osborne, Queen Victoria's Italianate mansion on the Isle of Wight, whereas Government House in Poona was apparently "a blend of the Renaissance, the Romanesque and the Hindu styles."[27] Lutyens's New Delhi, though, resembled Rome as an unmistakable symbol of might—completed, ironically, just as the Raj entered its terminal stage of decay. Here and elsewhere I dwell on statues, memorials and edifices of all kinds, relics of the past and ruins of the future.

Against this background unfolds a narrative that bridges the gulf between the foundation of the American republic and its emergence as the sole superpower—a situation from which some now descry its own decline. The presence of the United States is ubiquitous, though it is sometimes unspoken. Indeed, I lack the space, not to mention the knowledge, to treat all aspects of the history of the British Empire. Like Gibbon, I have had to represent some happenings with others. The development of the dominions, for example, is only a sketch, not least because they attained virtual independence so early and so easily. The text is lightly burdened with economics. The characters are, alas, predominantly male. Little is said about the colonial masses, who feature in what are now oddly called "subaltern studies." Little is said, too, about the "official mind" of the Empire as it functioned in Whitehall. Clerks talked to other clerks interminably and often contradictorily; and in any case their latter-day deliberations are comprehensively embodied in the many volumes of the indispensable *British Documents on the End of Empire Project*. I rely mainly on printed sources and, although most chapters are fleshed out with manuscript material, I could only sample the archival wealth available. Other omissions are not hard to detect.

Naturally I hope that the book will be judged by the story it does tell. This story contains many exciting episodes, though less emphasis is placed here on triumphs than on the disasters that undermined the fabric of the Empire. Among the topics covered are the slave trade, the Opium Wars, the Indian Mutiny, the Irish Famine, the Boer War, Gallipoli and Vimy Ridge, defeat in the Far East, the struggles for Irish and Indian independence, the morass in the Middle East, the Palestine imbroglio, the retreat from Suez, the Mau Mau uprising, the flight from Africa, and the imperial epilogue in the Falklands and Hong Kong. The deeds that won the Empire, and even those that lost it, were sometimes valiant. But I do not shrink from also dealing with the seamy side of the enterprise, especially as it is apt to be played down in the unhealthy neo-imperialist climate of today. Just as the collapse of Rome has a perennial relevance, so too has the decline and fall of (to employ the inescapable cliché) the greatest empire that the world has ever seen. In this book, above all, I try to convey the full fascination of that momentous saga.

Piers Brendon
Cambridge

THE
DECLINE AND FALL
OF THE
BRITISH EMPIRE

1781–1997

The World Turned Upside Down

The American Revolution and the Slave Trade

At about ten o'clock in the bright morning of 17 October 1781, a lone drummer boy dressed in shabby bearskin and red coat scrambled on to the ruined earthworks outside Yorktown and beat for a parley. From their trenches, which encircled the little tobacco port like a noose, George Washington's forces could see him through the smoke of battle. But they could not hear him because of the thunder of their hundred guns. Firing incessantly were 24-pound siege pieces which smashed the fortifications, 8-inch howitzers which dismembered their defenders, lighter cannon whose balls splintered the clapboard houses along the bluff overlooking Chesapeake Bay and sometimes skipped over the water like flat stones, and heavy French mortars whose 200-pound projectiles—black bombshells clearly visible in daylight, blazing meteors after dark—made the whole peninsula shake. Then, behind the boy, a British officer appeared, waving a white handkerchief. He bore a message from Lord Cornwallis, whose battered army had no means of escape, proposing to end the bloodshed. The barrage ceased, the emissary was blindfolded and the terms of the British surrender were negotiated. Washington, unbending in his role as the noblest republican of them all, administered a severe blow to imperial pride. Cornwallis's 7,200 troops were to become prisoners of war. They were to march, flags furled, between the ranks of their foes drawn up along the road from Yorktown, which passed through fields white with ripe cotton bolls, and lay down their arms.

It was a "humiliating scene,"[1] watched in dead silence by the Americans, clad in ragged homespun, some "almost barefoot,"[2] and their French allies, plumed and often mustachioed, immaculate in white uniforms and black gaiters, their pastel silk banners decorated with silver fleurs-de-lis. King George III's German mercenaries marched past steadily but the British "lobsters"[3] (as the Americans called them) were less dignified. Some were the worse for rum—the largest single item of expenditure borne by the British Army during the war. Others were disdainful, others defiant. A few flung down their heavy, smooth-bored Brown Bess muskets as though to smash them. Lieutenant-Colonel Abercromby, who had led the only serious sortie from Yorktown, chewed his sword in impotent rage. According to an American witness, the British officers behaved like whipped schoolboys. "Some bit their lips, some pouted, others cried,"[4] hiding such emotions beneath their round, broad-brimmed hats. Cornwallis himself remained in Yorktown, pleading indisposition but perhaps unable to face the triumph of revolution. Meanwhile, the bandsmen of his captive army played a "melancholy" tune on drums and fifes. It was the dirge of the British Empire in America, "The World Turned Upside Down."[5]

The Old World did regard the New World's victory as an ominous inversion of the established order. It was an unbeaten revolt of children against parental authority—the first successful rebellion of colonial subjects against sovereign power in modern history. How could a rabble of farmers in thirteen poor appendages, with a population of only 2.5 million, defeat the trained might of the mother country? Americans were divided among themselves and thinly spread along an underdeveloped eastern seaboard which shaded gradually into isolated pioneer settlements and virgin wilderness. They were opposed not only by white loyalists but by black slaves and "Red Indians." Washington's recruits, in a spirit of democratic "licentiousness"[6] (his word), were disinclined to take orders without discussion: as one senior officer complained, "The privates are all generals."[7] Their auxiliaries, until the advent of the French, were wholly undisciplined. The militia consisted of summer foot soldiers on furlough from the plough and, wrote one witness, a cavalry of round-wigged tailors and apothecaries mounted on "bad nags" who looked "like a flock of ducks in cross-belts."[8] These were supported at times by tattooed and buckskinned frontiersmen with tomahawks in their belts, bear grease in their hair and coonskin hats on their heads.

Yet this motley array often proved effective, particularly in guerrilla fighting. After the "shot heard round the world"[9] which had opened hostilities at Lexington in 1775, the redcoats made such a "vigorous retreat," quipped Benjamin Franklin, that the "feeble Americans could scarce keep up with them."[10] On other occasions British generals proved dauntlessly incompetent. "Gentleman Johnny" Burgoyne distinguished himself less as a professional soldier than an amateur dramatist—when his play *The Bloodbath of Boston* was performed the audience at first thought that American shelling was part of the show—and in 1777 his histrionic recklessness led to the British capitulation at Saratoga. By contrast, George Washington, though by no means a military genius, was a great leader. Tall and stately in his familiar buff and blue uniform, with a long pallid face dominated by a jutting nose, a broad mouth and steely grey-blue eyes, he looked the part. And he played it with courage and canniness. Formidably self-possessed, ruthlessly single-minded, incomparably tenacious, he made small gains and avoided large losses, staving off defeat until he could achieve victory.

Before Yorktown, after six years of war, that outcome still appeared remote, despite the support of Spain and Holland as well as France, which the Earl of Chatham described as a "vulture hovering over the British Empire."[11] Redcoat bayonets dominated the battlefield and Britannia still ruled the waves. General Clinton had an iron grip on New York. From there he wrote to Cornwallis in March 1781:

> Discontent runs high in Connecticut. In short, my Lord, there seems little wanting to give a mortal stab to Rebellion but a proper Reinforcement, and a permanent superiority at Sea for the next Campaign without which any Enterprize depending on Water Movements must certainly run great Risk.[12]

Cornwallis himself was subjugating the south. He was assisted by Colonel Banastre Tarleton, who boasted of having "butchered more men and lain with more women than anybody"—he should have said *ravished*, remarked the playwright Sheridan, since "rapes are the relaxation of murder."[13] Washington's forces had scarcely recovered from their winter agonies at Valley Forge and Morristown, where, as one soldier wrote, "It has been amazing cold to such a Degree that I who never flinched to old Boreas had t'other day one of my Ears froze as hard as a Pine gnut."[14] In the spring of 1781 Washington wrote,

> our Troops are approaching fast to nakedness and . . . we have nothing to cloath them with . . . our hospitals are without medicines, and our Sick without Nutriment . . . all our public works are at a stand . . . we are at the end of our tether . . . now or never our deliverance must come.[15]

It came with French men-of-war.

In August, Washington heard that Admiral de Grasse was sailing with a fleet of twenty-eight ships of the line and bringing three thousand more regular soldiers to reinforce the five thousand commanded by the Comte de Rochambeau. Washington seized his opportunity. In great secrecy he disengaged from Clinton and marched his army south through New Jersey. When he heard that de Grasse had reached Chesapeake Bay, cutting Cornwallis off from outside help, Washington abandoned his usual reserve. He capered about on the quay at Chester, waving his hat and his handkerchief, and embraced Rochambeau as he arrived. The young Marquis de Lafayette was even more effusive when he met Washington at Williamsburg. He leapt off his horse, "caught the General round his body, hugged him as close as it was possible and absolutely kissed him from ear to ear."[16] The news was a tonic to the whole army—it even cured General Steuben's gout. For everyone except the British believed that Cornwallis would be "completely Burgoyned."[17] "We have got him handsomely in a pudding bag," wrote General Weedon. "I am all on fire. By the Great God of War, I think we may all hand up our swords by the last of the year in perfect peace and security!"[18]

Washington personally ensured that his "mouse-trap"[19] snapped shut. He made meticulous preparations, even going so far as to pay his troops (with French gold). He surveyed Yorktown's defences from an exposed position where "shot seemed flying almost as thick as hail."[20] With a pickaxe he broke the ground for the opening trench and he put a match to the first gun in the cannonade. Washington pressed forward fast, puzzled by the sluggishness of the enemy. Although erratic, Cornwallis was an able commander. He was brave, tactically adept and adored by his men, whose hardships he shared. But apart from shooting starving horses and expelling hungry slaves (many of them ill with malaria, smallpox and dysentery), he took few initiatives at Yorktown. This was because, as he told Clinton, his army could only be saved by a successful naval action. However, de Grasse had seen off the British fleet in an indecisive battle on 5 September and Washington persuaded him to remain on guard. By the end of the month Clinton informed Cornwallis: "I am doing everything in my power to relieve you by a direct move and I have reason to hope from the assurance given me this day by Admiral Graves that we may pass the Bar by the 12 October if the winds permit and no unforeseen accident happens."[21] But the Royal Navy was in no state to break the French hold on Chesapeake Bay.

It was ill led by Lord Sandwich, First Lord of the Admiralty, who, the philosopher David Hume complained, spent several weeks trout-fishing at Newbury with "two or three Ladies of Pleasure . . . at a time when the Fate of the British Empire is in dependance, and in dependance on him."[22] It lacked necessities: in the West Indies Admiral "Foul-weather Jack" Byron had "a fleet to equip without stores, to victual without provisions, to man without men."[23] It also suffered from less obvious defects. Among them was a hidden canker caused by the new system of sheathing the bottoms of wooden vessels in copper. This eliminated marine growth, crustacea and plants which slowed ships down, and the teredo worm which honeycombed their oaken keels in tropical waters. However, until a technical solution was found to the problem (as it was in time to defeat the French during the

1790s), the copper rapidly corroded underwater iron fastenings. This sometimes led to sudden disasters: merely by firing her seventy-four guns during
the action against de Grasse, the *Terrible* almost shook herself to pieces and
the following day she had to be scuttled. So for a time England was evicted
from "the throne of Neptune."[24]

The naval situation determined both the fate of the thirteen colonies
and the shape of the British Empire. If Cornwallis had been evacuated the
French and perhaps even the Americans might have sued for peace on
George III's terms. As it was, his First Minister, Lord North, spoke for
nearly everyone in Britain, except the contumacious King himself, when he
exclaimed on hearing the news of Yorktown: "Oh God! it is all over!" He
repeated the words many times, throwing his arms about and pacing his
Downing Street room "under emotions of the deepest agitation and distress."[25] In relative terms Yorktown was a small defeat but its significance
was great: it threatened to eclipse "the empire on which the sun never set."[26]
The famous phrase was apparently first coined by Sir George Macartney in
1773 and down the years endless variations were played on it, often with
gloomy emphasis on the final stage of the solar trajectory. Lord Shelburne,
long a fierce opponent of coercing the colonies, feared that their independence would end imperial greatness and "the sun of England might be said
to have set."[27] In his first comment on Cornwallis's debacle he adorned the
image. Shelburne told parliament that the King had "seen his empire, from
a pitch of glory and splendour perfectly astonishing and dazzling, tumbled
down to disgrace and ruin which no previous history could parallel."[28]

Yet in truth the ramshackle imperial edifice had never been securely based.
From the first, when the English began haphazardly planting colonies and
setting up trading posts overseas during the sixteenth and seventeenth centuries, the mother country's sway had been challenged. Settlers, traders,
conquerors, dissenters, preachers, trappers, explorers, freebooters, treasure-
hunters, lawbreakers and others who ventured abroad were obviously wedded to independence. Moreover they carried its seed with them. At least as
warmly as their kith and kin at home, they cherished the ideal of "English
liberty."[29] And they cited natural law, scriptural authority, ancient precedent
and modern philosophy (notably that of James Harrington, John Locke and
David Hume) in defence of their freedom. They also worked for it, electing
assemblies to control the purse strings and to rival the mother of parlia-
ments in London. These "little Westminsters"[30] sought to dominate colonial Governors, who were disparaged as grasping rogues—here a "needy
Court-Dangler" or "a hearty, rattling wild young Dog of an officer,"[31] there

an "excellent buffoon" or a fellow who had distinguished himself "in the profession of pimping."[32] Bad government or no government at all—known as "salutary neglect"—the Americans could endure. But after 1765 the conviction that they had become the victims of tyranny overcame their instinctive feelings of loyalty to the old country and its King, dubbed by Tom Paine in his celebrated pamphlet *Common Sense,* "the Royal Brute of Great Britain."[33] The Stamp Act, which Boston greeted with flags flown at half mast and muffled peals of bells, was viewed less as a fiscal imposition than as a measure of political oppression. "No taxation without representation" became the rallying cry of Americans determined to enjoy "the rights of Englishmen."[34] Many at Westminster concurred, among them Chatham, Edmund Burke and Charles James Fox, who appeared in what looked like an American uniform, toasted Washington's forces as "our army" and spoke of an English victory as "terrible news."[35] Fox's quasi-treasonable vehemence reflected his commitment to a "tradition of liberty"[36] which led to "the final undoing of the entire colonial project in America."[37] *Imperium et libertas* later became the watchword of British imperialists and the motto of the Primrose League; but as W. E. Gladstone would famously point out, the phrase was a contradiction in terms. In the last resort, liberty was at odds with empire, its ultimate solvent.

There were other reasons for anticipating imperial decline and fall. Like the sunset, it seemed a natural phenomenon. It was part of a process of individual and cosmic decay that had been regarded as inevitable since the fall of Babylon, perhaps since the fall of Adam. Hesiod had even visualised that in the old age of the world babies would be "born with greying temples."[38] The logic of the process was confirmed by the recurring metaphor of maturity: Francis Bacon, Thomas Hobbes and many others had said colonies were "children" which, as they grew up, might expect to separate from their parent kingdom.[39] In similar vein, the French economist Turgot compared colonies to fruits which detach themselves from a tree when they are ripe, as provinces did from Rome. Both Joseph Addison and James Thomson compared ancient Rome and modern Britain, contrasting their glories with the decadence of contemporary Italy. Empires clearly evolved, vigorous new growth replacing rotten old fabric. What is more, as Bishop Berkeley memorably prophesied, "Westward the Course of Empire takes its way."[40] It advanced from corrupt Europe to pristine America—where, in a reverse version of the conceit, Thomas Jefferson said that a journey eastward from the frontier to the coast was "equivalent to a survey, in time, of the progress of man from the infancy of creation to the present day."[41] The idea that progress followed Apollo's chariot was heard from "Horace to Horace Greeley."[42] And its transatlantic course was dramatised in a futuristic *jeu d'esprit* published by *Lloyd's Evening Post* in 1774. It was set in 1974 and featured two visitors from "the empire of America" touring the ruins of London. These resembled Piranesi prints of Roman ruins—empty, rubble-strewn streets, a single broken wall where parliament once stood, Whitehall a turnip field, Westminster Abbey a stable, the Inns of Court a pile of stones "possessed by hawks and rooks," and St. Paul's, its dome collapsed, open to the sky. The sun had set on British greatness and, thanks to the exodus of merchants, artisans and workers, it had risen over "Imperial America."[43] After the loss of the thirteen colonies, the British did indeed fear that their Empire, however wide its bounds, was vulnerable to expanding America. They looked with apprehension and fascination at the Great Republic, seeing it as the wave of the future. That astute gossip Horace Walpole pronounced that "The next Augustan Age will dawn the other side of the Atlantic." Casting "horoscopes of empires" in the manner of Rousseau, he forecast that travellers from the New World would "visit England and give a description of the ruins of St Paul's."[44]

By far the most authoritative harbinger of imperial doom, though, was Edward Gibbon. According to his famous account, he was inspired to write *The History of the Decline and Fall of the Roman Empire* while musing amidst the ruins of the Capitol and listening to barefoot friars singing vespers in the Temple of Jupiter. No stones in history were more eloquent than those of the Eternal City, recalling as they did the melancholy evanescence of imperial power, and no book was more imbued with the *genius loci,* the spirit of the place. Here, on the seven hills beside the Tiber, lay the sepulchre of Roman greatness. The Palatine, cradle of Rome and imperial precinct, was now a rank wilderness of scattered pillars and crumbled masonry. The monumental Septizonium was an empty graveyard, its bones resurrected in the fabric of St. Peter's basilica.[45] The Forum, where senators had made laws and emperors had become gods, was a dung-filled corral for "swine and buffaloes."[46] The Colosseum, where gladiators had fought and Christians were thrown to lions, was now a stupendous carcass. Other scenes of ancient grandeur, the Temple of Apollo, the Baths of Caracalla, the Theatre of Marcellus, the Tomb of Romulus, were reduced to sublime remnants. A few noble edifices did survive, some utterly transformed: the Pantheon, Hadrian's Mausoleum, Trajan's Column, the Arch of Constantine. But Gibbon, reflecting on the disappearance of gold palaces, marble statues, porphyry altars, bronze tablets, jasper pavements and granite obelisks, foresaw the final annihilation of "all the monuments of antiquity."[47] No one projected this Ozymandian vision with such might and majesty.

To be sure, Gibbon did say that Europe had so advanced by the eighteenth century that it was probably secure from the kind of catastrophe visited on Rome. Arnold Toynbee, chronicler of the cyclical rise and fall of civilisations, even depicted Gibbon as a kind of Pangloss who thought that his own age was the fulfilment of history. In an extraordinary waking dream Toynbee saw Gibbon, an ungainly figure in "silver-buckled shoes, knee-breeches, tie-wig, and tricorne,"[48] gazing at damned souls swept into hell before the Georgian era of equipoise. But his assault does ill justice to Gibbon, whose work reflects a magisterial breadth of vision. Gibbon himself warned that future foes might appear who would carry desolation to the verges of the Atlantic. After all, when the Prophet breathed the soul of fanaticism into the bodies of the long-despised Arabs they "spread their conquests from India to Spain."[49] More to the point, Gibbon showed remarkably good timing for a man said to believe that time had come to an end. He published the third volume of his *magnum opus,* which described the collapse of the Roman Empire in the west (and might have concluded the whole work had he not decided to add the thousand-year-long Byzantine epilogue), a few months before Yorktown. There were many passages in the book which implied that the British Empire—overextended, given to luxury, attacked by barbarians, employing mercenaries—would follow suit.

Most piquantly, Gibbon described the revolt of the "Armoricans"—inhabitants of Brittany—against Rome. "Imperial ministers," he wrote, "pursued with proscriptive laws, and ineffectual arms, the rebels whom they had made." As a result the Armoricans achieved "a state of disorderly independence," while the Romans lost freedom, virtue and honour, as well as empire.[50] Gibbon could not resist the pun but this probably represented his true view of the American crisis. However, the vain little historian, with his chubby cheeks (which a blind woman literally confused with a baby's bottom) and his weakness for puce-coloured velvet suits and orange zigzag dimity waistcoats, was no less susceptible to patronage than were most Augustan gentlemen. In return for a sinecure from Lord North, he penned a pamphlet denouncing the colonists' bid for independence as a "criminal enterprize."[51] It outraged Horace Walpole, who damned Gibbon as a "toad-eater."[52] And it prompted Fox to assert that Gibbon, who had described the corruption which overthrew the Roman Empire, exemplified the corruption which would overthrow the British Empire. The comparison had become a commonplace. When Gibbon had politely refused an invitation to dine with Benjamin Franklin in Paris because he could not consort with the ambassador of an enemy country, the American apparently offered "to furnish materials to so excellent a writer for the Decline and Fall of the British Empire."[53]

Franklin had helped to give the British "empire" its new meaning—political and territorial dominion rather than seaborne commercial mastery—but he thought that the structure was as delicate as a "China Vase."[54] And Britons, proud to see themselves as latter-day Romans, were always conscious of imperial fragility. Classical education so reinforced the lesson that every setback suffered by their Empire seemed to augur its ultimate dissolution along Roman lines. Yorktown was especially portentous because it occurred at a time when cracks were everywhere appearing in the veneer. The Crown's power was under assault at home and its other possessions were menaced abroad. Constitutional reformers were active and only the previous year the anti-Catholic Gordon Riots had inflicted more devastation on London in a week than Paris would suffer (the demolition of the Bastille excepted) during the entire course of the French Revolution. Ireland was in ferment as its people proceeded on the long march towards nationhood. The Mediterranean was unsafe, with Minorca and Gibraltar besieged—the former fell and the latter came so close to falling that its capture was celebrated on the French stage and pictured on the fans of Parisian ladies. In the Caribbean only Jamaica, Barbados and Antigua would remain under the Union Jack. France was sweeping Britain from its forts and trading "factories" in Africa. In India Hyder Ali, ruler of Mysore, had invaded the Carnatic, routing British armies and burning villages within sight of Madras. The Empire, wrote one observer, "seemed everywhere to be collapsing by its own weight or yielding to external attack."[55] King George himself subscribed to an early version of the "domino theory": if Britain lost the thirteen colonies, "the West Indies must follow them," Ireland would soon become a separate state, and the Empire would be annihilated.[56]

Many shared his fears when the Americans inflicted such grievous wounds on the imperial body politic. The consequences, some immediate and others long term, were traumatic. Yorktown destroyed the North ministry, tearing apart what Dr. Johnson called that "bundle of imbecility."[57] The King's eventual choice as Prime Minister and First Lord of the Treasury, William Pitt the Younger, who remained in power from 1783 until 1801, was obliged to ratify a peace treaty by which the British Empire lost a quarter of its white subjects. To avoid further dismemberment, the remaining parts of the "shattered empire" must be united, Pitt told the House of Commons, "by bonds of affection and reciprocity."[58] But such bonds looked tenuous in the light of the American experience. The measures taken to pacify

Ireland—parliamentary independence, trade concessions and the repeal of penal laws against Roman Catholics—whetted the nationalist appetite for complete self-rule on the transatlantic model. Canada, despite British attempts to conciliate its majority French population, seemed set for disintegration—with the United States eager to pick up the pieces. The white inhabitants of the West Indies, though dependent on the mother country in the vital matters of sugar and slaves, were "Americans by connexion and by interest," observed Captain Horatio Nelson from his Caribbean station in 1785, and "as great rebels as ever were in America."[59]

India—"the brightest jewel that now remained in his Majesty's crown,"[60] to quote Fox's metaphor, later the dullest cliché in the imperial lexicon—should no longer be plundered by "the greatest tyranny that was ever exercised."[61] Once the East India Company's mercantile despotism was brought to an end, the subcontinent could be governed in the interests of its people. This ideal was advocated with Ciceronian power and Jeffersonian polish by Edmund Burke—whom Gibbon described as "the most eloquent and rational madman that I ever knew."[62] But it was an ideal that would cut at the root of the British Raj. Even the convict colony of New South Wales—the first fleet arrived at Botany Bay in 1788—would soon produce "a fresh set of Washingtons and Franklins" to wrest their emancipation from the mother country, forecast Sydney Smith in the *Edinburgh Review.* He gave a darkly comical account of Britain's future struggle in the Antipodes:

> Endless blood and treasure will be exhausted to support a tax on kangaroos' skins; faithful Commons will go on voting fresh supplies to support a *just and necessary* war; and Newgate [Prison], then become a quarter of the world, will evince a heroism, not unworthy of the great characters by whom she was originally peopled.[63]

In short, as Smith further suggested, after the escape of the American tiger Britain was doubtful about breeding colonial cubs which might grow up to be equally savage.

British doubts were reinforced when American trade actually expanded after the loss of the thirteen colonies. Indeed, the astonishing growth in commercial activity called the entire imperial enterprise into question. According to the prevailing economic theory of the time, the purpose of colonies was to supply the mother country with raw materials and to provide a market for her manufactured goods, all on an exclusive basis. The mercantilist system was given legal form by the Navigation Acts, which barred foreign vessels and thus promoted imperial shipping, securing the

wooden walls of the sceptr'd isle. Gibbon called these laws "the Palladium of
Britain."[64] Yet the United States, which had broken free of the restrictions,
now played an increasingly vital role in the mother country's industrial revolution, providing most of the raw cotton, for example, which enabled
Britain to become the loom of the world. And by the 1790s Britain was supplying four-fifths of America's imports while taking half its exports. The
extraordinary boom in transatlantic traffic supported the case which Adam
Smith advanced with dazzling cogency in *The Wealth of Nations* (1776), that
protection was altogether less profitable than free trade. Smith asserted that
colonies were "a cause rather of weakness than of strength" to Britain. They
provided no tax revenue, cost blood and treasure to defend, and diverted
investment from more fruitful domestic channels. They were, in fact, a huge
cartel set up for the benefit of the mercantile classes, an Empire of customers
suited to "a nation whose government is influenced by shopkeepers." The
Empire might have worked if the Americans had sent members of parliament to Westminster. They could thus have put into practice a representative principle which Rome had lacked, to its ultimate ruin. And they could
have enjoyed the bonus of winning big "prizes from the wheel of the great
state lottery of British politics" instead of "piddling for little prizes in . . . the
paltry raffle of colony faction."[65] In the absence of an imperial elected
assembly, said Smith, the old monopolistic order should be replaced by an
"obvious and simple system of natural liberty."[66] What he wanted was an
open market in which capital and labour would gain their due reward
through the unimpeded operation of the competitive mechanism—the fair
dealing of Smith's famous "invisible hand." Here was a gospel which spread
like pentecostal fire and was to form the basis of a new world order.

Pitt venerated Smith's work and it affected his policies. Fox paid it an
even more telling tribute: he quoted from Smith's "excellent book"[67] in the
Commons but confessed privately that he had not read it and could never
understand the subject. It is almost impossible to overestimate the influence
of *The Wealth of Nations*. The argument that Britain should restrict itself to
commercial dominance, cost-effective, humane, immune to rebellion, was
to recur again and again. Jeremy Bentham, the champion of utilitarianism,
elaborated it with characteristic vigour when urging France to

> give up your colonies—because you have no right to govern them, because
> they had rather not be governed by you, because it is against their interest to
> be governed by you, because you get nothing by governing them, because
> you cannot keep them, because the expense of trying to keep them would be
> ruinous, because your constitution would suffer by your keeping them,

because your principles forbid your keeping them, and because you would do good to all the world by parting with them.[68]

Smith gained a host of converts as Britain became the world's workshop, with a vested interest in free trade. But from the moment his book appeared it began to sap the theoretical foundations of the colonial Empire, and this was the very time when the structure itself was being shaken by the American cataclysm. Of course, the British Empire did not disintegrate when the thirteen colonies broke away. Nor were the fears of pessimists such as Lord Sandwich justified: "We shall never again figure as a leading power in Europe, but think ourselves happy if we can drag on for some years as a contemptible existence as a commercial state."[69] In fact the American war, reported throughout by the *Annual Register* under the heading "History of Europe," was to prove more immediately disastrous to France, which was virtually bankrupted by it. Pitt's effort to consolidate his country's position was largely successful and the wars against the French between 1793 and 1815 saw a colossal augmentation of British power and possession.

In the mother country reactions to the American Revolution were by no means uniform. They ranged from liberal to authoritarian, reflecting the huge complexity of the event. The Revolution was conservative as well as radical. It asserted the equality of men but ignored the rights of women. It was magnanimous yet murderous, especially towards native Americans. And nothing about it was more paradoxical than the fact that the land which had fought for freedom was also a land of slavery. Many Americans were profoundly troubled by the inconsistency between the exalted ideals of the Declaration of Independence and the cruel realities of the "peculiar institution." Quizzed about it in France, the slave-owning champion of liberty Thomas Jefferson could only exclaim: "What a stupendous, what an incomprehensible machine is man."[70] Less stupendous men were less equivocal. "Blush ye pretended votaries for freedom!" cried one, excoriating the "trifling patriots" who trampled on "the sacred natural rights of Africans."[71] The white monopoly of rights, it was said, meant that American blacks got less protection from the magistrate than Roman slaves got from the emperor. Adam Smith himself noted:

> When Vedius Pollio, in the presence of Augustus, ordered one of his slaves, who had committed a slight fault, to be cut into pieces and thrown into his fish pond to feed his fishes, the emperor commanded him, with indignation,

to emancipate immediately, not only that slave, but all others that belonged
to him.[72]

In the matter of slavery even the British could claim to be more enlightened
than the Americans. Whereas the colonists' wartime banners had borne
Patrick Henry's famous slogan "Liberty or Death," Lord Dunmore had
dressed his "Ethiopian Regiment" in uniforms emblazoned with the motto
"Liberty to Slaves."[73] And when the British departed they took thirty thousand slaves, about 5 per cent of the colonies' black population, out of
bondage.

As the Americans were quick to point out, all this was brazen hypocrisy.
The British West Indies, which relied on slave labour to fill their argosies
with *muscovado,* the raw brown sugar that fed the European sweet tooth,
were the most prized of all imperial possessions—in 1763 George III's government had almost swapped the whole of Canada for Guadeloupe. Moreover, Britain had been chiefly responsible for making African-Americans
slaves in the first place. It dominated the slave trade, carrying more "black
ivory," so-called, than all other countries combined. In 1781, indeed, the
captain of the English slave ship *Zong* had perpetrated one of the worst
atrocities in the annals of this human traffic. Bound from West Africa to
Jamaica, he ran short of water and threw 132 slaves overboard so that their
insurance value could be claimed, as it could not if they had died a "natural
death."[74] At the time this instance of mass murder caused no outcry. When
the insurers took their case to court (they lost) it turned entirely on the subject of property and Chief Justice Mansfield said that, although the case was
a shocking one, in law killing slaves was no different from killing horses.
However, the episode—its horror is memorably evoked in Turner's painting
Slave Ship—nagged at the national conscience. It helped give the mother
country a new will "to convince the world that the throne of the *British
empire* is established in righteousness."[75] Faced with republicans and demo-
crats, George III's realm needed to occupy the moral high ground. Surely
Britain, with its well-established social hierarchy, its constitution dating
back to Magna Carta, its Christian polity embracing the globe, was the
country best fitted to preserve human rights in the age of the American
(and, still more, the French) Revolution. Now was the time for Britain to
show that, despite its huge vested interest in slavery and the slave trade,
Burke's professions were worth more than Jefferson's. The Irishman had
famously proclaimed, "The British Empire must be governed on a plan of
freedom, for it will be governed by no other."[76]

It was governed by no plan, of course, but at its heart lay the "trade in human blood."[77] As soon as the American war ended slave trafficking revived and by the time of its abolition in 1807 half Britain's long-distance shipping was engaged in it. The human freight borne across the Atlantic was a vital component in a commercial network that stretched around the planet. For not only did English captains buy slaves with home-made man-ufactures—cloth, guns, metal-ware, glass, paper—they also traded in for-eign merchandise—Indian silks, French wines, Virginia tobacco, gold from Brazil, cowrie shells from the Maldives. Furthermore, slaves in the West Indies (whose native populations had been virtually wiped out by Euro-peans and their diseases) produced what was until the 1820s Britain's largest import, sugar. A spicy luxury in 1700, this addictive substance had become a sweet necessity by 1800. During the century consumption increased five-fold, to nearly twenty pounds a head—compared to two pounds a head in France. Sugar was an essential complement to the imported tea, coffee and chocolate, drunk from imported porcelain. It transformed puddings, con-verting them from savoury dishes to sweets and justifying their promotion to a separate course at the climax of a meal. "Hot puddings, cold puddings, steamed puddings, baked puddings, pies, tarts, creams, moulds, charlottes and bettys, trifles and fools, syllabubs and tansys, junkets and ices, milk puddings, suet puddings"[78]—John Bull ate them all, distending his belly and rotting his teeth. Sugar changed patterns of behaviour in other ways, making porridge more palatable and encouraging a taste for confectionery. Sugar gave energy to workers and its profits helped to fuel Britain's phe-nomenal economic growth.

This is not to say that the industrial revolution relied crucially on slavery. But Liverpool did become the pre-eminent slaving port, adorning its Nel-son monument with the figures of chained Africans and its town hall with "busts of blackamoors and elephants,"[79] because it was close to Britain's manufacturing hub. And the exploitation of the West Indies, by means of the slave trade, amounted to "a massive injection of resources into the British economy."[80] It is difficult to grasp the scale of what one former slave captain, John Newton, called this "disgraceful branch of commerce."[81] Between the sixteenth century and the nineteenth some twelve million Africans (of whom about 20 per cent died en route)[82] were forcibly taken to the Americas; it was the greatest involuntary migration in history and it established the largest slave empire since Roman times. In the decade after the American war, the British alone carried nearly forty thousand slaves annually to the West Indies, where perhaps a quarter died within eighteen months of arrival. By the end of the century two tons of Caribbean sugar cost the life of one slave. Each sweet teaspoonful dissolved was a bitter portion of African existence, each white grain spilled was a measure of black mortality. Furthermore, overseers who admitted to having "killed 30 or 40 Negroes per year" to increase their output of sugar by about the same number of hogsheads, were apt to claim that "the produce has been more than adequate to that loss."[83] No wonder that the artist Henry Fuseli, when invited to admire Liverpool's superb buildings, imagined seeing "the blood of negroes oozing through the joints of the stones."[84] No wonder that Dr. Johnson pronounced Jamaica "a place of great wealth and dreadful wickedness, a den of tyrants and a dungeon of slaves," and that he drank to "the next insurrection of Negroes in the West Indies."[85]

The horrors of the slave trade were naturally emphasised by those bent on its destruction. And modern popular accounts have drawn on eighteenth-century propaganda, augmented by twentieth-century anti-racist rhetoric, to liken the Middle Passage (from Africa to the Americas, the central stage on the triangular voyage which English ships made) to the transport of Jews to Nazi concentration camps. Recent scholars, though, reacting against narratives "filled with violence and exploitation,"[86] have concentrated on the commercial aspects of the story, presenting the slave trade as a "business venture, as an economic phenomenon."[87] They have pointed out that slaves were an increasingly expensive commodity, purchased from experienced dealers in well-organised African states. Africans were carried across the Atlantic (latterly) in purpose-built vessels. And being worth more, they generally suffered a lower death rate than the brutalised white crew, a fifth to a quarter of whom perished on each slaving voyage. Doubtless the academic case is sound. But mercantile statistics often discount morality. To focus on the price of slaves rather than the value of humans is to obscure the true cost of the trade. This is to be found in its devilish detail.

The typical late eighteenth-century "Guineaman" was a fast, lightly armed, copper-bottomed, square-rigged ship of about two hundred tons, sixty-eight feet long, twenty-four feet abeam, twelve feet deep. She was manned by about forty sailors, many sporting pigtails, "white slaves kidnapped in the slums of Liverpool and Bristol," where they fell victim to "painted girls" and grog.[88] They embarked on a voyage, lasting several weeks, to the Guinea Coast of West Africa. It stretched from Senegal to Angola and was arbitrarily divided into segments whose exotic names conjured up visions of El Dorado and Prester John. At its core lay the Slave Coast, the Gold Coast, the Ivory Coast and the Grain Coast, so called because it exported malaguetta pepper, the "grains of paradise." But Europeans found this steamy, low-lying littoral, fringed by jungle, swamp and savannah, an infernal region. The shore was beaten by huge waves and there were few safe havens, only occasional, shoal-choked streams into the heart of darkness. This was an alien wilderness filled with the scent of spices, the cries of animals and the sound of drums, "a sound weird, appealing, suggestive, and wild," Conrad memorably wrote, "and perhaps with as profound a meaning as the sound of bells in a Christian country."[89] The primeval vegetation was dominated by huge trees—mangrove, plantain, banana, fig, palm, pine—which seemed to float upon the water like a fleet of ships. White men hardly ever ventured into the interior: before Mungo Park's expedition in 1793 the Africa Association's geographer, when attempting to map the continent, "found himself relying heavily on Herodotus."[90]

The gaps in antique maps, to paraphrase Swift's famous quatrain, were filled with imagination and hearsay. Terrible stories were told of fierce tribes who practised cannibalism and human sacrifice, piling up human heads outside their village gates like pyramids of shot in an arsenal. Doubtless because they were once grist to the racist mill, these propitiatory practices have now been obscured by a "conspiracy of silence." Recent historians have also argued that they were relatively benign, limited in scale, expressive of religious zeal or filial piety, often voluntary and, where incontestably barbaric, a result of European contact. In fact, "enormous" and increasing numbers of Africans were ritually sacrificed in places such as Benin and Dahomey.[91] Each subject was "brought up in the idea that his head belongs to the king."[92] Nevertheless the tales from Africa did become hugely exaggerated in the telling—at a time when punishments such as disembowelling and burning alive were still on the British statute book, and a human sacrifice was the cynosure of the established Church. The white man's grave was represented as the black man's hecatomb. And Africa was deemed to live up to her ancient personification—a woman holding a cornucopia and a scorpion.

So the early slavers had clung to the shore like barnacles, building fortified trading posts. These were guarded by heavy guns and equipped with slave pens (barracoons). At Cape Coast Castle (their headquarters in what is now Ghana) the English, for example, cut from the rock an enormous underground dungeon which would "conveniently contain a thousand Blacks."[93] But such forts were not only hotbeds of corruption and debauchery, they were incubators of disease. Dysentery, sleeping sickness, malaria and yellow fever (often known as "black vomit") took an incredible toll. Whites were exterminated like brutes and, like other tropical empire-builders, they had no recourse but to treat the tragedy as a comedy—"very improperly," wrote a shocked visitor, they called their burial ground at

Whydah "the hog-yard."[94] As late as the 1830s six successive Governors of Denmark's Christiansborg Castle outside Accra died within the space of ten years. Not until mid-Victorian times did health matters improve, though in 1894 Frederick Lugard noticed piles of coffins in the dungeon of Cape Coast Castle "ready for the poor devils of white men who die like flies in these parts."[95] Thus slaving vessels from the Mersey and Severn estuaries hovered off the deltas of the Niger and the Volta, doing business with coastal communities whose caravan links with the Mediterranean dated back to Roman times. The local ruler might be a genial figure such as one mariner encountered in Sierra Leone, a fat monarch sitting on the beach "dressed in a suit of blue silk, trimmed with silver lace, with a laced hat and ruffled shirt, and shoes and stockings."[96] Or he might be an Ashanti king with filed teeth and scarred cheeks, enthroned under brass-handled velvet umbrellas and surrounded by attendants "carrying gold swords, silver and gold dishes, tobacco pipes and silk flags."[97] But African chiefs were masters of the slave trade and ships' captains had to pay them or their agents tribute. This might include a seven-gun salute, "washmouth" of rum and a present *(dashee)*— silk cloaks, firelocks, bracelets, brandy, gunpowder. There was also a customs duty *(comey)* on each transaction to make it all correct.

Those conducting a business that officially designated people as things (the Royal African Company's charter of 1672 bracketed slaves with commodities like gold, ivory and beeswax) were themselves dehumanised by it. Britons involved in the slave trade, which might be viewed as an obscene caricature of the imperial enterprise as a whole, convinced themselves that Africans were "a species of inferior beings."[98] They did not "have souls"[99] and were "much on a level with beasts."[100] They were a "brutish, ignorant, idle, crafty, treacherous, bloody, thievish, mistrustful, and superstitious people." They had "a covering of wool, like a bestial fleece, instead of hair" and a "noxious odour" appropriate to a race "very nearly allied" to the orangutan.[101] Even their vermin were distinctive, large black lice instead of the smaller white variety found on Europeans. Since slaves were subhumans, the argument went, they could be treated as such. Yet African rulers engaged in the trade were themselves shocked by the foul antics of their European counterparts. Before purchase they would appraise slaves like cattle, prodding their bodies, inspecting their teeth, making them jump or stretch, and to ensure that none were "pox'd" (as one ingenuous account had it) examining "the privities of both men and women with the nicest scrutiny, which is a great slavery."[102] The King of Congo thought this a great indignity and desired one trader, *"for decency's sake, to do it in a more private manner."*

Slaves, many of whom had been captured in wars or kidnapped in raids and transported for long distances in *coffles* (fettered gangs), were now bought, often torn from loved ones and branded, thrown naked and manacled into small boats, and taken to the vessels that would cross the Atlantic. A number made desperate last-ditch attempts to escape. They incurred fearsome retribution: traders might "cut off the legs and arms of some [slaves] to terrify the rest."[103] Most (particularly the children) were already terrified, reduced to a state of "torpid insensibility"[104] or psychic shock. They had never seen the sea; they thought they had been "seized on by a herd of cannibals";[105] they expected to be sacrificed to the whites' fetish and eaten as holy food. Olaudah Equiano, one of the few slaves to record his experience, was "quite overpowered with horror and anguish." Once embarked he felt imprisoned in a "world of bad spirits" and would have given ten thousand worlds of his own, had he possessed them, to exchange his condition with that of the meanest slave in his own country.[106] Equiano was lucky in being so young and ill that he was kept on deck with the crew. Most slaves were shackled below in tiers, packed like herrings in a barrel, so tightly that they often had to lie spoonways on their sides. According to one witness, they "had not as much room *as a man in his coffin.*"[107]

During the two-month voyage, particularly when it was extended by storms or calms, the slaves endured a kind of living death. They were stifled by the confinement, "breathing of a putrid atmosphere, and wallowing in their own excrement." The irons ate into their flesh, which was wasted by malnutrition and disease. The worst killer was dysentery. It was spread by the distribution of food in communal buckets, including such delicacies as *dabbadabb* (ground Indian corn), *slabber* sauce (palm oil, flour, water and pepper) and boiled horse beans, which were supposed to induce constipation. In bad weather a slave might find himself chained to a decomposing corpse, which would eventually be thrown to the sharks, the constant escort of slave ships. In good weather attempts were made to cleanse the lower decks, to scour them with vinegar and lime juice, to fumigate them with burning tar or brimstone in fire pans. Moreover, the slaves were sometimes given comforts—rum and tobacco—and exercised on deck where, if they proved sluggish, the cat-o'-nine-tails was applied. As one witness noted, "a delight in giving torture to a fellow creature, is the natural tendency of this unwarrantable traffick."[108]

Even the most "respectable" captains succumbed. John Newton, later the author of "Amazing Grace" and "How Sweet the Name of Jesus Sounds," thought nothing of employing thumbscrews. But he did condemn the "licence" permitted towards unchained female slaves (about a third of each cargo), who were often "exposed to the wanton rudeness of white savages."[109] A minority of vessels were "half bedlam and half brothel,"[110] the scene of brutal violence and drunken orgy worthy of the Marquis de Sade, whose disciples found West Indian slave society "an ideal testing ground."[111] The slaves frequently resisted. Sometimes they tried to starve themselves and were forcibly fed—"coals of fire, glowing hot, [were] put on a shovel, and placed so near to their lips as to scorch and burn them."[112] One voyage in eight saw a mutiny, almost always hideously punished. Often a slave would climb over the netting rigged up to prevent suicide and throw himself overboard, raising his hands as he sank "as if exulting that he had got away."[113] Europeans liked to say that Africans had no knowledge of freedom and therefore no passion for it, but the evidence is all to the contrary. In the words of Ottobah Cugoano, who escaped to England and acquired an education, the ideal "burns with as much zeal and fervour in the breast of an Ethiopian, as in the breast of any inhabitant of the globe."[114] One woman ate the dirt off an African yam, "seeming to rejoice at the opportunity of possessing some of her native earth." Slaves howled with anguish at their "loss of liberty."[115] None saw more clearly that servitude was the greatest form of evil because it fostered evil in all its other forms.

Jamaica, Britain's largest sugar bowl and slave depot, looked from the sea a kind of Eden. Its high purple mountains, capped with a sapphire haze and clad in an immense cloak of green, had the "appearance of a new creation."[116] In the Arawak language Jamaica meant a country abounding in springs; and every valley had its stream, every crag its cascade. Christopher Columbus hailed it as "the most beautiful island of any he had seen in the Indies."[117] The rolling hills were crowned with groves of pimento and tamarind, cocoa-nut and palmetto, orange and mountain cabbage. And these, as one visitor recorded,

> commixed with the waving plumes of bamboo-cane, the singular appearance of the Jerusalem thorn, the bushy richness of oleander and African rose, the glowing red of scarlet cordium, the verdant bowers of jessamine and grenadilla vines, the tufted plumes of the lilac, the silver-white and silky leaves of the portlandia . . . all together compose an embroidery of colours which few regions can rival, and which none perhaps can surpass.[118]

The sultry coastal plains sustained a host of crops, the king of which was sugar cane—a freshly planted field was said to be "one of the most glorious sights of the vegetable world."[119] Kingston Harbour, a vast landlocked expanse on which the entire Royal Navy could have ridden at anchor, was equally picturesque. The town itself, an oblong grid of streets laid out with geometric precision, consisted of about three thousand buildings. Many of them, higher up the hill, were elegant, two- or three-storey mansions, with green and white verandahs and first-floor balconies protected by "jalousies," moveable, large-bladed Venetian blinds. But appearances were deceptive.

Jamaica's principal port was surrounded by swamps and lagoons, and it was so unhealthy that European galleons seldom stayed long without burying half their crews. Other fertile areas were equally pestilential. The reek of stagnant pools tainted the atmosphere. The velvet night, spangled with fireflies, resounded to a tropical cacophony: "a loud humming noise, a compound of buzzing, and chirping, and whistling, and croaking of numberless reptiles and insects on the earth, in the air, and in the water."[120] Moreover, the island was subject to appalling natural disasters: thunderstorms, conflagrations, earthquakes, landslides, hurricanes, tidal waves, volcanic eruptions. So inhospitable was the colony that many whites aimed not just to get rich quick but to get out quick. Women, said one Governor of Jamaica, had to "*marry* and *bury*."[121] Men had to harry and hurry. Kingston, with a population of 28,000, most of it black, some mulatto, was a hive of furious energy. The broad, sandy streets, their potholes packed with offal and ordure, resounded to the creak of ox carts and horse drays. On the wharfs, where the town's sewage tubs were daily emptied, slaves manhandled boxes and bales. Straw-hatted, saffron-faced merchants did business with "gingham-coated, Moorish-looking Dons,"[122] all puffing cigars. Sweating planters in square, blue, brass-buttoned coats, white jean trousers and long Hessian boots waited to buy slaves. After the rigours of the Middle Passage, Africans who reached the West Indies looked more like shadows than men.[123] Most were skeletal, many were ill and a few had gone mad. So they were prepared for market, fed, washed, rubbed with palm oil until they gleamed, calmed with drams and pipes. Grey hair was shaved or dyed. To conceal signs of the "bloody flux" some ships' doctors plugged the anuses of slaves with oakum, causing excruciating pain. They also used a mixture of iron rust, lime juice and gunpowder to remove the external symptoms of yaws. Slaves were then subjected to further humiliating scrutiny and sold once again, sometimes individually, sometimes by auction, sometimes in a "scramble." The last was a ferocious melee in which purchasers seized what slaves they could, all at a fixed price. For Africans it was an apt introduction to an island that was pilloried as "the Dunghill of the Universe."[124]

Outnumbered by about 200,000 to 20,000, the whites dreaded the prospect of slave revolts, which occurred more often in Jamaica than elsewhere. So as far as possible Africans were separated from those who spoke the same language. They were given new names, often classical ones such as

Pompey, Caesar, Cupid and Juno, which seemed to mock their servile condition. Then they were placed under a harsh regime of toil and punishment. Woken before dawn by the blast of a conch shell and the crack of whips, gangs of semi-naked slaves were driven from their thatched, wattle-and-daub huts and set to work, with breaks for breakfast and lunch, until dusk. Producing sugar was a physically exhausting and technically demanding task, partly agricultural, partly industrial. Slaves were forced to dig the clay soil, then plant, manure, cut and carry the cane. Within forty-eight hours of cropping it had to be crushed, whereupon the juice was boiled (in a rural factory that became as hot as an oven), clarified, cooled into crystals and potted into hogsheads. Watching their "busy slaves . . . bring the treasure home," often to the accompaniment of a "wild chorus" of "unpolished melody," planters were apt to hail Jamaica as Utopia.[125] It is true that slaves, who were anything but passive, frequently did much to improve their lot: they formed new relationships, acquired fresh skills, cultivated their gardens, went to Sunday market in their best Osnaburg (coarse linen) clothes, and even lent money to their masters. Nevertheless their state was lamentable and their numbers were in permanent decline, only topped up by new imports from Africa. Matters got worse during and after the American war. It so disrupted trade, halting supplies of grain, rice, fish and meat to the West Indies, that famine prevailed. Attempts were made to alleviate it, notably through the introduction of alien "economic plants"[126]—the scarlet-flowered ackee tree from West Africa, the mango from Mauritius, the breadfruit from Tahiti—instances of a botanical diaspora that was one of the great works of empire, though it was accompanied by the spread of pests. But slaves had to keep hunger at bay by eating "cane-roots, cats, putrid fish and even reptiles and animals in a state of decomposition."[127] By the end of the eighteenth century 10 per cent of the slave population had starved to death.

At the same time the "plantocracy" was living more extravagantly than ever. In the words of Lady Nugent, wife of a Governor of Jamaica, "they really eat like cormorants and drink like porpoises."[128] Witness the dinner given by a small landowner, Thomas Thistlewood, for a couple of friends on 22 August 1786:

> stewed & fried mudfish, stewed crabs & boiled crabs, a plate of shrimps, a leg of boiled mutton & caper sauce, turnips, broccoli, asparagus, a roast whistling duck, a semolina pudding, cheese, water melon, pine[apple], shaddock [a kind of grapefruit], punch, brandy, gin, Madeira wine, porter, Taunton ale.[129]

Thistlewood also had a voracious sexual appetite and other entries in his extensive diary reveal that he satisfied it by turning his estate into a private bordello. Preying on the bodies of African women was just another form of exploitation and the practice was almost universal. In the words of a disapproving contemporary, planters rioted in the "goatish embraces" of their slaves, preferring them to the "pure and lawful bliss" of married love and ushering into the world a train of "adulterated beings." Miscegenation might have assuaged the most extreme rigours of imperialism and some black women did find that copulation resulted in manumission. But it is clear that brutality was an integral part of West Indian life. This was often attributed to the inveterate viciousness of the "lower order of whites," offspring of indentured servants kidnapped by Glasgow "man-traders," refugees from Kilmainham Gaol or the Tyburn tree, the "dregs of the three kingdoms."[130] Thistlewood was typical in being quite willing to flog those with whom he had fornicated. Indeed, his diary is a tattoo of flagellation.

Of course, the rod was seldom spared anywhere at the time. Redcoats were known as "Bloodybacks." British sailors were sometimes sentenced to "several hundred lashes," while the American Navy "flogged at least twice as much"[131] as the Royal Navy. Admiral Rodney, a supporter of slavery whose elaborate classical monument celebrating the victorious battle of the Saintes still dominates the square of Spanish Town, said that "he never saw any Negro flogged with half the severity that he had seen an English schoolboy."[132] But according to one of William Wilberforce's investigators, if English workers had been punished on the same scale as West Indian slaves they would have received between six and seven million lashings a year. Certainly Thistlewood beat his slaves incessantly and mercilessly; and he employed disgusting refinements of cruelty to boot. Having whipped one runaway, he "made Hector shit in his mouth." Another was put in the bilboes with locked hands, rubbed with molasses and exposed "naked to the flies all day, and to the mosquitoes all night, without fire."[133] Penalties could be still more severe—slit noses, cropped ears, castration. Rebels might expect an auto-da-fé. In the face of it Africans from the Gold Coast were especially courageous, displaying "what an ancient Roman would have deemed an elevation of soul." One of them, burned alive while staked to the ground, "uttered not a groan, and saw his legs reduced to ashes with the utmost firmness," even managing to throw a brand from the fire in the face of his executioner.[134] Yet perhaps more agonising than such physical torments were the psychological traumas of slavery. Deprived of humanity, robbed of identity, separated from family, perpetually exiled, their finer feelings constantly violated, slaves fell victim to a malady which, according to a medical report drawn up for the Colonial Office in 1833, was unique in "the annals of physic."[135] Unlike the slaves of Rome, they had almost no chance of attaining freedom; they were denied hope, which Gibbon called "the best comfort of our imperfect condition."[136] Many gave way to despair. Some tried to infect themselves with diseases such as leprosy "to avoid the general circumstances of their situation."[137] Thomas Thistlewood found his slave Jimmy "throwing the fire about the cookroom . . . saying if this be living he did not care whether he lived or died."[138]

After the American war, which had inspired such libertarian rhetoric in Britain, the slave trade was increasingly damned as an epic of cruelty. Its defenders sought to justify it in traditional terms, as "the foundation of our commerce, the support of our colonies, the life of our navigation, and first cause of our national industry and riches." Abolition would precipitate the loss of the West Indies, the collapse of the British Empire and the ruin of the mother country. A parliamentary opponent of abolition put the matter bluntly: if the slave trade was not an amiable trade nor was that of the butcher, "yet a mutton chop was, nevertheless, a very good thing."[139] But the argument of naked self-interest merely incensed the moralists and, under mounting pressure from them, supporters of the trade also tried to make out an ethical case. Slavery was sanctioned by Holy Writ and by classical civilisation. Profit and principle were two sides of the same coin, like the elephant and castle embossed on a golden guinea. Having rescued Africans from savagery and barbarism, those engaged in the traffic naturally wanted them to reach market in prime condition. So they took pains to ensure that the Middle Passage "was one of the happiest periods of a negro's life."[140] Similarly, owners treated their slaves—called "negroes," "assistant planters," even "the working class"[141]—with paternal benevolence in order to get the best out of them. Their condition was improving and would be the envy of "half the peasantry in Europe."[142] Though specious, the pleas of planters were not entirely spurious for the black and white communities, like servants and masters everywhere, were subtly symbiotic. They were "so intimately connected and blended together" that one visitor found it "almost impossible to divide them."[143] But the planters' protestations were increasingly drowned by the cries of slaves themselves.

This was because of the moral revolution that occurred during the latter part of the eighteenth century. John Newton was its embodiment: in the 1760s he had thought the slave trade a genteel and "creditable way of life";[144] in the 1770s he was haunted by doubts; by the 1780s he shuddered at the hellish enterprise, wished to wipe out the stain it had left on "our national character"[145] and converted William Wilberforce to the abolitionist cause. Potent forces brought about the change. Chief among them perhaps was the evangelical revival, whose preachers declared the saving power of a religion of the heart (thus implicating themselves, according to many moderate Anglicans, in a "conspiracy against common sense").[146] Convinced that Africans were original sinners with souls ripe for redemption, Quakers and Baptists had long been opposed to the slave trade; but no one was more influential in denouncing its "complicated villainy"[147] than the founder of Methodism, John Wesley. The French *philosophes* also attacked it. Candide remarked, when a slave had an arm and a leg cut off, that it was the price demanded for sugar sent to Europe (though Voltaire, the epitome of Enlightenment, apparently speculated in the slave trade and certainly agreed to have a slave ship named after him). Romantics idealised the "noble savage." Patriotism fortified humanitarianism, as Britain's national identity crystallised around the ideal of liberty.

In his account of the abolition of the slave trade, for which he fought so valiantly, Thomas Clarkson quoted a striking piece of verse by Richard Savage which prophesied a ruination of Roman proportions if the British Empire betrayed its principles. Conjuring up the prospect of retribution for anything less than a reign of justice and a charter of freedom, the personification of Public Spirit warns:

> Let by my specious name no tyrants rise,
> And cry, while they enslave, they civilize!
> Know, Liberty and I are still the same
> Congenial—ever mingling flame with flame!
> Why must I Afric's sable children see
> Vended for slaves, though born by nature free,
> The nameless tortures cruel minds invent
> Those to subject whom Nature equal meant?
> If these you dare (although unjust success
> Empow'rs you now unpunish'd to oppress),
> Revolving empire you and yours may doom—
> (Rome all subdu'd—yet Vandals vanquish'd Rome)
> Yes—Empire may revolt—give them the day,
> And yoke may yoke, and blood may blood repay.[148]

The lines were little less than a proleptic elegy for the British Empire.

The campaign against slavery, which formally began in 1787 when the Society for Effecting the Abolition of the Slave Trade was founded, became the first and most sustained popular movement in British history. Activated by the American Revolution, it was further stimulated by the outbreak of the French Revolution. This appeared to be a momentous victory for the sovereign people over hereditary despotism. It opened up a new world to the imagination, a millennium of freedom and justice in which the most extravagant Enlightenment dreams would be realised. More specifically, French revolutionaries denounced "aristocrats of the skin"[149] and in 1794 they abolished slavery. Across the Channel reformers made fresh efforts. Reports, meetings, petitions, appeals, sugar boycotts, speeches in and out of parliament, all helped to muster support. The self-styled "Vase-maker General to the Universe," Josiah Wedgwood, whose neo-classical designs were inspired by antiquities found during excavations at Pompeii and Herculaneum, devised the most celebrated form of propaganda. His own strictly regulated workforce produced thousands of cameos in black jasper on a white ground, modelled on the seal of the Abolition Society, depicting a kneeling slave in chains, the outer edge moulded with the legend "AM I NOT A MAN AND A BROTHER?"[150] The heart-rending appeal combined with the submissive posture proved irresistible to Britons of all sorts. The image decorated brooches, bracelets, snuffboxes and other ornaments of fashion. It also appeared on mass-produced chinaware, accompanied by simple verses reminding tea drinkers that their sugar was "bathed with Negr'es Tears."[151]

In the long run the gospel of emancipation, with its echoes of the revolutionary mantra "Liberty, Equality, Fraternity," would fatally erode Britain's faith in its Empire. No one preached that gospel with more fervour than Wilberforce, leader of the abolitionist "Saints," as they were dubbed, in parliament. It is true that he was deeply conservative as well as genuinely philanthropic. He was keen on suppressing vice, especially among persons whose income, as Sydney Smith said, "does not exceed £500 *per annum*."[152] He was eager to enforce virtue, particularly among the lower orders—he might easily have supported the organisation invented by Wilkie Collins to lampoon excesses of puritan social discipline, "the British Ladies' Servants' Sunday Sweethearts Supervision Society."[153] In consequence radicals such as William Hazlitt thought Wilberforce morally slippery: "he trims, he shifts, he glides on the silvery sounds of his undulating, flexible, cautiously modulated voice, winding his way betwixt heaven and earth."[154] Friends considered Wilberforce to be seraphic, a "winged being in airy flight."[155] Certainly his combination of pragmatism and magnanimity, of polished charm and unaffected zeal, captivated the Prime Minister.

William Pitt was seldom governed by emotion, even under the influence of two bottles of port: it was said to be one of the duties of the Secretary of the Treasury to hold out his hat so that the First Lord could clear himself before making a speech. In fact, the Prime Minister was formidably aloof and unbending—stiff, according to contemporary jokes implying his misogyny or homosexuality, towards all except women. Especially stiff was his "long obstinate upper lip"[156] (George III's description), while his turned-up nose gave him a supercilious air. He was notably unsympathetic to evangelicalism, having an Augustan distaste for "enthusiasm" or fanaticism. But he succumbed to the vehement eloquence of Wilberforce, a shrimp who (as James Boswell observed) could talk like a whale. Pitt agreed with Wilberforce that the slave trade, which had turned Africa into a "ravaged wilderness," was the "curse of mankind." It was "the greatest stigma on our national character which ever existed."[157] So on 2 April 1792, Pitt called for its immediate end. Fox and others considered his speech, delivered during an all-night sitting of the Commons, "one of the most extraordinary displays of eloquence ever heard in parliament."[158] And his peroration seemed inspired. Pitt said that modern Africans were no less capable of becoming civilised than ancient Britons, who had also been sold as slaves and had practised human sacrifice. Indeed, a Roman senator might have deemed Britons incurably barbarian, "a people destined never to be free . . . depressed by the hand of nature below the level of the human species." Now civilisation could redeem savagery. Restoring Africans to "the rank of human beings" would bring light to the "Dark Continent." According to a dramatic but perhaps apocryphal story, as the sun's first rays pierced the three round-topped windows behind the Speaker's chair, Pitt looked up and quoted Virgil: *"Nos primus equis oriens afflavit anhelis"*[159]—With the breath of his panting horses Apollo has first inspired us. It surely heralded a new dawn for Africa.

That dawn was postponed. The Commons would only move towards abolition via regulation of the slave trade and the Lords proved more cautious still. Then reform of any kind became almost impossible as the French Revolution took a fateful turn and "the gale of the world" began to blow with a vengeance. What had at first seemed to many of George III's subjects as an enlightened attack on autocracy, a Gallic version of Britain's Glorious Revolution, now unfurled its piratical colours. The September Massacres occurred in 1792. In January 1793, Louis XVI was guillotined. The next month Britain was at war with France. It was a struggle against a creed as well as a country, for the Jacobins were the Communists of their day. They threatened the world with political and social upheaval, with red terror and beggars on horseback. The British response was fierce, particularly among those whose early illusions had been shattered. "I will tell you what the French have done," wrote William Cowper, the poet and friend of John Newton:

> They have made me weep for a King of France, which I never thought to do, and they have made me sick of the very name of liberty, which I never thought to be. Oh, how I detest them! . . . Apes of the Spartan and the Roman character, with neither the virtue nor the good sense that belonged to it.[160]

The revulsion grew after a successful slave revolt in the precious French sugar casket of St. Domingue (named Haiti in 1804) led by Toussaint L'Ouverture, a latter-day Spartacus.

Mirabeau had warned that the colonists "slept on the edge of Vesuvius"[161] and when the eruption took place British planters in the West Indies quickly spread stories of the black (but not the white) terror. Theirs was a catalogue of horrors from hell: infants impaled on pikes, wives raped on the corpses of their husbands or fathers, and, amid an orgy of torture, "Madame Séjourné having a babe cut from her womb and fed to pigs in her own sight, and then her husband's head sewed up in the bloody cavity."[162] It was easy to believe those who blamed such depravity on a fiendish alliance of Jacobins and abolitionists, and called for a ruthless exercise of power to prevent its spread. As well as being more aggressive abroad, Pitt's government grew more repressive at home over the next few years. It prosecuted radicals, imposed censorship, suspended Habeas Corpus, suppressed trade unions, even ranked lecture rooms where an admission fee was charged with brothels. Talk of "the rights of man" became tantamount to treason and Tom Paine's best-selling book of that title (dedicated to George Washington) was banned. Its author, who admittedly did much to provoke the authorities, calling the unstable George III His "Madjesty,"[163] was accused of corresponding with Satan, burned in effigy and forced into exile. The King himself now favoured the slave trade, whereas he had formerly been wont to whisper at levees: "How go your black clients, Mr Wilberforce?"[164] Pitt's interest in getting rid of the trade waned, though Wilberforce tried to galvanise him and to make abolition respectable. It must be distanced, he insisted, from the schemes of "mad-headed professors of liberty and equality."[165] Any reference to revolutionary ideals, Wilberforce told Clarkson, would be "ruin to our cause."[166]

Pitt's government naturally gave priority to its own great cause, the titanic conflict with a reinvigorated France. What amounted to a "second hundred years' war"[167] between the traditional foes now approached its climax. This was essentially a struggle for power, fought on a global stage. But it was also an economic contest which Britain, financially, commercially and industrially strong, was well placed to win. However, the new republic was infused with a fresh spirit. It was animated by millenarian zeal and inspired by the example of antiquity. France developed its own Roman pretensions, with legions and tribunes, fasces and axes, victory columns and triumphal arches, and a wealth of classical iconography best represented by David's "martial and patriotic epics."[168] Napoleon, first Consul and then Emperor, even ordered that the Paris sewers should be modelled on those of Rome. As Britons ruefully acknowledged, his compact European empire much more resembled that of Augustus than did their own sprawl of territories. Yet George III's realm responded to the challenge of a resurgent France with an astonishing imperial revival of its own. The liberal concerns, the fears about decadence, the doubts about colonial coercion, which had all been in the ascendant since the American Revolution, were eclipsed by the French Revolution.

In their place emerged a pugnacious nationalism. It was heard in the slogan shouted by loyalist mobs, "Church and King." Titles of undergraduate essays were militantly patriotic: "The Probable Design of the Divine Providence in subjecting so large a portion of Asia to the British Dominion."[169] Satirical prints showed John Bull feasting on plum pudding and the roast beef of old England, while clog-shod, Phrygian-capped sans-culottes scavenged for scraps in the blood-stained gutters of Paris. Cowper's Druid chief prophesied that "other Romans," the posterity of Queen Boadicea, would arise to hold sway over "regions Caesar never knew."[170] A bellicose Britain, employing its time-honoured strategy of encouraging allies to fight on the Continent while using naval power to defeat France overseas, stamped its mark or raised its flag all round the globe. It made huge gains in India and smaller, more costly ones in the West Indies. It quelled Ireland. The British swept up bits of the Dutch Empire, in the Cape, Ceylon and Java. They advanced in the Mediterranean, the Indian Ocean and the Antipodes. British missionaries penetrated the Pacific and British traders beat at the doors of China and South America. Where there had been twenty-three British colonies in 1792, there were forty-three by 1816. The Empire had contained 12.5 million people in 1750: seventy years later it was 200 million strong.

Thus if the American Revolution had foreshadowed the decline of the British Empire, the French Revolution occasioned its rise to new heights. Napoleon's attempt to dominate Europe seemed to justify Britain's yet more ambitious self-aggrandisement. Gibbon's gloomy forebodings about eventual collapse were not forgotten. Indeed, there were constant fears that

Britain was too small to sustain a mighty overseas growth—the Empire was "an oak planted in a flower-pot."[171] But a new mood of militant expansionism prevailed. The "dreadful example" of Rome was now cited to show that "it is more difficult to preserve than to acquire: that whatever is won, may be lost: and that to cease to acquire is to begin to lose."[172] Only through combat could imperial decline be averted. Only by conquest could Britain match other empires—French, Spanish, Portuguese, Dutch, Russian, Austrian, Ottoman, Mughal, Chinese, even American.

Of course, dawn was only just breaking over America. When "the assembly of demigods"[173] signed the constitution at Philadelphia in 1787, Franklin declared himself happy to know that the painting on the back of the President's chair represented the rising—not the setting—sun. Washington saw a "New Constellation"[174] appearing in the western hemisphere. And the city named after him, when still an "Indian swamp in the wilderness,"[175] took Rome as its model because it aspired to be the "capital of a powerful Empire."[176] But whatever greatness lay in store for America it set Britain an early example of how diverse elements could be combined into a unified power, how antithetical principles could be embraced by a single constitution.

Naturally the British asserted that rival empires were despotisms, whereas their own colonies were founded on freedom. As Burke had said, the government of those unable to rule themselves, for whatever reason, was a *"trust,"* to be "exercised ultimately for their benefit."[177] Ultimately, too, these moral obligations would undermine an Empire gained and held by force. But in the crucible of the French wars Britain fused together its commitment to liberty and its will to power. A notable product of this was the abolition of the slave trade in 1807, the year after Pitt's death, accomplished by the "Ministry of All Talents." Parliamentarians were inspired by the humanitarian rhetoric of Fox and Wilberforce; they were convinced that, since Napoleon had reintroduced slavery, abolition was a patriotic act; for various reasons they believed it would no longer be economically damaging, particularly as America was also outlawing the trade and other countries were expected to follow suit. Above all, abolition was accepted because it established Britain's leadership of the civilised world, the champion of righteousness. It put the nation's fundamental principle of liberty into practice and realised "the idea of 'imperial trusteeship' for the betterment of native societies."[178] In the same year, moreover, the faltering settlement of Sierra Leone was established as a colony for liberated slaves—some of whom were unwilling to go there and had to be forced to be free. So, as Rousseau had seen, liberty could be compulsory. Britain would subjugate many lands in its name.

2

An English Barrack in the Oriental Seas

Britannia's Indian Empire

Having lost an empire in the West, Britain gained a second one in the East. Defeated on the continent "discovered" by Christopher Columbus, the British triumphed in the subcontinent laid open by Vasco da Gama. Eleven years after his capitulation to George Washington at Yorktown, Lord Cornwallis, now Governor-General of India, overcame Tipu Sultan at Seringapatam. For the modest earl and for his resurgent nation, this victory over their most determined enemy in the realm of the Mughals marked a singular change of fortune. It was celebrated with fierce jubilation, especially in Calcutta. The whole city was illuminated in "one of the most superb coup d'oeils" [sic] the *Calcutta Gazette* had ever witnessed, and an array of classical mottoes and allegorical motifs conveyed the sense of a Roman triumph. Government House, for example, was draped with a huge "transparent painting"[1] which depicted Fame blowing a trumpet over the bust of Cornwallis, while Tipu's sons give the treaty (which deprived their father of half his Mysore kingdom) to Britannia, herself supported by the figure of Hercules against a background of Seringapatam. This is not to say that the subcontinent was vanquished at a stroke as a compensation for the loss of the American colonies, though that loss did inspire the British to be more acquisitive in Asia. In fact, India was subverted over several generations. It was coerced and inveigled into collaboration according to no central plan and often by the initiative of men on the spot. This was a radically different form of empire-building from that carried out in America, a new model suited for regions deemed inhospitable to European colonists. British dominion in India rested on conquest rather than settlement. Like Rome's Empire, Britain's Raj was based on force of arms. As Lord Bryce said, its administration bore "a permanently military character."[2] Its atmosphere was permeated by gunpowder. The tiny white community was a garrison, all too aware that what had been won by the sword might be lost by the sword.

Nothing could have seemed more fantastic, when Queen Elizabeth I gave the East India Company its charter on New Year's Eve 1600, than that within two centuries it would be the paramount power in India. The Company's aim was to trade in spices, and it was permitted in due course to establish a few commercial outposts or "factories" on the fringe of the Mughal Empire. This was a byword for might, majesty and magnificence. Its court was a self-proclaimed paradise of gems, silks, perfumes, odalisques, ivory and peacock feathers. English visitors were humbled by its luxury: when "John Company" (as it was called) presented the Emperor Jahangir ("World-seizer")[3] with a coach, he had all its fittings of base metal replaced with ones of silver and gold. The Mughals' cities were larger and more beautiful than London or Paris. Their bankers were richer than those of Hamburg and Cádiz. Their cotton producers clothed much of Africa and Asia, and their hundred million population matched that of all Europe. Their elephant cavalry would have intimidated Hannibal and their trains of artillery would have awed Louis XIV. What is more, the seventeenth century was a golden age of Mughal art, poetry, painting and architecture.

During the reign of Aurangzeb, who wore an iron disembowelling claw on his arm and devoted his life to conflict, this gorgeous imperial edifice was strained to the limit. After his death in 1707 it disintegrated. His successors either engaged in power struggles or, in Macaulay's contemptuous words, "sauntered away life in secluded palaces, chewing bang [or *bhang*, cannabis], fondling concubines, and listening to buffoons."[4] There were internal revolts in Oudh, Mysore and elsewhere, while the Marathas, a confederacy of marauding clans based in Poona, devastated huge tracts of central India, reaching as far as the British trading post of Calcutta. Foreign invaders also took their toll. Delhi was sacked by the Persians in 1739 and by the Afghans in 1756, the former carrying off the Peacock Throne and the Koh-i-noor Diamond (the "Mountain of Light") as well as booty worth a billion rupees, the latter carrying out rape and massacre on an inconceivable scale. Britain and France, whose hostilities extended to India, exploited and exacerbated the disorder. They formed alliances with local rulers. And they fought increasingly for political as much as for commercial ends, though these ends were inextricably entwined since, according to the mercantilist orthodoxy of the time, wealth was crystallised power. Thus cash from commerce paid native troops (sepoys) to take territory which yielded tax revenues and opportunities for further gain. The British were more adept than the French in this endeavour, having better military leadership as well as greater naval strength. For all his imperial vision and diplomatic skill François Dupleix, the French Governor, was not a brave man—he avoided shot and shell on the grounds that tranquillity was necessary for the cultivation of his genius.

By contrast the genius of Robert Clive, the burly pen-pusher who emerged as the English conquistador, was for action. He combined terrific energy and suicidal courage. His bouts of activity were so furious that they seem to have brought on attacks of nervous derangement, which he calmed with opium. Although he spoke no Indian tongue, Clive won the devotion of sepoys by relentless dynamism and hypnotic charisma. He was also a master of what he once called "tricks, chicanery, intrigues, politics, and the Lord knows what."[5] In 1757 he defeated the huge army of France's ally Suraj-ud-daulah, Nawab* of Bengal, employing as much bribery as force. The British put a puppet on the throne of Bengal and within four years they had crushed French opposition. Clive claimed to be, in the words of his motto, *Primus in Indis.*

The claim was premature. Despite Clive's urgings, the East India Company was concerned with trade not empire. Like the British government, the Company had no wish to saddle itself with the administrative burden of ruling Bengal. This abnegation spelled catastrophe for India's richest province, that fertile alluvial plain watered by the Ganges and the Brahmaputra which the Mughals had called "the paradise of the earth."[6] Since the East India Company had the power but refused to take the responsibility, its servants were free to act as tyrants. They had always been "hybrid monster[s],"[7] private traders as well as public functionaries, and now they gorged on "Plassey plunder."[8] Clive himself garnered several hundred thousand pounds as well as a valuable *jagir* (annuity from land) and was famously astonished at his own moderation. Others extorted lavish presents, exacted vast profits and raised heavy taxes. They made fortunes comparable to those of great English proprietors or large West Indian planters. They outdid the "Roman proconsul, who, in a year or two, squeezed out of a province the means of rearing marble palaces and baths on the shores of Campania, of drinking from amber, of feasting on singing birds, of exhibiting armies of gladiators and flocks of camelopards."[9] Their opulence transformed Calcutta, denounced by Clive himself as a Gomorrah of corruption, into a city of palaces. In London, to quote Macaulay again, they inflated the price of everything from fresh eggs to rotten boroughs. The deluge of gold *mohurs*† shaken from the "pagoda tree" dazzled the whole world. In Corsica the young Napoleon Bonaparte dreamed of going to India and returning home

---

* Suraj-ud-daulah meant "Lamp of the State" (though one Company director did ask whether Sir Roger Dowler was really a baronet). Nawab meant "deputy" (for the Mughal Emperor). The word was corrupted into "nabob," a term also used to describe Britons who had made fortunes in the East.

† East India Company coins worth about fifteen rupees, thirty shillings or seven dollars.

a nabob. Bismarck in youth had much the same idea until he thought, "after all, what harm have the Indians done me?"[10]

Bengal was bled white. In 1765 its people were provoked into a desperate revolt, which ultimately enhanced the Company's power through the acquisition of a crucial tax-collecting right from the Mughal Emperor. Indian revenues (which perhaps amounted to a billion pounds sterling between Plassey and Waterloo) spelled the redemption of Britain, said the Earl of Chatham. They were "a kind of gift from heaven."[11] But in 1769–70 Bengal descended into a hell of dearth. Millions died of hunger and some were driven to cannibalism. The famine wiped out a third of the population, their unburied corpses sating the appetites of vultures, jackals and alligators. Yet, though relief efforts were made, British "bullies, cheats and swindlers"[12] continued to prey on the carcass of Bengal. Some profiteered in hoarded grain. Perhaps they were rendered callous by their own likely fate: about 60 per cent of the Company's appointees died before they could get back to England. As the saying went, "two monsoons were the life of a man."[13] One nabob told Clive, who tried to check the worst abuses, that having taken such risks he could not, when helping himself to a fortune, contemplate self-denial.[14] The Governor of Bombay was typically self-indulgent and, being "more arbitrary than the King of England," he had it in his power to "get as much money as he pleases." So wrote Francis Pemberton, an ambitious young Company servant, who estimated in 1770 that "with his trafficking and everything else he saves £40,000 yearly."[15] However, individual rapacity on such a sumptuous scale undermined the East India Company's own trade and threatened it with bankruptcy. Pressure mounted to establish a humane, honest administration in Bengal. In 1773 parliament passed a Regulating Act to bring the Company under partial government control. The new Governor-General, Warren Hastings, had the task of conjuring order out of chaos.

Although mocked as the clerk who sat on the Mughals' throne, Hastings was the ablest Indian leader since Aurangzeb. He admired Indian culture, studied Persian and Urdu, and founded the Asiatic Society of Bengal. He also founded a Mahommedan College (madrasseh) in Calcutta to "soften the prejudices . . . excited by the rapid growth of British dominions."[16] And Hastings supported translations of Hindu classics such as the *Bhagavad Gita*, which would survive, he said, "when the British dominions in India have long ceased to exist."[17] He respected Indians in a fashion that was still quite common at a time when Englishmen were not ashamed to smoke hookahs, drink arrack, chew betel, attend nautches (dances), grow moustaches, hold cows sacred, wear Indian dress, dye their fingers with henna, wash by splashing in the Hindu manner, keep native mistresses (and even, on at least one occasion, get themselves circumcised to meet the religious requirements of Muslim women). Furthermore, Hastings thought that the best way to govern India was through Indian officials and according to Indian customs. "The dominion exercised by the British Empire in India is fraught with many radical and incurable defects," he said. This was largely because distance made efficient control impossible. Only a system of indirect rule, through indigenous intermediaries, could extend what Hastings saw as Britain's "temporary possession" of the subcontinent and "protract that decay, which sooner or later must end it."[18] However, there was a fundamental flaw in Hastings's scheme—it diffused power. The only way to ensure good government, sound defence, fair tax-gathering and an equitable system of justice was to establish a strong central authority. Thus British involvement in Indian affairs increased willy-nilly and Hastings himself, a spindly figure with a bulging forehead, became something of an oriental despot.

He had no alternative in view of the host of difficulties which encompassed him. He got little but insatiable demands from home and had to endure prolonged opposition from his own Council, on which he could be outvoted. He faced the incompetence of insubordinate subordinates in Bombay and Madras, and the treachery of John Company's grasping employees, who "to get a rupee would sell an army."[19] He was also confronted by the hostility of formidable Indian states such as Mysore. Hastings knew that it was a question of conquering or being conquered and that the Company's trade depended on victory. So to preserve Britain's position in India he extended its stake, following and setting a trend. His tenacity matched Clive's audacity. And his methods were, if anything, more brutal. Hastings connived at the judicial murder of one maharajah. He despoiled rich provinces. To local rulers who could afford it, he even hired out his sepoy army, the best-trained force in India, equipped with firelocks and bayonets, obeying commands given in English, drilling to drums and fifes instead of tom-toms and trumpets, and clad in tasselled blue turbans, red jackets, white drawers and sandals. Hastings, it was said, would never "forgive an *enemy*" or "*desert* a friend."[20] Certainly he employed the patronage system to the full, making one crony "Persian translator to the Government"[21] though he knew not a word of the language. Hastings also acquired a small fortune (tiny by Clive's standards), sending £70,000 home in diamonds alone. The Governor-General was particularly indulgent towards his acquisitive and much-loved second wife Marian, who dressed like "an Indian princess,"[22] braided her auburn ringlets with gems, and amused herself by throwing kittens into a bowl full of enormous pearls which slid under their paws when they tried to stand up. Yet he himself avoided ostentation. His throne was a mahogany chair, his finery was a plain brown coat and his palace was a modest country house at Alipore (reputedly still haunted by him). Hastings lacked imperial pretensions but he secured Britain's empire in India.

On his return home, however, he fell victim to a change in the climate of opinion. The methods of the condottiere and morals of the nabob, which had produced ruin in America and spoliation in India, were now discredited in Britain. Hastings was impeached on charges of misgovernment and corruption. When his epic trial before the House of Lords began in 1788 there seemed every chance that he would be found guilty: "innocence does not pave his way with diamonds," remarked Horace Walpole, "nor has a quarry of them on his estate."[23] Accusing the former Governor-General were the three most spellbinding orators of the day. Fox prosecuted Hastings as Cicero had prosecuted the corrupt praetor Verres. Sheridan said that nothing equal to Hastings's criminality could be "traced either in ancient or modern history, in the correct periods of Tacitus or the luminous page of Gibbon."[24] Burke's invective, stoked by Gibbon's opinion that oriental luxury was fatal to empire, ran riot. Hastings was the "captain-general of iniquity," who had tortured orphans and widows, and never dined without "creating a famine." His heart was "gangrened to the core" and he resembled both a "spider of Hell" and a "ravenous vulture devouring the carcases of the dead." Burke invested all his passion and imagination in the indictment, but his virulence actually provoked sympathy for Hastings. William Cowper was shocked by the martyrdom of a man who had "been greater and more feared than the Great Mogul himself."[25] Furthermore, as Britain was menaced by revolutionary France, Hastings's achievement seemed more heroic than criminal. He had, as his counsel argued, preserved the British Empire "*entire* in India," where it had been "convulsed and torn to pieces in other parts of the globe."[26] Perhaps rough measures were necessary, though it was not clear just how rough Hastings's measures had been. This was due in part to witnesses such as his friend and client Mr. "Memory" Middleton, so nicknamed because of "his total want of recollection respecting any fact or circumstance which he conceived could tend to the prejudice of his patron."[27] Here was an early instance of the organised amnesia which so often obscured discreditable episodes in Britain's imperial history. Finally, in 1795, Hastings was acquitted.

News of his victory provoked rejoicing in Calcutta, but although Hastings won the case he had long since lost the argument. Pitt's India Act

(1784) took political control away from John Company and vested it in the British government. The Act also prohibited further conquest in India and attempted to ban peculation, obliging holders of offices of trust in India to disclose the size of the fortunes they brought home. Hastings's trial had dramatised Britain's guilt over colonial oppression and the nation's fear that it too might be corrupted by nabob methods and money. To enforce the reign of virtue Lord Cornwallis, held blameless for the surrender at York-town, was made Governor-General, with enhanced powers, in 1785. On him Henry Dundas, the Scottish minister known as "Harry the Ninth" who (it was said) stuck to Pitt as fast as a barnacle to an oyster shell and aspired to rule India from Whitehall, built all his hopes of the "salvation of our dying interests in Asia. Here was no broken fortune to be mended, here was no avarice to be gratified. Here was no beggarly mushroom kindred to be provided for—no crew of hungry followers gaping to be gorged."[28] Corn-wallis lived up to expectations as a conservative reformer who established lasting standards of official probity. He abandoned Hastings's scheme of partnership and tried to realise Burke's notion of trusteeship, excluding Indians from all government posts at once but implying that the ultimate goal of the Raj was self-government. He subordinated rulers and ruled alike to a code of law, an achievement which made him worthy to be entitled the "Justinian of India."[29]

As such Cornwallis was evidently bringing a kind of Roman order to barbarian chaos. Certainly Britons were more and more apt to regard Indi-ans as uncivilised. Where they had once admired Hindu temples and Mus-lim tombs, for example, they now damned them as dens of vice and shrines of idolatry. This change reflected the growth of aggressive nationalism and missionary zeal during the 1790s. But even a liberal with a rare appreciation of the culture of the subcontinent, such as the oriental scholar Sir William Jones, could declare that its inhabitants were "incapable of civil liberty" and must therefore be "ruled by an absolute power."[30] This became the standard rationale for the British Raj. But Cornwallis himself was more aristocrat than autocrat. While acknowledging that his primary duties were to ensure the "political safety" of Bengal and to render its possession "as advantageous as possible to the East India Company and the British nation,"[31] he adhered to the precept of *noblesse oblige*. Indians should be looked after, he thought, as befitted people who were backward, corrupt and incapable of much save low cunning. They were too far down in the human hierarchy to command respect or to hold any but minor offices—and even in such appointments, Cornwallis said, "preference should always be given to European settlers."[32] True, he awarded Indian *zamindars* (magnates) permanent tax-collecting powers in the settlement of 1793. But this was mainly because he reckoned, optimistically, that it would induce them to cherish rather than fleece the peasant cultivators (*ryots*, who were taxed directly in the south where the British hoped to make them yeomen farmers). In this, as in his other paternalistic endeavours, Cornwallis insisted, "the great object of our being here is to serve the [Indian] public at large."[33] Yet British interests must equally be served, as appears from Cornwallis's expression of relief when rains averted a famine: "there is now I trust no danger of losing the inhabitants, or of much failure in the revenue."[34] The Governor-General was blinkered, unimaginative, racist and dull. But he was also honest, brave, humane and just. He embodied the Roman ideal of fair dealing and the British faith that character counted for more than intellect. He established the principle, which would be held sacred by the Victorians, that imperial power involved moral responsibility.

Cornwallis took many measures, such as improving gaols, reforming the coinage and suppressing child slavery, to ameliorate the Indian condition. But he concentrated most on the improvement of the white community. He was determined to make Britons fit to rule "in a country where a handful of them are to hold millions in subjection." This meant cleaning out the "Augean stables" of the previous regime, which he denounced as "a system of the dirtiest jobbing."[35] And it involved a change in the prevailing opinion that every man who came poor from India was a fool, just as every man who came rich was a rogue. In place of "immense perquisites," he insisted, officials should receive "large salaries."[36] And Europeans should live modestly: Cornwallis publicly rebuked military officers for "indulging themselves in habits of dissipation and expense."[37] He set a high standard of rectitude, refusing requests for patronage from everyone including Warren Hastings and the Prince of Wales. To one peer's solicitation for a particular office the Governor-General responded tartly, "here, my Lord, we are in the habit of looking for the man for the place, and not the place for the man."[38] Yet even Cornwallis made judicious compromises. He did "little favours"[39] for William Burke, Edmund's cousin, and he relied on men with shady pasts. Among them was Charles Grant, who lauded "the goodness of God that [had given him] the power to get wealth" while damning "the offal of Hindoo morals," and was understandably considered a "canting Presbyterian."[40]

Nevertheless, Cornwallis succeeded in raising the tone of British society in Bengal where the East India Company had signally failed. It had long campaigned against the extravagance of its servants in India, their ostentatious chariots with outriders and running footmen, their gigantic meals serenaded by musicians and washed down with "an Atlantick of claret."[41] It had condemned sartorial excesses of the kind which prompted London friends of the silked and spangled diarist William Hickey to say that he looked like "the *Lord Mayor's Trumpeter.*"[42] The Company had even tried to inhibit the "sultanizing process" by imposing sumptuary regulations, which its employees evaded and ridiculed—one said that he did not think the ban on gold lace "was *binding.*"[43] As this suggests, few who worked for the Company, itself a byword for avarice, respected it. When its directors objected to Hickey's friend Bob Potts taking a "common prostitute" (his beautiful inamorata Emily) to India, he vilified them in standard fashion as "the cheese-mongering varlets of Leadenhall Street."[44] Cornwallis led by example. He ate and drank little, though he grew steadily more rotund. He worked hard and every morning he rode hard, following a routine like "perfect clockwork." Spartan and stoical, he disliked flummery, refusing a diamond star after the defeat of Tipu, "or any other present."[45] He embraced duty. Explaining the removal of a Collector from his post, Cornwallis wrote: "his official misconduct was of such a nature, that I could not save him without marking a partiality which must have destroyed all respect for my government . . . mine is the duty of a rigid judge."[46]

In fact, since the death of Cornwallis's beloved wife in 1779—she had been buried, according to her own morbid wish, with a thorn tree planted over her heart—a vein of melancholy had suffused his character. He seemed to have renounced worldly ambition and under his influence Calcutta began to change. There was less drinking and more dancing, since now the gentlemen could often stand up after dinner. There was also less gambling, duelling and roistering. Fewer people committed suicide. Even the game of cricket became better organised. Official corruption so diminished that Dundas could tell Cornwallis, "we never before had a Government of India, both at home and abroad, acting in perfect unison together, upon principles of perfect purity and integrity."[47] Cornwallis himself was less sanguine, informing Dundas that "there is scarcely a man to be found who has held any office of consequence, that has not been driven to make money in a manner which he ought to be ashamed of."[48] But there was plainly some improvement. After purveying supplies to General Abercromby's forces in the war against Tipu Sultan, Francis Pemberton congratulated himself on having increased his fortune to more than £30,000 "in the most honourable manner; commissaries to so large an army as I have been with formerly wd. have gained ten times that sum."[49] So young rakes aiming to make huge fortunes in India might well now cry "Alas and alack-a-day" in earnest, whereas they had previously drunk to a punning version of that traditional lament: "A lass and a lakh* a day."[50]

The fatherly governance of Cornwallis was most famously represented in Mather Brown's painting of his reception of Tipu Sultan's sons after the successful siege of Seringapatam, just north of the city of Mysore, in 1792. The Governor-General is shown, surrounded by a retinue of British officers, holding the boys' hands while they gaze at him trustingly and their Indian attendants tamely submit to the custody. Although Brown never visited India and was intent on producing a scene out of oriental romance, his grand canvas does contain some truth. Cornwallis genuinely regretted that the "mad barbarian Tippoo has forced us into a war" and he conducted it with uncommon restraint. When his own troops burned two villages, the Governor-General condemned the "disgraceful outrages" as being fatal to "all our hopes of success" and liable to "blast the British name with infamy."[51] He left Tipu his throne, an act of reconciliation which mortified his officers: one expostulated, "At this rate we shall all be Quakers in twenty years more."[52] But if Tipu had been deposed or killed, the Governor-General argued, "we must either have given [his] Capital to the Marattas (a dangerous boon) or to have set up some miserable Pageant of our own, to be supported by the Company's troops and . . . to be plundered by its Servants."[53] Moreover, Cornwallis really did treat the young princes with the "most benignant kindness."[54] As they arrived at the English camp outside Seringapatam, seated in silver howdahs on richly caparisoned elephants, escorted by outriders on camels, by their father's *vakils* (envoys), and by a hundred marching pikemen and standard-bearers with green Islamic flags, the boys (aged eight and ten) were fearful. But when they dismounted, exotic little figures in white muslin gowns and red turbans, with rows of pearls round their necks from which hung large ruby and emerald ornaments set amid clusters of brilliants, Cornwallis embraced them "as if they had been his own sons." At once their "faces brightened up"[55] and he led them by the hands into his tent, where they were further cheered with gifts of gold watches, accompanied by betel nut and attar of roses.

Here, it seemed, was the best of British paternalism in practice. One of the congratulatory commentaries on Brown's picture of the event salutes "the gallant Cornwallis" for "displaying to his captives a generosity which would have done honour to the brightest hero of the classic page of antiquity."[56] Yet Brown's imperial icon, like the many other

---

* A lakh (of rupees) was 100,000 (worth roughly £10,000), whereas a crore was ten million.

celebrations of this episode, is a fabulous piece of propaganda. It is imaginative in detail and idealised in concept, British moderation being contrasted with Asiatic extravagance. It also varnishes over the fact that Cornwallis was extorting vast territorial concessions plus a huge financial indemnity from Tipu. As the Governor-General himself reported to King George,

> although the formidable power of Tipoo has been so much reduced by the events of a war into which we were forced by the ungovernable ambition and violence of his character, as to render it improbable that he can be able for many years to come to give any material disturbance to the British possessions in India, yet in the selection of the countries that are to be ceded to us, my primary object shall be to fix upon those . . . best calculated for giving us a strong defensive position against the future attacks of any power whatever.[57]

In the guise of guardianship, Cornwallis was using the princes as human pawns in a ruthless game of *realpolitik*. This, critics declared, was the fraudulent essence of imperialism. The charge that their Empire was a system of hypocrisy was one which irked the British because it came so close to the truth; in the long run, paradoxically, the only way that they could refute it was to try to make the Empire a system of magnanimity. The ultimate logic of the myth disseminated by Mather Brown and his tribe was that Tipu's heirs would duly emerge from tutelage into a state of independence. But the immediate effect of unprecedented drum-beating over the defeat of Tipu, often called "the modern Hannibal,"[58] was to encourage greater British belligerence in India.

A European cataclysm further aggravated that belligerence. Over the next few years the French Revolution became (in Shelley's phrase) "the master theme of the epoch."[59] To check the spread of Jacobinism eastwards, the British felt bound to show less of the velvet glove in India and more of the iron fist. Otherwise, wrote Captain John Taylor in Bombay,

> Adieu to power, influence and respectability, and, finally, Adieu to our possessions in the East. Not only the Marattas and [the] Nizam [of Hyderabad] will detest our incapacity and presumption; but every state in India, from the Mountains of Thibet to the Southern Peninsula, will be justly roused, and the disaffection of our Native Troops will finally dismember the Colonies of India from the British Empire.[60]

So British proconsuls, notably Lord Wellesley,* elder brother of the future Duke of Wellington, used the Jacobin danger, later compounded by the Napoleonic threat to advance on India from Egypt, as an opportunity to augment British power. Wellesley, a man of Olympian pretensions and Jovian passions, was Governor-General between 1797 and 1805. With the assistance of his brother Arthur, he conquered more territory in India than Bonaparte did in Europe. He became, in the words of a contemporary, "the Akbar of the Company's dynasty."[61] Indeed, he ruled more of India than the Mughal Emperor had ever done, though this in itself caused concern at the East India Company's headquarters in Leadenhall Street. One of the directors, Charles Grant, noted dourly, "It was the unwieldiness of the Mogul Empire that accelerated its fall." He believed that "the wider British dominion in India spread, the more vulnerable it becomes."[62]

By contrast Tipu Sultan maintained that the English gained complete control wherever they "fix[ed] their talons."[63] Ever since his defeat by Cornwallis, Tipu had dreamed—literally as well as metaphorically—of a "holy war" (jihad) of vengeance. He also sought allies, making eager overtures to Britain's hereditary enemy and even permitting a Jacobin Club to be established at Seringapatam. Wellesley recognised Tipu's irreconcilable hatred. He maintained that perhaps the principal object of Napoleon's Egyptian expedition "was to satisfy the demand of Tippoo Sultaun for military assistance to the full extent of his wishes."[64] And he determined to make Tipu "renounce all connection with the French nation."[65] While honeyed words of signal insincerity passed between Calcutta and Seringapatam, Tipu was systematically demonised. The British represented him as a dangerous radical, the sympathiser with sans-culottes in France and the friend of "republicans in America." He was also a "remorseless savage,"[66] the oppressor of Hindus and the murderer of Christians. "The laws of Draco are tender mercies," wrote one of his accusers, compared to Tipu's legal code, which combined "the terrors of death with cold-blooded irony, filthy ridicule with obscene mutilation, the pranks of a monkey with the abomination of a monster."[67]

Certainly Tipu was capable of cruelty and fanaticism, especially against those who refused conversion to Islam. As one English officer stated, "I have myself witnessed a sight of barbarity unknown in any civilized nation, where the unfortunate Hindoos have been hanged by dozens on trees by the road side."[68] With his "tawny complexion," blazing eyes and "bloodthirsty"

*At this stage he was still the Earl of Mornington.

temperament, Tipu did much to earn his English nickname, the "Tiger of Mysore."[69] Indeed, he gloried in the alias, decorating his palaces and his furniture, his weapons and his armour, with tiger motifs. His troops wore striped uniforms and his walls were scarified by claw marks. His own throne, an octagonal *musnud* which rested on the back of a larger-than-life-size gold tiger, was embellished with jewelled tiger heads. The narrow passage to his bed chamber was guarded by four live tigers and Tipu often said that he would "rather live two days like a tiger, than two hundred years like a sheep"[70] (a sentiment later echoed by Mussolini). Nothing better demonstrated Tipu's ferocious nature, in British eyes, than his most celebrated artefact. This was a wooden tiger which, at the turn of a handle, roared while attacking a European soldier, who raised his arm and moaned despairingly. This monstrous mechanism was later put on show in London (where it may still be seen, at the Victoria & Albert Museum). Along with many other representations, such as theatrical versions of the "storming of Seringapatam,"[71] it proclaims the beastliness of Tipu and the heroic character of England's civilising mission.

Moral censure of Tipu Sultan did not come well from a nation which treated convicts and slaves so brutally and, in any case, it rather missed the mark. Seen in the context of South Indian kingship, the Tiger of Mysore was, if hardly tame, not altogether wild. Tipu was intelligent, cultured and witty. He possessed a library of two thousand volumes (carefully wrapped and placed in chests to protect them from white ants) which doubtless nurtured his passion for innovation. He was as fascinated by western technology as by eastern astrology, wearing on his person a gold fob watch and a magical silver amulet. His French-trained army was in some respects superior to that of the British. Tipu's artillery was "both larger and longer than ours," wrote an English officer, his "Rocket Boys are daring, especially when intoxicated by Bang." The Sultan was altogether "a respectable and formidable enemy."[72] He was also notably fastidious. His chin was cleanly shaved in oil of almonds, and his muscular body, tending to corpulence but distinguished by delicate wrists and ankles, was regularly "shampooed" (i.e. massaged). A fine white handkerchief, a black enamel vase of flowers and a silver spit-box were placed close to his *musnud*, which faced Mecca. Although the court elephants were trained to make obeisance to him, Tipu dressed plainly, ate with restraint (for breakfast "an electuary composed of the brains of male tame sparrows"), and spent little time in his zenana. A keen hunter, "an incomparable horseman, a gallant soldier, an excellent marksman,"[73] he was admired as well as feared. His subjects evidently did not see him as a tyrant or a bigot, and mourned his passing—many prostrated themselves before the bier and "expressed their grief by loud lamentations."[74] Even the caste-ridden inhabitants of Malabar's spice coast seem to have preferred his rule to that of the British.

Mysore, a broad plateau where fertile grain lands, paddy fields and coconut groves sustained populous villages, flourished under Tipu, who introduced silkworms and sericulture. Seringapatam, an island sacred to Vishnu in the Kaveri River, was "the richest, most convenient and beautiful spot possessed in the present age by any native Prince of India."[75] Magnificent buildings sprouted amid tropical fruit gardens. Overtopping the white ramparts of the fort were the fretted towers of temples and the banded minarets of mosques. Within its walls, too, stood Tipu's majestic new palace, embellished with zodiacal verses emphasising "the godlike superiority of the Sultan in his princely character."[76] Equally gorgeous were the floral arabesques adorning the teak interior of the Dauria Daulat Bagh, the Garden Palace of the Wealth of the Sea. This also contained a gigantic mural celebrating the victory of Hyder Ali, India's Vercingetorix, over the British at the battle of Pollilor. Close to Hyder's square, onion-domed mausoleum, with its arcade of polished hornblende columns and its ebony and ivory doors, was the Lal Bagh pavilion, set in a "garden of rubies." Its huge red audience chamber was especially splendid, decorated with gold texts from the Koran and supported by rows of fantastically shaped pillars on black marble bases. But it was the treasure housed inside these edifices that really amazed the British. For Tipu surrounded himself with exquisite works of art, talismanic gemstones, filigreed weapons, gilt furniture, silk carpets, eggshell porcelain and Malabar muslins so fine that they seemed to be, as a Roman writer had said, "woven wind."[77]

Thus Mysore was in every sense a prize when the British invasion culminated, on 4 May 1799, in the second and final victory at Seringapatam. To strike a blow against Tipu, the Governor-General had said, might "save crores of rupees and thousands of lives," for it would stop the Sultan forming an alliance with France, which aimed to revive its "ancient splendour"[78] in India. He stressed political rather than financial gains, victory not only winning sixty lakhs of rupees in additional revenue but establishing "on the most permanent foundations our power in the Deccan."[79] Yet lust for booty can hardly be overestimated as an imperial imperative—or as a source of native hatred. "Loot" was a Hindi word but the British soon adopted it. As the evidence has already suggested, most soldiers regarded plunder as a legitimate, if clandestine, perquisite. Their leaders set a bad example. Indeed, some of the Empire's greatest military heroes satisfied ravenous appetites for the spoils of war. During the Second Afghan War (1878–80) General

Roberts "sent off nine camel loads of loot before the Prize Agents were appointed."[80] After the second Ashanti expedition (1895–6) Major Baden-Powell carried away gold jewellery, a brass bowl supposedly used for catching blood in human sacrifices and King Prempeh's hat. Following the battle of Omdurman (1898) General Kitchener's men laid profane hands on even the most sacred objects, including the crescent from the dome of the Mahdi's Tomb, today preserved at the Royal Engineers' Museum in Chatham, and its copper-plated finial, which now adorns a turret at Blair Castle, seat of the Duke of Atholl. Kitchener himself instructed a subordinate to "loot like blazes. I want any quantity of marble stairs, marble pavings, iron railings, looking-glasses and fittings; doors, windows, furniture of all sorts."[81] In the chaos following the capture of Seringapatam, the army's rapacity was equally unconfined.

Soldiers ransacked the Tiger's fabulous lair. They raided the treasury, leaving a trail of gold pagodas across the floor. They stole rings, bracelets, necklaces and diamond aigrettes by the pocketful. They pillaged almost every dwelling. Tipu's throne was broken up, though a couple of the best pieces—the gold *huma* bird of paradise that had perched on the pearl-fringed canopy and the largest gold tiger head, with moveable tongue and rock-crystal teeth—finally found a home at Windsor Castle. It was said that a redcoat had shot Tipu for the jewel in his turban or the gold buckle in his red silk belt. When his body was found, still warm, under a heap of corpses there were no ornaments about his dress—"a fine white linnen jacket, Chintz Drawers and a Crimson Cloth round his waist."[82] But he was still good for a final souvenir: a British officer took a penknife and cut off half the Sultan's moustache. Arthur Wellesley, who himself defined plunder as "What you could lay your bloody hand on and keep,"[83] stopped the looting by flogging and hanging miscreants. However, he did discover subsequent instances of British "villainy" which "would disgrace the Newgate Calendar."[84] Among them was extortion by torture and even murder. Yet the official rewards were bountiful enough: the army received prize money of well over a million pounds, Colonel Wellesley's own share being £4,000. The Governor-General's wife, meanwhile, was urging him to take the lion's share of the Tiger's precious stones. He replied indignantly: "How like a woman! I have never yet met a woman who did not think that a great public position was an opportunity to thieve." Instead he struck a bronze medal showing the British lion overcoming the Mysore tiger. Eventually, though, he did accept a diamond star made from Seringapatam jewels and he permitted the Governor-General's crimson and gold throne in Calcutta to be ornamented with bits of Tipu's own *musnud*. Richard Wellesley was also rewarded with a step up in the peerage, though he remained permanently embittered by the fact that it was an Irish title, an "execrable Potato Marquessate." Still, he did incorporate the sacred *huma* bird in his coat of arms. And he took his motto from the *Aeneid: "Super Indos postulit Imperium"*—He extended the Empire over the Indians.[85]

No Roman proconsul had more vaulting ambitions than Richard Wellesley and no Indian Brahmin had a fiercer pride of caste. Building on his triumph in Mysore, where he annexed some territory, appointed a puppet ruler and tried to emasculate Tipu's sons politically by encouraging them to concentrate on concubines, Wellesley aimed to establish one paramount power in India. To a female friend he boasted, "I will heap kingdoms upon kingdoms, victory upon victory, revenue upon revenue; I will accumulate glory and wealth and power, until the ambition and avarice even of my masters shall cry mercy."[86] Wellesley would thus complete the rise of "an insignificant trading settlement to a mighty empire."[87]

His main enemy was now the Maratha Confederacy, which posed a constant threat to British domination. This was not only because of its French connections but, in Wellesley's view, because of "the treachery of the Maratta character." More to the point, the Marathas were skilled irregular fighters and brilliant cavalrymen whose empire was "the empire of the saddle."[88] But the British had the advantage of superior organisation, discipline, weaponry and credit. They also possessed a general of genius, Arthur Wellesley, and a commander of "matchless"[89] valour, Sir Gerard (later Lord) Lake. In one battle Lake had two horses killed under him as well as six or seven musket-ball holes in his hat and coat, and all this while being "four and twenty hours without claret," something, wrote William Hickey, it was hard to believe he survived.[90] Thanks to such heroism as well as diplomacy to match—a lot of it provided by Wellesley's quartet of protégés, Thomas Munro, John Malcolm, Mountstuart Elphinstone and Charles Metcalfe— the British were able to divide and rule. They got direct and indirect control over a huge region between the Ganges and the Jumna. They also brought the Mughal Emperor Shah Aulum under the Calcutta government's "protection." He was now a blind, bedraggled and aged figurehead but he was still known as "Lord of the Universe." In French hands, Wellesley wrote, his name might have been used "to justify exaction, violence and encroachment."[91] This was precisely what the Governor-General himself had in mind. In trenchant language the *Edinburgh Review* anatomised his "*Roman policy*":

to take part in every quarrel; to claim the lands of one party for assisting him, and seize the lands of the other after beating him; to get allies by force, and take care nobody shall rob them but ourselves; to quarter troops upon our neighbours, and pay them with our neighbour's goods.

Wellesley might represent his own aggression as a form of defence, the *Edinburgh Review* continued, but to warn that Napoleon was following in the footsteps of Alexander was like crying that "the Great Turk is come as far as Whitechapel." It concluded with the solemn hope that Britons "seduced into Roman schemes of conquest abroad, will never be *honoured with a triumph* at home." They should not be "permitted to suspend in temples of British structure, those inauspicious trophies which can be regarded as the spoils of British reputation."[92]

In fact British governments tried to impress on Wellesley that scarcely any "military success" could justify breaching the "sacred principle" that Company specie should not be diverted to "the purposes of war."[93] Lord Castlereagh, Secretary of State for War and the Colonies (a suggestively hybrid office, thus titled between 1801 and 1854, accused not only of making war for colonies but against them), acknowledged that the British had necessarily passed from being "traders" to being "sovereigns" in India. But it was better to improve the territory already gained than to subdue the Marathas. Far from achieving security, as Wellesley argued, further conquest would bring the British Raj, Castlereagh said, "in contact with neighbours much more troublesome."[94] But as often happened in imperial history, local authority proved stronger than central government. Private enterprise flourished in a raj administered by a commercial company half a world away: even getting news from the Mediterranean, one minister complained, was like getting news from the moon; and in 1801 Wellesley in India was "seven months without receiving one line of authentic intelligence from England."[95] So neither Downing Street nor Leadenhall Street could stop the Governor-General from marching down "the splendid road to ruin." A man of majestic littleness and "brilliant incapacity,"[96] he added insult to injury by spending the Company's money like water to establish himself in "Asiatic pomp."[97]

In his servants and equipages Wellesley was extravagant to a "superlative degree."[98] He rode around Calcutta in a gleaming coach and six, escorted by a bodyguard of dragoons and a posse of outriders. He sailed the Ganges aboard a fairy-tale yacht, the flagship of a small flotilla, whose green and gold livery contrasted brilliantly with the scarlet habits of its crew. He began to create a country house at Barrackpore, a "villa of the Caesars"[99] set in a beautiful pleasaunce, with such accessories as a theatre, a bandstand, an aviary and a menagerie. His most prodigal indulgence, though, was the new Government House on Esplanade Row, overlooking the *maidan*, the space cleared to give the guns of Fort William an open field of fire. Wellesley demolished the Governor-General's old official residence, as well as the Council House and sixteen private mansions, some recently constructed. In their place he built a palace, modelled on Kedleston Hall in Derbyshire. That neo-classical pile, designed by Robert Adam, was much admired, though Dr. Johnson's compliment was barbed—it would do excellently for a town hall. The new Government House, soon crowned with a huge, honey-coloured dome, was also too grand to make a comfortable home. Guests felt imprisoned or they got lost, since the living apartments were isolated in four vast colonnaded wings. Here they experienced space without room and luxury without comfort. There was not a water closet in the place and the food was always cold since the kitchens were situated two hundred yards down the road.

The building was, however, ideally suited to be the headquarters of an empire. The Marble Hall was modelled on a Roman atrium, with a coffered ceiling supported by Doric columns of gleaming white *chunam* (burnished stucco made from seashells), a grey marble floor and along the walls the busts of a dozen Caesars. Above it, on an equally impressive scale, was the pillared ballroom, floored with polished teak, flanked with huge looking-glasses and lit by "a profusion of cut-glass lustres."[100] The Augustan architecture was punctuated by coats of arms, captured guns, monumental lions and plaster sphinxes—two of the last had their breasts cut off when an aide-de-camp thought the Governor-General "might be shocked by their exuberance."[101] (This was a gross misjudgement, since Richard Wellesley was prone to such flagrant promiscuity that his brother Arthur, himself to be caricatured straddling an erect cannon, wanted him castrated.) The Directors of the East India Company did not go that far but the unexampled magnificence of Government House, which cost £170,000, caused exquisite pain in Leadenhall Street. Wellesley claimed that the building was essential to the Governor-General's health in a debilitating climate. He himself suffered from boils ("horrible leprosy") and haemorrhoids, complaining to his wife: "I have been reduced to a skeleton, yellow, trembling, without appetite, unable to sleep, too weak to walk twice round the room."[102] But he would undoubtedly have agreed with Lord Valentia's famous justification for the splendour of Government House. Effortlessly combining racial prejudice and social snobbery, Valentia took the standard view that orientals would despise revelations of a "sordid mercantile spirit" whereas they would be awed and dazzled by a theatre of power. "In short," he concluded, "I wish India to be ruled from a palace, not from a counting-house; with the ideas of a Prince, not those of a retail dealer in muslins and indigo."[103]

Wellesley had an even more pronounced contempt for the cheesemongers of Leadenhall Street since he was never hampered, as they supposedly were, by "the craven fear of being great."[104] On the contrary, he made every effort to enhance the Governor-General's quasi-regal status. He disdained even the most puissant maharajahs, calling the Nizam of Hyderabad "a twaddler of order high."[105] Yet he insisted that Indian potentates should receive him like a "Tutelary Deity,"[106] with the full panoply of gold *chobdars* (mace-bearers) and jewelled elephants. According to Charles Metcalfe, Wellesley entered Lucknow in such majestic state that he "completely beggared"[107] Gibbon's description of the Emperor Aurelian's Roman triumph, which featured the wealth of Asia, 200 exotic beasts, 1,600 gladiators, a vast train of barbarian prisoners and the captive Queen Zenobia chained with gold and swooning under the weight of diamonds. Wellesley also held durbars (levees) so that "the nobles of Hindostan [could] come in all their barbaric pomp to pay their respects at the Viceregal Court."[108] Otherwise he excluded Indians from social functions as Cornwallis had debarred them from official positions. Indeed, he held himself totally aloof. "I stalk about like a Royal Tiger," he wrote, in "magnificent solitude." The army of major-domos, butlers, footmen, bodyguards, silver stick carriers, fan wavers, bearers, messengers and other attendants was evidently invisible.

The Governor-General also shunned the society of his white subjects. They were "so vulgar, ignorant, rude, familiar, and stupid as to be disgusting and intolerable; especially the ladies, not one of whom, by the bye, is even decently [good-]looking." (The "want of a decent looking woman" was a frequent complaint in a climate that soon turned blooming girls into leathery memsahibs known as "painted corpses"; those in Calcutta were said to be "such a set of cats that have been withering away these last ten years.")[109] Anyway, Wellesley felt compelled to entrench himself "within forms and ceremonies, to introduce much state into the whole appearance of my establishments and household, to expel all approaches to familiarity, and to exercise my authority with a degree of strictness and vigour amounting to severity."[110] Wellesley also laid down the law in hectoring tones. He established Fort William College to instruct Company servants in their duties. He prohibited horse-racing on Sundays. He banned comfortable white linen in favour of formal cloth jackets—worn in such heat that diners longed, like Sydney Smith, to "take off our flesh and sit in our bones."[111] Wellesley's vanity and arrogance, reflected in the insolent tilt of his strong chin and the freezing glance of his blue eyes, alienated everyone but his acolytes, who extolled his charm. Yet in asserting his position at the apex of the social hierarchy, he was only doing to Britons what they were doing to Indians.

The growing estrangement of the two communities was symbolised by the gulf between the "princely" opulence of white Calcutta and the wretched condition of its so-called "Black Town." Most people sailing up the muddy, fast-flowing Hooghly for the first time were struck by "the stately forest of masts," worthy of the Port of London, and by the succession of "elegant classic built houses adorned with luxurious plantations." They also admired the handsome octagonal Fort, its flag flying and drums beating, which was reminiscent of Vauban's citadel at Valenciennes, "regular, majestic and commanding."[112] The Chowringhee, the main avenue across the *maidan* from Fort William, was "an entire village of palaces."[113] Most of them were constructed in the Palladian style with pillared verandahs and balustraded roofs, as well as "porticoes, domes, and fine gateways."[114] In Wellesley's time the buildings grew ever more imposing and when Bishop Heber arrived in 1823 he was reminded of St. Petersburg. Even the dead dwelt in style. Park Street Cemetery, a necropolis so busy that the chaplain from St. John's Church who conducted burials received a special palanquin allowance of thirty rupees a month, was an extraordinary architectural agglomeration. It was crowded with urns, obelisks, columns, sarcophagi, Ionic temples, mausoleums built in imitation of Muslim tombs, and pyramids, the tallest of which was modelled on that of the praetor Caius Cestius in Rome. (This "wedge sublime . . . Like flame transformed to marble," as Shelley called it in *Adonaïs*, overshadowed the English Cemetery where Keats lay and possessed a strong appeal to the Romantics; Turner's twilight picture of the pyramid illustrated the title page of Byron's *Life and Works*.) All told, European Calcutta was reckoned "not only the most beautiful city in Asia but one of the most beautiful in the world."[115]

Yet like other British enclaves it was also a city under siege. The Grim Reaper was always in attendance, especially during the hot season when the sun could broil meat on the cannon of Fort William and people sheltered under umbrellas even from the rays of the full moon. Nature constantly encroached. At night tigers padded behind the Chowringhee and by day they were "often bold enough to leap on boats"[116] plying near the shore. Jackals, hyenas, vultures and pariah dogs scavenged the streets, though none rivalled the strutting adjutant birds. These were giant cranes which disposed of "astonishing quantities of putrefactive offal"[117] and could swallow a calf's leg, iron-shod hoof and all; so vital was their cleaning role that cadets at Fort William were warned that anyone injuring them would be guilty of "gross misconduct."[118] Government House provided a roost for them, as for monkeys, civet cats, flying foxes, bats, crows, kites and flocks of bright green parakeets. Some of these creatures infested the house itself, especially during the monsoon, when they might be joined by frogs, lizards, snakes, ants, spiders, mosquitoes, moths, beetles and so many other flying, buzzing and stinging bugs that they covered surfaces like specimens on museum trays. There were no curtains in Calcutta lest they harbour scorpions or centipedes. Glasses were fitted with little pagoda roofs and candles were often placed in soup plates full of water in which myriad insects drowned. Guests whose imaginations were infected by the hypertrophy of the tropics complained of cockroaches "as big as mice" and rats the size of "small elephants."[119] Exposed to invasion from the animal kingdom, European communities seemed still more vulnerable to human incursions, and many saw the perils as twins.

Wellesley himself referred to the dusky swarms in white muslin overflowing from the native quarter. This was socially remote but physically and psychologically ever-present. In contrast with the Roman regularity of the white city as depicted by such painters as William Hodges and the Daniells, it was a chaotic labyrinth of narrow, unpaved streets, pot-holed alleys, and foetid courts. Occasionally these were flanked by elaborate *pukkah* (brick) houses, belonging to landowners, merchants or businessmen *(banias)*. But for the most part Black Town was a festering slum *(bustee)*. It was a cluster of ramshackle bazaars, mouldering godowns, dingy tenements, and huts made of mud, straw and bamboo, not superior to the Irish cabin or "the rudest wigwam."[120] Black Town, itself hemmed in by jungle and swamp, literally leaned against the British capital. It also impinged in other ways. Wellesley was especially concerned about the danger of disease and fire spreading from the native quarter. The stench of cow byres, slaughterhouses, stagnant tanks and open sewers tainted the atmosphere of the whole metropolis, as did the smoke of dung fires and the aroma of spices, coconut oil and *ghee* (clarified butter, the invariable medium of Indian cooking). Religious processions along the Chitpore Road attracted such Hindu multitudes that "Christian gentlemen driving their buggies amongst them" lashed out indiscriminately with whips, causing some to fall in ditches "while others were trampled under foot."[121] Residents of smart villas on Garden Reach had to employ a servant full time to push floating corpses away from the bank and into the main stream of the Hooghly. Here they "moved up and down with the tide," as many as a hundred passing any particular spot each day, "a prey to vultures perched upon them"[122] and to pariah dogs which dragged them ashore. Other "nuisances"[123]—an English euphemism for faeces—were unavoidable.

If the British community could not isolate itself topographically, however, it increasingly accomplished a degree of racial segregation. The race barrier, indeed, had always been present, even among admirers of the East. Sir William Jones, for example, likened the experience of being "forced to borrow from a *black man*" to that of "touching a snake or a South American eel."[124] Similarly, William Hickey had to overcome feelings of "disgust" and "horror" before having sexual intercourse with a "black woman."[125] But by Wellesley's time discrimination on grounds of race was becoming more institutionalised. A few eminent Indians continued to mingle "freely in the fashionable circles of Calcutta."[126] A handful of Britons felt that Hindu civilisation was not inferior to that of Europe and had "many native friends."[127] But most Indians, even those "who imitated the English by manners and rivalled them in literary attainments," were kept out of white society. Often the excuse was that their habits were incompatible with those of Europeans. In particular "their notions and customs in respect to women must for ever exclude them from that intimate association with the ruling race in their domestic and private relations."[128] Essentially, though, the British sought to distinguish themselves as the dominant race, the ruling caste. This also meant shunning half-castes, "that forlorn race of beings,"[129] as one missionary called them, then known as Indo-Britons or Eurasians (and later as Anglo-Indians). Eminent exceptions were admitted, such as the cavalry commander James Skinner. But there was no notion of Roman assimilation. There was no question of the Ganges flowing into the Thames as the Orontes had supposedly flowed into the Tiber. In this respect, as the historian R. G. Collingwood acknowledged, the British Raj was "utterly unlike the Roman Empire."[130]

Interbreeding might be "the first step in colonisation," as Lord Valentia said, "creating a link of union between the English and the natives."[131] However, it would be ruinous if continued and during the Regency period there was growing agreement that the products of miscegenation had to be ostracised. They could nevertheless remain "useful allies," wrote John Malcolm, because their pride in ranking themselves as Europeans would overcome their humiliation at "every instance of scornful repulse."[132] In some respects, such as the matter of growing moustaches and eating curry, the rulers did come to resemble the ruled. But certainly by the Victorian age anything liable to blur the lines between the races was anathema. "The extreme horror which European ladies entertained of appearing to imitate the natives" and to look like "nautch girls," wrote a visiting Englishwoman, caused them to banish "gold and silver from their robes."[133] Whereas a Frenchman among Indians says, "I am the first," wrote a Gallic observer, "an Englishman, a thousand times richer and more powerful, says, 'I am alone.'"[134] The British were not guilty of injustice or wilful oppression but of "foolish, surly national pride," said Bishop Heber. "We shut out the natives from our society, and a bullying, insolent manner is continually assumed in speaking to them."[135] British society took its tone from Wellesley, who treated even princely envoys with "mortifying hauteur & reserve."[136] Some Indians were intimidated by such overbearing behaviour. Many more were antagonised. In the words of an English visitor who believed that it was vital to conciliate the natives, "our proud and disdainful islanders . . . usually contrive to make themselves hated wherever they go."[137]

Wellesley had provoked almost universal animosity by the time he was recalled in 1805. Even the aged, amiable Cornwallis, who was sent out to save the subcontinent by replacing him, took umbrage at all the pomp and circumstance. William Hickey famously recorded his response to the dazzling cavalcade that greeted him at the Calcutta landing stage.

> CORNWALLIS (to his confidential secretary): "What! What! What is all this, Robinson, hey?"
>
> ROBINSON: "My Lord, the Marquis Wellesley has sent his equipages and attendants as a mark of respect and to accompany your Lordship to the Government House."
>
> CORNWALLIS: "Too civil, too civil by half. Too many people. I don't want them, don't want one of them, I have not yet lost the use of my legs, Robinson, hey? Thank God. I can still walk, walk very well, Robinson, hey; don't want a score of carriages to convey me a quarter of a mile; certainly shall not use them."[138]

Cornwallis went on foot, only to be appalled at the Byzantine splendours of Wellesley's palace. In the couple of months before his death Cornwallis tried to live less ostentatiously and, more important, he insisted on a reversal of his predecessor's expansionist policy. He deplored the "frenzy" for "conquest and victory," ordered a withdrawal from nearly all "territories on the west of the Jumna," and denounced the view, championed by General Lake, that "a system of power was preferable to one of conciliation."[139]

In practice the military authorities seemed bent on a system of exasperation. During the course of 1806 the Commander-in-Chief of the Madras army, Sir John Cradock, imposed fresh regulations on his sepoys, who were anyway ill treated and badly paid. In the name of smartness he ordered them to trim their moustaches "to a military pattern,"[140] and to cut off their beards—for as long as wigs were worn facial hair was an object of ridicule in England, where it was seen as tragically appropriate that in his mad state George III should remain unshaven. Sepoys were also instructed to wear a new turban with a leather cockade, and to remove caste marks and earrings while in uniform. This sparked off a mutiny at Vellore, the most powerful fortress in the Carnatic and the granite guardhouse of Tipu Sultan's sons. In the dead of night well-organised detachments of sepoys attacked the sleepy British garrison and killed a hundred officers and men. Britons were terrified that the instrument they had created to dominate the subcontinent would now destroy them. Eighty miles away in Madras the white community for "many nights together," said the Governor, Lord William Bentinck, "went to bed in the uncertainty of rising alive."[141] Colonel John Malcolm wrote home to Wellesley, "Your Lordship knows I am no alarmist. This is the first time I have ever trembled for India."[142]

The Vellore uprising was the most serious challenge to British power in India between the fall of Calcutta in 1756 and the Mutiny of 1857. It was quickly suppressed but the government agonised long and hard over what had caused it and who was to blame. The civilians accused the soldiers, who admitted that whiskers (though not the shape of moustaches) had "always been deemed sacred" in India.[143] Cradock also acknowledged that the dress reforms could have reinforced "the common cry 'that the next attempt will be to make the sepoys Christians.'"[144] Certainly it was the height of folly to offend Hindu and Muslim susceptibilities at a time when "violent and implacable"[145] missionary endeavour was persuading Indians that, as one put it, "you English have taken the whole country, & now you want the people to receive your religion."[146] It was, in any case, oft-expressed government policy "to adopt a system of universal toleration, and to yield to the local habits and religious prejudices of the several sects which compose our native army."[147] This did not prevent the founding of an Anglican diocese at Calcutta in 1813—it stretched from St. Helena to Sydney and its first bishop, Thomas Middleton, solemnly attacked the "fabric of idolatry,"[148] which gained him no converts but instead a marble tableau in St. Paul's Cathedral representing him blessing two young kneeling Indians. Nor did the Vellore Mutiny prevent the flouting of caste taboos in 1857, with far more disastrous results. But in 1806 the military could plausibly argue that the rebellion had much deeper roots. Evidence that it was, indeed, the fruit of a conspiracy in which Tipu's sons were implicated had been brandished over the moated battlements of Vellore itself when the mutineers ran up the Sultan's flag. This red and green banner, with the sun at its centre and its ripple of tiger stripes, was not an emblem of mutiny but an icon of independence. It represented what one of Cradock's senior officers called "that implacable hostile spirit against European Dominion."[149] After the official inquiry Bentinck and Cradock were sent home. The regulations were withdrawn, as the Resident of Hyderabad advised, "to avert by conciliation . . . the dreadful extremity of a general insurrection."[150]

It was a commonplace that Britain held India by a thread, which could snap at the slightest miscalculation. The colonial order, whereby Indians were denied economic advantage and political advancement, was deeply unpopular. Bengal villagers actually welcomed intolerant Baptist missionaries such as William Carey because they did not resemble other Europeans, "who were worse than tigers."[151] The brown man's burden was oppressive and his resentment was summed up in the chant of John Malcolm's palanquin bearers, whose meaning, when he discovered it, gave him wry amusement: "There is a fat hog—a great fat hog—how heavy he is—hum—shake him—hum—shake him well—shake the fat hog—hum."[152] Many Britons regarded the dominion of forty thousand Europeans over forty million Indians as not just precarious but "unnatural."[153] Some even detected in it "an element of the supernatural." Lord Bryce would illustrate the uncanny power of the Raj with a story about a tiger which, having escaped from its cage in Lahore Zoo and resisted all attempts to lure it back, returned when its keeper "solemnly adjured it in the name of the British Government."[154] But a less happy ending to this smug fable, an ending red in tooth and claw, must have suggested itself to all but the most credulous Britons. Charles Metcalfe, for example, thought that a sudden insurrection could quickly dispel "the impression of our invincibility," "unite all India," and make "short work" of white supremacy. "Empires grow old, decay and perish," he wrote. Britain's Indian empire had reached "premature old age" and its life could only be prolonged with care.[155] So for more than two decades after the Vellore Mutiny, the Raj was largely run according to Wellesley's formula, as a despotism tempered by paternalism. Its rulers combined the old ruthlessness of Warren Hastings and the new sense of responsibility introduced by Cornwallis. And they tried to instil the faith of Wellesley, who had said that India must be governed not as an empire "of which the tenure is as uncertain as the original conquest and successive extension were extraordinary; it must be considered as a sacred trust, and a permanent possession."[156] This involved taking occasional savage reprisals (for example, shooting men from guns) and invariable repressive measures, such as controlling the Indian press, limiting freedom of movement and subordinating the rule of law to the convenience of the administration. It also involved territorial expansion, mostly at the expense of the Marathas in the north and west.

Once again official plunder, in the shape of tax receipts, paid for the conquest. Taxation, which raised £18 million a year at this time (a third of the peacetime revenue of Britain itself), was much more important than trade. Indeed, before John Company lost its commercial monopoly in 1813, India was said to be about as valuable a trading partner to Britain as Jersey, though the Company was on the way to creating what has been called the world's first "narco-military" empire.[157] It did so through a new triangular trade: Indian opium sold to China covered the cost of tea imports to Britain, which found a market in India for textiles and other products of the industrial revolution. Meanwhile, a third of the Indian government's expenditure was devoted to the military, which gave Britain a priceless possession—a free foreign legion. India truly was "an English barrack in the Oriental seas."[158] The seas were entirely dominated by the Royal Navy after Nelson's victory at Trafalgar in 1805, though American privateers administered a few shocks. And during the Pax Britannica, the century of peace that followed Waterloo, this marine enterprise, described as "the first true multinational manufacturing corporation,"[159] was rightly judged to be John Bull's supreme weapon of war. But the power of his whale should not obscure the strength of his elephant. India contained a standing army that was financially independent of the parliament at Westminster. It consisted of 200,000 men: the same number as made up the twenty-five legions with which Marcus Aurelius defended the whole Roman Empire; a match for most contemporary European regular armies; thirty times larger than the force that the United States mustered to fight Britain in the war of 1812; but only a third of the size of Napoleon's Grand Army which invaded Russia in the same year. Despite concerns about losing caste by travelling across the ocean, sepoys were first sent to fight abroad (in Sumatra) as early as 1789. They were subsequently deployed in the Moluccas (1795), Egypt (1800), Macao (1808), Mauritius (1809) and Java (1811). Indeed they continued to augment Britain's military might, notably during the two world wars, until India achieved independence.

Preoccupied by the titanic struggle against the French Empire, the British naturally thought in terms of the mailed fist and the sinews of war. Anyway, military force seemed suited to a country which was, according to James Mill's influential *History of India* (1818), cursed from end to end by Asiatic barbarism and entirely unfit for self-determination. Yet some Governors-General preferred conciliation to coercion as a means of bestowing on India what Harriet Martineau called "the blessing of our rule."[160] If this cant phrase does not hide the cruelty, selfishness and ineptitude of that rule nor should it conceal its justice, efficiency and benevolence. In many ways the British Raj was preferable to the Indian rajah. At least one rajah agreed, the liberal-minded theologian Ram Mohun Roy. He even hoped that India would "for an unlimited period enjoy union with England, and the advantage of her enlightened Government."[161] But he did not give the Raj much more than half a century, the same sort of timescale as that contemplated by Thomas Munro, who also talked of its being "maintained permanently."[162] Roy concurred with many of its other leading figures who said "openly that English supremacy cannot be eternal, and that it is a duty to humanity to prepare India to govern herself."[163] Britain's civilising mission must have a finite goal and a positive outcome. So Roy favoured cooperation with those "far-seeing Englishmen" (many of them actually Scotsmen or Irishmen) who were promoting education and institutions in India to equip "the natives ultimately to take the government of their own country into their own hands."[164] Self-rule in India could no more be stopped in the long run than self-rule in Britain. Roy himself supported the extension of the British franchise so enthusiastically that he threatened to renounce his allegiance to the Empire if the Reform Bill of 1832 were not passed. Thus, even while the Raj grew as an armed autocracy, a microscopic strain of libertarian democracy was germinating within its frame. As a modern scholar writes, the Empire was "born with the genetic faults that would bury it."[165]

Whatever India's future, its crucial importance as Britain's Asiatic auxiliary was established by the end of the Napoleonic Wars. Oddly enough, this did not mean that the subcontinent captured the British imagination. London clubmen yawned at stories of tiger-hunting and pig-sticking. The India bore became a stock figure of fun in English life and literature. The vast majority of Englishmen neither knew nor cared about the difference between "commissioners and chilumchees [metal basins], magistrates and punkah-wallahs [fan-pullers], Indian colonels and brandy pawnees [brandies and water]."[166] Even at Westminster, it was said, the outcome of a by-election in Falmouth aroused more interest than the fate of the Raj. "Parliament despises India," wrote Mountstuart Elphinstone, "and would never dream of quarrelling with a Ministry about a few millions of black rascals who have no votes."[167] On the other hand, the value of the Empire's garrison state was beyond doubt. India was the most imperial element in John Bull's haphazard miscellany of overseas dominions, an empire within an empire.

Brobdingnag in thrall to Lilliput, the subcontinent confirmed Britain's position as a global power. It conferred unique prestige on the ruling race. It provided jobs for suitably qualified young men—in 1809 Haileybury was founded to educate them, though students thought the College "rather a farce as far as learning was concerned."[168] According to an adage fashioned in the mid-eighteenth century and repeated for two hundred years, the loss of India would fatally tarnish England's glory. It would reduce her to the status of a second-rate nation, on a par, it was sometimes said, with Belgium. It would render her "insignificant in the eyes of Europe and the world."[169] The danger of losing India, whether through internal revolt or external invasion, or perhaps as the result of a lily-livered abdication of imperial responsibilities, increasingly obsessed the British. As a result the so-called "defence" of the Raj became a matter of throwing out new ramparts and parapets, of occupying distant bastions and barbicans. Critics such as James Mill said that by extending its territory Britain was merely making new enemies. But the drive to safeguard India acquired a juggernaut momentum. And there seemed no limit to how far it could go. Disraeli would say that those who harped on threats to India consulted only small-scale maps (which was inevitable, as it happened, since there were as yet no large-scale maps of Central Asia). Lord Salisbury complained about soldiers who were intent on "garrisoning the Moon in order to protect us from Mars."[170]

So the enormous imperial advances made as the struggle with France reached its climax during the decades after the loss of the American colonies were largely intended to protect India as a vital source of Britain's strength. In response to John Company's oft-repeated axiom that the Cape of Good Hope was "the Gibraltar of India,"[171] Britain finally annexed it from the Dutch in 1806. The Mediterranean was another key route to be guarded—by means of "insular aggrandisement."[172] Malta, which Nelson thought "a most important outwork of India,"[173] was occupied in 1800. Added to it were Corfu, the Ionian Isles and Sicily, which its temporary dictator, the former Governor of Madras Lord William Bentinck, dreamed of making "the Queen of our Colonies."[174] The Royal Navy's influence spilled over the shores, from the Ottoman Empire to Tripoli, where the British Consul-General was the power behind the Pasha. Trade followed the flag and the Mediterranean virtually became Britain's *mare nostrum*. Britannia also ruled the Indian Ocean, securing the French naval base of Mauritius (1810) and the Dutch trading station of Ceylon. The latter island was finally quelled by 1818, after a war of horrific brutality: the King of Kandy sent one group of Britons back to Colombo with their severed ears, noses and hands tied around their necks, an atrocity which was amply repaid in kind. The main prize was Ceylon's superb harbour of Trincomalee, which looked like a tropical Lake Windermere and had a unique capacity to be "the grand emporium of Oriental commerce, the Gibraltar of India [another one], and the arsenal of the East."[175]

The only haven to equal it within striking distance of the Coromandel Coast was Singapore. Sir Stamford Raffles, who had risen from humble beginnings in the service of the East India Company to become master of Java in 1811, quickly discerned Singapore's unique potential. Raffles described himself as "meek as a maiden" but "insatiable in ambition,"[176] and his main ambition was to destroy the Dutch Empire on India's south-eastern flank. It was brutal and corrupt, he maintained (not without reason), whereas the extension of British influence served "the cause of humanity." As it happened Raffles himself was surprisingly indulgent towards Malay tribal customs that were by no means humane. The "Battas are not bad people," he wrote, "notwithstanding they eat each other." With apparent relish he reported that they sometimes grilled human flesh and sometimes devoured it raw, that they regarded the palms of the hands and the soles of the feet as "the delicacies of epicures," that they bottled the brains of their victims "for the purposes of witchcraft," and that he himself was forming a collection of the skulls of people who had been eaten.[177] Nevertheless, Raffles saw himself as an agent of civilisation. He treated his subjects as a family of which he was head or feudal overlord: "The Chiefs are my barons bold, and the people are their vassals." After 1815, however, Britain came to terms with the Dutch and returned Java. Simultaneously, for financial reasons, the East India Company drew in its horns. Raffles concluded that the only way to prevent the Dutch from regaining their old supremacy was to acquire Singapore, which he did (with the support of the Governor-General of India, Lord Minto) in 1819. Raffles had a vision that the little fishing village could become the crossroads of Asia, commanding the sea lanes between Europe and the Far East and opening up trade on an unparalleled scale. "I see no reason why China may not be, in great measure, clothed from England," he declared.[178] Singapore could be both a grand commercial *"entrepôt"* and a political *"fulcrum . . . what Malta* is in the West."[179] It became the key link, attached to others such as Penang and Malacca, in a chain fence protecting India. Moreover, diplomatic and commercial agreements from the Persian Gulf to the South China Sea provided the subcontinent with buttresses and bulwarks on an oceanic scale.

Wider still and wider were its boundaries set. Captain James Cook's voyages of exploration (1768–79) were also voyages of exploitation. Of course, his geographical and medical discoveries (notably the defeat of scurvy) were wonderful achievements, for which he was portrayed as the saint with the sextant. He was also made a Fellow of the Royal Society—an accolade, said the President at the presentation, equivalent to Rome's "civic crown."[180] But a major aim of Cook's odysseys was to steal a strategic and commercial march on Britain's European and American rivals in the Pacific. And one result of its being opened up was that European diseases killed over three-quarters of its population. Australia, furthermore, did not become a penal colony in 1788 just because America was no longer available as a dumping ground for felons. In the words of the Secretary of State, Lord Sydney, it would also "be a means of preventing the emigration of Our European Neighbours to that Quarter, which might be attended with infinite prejudice to the Company's affairs." Thus convicts would serve the Empire by deterring the French, outflanking the Dutch, providing naval supplies and strengthening the "strategic outliers about India."[181] In other words, Britain was "more interested in controlling Australian seas than Australian land,"[182] though the port of Sydney, named after the minister responsible for the settlement, might become a staging post on the trade route to China. Even the New World was called in to augment the security of India. Whereas America's motive for declaring war in 1812 was to protect its trading and shipping interests against the Royal Navy, which was blockading Napoleonic Europe, Britain defended Canada not only for its own sake but in order to preserve the éclat of empire. As Lord Elgin later said of the threat to Canada from the south: "Let the Yankees get possession of British North America with the prestige of superior generalship—who can say how soon they may dispute with you the Empire of India and of the Seas?"[183]

Expansion northwards did not interest Americans nearly as much as going west, stretching their own dominion to the Pacific. But the war of 1812 showed that they were already a formidable Atlantic power. And the Monroe Doctrine, promulgated in 1823, was not just a warning that European countries should keep out of North and South America: it was a declaration that the United States had imperial aspirations in both hemispheres. Considering the might of the Royal Navy, the British government regarded President Monroe's pronouncement as a rhetorical impertinence. Anyway Britain had no intention of colonising Latin America, aiming only to monopolise its trade. As the Foreign Secretary George Canning said in 1824, "Spanish America is free; and if we do not mismanage our matters sadly, she is English."[184] The idea that commercial penetration could secure political influence without the trouble and expense of imperial occupation and administration increasingly attracted leaders of the first industrial nation. The benefits of freer trade were already apparent in Britain's rapprochement with the United States, which was taking up to 40 per cent of its exports (and 80 per cent of its emigrants) by the 1840s.

What is more, the Great Republic, with its democratic institutions and its libertarian traditions, provided a model of how Britain's colonies of settlement could evolve. If India might expect to be self-governing inside a century, Canada might anticipate independence within decades. If mankind really did progress from east to west, as Thoreau said, Australia could eventually strike off its shackles. Its pioneers were certainly self-confident. In 1803 the British attempted to plant a penal colony near modern Melbourne, on the strategic Bass Strait. Enduring furnace heat, swarms of biting flies, near-starvation and near-mutiny, the tiny community of convicts and guards clung to the barren shore for only a few months before sailing to less inhospitable Tasmania. Yet during that time Lieutenant James Tuckey had a vision of how outcasts were building in Australia an empire which would supersede those now in the ascendant but doomed to decline and fall. "I beheld a second Rome rising from a coalition of banditti. I beheld it giving laws to the world, and superlative in arms and in arts, looking down with proud superiority upon the barbarous nations of the northern hemisphere."[185]

3

Exempt from the Disaster of Caste

Australia, Canada and New Zealand

Fifteen years after the Australian penal settlement had been established in 1788, and just as Tuckey was indulging in his fantasy, Sydney Smith also imagined a mighty future for the so-called "Colony of Disgracefuls." The time might come, he wrote, "when some Botany Bay Tacitus shall record the crimes of an emperor lineally descended from a London pick-pocket, or paint the valour with which he has led his New Hollanders* into the heart of China." As it happened the first Governor of New South Wales, Captain Arthur Phillip, did have imperial dreams. But "the Romulus of the Southern Pole,"¹ as Smith whimsically dubbed him, did "not wish convicts to lay the foundations of an empire." Phillip, a naval officer appointed to lead the first fleet (or sent to Botany Bay, his critics said, because he so nagged ministers for preferment), envisaged that felons would merely provide the sinew strength to tame the wilderness. They would not be slaves, said Phillip, because "there can be no slavery in a free land." But the convicts should be separated from the garrison and from free settlers who might later emigrate to Australia. They should also be subjected to strict discipline and severe punishment. Phillip, a thin-faced man with a large bald cranium and a missing front tooth (which may have endeared him to Aboriginal men, who ritually knocked out one of their own teeth), was a relatively benevolent despot. Yet he proposed to hand over anyone found guilty of murder or sodomy to the cannibals of New Zealand "and let them eat him."² Within two months of arrival he approved the execution of a youth aged seventeen for stealing property worth five shillings. As for an Irishman who protested "disrespectfully" that the papers setting the expiry date of his sentence had been left in England, he was given six hundred lashes and clapped in irons for six months.³ Only by coercing and deterring, Phillip believed, could his

---

*New Holland was synonymous with Australia (a name not officially sanctioned until 1817) for almost a century. Similarly Sydney was originally called Port Jackson and Tasmania was known as Van Diemen's Land until 1853. For convenience their modern names are used here, though the generic term for the settlement, Botany Bay, is also employed.

criminal community of some 750 souls (among them about 190 women and 18 children) be forged into an engine of empire.

Initially some effort had been made to select for transportation convicts who were "ingenious in every branch of English manufacture."[4] But this had been abandoned because of sheer weight of numbers—the mass of depraved and deprived humanity caged on the Thames threatened to turn their rotting prison hulks into literal as well as moral plague spots. In the event most of the convicts in the first fleet were young labourers who had committed minor offences, generally theft. Few of the "yokels" and fewer of the "townies" (to employ their own distinction) were qualified to be pioneers. None had any idea, as they sailed up the coast from Botany Bay, the site recommended by Captain Cook but found to be unsuitable, what it would take to establish a colony in the Antipodes. But hearts lifted as their stinking transports, three-masted, square-rigged, flat-sided, deep-bottomed vessels crammed with plants, seeds and animals like so many Noah's arks, passed through the "granite gates" of Sydney Harbour and entered a blue "paradise of waters."[5] Here, said Phillip, amid a labyrinth of islands, capes and bays, was the finest harbour in the world. It was, moreover, surrounded by meadows, crags and woods, among which the flight of green parakeets and pink cockatoos made the vista "appear like an enchantment."[6] In fancy one sailor even translated the rocky eminences into pavilions and palaces: he discerned "charming seats, superb buildings and grand ruins of stately edifices."[7] But it was a mirage of bliss. For the convicts were about to experience worse "hardships," one of them wrote, than any described in "the Crusoe-like adventures I ever read."[8]

At Sydney Cove, where disembarkation commenced on 27 January 1788, European order made its initial mark on Antipodean nature. For "the first time since the creation," wrote the implacable Judge Advocate, David Collins, the silence was broken by the rude sound of the labourer's axe. The stillness of the ages gave way to the "busy hum" of the land's "new possessors."[9] They cleared the ground and landed stores and livestock. They began work on a sawpit, a cookhouse and a blacksmith's forge. They laid out encampments and erected Phillip's portable canvas house, which had cost £125 and leaked. On 6 February the female felons came ashore and the males were given an extra ration of grog to celebrate. Efforts had been made to keep the sexes apart during the voyage since convict ships were reputed to be floating brothels. But sailors subscribed to the Georgian view that involuntary chastity induced gout and, as a recent chronicler says, in some vessels they had taken no risks.[10] Now, with the coupling of whore and rogue (as one convict put it), began the first white orgy to take place under the Southern Cross. The "scene of debauchery and riot" acquired a still more Dionysian character when it was overtaken by "the most violent storm of lightning, thunder and rain."[11] Felons shook their fists at the elements and cursed the terms of their captivity. Doubtless all this was a natural outburst of passion. But such defiance was also an incipient challenge to imperial authority, a primal cry of freedom inside a continental oubliette. The following day all (save nine absentees) assembled in a clearing to hear the Governor's supremacy proclaimed. Flags flew, the Marine band played and Phillip was formally invested with dominion over the eastern half of Australia and adjacent Pacific islands. His commission gave him a "plenitude of power,"[12] unlimited by an advisory council. Addressing his charges, the Governor promised to reward industry and virtue and to punish indolence and vice. The Marines fired volleys, toasts were drunk, and Phillip entertained senior officers to a cold collation.

The convicts, many suffering from scurvy, proved intractable. Despite having "experienced every indulgence from the Governor, whose humanity & attention to them whilst at sea & since our arrival here entitles him to their esteem as their best friend," they remained in general, wrote Lieutenant David Blackburn, "a set of hardened wretches."[13] They were reluctant to work. Some tried to escape, venturing into the bush (China was rumoured to be only one hundred miles away) or seeking passage on the two vessels of the French explorer La Pérouse which, to the amazement of the British, had coincided with them at Botany Bay. Others reverted to crime, ranging from petty larceny to serial murder. Incorrigible villains, as Governor Phillip called them, often made light of the heavy penalties. They displayed their flogging scars like war medals and one convict sentenced to death vowed to "create a laugh" by playing "some trick upon the executioner."[14] At home there was gloom, well expressed by William Cowper in a letter to John Newton: "We mourn for the mismanagement at Botany Bay, and foresee the issue. The Romans were, in their origin, banditti; and if they became in time masters of the world, it was not by drinking grog, and allowing themselves in all sorts of licentiousness."[15]

In Australia none seemed to share Phillip's bright vision that Australia could become "the Empire of the East." On the contrary, most were soon as disillusioned as the choleric Marine commander, Major Robert Ross. This was the worst country in the world, he said, "so hateful as only to merit execration and curses."[16] Far from offering a "virgin mould"[17] more fertile than the exhausted tilth of Europe, as one London journal had hoped, the soil was barren and food was scarce. The vegetation was sparse and unprepossessing: gum trees rotted and warped, while the ironwoods blunted steel.

The natives, who wore bones in their noses, fish oil on their naked bodies and dog teeth or lobster claws in their grizzled hair, were "to all appearance the lowest in Rank among the Human Race."[18] The animals were freakish, rivers flowed backwards, the seasons were topsy-turvy and all "nature is reversed."[19]

Europeans were strangers in a strange land. They wondered at the scentless flowers and the songless birds. They puzzled over the bronzed Sydney earth, which sustained huge myrtle, mimosa and eucalyptus trees but little undergrowth. What did flourish—wild celery, spinach, samphire, fig—seemed familiar; but "whole tribes of plants"[20] proved utterly alien, botanical nonpareils best sent for classification at Kew. Odder still were the fauna: black swans, flying foxes and fish that walked on land. There were weird antediluvian creatures which flouted every norm. The koala was not a bear, more a marsupial sloth. The emu was a flightless bird without a gizzard. The wombat resembled a rodent. The spines on the porcupine anteater (echidna) were really fur and it laid eggs like a bird, hatching them in its pouch. The prize sport in this outlandish bestiary was the platypus, with its mole body and beaver tail, its duck bill and webbed feet (the back ones also equipped with claws and poisonous spurs), to say nothing of its two penises (neither used for urination). The emblematic prodigy, of course, was the kangaroo. Everyone marvelled at this shy herbivore with its spring-heeled, twenty-foot leaps, the mouse-like joey in its pouch and its testicles "placed contrary to the usual order of nature."[21] For Britons, who were soon paying a shilling a head to view a live kangaroo, transported across the ocean and caged in London's Haymarket, this creature typified the anomaly that was Australia. Fantastic conceits were woven about the land that spawned it. And the kangaroo itself was variously categorised as a "divine mistake"[22] and a missing link in the great chain of being.

Scarcely to be distinguished from the wild animals, in the eyes of many Europeans, were the Aboriginal people. Captain Cook had deemed the natives happy because they possessed everything they needed and were free from the artificial wants of civilisation. Their world was all in all, so much so that when the 368-ton *Endeavour* had sailed into Botany Bay in 1770 the natives in their bark canoes simply ignored it. They were equally incurious about the white settlers led by Governor Phillip. He went out of his way to befriend them but these hunter-gatherers were unmoved by blandishments, indifferent to gifts, nonchalant about clothes (though amused by hats). They were anxious only that the visitors should "go away," as indicated by the frequent incantation "Warra, warra, warra."[23] Cook might have seen in this stubborn self-sufficiency the noble savage's commitment to the simple life. A generation later, Marine Captain Watkin Tench scorned philosophers who exalted "a state of nature over a state of civilisation." Far from enjoying Elysian felicities, the Aborigines were degraded by the nasty, brutish circumstances of their short lives. Paradoxically, though, Tench liked and admired them for their many virtues, notably courage, "humanity and generosity." Among the women, often the victims of male cruelty (though both sexes were horrified by the alien punishment of flogging), he found "innocence, softness and modesty." Furthermore, he acknowledged that Aboriginal attacks on Europeans were mostly a response to the "unprovoked outrages" of the more vicious convicts. There was truth in all these observations. But the crucial fact was that the whites had a fatal impact on the blacks. They invaded the sacred sites and the ancestral hunting and fishing grounds of the natives, destroying the essentials of their way of life. They also infected the Aborigines with smallpox, which killed perhaps half their number in the area around Sydney. The community that remained became dependent on the settlers, who prostituted its women and demoralised its men—they were sometimes encouraged to fight each other for buckets of rum. In short, the intruders began to assault the environment and to turn the Aboriginal world upside down. Nothing corrupted "savages" more effectively than "civilisation."

The European community, clinging to the rim of the continent like a clutch of limpets, was itself lucky to survive the first few years. It dwelt in a "few hundred hovels built of twigs and mud."[24] It was slow to become self-sufficient in food, despite the cultivation of more fertile ground a few miles inland at Parramatta. Meanwhile supplies from England failed to arrive. Rations were cut and there was little to eat except salt beef or pork, known as "mahogany," which shrank almost to nothing when cooked, and rice, every grain of which "was a moving body from the inhabitants lodged within it." By 1790, Tench noted, famine was "approaching with gigantic strides."[25] Men sold their convict garb, blue kersey jackets and raven pantaloons, to buy bread and worked as naked as the Aborigines; women traded sex for sustenance; some felons died of starvation. The advent of the second fleet, in June, scarcely improved matters. After a voyage which made the Middle Passage seem "merciful,"[26] it disgorged a convict cargo that was itself in desperate straits. Unlike slaves, these prisoners were worth nothing on delivery, so the owners and masters of the ships that transported them had "no interest in their preservation." On the contrary, "the dead were more profitable," they calculated, "than the living."[27] Their provisions could be saved and sold on arrival, as the Captain of the *Neptune* demonstrated. He had kept his five hundred convicts, who were shackled in solid slave irons which made movement a torture, on such short commons that about 170 died during the voyage. Survivors had stolen swill from the hogs, taken "chews of tobacco from the mouths of men that lay dead on deck,"[28] and concealed the fact that they were chained to corpses (until the stench gave them away) in order to get an extra allowance of victuals.

Some of those who lasted the course expired as they were brought ashore from their floating Devil's Island. Of the rest, living skeletons covered "with their own nastiness, their heads, bodies, clothes, blankets, all full of filth and lice,"[29] many could barely stand and few were fit to earn their keep. Governor Phillip accused commanders of the second fleet of "murdering"[30] their charges and he feared that the influx of such "helpless wretches" as remained would prove an intolerable burden to the colony. But by the time he returned home in 1792 more aid had arrived, the seeds of prosperity were beginning to germinate and a number of women, previously too debilitated to conceive, bore children. Everyone extolled the climate, if not the fruitful earth, and some now praised the exotic scenery. Among the "mangrove avenues" and "picturesque rocks" on the way to Parramatta, for example,

> Arcadian shades or classic bowers present themselves at every winding to the ravished eye. Overhead the most grotesque foliage yields a shade, where cooling zephyrs breathe every perfume . . . In short, were the benefits equal to the specious external, this country need hardly give place to any other on earth.[31]

The benefits accrued slowly and unevenly. Food supplies remained precarious for another twenty years, though the exploitation of nature and humanity became more ruthless. If every prospect pleased, the conduct of man became increasingly vile.

Phillip's successors were not of his calibre and they permitted officers of the New South Wales Corps to crack the whip. This force was raised to take over from the Marines, who refused to be warders. It consisted of soldiers and soldiers of fortune who were the dregs of their profession. Among them was a set of the "most atrocious characters," one Governor wrote, "superior in every species of infamy to the most expert in wickedness among the convicts."[32] Nevertheless, they gained legal powers. They were given land as well as seed, tools and convict workers. They were also encouraged to engage in trade. The aim was to spur on private enterprise in the public interest and to some extent it succeeded. But officers acquired commercial rights and established monopolies which earned them huge profits, sometimes more than 1,000 per cent. In particular the "Rum Corps," as it was aptly called, controlled the liquor traffic. Indeed, its officers turned rum into a currency, paying in gallons and stimulating an insatiable thirst for wealth. They aggravated what one Governor called the "passion for ardent spirits" that prevailed among all classes.[33] Antipodean society was said to consist of "those who sold rum and those who drank it."[34] In 1808 the officers even staged a rebellion against Governor William Bligh (survivor of the more famous mutiny on the *Bounty* and known in Sydney as Caligula), who had condemned the ruinous rum monopoly. Thus for almost two decades the Corps established an oligarchy in New South Wales, against which Governors struggled in vain. The military shaped and ordered society. High in the hierarchy came free settlers, who began to trickle in during the 1790s and were also given incentives—free land and labour. At the bottom were the convicts who, despite Phillip's good intentions, were virtual slaves.

There were, though, degrees of slavery. A convict assigned to work for a settler might fall into good hands. But "in ninety-nine cases out of a hundred," the *Sydney Gazette* reported, his employer would be a blockhead or a despot,

> cursing and abusing, and getting him flogged for no reasonable cause . . . He may be harassed to very death. He may be worked like a horse and fed like a chameleon. The master, though not invested by law with uncontrolled power, has yet great authority which may be abused in a thousand ways precluding redress.[35]

More hardened felons, fit for "double irons and single rations," were consigned to chain gangs, on which buggery was as inescapable as brutality. Irishmen, who made up a quarter of the convict population by 1801 and were detested as rebels and idolators, received especially rough treatment. Joseph Holt, leader of the revolt of the United Irishmen in Wicklow in 1798, compared the persecutors of his countrymen to "human tigers, who tortured and killed those within their power, according to the caprice of the moment." Like others convicted of additional crimes or deemed so vicious that they would only submit to terror, Holt was banished to one of the subordinate penal colonies which spread like a cancer across the face of the southern ocean. Norfolk Island, a thousand miles east of Sydney, had once been hailed as a vegetable "paradise."[36] Holt described it as "the dwelling place of devils in human shape, the refuse of Botany Bay, the doubly damned."

Its commandant, when he arrived, was Major Joseph Foveaux, whom Holt called an iron-fanged ogre worse than "the offspring of the Patagonians, that eat human flesh and drink blood."[37] It was Foveaux's sadistic delight to flay men alive and he found any excuse, or none, to hand out "feelers"—two hundred strokes of the cat. According to one flagellator, fifty strokes left a man's back resembling "a mass of bullock's liver,"[38] while two hundred exposed his shoulder blades "like two ivory polished horns."[39] Foveaux also enjoyed subjecting females to the scourge. But he would remit half their "Botany Bay dozen" (or twenty-five lashes) if they agreed to take their punishment unclothed. Women, immured in vice yet cursed for being "instruments of corruption,"[40] naturally occupied the first circle of this Pacific inferno. They were bought and sold for rum, passed from hand to hand and, under Foveaux's dispensation, forced to perform nude corybantics in the soldiers' barracks. They were the slaves of slaves.

Yet the system was less apt to break the convict spirit than to provoke implacable resistance. There were even instances of female insubordination, the most notorious of which took place in front of the Governor of Tasmania, Sir John Franklin, at the Hobart House of Correction. When the Rev. William Bedford began preaching to three hundred women, they all "turned round and at one impulse pulled up their clothes showing their naked posteriors which they simultaneously smacked with their hands making a loud and not very musical noise." At this spectacular piece of cheek, so to say, the Governor's aide laughed, the Governor's wife "pretended to faint" and the Governor himself raised his hands to heaven and concluded that most female convicts were prostitutes "in whose bosoms every spark of shame has perhaps long been extinguished."[41] Their treatment did not improve as a result and they were "often reduced to government-subsidized whoredom in assignment." The penal satellite of Tasmania was in some ways even more of a purgatory than Norfolk Island, especially under its most dictatorial governor, Franklin's predecessor, Sir George Arthur. He was a granite-faced Evangelical who established "the closest thing to a totalitarian society," wrote Robert Hughes, "that would ever exist within the British Empire."[42] He worked assiduously "to render transportation a painful punishment, and to make the convict feel his position to be a disagreeable and degraded one." Arthur supervised and regulated everything minutely, laying down seven levels of punishment. The fifth was the chain gang, whose torment continued from sunset to sunrise when batches of between twenty and thirty men were locked up in boxes "in which the whole number can neither stand upright nor sit down at the same time."[43] The seventh was double exile in hellish outstations such as Macquarie Harbour or Port Arthur on the Tasman peninsula, which was guarded by a line of ferocious dogs. Convicts stopped at nothing to escape. In the process some were driven to murder and cannibalism.

During Arthur's administration, moreover, the last serious resistance of the Tasmanian Aborigines was crushed. By now the victims of burgeoning racial prejudice against the "ignoble savage," they were destroyed like vermin. Sometimes they were hunted for sport and used for dog meat. "One European had a pickle tub of black men's ears, whom he had shot; another had the wife of a black carrying round her neck with a string the head of her own murdered husband, killed while defending his own pasture grounds." However, concluded the Hobart official who chronicled these atrocities against the "seven thousand" original inhabitants, "probably it is as well that they have, by the order of the Great Disposer of Events, given way to the white man in Tasmania, because it is too clear that they would never assimilate."[44] Seldom has the guilt of man been so smugly attributed to the will of God. And science would soon rival religion in supplying, through its evolutionary "laws," a specious justification for crimes against races deemed unfit to survive. Charles Darwin himself, while noting the "train of evil" involved, said that the colony now enjoyed "the great advantage of being free from a native population."[45] Actually some Aborigines did survive on nearby islands. But the myth of their complete extermination was a useful one. It offered a final solution to an awkward problem. And it raised "the value of Tasmanian skulls"[46] on the curio market. In any event, what took place in Tasmania amounted to "the only true genocide in English colonial history."[47] It confirmed the fact that Australia's penal archipelago was far more savage than the main settlement of New South Wales. Convicts sentenced to death on Norfolk Island actually thanked God that they would be delivered from further agony and sometimes "men committed murder in order to be sent to Sydney . . . with the certainty of being hanged." Noting this fact in 1837, Sir William Molesworth's parliamentary committee condemned the whole system of transportation and recommended instead free emigration. In Molesworth's words, Britain had emptied its "vast and fomenting masses" of moral filth into Antipodean pest-houses, which thus "stank in the nostrils of mankind."[48] The penitentiary should now become a colony.

In fact this transformation had been going on for some time, perhaps ever since 1791 when Governor Phillip gave selected convicts land grants and implored the British government to send out "a few honest, intelligent settlers."[49] But it was pushed forward by Lachlan Macquarie, who succeeded Bligh in 1810 and remained Governor until 1821. A simple Scottish soldier with a face like a claymore, Macquarie described himself as an "awkward, rusticated, Jungle-Wallah."⁵⁰ He had served in America, Jamaica and India, twice fighting against Tipu Sultan and acquiring from the final victory at Seringapatam seventeen ruby rings, worth £1,300. In Australia Macquarie found a community that was "barely emerging from infantile imbecility" and its development was impaired after the Napoleonic Wars by unprecedentedly large "annual importations . . . from Newgate, and other similar nurseries."⁵¹ Macquarie had no doubt that felons should be duly punished and, when provoked, he could even subject free settlers (illegally) to the lash. Sydney Smith deplored Macquarie's "Asiatic and satrapical proceedings."⁵² Others condemned an "absolutism"⁵³ compounded by gullibility, irritability and vanity. Macquarie commended Foveaux, was cordial only to those who agreed with him, and attached his name to an inordinate number of natural and man-made objects. But the colony's self-appointed poet laureate, Michael Massey Robinson, hailed Macquarie as an Augustus who was turning Sydney into "a second Rome."⁵⁴ And Macquarie certainly employed his power to achieve enormous improvements. He created a police force, constructed roads, erected public buildings, extended settlements, explored new territory and even tried to protect the natives. Under his aegis the wool trade began to flourish, sheep vastly outnumbering black sheep. Whalers and sealers benefited the economy (at the expense of the ecology, as even contemporaries lamented). Provisions were plentiful and if people grumbled about "sour *smiggins* (cold meat hash)" they were soon reminded of the hungry years when many an "ill-fated cat" was sent virtually "mewing down their throats."

Despite its noxious slums, Sydney was becoming a dignified metropolis. A square mile inhabited by ten thousand people, it was full of handsome residences and smart shops, neat cottages and extensive warehouses. Along its broad streets (not yet paved or lighted) walked fashionably dressed women as well as convicts in arrowed motley and naked Aborigines, known as "dingy dandies," wearing their trousers around their necks. Although the town awaited a theatre and a library, it contained churches, schools and civic amenities that would not have disgraced an English provincial city. America itself could not match such progress, wrote an enthusiastic English visitor, who was surprised to find "little crime"⁵⁵ in Australia. It was, and remained, a rough, tough frontier land, of course. It was a breeding ground for bushrangers and beachcombers, flotsam and jetsam that eventually polluted the entire Pacific. Australia's critics were candid. One called it "a sort of moral cloacina, debased, burglarious, brutified, larcenous and pickpocketous."⁵⁶ Another would describe its daughters as "dowdy hussies" and its sons as "lanky, lean, pasty-faced, blaspheming blackguards, drinking rum before breakfast, and living by cheating one another out of horses."[57] But Macquarie helped to civilise the country by accepting freed convicts as full citizens. Many of these "emancipists" were ambitious, productive and wealthy people, and the Governor promoted some to official positions. As the "champion of all meritorious persons who have been convicts," Macquarie tried to transform a province of "Satan's Kingdom"[58] (as the hellfire parson Samuel Marsden termed Australia) into a respectable part of Britain's Empire.

Only in a head-over-heels hemisphere, contemporaries carped, could vice be elevated into the position of virtue. Free settlers, known as "pure merinos," were outraged that ex-convicts, who still bore the stigma of bondage, should be treated as their equals. Nothing on earth, in the opinion of Marsden, could purge their sin. Many of Charles Dickens's contemporaries concurred, reckoning that a transported Artful Dodger would grow into a Magwitch rather than a Micawber. British ministers also had qualms about a policy which might diminish the "salutary terror"[59] of transportation. A punishment that ought to seem worse than death, said one Secretary of State for the Colonies, Edward Stanley, was being turned into a new lease of life. Moralists dismissed Macquarie's ambition to make Australia a Land of Promise as a dream. But they considered that the desire to make it a nation, cherished by colonial patriots such as W. C. Wentworth, was a nightmare. Think "what stuff this people will have been made of," exclaimed Archbishop Whately of Dublin, "and who is it that posterity will then curse for bringing this mildew on the social intercourse of the world?" Macquarie himself could not be blamed: he was an autocrat, not a democrat, and the idea of Australian independence was entirely alien to him. However, no emigrants lusted for liberty more than convicts and Governor Lachlan Macquarie encouraged them, once unshackled, to make the most of their emancipation.

By exporting a social problem, then, Britain created a colonial problem. Soon Australian delinquency seemed to be another version of American contumacy. As early as 1791 emancipists held a meeting to challenge the authority of Governor Phillip. By the end of Macquarie's time Australians were agitating for trial by jury, the rights of Englishmen and no taxation without representation. There was talk of an Australian Declaration of Independence, even a war of independence which "the United States of Australia" would fight in the Blue Mountains. Noting the spirit of Yankee revolt (to be exacerbated by the advent of more political prisoners, such as Chartists), the Supreme Court Judge Barron Field prophesied that Australia would "end in declaring itself a nation of freebooters and pirates."[60] Others made more optimistic forecasts. "Australia Felix" would arise, replace decaying empires and win, like Rome, immortal fame. Indeed, the convenient circumstance that the scum of the earth had "laid the foundations of the Eternal City" was mentioned so often that it became a cliché and a joke.[61] Nevertheless, by 1840, when convicts ceased to be transported to New South Wales (though the system survived in Western Australia until 1868), the colonies extending from the beachheads of Sydney, Brisbane, Hobart, Melbourne, Adelaide and Perth were making distinct progress towards self-government. It arrived at a gallop during the 1850s, when prospectors struck gold. The first response of the Governor of New South Wales was to conceal the discovery "or we shall all have our throats cut."[62] But the secret could not be kept and convicts as well as policemen joined in the rush. The Australian population tripled during the decade (to 1.1 million) and gold helped to pay for the separate elected assemblies which were established with Britain's approval, though federation had to wait until 1900.

For longer still Australians remained heavily reliant on, and fiercely loyal to, the mother country, unimaginably distant though it was—Charles Lamb said that writing to the Antipodes was like "writing for posterity."[63] Many emigrants, whatever their origins, aspired to create a down-under Britain. It would be socially hierarchical, culturally deferential and politically submissive. It would even be topographically imitative. In that arsy-versy landscape Barron Field rejoiced to find settlements which had become "so English . . . downs, meadows and streams in the flat—no side-scenes of eucalyptus."[64] But many other Australians took a radically different view of what was implied by their genesis and exodus. Emancipists tried to discard their origins with their chains, but insofar as the convict stain was indelible it denoted a passion for freedom. Large numbers of free settlers, who had supported a crusade for liberty in Britain during the era of reform, helped to create in Australia a "paradise of dissent."[65] Once new emigrants had landed they waxed mightily republican.[66] They no longer called gentlemen "Mr." or touched their hats to ladies. According to Dr. Thomas Arnold, headmaster of Rugby School, they became Jacobinical in the true sense of the term. They participated in a "culture of opposition"[67] spread around the globe by the French Revolution and epitomised by Victor Hugo's dictum, "Je suis contre."[68] By the mid-Victorian period the island continent was acquiring what it had hitherto lacked—a distinctive history, a comprehensive geography and a positive identity. Its people were beginning to espouse an Australian nationalism which would inevitably diverge from imperial patriotism. They were making a virtue of contrariness, even of bloody-mindedness, and looking forward to a golden age of independence.

If Australians found their passage towards self-government surprisingly easy, so did Canadians at much the same time; for throughout Britain's colonial history, even when enthusiasm for overseas expansion was at flood tide, there was always a strong countercurrent which threatened to erode the fabric of empire. During the 1830s, far from trying to hang on to the colonies at all costs, the political elite at Westminster was coming to the conclusion that they might as well leave the nest—preferably on more amicable terms than the South American fledglings of Spain and Portugal. As the Colonial Secretary Lord Grey later wrote to the Governor-General of Canada, "There begins to prevail in the House of Commons, and I am sorry to say in the highest quarters, an opinion (which I believe to be utterly erroneous) that we have no interest in preserving our colonies and ought to make no sacrifice for that purpose."[69] Among those who shared that erroneous opinion were both Peel and Gladstone. Even the permanent head of Grey's own department, Sir James Stephen, thought colonial emancipation both sensible and inevitable. Canada, for instance, would be "a good loss if parted with kindly and graciously."[70]

Nothing better symbolised these adverse sentiments, which require some explanation, than the Colonial Office itself. It was accommodated in 14 Downing Street, a large, dingy, ramshackle brick dwelling, built over an old sewer at the end of the prime ministerial cul-de-sac, which looked "less like a centre of State affairs than a decent lodging-house."[71] It became less decent during the Victorian age, when the furniture was sparse—an assortment of rickety chairs and old, baize-covered tables—and the fabric steadily decayed. Indeed, from the basement, so damp that it had to be pumped out twice a day, to the attic, which officials used illicitly as a fives court, this Hogarthian rookery was fundamentally unsound (and was condemned as such in 1839). The fives players were discovered because they shook the balconied house to its foundations—whereupon they took to darts, made from office pencils tipped with needles tied on by red tape and weighted with sealing wax. Paper was stored in the basement to prevent the building from collapse but it groaned and shuddered with the effort of standing upright. The Duke of Newcastle hoped it would "fall (for fall I believe it will) at night."[72] Actually, it was demolished in 1876. Meanwhile the staff, who numbered forty-eight by 1862, only worked in the afternoons. Appointed through jobbery, they regarded their posts as a kind of property. And often the confidential clerks as well as the lowly quill drivers lacked the most basic qualifications for their task: one recruit was given "a month's leave of absence that he may endeavour to learn to write."[73] Still, little effort was required in this "sleepy and humdrum office."[74] One man offered to bet that on a quiet day he could transact its entire business by himself, but nobody would take the wager. Another, Sir Henry Taylor, later "conducted his official correspondence from a convalescent home in Bournemouth."[75]

The rot started at the top. Colonial Secretaries were hard to find, frequently bored or incompetent (sometimes both), and they seldom stayed long in the department. Sir John Pakington's reluctant appointment in 1852 provoked ribaldry, not least when he allegedly expressed the hope that, wherever they were, the Virgin Islands were situated as far as possible from the Isle of Man. A predecessor, Sir George Murray, told parliament: "I have always supposed until this moment that to abstain from any extraordinary activity in the measures to be carried into effect with respect to the colonies was a merit rather than a defect." Even a diligent Colonial Secretary could hardly fulfil his far-flung responsibilities despite traversing the terraqueous globe, as Sir William Molesworth said in a famous philippic, like the Wandering Jew.

> For instance, one day the Colonial Secretary is in Ceylon, a financial and a religious reformer, promoting the interests of the coffee planter and casting discredit on the tooth and religion of Buddha; the next day he is in the West Indies, teaching the economical manufacture of sugar; or in Van Diemen's Land, striving to reform the fiends whom he has transported to that pandemonium. Now he is in Canada, discussing the Indemnity Bill and the war of races; anon he is at the Cape of Good Hope, dancing a war dance with Sir Harry Smith and his Kaffir subjects; or in New Zealand, an unsuccessful Lycurgus, coping with Honi Heki . . . or in Labuan, digging coal and warring with pirates . . . or in the Mauritius, building fortifications against a hostile population.[76]

The Colonial Office was only saved from complete chaos by a series of outstanding permanent under-secretaries.

Sir James Stephen (1836–47), for example, did much to shift his Tite Barnacles from the official practices satirised in Dickens's Circumlocution Office—the first title of *Little Dorrit* was *Nobody's Fault*. Wilberforce's nephew (and Virginia Woolf's grandfather), Stephen was imbued with a stern Evangelicalism. Being his child, said Stephen's daughter, was like being "brought up in a great cathedral."[77] His son Leslie, whom he reluctantly exposed to "the temptations and the impurities and the profaneness and the gluttony" of Eton,[78] called him "a living 'categorical imperative.'"[79] Stephen was neurotically abstemious, taking a biscuit and sherry for lunch, an egg for tea and nothing for dinner. He abhorred worldly vanities, despising "man milliner" colonial governors who were preoccupied with "coats and buttons and bows and all that sort of trumpery."[80] Red-haired, lofty-browed and sharp-nosed, Stephen had a mouth "compressed as if cut with a knife"[81] and he often appeared with a gashed face because even when shaving he refused to look at himself in a mirror. He shunned pleasure, abstaining from plays and balls. Finding his first cigar too agreeable, he never smoked another. Lonely, clever, modest and sardonic, Stephen laboured with unrelenting zeal, dictating so rapidly that shorthand writers could not keep up with him. He was equally voluble to visitors from the colonies, hiding his acute shyness behind a relentless monologue. Shutting his weak blue eyes and knitting his long clumsy fingers, he would talk without a pause, eventually rising, bowing, thanking them for their "valuable information,"[82] and ringing the bell to have them ushered out. Stephen was thus guilty of the conduct which he condemned in W. E. Gladstone, "the poorest and feeblest . . . of all my Downing St. Rulers," namely "bestowing his subtlety and fostering advice on [colonials], and treating them like children."[83] But even the resulting attacks on Stephen, to say nothing of the famous nicknames, "Mr. Oversecretary," "Mr. Mothercountry" and "King Stephen," were tributes to his dominance. Contemplating abuse heaped on him by *The Times,* agony to someone so sensitive that his wife called him a man "without a skin,"[84] he acknowledged to his journal that the Colonial Office was "in truth little more than a periphrasis for the noble JS and his bird of passage chief for the time being."[85]

Both Stephen's long-serving successors agreed with him that "the destiny of our colonies is independence."[86] The reason was simple: self-government was a natural adjunct of maturity. But the Colonial Office consensus also reflected the momentous change in the fortunes of John Bull, who could now stand alone without overseas appendages. Having become the globe's paramount power after the battles of Trafalgar and Waterloo, Britain was consolidating its position as the workshop of the world. The first and the only industrial nation, it reached the peak of economic pre-eminence in about 1860. Then Britons mined two-thirds of the world's coal and generated a third of its steam. British factories produced a third of all manufactured goods. This included half the iron and half the cotton cloth— it was said that the nation clanged like a huge smithy and that the sound of its mills was like the boom of the Atlantic. A third of the merchant ships plying the seven seas flew the Union Jack and they carried a fifth of all trade. London was the capital of an invisible financial empire, involving banking, insurance, brokerage and investment, which gave it a stake in almost every country on earth. This colossus no longer needed the protection of tariff barriers and colonial monopolies. It would be better served by free trade. Adam Smith's gospel gained new converts when preached by the charismatic Manchester radicals Richard Cobden and John Bright, who led a middle-class crusade against duties on grain imports during the hungry forties.

It triumphed when Sir Robert Peel's Tory government repealed the Corn Laws in 1846, just as the catastrophic Irish famine was raging. The repeal ushered in an era of cheap food for the masses and Cobden hailed it as the most important event since the coming of Christ. *Laissez-faire* was nothing less than "God's diplomacy."[87] It would accomplish a global revolution, Cobden thought, producing not only economic advance but peace on earth and goodwill towards men. Like every individual, every nation would cooperate through the global division of labour and harmonise competing interests in the open market. Free trade would act in the moral world, said Cobden, like "the principle of gravitation in the universe—drawing men together and thrusting aside the antagonism of race, and creed, and language."[88] Colonies, burdensome relics of the old coercive and corrupt order, would escape from Britain's planetary pull and describe new orbits of their own. They would thus, Cobden and his acolytes reckoned, follow the course of America, which in boom years took over a third of British exports. As one free trader said, "we have derived ten times more advantage from the United States"[89] since 1782 than before—and without drawbacks. Canada, by contrast, which cost the mother country £2.36 million in 1833–4, was a perpetual drain on Britain's exchequer.

Beside the U.S. behemoth, of course, British North America was a minnow in everything except geography. By 1860 the population of the United States (31 million) had overtaken that of the United Kingdom (29 million), while the provinces that would form the Canadian confederation contained 3.3 million people—fewer than the city of London. They took 3 per cent of Britain's exports and their own productions were not worth those of "the single island of Jamaica."[90] Canada's so-called "sedentary" militia could no more have resisted an American incursion than (as a Fredericton newspaperman put it) "a fish could walk up a beanpole."[91] The only way to create a compact and defensible border, a Canadian remarked, would be to tow Newfoundland and Prince Edward Island up the St. Lawrence and sink them in Lake Ontario. But was this "howling wilderness"[92] worth invading?

The radical journalist William Cobbett remarked that if the United States were to seize British North America it would be the act of a thief who should "steal a stone for the pleasure of carrying it about in his pocket." For the most part, indeed, the land was a frozen waste filled with monstrous natural barriers that separated one white community from another (the native peoples having largely succumbed to disease, drink and exploitation). The scattered outposts in British Columbia, on the prairies and around Hudson's Bay (where letters might arrive once a year) were virtually marooned. The impoverished maritime provinces were remote agglomerations of forest, swamp and rock. Their frugal inhabitants, mostly Scots and Irish, were reliant variously on lumbering, shipbuilding, fishing and farming, but they had to import food from Maine. These rugged territories were, to quote Cobbett's forthright opinion again, "the *offal* of North America; they are the head, the shins, the shanks and hoofs of that part of the world; while the UNITED STATES are the sir-loins, the well-covered and well-lined ribs, and the suet."[93]

Lower Canada was hemmed in by the Canadian Shield, that barren crust of pre-Cambrian magma contorted by volcanic fire and scarified by glacial ice which covered the north-eastern part of the continent. The French settlers hugged the St. Lawrence and its tributaries. Their strip farms stretched back from the riverside, where women could be seen beating clothes with large mallets in front of white-washed, rough-thatched, one-storey cottages dotted, every hundred yards or so, along the banks. The homespun-clad husbandmen carried on a subsistence agriculture which had hardly advanced from that of medieval Normandy. And during the worst years of the 1830s, years of "brass money and wooden shoes,"[94] some were reduced to eating their horses or leaving home to beg for bread. Only in the temperate, fertile crescent around Lake Ontario was there a degree of dynamism and prosperity. Upper Canada grew five-fold between 1830 and 1850 and its well-clothed farmers were "the most independent and contented people."[95] They had "food in abundance, including sugar from their own maple bush." And they drove their eight-spring wagons through improving townships such as Toronto, which had one gravelled street at the beginning of the 1830s, when it was transformed from wood to brick, and bore "a thoroughly Anglo-Saxon cast."[96] Nevertheless Lord Durham, who became Governor-General in 1838, contrasted the backwardness of the British province, most of which possessed "neither roads, post-offices, mills, schools or churches," with the "activity and progress" of the United States.[97] The difference was apparent to anyone who glanced at the opposite sides of the Niagara River. One was sleepy and stagnant, with a few stores, a tavern or two and natural landing places—the boundary of a colonial backwater. The other was a hive of industry, with new towns, ships, wharfs, warehouses, roads—the frontier of an empire in embryo. Visiting its nucleus, around Pittsburgh, in 1835, Richard Cobden forecast that "here will one day centre the civilisation, the wealth, the power of the entire world."[98] Yet while America was, for the most part, minding its own business, the Canadian provinces were a constant trouble to govern.

The main problem was a bone in the colonial throat which could neither be spat out nor swallowed. The French Canadians, 450,000 strong in 1837, could no more be absorbed into the British Empire than could the South African Boers, whom in some ways they resembled. Cut off from France, they were further isolated in Canada by race, religion and language—their speech was increasingly old-fashioned, harking back to the age of Louis XIV. They lived in a cultural cocoon, in a state of permanent alienation from their surroundings. They had no chance of escaping through a great trek into the interior. Nor could the British *"unfrenchify"* them, as some particularly wanted during the Napoleonic Wars, when "our arch-enemy is straining every nerve to Frenchify the universe."[99] And as Canadian solidarity weakened during the 1820s and 'thirties, in response to the fading of the American threat, so the huge influx of British immigrants strengthened the French sense of identity. This was a compound of peasant tradition and bourgeois aspiration. Most French Canadians were tillers of soil on which they paid feudal and ecclesiastical dues as heavy as those of *ancien régime* Europe. Few, including schoolteachers, could even sign their names and their Anglo-Saxon neighbours regarded them as pitiful primitives. Writing during the 1830s, a British officer described "the Canadian French" as

> the most wretched set I ever saw; they are a small, sallow, wizened, high cheeked, tobacco smoking race; their being so shrivelled I attribute to their stoves, which hot or cold are kept at their full power, so that it is really quite awful. They jabble out their patois, which of itself is horrid enough, in the most twangy stile imaginable.[100]

Yet, as Lord Durham wrote, it was vain to think that French Canadians had "enjoyed representative institutions for half a century, without acquiring any of the characteristics of a free people."[101]

French-Canadian discontent, though aggravated by racial hatred and rural hardship, was really the product of frustrated nationality. That malaise, indeed, afflicted the whole of British North America, where every province was more or less restive under its Crown-appointed Governor. The

Irish "Liberator," Daniel O'Connell, actually called the country "a miniature Ireland,"[102] identifying himself particularly with the champion of "La
Nation Canadienne,"[103] Louis-Joseph Papineau. It is true that both these
middle-class lawyers inspired their followers with a heavenly vision of
national independence expressed in brimstone phrases. But whereas
O'Connell aimed to achieve Home Rule under the British Crown without
bloodshed, Papineau belonged more to the American revolutionary tradition. He strove for democratic institutions, denouncing the legislative council (selected not elected, the colonial equivalent of the House of Lords) as "a
putrid cadaver."[104] He stirred up French republicanism, demonstrated in the
parish of Contrecoeur when worshippers walked out of the church in defiance of the Bishop of Montreal's order to celebrate Queen Victoria's coronation. The leader of the revolt, a radical merchant, pronounced: "It is painful
to have to sing the Te Deum for the damn Queen, damned whore with her
legs in the air."[105] If the episcopal flock was rebellious, the *patriotes* followed
Papineau so meekly that they were known as "moutons."[106] As he pursued
his campaign for French-Canadian self-determination, advancing from
increasingly bitter political dispute in the assembly to a Yankee-style economic boycott of British merchandise in the countryside, they rallied
against the government like the Sons of Liberty. The *patriotes* even designed
banners with American symbols, stars and eagles, as well as Canadian maple
leaves and pine cones, and French tricolours and red flags emblazoned with
the word "Liberté." Coercive measures, such as the Governor's summary
removal of office-holders and unauthorised seizure of revenue, provoked
protest meetings and declarations of independence. Violent disturbances
followed, culminating in armed insurrection. The last was soon quelled,
though Papineau himself managed to flee, disguised as a peasant, to the
United States—he was branded by history as "a braggart in the forum and a
coward in the field."[107] But French-Canadian exiles continued their struggle, prompting further conflict and greater repression north of the border.
There "bloodthirsty" British troops, as one of their officers acknowledged in
1838, "punished the rebels severely by burning and plundering."[108]

As if to demonstrate the need for conciliation throughout British North
America, the French *patriotes* took up their rifles at the very moment when
a miniature revolution occurred in ultra-loyal Upper Canada. This too was
prompted by a desire for more democracy, for the sovereign's Governor
effectively ruled as well as reigned, at the expense of the elected assembly.
So, as the writer Goldwin Smith observed, Canadian institutions of government, theoretically modelled on those of Britain, were "somewhat like
the Chinese imitation of the steam-vessel, exact in everything except the

steam."[109] Most Canadians wanted reform though extremists sought the grail of self-rule—"freedom from the baneful domination of the Mother Country." That phrase, which the radical MP Joseph Hume formulated in London, outraged United Empire Loyalists when it was published in Toronto. But it was used to rabble-rousing effect by the province's populist leader, William Lyon Mackenzie, who said that "our wrongs and those of the old thirteen colonies were substantially the same."[110] He too aspired to be "the O'Connell of Canada." But this astute, idealistic journalist-turned-politician, who as Mayor of Toronto had designed the city's arms and motto ("Industry, Intelligence, Integrity"), was also a wild-eyed pothouse brawler. He measured "five feet nothing" and looked "very like a baboon." He was too erratic and fanatical to inspire confidence. "You could trust him with your life but not with a secret,"[111] it was said and, according to the Governor of Upper Canada, Mackenzie lied "from every pore in his skin."[112] That such a firebrand could muster hundreds of rebels, armed with fowling pieces, pikes and cudgels, in Toronto's Yonge Street was a measure of the province's discontent. That the militia could disperse them with a whiff of grapeshot reflected its fundamental allegiance—though Mackenzie's force was little more than a mob and he himself was quick to gallop to the frontier. At any rate, this failed British coup, coming on top of the abortive French revolution, caused serious concern in London. Lord Brougham surmised that it had cost the lethargic Colonial Secretary, Lord Glenelg, "many a sleepless day."[113] Certainly Lord Melbourne's government felt that it must act to stop Canada going the way of the United States. It was not that the separation of the colony from the mother country would be a material loss, wrote Melbourne, but his ministry could hardly survive such "a serious blow to the honour of Great Britain."[114] Accordingly the Prime Minister appointed a troublesome rival, Lord Durham, as Governor-General of Upper and Lower Canada. Durham received such full powers that he was hailed as "the Dictator"[115] and the "great Mogul."[116]

"Radical Jack" and the "Dissenting Minister"[117] were other nicknames, for Durham was more left-wing than his colleagues, though he did not go so far as to support the Chartists. However, he managed to be at once a political democrat and a social autocrat. He advocated egalitarian reform while treating all humanity as his inferiors. Once the richest commoner in England—he was of the opinion that anyone should be able to "jog along on £40,000 a year"[118]—the Earl of Durham combined the arrogance of inherited wealth with the insolence of acquired rank. He assaulted waiters and insulted ministers with equal violence; once a tearful Grey protested that he would "rather work in the coal-mines than be subject to such attacks," on which the black-browed Durham muttered, "and you might do worse."[119] Melbourne said that there could be no peace or harmony in any cabinet to which he belonged. Yet if Durham was vain, overbearing and brutal, he was also shrewd, charming and high-minded. He took an enormous entourage to Quebec, rashly including a couple of notorious reprobates (one of whom, Edward Gibbon Wakefield, the champion of colonial emigration, had been imprisoned for kidnapping an heiress), and won the devotion of all its members. He arrived in splendid state—several days were needed to unload his luggage, which included a plethora of musical instruments whose purpose, Sydney Smith quipped, was to enable Durham "to make overtures to the Canadian people."[120] And he paraded through Quebec wearing the uniform of a full general embellished with silver lace and riding a long-tailed white charger. Yet despite subsequent displays of pride to match this pomp—Durham evicted all other guests from his Kingston hotel and refused to permit even the mails to share his steamer—he attained remarkable popularity in both provinces of Canada. Moreover his Report became "the Magna Charta of the Dominion."[121]

Even so, Durham's stint as Governor-General was a fiasco. He only lasted six months, ruining himself through a characteristic combination of liberality and autocracy. Keen to achieve reconciliation, he issued an amnesty to the rebel rank and file. But determined to mark the guilt of the ringleaders, whom juries would probably have acquitted rather than condemned to death, he banished them to Bermuda. Melbourne refused to endorse this just but illegal act and Durham at once resigned. Before quitting Canada, where his party had spent much time engaged in experiments with mesmerism, he issued a proclamation virtually accusing the ministry of betrayal. His hope had been dashed, he said, of conferring "on an united people a more extensive enjoyment of free and responsible government."[122] Durham's departure from Quebec, which took place before his resignation had been accepted, was even more ceremonious than his arrival. In freezing cold, under a sky that promised the first real snow of winter, his open carriage made its slow descent from the Château of St. Lewis to the Queen's Wharf. Spectators crowded the dirty narrow streets, lined with guardsmen, and filled the windows of the high stone houses. They watched in gloomy silence punctuated by occasional outbursts of cheering. As the lumber steamers towed Durham's frigate, the *Inconstant,* down the St. Lawrence, cannon boomed from the citadel in a valedictory salute. And through the dusk, when the ropes were finally cast off, echoed the strains of "Auld Lang Syne." Meanwhile, Durham himself, as one witness observed, was "inwardly nursing that corroding gangrene which terminated in his premature death,—the bitter consciousness that he was returning to England . . . A DEGRADED AND DISAVOWED GOVERNOR."[123]

Yet in 1839, the year before he died, the earl restored his reputation by publishing the Report that bears his name. It provided an incisive analysis of Canada's difficulties together with proposals for resolving them which were so universal in their application that the Durham Report became a handbook of white colonial development under the Union Jack. British settlers felt a natural pride in being part of the world's most powerful, civilised and glorious empire. But they also felt an understandable aversion to the tutelage of its rulers at Westminster, who denied them a proper say in their own affairs. Canadians contrasted their state with that of Americans, who had become masters of their own destiny. And like others throughout imperial history who were embittered by the apparent denial of their rights, some British North Americans were prepared to rebel against their mother country in the name of loyalty. That loyalty, supposedly to the true principles and real interests of Great Britain, was often excited by intransigent bodies such as the Orange Lodges exported from Ulster and pitched in place of the wigwams of the Iroquois. According to one die-hard loyalist whom Durham quoted, "Lower Canada must be English, at the expense, if necessary, of not being British." Durham's solutions to these problems were not especially original but, taken together, they were an ingenious attempt to combine colonial autonomy with imperial unity. In order to dilute the French, he recommended the merging of Upper and Lower Canada. He sought to bind the incipient nation together with blood and iron—state-aided immigration from Britain and inter-colonial railways. Finally he aimed to preserve transatlantic affection through "a veritable union of hearts."[124] This would be achieved by trusting Canadians to rule themselves, leaving London in control of external affairs, constitutional matters and public land administration. Durham believed that Canada would thus remain an intensely patriotic element within the British Empire. On the contrary, critics maintained, his Report prepared the way for complete independence. It assisted Canadian traitors and their American allies, who had already "engraved the name of Lord Durham on the blades of their bowie knives in demonstration of the certain result of 'Responsible Government.'" It was a "manual of treason."[125]

In fact Durham's "healing policy,"[126] which was partially implemented during the 1840s, helped to foster Canadian loyalty. It strengthened the colonial tie by easing the imperial yoke. It is true that the fusion of Upper and Lower Canada (1840) did not so much dispel French animus as compel French acquiescence, but unification and responsible government, introduced gradually and with difficulty, created an Anglo-French community of interest. One Premier, Sir Etienne Taché, declared that the "last gun in defence of English power in America would be fired by a French Canadian."[127] It was significant that he expressed solidarity in the face of an external threat, since the history of Canada—and, indeed, of the British Empire—can only be understood in the context of the United States. Nothing epitomised the tripartite relationship better than the medal struck in Upper Canada in 1813 featuring the British lion and the Canadian beaver guarding Niagara, which was menaced by the American eagle.

To be sure, after the conflict which that medal commemorated few Americans nursed designs against Canada. But disputes did occur, notably during the American Civil War, and they stoked fears that Uncle Sam intended to march to the "North Pole."[128] John Bull occasionally put his foot down. When William Seward, later Lincoln's Secretary of State, said that Britain would never dare to fight for Canada, the Duke of Newcastle replied:

Do not remain under such an error. There is no people under Heaven from whom we should endure so much as from yours; to whom we should make such concessions. You may, while we cannot, forget that we are largely of the same blood. But once touch us in our honour and you will soon find the bricks of New York and Boston falling about your heads.[129]

Seward remained convinced that, as he said at the time of the Alaska purchase in 1867, Nature intended the whole continent to come within "the magic circle of the American Union."[130] And he was determined to "cage the British Lion on the Pacific Coast."[131] Hostilities were avoided but rivalry was endemic. Well before the British Empire reached maturity, Victorians recognised that the United States was "a youthful empire,"[132] destined to supersede it. As a London journal wrote in the year of the Great Exhibition, "the superiority of the United States to England is ultimately as certain as the next eclipse."[133] One way of delaying the American rise was to create a counterweight north of the border in the shape of a Canadian confederation. Durham himself had wanted a provincial union and during the middle years of the century most British politicians came to agree.

Actually the federation of Ontario, Quebec, New Brunswick and Nova Scotia in 1867 (other provinces joined later) did little, if anything, to bolster Canada's defences. The consolidation, said the future Prime Minister Wilfrid Laurier, provided about as much protection against the United States as an eggshell against a bullet. Anxious not to provoke the Great Republic, the sceptr'd isle rejected the term "Kingdom" of Canada in favour of "Dominion"—the first of its kind. Empire loyalists, especially in Canada, convinced themselves that the confederation augmented both national and imperial might. Canadian politicians were distressed, though, by the manner in which the British North America Act was passed: it was treated as "a private Bill uniting two or three English parishes,"[134] the parliamentary clerk gabbled through the clauses and MPs took much more interest in a measure to tax dogs. Furthermore, as the former Premier of Nova Scotia, Joseph Howe, discovered, there was an "almost universal feeling" in England that "*uniting the Provinces was the easy mode of getting rid of them* . . . and the sooner the responsibility of their relations with the Republic is shifted off the shoulders of John Bull the better."[135] British views would change as competing powers prospered and the dominions came to seem more of a source of strength—integral parts, perhaps, of a federated empire that would master the globe. This was a dream; the reality was that Canada had taken a giant stride towards independence. As yet few Canadians wanted complete separation from the mother country. Their capital, Ottawa, retained the trappings of Britain's monarchical constitution, the mimic majesty of robes, ceremonies, titles and decorations. But those who pushed through the false front found inside a self-governing "federal republic after the American model."[136]

Just as Canada seemed set to leave the British Empire, New Zealand fell into its embrace. It was even said in April 1839, at a meeting of the New Zealand Company, which had been founded to advance colonisation in the Antipodes, that the sun of England's glory was setting in the west only to rise again in the south. Lord Durham, who was present, vehemently denied it. His Report recommended self-government in Canada to make its tie with the mother country "indissoluble."[137] Durham acknowledged that Britain's glory might be in eclipse across the Atlantic, but said he would rather lose his right arm than see British North America lost to the Crown. Edward Gibbon Wakefield, the promoter of the New Zealand Company, agreed. A distant relation of the historian, after whom he was christened, Wakefield deplored "the miserable despondency of those who contend that the decline and fall of England have commenced."[138] British power would be sustained, he argued, by judicious and systematic colonisation, by bringing (as Florence Nightingale later put it) "the landless man to the manless lands."[139] Nowhere was better suited to the planting of little Englands than fecund, salubrious New Zealand. Wakefield, who was bluff, burly and articulate, won influential converts. Lord Durham, who liked to get a return on his benevolence, was especially helpful, puffing the New Zealand Company because its object was "the civilization of a savage people & the acquirement of a fine field for the employment of British industry."[140] Despite the prevailing anti-colonial sentiment, Wakefield's advocacy of emigration had a potent appeal during an era of social unrest, high unemployment and Malthusian fears about overpopulation. These were so acute that Thomas Carlyle, the most influential social commentator of his day, ironically suggested the appointment of Parish Exterminators supplied with a reservoir of arsenic. In lieu of this fantasy, he insisted that the poor, some of whom preferred to starve rather than enter workhouses where conditions were akin to slavery, should seek salvation abroad. Carlyle pictured "a whole vacant earth" crying out to be reaped by Chartist "Sanspotatoes." They should be led, in the hierarchical spirit of Wakefield, by "briefless Barristers, chargeless Clergy, taskless Scholars" and "Half-pay Officers." So would the stream of world history flow towards a "BRITISH EMPIRE," gloated Carlyle; "Romans are dead out, English are come in."[141]

The Whig government, assisted by the Colonial Office, tried at first to divert the stream of world history from New Zealand. Scarcely anyone apart from Durham trusted Wakefield, who was as much a charlatan as a visionary. "His deceptiveness was ineradicable, and, like the fowler, he was ever spreading his nets; always plausible, and often persuasive, he was never simple and straightforward."[142] James Stephen refused to have anything to do with Wakefield, deliberately courted his enmity and opposed his colonisation scheme. Acquiring sovereignty over New Zealand, he said, would "infallibly issue in the conquest and extermination of its present inhabitants." However, even Mr. Mothercountry could not stop his compatriots sailing to New Zealand and, as Melbourne remarked in a delicious double entendre, Wakefield and Co. were "quite mad to go there." By 1839 at least two thousand settlers had preceded him and conflict with the Maoris, always endemic, seemed likely to result in another Aboriginal genocide. Warnings to this effect were exaggerated. But they were compounded by horror stories about cannibal feasts, the Maori worship of muskets, the spread of venereal and other diseases, and the trade in women and tattooed heads. The British nation's conscience was pricked at a time when its humanitarian impulse, focusing especially on the abolition of slavery in the West Indies and attempts to suppress it elsewhere, had reached its apogee. Even Melbourne acknowledged that something must be done: New Zealand afforded "another proof of the fatal necessity by which a nation that once begins to colonize is led step by step over the whole globe."[143] Nothing but annexation, apparently, could protect natives from whites and vice versa. In the event, however, it proved almost impossible to reconcile the interests of the races.

The Maoris, Polynesians who had voyaged across the Pacific during the Middle Ages to colonise *Ao Tea Roa,* the Long White Cloud, were a warlike people. When Abel Tasman discovered what he christened New Zealand in 1642 their unambiguous aim was to kill and eat him, not necessarily in that order. Captain Cook was greeted in the same spirit, though the Maoris thought his sailors gods, their gunfire thunderbolts and the *Endeavour* a white-winged whale. Europeans, who established tenuous contact with New Zealand after 1769 through explorers, traders, whalers, sealers and so on, also wove fantasies around the Maoris. With their blue scroll-worked faces and red ochre-daubed bodies, their white gannet feathers and greenstone ornaments, their Neolithic tomahawks *(meré)* and necklaces of human teeth, they became demons in a thousand South Sea romances, naked grotesques set in an exotic landscape of volcanic peaks, vertiginous fjords, belching fumaroles, matted forests, freezing torrents and grassy dales. In fact, the Maoris (whose population Cook estimated to number 100,000) were well adapted to their environment. Although wanting in political cohesion, they had developed tight kinship groups which could resist severe stress. They lacked script, metal, livestock and lucre. But they possessed abundant oral lore, practised incantatory rituals *(karakia),* respected the moral authority *(mana)* of their chiefs, and lived "from infancy to old age enveloped in a cloud of *tapu*" (or taboo, sacred injunction). Wooden spades, obsidian adzes, bone fish-hooks and spears tipped with the barbs of stingrays supplied their needs. Moreover, the Maoris proved adept at commerce, eagerly learning every trick of trade from Europeans and inventing some of their own.

They first sold timber and flax, then potatoes and pork, later several kinds of grain, much of it exported to New South Wales. Up to three tons of scraped flax would purchase an old Brown Bess, perhaps bearing the U.S. coat of arms stamped over the mark of the Tower of London, which indicated that it had probably been surrendered at Yorktown. Once armed with muskets, the Maoris were formidable warriors, none more so than Hongi, Napoleonic chief of the Ngapuhi, who fought in a suit of armour personally given to him by King George IV. They were accustomed to internecine conflict, spending their lives "in a scene of battle, murder, and bloodthirsty atrocities of the most terrific description, mixed with actions of the most heroic self-sacrifice and chivalric daring." But shooting wars were more destructive still, until a balance of power was reached in 1830. Maoris even involved whites in their hostilities. The Ngatiawa tribe forced the captain of the trading brig *Rodney* to take an invasion force to the Chatham Islands, 450 miles into the Pacific, most of whose inhabitants they murdered and devoured. However, the Maoris themselves had often fallen victim to the first European exploiters of New Zealand who, according to one pioneer, lived in "a savage-and-a-half state, being greater savages by far than the natives."[144] Most vicious of all were the foul-mouthed, rum-sodden, pox-ridden "knights of the harpoon,"[145] many from America, which possessed the largest whaling fleet in the world. Their work, spearing leviathans twenty-five times the size of elephants and extracting blubber oil for street lamps, spermaceti wax for candles, whalebone for corsets and ambergris (precious as gold) for perfumes, was inconceivably hard, dangerous and disgusting. Their whaling stations, where Maori men were enslaved and "aboriginal Messalinas"[146] were bartered, spread like chancres on the epidermis of New Zealand. Such "devil's missionaries"[147] were guilty of what the Rev. Samuel Marsden, self-proclaimed "beacon for the godly" in the Australian "brothel of felons,"[148] called "wanton cruelties, robberies and murders of the natives."[149] Early in his ministry this flogging parson concluded that New Zealand was entirely in thrall to the Prince of Darkness. Only the Gospel could save it.

Marsden evidently had a real regard for the Maoris who, despite their heathen abominations, were "a noble race."[150] One contemporary was surprised to find that he sat in their verminous huts, "inhaling their intolerable stench, and beholding their filthy habits with as much composure as if he had been in the midst of the most elegant circle of Europe."[151] Even their habit of eating human flesh he seemed to interpret as some kind of sacramental rite. However, Marsden did not share the view of many colonial officers that the pristine "savage" was spoilt by civilisation and that "the warrior who had eaten his man as a quasi-religious act was a far more estimable person than the town-bred, mission-educated native."[152] He was committed to the Maoris' conversion, initiating the process with a stentorian sermon preached in the open at the Bay of Islands on Christmas Day 1814. From an improvised pulpit made from part of a carved canoe, he addressed four hundred people seated under the Union Jack and the white missionary flag featuring a cross, a dove and an olive branch. He took as his text, "Behold I bring you glad tidings of great joy." But apart from prompting an instant war dance, the good news at first had little effect. The natives stubbornly insisted that their own god had created New Zealand, fishing it from the bottom of the sea with three hooks. They even managed to turn one of Marsden's grim-visaged, black-coated evangelists, the Rev. Thomas Kendall, "from a Christian to a Heathen," his mind having been seduced by the "apparent sublimity"[153] of their religious ideas and his "vile passions inflamed" by miscegenation. But Marsden, apparently believing himself to be the Moses of this new "Promised Land," was not discouraged. When Maoris fell asleep during divine service, of which they understood not a word, he said that he had never seen a more orderly congregation.

It was clear, though, that the surest way to their hearts was through commerce—that the Maoris would "buy and sell anything" confirmed Marsden's view that they were the lost ten tribes of Israel.[154] Commerce would bring civilisation in its train. And it would enable Marsden to lay up treasure on earth as well as in heaven. Once a blacksmith, this hammer-headed, barrel-bellied cleric had grown financially as well as physically fat in Parramatta, and he was not always scrupulous in his dealings. He probably sold the Maoris muskets, possibly rum. And on at least one occasion he bought a mummified human head—merchandise that was outlawed by the Governor of New South Wales in 1831 since traders had taken to bidding for finely engraved heads still attached to shoulders, which were duly delivered. Missionaries following in Marsden's footsteps, whom he frequently excoriated for their errors and crimes, were as impoverished as he had once been. Sydney Smith famously said that "if a tinker is a devout man, he infallibly sets off for the East"[155] and this was not just a joke; for, in the echoing words of the vice-consul in Tahiti, missionaries to the Pacific were "a set of Tinkers having no bread to eat in England."[156] Accordingly they did business with the Maoris to support their families, buying land with axes and cloth, guns and grog. In fact the missionaries, who numbered nearly a hundred in 1831, about a third of the white population, became colonists for Christ. And the Maoris, who were intent on acquiring everything of value that foreigners (Pakeha) had to offer, became devotees of a cargo cult.

However, the missionary position was by no means straightforward. It combined theocratic pretensions and exploitative inclinations with a genuine desire that "The word of the Lord may truly be . . . glorified among the New Zealanders."[157] The New Zealanders recognised the mixture of motives. They appreciated that the missionaries tended to consider them "an inferior race of beings"[158] and suspected that they had been sent "to tame the Maoris as we break in a wild horse."[159] They feared that the ultimate purpose of these foreign men of God was to sanctify their extinction. Certainly the gifts of the whites were as demoralising as they were enticing. Iron axes facilitated homicide, especially in the home—though it is hard to square horrifying reports of domestic violence with equally graphic accounts of the Maoris' happy family life, the "fun and gaiety" of their disposition, the "pleasing" manner in which they rubbed noses.[160] The blanket, which got damp, was less healthy than the flaxen cloak *(kakahu)*. This was particularly apparent when the Maoris moved from their hill-top fortresses *(pas)* to marshy lowlands in order to do business with Europeans, though distance may have helped to quarantine them from imported diseases that proved lethal elsewhere. Potatoes gave Maoris "prominent paunches." Christian ethics also undermined their way of life. The proscription of polygamy sapped male prestige and female security. The ban on cannibalism produced protein deficiency in their diet, though in truth Maoris disliked "salt and disagreeable" European flesh and chiefs had generally been content to eat only the left eye of their enemies, "the seat of the soul."[161] More seriously, the erosion of such core beliefs as *mana* and *tapu* weakened the foundations of their culture.

Still, as Charles Darwin noted when he visited New Zealand in 1835, "the lesson of the missionary is the enchanter's wand." He was particularly impressed by a children's Christmas party at the house of the Rev. Mr. Williams, never having seen "a nicer or more merry group"—and this in "the land of cannibalism, murder, and all atrocious crimes."[162] With uncanny speed such evangelists imparted scientific knowledge, technical skills and humane values. Darwin thought that they were good men working for a good cause and he suspected that those who "abused and sneered at missionaries, have generally been such as were not very anxious to find the natives moral and intelligent beings."[163] Actually the Maoris, who were shocked by white customs such as flogging and waltzing, quickly acquired literacy from the Scriptures. Perhaps they regarded the Bible as a talisman, though in subsequent wars they used its pages for gun-wadding, asking the missionaries for fresh supplies. But the New Testament, translated during the 1830s, was also their first recorded literature. And there is no reason to doubt Maoris' hunger for Holy Writ, which they paid for with food even when they were still unable to read. At Cloudy Bay, for example, the Rev. Samuel Ironside accepted six hundred "baskets of potatoes and Indian corn," each worth sixpence or more, in exchange for "the bread of life."

> I think I never shall forget the moment—that, indeed, would have been a great scene for a painter!—so many hundreds of once-cannibal New Zealanders straining their eyes towards me, and the heap of books, as the distribution was going on; looking as though they would devour the heap.[164]

Maori Christians, who numbered many thousands by the 1840s (though missionaries claimed more souls than the entire population), profited from their conversion. Sometimes they played rival denominations off against each other and sometimes they evolved cults of their own, one involving the ritual eating of lizards, another the sacrifice of an Anglican clergyman. But generally they gained the patronage of those who had redeemed them from paganism. Missionaries resisted *Pakeha* who tried to fleece their flocks, still more those who might slaughter them. Serving God as well as mammon, they were often deeply subversive to the colonising enterprise. In fact, "Christian imperialism" often proved a contradiction in terms.

At any rate, by the end of the 1830s Marsden's disciples in the field, like Stephen's minions in the Colonial Office, came to support Britain's annexation of New Zealand. The dual purpose of the missionaries was to assert their authority over the natives while protecting them from exploitation, for only a properly constituted government could secure law and order. Crucially, too, it would control any transfers of Maori land. To pre-empt the state's interference, the New Zealand Company, which had been refused a charter to colonise the country, rushed out a land-sharking expedition in May 1839. "Acquire all the land you can," Wakefield urged. "Possess yourselves of the soil & you are secure."[165] His brother William accordingly went through the form of purchasing twenty million acres (nearly a third of the whole country) for goods worth rather less than £9,000, including twelve shaving brushes and sixty red nightcaps. He knew perfectly well that the Maoris, who regarded humans not as owners but as guests of the earth, were unused "to any dealing in land according to our notions."[166] He was also aware that they had no conception of the number of settlers who would arrive as a result of organised emigration, promoted by a company which advertised a cheap stake in a land of limitless dreams, giant vegetables and immense "banana orchards."[167] However, the Colonial Office could also play the pre-emption game. It appointed as Governor of New Zealand a blunt sailor, Captain William Hobson, who habitually referred to the New Zealand Company "as if it were composed of rogues and swindlers."[168]

Charged with obtaining Maori assent to the establishment of British sovereign authority, Hobson arrived in January 1840. With missionary help he persuaded some five hundred chiefs to sign the Treaty of Waitangi (Water of Weeping). Effectively, this appropriated New Zealand for the Crown, though no compact in colonial history was more ambiguous. In essence, though, the British believed they were acquiring sovereignty in exchange for civilisation and protection, particularly the safeguarding of native land rights. The Maoris thought they were getting access to a white cornucopia while granting a vague overlordship. "The shadow of the land goes to Queen Victoria," concluded one chief optimistically, "but the substance remains with us."[169] Since the treaty relied on good faith rather than legal precision it turned out that, despite some early restoration of territory, the reverse was true. For the two principles that lay at the heart of Waitangi— white rule (initially from London but as soon as possible from Auckland) and guardianship of the natives—were impossible to reconcile. With the advent of more settlers (between 1841 and 1861 New Zealand's *Pakeha* population rose from 3,000 to 100,000) pressure mounted on the Colonial Office literally to give ground. The New Zealand Company stirred up opposition to "the 'Stephen' ascendancy in Downing Street," its Antipodean emanation in Hobson and their "paralysing influence" on colonial enterprise.[170] Gradually the Company gained its point, while Stephen fulminated in his diary, "I hate N. Zealand."[171] In 1846 the Colonial Office acknowledged that the land guarantee given at Waitangi could not be scrupulously observed because it was "a bar to sound colonisation."[172] Writing in the 1890s, a historian of New Zealand explained the situation with brutal simplicity: missionaries and officials could not be allowed to leave "a fertile and healthy Archipelago larger than Great Britain" in the possession of "a handful of savages—not more, I believe, than sixty-five thousand in all, and rapidly dwindling in numbers."[173]

Such greed prompted clashes during the 1840s. The antagonism hardened during the 1850s when the settlers got provincial autonomy under the forceful governorship of Sir George Grey—one said that he would rather be ruled "by a Nero on the spot than by a board of angels in London" since the former could be decapitated.[174] By now the whites outnumbered the Maoris and they acquired about half New Zealand's total area, paying a halfpenny an acre. This was a kind of Roman occupation of a country "much in the state that Britain was when Caesar landed." Moreover, readers of Gibbon discovered, the natives resembled the Attacotti, Caledonian cannibals who so delighted in the taste of human flesh that they attacked "shepherds rather than sheep."[175] Such creatures were hardly suited to the modern world and the Maoris' doom seemed imminent. A humanitarian remarked, "Our plain duty, as good, compassionate colonists, is to smooth down their dying pillow."[176] However, when war broke out in the 1860s, the Maoris showed themselves to be anything but moribund. They defended their *pas* with the skill of Vauban and invented a form of trench warfare which would have educated Sir Douglas Haig. In fact they easily matched British officers in "quality of leadership,"[177] inflicting a series of humiliating reverses on their foes. Ultimately they were not so much defeated as deluged and demoralised, facing as many as eighteen thousand British soldiers. These were sent in response to exaggerated accounts of Maori aggression, relayed by Sir George Grey (in his second term as Governor), a fierce paternalist who enjoyed provoking wild bulls and shooting them down as they charged. But London resented the expense, especially as the settlers seized further tracts of territory from the natives. So the troops were withdrawn (the last in 1870) while the *Pakeha* fused their local governments into a centralised state whose capital was Wellington. Its white citizens, "the most John-Bullish" of John Bulls, who considered their country "to be the cream of the British empire,"[178] felt utterly betrayed by the departure of the imperial legions.

Many of the new New Zealanders cherished a seminal myth, eagerly fostered by Edward Gibbon Wakefield, to the effect that their colony was a reincarnation of old England. As distant in time as in space from a motherland now blighted by dark satanic mills (on which New Zealand's wool-exporting economy depended), the Britain of the south was a rural Elysium. It had attracted "the most valuable class of emigrants"[179] since the foundation of "the Cavalier settlements of Delaware and Virginia." Among them were noble and landed families, members of the professions, merchants and tradesmen of good standing, as well as the occasional retired officer, a "'vieux moustache' of the line or Indian service."[180] Thus New Zealand, ethnically homogeneous, socially well ordered and morally wholesome, would resist the prevalent colonial tendency to "Americanise."[181] Such resistance was reflected in an unpublished letter from a hard-up British immigrant, George Thornhill, who commented on the "regular deluge of dukes" arriving in 1890:

> though people here pride themselves on being so democratic it is wonderful how much trouble they will take even to see a sprig of the nobility. Only yesterday a large crowd waited most of the afternoon to catch a glimpse of the Earl of Kintore who passed through on his way to Dunedin.[182]

New Zealand was, in short, a "gentleman's colony."[183] But this creation myth, which linked the country to its transoceanic parent while denying any bond with its felonious sibling across the Tasman Sea, was balanced by a powerful counter-myth.

Containing as much (if not more) truth, it represented New Zealand as "a new Great Britain,"[184] a Britain of the future not the past. Despite the "wooden boxes of houses"[185] that disfigured Christchurch, the crude "shedifices"[186] of the Canterbury settlement and the squalid gold-mining camps of Otago, here was a progressive paradise. Its pioneers, many of them stiff-backed Scots and hard-fisted Irish, others resembling "the Kentucky variety of the Anglo-Saxon race,"[187] were egalitarians. They were hostile to the practice of tipping and ill suited to the occupation of domestic service. This was not a colony for people who regarded "the flunkey as an institution, and who, like the Oxford man, would not save you from drowning because you had not been '*introduced*.'" Snobs were as out of place "as a dancing dog in a fox hunt."[188] Even ethnic pride was unacceptable to those who wanted to make all things new. The mixing of Caucasian and Maori blood would create a fine new people. For, as one advocate of interbreeding concluded, "it is every day becoming more probable that the once visionary hope of the illustrious Gibbon will be realised, and the Hume of the Southern Hemisphere spring from among the cannibal races of New Zealand."[189] Samuel Butler, who read the *Decline and Fall* on the voyage to New Zealand (especially recommending volumes two and three for anyone considering taking holy orders) and based his novel *Erewhon* (1870) on this southern Utopia, sympathised with the young radicals. On arrival they were

> so delighted with the prospect of the untrammelled life before them that they felt it necessary to make some gesture of contempt for the conventions they had left behind, so the first evening ashore they built a huge bonfire, piled on it their top hats and tail coats, and danced in a ring round the blazing fire.[190]

Such emigrants (like all colonists, according to Sir James Stephen, "exempt from the disaster of Caste")[191] naturally aspired to full nationhood for New Zealand. Paradoxically, though, they were all the more resentful when Britain left them to fight the Maoris alone. But the flight of the imperial eagles was a portentous event, which seemed to augur the sickness of the British lion. In his inimitable fashion the poetaster Martin Tupper conjured with the notion that a virile New Zealand would succeed it in a world turned upside down.

> Even should Britain's decay be down-written
> In the dread doom-book that no man may search,
> Still shall an Oxford, a London, a Britain
> Gladden the South with a Home and a Church![192]

Macaulay's famous trope about some future traveller from New Zealand taking "his stand on a broken arch of London Bridge to sketch the ruins of St. Paul's,"[193] first rehearsed on a Gibbonian visit to Rome,[194] was repeated so often that it became the subject of parody. When an earthquake wrecked Wellington in 1855, one Australian newspaper visualised a Cockney gazing on its ruins. The Positivist Frederic Harrison offered a particularly elaborate variation on Macaulay's theme. He advocated the creation of a British Pompeii, a subterranean city under Skiddaw or Stonehenge, to preserve the treasures and trivia of each century. This time capsule, to employ the modern term, would contain pictures, photographs, instruments, encyclopaedias, manufactured goods, Bradshaw Railway Guides, Whitaker Almanacs and the correspondence of Mr. Gladstone, which would require an entire vault to itself. All would entrance the globetrotter from New Zealand who, a millennium hence, might "moor his electric balloon on the last broken arch of London Bridge."[195] Seeing the dawn of a lambent destiny, New Zealanders, like white settlers elsewhere in British dominions, talked of issuing a declaration of independence. They even considered applying to join the more vigorous civilisation of the United States. Mid-Victorian Britain accepted the idea of a self-liquidating empire. When colonists insisted on "being independent in form and in name as they are already in truth and reality," said Sir James Stephen rhetorically, "is there a man among us who would discharge, I do not say a single cannon, but so much as a single lucifer-match, to resist it?"[196]

4

To Stop Is Dangerous, to Recede, Ruin

The Far East and Afghanistan

In September 1839 Sir James Stephen remarked that he had "been living for the last six months in a tornado."[1] Not only was he struggling with the creation of British New Zealand, against his better judgement, but he was beset by storms elsewhere in the Empire. Aden was annexed in January and Sind became a protectorate in February. Trouble was brewing in Gibraltar, Malta, the Ionian Islands, the Cape, Ceylon, Jamaica, Canada and Australia. War threatened in Burma and there were fears of a clash with France in the Persian Gulf. That danger was compounded by a crisis in the Levant resulting from Egypt's rebellion against the Ottoman Empire, now the "sick man of Europe." Furthermore, two conflicts were already in train. Britain was engaged in the opening skirmishes of the Opium War against China, designed to prise open the most populous market on earth. And the First Afghan War had begun, its purpose being to keep the Russian Bear at bay and to intimidate the Himalayan tribes. "It was felt," according to an article in the *Asiatic Journal*, "that the security of our Empire would be irrevocably compromised whenever we were obliged, like the Empire of Rome in its decline, to buy off the barbarians on our frontier."[2]

Defence invariably meant attack. By a curious paradox the first half of Queen Victoria's reign, the nadir of enthusiasm for colonies and dependencies, saw what one of her subjects called the greatest advances and conquests since the days of Julius Caesar.[3] During this period the British Empire grew on average by 100,000 square miles a year, almost the same rate of expansion as that in the late nineteenth century, usually reckoned the golden age of territorial aggrandisement. True, the forward policy was by no means consistent. Britain's Empire was won as it would be lost, in a haphazard, piecemeal fashion. Serious setbacks occurred, notably the Indian Mutiny, which seemed harbingers of imperial doom. Moreover, well-placed observers believed that the enlargement process was unsustainable as well as undesirable. Stephen himself wrote in 1843: "We are recklessly increasing and dispersing our colonial Empire in all directions and creating a demand for naval and military force which there is no means of meeting, except by weakening that force where its presence is most needed." For all the shrewdness of this analysis, though, a huge and heterogeneous Empire was coming into being, the like of which the world had never seen. Compared to this tangled motley, Rome wove a seamless web.

The British Empire was such a gallimaufry that some authorities say it never really existed at all. It was acquired by conquest, settlement, cession and in a bewildering variety of other ways: Bombay was part of a royal dowry; Freetown was purchased by a band of English philanthropists; most of Hong Kong was leased; Cyprus was held on licence; the New Hebrides were part of an Anglo-French "condominium." The Empire had no legal coherence: Englishmen carried their own law with them to settler colonies; but Roman-Dutch law was retained in the Cape, Ceylon and British Guiana; varieties of French law prevailed in Lower Canada, St. Lucia, Mauritius and the Seychelles; Trinidad had Spanish law, Heligoland Danish law, Malta the Maltese Code; Cyprus clung to old Turkish law even when Istanbul reformed it. Nor was there judicial impartiality. Naturally "all men are equal before the law" but, wrote one Colonial Secretary unblushingly, it was a mistake to suppose that "you can treat Chinese as if they were English."[4] The Colonial Office had no monopoly of power in the Empire and could at any time be overruled by the Admiralty, the War Office, the India Office, the Board of Trade, the Foreign Office or the Treasury. The last of these departments often had the final word, though its efforts to impose "stringent economy" were not always successful—when the Treasury tried literally to cut the Colonial Office's use of stationery, it penned a crushing riposte: "No gentleman writes to another on half a sheet of paper."[5] In practice, too, the man on the spot might prove more powerful than his theoretical masters at home. It has even been argued that the Empire was not so much pushed out from the centre as pulled out from the extremities, because there were so many cases of "the metropolitan dog being wagged by its colonial tail."[6] A particularly rabid example occurred in 1848 when, entirely on his own initiative, the half-mad Sir Harry Smith annexed "British Kaffraria," a huge region south of the Drakensberg Mountains, placing his foot on the neck of the Xhosa ruler and proclaiming, "I am your Paramount Chief, and the Kaffirs are my dogs!"[7] To emphasise the point he blew up a wagon packed with explosives in front of two thousand tribesmen.

Local administrations were sometimes as eccentric as local proconsuls. In different ways Canada, Australia and New Zealand virtually ran their own affairs. The East India Company nominally ruled the subcontinent and held economic sway between Cape Town and Cape Horn. It was "the strangest of all governments," said Macaulay, but it was "designed for the strangest of all empires."[8] For India also contained about 560 princely states, whose rajahs were often "advised" by British Residents. And its subordinate presidencies had additional responsibilities: for example, Bombay supervised Aden and the British Agency in Zanzibar; Bengal held sway from Peshawar to Rangoon. Other chartered companies would gain fiefdoms in Borneo, Nigeria and Rhodesia. "Crown colonies," obtained by war, treaty or occupation, such as British Guiana, Trinidad, the Falkland Islands, Malta, the Cape, and Ceylon, were directed more or less despotically by a British Governor. Protectorates, such as the Gold Coast, Uganda, East Africa and assorted Pacific Islands, represented a halfway stage between alliance and sovereignty, though even the Colonial Office did "not quite know what this means."[9] Tristan da Cunha, though it was administered by missionaries, had no form of government whatever.

Britain exerted a still vaguer dominion, thanks to its commercial and naval strength, over satellite states in South America, Asia and elsewhere. The Mediterranean, as earlier noted, was virtually a British lake. From 1814 until 1846 the Consul-General at Tripoli, Colonel Hanmer Warrington, was "to all intents and purposes the Pasha's Foreign Secretary."[10] Hailed as "the Great Elchi" (ambassador) in the Sultan's court at Constantinople, Lord Stratford de Redcliffe exercised nearly despotic authority between 1841 and 1857, dispensing his own law and having his own gaoler.[11] Even the United States was drawn into the British orbit during the nineteenth century: "We are part, and a great part," wrote the *New York Times,* "of the Greater Britain which seems so plainly destined to dominate this planet."[12] But though some historians have described the tenuous association of client countries as Britain's "informal empire,"[13] it was less a nexus of power than a sphere of influence. Its strength varied according to circumstances and often Britain exercised no more than a phantom hegemony. More substantial were direct forms of control, whether imposed by sweating consuls on the Niger, by the hereditary white rajahs of Sarawak or by the naval captains who commanded Ascension Island, which the Admiralty denominated a ship—a "stone frigate."[14] This was, in short, an empire of anomalies.

Nevertheless it was an empire. It acknowledged the supremacy of the British Crown in the Westminster parliament. And its purpose was to promote the nation's real interests on which, said Lord Palmerston, the sun never set. Britain was essentially interested in political advantage and commercial gain, which in turn enhanced strength and growth. Power and wealth were the warp and woof of empire. But the worldwide mesh was so loose that if any strand broke, Britons often thought, the whole fabric might unravel. Consequently empire-builders were always inclined to advance. They hankered to thrust out a bastion here, to nip off a salient there, to seize the initiative somewhere else. Like Sir Charles Metcalfe, they echoed Clive's dictum: "To stop is dangerous, to recede, ruin."[15]

Of course, they had high-minded justifications aplenty for imperial expansion. Christianity and civilisation followed the Union Jack, since on the long march to improve the world Britain had plainly been chosen to take the lead. Awed by the unparalleled grandeur of the country's imperial situation in 1843, *Blackwood's Magazine* believed that "Great Britain is destined by Almighty God to be the instrument for effecting his sublime hidden purposes with reference to humanity."[16] True, cynics like Sir William Molesworth said that people who talked of promoting humanity at the expense of barbarism generally meant "shells, congreve rockets and grapeshot, the burning and destruction of native towns and the wholesale massacre of their inhabitants."[17] But although such criticisms sometimes came painfully close to the mark, few doubted that the nation's destiny was bound up with the gospel of progress. Even radicals hostile to imperialism, such as Cobden and Goldwin Smith, did not want to dismantle the Empire. And politicians who deplored its trouble and cost believed that it was essential to the greatness of Britain. A significant colonial loss would "diminish our importance in the world," said Lord John Russell, "& the vultures would soon gather together to despoil us of other parts of our Empire, or to offer insults to us which we could not bear."[18] No one could bear them less than Lord Palmerston, the greatest champion of an aggressive foreign policy during the first half of the Victorian age. Sharing Macaulay's view that "To trade with civilised men is infinitely more profitable than to govern savages,"[19] Palmerston was keener to foster commerce than to acquire territory. But sometimes one enterprise involved the other. Whatever the case he had an infallible guide: "the interest of England is the Polar star."[20]

Palmerston, a Regency buck who dominated most early Victorian governments and remained Prime Minister for much of the decade before his death in 1865, was known in his youth as Lord Cupid. This was a tribute to an amorous disposition not always kept within the bounds of decency. In 1837 he attempted to seduce—perhaps even to rape—one of the ladies-in-waiting at Windsor Castle, which got him into serious trouble with the virgin Queen. The monarch also took exception to the high-handed way in which Palmerston conducted foreign affairs. A Whig grandee with populist leanings, he resisted royal interference, antagonised Prince Albert and advised the sovereign to confine her international correspondence to family gossip. Palmerston was equally brusque with his cabinet colleagues, who were often appalled by the violence of his language and the rashness of his behaviour. As Prime Minister, Lord Melbourne began many sentences in his letters to the Foreign Secretary with the words "For God's sake don't . . ."[21] The British electorate, though, enjoyed "Lord Pumicestone's" abrasive way with alien potentates. Among others he insulted the Pope, who so prized temporal rule, Palmerston suggested, that he "would not open the gates of Paradise" unless he could "make some little hell on earth."[22] Palmerston also caused offence by permitting military bands to play in parks on Sundays; churchmen complained that he "treated Heaven like a foreign power."[23] Incurably frivolous, he was also immensely industrious and boisterously patriotic. *Punch* said that he never slept, though occasionally "he rests his head on a loaded cannon."[24]

Edward Bulwer-Lytton, author of *The Last Days of Pompeii*, described Palmerston as "mamma England's spoilt child":[25] when he had a tantrum and smashed all the crockery, the mother proudly remarked on his high spirits. Jaunty, debonair and eupeptic, Palmerston combined patrician disdain for popular clamour and abuse with a raffish aptitude for playing to the gallery of public opinion. This he personified as "the man with the umbrella on top of the omnibus." He added that public opinion was "more powerful than a charge of cavalry or the thunder of artillery."[26] Palmerston was never more loudly applauded than when he bullied Greece into compensating an Iberian Jew called Don Pacífico, who claimed British citizenship because he had been born in Gibraltar, for damage done to his property in Athens during anti-Semitic riots. Concluding a bravura parliamentary defence of his gunboat diplomacy in 1850, Palmerston memorably pronounced that "as the Roman, in days of old, held himself free from indignity when he could say *Civis Romanus sum:* so also a British subject, in whatever land he may be, shall feel confident that the watchful eye and strong arm of England will protect him against injustice and wrong."[27]

Less well known is Macaulay's Commons peroration, which anticipated Palmerston's by a decade and also celebrated his country's achievement in making "the name of Englishman as much respected as ever had been the name of Roman citizen."[28] Macaulay, then Secretary at War, was attempting to justify Britain's policy towards China. This led to the Opium War (1839–42), a characteristic example of Palmerstonian pugnacity which resulted in a small addition of territory and a large accession of influence to the British Empire. The purpose of the war, according to the opposition, was to protect British dealers in an illicit drug that was demoralising countless Chinese. In his reply to Macaulay, the young W. E. Gladstone said that

England had been respected because its flag had always flown over the "cause of justice," whereas a war in defence of this "infamous contraband traffic" covered the entire country in disgrace.[29] He even suggested that since the Chinese had no armaments capable of expelling their foes they might reasonably resort to poisoning British wells. Palmerston exploited this gaffe in his own speech, adding that it was not his country's task to preserve "the morals of the Chinese people, who were disposed to buy what other people were disposed to sell them."[30] But it was right to preserve the legitimate business and lawful property of British merchants in Canton. The extension of commerce, the Foreign Secretary believed, was tantamount to the promotion of civilisation. From the perspective of Peking, the reverse was true. This was the contentious issue between the callow British Empire and the venerable Celestial Empire. A sublime irony lay at the heart of their long struggle: each empire thought the other utterly barbarous.

China, where Confucius taught philosophy when Rome was a village, where gunpowder was invented when Europe was in the Dark Ages, where Kublai Khan reigned over the largest empire ever seen when Edward I was wrestling with a disunited kingdom, now seemed to Britons hopelessly backward. It had been admired in the West as late as the Enlightenment period, when the fashion for *chinoiserie* was at its height. But subsequently it was condemned for its continental insularity, its Great Wall mentality. The Middle Kingdom had rebuffed every British overture since the first diplomatic mission, led by Lord Macartney, in 1793. In accounts of that famous embassy the Chinese appeared as infinitely polite and graciously hospitable Yahoos who spat on the carpet and openly searched themselves for vermin, which they then ate with relish. They had failed to appreciate the value of English gifts presented to the suave, ruthless, octogenarian Emperor Qianlong: the coach was never used because the Son of Heaven could not sit lower than his driver; the mechanical planetarium was dismissed as a stupid toy; the map of the world was rejected on the grounds that China was too small and not in the middle.* Claiming the globe, the "inscrutable Celestials"[31] were insufferably condescending towards the big-

---

*Cartographical pretensions were almost as common as racial ones. At the heart of the Mediterranean, Rome had been head of the world. Medieval Christians, whose *mappae mundi* were geometrically shaped like a T inside an O, had set Jerusalem at the hub of the *orbis terrarum*. Britain had taken pride of place since 1767 when the *Nautical Almanack* established Greenwich as the prime meridian of longitude, a convention internationally ratified in 1884; and imperial maps using Mercator's projection exaggerated the size of the United Kingdom. In 1944 Americans called for their maps to reflect the new distribution of power by placing the United States geographically at the centre of the world.

nosed, red-faced, tight-clothed "barbarians." Macartney and Lord Amherst, who followed him to the Forbidden City in 1816, clearly did not know how to behave for they refused to kowtow to His Imperial Majesty. Such uncouth visitors could not grasp that the Middle Kingdom, which held sway from the Caspian Sea to the Ryukyu Islands, from Lake Baikal to the gulfs of Bengal and Siam, was "the only Civilisation under Heaven."[32] Mutual misunderstanding aggravated interracial contempt. The British were disgusted by the Chinese diet, which included snakes, tortoises, dogs, cats, bats, new-born rats (known as "honey peepers") and raw monkey brains, but believed that they would readily buy tweed. The Chinese thought the British looked like devils, stank like corpses and probably had webbed feet. They also reckoned that a ban on the export of rhubarb from Canton could bring England to a halt via an epidemic of constipation.

Canton was the only seaway into the Emperor Tao-Kuang's sublimely self-sufficient universe. Foreigners were not even allowed to enter the city itself. Likened to merchants trying to do business in London but "placed in close confinement" at Wapping,[33] they were virtually imprisoned in a small, squalid factory ghetto set between Canton's granite walls and the Pearl River. This broad waterway was as busy as the Thames below London Bridge. It was "a floating world"[34] of hatched sampans, rakish lorchas (schooners), oval-roofed houseboats, barbers' skiffs, barrel-hulled lighters, beflagged mandarins' barges and red-and-black, single-masted, mat-sailed junks, with ramshackle poops, wooden anchors, rattan rigging and bows painted with enormous eyes to scare off sea serpents. On its forty-mile journey from Canton to the sea, the river wound through grey mud flats and green paddy fields, dividing into a maze of shallow channels. An early one was "Lob Lob Creek," from which silk-robed prostitutes would glide in gorgeously decorated "flower boats" to "satisfy the carnal appetites"[35] of foreign sailors, a transaction controlled by mandarins who took their usual "squeeze" of the profits. A few miles downstream, off Whampoa Island, the larger merchantmen moored. Among them were the fat-bellied, thousand-ton argosies of the East India Company with their black-and-white checkerboard colours and their red-and-white-striped flags flying over a forest of masts, struts and spars, as they disgorged cargoes of cotton, wool, tin, lead and silver, as well as watches, jewelled musical boxes and other clockwork curios known as "sing-songs." Finally, the main stream of the delta flowed between fortified headlands known as the Bocca Tigris, the tiger's jaws, before emptying into a vast estuary guarded by the Portuguese enclave of Macao and the rocky sentinel of Hong Kong. Bottled up in the single port of Canton, with its humid malarial summers and its damp rheumatic winters, exposed to restrictions, exactions and humiliations, British merchants were constantly at odds with their hosts. And by spitting, hooting and gesturing, the local people made it quite clear that they loathed, derided and despised the "foreign devils" *(Fan Qui)*.

Matters grew worse when the East India Company lost its monopoly to trade with China in 1834. Private traffickers, beating the monsoons in fast, new, three-masted clippers, said to be the finest boats in the world,[36] began to transport unprecedented amounts of opium from India. They were generally anxious to avoid smuggling themselves. So off China's coast they transferred the mango-wood chests (forty thousand of them by 1840, each packed with forty brown, human-head-sized cakes of opium) to narrow, streamlined craft known as "scrambling dragons" or "fast crabs."[37] These had three masts as well as fifty or sixty oars and sailed so swiftly, despite heavy armaments and iron nets designed to protect them from cannonballs, that they were said to have "glued-on wings."[38] They were crewed by Tanka boat people described as "vermin on land, veritable dragons afloat."[39] The Chinese purchased opium from the British with silver, the very same metal which the British paid to the Chinese for their own addictive drug—tea. This had become "a necessity of life"[40] in Britain, where thirty million pounds of tea were consumed each year at a cost of over £2 million. So the balance of trade in bullion, which had tilted heavily towards China before the 1830s, now swung in favour of the British. In the words of a contemporary pamphlet, this enabled India

> to increase ten-fold its consumption of British Manufactures . . . to support the vast fabric of British dominion in the East . . . and, by the operations of exchange and remittances in Teas and other Chinese produce, to pour an abundant revenue into the British Exchequer and benefit the British Nation to the extent of six millions annually.[41]

Tea duties provided a tenth of the national revenue, enough to finance half the Royal Navy. The British were, moreover, stimulated by congou and bohea while the Chinese were poisoned by the poppy.

It is true that opium, known as a soporific to the Egyptians, Greeks and Romans, had many properties. As well as being an anodyne it could act as an aphrodisiac, prolonging erection and ejaculation. It could also excite the imagination of those who, like Thomas De Quincey, plunged into the "abyss of divine enjoyment."[42] Certainly the British, who allowed opium to be sold freely at home, made light of the drug. They said that Peking's complaints about its corrupting effects were spurious, concealing fears about gains in British power and losses of Chinese silver—"the idol of their real worship."[43] Englishmen favourably compared the effect of opium on the Chinese to that of gin on their own countrymen. Some even claimed that it carried out the valuable "mission of soothing John Chinaman into a temporary forgetfulness" of the evils that beset him, "deluding his soul with visions of a Paradise where the puppy-dogs and rats run about roasted; where the birds' nests are all edible . . . and the women all [have] short feet."[44] This was humbug. Burke had rightly condemned the opium trade, which he called a "smuggling adventure," as "the great Disgrace of the *British* character in *India.*"[45] And Dr. Arnold of Rugby said that forcing the drug on China was "a national sin of the greatest possible magnitude."[46]

It usually had disastrous effects on smokers. They suffered from indigestion, emaciation and lassitude. Their skin turned sallow, their teeth blackened and their minds decayed. Eventually they became "walking skeletons."[47] Moreover, there was no escape from addiction without the "writhing, throbbing, palpitating, shattered" feelings that De Quincey experienced.[48] The Emperor Tao-Kuang (Heavenly Rectitude) feared that his realm would be impoverished and his subjects stupefied by the drug. Senior court eunuchs had succumbed to it, as had sections of the army, which proved incapable of fighting. The entire administration of the Celestial Empire was being corrupted since mandarins, if not addicts themselves, exerted such a huge "squeeze" that they were essentially in league with the drug traffickers. For over a century emperors had been trying to suppress opium smoking. In 1839 Tao-Kuang sent a new commissioner to Canton, Lin Tse-Hsu, to solve the problem once and for all. Short and stout, with a thick black moustache and a long thin beard, Lin announced his intentions in a letter (not delivered) to Queen Victoria. "The vice has spread far and wide," he wrote, and "we mean to cut off this harmful drug for ever." To acknowledge the superhuman power of the Son of Heaven, the Queen "must" at once forbid its manufacture throughout the British Empire.[49]

Lin followed up this missive by executing more Chinese addicts and by besieging the trading factories in Canton. He forced the *Fan Qui,* including the American "flowery flag devils," to surrender twenty thousand cases of opium worth £2 million, over a third of which belonged to the leading British *hong* (firm) Jardine, Matheson & Co. The so-called "foreign mud" was dissolved in lime pits. And the merchants fled to Macao where, after a "jollification on the Queen's birthday," one of them fired off guns which damaged a Chinese war junk and "created a great sensation."[50] They then decamped to Hong Kong, but the resumption of opium trafficking caused further friction in the Pearl River estuary. It culminated in two engagements between a 28-gun frigate of the Royal Navy and junks of the Chinese battle fleet, several of which were sunk. Lin reported a glorious victory to the Emperor. Palmerston was able to persuade parliament that, despite Gladstone's moralisings, Britain's honour was at stake in the defence of free trade. He rejected the notion that this had anything to do with safeguarding the "nefarious traffic"[51] in narcotics and historians tend to agree that opium was the occasion rather than the cause of the war. Yet Palmerston was disingenuous in his arguments and extravagant in his demands for compensation to British drug dealers. They lobbied him relentlessly and were "quite confident"[52] of his acquiescence despite his canny refrain, "My ears are open but my lips are sealed."[53]

Palmerston knew perfectly well that a victory for free trade would increase the opium trade, which accounted for 40 per cent of India's exports and was *the largest commerce of the time in any single commodity.*"[54] Indeed, the sale of that commodity, which he urged the Chinese to legalise, helped to pay for the war. It turned out to be a demonstration of Britain's overwhelming technological superiority. In particular, China met its *Nemesis.* This was an iron paddle steamer, the first one to round the Cape, on what had been an epic voyage. It fired shells and Congreve rockets, and though its flat bottom attracted more barnacles than the Colonial Office, the 630-ton *Nemesis* could tow men-of-war up rivers to wreak havoc deep inside the Celestial Empire. Commissioner Lin said that the wheeled "devil ship" used "the heads of flames to drive machines, cruising very fast."[55] Some of his countrymen thought that it was powered by windmills or oxen and they actually developed their own paddle wheelers which were propelled by coolies inside the hulls turning treadles. Otherwise the Chinese relied on magic charms, gruesome masks, bows and arrows, ancient matchlocks, rusty cannon and monkeys with fireworks strapped to their backs which were supposed, when hurled aboard British vessels, to explode their powder magazines.

Inevitably, therefore, the British won a series of crushing victories. When the Treaty of Nanking was signed in 1842, they were able to extort a colossal indemnity, including compensation for the destroyed opium, and commercial privileges in five ports, among them Canton and Shanghai. They also got sovereignty over Hong Kong (Fragrant Water). After some dithering the London government decided that this barren island was worth keeping as "an exception to ordinary rules." It was occupied, said James Stephen, "not with a view to Colonization, but for Diplomatic, Commercial and Military purposes."[56] Its Governor was well placed to watch and to penetrate China. Its harbour would make it a naval base second only to Singapore. As early as

1842, sixty-foot-wide roads were being built round the island. Houses, stores, brothels, gambling dens and opium booths were multiplying. An immense Chinese bazaar was in business. Despite typhoons, fires and malaria so murderous that the smart residential area of Happy Valley was quickly "converted into a cemetery,"[57] the new crown colony at once surpassed Macao, whose shopkeepers fled thither "like rats from a falling house."[58] Hong Kong promised to become, "next to Calcutta, the most important commercial town this side [of] the Cape."[59] *Punch* prophesied that its merchants would soon have "the Emperor of China clothed in a Manchester shirt, and . . . his court handling Sheffield knives and forks."

The drug trade also followed the flag. The first substantial stone building in Hong Kong was Jardine, Matheson's opium godown, and within a decade the entire island was "a kind of bonded warehouse . . . for the opium trade."[60] This remained illegal as far as China was concerned, which secretly gratified Alexander Matheson. As he told his Bombay supplier Sir Jamsetjee Jeejeebhoy, lawful competition would cut the profits they themselves made from the traffic: "*The more difficulties attend it, the better for you and us. We shall always find ways and means to carry it on in spite of every obstacle.*"[61] The first Governor of Hong Kong, Sir Henry Pottinger, abetted the strategy of these unscrupulous *taipans* (great managers). Matheson further wrote:

> Pottinger has published a most fiery proclamation against smuggling, but I believe it is like Chinese edicts, meaning nothing and only intended for the edification, or rather gratification, of the Saints [i.e. Evangelicals] in England. Sir Henry never meant to act on it, & no doubt privately considers it a good joke. It will, however, deter many parties from speculating in the drug, which will be so far well.[62]

From start to finish, in fact, Hong Kong's role was shrouded in official hypocrisy. Britons liked to say that the colony was a "vantage point from which the Anglo-Saxon race has to work out its divine mission of promoting the civilisation of Europe in the East." Sometimes spiritual and temporal endeavours were conveniently associated, and given added grandeur by reference to Rome. A brass plate on the foundation stone of St. John's Cathedral said that it was laid by the Governor, Sir John Davis, "bedecked with proconsular dignity, on the fifth day of the Ides of March in the tenth year of Queen Victoria, A.D 1847."[63]

Some people thought that by acquiring Hong Kong Britain had cut a notch "in China as a woodsman notches a tree, to mark it for felling at a convenient opportunity."[64] Indeed, toppling the Son of Heaven from the

Dragon Throne and enrolling the Chinese masses in Britain's service became perennial Victorian fantasies. For if yellow auxiliaries were to reinforce brown, the white Empire could rule the world. So visionary imperialists, Kipling among them, called for the conquest of China. Without doubt it seemed ripe for the chop. Plainly the Celestial Empire was in a state of terminal decline, with a decadent leadership, a moribund bureaucracy and a stagnant culture. China was afflicted by overpopulation, vicious land-lordism and incipient bankruptcy. It was plagued by natural catastrophes such as the flooding of the Yellow River, "China's Sorrow." It was ravaged by lethal convulsions such as the Taiping rebellion (1850–64), which killed more people than would the First World War. However, Palmerston wanted to exploit China not to precipitate its downfall which, he maintained, was by no means inevitable. The habit of identifying an ancient monarchy with "an old tree, or an old man," said Palmerston, was "an abuse of metaphors." To think that a nation would decay and die like an organism was an "utterly unphilosophical mistake."[65] China might seem to be the Far Eastern equiv-alent of Turkey, the sick man of Asia; but it was in fact a state that could be mechanically renovated. Commercial intercourse would restore and improve the Manchu Empire, as well as benefiting Britain. When the Chi-nese continued to be uncooperative Palmerston hoped to make them see reason with what he called the *"argumentum Baculinum"*—the argument of the stick.[66]

He got his chance in 1856 when the Canton authorities seized a British-registered lorcha called the *Arrow* "in open day in a crowded anchorage"[67] and imprisoned its Chinese crew. Probably they were smugglers or pirates, but their arrest prompted a characteristic outburst of belligerence from the Prime Minister, now too lightly dismissed as "an old painted pantaloon" with false teeth and dyed whiskers: "An insolent barbarian, wielding author-ity at Canton, has violated the British flag, broken the engagement of treaties, offered rewards for the heads of British subjects in that part of China and planned their destruction by murder, assassination and poi-son."[68] Sporadic hostilities followed (interrupted by the Indian Mutiny) and in 1860 a military expedition was sent to Peking. It included French forces and it was even supported by the supposedly neutral Americans—although critical of British imperialism, the United States took aggressive advantage of China's open door. With the help of new breech-loading Armstrong guns, the door was knocked off its hinges. The Chinese put up strong resis-tance, which was rewarded by corresponding carnage. Women were raped and men were ritually humiliated: their queues (long pigtails) were cut off and they were made to kowtow. When the Emperor's forces tortured and murdered prisoners, the British retaliated by burning down his Summer Palace. Its destruction reminded a French officer of "le sac de Rome."[69]

No doubt white soldiers indulged in an orgy of looting worthy of Visigoths or Huns. But the Summer Palace (*Yuanming Yuan,* Garden of Perfect Brightness) was actually less like Rome than like Versailles. It was a monument not to the Sun King but to the Brother of the Sun, an oriental divinity who eclipsed all other monarchs on earth. The Emperor's favourite palace, set in a park girdled with five miles of granite and containing a thousand bridges, was a proclamation of his majesty. It was a willow-pattern paradise of rockeries and waterfalls, terraces and temples, cedar groves and lotus-blossom lakes, jewelled pavilions and golden pagodas. It was an art gallery, a fantastic theatre, "an imperial museum."[70] Victor Hugo described the Summer Palace as a wonder of the world:

> Build a dream of marble, of jade and bronze and porcelain; cover it with precious stones; make it a sanctuary, a harem, a citadel; fill it with gods and monsters; varnish it, enamel it, gild it, adorn it . . . add gardens and ponds, fountains of water and foam, swans, ibises, and peacocks, a dazzling cavern of the human imagination.[71]

The sight of this Aladdin's cave seemed to drive the troops into a frenzy.

Body and soul, wrote Colonel Garnet Wolseley, they became "absorbed in one pursuit, which was plunder, plunder."[72] They swarmed through massive red gates guarded by gigantic yellow lions (untouched because no one realised that they were made of gold). They swept aside the few eunuchs left by the Emperor Hien-Feng, who had fled to Jehol. They broke into the marble-floored Audience Hall, streamed through the maze of courts filled with bonsai pines, fairy grottoes, purling brooks, zigzag bridges and scented parterres, and plunged into the treasure chambers. And they emerged laden with pearls, rubies, sapphires, silks, satins and furs. They carried off ivory fans, coral screens, sable cloaks, filigree necklaces, gold clocks, crystal chandeliers, vases inlaid with bloodstone and cornelian, silver sing-songs (there were four thousand musical boxes) and priceless art objects of all sorts. They stripped the private apartments, Frenchmen with riotous abandon, the English more methodically (retrieving in the process some of Macartney's neglected gifts, including the planetarium). They even stole Pekinese dogs, sacred to royalty, one of which was eventually presented to Queen Victoria, who called it Looty.

The *Fan Qui* did not stop at looting. They smashed furniture, ripped paintings, threw mirrors out of windows, took pot shots at bronze unicorns, capered about in imperial yellow robes, daubed moustaches on the faces of priceless statues. As Gibbon wrote about the fall of Constantinople, "the rapine of an hour is more productive than the industry of years."[73] Yet the head of the British mission, Lord Elgin, who directed the looting from the Hall of Probity, decided that only by burning the Summer Palace could he punish Hien-Feng personally. Elgin's father had despoiled the Parthenon of its marbles and news of the son's desecration caused widespread outrage in Europe. For Victor Hugo and others, British pretensions to being the standard-bearers of civilisation went up in the smoke of the Summer Palace.* Its gigantic funeral pyre, which shrouded Peking in a pall of ash and foreshadowed the doom of the Celestial Empire, merely confirmed Hien-Feng's subjects in their opinion of the barbarians. However, as their whole history showed, the Chinese were adept at appeasing and assimilating savage invaders. So they came to terms, opening up the interior of their country to foreigners, legalising the opium trade and permitting diplomats from abroad to reside at Peking. The Dragon lay down with the Lion. "We might annex the Empire, if we were in the humor to take a second India in hand,"[74] wrote Elgin contemplatively. But one India was sufficient. Palmerston wanted nothing more than a stable and commercially accommodating Manchu Empire. That way, indeed, as Alexander Matheson proposed, "China would be another *India* to us, while the enormous civil and military expenditure incurred in the latter would be saved in the former."[75] Meanwhile, it was enough that the brutal Tartars had been taught a lesson, though it might have been even more effective, the Prime Minister thought, if another palace had also been burned. Still, he was "quite enchanted"[76] by Elgin's conflagration. In the Prime Minister's view it was not an act of vandalism but another "exemplary drubbing."[77] It was a demonstration of might for all the world to see, such as Rome had visited on Carthage.

So John Bull established a hold over that third of humanity he was pleased to call "John Chinaman." Hong Kong was not yet of much value. It was now safer as a result of the acquisition of Kowloon, but its tiny white population was vulnerable to the thousands of Chinese who migrated there from the mainland, many of them pirates, outlaws, Triad gangsters and opium smugglers. The town of Victoria, a sea-side straggle set in a precipitous amphitheatre of hills, remained a backwater. One disenchanted British official likened the island's green highlands to "decayed Stilton cheese,"

---

*Despite the destruction, much of the fabric remained intact. But the Chinese plundered its wreckage and the stones, like those of the Colosseum, were quarried for other projects. Subsequent attempts at restoration caused further damage, as they did in Rome. The final stage in the downfall of the Summer Palace was its Communist resurrection as the "*Yuanming Yuan* Ruins Park."

while the tors across the water presented "the appearance of a negro streaked with leprosy."[78] Even Alexander Matheson had lost faith in Hong Kong as a colony: "It only adds immensely to our expenses, without adding in the least to the amount of our business." The island might be worth something as a military base, he thought, but as a commercial centre it was much less profitable than the treaty ports, especially those "great *Emporiums* of the Trade,"[79] Canton and Shanghai. Here small international communities, including Frenchmen, Americans and others, who enjoyed the extra-territorial privileges which Britain had won, existed in a strange, artificial, quasi-colonial state.

Shanghai soon overtook Canton as the most important of these hybrid settlements and expatriates lost no time in creating the usual appurtenances of empire: clubs, churches, Masonic lodges, race courses, tennis courts and public gardens. "Shanghailanders" did themselves proud. They were cosseted by a host of servants, whom they often kicked or cuffed. Many acquired Chinese mistresses, a fertile source of English-speaking girls being the Diocesan Native Female Training School at Hong Kong. Shanghailanders also indulged their appetite for food. They would

> begin dinner with rich soup, and a glass of sherry; *then* one or two side dishes with champagne; *then* some beef, mutton, or fowls and bacon, with *more* champagne, or beer; *then* rice and curry and ham; *afterwards* game; *then* pudding, pastry, jelly, custard, or blancmange, and *more* champagne; *then* cheese and salad, and bread and butter, and a glass of port wine; *then* in many cases, oranges, figs, raisins, and walnuts . . . *with* two or three glasses of claret or some other wine.[80]

Those who survived this regimen usually tried to preserve their health by taking violent exercise. Many physicians prescribed riding. So Shanghailanders galloped furiously through countryside fertilised with the city's night soil and, as an English diplomat wrote, sacrificed "their noses to their livers."[81]

The Chinese resented the behaviour and even the presence of these overbearing intruders. The sometime tributaries bearing gifts were now traders extorting profits—new recruits heeded the traditional advice "to keep the Sabbath and anything you can lay your hands on."[82] Xenophobia was endemic on both sides and the *Fan Qui* lived in a "chronic state of petty war with the natives."[83] British consuls tried to keep the peace. They were assisted by Cantonese compradors, shroffs, crimps and clerks with a knowledge of *pidgin* English. (*Pidgin* meant "business": a bishop, for example, was charmingly called a "No. 1 Heaven Pigeon.")[84] But it was hard to quell Chinese fury over, say, the British and American business of transporting coolies to work overseas, which bore a marked resemblance to the slave trade. Moreover Britain's representatives were beholden to the opium dealers, who carried their mails, cashed their bills and did them other favours. The drug corrupted everything it touched, including the consuls, whose salaries were subsidised by the government of India in return for their services to the traffic. Still, taking advantage of China's weakness, the British generally won the initiative and seldom lost face. They continued to sell opium until soon after The Hague Convention banned its export in 1912, though Lord Crewe, who supposed that "the Indian drug differs from the Chinese as '75 Margaux differs from Australian claret," could not "avoid an unholy regret that the traffic is doomed."[85] Britons even infiltrated the Emperor's own administration. For example, the maritime customs service, superintended from 1863 until 1906 by Sir Robert Hart, became "a chief financial pillar of the Chinese government."[86] Dictatorial yet diplomatic, Hart worked meticulously while living sumptuously—he kept his own band in Peking. Eventually he accumulated further responsibilities, from overseeing lighthouses to controlling the post office. Equally masterful during the 1920s was the British Consul-General, Sir Sidney Barton, who became "practically the autocrat of Shanghai."[87]

Yet such parasitic micro-colonies as the treaty ports had only a tenuous grip on the vast cuticle of China. Their host was a slumbering giant and they were soon shaken off when he awoke. After the fall of the Manchus in the early twentieth century, Nationalist China stirred and began to flex its muscles. Although racked by internal disorders, it took advantage of the fact that oriental technology was catching up with occidental and that the British Empire was too stretched, between the world wars, to back up prestige with power. Of course, the capitalist colony of Hong Kong survived for longer than the treaty ports, thanks to the symbiotic relationship it established with the Communist mainland. But the Chinese did not need Karl Marx to tell them that imperialism was based on exploitation. Just as Rome had, in Seneca's words, "exacted tribute from all Britain,"[88] so Britain had taken ruthless advantage of China. The Opium War, the sacking of the Summer Palace and the "unequal treaties" left the Chinese in no doubt about the true nature of the West's imperial enterprise. Ridding themselves of the bloodsuckers was only a matter of time.

This aspiration found an echo wherever red ink seeped across the map, from the newest conquest to the oldest colony, from Kiplingesque Kabul to Dickensian Dublin. For even at a time when Britain was virtually unchallenged as a world power, the Empire did not advance or stand still without sanguinary setbacks of one kind or another. Victorians anatomised them anxiously, seeking signs of present weakness and future collapse. They found plenty in the two greatest catastrophes of the 1840s. The military defeat in Afghanistan cast doubt on the virility of the imperial race and undermined British *iqbal* (prestige) throughout the subcontinent, a hopeful augury for Indian mutineers. The great famine in Ireland exposed the hollowness of propaganda about the blessings of British rule and spread implacable hostility towards the Empire, borne on a flood tide of emigration, all over the globe and particularly to the United States of America.

The First Afghan War (1838–42) was an opening gambit in the "Great Game,"[89] which lasted for more than a century. The stakes were high—control of the North-West Frontier of India. On its security, said Lord Curzon, rested "the domination of the world."[90] Russia was the principal opponent in this craggy contest and Tsar Nicholas I, the reactionary "Gendarme of Europe," seemed to be playing for keeps in Central Asia. He conducted diplomatic intrigues with Pathans and Persians, and exerted military pressure from the Caucasus to the Gulf. India could only be invaded from the north and Britons began to fear that the Tsar was another Alexander the Great. The approach of the Cossack seemed more menacing because the loyalty of the sepoy was doubtful. On the map, moreover, the Himalayas scarcely looked to be the earth's mightiest natural rampart. When Lord Ellenborough, who would succeed Lord Auckland as Governor-General of India in 1842, read a scare-mongering account of a possible invasion route from the Oxus to the Indus, he exclaimed, "the thing is not only practicable but easy, unless we determine to act as an Asiatic Power."[91] Palmerston was willing. And Melbourne agreed with him that "Afghanistan must be ours or Russia's."[92] So the government pushed forward with Auckland's scheme to replace the Amir of Kabul, Dost Mahomed, with a puppet ruler, Shah Suja. An invasion force achieved this coup in 1839, but the British, not to mention subsequent intruders, ignored the Duke of Wellington's warning that when the military difficulties are over in Afghanistan the real difficulties begin. Like Armenia between the empires of Parthia and Rome, as the writer Sir Alfred Lyall observed, Afghanistan learned to play off one powerful neighbour against another in a perpetual struggle to resist foreign ascendancy.

It was soon evident that Shah Suja, "an obstinate, proud, wrong-headed man," could only survive inside a ring of British bayonets. Thus the army of occupation became the common enemy of Afghan tribesmen who, in the absence of an alien foe, devoted their energies to fighting one another. "We and our King are extremely distasteful to the country," wrote an English subaltern. "We are not tyrants enough to be feared and have done little to be respected by a semi-barbarous country."[93] Its people were, a Scottish officer later declared, "a race of tigers."[94] Now they stalked their prey amid the labyrinth of narrow, sordid alleys flanked by flat-roofed, mud-brick houses that was Kabul. Every male among its sixty thousand inhabitants possessed "a sword and shield, a dagger, a pistol or a musketoon."[95] They insulted, assaulted and then murdered foreign infidels, their most prominent victim being the British envoy Sir William Macnaghten. He was struck down during negotiations with Dost Mahomed's vengeful son Akbar Khan, whose face, as he did the deed, twisted into a grimace "of the most diabolical ferocity."[96] Parts of Macnaghten's dismembered body were paraded through the streets while his torso was hung on a meat hook in the Great Bazaar. Yet the British garrison, whose officers had raced, skated, fished, played cricket, pursued Afghan women and jumped their horses over the cantonment wall instead of fortifying their position and foraging for supplies, did not retaliate. Instead, under the command of General William Elphinstone, an ailing incompetent who had last seen shots fired in anger at Waterloo, they beat the most disastrous retreat in British military history.

On 6 January 1842 a column of 4,500 fighting men (mostly sepoys) and 12,000 camp followers set off on the ninety-mile march through the mountains. Their goal was Jalalabad, held by General Sale in "the soldierlike spirit of an English gentleman" which was (according to *The Times*) as proud as "the noble spirit of an old Roman."[97] Deep snow hampered the progress of Elphinstone's force, as did an immense baggage train. One regiment had required two camels to transport its stock of cigars to Kabul and British subalterns, who might have as many as forty servants each, would as soon have left behind their swords and pistols as march without "their dressing-cases, their perfumes, Windsor soap and eau-de-Cologne."[98] Here was loot on the hoof and the Afghans tore at it like wolves harrying a flock of sheep. They cut down stragglers, drove off pack animals, ransacked bullock carts. At dusk on the first day Elphinstone's van had only gone six miles and his rearguard was still leaving the cantonment, which the Afghans burned to the ground. In the intense cold that night some sepoys, bivouacking in the open, made fires of their caps and equipment. Others woke up so badly frost-bitten that their legs looked like charred logs. One Englishwoman saw "men taking off their boots, and their whole feet with them."[99] Everywhere the weakest perished. "Firing from the enemy recommenced at sunrise," recorded Captain William Anderson in his unpublished journal. "Our people had become such a mass of confusion as I never witnessed—our own servants and followers plundering the camp in every direction while the officers were exerting themselves to get the troops out of the chaos."[100]

By the time Elphinstone's column struggled as far as the Koord-Kabul pass, narrow, precipitous, five miles long and threaded by an icy torrent that had to be crossed and recrossed twenty-eight times, it was a frozen, famished rabble. Caught in "the jaws of this terrible defile,"[101] it proved easy meat for Ghilzai and Ghazee marksmen perched on the rocky heights. Their long-barrelled matchlocks *(jezails)* were more accurate and had a longer range than English muskets, and they poured a devastating fire on their foes. The gorge became choked with corpses. Elphinstone tried to bribe his way out and Akbar Khan did take a few Britons into protective custody— wounded officers, women and children. But local chiefs said that they did not want gold: "nothing but blood could satisfy them." Among the white remnant, wrote Anderson, "despair with its usual extremes of passiveness and frenzy now prevailed."[102] The Afghans barricaded the next major pass and massacred the rest of the British array. A single European, Assistant Surgeon William Brydon, reached safety—on 13 January. He was wounded in several places and an Afghan knife had sliced a wafer of bone from his skull; it would have been worse, Brydon recorded, had he not had "a portion of Blackwood's magazine in my forage cap."[103] As his dying pony carried its blood-stained burden towards the walls of Jalalabad, a "shudder ran through the garrison." Brydon, depicted in Lady Elizabeth Butler's well-known painting of the scene, a vivid image of the Empire *in extremis,* looked like "a messenger of death."[104]

Brydon's news shocked Britons as much as tidings of the Parthian victory at Carrhae had shocked Romans "in the very *acmé* of their power."[105] The foundations of the British Empire seemed to tremble. The Afghans were undisciplined, disunited and backward, yet they had "utterly overwhelmed" a strong "force of civilised men."[106] They had inflicted, to quote *Blackwood's Magazine* itself, an "almost irreparable injury on the British nation—an almost indelible stain on the British character."[107] Some felt no anxiety, while others were actually reassured by the classical analogy. Dr. Arnold said that it would be now as it had been when the Romans were defeated in Spain: "the next year another consul and new legions go out."[108] Macaulay also remained confident though, mindful of the Empire's Muslim millions, he acknowledged that "a great Mahometan success could not but fall like a spark upon tinder and act on the freemasonry of Islamism from

Morocco to Coromandel."[109] The Duke of Wellington was also staunch, though he thought that every "Moslem heart from Pekin to Constantinople" would vibrate at the thought of European ladies being in the hands of Akbar Khan (who actually treated the prisoners quite well). However, Wellington did contemplate "the loss of this great Empire" and to save it from "Ruin and Disgrace" he advised withdrawal from the Himalayan wilderness. So, shaken by the financial as well as the human cost, Britain climbed down from the roof of the world. Lord Ellenborough accepted Dost Mahomed's restoration (Shah Suja having been murdered) and proclaimed that the Indian government was content "with the limits nature appears to have assigned to its empire."[110]

However, Britain could not leave as a worsted power and Ellenborough did sanction a brief punitive expedition to Kabul. It rescued British prisoners, destroyed the magnificent arcaded bazaar where Macnaghten's mangled body had been exhibited, pillaged on a spectacular scale and committed many "horrible murders."[111] In fact its "licensed assassins,"[112] as the future Field-Marshal Neville Chamberlain called the British soldiers, meted out enough retributive butchery to redeem present honour and ensure future enmity. Not satisfied with a show of force, Ellenborough also tried to wipe out the Afghan humiliation with a display of pomp. The Governor-General fancied himself as Aurangzeb, putting on such airs that Wellington reckoned he ought to sit on his throne "in a strait-waistcoat."[113] And at Ferozepore Ellenborough celebrated the army's return from Afghanistan with a grand pageant designed to appeal to the oriental imagination, which was thought to be peculiarly susceptible to such manifestations. It was much ridiculed in the West, not least because everything went wrong: "The troops were to march beneath a triumphal arch and between double lines of gilded and salaaming elephants, but the arch was a gaudy and tottering structure, and the ill-tutored elephants forgot to salaam and ran away."[114] Equally inept was Ellenborough's return of the sandalwood gates, supposedly carried off by the Afghans eight hundred years earlier, to the temple of Somnath. His bombastic announcement of their restoration offended Muslims, while Hindus regarded the gates, which turned out to be made of deal, as polluted by contact with Islam. However, Ellenborough possessed not just a "Napoleonic" style[115] but territorial designs to match.

Having been repulsed in the hills, he resolved to advance on the plains. In this endeavour, one critic remarked, he resembled "a bully who has been kicked in the street and goes home to beat his wife in revenge."[116] But Ellenborough believed that British power in India was now "in a state of constant peril"[117] and that only aggressive measures could preserve it. So in 1843 he sent General Sir Charles Napier up the Indus, lifeline of the north-west region and jugular vein of the rich, independent province of Sind. Napier was the archetype of flamboyant imperial heroes such as Nicholson, Gordon, T. E. Lawrence, Wingate, Thesiger. He was chivalric, eccentric, splenetic, ascetic and sadistic. Vain as a peacock and brave as a lion, Napier had a "beak like an eagle and a beard like a Cashmere goat." From topeed and bespectacled head to booted and spurred feet, he bore the scars of a lifetime's adventure among bullets, bayonets, sabres and shrapnel. He loved women and horses—his favourite charger, Red Rover, shared his tent on hot-weather campaigns and attended at his deathbed. Napier was no respecter of persons. He openly vilified the East India Company's directors at "Leadenhead Street,"[118] "godfearing scoundrels" who filled India with a "Galaxy of Donkeys." He dismissed Lord Ripon as "an idiotic fellow."[119] And he later quarrelled with Lord Dalhousie, who likened him to a vineyard on a volcano—he would have been "gay and genial but for the perpetual flames bursting out and blasting" all that was good in him.[120]

However, Napier revered Wellington and admired Ellenborough. The latter encouraged his piratical inclinations and Napier cherished no illusions about his new commission. In his diary he memorably acknowledged, "We have no right to seize Scinde; yet we shall do so, and a very advantageous, useful, humane piece of rascality it will be."[121] This was because the British would do more good and less mischief to the people than did their present rulers, the Amirs: "Not that we ever did good from 'liberality' or 'generosity' but simply because we can squeeze *more* money out of *rich* Sindeans, than out of *poor* Sindeans! And if damming up the Indus and drowning the whole race of Sindeans would give us more money still, we should dam the Indus accordingly."[122]

Napier succeeded against overwhelming odds, thanks to discipline, trickery, ferocity and a sublime faith in "that Mysterious Power which has ruled my destiny."[123] Visualising himself as another Moses in the desert, he placed at the head of his Camel Corps an elephant bearing a flag by day and a lantern by night. But Napier's famous punning message in Latin, *"Peccavi"* (I have sinned), expressed the truth of the matter—even though it was apocryphal, originating as a joke in *Punch*.[124] As his sometime subordinate Major James Outram confirmed, the acquisition of Sind was "positive robbery."[125] The *Edinburgh Review* agreed. The British had behaved like conquerors bent on founding "an empire more secure than that of the Caesars." But they had stored up so much hatred that the tribesmen "would eagerly join the standard of any new invading power for the sake of getting rid of us."[126] In fact the seizure of Sind was part of a dialectical process often (though not invariably) repeated throughout imperial history: a defeat at the hands of "natives" would provoke a belligerent British response, which in turn sowed the seeds of further discord and ultimate alienation.

5

Sacred Wrath

Irish Famine and Indian Mutiny

The process of alienation had been going on for centuries much closer to home. Ireland, which provided, ironically, a quarter of the officers in the British Army (including Napier himself) and half the white troops in India, was England's first real colony. It had been invaded by Henry II, subjugated by Henry VIII, "settled" by Elizabeth, "planted" by James I, ravaged by Cromwell and crushed by William of Orange. Each Irish rebellion was visited with fresh English oppression. Economic exploitation further aggravated the relationship between the two peoples, so much so that Dean Swift advised his countrymen to burn everything from England but her coal. Moreover, since the Reformation Ireland had been bedevilled by the mutual hatred of a Protestant ascendancy (with its English Pale around Dublin and its Scottish garrison in Ulster) and a Roman Catholic majority, subject to a penal code designed to keep it in a state of permanent inferiority. Thus Irish resistance was not just an expression of patriotism; it was, in more senses than one, an act of faith.

The American and French Revolutions sharpened nationalist aspirations, and England conceded measures of self-government and religious toleration. But in 1798 a radical peasant uprising took place in Ireland, with French backing. Pitt's remedy was brutal repression followed by attempted assimilation: the Act of Union (1800) incorporated Ireland into the United Kingdom of Britain. Catholic emancipation, the proposed reward to the Irish for sacrificing their legislative independence and sending MPs to Westminster, was put off until 1829. But for the "Liberator," Daniel O'Connell, and most of his compatriots this was no more than a step towards the goal of ending Saxon tyranny over Celt. As *The Economist* acknowledged, the English did not treat the Irish as part of the Empire but as "a conquered tribe." Consequently the Irishman merely existed in the present, whereas he *lived* in the past and in the future.

His imagination is filled with what Ireland was, and with what it may become. And you have but to touch on these two topics, the *past* and the *future,* in order to set fire to his mind, and to make him send up a shout that might rend the heavens, for a Repeal of the Union.[1]

More heartbreaking cries rent the heavens after 1845 as the Irish suffered famine, pestilence and exodus on a biblical scale. Here, spelled out in letters of blood, was the proof that Ireland must be master of its own fate.

Even in normal years Ireland hovered on the brink of starvation. By 1845 its population had risen to over eight million and pressure on the soil increased accordingly. Many families, rack-rented by landlords (a third of whom were absentees, Palmerston among them), survived on tiny plots of half an acre or less. They grew mainly potatoes, which sometimes constituted their entire diet—healthy enough to make Irish soldiers "consistently taller"[2] than English ones. But there were fatal dearths and for three months before each new crop was harvested a third of the people went hungry. Visitors to the wild western provinces of Munster and Connaught, where reliance on the potato was heaviest, were appalled by the want and squalor. On arrival they were assailed by hordes of beggars, all in the last stages of destitution, all vociferous in their appeals: "Won't yer ladyship buy a dying woman's prayers—chape!"[3] Inland they encountered ragged, Gaelic-speaking multitudes, "a harvest grown ready for the sickle of hunger."[4] Families shared bare, windowless cabins with any livestock they possessed. Evicted tenants and dispossessed squatters dwelt in burrows, bog-holes or turfed ditches known as "scalpeens." Many of them had never seen a tree and did not recognise a currency note. Englishmen of refined sensibilities likened Irish peasants to "white negroes,"[5] "apes"[6] and "human chimpanzees."[7] A Frenchman exclaimed, "I have seen the Indian in his forests and the negro in his irons, and I believed, in pitying their plight, that I saw the lowest ebb of human misery; but I did not then know the degree of poverty to be found in Ireland."[8]

Some parts of the island, especially the more developed east, were less badly afflicted. But Dublin itself contained slums, such as the Liberties, which made Tom-All-Alone's seem salubrious: "The entrance to the courts is very narrow—a sort of great stench valve, or over-ground sewer. As a general rule, there is a green slimy stream oozing from a surcharged and choked-up cess-pool, through which a visitor is compelled to wade."[9] Much of the city's sewage poured straight into the River Liffey, which was a sink of "contagion"[10] (though its black water supposedly had "miraculous properties"[11] that gave strength to Guinness's stout). According to William Cobbett, English hogs were "better lodged, and far better fed, and far more clean in their skins, than are thousands upon thousands of human beings" in the second city of the Empire. Yet with its broad Georgian streets and harmonious neo-classical squares, Dublin was as fine a metropolis, Cobbett acknowledged, "as almost any in the world."[12] One of its most splendid buildings, dominating the busy cobbled quayside, was the grey stone Custom House constructed on liquid ground by James Gandon, whose task would have been easier but for local advice given, as he sardonically remarked, freely and without a fee. It was domed, porticoed, topped with an immense statue of Commerce and decorated with other symbolic motifs and allegorical figures, among them Britannia and Hibernia embracing. Most poignant of all was the representation of Neptune banishing Famine and Despair.

This tableau was utterly confounded in 1845 when the fungal disease *Phytophthora infestans* turned a quarter of the potato crop into putrid black slime. Distress at once became acute, especially in the west. It was somewhat alleviated by government measures: public works, price controls and the import of yellow Indian corn, hard as flint and so indigestible that it was known as "Peel's brimstone."[13] However, after Peel split the Tory party by repealing the Corn Laws, which imposed duties on foreign grain, Lord John Russell's Whig ministry committed itself even more sternly to free trade. When the potato harvest failed again in 1846, this time almost completely, Britain relied on the panaceas of Adam Smith—private enterprise and market forces. So while peasants starved, ships full of Irish corn sailed for England, which sent troops rather than food to quell protesters. The Irish must look after themselves, maintained Sir Charles Trevelyan, the Treasury official in charge of coping with the catastrophe. Anything in the nature of a dole would sap the principle of self-reliance, cutting "like a canker into the moral health and physical prosperity of the people."[14] Nevertheless, England did provide some wholly inadequate relief, though even this was too much for the London *Times*. It inveighed against the dangers of conciliating and demoralising "Paddy," and preached the uncompromising gospel of *laissez-faire*.

For our part, we regard the potato blight as a blessing. When the Celts once cease to be potatophagi, they must become carnivorous. With the taste for meats will grow the appetite for them; with the appetite, the readiness to earn them. With this will come steadiness, regularity, and perseverance; unless, indeed, the growth of these qualities be impeded by the blindness of Irish patriotism, the short-sighted indifference of petty landlords, or the random recklessness of Government benevolence.[15]

Meanwhile, during the autumn and winter of 1846, Ireland was being consumed by the famine.

From the mountains of Donegal to the lochs of Kerry villages emptied, workhouses overflowed, evictions multiplied and crime rates soared—starving men saw transportation as a deliverance and prison as a reprieve, and some even tried "to break into gaol."[16] From the bogs of Mayo to the hills of Cork the countryside swarmed with human scarecrows, scavenging for blackberries, cabbage leaves, nettles, bark. Even a tough government inspector was "unmanned by the intensity and extent of the suffering I witnessed more especially among the women and little children." At Clare Abbey on Christmas Eve he saw crowds of them "scattered over the turnip fields like a flock of famishing crows, devouring the raw turnips, mothers half naked, shivering in the snow and sleet, uttering exclamations of despair while their children were screaming with hunger."[17] Then came reports of mass mortality. The hovels of Sligo were crowded with sick, dying and dead. The roadsides of Limerick were dotted with "emaciated corpses, partly green from eating docks, partly blue from cholera and dysentery."[18] The hamlets of west Cork contained a population of "famished and ghastly skeletons,"[19] naked adults huddled in filthy straw like doomed animals, children with the wasted limbs and shrivelled faces of premature old age. In Clare the dead were buried in mass graves without "sheet or coffin."[20] In Roscommon seven cadavers were found in a hedge half eaten by dogs. As late as May 1849 fifty-seven "wretched paupers" at the cholera hospital in Parsonstown "breathed their last on the same day."[21] The horrors were unevenly spread. The novelist Anthony Trollope, who crisscrossed the country as fox hunter and post office inspector, saw no "unburied bodies" and claimed that deaths from "absolute famine were, comparatively speaking, few."[22] It is true that about 90 per cent of the deaths were due to consequential disease, mainly typhus (known in America as "Irish fever").[23] But in terms of overall mortality as a proportion of the population, Ireland's "Great Hunger" was one of the most murderous famines in history.

By 1851, when the holocaust had burned itself out, perhaps a million had died and another 1.5 million had emigrated. The anguish of exile was commemorated in names given to points of embarkation: the Pier Head at Killaloe was christened the "Wailing Wall" while the Cove of Cork was known as the "Harbour of Tears." But there was no safety in flight for many took their sickness with them. They perished in Liverpool, which became known as the "City of the Plague."[24] They expired in the transatlantic "coffin ships," where death rates were often higher than those of slavers or convict vessels. They found graves in the hostile New World. At Grosse Isle in the

St. Lawrence, where immigrants were quarantined in dreadful conditions, stands a memorial to the tragic toll. It is a tall, granite Celtic cross, erected in 1909 by the Ancient Order of Hibernians in America and dedicated to the thousands who died of fever "on this island having fled from the laws of the foreign tyrants and an artificial famine."[25] Here, recorded on its ebony plaque in Gaelic (the English and French inscriptions are milder), is the unvarnished myth that has ever since inspired Irish nationalism. Leaders of the movement, such as John Mitchel, charged that the Irish had been "carefully, prudently and peacefully *slain* by the English government." The famine was, in the words of Charles Gavan Duffy, "a fearful murder committed on the mass of the people."[26] At home and abroad even today, according to Conor Cruise O'Brien, some Irish people equate this "man-made famine"[27] with the Nazi extermination of the Jews.

When the historian turns to Ireland, as Macaulay wrote, borrowing the image from a Roman poet, he steps on a "thin crust of ashes, beneath which the lava is still glowing."[28] Yet it must be said, *pace* a recent authority, that the Great Hunger was no act of "colonial genocide."[29] It was not manufactured. It was a natural disaster made more lethal by the chronic poverty of Ireland's subsistence farmers. Moreover, by restricting government interference to a minimum, English politicians and officials were responding in accordance with the received economic wisdom of the day. Trevelyan was no monster, deaf to pity as he sanctioned the export of grain from starving provinces. On the other hand, he was a ruthless ideologue. A stern Evangelical and a rigorous philosophical radical, he was prepared to make terrible sacrifices on the altar of what he saw as an ultimately beneficent historical process. In Trevelyan's opinion the famine was the "direct stroke of an all-wise and all-merciful Providence,"[30] apparently operating on Malthusian lines, to civilise the Irish. Yet Trevelyan was not the impotent victim of a monolithic orthodoxy. Many contemporaries favoured state intervention, damning *laissez-faire* when it meant "Liberty to die by starvation."[31] Others pointed out the shameful incongruity of spending vast sums to promote the opium trade or to conquer Sind, and paying £20 million to compensate West Indian planters for the emancipation of their slaves, while giving only £8 million (half of it in loans) to relieve Ireland. Even those engaged in carrying out government policies denounced the philosophy behind them. One experienced Poor Law Commissioner condemned the theory "that a person who permits the destitute Irish to die from want of food is acting in uniformity with the system of nature . . . I believe it is part of the system of nature that we should have compassion for them and assist them."[32] Contrary to some claims, then, Trevelyan and his political masters cannot be exonerated as the slaves of dogma. It is by no means anachronistic to say that, despite the difficulties, including a financial crisis at home and food shortages throughout Europe, they could and should have done much more to assist Ireland in its supreme hour of need.

The truth is that John Bull had scant sympathy for Paddy. The English gave little in charity yet accused the Irish of ingratitude. They liked to blame the famine on Hibernian fecklessness and to assert that the real cause of potato rot was Popery.[33] An American traveller, who heard English aristocrats describing the Irish as "a company of low, vulgar, lazy wretches, who prefer beggary to work and filth to cleanliness," concluded that it was a law of nature "to hate those we oppress."[34] The Irish recognised the animus and kicked against the pricks. But the famine, which provoked a revolt in 1848, also ensured that it was never more than a clash in a cabbage patch. Quixotic leaders of the "Young Ireland" movement, such as the green-uniformed William Smith O'Brien, could not rouse a peasantry too broken to try "to 'squelch' the 'bloody old British Empire.'"[35] Meanwhile, the British government, alarmed by Chartists in London and revolutionaries on the Continent, had filled Dublin with so many troops and guns that the Custom House had to be used as a barracks and an arsenal. Nevertheless, Irishmen had raised the Green Flag in opposition to the Union Jack and kept alive a tradition of political violence whose manifestations would be legion.

This is not to say that revolutionary organisations such as the Fenians (founded in New York in 1857 as the Irish Republican Brotherhood), still less terrorist splinter groups like the Invincibles, commanded significant support in Ireland, let alone throughout the Empire. Indeed, very few Victorian proponents of Home Rule for Ireland demanded complete separation from Britain, preferring some kind of dominion status. Still, the blood of famine victims was the seed of the nationalist cause. Its spillage on such a scale demonstrated that Irishmen at Westminster were not, as John Mitchel put it, "members of an Imperial senate" so much as "captives dragged at the chariot wheels of an Imperial ovation in the enemy's capital city." The "sacred wrath" which the Irish felt at the "horror and desolation" that had overtaken their country spread across the globe as the national diaspora continued: by 1860 there were 300,000 Irish in Canada, 250,000 in Australia and during the next ten years a million went to the United States. At home and in the wider Empire, Roman Catholic Irishmen were generally reckoned a subversive influence. But in the cellars of Boston, the slums of New York and the tenements of Chicago "bitterness against the English" was unconfined. The story of the famine, which grew in the telling, evoked such "hatred and horror," said Mitchel, that no U.S. citizen would have cause to "wonder hereafter when he hears an Irishman in America fervently curse the British Empire." That Empire would be buried, he prophesied, while "the passionate aspiration of Irish nationhood"[36] was still green. British politicians observed the same prospect, though of course from a different point of view. They bemoaned the hatred of England that was being carried abroad. And they feared that Ireland, along with other oppressed nations, would be the nemesis of the Empire.[37]

While Ireland was urged to shift for itself, Britain intervened more and more in India, for equally high-minded reasons but with correspondingly lamentable results. By the 1830s, when reform was all the rage at home, many whites (among them, ironically, Charles Trevelyan himself) aspired to extend the benefits of European civilisation to the subcontinent. Often they were animated by Utilitarian and Evangelical sentiments. They wanted to found "British greatness upon Indian happiness"[38] and to substitute revealed religion for the "filth and obscenity" of heathen idolatry, involving as it did "bull, peacock, monkey and other nameless objects of worship."[39] Lord William Bentinck, who served as Governor-General from 1828 to 1835 despite having been blamed for the Vellore Mutiny, led this drive to westernise. He banned suttee, the burning of Hindu widows—which Europeans sometimes attended as a spectacle, like the animal fights which rajahs staged for them. He suppressed thuggee, the ritual strangling of travellers—the British saw Thugs, none too clearly, as "a national fraternity of murderers."[40] He attacked corruption and encouraged the spread of "useful knowledge."[41] He reformed the judicial system and abolished flogging for sepoys, though not for white troops. He initiated a steamboat service on the Ganges. He instituted public works—drains, roads, bridges, irrigation schemes and the like. He even blew up and melted down the huge Mughal gun at Agra for its metal and it was rumoured (wrongly) that he proposed to sell blocks of marble from the Taj Mahal. At a time when the cheap cloth of Lancashire was destroying the hand-weaving industry of Bengal and superseding the muslins of Dacca, formerly the "Manchester of India,"[42] Bentinck promoted the first cotton mill, which soon undersold English products. Tall, aquiline and cold-blooded, the Governor-General regarded the subcontinent as a great estate to be improved. But only an "all-powerful" government could accomplish this, by ensuring the requisite security for property and persons. "This is civil liberty," said Bentinck. "Political liberty would turn us out of India."[43]

Summing up in his lapidary fashion, Macaulay wrote that Bentinck "infused into Oriental despotism the spirit of British freedom."[44] As this paradox suggests, the Governor-General, always a liberal conservative, was inconsistent. Like other westerners, he was alloyed by the East. In Government House he kept "royal and Asiatic" state but he dressed in a frock coat like a "Pennsylvania Quaker."[45] Seeing him on the way to the country with an umbrella under his arm, Englishmen talked "loudly of the dissolution of the Empire, and the world's end."[46] They were further scandalised when he invited "native gentlemen" of rank to feasts worthy of the Mughals. But he imported his pickles from London, his cookery from Paris and between courses his band played Mozart and Rossini. Bentinck travelled with an escort of three hundred elephants in the manner of Shah Jehan, his own beast was hung with *jhools* (broadcloth) of scarlet and gold, and his silver howdah was polished with cow dung. But he so neglected the menagerie begun by Wellesley that some thought its "own decadence signified that of the Empire"[47]—the British collected wild animals, as the prospectus for the London Zoological Society indicated, in deliberate imitation of "Rome at the period of her greatest splendour."[48]

There was nothing unusual about Bentinck's eclecticism. However convinced westerners were of the superiority of their own race, religion and culture, many found it hard to resist the influence of the Orient. Its most obvious attractions—hookahs, nautches, eastern costume (excluding pyjamas) and Indian concubines, or "sleeping dictionaries"—were less acceptable to sahibs than they had been to nabobs. Now anybody who showed signs of "going native" was open to contempt: one lieutenant complained that "27 years in this country" had made his commanding officer "a perfect nigger in thought and habits."[49] Yet the most prejudiced griffin (novice) soon acquired a taste for Indian food, especially curry, kedgeree and mulligatawny soup. Indian servants, a ubiquitous presence, often orientalised their masters. They groomed, shampooed and dressed them and, it was said, all but masticated their food for them. Moreover, they tended to run their employers' households according to Indian rhythms, turning "the colonial power relationship on its head."[50] Britons also learned polite Indian bathing habits and kept their *dhobi-wallah* (laundry-man) busy; generations of them, returning home, were revolted by the "un-washedness of English people's skin and clothes."[51] Sarees had once been recommended as oriental togas; but although English women stuck to Piccadilly fashions, they were not immune to those of Chowringhee. Honoria Lawrence "felt very awkward in [the] presence of natives with my uncovered head."[52] White women often now watched durbars (at which their menfolk doffed their shoes) from behind a screen, protected like the inmates of a zenana from the alien male gaze.

Also reflecting the customs of the country was the growth of "the Moustache movement."[53] Some British officers had begun to sport hair on their top lip during the Napoleonic Wars. They did so largely, it seems, in dashing imitation of coxcombical Frenchmen, who took the Spanish view that an "hombre de bigote"[54] was a man of resolution, their whiskers evidently being "appurtenances of Terror."[55] The mode became imperative in India, where beards were deemed sacred but the moustache was a symbol of virility. Indians looked upon "the bare faces of the English with amazement and contempt," regarding as "*na-mard,* unmanly," countenances emasculated by the razor. So in 1831 the 16th Lancers hailed with delight an order permitting them to wear moustaches. But the battle for this "war-like appendage"[56] was not yet won. In 1843 James Abbott's "large mustachios"[57] raised eyebrows, despite his gallant feats as a political officer on the North-West Frontier. Such hirsute handlebars, worn by "the vulgar clever,"[58] still seemed a foreign affectation. And when Lord Dalhousie, as Governor-General, disparaged "capillary decorations" in 1849 they fell "like leaves in October."[59] But they soon sprouted again when organs such as the *Naval & Military Gazette* and the *Agra Messenger* campaigned for them. In 1854 moustaches were made compulsory for European troops of the Company's Bombay army and they were enthusiastically adopted elsewhere. The Royal Durban Rangers at once ceased to shave their upper lip, for instance, and the *Mercury* complimented them on their improved appearance. Despite further opposition, the vogue became a fetish and a martial art.

Moustaches were religiously cultivated and subjected to severe discipline, enforced by Queen's Regulations. They were brushed and pomaded. The follicles were fertilised with patent unguents such as Ayre's Formula, Elliott's Tonic Lotion and Oldridge's Balm of Columbia. The topiary luxuriance was trained with iron curling tongs. During and after the Crimean War barbers advertised different patterns in their windows such as the "Raglan" and the "Cardigan," the latter "a remarkable affair, alternately billowing out and narrowing."[60] Moustaches were clipped and trimmed until they curved like sabres and bristled like bayonets. Their ends were waxed and given a soldierly erection. Imitating warriors, civilians too stiffened their upper lips: Friedrich Engels mocked Anglo-Irish aristocrats with "enormous moustaches under colossal Roman noses."[61] By the 1890s the manly fringe was "the mark of every successful masher."[62] For different reasons sailors and parsons eschewed the fashion but it was jealously guarded by the *beau monde*. Edwardian tuskers rebuked servants who aped the "fancy hairdressing" of their betters.[63] Nothing should be permitted to devalue these military insignia, which achieved their apotheosis in the crossed scimitars of Lord Kitchener and gained iconic status in the famous Great War recruiting poster. So the moustache became the emblem of empire, roughly coterminous with the Raj but largely derived from it— much as the Romans derived the habit of wearing trousers from the barbarians.

Nevertheless, the tiny British caste, itself temporary, official and divided into a strict hierarchy, became more assertively racist during the 1830s. As a French observer noted, the Englishman only appeared before the natives "on a footing of superiority and grandeur" and if one of them addressed him as "you" instead of "Your Highness" he had to be given a "very sharp lesson in manners."[64] Domestic servants were regularly beaten and high status was no protection against white violence elsewhere: any Indian was liable to be kicked by "any planter's assistant or sub-deputy railway contractor whose path he may chance to cross."[65] Matters would get worse after the Mutiny. An American visitor to India, who was "astonished to see everybody bowing to us in the streets," noted that a rich native had "narrowly missed a horse-whipping lately"[66] because he did not stop his carriage and make obeisance to a British officer riding on the same road. General Baden-Powell refined the convention, asserting that

> as a rule the niggers seem to me cringing villains. As you ride or walk along the middle of the road, every cart or carriage has to stop and get out of your way, and every native, as he passes you, gives a salute. If he has an umbrella up he takes it down, if he is riding a horse he gets off and salutes. Moreover they do whatever you tell them. If you meet a man in the road and tell him to dust your boots, he does it.[67]

Always prepared with a fatuous cliché, the founder of the international Boy Scout movement justified this custom on the grounds that before a man can rule he must learn to obey. Few things, indeed, could have inspired Indians with a more ardent desire to rule themselves than such public assertions of racial supremacy.

Henry Lawrence himself, who came to be revered as an imperial soldier-saint comparable to Horatius, treated brown men with studied arrogance. They left their shoes outside his tent, uttered many "Salaams" and "Sahibs," and remained standing while he "sat without a coat, waistcoat or jacket, his legs over the arm of a chair or his feet on the table." Furthermore, as his wife Honoria reminded him, he scarcely ever addressed an Indian without "an abusive epithet . . . [even] when you are not angry."[68] Often he was angry, alarming even friends by the gunpowder in his composition. Lawrence's acolytes were rougher still in their effort to establish "Christian civilisation in lands where Idolatry too often occupies the Temple, Corruption the Tribunal, and Tyranny the Throne."[69] John Lumsden's well-used shillelagh became a regimental totem, hung on his door and saluted. In fact, the great gulf fixed between Europeans and natives was widening remorselessly. Emily Eden, Lord Auckland's sister, could hardly find a comparison to illustrate the difference between them:

> An elephant and Chance [her dog], St Paul's and a Baby-Home, the Jerseys and Pembrokes, a diamond and a bad flint, Queen Adelaide and O'Connell, London and Calcutta, are not further apart and more antipathetic than those two classes. I do not see how the prejudice can ever wear out, nor do I see that it is very desirable.[70]

Still more striking was Thomas Babington Macaulay's alienation from India. Steeped in the classics and wedded to the notion that Britain was the modern embodiment of progress, he completely failed to appreciate this new world. Yet his response to it was constructive as well as instructive—as befitted this brilliant "book in breeches," this "Babbletongue" whose "occasional flashes of silence" made his conversation "perfectly delightful,"[71] this historian of genius, the only British rival to Gibbon.

Macaulay said that Europeans were attracted to India as tigers were to the hills: "They encounter an uncongenial climate for the sake of what they can get." He himself came to the subcontinent, as legal member of the Governor-General's Council, to make his fortune—in four years he accumulated over £20,000, which gave him the independence to write. What he found was a land of barbarism, sometimes ludicrous, often revolting, always exotic. The sight of the native boatman, entirely self-possessed though clad in nothing but a pointed yellow cap, who came aboard to land him at Madras, almost made Macaulay "die of laughing." Having surfed over waves like huge bolts of green silk, he was "quite stunned" by the scene on shore. "Such a land—nothing but dark faces and bodies with white turbans and flowing robes,—the trees not our trees,—the very smell of the atmosphere like that of a hothouse,—the architecture as strange as the vegetation."[72] Still more bizarre, in Macaulay's view, was the Rajah's palace at Mysore, a vast confection of jewelled knick-knacks and tinselled tat. Grotesque (and sometimes obscene) images were also, Macaulay observed, objects of worship:

> Having seen his Highness's clothes, and his Highness's horse, I was favoured with a sight of his Highness's Gods, who were much of a piece with the rest of his establishment. The principal deity was a fat man with a paunch like Daniel Lambert's, an elephant's head and trunk, a dozen hands and a serpent's tail.[73]

Macaulay might have been less dismissive of India if his Sanskrit dictionary had not fallen overboard and he had learned that language—said by Sir William Jones to be "more perfect than Greek, more copious than Latin, and more exquisitely refined than either"[74]—instead of Portuguese on the two-week voyage from Madras to Calcutta. For this squat, ungainly man, known as "Beast" at Cambridge, combined intellect with imagination. His mind, which seemed to bulge from his forehead, was astonishingly capacious: he could read as fast as he could turn pages and he remembered everything, from the whole of *Paradise Lost* to street songs heard once in childhood. He was also an ardent romantic. He once had to turn down a by-path to avoid other walkers because he was crying over the *Iliad*, "crying for Achilles cutting off his hair; crying for Priam rolling on the ground in the courtyard of his house; mere imaginary beings, creatures of an old ballad-maker who died near three thousand years ago." He might have responded with equal passion to the wealth of oriental legend, lore and literature even then coming to light. But, immersed in the treasury of European culture and beginning to write *The Lays of Ancient Rome,* an epic to republican virtue rather than imperial might, he let it make no impression on his heart or his head.

Actually he accommodated himself to India better than most. He found Calcutta, where the climate suited only insects and undertakers, less suffocating than the House of Commons. He learned to eat breakfasts of "eggs, mango-fish, snipe-pies, and frequently a hot beef-steak." As much as possible he shunned official dinners, where he had to sit next to the lady of the highest rank, "in other words, the oldest, ugliest, and proudest woman in the company," and where the conversation was "deplorable twaddle." He got used to the swift deterioration of his surroundings: "Steel rusts; razors lose their edge; thread decays; clothes fall to pieces; books moulder away, and drop out of their bindings; plaster cracks; timber rots; matting is in shreds."[75] Such corruption typified India, in Macaulay's view, contrasting with the solidity of British civilisation. Like Bentinck, who thought Macaulay a miracle, he believed that the subcontinent could only be saved "if it were remodelled on English lines."[76] Thus he promoted freedom of the press and equality before the law. Most particularly, as his famous minute stated, he believed Indians should receive a western education and learn the English language.

Needless to say, his assumption of the superiority of European learning has been roundly condemned, not least because it was expressed in such trenchant terms. Although brought up to believe in Goliath and Methuselah and a land flowing with milk and honey, Macaulay disparaged Indian history which abounded with "kings thirty feet high, and reigns thirty thousand years long—and geography made up of seas of treacle and seas of butter."[77] But his ultimate purpose has largely been obscured. He aimed to fit Indians for independence and to teach them to embrace European institutions of government. Thus British civilisation would triumph even when its power had vanished, just as the civilisation of ancient Rome had survived the passing of the Caesars. The Empire being an empire of opinion, conservatives such as Lord Ellenborough opposed the spread of western education precisely because it did undermine British rule. But Macaulay declared that the ending of the Raj would be "the proudest day in English history"—provided that his compatriots left behind an empire immune to decay, "the imperishable empire of our arts and our morals, our literature and our laws."[78] This was a legacy that many Indian nationalists were prepared to accept. What is more, they valued English as, so to speak, the *lingua franca* of the subcontinent and, thanks largely to America, the Latin of the modern world. It became the vernacular of emancipation.

The drive to reform India along European lines continued until 1857. Its pace was variable and so were its consequences. For westernisation, which eventually fostered liberal nationalism, initially provoked a conservative revolution. Of course, it was not that simple. The Indian Mutiny (to use its British name) was a mixture of military uprising, political coup, religious war, peasant revolt and race riot. It was a reaction against all sorts of grievances, some long-standing, others immediate. Ever since 1813, when Christian missionaries were admitted, the British had seemed bent on the conversion of India. Associated with this was the attack on native customs such as suttee, most forcefully conducted by General Napier who promised to act according to the custom of his own country: "when men burn women alive we hang them."[79] Many Indians regarded the "great engines of social improvement" which Lord Dalhousie championed—"Railways, uniform Postage, and the Electric Telegraph"[80]—as assaults on the caste system.

Caste segregated people, whereas they were brought together by these instruments of hell—villagers thought that locomotives "were driven by the force of demons trying to escape from the iron box" in which the *Feringhees* had imprisoned them.[81]

The Marquess of Dalhousie, the most masterful Governor-General (1848–56) since Wellesley, bore down opposition with patrician hauteur. He reformed the revenue system, alienating the tax-farmers *(talukdars)* who were dismissed as "drones of the soil."[82] He tried to improve the lot of women. He completed the conquest of the Punjab, golden "Land of the Five Rivers," proudly adding "four million subjects to the British Empire and plac[ing] the historical jewel of the Mogul Emperors [the Koh-i-noor Diamond] in the crown of his own Sovereign." He seized lower Burma to "secure our power in India." He annexed princely states in the subcontinent when the ruler left no direct heir, flouting the Hindu tradition of adoption; among the plums that Dalhousie pulled out of this "Christmas pie"[83] were Jaipur, Udaipur, Jhansi, Nagpur and Oudh. Moreover, he disregarded Napier's warning that the sepoys were close to mutiny. They were ill disciplined, badly rewarded, appallingly housed and squeezed into uncomfortable western uniforms. White officers often called them "nigger" or "*suar*" (pig), and General Anson, who became Commander-in-Chief in 1856, never saw an Indian sentry "without turning away in disgust." In the same year sepoys were obliged to go overseas (previously a voluntary service) if ordered to do so, even though crossing the "black water" broke their (usually high) caste. Still more abhorrent to both Hindus and Muslims was the grease used on the cartridges of the new Enfield rifles, which replaced Brown Bess muskets in 1857. With singular ineptitude the British ensured that it contained both cow and pig fat.

The army command at once withdrew the offending cartridges (which were never generally issued) but sepoys now saw pollution everywhere. Other rumours were rife during the first months of 1857, the centenary of Clive's victory at Plassey, among them prophecies that the Raj would only last for a hundred years. Equally ominous was the sudden appearance of chapattis, little grey cakes of baked flour, which men distributed throughout the northern provinces for reasons that remain a mystery. High-ranking figures plotting subversion in India, notably Nana Sahib, adopted son of a deposed Maratha ruler, took heart from Britain's setbacks during the Crimean War. Although cocooned inside their own society, some British officers sensed that a full-scale revolt was imminent. At Ambala on 5 May a Lieutenant Martineau wrote: "I can hear the moaning of the hurricane, but I can't say how, when, or where it will break forth."[84] It broke forth at the great military station of Meerut, forty miles north of Delhi, less than a week later. There eighty-five skirmishers of the 3rd Light Cavalry, who had been court-martialled for refusing to accept the cartridges, were mustered on the dusty parade ground in stifling heat under a leaden sky. They were ceremonially stripped of their uniforms, fettered and marched off to serve a ten-year gaol sentence, some lamenting, others cursing. Despite further warnings the British were completely unprepared when, at sunset the next day, three regiments mutinied. They killed about fifty officers and other *Feringhees,* including women and children, and burned and plundered at will. Then they marched on Delhi, soon capturing the ancient capital and modern arsenal of India.

Its loss could have been fatal to the Raj. For, as one missionary wrote, "Our Empire here has existed more upon the *opinion* that the people had of our strength than upon our force" and the natives would now be encouraged to "rise in a body with a determination to murder every European."[85] This happened in Delhi. The mutineers also proclaimed Bahadur Shah, the hook-nosed, white-bearded, octogenarian heir to the Mughals, Emperor of India. He was an improbable leader. A poet and a mystic (who believed that he could turn himself into a gnat), he dwelt amid splendour and squalor in the Red Fort in Delhi, stimulating himself with naked dancing girls and draughts of opium enriched with crushed pearls, rubies and coral. Yet he seems to have conspired with the mutineers and he certainly provided them with a figurehead. An avatar of decadence, he was also a living symbol of the past which they sought to restore. So the "Devil's Wind"[86] coursed through north India, along the Grand Trunk Road, down the brown Ganges and the blue Jumna, across the great swathe of territory stretching from the Punjab, via Rohilkhand, Oudh and Bihar, to Bengal. In the words of Lord Canning, Dalhousie's successor as Governor-General, the Mutiny was "more like a national war than a local insurrection."[87]

From Lahore to Calcutta panic gripped British society. Always a white froth on a brown tide, it was in danger of being blown away in the gathering storm. Indeed, seeing the flight of the capital's Europeans across the *maidan* to Fort William and ships in the Hooghly, one witness was reminded of the evacuation of Herculaneum after the eruption of Vesuvius. While larger communities concentrated on defence, smaller ones scattered, often with terrible consequences. Maria Mill's experience, recalled in her poignant unpublished account, was typical. Her husband, an artillery major, was killed at Fyzabad and she fled into the countryside with her three children. Deserted by their servants, they endured heat, thirst, hunger, illness, exhaustion and "unspeakable anguish." Occasionally brave villagers, "moved with compassion," helped them, even providing a wet nurse for her baby boy. Once a sympathetic rajah gave them shelter in a cow shed with other fugitives, three sergeants' wives and their offspring. Mrs. Mill found this a mixed blessing:

> I quite feared illness must be the result of so many being crowded together, beside the want of air, and proper food and, to be associated with these women, whose language was often dreadful to hear, was not the least of my miseries, for I was shocked that my children should hear it.

She was unable to breast-feed her baby, who died en route, and when she reached Calcutta after a four-month odyssey, she gave birth to a daughter who also died. Mrs. Mill and her two older children owed their own survival to luck, having been surrounded "by a fierce body of desperate men, who were apparently ready to murder us without any compunction."[88] Despite the sepoys' obvious disaffection, though, many British commanders insisted that their own regiments were loyal and refused to disarm them. Up and down country they paid for their faith with their lives.

Yet the mutineers were never able to transform the uprising into a war of independence. They lacked unified command, a coherent strategy and (for the most part) Enfield rifles. They were distracted by the sieges of Cawnpore, Lucknow and Agra. Their support was always confined to the north and even here it was patchy. Few princes or educated people joined them. Many of their countrymen fought against them, notably thirty thousand sepoys. They had to face formidable contingents of Sikhs, Punjab cavalry dressed in red turbans spangled with gold, dark blue tunics, scarlet cummerbunds, light yellow trousers and large top boots. They were also opposed by Gurkhas, valiant Himalayan infantry in green woollen overcoats (which they refused to discard in temperatures sometimes over 140 degrees) and black worsted headgear which was described as a frightful compromise between a puggaree and a Glengarry. Using steam power and the electric telegraph, the British were able to call in fresh white troops, some from abroad, others with Crimean experience. They included Scottish Highlanders, bag-piped and red-coated, bonneted, plumed and kilted, who were variously thought to be women, eunuchs and demons with a keen appetite for "curried black babies."[89] Certainly they were a terrifying array, once complimented by General Havelock for holding their fire until "you saw the colour of your enemy's mustachios."[90]

The mutineers got no assistance from Dost Mahomed in Afghanistan, while Herbert Edwardes recruited a North-West Frontier militia: "Every idle vagrant, every professional robber, every truculent student in the mosques, at whose finger-ends fanaticism was beginning to tingle, found a market for his sword."[91] Sir John Lawrence, who had succeeded his brother Henry as master of the Punjab, quelled sedition *(fissad)* by giving free rein to his implacable Christian soldiers. The most famous of them was General John Nicholson, a giant of morose temper and superhuman courage—his method of killing tigers was to ride round and round them on his horse until they grew dizzy and then strike them down with cold steel. Some tribal people literally worshipped Nicholson though when their devotions became too intrusive he had them flogged. With his bushy black beard and glittering grey eyes, Nicholson exercised a hypnotic sway over all who encountered him. Having stamped out manifestations of mutiny in the Punjab, he swept down from its russet plain like the "incarnation of vengeance."[92] The sign of his arrival was corpses swinging from newly erected gallows.

Other British commanders were equally homicidal. At Allahabad Colonel James Neill, exceeding the zeal of his Covenanting countrymen, executed six thousand people, more than were killed on his own side during the entire Mutiny. And he destroyed so many villages during the march towards Cawnpore that his officers protested: if Neill "depopulated the country he could get no supplies for his men."[93] In June the exhausted defenders of this dusty city surrendered when Nana Sahib, at the head of the rebels, promised them safe passage down the Ganges. Instead, they were massacred as they embarked on the boats. The following month, when the relief force closed on Cawnpore, Nana Sahib had the survivors literally butchered. The mutilated bodies of 197 women and children, some still breathing, were thrown into a well. This crime, aggravated by other atrocity stories, many alleging rape and nearly all spurious, maddened the British. Prior to it some officers expressed revulsion at the reprisals. "This hanging work is very sickening," Captain Campbell told his wife. "I cannot feel the pleasure that some seem to do now, in looking at the dead Mutineers. They are God's creatures."[94] But the murder of the so-called "angels of Albion"[95] sent a thrill of horror through the world. Many paid pilgrimages to the site of the killings: one officer found "blood on the walls, and marks of the sword cuts and bullets; locks of hair lying about, and a little child's shoe."[96]

Such accounts apparently licensed an insensate lust for revenge. Captain Garnet Wolseley took a vow that "most soldiers made . . . of having blood for blood, not drop for drop, but barrels and barrels of the filth which flows in these niggers' veins for every drop of blood" they had spilled at Cawnpore. There Neill flogged mutineers, or suspected mutineers, and made them lick blood from the slaughter-house floor before they were hanged.

Prior to dancing the "Pandies'* hornpipe"[97] or receiving a "Cawnpore dinner"[98] (a bayonet in the stomach), many were gleefully or casually tortured, and defiled with pork and beef. They were told that their corpses would be flung to the dogs so that "their souls would not rest."[99] Burning with holy rage, many clergymen approved that doom. They and their compatriots did so in part because the mutineers had shattered the myth of British invincibility, with incalculable consequences. As a British merchant in Calcutta wrote, "Another Cawnpore, and it is my firm belief that we shall be driven into the sea or massacred, and then India will be lost to the English."[100] But the pathological animus was primarily inspired by what seemed to be a hellish inversion of the cosmic order. The "peculiar aggravation of the Cawnpore massacres," wrote *The Times*'s war correspondent William Howard Russell, was "that the deed was done by a subject race—by black men who dared to shed the blood of their masters."[101]

At home the British denounced the mutineers as brutes and barbarians who deserved no mercy. Canning said that the prevailing sentiments compared in savagery to those of "an American Slave-state newspaper,"[102] though as it happened they were echoed in Boston and New York. The paean of hatred silenced organisations such as the Aborigines' Protection Society. Englishmen rejoiced in gory reports of the mass shooting of mutineers from guns, a punishment held long afterwards to be "a wonderful display of moral force."[103] One wrote, "I feel a portion of the Roman emperor's passion who wished that a nation had but one neck that he might be destroyed at a blow."[104] Martin Tupper wanted to cover India with "groves of gibbets."[105] John Tenniel produced a triumphalist cartoon entitled "The British Lion's Vengeance on the Bengal Tiger."[106] Londoners actually taunted the tiger at the Zoo, much as their descendants would kick dachshunds during the Great War. Even Macaulay succumbed to the hysteria: "I, who cannot bear to see a beast or bird in pain, could look without winking while Nana Sahib underwent all the tortures of Ravaillac."[107] The historian puzzled over his emotions. He acknowledged that sadism was injurious to the character and recalled his horror on reading that Fulvius had put the entire Capuan Senate to death during the Second Punic War. But, Macaulay concluded, he would not be sorry to hear that the sepoy garrison at Delhi had suffered the same fate.

Many Britons expected that the Mughal capital would be "taken like a pinch of snuff."[108] But the city, with its deep dry moat, thick red walls and

---

* The slang term for sepoy mutineers, derived from the common Bengal Brahmin surname, Pande.

1. MISSIONARY WITH TAHITIAN CONVERTS

Missionaries both sustained and undermined the Empire.
They also spread more than the gospel: Pacific Islanders called
TB *Christiano*, the disease of Christians.

2. WEDGWOOD ANTI-SLAVERY MEDALLION

During the 1780s it became fashionable to oppose the slave trade.
This jasper medallion is inscribed with the famous slogan,
"Am I Not a Man and a Brother?"

3. IMPERIAL INTERIOR, 1890

In India and elsewhere British clubs and bungalows were
stuffed with hunting trophies. They celebrated the courageous
spirit of the imperial race.

4. LORD AND LADY CURZON HUNT IN HYDERABAD, 1902

Tiger shooting was the sport of kings in India.
Photographs like this, taken when Curzon was Viceroy,
were icons of imperial power.

5. HYDERABAD'S ARMY POLO TEAM

As this early photograph shows, sport could transcend
racial boundaries. The games ethic was one of the great
legacies of the British Empire.

6. ABODE OF THE LITTLE TIN GODS

Sir James Grigg, the peppery Finance Member of the Viceroy's
Council, enters Simla in style, 1938.

7. Hong Kong Harbour Seen from Victoria Peak in about 1878

Within a few years of its acquisition by the British, Hong Kong became a thriving entrepôt. Its prosperity rested on the opium trade.

8. The Iron Horse

A Canadian Pacific Railway passenger train steams across Canyon Creek Bridge in the Rockies. Its trestles were later destroyed by fire, but the iron road united the nation.

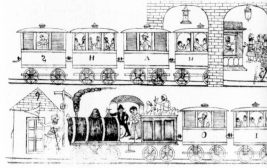

9. Indian Railway Engraving

Railways of the Raj, like Roman roads, had a military purpose. But Indians quickly took advantage of them—though some still believed locomotives to be hell in harness.

10. Tea-Time in Ceylon

Late-Victorian Britons enjoyed a far higher standard of living in outposts of the Empire than they did at home.

11. Ceylon Tea Harvest

Sacks of tea are sent by pulley to drying sheds on one of Sir Thomas Lipton's plantations. The coolies were hard-worked, ill-paid and harshly treated.

12. King Thibaw, Queen Supayalat and Her Sister

Despite attempts to modernise Burma, typified by the French
court photographer who took this picture of its revered royal
family, the British defeated and exiled Thibaw in 1885.

13. Christmas Day in Burma, 1885

Armed soldiers of the Hampshire Regiment attend Christmas
service outside a Burmese monastery. Buddhist monks were
leaders of national resistance.

14. Scots in the Land of the Pharaohs, 1882

After General Wolseley's victory over Egyptian forces at the battle
of Tel-el-Kebir, kilted troops pose beside the Sphinx, which they
also used for target practice.

15. On Top of the World, 1938

British tourists grace the last remaining wonder of the
ancient world. But Egypt, such a prized imperial possession,
also provided Ozymandian warnings of imperial decadence.

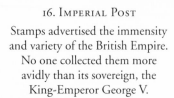

16. Imperial Post

Stamps advertised the immensity
and variety of the British Empire.
No one collected them more
avidly than its sovereign, the
King-Emperor George V.

strong green bastions, was well defended. As one British officer wrote, "The Pandies are exceedingly plucky and fight like fiends."[109] Moreover, thanks to the powerful glacis, the siege guns, 24-pounders drawn by elephants, could only make breaches high up in the fortifications. They failed to reduce Delhi to what military wits called a "Pandymonium." So the storming of the city, which began on 14 September, was a bloodbath. Nicholson led the assault and was mortally wounded at the Lahore Gate. A prolonged and ferocious battle followed through the narrow streets, walled gardens, white mansions, domed mosques and cypress groves. The British advance faltered as soldiers got drunk on pillaged alcohol—their Sikh allies, it was noted, took their "rum like true Christians."[110] "Even when the men were sober they behaved some of them with the most rank cowardice," one officer wrote, "having what we call, regularly got *funked*."[111]

Yet over a fifth of all the troops engaged were killed, as were thousands of civilians. The carnage shocked even a hardened young subaltern like Frederick Roberts, who described entering "a veritable city of the dead."

> We marched in silence or involuntarily spoke in whispers, as though fearing to disturb those ghastly remains of humanity. The sights we encountered were horrible and sickening to the last degree. Here a dog gnawed at an uncovered limb; there a vulture disturbed by our approach from its loathsome meal, but too completely gorged to fly, fluttered away to a safer distance. In many instances the positions of the bodies were appallingly life-like. Some lay with arms uplifted, as if beckoning, and, indeed, the whole scene was weird and terrible beyond description. Our horses seemed to feel the horror of it as much as we did, for they shook and snorted in evident terror. The atmosphere was unimaginably disgusting.[112]

Lieutenant William Hodson compounded the horror by murdering three of Bahadur Shah's sons, who had surrendered with their father at Humayun's Tomb. The princes were first stripped of their finery and later a Captain Williams sent "his wife all the rings and ornaments found on the King's sons when they were shot."[113] The city was sacked with the same ruthlessness and a vast amount of hidden treasure was unearthed. As usual, Queen Victoria (who deplored the unchristian spirit of vengeance) acquired some prize articles, including the evanescent emperor's jewelled hat and gilt chairs. Every man brought home enough spoil to make himself "a Croesus," wrote Herbert Edwardes. It was "like the return of the crusaders."[114]

The recapture of Delhi augured the defeat of the Mutiny, though the white terror continued after the final relief of Lucknow (where Henry

Lawrence had been martyred) in 1858. During the hard campaign to crush the last vestiges of resistance in central India the British "committed all sorts of atrocities." As Major Pemberton Campbell acknowledged, "Our men were very savage, treating these poor wretches like vermin. Some carried ropes on purpose to hang them with, which they did with great delight." Others told suspected mutineers "to run, and when they got about 20 yards shot them, as one would a hare in a battue."[115] British vengeance was sustained by an overwhelming sense of betrayal. Officers had been killed by their own men, families stabbed in the back by their personal servants. Yet the charges of "treason" and the cries of "treachery" were scarcely logical. Equally inappropriate was the word "mutiny," which helped to justify the vast catharsis. For as radicals like John Bright and Charles Dilke pointed out, the British had no right to assume the loyalty of a land taken and held by force, and governed for the benefit of conquerors alien in creed, colour and culture. Arguably they themselves, as vassals of the Mughal emperor, were in revolt. Moreover, their vindictiveness was bound to exacerbate race hatred and, in the long run, to undermine the Raj. Just as "Sarmatia fell unwept without a crime," mused William Howard Russell, as he contemplated the violence his compatriots had done to Hindustan, "so might we fall unwept with many crimes."[116] Canning attempted to avert ruin by means of policies that earned him the hostile nickname "Clemency." The first Viceroy, as he became, was less lenient than he sounded and took strong measures to increase British security. However, Canning did deplore the daily use of the term "niggers" in the newspapers, saying that it would "be a bad day for us when that word becomes naturalized in India."[117] But he could not stem the growth of racial prejudice.

The British government, which superseded the East India Company, also came to espouse appeasement in the wake of the Mutiny. That catastrophe, which marked an epoch in the history of the British Empire, had evidently been caused by the liberal reforms of Bentinck and Dalhousie. The new emphasis would therefore be on consolidation rather than improvement, on holding the subcontinent rather than preparing it to shed the foreign yoke. India would now be ruled according to the canons of conservatism. So Christian evangelism was discouraged. Hindu customs were respected. Annexations ceased. Bahadur Shah was deposed but Indian princes became lions under Queen Victoria's throne. *Zamindars* and *talukdars* were treated as "native gentry."[118] Leaning on them, a caste of firm, honest, efficient British officials would govern an inferior race and keep anarchy at bay. However, there were contradictions at the heart of the post-Mutiny Raj. For in some ways the British rejected what one Indian journal called

"Asiatic stationaryism."[119] As Sir James Fitzjames Stephen (son of the Colonial Under-Secretary) put it, they sought to make their Indian empire "the cradle of changes comparable to those which have formed the imperishable legacy to mankind of the Roman Empire."[120] For example, they continued to promote western technology and progressive education. As Kipling later wrote of his countrymen,

> They terribly carpet the earth with dead, and before their cannon cool,
> They walk unarmed by twos and threes to call the living to school.[121]

To be sure, learning was no longer fostered in the assimilative spirit of Macaulay and Charles Trevelyan, who had rejoiced that Indian youths, taught English literature, would "become more English than Hindus, just as Roman provincials became more Romans than Gauls or Italians."[122] Yet an educated elite, equipped with modern ideas, was bound to challenge the paternalistic Raj, especially when it was buttressed by the most reactionary elements in Indian society. Unlike the mild Hindu, the studious Hindu would pose a serious threat to white supremacy, a threat of cultural miscegenation as well as political subversion. In the European club and the *cutcherry* (office) no Indian was more bitterly vilified than the "sleek *babu*"[123] (clerk).

Meanwhile, all sorts and conditions of men continued to look for signs that the days of the Raj were numbered. One blazing portent appeared in Calcutta on 1 November 1858, at a ceremony marking the transfer of power in India from John Company to the British Crown. It included a proclamation (read out all over India) promising respect for native customs and religion, which Queen Victoria herself had made more conciliatory in an attempt "to draw a veil over the sad and bloody past."[124] The press praised this endeavour and the Calcutta *Englishman* denounced irreconcilables who uttered the "wicked and foolish cry of India for the English."[125] When darkness fell the capital was brilliantly illuminated. Esplanade Row, Chowringhee Road and Auckland Gardens were a dazzling constellation. The outlines of Government House, the Town Hall, the Ochterlony Monument, the Burmese pagoda and all the public buildings were picked out with coloured rows of oil and gas lamps. The ships on the river, "particularly the men-of-war, burning beautiful lights, held up by hundreds of jolly tars at the yard-arm in their white dresses, made the scene an exquisite bit of fairy land."[126] The evening culminated with a colossal firework display costing 30,000 rupees, which took place in front of an appreciative crowd on the *maidan*. But as the crackers, squibs, Catherine wheels, Bengal flares,

Roman candles, "serpents and cornucopias" were lit, everything got out of hand. Thousands of rockets "suddenly went off 'sky-larking' on their own account." Sparks ignited the "immense wooden edifice" representing Mount Vesuvius, which was "stuffed with combustibles" set to erupt. The tame volcano became a wild inferno, scorching and blasting its surroundings like the Mutiny itself. The conflagration spread to a large transparency of Queen Victoria, an icon not intended for the flames. As a British witness wrote, she was "burnt in effigy." This incendiary spectacle delighted "disloyal natives, who shouted 'Wah! Wah!' and seemed to see herein an omen."[127]

6

Spread the Peaceful Gospel—with the Maxim Gun

Towards Conquest in Africa

From palace to slum the British were also haunted by the Mutiny, which shaped the character of their empire in strange and contradictory ways. The Raj in particular became at once sterner and more emollient. This was a mode of government that Indian nationalists called "the knife of sugar"[1]—sharp but sweet, force made palatable. To adopt Theodore Roosevelt's adage, John Bull spoke softly and carried a big stick. Or, in Kipling's image, he wore knuckle-dusters under kid gloves. Queen Victoria herself came to espouse this twin strategy of imperial rule and even to embody it. One of her cardinal tenets was never to give up what she had, even if it was as hard to hold as Afghanistan. And she grew more belligerent with age. "If *we* are to *maintain* our position as a *first-rate* Power," she told Disraeli with characteristic emphasis, "we must, with our Indian Empire and large Colonies, be *Prepared* for *attacks* and *wars, somewhere* or *other* CONTINU-ALLY."[2] On the other hand, the Queen cherished a quasi-mystical bond with her subjects, especially Indians. When the handsome young Sikh Maharajah Duleep Singh was exiled to England, for example, she made a pet of him, arranging to have his portrait painted by "our dear Winterhal-ter" and urging him to wear warm woollen underclothes. (The two royalties shared a passion for Indian gems—the Queen possessed three portman-teaux full of them—but Duleep Singh could not forgive her for receiving the Koh-i-noor Diamond, that supreme emblem of might which he had once worn on his sleeve, and he later nicknamed her "Mrs. Fagin.")[3] After the Mutiny the Queen continued to press for reconciliation in the subcon-tinent.

She also aspired to the sceptre which had been torn from the frail grasp of Bahadur Shah and in 1876 she became Empress of India. The new title, suggesting as it did both despotism and evanescence, was initially unpopu-lar at home. Gladstone denounced it as "theatrical folly and bombast."[4] Benjamin Disraeli, the Tory Prime Minister, was happy to gratify his sover-eign's vanity, but he publicly maintained that the imperial style would please

Indian princes whose ancestors had occupied their thrones "when England was a Roman province."[5] An incurable romantic, Disraeli sensed that the magic of monarchy could win fealty to the Empire and thus avert its decay. As his novels reveal, he too had meditated on the ruins of the Capitol; and "the image of Rome as the power which declined and fell haunts even the sunlit dreamworld of *Tancred*."[6] Loyalty to the Crown could sustain Britain's Empire because it was an emotional bond stronger than the trembling allegiance given to the Caesars or the federal link uniting the states of America. Equally important, it disguised the true nature of the imperial relationship. As a means of government, to paraphrase Lord Salisbury, bamboozle was better than bamboo. The royal cult, with its rituals and fripperies, insignia and regalia, multi-gun salutes and intricate table of ranks, would fascinate the rajah class. And it would hide even from educated Indians, as Salisbury put it, "the nakedness of the sword upon which we really rely."[7]

Certainly the imperial diadem became a symbol of unity to millions of British subjects divided by creed, colour, race and space. This did not happen by chance. Sterling efforts were made to promote the sovereign as an imperial fetish. She was acclaimed in prayers, anthems, ceremonies and toasts. Her majesty was hailed at parades, festivals and pageants. There were jubilees embellished with every kind of theatrical display, from dazzling pyrotechnics to patent musical bustles which played "God Save the Queen" when the wearer sat down. There were durbars such as that held in Delhi to mark the Royal Titles Act, disparaged by its painter, Val Prinsep, as a "gigantic circus" full of gimcrack ornamentation which "outdoes the Crystal Palace in 'hideosity.'"[8] Huntley & Palmer produced "Royal Sovereign" biscuits, decorated with apricot jam crowns. The Queen's birthday, 24 May, which became Empire Day in 1904, was marked with celebrations and salutes, levees and soirées. The name Victoria became geographically ubiquitous, despite occasional worries that it would be insulted by association with barbarous places such as Africa. It was bestowed on mountains, lakes, rivers, waterfalls, harbours, beaches, provinces, districts, towns, hotels, hospitals, railway stations, botanical gardens, even cemeteries. Also called after her were several fabrics, a huge lily, a plum, a carriage, a pigeon, a medal and a heavenly body. The Queen's face was everywhere, appearing not only in portraits, photographs, lantern slides, advertisements and stained-glass windows, but on stamps, coins, badges, plaques, china, even condoms. Many abroad swore that they had seen her in the flesh. Some were doubtless inspired by the kind of semi-allegorical school-room picture entitled *The Jewel in Her Crown* which Paul Scott described in his famous novel, part of

The Raj Quartet: the Queen was represented sitting on a golden throne under a crimson canopy, heralded by angels above and receiving glittering princely tribute below. Others may have been impressed by the large portrait of the Queen conspicuously displayed in one of Bombay's best-known brothels. Just as people in remote parts of the British Isles rubbed her image on gold sovereigns to ward off sickness, Indians bowed before her likeness and sacrificed goats in front of her effigy (though goats were also sacrificed to the Judicial Committee of the Privy Council). Bishop Welldon of Calcutta could not understand why Queen Victoria appealed more to the natives than did Jesus Christ.

In Africa the Great White Mother was also idolised. Henry Morton Stanley worshipped her and in his dreams John Hanning Speke confused the sovereign with his real mother. The Bantu races felt the same respect for Victoria as they did "for their own departed chiefs."⁹ One Basuto king told the Queen that "my country is your blanket, and my people the lice upon it."¹⁰ Zulus called gin "the Queen's tears."¹¹ After attacking the Royal Niger Company at Akassa in 1895 the Brass people wrote to the Prince of Wales, saying that they were "now *very very sorry* indeed, *particularly* in the *killing* and *eating* of parts of its employees"; they threw themselves on "the mercy of the *good old Queen* . . . a most kind, *tender hearted,* and sympathetic *old mother.*"¹² True, the few Africans who actually met the monarch were disappointed to find that she was so short and stout. But art added cubits to her stature. Larger-than-life-sized sculptures of the Queen took pride of place in every imperial city from Accra to Adelaide, from Toronto to Calcutta— where Lord Curzon later designed the Victoria Memorial to reinforce the "overpowering effect" that the Queen-Empress had on "the imagination of the Asiatic."¹³ These manifestations of the monarch in marble and bronze were "as essential to civic self-respect as figures of equestrian Romans had been in antiquity."¹⁴ They were not always flattering: the statue opposite Leinster House in Dublin was known as "Ireland's Revenge."

Yet even after her death Queen Victoria remained an icon. When rioters broke off a finger of her statue at Amritsar before the massacre in 1919, someone in the mob averted further damage by shouting, "Do not attack her. She was a good Queen."¹⁵ An army officer drumming up support in Assam during the Second World War found that his interpreter was saying persuasively, "the British are of the same race as the great Queen . . . and Japan is therefore sure to be defeated."¹⁶ After the war, during which the Japanese looted royal statues from Hong Kong, the only one to be re-erected was that of Queen Victoria (though earlier party-goers had often committed sacrilege, "with someone putting a straw hat or a bowler on her crown").¹⁷

Well into the twentieth century black Barbadians revered her "as a good queen because she freed us."[18] As late as the 1950s chiefs in Nyasaland regretted that "Queen Victoria did not come herself to make the treaties."[19] Some Victorians, though, feared that as democracy blossomed the mystique of monarchy might wither. They did their utmost to prevent a loss of faith. Throughout the Empire children learned their history as a succession of English kings and queens, but in Nigeria Sir Frederick Lugard discouraged schools from teaching about the Stuarts since this might "foster disrespect for authority."[20] At the coronation durbar of Edward VII in Delhi, Lord Curzon banned the singing of "Onward! Christian Soldiers" because it contained the lines "Crowns and thrones may perish/Kingdoms rise and wane."

The crusading strain of imperialism after the Mutiny, which many saw as "a challenge to Christianity itself,"[21] was perhaps best conjured up by this parody of the popular hymn:

> Onward Christian soldiers, on to heathen lands,
> Prayer-books in your pockets, rifles in your hands,
> Take the glorious tidings where trade can be done,
> Spread the peaceful gospel—with the Maxim gun.[22]

Actually the Maxim was not patented until 1884, but its predecessor, the Gatling gun, was used during the American Civil War and, despite its notorious propensity to jam, in some of Britain's colonial conflicts. Like other instruments designed to bring scientific efficiency to death, such as the guillotine and poison gas, the Gatling was intended as a humanitarian device. If one soldier could fire as many shots as a hundred, its eponymous inventor reckoned, armies would be smaller and battlefield casualties fewer. In practice, of course, this weapon was the first serious attempt to mechanise mass murder. The machine gun cut down men by the bushel, being to the musket what the McCormick reaper was to the sickle. It was notably effective against Zulu assegais, Ashanti spears and Dervish* lances. And it was better still, according to *The Times,* if a British general were lucky enough "to catch a good mob of savages in the open." Much as that newspaper liked the idea of treating the Ashanti to "a little Gatling music," it thought that wholesale killing was less desirable than inducing "a regular 'skedaddle' among a set of savages."[23] Cecil Rhodes was more ruthless. Describing how each wave of

---

* Dervish means "beggar" in Persian and, by extension, member of an Islamic religious fraternity. Victorians applied the term to militant Sudanese Muslims and this usage is followed here.

Matabele *(Ndebele)* warriors "left a thick deposit of corpses on the ground," he remarked happily: "There is no waste with the Maxims."[24]

Similarly, new breech-loading rifles developed in the 1860s were more of an advance over the Brown Bess flintlock than it had been over the bow and arrow. They gave imperial troops an overwhelming further advantage in the "little wars" of Queen Victoria's reign, wars so frequent that anti-imperialists denounced the term Pax Britannica as "a grotesque monster of hypocrisy."[25] In 1869 the British army began to adopt the tough, accurate Martini-Henry, though its mule-like kick gave men nosebleeds as well as bruised shoulders. This rifle, which could fire six shots a minute and had an effective range of a thousand yards, turned colonial fighting into hunting. Soldiers actually referred to the "nigger" as "game" and Robert Baden-Powell thought that pursuing those "laughing black fiends" the Matabele was the finest "sport" in the world. The chase was all the more thrilling because the quarry also had guns, though these were usually European cast-offs or cheap trade flintlocks known as "Birmingham gas-pipes." Baden-Powell himself was hit on the thigh by a lead-covered stone bullet fired from a large-bore Matabele musket: it left a bruise. Empire-builders who enjoyed such superiority in arms were more inclined to coerce than to conciliate. Africans, to quote Baden-Powell again, had to "be ruled with an iron hand in a velvet glove" and if they failed to understand the force of it "you must take off the glove."[26]

Iron and later steel, its mass production made possible by the invention of the Bessemer converter (1850) and the development of open-hearth furnaces during the 1860s, were the sinews of imperialism. Manufacturing with these metals on a giant scale, Britons considered themselves the "titans of technology."[27] It was technology that enhanced their power to dominate huge regions of the globe, particularly at a time when major competitors were grappling with internal problems, Germany with unification, America with civil war. Commercially it gave them an iron grip and an unparalleled reach. They exported cutlery to Timbuktu, metal dwellings (known as "iron pots") to Melbourne and Kimberley, foundries to Chile, barracks to the Crimea. They forged a new mid-Victorian Montevideo: "over forty miles in iron pipes, with all the iron-work, machinery, rolling stock of railways, tramways, gasworks, and waterworks being English, as well as the iron work in the construction of houses, and stores, as also of two commodious iron built market-places."[28] They sent abroad prefabricated iron lighthouses, customs offices, hotels with verandahs and churches with steeples (known as "tin tabernacles"). Britain provided portable government residences from Simla to Fernando Po, the latter described by Sir Richard Burton as a "corrugated iron coffin or plank-lined morgue, containing a dead consul once a year."[29]

Metal technology also enhanced Britain's marine power. "Peacock's iron chickens,"[30] as gunboats were nicknamed, after their novelist-protagonist at the East India Company, had proved their worth in China and would open up other continents, notably Africa, to the British. This did not prevent the Royal Navy, which had learned little or nothing since Trafalgar, from declaring in 1851 that "iron does not appear to be applicable to ships of war."[31] As late as 1859 it launched a three-decker wooden battleship, named *Victoria*—though admittedly this was the last of its kind and it was steam-assisted. The Royal Mail was almost equally obscurantist, insisting until 1855 that the post must sail in wood. Indeed, from the mid-1830s, when Dr. Dionysius Lardner offered to eat the vessel that could cross the Atlantic entirely under its own steam (as the *Sirius* did in 1838), to the 1880s, when steamers overtook sailing ships in terms of tonnage, the revolution made haste slowly. Yet the *Great Britain*, built by Isambard Kingdom Brunel in 1843, provided an irresistible model of strength and speed. It was made of iron and its screw propeller was driven by steam generated from fossil fuel. "Coal, the stored-up sunlight of a million years, is the grand agent," wrote a Victorian enthusiast. "Liberty lights the fire and Christian civilisation is the engine which is taking the whole world in its train."[32] It was evidently the fulfilment of a plan whereby Providence (in the opinion of William Buckland, Professor of Mineralogy at Oxford) had wisely placed coal and iron deposits together near Birmingham in order to make England the richest country on earth. Leviathans constructed on the principles of the *Great Britain* secured the nation's rule over the waves, reinforced by a global accumulation of harbours and coaling stations. They also tightened its grip on the terrestrial empire. In 1830 an East Indiaman might take from five to eight months to reach Bombay, a voyage so long that it seemed "to turn seconds into centuries."[33] By 1869, when the Suez Canal halved the maritime distance between London and Bombay, Peninsular & Oriental Line steamers could do the journey in four weeks, giving Britain the power of rapid response in the event of another Mutiny.

Although obsessed by that peril, British governments had failed to take a proprietorial interest in the Canal. Indeed, they long opposed Ferdinand de Lesseps's colossal undertaking, which was built with French money and Egyptian muscle. As well as making Britain's Cape route to India redundant, Suez might have become a source of rivalry between the two great powers. So Palmerston dismissed the Canal as a "hoax"[34] and *Punch* derided it as an "impossible trench."[35] Their countrymen concluded that the project was as practical as steam balloons on the moon and that capital sunk in it would drain away like water in sand. But its value became obvious on the completion of the ninety-eight-mile channel, then the world's greatest engineering feat, involving the removal of nearly 100 million cubic feet of earth, enough to fill the Champs-Elysées to the top of its trees fifty times over. Furthermore, its triumphant opening by the Empress Eugénie of France was a humiliation to Britain, where Queen Victoria was opening Holborn Viaduct. Led by the imperial yacht *L'Aigle,* a flotilla of ships made the short passage from Europe to Asia. With elaborate ceremonial and amid *Arabian Nights* entertainments, Africa was declared an island. Religious leaders of various persuasions blessed the Canal as a passage to prosperity and a channel of grace. Finally the fireworks dump at Port Said blew up and "nearly demolished the town."[36] All told, the inauguration was felt to be the most spectacular event the region had witnessed since Moses parted the Red Sea. The Canal itself captured the contemporary imagination. It was a modern wonder of the world, grander than the pyramids. It stimulated new feats of travel, from Jules Verne's fictional round-the-world journey to Thomas Cook's real one. It encouraged the construction of further waterways, including the one at Panama. Apparently it even inspired the "discovery" of canals on Mars.

From London's viewpoint, though, the Suez opening looked like another Napoleonic expedition to the Middle East and thus a threat to India. So when the bankruptcy of Ismail, Khedive (ruler) of Egypt, forced him to sell his shares in the Canal Company in 1875, Disraeli snapped them up. To Queen Victoria he famously wrote, "You have it, Madam."[37] The purchase was extolled as a brilliant coup and the English press "joined in a shout of triumph as if the world were conquered."[38] Certainly Britain now had a large stake in what promised to be the greatest commercial artery in the world and the jugular vein of the Empire. Port Said was, a contemporary wrote, "our nexus—our nerve-centre—at which our lines of empire meet."[39] But from end to end the Canal was actually in the grip of Egypt, itself nominally subject to Turkey. So Britain, fearful of a strategic challenge, became increasingly concerned with the Land of the Pharaohs and what Victorians called the "Dark Continent." Newspapers intoned, "Egypt for the English."[40] Actually Disraeli seemed to take little interest in Egypt: his only reference to the country in discussion with one of its financial commissioners, Evelyn Baring, was to ask if there were many pelicans on the banks of the Nile. However, Gladstone rightly reckoned the Canal shares would lead Britain to colonise other parts of Africa, all in the name of defence. Others, even more far-sighted, prophesied that the national obsession with this vulnerable waterway would prove disastrous to British interests. John Bull was bent on *"Suez-cide!"*[41]

Meanwhile, the sea link to India was as secure as the iron hulls of the Royal Navy and the iron bands which riveted together imperial land masses. Victorians often compared the railways to Roman roads, whose chief object, as Gibbon had said, was "to facilitate the marches of the legions."[42] This was especially true in India. Here the lines, though built for profit and sometimes ill-planned, had a "primarily strategic"[43] purpose. They were intended, as Lord Dalhousie had written, to avert "the perpetual risk" of hostile attack and to enable the tiny British garrison to bring its "strength to bear upon any given point." Thus the narrow gauge was rejected for trunk routes because it did not permit cavalry horses to travel two abreast. "No line should be constructed in India," it was said, "which will not bear the transport of an Armstrong gun."[44] Bridges and tunnels had turrets with loopholes and gun ports. Military cantonments had separate stations and many stations were fortified to "stand a siege."[45] The most spectacular, admittedly, were soaring temples to the fire-breathing "iron cow"[46] or steam cathedrals, such as Bombay's fantastic Victoria Terminus, with its domes and spires, gargoyles and rose windows, marble columns and tesselated pavements. But in general, after the Mutiny, railway stations were to the British "what the motte and bailey and great stone keeps were to the Normans."[47] The red-brick edifice at Lahore resembled a medieval castle, complete with towers, machicolations, arrow slits, portcullises and drawbridge. The Charbagh Station at Lucknow incorporated a fort, an arsenal and a barracks. As happened elsewhere, passengers were treated like prisoners.

India's permanent way, which used rails, spikes, sleepers, trucks, carriages, locomotives and even coal brought from England, benefiting British investors and producers at the expense of Indian taxpayers and manufacturers, was the largest and costliest project of the colonial era. During the 1860s Britain sent 600 tons of material, a complete shipload, for each mile of track completed. Between 1850 and 1947 more than 40,000 miles were laid, involving heroic feats of embanking, tunnelling and bridging. To span the Indus at Sukkur, for example, took 3,300 tons of "awkwardly designed steelwork,"[48] riveted together in a latticework of girders, struts, ties, beams and trusses. By the 1890s a Scottish engineer could claim that England had stamped "more enduring material monuments" on a dependent land than any nation in history, not excluding "ancient Rome."[49] Of course many people shared Blake's hatred of England's "dark satanic mills" and sympathised with Ruskin, who deplored "the ferruginous temper"[50] of the time. Others pointed out that the permanent way was not much use in famine relief—it actually allowed merchants to transport grain from drought-stricken, riot-menaced districts "to central depots for hoarding."[51] But imperialists swelled with pride at the whole railway enterprise. Kipling said that "if a Briton wished to swagger—and at times this duty is incumbent upon him—he might challenge the world to match our achievements in this line."[52] The achievements were global in scope: by 1914 British investors owned 113 railways in twenty-nine countries. This gave their government indirect influence from Argentina to Mozambique, from China to Peru. Iron and steam unified immense dominions such as Canada, famously said to be "a railway in search of a state."[53] And because of its ability to concentrate its power in colonies of conquest, Britain could calm Victorian fears that "every extension of the empire diminished its stability and hastened its dissolution."[54]

That modern technology might save Britain from the fate of Rome was the central argument in J. R. Seeley's widely read book *The Expansion of England* (1881). Not just steamships and railways, he argued, but the electric telegraph (which played a vital role in defeating the sepoys) and the submarine cable (which reached India in 1870 and enabled Britain to manage the news) would tighten the bonds and widen the bounds of empire. Vitalised by this network of veins, nerves and fibres, it could grow in size yet not outgrow its strength. Britain could exert control even though, unlike Rome, it was not at the geographical heart of its empire. Seeley was alarmed by the rise of super-states such as America and Russia, which dwarfed the British Isles. But steam and electricity made it possible, in his optimistic assessment, to "realise the old utopia of a Greater Britain."[55] Other scientific advances would help too. Medical improvements gave Europeans a better chance of survival in the tropics. Particularly effective was the control of malaria by means of quinine, or "Peruvian bark,"[56] derived from the cinchona tree, seeds of which botanists at Kew Gardens distributed from Jamaica to Ceylon. High explosive shaped alien landscapes and barbed wire tamed them. Tinned food, telescopes, lucifer matches, magic lanterns—all assisted empire-building in their different ways. Mechanised book-binding, paper-making and printing presses helped to colonise native minds. The camera, "the pencil of the sun,"[57] captured images of the Empire all round the earth. Photographs were carefully selected, cropped (sometimes even retouched) and captioned to show their subjects in a suitably imperial light, whether commanding in topees or backward in beads. Many of these sepia scenes represented savagery being subjugated by civilisation. Framed and mounted, they were the pictorial equivalent of the stuffed animal trophies which testified to the prowess of white hunters in their conquest of the wild. Photographs celebrated shooting of every kind. One fanatic of the lens,

Colonel W. W. Hooper, even snapped Burmese robbers *(dacoits)* as they were shot by a British firing squad. He delayed the execution several times while preparing his apparatus to capture the prisoners' attitudes and expressions at "the moment the bullets struck them."[58]

Yet even the most callous illustration of Britain's power could not obscure the fact that it had no monopoly of technology. Other races could share in it. Indians made bombs, Zulus used modern rifles, Dervishes acquired artillery. Nationalists of all sorts travelled by train—including Gandhi, despite his hatred of modern machinery. Most colonial people embraced scientific progress, just as ancient Britons had embraced the baths, aqueducts and hypocausts of Rome. Tacitus wrote that this conquered race called such novelties "civilisation" when really they were a feature of its enslavement. In due course, however, technical novelties did afford a means of emancipation from the British Empire. They not only shifted the balance of power but transformed the temper of the time. As Karl Marx said, the locomotive was the engine of social as well as industrial revolution in Britain's colonies. The steam-breathing express and its mechanical cohorts girdled the globe at such speed that they rapidly diffused the secrets of their magic. In fact, the British Empire provided the tools that helped foes to finish it.

That outcome was dimly perceived during the mid-Victorian period, when most Britons still thought that their country's duty was to ripen colonial "communities to the earliest possible maturity—social, political and commercial—to qualify them, by all appliances within reach of a parent state, for present self-government and eventual independence."[59] However, technological ascendancy boosted British pride as well as power. It seemed to afford gleaming proof of the pre-eminence of the Anglo-Saxon breed. When Mary Kingsley returned home from exploring West Africa she felt like embracing "the first magnificent bit of machinery" she saw, since it was a "manifestation of the superiority of my race."[60] The corollary was that peoples with few mechanical achievements to their credit were inferior. Ironically, at the very time when Darwin's disquisition *On the Origin of Species* (1859) was teaching his contemporaries that *Homo sapiens* had evolved, anthropologists were asserting that "rigid and permanent differences in mental and physical capacity between the races could be scientifically demonstrated."[61]

Actually they did little more than codify the racial prejudices that had been accumulating since the eighteenth century and had intensified during the Mutiny. In his account of *The Negro's Place in Nature* (1863), for example, John Hunt stated that, apart from a crude knowledge of metallurgy,

Africans possessed "no art." Mentally dormant and morally undeveloped, they were also "indolent, careless, sensual, tyrannical, predatory, sullen, boisterous, and jovial." To sustain these stale and contradictory stereotypes, Hunt provided a gross physiological description of the Negro—his small brain had a "smoky tint" and his "unusually large" penis had "mammilated eminences"—which identified him with the "monkey tribe."[62] The case did not go unchallenged. A West African doctor, J. A. B. Horton, attacked the "grave errors" and "false theories" of the anthropologists in his *Vindication of the African Race* (1868). Stating that Africans had been for ages isolated from civilising influences, he compared their progress favourably to that of ancient Britons after the landing of Julius Caesar. In particular Horton recalled that Cicero had advised his friend Atticus not to buy slaves from Britain because these scantily clothed barbarians were "the ugliest and most stupid" creatures, quite incapable of learning "music and other accomplishments."[63] Nevertheless, Hunt's views remained eminently convincing to all who agreed with them. At best, it seemed, the black man must be a servitor if not actually a slave—slavery, wrote an Alabaman contributor to a London journal of anthropology, was "the normal condition of the Negro, the most advantageous to him."[64] At worst, he and his kind were doomed.

The theory of evolution itself, which gained swift acceptance during the 1860s, seemed to support that conclusion. The struggle for life, said Alfred Russel Wallace, co-formulator of the theory with Charles Darwin, would lead to "the inevitable extinction of all those low and mentally undeveloped populations with which Europeans come into contact."[65] The popular champion of what came to be called Social Darwinism, Herbert Spencer, stated that weeding out the weak was a "beneficent, though severe discipline"[66] to which humanity must be subjected for its own good. His view was echoed from Queensland to Florida. As late as 1883 one colonial Governor told Gladstone that he had heard Queenslanders

> of culture and refinement, of the greatest humanity and kindness to their fellow whites . . . talk, not only of the *wholesale* butchery (for the iniquity of that may sometimes be disguised from themselves) but of the *individual* murder of natives, exactly as they would talk of a day's sport, or of having to kill some troublesome animal.[67]

After meeting a Deep Southerner who favoured hunting Seminole Indians with bloodhounds ("sarves the pesky sarpints right, sah!"), Sir Charles Dilke declared that the "gradual extinction of the inferior races is not only a law of nature, but a blessing to mankind."[68]

The author-explorer Winwood Reade was more blunt still: "The law of murder is the law of growth."[69] Reade concluded his book *Savage Africa* (1864) by urging readers to look with composure on the benign extermination of the native inhabitants, picturing an idyllic white future for the dark colony.

> When the cockneys of Timbuctoo have their tea-gardens in the Oases of the Sahara; when hotels and guide-books are established at the Sources of the Nile; when it becomes fashionable to go yachting on the Lakes of the Great Plateau; when noblemen, building seats in Central Africa, will have their elephant-parks and their hippopotami waters; young ladies on camp-stools under palm trees will read with tears *The Last of the Negroes;* and the Niger will become as romantic as the Rhine.[70]

Aggressive imperialism was therefore justified on the grounds that it was working with the evolutionary grain. But some anthropologists were unhappy about the axiom that "to colonize and to extirpate are synonymous terms." They deplored that "thirst for blood which seems so mysteriously to come over civilised man when he is placed in contact with inferior tribes."[71]

Many other Victorians rejected altogether the tenets of both Darwinism and Social Darwinism. Like Disraeli, they preferred to believe that men were not risen apes but fallen angels. Or when, like the geologist Charles Lyell, they found Darwin's arguments persuasive, they hesitated to "go the whole orang."[72] They were still more reluctant to accept that biological progress depended on the heartless mechanism of natural selection. Even if it did, they said, morality remained the same and man's highest duty was to love his neighbour as himself. Like T. H. Huxley, they concluded that there was nothing ethical about the "cosmic process,"[73] which should be resisted, not assisted. Only thus could England's mission be civilised as well as civilising. So the humanitarianism of Wilberforce and Wedgwood survived into a harsher age. Ultimately the philosophy of racism on which the more aggressive forms of imperialism were based was indefensible—even among scientists. As Winwood Reade recorded sardonically, when the President of the Anthropological Society told a meeting of members of the British Association for the Advancement of Science that they were more intellectual than Negroes, his audience "endeavoured to prove the contrary by hisses."[74]

Nevertheless, in the years after the Mutiny Britain's knife of sugar gained a sharper cutting edge. The iron fist of empire struck harder blows. A notorious instance occurred in 1865 when a small-scale uprising occurred in Jamaica. Impoverished and unemployed ex-slaves in Morant Bay, wanting land as well as freedom, killed a score of whites. According to *The Times,* happily disillusioned about the civilising effects of emancipation, the blacks had reverted to barbarism:

> Like the old Gauls hewing down the *Patres Conscripti* [senators], the sable mob fired into the Court-house, and . . . revelled in blood, and in still more outrageous insult to the survivors; for days they indulged in a drunken dream of negro mastery and white slavery. It was Africa, hitherto dormant, that had broken out in their natures . . . They desired the extermination of their emancipators.[75]

Racked by memories of the Indian Mutiny and by fears of a general massacre, Governor Edward Eyre declared martial law. He then hanged and flogged many hundreds of black people, and burned over a thousand dwellings. He also accused a Baptist preacher, G. W. Gordon, of being responsible for the insurrection and had him executed. This was done on the principle that "although he might not be guilty, it served him right."[76] So said T. H. Huxley, who professed himself to be no negrophile but who regarded this as the worst case of political murder since the time of Judge Jeffreys.

At home, controversy about Eyre's actions flared "into white heat." Victorians, including the most eminent, divided into hostile camps. Each fortified itself with Roman analogues. The Governor's apologists, for example, were said to have been "drilled after classical models"[77] and only to know the brutal ways of Rome. Carlyle led the defence, calling Eyre "a brave, gentle, chivalrous and clear man, whom I would make dictator of Jamaica for the next twenty-five years."[78] As such, reckoned Carlyle, anticipating the language of fascism, Eyre could discipline the "idle Black gentleman, with his rum bottle in his hand . . . no breeches on his body, pumpkin at discretion, and the fruitfulest region of the earth going back to the jungle round him."[79] John Stuart Mill headed the opposition. The philosopher did not succeed in getting the Governor convicted; but Eyre was recalled and Jamaica came under direct rule as a crown colony, a significant early instance of white settlers being curbed by imperial authority. For his pains Mill was deluged with abusive letters, graduating from "coarse jokes, verbal and pictorial, up to threats of assassination."[80] The whole episode revealed what one contemporary called that hatred for the Negro which had sprung up in the space of a single generation and was "now so curiously characteristic of almost all Anglo-Saxons but the professional or sectarian philanthropists."[81] Coercion grew in the mire of racial prejudice. "We are too tender to our savages," Tennyson told Gladstone, "niggers are tigers, niggers are tigers."[82] Prejudice also fostered an insular arrogance, wrote Goldwin Smith, which was unfortunate in an imperial people. For it precluded "not only fusion but sympathy and almost intercourse with the subject races." Where Romans had rubbed shoulders with persons from all corners of the known world, the British shunned "lesser breeds." Whereas the Latin poet Claudian had written "we are all one people,"[83] Smith said that the gulf between the races "now yawns wider than ever."[84]

Many Victorian explorers, harbingers of empire who beat new paths through jungles, over mountains and across deserts, widened the gulf. They had "no idea of a naked savage being 'a man and a brother'"[85] and no intention of treating him as such. On the contrary, their efforts to subdue indigenous people were as ruthless as their struggles to overcome nature. But white pioneers were mavericks to a man. Not all were conquistadors, though even the gentlest of them had a disruptive effect on native cultures ill equipped to resist European incursions. Furthermore, discovery was not necessarily carried out with conquest in mind. Those who filled the blank spaces on contemporary maps were often freebooters, sportsmen, traders, missionaries, prospectors for gold or fame. Still, pushing out geographical frontiers did open up new spheres of influence, where the gospel, the market and the flag might eventually be established. The Royal Geographical Society, founded in 1830, became "virtually an arm of the imperial state."[86] When "America is filled up," wrote Henry Morton Stanley, there would be plenty of Anglo-Saxon "Hengists and Horsas"[87] eager to follow his trail into Africa. The Scottish explorer Joseph Thomson wanted his epitaph to record how he had pegged out "claims on the Dark Continent."[88] David Livingstone believed that Britain could introduce Africa to a golden age.

Exploration certainly opened fresh fields to the European imagination, flinging wide, as Rider Haggard said, the "gate of ivory and pearl which leads to the blessed Kingdom of Romance." Romance also shaped reality. When writing *King Solomon's Mines* (1885), Haggard drew on accounts of African landscape penned by Thomson, and the novel in turn supplied Britain's Foreign Office with the archaic language deemed suitable for treating with the Matabele monarch, Lobengula. Like many authors who set their stories on the margins of empire, Haggard believed "in the divine right of a great civilising people—that is, in their divine mission."[89] Better writers were less sure. Joseph Conrad's classic evocation of Africa's barely penetrated *Heart of Darkness* (1899) is highly ambivalent. On the one hand it portrays a green nightmare peopled by black barbarians in need of white civilisation.

On the other, Conrad exposes the fragility of civilisation and asserts that imperialism is mostly "just robbery with violence, aggravated murder on a great scale." Significantly, he begins the tale with a striking picture of empire-builders facing death and demoralisation in alien and incomprehensible wastes: "Land in a swamp, march through the woods, and in some inland port feel the savagery, the utter savagery . . . all that mysterious life of the wilderness that stirs in the forest, in the jungles, in the hearts of wild men." What Conrad describes here, though, is not Victorian explorers on the Congo but Roman legionaries on the Thames. This sketch of the conquest of Britain is an ambiguous prelude to the horror he unfolds in central Africa. It affirms both the power and the transience of empire. Conrad, who seldom let his prejudices narrow his perspectives, viewed imperial pioneers from an unusual angle. The farms and cottages of Kent would soon empty, he wrote, "if a lot of mysterious niggers armed with all kinds of fearful weapons suddenly took to travelling on the road between Deal and Gravesend, catching the yokels right and left to carry heavy loads for them."[90] It was a vivid insight into the impact of contemporary exploration on Africa.

Such a relative way of thinking was quite foreign to Samuel White Baker. He was the prototypical explorer who in 1864 discovered Lake Albert, a "sea of quicksilver" in the high savannah, one of the gigantic reservoirs that nourished Egypt. Baker had inherited a fortune derived from his family's sugar plantations and he was correspondingly brutal in his attempts to dominate nature and "natives." A great bear of a man, with a gruff, bluff manner and a shaggy black beard, he was primarily a hunter and an adventurer. No one was more dedicated to the massacre of game (unless it was John Hanning Speke, discoverer of Lake Victoria, who liked to eat the foetuses of pregnant animals he killed). No one knew better how to mend a gun stock with fish, crocodile or iguana skin; to thrash his boat captain *(reis)* for laziness; to quell fever with doses of potato whisky; to live off boiled hippo head (which, when served with chopped onions, salt and cayenne pepper, "throws brawn completely in the shade"); and to keep clean in the bush with the aid of a portable "sponging-bath, that emblem of civilisation."[91] During the 1850s Baker had tried to bring civilisation to Ceylon. He had set up an experimental village in the hills, with himself as squire, importing English craftsmen and labourers, plants and animals, among them a pedigree Durham cow and a pack of foxhounds. After many setbacks it flourished and Baker concluded that Ceylon, despite its contagiously lethargic colonial government and its bearded, petticoated natives, was a "Paradise of the East."[92]

During the 1860s he determined to win the source of the Nile for England. This he accomplished, partially and metaphorically at least, after an appalling journey south from Khartoum. It took him through the Sudd, the world's most stupendous morass, a product of the Nile's transcontinental incontinence. Clogged with reeds, papyrus and rotting vegetation, it was a Sargasso Sea in the desert. Alive with crocodiles, hippopotamuses and mosquitoes, it was a slimy, noxious spawning ground of pestilence and death. Baker and his beautiful, blonde Hungarian wife endured sickness, encountered cannibals and fought against mutiny and desertion among their porters. They were victimised by Arab slave-traders and despoiled by Bunyoro tribesmen. Baker raged against the humiliations inflicted on them by "these almighty niggers,"[93] whom he thought more brutish than monkeys and less noble than dogs. Attempting to Christianise them was futile, he believed. "You may as well try to turn pitch into snow as to eradicate the dark stain of heathenism."[94] Yet some advance could be made, as his experience in Ceylon had shown, through commerce and colonisation. Britain was "the natural coloniser of the world," Baker wrote, uniquely qualified "to wrest from utter savagedom those mighty tracts of the earth's surface wasted from the creation."[95] Nevertheless, a hint of doubt did creep into his paean to the nation whose standard "floated on the strongholds of the universe." For Britons themselves had once been Druid-ridden primitives. Might not Destiny decree "that as from dust we rose, so to dust we shall return"?[96]

Richard Burton, who discovered Lake Tanganyika (with Speke) in 1858, had even less faith in European efforts to better the lot of Africans. He was profoundly sceptical about their capacity for improvement and, like other misanthropists, Burton could find reasons to justify cynicism. For example, when the Royal Navy returned freedmen to Sierra Leone they were apt to enslave one another. The campaign to stop trade in slaves increased the number of human sacrifices in Ashanti. In Zanzibar many of those released from Arab dhows were sent to the Seychelles as indentured labourers, a fate worse than bondage. Burton was also sceptical about the value of Christian missions, which undermined tribal systems based on fetishes, witchcraft, polygamy and divine kingship. He thought Islam better suited to the needs of Africans, who were invariably demoralised by "intercourse with white men."[97] On the question of clothing indigenous people, Burton was a confirmed sans-culotte. Trousers became the defining article in the debate between Victorians eager to civilise Africans and those who favoured cultural *laissez-faire*, usually for the purpose of "keeping the native down." Missionaries were particularly shocked by the "frightful nudity"[98] of Africans and David Livingstone urged, to their amusement, that in lieu of more formal garb they should wear "grass."[99] Ideally, of course, the looms of Lancashire should cover their nakedness. Sartorial imperialism would overcome heathen depravity. Not only must Africans be "decently clad," intoned the *Daily Telegraph,* but English authority should be exercised to ensure that they did not "revert to their old terrible habits."[100]

On the contrary, romantics argued, the descendants of Ham were children of nature. They were essentially innocent, well adapted to tropical conditions and unfettered by artificial conventions. "There is a tendency to regard natives in the light of beauty spots," wrote Elspeth Huxley later, "and European clothes as paper bags and orange peel."[101] Furthermore, conservatives maintained, the white man's costume gave the black man ideas above his station. Maoris decked out in European apparel looked "snobbish," reported Burton. He himself, particularly when among nubile African women, always took care to secure "a seat in the undress circle." Nothing should hide or alter the character of these "beautiful domestic animals."[102] As for the males, the "quasi-gorillahood of the real 'nigger'" should be evident, to use a phrase he liked to repeat, "from scalp to scrotum."[103] (He was indignant when prudes secured the removal of the penises of the first stuffed gorillas exhibited in London, an absurdity on a par with the African custom of eating their brains as an aphrodisiac. Perhaps he felt it appropriate that the first live gorilla brought to London, named Mr. Pongo, turned its back on Charles Darwin.) At any rate, Burton thought that Africa, a scene "of bleared misery by day, and animated filth by night,"[104] could not embrace progress. Plainly the continent was best treated, preserved and run like an enormous zoo.

Burton himself reminded people of a caged black leopard. He had a muscular frame, a barrel chest and, wrote Wilfrid Scawen Blunt, "a countenance the most sinister I have ever seen, dark, cruel, treacherous, with eyes like a wild beast's."[105] Burton liked to boast that he had indulged in every vice and committed every crime. His traveller's tales grew ever taller: mocking them, an Argentinian newspaper reported that he had set out to explore the pampas armed with a cannon and torpedoes. Certainly, though, he was a ferocious character and his exploits matched his nickname, "Ruffian Dick." At Oxford, already an expert swordsman, he challenged another undergraduate to a duel for laughing at his moustache (which matured into the most prodigious walrus of the age). In India, where he won favour with the equally daemonic General Charles Napier, Burton rode alligators, charmed snakes and became the army's most brilliant linguist. He eventually mastered more than two dozen languages and many dialects, even trying to learn simian speech from a troupe of monkeys he installed in his house. Disguising himself as a Muslim, complete with circumcision, he made a forbidden pilgrimage to the holy places of Mecca. So comprehensive was his knowledge of the East that "he was able to become an Oriental."[106]

Burton was insatiably curious, studying mesmerism, mysticism, spiritualism, cannibalism and eroticism. His important ethnological research caused offence by its sexual frankness and his unexpurgated translation of the *Arabian Nights* included a dissertation on the Sotadic Zone, those sultry regions of the earth where sensuality flourished and sodomy was "popular and endemic."[107] Vindictive and self-destructive, Burton spent much of his life engaged in feuds, the most bitter of them with his fellow explorer Speke, who stole a march on him in 1858 by discovering the main source of the Nile. Ironically, Burton, the least diplomatic of men, was rewarded for his explorations with a billet in the consular service. Exiled to outposts such as Fernando Po, he behaved like a "caged hawk" and compared himself to "a Prometheus with the Demon Despair gnawing at my heart." Burton admitted that he was unusually well endowed with the Englishman's "eccentricities, his bizarreries, his hobby-horses, his whimsy-whamsies."[108] Increasingly he indulged rancorous prejudices that embraced most of the human race, Jews, Americans, Irishmen and so on. Although seldom consistent, he reserved his most poisonous invective for Africans. Like orientals, they had to be ruled by fear. For them the only effective form of government was "an iron-handed and lion-hearted despotism."[109]

Yet even Burton disapproved of the tyrannical methods employed in Africa by Henry Morton Stanley. He "shoots negroes as if they were monkeys,"[110] Burton complained. Stanley's most recent biographer denies this, pointing out that his hero was less racist than Burton and less bloodstained than Baker, and that he tended to "exaggerate the casualty figures"[111] for journalistic effect. Certainly Stanley's reports did severe damage to his reputation. He described his acts of violence with a callous insouciance which rendered them doubly odious. He praised the "virtue of a good whip," which restored lazy bearers "to a sound—sometimes to an extravagant activity."[112] Burning the villages of hostile tribesmen had, by contrast, a remarkably "sedative influence on their nerves."[113] Liberal opinion in England was outraged. The *Saturday Review* protested that Stanley had engaged in "wholesale and wanton homicide." Worse still, this Yankee newspaperman who made "war like a Napoleon," using long-range rifles and explosive bullets against frightened savages, flew the Union Jack as well as the Stars and Stripes.[114] Of course, Stanley was only a naturalised American. He began life, his many enemies insisted, as a Welsh bastard and was brought up in the workhouse at St. Asaph. But he always shrank from being publicly "branded with the hideous stigma" of his "parentless and abject condition."[115] Aged seventeen, in 1858, he escaped to a roving transatlantic life, managing to serve on both sides during the American Civil War. Afterwards he became a tramp reporter and eventually secured employment on the most jaundiced organ of New York's yellow press, the *Herald*. Its owner, James Gordon Bennett Jr., was the gaudiest beast in the newspaper jungle and he appreciated the tigerish qualities that were to make Stanley the greatest of all African explorers. Not that the young reporter was much to look at, being stocky, ugly and uncouth. But he gave "the impression of overwhelming and concentrated force" and his eyes, "pools of grey fire . . . , seemed to scorch and shrivel"[116] everything they lighted on. Before sending Stanley on the quest that would win him fame, Bennett ordered him to cover another British venture in Africa. It provided a perfect illustration of the way technology could be used to realise the increasingly aggressive ambitions of mid-Victorian imperialists.

In 1868 General Sir Robert Napier, a grizzled veteran of many wars, was sent to invade Ethiopia. The purpose of his expedition was to rescue some sixty European prisoners incarcerated by the Emperor Theodore. But it was also a parade of power. It was designed to uphold British prestige in Africa, to buttress the Raj in India and to show possible rivals elsewhere that Britannia's reach extended well beyond the waves. As America began to rebuild in the wake of Lee's surrender at Appomattox, as Germany moved towards unification after Bismarck's Prussia defeated Austria at Sadowa (1866), as Napoleon III's France, which had just acquired part of Cochin China, looked set to exploit the Suez Canal, Queen Victoria's subjects were painfully reminded of "the ephemeral nature of Britain's supremacy overseas."[117] Anxiety about decline, in the economic as well as the political sphere, was a root cause of British participation in the scramble for Africa—for which the Abyssinian adventure was a rehearsal. What immediately prompted Napier's mission, though, was the repeated cry of *"Civis Romanus sum,"* uttered by a public stirred over the plight of white captives in the hands of a "horrible barbarian."[118] This characterisation of the Emperor did not just stem from prejudice since Theodore, who had waded through blood to the throne, was an Ethiopian Caligula. He presided cruelly and capriciously over an isolated realm whose people had (as Gibbon said) "slept near a thousand years, forgetful of the world, by whom they were forgotten."[119]

Little had changed, indeed, since Augustus withdrew his legions. Ethiopians wearing white cotton *shammas* (togas) and dressing their hair in rancid butter continued to feast on *tej* (mead) and raw steaks cut from live cattle. Corpses swung from gallows trees and every cluster of dung-coloured conical huts *(tukuls)* had its quota of mutilated beggars. Civil war was as much a part of Ethiopian life as the translucent atmosphere, the majestic horizons and the primeval wilderness. Yet in some ways Theodore was a progressive ruler. He opposed slavery, defended the Coptic faith and made overtures to other Christian states—it was the Foreign Office's failure to answer his letter to Queen Victoria, who had earlier sent him a brace of silver pistols, that provoked his hostage taking. The Emperor also tried to modernise his feudal host, equipping his men with muskets and mortars, drilling them in European fashion, and going so far as to pay them. On Lake Tana he even constructed a large imitation paddle steamer from papyrus grass, "with a couple of wheels affixed to the sides . . . to be turned by a handle like that attached to a common grindstone."[120] It sank. Meanwhile, Napier mustered a formidable armada to supply his army, which consisted of thirteen thousand troops (mostly Indian) and fifty thousand camp followers, as well as eighteen thousand mules, seventeen thousand camels and forty-four elephants. This was an array that Hannibal would have recognised but it was sustained by machinery that would have staggered him.

Napier was an engineer—he had not only relieved Lucknow but radically redesigned the city to make it more defensible in case of another mutiny—and his Ethiopian campaign was an industrial enterprise. At Zula on the Red Sea he created a harbour complete with prefabricated lighthouses and tramways along the piers. On shore a new town sprang up with a railway track and locomotives, telegraph lines, an arsenal, warehouses for medical and other stores, meteorological apparatus, ice-making equipment, Norton tube wells, Bastier chain pumps, condensers to distil salt water into fresh and reservoirs to hold it. All this helped Napier to master his chief foe, geography. Ethiopia is a natural fortress, a mountainous plateau guarded by thickets of juniper, oak, tamarisk, acacia, sycamore and euphorbia. It is a chaos of crag, scarp and gorge, a tumult of basalt peaks and granite troughs like a vitrified sea in a storm. Sappers had to blast rocks and clear tracks up such formidable ascents as "the Devil's Staircase."[121] And, for much of its four-hundred-mile march, Napier's seven-mile-long column advanced in single file. Like an immense python it inched through precipitous defiles and slithered over boulder-strewn steeps. The sun gleamed on its scales, multi-coloured uniforms topped variously by crimson caps, silver helmets, red fezzes, white turbans, scarlet tarbooshes and emerald puggarees. One "young lordling," Stanley noted disdainfully, "wore kid gloves and a green veil."[122] (British officers returned the journalist's contempt, reckoning Stanley a howling cad and nicknaming him Jefferson Brick, after the *Rowdy Journal*'s brash war correspondent in Dickens's *Martin Chuzzlewit*.) In the thin, cold air, progress was slow. Hailstones fell, as big as marbles. The camels' roaring stampeded the mules. The beasts were additionally burdened with bottles of claret and casks of porter, which left "men drunk all over the place, and no end of stragglers." One miscreant got "50 lashes, and his back was well mauled."[123]

Eventually, on 10 April 1868, Napier encountered the Ethiopian horde below Theodore's volcanic stronghold of Magdala. When the yelling, red-clad warriors hurled themselves at the invaders, during a terrific thunderstorm, the result was not a battle but a massacre. Stanley exclaimed: "Against shell-vomiting cannon, and against a very wall of fire, discharging bullets by the hundred to their one, what could matchlocks and spears effect?" The British Army, itself scarcely touched, killed seven hundred Ethiopians. Theodore shot himself with one of Queen Victoria's silver pistols. British troops released the prisoners. Before burning down the palace they looted it, seizing the royal treasures in an "extempore pandemonium." Among them were gold crowns and mitres, jewelled crosses and goblets,

> robes of fur; war capes of lion, leopard, and wolf skins; saddles, magnificently decorated with filigree gold and silver; numerous shields covered with silver plates; state umbrellas of gorgeous hues, adorned with all the barbaric magnificence that the genius of Bejemder and Gondar could fashion; swords and claymores; rapiers, scimitars, yataghans, tulwars, and bilboes; daggers of Persia, of Damascus, and of Ind, in scabbards of crimson morocco and purple velvet, studded with gold buttons.[124]

Queen Victoria received her usual share of the booty, including priceless illuminated religious manuscripts and "Theodore's crown."[125] Disraeli announced that the standard of St. George was flying on the mountains of Rasselas. Perhaps that triumph justified the £9 million bill. One Tory minister said that Magdala was to Britain what Sadowa had been to Prussia—whereas Italy's defeat at Adowa in 1896 seriously damaged European prestige, preserving Ethiopia as Africa's last bastion against colonial rule and proving that black men too could win an "engineer's war."[126] Like the politicians, the British people received news of Napier's victory from the New York *Herald*. After the demolition of Magdala, Stanley had raced back to Suez (encumbered only by a bloodstained piece of Theodore's coat, a souvenir for his mother) and gained his scoop by the simple expedient of bribing the chief telegraphist to send his dispatches first.

Bennett rewarded Stanley by instructing him to find Livingstone. The Scottish missionary explorer, widely regarded as the moral suzerain of Africa and "the greatest of England's heroes,"[127] had not been seen by a white man since 1866. Tracking him down would give Stanley the story of the century. He started in Zanzibar, the island gateway to East Africa. This was a ruined Eden with an oily blue lagoon crowded with exotic craft, a steamy green jungle suffused with the scent of cloves, seafront mansions "whitewashed like sepulchres," and noisome slums, "a foul dense mass of dwelling-places, where the poor and the slaves pig together."[128] Stanley assembled a powerful and well-equipped caravan. Then he marched west, blazing a new trail a third of the way across the continent. It was a hellish journey through forest, swamp and sierra, punctuated by assaults from bellicose tribes, rebellious retainers, intermittent fevers and pestiferous insects, whose bites and stings produced festering sores and purulent ulcers. "Fatal Africa," Stanley later wrote,

> the torrid heat, the miasma exhaled from the soil, the noisome vapours enveloping every path, the giant cane-grass suffocating the wayfarer, the rabid fury of the native guarding every entry and exit, the unspeakable misery of life within the wild continent, the utter absence of every comfort, the bitterness which every day heaps upon the white man's head, in that land of blackness.[129]

Eventually, on 10 November 1871, Stanley's robed and turbaned train reached the straggling little port of Ujiji on Lake Tanganyika. Here he met his man and spoke the immortal words: "Dr. Livingstone, I presume."

It was an absurdly stilted formula, often mocked by others and always regretted by Stanley, who uttered it from "cowardice and false pride"[130] in order to ward off an expected rebuff. But instead of the prickly personage he had anticipated, Stanley encountered a benign father figure. Brought up in a crowded one-room tenement just outside Glasgow and sent to work in a cotton mill at ten (in 1823), Livingstone had endured juvenile hardships to match those of his visitor. Now in dire straits, his body "a mere ruckle of bones,"[131] he desperately needed Stanley's help. They established an immediate bond of sympathy. As Stanley poured out the news—the Suez Canal, the Pacific railroad, the transatlantic cable, Bismarck's armies around Paris, Napoleon III a fugitive—he began to study his listener. He noticed the worn bearded countenance, the keen hazel eyes and the gappy teeth which, Livingstone himself said, made his smile resemble that of a hippopotamus. Stanley observed Livingstone's heavy, stooping gait, his voracious appetite, his clothes—consular blue cap with faded gold band, red-sleeved waistcoat and grey tweed trousers. In due course the journalist perceived that the missionary had a tough, unforgiving disposition and an abrasive Carlylean wit—he was especially caustic about Glaswegian Freemasons who wanted to enrol him because membership of their order would do him so much good in Africa. Nevertheless, Stanley concluded that Livingstone was "a Christian gentleman" as nearly angelic as the fallen condition of humanity would allow. Stanley contrasted Livingstone's habitual (though not invariable) gentleness towards Africans with his own instinctive violence. He even recorded his servants' verdict: the Doctor was "a very good man" whereas their American master was "sharp—hot as fire."[132]

Despite his epic journeys, Livingstone's methods had not got him far in Africa. He gained only a single convert (who later lapsed) and his congregations lampooned his preaching and psalm singing by bellowing like bulls. His medical nostrums, which included pills called "Livingstone's rousers,"[133] were scarcely an improvement on those of local witch doctors. On his explorations, which had proved a killing ordeal for his young family, he certainly exhibited the Roman fortitude that Stanley admired. But he broke surprisingly little new ground and he made grave mistakes, notably when trying to navigate the Zambesi in 1858. This river, which he had dubbed "God's Highway"[134] to a commercial paradise in the interior, was blocked by cataracts and fatally fever-ridden. Livingstone blamed the steamer, "a wretched sham vessel" with an engine "evidently made to grind coffee." He claimed (absurdly) that "the rapids"[135] could be passed at high water. He fell out with other members of the expedition, advising dissidents to take aperients. One hurled his copy of Livingstone's inspiring but misleading *Missionary Travels* (1857) into the "turbid muddy weedcovered Zambesi" with the imprecation, "So perish all that is false in myself and others."[136] Livingstone's colonising ambitions in the Shire Highlands, south of Lake Nyasa, were also thwarted. He asked the Foreign Secretary, "Is it any part of my duty to take possession of new discoveries as of Her Majesty?" Lord John Russell's answer was more than usually arctic: "No."[137]

Nevertheless, as the herald of Africa's salvation Livingstone was without peer. No one dramatised the work of bringing light to the continent with such sublime conviction. This was not just a matter of preaching the Word. As well as the Gospel, he wrote, trade would save Africa. For the "fairy fabrications" of Manchester's cotton mills were as wonderful to the natives as the "silken robes of the East" had been to "our rude forefathers."[138] The flag would follow trade, Livingstone believed. In short, here was another trinity—Christianity, commerce and colonisation. It became an article of Victorian faith, a new Athanasianism. Recited like an incantation, Joseph Thomson said, it concealed the fact that European benevolence to Africa was "little better than an unmitigated curse."[139] But in Livingstone's eyes the supreme merit of this triple alliance was that it could rid Africa of its greatest evil, slavery. Stanley himself had seen slavers ravaging the land like locusts and driving off their captives in chains so heavy that they might have shackled elephants, the blood-red bunting of the Sultan of Zanzibar flying at the head of their caravans. And he helped Livingstone to pen an eloquent call for the suppression of the traffic. Citing the achievement of President Lincoln (after whom Livingstone had named a lake), they declared that freeing Africa from this scourge was far more important than the discovery of all the Nile sources. Bennett, to whom the appeal was addressed, gave it wide publicity. Some were sceptical about what Dickens had called in *Bleak House* "telescopic   philanthropy"[140]—good   work   in   Borrioboola-Gha matched by neglect at home. They dismissed Livingstone as a negrophile crank, his "poor naked mind bedaubed with the chalk and red ochre of Scotch theology, and with a threadbare, tattered waistcloth of education hanging round him."[141]

Livingstone strengthened this impression by the obsessive and ultimately suicidal wanderings which he undertook once he had bade farewell to Stanley, now a surrogate son, in March 1872. But in his famous account of finding Livingstone, Stanley canonised him. The Doctor's death on his knees in 1873 placed him in (what Samuel Baker called) "the noble army of martyrs who have devoted their lives to the holy cause of freedom."[142] The return of Livingstone's embalmed body, thanks to the heroic efforts of his African retainers Abdullah Susi and James Chuma, was deemed supernatural. At his lying in state, embowered by palms and lilies, in the Savile Row council rooms of the Royal Geographical Society, and at his funeral in Westminster Abbey, the whole nation mourned. Livingstone seemed to enshrine all the idealism of the imperial enterprise, all its nobility of purpose, all its evangelical zeal. As the *British Quarterly Review* wrote, "his death has bequeathed the work of African exploration and civilisation as a sacred legacy to his country . . . The life which Livingstone offered for the salvation of Africa, like a greater life, is a pledge and a prophecy of its redemption."[143]

He further inspired Victorians through his carefully bowdlerised *Last Journals*. Some followed him into the mission field. A few suffered martyrdom, among them James Hannington, Bishop of Eastern Equatorial Africa, whose own *Last Journals* were not bowdlerised and told how he gave his porters "hearty thrashings."[144] Nothing was recovered of him except a "skull without the lower jaw, the soles of his boots, a rubber hot-water bottle, and

the basin-lid of an Army and Navy canteen."[145] Many missionaries promoted Queen Victoria's empire as well as preaching the kingdom of Christ.
At the manse in Blantyre, the settlement in the Shire Highlands named after
Livingstone's birthplace, several sewing machines were kept busy producing
Union Jacks to present to local chiefs. Most Britons thrilled to his words
about the slave trade, which were incorporated into his Abbey epitaph, calling down "heaven's rich blessing" on everyone who would "help to heal this
open sore of the world."[146]

However, Livingstone's vision of the Empire as a humanitarian crusade
was hard to reconcile with Stanley's demonstration that it was a brutal
adventure. Despite his veneration for Livingstone, who had advised him to
treat the African as a "thorough gentleman,"[147] Stanley was convinced that
the world required mastery as well as charity. So, at least by his own
account, he turned exploration into a species of warfare. When setting out
in 1874 on his most daring odyssey, a voyage through Africa's virgin core
along its central waterway, he imposed military discipline on his own men,
flogging and chaining (later even hanging) at will. He also armed them with
Snider breech-loading rifles, which enabled his little fleet to run the gauntlet of riverine tribes on his descent of the Congo. They evidently took his
followers for slavers or raiders and Stanley seldom tried to persuade them
otherwise. Force was quicker than diplomacy. In any case, the canoe-borne
attacks of "cannibal butchers," parrot feathers in their hair, ivory bracelets
on their arms, poisoned darts in their hands, stimulated his blood lust.
Their "wild rancour" convinced him that, despite its equatorial allure, he
was traversing "a murderous world."[148] Gliding downstream, past spicy
islands and vernal shores, he saw a spell-binding panorama of teak, cotton-
wood and feathery palm,

> the bushy and many rooted mangrove which flourishes by the water side,
> here and there a low grassy bank from which the crocodile plunges into the
> brown depths, [while] the snorting and watchful Behemoth whose roar,
> echoed between tall banks of woods, has its volume redoubled. The terrors
> are rocks and rapids, the roaring, plunging, dreadful cataract, the sudden
> storms which wrinkle the river's face into a dangerous aspect, the savages
> which howled after us and required us for meat.

Among the trees birds screeched, baboons howled, elephants trumpeted and
the very insects seemed to drum for war: the humming of myriad mosquitoes "sounded to our half awakened senses like the noise of advancing savages."[149] After an epic final push, Stanley reached the Atlantic with 108

followers—he had started the expedition with 228, some of whom had deserted. All three of his white companions were among the dead.

Stanley had proved that Lake Tanganyika was the source of the Congo not the Nile. He had drained Africa of its essential mystery. He had dissolved its prodigies, ridding it of unicorns and manticores just as Columbus had emptied the Atlantic of the kraken and the sea serpent. He had consigned the land of Ophir and the kingdom of Prester John to the realm of fable. He had dispelled legends about Ethiopians feasting with the gods and about dawn battles between the pygmies and the cranes. He had become chief among the "conquerors of truth,"[150] as Conrad called explorers who both revealed unknown landscapes and wove heroic myths around themselves. But Stanley was the bridge between the golden age of exploration and the iron age of exploitation. He had established enough of the physical geography to invite political cartography, himself championing the new imperialism whereby European powers drew bold new lines on the map and coloured the areas they enclosed red (Britain), purple (France), brown (Germany), green (Portugal) or yellow (Belgium). Partition did not occur at once since most statesmen feared that the costs would outweigh the benefits. In fact, the most eager participant in the scramble for Africa was King Leopold of the Belgians. He employed Stanley, who earned his African nickname "Breaker of Rocks,"[151] to help build what became the most bloodthirsty colonial enclave in history. This was named, grotesquely, the Congo Free State. A "vampire growth, intended to suck the country dry,"[152] it was, of course, the setting for *Heart of Darkness*.[153] British territories in Africa were also won and run along lines evidently pioneered by Stanley. But their animating spirit was invariably that of Livingstone, whose life had been a sermon on the duty of "a superior race . . . to elevate the more degraded portions of the human family."[154] The two men, though portrayed respectively as the evil genius and the patron saint of empire, were not wholly antithetical. But they conveniently summed up vital conflicting elements in the imperial enterprise. In the long term the Snider was at odds with the Bible. To rule the British Empire with a rod of iron was to destroy it as a civilising mission. In short, the Empire was undermined by its own internal contradictions.

There was also a contradiction, as Queen Victoria's reign passed its halfway mark, between Britain's continuing reluctance to acquire overseas dependencies and its increasing colonial expansion. Successive governments echoed Sir James Stephen's view that even if, for example, the whole of Africa could be taken, it would be a worthless possession. Politicians were sceptical about the accounts of explorers, who conjured up visions of African wealth that might have dazzled the Queen of Sheba. Until its mineral riches were uncovered, Africa clearly had little to offer save palm oil, slaves and ivory. And by the 1870s hunters had slaughtered most elephants outside the tsetse fly belt to provide tusks for fans, piano keys, cutlery, bangles, statuary, chessmen, billiard balls, crucifixes, false teeth and dildoes. As late as 1884 the *Edinburgh Review* pronounced:

> No rational English statesman desires to extend the territorial limits of Empire, and we are well aware that the acquisition of new territories not only brings with it no increase in power and wealth, but on the contrary adds to the duties we have to perform and to the burdens which already overtask the strength of our Government.[155]

On the other hand, Britain enjoyed a paramount position in Africa, thanks to the Royal Navy, and sometimes responded to challenges, first from Boers in the south, later from Frenchmen and Germans further north. There were other reasons for intervention, which the Liberals themselves acknowledged. Gladstone's government annexed Basutoland in 1868 to protect it from the Afrikaners and Griqualand West in 1871 to control its newly discovered diamond fields. As Prime Minister from 1874 to 1880, Disraeli prosecuted a similar imperial policy, being equally reluctant to accumulate costly encumbrances, especially in the tropics. He was furious when "prancing proconsuls"[156] dragged Britain into wars with Zulus and Afghans. However, Disraeli would add to the Empire if he could thereby augment British greatness. Moreover, he sometimes responded to local circumstances, such as native disorders which threatened British merchants, missionaries or settlers. Thus in 1874 he extended British authority in Malaya and took control of Fiji—Queen Victoria was horrified by the prospect of admitting cannibals to the Empire but Disraeli assured her that "these Fijians were all Methodists."[157] The fidgety Colonial Secretary, Lord Carnarvon, known as "Twitters," considered applying a Monroe Doctrine to much of Africa but contented himself with making the Gold Coast a protectorate (in 1874) and annexing the Transvaal (in 1877). In 1878 Britain occupied Cyprus. The following year it got the Sultan to depose the spendthrift Khedive Ismail, who went into exile with his yacht, £150,000 in gold for immediate necessities, thirty large chests of jewels, twenty-two of the best dinner services from the Abdin Palace and the seventy most attractive members of his harem, and eventually died as extravagantly as he had lived, after trying to drink two bottles of champagne in a single draught. Britain then established, with

France as a junior partner, Dual Control over Egypt's finances. The rhetoric of imperial aggrandisement remained muted, even among Tories, but the work of empire-building carried on apace.

It accelerated at the very time when Britain seemed in danger of losing economic supremacy. Foreign competition had been increasing since the 1860s but with the onset of the "Great Depression" in 1873 it was clear that France, Germany and the United States were catching up with Britain. Whereas the first industrial nation produced nearly a third of the world's manufactured goods in 1870, the figure had shrunk to less than a quarter ten years later and by 1913 it was only 14 per cent. Why? Some historians blame a deep-seated cultural malaise caused by the microbe of gentility. In class-ridden Britain, their argument goes, captains of industry and merchant princes aspired not to beat the aristocracy but to join it. They sent their sons to public schools where boys acquired the character of gentlemen and empire-builders, learned to "play the game," to despise "trade"[158] and to value Latin and Greek above science. "Stinks" was taught at Rugby in the Town Hall cloakroom one hundred yards from the school and, T. H. Huxley discovered, an Oxford undergraduate could gain the highest honours without having "heard that the earth went round the sun."[159] When war broke out in 1914 the Rugby-educated Secretary to the Committee of Imperial Defence was reading Gibbon, whose account of the eighth-century defence of Constantinople suggested to him "the idea of recreating Greek Fire"[160] in the form of flame-throwers. But Germany had long been experimenting with the *Flammenwerfer* and first used it to surprise effect near Verdun in 1915. In short, classical learning sapped present enterprise and snobbery militated against industry. Yet this seductive explanation is not altogether satisfactory. Many members of the elite succumbed to "the romance of technology."[161] The sports-and-spats worldview of effete patricians by no means drove out the muck-and-brass attitudes of hard-faced businessmen, as Victorians often lamented. A. C. Benson, an Eton housemaster, said that the public schools had a vulgar goal—the "glorification of . . . self-interest."[162] When Tom Brown left Rugby for university he found that "the worship of the golden calf was verily and indeed rampant in Oxford."[163]

The fact is that in the long run economic rather than social forces caused Britain to lose its position as the workshop of the world. Britain had invested heavily in traditional industries while rivals inevitably made the most of new techniques and inventions. Germany's chemical industry pulled so far ahead, for example, that in 1914 the British Army discovered that all the khaki dye for its uniforms came from Stuttgart. Similarly, Germany's electrical generating plant soon eclipsed that of Britain, where it was initially assumed that "each parish should have its own power station."[164] America was still more dynamic, mass-producing Remington typewriters, Singer sewing machines and Yale cylinder locks. It also pioneered the construction of automatic tools. The island that had made steam engines by hand was bound to fall behind the continent that manufactured motor cars on assembly lines. America's economy overtook Britain's between 1870, when it was roughly equal in size, and 1914, when it was nearly three times larger. It is true that Britain's decline was both relative, and relatively slow. British capitalism remained resilient and innovative, assisted by good performances in shipping and textiles.

Still more vital were financial services and overseas investments. In the half-century before the Great War Britain supplied two-fifths of all exported capital. Its invisible empire stretched round the world, reflected in the names of banks, as one Chancellor of the Exchequer observed:

> There is the Anglo-Austrian Bank, the Anglo-Italian Bank, the Anglo-Egyptian Bank. There is the English and Swedish Bank; there is the London and Hamburg Continental Exchange Bank; there is the London and Brazilian Bank, the London, Buenos Aires and River Plate Bank, and even a London and South American Bank.[165]

As for the Imperial Bank of Persia, it was a company registered in London. So in absolute terms John Bull prospered. But this was little comfort to Britons accustomed to effortless superiority. Indeed, prophecies of economic doom strengthened intimations of imperial nemesis. As Henry James wrote to an American friend in 1877, "the 'decline' of England seems to me a tremendous and even, almost, an inspiring spectacle, and if the British Empire is once more to shrink up into that plethoric little island, the process will be the greatest drama in history!"[166] In the opinion of increasing numbers of Queen Victoria's subjects during the last two decades of her reign, imperial protection, consolidation and even expansion were essential to keep decadence at bay. The Empire must wax in power to compensate for its relative waning in pelf. It must rise to avert decline.

These were not the views of Mr. Gladstone, though he was characteristically ambivalent on the subject. Unlike Disraeli, who discerned the possibility of making royalty, empire and paternalism into a platform from which he could appeal to the enlarged electorate, the Liberal leader was wedded to peace, retrenchment and reform. This did not mean, as Disraeli claimed in his famous speech at the Crystal Palace in 1872, that the Grand Old Man (GOM) favoured imperial disintegration. On the contrary, Gladstone in office almost invariably kept territories—Fiji and Cyprus, for instance—whose acquirement he had condemned in opposition. Indeed, he was sometimes prepared to augment British sovereignty, notably to protect "the rights of the savage, as we call him."[167] Moreover, he later became "an active aggressor"[168] in Egypt, concerned about England's major economic interests there and perhaps mindful of the fact that 37 per cent of his personal portfolio consisted of Egyptian stock, which rose enormously after the British occupation. But Gladstone did believe, as his opponents did not, in the transcendent virtue of self-rule and he favoured ending British tutelage as soon as possible. He was profoundly suspicious of empire, fearing that Britain, like Rome, would be corrupted by holding sway in Asia. He could find nothing to say in favour of India except as a destination for Cook's tourists. And he forecast the deplorable implications of Britain's expanding its stake in Suez:

> our first site in Egypt, be it by larceny or be it by emption, will be the almost certain egg of a North African Empire, that will grow and grow until another Victoria and another Albert, titles of the Lake-sources of the White Nile, come within our borders; and till we finally join hands across the Equator with Natal and Cape Town, to say nothing of the Transvaal and the Orange River on the south, or of Abyssinia or Zanzibar to be swallowed by way of *viaticum* on our journey.[169]

Critics dismissed this prognostication as "a mirage of the desert."[170] But even Lord Derby, Disraeli's Foreign Secretary, who resigned in 1878, described his chief's policy as "occupy, fortify, grab & brag."[171]

Gladstone excoriated Tory flag-wagging and drum-beating with all the fervour of one who as a young man had wondered whether to become Archbishop of Canterbury or Prime Minister. The anti-imperial rhetoric that erupted from the deep craters of his personality was never more incandescent than during the campaign which won the Liberals victory in the 1880 election. On the stump in his Midlothian constituency, the People's William declaimed like a hell-fire preacher. He denounced aggression in pursuit of "false phantoms of glory."[172] He condemned conquest sustained by a spirit of jingoism, which the radical journalist W. T. Stead defined as "imperialism sodden with gin."[173] Gladstone called the Afghan War a crime against God. He attacked the annexation of the Transvaal. He inveighed against "the policy of denying to others the rights that we claim ourselves."[174] He censured Disraeli's habit of using Roman analogies as a guide to British policies, notably his conjuring with the slogan *Imperium et liber-*

tas." What this meant in a Roman mouth, said the GOM, was "Liberty for ourselves, Empire over the rest of mankind."[175] Disraeli famously thought Gladstone inebriated by the exuberance of his own verbosity and Queen Victoria threatened to abdicate rather than allow this *"half-mad fire-brand"* to become Prime Minister once again. But she could neither stop his advent nor predict its result. Ironically, Gladstone's crusade for international right-eousness both sapped the moral foundations of the Empire and justified its extension into Egypt.

Admittedly the GOM strove to escape that bondage. At first he even sympathised with the nationalist revolt of Colonel Ahmed Arabi in 1881, which itself prompted such rapture in Cairo that strangers hugged one another in the streets. The rebellion was directed against the corrupt Ottoman elite, against remorseless officials of the Anglo-French Dual Con-trol, who dominated the country's feeble new ruler, Khedive Tewfik, and against some ninety thousand "foreign adventurers,"[176] financiers, entrepre-neurs and concessionaires, protected by privileges and immune to taxation, who were bleeding the inhabitants dry. "Egypt for the Egyptians," intoned Gladstone, champion of peoples oppressed by "the unspeakable Turk."[177] But in June 1882 riots broke out in Alexandria which caused the death of fifty Europeans. At Westminster, as one Liberal imperialist wrote, "Our side . . . badly want to kill somebody. They don't know who."[178] A month later the ironclads of Admiral Beauchamp Seymour, known as "the Ocean Swell,"[179] bombarded Alexandria. This was a thriving port of 250,000 peo-ple, noted for an exotic cosmopolitanism. Its harbour was full of propeller-driven steamers from Liverpool, paddle wheelers from Marseilles, two-masted schooners from Genoa, long-prowed xebecs from Barcelona, lateen-rigged tartans from Constantinople, white light caïques from Limas-sol, streamlined feluccas from Cairo. The city itself, according to Sir Charles Dilke, surpassed "Cologne for smells, Benares for pests, Saratoga for gam-ing, Paris itself for vice."[180]

The shelling caused considerable damage to life and property, especially in the smart consular area. But it was predictably "ineffective against forts,"[181] as Jackie Fisher, whose battleship *Inflexible* blasted them with her 16-inch guns, should have remembered at the time of the Dardanelles. It also failed to quell Arabi. Britain's representatives in Cairo told London that he and his party were "a set of fanatical incendiaries who would burn down the Stock Exchange if they could get the chance, and who had already suc-ceeded in lowering the price of securities."[182] Aggressive imperialists in Gladstone's cabinet heard that Egypt was sliding into anarchy, which would harm British creditors and investors. Among them were the newly jingoistic

Joseph Chamberlain and the Whig magnate Lord Hartington, whose vigour was all the more impressive since he had raised somnolence to a political art, yawning during his maiden speech and later dreaming that he was addressing his peers, only to wake up and find that it was true. Already demanding coercion in Ireland, "Harty-Tarty" and his allies insisted that Britain should fill the vacuum left by ailing Turkey in the eastern Mediterranean. In Egypt it should restore political stability, impose financial probity and secure the Suez Canal. So Gladstone, like others before and since, went to war in the name of peace.

General Sir Garnet Wolseley was sent to Egypt with a force of forty thousand men. He arrived wearing a blue tunic, brown boots, gauntlets, a solar topee and large smoked goggles, an outfit that did not prevent his nose blossoming, in a climate "hotter than the furnace of Nebuchadnezzar,"[183] into "a sort of half fungus, half cauliflower." Nothing daunted, he promised his wife to obtain for their daughter the tip of Arabi's nose. He added that "Caesar has great confidence in his future."[184] Although some of his officers thought him a self-promoting "snob,"[185] his confidence was justified. Combining guile, audacity and speed, Wolseley conducted a brilliant series of manoeuvres. They culminated, on 13 September 1882, in a hazardous night march across the desert to Arabi's fortified position at Tel-el-Kebir. That nearly went wrong because of the unexpected appearance of the Great Comet, which one staff officer, William Butler, described as "a flaming broom sent to sweep the stars out from the threshold of the sun."[186] Despite this false dawn Wolseley surprised and routed Arabi's raw militia. Many of the wounded were shot on the battlefield and British troops quickly occupied Cairo. As their commander observed smugly, it was the tidiest little war ever fought by a British army.

However, its outcome, many Britons feared, would be an infernal muddle. For as Lord Randolph Churchill said (in a speech that his grandson would gleefully reprint with reference to Anthony Eden after the 1956 Suez invasion), the British people had been systematically deceived into thinking that Arabi had led a military rebellion. Yet it was clear that "he was the leader of a nation, the exponent of a nation's woes, and that the military rebellion was the desperate struggle of a race."[187] Egyptian nationalism could not be frustrated for long. Although Arabi was only exiled (Gladstone wanted him executed after a fair trial), he would "live for centuries in the people; they will never be 'your obedient servants' again."[188] So, at least, forecast General Charles Gordon, who elaborated his criticisms of imperialism in a characteristically shrewd and breathless letter to Sir Samuel Baker:

pity is it, that our Govt. always goes agst liberty of peoples . . . Agitators are fruits of existing seeds, does not Parnell represent Irish N[ationalist] feeling. These things are not chance they are the uprisings of peoples. This is my idea, and one sees the same thing here with the Basutos. They pretend only Musapha is resisting, whereas the whole nation is backing him up. Put your energetic mind and pluck into an Agyptian's body, would you have been content to be quiet, no, you would have been far more bitter than Arabi, and you know it. *What right have we to make ourselves guardians of Egypt with our pauper office seekers 397000 to year salaries. The people do not want us.*[189]

Baker disagreed but General Sir William Butler, as Wolseley's staff officer became, shared Gordon's radical views. According to Butler, the heavens had warned against hubris at Tel-el-Kebir. He saw the comet as a sinister portent of future British miscalculations and fatal conflicts in the shadow of the pyramids, for Egypt "has ever played a strange part in the destiny of empires."[190]

Gladstone wanted to let the Egyptians go, but he let the British stay. Caught on the horns of the liberal dilemma, he was keen to confer independence on the land of the Nile while at the same time affording it a stable, honest and friendly government. But as Sir Evelyn Baring pointed out, withdrawal and reform were mutually exclusive. So in 1883 Baring himself was appointed Consul-General and British Agent in Egypt. Gladstone reiterated that the British occupation was temporary, believing with sublime faith exactly what he wanted to believe. The Grand Old Man could persuade most men of most things, said his colleague W. E. Forster, but he could persuade himself of anything. Others noticed his marvellous ability to improvise convictions, to play fast and loose with his intellect. Like Cardinal Newman, wrote the contemporary historian William Lecky, Gladstone was "an honest man with a dishonest mind."[191] Yet the Prime Minister faced genuine difficulties in extricating Britain from Egypt, which were compounded by the difficulties of extricating Egypt from the Sudan.

Even its inhabitants regarded this vast, parched wasteland of scrub, sand, shale and stone as a cosmic sick joke for, according to the Arab proverb, "When God made the Sudan he laughed." But Egypt, which had conquered this territory in the 1820s, valued it as a source of prestige, water and slaves. Paradoxically the Khedive Ismail appointed both Samuel Baker and Charles Gordon Governors during the 1870s to root out the slave trade. But Ismail thereby aimed only to win international respectability and, being himself a huge slave-owner, he did little to assist their efforts. These were the stuff of legend. Baker's rule resembled "a prolonged Balaclava charge. It was magnificent, but it could hardly be called government."[192] Gordon characteristically bit the hand that fed him. "I am at war with nearly every one in Cairo," he wrote, "and my crest is the thistle."[193] However, Gordon showed all the brilliance as a leader of irregular forces that had won him distinction during the Taiping rebellion in China, where the government's "Ever Victorious Army" had been an oft-defeated rabble until he took command. In the Sahara he would appear like a mirage after prodigious camel rides, a small, umbrella'd figure dressed in a gold-braided marshal's uniform, his red fez contrasting with the "steel-like"[194] blue of his piercing, hypnotic, colour-blind eyes. "I shoot and do not hang," he wrote, "it is shorter work."[195] But Gordon could no more eradicate the slave trade than satisfy his appetite for oysters in the desert, or quench his thirst by pouring the Nile down his throat, or cure his fever with Werburgh's tincture, despite its capacity to "make a sack of sawdust sweat."[196] Indeed, he brought further turmoil to a region that had never really been subdued. One English visitor said that control of the Sudan "must be measured by the length of Charlie Gordon's sword."[197]

When he sheathed it Egyptian oppression increased and in 1881 a self-proclaimed messiah known as the Mahdi arose to lead a holy war against the infidels and foreigners who plagued his land. Gordon felt some sympathy for the rebels since, as he said, no people could like being governed by aliens in race or religion. Gladstone agreed, declaring that the Sudanese were "struggling rightly to be free."[198] So when the Mahdi's Dervishes wiped out an Egyptian army led by General Hicks in 1883, the GOM decided that Egypt must abandon the Sudan. No one seemed better qualified to withdraw the garrison, despite his cranky reputation, than General Gordon. His appointment was noisily puffed by W. T. Stead, editor of the *Pall Mall Gazette,* who was as eccentric as Gordon himself. Admittedly Stead took an interest in virgin girls (an interest so keen that he was nicknamed "Bed-Stead" and said to sweat sperm) whereas Gordon, though evidently chaste, was fond of urchin boys, whom he washed in the horse trough at Gravesend. But the two men shared many theological preoccupations—about the exact site of the Garden of Eden, for example, which the general had finally located in the Seychelles because of the striking similarity between the ripe fruit of its giant palms and Eve's pudenda and the no less singular resemblance between the breadfruit and Adam's sexual organ. The *Pall Mall Gazette's* support for Gordon may have been crucial. Certainly Stead was one of the first journalists to appreciate the circulation-building possibilities of imperial campaigns and he himself claimed, with his usual modesty, to be "running the Empire."[199] But he could hardly have been more wrong about Gordon, whose wild telegrams soon convinced ministers and officials in London that he was "quite mad,"[200] a "Christian lunatic."[201] In Cairo Sir Evelyn Baring, his official superior, arrived at the same conclusion, saying that "a man who habitually consults the Prophet Isaiah when he is in a difficulty is not apt to obey the orders of any one."[202] Far from obeying orders, especially the hurried and imprecise orders he had been given, Gordon resolved to defend Khartoum and smash the Mahdi. He thus helped to ensure that Britain remained in Egypt for seventy years.

With comical insouciance Gordon acknowledged that he was inconsistent and insubordinate: "I know that if *I* was chief, I would never employ myself, for I am incorrigible."[203] Nevertheless he was hailed in Khartoum as the "Saviour of the Sudan"[204] and feasted on turkey and Bass's Pale Ale. Having made a bonfire of tax records and instruments of torture, he proceeded to fortify the fifty-thousand-strong town, a warren of mud-brick huts clinging to the "elephant's trunk," the spit of land between the White and Blue Niles. Even Lytton Strachey's caricature of the general as a God-intoxicated charlatan with Bible in one hand and brandy bottle in the other cannot obscure his courageous and chivalric character—Wolseley said that he himself was "not worthy to pipe-clay Gordon's belt."[205] As the Dervish grip tightened around the city, Gordon drew on all his resources. He mounted aggressive sorties. He turned his steamers into warships, which got pock-marked with bullets and stank like badgers. He printed his own currency. He encouraged deserters by giving them a dollar each and showing them their "black pug faces" in a mirror. He inspired defenders with a charismatic gaze, a voice said to be as vibrant as a golden Burmese bell, and a personality that seemed to glow with the beauty of holiness. Gordon matched the Mahdi in claiming divine support for his cause—the Christian general said that he was just the chisel in the hands of the Carpenter. He also invoked secular support by cultivating the press. Frank Power, *The Times*'s correspondent in Khartoum, sent home telegrams which fired the public imagination and helped to make imperialism his newspaper's dominant theme for half a century.

By the spring of 1884 the government faced mounting pressure to assist Gordon, much to the exasperation of Gladstone. He believed that the mutinous man on the spot, a genie out of his jar, was trying to force Britain to annex the Sudan. The Prime Minister resisted, employing his unrivalled powers of procrastination and equivocation. He argued that Gordon was not so much surrounded as hemmed in. The general's admirers held mass meetings, offered prayers, raised funds and even proposed to send out a private army of big-game hunters, financed by Baroness Burdett-Coutts. They also hissed the GOM in the streets and sent him white feathers on cards, known as "Gladstone primroses." According to a pamphlet entitled *The History of the Decline and Fall of the British Empire,* purportedly written by Edwarda Gibbon from Auckland in 1984, Gladstone's "fatal supineness" began "the decay of what was once the cream of nations." (Other causes of rot were Indian revolt, European aggression, America's liberation of Ireland, temperance, spiritualism, the Salvation Army, the abolition of military flogging, the exhaustion of the coal mines and an Ice Age caused by a shift in the Gulf Stream. So the Empire's ancient centre became a haunt of polar bears while the new Gibbon was inspired to pen his elegy by contemplating the ruins of St. Paul's and "a broken arch of London Bridge.")[206] Eventually, to return from futuristic fantasy, Queen Victoria and Lord Hartington remonstrated and the Prime Minister capitulated. He agreed to dispatch a "Gordon Relief Expedition" led, inevitably, by Wolseley. Its blue-eyed beneficiary, scanning the desert through the £5 telescope he had set up on the roof of his palace in Khartoum, rejected the name. The purpose of this force was not to relieve him but to *"SAVE OUR NATIONAL HONOUR."*[207]

This echoed popular sentiment at home and the Sudan campaign became one of the epics of empire, all the more poignant for ending in tragedy. As usual Wolseley's preparations were meticulous, but circumstances conspired to thwart him. The eight hundred open boats called "whalers," which had been built to transport his fifteen thousand troops up the Nile, proved sturdy and manoeuvrable in the hands of the Canadian voyageurs and West African Krumen who were recruited to skipper them. But their advance from Assiout was delayed because the stout, "fizz"-drinking, lobster-pink Chief of Staff, General Sir Redvers Buller, had failed to order enough coal for Thomas Cook's steamers, which towed them up river. The cataracts also proved a serious obstacle, though the whalers were light enough to be portaged round the worst of them. Sometimes the boats carried the expedition, it was said, and sometimes the expedition carried the boats. Wolseley established a tented base at Wadi Halfa, known to the soldiers as "Bloody Halfway."

> Soldiers, sailors, black men and yellow men, horses, camels, steam-engines, heads of departments, piles of food and forage, newspaper correspondents, sick men, Arabs and generals, seemed to be all thrown together, as though the goods station of a London terminus, a couple of battalions of infantry,

the War Office, and a considerable portion of Woolwich Arsenal had been all thoroughly shaken together, and then cast forth upon the desert.[208]

It was so hot and the insects were such a torment that Wolseley thought Wadi Halfa a foretaste of Hades.

As soon as possible he drove forward his spearhead of "camelry." It seemed an impressive array, the men in white helmets, red serge jumpers, ochre breeches and blue puttees. But English soldiers, while regarding the horse as a gentleman, thought the camel a boor—the "Devil's Steed."[209] Moreover, the camels, morose and refractory, emitting strange groans and ghastly smells, proved to be anything but indestructible ships of the desert. Their riders seemed to take that metaphor at face value. They treated these beasts as engines and used oakum to caulk the fist-sized, maggot-filled holes made in their flesh by ill-fitting saddles. Many camels died. Dervish sharp-shooters and skirmishers also held up Wolseley's vanguard as it trudged across the desert south of Korti to avoid a huge loop in the Nile. The blood-iest attack occurred at Abu Klea where a mass of Dervishes charged into the British square, killing nine officers and sixty-five men before being repulsed. Kipling toasted their courage in his inimitable fashion, at once admiring and condescending:

> So 'ere's *to* you, Fuzzy-Wuzzy, at your 'ome in the Soudan;
> You're a pore benighted 'eathen but a first-class fightin' man;
> An 'ere's *to* you, Fuzzy-Wuzzy, with your 'ayrick 'ead of 'air—
> You big black boundin' beggar—for you broke a British square![210]

As a result of the setbacks Wolseley's men did not reach Khartoum until 28 January 1885, two days after the Mahdi's forces had overwhelmed its fam-ished garrison and killed Gordon.

How he met his end has never been definitely established, though it seems probable that he went down fighting. Victorians preferred to visualise him as the peerless hero in a scarlet tunic, staring with sublime disdain at his savage foes just before they hacked him to pieces, as pictured in George Joy's celebrated icon. Although the tragic news did not cause him to postpone a planned fancy dress ball, Sir Evelyn Baring expressed the view of his coun-trymen: "No Christian martyr tied to the stake or thrown to the beasts of Ancient Rome, ever faced death with more unconcern than General Gor-don."[211] Britain gave way to mob grief, a jingoism of lamentation instead of jubilation. It was expressed in tributes, threnodies, memorials, statues, books, poems dedicated to the warrior of God whose life was England's glory and whose death was England's pride. From Queen Victoria downwards, people blamed Gladstone for a disastrous blow to the prestige of the Empire that would echo down the years. The GOM became the MOG, the Murderer of Gordon. In his journal Wolseley wrote that the Prime Minister could not, "self-illusionist though he be, disguise from himself the fact that he is directly responsible for the fall of Khartoum & all the bloodshed it entails."[212] Wolseley turned his bust of the MOG to the wall and taught his dog to growl at the name of Gladstone.

The Queen herself snapped at the Prime Minister, who seemed bound to avenge Gordon's death. However, what he took to be a providential Russian incursion into Afghanistan gave Gladstone the excuse he wanted to withdraw from the Sudan. Eventually Gordon's blood did become the seed of its reconquest. Meanwhile, the legend of his sacrifice was woven into the imperial tapestry in threads of scarlet and gold. His spirit quickened the martial mood of late Victorian Britain. And ironically, his old enemy Sir Evelyn Baring, the tall, impassive, moustached Consul-General, became one of the beneficiaries of Gordon's imperialist legacy. For Baring, formerly something of a rake and a liberal, managed to ensure that Egypt was slowly and deviously incorporated into the Empire. His dialectical shifts were worthy of Gladstone. According to one estimate, Britain made sixty-six official declarations of intent to quit Egypt in the four decades after 1882, and no one repeated them with such ringing sincerity as the Consul-General. But his wish for withdrawal was as urgent as St. Augustine's prayer for chastity. Somehow Baring's arguments all came down on the side of long-term occupation.

First and foremost, Egypt had to be held against the Dervishes. Next, Baring maintained, British authority was "essential to the progress of orderly reform" in a land misgoverned for sixty centuries. Of course, he said, Egypt should be governed by the Egyptians—but for the insuperable difficulty of discovering who the Egyptians were. For their land was filled with a hotchpotch of Arabs, Copts, Bedouins, Turks, Syrians, Nubians, Circassians, Jews, Greeks, Maltese, Levantines "whose ethnological status defies diagnosis . . . [and] half-breeds of every description."[213] Baring also emphasised the strategic benefit of moving Britain's centre of gravity in the Middle East from Constantinople to Cairo. Lord Salisbury, who superseded Gladstone as Prime Minister in 1885, might lament that a greedy Britain had tasted the Egyptian "fleshpots and will not let them go." But Baring persuaded him to value the fleshpots. The financial and commercial advantages were huge. The capitalisation of the Cairo stock exchange rose from £7 million in 1890 to £100 million in 1901. Britain supplied nearly half Egypt's imports and took four-fifths of its exports, notably cotton. The Suez Canal was becoming ever more important as an imperial lifeline. A cornucopia of goods flowed along it in British ships: wheat from the Punjab, cotton from the Deccan, jute from Bengal, indigo from Bihar, rice from Burma, tea from Assam and Ceylon, dates from Mesopotamia, tin from Malaya, hemp from the Philippines, sugar from Fiji and Java, frozen meat from Australasia. Egypt was anything but an "incubus."[214]

So Baring established himself as master of what one of his officials, Alfred Milner, called a "veiled Protectorate."[215] Or as Kipling put it, "Here is a country which is not a country but a longish strip of market-garden, nominally in charge of a government which is not a government but the disconnected satrapy of a half-dead empire, controlled pecksniffingly by a Power which is not a Power but an Agency."[216] The Khedive remained a figurehead, theoretically subject to the Sultan of Turkey. But in practice he could not even leave Cairo without British permission and he was completely controlled by the "bearing-rein."[217] "Over-bearing" and "Evelyn the First" were other nicknames given to the curt, aloof Consul-General, who lived in splendid state and regarded his subjects as naughty children steeped in mendacity. The Egyptian, he thought, was as intellectually remote from the European as "an inhabitant of Saturn."[218] Baring did not go so far as the future ambassador to Turkey, Sir Nicholas O'Conor, who told his wife that "semi-orientals certainly do not feel physically or mentally as we do—they are of a lower nervous organisation like fungi or fish."[219] But the Consul-General was quite clear that the people of the Nile must long remain in a state of inferiority. British heads could direct Egyptian hands to good effect though, and British hands could impose a necessary discipline. Baring's attitude was less that of a pharaoh than a Roman prefect. In the words of a subordinate, he

> was permeated by the heroic spirit of antiquity; its frankly avowed thirst for fame; its neglect of the insignificant; its belief in strength and power; its admiration for achievement; its contempt for weakness, whether in individuals or nations. Essentially Roman in his conception of things, [his] attitude in a crisis was certainly inspired by what he believed appropriate to a Proconsul.

Baring was "Roman even in recreation,"[220] taking exercise for precisely two hours a day to obtain a healthy mind in a healthy body.

The rest of the time he exercised power behind the throne, like the

British Resident in an Indian princely state. It was important, wrote Lord Salisbury, that "Baring's position as 'maire du palais'" should not be "too plainly revealed."[221] So he did not give commands but advice, which had to be taken. He governed by subterfuge, though his annual reports, said Wilfrid Scawen Blunt, were couched in the style of the first chapter of Genesis. The disguised autocracy had disadvantages. It fostered cynicism and alienation in the land of the Nile, where no political charade could conceal the impotence of khedives, beys, pashas, mudirs, sheikhs, omdas, effendis and bimbashis, let alone win the allegiance of five million fellaheen. To British critics, moreover, this Egyptian mummery typified the humbug at the heart of empire. Imperialism was a crime, said the economist J. A. Hobson, that dare not speak its name. It employed instead what Ruskin had called "masked words" such as "rectification of frontier" and "emissary of civilisation." Worse than false, said Hobson, this kind of cant was what Plato had termed "the lie in the soul"—the lie that does not know it's a lie.[222] Deep-dyed hypocrisy was the prime target of *Eminent Victorians* and in the book's final essay Lytton Strachey exploited the flaws in Gordon's character to undermine both the era and the Empire. He concluded with a satirical swipe at Britain's victory over the Mahdi's successor at Omdurman in 1898, which conferred further benefits on the casuistical Consul-General: "it had all ended very happily—in a glorious slaughter of twenty thousand Arabs, a vast addition to the British Empire, and a step in the Peerage for Sir Evelyn Baring."[223]

Lord Cromer, to give him his new title, ruled in Egypt until 1907, becoming ever more haughty and gouty. His central endeavour was to modernise a land where, said Kipling, "time had stood still since the Ptolemies."[224] Cromer conceded that reform on European lines could only go so far, since it was impossible to make "a Western silk purse out of an Eastern sow's ear."[225] Still, he increased prosperity, lowered taxes, improved the administrative and judicial systems, and lifted the tyranny of the kourbash and the corvée. He also claimed to have stiffened "the invertebrate ranks of the fellaheen soldiery"[226] with English officers and sergeants, who miraculously (to quote Kipling again) "drilled a black man white and made a mummy fight."[227] However, the Consul-General's achievement was patchy. He prided himself on the vast irrigation works which nearly doubled the crop area during his period of power. But they added to the workload of the fellaheen, saturated and exhausted the soil and spread waterborne plagues in Egypt such as malaria and bilharzia. As Cromer uneasily acknowledged, they also made "scandalous profits"[228] for alien financiers such as Sir Ernest Cassel (whose closest business associate happened to be Lord Revelstoke, Cromer's brother). The Consul-General made a show of improving Egyptian education. But English teachers were not employed if they spoke a word of Arabic and they were correspondingly unsympathetic to their charges. The Egyptian schoolboy was deemed "parrot-like in his unintelligence, incorrigible in his inaccuracy, hopelessly fatuous in his dishonesty." In adolescence he would be claimed by "cafés and hashish and mistresses."[229] In adulthood he would become an Arab *babu,* useful as a clerk, dangerous as a nationalist, to be kept down at all costs. The "Egyptian has no mind," said a typical Briton: "no coloured man imitates the collars of Englishmen so accurately; but in intellectual capacity . . . he is not a white man."[230] Fundamentally, Cromer's paternalism was at odds with Egyptian nationalism. This emerged most clearly in 1906, when a number of people from the village of Denshawai were savagely punished for taking part in a fatal affray with British officers. Their sentences were condemned in Britain as well as Egypt, particularly as Cromer received the Order of Merit on the very day when four of the villagers were hanged. It was an Egyptian version of the Eyre controversy. Blunt claimed that the episode did "more towards shaking the British Empire in the East than anything that has happened for years."[231]

Still, as early as 1889 Egypt was said to be modernising so fast that "a telephone line runs almost to the ear of the Sphinx." One sign of progress was the boom in tourism, fostered by Thomas Cook, "Booking Clerk to the Empire," whose travel agency was the largest British business in Egypt. Previously visitors had endured hotels full of fleas and cockroaches, and Nile boats swarming with rats and scorpions. Now they could enjoy lavish caravanserais, notably Shepheard's Hotel in Cairo, which had lifts, electric lights and a sumptuous décor described as "Eighteenth Dynasty Edwardian." Cook's steamers, a miniature British fleet ruling the muddy waters of the Nile, were so luxurious that they "eclipsed Cleopatra's barge of burnished gold."[232] There were even respectable brothels—those near Shepheard's were owned by the Coptic Patriarch. By 1891, an Englishman remarked, Cairo resembled an English town which had retained oriental sights "much as the proprietor of a country place keeps a game preserve or a deer park for his own amusement."[233] But the picturesque had its limits. Certainly visitors were entranced by minarets and mosques, their domes rising like "great gilt and turquoise bubbles" above the palm trees and the house tops. They were charmed by Moorish arches and lattices, by carpet bazaars and spice markets, by street scenes filled with the "*dramatis personae* of the Arabian Nights."[234] They were dazzled by the abundant natural life and the kaleidoscope of colours in the Nile Valley.

However, Europeans were also horrified by the squalor and confusion that reigned in Egypt. They were assailed by touts, pimps and deformed beggars whining for baksheesh. They saw tattooed harlots and bastinadoed slaves, emaciated dogs and maltreated donkeys, garbage-strewn slums and fly-blown souks. They witnessed indigo Bedouin and blue-shirted fellaheen "living in filth and poverty unmatched even in India and China."[235] Still more shocking was the contrast between contemporary decadence and the stupendous relics of the first great civilisation. Living in the shadow of the Romantics, Victorians were awed by the Ozymandian ruins of Memphis and Thebes, by the majesty of the pyramids of Gizeh and the splendour of the temples of Luxor. Once "Mother of the World,"[236] Cairo now had an ashen look, seeming "to have been buried in lava, and like Pompeii to have just been brought to light."[237] In the opinion of one traveller, Amelia Edwards, the Hall of Pillars at Karnak, known to the ancients as the forest of eternity, was "the noblest architectural work ever designed and executed by human hand."[238] Yet the Egyptians, who had once summoned giants from solid rock, were now "a nation of slaves." Florence Nightingale thought it "good for British pride" to compare the titanic past with the present degradation and she wondered if England would "turn into Picts again . . . as Egypt has turned into Arabs."[239] Perhaps some violation of natural or divine law would cause this fall. At any rate, Egypt provided a memento mori of imperial greatness as sublime as the wreckage of classical Rome. It afforded an image of transient glory as brilliant as the opalescent sunsets over the Nile.

Cromer did not like to contemplate the decadence of Britain but he acknowledged that it could not govern Egypt indefinitely. For no benefits that he or his successors might confer on the inhabitants could stop the man in the turban or the tarboosh craving the departure of the man in the topee or the top hat. Cromer concluded the two-volume apologia for his stewardship, *Modern Egypt* (1908), by citing the experience of the Roman Emperor Theodosius, who found that "not even the wisest and most humane of princes, if he be alien in race, in customs, and religion, can ever win the hearts of the people."[240] He repeated the point in a book comparing the Roman and British empires, alike especially in being unsettled by expansionist proconsuls and native auxiliaries while searching for "defensible frontiers."[241] True, Cromer insisted that Britain should retain India for the foreseeable future since only the Raj gave unity amid religious, racial and linguistic diversity. But, he said, the slipshod Anglo-Saxon was always striving for two imperial ideals that were mutually destructive, "the ideal of good government, which connotes the continuance of his own supremacy, and the ideal of self-government, which connotes the whole or partial abdication of his supreme position."[242] In the long run this contradiction could hardly bode well for the Empire. Meanwhile, Gladstone's acquisition of Egypt, which mortified France and offended Germany, helped to precipitate an international scramble for other African territories. John Bull would get the lion's share. But the very fact that European rivals could mount a challenge in Africa indicated that Britain's imperial ascendancy was under threat.

7

A Magnificent Empire Under the British Flag

Cape to Cairo

Since the time of the American and French revolutions, when the Royal Navy came to dominate the oceans of the world, Britain had seen the Cape of Good Hope as the barbican of Africa. The blue granite walls of Table Mountain, first rampart of the great escarpment which rises in giant steps towards the arid veldt of the Karoo and the snowy crests of the Drakensberg, guarded the sea route to India, Australasia and the Far East. Seized from the Dutch during the Napoleonic Wars, the Cape was retained in 1815 as a strategic and commercial stronghold. To secure it Lord Liverpool's government assisted the emigration of five thousand settlers in 1820. Disembarking on the sands of Algoa Bay, with their tents, tools and boxes, they were a motley group, some elegant gentlefolk, more respectable farmers and tradesmen, most pale-faced artisans, weather-beaten labourers and ragged paupers plucked from the workhouse. Here was the nucleus of another British colony, though its development remained problematic. This was not just because Africans greatly outnumbered Britons, but because the new arrivals made up only an eighth of South Africa's European population.

The rest were Boers (farmers), descendants of seventeenth- and eighteenth-century Dutch pioneers. They had gradually pushed eastwards along the green coastal plain. They fought for possession of the land, demoralised the Hottentots *(Khoikhoi)* with brandy and smallpox, killed the Bushmen *(San)* like snakes, hunted the abundant game, and established tiny settlements and scattered homesteads. Many of the Afrikaners were nomads—"trekboers"—Calvinist patriarchs who packed their families into ox wagons and followed their flocks and herds. They relied on their rifles and Bibles, ate *biltong* (jerked venison) and *bokkems* (salted fish), made their own clothes from the pelts of animals and were self-sufficient in almost everything except ammunition. In fact their way of life differed little from that of the Hottentots, who existed in symbiosis with their cattle and anointed themselves with their fat and guts. The Boers greased their bodies to ward off fleas and covered their floors with cow dung to discourage other vermin.

They slept communally under buckskin karosses, like Africans in their kraals. And the men made free with "slave and Hottentot women." Thus the Boers created a new coloured race (one group adopting the name *Baastards*) while insisting on the purity and superiority of their own. They were correspondingly cruel. The first British reform was to abolish torture and breaking on the wheel. As the new rulers would find, however, the most recalcitrant community on the continent was the white tribe of South Africa.

The British also believed in white supremacy, but not on terms that would satisfy Afrikanerdom. They permitted an influx of missionaries and promoted humanitarian ideals. They rejected Dutch criminal law, made English the official language and gave limited rights to Africans. Finally, in 1833, the Empire emancipated its slaves, of whom there were nearly forty thousand in the Cape, paying compensation only in London. This attack on what Boers deemed the natural order prompted thousands of them to migrate across the Orange River, an odyssey later dramatised as the Great Trek. The *Voortrekkers* naturally asserted that theirs was a march to win freedom not to maintain bondage. Indeed, by casting off the British yoke they claimed to be acting "under a divine impulse."[1] The Great Trek was the exodus of a new chosen people in search of the Promised Land. It thus became enshrined at the heart of Boer mythology. Here was a faith powerful enough to bind together the impoverished, straggling, quarrelsome *Voortrekkers* on their prolonged venture into the interior, a journey in time whereby they sought to make their future in the past. They were also united against the Bantu, waves of whom had been rolling southwards for generations. The Boers damned them as Kaffirs (the Arab name for infidels) and smote them like Amalekites. No Bantu were more redoubtable than the Zulus, forged into a mighty war machine by their most ferocious ruler Shaka, who had drilled his barefoot warriors on a carpet of three-pronged devil-thorns, executing anyone who flinched.

Yet the Boer advance was remorseless, as a British officer later wrote:

> One thing is clear, that the white man wanted the black man's land—that he got leave from the black to graze his cattle in the first instance, then came over and put up a shanty, then a house. Then more Boers came, and so on, until, as the Zulus told us, the Boers were like a toad that comes hopping and hopping until it hops right into the middle of the house.[2]

In the lush grasslands of Natal massacres occurred on both sides. But Zulus armed with stabbing assegais and protected by ox-hide shields could make little impression on circles of lashed ox wagons defended by Boer rifles. Thousands fell before these laagers, their black bodies "heaped like pumpkins on rich soil."[3] Anxious to keep the peace and to land-lock the Boers, Britain annexed Natal in 1843. The British expanded to the Vaal and the Tugela, while the Boers retreated across the Drakensberg. There they seemed to pose no threat (except to their black neighbours, whose children they kidnapped and enslaved as "apprentices")[4] and conventions were signed giving them the right to run their own affairs in the Orange Free State and the Transvaal. The Cape itself acquired an elected assembly in 1853, voters being qualified by cash not race. And the British concentrated on engorging and exploiting what they had got. None suffered more from this policy than the Xhosa people in what had become British Kaffraria, north-east of the Great Fish River. Having seen their independence lost, their culture subverted and their labour extorted, they succumbed to a millenarian cult preached by their own soothsayers. In 1856–7, expecting to achieve national salvation through a stupendous sacrifice, they killed their cattle. Following this unexampled hecatomb, "an act of consummate despair,"[5] tens of thousands of Xhosas starved to death.

Native disarray seemed to be matched by Boer backwardness but British ministers concluded that South Africa should develop along the lines of Canada rather than India. In other words, it should not be a martial raj with a white garrison under orders from London but a "confederate and self-governed . . . dominion." The Boers would inevitably dominate it, wrote J. A. Froude, an emissary of Disraeli's Colonial Secretary Lord Carnarvon, as they dominated the Cape parliament. But, he reckoned, these shaggy farmers who had grown over two centuries "into the dimensions of Patagonians" would choose to remain under the British flag. There was just one condition, he concluded. They must be allowed "to extend to the whole country the more severe system [of native management] which they find to succeed excellently in the Orange Free State."[6] Sacrificing black interests for the sake of white unity had a perennial appeal. But British liberals opposed the attempt to "improve [Africans] off the face of the earth."[7] And Boer conservatives resented British incursions. They were particularly bitter about the loss of the diamond-rich blue ground around Kimberley, to which the Orange Free State had a fair claim. More galling still was the annexation of the Transvaal in 1877, when it was too weak to resist British pressure. The Boer republic was on the brink of bankruptcy: it had 12s 6d in its exchequer and was obliged to pay its Postmaster General in stamps. Moreover the Transvaal was beleaguered by hostile Bantu.

So Sir Theophilus Shepstone, Natal's minister for native affairs, marched into Pretoria, a raw frontier dorp enclosed by ancient rocky hills and new forests of eucalyptus and oleander, at the head of twenty-five blue-uniformed, spike-helmeted Natal Mounted Police. And on Queen Victoria's birthday, 24 May, the youngest member of Shepstone's staff, Rider Haggard, raised the Union Jack over the Transvaal for the first time. In the market square, where cattle grazed under the oak trees and cricket was played between the thatched church and the thatched parliament (*Volksraad*), Boers looked on sullenly. But they needed British protection, especially against the Zulus, whom Haggard dubbed "the Romans of Africa."[8] The new British High Commissioner in Cape Town, Sir Bartle Frere, was determined to protect them into subservience. The Boers, he informed Queen Victoria, were a "most interesting and very primitive people" who could be made "as loyal subjects to Your Majesty as the French Canadians."[9] It was an apt but inept comparison, since both communities fiercely resisted assimilation. Frere's policy, moreover, contained a fundamental flaw. Shepstone had gained Afrikaner acquiescence, but not allegiance, because the republic was in danger. Once Frere had kept his promise to give the Transvaal secure frontiers, the Boers would have no reason to remain under the Crown.

Frere made another miscalculation, imposing his own policy rather than that of his political masters, which would bring his illustrious public life to an inglorious conclusion. Able, energetic, cultured and punctilious to the tips of his exquisitely groomed moustache, he had distinguished himself in India. He had acquired several languages (learning en route to the subcontinent enough Arabic "to scold his way across Egypt")[10] and taken a sternly paternalistic line in "dealing with barbarous folk."[11] As Governor of Bombay he had also gained a sublime faith in his own judgement. At the Cape he bubbled with self-confidence, expelling an uncooperative ministry and earning Wolseley's nickname "Sir Bottle Beer." Actually Wolseley had mixed feelings about Frere, reckoning that he had "marked out for himself a great career of conquest to end in a magnificent African empire under the British flag . . . I have a great admiration for Frere, who under an oily, Pecksniff, almost old womanly manner and appearance has the heart of a man."[12] At any rate the new High Commissioner was bold enough to ignore the new Colonial Secretary, Sir Michael Hicks Beach, who told him in November 1878 that "we are *most anxious* not to have a Zulu war on our hands just now."[13] Frere insisted that King Cetewayo, Shaka's nephew, was an "aggressive despot" and that the history of his reign was "written in characters of blood."[14]

Without Beach's knowledge or approval, the High Commissioner issued an ultimatum demanding Zulu disarmament. The irascible Colonial Secretary complained that he could not control Frere without a telegraph—the submarine cable only reached Cape Town in December 1879—and that he probably could not control him with one. So a British army set off from Pietermaritzburg, white-helmeted redcoats, straw-boatered blue-jackets and slouch-hatted colonials, as well as nine thousand African levies, about half the total force. Wheels creaked, sjamboks cracked and the band played "I'm Leaving Thee in Sorrow, Annie," the tune that had sent Confederate troops off to fight in the American Civil War. General Lord Chelmsford's array, which advanced in three long columns and a vast plume of dust, made piti-fully slow progress. The Zulus, whose impis could move three times as fast as British infantry, nicknamed them "pack-oxen."[15] But it was the 27,000 four-legged oxen needed to pull his 2,500 supply wagons which really encumbered Chelmsford and he found it too time-consuming to form a laager each evening, as Boer leaders like Paul Kruger advised. The general, whom other senior officers thought unfit to be a corporal, believed in the invincibility of British firepower and worried only that the Zulus would avoid a pitched battle. He even divided his central column. With half his command he pursued detached war parties over the high plateau, a land-scape of grass, bush and boulder, broken by *kloofs* (ravines) and *kopjes* (hills). The rest he left in an exposed camp beneath a sphinx-shaped crag called Isandhlwana.

Here, on 22 January 1879, twenty thousand warriors who had hidden throughout the cold, dewy night in a nearby valley with little to sustain them but snuff, which they carried in gourds attached to their pierced ear lobes, launched the main attack. Frere called Zulus "celibate man-destroying gladiators"[16] but they were not animated by sexual deprivation, only by the impulse to defend their land, kraals and cattle. They swept for-ward, a dark wave breaking over the grey-green veldt. At a distance, said one trooper, the Zulu impi was "black as Hell and thick as grass."[17] Soon details appeared. The Zulus were big men, bigger on average than their British foes. Depending on their rank and regiment, they wore red feathers or white ostrich plumes in headbands of otter or leopard skin, earflaps of green mon-key skin, necklaces containing charms wrapped in snake- or lizard-skin pouches, white oxtails around their necks, wrists, knees and arms, fur kilts or tasselled capes. They loped forward hissing like so many mambas, drum-ming assegais against black or white shields, firing muskets wildly. Far more deadly were the volleys of the Martini-Henrys, their heavy, soft-nosed 45-calibre slugs "cutting roads"[18] through the ranks of the charging throng. But the Zulus adopted their usual taurine tactic, bearing the brunt of punishment on the "chest" of their impi while flinging out two "horns" to envelop the enemy.

Within minutes they were able to exploit gaps in the British line and shortages of ammunition. The battle disintegrated into scattered hand-to-hand encounters, bayonets against *iklwas*—razor-sharp blades, so named in imitation of the sucking sound they made when pulled from human flesh. Some of Chelmsford's men escaped. But in the growing darkness, caused by a partial eclipse of the sun, the Zulus "washed their spears" in the blood of more than seven hundred Europeans and nearly five hundred Africans, disembowelling their bodies to release spirits which would otherwise have haunted the killers. At least 1,500 Zulus also lost their lives, so theirs was a Pyrrhic victory. "An assegai has been thrust into the belly of the nation," cried Cetewayo. "There are not enough tears to mourn the dead."[19] Chelmsford waxed less eloquent, though he was said to be "awfully cut up"[20] by the defeat. Disraeli was prostrated, though he voiced reluctant admiration for the Zulus, who not only defeated British generals but converted British bishops—he referred to John Colenso of Natal, known as "Pen" because of the unorthodox views about the Pentateuch that he had adopted as a result of persistent Zulu questioning. Disraeli's government publicly censured Frere, who was soon recalled, and British newspapers expressed horror at the worst disaster inflicted on a British army by "savages" since the retreat from Kabul. The Boers, however, took heart from Isandhlwana, inferring that Britain's martial spirit was on the wane and that its Empire was in decline.

The British partially vindicated themselves at Rorke's Drift, though the eleven Victoria Crosses won in its defence were awarded not just for valour but for propaganda. And after further setbacks, both sides murdering and pillaging freely, they brought more organised firepower to bear on the foe. In July 1879 the Zulus, whose peace overtures had been ignored, suffered a crushing defeat at Ulundi. Wolseley, who replaced Chelmsford, then divided Cetewayo's realm into thirteen separate chiefdoms, nominally answerable to a British Resident, which led to civil strife and the disintegration of Zulu power. Cetewayo himself was imprisoned in Cape Town Castle, where he donned western clothes in place of his leopard skins and his necklace of lions' claws—this Wolseley claimed as his prize, having the claws individually mounted and engraved and sent to influential ladies in Britain. Even in a grey flannel suit Cetewayo retained his "regal bearing"[21] and he apparently sought to retain his royal prerogatives, offering fifty head of cattle for the attractive wife of the new High Commissioner, Sir Hercules Robinson. The offer was said to be "neither appropriate nor, probably, sufficient."[22] In due course Cetewayo visited England where he was feted by the public, received by Queen Victoria and welcomed by Mr. Gladstone, who invited him to stay in his house in Harley Street. By contrast, Paul Kruger, soon to be President of the Transvaal, had to put up at the Albermarle Hotel. Here, in his bushy whiskers and baggy trousers, his black hat and short Dopper (Baptist) jacket stinking of the pungent Magaliesberg tobacco from his Meerschaum pipe, he cut as incongruous a figure as the Zulu king.

Cetewayo won leave to return to Zululand (dying soon afterwards) whereas Kruger could not gain freedom for the Transvaal. Hicks Beach refused to give up anything on which the British Lion "had set his paw."[23] Gladstone, whose government was bitterly divided over other issues, notably the coercion of Ireland, went back on his word over the annexation he had so fiercely denounced. He was swayed by Wolseley's warning that the Boers were incapable of self-government and that an independent Transvaal might collapse. This could "reverse the relative positions occupied by the white man and the native generally throughout Africa, a result that may prove fatal to British interests." Wolseley tried to reconcile the Boers to their colonial fate, suppressing other Bantu and holding out the promise of a railway. But he was adamant about sovereignty. The Vaal would flow backwards, he declared, and the sun would cease to shine before the British flag was lowered. Frere had also said that the Union Jack would continue to fly over the land, to which the Boer leader Piet Joubert riposted: "Over the land possibly; over the people never."[24]

So, convinced that they must resort to force, the Boers raised their own banner, the Vierkleur, which had a green vertical stripe nearest the pole and three horizontal stripes of red, white and blue. The first shots were fired in December 1880. The British expected a prompt victory, regarding the Boers as cowardly peasants, little better than savages. But the "nation of deerstalkers"[25] was fighting for a cause, acknowledged Sir Robert Herbert, Under-Secretary for the Colonies, that "stimulates their 'Dutch courage.'"[26] And redcoats, obedient to "the dogmatic teachings of the barrack square,"[27] where bayonet drill ranked higher than marksmanship, were no match for these "mountain devils."[28] Wolseley's successor, General Sir George Colley, suffered two reverses in quick succession. In London the War Office plaintively asked how long the conflict would last, to which the Colonial Office wittily replied that it had not been endowed with the gift of second sight. Colley was confident that he could finish the Boers by occupying Majuba Hill, a volcanic peak (its name meant "hill of doves" in Zulu) overlooking their key position at Laing's Nek. Once at the top, seeing the enemy fires twinkling below him, Colley exclaimed: "We could stay here for ever."[29]

However, he had failed to bring up Gatlings or rockets and he did not order trenches to be dug on the rim of the saucer-shaped summit. The Boers resolved to attack. About 180 volunteers crept up the steep, scrubby, boulder-strewn slopes, making skilful use of the cover and directing a deadly fire at the defenders. Finally, they stormed the heights. They shot Colley in the forehead. They also killed, wounded or captured 284 of his 350-strong force (looting everything, right down to Colley's shoes) at hardly any cost to themselves. Majuba was hailed as the Boer Bunker Hill.

It was more a skirmish than a battle, but it compounded Gladstone's Irish and other travails, and he exclaimed in his diary: "Is it the Hand of Judgement?"[30] Whatever the truth of that, the reverse persuaded him that he should have trusted his conciliatory instincts towards the Transvaal. Majuba had stimulated pan-Afrikaner nationalism and the Cape Dutch seemed ready to make common cause with their rough cousins in the north. So the GOM showed what the press called "Majubanimity." Rejecting calls for revenge, enduring charges of surrender, swallowing pills of humiliation, Gladstone liberated the Transvaal. The Boers got partial independence at first and, in return for agreeing to stabilise their frontiers, complete Home Rule in 1884. But Britain, while leaving the Bantu at the mercy of the Boers, still claimed "suzerainty" over the Republic. This was a vague and contested term, implying that London retained control of Pretoria's foreign affairs. Actually it was designed to conceal Britain's loss of power and to obscure Gladstone's acknowledgement that President Brand of the Orange Free State was right when he said, "You cannot rule a people with bayonets."[31] Indeed, the Boers would probably have been left to their own devices had not Germany's "Iron Chancellor" suddenly changed his mind about colonies. Prince Bismarck had always maintained that they were an expensive luxury for poor Germany, "exactly like the silks and sables of the Polish nobleman who had no shirt to wear under them."[32] But now, for reasons of national prestige and economic protection, he decided to seek a place in the sun.

In 1884, taking advantage of the GOM's Egyptian embarrassment, Bismarck established a protectorate over South-West Africa. At first the British were unperturbed. They wanted profitable markets not more costly territory and Bismarck was welcome to this "sterile sand hole." If Germany became a colonising power, declared Gladstone, "all I can say is 'God speed her.'"[33] However, the German occupation gave the Transvaal a possible western outlet to the sea, through Bechuanaland. This barren region, embracing the Kalahari Desert, was also the "Missionaries' Road"[34] north, once trodden by Livingstone, and "the Suez Canal" of the Cape, which wanted the freedom to expand towards the Zambesi. Already, wrote Gladstone's secretary, the Transvaal Boers had been "boorish beyond measure," supporting murderous frontier freebooters and "encroaching onto Bechuanaland."[35] So in 1885 Gladstone once again resorted to force. He won the support of his ablest minister "Radical Joe" Chamberlain, who was now becoming "Jingo Joe," in part because he refused to be "cheeked"[36] by Bismarck, let alone by Kruger. General Sir Charles Warren travelled north with a small force (its transport organised at considerable cost by some of the very frontier freebooters who were causing the trouble) and annexed Bechuanaland to the Crown. Its acquisition was a classic exercise in defensive and reluctant imperialism, extending Britain's reach while straining its resources.

A year later the discovery at Witwatersrand of a gold reef so rich that it eclipsed even the diamond fields of Kimberley transformed the position of the Transvaal. Suddenly, from being a needy, rustic backwater, Kruger's republic became El Dorado. Johannesburg sprang up like a mushroom on the bare plateau, where even anthills yielded yellow dust. Prospecting and speculating made this canvas and tin shantytown, scarred by excavations and latrine trenches, bloated with saloons and brothels, "the biggest gambling hell on earth." But within ten years the focus for the greatest gold rush in history had become the largest city in South Africa—though until the arrival of the railway in 1892 every nail, plank and brick had to be hauled in by ox-wagon. By the end of the century over a quarter of the world's gold was being dug from Johannesburg's mines. The metal tilted the balance of power across half the continent, for by 1889 the Transvaal's revenue, £1.5 million, was equal to the Cape's. As a result, said one Cape politician, John X. Merriman, "The idea of a British Empire in South Africa is at an end, and that of the United States of South Africa, under the friendly protection and possibly in some undefined connection with Great Britain, takes its place."[37] Anything short of untrammelled independence was precisely what President Kruger could never accept. He used the Transvaal's new wealth to build a railway through Portuguese East Africa to the sea, at Delagoa Bay, and to angle for German help to challenge British supremacy. However, Kruger's position was undermined by the influx of foreigners, *Uitlanders*, many of them British. They were unruly and uncouth: the *Times* journalist Flora Shaw said that not one man in a dozen knew the difference between a violin and a vegetable. They were also multifarious, as the writer Olive Schreiner noted:

> Your household servant may be a Kafir, your washer-woman is a Half-caste, your butcher is a Hungarian, your baker English, the man who soles your

boots a German; you buy your vegetables and fruit from an Indian Coolie, your coals from the Chinaman round the corner, your grocer is a Russian Jew, your dearest friend an American.

The pick of the prostitutes, known as "continental women,"[38] came from Paris and Chicago. The President regarded Johannesburg as the City of the Plain, evil in itself and wicked in its implications. He called the *Uitlanders* *"assvoels"* (vultures) and clipped their political wings to retain Boer control of the Republic. But he could not stop Britain from continuing to fence in the Transvaal. Moreover, he met his match in the champion of aggressive imperialism and the Colossus of the diamond fields, Cecil Rhodes.

Kruger compared himself to an ox and Rhodes to a racehorse, hoping that strength would vanquish speed. The President was indeed a powerful figure, gruff, ugly, stubborn and brutal. In youth he could lift a laden wagon on his shoulders and when much of his left thumb was blown off in a gun explosion and the stump became infected with gangrene he cut it off with a jackknife, drawing out the poison by plunging his hand into the stomach of a newly slaughtered goat. But Kruger belonged to the era of the Great Trek, which he had taken part in as a boy. As President he wore an archaic uniform—top hat, frock coat, green sash and throat whiskers. Although capable of bestial rages, he usually played the bucolic Nestor, uttering gobs of folk wisdom and spittle in equal measure. He clung to the Old Testament, once assuring the round-the-world sailor Joshua Slocum that the earth was flat. Rhodes, by contrast, wished to annex the planets if possible. Certainly he believed that "we are the first race in the world, and that the more of the world we inhabit the better it is for the human race." He dreamed of bringing all its "uncivilised" territories, including Palestine, Japan, South America, and Africa from Cape to Cairo, under the Union Jack. He even envisaged recovering the United States and thus securing global peace "for all eternity."[39] At a time when the British were beginning to conjure with the special transatlantic relationship in order to compensate for their country's relative decline, he was willing to have the Empire "annexed to the American Republic" if that would secure a "union of the English-speaking peoples."[40]

In his view expansion abroad would avert revolution at home and, ever alive to Roman precedents, Rhodes read Gibbon rather than the Bible. Secretly he even paid impoverished scholars to translate all the original authorities which the historian had used, collecting them in two hundred morocco-bound volumes, with supplementary biographies of the Roman emperors. Rhodes believed that he himself resembled Titus physically,

Hadrian intellectually. His favourite quotation was "Remember always that you are a Roman."[41] "Rhodes was more Roman than any Englishman had ever been," said the writer Emil Ludwig, "a romanticist of distinction, a genius as a colonizer, an imperialist to the point of madness."[42] Relaxing in the shabby tweeds or flannels he liked to wear, Rhodes would sit in bright moonlight on the stoep of his low, white, gabled mansion, Groote Schuur (Great Granary), beneath the Devil's Peak of Table Mountain, talking about the grandeur that was Rome. (The house even contained a huge neo-Roman bath hollowed out of a single block of granite, in which its owner took a cold plunge every day.) Whereas Kruger, whose republic rested on gold, was the prophet of Boer survival, Rhodes, who became king of diamonds, was the visionary of British expansion. Oswald Spengler, author of *The Decline of the West* (1918), considered him a modern Caesar, "the first man of a new age."[43]

Born in 1853, Cecil Rhodes was the son of the vicar of Bishop's Stortford and he early proposed to found a secret society on Jesuit lines to promote Greater Britain. A tall, leonine figure with fair hair, blue eyes, cleft chin and weak lungs, he came to South Africa in search of health and found a fortune large enough to realise even his ambitions. In Rhodes's view diamonds were merely crystallised power. Once back from belated studies at Oxford, which his first prospecting had paid for, he spent hours gazing into the stupendous open-cast mine at Kimberley. It was the largest man-made hole in the world, carved into an extinct volcano which had secreted a cornucopia of diamonds in its throat. Twelve acres in area at the top and descending several hundred feet, the pit contained thousands of naked Africans filling one-ton iron buckets with blue earth. These were pulled to the surface on wires crisscrossing the crater like the web of a "Titanic spider"[44] or "the strings of some wonderful harp."[45] Offered a penny for his thoughts, Rhodes replied that he was calculating "the power that this blue ground would confer on the man who obtained control of it all."[46] Deploying his silver tongue, the spellbinding charm of his personality and every technique from cajolery to bribery, Rhodes consolidated rival companies into the virtual monopoly of De Beers. The last major entrepreneur to resist the amalgamation was Barney Barnato, a very rough diamond indeed—when, later, an aristocratic lady invited him to see her Watteau he assumed she was referring to part of her anatomy. But, after eighteen hours of Rhodes's shrill wheedling, at four o'clock in the morning Barnato said: "You have a fancy for making an empire. Well, I suppose I must give in to you."[47] Two years later, in 1890, Rhodes claimed that the wealth of De Beers was "equal to a quarter of that of the whole of the Cape colony."[48] But he was only interested in imperial dividends and milked De Beers accordingly. This provoked anguished but ineffective protests from its capitalist backers, who wanted profit before power—contradicting the thesis of J. A. Hobson and others that finance was "the governor of the imperial engine."[49] Lord Rothschild himself, who said that the history of De Beers was "simply a fairy tale," failed to prevent Rhodes from using the company to pay for "the dream of your life."

Rothschild considered Rhodes "an adventurer"[50] and there is no doubt that he was often ruthless, sometimes reckless. A sentimental cynic as soft as the Graces and as hard as Fate, Rhodes believed that the ends justified the means, that philanthropists deserved 5 per cent, and that every man had his price. As well as manipulating politicians, peers and Prime Ministers, he proposed to square the Mahdi over the Sudan and to "square the Pope"[51] over Ireland. In his drive to occupy the land that would bear his name, it was even said that Rhodes would "find means of squaring the tsetse fly."[52] His first major deal as a Cape politician was with Jan Hofmeyr, farmers' champion and leader of the Afrikaner Bond (League), who supported his imperial venture north of the Limpopo in return for Rhodes's promotion of dear bread, cheap brandy and African helotry. In 1888 Rhodes paid in guns for mining concessions from King Lobengula, whose gout his confidential agent, Dr. Leander Starr Jameson, treated with injections of morphine. When the Bishop of Bloemfontein protested about the devilry of arming the Matabele he was silenced by a contribution to his missions—Rhodes told a friend that the Bishop had repented. As a result of his tenuous, even bogus, agreement with Lobengula, Rhodes was able to secure a royal charter for his British South Africa Company (its board packed with venal functionaries and dim patricians) to exploit mineral resources north of the Transvaal. In 1890, playing up the prospect of gold discoveries that would beggar those of the Rand, he sent a Pioneer Column from Kimberley to Mashonaland. A mixed band ranging from peers to lumpenproletarians, it was seen off by General Methuen who told it to go to Siboutsi, though, he confessed nonchalantly, "I do not know whether Siboutsi is a man or a mountain."[53]

Transported by 117 ox wagons, which carried searchlights and Maxim guns, the Pioneers inched over the veldt, through dense bush, past bloated baobab trees, across sandy river beds and up into the rocky Shona plateau. This was an invasion masquerading as a mining expedition. It was a private enterprise, soon to extend across the Zambesi, blessed by the British government, which hoped for power without responsibility or cost. Rhodes, who became Prime Minister of the Cape in 1890, now aimed to form a huge political confederation, a British union of South Africa stretching from the

Cape to the Belgian Congo. He pushed so aggressively into Mozambique that the Foreign Office thought he proposed to make war on Portugal. He gave Jameson his head in Matabeleland and the doctor duly mowed down Lobengula's impis in 1893—when the Company's town rose on the site of his kraal at Bulawayo its hotel was named "The Maxim."[54]

Kruger, who had refused even to join a customs union and who damned Rhodes as "one of the most unscrupulous characters that have ever existed,"[55] remained the stumbling block. Rhodes, who had enclosed the Transvaal from the north, now determined to subvert it from within, using the *Uitlanders* as his Trojan horse. By 1895 they outnumbered the Boers (of whom there were fifteen thousand adult males) by about four to one and they paid nine-tenths of the Transvaal's taxes, yet they were denied the vote. They had other grievances, too. For example, Kruger tried to draft them to fight in his war against the Bagananwa, who took refuge in caves which the Boers blew up with dynamite. This was not only an "extravagant waste"[56] of state-controlled explosives needed in the gold mines but a threat to the Randlords' labour supply. Rhodes had long believed that the "diggers will never endure a purely Boer Government."[57] So, spurred on by an "innate Caesarism,"[58] he plotted an armed coup against Kruger's regime. Acting with the secret connivance of the Colonial Secretary, Joseph Chamberlain, who had deserted Gladstone over his policy of giving Home Rule to Ireland and was now the staunchest empire-builder in Salisbury's cabinet, Rhodes masterminded a fiasco so spectacular that it threatened to undermine the whole imperial enterprise.

Chamberlain himself warned that a "fiasco would be most disastrous." But he urged Rhodes to "hurry up"[59] (on account of Britain's impending dispute with the United States over Venezuela) and trusted that "The Napoleon of South Africa"[60] would live up to his popular title. In fact the conspiracy was worse than a crime, it was a series of blunders inspired by personal and imperial hubris. Rhodes kept changing his timetable: the insurrection was postponed because of Johannesburg race week and half-hearted efforts were made to call it off at the last minute. He let too many people into the secret: Sir Hercules Robinson "knew and did not want to be told"; the London *Times* knew and urged Rhodes not to commence action on a Saturday since it did not appear on Sundays. The Colossus entrusted command of the invasion to Jameson, the rashest of the male cronies on whom he doted with an apparently chaste passion. The poker-playing "Dr. Jim," who dismissed regular officers as machines evolved from an amalgam of red tape and sealing wax, was confident that he could defeat the Boers with a force of five hundred men armed with bull-whips. The arrangements he made in December 1895 reflected this boast. Jameson's private army, consisting mainly of a "harum-scarum regiment"[61] of grey-uniformed, smasher-hatted Mashonaland Mounted Police, was drunken, ill trained and badly equipped. The planned uprising of the *Uitlanders* in Johannesburg, as Rhodes said, "fizzled out like a damp squib." Dr. Jim carried on regardless, although unfit for a long ride since he was suffering acutely from piles. After a brief, bloody clash twenty miles from Johannesburg, he surrendered to the Boers who had been tracking him nearly all the way from the Bechuanaland border. As one of Jameson's men wrote, "we were simply caught like rats in a trap . . . and in a short time the whole of the gallant little band were marched off to Krugersdorp."[62]

Kruger was not only gross but also *slim*—cunning. Before the Jameson Raid he had said, "You must give the tortoise time to put out its head before you can cut it off."[63] Now, content with the moral and political harvest of victory, he showed mercy to the insurgents. But Kruger's magnanimity was nullified by the Kaiser's impetuosity. Having just proclaimed Germany a world empire, its Emperor sent a telegram on 3 January 1896 congratulating Kruger on maintaining the Transvaal's independence without calling on the aid of friendly powers. The British public reacted with an outburst of xenophobia and the government sent a naval squadron to Delagoa Bay, which encouraged Germany to build its battle fleet. Wilfrid Scawen Blunt deplored the furore: "The gangrene of colonial rowdyism is infecting us, and the habit of repressing liberty in weak nations is endangering our own."[64] But the press made Jameson a national paladin and he was greeted in London by a band playing "See the Conquering Hero Comes." He was hymned not only by the artless Poet Laureate Alfred Austin but by Kipling, who apparently based *If* on Jameson's character and called him "the noblest Roman of them all."[65] Briefly incarcerated in Holloway Prison, London, he also occupied a place of honour in the national pantheon at Madame Tussaud's.

Rhodes, though forced to resign as Cape Prime Minister, escaped everything but censure. He was too powerful to gaol and, said Olive Schreiner, too big a man to go through the gates of hell. In fact, Rhodes was soon being hailed as "the Abraham Lincoln of South Africa."[66] "When he stands on the Cape," wrote Mark Twain, "his shadow falls to the Zambesi." He was "the only unroyal outsider whose arrival in London can compete for attention with an eclipse."[67] Such was the effervescence that Chamberlain, who repudiated Jameson and cursed "amateur belligerents,"[68] managed to cover up his own complicity in the affair. Rhodes helped, suppressing the cables which showed that the Colonial Secretary was in "up to his neck"[69] in the conspiracy. Jameson "played the game loyally . . . and deceived the Committee"[70] of Inquiry, which earned its famous nickname, the "Lying in State at Westminster."[71] Treachery compounded by hypocrisy outraged the Boers and helped to unify them against the British. Kruger said that they had punished the dogs and let the masters go free. He began importing arms on a large scale, among them thousands of Mauser rifles from Germany, which shared his hostility to Britain. In *The World Crisis* Winston Churchill dated the "growth of the great antagonisms abroad"[72] to the Jameson Raid. This ignominious episode was a prelude to the Boer War and a foreshadowing of the Great War, the first damaging, the second almost fatal, to the British Empire.

The scramble for tropical Africa was also an expression of European rivalries. North and South Africa had their obvious value but the core of the continent hardly seemed to merit the cost of conquest—before 1914 its annual trade with Britain was worth only £14 million. As the British Foreign Secretary told the French ambassador in 1895, these vast areas were nothing more than "barren deserts or places where white men cannot live, dotted with thinly scattered tribes who cannot be made to work."[73] This was also the view of the Marquess of Salisbury, Prime Minister for most of the time between 1885 and 1902, who joked that Europeans were haggling over bits of central Africa which they could neither pronounce nor locate on the map. However, these remote regions were useful make-weights in the international balance of power. They sustained Britain's political position at a time when its economic weakness was becoming palpable, helping to preserve an equilibrium from which John Bull was the chief beneficiary. Salisbury, who as Prime Minister added two and a half million square miles to the British Empire, saw the partition of Africa as a means of keeping the peace in Europe. And since no major war took place between 1870 and 1914, it is arguable that his policy succeeded, that national animosities were diverted into imperial channels, that European poisons drained away in the swamps, sands and jungles of tropical Africa.

On the other hand, colonies became such a focus of antagonism, especially after Britain's occupation of Egypt, that they often increased European tensions. France sought revenge in the Sahara for the lost provinces of Alsace and Lorraine, and tried to emulate its maritime neighbour by seizing Madagascar, "an Australia all of our own."[74] Germany, unable to expand any more at home but confronted and affronted by Britain everywhere abroad, acquired territory three times larger than the Reich—from the Cameroons to East Africa. Lesser powers tried to prove that they were greater by staking claims in the heart of the continent. Italy craved an African empire "in a spirit of imitation . . . for pure *snobisme*."[75] King Leopold of the Belgians was equally keen to demonstrate his people's virility and to enhance his country's prestige: as early as 1861 he inscribed on a paperweight made of marble taken from the Parthenon the motto, *"Il faut à la Belgique une colonie."*[76] The British themselves reacted sharply to the European challenge in Africa. In 1884 Salisbury observed that the public took no notice of imperial matters unless "some startling question appealing to their humanity arises."[77] But the following year excitement about Gordon and Africa had risen to fever pitch—it prompted Frederic Harrison to repudiate with his whole soul "the code of buccaneer patriotism."[78] And by 1890, in answer to alien advances, it was possible to talk of a "popular outcry for extending our Empire into Central Africa."[79] Flag-wagging and drum-beating so increased that by 1893 Gladstone could exclaim, "Jingoism is stronger than ever. It is no longer war fever, but earth hunger."[80] The national mood was erratic. It responded most fiercely to issues near at hand, such as Home Rule for Ireland. But it could also react to a small Cossack incursion at Buzai Gumbaz: although the Foreign Office had to cable India to ask where this was (in fact, just inside Afghanistan) the Foreign Secretary soon stated that Buzai Gumbaz was "the Gibraltar of the Hindu Kush."[81] People recognised that distant friction could spark a conflagration on their doorstep. And they were particularly fearful that "by sowing dragon's teeth in Africa we may reap a most bloody crop of armed men in Europe."[82]

Salisbury tried to avert that catastrophe by hard-headed calculations about where Britain's true interests lay. Although he was as keen a High Churchman as Gladstone, Salisbury had none of the imperial idealism espoused by the GOM—initials that at Hatfield stood for "God's Only Mistake."[83] A thick-skinned, short-sighted, cross-grained reactionary, known as "the Buffalo," Salisbury was as cynical about high-minded justifications of empire as he was about all schemes of political improvement. He was invariably sceptical and sometimes ribald about philanthropic endeavours, such as the organised emigration of "distressed Needlewomen"—they were seduced on board ship to the Cape, there consigned to the Church's care, and then known as "the Bishop's women."[84] Salisbury denounced missionaries as vulgar radicals. He dismissed phrases like "advance of civilisation" as humbug. "If our ancestors had cared for the rights of other people," he declared, "the British Empire would not have been made."[85] Its purpose was not to spread sweetness and light but to increase Britain's wealth and power. Exploitation involved computation: "as India must be bled, the bleeding should be done judiciously."[86]

British rule must be imposed by persuasion if possible, by force if necessary. The carrot was usually more effective than the stick, Salisbury thought,
for most colonial people were easily led and quite incapable of governing
themselves. Irishmen, he declared, were no more fitted for self-rule than
Hottentots. Equally unfit for government were leaders such as Kruger, a
"frock-coated Neanderthal."[87] Indeed, a prime function of alien potentates
was apparently to provide amusement at Hatfield: nothing delighted Salisbury more than hearing that the uxorious Sultan of Turkey had awarded one
of his wives the Order of Chastity (Third Class), or that the ailing Emperor
of Ethiopia, fed pages of the Bible by his doctors, had expired eating Kings.
However, he was as fearful of sedition in the Empire as he was of insurrection at home. This hulking, hirsute figure suffered from "nerve storms"[88]
which invaded even his dreams; he was once discovered sleepwalking in
front of an open second-storey window preparing to repulse a revolutionary
mob. In an article entitled "Disintegration" he dwelt on the danger of losing
"large branches and limbs of our Empire"[89] such as Ireland, Egypt and
India. Elsewhere, he warned, white settlers were too prone to "nigger-
despising" and in due course native peoples would revolt effectively instead
of just "testing our Armstrong guns."[90] Thus Salisbury was reluctant to get
sucked into tropical Africa, except to counter other great powers or to buttress Britain's key positions in the north and south. Even here he was wary of
prodigal proconsuls keen to annex places with "unrememberable"[91] names
or ambitious generals equipped with small-scale maps and large appetites
for conquest.

The most compelling of the consular scramblers for Africa, in Salisbury's
view, was Harry Johnston. Beginning his career as a painter, explorer, philol-
ogist and naturalist, Johnston became a freelance agent of imperial expansion. A colourful little adventurer of rare wit and ability, he always exuded a
whiff of charlatanism. And he sent the Foreign Office voluminous reports of
his exploits which might have been penned by Rider Haggard or G. A.
Henty. In Old Calabar, for example, he described a palaver with "inveterate
cannibals":

> Almost over my head, hanging from the smoke-blackened rafters of the
> house, was a smoked human ham, and about a hundred skulls were ranged
> round the upper part of the clay walls in a ghastly frieze . . . the old chief pre-
> sented me with a necklace of human knucklebones from off his own neck.

However, Salisbury was amused by this sort of thing and he invited Johnston to Hatfield, where the consul in turn enjoyed the charades—Lady

Gwendolen Cecil (the marquess's daughter), wearing an enormous moustache, played Lord Randolph Churchill (Winston's father). Salisbury was unconvinced by Johnston's high-pitched schemes for exploiting tropical Africa along the lines of India or treating it as a New World, the modern equivalent of what America had been to Europe in the sixteenth century. But he favoured the consolidation of British interests and he used Johnston to limit Portuguese pretensions, notably by making treaties with local rulers in the Shire Highlands and establishing a protectorate over Nyasaland (modern Malawi) in 1890. Rhodes paid for this undertaking though Johnston, appointed British Commissioner for South Central Africa in 1891, had a stormy relationship with him.

They agreed over painting the African map red and at their first meeting they stayed up all night discussing the project. They also agreed over methods. Johnston thought nothing of burning native villages and confiscating grain and livestock, marching into battle under a white umbrella that was never furled. And around his sailor's straw hat he sported a white, yellow and black ribbon, a tricolour replicated in the specially designed uniforms of his few Sikh troops and symbolising his faith that Africa would be governed by Europeans, developed by Indians and worked by Africans. However, Johnston resented Rhodes's ruthless exercise of power through the purse strings: "I can scream and write frantic articles, but you move on with your armies and your gold with all the quick, majestic, resistless advance of an elephant through brushwood."[92] In 1894, when Rhodes's demands for land and mineral rights became exorbitant, Johnston persuaded the British Treasury, whose Scrooge-like functionaries he wanted to hunt from room to room at bayonet point, to substitute a grant (£28,000 for 1895–6) in place of the British South Africa Company's subvention. All told, the colonisation of Nyasaland was a characteristic imperial enterprise. A Prime Minister concerned to counter European rivals gave free rein to an amateur empire-builder who was subsidised by a private company, supported by a tiny imperial force and sustained by agreements with client headmen, and the haphazard arrangement was eventually put on an official footing. Johnston himself was sanguine about the process but he feared that a white despotism might not long remain benevolent. The time would therefore come when the Negro, "a man with man's rights" despite his almost "ape-like" existence, "will rise against us and expel us" from the land he originally owned.[93]

Elsewhere in Africa, a continent "created to be a burden to Foreign Offices" in Salisbury's opinion, commercial companies were encouraged to take on responsibilities of colonisation that successive British governments refused to accept. In 1886 Sir George Goldie's Royal Niger Company gained a charter to administer the vast hinterland north of the delta. Economic advantage was always a factor in imperial reckoning and no one pursued it more ruthlessly than Goldie, who had a mind like a calculating machine. It was matched by a personality which he himself compared to "a gunpowder magazine." Gaunt to the point of emaciation, he was fierce in his rages and uncompromising in his rationalism—he left England to escape the sound of church bells. Goldie was also "rapid and violent in his movements, his nervous force extraordinary, the nose the beak of an eagle, the eyes blue rapiers."[94] In London he rented a room off the Strand, where he set up a Gatling gun, teaching himself how it worked and aiming it across the Thames. On the Niger he amalgamated rival concerns (including French ones), excluded African middlemen and established an unauthorised but effective monopoly. Trading firearms and firewater for palm oil, used in soap, proved profitable to an efficient company "free from gas and bunkum."[95] But Goldie, like Rhodes, aimed at empire.

It was here that the new companies differed from the old, which had put trade before the flag. They thus attracted radical attacks on "stock-jobbing Imperialism."[96] Goldie paid no heed, envisaging a British dominion that stretched from the Niger to the Nile. He pushed northwards through the thick rainforest of Yoruba and Ibo pagans into the scrubby savannah of Fulani and Hausa Muslims. The Islamic states contained walled red cities, thriving mosques, crowded bazaars, well-tilled fields, literate mullahs, learned jurists, cosmopolitan merchants, craftsmen in leather and metal, and a cavalry out of medieval romance. Its indigo-turbaned, chain-mailed warriors rode long-tailed ponies with silver bridles, embroidered trappings, high double-pommelled saddles, and enormous moon-shaped brass and iron stirrups. They galloped into battle "waving their swords or spears in the air, with their white robes flying in the wind . . . [encouraged] by the clamour of their small drums and deep bassed horns."[97] Of course, they were no match for Sniders, let alone Maxims. But Goldie's aim was diplomacy rather than conquest and he tried to persuade local rulers to sign treaties ceding jurisdiction in return for protection. The treaties were often spurious and the protection was usually nebulous. For the British relied on water transport—on Sanders of the River—and whites always remained thin on the ground. Indeed, the Emir of Kontagara asserted that Europeans were a species of fish and would die if they strayed far from the Niger.

Goldie's most effective agent was Frederick Lugard, an army officer who had been jilted in India and had won his spurs in East Africa. Here, after freebooting in Nyasaland, he had done important work for another private concern. This was Sir William Mackinnon's Imperial British East Africa

Company, given its charter in 1888 to protect Britain's position in what would become Kenya and Uganda. Mackinnon was a shipping magnate, devout, philanthropic and keen to spread civilisation to Africa. But although he had a heart of gold he lacked Goldie's will of iron. Soon his "one horse Company"[98] (Lord Rosebery's term) collapsed. It found too little trade and accepted too many responsibilities, notably that of commanding the headwaters of the Nile. Germany was the rival here and in 1890 Salisbury bought off the Kaiser by renouncing the "red" Cape-to-Cairo corridor and ceding Heligoland, giving up that inhabited island, W. T. Stead complained, on the principle whereby "Russian grandees of olden times" paid their gambling debts with serf-populated estates.[99] France complained about the flouting of its rights in Zanzibar (now made a British protectorate) and the Prime Minister replied airily that he and Bismarck had grown used to squeezing the Sultan "as though he were a rubber doll."[100] Gallic pressure continued and fear of France became "the mainspring of British policy in Africa."[101]

Lugard imposed a measure of control on Uganda, which was lacerated by civil and religious strife, Catholic against Protestant and Muslim against both. And to secure the Upper Nile, Salisbury gave France ground from Algeria to Timbuktu; seldom able to resist a blazing indiscretion, particularly one to cause mortification across the Channel, he described this Saharan acquisition as "'light' land."[102] Having helped to ensure that the government took over from the Company in Uganda, which became a British protectorate in 1894, Lugard went on to oppose the French challenge in what would soon be Nigeria—refusing to emulate Rhodes, Goldie rejected the name Goldesia. With a tiny, ill-trained force, whose language he could not speak, Lugard marched north-west into Bornu country. He secured treaties from rulers who feared that signed papers might be used to cast evil spells on them, cured himself of fever with "10 grains antipyrine and 13 miles marching in a blazing sun," and beat off attacks of hostile warriors firing poisoned arrows. One, tipped with iron, penetrated a quarter of an inch into Lugard's skull. His hunter wrenched it out, putting his foot on his master's head to get the necessary leverage, and Lugard swallowed various disgusting antidotes. In the spirit of the legendary British empire-builder whose wounds hurt only when he laughed, he continued throughout to bark orders. No wonder Sir Harry Johnston hailed him as the Clive of Uganda and the Warren Hastings of Nigeria.

Lugard was a small man with a large moustache who professed a "woman's"[103] aversion to violence—though he once broke a finger striking an Indian trader and he nearly knocked out the eye of an impertinent servant in the interest of maintaining white prestige. However, he did possess humane instincts and he exercised command chiefly through force of personality. Indeed, never having more than a handful of British subordinates, he adopted Goldie's method of delegation. This had worked triumphantly during the Niger Company's war against the people of Nupe and Ilorin in 1897, assisted by Maxims, flares, searchlights, tinned food and barbed wire. Goldie was so impressed by the performance of his black levies that he recommended that West Africa, rather than India, where nationalism was sapping loyalty, should provide "a reservoir of military manpower"[104] on which the Empire could draw to forestall its decline. Paradoxically, further French incursions convinced Joseph Chamberlain, the first major politician whose mission it became to develop the nation's great colonial estates, that Britain must no longer govern Nigeria by proxy. So the Company's charter was revoked in 1899 and the Crown took over its rights for the sum of £850,000. Goldie protested that the Empire was buying a great province for "a mess of pottage."[105] He likened the government to a highwayman who not only robbed his victim but stole his clothes.

However, Lugard himself became High Commissioner for northern Nigeria in 1900. He was still devoted to Goldie (though their friendship faded after 1902, when Lugard married the journalist Flora Shaw, who had been in love with Goldie) and refined his methods, recruiting local chiefs as the "'collaborators' of colonialism."[106] This was the term which African nationalists later used, whereas Lugard himself understandably regarded the "dual mandate" as the quintessence of imperial wisdom. He also penned its classic justification:

> As Roman imperialism laid the foundations of modern civilisation, and led the wild barbarians of these islands along the path of progress, so in Africa to-day we are repaying the debt and bringing to the dark places of the earth, the abode of barbarism and cruelty, the torch of culture and progress, while ministering to the material needs of our own civilisation . . . British rule has promoted the happiness and welfare of the primitive races . . . We hold these countries because it is the genius of our race to colonise, to trade, and to govern.

In fact, Lugard's system, which seldom did more than scratch the surface of Nigerian life, was doomed by its complacent conservatism. He failed to grasp the logic of the progress he praised let alone the education he espoused, which produced westernised Africans who "would appeal successfully to the masses and lead them to independence across the ruins of chieftainship." Furthermore, indirect rule only worked passably where distinct local authorities already existed, which was not the case among the fragmented Yoruba kingdoms and the autonomous Ibo forest dwellers of the south. Powerful, wealthy emirs among the supposedly virile races of the north made effective officers of state but, with British support, they often became more tyrannical than ever.

Lugard's own dictatorial proclivities were checked by his need to delegate. But he frequently gave way to grim moods. He thought that education not only changed the mental outlook but damaged the physical health of the African, making him less fertile and more prone to "disabilities which have probably arisen from in-breeding among a very limited class, and to the adoption of European dress."[107] He also harped on the inveterate evils of "primitive people." These could never be eradicated by "a negrophile kowtowing policy."[108] Instead Lugard tried to impose order with the whip, the stocks and the pillory. He also mounted "punitive expeditions" which soldiers seemed to take as a licence for lechery as well as butchery. "Bull Pup" Crozier, who later became a general, told in his memoirs how one young brother officer, Bellamy by name, carried off the under-age daughter of a Sokoto chieftain. But the British Resident, "such a sport," hushed up the scandal for fear of what "psalm-singing ——s at home" would make of it and a "topping new verse" caused mirth in the mess:

> She was a Mallam's daughter,
> She lived at Sokoto,
> She didn't know what she ought to
> Till Bellamy taught her to.

Crozier also recorded that British officers were apt to "'finish off' the wounded with sporting rifles" and to cut limbs from the dead for the sake of bracelets and anklets: "whack—whack—two strokes and it's done."[109] As a young Liberal minister at the Colonial Office in 1906, Winston Churchill commented ironically on Lugard's so-called "pacification" of northern Nigeria: "the whole enterprise is liable to be misrepresented by persons unacquainted with Imperial terminology as the murdering of natives and stealing their lands."[110]

Lord Salisbury might have been more amused than shocked by this observation since he believed that living nations were destined to take the place of dying ones. But his Colonial Secretary Joseph Chamberlain, though hard and sharp as the screws he had once manufactured, took a more positive view of imperial endeavour. Its aim was to spread civilisation and commerce abroad in order to promote prosperity and social reform at home. Like Rhodes, Chamberlain believed that imperialism was "a bread and butter question."[111] By providing markets, raw materials and outlets for surplus population, colonies could alleviate hardship and take the sting out of socialism in Britain. No one advanced the commercial case for empire with more vigour and brilliance than Chamberlain. It became a revised version of the radical gospel he had preached and practised as mayor of Birmingham during the 1870s and it attracted corresponding brickbats. *Punch* memorably jibed, "The more the Empire expands, the more the Chamberlains contract."[112] The Liberal John Morley described Chamberlain's imperialism as "killing people because it is good for trade."[113] Others regarded Chamberlain as a political Lucifer and claimed to detect a whiff of sulphur whenever his name was mentioned. Tories, though, were glad to have as an ally the statesman who, as Winston Churchill said, made the weather. Blunt's cousin, George Wyndham, appreciated him as "the grandest specimen of the courageous, unscrupulous schemer our politics have ever seen."[114] Salisbury's nephew, Arthur Balfour, especially admired Chamberlain when he was "drawing blood with his back to the wall; then his bad taste is less conspicuous."[115]

Persons of refinement disparaged Chamberlain, his parvenu origins imperfectly disguised by smart tailoring, monocle and orchid. H. H. Asquith, the future Prime Minister, said that he had the manners of a cad and the tongue of a bargee. Beatrice Potter (later Webb), who was in love with him, remarked on visiting Chamberlain's house that "there was a good deal of taste, and all of it bad."[116] Vulgarity, too, was sensed in his expressionless face, his slicked black hair, his long questing nose. Salisbury dubbed his Colonial Secretary "the Cockney."[117] There was, indeed, a "patient subtle antagonism"[118] between Hatfield House and Birmingham Town Hall. But the diehard patrician exploited the progressive tribune's unique popular appeal. He made use of Chamberlain's Svengali-like personality, vividly evoked by Lugard, who said that when he screwed in his eyeglass "you felt as if you were going to be sifted to the marrow."[119] Salisbury also tried to prevent him from dominating the government. This was not always possible. At the end of 1895, for example, Chamberlain took it upon himself to crush the Ashanti and stake a claim to the hinterland of the Gold Coast. The operation was swift and bloodless. It resulted in modest spoils for the victors, among them Baden-Powell, and the exile of King Prempeh, who eventually returned to become President of the local Boy Scouts Association. It also justified Chamberlain's newspaper nickname, "Josephus Africanus," and his sobriquet at the Colonial Office, where he replaced candles with electric light—"The Master." According to Salisbury, Chamberlain "wants to go to war with every Power in the World, and has no thought but Imperialism."[120]

Soon afterwards Wilfrid Scawen Blunt made a similar charge from a different point of view, noting that in six months Britain had quarrelled with China, Turkey, Belgium, Ashanti, France, Venezuela, Germany and the United States. It was a record performance which, he hoped, would break up an empire that was "the great engine of evil for the weak races now existing in the world."[121] Actually the imperial temper, particularly as regards racial chauvinism, commercial rapacity and strategic aggression, had never been fiercer. In Africa British hostility was still mainly directed against the French. Their designs on Egypt's lifeline were well known and it was feared that they might destroy the land of the Nile by damming it at Fashoda—a paranoid fantasy since there was no stone within miles of the place. Nevertheless, when Italy was defeated at Adowa in 1896 and the Ethiopians seemed poised to support France in Equatoria, the British government resolved to reconquer the Sudan, avenge Gordon and secure Egypt for good.

Two railway tracks were thrust towards Uganda, one from the east and one from the north. From Mombasa what became known to Europeans as the "Lunatic Line" and to Africans as the "Iron Snake" crossed deserts, mountains, valleys, ravines, forests, and quagmires on its six-hundred-mile journey to Lake Victoria. Sometimes the ground was so swampy that the train would rock like a ship in a choppy sea, "squirting liquid mud for ten feet each side of it, from under the sleepers, after the manner of a water cart."[122] The Line's bridges were named after the likes of Salisbury, Chamberlain and Devonshire but, as Harry Johnston wrote, it "drove a wedge of India two miles broad right across East Africa." Thirty thousand coolies from the subcontinent, aided by hundreds of clerks, draughtsmen, mechanics, surveyors and policemen, brought the Hindustani language and the Indian coinage, clothing, penal code and postal system to wastes hitherto tenanted by "native savages or wild beasts."[123] Meanwhile, southwards through the Sahara from Wadi Halfa, with Roman precision, General Kitchener (the Egyptian Sirdar, or Commander-in-Chief) pushed his single-track railway towards Khartoum at the rate of a kilometre a day. It had the same gauge as Rhodes's South African lines and so penny-pinching was Kitchener that he used wood from Dervish gallows as sleepers. Imperious and impatient, the Sirdar drove his men hard in temperatures so high that thermometers burst. When no engineer could be found he even drove his locomotives (the best of them bought in America, to the chagrin of patriotic Britons), racing them down the track at more than the permitted twenty-five miles per hour. Kitchener made war with "rivets and spindle-glands."[124] In the words of Winston Churchill, who as an ambitious subaltern had inveigled himself into the Khartoum expedition against the Sirdar's will, "Victory is the beautiful, bright-coloured flower. Transport is the stem without which it could never have blossomed."[125] The River War was won on the iron road.

Horatio Herbert Kitchener was the most ruthless technician of empire. This is not to say that he was the Sudan Machine of legend, the metalled titan who "rarely opened his mouth save to order an execution." He did have finer feelings. He collected ceramics, though he was reluctant to pay for them. He possessed a "feminine sensitiveness to atmosphere."[126] He could ingratiate himself with the great: "Lord Cromer is a splendid man to serve under."[127] He won the approval of Wolseley, who admired his "pluck, energy and able leadership."[128] He enjoyed a roguish relationship with good-looking young men on his staff. Moreover, after a victory, it was said, he could be quite human for as much as a quarter of an hour. But Kitchener had little imagination and less education—his letters were illiterate where they were not illegible and as late as 1916 he had never heard of Wordsworth. He treated troops as mere cogs in a military machine. Indeed, he was "never seen to address or even notice a private soldier"[129]—though it was hard to tell what he noticed because his china-blue eyes, which glittered strangely between bulging forehead and brick-red cheeks, had a disconcerting squint. Towards most of his officers Kitchener was unbending, ungracious and uncouth. They were said to have the look of hunted animals.

He trusted so few of them that he could hardly bear to delegate. In North Africa he acted as his own Chief of Staff, writing telegrams from a stock of forms which he kept inside his helmet. In India, later, he had the files of the military department pounded into papier-mâché and used for mouldings on the ceiling of his new dining hall. Nursing "a profound contempt for every soldier except himself"[130] (which inclined Arthur Balfour to think well of his brains but not his character), Kitchener seldom inspired loyalty. General Hunter, his right hand man in the Sudan, wrote:

> I have plumbed to the bottom of Kitchener now—he is inhuman, heartless; with eccentric and freakish bursts of generosity specially when he is defeated: he is a vain egotistical and self-confident mass of pride and ambition, expect-

ing and usurping all and giving nothing; he is a mixture of the fox, Jew, and snake and like all bullies is a dove when tackled.[131]

Despite quoting this, Kitchener's most recent biographer reaches a surprisingly favourable verdict on his subject. Yet the weight of contemporary evidence is against Kitchener. Churchill said that he might be a general but would never be a gentleman. Francis Younghusband thought him "a coarse blob of a man."[132] T. E. Lawrence reckoned that he was "not honest according to ordinary men's codes."[133] Lord Esher, who probably knew that Kitchener was seen cheating at billiards in Balmoral, surmised that he would "walk over the body of his best friend."[134] Kipling called him a "fatted Pharaoh in spurs" and hated his "butcherly arrogance."[135]

This was gruesomely displayed when he encountered the Khalifa's white-robed host at Omdurman on Friday 2 September 1898. With superhuman courage a vast array of "chocolate-coloured men on cream-coloured camels"[136] charged Kitchener's rifles, Maxims and artillery. They were cut down like chaff. Indeed, at one point Kitchener was reduced to repeating, "Cease fire! Cease fire! Cease fire! Oh, what a dreadful waste of ammunition!"[137] At a cost of fewer than fifty British and Egyptian dead, eleven thousand Dervish corpses, perhaps a fifth of the Khalifa's army, littered the battlefield, "spread evenly over acres and acres."[138] Worse still, many of the wounded were either shot or left to die. Winston Churchill condemned this "inhuman slaughter"[139] and humanitarians at home denounced an empire won and run with such cruelty. The British in Africa, like the Romans in Britain according to Tacitus, had made a wilderness and called it peace. (In Berber, as if to confirm the analogy, Kitchener held something like "a Roman triumph,"[140] riding in front of a vanquished emir who was shackled, yoked and scourged.) But Kitchener's ADC and Salisbury's son, Lord Edward Cecil, spoke for many when he declared that it was "rot" to sympathise with the Dervish "brutes."[141] And war correspondents thought that Omdurman deserved a quasi-divine punishment: "The reek of its abomination steamed up to heaven to justify us our vengeance."[142] The Queen's strictures, also appealing to piety, were less easy to dismiss. Herself the recipient of much Omdurman loot,[143] she was shocked to hear that the Sirdar had demolished the tomb of the Mahdi, a religious leader, with lyddite shells and thrown his bones into the Nile. Kitchener explained these acts of desecration as attempts to purge a nationalist cult of its magic. But he was further excoriated for his plan to make a drinking bowl out of the Mahdi's skull—something General Reginald Wingate later did, more discreetly, with the Khalifa's.[144] Churchill for one did not believe Kitchener's claim that he had sent the Mahdi's skull back for burial in the Sudan in a kerosene tin, saying that the tin might have contained anything, perhaps ham sandwiches.

However, Kitchener won nothing but praise for his tactful handling of Major Jean-Baptiste Marchand, whose heroic trek from the Congo to stake his country's claim on the Nile brought France and Britain to the brink of war. Admittedly Kitchener had gunboats and bayonets where Marchand only had a solid-wheeled bicycle and a flag—and his flagpole snapped when he tried to fly it at Fashoda. During his courteous confrontation with Kitchener, Marchand was completely isolated in "a landscape of dessication and rubble populated by scorpions."[145] The Sirdar, by contrast, could keep in touch with London via a telegraph cable on the bed of the Nile. France was inevitably defeated in what Blunt described as this "wrangle between two highwaymen over a captured purse."[146] Marchand withdrew and the Sudan became an Anglo-Egyptian condominium. It thus added a further anomaly to the region and the Empire. What mattered, though, was British control. This was not secured by means of delicate diplomacy. It was accomplished, to quote Churchill's characteristic summation, through the most signal triumph ever won by the arms of science over barbarians.

As it happened, Churchill had curiously mixed feelings about the victory. He was thrilled to have taken part in what would be the British Army's last great cavalry charge but disappointed that the 21st Lancers did not incur enough casualties to make it a truly historic engagement. He rejoiced in the advance of civilisation over savagery but justified the use of dum-dum bullets. He said that surrendering Dervishes had no right to clemency.[147] But he blamed Kitchener for encouraging his troops "to regard their enemy as vermin—unfit to live."[148] More significantly, Churchill was also ambivalent towards the Empire itself, at a time when it had become a "positive intoxication"[149]—Omdurman not only avenged Gordon and set the seal on Britain's scramble for tropical Africa, it provided a fairy-tale finale to Queen Victoria's 1897 Diamond Jubilee. In that year, fresh from reading Gibbon and Winwood Reade and from fighting on the North-West Frontier, Churchill had become imbued with a curious blend of long-term historical fatalism and short-term evolutionary optimism. On the one hand he thought that civilisations were doomed to decadence and that imperial entropy was inevitable. En route for home he paused in the Capitol at Rome and fell into grim Gibbonian musings about the decline and fall of the British Empire. Back in India, where he had become besotted with

Macaulay, Churchill speculated about future travellers visiting the sub-continent and finding nothing to remind them of the Raj but a "few scraps of stone and iron."[150] On the other hand Churchill believed that "might is a form of fitness"[151] and that the strong would win in the struggle for survival. He altered the manuscript of his first book to insist on white supremacy in India: "the prestige of the dominant race enables them to ~~keep up appear-ances~~ maintain their superiority over the native troops."[152]

In public Churchill quelled his private doubts. More than that, he beat the imperial drum in the spirit of his Harrow headmaster, J. E. C. Welldon, the model for "the Jelly-bellied Flag-Flapper"[153] in Kipling's *Stalky & Co.* In his first political speech, delivered a month after the Jubilee, Churchill casti-gated the "croakers" who prophesied that the British Empire, now at the height of its glory and power, would decline like that of Rome. We should, he said,

> give the lie to their dismal croaking by showing by our actions that the vigour and vitality of our race is unimpaired and that our determination is to uphold the Empire that we have inherited from our fathers as Englishmen, *[cheers]* that our flag shall fly high upon the sea, our voice be heard in the councils of Europe, our Sovereign be supported by the love of her subjects, then we shall continue to pursue that course marked out for us by an all-wise hand and carry out our mission of bearing peace, civilisation and good gov-ernment to the uttermost ends of the earth. *[Loud cheers]*[154]

This litany was familiar to the point of platitude. But the last and most sonorous of the Whigs would invest the imperial theme with unique elo-quence, notably during the Second World War. Then Churchill conjured up a vision of the past glory and future victory of Greater Britain, of an imperial climb to broad sunlit uplands with himself providentially in the van. In the nation's darkest hour realists might well have regarded this as lit-tle more than inspiring verbiage. Ironically, his first speech had been a piece of rhetorical afflatus; for his faith in the Empire's manifest destiny, like that of many Britons at the conclusion of Queen Victoria's reign, was far from being secure.

Nevertheless, the years between the Diamond Jubilee and the Relief of Mafeking probably witnessed the most fervent devotion to the Empire ever manifested in Britain. All nations tend to think that they are the heaven-born but the British were now more than ever inclined to believe themselves anointed as the imperial race. Some affirmed that they were literally the chosen people: British Israelites claimed descent from the lost ten tribes sired by Abraham. Others, especially among the bourgeoisie, adopted the Jewish practice of circumcision in order to improve the health and "manliness of the future custodians of empire"[155]—the rise of the moustache complemented the fall of the foreskin. However shaven or shorn, late Victorians felt uniquely endowed by their creator with a genius for governing lesser breeds. These Kipling bracketed with the Gentiles, perennial outsiders; whereas insiders such as public schoolboys were the beneficiaries of both natural selection and celestial dispensation. "God has arranged that a clean-run youth of the British middle class," said Kipling, "shall in the matter of backbone, brains and bowels, surpass all other youths."[156] The British were the Praetorian Guard of the world. They had inherited the earth and theirs was the kingdom of heaven. The Empire was over four times larger than that of Rome, comparisons with which were now usually intended to boost confidence in Britain. Discussing "The Fall of the Roman Empire and its Lessons for Us," the historian Thomas Hodgkin concluded that Britain's Empire would survive thanks to its innate "sense of fair play."[157] Another historian, Sir Alfred Lyall, recalled how St. Augustine, looking out from the City of God at the still vast domain of Rome, had concluded that for such an empire to extend its rule over uncivilised nations "seems to bad men felicity, but to good men a necessity."[158] Plainly Britain's huge constellation of territory—eleven million square miles containing four hundred million people—was sanctioned by the Almighty. Lord Rosebery, who was briefly Liberal Prime Minister in the mid-1890s and kept cheerful by humming "Rule, Britannia!," characteristically maintained that the Empire was "Human, and yet not wholly human, for the most heedless and cynical must see the finger of the Divine."[159]

It was apparent in the work of ten thousand overseas missionaries. Freemasonry, that ubiquitous feature of the colonial scene, helped (among other things) to give a mystical unity to Greater Britain. So did new organs of the Beefeater press, such as the *Daily Mail,* for which the expansion of England was a secular religion. Still more did the rediscovery of the Crown and the fresh awakening of imperial sentiment at the Diamond Jubilee. Of course, royal festivals had occurred before and everyone recognised that the first article of empire patriotism was loyalty to the sovereign. Yet, as W. T. Stead observed, in 1897 the British people were as thrilled to discover what they already knew as Molière's hero was to find that he had been talking prose all his life without realising it. For the Jubilee resembled nothing so much as a conversion experience during an evangelical revival. Stead wrote:

The uncontrollable outburst of intense emotion that is witnessed when . . . a poor, lost, hell-deserving sinner puts forth the hand of faith, and grasping the finished work of Christ, passes in a moment from death into life, is the nearest analogy which can be adduced to explain the hitherto unknown spirit of exultant joy and unspeakable gratitude which culminated in the Jubilee.[160]

Others were equally apocalyptic. The *Daily Mail* said it was fitting that the Queen should pay homage to God at St. Paul's since He was the one being more majestic than she. Mark Twain found the sight of so many nations marching past on 22 June indescribable, "a spectacle for the kodak, not the pen," but it provided him with "a sort of allegorical suggestion of the Last Day."[161]

Everything was done to enhance the solemnity of "one of the most brilliant pageants in history."[162] Chamberlain's biographer, quoting Gibbon, compared the Queen's Jubilee to the secular games in Rome: these had "dazzled the eyes of the multitude"[163] by their splendour and inspired reverence like any "great spectacle which the oldest have never seen before and the youngest will never see again."[164] A quarter of a million pounds was spent on decorating London as befitted the imperial capital. The streets were festooned with garlands, banners and bunting. Buildings were adorned with huge VRI emblems, many wrought in metal and coloured glass. Patriotic and imperial slogans abounded, often employed by manufacturers to advertise products such as Bovril, Colman's Mustard, Eno's Fruit Salt and Willson's Sparkling Stomach Tonic. The Bank of England, which dominated the forum often called the "heart of the empire,"[165] bore the illuminated legend "SHE WROUGHT HER PEOPLE LASTING GOOD."[166] Electricity augmented gas in shedding lustre on the imperial monarchy during what *The Times* called its first pan-Britannic festival. Before setting off for St. Paul's, Queen Victoria pressed a button telegraphing this message to the Empire: "From my heart I thank my beloved people, May God bless them!"[167] Eleven colonial Premiers took part in the procession. So did jewelled satraps of empire, none more glittering than the Indian maharajahs, who illustrated Kipling's aphorism that they had been created by Providence to offer mankind a spectacle.

Still more impressive was the assortment of military might. Some 46,000 men, the largest force ever mustered in the capital, marched past to the sound of clattering hooves, jingling accoutrements, blaring bands and stamping boots, boots, boots. But this was not just a familiar array of scarlet uniforms and gold breastplates, white plumes and gleaming lances, silver kettle drums and brass naval guns. It was an imperial phalanx, described most vividly by the *Daily Mail*'s star writer G. W. Steevens.

> Lean, hard-knit Canadians, long-legged, yellow Australians, all in one piece with their horses, giant, long-eyed Maoris, sitting loosely and leaning back curiously from the waist, burned South Africans, upstanding Sikhs, tiny lithe Malays and Dyaks, Chinese with white basin turned upside-down on their heads, grinning Hausas, so dead black that they shone silver in the sun—white men, yellow men, brown men, black men, every colour, every continent, every race, every speech—and all in arms for the British empire and the British Queen. Up they came, more and more, new types, new realms at every couple of yards, an anthropological museum—a living gazeteer of the British empire. With them came their English officers, whom they obey and follow like children. And you began to understand, as never before, what the empire amounts to.[168]

However, it was in Queen Victoria, according to Mark Twain, that the British "public saw the British Empire itself."[169]

Modestly dressed in black moiré embroidered with silver, crowned by a bonnet trimmed with white ostrich feathers, and riding along the six-mile route in the open State landau drawn by eight cream horses, she was greeted on that grey day with ecstasy. "The cheering was quite deafening," she wrote in her journal, "and every face seemed to be filled with real joy."[170] At St. Paul's, where the service took place outside the cathedral on account of the Queen's lumbago, the Church bestowed a divine blessing on earthly majesty. The gorgeously coped, croziered and mitred Bishop of London, Mandell Creighton, known as "the Admirable," declared that the nation's imperial destiny had been conceived during Victoria's reign. According to one witness, the Queen "became visibly transfigured before the eyes of her subjects." The host of other Jubilee events confirmed her apotheosis. The most awesome was the Spithead Naval Review—more than 160 warships arrayed in three lines almost thirty miles long. It convinced even French observers that the British had totally eclipsed the Empire of Rome. This incomparable armada signified that "the express decree of the Eternal had conferred on them the command of the sea."[171]

Yet the Diamond Jubilee, which took myriad forms in far-flung places, did not win universal acclaim even among leaders of British society. Mr. Gladstone, a Little Englander to the last, shunned the proceedings, railed against "the spirit of Jingoism under the name of Imperialism"[172] and privately suggested that the best way the Queen could celebrate her sixty years

on the throne was by abdicating. The radical MP Henry Labouchere recommended that Buckingham Palace should be turned into a home for
fallen women. Lord Salisbury acknowledged that the multitude needed cir-
cuses as well as bread. But he found them vulgar and absurd, from the sham
of making knights who knew nothing of cavalry or chivalry to the regal theatre that seemed doomed to become farce. His prognostications on that
score proved accurate. During the processions the crowd booed the Cypriot
Zaptiehs, who were wearing fezzes, under the impression that they were
Turks. The Lord Mayor lost his hat as his horse galloped off with him. And
Colonel Lord Dundonald of the Life Guards, riding behind the monarch's
carriage on a spirited mare, kept repeating, "Steady, old lady! Whoa, old
girl!"[173]—calls which the Queen at first thought addressed to her. The Prime
Minister also mocked the lust for stars and garters, which raged with particular ferocity among colonial dignitaries—all the Premiers became Privy
Councillors, entitled to wear a uniform something between that of "a pos-
tilion and a buffoon."[174] Salisbury was almost as scathing about royal ritual
as Frederic Harrison, who regarded it as "sublime hocus"[175] like the Roman
Lectisternium, the placatory feast offered to images of the gods, or the beating of gongs and tom-toms by savages to ward off an eclipse.

The Diamond Jubilee was, indeed, a fanfare designed not just to exalt
the imperial spirit but to subdue national fears about the end of the "British
century."[176] It was a roar of reassurance at a time when Britain's kingship of
the international jungle seemed increasingly under threat. It was a parade of
unionism, challenged in Dublin by marchers with black flags, Home Rule
slogans and a coffin bearing the legend "British Empire," which they threw
into the Liffey. It was a triumph that betrayed unease, signified weakness
and caused disquiet. Kipling, who marvelled at Spithead but thought jubilant London "unspeakable Tophet,"[177] classically warned about present
pride and future peril:

> Far-called, our navies melt away;
> On dunes and headlands sinks the fire;
> Lo, all our pomp of yesterday
> Is one with Nineveh and Tyre.[178]

The theme of *Recessional* was rehearsed again and again as imperial growth
failed to stem "industrial decline."[179] Britain was compared to Rome, gorged
with distant conquests, provincial tributes, oriental luxury and alien corn,
while Cato thundered in vain about the dissolution of its economic fabric
and was called a "Little Italian" for his pains.[180]

Ironically, even the *Daily Mail*'s chief trumpeter of the Jubilee discerned "in the public felicity the latent cause of decay and corruption." Writing in *Blackwood's Magazine* in July 1897 under the pseudonym "the New Gibbon" and mimicking the historian's style with some panache, Steevens declared that Britain relied too much on "the martial virtue of subject barbarians." The imperial race was losing its force under the "enervating influence of industrial civilisation" and a narrowly commercial spirit. Vulgarity was sapping vitality. Hunting, shooting and fishing, sports in which man matched himself against nature, were giving way to "plebeian exhibitions of mere brute strength and agility" such as bicycling and tennis. Still more demoralising was spectatorship. Watching games of football and cricket, "lazy recreations which were fondly called national," stunted people's growth. A puny breed was emerging that would fail at the first crisis. It was deaf to the mutter of the coming earthquake, blind to the prospect of imperial ruin. Yet, Steevens concluded, "decline was already accomplished and irremediable, and fall was but too surely impending."[181]

There was much on the international scene, at a time when Britain's diplomatic isolation seemed perilous rather than splendid, to confirm Steevens's gloom. Indeed, for twenty years or so the nation had been anxiously attempting to reinforce the imperial panoply. Defensive bodies proliferated, such as the Royal Colonial Institute (1868), the Fair Trade League (1881) and the Imperial Federation League (1884), which propagandists such as George Parkin ("the bagman of Empire")[182] proclaimed the sovereign antidote to disintegration. Others sought to sustain Britain's economic position by means of an Imperial Zollverein, or customs union. Still others formed societies promoting emigration to the Empire. Youth was rallied in organisations such as the Boys' Brigade (1883), the Church Lads' Brigade (1891) and the Jewish Lads' Brigade (1895). The last aimed to "Anglicise" the "narrow-chested, round-shouldered sons of the Ghetto."[183] All found inspiration in militantly patriotic literature such as the *Boy's Own Paper*, begun in 1879. In 1884 Stead started the first of several scares about the fragility of the Empire's iron walls. So efforts were made to improve and expand the Royal Navy, which adopted the "two-power standard" (making it more than a match for any pair of foes) in 1889. Yet the speed of technological advance assisted Germany, France, America and Japan, which lacked such shoals of obsolescent leviathans. Moreover, the Admiralty was slow to abandon muzzle-loaders, to adopt grey paint, to build submarines and to design ships more like the *Dreadnought* than the *Victory*—the Senior Service still looked back to Nelson and, said Admiral Fisher, might just as well have looked back to Noah. As Fisher further observed, "The British Empire floats on the

British Navy."[184] So at its jubilant apogee some observers forecast that Britain was "about to sink into the position of a second-rate Power."[185]

The challenges it faced on land seemed even more acute. Ireland threatened to blow a hole in the heart of the Empire. Russia and Japan were leading the "scramble for China," where other powers also established footholds—to Britain's disadvantage. France continued to press in North Africa. London had to make concessions to Berlin in Samoa, though neither side thought the transaction worth the stamps. John Bull also felt obliged to give ground to Uncle Sam in Alaska and elsewhere. Of course, despite traditions of liberty going back to 1776, America had been an imperial competitor in embryo at least since the promulgation of the Monroe Doctrine. It looked far west as well as north and south. Commodore Robert Shufeldt, for example, who opened up Korea in 1882, as Commodore Perry had earlier opened up Japan, declared flamboyantly:

> The Pacific is the ocean bride of America. China and Japan and Korea, with their innumerable islands hanging like necklaces about them, are the bridesmaids. California is the nuptial couch, the bridal chamber, where all the wealth of the Orient will be brought to celebrate the wedding. Let us as Americans . . . determine while yet in our power, that no commercial rival or hostile flag can float with impunity over the long swell of the Pacific.[186]

The United States' victory in the war over Spain in 1898 and the annexation of its colonies (Guam, Puerto Rico and the Philippines) indicated not just the waxing of America but the waning of Britain.

This was reflected in the many appeals from the Old World to the New for a tightening of transatlantic bonds, an Anglo-Saxon alliance, a coalition of English-speaking peoples. Kipling, now established as the laureate of empire, urged Americans to "Take up the White Man's burden."[187] Andrew Carnegie promoted race patriotism. Chamberlain pleaded that "the Stars and Stripes and the Union Jack should wave together."[188] They did so on many occasions. At the Lord Mayor's Show in 1898, for example, the two flags flew on top of a float in the form of a ship representing "Sea Power," which bore mottoes such as "Blood is thicker than water"[189] and carried on deck the figure of Britannia extending the hand of friendship to Columbia. Londoners cheered. On both sides of the ocean people forecast an Anglo-American reign of global peace, plenty, justice and progress. In the United States, however, many invoked traditions of liberty going back to Jefferson. These were always to play a part, and ultimately perhaps a dominant one, in the relationship between Britain and America. But they had been flouted by the cruel conquest of the Philippines. Mark Twain said this colonial conflict, which caused the death of some 220,000 Filipinos, had "debauched America's honour and blackened her face before the world." Henry Adams turned "green in bed at midnight if I think of the horror of a year's warfare." Members of the Anti-Imperialist League parodied Kipling:

> Pile on the brown man's burden
> To gratify your greed;
> Go, clear away the "niggers"
> Who progress would impede;
> Be very stern, for truly
> 'Tis useless to be mild
> With new-caught sullen peoples,
> Half devil and half child.[190]

Goldwin Smith denounced America's putative "partnership with British Jingoism." Behind it was a fresh spirit of force in the world, exemplified by the fact that women now attended prize fights. But modern imperialists also imitated Rome, he said. They aspired to build a new civilisation while actually crushing nations in order to create a "central despotism." Smith quoted Gibbon's classic caveat: "There is nothing more adverse to nature and reason than to hold in obedience remote countries and foreign nations, in opposition to their inclination and interest." This was an eternal truth about empire. In the meantime, though, since America was imposing its will by force in Asia it could hardly object to Britain's doing the same in Africa. Protests about the bullying of the Boers were muted in the United States, said Smith, because the "blood of the Filipinos chokes us."[191]

8

Barbarians Thundering at the Frontiers

The Boer War and the Indian Raj

The Boer War blighted the end of Queen Victoria's life and tarnished the gilt of empire during her son's reign. Despite outbursts of jingoism at home and expressions of loyalty in the dominions, there was widespread unease that David seemed to be matched against Goliath and that white men should be fighting one another on the veldt. The British gave every indication of having provoked the conflict. The Afrikaners saw it as the bloody "last act in the great drama"[1] of *A Century of Wrong*—the title of Jan Smuts's pamphlet, written on the eve of hostilities in September 1899, denouncing the protracted British attempt to crush Boer liberties. Moreover, the war appeared to stem from the root of all evil. Politicians such as David Lloyd George, journalists such as W. T. Stead and economists such as J. A. Hobson all accused their government of resorting to arms from a lust for gold. Its aim, they said, was to monopolise the mines, to secure cheap black labour for the owners and to enrich their financial backers. A number of critics went further, some odiously so. Henry Hyndman, a silk-hatted, frock-coated Old Etonian who allegedly became a socialist "out of spite against the world because he was not included in the Cambridge [cricket] eleven,"[2] saw the war as part of a conspiracy to plant "an Anglo-Hebraic Empire in Africa." Its beneficiaries would be the Randlords—generically pilloried as Hoggenheimer—and its capital would be "Jewhannesburg."[3] If the cause of the war appeared disreputable, its course was plainly disastrous. An imperial army of 250,000 men, swollen by contingents from Canada, Australia and New Zealand, took almost three years to subdue a colony of farmers whose population, as Lloyd George scornfully remarked, did not exceed that of Flintshire and Denbighshire. During this time the Boers inflicted a series of reverses on their foes so humiliating that Lord Salisbury wondered whether he might not do better with "an army of Red Indians."[4] To defeat the Boers the British employed against innocent civilians what the Liberal leader Sir Henry Campbell-Bannerman called "methods of barbarism."[5] In fact, the

South African conflict was the greatest catastrophe to overtake the Empire since the loss of the American colonies.

Yet the war was not the culmination of a hundred years of creeping aggression, as Smuts asserted in his war cry. Nor was it the product of a capitalist, still less a Jewish, plot. Of course many mining and railway interests (harmed by the new line to Delagoa Bay) did want to modernise the Transvaal. In particular, they wanted a streamlined, low-cost economy, something unlikely to be achieved in a "mediaeval race oligarchy"[6] led by a "palaeolithic"[7] President. They therefore urged the righting of *Uitlander* wrongs and hoped that a British South Africa would swallow the Boer republics. But Marxist historians are incorrect to claim that "the motive force for the Boer War was gold."[8] Some "gold-bugs," having learned their lesson from the Jameson Raid, sat on the fence. Others preferred peace and profit with Kruger. What is more, Salisbury and Chamberlain, like their new South African High Commissioner, Sir Alfred Milner, were primarily concerned with political and strategic power. Control of all South Africa was essential, they believed, for without it Britain would lose the key naval base at Simonstown. This sat astride one of the world's most vital trade routes and, as the War Office said, it would be impossible "to create a Gibraltar out of the Cape Peninsula."[9]

Milner, in particular, was a "British Race Patriot"[10] with a passion for imperial consolidation. Half German and wholly unscrupulous, he had been brought up in shabby-genteel circumstances, had won nearly all the glittering prizes at Oxford and had equipped himself for proconsular life by stints as a barrister, a journalist and a civil servant. Before becoming chairman of the Board of Inland Revenue at home, Milner had administered the finances of Egypt. He seemed to be a model of moderation, "the safe man with the crossbench mind."[11] But underneath his dignified exterior—the tall spare figure, narrow moustached face, close-set grey eyes and winning smile—seethed an ardent spirit. Chamberlain later wished that he would remember the advice given to the lady whose clothes had caught fire, "to keep as cool as possible."[12] In London Milner kept a secret mistress with whom he went on bicycling expeditions and, assisting with the *Pall Mall Gazette*'s crusades, he would exclaim: "What larks!"[13] In Cape Town he pursued imperial interests in "the spirit of Torquemada, ruthless, unbending, fanatical."[14] He learned Dutch, which enabled him to misunderstand the Afrikaner position comprehensively. He notified Boer leaders that war must come.[15] He told Chamberlain that the High Commissionership was "a *fighting post*."[16] Milner also helped to convince the Colonial Secretary that the mineral-rich Transvaal, perhaps assisted by Germany or even France, represented a threat to British supremacy in South Africa. In view of the Lilliputian dimensions of the Boer republics this fear might seem absurd. But empires tend to suffer from a paradoxical form of paranoia: anxieties about their vulnerability increase in proportion to their size. As Stead shrewdly remarked, the more wolfish John Bull became the more he worried that "people will mistake him for a sheep."[17]

Since the Jameson Raid, however, the Transvaal had been purchasing "arms and ammunition enough to shoot down all the armies of Europe."[18] And Kruger's answer to the question of why he needed such an arsenal was scarcely reassuring: "Oh, Kaffirs, Kaffirs,—and such-like objects."[19] At the very end of the last year of peace William Butler, now the Commander-in-Chief of British troops in South Africa, saw another fearsome portent in the sky. He witnessed a total eclipse of the moon, which "seemed to have been washed over with a blood-stained cloth" and shed such an eerie light that it made the earth look "like a nocturnal graveyard."[20] But in 1899 Milner, whom some saw as an ironclad Bartle Frere and others as a pocket Bismarck, needed no astral help to plot a course towards aggression. His tactic was to use the *Uitlanders* to win control of the Transvaal, either by securing them votes or by resorting to force. During a conference at Bloemfontein in June, which one of Milner's officials likened to a "palaver with a refractory chief," Kruger perceived their intent. With tears in his eyes he exclaimed, "It is our country you want."[21] The Prime Minister and the Colonial Secretary would have preferred the President to capitulate. But as Salisbury said, they were forced to confront Kruger on "a moral field" skilfully prepared by Milner and "his jingo supporters."[22] Nevertheless, the High Commissioner, who did more than anyone to start the war, was only just in advance of his political masters at home. Chamberlain, who wanted a convincing *casus belli,* endorsed his inflammatory dispatch asserting that the *Uitlanders* were being treated as helots. Salisbury let Milner know that "the real point to be made good to South Africa is that we not the Dutch are Boss."[23]

Salisbury and Chamberlain were worried, though, that Milner's pugnacity would offend public opinion at home. So when the Transvaal's President, recognising that hostilities were unavoidable, issued an ultimatum in October 1899, the British Prime Minister was glad to have been relieved of the task of explaining to his people why they were at war. By allowing Britain to present itself as the victim of aggression Kruger sacrificed a permanent propaganda advantage for a temporary military gain. The Boer plan of campaign, as formulated by Jan Smuts, was to mobilise the nation (the two Boer republics could muster 45,000 armed burghers) and thrust into Natal before British reinforcements arrived. Smuts, successively lawyer, soldier and statesman, told Kruger that their country was facing "a terrible blood-bath, from which our people will emerge either as an exhausted remnant, wood-cutters and water-carriers for a hated race, or as victors, founders of . . . an Afrikaner republic . . . stretching from Table Bay to the Zambesi."[24] Victory would occur, he hoped, through foreign help and British demoralisation. However, Boer strategy, after triumphant advances which left British garrisons besieged in Mafeking, Kimberley and Ladysmith, soon veered towards the defensive. The Boer high command, led by Piet Joubert, was cautious—only one general had any real military knowledge, and he had gleaned that from Carlyle's life of Frederick the Great. Still, their opponents proved even more inept, so much so that it was rumoured among Boers that shooting a British general carried the death penalty. And Milner privately lamented the evident immunity of the most senior officers to enemy bullets.

Such a gallery of martial grotesques has proved impervious to historical rehabilitation. There was the bovine Buller, with his ox carts full of domestic accessories, including a sumptuous kitchen and an iron bathroom. There was the cadaverous Gatacre (known as "Back-acher") who wore out his soldiers with harangues and fatigues. There was the eye-glassed Warren, who thought his men ought to be "introduced"[25] to the enemy before being permitted to fight. There was the insomniac Hart, whose fatal manoeuvres reflected, said one subaltern, "the fidgety unrest of a doting old fool."[26] Nothing was more astonishing, wrote Leopold Amery in *The Times History of the War in South Africa,* than the contempt which the Boer generals showed for their adversaries except the fact that it was almost invariably justified. Amery blamed the promotion by seniority of parade-ground officers who had won cheap laurels by "shooting down ill-armed savages."[27] Now they exposed their own troops to massacre. They completely underestimated the lethal impact of modern firepower, which had been displayed so decisively at both Majuba and Omdurman. Here was a disastrous failure to recognise the changed nature of warfare, a failure which boded ill for any greater test of imperial strength.

No battle illustrated Britain's military shortcomings more dramatically than the third defeat of "Black Week" in December 1899. It took place at Colenso, a cluster of corrugated-iron shacks around a railway station twelve miles south of beleaguered Ladysmith. This sordid dorp was a paltry monument to the Bishop but its setting was sublime. Looped by the Tugela River, a silver serpent slithering down from the Drakensberg, purple in the distance, Colenso was overlooked from the north and west by a semi-circle of copper-coloured kopjes, six miles in diameter, rising in tiers like seats in an amphitheatre. Its pit, to the south, consisted of open veldt rolling down to the river in green-brown billows. Into this arena, following the railway line towards Ladysmith, marched Sir Redvers Buller's army, up to its khaki waist in powdery grey dust. It consisted of eighteen thousand men, the strongest force Britain had put into the field since the Crimean War: infantry, cavalry, guns, ox wagons, mobile kitchens, mule-drawn ambulance carts and camp followers of all sorts. The troops lusted for glory. They had full confidence in their gallant, if taciturn, chief, whose leadership qualities Gladstone had rated above those of Joshua. They rejoiced in the jaunty nicknames of their various units—"Bethune's Buccaneers," the "Imperial Light Looters" and, because the South African Light Horse sported cocks' feathers in their smasher hats, the "Pipe-Cleaners."[28] Meanwhile, the Boers, about five thousand shabby, whiskery men commanded by one of the best of their young generals, Louis Botha, were silent and invisible in their fortified position across the Tugela. The steep-banked river was their moat. The scrubby ridges were their parapets. The rocky earth hid their trenches and artillery emplacements. In fact Botha had transformed the Colenso heights from colosseum into capitol. He rightly expected that his enemy would fail to recognise this and try to stage a spectacular gladiatorial performance. True to form, Buller neither probed the Boer lines nor launched a serious flanking attack. He ordered a long-range bombardment, but the crashing salvos did nothing except throw up clouds of red dirt mixed with green lyddite fumes. Then followed a frontal assault.

It proved fatal from the start, for Colonel Long's 12-pounder guns advanced too far ahead of the infantry. They presented Boer marksmen with a perfect target spot-lit by a hot sun in the limpid morning air. When the Mausers opened fire it was as though "someone had pressed a button and turned on a million electric lights."[29] With a staccato crackle, myriad tongues of flame darted from the trenches. Boer bullets flew "in solid streaks like telegraph wires."[30] Using smokeless cartridges, the riflemen were hard to spot. They cut the British gunners and their horses to ribbons. They also inflicted terrible punishment on Hart's Irish brigade, which had marched forward in close order with fixed bayonets and, unable to locate a ford, was confined by an oxbow in the river. Buller's rightward push, which might have won him a vantage point from which to enfilade the Boer redoubt, fared no better. Before noon, unwilling to countenance further carnage, he withdrew, leaving ten guns to the triumphant Botha. The Boers had suffered 29 casualties, of whom 7 died, whereas the British lost 143 killed and 1,002 wounded. Comparing the Dervish defeat on the Nile to the Afrikaner victory on the Tugela, General Lyttelton said: "In the first, 50,000 fanatics streamed across the open regardless of cover to certain death, while at Colenso I never saw a Boer all day till the battle was over and it was our men that were the victims."[31] The Empire's enemies rejoiced: when told that the cream of the British Army had gone to South Africa, the American artist James McNeill Whistler retorted, "Whipped cream."[32] But at home the cruel climax to Black Week induced "hysterical alarm."[33] On the first day of 1900 one trenchant commentator warned that unless root-and-branch military reforms took place "the historian of the future will have to summarise the causes of the decline and fall of the British Empire in three pregnant words—suicide from imbecility."[34]

On the evidence of Sir Redvers Buller's proceedings in the aftermath of this bloody repulse, that was hardly too harsh a verdict. He at once telegraphed London to say that Colenso was impregnable to anything but a blockade. He also heliographed Ladysmith advising Sir George White to "burn your ciphers, destroy your guns, fire away your ammunition, and make the best terms possible."[35] These were tragic testaments not to a loss of soldierly nerve but to a lack of military intelligence. Buller also lacked drive for his energy had been sapped by his appetite. As William Butler said, Colenso was lost on the war-game fields of Aldershot, where Buller had apparently "regulated the movements of his brigade by the direction which the refreshment carts took in the commencement of the fray."[36] So White kept the flag flying while Buller was superseded as Commander-in-Chief. But Buller was left to persist with those valiant blunderings on the Tugela, notably at Spion Kop and Vaal Krantz, which earned him the nickname "Sir Reverse." Field-Marshal Lord Roberts, with Kitchener as his Chief of Staff and copious reinforcements, many of them volunteers from the dominions, sailed to replace him. A "cute, little, jobbing showman,"[37] in Wolseley's opinion, the dapper "Bobs" became the national saviour. Despite the shock of having lost his only son at Colenso, he acted decisively to exploit the Boers' defensive strategy. Roberts advanced from the Cape, outflanking the Boers with forty thousand men and one hundred guns. It was a dreadful march, accompanied by surprise attacks, sandstorms, rain, cold, hunger, enteric fever, plagues of flies and the unbearable stench of decomposing horses, mules and oxen. As Kipling wrote:

> The trek-ox when alive can haul
> Three-quarters of a ton per head.
> But he can shift you camp and all,
> Once he is dead.[38]

Despite a hopelessly disorganised transport system, Roberts's juggernaut was irresistible.

First he relieved Kimberley where Rhodes, guarding his assets, had tried to keep calm by reflecting on "what the old Roman emperors must have felt when (as often happened) their legions were scattered."[39] Then Roberts trapped four thousand Boers under Piet Cronjé at Paardeburg. Kitchener tried to smash their laager, earning a reputation for being "the most talented murderer [of his own men] the war has produced."[40] But Roberts forced a surrender that was the turning point of the conflict. Buller liberated Ladysmith, which the Boers had hoped would be another Yorktown—its defenders, who had survived on a Bovril-like soup called Chevril, so equine that it was said to kick, were as "gaunt as ghosts."[41] Roberts marched into Bloemfontein, its fall celebrated with a dinner at which Kipling proposed a toast to President Kruger, "who had taught the British Empire its responsibilities."[42] Among other manifestations of delight was a booklet entitled *Thrilling Experiences of the First British Woman relieved by Lord Roberts*. On 17 May 1900 Mafeking was relieved. The siege of this dusty railway junction on the veldt had been elevated into an epic of heroism, thanks in part to Colonel Baden-Powell's plucky "Kaffirgrams": "All well. Four hours bombardment. One dog killed."[43] When news of its relief reached England flag-waving crowds celebrated with such wild abandon that they gave a new word to the language, "mafficking." In London and elsewhere "streets were blocked by a shouting, singing, cheering multitude, composed of both sexes and all classes—a multitude that seemed literally to have gone mad with joy."[44] Actually the danger to Mafeking had been slight (though under Baden-Powell's regime seven hundred Africans died from starvation) and its strategic importance had been exaggerated. Afterwards Kitchener liked to explain that the town had been held "because the War Office believed that it was the nearest sea port to Pretoria."[45] But the public demanded a catharsis in the form of a carnival. This was not an "orgy of rowdyism"[46] stirred up by jingoists of press, pulpit, stage and soapbox, though they undoubtedly contributed to war fever in the following days. It was a spontaneous response to glad tidings after the despair of Black Week, a proclamation of imperial triumph and an anticipation of final victory. Roberts apparently achieved that when he marched into Pretoria in June. Despite large-scale surrenders, though, the exultation was premature. For the struggle had merely entered a new and more deadly phase.

The Boers embarked on a guerrilla campaign in the real hope of exploiting their unrivalled mobility and the vain expectation of capitalising on the profound international sympathy felt for their cause. Scattered units of mounted infantry raided British outposts, ambushed columns, plundered convoys and cut railway lines. They also carried out major forays into the Cape Province which, torn between loyalty to the Crown and blood-brotherhood with the Boers, remained largely passive. The commandos were led by commanders of genius such as Koos de la Rey, the Stonewall Jackson of the resistance, and Christiaan de Wet, whose mastery of butcher-and-bolt tactics won the admiration of the British themselves. One of those pursuing him, Walter Guinness (later Lord Moyne), wrote in June:

> it is like catching quicksilver with a pair of tongs . . . My belief is that the war in the Free State has barely begun as yet. De Wet is a great deal cleverer than our generals, and only fights when he can injure us with impunity. When the papers say that the Boers "ran away" they express the fact that they have the sense to clear out when they have attained their object . . . unless we burn every farm in the country, and Europe will hardly stand that, this state of things will go on indefinitely.[47]

Roberts was less perceptive. Belying his reputation for leniency, he initiated a scorched-earth policy so ferocious that it seemed set to expunge (though it actually stiffened) resistance. After Kruger's autumn escape to Holland, "Bobs" returned to England convinced that Kitchener would quickly put an end to so-called "bitter-enders." This was the common opinion, which Salisbury had just exploited to win the Tories another term in office at the so-called "Khaki" election. But Kitchener was hampered by the fact that the "Boers are not like the Soudanese who stood up for a fair fight, they are always running away on their little ponies." He hunted them relentlessly, commandeering ambulance horses, employing five thousand so-called "Judas Boers" and arming thirty thousand Africans in what was supposed to be a white man's war. He harried his own forces almost as much as those of the enemy, earning the title "K of Chaos."[48] He built a chain of blockhouses, eventually numbering eight thousand, and connected them by barbed wire. But the Boers usually managed to break though this cordon and escape, blending into the background like guerrillas throughout the ages. They were sometimes fighters, sometimes farmers—fish swimming in the sea of the population. With the full approval of Salisbury, who favoured the branding of recalcitrant Boers, Kitchener tried to drain the sea.

Not so much a fully fledged martinet as an embryo dictator, he destroyed thirty thousand farms and dozens of villages. He burned crops and cut down trees. He killed or confiscated livestock. This not only deprived the burghers of food and shelter, it drove 160,000 of their wives and children into the fifty concentration camps established along lines pioneered by Roberts but not, apparently, in imitation of those created in Cuba by General "Butcher" Weyler. Here 28,000 inmates, mostly children, succumbed to disease and malnutrition caused by conditions almost as bad as in the separate camps set up for Africans, where the mortality rate was probably even higher. Then and later, attempts were made to justify the camps or at least to mitigate their horrors. They were said to be a military necessity. The female of the species had to be quelled too: according to Rhodes's brother Frank, "as we approached farms the women hopped into bed with Mauser rifles, a curious choice but a fact."[49] In any case, some Boer women and children lived worse at home than in the camps and all would have suffered more on the veldt. Sanitary conditions in British barracks and military hospitals were equally poor. The Boers were their own worst enemies, dosing themselves with "Kaffir" remedies such as dog's blood and horse dung, but the British did their best to help them. In *The Times* Flora Shaw even rejoiced in "the happy faces of the thousands of children who cluster round the schools and soup kitchens."[50]

Yet for all the special pleading there are few uglier blots on the imperial escutcheon than these camps. In them the authorities deemed mattresses, candles and soap luxuries; the families of "bitter-enders" received less food than those of "hands-uppers" (burghers who surrendered); the children looked like "little old men and women."[51] Altogether a sixth of the Boer population died in what the British claimed to be places of refuge, a claim which Stead denounced as "the very superlative of audacious hypocrisy."[52] There were further accusations of deliberate genocide, a planned massacre of the innocents. These were wide of the mark. However, Lloyd George plausibly charged Salisbury's government with carrying out what was *in effect* "a policy of extermination," one that would rouse "the deepest passions on the human heart against British rule in Africa."[53] Emily Hobhouse, a relief worker who investigated the camps, also talked of "a war of extermination."[54] Thanks to her and others, conditions improved. But the conflict as a whole became more vicious. Atrocities, reprisals and executions took place on both sides. Africans were sometimes perpetrators, usually victims, for the Boers "look upon Kaffirs with extreme contempt and treat them like dogs."[55] Chivalry was in short supply: when British officers wore out the dance floor at the Bloemfontein Residency they sold the old floorboards for 1s 6d each to incarcerated Boer women to make coffins for their children. The rules of war were freely broken: even Conan Doyle acknowledged that the British fired dum-dum bullets, which "were never intended to be used against white races."[56] The quality of mercy was thin on the ground: Irishmen "skewered"[57] Irishmen fighting opposite and the story was told of one, belonging to a regiment that took no prisoners, who "went in with steel. The Boer threw down his arms and held up his hands and prayed for mercy—said he was a Field Cornet. The Irishman said it would make no difference if he were a whole bloody brass band and he had got to have it."[58] All in all, this was not "the last of the gentlemen's wars,"[59] let alone (in Churchill's phrase) the last enjoyable war or (G. K. Chesterton's verdict) a very cheerful war. It was more akin to total war. Kipling called it a "dress-parade for Armageddon."[60]

Ironically, no one was keener to end it than the Boers' most implacable foe, Lord Kitchener himself. Milner, by contrast, who deplored the "barbarous" treatment of the Boers, demanded their unconditional surrender. He detested Kitchener's "absolutely autocratic" manner, despised his "very crooked"[61] methods, and resented his attempts to find a compromise. But short of exiling half the population overseas, something he considered, the general could see no end to hostilities. The best chance was to seek a peace of reconciliation whereby the Boers lost their independence but gained a stake in the British Empire as well as mastery over the black man. This might prove acceptable to the exhausted burghers, who were harassed by Africans, anxious about their families in the camps and on the veldt, and pitiably short of horses, ammunition, supplies and clothes. Many were reduced to wearing garments of sacking, blanket or green baize, and the skins of deer, leopard, monkey or sheep—those who donned stolen British uniforms were liable to be shot on the spot. Commenting on the ragged, wretched state of his division, De la Rey himself acknowledged that they had reached the bitter end.

Peace terms were hammered out inside a marquee at Vereeniging, a small town just south of Johannesburg, in May 1902, just after Rhodes's demise. (His famous last words were "So much to do, so little done!"[62] But cynics asked what he hoped to gain by dying at this point and suggested that he had really said, "So many done, so few to do.") It was agreed that the Boers would become subjects of the new King, Edward VII, and would soon, like Canadians and Australians, obtain self-government. They would also receive an amnesty and £3 million to rebuild their devastated land; Milner wanted to haggle but Chamberlain overruled him, pointing out that the war was costing a million pounds a week. The question of giving Africans the vote was postponed until the Transvaal and the Orange Free State got independence. Chamberlain had promised not "to purchase a *shameful peace*" at the expense of "the coloured population";[63] but Milner had privately noted that to win the game in South Africa "You have only to sacrifice 'the nigger' absolutely."[64] In fact, British Liberals did try to safeguard "African interests."[65] Nevertheless, Africans were the prime victims of the Vereeniging settlement, being subjected to a system of segregation which was eventually transformed into full-blown apartheid. Kitchener was the chief beneficiary. Parliament gave him a £50,000 grant, which he promptly invested in Rand gold shares. He returned to England in triumph, taking with him masses of loot, including life-sized statues of Kruger and other Boer leaders which he had removed from public squares in Bloemfontein and Pretoria. He planned to erect them in his park, but the Colonial Office eventually made him send them back to South Africa.

Worthier memorials to the Boer War went up all over Britain during the next few years, among them, in Exeter, an equestrian statue of Buller which bore the legend "He saved Natal." Some nine hundred monuments, pre-monitory symptoms of the commemorative epidemic that occurred after 1918, honoured the twenty thousand patriots who had given their lives in the defence of country, empire and civilisation. Lapidary inscriptions to that effect probably also expressed the common view throughout the dominions. There many believed that the blood of Boer War martyrs was the seed of both colonial nationhood and imperial consolidation, then by no means a contradiction in terms. At home the victory was hailed as a vindication of British enlightenment over Boer obscurantism. Even the radical Fabian Society cheered the outcome of this "*wholly* unjust but wholly necessary"[66] war, having adopted Bernard Shaw's "extra-ultra-hyper-imperialist"[67] mani-festo which declared that the British Empire, as the nearest thing to a world government, should rule backward societies in the interests of progress. This was a classic notion which, with appropriate variations, had (and still has) its proponents in the United States. Despite widespread American sympa-thy for the Boers, shared partially by Theodore Roosevelt and wholly by his cousin Franklin, the President had complete faith in the Anglo-Saxons' civilising mission and thought it to the "advantage of mankind to have Eng-lish spoken south of the Zambesi."[68] Roosevelt considered the Boers to be as medieval as the Spaniards, against whom John Bull had given Uncle Sam warmly appreciated moral support in 1898. So, mindful of American busi-ness and strategic interests too, he reciprocated, even covertly providing detectives from the Pinkerton agency to sniff out Irish–Boer collaboration. The other great powers, though their populations were overwhelmingly indignant about the Lion's mauling of the Springbok, resisted any tempta-tion to intervene. This was an implicit tribute to Britain's continuing strength, which actually increased thanks in part to further imperial integra-tion in matters of defence and trade. Despite the worst setbacks in the greatest war the country had fought since Waterloo, declared the *National Review,* no foreigner could describe "the British Empire as a Colossus with feet of clay."[69]

Nevertheless, the image of the Colossus had been defiled by Boer blood. The concentration camps had shocked the world, implying the moral doom of the Empire. Deciding that "Heaven was against us," Churchill himself had briefly "despaired of the Empire"[70] during "this miserable war—unfortunate and ill-omened in its beginning, inglorious in its course, cruel and hideous in its conclusion."[71] But the damage to the Empire's character as a bastion of freedom and fair play was lasting: Nazi Germany justified its own concentration camps as being a British invention. The South African camps left an indelible legacy of bitterness. They filled Afrikaner nationalism with hate as the Great Trek had filled it with pride. They "seared into the very soul of the Boer people,"[72] a people increasingly inclined to identify with the children of Israel, who were purified by suffering "as by fire."[73] Memories of the camps impeded reconciliation for generations after Britain granted the two republics independence and (in 1910) formed the Union of South Africa. In the other dominions, where some of the apparently spontaneous enthusiasm for the war had been the product of propaganda, faith in the Empire was shaken. Settler communities overseas were always inclined to think that it was based on exploitation and nothing did more to confirm this than Milner's post-war sanctioning of indentured Chinese labour on the Rand. Widely denounced as "slavery," it seemed to confirm that the South African conflict had been a "colossal fraud" engineered by "bloodthirsty money grubbers." Far from being fought to defend the Empire, "the war was a sweater's war, a war for cheap labour."[74] Colonial alienation fed on the suspicion of British greed. When Chamberlain appealed to the dominions for help with imperial defence in 1902, they saw not a "weary Titan" staggering under the "too vast orb of its fate," to use the metaphor he borrowed from Matthew Arnold, but a "Falstaff, gorged beyond digestion."[75]

Actually the South African conflict was Britain's last major war of imperial expansion and it provided humiliating evidence of physical decrepitude as well as moral turpitude. The British Army seemed to epitomise the national deterioration that obsessed the Edwardian age. Patriots such as Arthur Conan Doyle lamented that its men were less virile than their foes and even their colonial allies. Irish nationalists such as James Connolly rejoiced that the Boers had "pricked the bubble of England's fighting reputation," thus marking the "beginning of the end"[76] of the British Empire. The rot could be seen everywhere and efforts were made to shore up the edifice. A prime concern was the security of Britain's iron walls. While its dockyards bulged with archaic vessels, "a miser's hoard of obsolete junk,"[77] could the nation survive "a naval Colenso"?[78] No one warned more urgently than the daemonic Admiral Jackie Fisher about the loss of supremacy at sea on which Britain's Empire rested. The alliance with Japan (1902) relieved pressure in the Far East just as the rapprochement with the United States had done in the Caribbean. And Fisher augmented the fleet's strength closer to home, building great ships such as *Courageous, Furious* and *Glorious*, which his officers called *Outrageous, Spurious* and *Uproarious*. But foreign armadas grew remorselessly, especially across the North Sea. Before the Great War it was a commonplace that "We are in the position of Imperial Rome when the Barbarians were thundering at the frontiers."[79]

Arthur Balfour, the silky aesthete who succeeded his uncle Lord Salisbury as Prime Minister in 1902, had no difficulty in recognising decadence when he saw it. It was one of the most potent "forces which silently prepare the fate of empires."[80] He took several fortifying measures, reforming the education system, establishing the Entente Cordiale with France and founding a permanent Committee of Imperial Defence to collate military matters on scientific lines. Joseph Chamberlain saw "signs of decay"[81] in the once-glorious fabric of British trade, comparable to cracks in the walls of the Campanile of St. Mark's in Venice which had just collapsed in ruins. In 1903, tapping anxieties about the further advance of commercial rivals, as expressed in popular books such as *Made in Germany* (1896) and *The American Invaders* (1901), he launched a campaign for the erection of tariff barriers. Chamberlain hoped that economic protection would go hand in hand with imperial federation. As it happened, the nation would not abandon free trade and the dominions would not abandon independence. Yet the Boer War, so disastrous to Britain's standing in the world, did encourage the growth of a laager mentality.

Governments aimed to improve social defence and to increase national efficiency. "I see little glory in an Empire which can rule the waves and is unable to flush its sewers,"[82] said Winston Churchill, who during the years after the Liberal victory in 1906 helped to lay the foundations of the welfare state. Kipling thought that the lesson taught by the war was that flannelled fools at the wicket and muddied oafs at the goal should learn to shoot and ride. Roberts crusaded for national service. The Victoria League issued female imperial propaganda. In 1906 the Junior Imperial League (known as the Junior Imps) was formed. Two years later Baden-Powell founded the Boy Scout movement to transform "pale narrow-chested, hunched-up, miserable specimens"[83] who smoked, loafed, soaked and practised self-abuse, the sort of duffers who had caused the downfall of the Roman Empire, into a healthy master race. Many novels of the time centred on invasion scares—the *Daily Mail* serialised one in which the German army's route through England was determined by a desire to boost the paper's circulation in certain towns—and in several of them manly Boy Scouts saved the day. For example, the plucky refusal of "the Janissaries of Empire" to march past the victorious Kaiser in Saki's *When William Came* (1914) destroyed the conqueror's prestige. There was an element of farce in the attempt to rejuvenate the nation by juvenile means, compounded by Baden-Powell's callow personality and adolescent language. But he was typical of his time in nursing terrible doubts about the continuing superiority of the imperial race.

This was invariably regarded as the key element in British greatness. As G. K. Chesterton said, "in the last resort, all progress, all empire, all efficiency, depends upon the kind of race we breed."[84] It was the prime article of faith for imperialists such as Joseph Chamberlain:

> I believe in this race, the greatest governing race the world has ever seen; in this Anglo-Saxon race, so proud, tenacious, self-confident and determined, this race which neither climate nor change can degenerate, which will infallibly be the predominant force of future history and universal civilisation.[85]

Yet the spectre of racial deterioration stalked the land. Many sought to exorcise it by conjuring with pauper emigration, racial hygiene (i.e. birth control), labour colonies for wastrels, sterilisation of the unfit. Eugenics became fashionable and Beatrice Webb even toyed with the idea of polygamy because it opened up vistas of "scientific breeding."[86] Nevertheless, a general mood of pessimism prevailed. Books were published bearing titles such as *What Should England do to be Saved?* and *Will England last the Century?* In 1905 a new tract appeared entitled *The Decline and Fall of the British Empire.* It purported to be the translation of a text written for the instruction of Japanese schoolchildren in 2005 and its author's ideograph *nom de plume* was rendered thus: "FOR THE GOOD OF THE RACE."[87] Drawing on Gibbon, the pamphlet made much of the morbid symptoms common to Britain and Rome. For example, it likened the British Army's adoption of a lighter rifle to the Roman legions' abandonment of the heavy short sword. The British Empire's collapse was attributed to physical as well as moral decadence.

So vital was it to preserve the myth of British race superiority in India that, despite Kitchener's pleas, no sepoys were sent to the Cape. The London government feared that if brown soldiers defeated whites in the "Dark Continent" they might be emboldened to attempt another uprising in the sub-continent. The distrust was as endemic as malaria. After the Mutiny, indeed, it was seriously suggested that "we might do well to imitate the Roman policy, which jealously excluded the employment in the conquered provinces of troops native to the place," and garrison India with "Hottentots, Caffres, Negroes, etc."[88] Sepoys therefore fought Boxer rebels in China but not Boer commandos in South Africa. Many Indians resented this slur on Indian loyalty and genuinely wanted an imperial victory. But the despised *babus* often rejoiced at Boer successes. And militant nationalists such as Bal Ganghadar Tilak, quoting the Pathan dictum that the Raj was "the reward given to the British by Allah sitting in the barrel of a gun," noted how vulnerable they were to "guerrilla warfare."[89] The ambivalence of the Indian position was embodied in the slight person of a radical young lawyer called Mohandas Gandhi, who was known in South Africa as a "coolie barrister."[90]

Gandhi, which means "grocer" in his native Gujerati, was the son of the chief minister *(dewan)* of the small princely state of Porbandar and aged thirteen, in 1882, he had married a child bride chosen for him by his father. Later he qualified at the Inner Temple in London, where he adopted metropolitan ways, took lessons in ballroom dancing and dressed like a Wildean dandy. He was once seen in Piccadilly wearing a silk top hat, starched collar, rainbow-coloured tie, silk shirt, morning coat with striped trousers, patent leather shoes and spats, and carrying gloves and a silver-mounted stick. In the ungainly little figure of Gandhi East met West. He imbibed Hindu transcendentalism from such classics as the *Bhagavad Gita* and he assimilated the ideals of the "Victorian gentleman"[91] from his legal studies in England. Bridging this gulf were sages such as Tolstoy, Ruskin and Thoreau, who exercised a powerful influence over his mind. Moreover, Gandhi participated in eclectic movements such as theosophy and vegetarianism. He read voraciously and ate sparingly, becoming less a faddist than a fanatic about food—when his son was on the point of death his main fear was that the doctor would give him beef tea. Eventually Gandhi insisted that his own meals should cost no more than three annas (threepence) a day. Since nothing complicates life like the quest for simplicity, this restriction caused inordinate trouble and expense, particularly as he refused cow's milk because it excited concupiscence and would only drink the milk of "the chastest" she-goat.[92] As well as being a dietary evangelist Gandhi was a sartorial pilgrim, gradually reducing his dress until he reached the sans-culotte state. Europeans "wear plus-fours," he would famously quip, "but I prefer minus-fours."[93] Like Edward Carpenter, who "preached the gospel of salvation by sandals" on the grounds that shoes were "leather coffins,"[94] Gandhi learned to make his own sandals. He even presented a pair (fashioned at Tolstoy Farm, the Utopian community outside Johannesburg which he founded in 1910) to General Smuts. In sum, the mature Gandhi was a compound of oriental mystic and occidental crank, humble *sadhu* and astute advocate, visionary and revolutionary.

In South Africa during the 1890s he was still developing his ideas and refining his tactics. He himself felt the weight of discrimination when he arrived at Durban, being pushed around by railway officials and policemen, and once severely beaten. Soon he took the lead in resisting the race laws of Natal, where Indians outnumbered Europeans who, said Gandhi, "desire to degrade us to the level of the raw Kaffir." When the war broke out, he sympathised with the brave, patriarchal Boers. But as an imperial subject he supported the British and hoped that his compatriots would reap a political reward for their loyalty. Indeed, Gandhi helped to form an Indian Ambulance Corps. He served in it himself, wearing a khaki uniform, a Red Cross armband and a moustache, and came under fire at Spion Kop, for which he won a medal. When Queen Victoria died he led a procession of Indian mourners in Durban and telegraphed the community's condolences to the royal family, "bewailing the Empire's loss in the death of the greatest and most loved Sovereign on earth."[95] But far from being treated better after the war, South Africa's Indians suffered worse disabilities simply "because they wear a brown skin."[96] In the Transvaal, for example, the Boer pass laws, which Milner had earlier condemned as a malign manifestation of Krugerism, were enforced with new rigour. Gandhi was shocked as much by the hypocrisy as by the injustice. He himself embraced poverty, chastity and civil disobedience. He campaigned actively for Indian rights by means of passive resistance. This he called *satyagraha,* or "soul force," a blend of Christian pacifism and Hindu non-violence. By his inspiring championship of his countrymen abroad he revitalised the nationalist movement at home, a movement whose roots went back to the Mutiny and beyond.

Since 1857, the British in India had themselves been caught on the horns of an East/West dilemma. In order to maintain stability they felt obliged to rule an oriental despotism by the sword and to support the old order up to the hilt. They expressed scepticism about improving the lot of their native subjects, such progress being "utterly at variance with every Eastern idea." Two thousand years more "will not change them," declared Sir William Denison, Governor of Madras, "or make a white man of an Hindoo."[97]

Independence might be the goal but most Britons felt that it could only be reached, if at all, after painstakingly slow reform. Lord Elgin, who succeeded Canning as Viceroy in 1861, could scarcely expect to amend the condition of people whom he treated "not as dogs, because in that case one would whistle to them and pat them, but as machines with which one can have no communion or sympathy."[98] Elgin, who was said to talk platitudes on principle, gave fastidious expression to the policy of gradualism. "We must, for a time at least, walk in paths traced out by others," he said, "filling up here a little hole, removing there a bit of dirt—confining ourselves in short to a sort of scavenger's work—all of it very humble and some rather nasty."[99] On the other hand, enlightened Victorians could hardly deny that good government was the *raison d'être* of the Raj. "Sanitation, Education, Hospitals, Roads, Bridges, Navigation," intoned Lord Mayo, who became Viceroy after Sir John Lawrence in 1869. "We are trying to do in half a century what in other countries has occupied the life of a Nation."[100] The final object of this advance was inescapable, not least because in 1867 Britain itself shot Niagara (as Carlyle put it), taking the plunge towards democracy. Britain's aim should be, said Lord Ripon, a later Viceroy, to help Indians acquire "a larger share in the management of their own affairs."[101] Needless to say, policies do not fit squarely into boxes and the Kiplingesque dichotomy between East and West is too simple. Like Gandhi, British rulers drew freely on the traditions that suited them. Moreover, conservative as well as liberal Viceroys helped to foster the growth of Indian nationalism.

This was partly because the British, despite their proclaimed genius for government, ruled India badly. According to myth the Grand Ornamental on top was as able, assiduous and high-minded as "the heaven-born" beneath—those thousand members of the Indian Civil Service who were sometimes likened to Plato's "Guardians,"[102] a specially trained elite whose composition the gods had alloyed with gold. But if the intentions were benevolent, the results were dispiriting. Sir John Lawrence, for example, was a dedicated paternalist who emphasised to Mayo, on his arrival in Calcutta, the importance of treating natives kindly, only to leap out of their carriage and pull the ears of a tardy groom *(syce)*. Mayo himself, a hearty, burly Tory, promised India an "age of improvement"[103] and spared no pains to achieve it. He took advice from Florence Nightingale, who prided herself on being "Governess to the Governor of India."[104] He promoted public works such as ports, railways, canals and irrigation schemes. He encouraged his lonely officers, toiling amid heat, dust and disease, to establish a "pure, powerful & just" regime.[105] Each year Mayo travelled thousands of miles through the countryside *(mofussil)* to take a personal lead in "the magnificent work of governing an inferior Race."[106] A lot of the distance he covered on horse-back, wearing out his breeches and wondering why nobody paid him the compliment once addressed to the hard-riding George Canning: "Under any circumstances Sir, but especially at the present, I'd rather be the owner of your head than your a[rse]."[107] Yet the evidence of Mayo's own correspondence, much of it unpublished, suggests that he involuntarily presided over a subcontinental muddle.

State intervention was minimal since London instructed him "to make bricks without straw, to reduce taxation & to increase expenditure."[108] Even during the famines that ravaged India between 1860 and 1908, costing at least thirty million lives, humanity was sacrificed to economy—Lord Curzon later acknowledged that an Indian famine excited no more attention in Britain than a squall on the Serpentine. In the Presidencies of Bombay, Bengal and Madras, which (to Mayo's chagrin) invariably obstructed the employment of Indians, bitter jealousy and divided authority paralysed control. British civil servants, often pig-sticking, gin-swigging, public-school men impossibly remote from their subjects, "look on India as a milch cow."[109] There were so many military sinecurists, inspecting officers with nothing to inspect and duty officers with no duties to do, that the army had become a "laughing stock."[110] The Public Works Department was a byword for villainy—the initials PWD allegedly stood for "Plunder Without Danger" and Mayo waxed indignant about the use of English wood for telegraph poles "put up in one of the finest forests in India."[111] The unofficial European community, which grew rapidly after the Mutiny, "do not care a farthing for the country . . . [and] come here to get as much money out of the blacks as they can,"[112] an ambition which British policies largely assisted. Such hopes of amelioration as the Viceroy may have retained were cruelly extinguished in 1872. While inspecting a penal colony in the Andaman Islands, he was assassinated by a convict. Mayo's body, enclosed in a two-ton coffin, was received in Calcutta with pomp and passion. The procession passed in silence. Nothing was heard but the rattle of the gun carriage, the tramp of horses and men, among them an escort of giant, white-clad sailors, and the firing of minute guns from Fort William and from the two-mile line of ships in the Hooghly, their flags at half mast and their yards tossed into a state of disarray. The atmosphere was "excited and half-electric." Every white face looked as "grim as death." Every European heart seemed possessed by murderous fury of a kind not experienced since the Mutiny. Fitzjames Stephen wrote to his mother, "When Lord Mayo was stabbed, I think every man in the country felt as if he has been more or less stabbed himself."[113]

Mayo had been especially keen to end the condition of "chronic anarchy"[114] prevailing in Jaipur, Udaipur, Alwar and a number of the other quasi-independent native states that occupied a quarter of the subcontinent. He complained that in these kingdoms corruption and intrigue were as rife as during Mughal times, and there was a vast amount of female infanticide to add to other social evils. By contrast, Lord Lytton, who was Viceroy from 1876 to 1880, conciliated what he saw as India's great hereditary aristocracy. He thought officials wrong to believe that "we can hold India by what they call good government" and he put his trust in princes. They should be given no real power, of course, but fortunately they were "easily affected by sentiment, and susceptible to the influence of symbols."[115] In particular they could be captivated by the magic of the new Empress of India, and attached to the throne by feudal ties, gold medals, silken banners, multi-gun salutes and all the paraphernalia of majesty. Lytton was a minor poet and a major popinjay, who was himself dazzled by jewelled visions of the East—by gorgeous palaces, elephant parades, royal tiger hunts and "emeralds to make your eyes water."[116] But this picture was already a romantic anachronism. Not all maharajahs thought only of nautch girls and polo ponies, and some were remarkably progressive, so much so that the British held them back. Furthermore, princely influence over the supposedly inert peasantry was more limited than Lytton imagined. In a land of nearly two hundred languages and six hundred dialects, as the Parsee politician Dadabhai Naoroji said, English was creating "strong bonds of nationality" and educated members of the middle class were becoming "the natural leaders of the masses."[117] Doubtless Lytton had an inkling of this for he grumbled about *babus* learning to write sedition. And he became all the more determined to secure the loyalty of the Indian princes to the Kaiser-i-Hind, to give Queen Victoria her new title, at the Imperial Assemblage in 1876.

This took place in a tented city of 84,000 people erected on the red clay plain, cleared of a hundred villages, just beyond the ridge occupied by the British forces during the siege of Delhi. At its centre was the Viceroy's gas-illuminated canvas pavilion and the focus of the pageant was his eighty-foot-high daïs, a scarlet temple embellished (by Lockwood Kipling, Rudyard's father) with so much tinsel and glitter that it looked like a huge Christmas cake. There were battle-axes, silver shields, gold imperial crowns, festoons of red and white satin embroidered with gilded fleurs-de-lis, and multi-coloured silken standards adorned with heraldic devices—a mock-baronial melange reminiscent of Lytton's ancestral home, Knebworth. The decorative details were as vital, Lytton told Disraeli, as the entrails from which "augurs draw the omens that move armies and influence princes."[118]

An elaborate ceremony took place, at which British officers joked audibly about cutting off the ears of the brilliantly attired maharajahs for their diamonds. The Viceroy, a small, robed figure in a blue-velvet, ermine-bordered, star-spangled, gold-tasselled cape, presented them with concocted coats of arms—the most useless of all coats, according to Gibbon. A proclamation was read, trumpets sounded, guns fired, elephants stampeded and, as Val Prinsep noted coolly, "killed a few natives."[119]

Meanwhile, over five million more were dying in the worst famine of the century. Lytton was criticised for holding this public display of magnificence at such a time and caricatured as Nero fiddling while Rome burned. Perhaps he fancied himself more as Diocletian, who had maintained that "an ostentation of splendour and luxury would subdue the imagination of the multitude."[120] At any rate, he was unabashed. Malnutrition was a fact of life in India. Over a fifth of Bengalis did "not know the feeling of a full stomach except in the mango season"[121] while the "nearly naked"[122] peasants on the burning plains of the Deccan ate little but millet flavoured with red peppers. As starvation bit deeper, producing scenes of horror that made the blood of witnesses run cold, Lytton condemned "humanitarian hysterics."[123] Instead he treated the famine as an official secret and enjoined strict economy over state aid. He wanted grain prices kept high to encourage imports, failing to recognise that people were dying from poverty rather than scarcity. Despite a recent operation for piles, which caused him to sit uneasily on the Viceregal throne, Lytton did inspect the hard-hit area around Madras. But he found the relief camps "swarming with fat, idle, able-bodied paupers."[124] His priorities had been clearly stated when the Governor of Bombay said that he could not come to the Delhi durbar because he was tackling the food crisis. Lytton summoned him peremptorily, insisting that "the failure of the Assemblage would be more disastrous to the permanent interests of the Empire than twenty famines."[125]

Such Bourbon insouciance not only precipitates revolution but accelerates the death of empires. There were indeed widespread protests and grain riots in 1877. Despite traumatic memories of the post-Mutiny terror, there was even a Maratha conspiracy "to destroy British power in India by means of an armed rebellion."[126] But Lytton remained a self-indulgent seigneur posing as a bearded bohemian. He wrote erotic verse and dawdled away whole evenings flirting with pretty women, occasionally availing himself of their company by promoting their husbands. He kept people waiting in the sun while he finished his cigar. He preened himself in velvet smoking jackets, floppy cravats, bell-bottomed trousers, square-toed shoes and flashy jewellery. He succumbed to hysterical depressions, hardly alleviated by his

French chef, his Italian confectioner and his German band. Although he consorted with Indian chiefs to such an extent that his reign was known as the "Black Raj," his policies alienated the emerging middle class. He tried to create a two-tier civil service whereby Indians would be excluded from top levels, arguing that race distinction was fundamental to Britain's position as the conquering power. The India Office preferred the system which permitted a handful of natives to join the ranks of the "heaven-born," but it did sanction other discriminatory acts. Lytton removed duties on imported coarse cotton goods, thus further sacrificing Indian manufactures to those of Lancashire. He imposed a Vernacular Press Act (1878), modelled on Irish legislation, to gag criticism in non-English newspapers—as Jawaharlal Nehru would point out, the word "vernacular" came from the Latin *verna,* meaning home-born slave. Lytton simultaneously appointed a Commissioner to feed journalists official information and if necessary to bribe them with Secret Service money. Finally, he plunged India into a bloody, expensive and needless war.

Disraeli and Salisbury, impatient with the policy of "masterly inactivity," had encouraged him to assert British sway over Afghanistan in order to check the alleged ambitions of Russia. But this was not enough for Lytton. He thought that his compatriots were "fast losing the instinct" of empire, demoralised by the democracy enshrined in "that deformed and abortive offspring of perennial fornication, the present British Constitution."[127] "Really," he exclaimed, "England seems to be under some fate as inevitable as the doom of the House of Pelops."[128] Lytton therefore became more aggressive than his instructions allowed, trying to force an unwelcome diplomatic mission on the Emir Sher Ali, the son of Britain's former enemy Dost Mahomed. In cabinet Salisbury declared that the Viceroy was attempting to dictate the government's foreign policy and that unless curbed he would bring about a disaster. However, the Emir's rejection of the British envoy dealt a blow to Britain's prestige that could not be ignored. So Lytton ordered the invasion of Afghanistan. His aim was not to annex the country, which contained "nothing but stones and scoundrels,"[129] but to punish and secure it. A superstitious atheist, the Viceroy spent much of his spare time "making fire-balloons which he launched at intervals, auguring from their quick or slow ascension good or bad fortune to his army."[130]

At first it achieved success and the British minister, Sir Louis Cavagnari, duly arrived in Kabul. But in September 1879 he and his staff were murdered, an event widely predicted yet as shocking in its way as Isandhlwana. The conflict resumed and Sir Frederick Roberts proved as victorious in battle as he was vicious in repression. According to one of his generals, he shot at least six men "in cold blood" and hanged dozens more, some of them in pig-skin hoods, "for fighting against us."[131] Lytton told Fitzjames Stephen that he would support Roberts "through thick and thin, yet between ourselves, I think that some of his arrests and executions were political mistakes."[132] However, Roberts enabled the British to extricate themselves and in due course to establish an uneasy détente with Afghanistan. Meanwhile, Lytton was almost universally execrated. Gladstone thundered about the irredeemable guilt of unnecessary war. And the Duke of Argyll, formerly Secretary of State for India, became so incandescent with rage that (as Lytton imaginatively phrased it) he set himself on fire with his hair. In the subcontinent itself the Viceroy was blamed for adding war to famine. All told, he significantly sharpened the differences between white rulers and educated Indians, who in 1857 had generally identified with the Raj and by the end of the century generally opposed it.

The hostility grew still more acute after 1880 even though Lytton's successor, Lord Ripon, was a Gladstonian Liberal who governed India with unprecedented sympathy. Ripon, the high-minded, long-winded son of Britain's most insignificant Prime Minister, Lord Goderich, believed that it was vital to make "educated natives the friends, instead of the enemies, of our rule."[133] Thus he introduced a measure of local self-government that provided Indians with a means of political expression. Admittedly it was limited—Evelyn Baring called it a safety valve for the *babu,* who would soon be shut up if he spouted on any topic more important than roads and drains. But Ripon regarded it as a stage on the path to independence. From that path he removed the block of censorship, repealing Lytton's Vernacular Press Act. He opposed foreign adventures, refusing to annex Upper Burma, for example, though this task was merely postponed. Other reforms were thwarted. Traditional evils continued. Indian policemen, sometimes "more moustache (!!) than brain,"[134] went on using torture with the connivance of their British superiors. Ripon lacked the strength and the ability to get his way, notably in the *cause célèbre* of his reign. This was his endeavour to permit Indian judges to try Europeans, which they had recently been prohibited from doing in violation of the principle asserted by Macaulay and others that the law was colour-blind.

Known as the Ilbert Bill, after the legal member of the Viceroy's Council, the proposal outraged almost the entire British community. Especially incensed were the twenty thousand non-official Europeans—traders, engineers, planters and so on. These were the lowest castes in the white hierarchy and they only maintained that status by asserting their dominance over Indians, often rudely, sometimes brutally. One tea planter advised Wilfrid

Scawen Blunt to strike natives hard but not too hard, since "they are capable without any exaggeration of dying to spite you."[135] Opponents of the bill conducted a fierce campaign, the hubbub of their first great protest meeting, held in Calcutta Town Hall on 28 February 1883, being audible in Government House. They asserted that this malign measure would wreck the whole basis of British rule in India. Among other things they exploited the most lurid fears of their countrymen, declaring that inveterately corrupt Indian magistrates would abuse their powers and fill their harems with the flower of English womanhood. Ripon and Ilbert were denounced as race traitors. Kipling, who as a cub journalist inadvertently endorsed government policy, was hissed in the Lahore Club. He quickly changed tack, reflecting European paranoia in this grotesque depiction of India's urban throng as a "human menagerie": "Faces of dogs, swine, weazles and goats, all the more hideous for being set in human bodies, and lighted with human intelligence . . . all giving the on-looker the impression of wild beasts held back from murder and violence, and chafing against the restraint."[136] Racial passion threatened to boil over into a "white mutiny,"[137] so Ripon abandoned the bill. Nevertheless, Indians respected him above all other Viceroys and when he left in 1884 they saluted him with well-planned demonstrations. Amritsar deluged him with rose petals. Calcutta blazed with illuminations in his honour. Bombay, which was decorated not only with "banners and bands, flags, streamers, mottoes, garlands,"[138] but with pearls and diamonds, gave him a triumph. Now, though, many of the country's well-educated Indians felt that friendship between the races had become impossible. The British had shown their true colours. They had also provided a lesson in organised agitation. The Indian National Congress rose from the ashes of the Ilbert Bill.

Nothing better reveals the initial weakness of this nationalist association, consisting mainly of Hindu lawyers and journalists, than the fact that its leading spirit was a Scotsman. Allan Octavian Hume, the son of a radical MP, had been a high official whose fatherly rule was popular in the North-West Provinces. He had even devised a patent drop to reduce suffering on the gallows and it was said that men prayed to be tried by Hume and, if found guilty, to be hanged by him. His career had come to a premature end, partly because of his insistent warnings that the fate of the Empire depended on the inclusion of more Indians in the government. This was the modest aim of Congress, which first met in 1885 and hoped to be "the germ of a Native Parliament."[139] But having no widespread organisation, no substantial funds and no popular appeal, it made virtually no progress. In India the walrus-moustached Hume, who referred to Indian colleagues as his children,[140] raised the spectre of revolution. In Britain, Naoroji and other emissaries flirted with Charles Parnell's Irish Home Rulers and took counsel with English anti-imperialists such as Blunt. The latter urged Indian nationalists to "frighten and coerce the English people into giving them their rights."[141]

Blunt gave bad advice for at this time coercion was a British prerogative, as Ripon's successor, Lord Dufferin, demonstrated on the road to Mandalay. In two earlier wars Britain had reduced Burma to an impoverished and unstable rump. It had been shorn of its coastline and deprived of the fertile Irrawaddy delta, which raised the price of its staple foodstuffs, rice and fermented fish or shrimp paste (ngapi). Now, in 1885, Lord Randolph Churchill, Secretary for India, became concerned about French advances in Indo-China and disorder inside King Thibaw's diminished realm. So, in his "easy-going jaunty way,"[142] he approved the conquest of Upper Burma. General Prendergast advanced with rifles and a Burmese phrase book "laboriously compiled by a gentleman unacquainted with the language."[143] One battle achieved a capitulation, opening the path to the golden pagodas and teak lacquer pavilions of Mandalay. Thibaw, a keen cricketer as well as "Lord of All Umbrella-Bearing Chiefs,"[144] was brought by bullock cart amid lines of his weeping subjects to the Irrawaddy steamer that would take him into exile. His palace became Fort Dufferin and its main throne rooms were turned into the garrison chapel and the Upper Burma Club.

On the first night of their occupation drunken British soldiers burned the royal treasury, which contained the genealogical records of the hereditary nobility, written on gold-bound palm-leaf manuscripts wrapped in figured silk cloths. A few days later the revered white elephant that was kept in the palace died and Indian troops dragged its carcass through the inauspicious west gate. Thibaw's throne, supposedly situated at the centre of the universe, was removed to a museum in Calcutta and Queen Victoria received the pick of his gems, including a "necklace with diamond peacock and gold comb" as well as his "best crown."[145] Reckoning that the stubborn Burmese would not provide pliable puppet rulers, Dufferin destroyed the old framework of government and imposed a wholly alien administrative system on the country, incorporating it into the Indian Raj. These and other affronts provoked a long and fierce guerrilla war against the invaders, conducted by princes, peasants, brigands and even Buddhist monks (pongyi). British "pacification" aimed to instil terror. It included flogging, village burning, pagoda looting, summary execution and the employment of Karen tribal people, many of them Christians, to hunt for pongyi heads. Nothing was better calculated to entrench Burmese hatred for the imperial power. "No trumpet of sedition has such an infuriating effect on a population as the shrieks of the women in the villages," wrote an eyewitness, "lamenting brothers and husbands slain not in battle, but as examples of the power and sternness of the conqueror engaged in 'establishing a funk.'"[146]

The Indian National Congress had no wish to face a similar trial and kept to the constitutional path. But the indolent Dufferin, who had at first been sympathetic, was now alarmed. Told that Hume aspired to become an Indian Parnell, Dufferin damned him (with some justice) as a vain, mendacious eccentric. And he dismissed Congress (with more justice) as the representative of a "microscopic minority," adding the unwarranted claim that the Raj was the defender of the "voiceless millions."[147] The British did make concessions, notably by extending native participation in provincial government. They even made gratuitous gestures, for example allowing Indian cricketers to use the Bombay esplanade, previously consecrated to European polo. It was hoped that cricket matches between the races would "conduce to the solidity of the British Empire." But when a Parsi side beat a team from England in 1890, the "lowing, multi-coloured throng" celebrated its triumph, wrote a white observer, by surging to and fro "gibbering and chattering and muttering vague words of evil omen."[148] Such manifestations ensured that the British also pursued their traditional policy of exploiting the "ready-made fissures"[149] within Indian society. Congress could not speak for the nation, they said, because there was no nation. There was only a mosaic of competing races, religions, castes, customs, languages and scripts. India was (to quote Winston Churchill) "no more a united nation than the equator."[150]

Congress itself illustrated the point by splitting over the deepest rift, that between Hindus and Muslims. Its unity was also threatened by contentious issues such as child marriage. In 1891 the Viceroy proposed to raise the age of consent after an eleven-year-old wife died as a result of sexual intercourse with her mature husband. The reform was carried out in the name of western enlightenment (though until 1929 twelve remained the legal age at which girls could marry in Britain) and it provoked a violent response from renascent Hinduism under the leadership of the Chitpavan ("Purified by Fire") Brahmin B. G. Tilak. To keep him within the fold, Congress temporised, trying to focus attention on an all-Indian cause. That was provided after 1895 by outbreaks of plague and famine so grave as significantly to decrease the population. Nationalists, who made political capital out of what they claimed to be the "constant drain of wealth" from the subcontinent to the United Kingdom, plausibly asserted that "India is bleeding to death."[151] So Congress grew stronger, accommodating for a time two rival leaders: the revolutionary firebrand Tilak and the social reformer Gopal

Krishna Gokhale. Tilak inspired a large Hindu following by conjuring with India's past glories as embodied in the Maratha ruler Shivaji, whose violence he found congenial—he himself was implicated in the assassination of a senior British official during the Diamond Jubilee celebrations in 1897. By contrast, Gokhale was a liberal humanitarian who drew on western traditions which had a special attraction for educated Bengali youths, some so dissident that they ate meat, drank beer and greeted the ferocious goddess Kali with "Good morning, Madam."[152] Most had a passion for freedom stimulated by their classical studies: as the writer Nirad Chaudhuri said, "we seemed to feel on our shoulders the weight of an unseen toga."[153] Gandhi compared Tilak to the turbulent, mysterious ocean and Gokhale to the smooth, inviting Ganges. In him they merged, forming a single flood from the crosscurrents of Indian nationalism. Gandhi had a "unique capacity" to combine Tilak's mass appeal with Gokhale's moral example.[154]

Meanwhile, though, the most industrious, ambitious and ostentatious of all the Viceroys, Lord Curzon of Kedleston, tried to kill Congress by kindness—by giving India the best government it had ever enjoyed. The subcontinent had excited Curzon's imagination ever since, as a boy at Eton, he heard Fitzjames Stephen talk about Britain's possession of an eastern empire "more populous, more amazing and more beneficent than that of Rome." Stephen's address was full of "school book commonplaces,"[155] Curzon remarked with characteristic loftiness, but it inspired him with a vision of India as the axis of imperial glory and the talisman of British greatness. So he prepared himself for a historic role in the Raj. He excelled at Oxford. He married an American heiress. He travelled widely in the East, having first hired from a theatrical costumier a galaxy of foreign decorations, huge gold epaulettes, enormous Wellington boots with spurs, and a gigantic curved sword. He then established himself through his pen as the prime parliamentary authority on Asia.

The young George Nathaniel Curzon, who was said to have the habits of minor royalty without its habitual incapacity, made it plain that he was destined to ascend the Viceregal throne—conveniently situated in a Government House modelled on his own ancestral home. He was duly mocked as a "most superior person," as "George the Fifth," as "God's butler." But the grand manner was as natural to him as the air he breathed. Pomp was his essential medium and pomposity his instinctive mode, though he sometimes pricked both with shafts of ribaldry. Lord Beaverbrook could not understand how he managed to be at once a wit and a bore. Curzon behaved with "enamelled self-assurance,"[156] not to say brazen arrogance—

late in life, when the chimes of Big Ben disturbed his rest, he tried to have them silenced. Conscious of Britain's world responsibilities, he personified "the old Roman quality of *gravitas.*"[157] He wrote incessantly, never pausing for thought and once sending his wife a letter a hundred pages long. He spoke with orotund magniloquence, though (a friend observed) his words were always a size too big for his thoughts. "He lisped in Gibbon," said Lord D'Abernon, and gave orders "in language that would not have disgraced Cicero addressing the Roman Senate . . . 'Housemaid, throw wide the casement,' 'Footman, add fuel to the flame.'"[158]

When he did become Viceroy in 1899, just before his fortieth birthday, Curzon was equally imperious towards Indians, whatever their rank—he treated the princes as a pack of ignorant, unruly schoolboys who had to be disciplined for their own good. They were also to be awed by assertions of power. Curzon chose as the epigraph for his book *British Government in India* the invocation which another conqueror of Delhi, Tamerlane, addressed to the Ottoman successor of the Roman emperors in Constantinople. As quoted by Gibbon, it reads:

> Dost thou not know, that the greatest part of Asia is subject to our arms and our laws? that our invincible forces extend from one sea to another? that the potentates of the earth form a line before our gate? and that we have compelled fortune herself to watch over the prosperity of our empire?[159]

Yet although Curzon was the shadow-sovereign of what he hoped would be a thousand-year Raj, he nursed Gibbonian doubts about whether it would last a century. He recognised the growth of national feeling that could "never be wholly reconciled to an alien government." He repeated the cliché that Indians would rather rule themselves badly than be well ruled by the British. And he determined "to postpone the longed-for day of emancipation" by denying Congress what it craved, "an open sore which can always be kept angry by the twist of the goad."[160]

If toil was the criterion, Curzon's administration lived up to his exalted aspirations. His Viceregal existence was "an endless typhoon of duty."[161] To paraphrase *The Times,* he took to government as other men take to drink.[162] He laboured with indefatigable zeal (and interminable, self-pitying complaint) to give India measures of justice, reform and public welfare. In his efforts to foster commerce, improve communications, develop irrigation, relieve famine, spread education, strengthen defence, increase security and promote efficiency, Curzon virtually reconstructed the Raj. He made himself almost as unpopular as Ripon with the white community (and initially popular with Indians) by condemning instances of racial violence on the part of British soldiers and civilians. He resisted Britain's "Shylock" exploitation of India,[163] writing to Whitehall as though he were the ruler of a foreign power. He restored the Taj Mahal and other monuments, aiming to build a golden bridge between East and West, as he put it, which even the roaring floods of time would not sweep away. In Calcutta he initiated his own version of the Taj in the shape of the Victoria Memorial, a white marble Valhalla of British-Indian heroes (some dressed in togas) with the Queen at its centre. It was designed to immortalise the Raj and, like the gardens at the northern end of the maidan which Curzon remodelled in the shape of a Union Jack, to stimulate imperial patriotism. This task was beyond him, not least because he tried to rule alone. Incapable of delegation, he dissipated his energies in minutiae. He kept his own household accounts. He criticised his subordinates' punctuation and wardrobe. He complained about pigeon droppings in Calcutta's Public Library and the state of the lion's cage at the Zoo. He banished European barmaids from India lest they impair white prestige. He arranged every detail of the 1903 Delhi durbar to mark King Edward's coronation, "the width of a road, the pattern of a carving, the colour of a plaster,"[164] right down to the sale of Indian artefacts through the agency of Thomas Cook. This extravagant pageant, known as the "Curzonation,"[165] was another attempt to dazzle the supposedly susceptible masses. Educated Indians pilloried it as "government by entertainment."[166]

Personally and politically, Curzon was at once unbending and condescending. His clean-shaven features seemed to have been chiselled into a patrician mask. He was physically aloof, partly as a result of wearing a steel corset to combat painful curvature of the spine—he moved, said Harold Nicolson, as if he were carrying his own howdah. He was also socially distant, in the manner of Wellesley. Since the Mutiny the Olympian character of British rule had been best symbolised by the regular summer migration of the government to the Himalayan village of Simla. This cool "Capua in the hills,"[167] as Curzon called it, became more accessible in his time thanks to the construction of a narrow-gauge railway from Kalka. Costing over £1 million, it was a marvellous feat of engineering, including two miles of viaducts and 107 tunnels, traversed in only six hours by a puffing-billy that R. A. Butler christened "the Little Ill Train."[168] Nevertheless, India's summer capital was as remote as it was precarious—an avalanche of villas, faintly reminiscent of Tunbridge Wells, poised to cascade off its ridge. "Beyond the beyond" was the architect Edwin Lutyens's verdict on the ramshackle, tin-roofed hill station which might have been built by clever monkeys, he suggested, who "must be shot in case they do it again."[169] Curzon appreciated the bracing atmosphere. His imagination soared as he contemplated the snowy peaks and he resolved that the English should climb them and become "the first mountaineering race in the world."[170] But he would have agreed with Lytton that Simla was "a mere bivouac."[171]

Curzon looked down on the society of what had always been "a very gay and worldly place—full of scandalous people and gossiping tongues who make much mischief."[172] He disdained the Arcadian frivolities of the little tin gods (and goddesses), evoked for the ages by Kipling—the archery and axe-grinding, the croquet and tennis, the skating and sketching, the steeple-chases and gymkhanas, the amateur dramatics and fancy dress balls, the games of riddles and forfeits, and the picnics made exotic by the scent of deodar and rhododendron, and by the taste of wild strawberries and fresh lemon sherbet. Curzon disparaged the Maples furniture in the grim new Viceregal Lodge on Observatory Hill (though King George V, Tsar Nicholas II and Georges Clemenceau were among many global notabilities who did not scorn to furnish their houses from the Tottenham Court Road). With its mock-baronial porches and its pseudo-feudal towers, the Lodge was indeed stunningly hideous, fit only, in the view of a future Vicereine, to be an inebriates' home or a lunatic asylum. Curzon compared banquets there to dining in the housekeeper's room with the butler and the lady's maid. He preferred to retreat to a luxurious tented camp set in magic mountain scenery, the most elevated of all imperial belvederes. From here he kept in touch with the Raj by heliograph during the day and flash-lamp at night.

If Curzon's *de haut en bas* attitudes offended Europeans in the subcontinent, who were used to protocol so rigid that it astonished even Edward (VIII) Prince of Wales, they infuriated Indians. The Viceroy affirmed that not a single native was fit to occupy a seat on his Executive Council. The hierophant of Asia suggested that truth was a western concept. The blue-blooded reactionary favoured his own kind in India and seemed to impose a stranglehold on the educated bourgeoisie by increasing government control of universities. Worried about the glacier-like advance of Russia (itself soon to be defeated by Japan, a victory which made all eastern hearts beat faster), Curzon involved India in another needless war. This time Tibet, allegedly succumbing to Russian influence, was the target. The Viceroy dispatched Colonel Francis Younghusband's military mission to Lhasa on the flimsiest of pretexts, such as attacks by Tibetan troops riding "Nepalese yaks on the frontier."[173] Worst of all, in 1905 Curzon partitioned the province of Bengal without consulting any of its eighty-five million inhabitants. The creation of a Muslim-dominated east and a Hindu-controlled west was administratively convenient but politically provocative. It was a flagrant instance of divide and rule all the more galling for being so successful. It helped to create the Muslim League in 1906, whose members claimed to represent a nation within the nation, a claim partially acknowledged by the provision of separate electorates. And, fifty years after the Mutiny, it split Congress between Gokhale's moderate majority and Tilak's angry dissidents.

They staged huge demonstrations. They also tried to promote a nation-wide boycott of all things British, though the initial plan to drape Calcutta Town Hall with black in order to mourn partition was dropped when it turned out that the only cloth available was made in England. Furthermore, as acts of terrorism multiplied, Tilak invoked Kali, the sharp-fanged, blood-stained goddess of death and destruction. Gokhale, by contrast, advocated pacific forms of protest. He encouraged Indians to buy *swadeshi* (home-produced) goods, which advertised the need for *swaraj* (home rule), now the official policy of Congress. Over the next few years British cotton exports to India fell by a quarter and home-spun *(khadi)* garments became the livery of nationalism. Curzon, vilified as an obscurantist ogre, was surprised by the uproar. Soon afterwards he was appalled to be jockeyed off his throne as the result of an unscrupulous intrigue by the new Commander-in-Chief, Lord Kitchener, whom he described as "a molten mass of devouring energy and burning ambitions."[174] Steaming away from India, Curzon kept the Viceregal flag flying until he reached Suez but he drained the cup of disappointment to its dregs. No Viceroy had regarded his mission in such an elevated light. "The sacredness of India haunts me like a passion," he intoned. "To me the message is carved in granite, hewn in the rock of doom: that our work is righteous and that it shall endure."[175] But no Viceroy had stirred up such a spirit of national revolt. It would, with startling speed, reduce Curzon's whole enterprise to dust.

The Liberal government's response to the crisis in the subcontinent was conservative. This was surprising since John Morley, who became Secretary of State for India in December 1905, was an old-fashioned radical. He was the free-thinking disciple of Mill and the hero-worshipping biographer of Gladstone—reserving the capital G for his name, it was said, while spelling god in lower case. "Honest John" was also the heir of Cobden, sharing his conviction about the ultimate futility of the Raj and adding to it the contemporary belief that "old England is played out in all respects."[176] Moreover, he was the guru of Gokhale and other progressive members of Congress. But once in power Morley reminded them of "Ariel in the hateful bondage of Sycorax."[177] He succumbed to officialdom and he was further hampered by having to work through Curzon's successor, Lord Minto. The new Viceroy was an ardent rider and huntsman, known on turf as "Mr. Rolly," whose writ was said to run no further than the stables. But he resisted positive action, maintaining that "many a race has been won by giving the horse a rest between the gallops."[178] Morley himself baulked at the first hurdle, refusing to revoke the partition of Bengal. He also ignored Congress when it proclaimed that the day of India's emancipation, foretold by Macaulay, was nigh and that if England granted it "her name will continue to shine with undimmed glory, even when the New Zealander sits on the ruined arches of Westminster Bridge."[179] An indecisive autocrat, Morley was half-convinced by the Edwardian maxim that "A democracy cannot keep an Empire."[180] He dithered unhappily between his own liberal instincts and the stern exigencies of the Raj. He worried about the "tide of strong opinion"[181] rising in the United States against Britain's Indian despotism yet compared himself approvingly to Cromwell. Everyone said that Morley was a perfect gentleman (except Lord Rosebery, who thought him "a perfect lady")[182] but he swung between high principle and sharp practice. Liberal policy towards India before the First World War is therefore best summed up in a tripartite formula: repression, concession, procession.

First, then, police and troops cracked down on violence and civil disorder throughout the subcontinent. In July 1908 Tilak was arrested and charged with sedition, having extolled the bomb as "a kind of witchcraft, a charm [mantra], an amulet."[183] He was tried by a jury containing not a single Hindu and sentenced to six years in a Mandalay prison, which prompted more riots and strikes. The press was controlled, though Morley described this cure as a "pill for an earthquake."[184] Secondly, an Indian member was introduced into the Viceroy's Executive Council (where Kitchener insulted him) and further Indian representation was provided on the advisory Legislative Councils, especially in the provinces. This was more a measure of conciliation than a serious move towards representative government, though many in Congress interpreted it as such. Certainly it was an advance on anything Curzon had envisaged and there was some justification for thinking that Morley had taken "a real step forward."[185] It was even said that he had "crossed the Rubicon."[186] Yet Morley himself told Gokhale that an independent India was "a mere dream."[187] And Lord Crewe, who took over at the India Office in 1910, made the same point to Minto's successor, Lord Hardinge, when he reunited Bengal. Crewe wanted to dispel "the hallucination that any of us are working for an ultimately self-governing India. It is an idle dream, where it is not a revolutionary project."[188]

Thirdly, the British staged a magnificent durbar in 1911 to mark the coronation of George V, the only reigning King-Emperor to visit India. It was deliberately designed to eclipse the efforts of Lytton and Curzon. Outside Delhi a camp consisting of ten square miles of canvas was erected for a quarter of a million people. It was the setting for a "unique, splendid, and gorgeous scene," as one witness recorded, "the like of which has probably never been seen before in the world."[189] At its culmination the King and Queen, preceded by attendants bearing peacock fans, yak tails and gilt maces, flanked by brilliantly caparisoned dignitaries, and followed by ten Indian pages carrying their heavy purple trains, processed to a tented pavilion with a golden cupola set in a vast amphitheatre. With elaborate ceremony they took their places on raised silver thrones. There the monarch, wearing a new crown (an involuntary gift from the people of India costing £60,000), accepted the homage of a glittering constellation of princes. According to the British press, nothing was better calculated to win oriental devotion than this apotheosis of imperial sovereignty. American newspapers were more sceptical, discerning in the very extravagance of the pageantry an attempt to compensate for the increasing vulnerability of the Raj. As a modern scholar observes, "Imperial propaganda grew as Britain declined."[190]

It is true that the durbar visit prompted many loyal ovations. In Calcutta, as one witness recorded, the people surged round the royal carriage and "did what the Bengalee Baboo never does—salaamed to the ground, threw dust on their heads, and the women made a guttural sound in their throats which is always kept for the temple."[191] But critics were also vocal. They said that festivity insulted poverty and that frivolity diminished dignity. Crewe himself acknowledged that the priority given to shooting, which seemed to exercise "an unholy fascination" over the King's mind, gave "an air of flippancy to the tour."[192] There were also contretemps during the durbar itself. When the Gaekwar of Baroda failed to pay obeisance according to the prescribed etiquette Hardinge rebuked him for a shocking lack of respect, whereupon this "disloyal and conceited ass," an equerry wrote, "cringed and crawled."[193] Furthermore, although the news of the reunification of Bengal pleased Hindus, Muslims were horrified by it and rivalled them in violence. The Viceroy himself was badly injured in a bomb attack as he made his state entry into Delhi on elephant back in 1912. He displayed impressive sang-froid, ordering the procession to continue, but his pith helmet had been blown off and his wife insisted, "You cannot go out in India without a topee."[194] When his stand-in as Viceroy inadvertently wore his topee back to front at an investiture, officials said that the unexpected elevation had quite turned his head.

Hardinge felt increasingly embattled as nationalist pressure continued. It was supported at home by a few faddists and factions, as he called them, who did not seem to appreciate that India was a hugely profitable field of investment and now Britain's greatest export market, a nucleus of its economy as well as the fulcrum of its Empire. Even Crewe's India Office seemed bent on compromise, on showing that it was not full of "blood-and-iron bureaucrats."[195] To the Viceroy's fury it forced him to accept Gokhale as a member of a royal commission on public services. Publicly Hardinge appeared sympathetic towards Congress but privately he regarded Gokhale as "the most dangerous enemy of British rule in this country."[196] In fact that enemy was still at work in South Africa. Here Gandhi made such an issue of Indian grievances that before 1914 they became the focus of the nationalist struggle in the subcontinent. "Ghandi," whom Crewe spelled thus and described as "a straight and rather high-charactered person, but an undoubted fanatic,"[197] persuaded Gokhale to help him in South Africa. Even Hardinge protested about its ill treatment of Indians, who were indeed the helots of empire, their labour exploited from Malaya to Fiji, from East Africa to the West Indies. The success of Gandhi's campaign (which relieved his countrymen of various disabilities, though it did not win them the vote) established his credentials as Gokhale's heir. On the eve of the First World War he left South Africa to make his tryst with destiny in India.

There the British had just embarked on a vain attempt to enshrine their sovereignty in stone, teak, marble and bronze. To complement the King's other durbar announcement—that the capital would move from Calcutta to Delhi—they began to build a new city. The ancient walls of Delhi enclosed the remains of seven previous cities, encompassing an imperial tradition, as Crewe said, comparable to that of Constantinople or Rome. New Delhi would overshadow the seats of Akbar and Aurangzeb, and it would overlook the relics of Hindu dynasties lost in the mists of time. Fascinated by this majestic panorama of the past, the explorer Gertrude Bell exclaimed: "A landscape made up of empires is something to conjure with."[198] The new city, of course, would symbolise the lasting supremacy of the British Raj. The architects Sir Edwin Lutyens and Sir Herbert Baker designed it along classical western lines, though with Hindu, Buddhist and Mughal features such as water gardens with lotus-petal fountains, lattice casements *(jalis)* and extended cornices over windows to provide shade *(chujjas)*. Thus New Delhi was to present an orderly contrast to the confusion of Old Delhi, to smack of Roman discipline amid oriental decadence. It was an exercise in hierarchy and geometry. From the position of each building in relation to the Viceroy's House, crowning Raisina Hill, could be determined the exact status of its occupants. With its spacious vistas, imposing façades, triumphal arches and processional boulevards, New Delhi suggested, as one commentator said, the setting for a perpetual durbar.

The stateliness was matched by the minutiae. The Viceroy's House, for example, was a palace larger than Versailles, its façades made with red and cream sandstone hewn from Mughal quarries, its floors and walls gleaming with multi-coloured marble such as adorned the Taj Mahal. So vast was this 285-room bungalow masterpiece that servants rode the length of its basement corridors by bicycle. Yet Lutyens also designed the chairs, the nursery furniture, the intricate chimneypieces, the coffered ceilings and the door handles in the form of lions couchant wearing the imperial crown. Not everything went according to plan in the new city. As committees quibbled and costs were cut (though they eventually reached £10 million), Lutyens complained that he was struggling with "Bedlampore"[199]—crazier even than Edward Lear's "Hustlefussabad."[200] Inferior workmanship prompted the architect to assert that Indians should "be reduced to slavery and not given the rights of man at all."[201] Even that most snooty of memsahibs, Lady Grigg, who thought Indians subhuman, was embarrassed when the streets were all "named after us"—Queen Victoria Road, Freeman Terrace, "Willingdon Crescent and Curzon tiddly-um-pom." She felt that New Delhi was a "triumph of egotism."[202] Dissatisfied officials called their houses "Baker's Ovens." And Sir Herbert was also responsible for giving the Rajpath such a steep gradient that those who approached the Viceroy's House along this route witnessed its partial disappearance. Lutyens memorably said that he had met his Bakerloo.

Still, New Delhi was the grandest monument ever erected to the British Empire. From the Viceroy's House, its great copper dome modelled on Hadrian's Pantheon, to the Jaipur Column, a pillar of victory inspired by that of Trajan, it was an image of dominion. From the avenues of British lions to the clapperless stone bells, intended to counteract the Hindu belief that bells tolled the knell of dynasties, it was a metaphor of enduring strength. Lutyens spelled out its purpose graphically in 1914, when he proposed that the inscription on the Viceroy's House should read: "Govern them and lift them up for ever." It was a matter of supreme irony that the whole concept was formulated at a time when the Empire stood on the brink of Armageddon. Moreover, as New Delhi rose over the next two decades the imperial ideal it stood for grew increasingly moribund, as if to fulfil Curzon's prediction that the city would become a "gilded phantom"[203] of the Raj. The administrator Sir Montagu Butler, mindful of the Indian prophecy that he who built a city at Delhi would lose it, and aware that nothing could withstand the surging tides of nationalism, called New Delhi "the ruins."[204] "Tiger" Clemenceau, who visited India to shoot tigers after the war, said that it would be "the finest ruin of them all." By mistake George V had laid the foundation stone of the new capital in a cemetery. The city's formal inauguration two decades later—in 1931, the year in which Gandhi (to Churchill's disgust) strode up the steps of the Viceroy's House to parley on equal terms with the representative of the King-Emperor—was less a fanfare than a requiem. One witness described it as "the funeral of our Indian Empire."[205]

9

The Empire, Right or Wrong

Flanders, Iraq, Gallipoli and Vimy Ridge

The Rajpath in New Delhi, like Whitehall in London, would soon be the scene of a still more poignant commemoration of mortality. As it happened Lutyens designed both the India Gate, which bore the names of the seventy thousand Indians who lost their lives in the Great War, and the Cenotaph, "the reverent salute of an Empire mourning its million dead."[1] The two monuments make a striking contrast. The colossal red arch, engraved with radiant suns and topped with a domed bowl to hold burning oil on anniversaries, is an exclamation. The empty white tomb on its tapered stone pylon, a work of such sublime simplicity that it seems to point towards the infinite, is an ellipsis. As this suggests, London was less emphatically an imperial city than New Delhi. The Anglo-Indian architecture there affirmed despotism, whereas the British capital was, in its very lack of grand design, an assertion of liberty. Admittedly, feeble municipal government and high property prices constrained comprehensive development in London. So did dyed-in-the-wool conservatism. "Do away with the congestion of traffic at Hyde Park Corner?" exclaimed Disraeli to the Commissioner of Works. "Why, my dear fellow, you would be destroying one of the sights of London."[2]

Thus the city always resisted the drastic reconstruction that transformed Franz Joseph I's Vienna and the "Haussmannisation" which destroyed the compact revolutionary faubourgs of Napoleon III's Paris. The East End of London remained, in the words of one local newspaper, "a vile, malodorous irreclaimable thing, a dumping ground for undesirables, a dust bin, a forgotten garret, a neglected basement, creepy, smelly, stifling."[3] The West End was also unamenable to discipline. Despite the opportunities offered by the completion of the Thames Embankment in 1870 and the construction of the Mall before the First World War, state-sponsored schemes for a truly imperial metropolis came to nothing. Delay was endemic. The sculptor Thomas Thornycroft began his equestrian statue of Boadicea in the mid-Victorian period, using as models horses in Prince Albert's stables (which

made them far larger than the ponies that pulled the warrior queen's chariot). But the tableau did not find a permanent home, near Westminster
Bridge, until the Boer War replenished "the ancient fires of British valour
and patriotism."[4] Diversity was ubiquitous. In fact, as one authority says,
Queen Victoria's London witnessed a uniquely "exuberant, even anarchic,
proliferation of styles, materials, constructional techniques, colours, outlines, ethical and intellectual statements." It was "a proud expression of the
energies and values of a free people."[5]

Nevertheless, there were piecemeal attempts to make the city worthy of
a pre-eminence summed up in H. G. Wells's novel *Tono-Bungay* (1909):
"The richest town in the world, the biggest port, the greatest manufacturing
town, the Imperial city—the centre of civilisation, the heart of the world!"[6]
To deserve such encomiums, London had to imitate Rome—Paris being
usually deemed the heir of Athens. Thus in 1843 Nelson's Column was modelled on a pillar in the Temple of Mars. In the mid-century new government
buildings along Whitehall reflected imperial glory, notably the neo-classical
Foreign Office. Its design was the subject of a celebrated dispute between
the architect, Sir George Gilbert Scott, champion of Gothic, and Lord
Palmerston, who rejected both his proposed "monastery" and a "mongrel"
compromise. Palmerston also disallowed pleas for a genuinely indigenous
style, asserting that "the real aboriginal architecture of this country was mud
huts and wicker wigwams."[7]

So he got an Italianate "national palace"[8] replete with marble balustrades, majolica friezes, bronze medallions, mosaic pavements, ormolu
chandeliers, Corinthian columns and statues of imperial heroes such as
Clive dressed in Roman garb. It incorporated a noble quadrangle, a grand
staircase flanked with effigies of previous ministers, a gilded dome with the
sun at its centre and eventually allegorical frescoes in Venetian red and
cobalt blue portraying the "expansion and triumph of the British Empire,"[9]
one of which appeared to depict a rape. There were vast salons such as the
great barrel-vaulted Locarno Room (as it was named in 1925) and chambers
so echoingly cavernous that they were suspected of being Scott's acoustic
revenge on officialdom. The new Colonial Office was similarly embellished,
notably with representations of the continents and their explorers and proconsuls. The India Office was adorned with images of the rivers, cities and
people of the subcontinent. It boasted the magnificent granite-pillared Durbar Court and the Muses' Stair leading to an octagonal glass lantern decorated with goddesses of plenty supported by cherubs representing the
Roman virtues. It also included nabob furniture, mahogany doors and a

marble chimneypiece depicting Britannia receiving the riches of Asia, all taken from the East India Company's headquarters in Leadenhall Street, together with Persian miniatures looted from the Red Fort.

Finally, the Mall, paved with wood on its completion in 1904, provided a "public axis of imperialism." It was a huge proscenium on which majestic pageants were staged to dramatise the Empire's sovereign institution. Each wing of this outdoor theatre was duly improved. Buckingham Palace acquired a Renaissance façade. And Admiralty Arch, an "essentially Roman"[10] creation, was ornamented with figures representing Gunnery and Navigation. Imperial heroes such as Captain Cook took their proper places and, of course, the late monarch was ubiquitous. Yet the Victoria Memorial itself, on which colonies were characterised by cherubs carrying national symbols, was curiously muted about the Empire, though the watery basin was designed to suggest its maritime foundations. India was entirely absent, having its own (or rather Curzon's) memorial to the Empress in Calcutta. Prominent were effigies of Courage, Constancy and Motherhood as well as Justice and Truth—*The Times* regretted that they were conventionally represented in angelic form since, as T. H. Huxley had said, the angel was "a morphological monstrosity."[11] The sculpture was more an accolade to regal virtue than to imperial victory. Unlike the bombastic Victor Emmanuel monument in contemporary Rome, it was neither the "national anthem in marble" nor the "Altar of the Fatherland."[12]

In fact, the Victoria Memorial was an expression of eclecticism—like London itself. The capital was less than an imperial city because it was more than an imperial city. Like Washington, which modelled itself on ancient Rome yet cherished the structures of democracy, London was a megalopolis of varieties. Compared to the Rome of the Caesars, it was but sparsely furnished with the spoils of empire. It showed surprisingly few signs of attachment to Britain's overseas possessions, which many still deemed burdens rather than assets. Nevertheless, as Henry James noted at the beginning of *The Golden Bowl* (1904), if one wanted a sense of the imperial city to which the world paid tribute it was to be found in contemporary views of the Thames not the Tiber. Such comparisons were commonplace. The ghost of imperial Rome haunted London, sometimes as a hopeful spirit of unity, sometimes as a grim portent of disintegration.

The Festival of Empire, for example, which took place at the Crystal Palace in May 1911, was the most elaborate attempt hitherto devised to strengthen the tenuous bonds holding together the worldwide British family. George V opened it, the first public event he attended as King, and received a rapturous welcome. It included a ceremonial greeting from Maori warriors, described by the *Illustrated London News* as "New Zealand's primitive inhabitants."[13] More than three hundred buildings had been erected to represent every part of the Empire, filled with exhibits and linked by an electric railway travelling on an "All-Red Route."[14] Among them were two-thirds-size replicas of the parliament houses of Ottawa, Melbourne, Wellington, Cape Town and St. John's, Newfoundland. There were contemporary scenes, everything from a Jamaican sugar plantation to a Malayan village on stilts, from Newfoundland fisheries to South African diamond mines, from the Blue Mountains to the Himalayas. Nothing was better calculated to promote emigration and advertisements puffed what the *Standard of Empire* called "one of the most stupendous movements of modern times—the exodus from the Motherland to the Dominions overseas."[15]

Moreover, there were forty historical tableaux, ranging from Stanley's meeting with Livingstone to the arrival of a Roman Emperor at the Temple of Diana in a scarlet and gold chariot drawn by four white horses. Yet this panoply of propaganda hid real concerns about the relative decline in Britain's global position. It also concealed worries about the meagreness and fragility of imperial consolidation—justified, as it happened, by the fact that the first British Empire Games, held as part of the Festival, were confined to the dominions. According to Winston Churchill, people feared that the Empire was by then so rickety that "a single violent shock would bring it clattering down and lay it low for ever."[16] The anxieties appeared even in this drum-beating verse of the time:

> Though cowards fear its giant size
> And croak of its decay
> And nations, envious of the prize,
> Would filch its wealth away . . .
> And broader far, and stronger yet,
> And grander grows the tree
> Whose branches are in justice set,
> Whose roots in liberty.[17]

The organisers of the Festival took particular care to exhibit alternative imperial models (Tudor ones, for instance) to that of Rome. They were determined to avoid "any suggestion of the inevitability of decline and fall."[18]

The Great War, the tragic climax of European rivalries which had long been regarded as (in Bergson's phrase) probable but impossible, at first seemed to avert that threat. Admittedly, the balance of power favoured the foe. Germany, with a conscript army that in 1913 numbered 660,000, dwarfed Britain in terms of military might. Bismarck had quipped that if the British Army invaded the Reich he would send the police to arrest it and the Kaiser held the British Expeditionary Force, consisting of 160,000 troops, in equal contempt. He assumed, moreover, that Britain's difficulty would become the opportunity for dissidents within the Empire to raise the standard of revolt. In fact, to the astonishment of the British government itself, which declared war (on 4 August 1914) on behalf of all the King's subjects without consulting them, nationalist leaders at once rallied round the Union Flag. The revolutionary Tilak pledged unswerving loyalty to the British cause and the pacifist Gandhi drummed up recruits for the army, to which India eventually supplied nearly one and a half million men. Although the Home Rule Bill would not come into effect until the war was over, the Irish leader, John Redmond, promised a united front against the common enemy. He even offered to form a separate army of his countrymen. Kitchener, the new Secretary for War, rejected the scheme, but 160,000 Irish volunteers swelled the ranks of more than two million Englishmen who flocked to join the colours. The former Prime Minister of Canada, Sir Wilfrid Laurier, despite his long championship of autonomy, supported Sir Robert Borden's government in 1914, declaring that "when Great Britain is at war we are at war."[19]

After an initial burst of enthusiasm, French Canadians were less accommodating; yet 30,000 of them enlisted, along with 600,000 British North Americans. Australia and New Zealand reiterated Laurier's formula. South Africa, alone among the dominions, witnessed a revolt against participation in the war. Boer fought Boer and Prime Minister Botha defeated the rebel General de Wet. Yet South Africa contributed more than 135,000 soldiers to the wider fray. Recruits flooded in from all parts of the Empire and beyond: Maoris and Fijians, West Indians and Falkland Islanders, Moosejaw frontiersmen and Khyber Pathans, Chinese coolies and African askaris, Dutch farmers from the Cape and Scottish shepherds from Patagonia. The Dalai Lama even offered a thousand Tibetans. Patriots were thrilled by this international rush to the colours. Julian Grenfell, the golden boy of the lost generation, said that it reinforced his belief in the Old Flag and the Mother Country and the Heavy Brigade and the Thin Red Line and all the Imperial Idea. Also vital were the overseas contributions of money, munitions and raw materials. Flung into the scales of war, the imperial sword may well have tipped the balance. It probably averted defeat in 1917 and certainly helped to secure victory the following year. That triumph, along with the new territories which Britain acquired in its wake, seemed to fulfil the dream of a united empire. John Buchan, a member of Milner's "Kindergarten," his band of young disciples, wrote lyrically on the subject. The war revealed that wonderful thing for which the makers of empire "had striven and prayed—a union based not upon statute and officialdom, but upon the eternal simplicities of the human spirit."[20]

On the other hand, the world war caused an irreversible change in the political weather. It precipitated the collapse of the Russian, German, Austro-Hungarian and Ottoman empires—Churchill complained of a "drizzle of empires falling through the air."[21] And it had a profoundly destructive impact on the British Empire. At its simplest the mother country suffered a terrible haemorrhage of blood and treasure. Some 725,000 Britons were killed, 9 per cent of males under the age of forty-five, and 1.7 million were wounded. Young officers suffered disproportionate casualties, 30,000 sacrificing their lives—a lost generation of empire-builders. The war cost £9 billion, which increased Britain's national debt fourteen-fold and ensured that future expenditure on the Empire would be ferociously squeezed. Further constraints stemmed from lost markets and the gains of competitors such as Japan and the United States. The appalling casualty rates shook colonial (and domestic) confidence in Britain's leadership, particularly as the Central Powers proved to be "at least a third better at mass slaughter"[22] than the Allies. The dominions suffered, proportionately to their population, almost as badly as Britain. As a result their people felt a fierce pride in their national contribution to victory and their Premiers acquired more influence over imperial foreign policy. According to the pugnacious Australian Prime Minister Billy Hughes, there was "only one Caesar" in the Roman Empire, but in "the British Empire there are many."[23]

Military setbacks, such as those in Gallipoli and Mesopotamia, undermined the prestige upon which, said Maurice Hankey, the Secretary to the Committee of Imperial Defence, "our Eastern Empire depends."[24] The Easter Rising in Ireland and the Bolshevik Revolution in Russia inspired independence movements throughout the Empire. The Allied war aims, especially as enunciated by the high-minded American President Woodrow Wilson, had a still wider appeal. When Wilson preached the gospel of liberty, democracy and nationality, those chafing under the imperial yoke hailed him as a saviour. And they regarded the peace settlement as a hideous betrayal. Arabs, encouraged by T. E. Lawrence "to build an inspired dream-palace of their national thoughts,"[25] merely swapped one imperial power for others, with the added mortification of having Christian suzerains and a Jewish homeland in Palestine. India was bitterly disappointed that its immense contribution did not receive a just reward, especially as the Montagu Declaration in 1917 had promised "the progressive realisation of responsible government."[26] In Africa, the conflict caused widespread disruption and, as Sir Harry Johnston wrote, marked the "beginning of revolt against the white man's supremacy."[27]

In short, like all major events, the Great War had complicated and contradictory results. It tightened "the crimson thread of kinship"[28] between the mother country and the dominions. Yet in a sense Canada really *was* born, as the conventional wisdom has it, amid the carnage of Vimy Ridge.[29] Similarly, Australia and New Zealand did proceed to forge their separate identities in the crucible of Gallipoli. Elsewhere the conflict both promoted imperial solidarity and stimulated hopes of self-determination. The *esprit de corps* of Indian troops survived the holocaust of Ypres. But as the struggle continued Britain's alien auxiliaries, like those of Rome as described by Gibbon, learned to despise her manners and to imitate the arts "by which alone she supported her declining greatness."[30] Despite the defection of Eire, the war increased the bulk of the British Empire, adding nearly two million square miles and some thirteen million subjects, mostly in Africa and the Middle East. Of course the new colonies were disguised as mandated territories, reflecting the high moral tone adopted by the peacemakers and the disrepute attached to imperialist annexation. Until ready for independence, these territories were to be held as a sacred trust on behalf of the League of Nations. But they were coloured red on the map and they appeared to make the Empire, which reached its geographical apogee between the wars, more formidable than ever. However, with the rise of fascism and the advent of the Depression it seemed more of a charge on, than a benefit to, Britain itself. Many felt that the Empire had become a gorged giant, gouty at the extremities, whose very size sapped its strength. Some quoted the maxim attributed to Napoleon that "great empires die of indigestion."[31] Others recalled Gibbon's famous conclusion that "the decline of Rome was the natural and inevitable effect of immoderate greatness" and that once "time or accident had removed the artificial supports, the stupendous fabric yielded to the pressure of its own weight."[32]

On 26 September 1914 a procession of vessels entered the harbour of Marseilles to a noisy welcome, including sirens, gun salutes and brass bands giving endless renditions of the "Marseillaise." The convoy contained the first of 138,000 Indians who came to help prop up the tottering Western Front. They were drawn from those races which the British designated "martial"— Punjabis, Baluchis, Afridis, Sikhs, Jats, Dogras, Gurkhas, Pathans, Garhwalis. There were also contingents from the princely states, whose rulers contributed lavishly to the British cause, giving cash, jewels, horses, camels and a hospital ship called the *Loyalty*. Despite his seventy years, Sir Pertab Singh, the Regent of Jodhpur, enrolled for active service in person, as if to confirm Hardinge's view that he was "truly 'a white man' among Indians."[33] About a month after disembarkation battalions of the Lahore Division were fed into the line, just as the invading Germans, driven back from the River Marne, attempted to outflank the Allies in Flanders. So on that low coastal plain crisscrossed by ditches, drains and canals, and dotted with farmsteads and copses, the Indians witnessed the last gasp of the war of movement which had well-nigh destroyed the British Expeditionary Force. They also experienced the first battle of Ypres, a sickening foretaste of static combat in the trenches. Their courage was apparent from the start. While driving off an enemy assault, Sepoy Usman Khan stuck to his post although twice wounded by rifle fire, only allowing himself to be carried back when a shell splinter cut large chunks of flesh from his legs. Soon Indian units took part in a counter-attack against barbed wire and machine guns. By 1 December their casualties numbered 133 British and 95 Indian officers and 4,735 other ranks. Despite the shock, many sepoys were thrilled to be participating in the great European *"tamasha"* (spectacle).[34] They were impressed by western wonders such as "flying steel birds"[35] and thought that Europe, with its knowledge, wealth and beauty, was living in "the first Golden Age." They were also proud of their own warrior spirit. Death in battle "for us of the Rajput caste," wrote one, "is an open door to Paradise." The Pathans seemed throughout "actually to enjoy the fighting."[36] The Gurkhas also showed a grisly relish for getting to grips with the foe—they had sharpened their *kukris* on the train to Calcutta "under the impression that they were about to engage the enemy."[37] In France one Gurkha paraded as a trophy "the face of a German—not his head, just his face, clean sliced off."[38] To judge from sepoy letters, there was much real and lasting imperial patriotism. One Indian officer thought it "a great honour that we have an opportunity of showing our loyalty to our great Emperor by the sacrifice of our bodies."[39]

However, Indian troops were quite unprepared for the bone-chilling, gut-wrenching, soul-destroying shambles of the Western Front. They belonged to what was little more than a frontier constabulary, infantry trained for bayonet charges along lines familiar to Wellington, cavalry armed with sabres and lances. The two Indian divisions (Lahore and Meerut) lacked modern equipment. They took barbed wire from farm fences, made grenades from empty jam tins, employed 13-pounder horse batteries as artillery, and improvised mortars from wood and cast iron. They endured rain and snow in cotton khaki uniforms designed for the tropics. Accustomed to snakes, scorpions and mosquitoes, they were appalled by infestations of lice whose bite was "worse than a rifle bullet."[40] In water-logged trenches, where the living mingled with the dead and all taboos were broken, they suffered perpetual pollution. "Fragments of human beings"[41] were everywhere, providing a feast for millions of enormous rats which ran over everything, even the face of General Sir James Willcocks, the com-manding officer of the Indian divisions, as he slept in a dugout: "I jumped as if shot, with the result that I knocked my head against the supporting timber."[42] And nothing compared with the sheer scale of the butchery. One Garhwali rifleman wrote:

> When we reached their trenches we used the bayonet and the kukri and blood was shed so freely that we could not recognise each other's faces; the whole ground was covered with blood. There were heaps of men's heads, and some soldiers were without legs, others had been cut in two, some were with-out hands and others without eyes.[43]

The Germans retaliated with murderous firepower, turning Neuve Chapelle into an "oven"[44] and Loos into an inferno. Indian troops huddled under the deluge of metal like "beggars in a monsoon."[45] When poison gas was used some gave way to panic, screaming as they fled, "We have come to hell!"[46] "This is not war," wrote a Punjabi familiar with the prophecies of the *Mahabharata*. "It is the ending of the world."[47]

Morale grew increasingly shaky—there had already been an epidemic of self-inflicted wounds, mostly in the left hand. Sepoys' spirits sank still fur-ther because they got no home leave. Wounded men were sent to Brighton Pavilion, which was converted into a hospital for Indians despite anxieties about their "possible encounters" with British women.[48] Here, according to different accounts, they were either tended like flowers or treated like con-victs. As casualty lists lengthened, desertions multiplied. Although General Willcocks's senior subordinates were incompetent even by the usual brass-hat standards, the death of so many junior British officers undermined the Indians' will to resist. For each one was a linguistic lifeline in a military Babel of at least ten tongues. Moreover, Indian officers lacked the prestige to provide effective command, a situation caused by racial prejudice but blamed on racial inferiority. "The Indian is simply not fit to lead his men against Europeans," wrote Willcocks. "He will lead a charge or cover a retirement, but if he has to think he fails."[49]

In fact sepoys thought a lot about being used as cannon fodder in defence of an empire which had subjugated their own people. And such thoughts prompted disaffection, indiscipline and even mutiny among men whose horizons had been widened by their European experience. One sepoy told a British officer, "If the Germans allied themselves with us Afridis we could lick the world."[50] Others sent home seditious letters. Sometimes they were written in code to elude the censor: for example, bullets were referred to as "rainfall" and Indian troops as "black pepper." Occasionally these missives contained obscene abuse: the English were called *salas*.* Gandhi hoped that India's freedom would burst from the battlefields of France which he had helped to crowd with "an indomitable army of Home Rulers."[51] But the process was one of germination not revolution. The blood of sepoys was the seed of independence. Nothing less than a sacrifice of power in the subcontinent could atone for the hecatombs of the Western Front. The British would give as little, and as slowly, as they could. But they saw concession as the price of collaboration, if not allegiance. When the Lahore and Meerut Divisions were withdrawn from Flanders in 1915 they were not sent home for "fear of unrest."[52]

Indian troops were, anyway, in demand elsewhere and they duly served in many other theatres of war—Gallipoli, Salonika, various parts of Africa and the Middle East. Their main field of operations was Mesopotamia. Here nearly 700,000 sepoys fought the Turks, even though the Ottoman Caliph, whom Muslims believed to be the shadow of God upon earth, had declared a *jihad* against enemy infidels. But defections inspired by Islamic faith proved less fatal than defeats caused by British ineptitude. To secure Mesopotamia's supply of oil it was enough to hold the region around Basra, the squalid river port said by an English officer to be "sixty miles up the world's arsehole."[53] The delta of the Tigris and Euphrates was so humid that "the very air seems to sweat."[54] But compared to the burning fiery furnace of the northern desert, this green spot beside the Persian Gulf, with its vines, pomegranates and fig trees, could well have been, as religious tradition claimed, the Garden of Eden. Especially alluring were the millions of date palms, with diamond-shaped striations on their trunks, golden clusters of fruit and an emerald whorl of fronds sussurating in the breeze. Nevertheless, the minarets of Baghdad were an irresistible temptation and General Charles Townshend, a banjo-strumming joker to compare with Gordon or Baden-Powell, advanced into the wilderness. No bloodhound, he boasted, could have pursued the Turks with more tenacity. However, his force was weak and ill supplied: the medical services were comparable to those of

---

* *Sala* meant brother-in-law but implied sister-fucker.

Scutari and much of the ammunition was labelled "Made in the USA. For Practice only."[55] After a Pyrrhic victory at Ctesiphon, Townshend had to withdraw to the sordid mud-brick town of Kut, looped by the Tigris, where he allowed himself to be invested. Efforts to relieve him, supported by the refitted Lahore and Meerut Divisions, were bloodily repulsed.

So on 29 April 1916, worn out by heat, stench, disease, inundation and starvation, not to mention hosts of fleas that darkened the ground and clouds of flies that bit like bulldogs, Townshend surrendered. His garrison had endured the longest siege in British history (147 days) and he had suffered a greater defeat than that of Cornwallis at Yorktown. But worse was to come. The Turks stripped the prisoners of most of their possessions, including water bottles and boots. Then they herded the men (separated from their officers) northwards, driving them through the desert with the bayonet and the bastinado. Stragglers were raped or murdered. Many others died of hunger, thirst and sickness before they reached Baghdad. There the remnant was paraded, a legion of scarecrows derided by the people but pitied by the American consul, who came to their aid at the cost of his own life. As the prisoners stumbled onwards to Anatolia they were subjected to what one private called "an extended massacre."[56] When set to railway work in chain gangs they had to endure further brutalities. Only 837 of the 2,592 Britons taken at Kut saw the end of the war, while 7,423 out of 10,486 Indians survived. The sepoys, especially the Muslims, were treated less harshly and coped better with captivity than the British, whose self-confidence suffered accordingly. So did their prestige—the reflection of power that was, to repeat the mantra ceaselessly intoned by India pundits, the bedrock of the Raj.

Nationalists seized the moment to demand, in return for India's largesse, the "priceless blessing" of liberty.[57] They exploited growing popular discontent. Two years of conflict had raised the cost of food by nearly a third and fodder was exported to the Middle East while the Deccan starved. Also, as one Indian leader said, the war had put the clock fifty years forward.[58] It had shortened patience and quickened expectations. The time was ripe, as the government took repressive war powers, for spreading the gospel of independence. One of its most powerful preachers was Annie Besant, now nearing the end of a strange pilgrimage which had led her from Anglicanism, via atheism, socialism and neo-Malthusianism (i.e. contraception), to Indian nationalism. This she combined with devotion to Theosophy and to the Boy Scout movement—wearing a green turban, purple scarf and khaki sari with emerald borders, she later took an oath of loyalty in front of Baden-Powell. In 1916 she formed a Home Rule League and proclaimed herself "an

Indian tom-tom waking all the sleepers so that they may work for their Motherland."[59] Tilak, back at the helm of Congress after Gokhale's death, and Mohammad Ali Jinnah, the austere lawyer who had recently become President of the Muslim League, needed no such summons. At Lucknow they made a pact to fight for self-government by constitutional means. The Muslim position was safeguarded through separate electorates and Jinnah announced that "the Promised Land is within sight."[60]

The following year Britain at last seemed prepared to let his people go. For then Russia succumbed to revolution and defeat, and India rang with Besantine pronouncements about the "awakening of Asia."[61] So Indian leaders were invited to attend the Imperial War Conference. Indian soldiers were granted the King's Commission, though the military took care that brown officers should not command whites. And the new Secretary of State for India, Edwin Montagu, issued his momentous declaration that self-governing institutions would gradually be developed in the subcontinent. He and the Viceroy, Lord Chelmsford (son of the Isandhlwana general), honoured that pledge in 1918 by proposing a system known as dyarchy. This broadly meant devolving control over matters such as health, education, agriculture and public works to Indian provincial authorities, while leaving a slightly more representative central government in charge of foreign affairs, security and taxation. But the scheme annoyed conservative Britons, who denounced it as "a spider's web spun out of the brain of a doctrinaire pedant."[62] And Indians damned it as an unsatisfactory interim measure, though it did bring them enough autonomy to sound the "death-knell of the Raj."[63] Jinnah, "armed to the teeth with dialectics," made mincemeat of the scheme and Montagu privately admitted it was outrageous that such a clever "man should have no chance of running the affairs of his own country." Violent agitation continued, as did racial antipathy—the *Times* correspondent disliked Bombay because it was "overrun by Indians."[64] Montagu queasily agreed to help Chelmsford stamp out rebellion. So in 1919 the Rowlatt Act was passed whereby those accused of sedition could be arrested without warrant and tried without jury. It caused a storm. Jinnah denounced it as a "Star Chamber" decree which violated "the principles for which Great Britain fought the war"[65] and he resigned from the Legislative Council. Gandhi mounted a campaign of passive resistance to unjust laws, beginning with a *hartal,* or general strike, a stratagem which had been suggested to him in a dream. Civil disobedience proved a far more effective form of opposition than anything envisioned by Jinnah. It thrust the Mahatma ("Great Soul"), as he was now called, into national prominence and won him a unique place in the leadership of Congress. Chelmsford wrote to Montagu, "Dear me, what a d . . . d nuisance these saintly fanatics are!"[66]

Revolt against the Rowlatt Act was especially explosive in the Punjab, the garrison province of India now writhing in the iron grip of its diehard Lieutenant-Governor, Sir Michael O'Dwyer. He authorised the arrest of two opposition leaders in Amritsar, which means "Nectar of Immortality," the holy city of the Sikhs. This provoked a riot which culminated in murder, looting and arson. It prompted white fears of another Mutiny and gave Indians "some excuse for their belief that the British *raj* was over."[67] After such a "display of Gandhi's 'Soul Force,'"[68] as O'Dwyer sarcastically put it, strong measures were deemed essential. One colonel advocated using aeroplanes to bomb the mob, a tactic employed elsewhere in the Punjab. Instead "a fire-snorting General"[69] called Reginald ("Rex") Dyer was sent to restore order. He was a martinet of the old school, with cropped grey hair, a brick-red complexion and blue eyes which the *Daily Mail* later described as "kindly."[70] His hot temper was aggravated by the constant pain he suffered from injuries sustained in the hunting field—he tried to soothe himself with aspirins, brandy and cigarettes, and sometimes he wrapped his head in wet towels. Dyer put on a show of force in Amritsar. With a convoy of soldiers and armoured cars he toured streets flanked by gutted ruins and smouldering with resentment. He also banned further assemblies on pain of instant dispersal, if necessary under martial law.

The proclamation was repeated the following day, 13 April 1919. But this was a Sunday of religious festival and, as the sun beat down on Amritsar through a pewter sky, many came to worship at the Golden Temple and to bathe in its sacred pool. Others attended a horse and cattle fair and by the afternoon some fifteen thousand people had gathered in the walled space near the Temple, known as the Jallianwala Bagh. A garden by name, it was actually a five-acre courtyard of baked earth scavenged by pariah dogs and mud-stained buffaloes. It contained a few trees, a well, a shrine and a stage from which a political speaker addressed the crowd, most of whom were dozing, chatting or playing cards or dice. Towards sunset, Dyer marched through one of the Bagh's narrow entrances with a detachment of ninety Gurkhas and Baluchis armed with rifles. He lined them up on a slight eminence and, without warning, gave the order to fire. As they shot at will, steadily emptying and reloading their magazines, the Jallianwala Bagh became a blood-soaked pandemonium. The crowd surged to and fro like hunted animals, screaming, falling, dying. The general directed the fusillade towards places where the throng was thickest, notably in front of the alleys offering the only escape routes, which were soon clogged with corpses. After ten minutes, during which 1,650 rounds were discharged and ammunition was running low, Dyer ordered a cease-fire and withdrew. He did nothing for the 1,500 wounded and, according to the official estimate, he left behind 379 dead, many of them children. "It was a merciful though horrible act and they ought to be thankful to me for doing it," he later said. Claiming that the massacre had saved the Punjab from a still worse fate, he added, "I thought it would be doing a jolly lot of good."[71]

Not content with doing good on such a scale, Dyer sought to punish those who had been responsible for the disturbances in the first place. He employed various expedients: curfew, blackout, expropriation, torture, arbitrary arrests and trials held in camera at which defendants were summarily convicted on false evidence. In due course the government extended clemency to most of those found guilty, but not before eighteen had been publicly hanged and hundreds flogged. Dyer also imposed a number of ritual humiliations on the citizens of Amritsar. He ordered them to salaam white officers, made lawyers do coolie work and, notoriously, forced passers-by to crawl on their bellies down an offal-strewn lane in which a European woman had been beaten and left for dead. O'Dwyer stopped this but otherwise supported Dyer. He also tried to suppress news of the massacre and its aftermath. Chelmsford connived weakly in the interests of firm government. He was also intimidated by white opinion in India. This was so rabid that a magistrate in Lahore, Malcolm Darling, felt constrained to write to his sister in French about Dyer's "crime contre l'humanité"[72]—when Darling condemned it at the club, fellow members said that he should be court-martialled. In fact some agreed with him that Amritsar had fatally eroded the ethical buttresses of the Raj. Amritsar sapped the superb self-confidence of Englishmen in India, who were accustomed to behave, E. M. Forster noted, as though they were part of an army of occupation. Malcolm Darling, a friend of Forster's who believed that to give three hundred million illiterates independence would be an act of Gadarene folly, nevertheless told the novelist soon after the massacre: "Home Rule is so much in the air, that now the only way is to let them have it."[73]

Montagu vainly attempted to recapture the moral high ground, setting up an official inquiry which duly censured Dyer. In 1920 the House of Commons endorsed that conclusion. Churchill, then war minister, confirmed that Dyer would receive no further military employment and memorably pronounced, "Frightfulness is not a remedy known to the British pharmacopoeia."[74] Montagu stated that the Raj could only be maintained by goodwill. Citing Gibbon, the radical MP Josiah Wedgwood said that the British Empire must not be a stern "replica of the Roman" but should invite all its people to become citizens "on equal terms with ourselves." Such mild opinions did not assuage Indian anger and they provoked bitter parliamentary opposition. Especially virulent were critics who associated conciliation in India with concession in Ireland. But the debate was also tainted by racial prejudice. In the Commons chamber itself Tories gave an "astonishing exhibition" of anti-Semitism, taunting and barracking Montagu, whose speech was said to be "Yiddish in screaming tone and gesture."[75] *The Times* further stated that, as a Jew, he was imbued with "the mental idiom of the East."[76] The *Morning Post* thought that Montagu, not Dyer, should have been in the dock and it serialised *The Protocols of the Elders of Zion,* the infamous forgery describing a Jewish plot to dominate the world. Furthermore, the House of Lords vindicated Dyer—when the Indian Lord Sinha made the case against him one backwoods peer was heard to mutter, "If they are all like him the more they massacre the better."[77] Over £26,000 was raised for Dyer by public subscription. He was presented with a jewelled sword inscribed with the legend "Saviour of the Punjab." When he died in 1927 flowers were laid at the Cenotaph.

If Dyer saved the Punjab, which did subside under the mailed fist, he significantly loosened Britain's grip on the subcontinent as a whole. For Indians saw him as the id of the Raj. The young Jawaharlal Nehru arrived at this view towards the end of 1919 when he happened to share an overnight train from Lahore with the general and several of his staff. Nehru was shocked by Dyer's pyjamas, which he flaunted on Delhi station despite their bright pink stripes, and still more shocked by overhearing his boast that the Jallianwala Bagh "would teach the bloody browns a lesson."[78] Dyer's compatriots, by their sympathy for him, plainly shared his attitude. Nehru concluded that Amritsar was not an isolated incident, as Churchill had maintained. Instead it typified the "brutal and immoral" nature of imperialism, which "had eaten into the soul of the British upper classes."[79] The Nobel Prize–winning poet Rabindranath Tagore used similar language, saying that English souls had been poisoned by the power they wielded in India and that Amritsar "conclusively proved that our true salvation lies in our own hands."[80] Jawaharlal's father, Motilal Nehru, agreed. At a meeting of Congress which condemned Dyer's "demoniac deeds," he had coolly observed that "repression and terrorism have never yet killed the life of a nation."[81] But his blood boiled when he heard how British politicians responded to the official report on the massacre and he wanted to "raise a veritable hell for the rascals."[82]

Gandhi, ever concerned to avoid violence, reacted more cautiously. He did not at once turn Congress into a mass party. And he could not sustain either popular protest or Hindu–Muslim unity. But he did ride the tidal wave of anger over Amritsar, which "shattered the tradition of loyalty" to the Raj[83]—to such an extent that General Lord Rawlinson, appointed in 1920, thought he would be India's last Commander-in-Chief. Gandhi declared that it was essential to change the system which had produced Dyer. He advocated *swadeshi* as urgently as *swaraj,* saying that the spinning wheel (or *charkha,* which he proposed as a motif for the flag of India) was a means of salvation. He even persuaded the Nehru family to burn their western clothes—Jawaharlal was content to cast off his silk underwear but worried about walking around in *swadeshi* socks. Having lost his faith in Britain's good faith, the Mahatma renounced his medals and announced that it was sinful to cooperate with a satanic government. Having cast out fear himself, he inspired acts of disobedience in all sorts and conditions of people—Gokhale had said that Gandhi was "capable of turning heroes out of clay."[84] Among other things, he organised boycotts of the Prince of Wales's 1921 tour, which were quite effective despite government bribes of free food and elephant rides. Although warned by officials and soldiers that India was "no longer a place for a white man,"[85] the future Duke of Windsor thought only a "lunatic" could believe that the "brightest jewel" in the British crown would be lost during his lifetime.[86] Gandhi was obviously a holy fool. Plassey had laid the foundations of the British Empire, he said, but Amritsar had shaken them.

Gallipoli also shook them, according to a legend engendered under the Southern Cross. This maintained that when the Australian and New Zealand Army Corps took part in the assault designed to knock Turkey out of the war in 1915, the convulsions which racked the peninsula rocked the Empire. Antipodeans revolted against British leadership which had done for so many of their comrades, it was said, and colonial independence sprang fully armed from Anzac helmets. Here was a seductive notion. It appealed particularly to radical Australians who had long expressed antagonism towards "the British Vampire" and "the Union Jackals."[87] From late Victorian times the Sydney *Bulletin,* which coined those phrases, had been the prime medium of that hostility. It fostered "violently anti-British" attitudes in the sheep shearer's hut and the gold miner's tent, beside the billabong and under the coolibah tree, and its pink cover was seen as far afield as New Zealand. It spread the derogatory new term "Pommy," a wordplay on pomegranate/immigrant. It scorned John Bull's affected airs and patronising manners, his fondness for frills and gold lace, and his "military spirit"[88]—which turned out to be rum. In the new Commonwealth, where local brand names such as Billy Tea, Boomerang Brandy and Dingo Eucalyptus Oil proved increasingly popular, it inveighed against "Australian groveldom."[89] It stimulated the growing but still often subterranean estrangement from "an effete, poverty-stricken and caste-ridden England."[90] The *Bulletin* also glorified a white Australia, damning the British Empire as "a nigger empire, run by Jews."[91] It championed other populist notions, among them democracy and equality, republicanism and socialism. And it raised the outback nomad, the jolly swagman with his tucker bag and even the defiant bushranger in his cabbage-tree hat, to the status of folk hero—hymned for the ages by Andrew ("Banjo") Paterson and Henry Lawson.

> They tramp in mateship side by side—
> The Protestant and Roman—
> They call no biped lord or sir
> And touch their hat to no man![92]

The ideal of mateship, perhaps originating on the chain gang and eventuating in a spirit of national solidarity, achieved its apotheosis at Gallipoli.

That, at any rate, is a central tenet of the Anzac legend. It was spawned by propaganda at the time and later sustained by Australia's official war historian, Charles Bean, the prime author of Gallipoli hyperbole. Slight, with bespectacled blue eyes and bright red hair that earned him the nickname "Captain Carrot," he witnessed the Gallipoli campaign from the front line and formed an intense admiration for the "Diggers" who fought in it. He shared John Masefield's lyrical opinion that these bronzed giants, who "looked like the kings in old poems,"[93] were the finest body of young men in the world and died as they had lived, owning no master on earth. Bean attributed their virility to the Anglo-Saxon stock from which they sprang and to the wholesome influence of the frontier, which had percolated through to the city men who made up the bulk of the Australian Imperial Force (AIF). He explained their chivalry as a product of the bush creed, which held that "a man should at all times and at any cost stand by his mate." In consequence of this they exhibited an "unsurpassable heroism."[94] From the courage and sacrifice of ordinary Australians, Bean concluded, the "nation came to know itself."[95] By the same token, many New Zealanders believed, their own country discovered its unique identity.

From the start journalistic snipers shot holes in this creation myth and subsequently academic big guns tried to blow it to pieces. Charles Bean was deemed a "brilliant myth-maker,"[96] whose history, for all its ability, humanity and integrity, presented the Anzacs in a rose-tinted light. Often emollient and sometimes evasive, it dramatised their valour and ennobled their suffering. Bean exaggerated the "breezy egalitarianism of the 'Digger' officers,"[97] which supposedly fostered resourcefulness and teamwork that could not be matched by slum-bred Tommies under the command of monocled and moustached toffs. It was impossible to sustain Bean's argument that military virtuosity was the natural product of "an open society":[98] German soldiers, shaped by a state far more hierarchical than Britain, were generally agreed to be the best in the world.

Moreover, it was easy to show that before, during and after the war most Australians and New Zealanders were devoted to the Empire. They prided themselves on their common blood and culture. They cherished the political ties, commercial links and martial bonds that united them with the mother country. They intoned Tennyson's line, "One life, one flag, one fleet, one throne"—the motto of the Imperial Federation League, not yet desecrated by the Nazi slogan. They also believed that the Empire had a single destiny. A model imperial patriot was the Australian journalist John Adey, who noted that Thornycroft's statue of Boadicea bore Cowper's famous lines:

> Regions Caesar never knew,
> Thy posterity shall sway.

An overseas descendant of Boadicea, wrote Adey, "is not an Englishman perhaps; but he is something greater—he is an Empire man, one of the children of silence and slow time, returned in the eternal cycle to worship at this shrine. It is his." Worship implied fealty. In case of war Australia's watchword would be, said Liberal Prime Minister Alfred Deakin, "The Empire, right or wrong." When his Labor successor, Andrew Fisher, told W. T. Stead in 1911 that were Britain to involve Australia in an unjust war "we should have to haul down the Union Jack,"[99] he was forced to eat his words. Thus in 1914 the Antipodes eagerly answered Britannia's call and volunteers rushed to the colours, as they did again in 1939. Then the Gallipoli spirit was once more invoked. It inspired empire loyalty in both Australia and New Zealand, which were, according to the likes of Billy Hughes, as much a part of Britain as was Middlesex.

What truth is there in the fecund Anzac mythology and how do conflicting views about Gallipoli square up to the evidence? From its inception the entire venture was an imperial tragedy. Imaginative, ambitious and rash, it bore the unmistakable hallmarks of its empire-minded champion, First Lord of the Admiralty Winston Churchill. He was appalled by the spectacle of Allied soldiers chewing barbed wire in Flanders. As an alternative to the western stalemate he conjured up an eastern expedition, Homeric in hero- ism and Napoleonic in scope. Churchill proposed to seize the Golden Horn, unite the Balkans, join forces with Russia and outflank the Central Powers on a continental scale. At first he urged that ships alone could blast their way through the Dardanelles—the ancient Hellespont, which led to the city founded by Constantine at the confluence of Europe and Asia as "an eternal monument of the glories of his reign."[100] With characteristic perti- nacity Churchill even persuaded doubting admirals to support the plan: Jackie Fisher, the First Sea Lord, later complained that Winston had "miasma-ed" him. But mines sank several battleships, whose bombardment of the Gallipoli forts merely warned the Turks of Allied intentions. Kitch- ener nevertheless agreed to send troops, British, Indian and Anzac. To com- mand them he appointed General Sir Ian Hamilton, a lean, courageous paladin of many conflicts—a Boer bullet had shattered his left hand at Majuba Hill. An unusually progressive and articulate soldier, Hamilton had literary aspirations and Kitchener once described him as a "bloody poet."[101] Thus he appreciated the trials of Xerxes, who briefly bridged the Helles- pont, and the tribulations of Agamemnon, who spent "ten long years in tak- ing Troy."[102] But, awed by his basilisk-eyed chief, Hamilton never demanded sufficient resources to carry out what was then the largest amphibious invasion in history. Instead of exerting a grip on the battle he lamented the plight of his soldiers in purple passages. After Rupert Brooke's death en route to Gallipoli he wrote that God had "started a celestial spring cleaning, and our star is to be scrubbed bright with the blood of our bravest and our best."[103] Hamilton underestimated the enemy, essayed no new tac- tics, made suggestions instead of giving orders, and remained both literally and metaphorically at sea.

The Anzacs, whose first convoy had docked at Alexandria in December 1914, got an introduction to the British high command during their training in Egypt. General Godley instructed his New Zealanders that the Egyptians belonged to "races lower in the human scale" than the Maoris and that "the slightest familiarity with them will breed contempt."[104] The New Zealan- ders proved more tractable than the Australians, who refused to salute supercilious staff officers and so wallowed in the fleshpots of Egypt that they allegedly turned Cairo into a "vaudeville of devils."[105] The Anzacs' training consisted mainly of long marches in the desert, as if to fit them for another fight on the veldt rather than for trench combat. Further war games they regarded as "a pure farce and an insult to our intelligence."[106] Security was so lax that letters were addressed to "The Constantinople Expeditionary

Force" and the *Egyptian Gazette* helpfully confirmed that this was their destination. One transport bore the chalked inscription "TO CONSTANTINOPLE AND THE HAREM."[107] In the early hours of 25 April 1915, apparently confused by the strong Aegean current and the dark coastline, the Royal Navy took the Anzacs to the wrong place, opposite a headland on the western waist of the Gallipoli peninsula christened Hell Spit. The troops of the 3rd Brigade, wearing pea-soup khaki uniforms (brass buttons and rising sun badges oxidised to black), green webbing packs, pouches and belts, and wide-brimmed felt hats, held their breath as the crammed picket boats slid through the velvet night and over the satin sea. Nothing showed except gleaming eyes and splashes of phosphorescence at the bows. But the Turks were awake. When the boats grounded on the shingle they unleashed a firestorm. It killed so many Australians as they struggled ashore that, "looking down at the bottom of the sea, you could see a carpet of dead men."

The survivors faced an unexpected line of cliffs. They clawed their way upwards in a hail of lead, waving their bayonets, "berserk with fury"[108] and "'cooeeing' like mad."[109] As dawn broke knots of Anzacs breasted the first ridge and scattered the two companies of Turks confronting them, a feat which, according to the Rev. W. H. Fitchett, author of *Deeds that Won the Empire*, surpassed in daring that of Wellington's troops at Waterloo. Then they plunged into a labyrinth of which they had no conception. Neither officers' coloured maps, which were of Crimean War vintage, nor the guidebooks bought in Egypt to supplement them, gave an accurate picture of a terrain which seemed to have suffered an epileptic fit. It was a convulsive jumble of jagged hills and crooked valleys, crisscrossed by razor-backed spurs and knife-edged ravines, all covered with a thick pelt of prickly scrub. Here was a landscape that seemed to have been devised by nature for defence and the Turks took full advantage of it. They were ably commanded by General Liman von Sanders—Germany so dominated its Turkish ally that wits quipped, "Deutschland über Allah."[110] And General Mustapha Kemal, who went on to rule and modernise Turkey, combined efficiency with ruthlessness. On 25 April he famously told his men: "I do not expect you to attack, I order you to die."[111] So the Turks clung to the high ground and pinned down the Anzacs in a four-hundred-acre triangle of tortured soil whose apex was never as much as a mile from the sea. Within a matter of hours the British commander, General William Birdwood, was considering disembarkation. For the virgin Anzacs had experienced not just a triumphant baptism of fire but a traumatic loss of military innocence. As the British official historian wrote, "a disturbing number of leaderless men" soon began to quit the front line, searching for food, drink and rest, or helping wounded mates.[112] Whether they were "stragglers" or "shirkers," their dereliction of duty undermined the myth quickly put into circulation that "Anzac troops did magnificently against amazing odds."[113] Certainly Birdwood feared a fiasco.[114] But Sir Ian Hamilton thought it better to resist than to be butchered on the beach like the fleeing Persians at Marathon. He told the Anzacs to dig in for their lives. Overnight the invasion became a siege. Hamilton, conveyed to the eastern Mediterranean in a vessel named HMS *Foresight,* had prepared for a Turkey shoot, a revised version of colonial conflict. Instead, he got a pocket edition of Flanders.

During the first week, the Anzacs suffered 8,100 casualties, 2,300 of them killed. As the fierce struggle for position began to subside, young soldiers who had expected the war to resemble a game of rugby learned the grim rules of attrition. They were showered with shrapnel which landed "as thickly as plums in a pudding."[115] They were pulverised with high explosive—so insistent was the shriek of shells that cuckoos changed their note in response to it. The Anzacs were relentlessly sniped and sapped, bullets flying so densely that they shaved the scrub bare, mines turning their trenches into cemeteries. Sudden death on this scale seemed all the more incongruous amid the weird beauty of Gallipoli: the clouds of brilliantly coloured butterflies, the song of larks, the scent of wild thyme, the carpets of magenta flowers, the sapphire sea dotted with steel-grey leviathans, the golden dawns above the fields of Troy, the crimson sunsets over snow-capped Samothrace. Macabre incidents punctuated the conflict: a direct hit on a dentist's dugout sowed an entire hillside with false teeth; a corpse leaning against a rock on Anzac Beach so deceived snipers that they had encircled its skull with "a silvery halo of lead."[116] The beach was a perpetual target. As narrow as a cricket pitch, it was so crammed with mules, men, ammunition and stores that it looked like "a gigantic shipwreck."[117] A rookery of bivouacs pitted the cliff face. But these "funk holes" gave little more than psychological protection and they often turned into premature graves.

Australians, even more than New Zealanders, became demoralised by the squalor and monotony of trench life. They hated the filth, the lice and the maggots spawned by acres of corpses. They complained of thirst assuaged by "fly tea," hunger alleviated by "fly stew"[118] and the resulting "gyppy tummy," sometimes known as the "Gallipoli gallop." They choked on the stench of death, which was almost tangible, said Compton Mackenzie, and "clammy as the membrane of a bat's wing."[119] There were frequent instances of desertion, self-mutilation, "cowardice and treachery." Charles Bean himself privately acknowledged that "our force contains more bad hats than the others."[120] In the opinion of a British colonel, George Napier Johnston, whose unpublished diary has recently come to light, all the Anzac soldiers lacked stamina. He attributed this to affluence, good living and racial deterioration.

> New Zealanders and Australians don't last well. They are going sick by hundreds, much of it due to wanting to get away. I believe it to be the characteristic of overseas troops that when the show was new and when they had to justify all the boasting they were guilty of, they did well. But it needs men of sterner stuff to last month after month on the same food, living in trenches in heat, dust, flies, dysentery, diarrhoea. But it should be done: this is where one's race shows its superiority over others.

Johnston's diary is full of such censure. He deplored Anzac "indiscipline, wasteful habits and bad conduct." And he was appalled by the brutal way in which they stripped dead comrades of money and other valuables: "The Australians are the biggest culprits in this respect—they are very callous." Despite all this, he thought that the Anzacs were the best soldiers the Allies had. They "would be very hard to beat in a straight out-and-out fight" and they possessed incomparable "pluck" under fire.[121]

This they demonstrated daily on Anzac Beach. There the convention was established that "no one must pay heed to shell fire even by so much as turning a head"—though it was permissible to pause when a large projectile landed and call it a bastard. A British officer from the Western Front reckoned that such disregard for the torrent of shrapnel was "absolute madness." According to Charles Bean, however, the Australians, who lost a higher proportion of troops than any other Allied contingent, saw it as a "natural expression of the men's self-respect."[122] So was the Anzacs' most famous exploit, bathing amid flying metal and rotting flesh—the sea was full of dead mules floating on their backs, whose legs were sometimes mistaken for submarine periscopes. The freemasonry of the nude encouraged Antipodean irreverence, even towards Birdwood. "Duck, you silly old dill," one soldier shouted as a shell screamed over the water.[123] Observing the general's pot belly, another exclaimed: "My bloody oath mate, you 'ave been among the biscuits."[124] Such familiarity, wrote a British war correspondent, would have caused "apoplexy at Aldershot."[125] But Birdwood took it in his stride, currying favour with the Anzacs in the hope of forming them into a separate army which he would command. He believed, too, that rigid military discipline might inhibit the individual initiative and mutual assistance which produced such an outstanding battlefield performance.

There were frequent encores as Hamilton, eager to justify his optimistic communiqués, tried to break the deadlock in the several Allied beachheads gouged from the flanks and foot of Gallipoli. For example, the British had secured a toehold on Cape Helles at hideous cost—corpses covered the shore like a shoal of stranded fish and fifty yards from the land the sea was stained red with blood. Here, on 8 May 1915, Australian troops were ordered to make a frontal attack on the Turkish trenches. A British major described their charge with the kind of rhetorical afflatus which the Great War itself eventually exploded.

> The enemy's shelling was shifted on to them in one great concentration of hell. The machine-guns bellowed and poured on them sheets of flame and of ragged death, buried them alive. They were disembowelled. Their clothing caught fire, and their flesh hissed and cooked before the burning rags could be torn off or beaten out. But what of it? Why, nothing! They were as devils from a hell bigger and hotter. Nothing could stop them. They were at home in hell-fire, and they caressed it back when it licked and caressed them. They laughed at it; they sang through it. Their pluck was titanic. They were not men, but gods, demons infuriated. We saw them fall by the score. But what of that? Not for one breath did the great line waver or break.[126]

Later in the same month the Turks themselves demonstrated the futility of these tactics. As they stormed forward the Anzacs shot them down in thousands, saying that it was better than a wallaby drive. Nevertheless, Hamilton and his generals, sometimes abetted by Anzac officers, persevered with such attacks. The consequences were invariably disastrous, but the Anzacs took it in their stride. In one race over poppy-strewn no-man's-land, a member of the Canterbury Battalion pictured rugby players on Christchurch park "who might be playing the game of life here with . . . rifles and bayonets for weapons, and freedom for the goal."[127] Feats of astonishing courage were commonplace. Men who had one hand blown off threw grenades with the other. One private, as he was being carried from the front line with half his face shot away, tried to sing "Tipperary." Another reported to the doctors after months of pain that he was having a little trouble, which turned out to be dysentery, a fractured arm, two bullets in the thigh and bullet wounds in the stomach. Seeing a batch of wounded men, some terribly mutilated, others plainly dying, but all with a "stiff upper lip," Hamilton wrote: "In fullest splendour the soul shines out amidst the dark shadows of adversity."[128]

This brand of uplift sounded increasingly fatuous to soldiers who had endured medical services that gave trench warfare an extra dimension of horror. Their disenchantment was summed up in an exchange between a transport vessel bringing in fresh troops and a hospital ship taking wounded from Gallipoli. As they passed the new boys shouted in unison, "Are we downhearted?" After a pause, a single croak sounded across the water: "You bloody soon will be."[129] To Anzacs (and others) Gallipoli seemed a gigantic mincing machine. And those who put them through it did not hide their readiness to purchase victory at a high price in mangled flesh and crushed bone. For all the cheery pieties uttered by British commanders, many of them thought that an acceptance of heavy losses was a test of their military virility. "Casualties?" exclaimed General Hunter-Weston, eyes flashing, moustache bristling, aquiline nose quivering. "What do I care for casualties?"[130] When Anzacs told another senior British officer that they could not bury putrescent corpses in front of their trenches because men got killed in the attempt, he shocked them by replying: "What is a few men?"[131] Such carelessness with lives compounded the consistent failure of the British high command at Gallipoli. Australians joked that the red-tabbed staff officers planning military mayhem on their Greek island headquarters would receive three clasps on their war ribbons, "for Imbros, Mudros and Chaos."[132] Doctors who witnessed unnecessary suffering and death caused by inept medical arrangements were less indulgent. One wrote that the generals responsible should be incarcerated in a "Hospital for senility."[133]

No one did more to publicise British bungling than Keith Murdoch, a brash, ambitious Australian journalist who was described by Maurice Hankey as "a horrible scab."[134] His revelations caused a sensation because of the tight censorship imposed at Gallipoli by intelligence officers such as Colonel Tyrrell, who thought that a properly organised government "does not need war correspondents" but should tell the people anything conducive to victory, whether truth or lies.[135] But Murdoch achieved the remarkable feat of grossly exaggerating the culpability of the British top brass; and his son Rupert, the media magnate, continues to claim that by raising the matter he "got our boys out of Gallipoli."[136] In fact, they were evacuated because almost everyone except Winston Churchill came to the conclusion during the summer and autumn of 1915 that the campaign was, in Lord Cromer's words, a "colossal blunder."[137] Hardly better, it seems, was the overarching strategy. Even if the Allies had marched in triumph to Constantinople they stood little or no chance of taking Europe from the rear— Germany itself won in the east and lost in the west. As one veteran of the Dardanelles said, war produces two kinds of muddle: the "Ordinary Military Cock Up" (OMCU) and the "Inextricable Balls Up" (IBU).[138] In every respect apart from the final withdrawal, conducted with stealth and speed at the end of the year, Gallipoli was an IBU. The campaign cost the lives of

21,255 Britons, 10,000 Frenchmen, 8,709 Australians and 2,701 New Zealanders. For all the drum-beating about the Anzacs' contribution, there is no escaping the fact that they played a subsidiary role in a peripheral field of conflict.

It is also clear that the war was not won by glorious failure in a sideshow but by success gained at unimaginable cost in the main theatre of operations. The torment the Anzacs suffered at Gallipoli did not compare with their prolonged agony in France, where six times as many of them were killed. A single hour of the battle at Pozières subjected them to greater stress than "the whole of the Gallipoli campaign,"[139] as Charles Bean later acknowledged—though at the time he told the public that they went through the German barrage "as you would go through a summer shower."[140] Lieutenant Alec Raws, a newspaperman in civilian life who was killed in 1916, vividly described the bloodbath at Pozières: the tornado of bursting shells, the mad shambles of no-man's-land, the shock of being buried alive amid corpses in all stages of decay. "I saw strong men who had been through Gallipoli sobbing and trembling as with ague," wrote Raws, "men who had never turned a hair before."[141] In the face of this dazing and deafening experience the Anzacs became ever more cynical about their British commanders. As shells exploded all round him one corporal wrote, "I have seen things here that will make the bloody military aristocrats' name stink for ever."[142] Birdwood roused especial ire, pontificating about the Anzacs' eagerness to drub the Huns and then sending them on further suicidal missions. Disillusioned survivors declared that their mates had been "murdered" through the "incompetence, callousness and personal vanity of those high in authority."[143] Such views, repeated and refined, acted as a slow poison in the heart of the imperial relationship.

Ardent empire loyalist though he was, Billy Hughes provided no antidote. Indeed, he divided opinion in Australia and split his own Labor Party over the issue of conscription. William Morris Hughes was a hyperactive dyspeptic who lived on little but tea, toast and tomato sauce. He looked like a wizened gnome. To a portrait painter who said that he would try to do him justice, Hughes replied: "I don't want justice, I want mercy."[144] But the spirit of a warrior animated that puny frame. When he visited the Anzacs in France they joked that Australia had sent its last man; yet, as General Birdwood noted, Hughes "gives orders like a centurion."[145] The "Little Digger," as he was nicknamed, had fought his way up from humble Welsh origins via trade union work on the Sydney docks. He called everyone "brother" but won the Premiership (1915–23) thanks to a despotic will, an acerbic wit and a Machiavellian guile. Hughes also possessed a ferocious capacity for invective, rapping out insults in a harsh, metallic voice that stunned his enemies, one of whom, he said, had "abandoned the finer resources of political assassination and resorted to the bludgeon of the cannibal."[146] Like Lloyd George, whom he in some ways resembled, Hughes sacrificed his radical principles on the altar of the war god. He repressed dissenters, imposed censorship and promoted xenophobia. Thus Australians shunned lager and frankfurters. They also changed names such as German Creek (to Empire Vale) and Mount Bismarck, which (like Berlin, Ontario) was rechristened Kitchener. Hughes insisted that Australia—white Australia—could only be free if it was part of a victorious British Empire. It must therefore mobilise all available men. Those opposed to conscription—trade unionists, Irish Catholics (incensed by Britain's execution of leaders of Dublin's Easter Rising) and most Australians fighting in France—said that he wanted to send his compatriots overseas in order to import cheap Asiatic labour. They won both referendums on the issue, in 1916 and 1917, with a slogan that was deeply subversive to imperial solidarity: "Put Australia First."

Paradoxically, Hughes did just that in the counsels of the Empire and the councils of the nations. Remaining leader of a national coalition at home despite his double defeat, he asserted himself abroad. Indeed, Hughes became so aggressively imperialist that he sounded like the spokesman of a separate and not altogether friendly power; or like an outback prophet, the voice of one crying in the spinifex. He disparaged dull-witted British generals and insisted that the mother country should treat Australia as an ally instead of an auxiliary. He demanded a Monroe Doctrine for the Pacific and forged new diplomatic ties with the United States, warning that Japan might change sides in the next war. After the Great War Hughes obtained independent representation for Australia (as did the other dominions) at the Paris Peace Conference.

Here he ridiculed the vapourings of visionary conciliators such as Woodrow Wilson, calling him the "Heaven-born"[147] and being himself dubbed by the President "a pestiferous varmint."[148] Hughes tried to extort large indemnities from Germany and to impose Anglo-Saxon control over its Pacific colonies. He did obtain an Australian mandate over German New Guinea, though when Wilson asked if the natives would have access to missionaries Hughes assured him that they would because as it was "these poor devils do not get half enough . . . to eat."[149] But the distribution of Far Eastern spoils became a bone of contention between Hughes and Lloyd George, who felt bound to honour British pledges to Japan. Eventually the two Prime Ministers began to abuse each other in Welsh. It must have been an odd sort of altercation since Hughes apparently spoke little of that language and skilfully manipulated his deaf aid, an "electric ear trumpet," to cut out remarks he did not wish to hear. But Lloyd George fumed that he would not be bullied by "a damned little Welshman."[150] Hughes was equally abrasive about the League of Nations. Supported by Sir William Massey, the New Zealand Premier, he helped quash the Japanese proposal to include a clause enshrining racial equality in its covenant. Sooner than agree to it, Hughes vouchsafed, he would appear naked in the Folies-Bergère. But while denying claims based on Japan's war effort, he championed those of Australia, whose sixty thousand dead entitled it to enter the family of nations on a footing of equality. By the same token, during the next decade or so, the white dominions attained formal equality and autonomy within the imperial framework. Thanks to Anzac prowess, Hughes declared, Australians had "put on the toga of manhood."[151]

They did not immediately or completely cast off the garments of tutelage. For another generation Australians and, still more, New Zealanders clung to the mother country's leading strings, especially in the sphere of foreign policy. Indeed, as late as 1975, when a Governor-General ousted a Prime Minister, the novelist Patrick White could complain that his "supposedly sophisticated country is still, alas, a colonial sheep-run."[152] In many ways Gallipoli strengthened empire loyalties in the years between the two global conflicts. The iconography of Antipodean war memorials is particularly telling. Most paid tribute to an imperial oblation which included the national offering: thus classical obelisks outnumbered Digger statues, laurel wreaths were more common than fern leaves, and inscriptions showed that "independent Australians were still Britons."[153] So, more fervently, were New Zealanders. The memorial on Brooklyn Hill overlooking Wellington bore a typical sentiment: "The Motherland called, and they came."[154] Similarly, Anzac Day was celebrated as Australia's most sacred festival in the context of Greater Britain. In Victoria on the first anniversary of the Gallipoli landings an archiepiscopal pronouncement, no less, established that Australia, formerly a distant settlement in the southern seas, was now "a real part of the Empire."[155]

On the other hand, the Anzac myth contained sufficient truth and strength to generate purely nationalist emotion, especially among radicals. It became a commonplace to declare that Australia was born again at Gallipoli, a new nation created in a spirit of sacrifice and redeemed by the blood of martyrs. New Zealand, too, was said to have experienced a blessed nativity, discovered an independent character and received an irresistible impulse towards national consciousness. Its people had now matured into "Kiwis" and, according to one Methodist chaplain, "the average man is not an Imperialist because New Zealand had been treated, not as a partner, but as a child."[156] The two Antipodean dominions now had their own military traditions. They had a self-respect that matched the disdain, sometimes alloyed with bitterness, which many felt for British leadership. They had heroes whose gallantry deserved to be hailed, as Compton Mackenzie had said, not in headlines but hexameters. They had feats of arms to their credit which were not always properly appreciated by the mother country—the most bizarre tribute, to the sailors of HMAS *Sydney* which sank the German cruiser *Emden,* was paid by the imperialist versifier Sir Henry Newbolt:

> Their hearts were hot, and, as they shot
> They sang like kangaroos.[157]

Australia and New Zealand were increasingly apt to contrast their own advance with British decline. They compared the achievements of the Anzacs in the glad confident morning of their initiation to those of stunted, spiritless Tommies and their snobbish, nonchalant officers and came to accept Bean's view that their own force possessed a "unity of spirit almost impossible under a more feudal tradition."[158] They detected in the old country a pervasive air of decadence. The seed of alienation had been sown and it grew as Britain's power withered. By the late 1920s Billy Hughes himself considered that the splendid glow which the British Empire cast on the earth reflected not its noon-day greatness but the fading hues of sunset. He was not alone in thinking that the "United States is destined to assume the hegemony of the world of tomorrow."[159]

The rise of the American empire was watched with particular alarm in Canada. Between the confederation of 1867 and the outbreak of the Great War its own population barely doubled, to eight million, whereas by 1914 the United States could boast nearly one hundred million citizens. After the Civil War, moreover, Americans went west so swiftly that in less than three decades the young historian Frederick Jackson Turner was able to declare an end to the golden age of expansion from sea to shining sea. But could the great republic, now poised to become an imperial power, open a new frontier to the north? Most Americans continued to think of the whole region above the forty-ninth parallel—when they thought of it at all—as a glacial wilderness. In 1869 the Ottawa government bought the vast central tract known as Rupert's Land from the Hudson's Bay Company for a mere

£300,000 (plus additional territory). Canada was a corpse shrouded in snow. There was no point in capturing it, said one U.S. army commander: "New York is worth a hundred Canadas."[160]

On the other hand, the empty immensity of *The Great Lone Land,* as Wolseley's protégé William Butler famously called it in 1872, offered limitless potential. Canada's mineral wealth might eclipse the treasure of the Yukon. Its forests darkened the earth and their clearance was expected to produce not only enormous profit but a warmer climate. (The authority for this unscientific notion was Edward Gibbon, who said that Germany, on the same latitude as Canada, had become "more temperate"[161] since Roman days because of the destruction of its canopy of trees.) Canada contained oceans of grass, which had sustained huge herds of buffalo, now fast being annihilated along with the plains Indians who lived in symbiosis with them. To Butler and others it seemed "impossible that the wave of life which rolls so unceasingly into America can leave unoccupied this great fertile tract."[162] Canadians averse to the French connection occasionally mooted an Anglo-Saxon reunification in North America. And sometimes Uncle Sam seemed keen to extend his bony reach to the Pole. That the "blue-bellied" Yankees, having defeated the Confederacy, might set their sights on the Confederation, whose red-coated North West Mounted Police were only a symbolic deterrent, appeared most likely before Canada completed its transcontinental railway in 1885. The opening of an American line just south of the border, a U.S. Senate committee had reported in 1869, would seal the fate of "British possessions west of the ninety-first meridian. They will become so Americanised in interests and feelings that they will be in effect severed from the new Dominion." Annexation would then be only "a question of time."[163] So the Canadian Pacific Railway was much more than a gigantic commercial enterprise and a prodigious feat of engineering. It was a first line of defence. It was an exercise in nation building, an endeavour to bind together all British territories in North America with "sinews of iron."[164]

The Conservative Prime Minister Sir John Macdonald inaugurated the project in 1871 specifically to secure the entry of British Columbia into the Confederation. The fifty thousand inhabitants of this far western colony were immured behind the mighty barricade of the Rocky Mountains and, hungry Americans boasted, "sandwiched" between Alaska and Idaho.[165] Macdonald, a flamboyant figure with silver-topped cane and fur-collared coat who talked like a Highland laird and drank like a railroad navvy, promised British Columbians a steel highway to Ottawa by 1883. In view of the stupendous financial and geographical obstacles, this smacked more of alcoholic delirium than national dream. All too soon the railway was bedevilled by a series of false starts, cash crises, disputes, scandals and setbacks. In 1873, for example, Macdonald himself lost office for five years when stolen documents revealed that the company bidding to build the railway had contributed lavishly to his party's election expenses. Not until 1881, when a new consortium appointed William Van Horne to manage the undertaking, did the Canadian Pacific build up a full head of steam.

Born in an Illinois log cabin, Van Horne owed his promotion to an irresistible combination of energy, ability and brute strength. In body he came to resemble King Edward VII but in character he was "a first-class tyrant."[166] His sceptre was a foot-long cigar and his cobalt-blue eyes seemed to bore into minions like a Burleigh rock drill. No one else could have so brilliantly commanded the twenty-thousand-strong army of labourers, teamsters, muleteers, blacksmiths, loggers, carpenters, bridge-builders, engineers, surveyors, cooks, clerks, dispatchers, trainmen, telegraphists and operatives of all sorts required to girdle the continent. Among this human "refuse," wrote one of Van Horne's lieutenants, were "some of the worst cut throats and thieves I ever met."[167] They were especially given to mayhem when sold whisky by illicit traders, whose brew was "a mixture of blue ruin, chain lightning, strychnine, the curse of God and old rye."[168] Yet the advance of Van Horne's legions was likened to General Sherman's march to the sea. The discipline and drive owed much to the skill and experience of his construction supervisors and gang bosses, many of whom were American. Much of the capital that kept the enterprise on the rails also came from the United States, and from Great Britain—which supplied, too, most of the rails. In fact, Canada's national lifeline owed its existence to international endeavour.

This irony counted for nothing as the Canadian Pacific Railway (CPR) embarked on its titanic struggle with the forces of nature. The first great barrier was the Canadian Shield itself, that pre-Cambrian carapace of gneiss and granite that stretches down to the tempestuous shores of Lake Superior. The earth's most ancient armour, this hard, grey, ridged rock presented Van Horne with "200 miles of engineering impossibilities." For months his men blasted their way through it using three tons of dynamite a day and causing many fatal accidents. Next they faced a three-hundred-mile tract of sphagnum bog, guarded by walls of black flies and mosquitoes which (according to Butler) made the insects of India seem almost benign. The muskeg, as this marshland was called, devoured locomotives at a gulp and could have ingested the entire CPR. It also swallowed mountains of gravel and ballast while remaining so spongy that the line was liable to undulate or sink. Next came the prairie, an arid expanse white with buffalo bones—the CPR took the less fertile southerly route, probably to fend off competition above and below the border. Every stick, plank, sleeper and telegraph pole had to be hauled from Winnipeg into this 850-mile-wide steppe along a causeway created by the excavation of ten million cubic yards of earth. So did every rail, spike, fishplate and load of provisions—a logistical operation to baffle any general. But assembly-line organisation caused the steel to roll westwards at nearly three and a half miles each day. Its progress reminded Father Albert Lacombe of "a flight of wild geese cleaving the sky."[169]

The Blackfoot people, to whom this black-robed Oblate ministered, believed that beyond the "Mountains of the Setting Sun"[170] lay paradise. Van Horne might have agreed as he strove to thread his way through the monstrous cordillera at speed—before the CPR was engulfed by bankruptcy. The route, via the Kicking Horse and Rogers Passes, was serpentine, precipitous and choked by an icy jungle. Temperatures fell below minus 30 degrees, when metal burned flesh and boiling tea froze as it was drunk; and rails laid in these conditions expanded and buckled as the weather warmed. Sometimes forest fires halted the work. Sometimes the track was buried under thirty feet of snow. Million-ton avalanches thundered down at a hundred miles an hour, generating their own cyclones and reducing cheap trestle bridges and timber viaducts to matchwood. Many workers perished during the final push, including a disproportionate number of Chinese. Tradition has it that each foot of railroad built through the Fraser Canyon cost a coolie's life—a gross exaggeration though, since Chinese did not count, their deaths were not counted. Finally, as the sign erected at Craigellachie announced: "Here on Nov. 7, 1885, a plain iron spike welded East to West."[171]

That legend commemorates a political achievement to match the stupendous human effort. Macdonald's feat of nation creation through railway construction ranked with those of Bismarck, Cavour and Grant. This is not to suggest that the CPR was anything other than a commercial venture. It was founded to make money, as Van Horne acknowledged, "and for no other purpose under the sun."[172] It profited spectacularly once the line was complete. The CPR ruthlessly exploited its government grant of twenty-five million acres. It sprouted branch lines. It diversified into luxury steamships and grand hotels resembling medieval castles and French châteaux. It promoted tourism in the "Canadian Alps," urging its customers to see this world before they saw the next.[173] However, the main result of the railway's economic success was to people the prairies. By 1911 the CPR had brought in 1.3 million inhabitants, which could not have been accomplished by squealing Red River ox carts lashed together with shaganappi, strips of buf-

falo hide used in lieu of expensive nails. New habitations burgeoned beside
the trail of the iron horse.

At first they were shantytowns apparently "laid out on designs made by a
colony of muskrats."[174] Soon they expanded in size and civic dignity. Winnipeg, which had attracted the CPR with concessions amounting to bribes
and flourished with the Edwardian wheat boom, resembled "a great mushroom sprung up in the night out of the prairie."[175] Regina, "a double-barrelled
forty-horse-power fool of a name"[176] chosen by the Governor-General's wife
Lady Lorne (Queen Victoria's daughter) to replace the coarse appellation
Pile O' Bones, rose to become the capital of Saskatchewan. A street of
shacks in 1885, Calgary "grows while you watch it," wrote an English visitor
in 1910, noting that the Canadian Pacific was "willing to give 'ready made
farms'" to suitable British settlers.[177] Vancouver, which granted the CPR
6,458 acres in the heart of the future city, thrived as its western railhead. By
creating, linking and developing such centres, the Canadian Pacific realised
Macdonald's vision of transforming the dominion from a "geographical
expression" into "one great united country with a large inter-provincial
trade and a common interest."[178] It is true that the Prime Minister, like most
of his compatriots, regarded the transcontinental connection as an "Imperial Highway." It was an "All-Red" route linking the mother country to the
Antipodes.[179] However, the further Canada travelled towards the terminus
of full nationhood the more prone it was to diverge from the line of empire.
Macdonald himself, though he always honoured the Crown and saluted
the Union Jack, put Canada first when it came to assisting in the rescue
of General Gordon and raising a national tariff barrier. Imperial federation
was a will-'o-the-wisp beside a Canadian Confederation forged with blood
and iron.

Of course, confederation was anything but complete. Regional differences were acute and not until 1949 did Newfoundland, Britain's oldest
colony, become Canada's last province. Moreover, immigration added to the
diversity of the dominion, making it more like South Africa than Australia
or New Zealand, where the white population was nearly all of British stock.
In 1870 a quarter of Canada's population spoke with an Irish accent—
despite the Emerald Isle's reputation for lack of industry, said William Butler, it manufactured nations. Among subsequent settlers were Icelanders,
Jews and German-speaking Mennonites from the Ukraine. Their numbers
were later swollen by Scandinavians and East Europeans, many fleeing from
the Cossack knout and the Habsburg yoke. Anglo-Saxon critics characterised them as the "scum and dregs of the old world."[180] But the "stalwart
peasant in a sheepskin coat,"[181] to employ the phrase coined by Canada's

Minister of the Interior, proved his worth as a pioneer. The bitter cold, the sod hut and the peat fire held no terrors for him. He and his ilk were used to back-breaking toil. Doukhobors (Russian nonconformist Christians) who lacked horses thought nothing of harnessing a score of their women to the plough. Many of the million Britons who moved to Canada in the decade before the Great War seemed feeble by comparison. Farms in what was advertised as "The Last Best West" often displayed signs on their gates saying, "No Englishman need apply." Some who could not find jobs drifted into Canada's growing urban slums and became a "drain on public relief moneys."[182] The mother country was mortified.

Eminent Edwardians, from General Baden-Powell to General Booth (founder of the Salvation Army), set up training schemes to prepare the "depraved and destitute" of British cities for the regenerative experience of tilling the virgin prairie.[183] These were works of practical imperialism designed to strengthen Canada as a member of the extended British family. Doubtless they had some effect. Probably they helped to reinforce Canadians' sense of themselves as virile "new Britons" tempered by frontier and climate.[184] This was a chilly version of Antipodean folklore about the saving power of the wilderness. The idea was that decadence blossomed in the warm south whereas long winter nights encouraged a wholesome fecundity. As Joseph Howe said, "Large, vigorous, healthy families spring from feather beds in which Jack Frost compels people to lie close."[185] Canadians identified with Gibbon's "hardy children of the North," with robust backwoodsmen like the Teutonic Cimbri who, "by way of amusement, often slid down mountains of snow on their broad shields."[186] Yet such transplanted Britons, having bidden "farewell to feudalism" in the old country, inevitably aspired to "perfect independence" in the New World.[187] Moreover, the advent of so many aliens, nearly all Protestants who became part of Anglophone society, widened the great national schism. French Canadians, themselves deemed to be descendants of rugged northern Gauls, felt threatened by the influx. Despite their high birth rate, it reduced them, as a proportion of the population, to just over a quarter. As a result they fought all the more fiercely for political and cultural survival. Their existence depended on resistance to the integration of Canada as a nation.

Wilfrid Laurier, the handsome curly-haired lawyer who in 1896 became the country's first French-Canadian Prime Minister, sought unity in diversity. "My object is to consolidate Confederation, and to bring our people long estranged from each other, gradually to become a nation," he wrote. "This is the supreme issue. Everything else is subordinate to that idea."[188] To realise the idea Laurier had to perform a tightrope act worthy of Blondin over Niagara. Thus he revived the Liberal Party while mollifying Quebec's Roman Catholic bishops, who still itched to damn it as the spawn of Beelzebub. He expressed pride in the Empire while politely obstructing, for the sake of Canadian autonomy, British attempts to centralise it. In 1897 he frustrated Chamberlain's endeavour to set up an Imperial Council, accepting instead the more intermittent Imperial Conference. But he played a prominent part in the Diamond Jubilee procession, wearing the cocked hat, gold-frogged tunic and white silk stockings of a Privy Councillor and sporting the seven-pointed star of the Knight Grand Cross of the Order of St. Michael and St. George. At home anti-imperialists complained that British titles sapped colonial virtue. But though Sir Wilfrid was fascinated by the glitter of rank, he was not seduced. He showed little enthusiasm for helping Britain during the Boer War, though he believed the Empire's cause was just. In fact he was so suavely evasive about contributing to imperial defence that Chamberlain said he would rather do business with a straightforward cad. Dr. Jameson said that Laurier was a "damn dancin' master" who had "bitched the whole show."[189]

The question of whether and when Canadians should be prepared to shed their blood for the Crown split the dominion to its foundations. Those of British descent had, in Kipling's words, "a certain crude faith in the Empire, of which they naturally conceive themselves to be the belly button."[190] The Boer War, many of them thought, provided an opportunity to strengthen the cord of loyalty that still bound the infant land to the mother country. Sending a Canadian contingent to fight on the veldt would also be a move towards political maturity, towards toughening the Confederation's moral fibre, forging the national character and summoning up a new spirit of patriotism. According to the most ardent jingoists, that spirit was best expressed in the slogan of the Orange Order: "One race, one flag, one throne." Some also demanded one tongue and one faith, asserting majority rights in Canada just as vehemently as they asserted minority rights in Ireland. The Orangemen were powerful, having nine hundred lodges in Ontario alone and helping to impose a dour Puritanism that made it possible, according to the old joke, to spend a week in Toronto on a Sunday. To counter the sectarianism of Canadians, *Canadiens* often professed a willingness to fight for the Empire, which offered the best chance of preserving the dualism of the dominion and thus protecting their identity. But the Boer War presented them with the brutal spectacle of Great Britain attempting to coerce into conformity another small people. No one expressed Quebec's indignation with more eloquence than Henri Bourassa, a zealot to match his revolutionary grandfather Jean-Louis Papineau. He denounced "the military frenzy which is the means of grabbing and maintaining foreign territory"[191] and declared that patriotism of this kind was the last refuge of a scoundrel.

Laurier had to find a compromise that would mollify, though it might not satisfy, each community. He did so by authorising the dispatch to South Africa of a Canadian force made up of volunteers. As the Prime Minister told Bourassa, he thus avoided "a cleavage in the population of this country upon racial lines. A greater calamity could never take place in Canada."[192] Laurier made the most of Canadian achievements in this conflict, announcing that a new power had arisen in the West. But it was not powerful enough to chart a truly independent course, even under the direction of Laurier, who shunned both imperialism and anti-imperialism and kept before him "as a pillar of fire by night and a pillar of cloud by day a policy of true Canadianism."[193] His steps were tentative. Canada took over all its own defences and in 1909 established a Department of External Affairs—above a small barber's shop in Ottawa. The country hovered uneasily between its growing American neighbour and its fading European mother, negotiating a controversial trade agreement with the United States and seeking an acceptable way to augment Britain's naval strength. Eventually, despite Laurier's efforts, Canada was sucked into the vortex of militarism. This had paradoxical consequences. The Great War ultimately divided Canadians. Laurier himself, who memorably declared in 1914 that all his countrymen were "Ready, aye, ready,"[194] was by 1917 supporting the bitter French-Canadian campaign against conscription. Yet the war helped to create a nation united in its determination to shake off the last vestiges of Britannic tutelage, a nation eager to exchange its subordinate place in an old Empire for equal membership of a young Commonwealth.

In early August 1914 all Canada rejoiced at the prospect of a death grapple with Germany. Echoing to the sound of the "Marseillaise" and "Rule, Britannia!," the streets of Montreal and Quebec, like those of Vancouver, Winnipeg and Toronto, blazed with banners and overflowed with parades. In the province of Quebec prelates and press supported the war, with the solitary exception of *La Vérité* which warned that France's greatest foe was not Germany but Freemasonry. But Bourassa soon changed his own tune and that of most other French Canadians. They focused on domestic issues and enemies, at first discouraging enlistment into an army which used only English as the language of command and later putting up violent resistance to conscription. The conflict stirred atavistic passions. Irish Catholics, loyal Canadians who were keen to distinguish themselves from Francophone "hooligans," responded eagerly to the slogan (blessed by their bishops),

"Join the Buffs and Hunt the Huns."[195] French Canada could not be assimilated or accommodated or assuaged, and nationalist opposition to Anglo-Saxon imperialism in all its forms became more deeply entrenched. "They fly the Tricolor everywhere," wrote an indignant English visitor, "even over His Majesty's Post Office!"[196] In Ontario "Von Bourassa"[197] was denounced as a traitor. No one did more to foster xenophobia than "Drill Hall" Sam Hughes, the Minister of Militia in Sir Robert Borden's Conservative government, who had once attributed an outbreak of smallpox in Montreal to the prevalence of popery.

Hughes was a foul-mouthed bully who drummed up recruits with speeches described as "a medley of blatherskite and rodomontade."[198] He was, furthermore, incompetent, corrupt and probably more or less mad. His training schemes were the stuff of comic opera. He insisted (until 1915) that wives should give written permission for their husbands to depart. He bestowed contracts on cronies who produced defective equipment, such as the Ross rifle which was fatally liable to jam. He also tried to augment his own authority by appointing three generals to the same post, more than violating Lloyd George's principle that although one general might not be better than another, "one General is better than two."[199] In 1916 Borden dismissed Hughes, his antics becoming unacceptable as the dominion's forces grew ever more professional. Like the Anzacs, Canadians were hailed as natural soldiers. They were supposed to be instinctively aggressive, hardened by the wilderness and inspired with the democratic spirit. There was a grain of truth in the myth. Major Edison Lynn, MC, wrote: "I am sure Napoleon at the zenith of his powers had not men more keen than ours."[200] But only a quarter of Canadians could be classed as backwoodsmen and the conflict took its toll on the toughest. Having been buried five times at Festubert by "Jack Johnson" shells and lost 250 men in "a senseless attack," the commander of the 8th Canadian Infantry Battalion wrote home: "I am pretty well all right now but am scared of my nerves going, as I seem to be getting confoundedly jumpy . . . if I get sent back to England for putting straw in the corner for the crocodile to sleep on, don't be surprised."[201] Again like the Australasians, Canadians had to learn the business of modern warfare through trial and error, "in a bloodbath of confusion and misdirection."[202]

The most terrible carnage occurred on the Somme. Unforgettably, on the first day of that battle, 1 July 1916, the British suffered sixty thousand casualties, nearly a third of them killed. Many were shot down in ranks as they walked with rifle and sixty-pound pack into the mouths of the German machine guns. In forty-five minutes the 1st Battalion of the Newfoundland

Regiment lost 684 out of 752 men, a casualty rate "which can scarcely have been equalled by any unit during the war."[203] The Canadians themselves lost over 24,000 men during subsequent months of attrition. They became understandably disillusioned about British generals. The Commander-in-Chief, Sir Douglas Haig, for example, felt that every step in his Somme plan had been taken with divine help but disparaged Canadians who suffered a reverse: "men with strange equipment and rugged countenances and beards are not all determined fighters."[204] Attempting to instil "blood lust" into the 5th Army, Sir Hubert Gough told his staff, "I want to shoot two officers."[205] In the 3rd Army "Bull" Allenby even demanded obedience from the dead, once complaining that a corpse was not wearing regulation uniform. He sometimes intimidated living subordinates so as to make them physically sick. A cynical captain said that the best sight he saw on the Somme was "two Brigadier Generals lying dead in the same shell hole."[206] Afterwards the authorities made one change in the British infantry handbook, deleting an instruction to "close with the enemy, cost what it may."[207]

By 1917 the four Canadian divisions, now fighting together for the first time, had acquired the experience to achieve their historic victory at Vimy Ridge with a smaller investment of flesh and blood. This battle, for all the significance later attached to it, was actually just part of a British diversion to assist a major French offensive against the Hindenburg Line. But it occurred at a crucial moment, three days after the United States entered the war and a week before Lenin arrived at the Finland Station in Petrograd. Since the Americans would take months to mobilise, whereas a Russian collapse would speedily release 1.5 million German troops to fight on the Western Front, the Allied position was precarious. Moreover, Vimy Ridge was important because it dominated the Flanders plain. From its 450-foot eminence, said one observer, "more of the war could be seen than from any other place in France."[208] The Ridge was a fortress of long standing. "To all outward appearances it is only a huge mound," wrote Major Lynn, "but it is as full of galleries and chambers as a field would be full of moles." Tacitus, he noted, had told how the Germans, when fighting against Rome, had "built shelters in the chalk" as they were doing now.[209] Honeycombed with trenches, tunnels, deep bunkers, concrete pillboxes and camouflaged machine-gun nests, all protected by forty-yard-wide belts of barbed wire, the Ridge had become a German Gibraltar. To capture it the Canadians developed tactics which ultimately helped to win the war.

They studied French methods and trained on a replica of the battlefield based on ground reconnaissance and aerial photographs, obtained at great cost. They assembled vast quantities of stores, rations and ammunition.

They constructed twenty-five miles of new road, twenty miles of tramway and four miles of tunnels to transport men and supplies to the front, connected to the rear by eighty-seven miles of telephone cable. They orchestrated a bombardment weighing fifty thousand tons which smashed the German fortifications, cut their wire and destroyed most of their hidden batteries, pinpointed by new sound-ranging techniques. At dawn on Easter Monday the explosion of mines was heard above the deafening roar of nearly a thousand guns and the dark Ridge became enveloped in multicoloured smoke. Then, as the Canadians went over the top, it was illuminated by a golden rain: the Germans fired amber flares which burst in clusters of sparks and stars to summon their own artillery support. Unencumbered with packs or even greatcoats, despite the snow, the dominion's army advanced under a barrage that rolled forward one hundred yards every three minutes. The shells thrashed the earth in front of them like a giant flail. The heavy machine-gun bullets flew so thickly that they beat the strands of barbed wire into solid chunks of metal. Under this "cupola of lead,"[210] this "solid ceiling of sound," the weaving and ducking Canadians seemed to execute a "mad macabre dance."[211]

They crossed the enemy's first trench without even recognising it amid the chaos of craters. They dashed through flurries of sleet and streaks of flame, using cover and infiltrating in small, specialised groups, every man his own general. They bombed dugouts, captured grey, dazed prisoners and outflanked German strongpoints. From them the defenders crawled once the first wave had passed and so many Canadians got bullets in the back that the water in shell-holes turned red with blood. But the attackers, conscious that they had done "wonderfully well,"[212] exulted in the unfamiliar sense of victory. Even the wounded appeared euphoric. One man who had both legs shot off tried to lever himself forward with his rifle: "You would think he was sitting in a canoe trying to paddle with his gun."[213] In two hours the first Canadians crested Vimy Ridge, later followed by supporting brigades. In mid-morning the heavens themselves shone forth their triumph, for suddenly the sky cleared and the sun lit up the pock-marked shambles. Groups of soldiers stood about admiring the panorama, officers waving their swagger sticks, as the enemy beat a retreat. The thrill was palpable. "For a few minutes the artillery fire almost ceased on both sides and complete silence fell as if all were lost in wonder," wrote a witness. "The battle itself seemed to hold its breath."[214]

After that pause the Canadians secured their hold on the Ridge, with the assistance of new Livens projectors which could fire fifty-pound drums of mustard gas over half a mile. But tanks were too cumbersome and cavalry were too vulnerable to achieve a breakthrough. Well out in the Arras plain the German line solidified once more and the bloody stalemate resumed. Still, the assault had captured more guns, prisoners and ground than any previous British offensive on the Western Front. The Canadian volunteers—Klondike prospectors, Alberta cattlemen, Saskatchewan wheat farmers, store clerks from Manitoba, businessmen from Ontario, labourers from Quebec, lumberjacks, steel workers and fishermen from the Maritimes—had proved themselves the equals of any soldiers fighting for the Allies. Indeed, as Lloyd George said, for the rest of the war they were used as "storm troops . . . to head the assault in one great battle after another."[215] As such they stayed together (despite Haig's attempt to employ them piecemeal) under the command of a Canadian, Sir Arthur Currie. He was ungainly and unpopular, once welcoming survivors from a battered unit with the words: "That's the way I like to see you, all mud and blood."[216] But he was parsimonious with their lives and he led them to success. Their achievement transformed Borden from a distant auxiliary, reliant on newspapers for information about the conflict, to a full ally with a seat on the Imperial War Cabinet. This body recognised the principle, which Borden formulated in 1917, that the dominions were the "autonomous nations of an Imperial Commonwealth." The crucial change in status and title reflected the way in which Canada, like the other dominions, had entered "the portal of full nationhood."[217]

Borden's cliché was repeated in many forms for it summed up a general view. As early as 1915 Canadians could hear a "new birth-song" for their country "filling the sky."[218] A year later Bourassa's cousin, Captain Talbot Papineau, rebuked him for his anti-imperial views and said a true nationalist would have felt that "in the agony of her losses in Belgium and France, Canada was suffering the birth pains of her national life."[219] An Englishwoman on a visit to Ottawa, observing the contempt felt for "those horrible Yankees" who were only interested in profiting from the war, concluded: "To a very great extent Canada is finding her soul, and like most of us, through suffering."[220] The artist A. Y. Jackson said in 1919, "We are no longer humble colonials, we've made armies. . . ."[221] So Canada asserted itself during the peace-making process, the decimation of its army providing sixty thousand reasons why Borden's arguments should prevail. Canada became a sovereign member of the League of Nations, which Borden supported even though he considered it "absolutely impracticable."[222] Canada also took a grip on its own foreign policy, notably refusing Lloyd George's appeal for help in a further confrontation with Turkey in 1922. Since the war had beggared Britain, Canada sought closer cooperation with the United

States, which bought ten times more of its exports than did the mother country. Armageddon was in crucial respects a "modernising experience."[223] Thus Canada rejected hereditary titles for its citizens and strove to define its destiny at home, an endeavour complicated yet stimulated by the French component, as well as abroad. The dominion's memorials to the glorious dead spoke most eloquently about what had been its war of independence. At Vimy Ridge two lofty pylons, made of marble hewn from the quarry in Dalmatia which the Emperor Diocletian had used to build one of his palaces, symbolised France and Canada, allies in arms, partners in grief and equals in status. The Ottawa monument consists of twenty-two bronze soldiers, a group designed to embody the nation, passing through a triumphal arch. That represents death being swallowed up in victory, the individual sacrifice which redeems and liberates an entire people.

10

Aflame with the Hope of Liberation

Ireland and the Middle East

In stark contrast to the Canadian monuments, Dublin's main war memorial was a symbol of national amnesia. Originally the shrine to the 49,400 Irishmen killed in the Great War was to be erected at Merrion Square in the centre of the city. But in 1923 the government of the newly independent Irish Free State rejected this location because it would provide too prominent a reminder of a war fought for the British Empire. Eventually a site was chosen at Islandbridge on the western outskirts of the capital between the Zoo and Kilmainham Gaol, twenty-five acres on the south bank of the Liffey— it might as well have been the Lethe. Sir Edwin Lutyens, inevitably, designed the memorial park. It contained a tall Celtic cross of sacrifice and a stone of remembrance, said to have "the appearance of a shop-counter,"[1] which was inscribed with the words chosen by Kipling: "Their Name Liveth for Evermore." These images stood amid fountains, pergolas and hand-carved limestone pavilions. But although the British Legion conducted Armistice Day ceremonies, and women (some of them widows living on John Bull's pension) sold poppies, and veterans sang "God Save the King" in Dublin as well as Belfast, Irish nationalists were determined to consign the Great War to oblivion. Islandbridge received no official opening on its completion in 1938 because the Taoiseach (Prime Minister), Eamon de Valera, refused to countenance the flying of Union flags, the parading of regimental standards or any other "display likely to give offence to national sentiment."[2] Subsequently the memorial was permitted to decay. The pergolas rotted. The rose gardens withered. Vandals sacked the pavilions, smashed the fountains and defaced the obelisks. Whereas Canada reverently maintained its colossal altar on the "hallowed ground"[3] of Vimy, Islandbridge suffered dereliction amounting to desecration. Other war memorials in the Free State were also slighted. The one in the centre of Sligo was superseded by a bronze statue of W. B. Yeats. The one at the main entrance of Dublin's Connolly Station was relegated to the obscurity of Platform 4. "Let Us Forget" might have been a suitable legend for plaques in twenty-six of Ireland's thirty-two counties. Those loyal to the green wanted no green memories of the sacrifice their countrymen had made in an irrelevant and erroneous war. They wished to recall instead the terrible beauty born at the Easter Rising in 1916, the glorious struggle for national freedom and the Irish achievement of blasting the widest breach in the ramparts of the British Empire since Yorktown.

All nations cut and shape their history to meet current requirements, but the new Irish state mutilated its past. This was understandable in view of its urgent need to fashion a separate identity, to efface the stigma of being John Bull's other island, to rip the harp from the crown. Moreover, it was easy to blot out the episode of Irish participation in the Great War when contemplating the saga of English domination and the end of what the Republicans' 1919 Declaration of Independence called the "long centuries of a ruthless tyranny."[4] That description itself ignores progress made in the half century after the Famine: the doubling in the number of schools, the building of 3,500 miles of railway, the development of health and welfare services, improvements in housing, significant economic advances and increased opportunities for gain in outposts of the British Empire. But none of that counted for much because galling grievances remained, notably over land, education and religion. British governments tried to alleviate them, assisting small farmers, sanctioning denominational instruction and disestablishing the Irish Protestant Church. Yet such concessions could never satisfy Ireland. The trouble was not that, whenever Gladstone found an answer to the Irish question, the Irish changed the question. The trouble was that the Irish question always remained the same—how to get rid of the Union? What obsessed the Irish mind was the unbearable tragedy of lost liberty. It was a wrong that poisoned every problem and infected every solution. Abroad, especially in urban ghettos of America where blood ran green, it bred an "embittered 'buy-the-dynamite,' 'God-free-Ireland' nationalism."[5] In the British Isles it engendered not just Fenian revolutionaries but Home Rule politicians at Westminster who sought, in Gladstone's charged words, to march "through rapine to the dismemberment of the Empire."[6]

In the wake of the Famine, of course, most Irish families were preoccupied with the struggle for survival. Many were still mired deep in poverty. Many others, those not altogether destitute, emigrated. England approved. "Ireland is boiling over," wrote the *Saturday Review*, "and the scum flows across the Atlantic."[7] But Irish-Americans, especially, looked on economic exile as political banishment. Many refugees were tillers of the soil whose small potato patches had been consolidated into large pastures—cattle and sheep drove out men. A quarter of Ireland, five million acres, changed hands in the years after the Famine. And the new proprietors gained the reputation of being "cormorant vampires" and "coroneted ghouls"[8] who took a fiendish delight in rack-renting and evicting their tenants. Few lived up to this description. In fact, the 150,000 tenant farmers occupying thirty acres or more (a total of three-quarters of the agricultural land in the country) enjoyed a modest prosperity until the depression of the late 1870s. They formed the core of an emergent middle class which sought parliamentary solutions to the ills of their island. But the Irish Party at Westminster, led by Isaac Butt and campaigning for limited Home Rule within the imperial framework, was ineffective. So were the Fenians, who in 1867 pitted pikes against Enfield rifles and got little in the way of trans-atlantic help apart from several dozen Irish-Americans who arrived in a ship called *Erin's Hope*.

The Fenian uprising was hopelessly organised and speedily crushed. In a land where Christ and Caesar were hand in glove, as James Joyce said, it was also memorably anathematised. The Roman Catholic Bishop of Kerry called down upon its managers "God's heaviest curse, his withering, blasting, blighting curse," and declared that eternity was not too long for their punishment "nor hell hot enough."[9] Their earthly fate was the gallows or the penitentiary. This all seemed to confirm the aphorism of one constitutional nationalist, J. P. Curran, that the Irish made bad subjects but worse rebels. However, these rebels kept alive the physical-force tradition, caught the imagination of compatriots and inspired a new drive to solve the Irish problem. Gladstone, who thought that the only danger to the Empire lay in Ireland's combining with America and Canada, revoked Anglican privileges and reduced landlord rights. Charles Stewart Parnell, who defended the Fenians in the House of Commons and became the "Chief" of the Irish Party in 1880, tried to maintain a balance between revolutionary and constitutional forces. In the spirit of James Fintan Lalor, the rebel of 1848 who believed that the Famine had dissolved the bonds of society, Parnell flirted with violence over the land issue as a means of attaining Home Rule. "If we had the farmers the owners of the soil tomorrow," he said, "we should not be long without getting an Irish parliament."[10] Only Parnell possessed the genius to create an alliance which, in the words of an admiring biographer, "brought Ireland within sight of the Promised Land."[11]

Parnell was the antithesis of the genial, emollient, leonine Butt. He was aloof, implacable and tigerish. As Butt himself said just before Parnell entered parliament, aged twenty-nine, in 1875: "the Saxon will find him an ugly customer, though he is a good-looking fellow." The Fenians themselves recognised that Parnell "was the man to fight the English; he was so like themselves, cool, callous, inexorable."[12] A cricketing squire from Wicklow, he had been to school in England, spoke with an English accent and had learned to hate the English on his American-born mother's knee. He especially loathed their assumption of effortless superiority. Arrogance was much in evidence at Magdalene College, Cambridge, which was well known for the social rather than the intellectual distinction of its undergraduates. Here Parnell refused to join the Boat Club, which provoked quarrels "resulting in blows."[13] Contrary to myth, however, he seems to have fitted into the college quite well. Despite attending intermittently, he acquired some education—though a later associate claimed that the only book Parnell ever read was William Youatt's *The Horse*. And fellow students gave him an alcoholic send-off when he was rusticated for brawling with a manure merchant. It was Parnell's unflinching resolve to stand up to the English in the Commons that made him such a formidable leader. His cold-blooded courage eclipsed obvious political defects such as inaccessibility and inarticulacy. Almost equally disadvantageous was his dislike of funerals, the black propaganda of nationalism. Worse still, Parnell had a superstitious aversion to the colour green.

Moreover, he constantly risked exposure on account of his illicit affair with Katharine O'Shea, though he was strangely unmoved by the dangers. When Captain O'Shea threatened him with a duel because he had found Parnell's portmanteau at his wife's house in Eltham, Parnell only asked what the Captain had done with his luggage. His frigid reserve barely concealed jangling nerves and seething passions, akin, some said, to the madness that ran in his family. Parnell was fire in ice. More even than his ruthless filibustering, his "superb silences"[14] impressed the people of his native land where, one Fenian remarked, all agitators talked. Parnell's "sphinx-like"[15] secretiveness came naturally to him—he would wave cheques in the air to dry the ink rather than risk leaving a replica of his signature on blotting paper. But inscrutability also enabled him to preserve the essential ambiguity of his political stance. He refused to define: despite his public Protestantism and his private agnosticism, he conciliated Roman Catholicism. He was devious to a fault: on adulterous business he sometimes adopted the alias "Mr. Fox." He behaved, though, with autocratic assurance and had horses called President and Dictator. His pale, bearded countenance was majestic and his flinty, red-brown eyes were hypnotic. He was a visionary who attracted adamantine metaphors—a "man of bronze,"[16] a bit of granite "encased in steel."[17] And he was a prophet whose assault on the integrity of the British Empire inspired sovereign salutations. Like the Liberator, Daniel O'Connell, Parnell was hailed as "the uncrowned king of Ireland."[18]

He gained this title to the country at a time when many Irishmen were losing their title to the land. As agrarian distress worsened during the late 1870s, the result of cheap food from America and more crop failures in Ireland, evictions multiplied. So did cases of arson, murder and other kinds of rural terror—"Captain Moonlight" and his minions indulged in cattle-maiming and the "'carding' of humans, whose backs were lacerated with nail-studded boards."[19] Parnell exploited the vital issue of land, for which, he was told, tenants were prepared to go to hell. He drew on the support of Fenians such as Michael Davitt who, having freed themselves from "the strait-jacket of intransigence,"[20] campaigned to restore the land to the people as a means of giving Ireland to the Irish. As President of the Land League, Davitt's organisation to help small farmers, Parnell urged resistance to high rents and evictions. He said that those who occupied properties from which the previous tenants had been expelled should not be shot but shunned as if they were lepers, morally excommunicated like Captain Boycott, who gave his name to the process. Yet such was the vehemence of Parnell's language and the menace of his demeanour that he satisfied all save the most fanatical nationalists. He formed a mass movement among people who wryly acknowledged that disunity was "the primeval curse of our race."[21]

As famine and crime paralysed the west, the new Liberal government (elected in 1880) prosecuted Parnell and his colleagues in Dublin for conspiring to create ill will among Her Majesty's subjects. Predictably, it failed to obtain a conviction. The foreman of the jury amused the court by declaring, "We are unanimous that we cannot agree."[22] Gladstone then combined coercion with conciliation. He repealed the Habeas Corpus Act, a move fiercely resisted by Parnell's increasingly well-disciplined party in the Commons. And he passed a Land Bill which gave tenants much of what they had long craved: the famous "three F's"—fixity of tenure, fair rents and free sale. Playing for higher stakes, Parnell continued to be obstructive. In October 1881 he was locked up in Kilmainham Gaol, a grim panopticon of glass, iron and granite run with "clockwork discipline" in "stupefying silence."[23] He thus became a martyr and a superhuman being—awed peasants noted that his incarceration coincided with the worst storm in half a century. Imprisonment clinched Parnell's ascendancy in Ireland, as it would clinch the ascendancy of many other leaders of struggles for national independence throughout the Empire. It also won valuable support in the United States, which deluged him with dollars. They were subscribed, wrote the novelist George Moore sourly, by Irish-American "nursemaids and potboys," who held the destiny of the British Empire in their hands just as "the Goths and Visigoths held the destinies of the Romans."[24]

Certainly Gladstone felt obliged to negotiate with Parnell, continuing a pattern of British behaviour towards Ireland known as "kicks and ha'pence," sticks and carrots.[25] They reached an informal agreement, misleadingly named the Kilmainham Treaty and denounced by the Tories as a pact with treason. It stipulated that the Grand Old Man would make up tenants' arrears of rent while the liberated Chief would use his influence to stop the land war. On 6 May 1882, however, a terrorist splinter group called the Invincibles murdered the Chief Secretary for Ireland, Lord Frederick Cavendish, and a leading official within sight of the white Ionic columns of the Viceregal Lodge in Phoenix Park. The assassination, carried out with long surgical knives, sent a pulse of horror through the United Kingdom. The loudest cry for vengeance came from Printing House Square. *The Times* not only tried "to fasten this hellish crime on the Irish people,"[26] a charge which Gladstone thought diabolical, but it also suggested that the Irish population in England should be massacred. Even Parnell's arctic composure was shattered by the crime. He offered to resign and, "white and apparently terror-stricken," he told Sir Charles Dilke that the blow had been directed against him.[27] Actually it was not a personal threat, though he took the precaution of carrying a revolver in the pocket of his overcoat. But it was an assault on Parnell's policy, which had now veered strongly in the direction of a constitutional settlement. Gladstone, although he had to impose another measure of coercion after the Phoenix Park murders, moved towards the same goal. It was the realisation of his long-held belief that "England owed a debt of justice to Ireland."[28]

Imbued with a spirit of magnanimity stronger even than his bent for casuistry, the GOM had for years sympathised with small nations struggling to be free. Recently he had acknowledged that the Union had no moral force behind it. And he aspired to make "the humblest Irishman . . . a governing agency"—not an idea that appealed to Lord Salisbury.[29] By 1885 Gladstone faced an Irish phalanx in parliament (itself now elected on a wider franchise) and a nation whose turbulence (extending to acts of terrorism in England) not even royal magic could assuage. When Edward Prince of Wales visited Ireland he was greeted in some districts with black banners bearing the words, "We will have no Prince but Charlie."[30] For a time the GOM, who was also groping for an issue to unite the factions in the Liberal Party, kept his own counsel. And the Chief embarked on a fleeting liaison with the Tories. But when it emerged that Gladstone did support Home

Rule, as the only means of pacifying Ireland, Parnell entered into a firm alliance with the Liberals. Gladstone's first Home Rule Bill (1886) provoked uproar in Protestant Ulster, drove Whigs such as Lord Hartington and Liberal imperialists such as Joseph Chamberlain into the arms of the Tories, and failed to secure a majority in the Commons. Nevertheless, the fact that a great British party had acknowledged the validity of Ireland's national aspirations was of momentous importance. It signified not only that the Union was doomed but that the days of the Empire were numbered. This was not because Gladstone was proposing, as Lord Randolph Churchill charged, to plunge his "knife into the heart of the British Empire."[31] The GOM aimed to secure the Empire on the foundation of consent. But that implied the option of dissent. If Ireland defected, as empire-builders always warned, India could hardly be retained, for India was "a larger Ireland."[32] The Conservative and Unionist Party, which now took power for two decades (with a Liberal interlude between 1892 and 1895), was determined to prevent this catastrophe. "Ireland must be kept, like India, at all hazards," declared Lord Salisbury, "by persuasion if possible; if not, by force."[33]

In 1887 Salisbury commissioned his nephew, Arthur Balfour, to govern Ireland along these lines as Chief Secretary. Almost everyone derided the appointment, not just because of the flagrant nepotism but because Balfour seemed so ill suited to the post. To consign such a languid sybarite to the hurly-burly of Irish politics seemed, as his soul mate George Curzon remarked, "like throwing a lame dove among a congregation of angry cats."[34] But Balfour shared his uncle's patrician disdain for the Irish, regarding them as no more fitted for self-rule than Hindus or Hottentots. There was something perverse about people who starved in bogs and mountains when they might have emigrated or grown lentils, which were less susceptible to disease than potatoes. The Irish had to be disciplined, otherwise, as the *Edinburgh Review* warned, the colonies would lose respect for the mother country and England would "cease to be regarded as the dominant nation."[35] Nevertheless, Balfour promised to be fair as well as firm. "I shall be as relentless as Cromwell in enforcing obedience to the law," he declared, "but, at the same time, I shall be as radical as any reformer in redressing grievances."[36] So Balfour sustained the landlords and suppressed the "Plan of Campaign," or rent strike—which Parnell himself repudiated. The Chief Secretary paid for bailiffs' battering rams out of secret service funds. He supported the police when they shot down rioters at Mitchelstown in September 1887. He resisted the amelioration of gaol conditions likely to kill political prisoners in poor health, privately complaining that there was "some mysterious connection between diseased lungs and Irish patriotism."[37] Irish MPs likened "Bloody" Balfour to the Roman Emperor Heliogabalus, "who was in the habit of recruiting his debilitated energies in a bath of children's blood."[38] He remained serenely indifferent to abuse, greeting taunts with quips and responding to threats with a nonchalant twirl of his pince-nez. For a time his brand of repression, though by no means Cromwellian in its severity, did manage to quell Ireland. But its long-term effect was to exacerbate a Celtic hatred for the Saxon as fierce, said George Moore, "as that which closes the ferret's teeth on the rat's throat."[39]

Balfour's panaceas, even when assisted by economic recovery, did little to improve race relations. It is true that he continued the process of assisting tenants to purchase their holdings, which would in due course solve the land problem. But he hedged it about with so many conditions that it became known as "Mr. Balfour's Puzzle." Most of his other reforms were still less successful. His project for a Catholic university collapsed. He wasted resources in the west and failed to invest enough in the east. He got little credit for light railways that were accompanied by heavy punishments. Finally, like other British imperialists, he never understood that administrative nostrums could not cure the ills of a conquered nation. Neither the lance of coercion nor the poultice of conciliation could draw the poison from the Irish body politic. Only Parnell's remedy, though it never took Ulster into proper account, would do. By 1889 the Chief reckoned that he might soon accomplish Home Rule, for his prestige reached its zenith when *The Times* was exposed for using forged letters to implicate him in the Phoenix Park murders. But the following year disaster struck. Parnell's adultery with Katharine O'Shea, which had complicated his life for a decade, was revealed when her venal husband cited him as co-respondent in a divorce action. Wishing to marry his mistress, Parnell offered no defence and his character was duly blackened. But he tried to hold on to his leadership, thus alienating custodians of morality, splitting the Irish Party and gravely damaging the Home Rule movement.

Within twelve months Parnell was dead, leaving Ireland a bitter legacy of frustration and division. Some said he fell like Lucifer, others that he was crucified like Christ. Whatever the verdict, the passing of its uncrowned king became a key episode in the nation's history. Yeats mourned him, visualising Parnell guiding Eire from the tomb:

> His memory is now a tall pillar, burning
> Before us in the gloom.[40]

James Joyce harped still more poignantly on the loss, identifying himself with the betrayed Caesar. And he too juggled with the idea that Parnell's "spirit may/Rise like a Phoenix from the flames"[41] and free his native land from the "brutish empire."[42] It was an alluring conceit for Parnell had embodied hope, instilled confidence and made Irish independence a living issue. What is more, he did rise again—on a fifty-seven-foot obelisk erected in O'Connell Square shortly before the Great War. Perhaps because it stirred "some instinctive memory of ancient priapic cults"[43] or seemed a tribute to the virility which had captivated Mrs. O'Shea, Dubliners used the word "parnell" as slang for penis. Respectable votaries at this shrine dwelt not on phallic symbolism but on the lapidary inscription of Parnell's most celebrated sentence. It inspired enemies of the British Empire all round the world: "No man shall have the right to fix the boundary to the march of a Nation."

The nation changed course after Parnell's death, marching to the beat of a different drum. Conspicuous in the 150,000-strong crowd at his funeral were those emblems of revolt, low-crowned, broad-brimmed hats known as wide-awakes. They belonged to leading Fenians, who asserted that the constitutional method of achieving emancipation was as lifeless as the corpse now being interred in Glasnevin Cemetery—under a sky filled with "strange lights and flames" that reflected the "electrical and high-wrought" sentiments of the mourners.[44] Irish MPs in disarray could not revive that method: in 1893 the House of Lords snuffed out Gladstone's second Home Rule Bill by 419 votes to 41. Not until 1900 did the Irish Parliamentary Party reunite. But it never regained its former cohesion under the leadership of the able, amiable John Redmond, who resembled Butt rather than Parnell. Meanwhile, the Tories promoted self-help and continued to extend peasant proprietorship. Adopting a technique that would be increasingly used in an effort to keep the Empire intact, they also gave Ireland a large measure of local self-government. This knocked the Protestant Ascendancy off its perch and, according to Redmond, "worked a social revolution."[45] Although such concessions could never satisfy the aspirations of subject peoples, Irishmen feared that Englishmen might succeed in killing Home Rule by kindness. So they challenged constructive Unionism with cultural nationalism. This was the campaign to show that Ireland, light of the world while England was in the Dark Ages, possessed a historic civilisation which entitled it to be master of its own fate. It was the endeavour to burnish heroic myths, notably that of "Cuchulainn the Valiant," who shed his blood for his homeland. It was the effort to embellish the superstructure of fable raised by Irish bards and monks, "two orders of men," as Gibbon wrote, "who equally abused the privilege of fiction."[46] It was the attempt to replace the caricature of the poor, ignorant, brutal, feckless Paddy with the character of the pure, spiritual, vigorous, imaginative Gael. Many organisations and impulses helped to create this ideal, which was deeply subversive to the Empire.

The Gaelic Athletic Association was founded in 1884 to encourage the playing of native games, especially hurling and Gaelic football, and it became "a central pillar of Irish nationalism."[47] Two thousand hurlers marched at Parnell's funeral. And with their fellows they opposed English sports like cricket, which was intended, as W. G. Grace said, "to knit together the various sections of the British Empire."[48] The National Literary Society, set up in 1892, was one of many expressions of the *fin-de-siècle* efflorescence of Irish literature, W. B. Yeats (who also helped to establish the national theatre) being its presiding genius. The stifling of the Irish voice after the Famine complicated the task of nationalist writers since most of them had been educated in English. But the Gaelic League, formed in 1893, was dedicated to the revival of the native language since, as George Moore said, "the soul of Ireland was implicit in it." Moore satirised many aspects of the cultural renaissance in which he himself participated, notably Yeats's saga-inspired vision of mystic peasants, his occult superstitions as a Hermetic Student of the Golden Dawn and his fairy fantasies as High Priest of the Celtic Twilight.

Moore was not afraid to speak ill of the Druids, to suggest that "gossip was Dublin's folklore" or to mock Douglas Hyde, President of the Gaelic League, who frothed Irish "like porter"[49] through a drooping tawny moustache that resembled an abandoned bird's nest. Actually, according to the Provost of Trinity College, Dublin, he spoke only "Baboon Irish."[50] But Hyde, though a serious writer, made a broad butt. He talked in a "pigeon-cautious coo," according to Sean O'Casey, and assisted with the worship of crepuscular gods such as "Aeonius Pure Bolonius."[51] His revolt against British sartorial imperialism was particularly risible. He urged Irish women to spin knee-breeches (a Celtic equivalent of Gandhi's *dhoti*) for their men and his rallying cry was "down with trousers."[52] How effectively the diffuse, white-collared cultural movement fostered an aggressive national consciousness is a matter of debate. But anti-British feelings certainly ran high during the Boer War, when the Empire's forces were kept at bay in South Africa by "about as many able-bodied men as one would find in the province of Connaught."[53] The League did much to propagate "Gaelic ideas of equality and democracy."[54] And the titular leader of the Easter Rising, Patrick Pearse, concluded that history would recognise the Gaelic League as "the most revolutionary influence that has ever come into Ireland."[55]

Pearse, a schoolmaster and poet who revered Ireland's past paladins and present peasants, was apt to read history backwards. He subsequently interpreted his endeavour to promote the integrity of the Irish folk as a deliberate apprenticeship for the fight to win independence for the Irish nation. In fact, he was a late convert to physical force since favourable conditions for its use were slow to materialise. Arthur Griffith, a prickly controversialist, founded Sinn Féin (Ourselves) in 1905 to foster self-reliance in Ireland and non-cooperation with England, but it soon languished. More effective was militant trade unionism led by James Larkin, a fiery syndicalist in a dark, wide-brimmed hat that was allegedly never removed because it hid the third eye of Antichrist in the middle of his forehead, and by James Connolly, an intellectual who found it easier to explain his socialism to the Irish than to explain the Irish to socialists. Exploiting social conditions that made Dublin unhealthier than Calcutta, they generated a wave of strikes, lockouts and disturbances. By 1911, though, when H. H. Asquith's Liberal government restricted the legislative veto of the House of Lords, there seemed a real prospect of attaining Home Rule by constitutional means. But Ireland's opportunity was England's difficulty. It now had to confront a Protestant community in Ulster which damned Home Rule as Rome rule, mustered behind the banners of loyalist Orangemen and prepared to resist it whatever the cost. Furthermore, the brusque new Conservative leader, Andrew Bonar Law, played the Orange card. He pledged to support Ulster by all necessary means rather than submit to what he saw as a crooked parliamentary deal between Asquith and Redmond. Although born in Canada, Law came from Presbyterian Ulster stock. He was alert to what Louis MacNeice called "the voodoo of the Orange bands"[56] and believed that the Catholic "Irish were an inferior race."[57] On Easter Tuesday 1912, standing on a platform at Belfast's Balmoral show grounds with Tory MPs, churchmen and other dignitaries, in front of what was supposedly the largest Union Jack ever made, Law told an Ulster multitude that "you hold the pass for the Empire."[58]

So, as Asquith's Home Rule Bill began its progress through parliament, Ulstermen, whose own uncrowned king was the charismatic Sir Edward Carson, pioneered a course that would be followed by other menaced minorities within the Empire. They threatened rebellion for the sake of loyalty and plotted treason in the name of the King. They pledged, mobilised, drilled and armed. The Ulster Volunteers seemed to intimidate the government (though Winston Churchill, saying that there were "worse things than bloodshed,"[59] professed his readiness to bombard Belfast). And the Secretary for War capitulated entirely to the so-called "Curragh Mutineers."

These were fifty-eight officers in the British Army who extracted an assurance from him that there would be no military coercion of Ulster.

Southern nationalists could do no other than respond with their own mailed fist. Irish Volunteers mustered in scores of thousands, supplemented by a tiny Citizen Army. Organised by Connolly, this was a proletarian Praetorian Guard wearing slouch hats and dark green uniforms and serving under a blue banner adorned with a plough and stars. The Irish Volunteers also equipped themselves by gun-running as, on the eve of the Great War, party leaders in London reached deadlock over the Ulster problem and what seemed to be its only feasible solution—partition. Like Parnell and Redmond, Patrick Pearse completely underestimated the intransigence of the Protestant north. Once armed, he thought, Irishmen would abandon sectarian strife to fight for national emancipation. They would propel Ireland, no longer divided and ruled, towards "a destiny more glorious than that of Rome."[60] Pearse had few scruples about what might be involved in the liberation struggle:

> We may make mistakes in the beginning and shoot the wrong people; but bloodshed is a cleansing and a sanctifying thing, and the nation which regards it as the final horror has lost its manhood. There are many things more horrible than bloodshed; and slavery is one of them.

But he was also willing, even eager, to shed his own blood in order to save his people. As Yeats observed, Pearse was a dangerous man, giddy with "the vertigo of self-sacrifice."

The Great War showed Pearse the way to his personal Calvary. He was inspired by the example of millions laying down their lives for their countries and, in the spirit of fascist patriots like Gabriele D'Annunzio, he intoned: "The old heart of the earth needed to be warmed with the red wine of the battlefields." Anyone who thought like that, said James Connolly, was a "blithering idiot."[61] He himself aimed to spark off a social revolution, believing that the beleaguered British Empire was now uniquely vulnerable. "Ireland," he declared, "was in the position of a child that might stick a pin in a giant's heart."[62] Yet early in 1916, during a secret meeting with leaders of the revived Irish Republican Brotherhood who had infiltrated the Volunteers and were planning the coup, Connolly succumbed to Pearse's dizzying rhetoric. He concluded that freedom could be achieved by "no agency less powerful than the red tide of war on Irish soil."[63] Others shared this vision, scurrying after Pearse, as Sean O'Casey observed, to keep their "rendezvous with Death."[64] But most hoped that a small band of rebels would stir into a blaze the embers of mass hatred for England, which Pearse called a "holy passion."[65]

Although prosperity was increasing and there was no obvious discontent, after two years of war the auguries appeared favourable. Home Rule was in suspense for the duration and it seemed as if Englishmen would help Ulstermen to mutilate Ireland. Many nationalists resented Redmond's support for the British war effort. Dubliners scorned posters appealing for recruits to defend the rights of small nations and the flow of volunteers had soon become a trickle. "Enlist?" one young man was supposed to have said. "Is ut me enlist? An' a war going on!"[66] Conscription therefore loomed, which Irishmen would contest. However, Pearse and his fellows did nothing to ready the nation for action. Hardened conspirators like Sean MacDermott and Tom Clarke feared the English sword less than the Irish tongue. They planned the Easter Rising in such secrecy that even Eoin MacNeill, commander of the small section of Volunteers not under Redmond's control, was duped. When he discovered the deception he countermanded the orders. Insurrection seemed hopeless, especially after the capture of the German ship *Aud,* with its twenty thousand rifles, and the arrest of their envoy to Germany, Sir Roger Casement. There were other setbacks and muddles, which virtually confined the rebellion to Dublin, delayed it until Easter Monday and limited the number of rebels to 1,600. MacNeill himself was as bemused by the current confusion as only a professor of history could be. He could not decide whether to support the Rising in uniform or plain clothes—and it was over before he had made up his mind. Connolly and Pearse were unperturbed by the chaos. "We are going to be slaughtered," said Connolly. But without bloodshed, as Pearse agreed, there could be no redemption.

So on the sunny Monday morning after Easter, as Irish Volunteers and troops of the Citizen Army assembled at Liberty Hall, Connolly's headquarters, Pearse ignored his sister's embarrassingly shrill plea: "Come home, Pat, and leave all this foolishness!"[67] Instead he marched off with his men. The various units, some going by electric tram and paying the fare, moved to seize key points in the city. Pearse's company resembled a legion of the lost. Some Volunteers wore plain clothes and had yellow armlets on their left sleeves. Others carried picks and sledgehammers as well as bandoleers and haversacks held together by straps and string. Their weapons were various— Mausers, shotguns, Sniders, sporting rifles, Martini-Henrys, Lee Enfields, pikes and home-made bombs. However, they quickly invaded the General Post Office in what is now O'Connell Street. The GPO, a massive, colonnaded block of granite, constructed in 1818 and recently refurbished, became their command centre. From its roof they flew the orange, white and green tricolour of the Young Ireland Movement and a huge green flag bearing the legend in white letters, "Irish Republic"—which did not stop the occasional British officer from coming in to buy stamps.

The insurgents also secured a ring of other large buildings, including the Mendicity Institution, the South Dublin Union, Jacob's biscuit factory, the College of Surgeons, Boland's Mills, City Hall and the Imperial Hotel, which were duly fortified. Dublin Castle itself might have been taken if anyone had known how weakly it was held. As it was, the first rebel to die, the actor Sean Connolly, shot the first policeman at the entrance to the Castle's Upper Yard—a baroque gateway topped by a statue of Justice which, as Dubliners cynically remarked, faced away from the city. Outside the GPO Pearse proclaimed the Irish Republic. He asserted Ireland's right to nationhood in the name of God and dead generations of fighters for freedom. He also declared that the egalitarian Republic was supported by Ireland's "exiled children in America and by gallant allies in Europe"[68]—a provocative and imaginative reference to Germany. There were a few thin cheers. But the onlookers, shabby men in broken boots, shawled women in patched dresses, barefoot children in ragged hand-me-downs, were puzzled and largely hostile. Some shouted, "Shitehawks! Lousers! Bowsies!"[69] Others pushed against the barricades, to be driven off by a Volunteer who hit them over the head with a lady's umbrella. When a company of Lancers galloped down O'Connell Street, to be sent racing back by a fusillade from the GPO, the crowd expressed its sympathy for the horses. A British cavalry charge against a heavily defended building, said Connolly, signified that "there was great hope for Ireland still."[70]

Connolly's buoyant courage did more than anything to animate resistance. The young firebrand Michael Collins, formerly a postal clerk, said: "I would have followed him through hell."[71] But the round-headed, pot-bellied, bandy-legged Connolly was no strategist. He had stated confidently that heavy guns would not be used since a capitalist government would never destroy the capital. So instead of imitating the guerrilla methods of the Boers, the insurgents tried to hold their scattered strongpoints. This made them sitting targets for the superior fire power which the British did not hesitate to deploy once they had recovered from their initial shock. They garrisoned the Castle and summoned reinforcements, which did engage in some fierce street fighting. At Mount Street Bridge, for example, their advancing khaki serpent was bloodily attacked by a handful of Republican riflemen. For the most part, though, the British masked hostile enclaves south of the Liffey and kept rebel heads down with sniper fire from tall buildings like the Custom House. This did not stop widespread looting: at one point Dublin's "slum lice,"[72] as a character in *The Plough and the Stars* called them, carpeted the cobbles of O'Connell Street with the unwanted starched collars of shirts plundered from Clery's department store. But the looters vanished as the British blasted their way towards the GPO with machine guns and artillery. The gunboat *Helga* fired shells from the river, pulverising "Liberty Hall, that 'nest of sedition.'"[73] By Wednesday the cordon had tightened and defenders in the Post Office were cooling their rifles with oil from sardine tins. Elsewhere the strain told on even the hardiest Volunteers. During one night-time foray de Valera was so overcome by nervous exhaustion that he went to sleep in a railway carriage at Westland Row Station. He awoke surrounded by nymphs, cherubs and angels, believing that he had died and gone to heaven. In fact he was in the Royal Coach, decorated in celestial style, which he later used as President of Ireland.

On Thursday incendiary shells and tracer bullets created a firestorm opposite the GPO in O'Connell Street. It engulfed the Imperial Hotel and the Dublin Bread Company. It melted Clery's plate glass windows and turned Hoyte's chemist's shop into a roaring inferno. The heat was so intense that sacks of coal used to barricade the GPO windows ignited and the water that sooty rebels poured on them hissed into steam. From a distance the flames soared so high that "the heavens looked like a great ruby hanging from God's ear."[74] Inside the postal redoubt the consumptive poet Joseph Plunkett, still immaculate with spurs, sabre and jewelled fingers, rejoiced: "It's the first time this has happened since Moscow! The first time a capital city has burned since 1812!"[75] But once the roof of the GPO caught fire the rebels faced defeat. Connolly was severely wounded in the left ankle and Pearse now strode to the centre of the stage. Small, proud and reserved, with a cast in one of his blue eyes, he was no great captain of men. He wore an officer's sword but he could hardly slice a loaf of bread. He forbade the use of explosive bullets. Devoted to Mother Church, Mother Ireland and Mother (to whom he wrote a moving poem from the condemned cell), he hated the sight of suffering and agreed to end it. So, on Saturday afternoon, wearing a slouch hat and a long coat over his thin, grey-green uniform, Pearse marched through an "arena of tragedy"[76] that resembled, according to one witness, a vast, shattered Roman amphitheatre. He surrendered unconditionally. Magnetic but repellent, he had been the Savonarola of the Irish independence movement. Now, knowing that he would be shot, he hoped to be the saviour of the nation.

This seemed unlikely at first. As the rebels were escorted through the crowd, Dubliners cursed, spat, hurled rotten vegetables and cried, "Bayonet them! Bayonet them!"[77] They were angry at the destruction of their city, the centre of which was now said to be a ruin "more complete" than war-torn Ypres.[78] They mourned the dead, 300 citizens as well as 70 insurgents and 130 British combatants. Amid much rumour and speculation there was also some sympathy for the rebels. But if the Easter Rising was propaganda from the barrel of a gun, it had evidently misfired; if it was street theatre, most of the audience was disgusted. Within weeks, though, the situation changed utterly. Although the British had regarded the Rising as a stab in the back, wantonly delivered at the time of the fall of Kut, they had played it down as a mere riot. So their retaliation, severe in itself though mild by the standards of Drogheda or Amritsar, seemed fair to them but savage to the Irish. They were still more embittered since it came on top of the British murder of five civilians during the Rising itself—one was the pacifist Francis Sheehy-Skeffington, who had condemned it as "noble folly."[79] But General Sir John Maxwell, who had imposed martial law, felt that he could not show weakness, particularly as Kitchener had advised him to "decimate" the prisoners.[80] He told Asquith that because of

> the gravity of the Rebellion and its connection with German intrigue and propaganda, and in view of the great loss of life and property arising therefrom, [he had] found it imperative to inflict the most severe penalties on the known organisers of this detestable rising.[81]

As well as imprisoning and interning nearly two thousand suspected dissidents, courts martial held in secret sentenced ninety to death. Most were reprieved. One or two escaped fortuitously, de Valera perhaps because of his alleged American citizenship and Countess Markievicz because she was a woman—the British had condemned the German execution of Nurse Cavell. But between 3 and 12 May 1916 fifteen rebels were shot, including Pearse, Connolly, Plunkett, Clarke and MacDermott. As invariably happened in imperial history, British reprisals prompted a fatal reaction.

The most impassioned parliamentary protest came from John Dillon, Redmond's trusted colleague, who accused an insane government of "letting loose a river of blood."[82] Americans were also outraged, equating the killing of prisoners of war with German frightfulness. The British ambassador in Washington wrote home, "The Irish question is poisoning our relations with the United States."[83] Some, like the Bishop of Limerick, contrasted the cruelty visited on the Easter rebels with the mercy extended to the Jameson Raiders. Bernard Shaw said that Maxwell's punishments resembled those inflicted by Lord Cromer on the unruly villagers of Denshawai. By their policy of blind retribution the British authorities had "worked up a harebrained adventure into a heroic episode in the struggle for Irish freedom." Nothing more "stupid and terror-mad could have been devised by England's worst enemies."[84]

The hanging of Sir Roger Casement in August provoked more fury, for it was vengeance served cold. Moreover, he had won fame as an anticolonial humanitarian, denouncing Belgian rule in the Congo, for example, as "a tyranny beyond conception save only, perhaps, to an Irish mind alive to the horrors once daily enacted in this land."[85] So he was discredited by unavowable methods. Extracts from Casement's diary revealing homosexual exploits were privately shown to influential people in England such as the Archbishop of Canterbury and the American ambassador. In most of Ireland, through the familiar Christian paradox, the Easter rebels triumphed through failure. The erstwhile pariahs won their martyrs' crowns. "Kings with plumes may adorn their hearse," ran a current jingle, "but angels meet the soul of Patrick Pearse."[86] Yeats wrote of the haunting impact of the sixteen sacrifices:

> But who can talk of give and take,
> What should be and what not
> While those dead men are loitering there
> To stir the boiling pot?[87]

Irishmen had worse civil strife to endure before they achieved Connolly's ambition to break the link with the "Brigand Empire."[88] But at Easter 1916 they had struck the vital blow which, as Lenin said, was "of a hundred times greater political significance than a blow of equal weight in Asia or in Africa."[89] It was a blow at the heart of the Empire and it inspired nationalists everywhere, especially in India and Egypt. As Gandhi later said, Irishmen had not purchased freedom with the blood they had taken but with "the gallons of blood they have willingly given."[90]

At first it seemed that the Rising had reinvigorated the Home Rule movement. But it foundered once more on the rock of Ulster. Loyalists there (and in the south) contrasted the noble sacrifice of Irishmen on the Somme with murderous treason in Dublin. Yet again grandees in England insisted that there must be no surrender. The lackadaisical Balfour went so far as to repeat Lord Randolph Churchill's baleful warning: "rather than submit to Nationalist rule Ulster would fight—and Ulster would be right."[91] So Redmond and his followers were made to seem still more irrelevant and the ultimate beneficiary of the Rising was Sinn Féin. This was not because Griffith had taken part in it, though he had offered to, but because the British blamed his party, which alone was identified with the cause of total independence. Martial law encouraged recruitment and the rat-infested internment camp for Irish prisoners at Frongoch in Wales was accurately known as the "University of Revolution."[92] In July 1917 Sinn Féin scored a stunning victory when de Valera, outspoken in his "wish that the British Empire will be blown into ruins,"[93] won at the East Clare by-election.

Tall, bespectacled, aloof and austere, this former teacher of mathematics was described by Yeats as "a living argument rather than a living man."[94] He was, indeed, so preoccupied with the nationalist case that in discussion with the Ulster leader Sir James Craig it took him half an hour to reach the era of Brian Boru and when negotiating with Lloyd George he only seemed interested in talking about Oliver Cromwell. At this early stage, though, de Valera was not clear about how the Republic was "to be raised on the ruins of the British Empire."[95] But the British themselves came to his assistance. They cracked down on minor instances of sedition such as drilling, wearing uniforms, whistling nationalist songs and displaying the green and black "Sinn Féin mourning badge."[96] Then, in September 1917, a Volunteer hunger striker named Thomas Ashe died as a result of forcible feeding in Mountjoy Prison, provoking a funeral procession that was a tableau of national defiance. A volley fired over the grave, said Michael Collins, was the only proper tribute to pay a dead Fenian.

Sinn Féin also benefited from Britain's apparent resolve to impose conscription on Ireland. The party reacted as though to a declaration of war, whereupon de Valera and his senior colleagues were arrested. Further repressive measures followed, such as the Sunday ban on Gaelic games, which was widely flouted. Michael Collins, who had evaded capture, favoured rifles over hurleys. Violent resistance was the only alternative, he declared, to remaining "a vassal state of John Bull."[97] So while on the run he organised Volunteers into what by mid-1919 became, with the initial connivance and the subsequent support of Sinn Féin, the Irish Republican Army (IRA). There was always an ambiguity in the relationship between the two organisations, confused still further by local loyalties and personal rivalries. Collins himself, jovial, handsome and audacious as well as ruthless, vain and homicidal, attracted hero-worship and hatred in almost equal measure. De Valera, known as the "Long Fellow," distrusted Collins, who was called the "Big Fellow" more on account of his pretensions than his size. They were at odds personally, politically and tactically. Amber-eyed with rage, Collins would let fly volleys of violent, grotesque and obscene oaths; de Valera was invariably cool and courteous. Lecturing about the role of the Catholic hierarchy in Irish history, Collins finished with the cry "Exterminate them"; when de Valera visited the assembled hierarchy, one bishop said, "it was as the descent of the Holy Ghost upon them."[98] Collins was an irregular fighter of rare skill. De Valera did not "object to slaughter so long as it was organised,"[99] but he preferred to rely on votes before rifles. At the post-war general election, based on a large new franchise, he received democratic endorsement: Sinn Féin got 73 of 105 seats and virtually annihilated the old Home Rule party. Boycotting Westminster, the twenty-seven Sinn Féin members who were still at liberty met in Dublin's Mansion House on 21 January 1919 to form the Dáil Eirann, or Irish Parliament. It did not seem a momentous assembly, particularly as the Lord Mayor had that day welcomed home four hundred Dublin Fusiliers who had been prisoners of war and the place was ablaze with Union Jacks—a flag James Connolly had dubbed "the butcher's apron."[100] But the Dáil took up where the Rising had left off and at once issued a Declaration of Independence proclaiming that the Irish were a free people.

On the same day, Volunteers shot two policemen in County Tipperary, the first they had killed since the Rising. This began a process of terrorism designed to make Ireland ungovernable. Collins and his militants forced the pace. Being their leader, de Valera followed them. As the British hit back, Sinn Féin first encouraged and then organised further attacks on the Royal Irish Constabulary (RIC). The party was duly proscribed, Lloyd George condemning as crimes what Collins deemed acts of war. De Valera took other initiatives. He fostered an alternative system of administration, complete with its own courts and taxation system, which by 1920 superseded British rule in many areas. He also tried to gain the support in the United States of President Woodrow Wilson, patron of the rights of small nations. This was a shrewd move since, as the journalist A. G. Gardiner wrote, "The Atlantic bridge that Anglo-American good will must erect, must have Ireland as the keystone of its central arch." But Wilson, a Presbyterian minister manqué, had little sympathy for Sinn Féin. He refused, as a Chicago priest said, "to take poor Ireland down from the Cross on which she has been hanging for seven long centuries."[101] Moreover, de Valera's eighteen-month absence in the United States enabled Collins to accelerate the vicious cycle of outrage and retaliation. It was conducted with particular ferocity where green clashed with orange. When Lloyd George attempted to find a compromise in 1920 with his complex Government of Ireland Act, the six northeastern counties of Ulster got a parliament of their own, eventually housed at Stormont. This made partition a fact on the ground. But Sinn Féin rejected Britain's right to interfere in Irish affairs and repudiated any parliament in the south except the Dáil, its authority soon strengthened by another election. By the autumn of 1920, though, a widespread guerrilla war was raging. The IRA tried to fight their way out of the Empire, which struck back. Having defeated the Huns, said Winston Churchill, the British Empire would not surrender to "a miserable gang of cowardly assassins like the human leopards of West Africa."[102] With his fire-eating colleague Lord Birkenhead, who damned Ireland as "a plague-spot" of sedition at the heart of the Empire, he insisted on "coercion full-blast."[103]

So the government augmented their forty-thousand-strong contingent of constabulary and soldiery with a force known from their dark caps and belts and their khaki uniforms as the Black and Tans. Many of these mercenaries, together with an Auxiliary officer corps, had been toughened in the trenches. But their training for police work was inadequate. They found that their new enemies dispensed sudden death with military incontinence. But since the IRA wore plain clothes and were indistinguishable from civilians, the Black and Tans exacted vengeance on the population at large. When the IRA bombed and burned RIC barracks, which were described as "the blockhouses of imperial rule in Ireland,"[104] the Black and Tans incinerated factories, farms and houses, smashing, looting and driving people to take refuge in hedgerows and haystacks. IRA flying columns ambushed Crossley lorries used by the Black and Tans, who responded with night-time raids and arbitrary arrests. Both sides practised intimidation, the IRA shooting collaborators and shaving the heads of women alleged to have consorted with soldiers, the Black and Tans torturing and executing suspects in front of their families. Two bayoneted corpses discovered after a particularly barbaric attack on Balbriggan, County Dublin, "looked as though they had been killed not by human beings but by animals."[105] Commenting on the proliferation of atrocities, one Black and Tan volunteer wrote, "The real sufferer in this fratricidal war was the non-combatant."[106] The material fabric of Ireland also suffered. On a lovely May day in 1921 a large active service unit of the IRA, operating at the behest of de Valera himself, made a costly assault on the British local government office at Dublin's Custom House. The crowd gazed in fearful silence at the scene, which culminated in a fire and the collapse of the massive copper dome. John Dillon wrote despairingly: "the most beautiful building in Ireland a mass of flame and awful clouds of black smoke . . . deliberately destroyed by the youth of Ireland as the latest and highest expression of idealism and patriotism."[107]

Such a guerrilla army could not hope for military victory but it possessed certain advantages over a state wedded to liberal principles and constrained by democratic pressures. The imperial authorities might inflict violence, take hostages, impose curfews, place selected areas under martial law and hang terrorists, but they were not able, as Lloyd George wished, to grab murder by the throat. In deference to public opinion at home and abroad, Britain was inhibited from exerting its full power. It could not, as Lord French proposed, set up concentration camps. It could not, as recommended by Field-Marshal Sir Henry Wilson (assassinated on Collins's orders in 1922), shoot the enemy "by roster."[108] Nor could it, as Churchill suggested, machine-gun Sinn Féin meetings from the air. The government vacillated about retaliation, both defending reprisals and denying that they had occurred. It maintained, as Lord Hugh Cecil said, that "There is no such thing as reprisals, but they have done a great deal of good."[109] Meanwhile, the death of Irish hunger-strikers made more telling propaganda than British claims that they themselves were engaged in a life-and-death struggle for the Empire. In the American press the news that Terence MacSwiney, the Republican Lord Mayor of Cork, had died in Brixton Prison after a fast of seventy-four days eclipsed reports of the presidential election. Furthermore, respectful Londoners lined the route taken by his bier, which was draped in the Republican tricolour.

Such events pricked the British conscience. So did mendacious denials at Westminster about the depredations of Crown forces: the assertion, for example, that "the citizens of Cork had burnt their own city."[110] In fact, the hostilities were sporadic and the total number of lives lost amounted to no more than 1,500—an average day's casualties for the British Army during the Great War. But the *Irish Times* doubtless summed up the general view of the conflict: "The whole country runs with blood. Unless it is stopped and stopped soon every prospect of political settlement and material prosperity will perish and our children will inherit a wilderness."[111] There was also popular revulsion in England against the increasing use of "blackguardism" to defend the Empire. Protests were heard from Ottawa to Delhi, from Cape Town to Sydney, from Rome to Washington—the American agitation being a matter of particular anxiety to Lloyd George and Churchill. The writer Sir Philip Gibbs was struck by the universal

amazement and indignation that England, the champion of small peoples, the friend to liberty, pledged to the self-determination of peoples, should adopt a Prussian policy in Ireland after a war in which, after all, hundreds of thousands of Irishmen had fought for the Empire.[112]

"Bloody" Balfour himself wished "to end this uphill, sordid, unchivalrous, loathsome conflict."[113] On a visit to Belfast in June 1921 George V appealed for reconciliation and peace among all his subjects.

To the astonishment of Collins, whose fighting men were reaching the end of their resources, the British government executed an abrupt volte-face. Heeding Field-Marshal Wilson's warning that a still greater military effort would be required to crush the IRA, Lloyd George proposed instead to negotiate. In July a truce was arranged and de Valera himself took part in the initial discussions, stage-managed by the Prime Minister in front of a large map of the world, with the Empire marked in red. The confrontation ended in frustration. Arguing with this Catholic conservative nationalist, said the Welsh Wizard, was like trying to pick up mercury with a fork. Certainly the Irish President was a student of Machiavelli as well as a follower of Christ. Realising that compromise was unavoidable, he returned to Ireland and sent a team to London led by Collins and Griffith. Months of hard bargaining followed, culminating in the Prime Minister's threat to resume the war. So, on 6 December 1921, the two sides agreed terms. Collins correctly forecast that he had signed his own death warrant. In part this was because the Sinn Féin delegation had accepted the partition of Ireland, though it expected that a Boundary Commission would reduce Ulster to a rump which could not survive on its own. But the main count against Collins and his colleagues was that the treaty failed to produce a Republic, the sacred focus of what one Irish writer has called "a mystical, hysterical, neurotic worship."[114] Instead the new Irish Free State remained within the British Empire, accepting an oath of allegiance to the King. Those on the British side who had worked for a settlement regarded this as "the miracle of Anglo-Irish reconciliation, the resurrection of a nation, the redemption of the Commonwealth"[115]—General Smuts's term, which had just been officially adopted. Die-hards said that England's cowardly surrender to gun and bomb had doomed the Empire.

After bitter debates in the Dáil the treaty was ratified by a handful of votes, de Valera himself opposing it and Griffith forming a provisional government. The issue split the IRA as well as Sinn Féin and in 1922–3 Irishmen fought each other in a civil war that was far more ferocious than the conflict with England. Collins was shot, a victim of his own organisation. Yet his argument prevailed. The treaty achieved Parnell's dream of ending the Union. It afforded the new state a degree of independence—dominion status on the Canadian model—which permitted the evolution of a Republic as envisioned by Pearse. It gave "not the ultimate freedom to which all nations aspire," as Collins said, "but the freedom to achieve it."[116] De Valera lived to take advantage of that freedom, shaping the nation's past as well as its future. As Taoiseach he unveiled a memorial to the Easter martyrs at Dublin's General Post Office, deemed holier ground than Islandbridge. Set on a base of Connemara marble, inscribed with the proclamation of 1916, it was a representation of the death of Cuchulainn, the ancient Gaelic hero who symbolised "the dauntless courage and abiding constancy of our people."[117] Two years later, in 1937, de Valera introduced a new constitution for the Irish Free State that rejected the Crown. This was political apostasy in the view of imperialists such as Winston Churchill, who took to pronouncing his name "D'evil Éire."[118] But it was a crucial move towards breaking the last links with the British Empire. Ireland freed herself by her exertions and would help to free others by her example.

While the British tried to crush one nationalist rebellion in Ireland, they tried to foster another in the Middle East. The Turks had dealt the Allies crushing blows at Gallipoli and Kut, and by the beginning of 1916 they were poised to strike across Sinai at the Suez Canal. So Britain encouraged the Arabs to rise against their Ottoman masters. The nominal leader of the rebellion, which began in the Hejaz, the rocky province bordering the Red Sea, was Sherif Hussein of Mecca, a vicious local ruler who traced his descent back to Mohammed and to Adam, and liked to recite his genealogy. The campaign that followed became an imperial epic, glittering with oriental romance amid the gloom of Armageddon and correspondingly puffed in the western press. Its hero, Lawrence of Arabia, shaped his own legend by art as well as by action. T. E. Lawrence's book *The Seven Pillars of Wisdom* (1926) is a huge, complex, richly textured saga of the Arab revolt, in whose leaders he kindled a "flame of enthusiasm, that would set the desert on fire."[119] It is still not clear how much Lawrence's sumptuous account owes to his imagination, for even admirers considered him untrustworthy. Bernard Shaw noted that he was no "monster of veracity."[120] John Buchan said that he had a "crack in the firing."[121] Aubrey Herbert thought him "an odd gnome, half cad—with a touch of genius."[122] Even General Allenby reckoned him a brilliant poseur. Certainly Lawrence dramatised himself as a warrior-sage, an Arabian knight with a Stoic philosophy. In passages of modest-jaunty prose, he appears as a condottiere of cut-throats, who "cut throats to my order." He also features as an ascetic in the wilderness, doing without food and sleep, shunning the "unhygienic pleasure" of sex and driving his body with his mind. Adding layers of paradox to the self-portrait, Lawrence acknowledged that he was a man of masks.

He was a compulsive actor, a modern Hamlet (with a pinch of Puck) always eyeing his own performances "from the wings of criticism."[123] He yearned to occupy the centre of history's stage but would only back into the limelight. He courted fame but shunned publicity. Ostentatiously anonymous, he concealed himself behind flamboyant gestures and meretricious revelations. A slight, blonde figure, he enjoyed flaunting his white, silken Sherifian robes and relished Arabs' aversion to his blue eyes, which looked to them like the sky shining through the sockets of an empty skull. He presented himself as a flawed protagonist tormented by pride, remorse, doubt and degradation. But in his book, as in his career, mummery shades into mendacity. His various reports of his adventures do not tally. Lawrence admitted to inflating "dull little incidents" into "hair-breadth escapes" and acknowledged that he was "imprisoned in a lie."[124] Championing the Hashemite dynasty, he misrepresented the Emir Feisal, Hussein's timid and unreliable third son, as the Saladin of the Arab forces. Lawrence's celebrated account of being captured, tortured and raped by the Turks at Deraa is evidently a sado-masochistic fantasy. Such deception has prompted stern critics to denounce him as a charlatan engaged in a charade. One described Lawrence as "our Sodomite Saint" about whom everything is true except the facts.[125] Another damned the *Seven Pillars* as a "corrupt work" which transformed "a *fronde*" executed by loot-hungry tribesmen into a national uprising.[126]

Although Sherif Hussein proclaimed himself "King of the Arab nation,"[127] the Arab nation was a mirage. It lacked political, geographical and even linguistic coherence. It was a congeries of cultures. Islam had split into sects. Educated urban Arabs, whom the British (Lawrence included) tended to despise as the *babus* of the Middle East, afforded little unity. The nomadic clans of the desert existed to feud and raid. Although Lawrence complained about "the beastliness of living among the Arabs,"[128] he idealised the Bedouin as Pearse idealised the peasants; but they were capricious in their loyalties. They yearned for the "carnal paradise,"[129] replete with banquets, jewels and *houris,* promised by the Prophet Mohammed and proffered by the Ottoman Caliph. Yet they also desired the gold sovereigns which Lawrence distributed with such cavalier munificence. Without them, together with British ships, aeroplanes, armoured cars, explosives, weapons and supplies, the Arab revolt would have fallen to pieces. As it was, the Turks dismissed Arab attacks as "pinpricks" beside the "sledgehammer" blows of the British.[130]

Yet guerrilla raids on the railways and mass assaults on isolated garrisons forced the Turks to concentrate on defence and assisted General Allenby in his drive through Palestine. A modern army joined a feudal host which, as Lawrence described, advanced in barbaric splendour:

> Feisal in front in white. Sharaf on his right, in red headcloth and henna-dyed tunic and cloak, myself on his right in white and red. Behind us three banners of purple silk, with gold spikes, behind them three drummers playing a march, and behind them a wild bouncing mass of 1,200 camels of the bodyguard, all packed as closely as they could move, the men in every variety of coloured clothes, and the camels nearly as brilliant in their trappings—and the whole crowd singing at the tops of their voices a war song in honour of Feisal and his family! It looked like a river of camels, for we filled up the Wadi to the tops of its banks, and poured along in a quarter-of-a-mile-long stream.[131]

The Arabs themselves were astonished by the military force they could muster. Lawrence reported a remark of the brigand-like sheikh of the Howeitat tribe, Auda abu Tayi: "It is not an army but a world that is moving on al Wajh." A confederate replied, "Yes, we are no longer Arabs but a nation."[132]

Although the march on al Wajh, like many of Feisal's manoeuvres, actually proved to be a fiasco, some measure of Arab solidarity did emerge from the struggle against the Turks. The British even declared it to be a war of independence. Such assurances did not "matter much," according to Lord Grey, the Foreign Secretary, since an Arab state was "a castle in the air which would never materialise."[133] It was more sensible to consider what advantages the British themselves could extract from the disintegration of the Ottoman Empire. Having long sustained the sick man of Europe in order to keep the Russian bear at bay, they now aimed to kill him off and split up his inheritance. Perhaps they were inspired by Gibbon's account of the division of the spoils after the first crusade, whereby "the Latins reigned beyond the Euphrates."[134] Certainly they schemed for key territories on the road to India, to be ruled more or less directly according to circumstances. Officials ranging from Lawrence himself to Sir Reginald Wingate, who governed first the Sudan and then Egypt, wanted to create "a federation of semi-independent Arab states . . . looking to Great Britain as its patron and protector."[135] However, it was impossible to ignore France's historic interests in the region. So in 1916 the Sykes–Picot Agreement, named after the two diplomats who signed it, secretly carved Arab territories into spheres of influence, allotting their own countries the Fertile Crescent. The French would control Syria, the British Mesopotamia and southern Palestine, while the Arabs would be left with a desert almost the size of India. Lawrence, a British empire-builder with an "almost mystical zeal for the Arab cause,"[136] took this as a betrayal of those he was encouraging to fight. A divided self with divided loyalties, he was riven by guilt: "I was almost the chief crook of our gang."[137] Yet from his illegitimate childhood upwards, ambiguity had been the essential dimension to Lawrence's existence. So he connived at the intrigue, revealed the agreement to Feisal and relished the singularity of his double life.

In 1917 the Allies added new strands to the web of equivocation being spun around the Arabs. Carnage and mutiny on the Western Front, the Bolshevik Revolution in Russia and unrestricted submarine warfare in the Atlantic all made it seem that Germany might win before America could mobilise. So Lloyd George calculated that "the Jews might be able to render us more assistance than the Arabs."[138] Because of the Russian pogroms, Jews all over the world tended to favour the Central Powers. By satisfying the Zionist aspiration that the Children of Israel should return to the Promised Land, the Allies hoped to win their support. Many British leaders, brought up on the Bible, had listened sympathetically to Chaim Weizmann's account of "the tragedy of Jewish homelessness."[139] Weizmann, allegedly the controller of "universal Zionism," combined an "almost feminine charm . . . with a feline deadliness of attack."[140] So pro-Zionist members of the British government concluded that now was the time to right a historic wrong. But having swallowed the myth about the pervasive power of International Jewry, they were also animated by more sinister notions. Arthur Balfour, for example, accepted some of the "anti-Semitic postulates" of Cosima Wagner, herself later admired by Hitler. Although Balfour acknowledged that western civilisation owed the Jews a debt it could never repay, he wanted to alleviate the "age-old miseries"[141] which their alien presence caused in Gentile society. Many Jews suspected that the proposed refuge was a prelude to their compulsory repatriation and Balfour was not alone in thinking that "rootless cosmopolitans"[142] were best planted in the land of Israel. Any such initiative, though, might lead the Turks to massacre the 85,000 Jews of Palestine as they had massacred a million Armenians. Edwin Montagu wrote a cogent and perceptive paper entitled "The Anti-Semitism of the Present Government." His objections were ignored, as were those of Lord Curzon, who said that Jewish claims to Palestine were weaker on historic grounds than English claims to parts of France.

On 9 November 1917, the very day of the Bolshevik coup in Petrograd, the Balfour Declaration was made public. It committed the British government to "the establishment in Palestine of a national home for the Jewish people . . . it being clearly understood that nothing shall be done which may prejudice the civil and religious rights of existing non-Jewish communities."[143] No one knew how these antithetical aims could be reconciled. But Balfour, who exaggerated the propaganda impact of the Declaration in Russia and America, soon added a gloss to it. Zionism, he said, "is rooted in age-long traditions, in present need, in future hopes, of far profounder import than the desires and prejudices of the 700,000 Arabs who now inhabit that ancient land." Since Britain had freed them from Turkish tyranny, they would not grudge a "small notch" being taken out of "what are now Arab territories."[144] This proved to be a tragic miscalculation. Equally misguided was the idea that Jewish settlement would be British colonisation by proxy. But it was an idea shared by American Jews, who were thus alienated from Zionism, as well as by British leaders. The government in London reckoned that a Jewish Palestine, which it controlled but justified on the impeccable basis of self-determination, would guard Suez from the French in a diminished Syria. It would also secure British supremacy, challenged by the force of local nationalism, in the entire region. Palestine was the cornerstone of the Middle East and thus vital, in the Foreign Office's view, "to the security and well-being of the British Empire."[145] Instead of relying on treacherous Arabs, adept only at looting, sabotage and murder, wrote Richard Meinertzhagen in an influential memorandum, Britain should garrison the Holy Land with loyal Jews, a people who had "proved their fighting qualities since the Roman occupation of Jerusalem."[146]

British antipathy to the Arabs grew as Allenby prepared to mount the most spectacular advance of the whole war. Having earned his nickname in France largely by dint of bellowing, "the Bull" found scope in the Middle East to charge and gore. In 1917 Allenby became the first Christian soldier to capture Jerusalem since the Crusaders and he entered the city during the Maccabean feast of Hanukkah—achievements that offended Muslims but were otherwise much celebrated, not least by the first wartime ringing of the bells at Westminster Abbey. In 1918 he planned the final defeat of the Ottoman Empire, using Arab forces on his right wing. Although Lawrence, one of a number of Allied officers who fought with them, set an inspiring example of courage and élan, they still proved quick to retreat and desert. Nevertheless, in a series of daring forays they cut the Turks' railway link with Medina, an iron welt across the sand which the Bedouin regarded as an industrial assault on their pastoral existence. Allied air power was the key to these piecemeal successes. Arabs were particularly impressed by the huge Handley-Page bomber, which they saw as a stallion that had sired the smaller British fighters. Still more stirring was the breakthrough of Allenby's ground troops. Among them were British, Anzac and Indian cavalry, as well as French, Jewish and British West Indian units, which attacked in September, surprising and enveloping the enemy. Mounted men even managed to charge down Turkish and German machine-gunners. They swept over the hills of Judea and through the town of Nazareth, forcing General von Sanders to flee in his pyjamas. They cantered across the Plain of Armageddon and past the Sea of Galilee. East of the River Jordan, Arab forces made their own dash for Damascus. They inflicted hideous cruelties on the shattered Turkish columns, which Lawrence either glossed over in the *Seven Pillars* or condoned as a reaction against centuries of tyranny. The Anzacs, who themselves committed war crimes against hostile Arabs, a "race they despised," likened their native allies to jackals and vultures, scavenging ravenously over this "old blood-drenched land."[147]

In the hope that Feisal might "biff the French out of all hope of Syria,"[148] Lawrence urged him to beat Allenby to Damascus. He stressed the magic character of the oldest living city in the world, where the Omayyad caliphs had ruled over an empire stretching from India to the Atlantic. Here Abraham fought, here Trajan built, here Saladin lies. With its white minarets and gilded domes, its fountained courts and latticed caravanserais, its groves of palm and orchards of pomegranate, Damascus from a distance resembled "a pearl in the dancing sunlight."[149] Closer inspection revealed a warren of narrow streets filled with offal, patrolled by starving dogs and so dilapidated that in places the tram lines were nearly a foot above the ground. Still, the "queen city of the Levant"[150] was for the Arabs the glittering prize in the war. So Lawrence was mortified when the Australian Third Light Horse entered Damascus first. The inhabitants showered them with confetti and rose-water, kissing the men's stirrups and "becoming hysterical in their manifestations of joy."[151] Lawrence claimed that the Bedouin had earlier infiltrated the city. He also said that the Damascene welcome was really sparked off by the appearance of Feisal's main force, hundreds of dust-covered men riding camels and ponies and shooting their rifles in the air as fast as they could empty the magazines. Lawrence himself could not suppress their appetite for blood and spoil, and he had to call in Australian troops to restore order. But Arabs, whether citizens or soldiers, exulted over the smashing of the Ottoman yoke. All were "aflame with the hope of liberation and national independence."[152]

In the final week of the war the British and French fanned the fires of hope with another paper pledge. They declared that the peoples of the Ottoman Empire could freely establish national governments. Lloyd George aimed to discredit Bolshevik propaganda by thus endorsing the twelfth of Woodrow Wilson's Fourteen Points. He was also moved by a visceral hatred of the Turks, "a human cancer, a creeping agony in the flesh of the lands which they misgovern, rotting away every fibre of life."[153] Now nationalities liberated from Ottoman rule seemed to have an unmolested opportunity for self-development, a dispensation that excited an almost spiritual fervour throughout the region. A wounded Kurd in a Baghdad hospital was found to have had the promise translated on flyleaves of the Koran and "strapped like a talisman to his arm."[154] Yet acceptance of the Wilsonian point added to the tangle of British commitments in the Middle East. Moreover, ministers such as Curzon and Milner, encouraged by victory in the Levant and in the Caucasus as well as in Europe, now aimed to found a new empire between Egypt and India—tightening the golden thread of self-interest that made the entire mesh impossible to unravel. Luckily for Lloyd George, the Versailles Peace Conference cut this Gordian knot.

The mandate system was devised to enable winning powers to hold the colonies of the losers in the name of the League of Nations. The Americans took a Burkean view of mandates as "a sacred trust on behalf of civilisation."[155] The British regarded them as a method of draping "the crudity of conquest . . . in the veil of morality."[156] Curzon, for example, envisaged that "British influence in the Arab Middle East should be as self-effacing as possible and discreetly veiled by a façade of self-determination."[157] Mandates were thus a continuation of imperialism by other means. But it was a more emollient, apologetic, mealy-mouthed kind of imperialism, watered down by the ideals of Wilson and Lenin. As Sir Mark Sykes (of Sykes–Picot fame) wrote in 1918, "imperial annexation, military triumph, prestige, white man's burdens have been expunged from the popular political vocabulary."[158] However, Arabs exposed the euphemism, translating the word mandate as sovereign power. And from the Mediterranean to the Persian Gulf they resented the alien intrusion. Thus when France acquired the mandate over Syria, ousting Feisal, who had been proclaimed king, it faced a long rebellion. Britain, now ruling more than half the world's Muslims, obtained the mandates for Palestine and Mesopotamia, where a justified sense of betrayal also led to trouble. Arabs were particularly resistant to European domination after the Great War. Gertrude Bell, the intrepid desert traveller who worked for the British High Commission in Baghdad, noted that the West had lost all credit among Iraqis. They naturally revolted against a civilisation that had, she said, relapsed into barbarism during the conflict—"the end of the Roman empire is a very close historical parallel."[159]

Although sometimes a prey to doubt and division at the end of the war, the British had reason to feel confident. "We are the victors," declared King George V, "we are the Top Dog."[160] Curzon expressed the same sentiments more majestically. Ringing down the curtain on one of the most stupendous dramas in history and heralding the dawn of a golden age, he declared: "The British flag has never flown over a more powerful and united empire . . . Never did our voice count for more in the councils of nations; or in determining the future destinies of mankind."[161] The destiny of the land of the Tigris and Euphrates, Britons on the spot surmised, would be rather similar to that of the land of the Nile. Mesopotamia would be a disguised protectorate with the added advantage that there was apparently no need to divide in order to rule. For the three million inhabitants of Iraq, to give the country its Arabic, nationalist name, could hardly be regarded as a nation. It was a "skein of tribes"[162] on a frieze of sheikhdoms. Iraq had porous borders, roads that were either dust or mud, and a social structure so confusing that the British recreated it in their own image: urban effendi were seen as a corrupt aristocracy, sheikhs as loyal gentry, and tribesmen and fellaheen as sturdy peasants. Half the Muslim population were Sunnis, owing allegiance to Mecca, while half were Shias, looking towards Persia. The 700,000 Kurds in the mountainous north, a fierce Indo-European people in baggy trousers, coloured boleros and bandoleers, resisted all attempts at assimilation. Adding to the diversity were other communities, Jews and Assyrians, Sabaeans, whose religious duty was to live near running water, and Zelidis, who revered Satan.

One English visitor gauged the cosmopolitan confusion by the variety of headgear—"tarbushes, topees, turbans, straw hats, skull-caps, the Arab's *aagal* and *kefieh* [cord and the headdress it holds in place], the elongated felt coal-scuttle of the Lur or Kurd, the brimless top-hat of the Bakhtiari, the black astrakhan of the north."[163] But underneath this medley of coverings Iraqi minds concentrated on the fashion as well as the fact of infidel control. The acting Civil Commissioner in Baghdad, Sir Arnold Wilson, determined to encase the country in a "steel frame" of British officialdom.[164] Its authority buttressed by a fraudulent "plebiscite" and its power manifested in regular tax collection, his regime became "increasingly dictatorial."[165] Accustomed to Turkish flexibility and fired by Syrian appeals to "the Unity of Islam and the Rights of the Arab Race,"[166] Iraq rebelled. By the summer of 1920 tribal cavalry, flags waving to signify *jihad,* was ravaging much of the countryside. Baghdad itself was threatened and strengthened its citadel. Wilson, who flew from place to place variously dropping bombs and British officials, concluded that the revolt was caused by the "new wine" of nationalism fermenting in the "old bottles" of imperialism.[167] In essence it resulted from the attempt to create a unitary state from such diverse elements that they could only be fused together by force. Shocked by the explosion of ferocity, General Sir Aylmer Haldane called for reinforcements and urged his men to "be as rough as nutmeg-graters." They burned villages, destroyed crops, slaughtered livestock, killed some nine thousand people and executed ringleaders without trial. Within three months Haldane quelled the insurrection. He also disarmed tens of thousands of tribesmen, forcing them, as he put it, "to pass beneath the Caudine Forks."[168]

Since humiliation was likely to exasperate nationalist sentiment still further, the British government plumped for collaboration. Wilson was superseded by the hatchet-faced Sir Percy Cox, a man renowned for "his ability to keep silent in a dozen languages."[169] Called "Kokkus" by the Arabs, he was regarded by his compatriots as "a political officer with a gift for handling fickle and turbulent African barbarians."[170] Cox's task was to transform "the façade of existing administration from British to Arab."[171] This he did by establishing a new Council of State and replacing hundreds of imperial functionaries with Iraqis. At the behest of Winston Churchill, who as Colonial Secretary took advice from Lawrence, Cox also managed "to secure the early choice" of Feisal as King of Iraq in 1921.[172] In theory he was the people's sovereign, acclaimed in a referendum which gave him 96 per cent of the votes. In fact Feisal was a puppet foisted on the country and elected by ballot-rigging on a dictatorial scale. It was typified by an Arab prefect in the Kirkuk region who organised a petition supporting Feisal's candidature and then heard a rumour that the British had changed their minds; so he provided a petition opposing Feisal, complete with signatures, and presented both to his superior.

Still, the Hashemite King at least looked the part. Despite occasional manifestations of hatred for the imperial powers—during the Peace Conference he and Lawrence had flown over Paris dropping cushions in lieu of bombs—Feisal bore himself with regal dignity. Slim, bearded and aquiline, he liked to speak in proverbs: "everybody thinks their own lice gazelles."[173] The American Secretary of State Robert Lansing wrote, "his voice seemed to breathe the perfume of frankincense and to suggest the presence of richly coloured divans, green turbans, and the glitter of gold and jewels."[174] Gertrude Bell was dazzled by his appearance: the white gold-edged robes, the fine black *abba* (cloak) over them, the flowing white headdress and silver cord. But behind the exotic exterior, Feisal remained a slippery customer. Like other clients uncertain about where their best interests lay, he intrigued with his subjects and dissembled with his patrons. As a result everyone distrusted him. Gertrude Bell, usually as sweet as the roses around her beautiful little villa (known as "Chastity Chase") beside the Tigris, told Feisal that she "did not believe a word he said."[175] Meanwhile, the state threatened to disintegrate from internal feuds and external pressures, the latter mainly from a renascent Turkey. Lloyd George suggested handing Iraq (and Palestine) to America. Churchill was incensed by Feisal's procrastination over the treaty of alliance that would confirm Britain's paramount position in Iraq. Asking whether the King did not have some wives to keep him quiet, the Colonial Secretary threatened deposition: "He will be a long time looking for a third throne."[176] By dint of further menaces and manoeuvres High Commissioner Kokkus got the treaty accepted in 1922. Feisal's role as shadow sovereign was confirmed whereas, wrote Curzon, Cox had made himself "King of the Gulf."[177]

The Gulf states generally deferred to guns and gold, but Cox and his successors reigned with difficulty in Iraq, where eventually they themselves had to fade into the background, retaining substantial power but ceding formal independence. During the 1920s, though, the British fought for their position. They did so for the sake of prestige, an evanescent commodity, and oil, vast deposits of which were then discovered. They wanted to keep the Turks and the Bolsheviks at bay. They aimed to reverse the "moral degeneration" of Iraqi townsfolk, exemplified by their addiction to "certain unmentionable indoor sports."[178] This would be accomplished through education, organised games and the Boy Scout movement. The British also valued Iraq as a staging post in the new Empire Air Route and as a training ground for the Royal Air Force. At the 1921 conference that he held in Cairo to settle his policy for the Middle East, Churchill was primarily concerned to cut imperial expenses and he put his faith in aeroplanes. They came to be seen as the cheap, efficient, modern method of colonial control. They could deliver the high explosive that would stop Iraq from falling to pieces. Twenty-pound bombs dropped by low-flying, 114-mph De Havilland biplanes (all struts and spars, fixed wheels and open cockpits) would also induce impoverished desert dwellers to pay tax. There was a surreal quality about the enterprise. While enjoying the hospitality of Sufran tribesmen who were little more than beggars, Special Services Officer John Glubb "candidly told them that I was preparing the map to be used for the bombing, and that I myself would have to be in the leading aircraft."[179]

Most contemporaries seem to have been more impressed by the technical virtuosity of air control than by its moral deficiencies. The RAF gave demonstrations of bombing "native villages"[180] in Baghdad and at the Hendon Air Show in London, though these did not reveal the devastating effect of incendiaries on the vaulted reed houses of the marsh Arabs. Winston

Churchill was "strongly in favour of using poisonous gas against uncivilised tribes."[181] In fact, aerial repression was often used as a convenient alternative to terrestrial administration. The RAF privately acknowledged that "we rely on 'frightfulness' in a more or less severe form"[182] and at Westminster left-wing MPs protested about "this Hunnish and barbarous method of warfare against unarmed people."[183] Certainly bombs helped to entrench Iraqi hatred of alien authority, a hatred liable to concentrate opposition and to express itself in terrorism. Despite the factional rivalries and ministerial convolutions that punctuated Feisal's reign, Iraq continued to agitate for a measure of national sovereignty. Ramsay MacDonald's Labour government granted this by the treaty of 1930, which came into force two years later when Iraq entered the League of Nations. Britain would retain control over defence and some administrative matters for a quarter of a century, it was agreed, but Feisal's oligarchy would exercise much more sway within the country. Iraq was far from being free but it had significantly weakened the imperial hold.

A similar process went on in Egypt, where post-war rebellion *(thaura)* also became the catalyst that precipitated nominal independence. "A witch's cauldron had been brewing," said Lord Milner, "almost ever since Cromer left."[184] It reached simmering point in 1914, when the British stripped the veil from Cromer's protectorate. They renounced Ottoman overlordship. They replaced the Khedive with a Sultan. And they openly incorporated Egypt into the British Empire. Having broken all promises to let the Egyptians go, Britain had to hold the lid on the cauldron throughout the Great War. A large garrison assisted, including units that boasted such nicknames as the Jordan Highlanders, the Royal Jewsiliers and Pharaoh's Foot. The imperial power imposed martial law, tight controls on newspapers and stern rules of assembly. Bars and cafés had to close early. Restrictions were placed on gatherings of all sorts, among them weddings, funerals, and feasts for local saints. The authorities even suppressed "snake charmers, acrobats, wandering conjurors, and suchlike Oriental accessories."[185] The conflict itself caused extra hardships such as high prices and a shortage of imports. "Volunteers" were forced to labour, which effectively revived the corvée and broke a British promise that Egypt would not have to bear any burden of the war. Furthermore, camels were conscripted and farmers had to grow grain rather than the more lucrative crop of cotton. The 1,600 British officials hardly sensed the mounting head of steam. Indeed, they sometimes augmented political provocation with personal affront. At the British Residency, a large, uncomfortable, verandahed house built for Cromer overlooking the Nile, one senior man apparently interviewed Egyptian notables with a dog (unclean to Muslims) perched on his shoulder. Yet the British prided themselves on giving Egypt the best government since a "Roman prefect was seated on the splendid throne of the Ptolemies."[186]

In fact, civil servants such as Ronald Storrs, an aesthete whose silky auburn moustache conveyed "a hint of dilettantism in the way it curled up slightly at the ends,"[187] were inveterately idle. Storrs, known as "Oriental Storrs" after an untrustworthy emporium of that name in Cairo, claimed that he and his colleagues were "hard and honourable" workers.[188] But he acknowledged that they only worked until noon. They spent the rest of the day at the Turf Club or the Gezira Sporting Club, where any Egyptian presence was "ground for indignation."[189] Wartime recruits to the service, often "temporary gentlemen," were still less likely to make contact with the natives. In any case, the British were deceived about the effervescence of opinion by their own censorship—the muzzled press did not growl. Portents of trouble might have been discerned in the manoeuvres of the new Sultan, Ahmed Fuad, who in 1917 attempted to assert his prerogative of appointing ministers. The following year, just as the war was ending, the Anglo-French declaration encouraged Egyptian politicians to demand a programme of complete self-rule. The High Commissioner, Sir Reginald Wingate, realised that nationalist sentiment was now coming to the boil: crowds of men in white gallabeahs, inspired by Woodrow Wilson's "twelfth commandment," haunted the American embassy in Cairo as if seeking a sign. Wingate urged the Foreign Office to respond favourably to reasonable Egyptian wishes. But the instinct of its chief, now Lord Hardinge, was merely to give brown politicians "a good dressing-down."[190] It ignored Wingate, just as his own officials ignored the discontent about to engulf Egypt. Warned that a conflagration was imminent, Wingate's Financial and Judicial Adviser Sir William Brunyate said that he "would put out the fire by spitting on it."[191]

Wingate himself struck the spark that kindled the blaze. Immediately after the armistice he prohibited the foremost nationalist politician, Said Zaghlul, from leading a delegation to put the case for Egyptian independence in London and Paris. Zaghlul thereupon formed his own delegation, or *Wafd*. This was a political party (though he preferred to call it a national movement) dedicated to breaking the imperial bond. Like de Valera and Feisal, Zaghlul was a complex and inscrutable figure. Tall, white-moustached and red-fezzed, with a wrinkled Mongolian visage, he was a lawyer from a prosperous peasant background who had been a minister under Cromer and later navigated cannily through the shoals of court cabal and pasha faction.

The British now viewed him as an opportunist and a demagogue. By contrast, the American ambassador characterised him as Egypt's Theodore Roosevelt. Zaghlul possessed a stubborn will and a flamboyant personality. Ruthless, charming, eloquent and vain, this ailing old man came to dominate both the Wafd and the nation. Furious that Feisal was at the Peace Conference while Egypt was unrepresented, Zaghlul organised petitions and stirred up anti-British agitation. On 9 March 1919 he and three associates were arrested for sedition and deported to Malta. This provoked an explosion of wrath. Protests and demonstrations rocked Cairo. Chanting "Free Egypt" and "Death to the English," students poured through the gates of el-Azhar, the radiant mosque revered as the most ancient seat of learning in the Muslim world. For the first time women engaged in political action, casting off their veils and waving banners as they marched through the streets. Crowds attacked Europeans, burned houses, smashed trains and looted shops.

Over the next few weeks riots, strikes and killings multiplied. The Commandant of the Cairo Police described his confrontation with thousands of men carrying staves, spear heads, chisels, adzes and jagged bits of cast-iron gratings.

> The whole mob was shrieking and yelling and waving their weapons in the air. If you can imagine a drawing by Hogarth of a scene made up of Dante's Inferno and the French Revolution, add to that mad oriental fanaticism—and you have something like this mob.[192]

Hideous instances of murder and mutilation occurred, often carried out by terrorists who were promised paradise in return for martyrdom. When a British police officer was shot in front of the Abdin Palace men and boys danced in his blood, shouting "Allah, Allah," and women urinated on his corpse. Moreover, violence spread to the provinces. The fellaheen, the "Tortured on Earth,"[193] who had not been regarded as politically combustible, took fire. Fearing another Indian Mutiny, the British fought fire with superior firepower. They employed aircraft and armoured cars. They bombed and machine-gunned crowds. They imprisoned and flogged villagers. Imperial troops, Indians as well as Australians, reacted ferociously against a race for which they had the utmost contempt. But while taking punitive measures, top British officials recognised that "the principles of Nationalism and the desire for independence have bitten deep into all classes." They believed that imperial policy towards Egypt must change to reflect an "increased sympathy with national aspirations so far as they keep *within* legitimate limits."[194]

The struggle to define those limits continued for more than three decades, but the essential decision was made by "Bull" Allenby, who replaced Wingate in April 1919. That rarity, a general who had won laurels in the Great War, he was appointed High Commissioner to restore order to Egypt. This he did during the following months though intermittent disturbances persisted and discontent remained at fever pitch among all classes, from effendi to fellaheen. The Wafd organised opposition ranging from boycotts to assassinations. Secret societies such as the "Black Hand" and the "Red Eye," some fostered in el-Azhar, practised intimidation, sabotage and murder, often by garrotting. In the familiar British manner Allenby leavened severity with appeasement. He released Zaghlul and permitted him to go to Paris, where his delegation achieved little—President Wilson privately advised Arabs to imitate the Americans of 1776 but publicly recognised Egypt as a British protectorate. Allenby also accepted a commission of inquiry into the disorders. It was led by Lord Milner and charged with the task of devising a constitution that would secure peace and prosperity. The Wafd instigated further violence and ostracised Milner's mission. They picketed the Hotel Semiramis, the new marble and bronze monstrosity where Milner and his colleagues were staying, so that they could only consult Egyptians in secret. Zaghlul refused to meet the mission in Cairo even after dark. Despite present rejection and his own proconsular past, Milner rapidly came to adopt Allenby's view of the situation. Nothing but self-government could pacify Egypt, which was currently a thorn in Britain's side as sharp as India, Ireland and Iraq.

Of course it would be the shadow of self-government not the substance, about which, he thought, orientals cared less. Milner told Lloyd George,

> The difficulty is to find a way of making Egypt's relation to Great Britain *appear* a more independent and dignified one than it ever really can be without our abandoning the degree of control which, in view of native incompetence and corruption we are constrained to keep.[195]

He tried to overcome this difficulty by producing a plan for Egypt (but not the Sudan) to receive formal independence while Britain retained control of defence and other administrative matters, mainly to do with finance and foreign residents. Negotiating an agreement along these lines was complicated by rivalries in both Cairo and London, where politicians were anxious not to be accused of betraying their country's interests. Zaghlul was so uncompromising that he provoked outbreaks of communal strife. Winston Churchill, who feared imperial dismemberment at a time when "Red Bruin" was on the rampage and regarded Arabs as barbarians who lived on camel dung, also opposed Milner's scheme. So did Lloyd George, who was simultaneously trying to conciliate Ireland. But the Prime Minister heeded the warning that unless a settlement were reached in Egypt "Zaghlul will begin to create a Pan-Islamic Sinn Féin machine making mischief every-where and linked up with Turks, Indians etc. all over the world."[196]

To preserve the Empire, coercion must give way to cooperation. Allenby clinched the matter by exiling Zaghlul to the Seychelles and then threaten-ing to resign if the protectorate were not brought to an end. Exactly forty years after the occupation, therefore, Britain unilaterally declared Egypt independent—on limited terms acceptable to Lloyd George. They were anathema to Zaghlul. Hard-line British imperialists also condemned the grant of liberty, which they took to be a capitulation to violence. And it has subsequently been represented as another instance of a post-war "weakening of the will to rule . . . which was to make the dissolution of the British Empire so ugly and ruinous."[197] There is no doubt that by ceding autonomy Britain had cut at the root of its position in Egypt. But the concession resulted not so much from a failure of nerve as from a change of mind. The British government recognised that it lacked the military strength and the moral authority to run the Empire in the manner of old Cromer or young Milner. Times had altered. Money was tight. Fresh ideals were in the air, perhaps to be realised if Ramsay MacDonald's Labour Party took office. White domination of coloured races was ceasing to be respectable. As one Whitehall mandarin said, the traditional type of imperial rule was "dying in India and decomposing in Egypt."[198]

However, the new type of imperial rule, dressed up in liberal language and presented as a form of trusteeship, enjoyed a certain vigour during the course of its short and troubled life. This was because hard-headed British practice belied high-minded British professions. The High Commissioner made full use of his remaining powers, which could always be backed up by force. As one official wrote, all the Egyptian army's "ammunition is in the Citadel with a perfectly good British battalion sitting on it."[199] At the bosky fifteenth hole of the Gezira golf course Lord Lloyd, who succeeded Allenby in 1925, was sometimes prompted to draw on heavier metal. "When I see those jacarandas in bloom," he said, "I know it's time to send for a battle-ship!"[200] Lloyd's mission in life was to advance himself and to prevent an imperial retreat. He had deplored Milner's truckling to Egypt and said that "we all know what happens to Empires when they begin to withdraw their legions." He came to believe that the spirit of compromise was rotting the soul of the Tory party at home. Indeed, he dreaded the slow, voluntary disintegration of Greater Britain abroad, preferring some kind of imperial Götterdämmerung, when the Last Post would ring out "on the flaming ramparts of the world." A dapper, monocled little misogynist, with oiled hair and an olive complexion, Lloyd had been an authoritarian Governor of Bombay. Now he longed to administer the smack of paternal government to the Egyptians, described by his wife as "childish, half-baked people."[201] The Lloyds' hauteur was as pronounced as their hostility. He particularly disdained the citified Arab in bowler hat and brown boots who lived as "a parasite upon the fringes of Western civilisation."[202] He thus alienated most Cairo politicians, including Zaghlul. In 1929 the Foreign Office actually negotiated with the nationalists behind Lloyd's back in order to secure his departure.

Nevertheless, Lloyd and his two successors, Sir Percy Loraine and Sir Miles Lampson, were adept at playing the King (as Fuad became in 1922), the Wafd and the sectional parties against one another. Fuad himself was no cipher despite a family weakness for Italian mistresses and an unusual handicap. He had a bullet lodged in his throat, put there by his brother-in-law, which made him bark like a dog—meeting him in 1922 Edward Prince of Wales was almost reduced to convulsions by the "royal yappings."[203] Fuad, whose moustache waxed so spiky that he seemed to have sprouted tusks, was a Machiavellian monarch. Austen Chamberlain described him as "sly, scheming, corrupt and autocratic."[204] Fuad pulled the strings of his court marionettes, as he called them. He also exploited the new constitution to acquire as much power and wealth as possible, while condemning Egyptian politicians for trying to get rich too quickly. This did not make him popular. Zaghlul was right in saying that although Fuad was "the King of Egypt, I am the King of their hearts." But, opposed both by the Residency and by the Palace, as well as by other influential interests, the Wafd could seldom hold office for long despite overwhelming majorities at the polls. It was, moreover, badly led after Zaghlul's death in 1927. His successor, Mustafa Nahas, was volatile to the point of madness. Described as "a cross-eyed albatross,"[205] he presided over a party that succumbed to faction, corruption and ossification. During the years of economic crisis caused by the Great Depression, therefore, political intrigue and royal repression prevailed in the land of the Nile. The British High Commissioner held the ring, usually in an intimidating manner—Loraine regarded Egyptians as "wretched brutes"[206] and habitually stared at those he invited to his study "without a word, his large lack-lustre eyes revealing no flicker of interest."[207] Fuad complained in 1935 that the Egyptian Prime Minister "dared not move a pencil on his desk without Residency advice."[208]

Yet the British position was steadily weakening in the Levant. This was largely because of the rise of potent foes in Europe and Asia, which stretched the Empire's defensive resources to breaking point. Mussolini's invasion of Ethiopia in October 1935 sharply exposed the extent of British feebleness. Having failed to buy off the Duce, whom the Admiralty thought liable, if thwarted, to carry out a "mad-dog act,"[209] Stanley Baldwin's government would not even close the Suez Canal to Italian ships. When General Badoglio marched into Addis Ababa in May 1936, Egypt seemed still more vulnerable to Fascist aggression, situated as it was between the Libyan hammer and the Ethiopian anvil. So in that year another Anglo-Egyptian treaty was signed, stipulating (among other things) that Egypt would join the League of Nations and that British troops would only garrison the Suez Canal zone. Britain's prestige was also seriously damaged by its conduct in Palestine. By carving the Arab state of Transjordan from the Promised Land and putting Feisal's brother Abdullah on its throne, it offended the Jews. By appointing Sir Herbert Samuel as High Commissioner in 1920, "the first Jewish ruler in Palestine since Hyrcanus II, that last degenerate Maccabean,"[210] in about 40 BC, it offended the Arabs. When he opened the door to Jewish settlement, in the spirit of the Balfour Declaration (which officials refused to publish in Palestine), Arabs were still further alienated. As will appear, the problems of Palestine were uniquely intractable. They were epitomised by the fact that Jerusalem was at once the city of David, the sepulchre of Christ and the site of Mohammed's ascent into heaven. So the holy ground, which the Romans ploughed up after they had destroyed the Temple of Solomon, was always polluted by the presence of infidels and always a scene of conflict.

Lloyd George and Baldwin could not succeed where Hadrian and Titus had failed. They were anyway preoccupied by trying to build a nation fit for heroes to live in at home, by attempting to satisfy the demands of a democracy that now gave most women the vote. Moreover, Britain was on the defensive elsewhere in the Middle East, the broadness of its grasp concealing the fragility of its grip. In 1919 Afghanistan declared war and Britain signed a treaty that allowed the Emir Amanullah to pose as the liberator of his people. Simultaneously the "Mad Mullah" was again on the attack in British Somaliland. In 1921 the new military dictator of Persia, Reza Khan, abolished Britain's traditional sphere of influence. The following year Lloyd George nearly spilt more British blood at the Dardanelles by supporting

Greece in its war against Turkey. But he got little support from the Domin-ions and his coalition ministry was brought down by the Tory leader, Bonar Law, who declared: "We cannot act alone as the policeman of the world."[211] Violence flared up in the Yemen and Transjordan, where the Arab Legion was formed under British officers. During 1924 mutinies occurred in the Sudan. At the same time Ibn Saud of Riyadh defeated Britain's Hashemite client Hussein and in 1932 he created the kingdom of Saudi Arabia. The post-war setbacks to the British Empire, particularly those in India and Ire-land, were all the more serious because of its economic stagnation and its exposed position on the international scene. It could expect little save dis-tant rumbles of thunder from the United States, now withdrawing into iso-lation. But it anticipated bolts of lightning from the other incipient superpower, Communist Russia, which purveyed throughout the world an ideology profoundly hostile to colonialism. In the apocalyptic words of Lord D'Abernon, the Soviet Union threatened Great Britain and its stupen-dous possessions with a "cataclysm equalled only by the fall of the Roman Empire."[212]

11

Englishmen Like Posing as Gods

West and East

Despite the Great War and its troubled aftermath, the British Empire continued to bestride the world like a colossus. Chiefly because the United States and the Soviet Union were so bound up in their own affairs—especially during the Depression, when there seemed little to choose between anaemic capitalism and bloody Communism—Britain remained the sole superpower. It dominated the League of Nations. Through the Locarno Pact (1925) it pacified Europe until the rise of Nazi Germany. Its imperial bounds reached their widest extent, encompassing, as geographers liked to boast, "one continent, a hundred peninsulas, five hundred promontories, a thousand lakes, two thousand rivers, ten thousand islands."[1] It evolved new methods of colonial control, putting more reliance on indirect rule through local elites. It found a way to run the Empire on the cheap, not just by using aircraft and armoured cars but by limiting the construction of capital ships. The Washington naval agreement (1921–2) led Britain to renounce its alliance with Japan and to share the "sceptre of Neptune" with the United States, "the one nation with which, above all things, we wish to live on terms of friendship."[2] In 1926 Balfour bound the dominions to the mother country with a final piece of verbal gossamer: they became "autonomous communities within the British Empire, equal in status . . . and freely associated as members of the British Commonwealth of Nations."[3] This indefinite definition was affirmed by the Statute of Westminster in 1931. After the violence in Ireland, the Levant and India, a lull occurred. Then it was possible to believe that the Free State would stay in a more closely united Empire, that Britain could establish a "Monroe Doctrine" for the Middle East and that the subcontinent would continue to glitter in the royal diadem.

Elsewhere bearers of the white man's burden supposedly exhibited a "genius for colonisation which has made the British Empire the greatest ever known."[4] This enormous edifice, apologists claimed, was a monument to the highest type of civilisation. It was the "greatest political experiment ever attempted," said Sir Evelyn Wrench, founder of the Over-Seas League. It could pioneer a way towards "the federation of mankind,"[5] he thought, just as Rome should have aspired to become, according to the elder Pliny, the common fatherland to all the peoples of the earth. In its might, majesty, dominion and power, the British Empire even appeared to prophets such as Leopold Amery and Lionel Curtis to be part of the divine order. In the gospel according to Amery the Empire was no mere super-state; it was, "like the Kingdom of Heaven, within us."[6] Curtis, who founded the quarterly *Round Table,* Chatham House (the Royal Institute of International Affairs) and other bodies designed to promote imperial union, collected "not more than 12 disciples"[7] and preached that the Empire was "the Kingdom of God on earth."[8] Foreigners were impressed against their will. On a journey round the world in 1922 Lord Northcliffe met an American who reluctantly acknowledged that "travelling in the Far East is a revelation as to Britain's greatness, and our vast possessions make Uncle Sam 'sit up and take notice.'"[9] Adolf Hitler himself was riveted by Britain's global hegemony and in *Mein Kampf* he called it "the greatest power on earth."[10]

This was a representation that Whitehall mandarins did not scruple to embellish. They had earlier invited Sigismund Goetze to paint a series of allegorical murals for the Foreign Office and soon after the armistice he completed his final panel, entitled "Britannia Pacificatrix."[11] Designed to show a victorious Britain upholding peace with the aid of far-off sons and allies, it is set against a marble colonnade topped with a Latin inscription. At the centre Britannia, magnificent in a plumed helmet and red, white and gold draperies, shakes hands across the sea with America, wearing the cap of liberty and holding the scales of justice. She is flanked by Italy, with axe and fasces (symbols of Roman law), and France, grasping a short sword which points down at the wreckage of Germany's war machine. In a supporting role are the dominions, Newfoundland with its trident, South Africa in its lion skin, Canada crowned with wheat and girded with maple leaves, Australia in its Digger's hat and New Zealand with its golden fleece. India appears in a suit of armour. Feisal embodies the epic of Arabia. Greece carries a statue, Romania an oil jar and Japan cherry blossom, while a black boy with a cornucopia of fruit on his head signifies the potential of Africa. Sheltering under Britannia's mantle are the naked victims of the conflict, notably Belgium, emerging from the horrors of war with broken sword but unsullied flag. Here, dignified by its classical iconography, was a triumphant image of Britain's post-war might and magnanimity. Curzon said that the painting was not art but melodrama. Really it was propaganda. It was an emblem of the endeavour, which intensified between the wars, to enhance British prestige in order to compensate for the relative decline of British power.

To be sure, the promotion of Empire was almost as old as the Empire itself. But Northcliffe and others had developed techniques for manipulating public opinion during the Great War when "propaganda, like a gigantic upas tree, dripped its poison over all nations."[12] Afterwards Britain made an unprecedented effort to rally democracy behind the imperial standard, so much so that inter-war governments were accused of "tampering with the human will,"[13] engendering a herd instinct and placing the mass "mind in chains."[14] New media were exploited. The cinema, more thrilling than the magic lantern show and easier to censor than the music hall, overtook the theatre as a means of fostering imperial sentiment. Films ranged from documentaries such as *Palaver,* which showed a British District Officer "administering justice, building roads and bridges, teaching the natives to develop the country and live peaceably together,"[15] to epics such as *Lives of a Bengal Lancer,* which Hitler used to teach the SS how a tiny elite could subjugate an inferior race. The wireless and the gramophone conveyed better pictures still, bringing the Empire vividly to life in the imagination of listeners. The British Broadcasting Corporation filled the nation's homes with "aural pageants"—royal ceremonies, military parades, religious services and the like.[16] It gave weight as well as wings to the imperial message, intimating that the plummy accent of the Establishment was the voice of objectivity. Traditional methods of advertising Greater Britain, everything from chocolate boxes to brass bands, from royal tours to popular songs, also flourished during the 1920s. Cigarette cards were never more popular or more patriotic. Scouting boomed and with it exhortations to khaki-shorted youth not to "be disgraced like the young Romans, who lost the Empire of their forefathers by being wishy-washy slackers without any go or patriotism in them."[17] Comics encouraged what George Orwell called "gutter patriotism." Juvenile literature depicted a timeless Britain where the King is on his throne, the pound is good as gold and the fleet is in the Channel, while comic foreigners jabber on the Continent and at the outposts of the Empire "monocled Englishmen are holding the niggers at bay."[18] The Beefeater press purveyed stereotypes that were scarcely less crude, as did schools, men's clubs, women's institutes and other organisations.

Yet it is doubtful whether they had much impact. Old colonial hands continued to complain that no one at home took the slightest interest in their affairs. One Viceroy, Lord Reading, observed that English people only listened to talk about India out of politeness. Another, Lord Willingdon, declared that lack of awareness about India was especially marked at Westminster: "He was amazed at Baldwin's ignorance; & still more amazed that he should not *want* to know."[19] Intellectuals said that the writings of Kipling, Haggard, Henty and their ilk no more won converts to the cult of Empire than Gothic melodrama inspired "a belief in ghosts."[20] Experts acknowledged the difficulty of influencing the public mind. For it was not a *tabula rasa* or blank sheet on which the imperial creed could be inscribed; it was a palimpsest of differing opinions and a "phantasmagoria of conflicting values."[21] Propaganda, which became a dirty word as wartime atrocity stories were exposed as lies, seemed less to direct popular views than to reflect official policy. In fact, Britain's drumbeat sounded louder as its Empire grew more hollow.

Nothing illustrated this better than the British Empire Exhibition at Wembley, the most ambitious show of its kind ever staged. When George V pressed the button on a golden globe to open it on 24 April 1924, amid scenes of dazzling ceremonial, he telegraphed a message of imperial power round the world in eighty seconds. The audience cheered the boy who delivered the telegram to His Majesty confirming this electronic feat almost as rapturously as it greeted the King, whose amplified voice, according to the *Daily Mail,* caused an African chief in the crowd to exclaim: "This is magic!"[22] Commentators were equally awed. They hailed the exhibition as "the greatest co-operative effort for peaceful ends the British Empire has ever made."[23] Of the fifty-eight countries in an Empire of four hundred million people covering fourteen million square miles—seven times larger than the territories of Rome at their greatest extent—only two or three failed to contribute. At a cost of £12 million the rest filled the 220 acres at Wembley with a bonsai version of this great association, as rich in detail as Queen Mary's doll's house (designed by Lutyens) which was also on display. The twin-towered sports stadium and the huge pavilions around it were erected at astonishing speed by the use of concrete. Indeed, the Palace of Engineering, covering a space over six times the size of Trafalgar Square, was the biggest concrete building on earth. But nothing seemed more to merit the eulogy of its builder, Sir Robert McAlpine, "the Concrete King," than the stadium itself, the finest in the world.

> When Titus of Ancient Rome built the vast Amphitheatre, known on account of its colossal size as the Colosseum, taking sixteen years to do the job, it probably did not enter his imperial mind that one day a stadium

almost three times as large, and infinitely more enduring, would be constructed in less than a tithe of the time by a nation he and his forebears thought it scarcely worth while to conquer.[24]

The twin towers, which scarcely survived the British Empire, were a Mughal excrescence on a Roman base and they typified the eclecticism of Wembley's architecture. Canada and Australia favoured the neo-classical. South Africa built a traditional Dutch mansion with stoep, loggia and pantiled roof. India amalgamated its largest mosque and its finest tomb, the Jami Masjid and the Taj Mahal, to create an alabaster palace. West Africa raised a three-acre, red-walled city encompassing a terracotta fort. Burma constructed an old Moulmein pagoda and Ceylon a Kandian temple. The Palace of Beauty was a melange of cream stone, Siena marble and lapis lazuli.

Laid out amid lakes and gardens, connected by the "Never-Stop Railway" and illuminated after dark by three million lights, these edifices were an imperial treasure casket. They contained gold, diamond and coal mines; furs, forests and fisheries; coffee, tea, sugar and rubber plantations; timber mills, ostrich farms, sheep stations, rice paddies, cotton fields, palm groves, oil wells, chocolate factories. Craftsmen from India to the West Indies wove cloth, worked leather and beat metal. Hong Kong offered a picturesque street of shops. Egypt provided a replica of Tutankhamun's tomb, complete with dragomans. Bermuda showed "Old Glory" being hoisted when America took over part of the dockyard during the war. England presented famous naval battles fought with model ships and a gigantic map of the world set in water. In front of its pale grey pavilion Australia placed an equestrian statue of Apollo in the chariot of the sun. Along with Mounties, Canada contributed a statue of the Prince of Wales carved in butter. Prince Edward himself said that the exhibition was "the Empire's shop window."[25] It did indeed promote sales of an exotic range of goods: everything from Canadian hockey sticks to Australian eucalyptus oil, from Malayan copra to Gold Coast cocoa, from Fijian turtle shells to Hong Kong human hair commodities, from New Zealand artificial limbs to Newfoundland eelgrass. Moreover, it led to the establishment of the Empire Marketing Board, designed to "sell the idea of Empire production and purchase . . . as a co-operative venture."[26] Yet as appears from the historical pageants and torchlight tableaux, the Scout jamborees and martial tattoos, the music by Elgar and street names by Kipling, the Exhibition was much more than a trade fair. It was, insisted *The Times,* "a true shrine of Empire." Its purpose was to make the imperial faith burn more brightly, to renew communion between all the King's subjects in the aftermath of the war and thus to win the peace. Majesty was the essence of the imperial saga, "'majestas' in the full Roman sense, but loftier and purer than all the majesty of Rome."

However, as *The Times* further observed, since the Crown was the sole bond of Empire "the weakness and dangers of the system are manifest."[27] So despite the pomp and circumstance, which Elgar himself found "irredeemably *vulgar,*"[28] the Exhibition bore involuntary witness to the frailty of the system. Plagued by labour troubles, it was not completed on time and stucco façades concealed a litter of tangled wires, twisted pipes and broken packing cases. It attracted twenty-seven million visitors but lost £600,000. It proved too expensive for many workers though the hard-pressed waitresses in its cafés and restaurants were woefully underpaid. Its fifty-acre amusement park seemed to be "a Roman circus where the populace could . . . seek a refuge from reality."[29] It confirmed racial prejudice: Zulu clerks in European employment were "painfully endeavouring," said *The Times*'s final Wembley supplement, "to assimilate the lessons of a man to the mind of a child."[30] It was politically divisive. The short-lived Labour ministry endorsed the Exhibition and the Empire, despite Ramsay MacDonald's earlier insistence that imperial expansion was "only the grabbings of millionaires on the hunt."[31] But many socialists still held such views and they disparaged the Wembley carnival. The left-wing *New Statesman* snubbed it. The *Daily Herald,* which was subsidised with tsarist jewels by Bolsheviks who identified the colonies as the "Achilles' heel" of British capitalism,[32] virtually ignored it. Instead the paper printed a hagiography of Lenin and publicised George Lansbury's confession that the minority Labour government could not implement a true socialist policy towards the Empire, "even if any of us were quite sure what that policy should be."[33] The closing speech by the Duke of York (the future King George VI) was a stammering embarrassment. All told, the Exhibition scarcely restored confidence in the British Empire's capacity to develop and, in the wake of the war, to undertake "the biggest rebuilding job our planet has ever seen."[34] Yet Britons believed that the Empire "must grow or it must decay."[35] So, for all its splendour, symbolised by the six lions at the entrance to the British Government pavilion, the Exhibition also suggested that the imperial structure was infected by decrepitude. Ravaged by conflict and bloated by mandates, the Empire was suffering from what Beatrice Webb called "a sort of senile hypertrophy."[36]

.   .   .

What kept the gigantic enterprise of empire going was something of a mystery, for the officials who conducted it were astonishingly thin on the ground. The Indian Civil Service was only 1,250 strong. Its Malayan equivalent numbered 220 and its Ceylonese a hundred. Britain ruled the forty-three million people in the two million square miles of its dozen or so African colonies with 1,200 administrators, two hundred judges and legal officers, and a thousand policemen and soldiers (not one above the rank of lieutenant-colonel). About forty Englishmen governed Sarawak. Sometimes a man in his twenties might take charge of a piece of Africa as big as Yorkshire or, like Leonard Woolf in pre-war Ceylon, a jungle district of four hundred square miles containing not one other European. Of course, any sudden upsurge of violence could overwhelm this "thin white line."[37] So the British augmented their power by collaborating with local elites and enhanced their prestige by insisting on white superiority. Keeping up appearances was deemed vital. Probably the single most evocative vignette of empire is George Orwell's account of how, as a policeman in Burma, he shot an elephant that had gone on the rampage, in order to sustain the dignity of his own race. The animal no longer posed a danger yet, equipped with his rifle, Orwell had to do what was expected of him "to impress the 'natives.'" As he wrote, "A sahib has got to act like a sahib."[38]

Come what may, the servants of empire must present a bold front. Indeed, so much effort went into a display of ascendancy that it was often to the detriment of efficiency. Soldiers paraded in polished array but the army remained little more than an imperial gendarmerie. Even after mechanisation the War Office allowed cavalry officers two free chargers each and regiments that received self-propelled guns slowed down their firing rate by retaining elaborate procedures for controlling non-existent horses. Sailors showed the flag with Nelsonian panache but the navy's inter-war sloops were "under-armed and under-powered"[39] because they were built more for their impressive silhouette than for their fighting capacity. Airmen put on a wizard show but the RAF was so starved of cash that in India it could not afford tyres for some of its aged Bristol planes, which had to take off and land on the metal rims of their wheels. District Commissioners dressed for dinner in the jungle "to maintain the proper pride" that a white man should have in himself, wrote Somerset Maugham, who noted the discomfort and inconvenience caused by such formalities.[40] Everything was done to elevate rulers above the ruled, to establish them as a separate order of beings. Each according to his place in the imperial hierarchy enjoyed a portion of the divine authority supposed to flow down from a theocratic King. Servants of the Crown became local deities. Eventually, as E. M. Forster wrote in his novel *A Passage to India* (1924), they would "retire to some suburban villa, and die exiled from glory." In the meantime, to quote one of his characters, "Englishmen like posing as gods."[41]

Those who ran the Empire between the wars were, at least, brought up to command. Half of them—those most likely to succeed—came from public schools which prided themselves on turning out the leaders of the future. By now the cult of athleticism was entrenched and games had definitively superseded godliness and good learning as the prime means for "the training of character."[42] Of course the colonial service also accommodated savants and classical scholars who felt "dreadfully Rome-sick."[43] But it was "qualities of character"[44] that chiefly recommended candidates to the ineffable Sir Ralph Furse. The incarnation of snobbery and jobbery, he was long responsible for recruitment at the Colonial Office, where as a young man he had played cricket in the Colonial Secretary's room, bowling from the great door and using the fireplace as a wicket. Furse, a product of Eton (which by itself provided over a quarter of those joining the Foreign Office during the early 1930s), gloried in the old boy network. He preferred men who came from "stock that has proved its worth"—though there might be a place for rougher types, the sort not afraid to tell smoking-room stories to tribal elders, in more uncouth outposts of the Empire such as the Gold Coast. And the methods of selection he employed during his term of office (1910–48) were simple to the point of naïveté. Indeed, the Colonial Office's *Appointments Handbook* sometimes seems to echo the Boy Scouts' *Handbook*: "Weakness of various kinds may lurk in a flabby lip or in averted eyes, just as single-mindedness and purpose are commonly reflected in a steady gaze and a firm set of the mouth and jaw."[45] Monocles were no impediment to the steady gaze but Furse took a dim view of "the spectacled chap."[46]

Still, his criteria had a wide appeal at the time, especially to traditionalists who thought that the Empire was best managed by solid, patriotic gentlemen committed to playing the game. As one senior administrator in Malaya wrote, "What we require out here are young public school men—Cheltenham for preference—who have failed conspicuously at all bookwork and examinations in proportion as they have excelled at sports."[47] On the whole such officials did sterling service, being honest, brave, responsible and industrious. They did much to earn the most fulsome encomiums. According to that scourge of imperial wrong-doing, E. D. Morel, they were "strong in their sense of justice, keen in their sense of right, firm in their sense of duty."[48] In his unpublished memoir an Irish lawyer, who was usually scathing about the English, had nothing but praise for the District Officers he met in Nigeria: "Their concern for the native people they governed was wonderful." He added that the philosopher George Santayana was thinking of such men when he said that the world had never had such "boyish masters." It would be a tragedy, Santayana added, when they were replaced by "the churl and the bully."[49]

On the other hand, despite much local partisanship their first duty was not to the inhabitants of the colonies but to the Empire. As an Acting Governor of Nigeria told the young James Callaghan, it would help him and his colleagues if Britain ceased its "hypocritical emphasis on being in Africa for the benefit of the Africans" and acknowledged that "we stayed there for our own good," though this might also profit the natives, who would otherwise revert to cannibalism in a "disease-ridden malarial swamp and jungle."[50] Furthermore, officials often had the vices of their virtues. Many were priggish, boorish, aloof and stultifyingly conventional. Leonard Woolf said that those in Ceylon never rose above the level of "the lowest Cambridge pseudo-blood" and that no one talked about "anything more interesting than 'the service' or whether Mr. A is really engaged to Miss B."[51] Margery Perham complained of a colonial civil servant whose conversation was "confined to sport, public schools and regiments, including the colour of their ties."[52] He and his kind were frequently smug, intolerant and reactionary. Given such power and such freedom, they were all too liable to develop "the failings of irresponsible rulers."[53] At home critics such as H. G. Wells increasingly damned the public schools for producing a cadre of narrow-minded Philistines dedicated to the defence of class and race privilege. Bernard Shaw declared that Eton, Harrow, Winchester and their cheaper imitations "should be razed to the ground and their foundations sown with salt."[54] Shocked by the habitual rudeness of expensively educated sahibs towards Indians, E. M. Forster wrote in 1922: "Never in history did ill-breeding contribute so much towards the dissolution of an Empire."[55]

Such hostile opinions might have been confirmed on a voyage out to Britain's Asian possessions aboard the floating caravanserais of the Peninsular & Oriental Steam Navigation Company. Its fleet, immaculate in black and white livery, the rising sun emblem loftily displayed, was a monument to imperial pride. Young men going to their first postings began to learn the ropes as they travelled in style with the P&O, which had always insisted on quasi-naval protocol and the "proper subordination" of second-class passengers.[56] Kipling complained that it imposed "chain-gang regulations" and acted as though it were "a favour to allow you to embark."[57] The new boys found that they must respond to the sound of bugles, which signalled such important events as huge meals, deck tennis competitions and dances to popular tunes played by the ship's band. In the punkah-stirred dining room, where "social level-finding"[58] was an art, they were soon put in their place and, as Talleyrand said, the place at table never lies. In the green-tiled smoking room, which resembled "a bedroom suite in the Tottenham Court Road,"[59] they discovered that it was good form to talk about sport—not money, like Americans, or beer, like Germans. Soon they were parroting the standard view that "kindness was absolutely wasted on black men; the one ethical quality necessary in a representative of Great Britain was firmness."[60] In the saloon they were initiated into the business of signing chits for drinks—payment settled weekly. In fact they signed chits for everything, including church collections, since Europeans seldom carried cash in the East—one Viceroy of India, Lord Linlithgow, confessed to never having seen a rupee. In their cabins it was ordained that the "precise, imperturbable, Imperial Englishman . . . goes to bed cleanly in his pyjamas . . . shaves religiously each morning, and carefully brushes his clothes."[61]

After Port Said, supposedly the Clapham Junction of the Empire, virgin sailors found that the tuxedo gave way to the white mess jacket, known as the "bum-freezer." This was worn with boiled shirt, stiff collar and black trousers. Despite the formality high jinks sometimes occurred and other barriers were breached thanks to "the promiscuity of ship-board."[62] But conventions governed even seductions: young women going out to look for husbands ("the fishing fleet") were forbidden fruit but those already married were fair game. Amid the spiced zephyrs of Ceylon it was permissible to succumb to the magic of the Orient, to the enchantment of crystal waters, coral strands, jewelled skies, jade foliage, bronze skins. No one conjured up the gorgeous East more vividly than Joseph Conrad, but he did warn that "a stealthy Nemesis" lay in wait for proud members of "the conquering race."[63] George Orwell, aged nineteen and en route for Rangoon, received a portent of this in 1922 when his ship called at Colombo, fabled "Queen of the Tropic Seas." On the dock, to his horror, he saw a police sergeant kicking a coolie. His fellow passengers watched the scene with "no emotion whatever except a mild approval. They were white, and the coolie was black. In other words, he was subhuman."[64] Ironically, as a policeman in Burma Orwell himself resorted to physical abuse. But violence inevitably provoked a hostile reaction, in perpetrators as well as victims. Orwell grew so disgusted by colonial dirty work that, to judge from his novel *Burmese Days* (1934), he burned with hatred for his own countrymen and longed for "a native rising to drown their Empire in blood."[65]

Few of his compatriots shared that hope but those bound for the East

often did discuss how long the Empire would last. It was still quite possible
to take the view that it "would go on for ever and ever."[66] Politicians at
home proclaimed the solidity of its structure, none more vehemently than
Winston Churchill, who had reverted to Toryism and sounded like "the
head of a True Blue Committee of Public Safety."[67] Proconsuls abroad continued to "doubt if Asiatics can ever be taught to govern themselves."[68]
Colonial statesmen such as Jan Smuts declared that the greatest political
organisation of all time, founded on freedom rather than force, had passed
through the "awful blizzard" of war and "emerged stronger than before."[69]
British soldiers snorted that they would preserve the Empire by flogging or
hanging nationalists—or, as Orwell's Colonel Bodger suggested, by boiling
them in oil. However, the Victorian illusion of permanence had largely vanished in the shambles of the Western Front. A view commonly heard on
P&O steamers between the wars was that the Indian Raj might last another
twenty-five years, long enough for new recruits to serve their time and earn
their pensions. The attractions of the service were not what they had been
before the war. To compensate for heat, solitude, fever, monotony and
tragedy, it still offered "cheap servants, cheap horses, cheap houses, cheap
sport, cheap social amenities."[70] But some warned that the progressive Indi-
anisation of the ICS made a posting outside the subcontinent more secure.
Burma, where disturbances led to power-sharing in 1935, was not an inviting
alternative. Nor, save to incurable romantics, were the remote islands of the
South Seas. For all their allure these were tropical slums run on a shoestring,
often by quaint characters like George McGhee Murdoch, whose will to
dominate was betrayed by "the deliberate, waxed bristle of his sergeant-
major's moustache."[71] Ceylon had merit, being peaceful, prosperous and
politically sophisticated. But the most attractive country in South-East Asia
was Malaya. Penang, for example, was the sort of place in which an Englishman might actually choose to live, remarked the patrician globetrotter
Patrick Balfour, whereas the "idea of anyone *choosing* to live in India would
be grotesque."[72] Malaya was "a Tory Eden in which each man is contented
with his station."[73]

Actually the British held sway because they controlled the local elites
through a variety of administrative systems and kept a balance between the
three races—Malays in the paddy fields, Indians on the plantations, Chinese in the shops and mines. Tin and rubber, of which Malaya was by far the
greatest producer in the world, brought wealth to the country. Furthermore,
a government monopoly in the manufacture and sale of opium provided
around half its income. One Governor explained the situation to the Colonial Secretary in terms redolent of Lord Palmerston:

Opium smoking in Malaya is not the awful scourge believed in by western sentimentalists . . . [it] is not doing as much harm as drink in England. It can never be stopped in Malaya . . . Smuggling is impossible to prevent, and the money now coming into revenue would go to the smugglers. Any attempt to earmark our opium revenue . . . to humanitarian works of supererogation would play the devil with our finances.[74]

If the Chinese suffered, British officials benefited from this bounty and could afford to send their sons home to public schools. By the 1920s the Malayan Civil Service (MCS) had become highly professional. Gone were the days of Victorian patriarchs such as C. F. Bozzolo, who had ruled Upper Perak from elephant back wearing only a hat and a sarong, disregarding government missives and maintaining a large harem. Admittedly his successor, Hubert Berkeley, also tried to keep the modern world at bay. He refused to build roads, invited guests who had not "dunged"[75] to share his two-seater latrine (decorated with pictures of other officials, including the Governor) and exercised *droit de seigneur* over the girls of a local orphanage. He even obtained a superior "sleeping dictionary,"[76] a Malay schoolteacher, for a new recruit to the service.

However, the advent of white wives caused an exodus of brown concubines. Once they had been thought so essential to health that when (in 1890) the Chief Commissioner of Burma issued a confidential circular against native mistresses, the Rangoon Turf Club ran a horse called Physiological Necessity. Now there was merely a jovial nostalgia for "the good old feudal times [when] the planter was always metaphorically and occasionally (bad luck, sir!) literally the father of his flock."[77] And now young men joined a civil service with a "distinctive *esprit de corps*."[78] Yet its members also held more aloof from the population. They took note of that distinguished champion of miscegenation, Sir Hugh Clifford, Governor of the Straits Settlements for two years before being shipped home in 1929, who constituted a terrible warning of its dangers. As a youth he had apparently contracted syphilis in Malaya and back in England, before being confined to a private asylum, he would sit in a sarong on the steps of the Colonial Office giving his former colleagues advice on imperial problems of the day as they went in and out of the building. Robert Bruce Lockhart, who had worked in Malaya as a young planter and returned in the mid-1930s as a journalist, reported that "over-bureaucratisation" was undermining initiative and destroying the efficiency of Britain's imperial administration. The same fate, he observed ominously, had overtaken Rome. Lockhart called the final section of his account "White Man's Twilight."[79]

This is not to say that MCS cadets were idle. Effectively prevented from marrying until their superiors gave the nod, they were set to work. Over the next few years they learned the range of duties that earned them promotion. The District Officer had to be omnicompetent. He collected taxes, presided in court, supervised the police, oversaw public works, advanced agriculture, promoted health, inspected schools, fostered sport, encouraged Boy Scouts, arbitrated in disputes and fulfilled endless social functions, from attending royal jubilee celebrations to introducing *wayang kulit* (shadow puppet) performances. Despite economic fluctuations and the Great Depression itself, which hurt primary producers much more than manufacturers, Malaya's relative prosperity enabled the British to improve the fabric of life. They took direct action, every Resident being, as one official put it, "a Socialist in his own state."[80] They invested in education, sanitation, irrigation and power generation. They erected buildings and created enterprises, notably the tin-smelting industry. They constructed roads and railways. The most spectacular railway station was the white and gold fantasy at Kuala Lumpur, supposedly built to the British specification that its roof should be capable of bearing the weight of three feet of snow. It was embellished with minarets, spires, cupolas, scalloped eaves and keyhole arches, an architectural style described as "Late Marzipan."[81]

Yet many of these achievements helped to widen the gulf between Europeans and Asians. New means of communication led to segregation. Whites now played games among themselves, "the hall-mark of British civilisation in the East [being] a bag of golf clubs."[82] They established exclusive districts in Kuala Lumpur and avoided fraternisation. They isolated themselves in hill stations of pebbledash and mock Tudor, making Home Counties residences out of bungalows in the Cameron Highlands. Above all, sahibs consorted with memsahibs, who encouraged a laager mentality and for the most part remained in a kind of European purdah.

Of course, as feminists have argued, women faced almost insuperable difficulties throughout the Empire. With notable exceptions, they lacked both essential work and an independent role. They were deterred from learning local languages by their alleged impropriety. They were fed lurid stories of coloured lust, doubtless intended to increase their dependence on white males, for whom violence against white women was "a potent symbol of political revenge against the ruling group."[83] They found themselves in an alien, sometimes hostile and often incomprehensible world. Like the wife of the District Officer in Joyce Cary's novel *Mister Johnson* (1939), set in Africa, they could often derive "no meaning" from the picturesque or squalid scenes around them.[84] In the Pacific, according to one official, British women knew islanders only as servants and "were unable to conceive that there could be any difference in rank between one 'nigger' and another."[85] Minds remained closed in the subcontinent. "The Indians!" exclaims Mrs. Bristow in Joseph Ackerley's *Hindoo Holiday* (1952), "I never think of them."[86] Indeed, according to Iris Portal, "The tragedy of British India was the unpreparedness of the memsahibs."[87] Even well-prepared memsahibs could develop an invincible aversion to Asians. "I really think I hate the women more than the men!" wrote Lady Grigg. She found them "semi-civilised & wholly revolting." And she was particularly disgusted by tinselly saris and matronly bodies, "so rude & shapeless & corsetless."[88]

Needless to say, some European women were sympathetic and selfless. They were keen to express "woman's love for her sister woman of other hue."[89] They preferred to build bridges with local people than to play bridge with their own kind. In Khartoum one tried to teach Sudanese girls Scottish glees. In Lagos a Ladies' League gave instruction in cookery, hygiene and needlework. But many who called themselves ladies were lazy, arrogant "vixens"—Nirad Chaudhuri's word.[90] The "poker-backed white woman, all whipped up in whalebone,"[91] was no mere stereotype invented by masculine prejudice. She was ubiquitous, a bored, aimless prig with nothing to do but curse the country, scold her servants, write letters home, play tennis and gossip with friends over gin *pahits* (bitters) or whisky *stengahs* (half-measures—also an offensive term for Eurasians). If you met her at the Colombo Garden Club, said Leonard Woolf, she could "tell you what you had for dinner two weeks ago in Jaffna."[92] She fussed inordinately about distinctions of status and refinements of etiquette—it was said that "the appearance of the first silver coffee-pot changed the face of Nigeria."[93] In Malaya she helped to draw between the races "an iron curtain of ignorance."[94]

Paradoxically, cultural harmonisation also aggravated racial alienation. The spread through Malaya of western dress, education, cinema, sport and habits prompted the British to insist on their own singularity. This was marked in various ways. The government ensured that whites never suffered what was regarded as the indignity of serving under Asians. Britons complained that the Chinese were not suitably deferential, refusing to step aside for them on the pavements of Kuala Lumpur, and they tried to insist that their Chinese servants kept their pigtails as a sign of respect and a token that they were unspoilt by civilisation. The authorities deported white engine drivers, bootblacks, prostitutes and others engaged in menial occupations. Sporadic attempts were made to keep the races apart: for example, non-Europeans could use Singapore's Raffles Hotel but they were not allowed on to the dance floor. Incipient rivalries gave new stimulus to ancient antipathies. On his tour round the world Lord Northcliffe inveighed against

> the swaggering, boastful, whisky-and-soda drinking, horn-spectacled, and fountain-pen-wearing Babu, who likes to think that because he has the imitative and blotting-paper mind that enables him to pass examinations, he is the equal of the Anglo-Saxon, and, *knowing* his own inferiority, is bitter and dangerous.[95]

Northcliffe was sensitive about examinations—it was said that the only one he ever passed was the Wassermann test for syphilis. But his characteristic commination might have been heard throughout South-East Asia during the inter-war years.

Nothing insulated the British more definitively from their imperial subjects than that omnipresent institution, the club. Wherever the map was painted red, Britons created more or less accurate imitations of the palaces of Pall Mall. Their aim was to exclude as well as to include, on the metropolitan model. In London, for example, Pratt's not only barred women but forbade them to telephone the club; while to get into the Beefsteak one had to be a relation of God and, members intoned, a damned close relation at that. Colonial clubs arose as social bastions and whites were encouraged to attend in order to maintain solidarity, as appears in Forster's *A Passage to India*. Early ones might consist of a thatched hut furnished with two benches and a plank. When the monsoon left the ground too wet for polo, members would make a bonfire of the entire structure, along with the club accounts, only to start again the following year. Soon more permanent establishments arose, though many remained down-at-heel. The Kandy Club in Ceylon was "poky, gloomy, and even rather sordid."[96] The European Club in Accra looked like, and perhaps was, "an out-of-date railway station"[97]—according to legend it had originally served Balmoral and was donated to West Africa when Queen Victoria required a smarter stop. With its faded wooden jalousies, its rusting wrought ironwork, its tattered green baize notice boards and its sagging verandahs, Aden's Union Club "reeked of the decay of Empire."[98] More cheerfully, tropical clubs were often embowered in English gardens. These were full of petunias, hollyhocks and roses, which grew dropsical in the heat and swooned under a riot of crimson hibiscus, silver frangipani, vermilion poinciana and purple bougainvillea. The clubs had high, barrack-like rooms cooled by punkahs, later by ceiling fans. They were furnished with rattan mats, bamboo tables and reclining cane chairs popularly known as Bombay Fornicators. The walls were adorned

with animal horns and heads—the British passion for *shikar* made taxi-
dermy big business.

Women were confined to separate enclaves, usually known as the "Hen
House," or *moorgi-khanna* (though the Sind Club in Karachi called this area
the "Shallow End"),[99] and sometimes they were banned completely. A proposal to equip the Madras Club with a ladies' pavilion in 1892 was regarded
as "revolutionary."[100] In 1930 the Hong Kong Club turned a redundant
cubicle into a Ladies' Room, which one beneficiary dismissed as "a mangey
[sic] concession very grudgingly given"[101] by members who still forbade
women to use the library. The Hill Club at Nuwara Eliya in Ceylon
imposed a range of petty restrictions on women, whose luggage was permitted to go through the front door while they themselves had to use a side
entrance. When a lost female strayed into the "sacred precinct" of the
United Services Club in Simla between the wars its horrified major-domo
"snatched a notice from the wall and, holding it in front of him, barred further progress to the intruder. The notice ran: 'Dogs and other noxious animals are not allowed in the Club.'"[102] Actually, such institutions were not
good at repelling the brute creation. At different times the Hill Club was
afflicted by a "plague of flies," its meat was "alive with maggots" and its billiards room swarmed "with fleas—one member caught 13 in a few minutes."[103] Other pests were rampant, as revealed in the unpublished
"Complaints and Suggestions Book" of the Bombay Club.

> The attention of the Committee is drawn to the daily increasing number of
> rats, bandicoots, mice, and other vermin in the Club. Can nothing be done
> to improve the state of things, in this respect? The Mongoose is evidently a
> fraud and a failure. We beg to suggest *cats* or *traps*. The undersigned have this
> evening seen a large rat seated on the gruyère cheese.

Still, clubs were Englishmen's castles—the Bombay Club, which prohibited
the use of foreign languages on its premises, even wondered "whether
Scotchmen are to be allowed to speak Scotch."[104]

Clubs were homes away from home. They supplied refreshment. This
was often deplorable, menus boasting English dishes such as tapioca pudding and spotted dick with custard. When a member ordered fresh papaya
at the Singapore Club he received tinned apricots because "the club did not
serve native food."[105] Exceptions were made. Curry *tiffin* (lunch), along with
brandy *chota pegs* (small measures), satisfied the inner man. And they were
sometimes taken as a kind of secular sacrament, especially at havens like the
Madras Club, which acquired a "qualified artist" as chef.[106] Clubs provided

recreation. Games of all sorts were treated with more than religious zeal, promotion at work often depending on proficiency at play. In one Indian club members complained that church services held next to the billiards room put them off their stroke and the Ootacamund ("snooty Ooty") Club even devised its own cult, snooker. Clubs offered entertainment. There were Burns Nights and St. Andrew's Nights. There were dances, fancy dress parties and lantern slide shows. There were amateur theatricals, featuring productions such as *Lord Richard in the Pantry* and *The Rotters' Farewell.* There were charades known as "Geographical Teas": at the Gorakhpur Club one ICS man "went as 'Lucknow' with a picture of two dice, with the sixes uppermost, over my open watch; and only two guessed it."[107] There were libraries full of mildewed Edgar Wallace thrillers, tattered stacks of *Punch* and *The Field,* and old copies of *The Times* which traditionally served as shrouds for comatose members. Little energy was devoted to reading: when Richard Burton, as a founder member, gave the Sind Club a copy of his unexpurgated translation of the *Arabian Nights,* it was placed among the children's books in the library where it remained, evidently unopened, for two generations. Larger clubs, like those at Malacca, Bangalore and Mombasa, were a little more sophisticated. And at the top were Athenaeums abroad.

The grand clubs of Calcutta were the Bengal, the oldest in India, dating from 1827, and the rustic Tollygunge. Their equivalents in Bombay were the Royal Yacht Club, which resembled a maharajah's castle in the air, and the Gymkhana Club, whose marble lavatories were "more magnificent than the High Courts."[108] The superb Singapore Club dominated the harbour. Kipling likened the Hong Kong Club, as reconstructed in 1860, to "a small palace";[109] built afresh in 1897, it resembled a large palace, in the style of Fatehpur Sikri, though a majestic entrance was sacrificed to accommodate no fewer than four bowling alleys on the ground floor. The United Services Club at Lucknow seemed to be a monstrously inflated cricket pavilion. Although its "premises did not match the glory of its occupants,"[110] the Lake Club in Kuala Lumpur was aptly known as the "Tuan Besar," or "Brass Hat" Club. In such temples of fashion the high priests were usually "die-hard reactionaries."[111] They preserved the spirit of London's eighteenth-century Warble Club, which had ruled that "any member who has two ideas shall be obliged to give one to his neighbour."[112] They spoke, as at Dublin's patrician Kildare Street Club, "in a sort of dialect, a dead language which the larva-like stupidity of the club has preserved."[113] Like public schoolboys, they relished esoteric shibboleths and arcane anathemas. They enforced rules and regulations with more-than-metropolitan severity. Indeed, they so worshipped convention that senior figures in Calcutta formed an Unceremoni-als Club to flout it; but members did nothing more outré than "wear a red cap playing tennis and a red smoking jacket at Club dinners."[114] Above all, British clubs determined their intake according to inflexible social and racial canons. This gave particular offence to indigenous elites. Motilal Nehru refused an invitation to stand for election to the Allahabad Club because he would not risk the insult of being blackballed. One chastened ICS man, though, was glad "for the sake of my own race"[115] that Indians did not wit-ness the intricate snobberies of British club life.

Eminent Asians did gain entry to some clubs, such as the Selangor Club in Kuala Lumpur, a mock-Tudor edifice which for its pains was nicknamed the "Spotted Dog." Similarly, a few Britons joined the Mohamed Ali Club in Cairo, a voluptuous sanctuary of deep carpets, velvet curtains, billowing divans and enormous chandeliers. Moreover, some clubs, such as the Island Club in Nigeria and the Cosmopolitan Club in India, were formed to mix the races. It was to encourage integration that Lord Willingdon founded the clubs that bore his name in Bombay, Madras and Delhi. Paradoxically, the first of these turned out to be the last word in hauteur. It included only maharajahs and their ilk, while banning Japanese, and it sanctioned a patri-cian superciliousness among its members, who might stand impassively near the showers until a servant arrived to take off their trousers. Moreover, Lady Willingdon did her bit to sabotage the enterprise: in the manner of Queen Mary, she admired the diamonds worn by princely members so effu-sively that they felt obliged to make her presents of them. Still, it was obvi-ous that such advice as the secret memorandum handed to new ICS officials about their social relations with "Indian gentlemen,"[116] which contained an appendix written in 1821, was no longer likely to sustain British rule.

So everywhere pressure increased to lift the racial bar to club member-ship. This was not always successful. As late as the Second World War, Cey-lonese were not even permitted to enter the Colombo Club as guests, though they often invited Europeans to the Orient Club. The Hill Club at Nuwara Eliya refused to admit Sri Lankans until 1966 when, facing financial extinction from a haemorrhage of European members, it was known as "The Morgue."[117] The Lahore Club followed a similar course. The Accra Club, which admitted Turks but not Syrians or Cypriots, continued to keep out Africans after the Gold Coast became independent. A senior official in West Africa who tried to promote racial mingling stated flatly, "Clubs are rarely an asset to a station."[118] But there was change, sometimes cheerfully embraced. Typically, the High Range Club at Munnar in Kerala accepted its first (very distinguished but essentially token) Indian member in 1934, though its social policy remained intact and it excluded Royal Air Force NCOs even during the Second World War. Nevertheless, the struggle for admission provoked bitter disputes throughout the Empire. It also became the theme for several novels, notably *Burmese Days,* in which a character warns that by giving way over small things "we've ruined the Empire."[119] Resistance was sometimes violent. At Nairobi's Muthaiga Club, where Edward Prince of Wales was wrestled to the floor by the amorous Lady Delamere, members set fire to the grand piano in protest against a proposal to admit Jews.

In fact, for all their emphasis on gentlemanliness, clubs often became the scene of hooliganism. Members insulted and assaulted servants. They indulged in high jinks and horseplay. In New Delhi's Gymkhana Club during the war one colonel tried to crack walnuts by hurling them at a portrait of the King-Emperor and shattered the glass instead. Clubmen bombarded each other with bread rolls though, unlike habitués of St. James's, they do not seem to have invested in "throwing port." They engaged in vicious feuds. Quarrels in the Hong Kong Club during the 1860s poisoned the social life of the entire European community. During a dispute over whist in the Bombay Club, a Mr. Ashburner directed a torrent of Billingsgate at the Secretary, Captain Walshe, whom he threatened to strike. Ashburner repeated with "gusto the obscene native term of abuse 'Barnshute' [mother-fucker], also adding thereto that coarse English expletive so dear to his foul mouth—'bloody.'"[120] The drinking of vast quantities of hard liquor, evidently the prime purpose of institutions such as the Lagos Club, known as the "Gin Tank,"[121] often led to the "frenzied destruction of property." The High Range Club, which was decorated not only with antlers but with the headgear of retired tea planters who had literally hung up their hats, cherished "a tradition of members wilfully breaking glasses,"[122] smashing furniture and destroying billiards tables. An entertainment at the Screechers' Club, formed by RAF officers in India during the war, was the "Prang Concerto" which concluded with "the complete demolition of the piano."[123] Such behaviour was unlikely to convince colonial people that they were governed by a superior race. It gave ammunition to critics at home: Bertrand Russell called the Empire "a cesspool for British moral refuse."[124] And it typified the brutality which the British could bring to the task of preserving their monopoly both in microcosm, at the level of the colonial club, and in the wider realm of the Empire.

This was much in evidence at Shanghai, Britain's richest citadel in the Far East. Strictly speaking, China's commercial capital, the cosmopolitan gateway to the interior situated at the vast yellow mouth of the Yangtse, was not part of the Empire. But the British, although they were outnumbered by Japanese, controlled the treaty port's International Settlement through the Shanghai Municipal Council. And they behaved with autocratic arrogance. For example, they barred both dogs and Chinese from Huangpu Park, the public gardens opposite the British Consulate on the Manhattan-style waterfront.[125] The "Shanghailanders," as they called themselves, enjoyed a spectacularly privileged mode of life. They drove gleaming Buicks and shopped for the latest fashions in neon-lit department stores like Sun Sun's. They gambled illegally at "The Wheel" on North Honan Road or followed pink-coated huntsmen in the Shanghai Paper Chase. They smoked cigars and drank cocktails beneath the Venetian campanile of the art deco Cathay Hotel, which was also the rendezvous of quasi-imperialist Americans "imitating the la-de-da manners of the British and 'cheerioing' one another."[126] But the *taipans* inhabited "a heaven on top of hell."[127] Stretched out beneath the grey skyscrapers of the Bund were the noxious slums, sweatshops, bazaars, brothels, factories, godowns and opium hongs of the city's three million Chinese—they even had a leper colony. At best most Shanghailanders regarded these nether regions as a grim backdrop to their own dazzling existence. At worst they thought that deformed beggars, diseased prostitutes, tubercular coolies, drug addicts and slave children were "refuse"[128] to be swept from the streets.

The authorities often burned down the verminous Chinese shantytowns and they exercised day-to-day control over the underworld through the Shanghai Municipal Police (SMP). As police forces go, this was a more than usually criminal organisation, at least half its officers being involved in the opium traffic. In other ways the SMP resembled the Black and Tans, for its middle ranks were staffed by British NCOs toughened in the trenches. Facing gangsters liable not just to kill them but to eat their Alsatian police dogs, they had few scruples about torture and murder, not even bothering to record the shooting of coolies. A recent biography of one such NCO, Maurice Tinkler, gives a graphic account of his fascist attitudes towards "these yellow Chinese swine." As a result of police brutality in the early 1920s, he recorded, "They hate the foreigners now far worse than they did at the time of the Boxer rising." For different (though associated) reasons, the Japanese shared their hatred of British dominance. In 1939 Tinkler himself, by then the labour superintendent of a cotton mill, was killed in a clash with the forces of Nippon—their official report stated that he "came into contact with" a bayonet.[129]

At breathtaking speed Japanese bayonets were to inflict lethal damage on British power in the Orient. This was because it had become a hollow shell.

Britain was still wealthy, owning more than half the foreign investment in China, worth £250 million. But it was no longer strong—during the Ethiopian crisis of 1935–6 one old cruiser and four destroyers had to put on a show of being the China Station Fleet. In fact, Britain's ostentatious but insubstantial position in Asia was symbolised by the Shanghai Club. This splendid edifice had a colonnaded façade of Ningpo granite crowned by Italianate cupolas, a black and white marble hall, an oak-panelled Jacobean room and, of course, the longest bar in the world—Noël Coward said that if you laid your cheek to it you could see the curvature of the earth. Yet from the Club the British could only watch—gleefully in 1932 but fearfully in 1937—as Nippon bombed and shelled the "native city." The Land of the Rising Sun seemed poised to eclipse the Empire on which the sun never set. Without American support, as a leading British diplomat said, "we must eventually swallow any & every humiliation in the Far East."[130] Impotence sapped self-assurance, a vital element in prestige. It fed the growing unease about the validity as well as the techniques of white rule. Some Britons were even alienated from club life itself, which was, with its comprehensive system of totems and taboos, the epitome of imperial existence. George Orwell was by no means alone in reacting against the "pukka sahib's code."[131]

During the inter-war years a surprising number of imperial officials came to deplore it as a form of organised humbug. It stifled thought and sapped integrity. It also imposed a canon of silence. Such was the pressure to conform that whites usually concealed their sentiments. Orwell memorably described a railway journey in Burma with another anti-imperialist, who was a stranger to him:

> Half an hour's cautious questioning decided each of us that the other was "safe"; and then for hours, while the train jolted slowly through the pitch-black night, sitting in our bunks with bottles of beer handy, we damned the British Empire—damned it from the inside, intelligently and intimately. It did us both good. But we had been speaking forbidden things, and in the haggard morning light when the train crawled into Mandalay, we parted as guiltily as any adulterous couple.[132]

Doubtless influenced by American as well as Russian rhetoric, some functionaries concluded that the colonial Empire was "a racket."[133] It was a benevolent "despotism with theft as its final object."[134] The official held the native down, Orwell said, while the businessman went through his pockets. But liberal officials were trapped in an authoritarian system, serving the inhabitants of their districts yet lording it over them. This fostered a disturbing ambivalence. Roger Pearce, a District Officer in Sind, had to act in the name of the Raj though he "believed that India should be independent."[135] Quite a few of Pearce's contemporaries would have sympathised with Leonard Woolf, who had become "politically schizophrenic, an anti-imperialist who enjoyed the fleshpots of imperialism, loved the subject peoples and their way of life, and knew from the inside how evil the system was."[136] Travelling through South-East Asia during the 1920s, Somerset Maugham met "judges, soldiers, commissioners who had no confidence in themselves and therefore inspired no respect in those they were placed over." Their will to rule was impaired. And the master whose conscience was troubled could scarcely be master for long. The whole situation presaged "the Decline and Fall of the British Empire." Maugham even presumed to counsel its future historian (assumed to be male) on the style that he should adopt for this "great work": "I would have him write lucidly and yet with dignity; I would have his periods march with a firm step. I should like his sentences to ring out as the anvil rings when the hammer strikes it."[137]

12

White Mates Black in a Very Few Moves

Kenya and the Sudan

Certainly the tones of British officialdom rang out boldly in distant lands and dark continents. However corrosive its private anxieties, its public pronouncements invariably struck a note of sublime self-assurance; and nothing seemed more sure than that Europe must govern Africa or that Kenya should become "a white man's country."[1] Thus spoke Sir Harry Johnston and Sir Charles Eliot, second Commissioner of what was (from 1895, after the failure of Mackinnon's chartered company, to 1920, when it became a crown colony) Britain's East Africa Protectorate. The declaration became a mantra for the European settlers whom Eliot did so much to introduce to the highlands bordering the Rift Valley east of Lake Victoria. This was a cool, mosquito-free zone, burned by the equatorial sun, watered by sparkling streams, shaded by juniper, mimosa and acacia. Eliot thought that this healthy, fertile country could become another New Zealand. Furthermore, he maintained that colonisation would not be "destroying any old or interesting system, but simply introducing order into blank, uninteresting, brutal barbarism." This was certainly the view of the immigrant community, to which Eliot was subservient. In the words of Elspeth Huxley, who spent much of her childhood amid the flame trees of Thika, near Nairobi, the idea that the interests of

> untutored tribesmen, clothed in sheep's fat, castor oil or rancid butter—men who smelt out witches, drank blood warm from the throats of living cattle and believed that rainfall depended on the arrangement of a goat's intestines—should be exalted above those of the educated European would have seemed to them fantastic.[2]

Eliot, an expert on sea slugs who was himself described as "invertebrate, with an icy cold nature,"[3] declared bluntly: "European interests are paramount."[4] He coined a metaphor and a motto from chess: "white mates black in a very few moves."[5]

As it happened, by the beginning of the twentieth century natural disasters had taken a fearful toll on the people of Kenya, who had numbered three million in 1890. Smallpox, rinderpest, locusts, jiggers, drought and famine had reduced the population by a third and weakened its power to resist incursions. Particularly affected were the black inhabitants of what became known as the White Highlands, most of this region an immense grazing ground for the cattle of the nomadic Masai, who lived on their milk and blood. According to one traveller, "There were women wasted to skeletons from whose eyes the madness of starvation glared."[6] Yet the tall, spear-carrying warriors, with their shining crimson bodies and their long braided hair, remained an impressive force. The British regarded the Masai as the Spartans of East Africa and did their best to conciliate and recruit them, even when they stole telegraph wire to adorn their women. Indeed, African levies enabled the white intruders to conquer the country by crushing opposition piecemeal among the Kikuyu, Kipsigis, Kisii, Nandi and others. The Europeans conducted a sporadic war of attrition, killing natives, burning villages and seizing livestock. The "nigger hunt,"[7] as it was popularly called, bore marked similarities to the Masai raid. The participants, one London official observed, "thoroughly enjoy themselves and get loot."[8] Retaliation was inevitable: Kikuyu villagers murdered one settler by pegging him down and all urinating into his mouth. In revenge Lieutenant Richard Meinertzhagen, then aged twenty-four, ordered his men to take no adult prisoners when they attacked the village. They left not a soul alive and their commander seemed to relish the operation as a "form of blood sport."[9] The local authorities countenanced such methods. In the words of Eliot's predecessor as Commissioner, Sir Arthur Hardinge, "These people must learn submission by bullets—it's the only school."[10] He said that a more modern and humane form of education could be essayed later. Meanwhile, the men on the spot minimised the casualties in their reports and represented the violence as "punishment" for a "revolt." London was not deceived. In 1904 the Foreign Office (shortly before it relinquished control to the Colonial Office) sent the Commissioner a stern warning: "It is only by a most careful insistence on the protection of native rights that His Majesty's Government can justify their presence in East Africa."[11]

These were fine sentiments, repeated more or less sincerely until Kenya became independent in 1963, but they were at odds with the government's other concern—to make the colony pay. The "Lunatic Line," the costly rail link between Mombasa and Kisumu on Lake Victoria, opened in 1901. But although Thomas Cook was soon selling tickets from London to the source of the Nile, the trans-Kenya train service seemed to be little more than a

locomotive white elephant. Its main station, situated at a place called
Nairobi, which meant "cold stream" in the Masai language, exemplified the
poverty of the railway. The pioneers had no idea of pitching a capital in a
papyrus swamp; Nairobi merely provided the last piece of flat ground for
shunting before the escarpment that rose to form the twisted lip of the Rift
Valley. What they raised was a wooden platform roofed with corrugated
iron and surrounded by a huddle of tents and tin sheds. From this grimy
nucleus a squalid shantytown spread over the rust-coloured earth. It was at
once divided into districts. To the west bungalows, warehouses, offices,
stores, a hotel and a European club sprang up along the main thoroughfare,
inevitably named Victoria Road. To the east sprawled an Indian bazaar, full
of rotting garbage, open sewers and vermin, looking and smelling much like
Calcutta. A missionary wrote,

> It is turbulent and as vivid as a box of paints. Arabs sweep by in their long
> robes, turbaned Sikhs stalk imperiously, Zanzibaris and Chinese, Baluchis
> and half-castes, soldiers and railway gangers, all jostle through the lantern-
> light and shadow in a medley of silks, sashes, brass buttons and bracelets,
> topis and rags.

Intoxicated by bhang or pombe, men staggered through vile "alleys where
perfume sickens the senses, where eyes glittering with kohl throw an invitation," into the arms of prostitutes.

In a drastic attempt to suppress outbreaks of bubonic plague, Britons
twice burned down the Indian quarter. The first conflagration was started
by Colonel J. H. Patterson, the formidable lion-hunter, whose "Kaiser
moustache was pomaded into two imperious curls."[12] And in 1902 the principal medical officer again torched the bazaar—partly, it seems, because he
did not like the look of it. The resurrection was swift. Equally rapid was the
replacement of Masai kraals with "native locations," suburban clusters of
(mostly) Kikuyu huts made from packing cases and flattened paraffin cans.
White Nairobi also grew apace. But it long remained a frontier dorp, known
as "Dead Horse Gulch"[13] before 1914 and described by a post-war Governor
as a "Buffalo-Bill" railway halt redolent of "poor-white sloppiness."[14] It was
an ugly rash of wood and metal extending over a grid of dusty streets
planted with eucalyptus trees and roamed at night by hyenas, jackals and
leopards. There were also a few good stone buildings and by the 1920s the
best of these belonged to the railway. Its prosperity, according to white
dogma, owed everything to colonisation.

From the first it had seemed axiomatic that only European settlers could produce the goods that would make a profit from the iron road. Furthermore, they and their capital could only be attracted by generous land grants. By 1903, therefore, Eliot was disposing of large chunks of territory around Lake Naivasha in the Rift Valley without regard for native claims and without the full approval of his masters in Whitehall. The stated price for additional holdings was two rupees (2s 8d, or 75 U.S. cents) an acre, but this sometimes fell to a halfpenny or even to nothing. Hundreds of applicants arrived, some English gentry from the shires, others Boers from the veldt, many squatting outside Nairobi in a scrofulous encampment known as "Tentfontein." Among the newcomers was Lord Delamere, soon to be the unofficial leader of Kenya's European community. An aristocratic ruffian who wore shorts, pistol, flannel shirt, and long ginger hair under a topee so vast that it almost concealed his beaky nose, he thought nothing of brawling, shooting out street lights or locking the manager of the Norfolk Hotel in his own meat safe. Delamere lived on an extravagant scale: he conducted his correspondence by telegram and kept three Morse code operators busy day and night, "calling them baboons and idiots" one minute and the next giving them generous "cash hand-outs."[15] Having acquired 100,000 acres on the western slopes of the Rift Valley, he told Meinertzhagen that he was going to prove that "this is a white man's country." Meinertzhagen replied: "But it's a black man's country; how are you going to superimpose the white over black?" Delamere said, "The black man will benefit and co-operate." Despite his own authoritarian bent, Meinertzhagen was unconvinced. He thought that the land grab would eventually lead to racial conflict, for he could not see educated Africans in flannel suits "submitting tamely to white domination."[16]

Meanwhile, the black man was forced to cooperate and he did benefit from the Pax Britannica, though this merely replaced African anarchy (caused by constant raiding) with European tyranny. As Eliot's Deputy Commissioner reported, Kenya was a country of "'nigger-' and game-shooters."[17] Indeed, according to one Foreign Office mandarin, there was almost "no atrocity in the Congo—except mutilation—which cannot be matched in our Protectorate."[18] The new settlers were forever threatening to take more land by force while demanding government protection against the native uprising they expected to provoke. Expressing prejudice against dark-skinned races with seigneurial arrogance, they were particularly aggressive towards the authorities. Captain Ewart ("Grogs") Grogan, an adventurer who thought Kenya needed a good dose of slavery, challenged them by flogging three allegedly insolent Kikuyu in front of Nairobi's courthouse. He was found guilty of unlawful assembly and sentenced to a month's imprisonment in a private house, settlers remarking on how civilised they were compared to American Southerners, who would have lynched the Negroes. Many local officials (though by no means all) were fearful of being criticised as pro-black, or even pro-Red, in such a tiny white community. They were subject to insult: one coffee planter entered his bulldog Squeak for a government job. They were blackballed at the Muthaiga Club. They were vulnerable to settlers who could "pull strings in London and make the puppets in East Africa jump and run."[19]

Often the puppets sided with the settlers automatically, regarding their African charges as "bloody niggers."[20] Officials in Kenya had a poor reputation, notoriously in the sphere of sexual misconduct. One District Commissioner was said to combine "tax collection with rape." And an Assistant District Commissioner called Hubert Silberrad caused such a scandal over concubinage that Lord Crewe issued his famous Circular (1909) warning members of the Colonial Service that they faced professional ruin for having "immoral relations with native women."[21] The settlers mocked their plight in a verse set to the tune of "The Church's One Foundation":

> Pity the Poor Official
> Whene'er he gets a stand,
> He may not have a bibi [mistress],
> He has to use his hand.[22]

Self-abuse certainly caused less harm than other official endeavours. Colonel Montgomery, a Land Commissioner, complained that "natives did irretrievable damage to forests, and whilst the natives themselves could always be replaced, with trees it was different, for it cost much money to plant a forest."[23] Such men had no scruples about moving the Masai from their richest pastures to make way for the European pioneers of civilisation. Eliot himself thought that they and "many other tribes must go under."[24] He compared the Masai to lions, strong and beautiful but "never of any use, and often a very serious danger."[25] By the time of the First World War the Masai had become, according to Baroness Blixen, who owned a coffee plantation in the Ngong Hills, "a dying lion with his claws clipped."[26] Expectations of its demise were premature. Equally misplaced were hopes that the settlers could establish themselves as the master race. Their brutal expropriations had kindled a slow-burning anger that would eventually burst into flame.

Other grievances multiplied, mainly to do with labour. The Englishman could not himself plough or dig in the uplands without sacrificing his prestige or "falling a victim of nervous collapse." Luckily he did not have to get his hands dirty. For Kenya was not just a white man's country; it was, according to the pioneer Lord Cranworth, "essentially an overseer's country."[27] Most of the new settlers, notably those from Britain, preferred to supervise. They were, as Afrikaners observed, "verandah farmers."[28] They wholeheartedly adopted the German maxim, condemned by Lugard: "Colonising Africa is making the negro work."[29] As Grogan said of the Kikuyu, "We have stolen his land. Now we must steal his limbs."[30] To this end hut and poll taxes were imposed so that the Africans (who initially proffered ivory, goats and even crocodile eggs in lieu of cash) would have to earn wages in order to pay them. The levy had the added advantage of helping to fund the administration, for white taxation was kept disproportionately low. Nevertheless, black people had an understandable aversion to becoming migrant labourers on white estates. There they were ill fed, ill housed, ill paid and otherwise ill treated. The unpublished letters of a typical settler, Arnold Paice, catalogue the punishments he inflicted on his "boys," which ranged from giving them "a pretty good thumping" to shackling them by the enlarged lobes of their ears. On one occasion he attached the ear of a sleepy herdsman to his saddle: "Then I shoved my heels in to the pony and set off at a canter; of course the nigger had to canter too as it would have been painful to have his ear pulled off." Relations between the races were by no means always hostile and could be benign. Paice himself acknowledged, "One can't exactly make friends of the 'black men' up here but some of them are pretty decent."[31] Yet exploitation was endemic and women workers were often sexually abused. Exiled from family life, African men faced a choice between "celibacy and syphilis." Frequently they deserted, breaking the law and leaving more than one employer in "a red-hot state bordering on a desire to murder everyone with a black skin who comes in sight."[32] Incensed by the departure of "beastly niggers" whom he had chastised, Paice exclaimed: "It's all rot about slavery—*these natives ought to be slaves*, treated humanely of course, but not spoiled for want of the rod."[33]

Although settlers extolled the merits of the corvée and the *kiboko* (hippopotamus-hide whip), they also offered Africans an advantageous form of service. In return for working for the white man for 180 days a year for a nominal wage, they were allowed to become "squatters" on his land and to cultivate their own *shambas* (farms). This freed them from the domination of chiefs on their own reserves and gave them scope to exercise their considerable agricultural skills. In fact the squatters, who were mostly Kikuyu and eventually numbered more than 200,000, became victims of their own success. Settlers feared that "Kaffir farming" might become a "peasant Trojan horse threatening estate production."[34] Worse still, squatters might establish rights to the soil. The High Court later quashed this menace by designating them as tenants who could be evicted. But there was always acute tension over the land question. Squatters suffered with their kin on the reserves, who also endured a succession of disabilities including the denial of a title to their holdings. Additional imposts (such as having to buy an annual licence to grow coffee) aimed to stop them from competing with whites. And there were frequent clashes, especially over livestock grazing on the open range. After the disappearance of eighteen of his sheep Paice expressed the gut sentiments of his kind, telling his mother that he would shoot dead the first thief he encountered. "You may think this is bloodthirsty nonsense. But it isn't. I should be delighted to shoot a leopard (whose natural instinct teaches him to steal) therefore I should be far more delighted to shoot a Kikuyu who *knows* it is wrong to steal."[35] A few local officials might have sympathised but the Colonial Office, as the watchdog of "imperial paternalism," endeavoured to protect "native rights."[36] Winston Churchill was particularly vigilant. He condemned the "butchery" of the defenceless Kisii.[37] A single principle should govern Britain's rule of subject people, he declared, the principle of justice. Although he regarded the "native races" of East Africa as "brutish children" who should respect the white man, Churchill said that it would be an ill day for them were their fortunes to be removed from "the impartial and august administration of the Crown and abandoned to the fierce self-interest of a small white population."[38]

That population amounted to fewer than 5,500 by 1914 and under pressure it became ever more fierce. Before the Great War, as Elspeth Huxley wrote, the Europeans had had a marked impact on the animal and vegetable, as well as the human, life of the Rift Valley. Arriving with their ox carts, tents, rifles, chop (food) boxes, tin baths and steel ploughs, they had put up fences, driven off the herds of zebra, darkened the land with their *shambas* and cattle *bomas* (enclosures), which rose "like tattoo marks on a warrior's cheek."[39] But the fighting in East Africa arrested this development, depriving many estates of their menfolk. Among those killed were a fifth of the tens of thousands of black workers who were press-ganged into the Carrier Corps "as if the days when Arab slave-raiders would descend on the tribes of the interior had returned."[40] The Governor, Sir Henry Belfield, deplored the way in which his colony had been dragged into a war not of its own making. Soon, though, the post-war slump further strained the finances of the white community. The situation got much worse during the Great Depression, when some settlers were reduced to "a diet of posho [maize meal] porridge and skim milk."[41] Their automatic response was to crack down on the Africans.

Between 1919 and 1922 the whites passed a series of harsh measures to strengthen their control over blacks. More labour was extorted from them under conditions that, according to a caustic but well-informed critic of the colony, Dr. Norman Leys, replicated "some of the evils of slavery."[42] Their wages were reduced, their taxes were increased and their movements were restricted. They were forced to carry identity cards bearing their finger-prints, each encased in a metal box called a *kipande,* worn round the neck on a string like a goat's bell *(mbugi)*. They set up several organisations to concert resistance. The most effective was the Young Kikuyu Association led by Harry Thuku, a so-called "mission boy"—a type who attracted as much white venom as did the Indian *babu*. His arrest in 1922 sparked off a demon-stration in Nairobi at which police reportedly shot twenty-five unarmed protestors dead, though the true figure may have been much higher. There was "talk of hundreds being killed by the police and being shot on the roads back by civilian Europeans in cars and on horseback," wrote a contempo-rary, and "several white men I knew boasted about it."[43] Thuku later claimed that he was objecting to unfair treatment not asserting that "we should get self-government."[44] But, as one former official wrote, his move-ment was the "genesis of a revolution." It heralded the emergence of "a poly-glot *nation*."[45] The ruthless exploitation of Africans also pricked consciences in Britain, where Kenya was depicted as the "Bluebeard of the Empire."

Meanwhile, the Europeans were also trying to put the Indians in their place. Having arrived in force with the railway, they now outnumbered the whites by six to one and played a major role in the commercial life of Kenya. Indians were denied political rights. They were forbidden to acquire prop-erty in the White Highlands, where 0.07 per cent of the population held a fifth of the country's best land. They were refused free entry to Kenya—which some of them wanted to turn into a colonial extension of the Raj, ruled by the Viceroy from Delhi, just as some Europeans wanted it to be incorporated into a South African federation centred on Cape Town. Fur-thermore, Indians had to endure a colour bar imposed on grounds of their "moral depravity" and their "incurable repugnance to sanitation and hygiene." Diplomatic overtures from the India Office and angry protests from the subcontinent achieved a modest improvement in their lot. But Lord Delamere and his friends denounced this as a capitulation to India and plotted a coup of their own. In the loyalist spirit of Belfast, they formulated the slogan: "For King and Kenya."[46] In the rebellious spirit of Boston, they planned to seize the railway, the telegraph and the post office, and to kidnap the Governor, who would be confined to a remote farm sixty miles from Nairobi but close to some excellent trout fishing.

Anxious to avoid violence, the Colonial Office held a conference in 1923. It was attended by delegations of Kenyan Asians and white settlers, the latter under the leadership of Lord Delamere, who shocked London society by pointing to his Somali servants and saying, "My sons."[47] Africans were not invited but they provided the new Colonial Secretary, the Duke of Devonshire, with a convenient means of neutralising the two rival factions. He announced that Kenya was primarily an African territory and that "the interests of the African natives must be paramount."[48] This angered the Indians, though Devonshire ended segregation in townships and increased their representation on the Legislative Council. But they could hardly object to his high-minded re-statement of the principle of imperial trusteeship. Nor, as Delamere realised, could his supporters. For they had posed as the champions of African interests against Indian incursions and anyway got most of what they wanted. However, the Devonshire Declaration did prevent the settlers of Kenya from establishing a self-governing colony within the Commonwealth, as those of Rhodesia did in 1923, based on minority white rule. And in the long run it proved fatal to their cause.

Between the wars, therefore, they struggled to change minds in London and to establish control in Nairobi. The Colonial Office responded by formulating a series of shifty and shifting policies about Kenya's future. It considered setting up an East African Federation, consisting of Kenya, Uganda and Tanganyika. It toyed with the notion of dividing Kenya into separate black and white regions. It edged towards accepting that Africans should eventually be represented in the Legislative Council. It resisted the more extreme demands of the settlers, whom Harold Macmillan, Devonshire's son-in-law, described as "turbulent bigots and potential traitors."[49] They were so troublesome, indeed, that the Colonial Office considered buying them out and bringing them home. This was a cheaper option, said Macmillan, than civil war. However, the boorish intransigence of the settlers proved more effective in Kenya, where they intimidated nearly all Governors and stamped their personality on the colony. In the long run this did them more harm than good because, thanks to the settlers' unbridled behaviour, the White Highlands earned a global reputation for decadence. Lurid tales were told of a community that drank sundowners until sunrise, took cocaine like snuff and swapped wives so often that no one could remember the ladies' latest surnames. It was said that the Wanjohi River ran with cocktails. The Muthaiga Club, a low, pink stone building decorated with hunting scenes by Sir Alfred Munnings, was supposed to be a hotbed of vice, the Moulin Rouge of Africa. King George V heard sinister rumours that dinner parties were being thrown to which guests were invited to wear "Tiaras or pyjamas, whichever you like."[50] Such people ought to have known better, he said, and instructed Sir Edward Grigg, Governor between 1925 and 1930, to put a stop to it.

Doubtless the reports were exaggerated. Kenya was advertised as a rich man's playground, a sportsman's paradise, the officers' mess as opposed to the Rhodesian sergeant's mess. But many whites were by no means affluent let alone aristocratic. A few barely scraped a living. Snubbed by Colonel Montgomery, Arnold Paice thought "he was afraid of his blessed daughter meeting with a sort of wild man of the woods who might turn up to dinner . . . in native costume."[51] Some of the post-war soldier-settlers seemed doomed to fail: one planned "to start a dairy farm and stock it with fifty bulls and fifty cows, that were, presumably, to pair off like partridges."[52] In 1929 Margery Perham was shocked to find Nairobi full of impecunious young white men, some with revolvers in their belts, wearing shorts or corduroy plus-fours, "green, orange, blue and purple shirts, and Stetson hats."[53] Nevertheless, there is abundant evidence to show that stories of settler profligacy were far from being baseless. Lord Delamere gave a dinner at which 250 people consumed six hundred bottles of champagne. Lady Northey, a Governor's wife, danced on the tables of the Muthaiga Club. Frank Greswolde-Williams offered drugs to the Prince of Wales and later his brother, Prince George, got cocaine from Kiki Preston, who was "clever with her needle."[54] Every time Beryl Markham (as she became) took a new lover, one of them being another royal brother, Prince Henry, her first husband knocked a six-inch nail into a post by their front door and soon there was quite a long row. Roman Catholic missionaries evidently succumbed to the general depravity—Meinertzhagen doubted whether some White Fathers were white but he was sure that they were fathers. Elspeth Huxley's mother learned Swahili from a handbook issued by the Society for the Propagation of the Gospel which contained such sentences as, "The idle slaves are scratching themselves" and "Six drunken Europeans have killed the cook."[55] Some blamed the equatorial sun for unsettling the settlers' nerves and Llewelyn Powys said that all hearts were turned to stone by the blazing "Gorgon's head of Africa."[56] Others thought that the altitude encouraged adultery. Still others believed that white scandal encouraged black disaffection.

In fact, Europeans were more likely to antagonise Africans by lashing out with fist, boot and whip. Between the wars assaults and even killings were "far from rare"[57] and settlers were liable to maintain that "If white murders black a laudable object has been achieved."[58] Their conduct in the Legislative Council was also aggressive. Here, often egged on to further extremes by Lord Delamere, they savagely denounced the enemies of the white community. Margery Perham, who witnessed one such outburst, decided that Kenya was a pathological case. This was partly because it possessed such a minuscule European population—21,000 by 1939, or 1 to 175 Africans, compared to Southern Rhodesia's 63,000 whites, 1 to 25. Kenya's Europeans lived in a perennial state of insecurity and defensiveness. Their world was a bubble and the rarefied air they breathed inside it was tainted with paranoia. During the 1920s, for example, the local press ran a hysterical campaign about the sexual "Black Peril" threatening white women. Yet it could quote scarcely a single instance of rape, even though the memsahib was apt to regard her black servant as "a piece of wood, and . . . call him into her disordered bed-room when she herself is practically nude."[59] In the following decade the white community also became neurotic about the Jewish peril— an influx of refugees from persecution in Europe as earlier proposed, ironically, by Joseph Chamberlain. Lord Erroll so disliked the "dirty foreigner" that he advocated British fascism for Kenya, finding a favourable climate for it—Sir Edward Grigg so admired Mussolini that he publicly appeared in a Blackshirt uniform of his own design. Erroll's fascism involved "super loyalty to the Crown" and an "insulated Empire."[60] Eventually the Settlement Committee agreed to admit a few "Jews of *nordic type*."[61] But white Kenyans mocked Lord Passfield, the Colonial Secretary who encouraged the Kikuyu Central Association, Thuku's renamed movement, as Lord Passover. And the Association's new leader, Jomo Kenyatta, who studied in the Soviet Union, compared the treatment of Africans by Britain's colonial fascists to that of the Jews by the Nazis.

It was a charge to concentrate minds in the Colonial Office, where the old confidence in Britain's power and pelf was wearing ever more thin during the 1930s. For years a few of the more perceptive British officials had been warning about the rise of nationalism in Africa. Sometimes they sought analogies in the history of the Roman Empire, which had also aimed to control and civilise a plethora of rival tribes. Charles Hobley, for example, wrote that the Romans had made a profound impact on their British subjects in four hundred years and that, although Britain had occupied Kenya for only a tenth of that time, the African was surely "capable of playing a great part in his own government."[62] Norman Leys, citing the 1915 millenarian uprising in Nyasaland, which had been sparked off by injustice and put down with ferocity, said that Britain faced Christianity and Islam in Africa, the two militant creeds which had triumphed over the Roman Empire. Rome had for a time maintained the loyalty of its subjects by sharing with them "such political rights as the age conceived."[63] Britain should apply the principles of guardianship and democracy, eradicating racial discrimination and giving representation to Africans. Questions remained about how soon this could be done and whether multi-coloured partnership or black para-mountcy would emerge. But between the wars it became clear, at least in the Colonial Office, that Kenya's whites could not hold on to their monopoly forever, especially as Africans were acquiring the education that would enable them to make informed use of the vote. By 1944 the editor of the *Kenya Weekly News* became the first prominent settler to acknowledge pub-licly that the government would have to be run by "all races co-operating."[64] In the same year the first African, Eliud Mathu, became a member of the colony's Legislative Council. He was the son of a Kikuyu "witch-doctor" who had been to university at Balliol College, Oxford.

If blue-blooded Englishmen led Kenya's whites, the Sudan was famously "a Land of Blacks ruled by Blues."[65] In fact less than a quarter of the four hun-dred officials who constituted the Sudan Political Service (as it came to be called—SPS) over fifty years won the accolade of athletic distinction at Oxford and Cambridge. Moreover, a tenth of them gained first-class degrees and in the Anglo-Egyptian condominium brains were at least as highly regarded as brawn. Nevertheless, sport was a vital element in forming the *esprit de corps* of the SPS. Taking violent exercise in furnace heat was believed to produce healthy minds in healthy bodies, to foster individualism as well as team spirit, and to train the character for the rigours of life off the beaten track. Having learned to play the game at public school and univer-sity, officials went on playing it in the wilderness. As one of them said, skill at golf, squash, tennis, rugby, rowing or cricket "gave us the self-confidence to cope with loneliness and being on our own in charge of large areas of population."[66]

Certainly the Sudan Political Service, which evolved from a military to a civilian body, came to rival the "heaven-born" elite of India. Even Odette Keun, a left-wing journalist who loathed the brutality of Britain's "obsolete empire," described the SPS as "an order of Samurai." According to her account, its members (a third of whom were clergymen's sons) possessed a high standard of honour. They bore the white man's burden instead of clamping themselves to the native back like the Old Man of the Sea. Settler colonies, Kenya being a prime example, were ripped open for such wealth as they contained. They were, she said, a "happy hunting-ground of the adventurer, the gold-digger, the industrial or commercial brigand, the ten-thousand-times-accursed concessionaire." The Sudan, which Kitchener had rescued from the chaos, rapine, famine and misery of the Khalifate at the battle of Omdurman, was by 1930 a model of good order. The SPS, never more than 125 strong yet governing an area four times the size of Texas, had abolished slavery, fostered prosperity, improved health, promoted education and preserved peace. In fact, Odette Keun concluded, the Sudan was a startlingly successful experiment in colonisation, having at its heart a unique and "incredible objective—the welfare of the conquered."[67]

The British naturally maintained that the purpose of all their colonies was to benefit the native people but they were gratified by "eulogies"[68] of their stewardship in the Sudan from such an unexpected source. Odette Keun was a pertinacious reporter—after interviewing H. G. Wells she apparently went to bed with him "to fill out her impressions."[69] Other witnesses, notably Margery Perham, confirmed her view of the condominium. But were they right? Khartoum, at least, seemed to vindicate their judgement. Kitchener at once began its reconstruction, allegedly planning the layout on the pattern of a Union Jack. There is no evidence for this, or for the claim that he designed its grid of streets for ease of firing Maxim guns. But in due course broad boulevards, shaded by banyans and wild fig trees, lit by electricity, traversed by trams, and bearing names like Victoria Avenue, did crisscross the city. Kitchener raised money for the Gordon Memorial College and he was so keen to rebuild the Palace where Gordon was martyred that he refused to allow camels to be diverted from hauling bricks to carrying grain for famine relief. In 1899 General Sir Reginald Wingate succeeded Kitchener as Governor-General and during his long tenure he presided over a substantial modernisation of the capital. The Nile was embanked and bordered by a spacious esplanade. Fine bungalows set amid lawns and palms also overlooked the water. New squares arose and with them government and business offices. Tennis, squash and fives courts appeared. So did a zoo, a railway station, a dockyard, a School of Medicine, a shooting range, a polo ground and a golf course, though its fairways were sandy and its greens were brown. Near the Anglican cathedral a statue of General Gordon riding a camel was floodlit every Sunday night—it shone with a silvery white radiance, a ghost of the martyr who died to save the city.

At the cool, verandahed Sudan Club, "that Mecca of social life among the British upper crust," embowered in riverside gardens complete with swimming pool, waiters in white robes and green cummerbunds served top officials with afternoon tea or iced lime soda. At the Palace, an icing-sugar-coloured confection known as "the Christmas cake,"[70] which was girdled with fountains and flowers, Wingate lived in regal state. His progress through the city, attended by a gorgeously uniformed staff and escorted by a glittering cavalcade of black lancers, reminded one witness of "a Drury lane Melodrama."[71] Khartoum even became a smart tourist resort with shops and hotels run by Levantines and Italians, a kind of African Riviera. In due course it attracted its own "fishing fleet." Wingate complained about having to entertain so many dignitaries and he often took refuge at Erkowit, a hill station near the Red Sea which aspired to be "the Simla of the Sudan."[72] An inveterate snob, though, he really appreciated the value of influential European visitors to what was advertised as the "Sunny Sudan." Thanks to them and, still more, to Egyptian subventions, Khartoum began to look like the capital of a flourishing country. Yet one influential visitor, Rudyard Kipling, discerned the doom of the Empire in the progress of the city. Furnished with an education and an easy life, its people would soon demand "Soudan for the Soudanese," he declared. "It is a hard law but an old one—Rome died learning it, as our western civilisation may die—that if you give any man anything that he has not painfully earned for himself, you infallibly make him or his descendants your devoted enemies."[73] This was the characteristically crusty view of a writer who, in his frequent identification of British and Roman imperial decline, once acknowledged that Gibbon was "the fat heifer I ploughed with."[74]

Nevertheless, Khartoum did in some ways symbolise the fragility of British rule, for the edifice of imperial order was lapped by waves of indigenous discord. Across the river, its foreshore heaped with gum, dura and hides, was the grey-brown jumble of Omdurman, a menacing labyrinth of narrow, sandy streets with open drains flanked by poky, flyblown shops and mud hovels plastered with dung. And behind the European façade in Khartoum itself the Sudanese dwelt in dusty rows of box-like abodes bereft of amenities such as running water and much inferior to the humblest SPS dwellings, which were later called "Belsens." Just as the river crossing was said to be a journey back in time, the architectural divide signified a social gulf. Except on business rulers seldom met ruled, regarding them less as human beings than as gaudy or unsightly components of the alien scene. As a young official Harold MacMichael found the women of Khartoum "the most repulsive objects of hideosity I *ever* saw: they carry themselves very well because of always having pitchers or bricks on their heads, but their faces are like gargoyles and they smell appallingly of unguents."[75] Sometimes members of the SPS were facetious at the expense of the Sudanese, one wag guying their (sensible) habit of riding on the hindquarters of their donkeys:

As I sat on my ass on the ass of my ass
This thought came into my mind,
That though three parts of my ass was in front of my ass
The whole of my ass was behind.

So at best race relations were "cordial but not very close."[76] The British, as always, kept to themselves. In the mordant words of Douglas Newbold, Governor of Kordofan for most of the 1930s, they seemed to think that their imperial mission involved herding like fatted cows "on each others' lawns or verandahs, drinking murderous cocktails and talking unadulterated bilge to unknown people."[77]

Members of the SPS were generally as starched and conventional as their evening dress, though they could unbend, sometimes getting "squiffier and squiffier" at dinner until the evening ended in "a drunken brawl."[78] They scorned the effendi class of Sudanese as semi-educated and half-baked, imitative in trousers and shoes but outlandish over food and drink. These exotic proletarians were certainly presumptuous and probably seditious, always to be slapped down and sometimes merely to be slapped. The tiny Arab intelligentsia resented living in a state of subordination and some enlightened whites predicted that the British reluctance to mix would destroy their administration. An augury of its fate was the nationalist White Flag League, formed in 1923, which demonstrated and agitated for freedom. The movement, which spread to the military, drew strength from a nominally independent Egypt. So when Wingate's successor as Governor-General of the Sudan, Sir Lee Stack, was assassinated on a visit to Cairo in 1924, the British took the opportunity to send home the Egyptian army along with many Egyptian civil servants, teachers and others. While maintaining the fiction of the "Anglo-Egyptian Condominium," they turned the Sudan into a virtual mandate. This provoked a mutiny among Sudanese forces, which was quickly crushed. A new Governor-General, Sir John Maffey, tried to insulate the country from dangerous modern influences. He aimed to sterilise any political germs floating up the Nile to Khartoum and to make the Sudan "safe for autocracy."[79]

The British also strove to prevent the predominantly Arab, Muslim north from infecting the largely African, pagan south. The vast basin of the Upper Nile was the province of the so-called "Bog Barons," white officials who aspired to become local patriarchs, even paramount chiefs. They were often idiosyncratic characters. One trekked with a handkerchief hanging from the corner of his mouth. Another walked away if he saw a white man, ran if it was a white woman. Another dressed the crew of his private Nile boat in uniform jerseys bearing the motto *"Ana muzlum"*—I am oppressed. Yet another kept two files for communications from Khartoum, one marked "Quite Sensible," the other "Balderdash."[80] Still others succumbed to the charms of "the most attractive, friendly, black, naked pagans you could wish for," though one of them, "Tiger" Wyld, said that to reveal such liaisons was to "let down the side."[81] Mostly tough ex-soldiers, the Bog Barons were sometimes brought to the capital to take instruction from "the super cock-angels" of the SPS, a facetious observer wrote, in "higher culture, advanced purity and semi-teetotalism."[82] But they faced almost insuperable difficulties in and around the primordial Sudd. There they encountered a world of what Sir Harold MacMichael, when Civil Secretary (i.e. top official) in Khartoum, deemed "semi-simian savagery." It was a "Serbonian bog into which had drifted, or been pushed, all the lowest racial elements surviving north of the equator and a great deal of equally decayed vegetation."[83] Certainly it was home to a host of peoples, among them Shilluk, Nuer, Anuak, Bari, Dinka and Zande. Strangers to the plough, the wheel and the pen, they were a prey to famine, violence and disease. Most were nude—the ritually cicatriced Nuer, whose ash-covered bodies gave them "the appearance of living skeletons,"[84] regarded clothes as the livery of servitude. Many embraced witchcraft, worshipped fetishes and possessed what Christians called a "ju-ju mentality."[85] Some practised cannibalism. They lived in atomised groups, often without headmen, and spoke some eight hundred languages.

As such they were hard to control and for thirty years the Bog Barons concentrated on suppression rather than administration. British punitive expeditions in the Sudan were even more brutal than those in Kenya, at times amounting almost to genocide. Certainly, as one District Officer acknowledged, they produced a crop of "regular Congo atrocities."[86] Supplementing ground forces with aircraft, since the RAF wanted to test "the moral effect"[87] of bombing and strafing in an ideal proving ground, MacMichael was apparently content to employ the methods of "Tamburlaine or Genghis Khan."[88] For he believed that only those speaking Arabic were susceptible to proper government. The best that could be done for the polyglot people of the south was to look after them "on a care and maintenance basis."[89] This involved little in the way of social welfare. Typically, the Director of Medical Services refused to post a Senior Medical Officer to the Fung District until its Commissioner had "got the place healthy enough for him."[90] Most Bog Barons accepted that they were keepers in "an anthropological zoo."[91] But less conservative officials rejected the idea of setting up a "human Whipsnade"[92] or "zoological gardens where black men are to be carefully fenced off to develop 'on their own lines.'"[93] They tried to raise Africans "to a higher standard of living and culture" on the grounds that "nations colonised by Rome still display advance over those who were not so fortunate." They made piecemeal attempts to strengthen tribal units and leaders. Thus Catholic and Protestant missionaries were allowed to teach and preach to the heathen, using English as the official language. Nevertheless, so long as order prevailed the British found it easy (and cheap) to neglect the Upper Nile. Indeed, they had a vested interest in southern stagnation.

Nor were they averse to northern backwardness. Of course the Khartoum government sought to develop the economy. In order to grow cotton between the White and Blue Niles, for example, it built the Sennar dam and irrigated the Gezira peninsula—a pharaonic enterprise which saddled the Sudan with a huge debt. Agricultural experts monitored progress, as suggested by this contemporary pastiche of John Masefield:

> Sweaty Block Inspector with gin-soaked arm-pits
> Trotting through the cotton on an old brown mare,
> With a cargo of horse-whips,
> Whisky-flasks, monocles,
> Polo-sticks, poker-dice, and Lotion for the Hair.[94]

The British also improved communications, threading the country with roads, railways and telegraph wires. They remoulded Omdurman. They built Port Sudan on the Red Sea. They fostered veterinary and medical services. To produce a cadre of clerks and technicians, they even approved a modest amount of vocational training. But although paying lip service to learning, they thought it wasted on the ignorant. They equated liberal education with political subversion—some medical opinion even deemed it a cause of African insanity. They favoured the old-fashioned culture of the country, uncontaminated by western ideas. Wilfred Thesiger, an Oxford boxing Blue and a District Officer in Darfur between the wars, was typical in this respect. He disapproved of educating tribal people and "questioned whether it was right to try to impose on the Sudanese the conventions and values of our utterly alien civilisation."[95] Among Sudanese conventions was an acceptance of slavery, something the government tolerated and even encouraged (through taxation) until the end of the 1920s. Even then it tried to settle slaves gradually "within their masters' tribes"[96] rather than freeing them, one District Officer wrote, to become thieves and harlots.

As in India and other imperial territories, the British identified with the most conservative elements of native society. But, like Burton, Doughty, Lawrence, Philby and Gertrude Bell, many members of the SPS also felt a powerful affinity for pastoral Arabs and the wild places in which they dwelt. Douglas Newbold was typical in having a quasi-mystical veneration for the desert, "the abode of jinns and efreets, of the basilisk and the cockatrice." Man's soul was purged, he said, amid its singing sands and quivering mirages. Vast, silent and clean, it was enough to "make the pygmy wayfarer tread as softly as in an empty cathedral."[97] Newbold and his colleagues admired the nomads as warriors, hunters, noble savages, nature's gentlemen. On safari the British enjoyed the intimacy of the oasis and the camaraderie of the camp fire, a contrast to their constraint with educated, urban Sudanese. No doubt some SPS men, both Thesiger and Newbold, for example, felt a homosexual attraction to desert Arabs, usually sublimated. Others relished the adventurous life, exploring, shooting big game, subduing turbulent tribesmen. Still others valued the early responsibility, the paternalistic oversight of everything from wells to latrines, from herd taxes to village petitions, from gun licences to marital disputes, from plagues of locusts to pedlars of subversion, from pulling out teeth to casting out devils. Nearly all accepted the need for indirect rule, which became official policy after the Great War, whereby colonial administration operated through native chiefs. Unlike effendi, who espoused progress, sheikhs personified the past. They might be fools or knaves, brigands or zealots, but they were surely wedded to tradition. The British saw them as a kind of rural gentry through which the SPS patriciate could best maintain control of this antique land.

In fact, indirect rule never worked well and sometimes hardly worked at all, its failings being particularly obvious in the Sudan. The system was beset by contradictions. It relied on the compliance of chiefs whose authority rested upon their independence from the British. It kept colonial people in a condition of tutelage yet purported to be preparing them to stand on their own feet. It imposed an archaic order on societies that could not be isolated from modernity. Newbold compared the erosion of feudal loyalty in northern Sudan during the 1930s to "the passing of the squire" at home and put both down to "the inexorable march of events."[98] Among the Africans of the south the entire process of devolution was bedevilled by uncertainty about who, if anyone, ruled whom. Whereas the Shilluk had a king, the Nuer had prophets and in one district, its Commissioner noted despairingly, the Dinka were represented by "47 different individuals, each called 'chief.'"[99] As a result indirect rule was never comprehensively adopted. What is more, no sooner had it become an orthodoxy than critics began to harp on its reactionary character. Sir Stewart Symes, who was Governor-General from 1934 to 1940, said that it held back educated Sudanese, who were acting as bottle-washers when they should be senior officials. However, Symes, formerly Wingate's ADC, was more prone to caution than to innovation. He believed that the Sudanese were in a state of political infancy and did little to lead them towards maturity. He encouraged modest "Sudanisation" during the Depression largely in order to save money and his educational reforms were more a matter of aspiration than achievement. In the south scarcely anything was done. Its people appreciated the Pax Britannica which prevailed for a quarter of a century but they later said that the main mistake the British made was that "they did not educate us."[100] As a later Civil Secretary, Sir James Robertson, reluctantly concluded, his countrymen in the Sudan had failed to carry out the government's avowed policy, "i.e. to further the interests of the Sudanese."[101]

Nationalists had felt this acutely at least since 1936, when the makers of the Anglo-Egyptian Treaty incensed them by deciding the fate of the Sudan without consulting its people. In effect the treaty maintained the status quo: Egyptian officials did return to Khartoum but British rule continued. So in 1938 the Sudanese intelligentsia formed the Graduates' General Congress and sought to exploit the rivalry between London and Cairo. They did so with some skill, assisted by a gradual erosion of confidence inside the SPS. Its officials recognised that Egypt, which Newbold described as "staggering in its vomit like a drunken man,"[102] might gain control of the Upper Nile. And this horrid prospect helped to reconcile them to eventual Sudanese independence (though they could scarcely have anticipated that their immaculate Club would later become home to the Sudan Socialist Union). When the Congress took advantage of the war to demand self-determination, Newbold, now Civil Secretary, who dismissed the Italian attack from Ethiopia as an "ice-cream blitzkrieg," issued a public rebuke. The Congress had fallen into "errors," he declared, and it should renounce any claim "to be the mouth-piece of the whole country." Privately, however, Newbold, likened by a colleague to "one of Plato's philosopher kings,"[103] moved to meet "reasonable aspirations of the enlightened Sudanese."[104]

Failure to do so might result in such troubles as had afflicted Ireland or India, he thought, and the Sudan was not hampered like Kenya with its white settlers or like Palestine with its community feuds. It should implement Britain's wartime imperial policy of supporting the "progressive evolution of self-governing institutions." In 1944, therefore, the Governor-General convened an Advisory Council which he hailed as the "first concrete expression of a Sudanese nation."[105] It was also an attempt to divide and rule. In the twenty-eight-strong Council, graduates were outnumbered by tribal leaders, nazirs in white togas, muftis in purple vestments, sheikhs in robes of scarlet and blue embroidered with gold. Neither the southern Sudan nor Egypt was represented, which widened the split inside the Congress itself. Followers of the Mahdi's posthumous son, Abd al-Rahman al-Mahdi, wanted "Sudan for the Sudanese." Their opponents, led by Ismail al-Azhari (later the Sudan's first Prime Minister), aimed to eject their white masters with Egyptian help and campaigned for the "Unity of the Nile Valley." These slogans were the writing on the wall for the British. But if the divisions that the SPS fostered could not prolong the rule of Blue over Black, they did help to foment civil war in the Sudan after independence. Al-Azhari's conclusion was harsh. To maintain its tyranny the imperial power had "sat heavily upon the land," he said, "spreading hatred and separation between its people."[106]

This verdict was heard in other parts of Africa painted red on the map. Settler colonies in particular seemed bent on following the Boer example: one Cewa chief complained that Southern Rhodesians did not look on black people as humans, "they just treat them as dogs."[107] In his impassioned account *How Britain Rules Africa* (1936), George Padmore, a Trinidadian Marxist, said its colonies were a "breeding-ground for the type of fascist mentality which is being let loose in Europe to-day."[108] Yet Britain's record in Africa was better than that of other European states and on the whole, once in place, its yoke was easy. It lacked the manpower, the resources and the will to govern its tropical dependencies by main force, ruling through native collaborators and relying on white prestige. Indeed, one colonial judge, remarking on how a single District Officer with half a dozen askaris might be in charge of 100,000 Africans, said that Britain's "whole position rests on bluff."[109] In settler colonies, limits were imposed on the exploitation and coercion of blacks by the poverty and paucity of whites, to say nothing of interference from London. True, the British squeezed where they could, as in the copper belt of Northern Rhodesia. There, between 1930 and 1940, they took £2.4 million in taxes and gave only £136,000 in development grants. They thus starved the colonial government of funds for roads, agriculture, housing and essential social services, which remained "very backward."[110] Development was also limited elsewhere, particularly when times were hard. Between the wars West Africa, though politically quite advanced, was economically stagnant. Basutoland was hardly touched by government. Such tiny sums were spent on Nyasaland that workers emigrated to the more racially hostile environment of Rhodesia and South Africa. A Governor of Tanganyika said that his territory was kept "in mothballs."[111] A Governor of Nigeria said, "The great merit of British rule is that there is so little of it."[112] Only in the Union of South Africa did the European community have the numbers, the wealth and the independence to impose thoroughly repressive policies based on colour. It duly laid the foundations of the apartheid system, confining the black two-thirds of the population to 13 per cent of the land, discriminating against Africans in the workplace, depriving them of votes and passing other racist laws. This prompted the creation of the African National Congress, with its haunting anthem, adopted in 1925, *"Nkosi sikeleli Afrika"*—"God Bless Africa."

Across the continent, though, other such bodies sprouted as opposition to imperial overlordship grew. The process was gradual, intermittent and by no means preordained. There was nothing inevitable, either, about progress towards the ultimate goal of self-government. Trusteeship, in any case a slippery concept, was supposed to become partnership with native peoples, which would eventually lead to their independence. However, as a liberal settler said, "Those of us who live in Central Africa know very well that partnership between black and white . . . is at best a pious hope, at worst a disingenuous myth propagated for political purposes."[113] Among other things, tribal divisions suggested that African nations would be slow to evolve. Smuts thought it would take Europeans an age to school "peoples who have slumbered and stagnated since the dawn of time."[114] Many British officials agreed. Sir Philip Mitchell, who became Governor of Uganda in 1935, reckoned that the Africans of 1890 were centuries behind the Britons of Julius Caesar's day. Their swift advancement was impossible because there was nothing in the continent between the Stone Age and Dr. Livingstone—"not a ruin, not a tomb, not an inscription."[115] (Mitchell did not mention iron-working and he believed that the stone structure at Great Zimbabwe was a colonial edifice.) In any case Africans who were "labouring in the throes of nation-birth" often wished to cooperate with colonial governments. The National Democratic Party in Lagos told the Governor that it wanted to preserve Nigeria "not only as an integral part of the Empire, but also as a bright jewel within the imperial panorama."[116] Nevertheless, as the examples of Kenya and the Sudan indicate, the tide of hostility to colonialism was rising in Africa and only the pace of the resulting political change was still in doubt.

Native elites were everywhere emerging, their consciousness shaped by the blackboard, the pulpit and the press—as early as 1900 there were nineteen newspapers in the Gold Coast and thirty-four in Sierra Leone. Frustrated by the limited opportunities available to him under white rule, the "accursed educated African" was angry at the advance of race prejudice and bitter that his colonial masters regarded him as "a worse evil than the primitive savage."[117] Africans without the benefit of schooling learned practical lessons from the demands for land, labour and tax made on them by the self-proclaimed purveyors of civilisation. Also instructive were the methods of white politicians and trade unionists. Many black people just wanted a redress of grievances. But some demanded more say in their own affairs and no taxation without representation. And others gave utterance to what Lord Hailey called that "pestilent polysyllable, self-determination."[118] They were emboldened by Britain's loss of prestige as a result of the Great War, which presented Africans, over a million of whom took part in the conflict, with the shocking spectacle of Europeans fighting one another. The Depression further weakened imperial power, particularly as Japanese goods drove British products from marketplaces in their own colonies; before the end of the decade, for example, Nippon supplied 93 per cent of East Africa's cotton cloth. African disillusionment grew when Britain responded so feebly to Mussolini's rape of Ethiopia in 1935 and tried to find ways of appeasing Hitler, perhaps by restoring Germany's colonies. But hope sprang from a growing international acceptance of the ideal of racial equality, which presented the Empire with an "unprecedented crisis of conscience."[119]

Many who shared that ideal helped to support African nationalism, whether through the advancement of human rights, local loyalties or black pride. Promoted by the American socialist W. E. B. Dubois, Pan-African conferences attacked colonialism. Marcus Garvey's militant Universal Negro Improvement Association "made Harlem felt around the world."[120] And the slogan of his Back-to-Africa movement—"Africa for the Africans"—not only influenced aspirant leaders such as Kwame Nkrumah but reverberated through the continent. It reached, for example, a remote corner of northern Nigeria, four days' journey from a telegraph office and eight from a railway, where many had never seen a white man let alone a white woman. Here, Joyce Cary wrote, village markets were excited by rumours of a black king coming in a great iron steamship full of black soldiers "to drive all the whites out of Africa."[121] Before the Second World War Indian protests about the disabilities suffered by their compatriots in South Africa, Kenya and elsewhere also stimulated African resistance to white domination. Gandhi encouraged it and the Indian National Congress demonstrated the need for political organisation. Nehru and other nationalists, such as Subhas Chandra Bose, were sympathetic. Nehru wrote that Negroes he met at the International Congress against Colonial Oppression and Imperialism (organised by the ubiquitous Communist agent Willi Münzenberg in Brussels in 1927) bore traces of the unique and "terrible martyrdom which their race has suffered."[122] But he thought that Africans would not gain freedom without a universal emancipation from imperialism. Thus *swaraj* and embryonic African independence movements were part of the same cause, drawing strength from one another. Africa learned much from India's campaign for Home Rule. India could only help Africans and Asians to win their liberty by triumphing in its struggle against the British Empire.

13

Spinning the Destiny of India

The Route to Independence

During the years after the massacre at Amritsar, India's struggle was dominated by Motilal and Jawaharlal Nehru and Mahatma Gandhi—sometimes termed Father, Son and Holy Ghost. In this nationalist trinity the last was unquestionably first. Gandhi's god-like moral stature, which transfigured his wispy frame, gave him unique authority both inside and outside Congress. Noting the calm depth of his eyes, the limpid clarity of his voice and the beguiling charm of his manner, Jawaharlal said that Gandhi had "a kingliness in him which compelled a willing obeisance." Motilal Nehru himself became a disciple, despite his worldly success as a lawyer under the Raj and a masterful character that was visibly etched upon his countenance. "With a broad forehead, tight lips and a determined chin," wrote his son, "he had a marked resemblance to the busts of the Roman Emperors in the museums of Italy."[1] Motilal's similarity to the Caesars became still more pronounced, others observed, when he gave up his velvet smoking jackets and gold-embroidered shoes for white, home spun, toga-like *chadders* and sandals. Jawaharlal, sophisticated, secular, progressive and so westernised that he spoke Hindi with an English accent, was still more of an antithesis to Gandhi.

Indeed, this fastidious aesthete puzzled over the affinity he felt for the loin-clothed ascetic who sat cross-legged on the ground and ate with his fingers. The rationalist could not comprehend the thought processes of the *sadhu*, who was directed by an Inner Voice, sometimes heard in the lavatory. The young philanderer had no sympathy with the sage who aspired to be "God's Eunuch."[2] But he concluded that personality has "a strange power over the souls of men."[3] Despite their differences, Gandhi appealed to the smouldering idealism in Jawaharlal, who for years gave him "humble, unquestioning allegiance."[4] His loyalty burned most brightly when he and Motilal joined the Mahatma in the non-cooperation campaign of 1920–22. Intended as a reasoned response to the bloodshed of the Jallianwala Bagh, this was Gandhi's endeavour to liberate the nation through the greatest manifestation of soul force hitherto seen in India. It turned out that he could not defeat the Raj through boycotts, *hartals* and peaceful protests. But the *satyagraha* did sap its claims to legitimacy and undermine its moral foundations. Those who took part offered themselves as a willing sacrifice and endured much suffering. None bore it with such redemptive zeal as Motilal Nehru's beloved son.

Jawaharlal's devotion to the national cause was unexpected, since he had long seemed little more than a dilettante. Born in 1889, he was brought up in the Anand Bhavan, or Abode of Bliss, the most palatial mansion in Allahabad. It was set in ten acres of luxuriant gardens complete with tennis courts, riding ring, indoor swimming pool and a courtyard fountain filled with ice and flowers that cooled and scented the whole house during the hot weather. He was surrounded by nurses, servants, governesses and tutors. His doting mother indulged him while his fiercely possessive father intimidated him. A Kashmiri Brahmin by origin, Motilal was determined that "the boy"[5] should be educated like an English gentleman and should enter that nirvana of respectability, the Indian Civil Service. So in 1905 Jawaharlal went to Harrow, where he was pursued by paternal exhortations to excel, not least in the matter of growing a moustache. He looked a fool without one, said Motilal, who himself sported a Kitcheneresque appendage at the time. But Jawaharlal had no more success in this respect than did his fellow Harrovian, Winston Churchill, and he soon shaved off the callow growth with the plea that it was "all awry and it spoils the whole look of the face."

He made scarcely any other mark at school and proceeded to Trinity College, Cambridge, where his career was also undistinguished. In fact, Jawaharlal lived the life of a young man of fashion, running up debts for Savile Row suits and Montmartre jaunts. There were signs of a political bent: he admired Sinn Féin, listened to Bernard Shaw and questioned his father's faith in John Bull. But Jawaharlal was a study in aimlessness and he got such a poor degree that he was unable to enter the ICS. He toyed with other options, telling Motilal that he wanted to read law at "a decent Oxford College" because Cambridge was "too full of Indians."[6] Eventually, without enthusiasm, he qualified for the bar at the Inner Temple in London. He was equally lukewarm when practising as a lawyer on his return to Allahabad, deciding that his profession aimed to "exploit others."[7] Nor did he seem keen on the marriage that Motilal arranged for him in 1916, an extravagant ceremony in which his seventeen-year-old bride, Kamala, was almost borne to the ground under the weight of her jewellery. Jawaharlal remained cool and detached. Although hot-tempered he cultivated cold-bloodedness, according to a later confession, because he feared being swept away by passion. That emotional avalanche occurred after the war, when Gandhi converted him to become "an ardent believer in non-cooperation." Only this form of protest would end India's slavery and bring victory over its oppressors, Jawaharlal declared. "That victory may not come in a day or a year, but come it must, *ruat coelum*"—though the heavens fall.[8]

Motilal dreaded such a cataclysm and tried to restrain Jawaharlal. But Amritsar worked a revolution in Motilal's views and he too "felt an irresistible call to follow the Mahatma."[9] What is more, the father knew that he must follow the son or lose him to Gandhi, whom Jawaharlal often addressed as *Bapu,* little father. So in 1920 Motilal threw in his lot with the *swarajist* non-cooperators. A pillar of the law, he supported a campaign of civil disobedience that led to some thirty thousand arrests, braving gaol himself. He was even to be seen, a refined, white-haired patrician, hawking *khadi* cloth in the grimy streets of Allahabad. But Motilal did not altogether renounce luxury. His Gandhi cap was fashioned in silk by Lock of St. James's in London. He drank alcohol when he felt like it, telling the Mahatma that he would not "yield to the puritanism affected in Congress circles." And he staggered the Governor of Yeravda Prison in Poona, who was used to feeding Gandhi on goat's milk, a few dates and the occasional orange, by requesting a "simple" menu such as only the Ritz could have supplied. Meanwhile, Jawaharlal experienced a fresh revelation in the countryside, learning to address peasants and discovering a depth of poverty that made him ashamed of his own affluence. "A new picture of India seemed to rise before me," he wrote, "naked, starving, crushed and utterly miserable."[10] He attributed the people's degradation to the Raj and took the lead in encouraging further strikes and protests. The crusade, as he called it, consumed and thrilled him. Congress now had two million members. Convinced that it was shaking the fabric of British rule, he succumbed to the bliss, or *moksha,* of martyrdom. When imprisoned, Jawaharlal wrote: "Jail has indeed become a heaven for us, a holy place of pilgrimage since our saintly and beloved leader was sentenced."[11] To serve under Mahatma Gandhi doubled the honour of fighting for India's freedom.

Jawaharlal was therefore bitterly disappointed when Gandhi called off the *satyagraha* early in 1922 because it was leading to bloodshed. This, at least, was the official reason but really the campaign was running out of steam. Although successful in some regions, particularly where stimulated by local grievances, it could not mobilise the whole of India. Inconceivably vast and variegated, cleft by deep social and religious fissures, riven by political divisions, freighted with an impermeable peasantry, the subcontinent resisted unification. In particular, the alliance that Gandhi had forged with

Muslims, who were concerned about the fate of the Islamic holy places and their protector the Caliph, began to collapse. Jinnah, howled down at one Congress meeting for addressing Gandhi as Mr. instead of Mahatma, had opposed the alliance. Now his supporters took alarm at adoring pictures of Gandhi as Krishna under a Muslim flag. Communal violence flared and when Mustapha Kemal abolished the caliphate in 1924 Muslims no longer needed Hindu help. The Muslim League, that year meeting separately from Congress, began to plan for a federal India containing provinces which it could dominate. At the same time Congress was waning and dyarchy was working—after a fashion. In 1923 five million Indians elected representatives to expanded provincial councils and to the national Legislative Assembly. The power of these bodies was limited and they had almost no scope, as Subhas Bose said, "to undertake nation-building work."[12] But they wore away British control at the edges and they taught Indian politicians valuable lessons, particularly in the arts of negotiation and obstruction. However, the issue of participation in constitutional bodies divided Congress. Gandhi went his own way, concentrating on the championship of Untouchables and the *khadi* campaign, in the "conviction that with every thread that I draw, I am spinning the destiny of India."[13] Motilal believed that Congress should exploit the councils, telling Gandhi that rather than resume a programme of boycott he would retire to a thatched hut *(kutiya)* by the banks of the Ganges. Jawaharlal opposed his father, wanting to adopt Sinn Féin tactics towards the institutions of the Raj. Thwarted, he went to Europe with his tubercular wife (who died in 1936) and their young daughter, Indira, where he acquired new reasons for disagreement with his conservative elders.

Like many other nationalist leaders, Jawaharlal had continued his education in prison. Inside the grim, square barrack at Lucknow Gaol he had devoured books, finishing, for example, six out of seven volumes of Gibbon. (His literary marathon irritated the British colonel in charge of the prison, who said that he had practically completed his own reading at the age of twelve, which no doubt helped him, Jawaharlal reflected sardonically, "in avoiding troublesome thoughts.")[14] Now, particularly when attending the Brussels Congress against Colonial Oppression, Jawaharlal imbibed the gospel of socialism. He associated with Leninist intellectuals who thought that the Indian proletariat had "grown up sufficiently to wage a class-conscious and political mass struggle" against the lackeys of the British Empire.[15] He concluded that western capitalism, engaged in an increasingly vicious effort to plunder colonies, was digging its own grave. A global revolution against imperial tyranny was in train, quickened by the Soviet Union.

Jawaharlal even forecast that, in order to save itself from extinction, Britain would "become a satellite of the United States," helping to form "a powerful Anglo-Saxon bloc to dominate the world."[16] Fearing Bolshevik Russia and mistrusting the British Labour Party, Nehru was never as Red as he was painted. He was certainly gullible about Stalin's purge trials and naïve in assuming that the Soviet Union was a new civilisation. He adopted a few Communist mantras, often saying that religion was the opium of the people. But he was less wedded to Karl Marx than to Kingsley Martin, volatile editor of London's left-wing *New Statesman*. Above all he was devoted to Gandhi, whose Utopian schemes for uplifting the masses he tried to combine with Fabian plans for state control of land and industry. The endeavour involved a long "mental tussle"[17] and occasional crises of allegiance which almost reduced him to despair.

Although the Mahatma disliked, and Motilal sometimes damned, Jawaharlal's new radicalism, the three of them united in opposing the Simon Commission. This was set up late in 1927 to reform the system of dyarchy. The bibulous Conservative Secretary of State, Lord Birkenhead, who could not take "Indian politicians very seriously" and found it "inconceivable that India will ever be fit for Dominion self-government,"[18] wanted to devise a constitutional framework that would preserve British supremacy. That, too, was the aim of the Viceroy, Lord Irwin. Believing that Indian psychology was "composed in equal parts of vanity, inferiority complex and fear of responsibility," he sought "some façade which will leave the essential mechanism of power still in our hands."[19] So, at Irwin's behest, Birkenhead appointed a Commission which included not a single Indian. This guaranteed Sir John Simon, the cold, serpentine lawyer who led it, the kind of reception that Milner had faced in Egypt. He and his "seven dwarfs" were duly met with black flags and cries of "Simon Go Back!"[20] The cries seemed to go on all night outside the Western Hotel in Delhi where the commissioners were staying, but they actually came from the jackals which still infested the waste places of the capital. Irwin compared the Indian response to a child's refusing to eat its supper but he had served up such a racist dish that Muslims joined Hindus in spurning it. "Jallianwala Bagh was physical butchery. The Simon Commission is butchery of the soul."[21] Not since the Ilbert Bill had there been such outrage. Furious demonstrations took place, notably in Lahore and Lucknow, where Jawaharlal experienced a police *lathi* charge. The European sergeants, he noted, were the most brutal of all, their faces suffused with "hate and blood-lust."[22] But according to Lajpat Rai, a nationalist who was killed in the disturbances, every *lathi* blow was "a nail in the coffin of the British Empire."[23] Clement Attlee, one of two

Labour members on the Commission, was vouchsafed another insight into the nature of the imperial relationship. His "excellent bearer" insisted on dressing him although, Attlee said, "I rather bar not tucking in my own shirt."[24] Nobody at the time could have envisaged that this modest man, who had (as Churchill unforgettably remarked) much to be modest about, would become Prime Minister and give India its independence.

Simon's Report, which recommended further provincial devolution (favoured by Muslims) but the retention of British power at the centre, was a dead letter before it appeared. This was because Irwin tried to allay Indian hostility by declaring in 1929, on behalf of the new Labour government, that the natural outcome of India's constitutional progress was dominion status. Congress was divided between those, led by Motilal, who accepted this as the next step towards *swaraj* and those, led by Jawaharlal, who demanded full national independence. Gandhi found a compromise and reined in the Nehru son, calling him a young hooligan. Inspired by his socialist creed, Jawaharlal had become (as he himself acknowledged, with considerable understatement) "a little bit autocratic in my ways, just a shade dictatorial." Writing an ironical but anonymous criticism of himself in the *Modern Review,* he said that his conceit, inflated by people who hailed him as "Jewel of India" and "Embodiment of Sacrifice,"[25] should be checked. "We want no Caesars!"[26] Jawaharlal's state was summed up in Byron's lines, which he transcribed in prison, saying that total dedication must be the lot of "those who are called to high destinies/Which purify corrupted commonwealths."[27] Yet Jawaharlal's vaunting ambitions and violent inclinations, expressed in rages to match those of Motilal, sometimes ending in blows, were curbed by a spirit of self-denial. Recognising this, the Mahatma ensured that he was chosen to follow his father as President of Congress in 1929. "He is pure as crystal, he is truthful beyond suspicion," said Gandhi. "The nation is safe in his hands."[28]

The nation was divided over the Viceroy's promise of dominion status which, according to one British report, had given "moral leadership in Indian politics to Lord Irwin."[29] In an attempt to safeguard their position if and when the promise was kept, representative Muslims, maharajahs and others accepted his invitation to attend a Round Table Conference in London. Congress boycotted it. But Gandhi needed a more positive and dramatic strategy both to unite his movement and to challenge Irwin, whose prestige was enhanced by a bomb attack on his train near Delhi. The patrician Viceroy responded to the explosion with his usual sang-froid, telling a friend that he was "inured to that kind of thing by the Cona Coffee machine which was always blowing up."[30] So Gandhi, who chided Irwin for accepting a salary five thousand times larger than the average Indian income, advocated a return to peaceful non-cooperation in pursuit of freedom from foreign rule. In Lahore, where Congress adopted this policy, Jawaharlal declared independence from an Empire that was "undergoing a process of political dissolution."[31] At midnight on 31 December 1929 he headed a large crowd which raised the saffron, white and green flag of freedom in the Lajpatnagar. Then, in the teeth of a chill wind blowing across the Ravi River, he led them on a wild dance round the flagpole to cries of *"Inquilab Zindabad"*—"Long Live Revolution." Nehru's revolution, with its talk of the inalienable rights of the Indian people, smacked more of Jefferson than of Lenin. Gandhi's revolution was the very antithesis of terrorism, which Nirad Chaudhuri defined as "political rabies."[32] It took the form of a non-violent pilgrimage to the sea in order to gather salt without paying the tax levied on "the only condiment of the poor."[33] It was a march that was compared to Rama's epic odyssey to Lanka and Moses' biblical journey to Canaan.

In the grey dawn haze of 12 March 1930 Gandhi set off from his ashram, a cluster of whitewashed huts amid a grove of trees on the sandy banks of the River Sabarmati, just within sight of the cotton-mill smokestacks of Ahmedabad. His goal was the remote coastal hamlet of Dandi, 240 miles to the south. Wearing his *dhoti* and holding a lacquered, iron-tipped bamboo staff, he was accompanied by seventy-eight *khadi*-clad disciples. Around him was a "vast sea of humanity"[34] including journalists, film crews and a brass band which struck up "God Save the King" before realising its inappropriateness and subsiding in confusion. Some people climbed trees to get a better view. Others waved flags and cracked coconuts to ensure good fortune. Still others, some in tears, strewed the Mahatma's path with water and green leaves. He set a fast pace in searing heat and soon left the first spectators behind. But thousands more lined the route, showering the marchers with flowers, coins, currency notes and *kum kum* (red powder, signifying reverence). And at each village fresh crowds assembled to greet him with garlands, banners, pipes and drums. So many people tried to wipe the dust from his feet that they had to be massaged with vaseline. At night, by the flickering glow of kerosene lamps, he preached the duty of disloyalty to the satanic government. He urged the inhabitants of all India's 700,000 villages to break the "inhuman monopoly"[35] on salt—which he himself, ironically, had for years banished from his diet.

His disciples, who carried their own bedding, slept in grass bivouacs and ate almost as sparingly as their guru, maintained a strict routine of praying, spinning and keeping a daily diary. A few fell out and had to be carried in bullock carts. But Gandhi, at the age of sixty-one the oldest of them, seemed imbued with superhuman energy. Having spent a day crossing the coastal plain, ten miles of dirt roads, paddy fields, marshes and rivers, he could sometimes be seen writing letters by moonlight at four o'clock in the morning. One of the newspaper correspondents charting his progress claimed that he was in a dangerously hyper-active "state of nerves."[36] On 5 April the Mahatma reached Dandi. "Never was there a more forlorn setting for a drama than the tiny, straggling village, perched on hummocks above the beach and the long rollers of the Arabian Sea," reported the *New York Times*.[37] The next morning Gandhi stepped from his hut and walked over the black sand, littered with jellyfish, towards the ribbon of surf. Watched by a huge crowd, many of them women, their saris making splashes of scarlet, pink and purple on the grey mud flats and the parched, dun-coloured shore, he picked up a handful of natural salt. It crystallised opposition to the British Raj. Beside him, the poet Sarojini Naidu, the first female President of Congress, cried out: "Hail, Thee, Deliverer!"[38]

The British themselves tried to play down the whole campaign, taking their line from the Viceroy, who had refused to arrest the Mahatma because he judged that the march would be a fiasco. The London *Times,* edited by Irwin's friend Geoffrey Dawson, ridiculed Gandhi's Dandi performance. It was a farce that "fell flat" and a melodrama deprived of vital members of the cast, the police. *The Times* further scorned the "Babu eloquence" of the pro-Mahatma press, which "would make intensely amusing reading were it not so tragic." And it sneered at Gandhi's "puppet-President" of Congress, Jawaharlal Nehru, a "quaint product of pre-war Harrow and post-war Moscow," who had "made a pathetic attempt to steal a little limelight" by manufacturing some of his own salt. Yet even the most partisan journalists acknowledged that to the peasants Gandhi was "more than a leader. He is a legend."[39] His *satyagraha* fired the imagination of Indians, who regarded salt as a gift of God. Equally inflammatory was Gandhi's appeal that every woman should clutch her lump of illicit salt as she would a fond child being wrenched from her by evil-doers. All over the subcontinent millions of Hindus (and some Muslims) collected salt illegally, relishing the savour of defiance. Packets of contraband salt were sold openly and a pinch of Gandhi's own lump was auctioned for 525 rupees. In Bombay, the cockpit of disaffection, a party of salt-gatherers processed up the steps of the "Gateway of India" and sang *"Bande Mataram"* ("Hail Mother," the Hindustan anthem) and other nationalist songs on the Apollo Bundur quay. Their protest encouraged a party of young Americans in a nearby hotel to don Gandhi caps. And it spread ripples of alarm across the peninsula, from the Yacht

Club to the Breach Candy Swimming Club, where members protected their privacy with a sign saying "No Dogs or Indians Allowed."[40]

The government responded forcefully to the demonstrations, producing a vicious cycle of aggression. Riots in Calcutta and Karachi were quelled by rifle fire. Garhwali troops mutinied after similar disturbances on the North-West Frontier, which were eventually put down with bombs, tanks and machine guns. Crowds stoned the police in Poona. Terrorists raided an arsenal in Chittagong. Gandhi condemned the violence that he involuntarily provoked. On the Bombay *maidan* a pack of white Cub Scouts witnessed the effect of his presence:

> In the distance, across the brown grass, we saw a vast crowd of natives with white Congress caps on their heads, listening to a bespectacled figure on a soap-box. In the further distance there were rows of Indian policemen, in blue and yellow uniforms with flat round frisbee-like caps, holding lathees. Little puffs of white dust where the mounted English police, wearing white topees, kept watch. We looked on in silence, not understanding the speaker's words or the chanting cries of the crowd. Suddenly the lines of Indian police advanced, lathees turning like propellers through seaweed. Soon the shrieks and cries from the panic-stricken mob and clouds of dust curdled our blood. The mounted police charged in. There was chaos as the crowds broke up and hordes of rioters streamed . . . past us.[41]

In May Gandhi was arrested.

This prompted a fresh outburst of civil disobedience, which took the form of *hartals,* strikes, boycotts and picketing. Sometimes the agitation got out of hand, notably in Bombay where for a time the mob ruled. But often the authorities encountered no resistance. When Sarojini Naidu's marchers advanced on the salt works at Dharasana, 150 miles north of Bombay, they did not even raise a hand to ward off the blows that the police rained "on their heads with their steel-shod *lathis.*"[42] In a single morning an American reporter counted 2 dead and 320 wounded *satyagrahis,* while another witness said that by 10:30 a.m. "nearly seven hundred men had been injured."[43] And the struggle went on for days. Writing to the King-Emperor, the Viceroy said that he could "hardly fail to have read with amusement the accounts of the several battles" at Dharasana, but assured him that "those who suffered injuries were as nothing compared with those who wished to sustain an honourable contusion or bruise." Irwin had a curious sense of humour: he found the suggestion that Afghans lived in trees "delicious."[44] However, the Viceroy was a kindly man (going so far as to give the constipated Congress strongman Vallabhbhai Patel his own bottle of Petrolagar) and he appreciated the limits of force. By the summer of 1930 the government had outlawed Congress. It had locked up well over sixty thousand of the staunchest nationalists, among them both Nehru men and several hundred women, whose emergence from seclusion marked a revolution. And it quickly regained possession of the streets. But Gandhi had won hearts and minds. Irwin recognised his moral victory, admitting that the authority of the Raj had suffered. Jawaharlal sensed that Congress was emerging as a shadow authority. It was a regime in waiting, just as India was a nation in waiting.

The traditional British strategy was to keep the Indian nation at bay by emphasising the variety of the Indian peoples. Conservatives such as Lord Birkenhead and Winston Churchill continued to play up the schisms within the subcontinent in order to demonstrate the perennial need for the high-minded and even-handed Raj. Birkenhead publicly exaggerated and privately welcomed sectarian antagonisms because they indicated that "we, and we alone, can play the part of composers."[45] Churchill later confessed that he "regarded the Hindu-Moslem feud as a bulwark of British rule in India."[46] No one exploited splits in the Indian ranks more forcefully than Churchill, but his efforts to challenge Congress's claim to speak for the nation were assisted by the prospect of independence itself. As it loomed larger, different segments of Indian society tried harder to protect their position in the coming democracy. After all, as Jawaharlal Nehru freely admitted, democracy "means the coercion of the minority by the majority."[47] So the six hundred princes, who had acquired an advisory Chamber in 1921, struggled to safeguard their feudal privileges. Dr. B. R. Ambedkar demanded a separate electorate for the fifty million Untouchables he represented, a demand rejected by Gandhi on the grounds that it would destroy the unity of India's 250 million Hindus. Nearly eighty million Muslims and five million Sikhs had already got a reserved franchise and both communities sought further advantage. Thus Jinnah attempted to entrench the power of Muslims in the provinces and in the future parliament, wanting a third of the seats plus a veto on laws harmful to their interests. When Congress spurned this proposal Jinnah announced a parting of ways and set off on a journey that would lead to Pakistan.

It was marked by an upsurge of communal violence. This was partly a reaction to Hindu revivalism, partly an expression of Muslim militancy, partly a response to local provocations—the din of gongs in front of mosques, the ritual sacrifice of cows, the clash of religious processions. Such a divide actually threatened to subvert British rule, which would culminate, Irwin hoped, in the establishment of India as the greatest dominion of all. He himself pleaded for a combined effort to stop the strife in order to build "the Indian nation." Although an old-fashioned Tory, Irwin agreed with the Liberal Simon that the subcontinent possessed an "essential unity in diversity."[48] If anyone embodied that unity it was Gandhi, whose spiritual sway transcended factional differences. He alone offered a way out of the Indian impasse. So the Viceroy sought to conciliate the Mahatma, releasing him unconditionally at the end of January 1931. Meanwhile, Motilal Nehru was dying in characteristic style. Since his relations with the Almighty were cordial he expected to be ferried across the Vaitarmi River, the Hindu Styx, in "a motor launch with a high-powered Rolls-Royce engine."[49] His last words to Gandhi were: "I shall not be here to see swaraj. But I know you have won it and will soon have it."[50]

As Churchill would bitterly observe, first Irwin grovelled to Gandhi and then (as Lord Halifax) he grovelled to Hitler. "Irwin?" he expostulated privately. "Lord worming and squirming is a better name."[51] Wrong though Churchill was about India, he was partially right about Irwin. For the Viceroy was not only one of nature's appeasers, he was so out of touch with reality that he later likened the Mahatma to the Führer—even though Hitler told him that the way to control India was to shoot Gandhi first and then his supporters in batches. Socially remote and intellectually detached as well as (at six foot five) physically aloof, this aristocratic High Churchman had almost no conception of either man. It was said that he established a rapport with Gandhi because both had such strict religious principles, the one taking his chaplain on his honeymoon, the other asserting that sexual intercourse without the desire for children was a crime. But at their first meeting Irwin felt as if he were "talking to someone who had stepped off another planet."[52] He had expected to woo Gandhi as he would woo a vain and capricious woman. Instead he faced a man whom Nehru likened to Socrates, a moral paragon and a dialectical virtuoso.

To give Irwin his due, he persevered despite flouts and doubts from home. Churchill, of course, condemned his nauseating negotiation with the half-naked fakir, convinced that making concessions to Gandhi was like feeding cat's meat to a tiger. But the King also expressed concern that the rebel fakir, in his very abbreviated clothing, should enter the Viceroy's beautiful new house. Nevertheless, Irwin invited Gandhi to eight meetings there and, on 5 March 1931, they signed an agreement. The Mahatma would discontinue non-cooperation and attend the second Round Table Conference. The Viceroy would release non-violent prisoners, relax repression and permit the collection of salt in coastal districts. Accused of drinking tea with treason, Irwin suggested that they should toast the accord in that beverage. Gandhi produced a pinch of illegal salt from the folds of his *dhoti* and said that he would put it in his tea "to remind us of the famous Boston Tea Party."[53] Indian radicals, like British reactionaries, denounced the pact as a betrayal. Jawaharlal Nehru deplored an ignoble compromise which took pressure off the government; yet he helped to persuade Congress to ratify it out of loyalty to Gandhi. This was, indeed, another moral victory for the Mahatma. His prestige had never been greater for, as Churchill said, he had treated on equal terms with the representative of the King-Emperor. One of Gandhi's early biographers noted the essential irony of their confrontation. Almost the first official act to take place in the Viceroy's House, symbol of British power, marked "the beginning of the end of that power."[54]

This was precisely what caused Churchill and his right-wing allies such anguish. They saw India as the essence of the Empire and they were haunted by the spectre of international impotence. Lord Lloyd's distress was palpable. "You see, if India goes, everything goes: our honour, our wealth, our strategic security and our prestige."[55] Churchill himself was still more apocalyptic. He described British policy towards India as "a hideous act of self-mutilation"[56] and declared that "Irwinism has rotted the soul of the Tory party."[57] He wanted Conservatives to identify themselves with "the majesty of Britain as under Lord Salisbury and Lord Beaconsfield"[58] and to crush "Gandhi-ism."[59]

> Our continued existence as a great power is at stake. The loss of India would mark and consummate the downfall of the British Empire. That great organism would pass at a stroke out of life into history. From such a catastrophe there could be no recovery.[60]

Churchill left the shadow cabinet over this question and stirred the Tory rank and file with many a "thrilling peroration about the Empire."[61] In parliament he recalled Gibbon's account of how the Senator Didius Julianus had bought the Roman Empire at auction, paying the Praetorian Guard £200 per head—cheap beside the terms on which Gandhi was acquiring the British Empire.

To his wife Clementine, Winston deplored the fact that the Conservative leader, Stanley Baldwin, "felt that the times were too far gone for any robust assertion of imperial greatness."[62] Baldwin said that Churchill had reverted to being the subaltern of hussars of 1896. On the Indian issue, Baldwin further remarked, he was like George III "endowed with the tongue of

Edmund Burke."[63] Employing a more contemporary comparison, Sir Samuel Hoare, the new Secretary of State for India, reckoned that Churchill wanted to rule India as Mussolini ruled North Africa. Birkenhead might dismiss the prissy Hoare as "the last of a long line of maiden aunts,"[64] but it was a fair point. For at this time Churchill admired the Duce and shared his old-fashioned view that colonial possessions were the measure of national greatness. He decried the Indian policy of liberal Tories such as Irwin, Baldwin and Hoare as feeble and defeatist, correctly regarding it as a further step (after Ireland and Egypt) in a long imperial retreat. They thought, also correctly, that the day had gone "when Winston's possessive instinct can be applied to Empires and the like." As Irwin wrote, "That conception of Empire is finished."[65]

It was finished for a variety of reasons. India was changing in ways that Churchill could not grasp—he had not been there since the Victorian age and he refused to have the beautiful clarity of his thought muddied by talking to "any bloody Indian," including Gandhi. Unprecedented population growth, from 306 million in 1921 to 400 million in 1947, increased social tensions and eroded British control, especially in the teeming cities of the subcontinent. By the end of the 1930s, 15 per cent of the people, mostly men, were literate, which gave them access to nationalist propaganda. Britain still had large financial interests in India, which were particularly valuable during the Depression. So was the influx of gold from the subcontinent. Peasants sold the precious metal to compensate for the low price of their crops—to the joy of the Chancellor of the Exchequer. As Neville Chamberlain wrote to his sister in February 1932, "The astonishing gold mine we have discovered in India's hoards has put us in clover."[66] At the same time, however, economic ties between the two countries were unravelling. Indian business was developing independently of Britain and commercial captains increasingly gave money to Congress. Between the wars it became clear to the British that, despite fluctuations in benefits conferred and costs incurred, India was a "declining asset."[67] In particular, the subcontinent was manufacturing its own cotton goods as well as importing cheap fabrics from Japan and it no longer provided a huge captive market for the products of Lancashire.

Moreover, threatened with resignations from the Viceroy's Executive Council, Britain could not even prevent India from imposing a protective tariff on English textiles. By the same token the Delhi Legislature prevented the British from exploiting the Indian army as they had done in the past and London had to pay for its re-equipment before the Second World War. Furthermore, the promotion of Indian officers caused resentment on both sides of the colour line: one Sandhurst-trained Indian said, "I was called a wog in my own mess."[68] The export of indentured workers had been prohibited in 1917 so the subcontinent no longer provided a reservoir of imperial labour. Nor was it such a rich field of employment for whites, since administrative posts increasingly went to Indians. By 1940 they constituted a majority in the ICS, applications from the United Kingdom being discouraged by fears about the imminent demise of the Raj. There was an undeniable slackening of Britain's grip on its prize possession. Nehru employed a different image: the alien government was a tooth still strongly embedded but in an advanced state of decay.

Lord Willingdon, who succeeded Irwin as Viceroy in April 1931, intended to stop the rot. An old India hand, he believed in the smack of firm government. He would take no "damn nonsense" from the nationalists, treating them to "a blitz of *lathis*" in the streets and floggings with "knotted ropes"[69] in the cells. Nor would he negotiate with Gandhi, reckoning that the saint in him was eclipsed by the *bania* (trader) and saying that he was "the most Machiavellian bargaining little political humbug I have ever come across." Thus, when the Mahatma returned empty-handed from the second Round Table Conference in London, where the East End had welcomed him though in Buckingham Palace King George had glared at his bare knees, he was once again arrested. So were eighty thousand of his adherents: Congressmen had been helping the wretchedly impoverished tenants of the United Provinces to resist the exactions of their landlords. Willingdon not only introduced internment but tighter censorship, identity cards, heavy fines, curbs on assembly, restrictions on movement (such as bicycle bans) and even dress decrees (a prohibition on Gandhi caps). According to Jawaharlal Nehru, the authorities had turned the subcontinent into a vast prison of the human spirit. The Viceroy himself confessed that he was "becoming a sort of Mussolini of India."[70]

Badgered by Churchill's legion of Blimps and battered by the economic blizzard, Ramsay MacDonald's new National Government backed Willingdon. After all, his methods were effective. He had clamped the lid on dissent. Gandhi, who was keener to convert than to confront the British, first limited and then (in April 1934) suspended civil disobedience. This angered Nehru, who noted the British knack of accommodating their moral values to their material interests and wanted to increase resistance. He threatened to break with the Mahatma, who resigned from the Congress Party (though he continued to dominate it). So Willingdon managed to weaken and divide the nationalists. Yet he himself resembled nothing as much as a Bourbon monarch in the last days of the *ancien régime*. Dim, idle and arrogant,

17. SIKH OFFICERS AND MEN, 1858

Britain's formidable Sikh allies played an important part
in quelling the Mutiny. They confirmed the need
to divide in order to rule India.

18. AFTER THE MUTINY

Lucknow's Chattar Manzil (Umbrella Palaces) were damaged
during the long and bloody siege. Afterwards the city was
reconstructed to make it more defensible.

19. British Camp in Afghanistan

British forces made sporadic and costly efforts to secure
the north-west frontier of India, but fierce Afghan resistance
invariably put them on the defensive.

20. Afghan Riflemen on the Khyber Pass

Afghan marksmen took a fearsome toll in border skirmishes.
Kipling wrote, "Two thousand pounds of education/Drops to
a ten-rupee jezail" (musket).

21. Irish Peasants in the 1880s

Despite grinding poverty, Ireland's burning grievance was
political. As Yeats said, its people lived in hope of driving the
English stranger out of their house.

22. Ruin of the Rising

Dublin's gutted Post Office signified the extinction of the Easter
Rising in 1916. But the execution of its leaders gave new life to
Ireland's independence movement.

23. THE RHODES COLOSSUS

This cartoon did not exaggerate the grandiose ambitions of Cecil Rhodes. Aspiring to be a modern Caesar, he wanted an English-speaking empire to dominate the earth.

24. AFTER THE BATTLE, 1879

Like other victories by "savages" over "civilised men," suggested *The Times*, Isandhlwana threatened the "supremacy of our race, nay, our very existence."

25. GOLD MINERS IN DE KAAP, SOUTH AFRICA

The vast gold discoveries of 1886 tilted the balance of power in southern Africa towards the Transvaal. And it was primarily for power that the British fought the Boers.

26. BOERS AT SPION KOP, 1900

The Calvinist burghers "were all of the seventeenth century,"
said Conan Doyle, "except their rifles." They inflicted
humiliating defeats on imperial forces.

27. A MEAL DURING THE SIEGE OF LADYSMITH

Despite hunger and hardship, Ladysmith's garrison kept the
Boers at bay. Its commander, Sir George White, said: "I thank
God we have kept the flag flying."

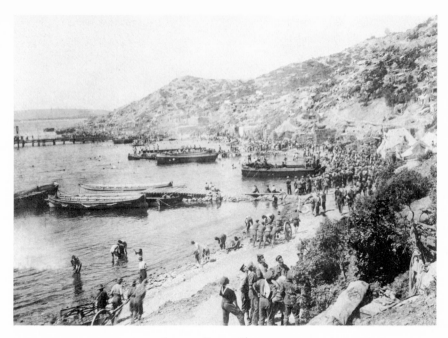

28. ANZAC COVE, GALLIPOLI, 1915

The Anzac beachhead, just north of Hell Spit, was only six
hundred yards long and always under fire. Charles Bean described
the dugouts as a mixture of cave and grave.

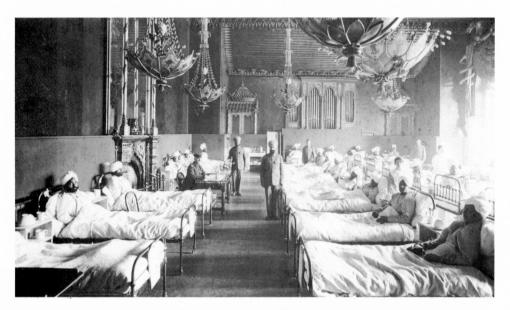

29. INDIAN MILITARY HOSPITAL, BRIGHTON

Brighton Pavilion became a well-run hospital for Indian troops,
though female nurses were excluded. Honourably wounded
sepoys resented being sent back to the trenches.

30. The Japanese March on Rangoon, 1942

Many Burmese saw the Japanese invaders as liberators.
Although Asian rule proved far more brutal than European,
Nippon's victories spelled the end of Britain's Empire in the East.

31. Nigerian Sergeant in Burma, 1944

African soldiers fought ferociously in Burma. Japanese troops
thought they were cannibals and, duty-bound to bury at least
a finger of dead comrades, took few black prisoners.

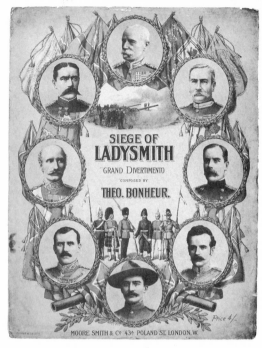

32. Trade Follows the Flag

Commerce beat the drum of militant imperialism in order to sell its products. But some Britons (to Kipling's fury) mocked the "uniforms that guard you while you sleep."

he was also suave, affable and elegant, a Grand Ornamental who staged pageants worthy of Versailles—at one fancy-dress ball he even appeared as Louis XVI accompanied by his wife as Marie Antoinette. Willingdon performed with particular grace in the new Durbar Hall with its white marble walls, its red porphyry floor and its yellow jasper columns. His gold lace, diamond-studded insignia and jewelled sword were matched by Lady Willingdon's glittering tiaras, lustrous pearls and lilac brocade dresses. She was, indeed, addicted to lilac and redecorated many rooms in the Viceroy's House—to the distress of Lutyens, who called her "a mauvey *sujet*"[71] and said that she would put bay windows on the Parthenon. The Vicereine even got the Maharajah of Patiala to supply her with lilac lavatory paper—but the colour ran. Combining ostentation with repression, Willingdon's regime aroused bitter enmity among nationalists. One described it as "Masked Balls and Black Terror."[72]

As usual, though, the British tried to temper coercion with conciliation, notably through the 1935 Government of India Act. This separated Burma from India and gave the eleven Indian provinces self-rule, though in extreme circumstances Governors could still frustrate the will of the thirty-six million electors. At the centre two all-India federal assemblies, seats allocated to princes, Muslims, Sikhs, Untouchables, women and others, would control everything except finance, defence and foreign policy. Actually the scheme of national federation foundered because the princes, intent on retaining their privileges, refused to participate. But even if it had worked the Viceroy retained ultimate control: he could veto laws, dismiss ministers and suspend the constitution. The Act was thus intended to divide and outflank Indian nationalism, not to be a stage in a "slow unending retreat"[73] from the Raj. It was designed, in the words of Willingdon's successor, Lord Linlithgow, "to hold India to the Empire."[74] However, die-hards at home thought it a fatal surrender and Churchill famously pronounced it "a monstrous monument of sham built by pygmies."[75] He prayed that in the crashing cheers for the India Bill "there may not mingle the knell of the British Empire in the East."[76] Many Britons in India shared these views, no one more fiercely than Churchill's former private secretary Sir James Grigg, now Finance Member of the Viceroy's Council. He said that independence was now inevitable and that "if England wants to keep India it will have to be at the point of a sword. A reconquest followed by autocracy."[77]

The Act was unpopular in India precisely because it seemed to invent new means of perpetuating British rule. Nehru called it a charter of slavery. Apprehensive that the British were undermining Indian unity by entrenching minority and reactionary interests, he urged his fellow Congressmen to refuse to participate in government. But Gandhi disagreed and Nehru was outvoted. The lure of power, even shared power, proved irresistible. So, all too often, did the spoils of office. In the local elections of 1937 Congress took control of six provinces at once, gaining two more within a couple of years. But although Nehru was buoyed up by victories at the polls his anxiety about national fragmentation proved justified. Jinnah had returned to the fray and he now asserted that Congress represented Hindu fascism. He abandoned his monocle, symbol of white sahibdom. He doffed his Savile Row suits (two hundred of them), silk ties (a fresh one every day) and sola topee for the Muslim *sherwani* (long black coat), *shalwar* (baggy trousers) and black *karakuli* sheepskin cap. He raised the green crescent-and-star flag and rallied his co-religionists with the cry "Islam in danger"—though privately he scorned sectarian zealotry and indulged a taste for whisky and ham sandwiches. Tall, gaunt, aquiline, lucid and implacable, with an ominous cough from the fifty Craven A cigarettes he smoked each day, Jinnah faced the facts. He told the Viceroy that if Britain "really had it in mind to abandon control of this country then it was quite obvious that Muslims must bestir themselves and be ready to fight."[78] Those who hailed Jinnah as their *Quaid-i-Azam,* or Great Leader, began to conjure with the punning acronym Pakistan. It stood for Punjab, Afghanistan, Kashmir, Sind and the last letters of Baluchistan, and in Urdu it meant "Land of the Pure." Critics called it Jinnistan.

Provincial governments run by local Congress politicians were equally divisive, favouring the Hindu majority and antagonising the Muslim League. Some of those enjoying power for the first time were quite uncontrollable. In Bihar the authorities suppressed a radical peasant movement. Elsewhere they were quicker than the British to shoot down rioters. The Prime Minister of Madras, C. Rajagopalachari, arrested left-wing members of his own party. Indeed, he proved to be more of a Tory than the British Governor, who complained that Rajaji, as he was called, wanted to go back two thousand years and "to run India as it was run in the time of King Asoka."[79] Yet Nehru himself had to concede that the successful Congress ministries brought a "breath of fresh air into the turgid and authoritarian atmosphere of India." Even the poorest stood up straighter, whereas under British rule they "had a hunted look about them and fear peeped out of their eyes."[80] Moreover, as Nehru's Congress rival Subhas Bose acknowledged, the prestige of the party "went up by leaps and bounds."[81] So did its membership, which rose from 473,000 in 1935 to 4.5 million in 1939. The *izzat* of the Viceroy's administration underwent a corresponding decline, while the London government was simultaneously discredited by Neville

Chamberlain's policy of appeasing the fascist dictators. By the time war broke out in Europe, Congress had become an "alternative *raj*."[82]

Yet on 3 September 1939 Linlithgow provided a brutal reminder of British mastery by declaring that India was at war with Germany. The Viceroy consulted neither party leaders nor provincial governments. Six foot five inches tall, with a long horse face that could look "desperately unpleasant"[83] on official occasions, bored, sulky and scowling, he was (because of an attack of polio in youth) literally as well as metaphorically stiff-necked. Gandhi was more flexible. He initially gave Britain moral support, moved to tears over the prospect that Westminster Abbey would be bombed. Nehru, who said that fascism and imperialism were twins, was unsympathetic. He had long warned that Chamberlain's policy of appeasement encouraged "international blackmail and gangsterism of the worst type."[84] And he had said that his country would not back a war for democracy unless its people gained the right to rule themselves. It was absurd for a subject India to fight for the freedom of Poland. Slaves would not shed their blood to keep their chains. Britain, argued Nehru, must not be permitted to thrust India into a conflict in which victory would be as bad as defeat. Of course, many Indians did contribute to the war effort. The princes were all for it—autocracy on the side of liberty, Congress sneered—and they shed diamond-studded satin for red-tabbed khaki. Military officers were generally true to their oaths and the wartime army recruited 2.5 million men. Jinnah took an equivocal line, using the conflict to promote Muslim interests.

Even Congress was divided. Rajagopalachari complained that the scrupulous British were fighting the war according to High Court rules. Bose urged revolt, saying that "Britain's difficulty was India's opportunity."[85] Gandhi espoused non-violence. But Nehru dominated the argument. His prestige had been augmented by seven prison terms and he was Gandhi's anointed successor. Tagore himself had extolled Jawaharlal's "majestic character," which gave him an "undoubted right to the throne of young India."[86] So Nehru, inspired by magnanimity towards imperial Britain and enmity towards Nazi Germany, made a personal appeal to Linlithgow. If the Viceroy would state that India could determine its own destiny after the war, he would help to mobilise all its forces on the side of the Empire. Linlithgow, who found it inconceivable that Britain would leave India "in any measurable period of time,"[87] could only repeat vague promises about post-war constitutional reform and dominion status. Proud and inflexible, he had a rooted aversion to "running after Congress."[88] Angry and disappointed, Nehru stigmatised this old-fashioned British aristocrat as the least emotional of men. He was "heavy of body and slow of mind, solid as a rock and with almost a rock's lack of awareness."[89] This hardly matched Grigg's verdict on the Viceroy, a man of "Messianic conceit" modified by "feverish lapses into depressed lassitude."[90] But Nehru plausibly indicted Linlithgow for lack of vision. Only one so blind could imagine that "the present-day world of empires and colonies and dependencies will survive the holocaust of war."[91]

For the time being, though, war augmented British power. This was because Congress resigned its ministerial offices in protest against Linlithgow's intransigence. Many were reluctant to leave their posts, partly because of the rewards and partly because the provincial governments demonstrated that Indians were able to rule themselves. However, by mid-November 1939 British Governors had taken over in all but the Muslim-controlled provinces of Bengal, Sind and the Punjab. Jinnah was delighted. He decreed a Deliverance Day (22 December) to celebrate freedom from the "tyranny, oppression and injustice" which Muslims had suffered under the heel of Congress.[92] Other minority groups, such as Untouchables, rejoiced with them. Nehru was furious. Just as Jinnah regarded him as a socialist atheist, he regarded Jinnah as the spokesman of feudal landlords and obscurantist mullahs. Nehru believed that the Muslim League was sacrificing Indian unity on the altar of sectarianism and helping the British to play the "same old game"[93] of divide and rule. He refused to recognise the League as the voice of all Muslims since this would be to repudiate other Muslim organisations, to disown Muslims in his own party and to deny Congress its position as the national mouthpiece. Nehru could not appreciate that the League, which opposed the introduction of democracy to India, reflected genuine fears about the security of the Muslim community. Still less did Nehru accept Jinnah's claim that the Muslims were a separate nation.

This Jinnah announced at the League Conference held in Lahore on 22 March 1940. The event was staged in the huge amphitheatre of Minto Park, in front of Aurangzeb's Badshahi Mosque and amid poignant relics of Mughal glory—Akbar's Gate in the Fort, the marble tomb of Jahangir, the three hundred fountains in Shah Jahan's Shalimar Gardens. Delegates pitched their white tents around the park. At its centre stood a colossal marquee *(pandal)* holding sixty thousand people, who entered through an archway decorated with bunting and green flags. Another forty thousand waited outside—Punjabis, Sindhis, Bengalis, Pathans and Baluchis. Jinnah, clad in the local garb of black *achkan* and *choridor* pyjamas and flanked by guardsmen in green and khaki uniforms, spoke for a hundred minutes. But though loudspeakers amplified his voice, few could comprehend what he said since he talked mostly in English, not Urdu, for the sake of the press. Even so the audience, hypnotised by his personality and electrified by his delivery, understood his message. Jinnah proclaimed that India was an artificial unit maintained by British bayonets. It was a dream that its disparate peoples could always be yoked together in a single state. Avoiding mention of Pakistan and keeping his demands vague, he said that when the Raj ended the subcontinent should be divided into "autonomous national states."[94] He spat on the grave of the old ideal that India was a beautiful woman with one eye Hindu and the other Muslim.

Many Muslims condemned Jinnah's assault on the unity of India. Hindus denounced him as the Viceroy's stooge just as they denounced the maharajahs as Britain's Fifth Column in India. But Jinnah had now made it impossible for Congress to pose as the sole avatar of Indian nationalism. Nor could Congressmen claim to be engaged in a straight fight with the British Empire. Hitler's triumphs in Europe and Churchill's accession to power in London compounded their difficulties. Nehru and his colleagues were torn between hatred for the swastika and hostility to the Union Jack. Churchill's new Secretary for India, Leo Amery, raised in Milner's kindergarten, wanted to exploit their anti-fascism to augment the war effort. Short, voluble and bouncy, he prompted the lofty, laconic and sluggish Viceroy, who was ultimately galvanised by the German *Blitzkrieg*, to make an overture to India. But while it was being formulated the Prime Minister intervened. Churchill had not changed his views about India since 1935 . . . or 1896. He still believed that its possession made Britain a great power and he wanted the "Empire preserved for a few more generations in its strength and splendour."[95]

Yet he was still haunted by Gibbonian apprehensions that the "shores of History are strewn with the wrecks of Empires."[96] As First Lord of the Admiralty in 1939, he had evinced a fierce "determination to support and maintain the most full-blooded British imperialism."[97] And at the outset of his Premiership he had famously declared that Britain's aim was victory, for without victory there was "no survival for the British Empire."[98] Now, in the summer of 1940, Churchill seemed almost as vehement about retaining India as about defending Britain. He damned suggested concessions and told Amery that "he would sooner give up political life at once, or rather go out into the wilderness and fight, than to admit a revolution which meant the end of the Imperial Crown in India."[99] As Amery concluded: "India, or any form of self-government for coloured peoples, raises in him a wholly uncontrollable complex."[100] The Prime Minister did control the content of Linlithgow's so-called August Offer. This invited Indians to frame their own constitution after the war, subject to various conditions, including the possible veto of minorities such as Muslims and maharajahs. It also proposed to appoint a few "representative Indians" to the Viceroy's Executive Council, by which, of course, Churchill meant a few unrepresentative Indians. Nehru was scathing about the offer, which aimed to prolong the Raj by denying India democracy. It signalled the parting of ways, he wrote, and "the ending of all hope that we shall ever march together."[101]

Yet neither side wished to march against the other. Gandhi refused to sanction a mass campaign of civil disobedience, saying that it would not remain civil for long, though he did permit individual non-cooperation. While millions of Indians were contributing to the war effort, many of them prospering in the process, these acts of defiance seemed mere pinpricks and Amery would not let Linlithgow go ahead with his plans for the "total extinction"[102] of Congress. But the Viceroy did respond firmly and by 1941 the police had arrested some 26,000 volunteers. Among them was Nehru, who told the court that the British Empire, not he, was on trial before the bar of the world. He was sentenced to four years in gaol. Despite an appeal from Churchill, Linlithgow ensured that he was treated as a common criminal. Before his early release in December 1941 (this time opposed by Churchill, who suggested that it would be fatal to the Empire), he had suffered much petty persecution. As Nehru wrote to his daughter Indira, he retreated into the "mighty Maginot Line" of his shell, reading, writing, dreaming and practising yoga. He lived "in the mind"[103] and stood on his head.

The political situation was equally static. Bose escaped to raise the standard of revolt in Germany, but the Nazis did not yet know what to do with him. Gandhi was caught in a crisis of faith, struggling to defend pacifism during a war against fascism. Congress lost momentum, still deadlocked with the Muslim League. Linlithgow always preferred to lie back and do nothing, though he did bring more Indians into his Executive Council. The status quo suited Churchill, but it did not suit the man on whom he looked as the likely saviour of Britain, Franklin D. Roosevelt. The President was a Wilsonian liberal committed to colonial emancipation, not least in the Philippines. When the two leaders first met, at Placentia Bay, Newfoundland, in August 1941, they were soon at odds over this crucial question. Churchill became apoplectic when Roosevelt said, with reference to India, "I can't believe that we can fight a war against fascist slavery, and at the same time not work to free people all over the world from a backward colonial policy."[104] The Prime Minister thought it "pretty good cheek" for the Americans to try "to schoolmarm us into proper behaviour"[105] towards the

Empire. But he did not let the issue mar his friendship with the President, who decided to treat Churchill on the subject of Indians as he treated southern senators on the subject of blacks.

Accordingly, they issued the Atlantic Charter. This was a high-sounding affirmation of Anglo-American principles which included a pledge to "respect the right of all peoples to choose the form of government under which they will live."[106] On his return to England, however, Churchill told the House of Commons that the Charter's promise of self-determination did not apply to the Empire. Later, in order to counter stories that his "reactionary, Old World outlook" had upset Roosevelt, Churchill claimed that the Charter had been "cast in my own words."[107] But Roosevelt had edited Churchill's draft and he desired a universal Charter. The President, who thought the British people decent, law-abiding and freedom-loving, privately inveighed against their government. It ran "a world tyranny compounded of imperialism, colonialism and power politics which violates all political morals and in particular denies the elementary human rights of all peoples to be independent like the United States."[108] Outraged by Churchill's emasculation of the Charter, Indian nationalists were still more vituperative. Nehru, who corresponded with Roosevelt and hoped for his support, said that almost alone America kept "the torch of democratic freedom alight."[109]

America became directly involved with Asia after the bombing of Pearl Harbor on 7 December 1941—an act carried out, Roosevelt stressed, by the "Empire of Japan."[110] It advanced with ferocious speed, ripping huge holes in the flimsy fabric of western empires in the East. Everywhere the British, still apt to dismiss their oriental foes as "coolies in uniform,"[111] were taken by surprise. White confidence and prestige plummeted with each defeat. The Japanese landed in Borneo. They seized Hong Kong. They rampaged through Malaya. On 15 February 1942 General Yamashita forced the capitulation of Singapore. The conquest of Burma followed, along with attacks on cities ranging from Calcutta and Colombo to Darwin. As Japan expanded in Asia and Germany invaded the Caucasus, the jaws of the Axis seemed set to close on India. So from America to China influential voices urged Churchill to give the subcontinent such measures of freedom and democracy as would rally its people to fight for those ideals in the global conflict. Roosevelt himself, in his first public pronouncement about India, said that the Atlantic Charter applied to the whole world. Labour members of Churchill's government, Clement Attlee and Ernest Bevin, argued that Linlithgow's "crude imperialism"[112] was impeding India's war effort.

Churchill tried to stick to his guns. As Amery told King George VI,

Winston "hated the idea of giving up all his most deeply ingrained prejudices merely to secure more American, Chinese and Left-Wing support. He
was undergoing all the conflicting emotions of a virtuous maiden selling
herself for really handy ready money."[113] But under pressure the Prime Minister acquiesced to a declaration that after the war an elected body would
frame a new constitution for the whole of India (individual provinces being
able to opt out), to be followed by "the complete transfer of responsibility
from British to Indian hands."[114] If this were agreed the Viceroy would at
once invite leaders of the principal sections of the Indian people to join the
counsels of the nation. Churchill wrote tartly to Mackenzie King in Ottawa,
"We have resigned ourselves to fighting our utmost to defend India in order,
if successful, to be turned out."[115] In fact, Attlee wanted the subcontinent to
become a dominion, like Canada. He hoped that Sir Stafford Cripps, who
was dispatched to Delhi in March 1942 to persuade nationalists to accept
the declaration, would become the Lord Durham of India.

Cripps, who had just entered the war cabinet after serving as ambassador
in Moscow, seemed an ideal choice. A Communist fellow-traveller during
the 1930s, he was on good terms with Nehru. As a barrister he matched Jinnah in brilliance and opulence. A purse-mouthed teetotaller and a wire-
spectacled vegetarian, Cripps was a faddist to rival Gandhi—he espoused
nudism and knitted his own ear muffs. Yet Cripps managed to alienate
Britons as well as Indians. One MP, "Chips" Channon, thought him a
"modern Savonarola," saying that the air chilled as he passed and "I felt as if
I had breathed the dark, fetid atmosphere of beyond the tomb."[116] Cripps's
Puritanism irked Churchill. "He has all the virtues I dislike and none of the
vices I admire," said the Prime Minister,[117] who called him "Sir Stifford
Crapps."[118] The Viceroy distrusted him and said that he was "crooked when
up against it."[119] According to Nehru, Cripps knew nothing about India but
the more information he got the more confused he became. In fact,
notwithstanding his forensic skill, Cripps had a head of feathers to go with
his heart of gold. He was curiously naïve and obtuse. He regarded apple-pie
beds as the acme of wit and, it was said, he saw more demanding jokes by
appointment only. In particular he did not recognise the atavistic hostility
of Churchill and Linlithgow to conceding significant power to the Indian
nationalists even to gain their help in the war. Yet the Viceroy warned
Cripps not to "steal his Excellency's cheese to bait his own trap."[120]

He came close to doing just that. Cripps stretched his brief to the limit
by offering Congress an Indianised Executive Council that approximated to
a ruling cabinet. Complex negotiations took place over whether an Indian
could hold the defence porfolio and, with the intervention of Roosevelt's

emissary Colonel Louis Johnson, they might even have succeeded. But Churchill reined in Cripps and Congress rejected the British declaration because it did not provide for a free and united India. Gandhi protested about the mutilation of the subcontinent and refused to accept "a post-dated cheque" on (a journalist added) "a failing bank."[121] However, the momentous fact was that Cripps had signed the cheque and it was bound to be honoured after the departure of Churchill. Independence was therefore imminent. For the time being, though, Cripps had not been able to offer India enough. So, amid mutual backbiting, his mission failed. Echoing a newspaper headline, Linlithgow remarked, "Goodbye, Mr. Cripps."[122] Amery said that if Congress were offered the moon it would reject it because of the wrinkles on its surface. Churchill celebrated the debacle by dancing round the cabinet room and chanting, "No tea with treason, no truck with American or British Labour sentimentality, but back to the solemn—and exciting—business of war."[123]

Roosevelt made a belated attempt to rescue the initiative, protesting about the British refusal to give "Indians the right of self-determination." This infuriated Churchill. According to the President's envoy, Harry Hopkins, his "string of cuss words lasted for two hours in the middle of the night."[124] More formally the Prime Minister warned the President that an independent India would come to terms with the Japanese and threaten the Middle East. As General Alexander fell back from Mandalay and General Rommel captured Tobruk, this caveat became more persuasive. Gandhi reinforced it by declaring that India had no quarrel with Japan. Public opinion in the United States turned against the Congress Party. Americans particularly resented the Mahatma's attacks on racism in the South, where blacks were lynched, visiting Indian officers were excluded from restaurants, and hotels displayed signs saying, "No Dogs or Jews."[125] The transatlantic change of heart blighted Nehru's hope of hitching "India's wagon to America's star and not Britain's."[126] Instead, after anguished debate, Congress embarked on another mass disobedience campaign. It was summed up in Gandhi's ubiquitous slogan, *"Bharat Choro!"*—"Quit India!"

The government was well prepared and on 9 August 1942 it arrested the leaders, incarcerating Nehru until 15 June 1945. Despite the decapitation of Congress, its rank and file tried to disrupt the administration and dislocate the war effort. They went beyond strikes and *hartals,* and their efforts were often aggravated by the participation of *dacoits* and *goondas* (hooligans). Protesters sabotaged railways, cut telephone wires, and attacked police stations, post offices and government offices. Major disturbances rocked Bombay, Calcutta and Madras. Bengal, Bihar and the Central Provinces witnessed riots worse than those that had occurred in the Punjab at the time of the Amritsar massacre. Troops and aircraft helped the police to quell them. Several thousand people were killed and wounded. Moreover, notwithstanding genuine endeavours to put liberal principles into practice since 1919, there were occasional atrocities reminiscent of 1857. In the Central Provinces a senior official "boasted at the club in the evening that he had jolly good fun having shot down twenty-four niggers himself."[127] Sixty thousand Indians ended up in gaol. By autumn the authorities had established peace and they used a battery of weapons to keep it. Among them were public floggings, village burnings and a crushing censorship, which produced its usual crop of absurdities—books from the All-India Progressive Writers' Association were banned while Hitler's *Mein Kampf* was freely available. Linlithgow had no scruples about employing repression since this had been, he thought, the most serious revolt since the Mutiny.

Congress had failed to remove the British. Furthermore, the imprisonment of its chiefs left a power vacuum that was filled by the Communist Party and by rival Hindu organisations. The Muslim League also took full advantage of it. Yet despite the setbacks to Congress, the issue of India continued to plague Churchill. Reflecting a momentous swing in British opinion, the newly liberal *Times* argued that a political settlement might multiply India's war effort tenfold. Americans insisted that they were not fighting to preserve the British Raj and Roosevelt virtually endorsed the opinion of his Republican challenger, Wendell Willkie, that the aim of the war was to end imperial domination. Privately Churchill fumed. Sometimes he got into a "frantic passion on the whole subject of the humiliation of being kicked out of India by the beastliest people in the world next to the Germans."[128] In public, buoyed up by Montgomery's victory at El Alamein, he famously pronounced: "We mean to hold our own. I have not become the King's First Minister in order to preside over the liquidation of the British Empire."[129]

This shocked opinion across the Atlantic, where a poll found that 62 per cent of Americans favoured Indian independence (as did 77 per cent of Britons, if Gallup's sample in November 1939 is to be trusted). Churchill's intransigence also flouted hopes that the United States would be able to forge a new global order from the crucible of conflict. "America," wrote *Fortune* magazine, "owes the world a substitute for the *Pax Britannica,* which is dead."[130] Whatever the peace might bring, the war strengthened American antagonism towards the Raj, particularly as more and more GIs and journalists saw it for themselves. Eric Sevareid, for example, reported that the morally sick atmosphere of Delhi "was not unlike what I had experienced in Nazi Germany after the pogrom against the Jews." He disparaged the "second-rate" British officials and condemned the Viceroy's House, a symbol of might "looming over vistas of wretchedness." And he concluded that "no compromise within the framework of imperialism could ever put this country on the road to health."[131] But Churchill himself was in no mood to compromise. In November 1942 he told the Teheran Conference that Britain would resist any loss of colonial territory after the war by force, though it might in due course voluntarily give up portions of its Empire. This remained his position throughout the war. "'Hands off the British Empire' is our maxim and it must not be weakened or smirched to please sob-stuff merchants at home or foreigners of any hue."[132]

That ringing declaration was part of a personal minute sent to the Foreign Secretary, but Churchill also wrote an elaborate speech in which he proposed to justify his imperial policies to the House of Commons. In it he acknowledged that there had been a time of

> wicked and brazen exploitation of colonies and conquests. But the broad, shining, liberating and liberalising tides of the Victorian era flowed across this scene. The exploitation of weaker and less well-armed peoples became odious, together with the idea of subject races.

For at least eighty years Britain had served India, he said, bringing peace, trade and progress. "Our stewardship and our mission may come to an end but to India it may well be the age of the Antonines."[133] This was the delectable epoch, classically described by Gibbon, when the Emperors convinced mankind that Roman power "was actuated only by the love of order and justice."[134] However, Churchill did not deliver his speech. Perhaps he doubted whether the historical allusion was sound or feared that it would conjure up the spectre of imperial decline and fall. Certainly he was conscious of the danger of "stirring up controversy" in the Commons by raising "big issues" about the subcontinent.[135] For by the end of 1942 there was a big issue on the horizon, which nationalists could plausibly present as the hideous "fulfilment of British rule in India." This was the "man-made famine"[136] that ravaged Bengal for over a year. It was much worse than anything experienced since the 1770s, wrote one ICS officer, Philip Mason, who said that the heart-rending scenes he witnessed in the towns were "a shame and a reproach to men of English blood."[137]

Acts of God caused the dearth of food in India but mammon created the

Bengal famine. Failed monsoons and poor harvests had raised the price of grain. Rice imports from Burma had dried up, replaced by a flood of refugees. Although many Indians prospered during the war, inflation had sapped the slim resources of the poor—that third of the population always on the brink of starvation. However, the provincial administration was hopelessly unprepared for the catastrophe. The British Governor was myopic and moribund; the Bengal ministry was corrupt and inept. Instead of procuring food themselves, the authorities advised people to keep two months' stock, which encouraged hoarding, increased prices and produced a "psychosis of shortage."[138] The authorities were also slow to introduce rationing, to prevent profiteering and to supply needy districts with such food as they did obtain, which was stored under tarpaulins in Calcutta's Botanical Gardens. Indeed, they impeded the distribution of provisions. In a panic measure they destroyed some fifty thousand coastal craft in the Ganges delta to deny their use to the Japanese and their allies, the 25,000-strong Indian National Army (INA), recruited from sepoys captured at Singapore and commanded by Subhas Chandra Bose. He seemed to be the real menace. Uniformed and bespectacled, the aspirant Führer of India had adopted the tiger emblem of Tipu Sultan and the watchword of the 1857 mutineers, *"Delhi chalo!"*—"Onward to Delhi!"

Meanwhile, a legion of the destitute marched on palsied limbs to Calcutta. In that city and in provincial towns some aid was available but it could never meet the needs of the famished multitude. So emaciated men in rags scavenged for scraps through filth-strewn *bustees* and collapsed in the doorways of blacked-out shops and offices. Clutching infants of skin and bone, skeletal women cried for alms on the pavements of Chowringhee and the platforms of Howrah. Fighting for offal in the dustbins of clubs and hotels, where affluent Indians as well as Europeans continued to eat substantial meals, stray waifs reverted to the wild and "got into the habit of feeding like dogs."[139] Every morning corpses, decomposing in the steamy heat and often gnawed by rats or jackals, littered the streets. The Calcutta *Statesman* printed gruesome pictures of the shambles. But censors changed the word "famine" to "grave food shortage"[140] and an official spokesman for the Viceroy accused the press of dramatising the situation. The Delhi government, which was ultimately responsible for the welfare of the subject people, gagged its critics and dragged its feet. Linlithgow professed concern. But unlike his successor, Field-Marshal Lord Wavell, who galvanised the relief work, he did not visit Bengal. One ex-member of his Council said that Linlithgow had shown a "callous disregard of duty."[141]

Indeed, the Viceroy seemed less preoccupied by mass starvation than by a single hunger strike. Early in 1943 Gandhi embarked on another fast and Linlithgow's anxiety was reflected in the code word chosen to telegraph the news of his death—RUBICON. Officials secretly imported several hundred pounds of sandalwood so that he could be privately cremated in the grounds of the Aga Khan's beautiful palace at Poona, where he was being detained. But having served God through mortification of the flesh, the Mahatma survived. Linlithgow suspected that the doctors had been spiking his lime juice with glucose, which may have been true since his weight, which fell from 109 pounds to 90 pounds, apparently rose by one pound towards the end of the three-week fast. In an undelivered broadcast Churchill described the episode as "fast or farce—because I understand there is some doubt about whether he kept to his own rules."[142] This kind of moral blackmail incensed the Prime Minister and, when it was repeated, he sent the Viceroy "a peevish telegram to ask why Gandhi hadn't died yet."[143] Actually the Mahatma was an artist in anorexia. He recovered from these wasting ordeals with remarkable speed, reminding Amery of what Byron had said about his mother-in-law—she had been "dangerously ill; now she is dangerously well."[144]

Meanwhile, conditions in Bengal had deteriorated, reaching a ghastly nadir during the autumn of 1943. Altogether malnutrition and diseases stemming from it killed some three million people. But Churchill's chief scientific adviser, Lord Cherwell, who thought that Africans and Indians were subhuman, dismissed the famine as a statistical invention—just as he likened Gandhi's "change of diet" to taking the cure.[145] Despite pleas from Amery, the Prime Minister refused to divert scarce shipping to Calcutta and little was done to bring relief when it was most needed, though American aid came later. Churchill regarded the dispatch of food to India as an appeasement of Congress and he believed that "the starvation of anyway underfed Bengalis is less serious [than that of] sturdy Greeks."[146] He added that despite the famine Indians would go on breeding "like rabbits."[147] The Prime Minister continued to harp on this theme at the very time when the new Governor of Bengal, an able Australian administrator called Richard Casey, was sending Wavell a shocked indictment of accumulated British failures in his province:

> Bengal has, practically speaking, no irrigation or drainage, a medieval system of agriculture, no roads, no education, no cottage industries, completely inadequate hospitals, no effective public health services; consequently there

is no real attempt to deal with malaria, which is the province's principal scourge and killer, and no adequate machinery to cope with distress. There are not even plans to make good these deficiencies.[148]

The Prime Minister's view seemed to be that it served them right. In February 1945, recorded his private secretary Jock Colville, Churchill described Hindus as a "foul race 'protected by their mere pullulation from the doom that is their due' and he wished [Air Marshal] Bert Harris could send some of his surplus bombers to destroy them."[149] Amery was once bold enough to tell the Prime Minister that he had a "Hitler-like attitude" to India, for which, according to Wavell, he "got a first-class rocket."[150]

Churchill was increasingly desperate to hang on to India because Britain was slipping from its position as a great power as the United States and the Soviet Union came to dominate the wartime alliance. He had long said that only the Empire enabled the two English-speaking nations to "meet on those terms of perfect equality which alone can be the foundation for a still higher synthesis and a still more important destiny."[151] At the Yalta Conference the little British donkey, he complained, was squeezed between the mighty American buffalo and the great Russian bear. Churchill resented Roosevelt's nuzzling up to Stalin. He even rebuked Anthony Eden for using the term "Big Three" because it was a "reminder of the Roman triumvirate, and Winston does not like to be regarded as Lepidus."[152] So, the Prime Minister told the cabinet, Empire solidarity was vital. Wavell, a brave warrior who had lost an eye during the Great War, took a different view. He believed that a disaffected India might become "a running sore which will sap the strength of the British Empire."[153] Public opinion at home, he said, would not allow him to hold down the subcontinent by force. The only alternative was to reach a settlement in line with the inter-war reforms by which India could become a friendly partner within the Commonwealth. Such advice ran counter to the Prime Minister's cherished creed. Handing India to a "Brahmin oligarchy" would "open the floodgates alike to corruption and carnage."[154] It would also demonstrate that "we are a broken, bankrupt, played-out power."[155]

So Churchill resisted the Viceroy's counsel, though all eleven Governors of the Indian provinces endorsed it. He habitually undervalued the taciturn, poetic Wavell, regarding him as prone to "oriental lassitude"[156] in military matters and best suited to be the chairman of a golf club or a Conservative association. Churchill kept putting him off and Labour ministers, alienated by the stubborn enmity of Congress, did not press for progress. Indeed, Attlee opposed Wavell's initiatives, saying that he was "frankly horrified" by the prospect of ceding power to a "brown oligarchy."[157] But by the spring of 1945 an exhausted Britain had to confront the problem of dealing with the subcontinent after the war and Churchill needed to show the British people, before a general election, that he was not wedded to obstruction. So he authorised Wavell to convene a conference of political leaders (among them the newly released Nehru) in Simla to "advance India towards her goal of full self-government."[158] Churchill only made this overture because he was confident that it would come to nothing. Sure enough, Jinnah's insistence that the League alone must represent the Muslim nation, which denied Congress's claim to speak for all India, prevented any agreement. Still, the Simla conference was a clear sign of Britain's weakness. During the course of it Sarojini Naidu said that the Empire now gleamed with "the iridescence of decay."[159] Less than a fortnight later, on 26 July 1945, Churchill had to resign after Labour's unexpected victory at the polls. By the following month he was reduced to begging Wavell to "Keep a bit of India" for the Empire.[160]

Paradoxically, Nehru had more respect for Churchill, whom he considered an honourable foe, than for the "humbugs of the British Labour Party."[161] Many of them were humbugs. They were staunch enemies of imperialism yet (in Herbert Morrison's classic phrase) "great friends with the jolly old Empire."[162] They opposed racial discrimination yet proposed to sustain white supremacy in Africa for "a considerable time."[163] They were committed to Indian self-government but vague about how and when it would be achieved. Yet if Labour politicians were more apt to prate about principles than the Tories, they scarcely differed from them in practice. Socialists were unwilling to sacrifice Britain's global position to anti-colonial dogma. In the words of Ernest Bevin, the hard-boiled Foreign Secretary, "if the British Empire fell, the greatest collection of free nations would go into the limbo of the past."[164] India had made a stupendous contribution to the war in men, materiel and money (London now owed the subcontinent £1,375 million) and its loss would involve an irreversible decline of imperial power and pelf.

When it came to the point, therefore, as Nehru sourly observed, Labour ministers were reluctant to speak plain about Indian independence. Bevin actually wanted to stand firm and draft in younger men to hold India. So Nehru was not alone in anticipating, at best, another round of procrastination. However, as the idealistic new Secretary for India, Lord Pethick-Lawrence, told the Viceroy, the Labour Party was bound by its previous pronouncements to reach an accommodation with India. Foreign opinion had to be placated, especially in the United States, at a time when Britain desperately needed dollars to rescue it from what Maynard Keynes called "a financial Dunkirk."[165] And American aid must be devoted to the creation of a welfare state at home rather than the perpetuation of the British Raj in India. Wavell now found himself lamenting that his countrymen had lost the courage to govern and resisting pressure from London for a quick transfer of power. Nehru also applied pressure, reinforced by threats of revolution. But as communal violence seethed and flared, the Viceroy remained intent on avoiding a settlement that would "throw India into chaos and turmoil."

In his desire to maintain discipline, however, Wavell himself contributed to the growing disorder. He approved a trial in the Red Fort at Delhi of the guiltiest men who had served in Bose's Indian National Army, the first accused being a Hindu, a Muslim and a Sikh. This even-handed selection united all three communities against him, for peace had transformed rebels into patriots. The prosecutions were a gratuitous blunder of the kind that always seems to attend the death of empires. Before being called off they provoked widespread riots, notably in Calcutta where dozens of people were killed. Rising prices, delays in demobilisation and other matters aggravated the unrest, which became acute during the national and provincial elections of 1945–6. They were the acid test for the Muslim League. Possessing built-in electoral advantages as a favoured minority, it had enormously strengthened its position during the war. Jinnah whipped his cohorts into action. As Wavell put it, he inflamed the minds of his "impressionable followers with the idea of Pakistan as a new Prophet's Paradise on earth and as their only means of protection against Hindu domination."[166] Jinnah apparently said that he "cared not a whit if Muslims voted for a lamp-post provided the lamp-post was painted in the League's colours."[167]

Thus he won the vast majority of Muslim seats and established the League as the unrivalled representative of his co-religionists. After an equally ferocious campaign, Congress gained over 90 per cent of the non-Muslim seats in the Legislative Assembly as well as control of eight provinces. Nehru might continue to dismiss Pakistan as a fantasy, but now Britain clearly had to reach a settlement acceptable to Muslims as well as Hindus—or risk civil war. The task became increasingly urgent as its hold on India slackened. More brown officials replaced white, leaving only five hundred British civil servants and five hundred police officers. The ratio of British to Indian troops fell dramatically: having been 81,000 to 152,000 during the 1930s, it stood at 64,000 to 389,000 after the war. Several mutinies took place, the most serious in February 1946 when sailors sparked off riots in Bombay. Wavell warned that if Congress started a revolution he might not be able to stop it. Attlee's cabinet decided that since coercion was impossible negotiation was essential. So at the end of March 1946 it sent three of its members on a mission to India, Pethick-Lawrence, Cripps and A. V. Alexander, First Lord of the Admiralty. Wavell called them "the Magi."[168]

As Cripps announced on their arrival, they brought a single gift—independence. But who should receive it and how should it be bestowed? Congress answered that power must at once be handed to a democratic government which, since communal strife stemmed from Britain's divide-and-rule policy, would successfully unite India. The Muslim League replied that such a regime would be a Hindu tyranny, which only an autonomous Pakistan could prevent. For three hot months the three wise men engaged in a tortuous endeavour to please everyone. They so deferred to Gandhi that Wavell longed to bash the bald pate of the woolly-minded Pethick-Lawrence (inevitably nicknamed Pathetic-Lawrence) with a knobkerrie. The Viceroy regarded the Mahatma as the "evil genius" of Congress, "an exceedingly shrewd, obstinate, domineering, double-tongued, single-minded politician." The single eye of the soldier glazed over as he listened to the oracular pronouncements of the sage. And Gandhi's activities, which ultimately wrecked the chance of an accord, provided some justification for Wavell's bile. At one interview, the Viceroy said, the apostle of *ahimsa* thumped the table and declared, "If India wants her blood bath she shall have it."[169]

During the negotiations Nehru, whom Wavell thought a quixotic fanatic, likeable but unstable, matched his old mentor in truculence. Nehru bitterly inveighed against Jinnah, who had elevated rudeness into a political art and found a problem for every solution. The *Quaid-i-Azam* confirmed the Congress view that he was Lucifer, the fallen angel of Indian harmony. Yet it was Jinnah who finally accepted the cabinet mission's complex scheme, which gave the provinces virtual sovereignty (excepting defence, trade, communications and foreign relations) but kept the subcontinent in one piece. This indicated that, as both Linlithgow and Wavell surmised, Pakistan might have been a bargaining counter. Its intrinsic value was questionable. For as a fully independent state Pakistan, with sixty million people, would be unable to protect the forty million Muslims left in India. And because of the predominance of Hindus in east Punjab and west Bengal, Jinnah feared he would get "a shadow and a husk—a maimed, mutilated and moth-eaten Pakistan."[170] So he plumped for the federal system, provided that its structure was set in stone. But in July Nehru, who disliked the agreement because it deprived India of a strong central authority, said that

Congress was not committed to the framework of devolution. Livid at what he took to be a flagrant betrayal, Jinnah concluded that there was no alternative to partition. He declared that the Muslim League bade goodbye to constitutional methods and would create Pakistan through direct action. The cabinet mission, which had shown that the British were now "determined to quit India,"[171] failed to provide a means by which they could do so without bloodshed.

In fact, through swathes of north India disorder was already rife during the spring and summer of 1946. The Punjab was worst affected. Cities, towns and villages were devastated by the largest explosion of violence seen since the Sikh wars a century earlier. The Sikhs, indeed, were once again a target of attack. Muslim mobs bent on murder and plunder set their beards as well as their houses on fire. They also assaulted Hindu enclaves, killing, raping and pillaging with only sporadic resistance from the forces of law. Often British officials could not rely on their Muslim police, but sometimes they neglected their duties, cynically referring panic-stricken Hindu refugees to the protection of Gandhi or Nehru. Ironically, the most shocking failure occurred in Amritsar. Here arsonists and looters destroyed the two main bazaars and many other buildings throughout the city, often butchering the inmates as they ran from the flames. Local people contrasted the ferocity of the British in defence of their Raj with the way in which they "appeared content to stand aside and do nothing" to defend the victims of its dissolution.[172] Jinnah's "Direct Action Day," 16 August 1946, multiplied the victims. In Bengal, especially, Muslims embarked on a pogrom, shouting "*Jihad*" and slaughtering thousands. Hindus and Sikhs, many of them taxi-drivers, retaliated with still more lethal force.

Calcutta became a battlefield reminiscent of the Somme. But the carnage was more frenzied—men, women and children were cut to pieces. It was "unbridled savagery," wrote a British general, "with homicidal maniacs let loose to kill and kill and to maim and burn."[173] Vultures feasted on mounds of corpses, apparently preferring human to animal flesh. The clean-up was called Operation Grisly and until its completion no one could escape the stink of putrefaction. As troops struggled to restore order, a stream of refugees poured from the city. Some bore wounds and all had atrocity stories which inflamed their brethren elsewhere. With incendiary speed bloodlust raced from Dacca to Bombay, from Ahmedabad to Rawalpindi. The fiercest conflagration raged in Bihar, where more than seven thousand Muslims were slain. "Murder stalks the streets and the most amazing cruelties are indulged in by both the individual and the mob," wrote Nehru. "Riot is not the word for it—it is just a sadistic desire to kill."[174] Now Prime Minister of the provisional coalition government that Wavell had formed in the vain hope of resolving communal differences, Nehru suggested bombing the rioters. Faced with strife similar to that brewing in Palestine, the Viceroy said that he now had responsibility without power. At the end of 1946 he warned that the British could no longer control events and that "we are simply running on the momentum of our previous prestige."[175] His two plans for an evacuation of the subcontinent, devised to meet a more or less serious threat to the rearguard of the Raj, were respectively code-named "Operation Bedlam" and "Operation Madhouse."

They smacked to Attlee of Operation Scuttle, an Asian Dunkirk. Churchill himself was quick to accuse the Labour government, now "genuinely committed to the principle of Indian independence,"[176] of conducting an ignominious imperial retreat. And it was partly to turn away his wrath that the Labour Prime Minister decided to sack Wavell. His replacement was his antithesis—reckless, flamboyant, egotistical, outspoken, ingratiating, vain, shallow, flagrantly handsome and pathologically ambitious. Admiral Lord Louis ("Dickie") Mountbatten had other qualifications to be the last Viceroy of India and to preside, as Attlee announced in February 1947, over Britain's orderly withdrawal from the subcontinent by June 1948. He was royal, a great-grandson of Queen Victoria, which enabled him to talk to maharajahs on equal terms. He had personal allure: if he put his mind to it, wrote one general, "he could charm a vulture off a carcass."[177] He was a war hero who had treated his destroyer like a cavalry charger and, despite suffering "one glorious defeat after another,"[178] won Churchill's esteem. He was a brilliant self-publicist, flashing his medals, polishing his genealogy and burnishing his myth at the expense of the facts. General Sir Gerald Templer once told him, unoriginally but not unfairly, "You're so crooked, Dickie, that if you swallowed a nail you'd shit a corkscrew."[179] Certainly he neglected his wartime duties to help with Noël Coward's film *In Which We Serve,* an exaltation of his naval adventures that he saw time and again. Priding himself on his panache, Mountbatten "was never afraid to take risks."[180] As chief of Combined Operations in Europe he had been "willing to experiment with lives"[181] during the disastrous Dieppe Raid. And in order to speed up the advance in Burma he offered to take personal responsibility, as head of the South-East Asia Command (SEAC), for "getting anything up to 3000 men killed."[182]

Nevertheless, he was an astonishingly popular leader. Much more than the "Glamour Boy" sneered at by Stilwell, Mountbatten was a showman to rival Montgomery. He possessed just the kind of flair and dynamism to win what he called Britain's "last chukka in India."[183] He had instilled a new spirit into troops engaged in jungle warfare against the Japanese—an enterprise that Churchill likened to going into the water to fight a shark. Moreover, at SEAC—Americans claimed that the initials stood for "Save England's Asian Colonies"—Mountbatten had actually favoured post-war colonial independence. An egalitarian besotted with the trappings of grandeur, he flew over a personal barber from the Mayfair salon Trumper's to avoid having his hair cut by an Indian but he liked to cause consternation by shaking hands with Untouchables. His attractive wife Edwina, who Attlee thought would make a brilliant Vicereine, was also politically pink. But, grand-daughter of the Jewish millionaire Sir Ernest Cassel, himself such a close friend of King Edward VII that he earned the nickname "Windsor Cassel," she was less socialist than socialite. Until she took up good works during the war, her life had been devoted to the frenetic pursuit of pleasure. She had spent hours with hairdressers, manicurists, couturiers. She had had her ear lobes pulped and remodelled. She had acquired a male harem, swapping one playboy lover for another and saying that her husband, himself unfaithful and known to his intimates as "Mountbottom," regarded sex as "a mixture of psychology and hydraulics."[184] Together, though, the Mountbattens were a formidable, if not always a harmonious, couple. Among other things they forged a powerful bond with Nehru, who apparently fell in love with Edwina. He later told her that they had been drawn together by "some uncontrollable force."

Granite-faced and ice-cool, Jinnah alone remained impervious to their fascination. Mountbatten employed his most seductive wiles and, when unsuccessful, concluded that Jinnah was a megalomaniac. The Calcutta *Statesman* added a wry comment to its report of a meeting between them: "Other riot news on page 4."[185] The *Quaid-i-Azam*, whose ideas were "diamond-hard, clear-cut, almost tangible,"[186] would not be deflected from the goal of Pakistan. At first the Viceroy thought this sheer madness. But Mountbatten, who was charged with handing power to a united India (along the lines of the cabinet mission's federal scheme) if possible, soon saw that partition was inevitable. In fact both the British government and the Congress Party had already come to terms with it. India was succumbing to the gangrene of communal violence. League gains in the Punjab and the North-West Frontier Province encouraged its spread. Rawalpindi and Multan were infected. As large parts of Lahore went up in flames and Amritsar became "a veritable inferno,"[187] Nehru lamented to Mountbatten, "horror succeeds horror . . . [until] our senses are dulled."[188] The toughest Congress leader, Vallabhbhai Patel, said that partition was the amputation of "a diseased limb."[189] As that metaphor suggests, he doubted whether Pakistan could survive on its own. Nehru agreed, though his own image was a medical mare's nest—he wanted to cut off the head to get rid of the headache. Mountbatten's task was to save as much of the body as he could. Facing an "incredibly explosive" situation, he worked with "a terrific sense of urgency."[190] And he relied heavily on a dedicated staff ("the Dickie Birds") led by General "Pug" Ismay, known during the war as Churchill's khaki eminence.

Arriving at Delhi, where the tension was palpable, Ismay felt as though he had boarded "an ammunition ship which was on fire."[191] Dressed in traditional tropical uniform, he was further shocked to be greeted at the airport by Field-Marshal Auchinleck wearing a beret. "Have you gone mad, Claude?" he exclaimed. "Where is your topee?"[192] Ismay learned with astonishment that this headgear was now outdated. Its abandonment presaged more momentous change. Mountbatten, who lacked precision in thought and writing, Ismay found, first recommended a radical but impractical scheme that would have balkanised India. By May, however, after intensive negotiations, he got agreement to a plan, suggested by a brilliant Indian official called V. P. Menon, to transfer power to two dominions which would stay within the Commonwealth—India and Pakistan. Each state would receive not only the provinces which chose to accede to them but appropriate areas of Bengal and the Punjab. This split was bound to be bloody. In particular it left the Sikhs, who "felt for the Punjab as Jews felt for Palestine,"[193] as their leader Master Tara Singh said, "like no man's children in no man's land."[194] Nobody liked partition. Gandhi said that it would happen over his dead body and preached against "the vivisection of the motherland."[195]

Yet the motherland was already tearing itself apart, as if to illustrate Robert Byron's verdict that India had a "genius for disintegration."[196] Mountbatten said that only partition could avert full-scale civil war and Gandhi paid a smiling tribute to his persuasive powers: "you and your magic tricks."[197] So the Viceroy announced that Indians would get their independence on 15 August 1947, the time being changed to midnight on the more auspicious 14th to satisfy astrologers fearful of the malign conjunction of Saturn, Jupiter and Venus. Here was a retreat as historic as that of Honorius, the decadent Emperor chiefly devoted to "feeding poultry,"[198] who sanctioned the independence of Britain and Armorica. It was duly saluted in this contemporary verse:

Lay down the white man's burden:
An Empire great as Rome
Sends back its tired servants
And calls its legions home.
Four hundred puzzled millions
With bated breath await
The dawn of India's freedom,
The last and fateful date.[199]

The British Raj, which had taken two hundred years to construct, was to be dismantled in seventy-three days.

Mountbatten said that speed was essential to save India from "complete breakdown"[200] but it actually helped to precipitate a holocaust. The Viceroy promised to nip "trouble in the bud."[201] He would use tanks and aircraft if necessary to ensure that any communal violence was "utterly and ruthlessly crushed."[202] In the event the very imminence of Indian independence gave him an excuse to avoid effective action. Although warned that Sikhs were planning a ferocious revenge for massacres they had suffered at the hands of Muslims, he detailed only 23,000 men to act as the Punjab Boundary Force. It understandably failed to keep the peace in an area larger than Ireland containing fifteen million souls. British officials, poised for sudden departure, lost their last vestiges of authority. One wrote, "The civil administration was by this time completely paralysed and I knew that it was pointless to attempt to restore it in the name of the dying British Raj."[203] As Ismay later said, "The sand was running out of the doll hour by hour."[204]

Mountbatten spent much of the time on the ceremonial aspects of the handover while his minions concentrated on the complex business of dividing assets, roughly in a ratio of four to one, between India and Pakistan. Everything had to be apportioned—from rolling stock on railways to books in libraries, from weapons in arsenals to furniture in offices, from ingots in vaults to lunatics in asylums. The army, navy and air force were sundered. Similarly the princely states had to be bullied and cajoled into acceding on privileged terms to one country or the other. Once again Mountbatten demonstrated his powers of persuasion, abrogating with regal nonchalance commitments to a feudal order that had been Britain's "sheet anchor in India"[205] since the Mutiny. As one ICS man put it, the Viceroy induced the princes "to sign what proved to be their own death warrants on the assurance that this afforded them the best chance of survival."[206] He failed over Hyderabad (which India seized in 1948) and Kashmir, whose Hindu ruler soon took his largely Muslim subjects into India, a source of bitter conflict to this day. Deeply mortified by Jinnah's refusal to let him become Governor-General of Pakistan (to match the office he would hold in free India), Mountbatten also seems to have made a secret and personal contribution to the discord. In response to Nehru's anxieties, he evidently put pressure on Sir Cyril Radcliffe's boundary commission to award India key Muslim-majority regions in the Punjab, notably the Ferozepore district and the Gurdaspur corridor to Kashmir. Fearing a boycott of the independence celebrations, his hour of glory, Mountbatten delayed announcing the particulars of Radcliffe's iron surgery until the following day.

In fact, the inauguration of Pakistan was a surprisingly muted affair. Around the new capital of Karachi, a bursting city set between desert and ocean, had blossomed an eczema of temporary dwellings, red-roofed hutments, sand-coloured shanties and white tents. The atmosphere was taut as Sikhs reportedly planned to assassinate Jinnah, perhaps during his processional ride with the Viceroy in an open car. No bomb was thrown and the ceremonies were a damp squib, greeted with "public apathy."[207] Mountbatten still regarded Jinnah, now a wraith dying of cancer, as a "psychopathic case."[208] Moreover, the last Viceroy complained, he had to attend a reception for 1,500 leading citizens of Pakistan that "included some very queer looking 'jungly' men." The celebrations at Delhi, by contrast, provided him with the "most remarkable and inspiring day of my life."[209] With the impromptu magniloquence that came so naturally to him, Nehru began by broadcasting his famous proclamation:

> Long years ago we made a tryst with destiny, and now the time comes when we shall redeem our pledge, not wholly or in full measure, but very substantially. At the stroke of the midnight hour, while the world sleeps, India will awake to life and freedom. A moment comes, which comes but rarely in history, when we step out from the old to the new, when an age ends, and when the soul of a nation, long suppressed, finds utterance.[210]

When Independence Day dawned, India's "joy was almost delirious."[211]

From the countryside a multitude streamed into the capital, its trees and grass verdant from early monsoon rain. They came on foot or bicycle, by donkey or lorry, aboard rattling tongas or creaking ox carts painted saffron, white and green. Some laughed, others wept and still others filled the air with cries of *Jai Hind.* Muslims, Sikhs and Hindus embraced amid manifestations of "intense popular enthusiasm."[212] The British themselves were cheered—at last, it was said, they had conquered India. In the Durbar Hall at the Viceroy's House, enthroned with his wife, who wore a silver-lamé gown, long white gloves and a coronet, Mountbatten, in white admiral's uniform, gleaming decorations, Garter sash and sword, took part in a ceremony of "the utmost pomp."[213] He had designed it himself. After being sworn in as Governor-General, he administered oaths of office to the white-jodhpured, Gandhi-capped Nehru and his ministers in front of five hundred leaders of the new India. Then the Mountbattens processed through Delhi in the black and gold state carriage made for George V's coronation durbar, which was drawn by six chestnut horses. They were attended by a bodyguard in blue and gold turbans, white uniforms splashed with scarlet, and long black boots. Only this glittering cavalcade, with its bugles, pennants and lances, could have forced a way through the tumultuous throng, a maelstrom of noise and colour. In fact, the weight of humanity almost crushed the Governor-General's party at the climax of the day. This was the flag-raising ceremony at the India Gate, which took place amid "scenes of the most fantastic rejoicing."[214] Here was unfurled the tricolour of the new dominion, with the Emperor Asoka's twenty-four-spoked wheel of cosmic order (preferred to Gandhi's *charkha*) at its centre. Simultaneously, at the other end of the Rajpath, in the black clouds louring over the Secretariat Buildings, appeared a rainbow. It seemed to echo the hues of India's flag, like some garish special effect created in Hollywood. But as Mountbatten's press attaché remarked, "it would have taken a man of iron scepticism to be unimpressed by such an augury at such a moment."[215]

For Indians the heavenly arc symbolised the blessings of freedom; for Britons, who wished the death of the Raj to be swallowed up in victory, it marked the fulfilment of a covenant. According to a myth even then being concocted, Britain's withdrawal from India was not a sign of national weakness, still less a portent of imperial collapse. It was a triumph of statesmanship, a logical conclusion to the process of tutelage and, as Macaulay had forecast in 1833, the proudest day in English history. There was an element of truth in this fabrication. The end of empire was in its beginning and the British had frequently said that their goal was colonial self-government. But the myth was designed to conceal the fatal damage that the war had done to Britain's position as a great power. It aimed to obscure the overwhelming strength of Indian nationalism, the prospect of administrative breakdown in the subcontinent, the diminishing returns of the Raj and the erosion of Britain's will to occupy the seat of the Mughals.

So London played down the abdication of the last Emperor of India while trumpeting the emancipation of a fifth of the human race. It placed less emphasis on the curtailing of imperial commitments at a time of economic crisis than on the benefits that would accrue to the Commonwealth from the adherence of two voluntary members. "The Indian Empire disappears from the political map," pontificated *The Times*, "and the circle of the Dominions is enlarged."[216] Indian independence marked the end of the era initiated by Vasco da Gama and it breathed life into nationalist movements that seemed "likely to make the coloured man of Asia the master in his own house for the first time in several centuries."[217] Some people were appalled by this mighty caesura. The young aspirant Viceroy, Enoch Powell, believed that "the British were married to India, as Venice was married to the sea."[218] On their divorce he felt that his world was "coming apart," walked the streets all night and finally "sat down in a doorway, my head in my hands."[219] But in general the British, basking in the afterglow of their finest hour, liked to think that little had changed. An almost empty House of Commons had nodded through the independence legislation. The *Daily Mail* merely replaced on its masthead the legend "For King and Empire" with "For King and Commonwealth." Politicians at Westminster stressed the continuity and amity of relations with India and Pakistan. They claimed that everything had gone according to plan and that nothing became the British Raj like the leaving of it.

Yet even as London indulged in congratulation and Delhi revelled in celebration, the Punjab was inundated by "rivers of blood."[220] Mountbatten himself had seen signs of the carnage when flying back from Karachi, billowing clouds of smoke and a vast panorama of burning villages. Even as Nehru took part in what some saw as his coronation, he was cast down by reports that Lahore was experiencing the "bloodiest orgy of violence and fire in five months of communal rioting." As news of Radcliffe's boundary award reached the Punjab, where Muslims denounced it as "territorial murder," sporadic attacks turned into "a systematic war of extermination."[221] Everywhere majority communities assaulted and expelled minorities, in a vicious cycle of reprisal and counter-reprisal that went on for many weeks. None were better disciplined than the Sikhs, a perpetual minority whose gangs *(jathas)* armed with swords *(kirpans)* and other weapons behaved with "pre-medieval ferocity."[222] But Muslims and Hindus also perpetrated every outrage summed up in that grotesque modern euphemism "ethnic cleansing." They roasted babies on spits, impaled infants on lances, boiled children in cauldrons of oil. They raped, mutilated, abducted and killed women, sometimes hacking off the penises of their dead husbands and stuffing them in their mouths. They subjected men to frenzied cruelties, burning them alive in their houses, stabbing them in the streets, butchering them in hospitals, strangling them in refugee camps, torturing and forcibly converting them in desecrated temples, mosques and *gurdwaras* (Sikh places of worship). They poisoned their enemies, drenched them in acid, blinded them by throwing chilli powder in their eyes.

The atrocities totally eclipsed those of the Indian Mutiny. Perhaps they reflected the brutal finality of partition. But many witnesses found the violence inexplicable save in terms of evil and madness. One official observed a man being sawn into "several pieces in a diabolical manner that baffles comprehension."[223] Neighbours who had lived on friendly terms for years suddenly went berserk and slaughtered one another. Some of the worst massacres took place on the railways, formerly vehicles of British military control freighted with hopes of Indian communal harmony. Taking advantage of a system already seriously disrupted, bands of *goondas* held up trains packed with people trying to escape the terror. Often they left nothing but coaches full of corpses, which arrived at their destinations, in the charge of Eurasian engine drivers, with gore seeping from every aperture. British officers said that the spectacle was a "thousand times more horrible than anything we saw during the war."[224] Some of the mobile charnel houses bore chalked messages, "A Present from India" or "A Present from Pakistan."[225] Lahore railway station and others like it, once white fortresses, became brown death traps. Hordes of refugees travelling by road, some in columns up to fifty miles long, became a still larger target for rapine and murder.

Delhi itself was infected by the violence and citizens saw "a whole social order haemorrhaging before our eyes."[226] Nirad Chaudhuri found it literally indescribable.

> I have weighed nearly all the words and phrases which the murderous ferocity of man, as distinct from his warlike ferocity, has contributed to the vocabulary of European peoples: massacre, pogrom, lynching, fusillade, noyade, St. Bartholomew, Sicilian Vespers, Bloodbath of Stockholm, Bulgarian atrocities, Armenian massacres, Belsen, genocide, etc., etc., but find them all inadequate.[227]

Yet troubles in the capital scarcely compared with the havoc in the frontier region. There cities such as Amritsar looked as if they had been bombed. Towns were ravaged by arson and looting. The countryside was a vast crematorium, with thousands of villages reduced to ashes. The Punjab Boundary Force was itself lacerated by communal hatred and soon had to be disbanded. By the time the convulsion subsided a million had died and eleven million had been driven from their homes, one of the largest migrations in history. A Punjabi magistrate remarked wryly, "You British believe in fair play. You have left India in the same condition of chaos as you found it."[228]

Bengal was less turbulent largely because Gandhi, ignoring the Delhi festivities, exercised a seemingly miraculous influence there. Even though the East Pakistan frontier was just as arbitrary as that with West Pakistan—jute-exporting Calcutta was severed from its jute-growing hinterland—there was a further movement of only 1.25 million refugees. And when communal rioting did break out in the city, the Mahatma fasted for peace. Much of the police force went on sympathetic hunger strike and within days thousands of Muslims and Hindus were mingling together in friendship on the *maidan.* Gandhi would pay for his saintliness with his life—a Hindu fanatic, who could not bear what he took to be his partiality to Muslims, shot him in January 1948. Meanwhile, the Governor-General extolled the Mahatma as a "one-man boundary force."[229] Keen to minimise the damage done by precipitate partition, Mountbatten also said that most of India had remained calm and that "only" 100,000 people had died in the north. Ismay was horrified by his speech since it obscured the essential fact that "there is human misery on a colossal scale all around one."[230]

Yet Indians themselves were reluctant to dwell on the agonising birth pangs of nationhood and many said that parting with their former rulers was such sweet sorrow. The feeling was mutual. It was displayed at many farewell ceremonies, notably the exodus of the last regiments: the Black Watch from Karachi on 26 February 1948, the Scots "blubbing like babies," and the Somerset Light Infantry from Bombay two days later. That parade was an emotional affair with guards of honour, slow marches, royal salutes; flags raised and lowered, formal presentations and speeches about "the manly comradeship existing between the soldiers of our two countries." Finally, the colour party and escort of the Somersets, dressed in green berets, drill shirts and shorts, white belts and gaiters, trooped the colours through the Gateway of India. Witnesses "could see tears in everyone's eyes."[231] The band played "Auld Lang Syne," the Scottish refrain being taken up by thousands of Indian voices, as the English embarked on the *Empress of Australia* and sailed home for good.

Yet such nostalgic valedictions, which were to become familiar over the next few years, projected on cinema screens in a thousand flickering newsreels, could not hide the fact that the British Raj had ended in blood as well as tears. To that extent the prophecies of Churchill and his ilk were fulfilled. Indeed, it became a commonplace to warn, as Norman Angell did, "When the Roman Empire, which was full of imperfections, fell, it was not followed by something better, but by something worse, the Dark Ages. Something equally unhappy could so easily follow the complete break-up of the British Empire."[232] It was hard to deny, though, that the end of the Raj heralded the dawn of freedom in the subcontinent. Nor was it easy to escape the conclusion that the British themselves bore a significant share of the responsibility for the disaster of partition. In the short term Mountbatten, despite lifelong attempts at self-vindication, was much to blame. Had he stuck to Attlee's timetable and taken proper precautions, a reconstituted army might have kept relative peace in the Punjab. This was certainly the view of Field-Marshal Auchinleck, who was in the best position to judge. In the longer term, however, the fault lay in the character of British imperialism itself. Such was the British impact on India that ever since the Victorian era both Hindus and Muslims had been forced to "raise mental and moral defences around themselves."[233] Economic and educational differences had helped to crystallise separate communal identities. And the British, by dividing in order to rule and by favouring the Muslim martial races, exacerbated the growing religious antagonism. This culminated in the hecatombs of the Punjab. Far from quitting India with honour and dignity, the British left amid the clamour of homicide and the stench of death. Auchinleck's private secretary, Colonel Shahid Hamid, believed that "The British Empire, which tried to build India over centuries, can never live down this great tragedy."[234]

14

That Is the End of the British Empire

Singapore and Burma

Certainly the blood-soaked partition wrecked hopes that the British might in fact strengthen their eastern empire by setting India free. Wavell and others had claimed that "Britain should not lose, but on the contrary, may gain in prestige and even in power, by handing over to the Indians."[1] The idea was that partnership would succeed trusteeship. There would be co-operation in matters such as trade, finance and defence. Both new dominions would have a common loyalty to the Crown. But none of this came to pass. Partition alienated Pakistan and India from Britain and entrenched enmity between the two fledgling states. Nehru made India a republic and it only remained in the Commonwealth because that body, the ghost of empire, could change its shape at will. So, lamented Lord (formerly Sir John) Simon to Winston Churchill in 1949, Nehru and Cripps had won after all. Nehru had got advantages without responsibilities, thus enabling Cripps to achieve "his ambition to 'dissolve the British Empire.'"[2] The Islamic Republic of Pakistan broke in two, the eastern wing becoming Bangladesh, and their governments forged links with other Muslim countries. As India's economy developed, commercial ties frayed along with bonds of sentiment. Nehru kept his country neutral during the Cold War, seeming more hostile to capitalist than to Communist imperialism. Most important of all, after the Indian army was split between India and Pakistan, the subcontinent could never again be an English barrack in the oriental seas. When the Raj ended, said Field-Marshal Lord Alanbrooke, "the keystone of the arch of our Commonwealth defence was lost and our imperial defence crashed."[3] The earth shook. Neighbouring colonial edifices in Malaya, Burma and Ceylon were no longer safe. Unlike the Roman Empire, which survived in the east for a millennium after it had vanished in the west, the British Empire in Asia crumbled first. Its swift collapse, which resulted as much from war as from decrepitude, began with the fall of Singapore—an event comparable to the sack of Rome by Alaric the Goth.

Singapore, which means Lion City, was a byword for strength. An emerald pendant at the tip of the Malayan peninsula, it had been acquired by Sir Stamford Raffles because of its strategic position. About the size of the Isle of Wight or Martha's Vineyard, it guarded the Malacca Strait, the main route from the Indian Ocean to the China Sea. By the inter-war period it had become the fifth largest port in the world, supporting a business community of more than half a million people. Chinese, the women in cheongsams but the men quick to adopt western dress, outnumbered native Malays, in their sarongs, *bajus* (blouses) and songkok caps, by three to one. But the city, its skyline of spires, domes, minarets and towers dominating the southern shore, pullulated with alien nationalities. Indians, Ceylonese, Javanese, Japanese, Armenians, Persians, Jews and Arabs filled the streets with a cacophony of accents and a medley of colours. Wearing blue cotton pyjamas and conical straw hats, barefoot coolies pulled rickshaws under bamboo poles hung with washing and between the bicycles and bullock carts of Orchard Road to Asian markets smelling of squid and garlic. Turbaned Sikhs in yellow Ford taxis dodged green trolleys along Serangoon Road, its pavements splashed crimson with betel juice, en route to Indian bazaars scented with coriander, cumin and turmeric. In slums foul with poverty, malnutrition and disease, rickety children in rags scoured the gutters for cabbage leaves and fish heads. British officials in dinner jackets drove their Buicks from rustic bungalows wreathed in jasmine to the creamwalled, red-roofed Raffles Hotel, standing among palm trees near the waterfront "like an iced cake." Here they were greeted by a head waiter with the "manners of a grand duke." Here they dined and danced amid whirling fans and rustling ferns. Here they called repeatedly, "Boy . . . Tiga whisky ayer."[4] European *tuans besar* (big bosses) wore their confidence like a cuirass. They had some reason to do so. For in Singapore they possessed an "impregnable fortress,"[5] newspapers reiterated, the greatest naval base in the southern hemisphere. They were masters of the "Gibraltar of the East . . . the gateway of the Orient . . . the bastion of British might."[6]

Since ending the alliance with Japan in 1922, governments in London had spent over £60 million on reinforcing Singapore. Admittedly the cash had come in dribs and drabs. This was because of the post-war disarmament, the pre-war Depression and what the cabinet secretary, Maurice Hankey, called the inter-war "orgy of extravagance on social reform."[7] Hankey asserted what became the conventional wisdom: the loss of Singapore would be "a calamity of the first magnitude. We might well lose India and the faith in us of Australia and New Zealand would be shattered."[8] If Britain ceded mastery in the East to Japan, General Smuts warned the Dominions Office in 1934, she would "go the way the Roman Empire had gone."[9] But by 1939 it seemed that the immense naval station constructed on the north-eastern side of the island, facing the Johore Strait which provided twenty-two square miles of deep-sea anchorage, could counteract the local superiority of the Japanese fleet.

To build it a major river had been diverted. Mangrove forest enmeshed in dense foliage was cleared. Millions of tons of earth were moved and thirty-four miles of concrete and iron piles were driven though mephitic swamp to meet bedrock at a depth of one hundred feet. Inside the base, which was ringed by high walls, iron gates and barbed wire, were barracks, offices, stores, workshops, boiler-rooms, refrigeration plants, canteens, churches, cinemas, a yacht club, an airfield and seventeen football pitches. There were huge furnaces, vast crucibles and troughs for molten metal, enormous hammers, lathes and hydraulic presses, massive underground fuel tanks, a crane capable of lifting a gun turret out of a battleship, and a floating dock large enough to accommodate the *Queen Mary*. This arsenal of democracy was bursting with ammunition, gun barrels, propellers, hawsers, radios, sandbags, aeronautical equipment, steel loopholes for pillboxes and spare parts of every kind. Some thirty batteries protected the position, the most powerful of which were five 15-inch guns capable of blowing Japan's heaviest warships out of the water. Contrary to myth, these guns could be swivelled to face the land (though their shells, armour-piercing rather than high explosive, were ineffective against troops). But the jungles of Malaya were supposed to be impenetrable. Almost everyone expected that an assault on Singapore would be seaborne and thus easily repelled. In the thirteen-storey Cathay Building, known as "Propaganda House," British broadcasters, who were encouraged by the Ministry of Information at home to play up the potency of Singapore, fostered popular contempt for the Japanese. If they arrived it would be in sampans and junks. Their aircraft were made of bamboo shoots and rice paper. Their soldiers were bandy-legged dwarfs too myopic to shoot straight. All told, the sons of Nippon were mimetic products of a counterfeit civilisation.

Further confirmation of the island's invulnerability was the British government's pledge to dispatch a fleet there in the event of hostilities with Japan. When Churchill became First Lord of the Admiralty in 1939 he emphasised that Singapore was a "stepping-stone" to Australia and New Zealand.[10] It was also the linchpin between the Antipodean dominions and India. As the war threatened to encompass the world, General Sir John Dill, Chief of the Imperial General Staff, said that Singapore was "the most important strategic point in the British Empire."[11] So although Churchill was by now giving priority to the Middle East, he overruled the Admiralty and dispatched two capital ships, *Prince of Wales* and *Repulse,* accompanied by four destroyers, to the Far East. This flotilla, code-named "Z Force," arrived in Singapore on 2 December 1941. Its task was to deter the potential foe and it seemed to those on the quayside "a symbol of absolute security."[12] The powerful new battleship *Prince of Wales,* which had been damaged in action against the *Bismarck,* was known as HMS *Unsinkable.* The advent of Z Force encouraged the Commander-in-Chief in the Far East, Air Chief Marshal Sir Robert Brooke-Popham, to announce that Japan did not know which way to turn and that "Tojo is scratching his head."[13] But the Japanese Prime Minister, Hideki Tojo, had already made his fatal decision. On 7 December aircraft from carriers in Admiral Isoroku Yamamoto's Combined Fleet bombed Pearl Harbor and the first troops of General Tomoyuki Yamashita's 25th Army landed on the north-eastern shores of the Malay peninsula. The following day, stating that Britain was at war with Japan, the London *Times* printed an article headlined "Singapore Prepared." The island's garrison consisted of soldiers from many parts of the Empire. There were "sturdy British infantrymen, Scottish Highlanders, bronzed young giants from Australia, tall, bearded Sikhs, Moslem riflemen fresh from service on the North-West Frontier, tough little Gurkhas, Malays from the Malay Regiment." The uniforms in the streets, the persistent drone of aeroplanes overhead, the wail of sirens to signal air raid drills, the nocturnal spectacle of searchlights playing over the water, the overwhelming presence of the Royal Navy—all proclaimed that Singapore was "the core of British strength in the Far East."[14]

It soon became apparent that the core was rotten. This was partly because the British community in Singapore had been softened by imperial self-indulgence. They dwelt in a world of servants, curry tiffins requiring two-hour siestas, lazy afternoons of golf, cricket or sailing, cocktail parties and fancy-dress balls. Despite its nickname, "Sin-galore," the city was not as much given to vice as Shanghai. Brothels were illegal and cinemas were far more popular than opium dens. Luxury was preferred to profligacy. Singapore was a place of "high living and low thinking,"[15] where the idea of rationing was to serve game on meatless days. It was a "cloud-cuckoo island"[16] in which it seemed perfectly natural for a woman to refuse to assist with war work because she had entered a tennis tournament. It was an enclave of smug inertia, summed up in the Malayan term *ti'd-apa* (why worry). The prevailing torpor was often attributed to the overwhelming humidity—Kipling had said that even the plants perspired and the tree ferns "sweated audibly."[17] But Duff Cooper, whom Churchill sent to Singapore as Resident Minister in 1941, attributed its malaise more to illusion than to accidie. He reported that

> the civil population appears to have been asleep in a comfortable dream that the Japanese will not dare to attack and have been lulled into a sense of false security by misleading reports of their impregnable fortress from the effete and ineffective Military Intelligence.[18]

In fact, Duff Cooper himself was hardly aware of the imminent peril hanging over the island and, frustrated by his relative powerlessness, he entertained dinner parties with ribald imitations of its bickering leaders. However, he was not far wrong about Brooke-Popham ("Old Pop-Off"), whom he thought "damned near gaga."[19] The Air Chief Marshal, supposedly the first man to fire a gun from an aeroplane (in 1913), was "pretty tired"—General Pownall's euphemism—and "quite out of business from dinner-time onwards."[20] Duff Cooper was equally disparaging about the Governor of the Straits Settlements, Sir Shenton Thomas, who was "the mouthpiece of the last person he speaks to."[21] Again this was a fair verdict. Others thought that the convivial Thomas, "sanguine to the verge of complacency,"[22] was best suited to be the headmaster of a preparatory school. Having insisted that proper authorisation must be obtained for taking air raid precautions, so as not to cause unnecessary alarm, Thomas ensured that no sirens sounded and no blackout occurred when the first Japanese bombers struck Singapore on the night of 8 December. Duff Cooper experienced another enemy bombardment a few weeks later, just as he was about to fly home. In what seemed a suitable ending to his mission in Singapore, he was hustled into "an air-raid shelter made entirely of glass."[23]

The *Prince of Wales* and the *Repulse* might just as well have been made of porcelain, for they sailed to intercept Japanese transports without fighter protection against dive-bombers and torpedo bombers. Z Force's commander, Admiral Sir Tom Phillips, was a diminutive and pugnacious sailor whom Winston Churchill nicknamed "the Cocksparrow." He had so little sea experience that a fellow admiral, Andrew Cunningham, said that he hardly knew one end of a ship from the other. Moreover, Phillips took the traditional naval view (shared by Churchill himself) that armoured leviathans were more than a match for mechanical harpies. On 10 December 1941 that belief cost him his life—having called for his best hat, he went down with his ship—as well as the lives of over eight hundred seamen. Undaunted by the radar-controlled pom-poms, known as "Chicago pianos," Japanese aircraft sank both his great vessels. Their loss gave Churchill the greatest single shock of the war and filled Singapore with a "sense of utter calamity."[24] This was "a catastrophe of gargantuan proportions," wrote an English serviceman, and "we felt completely exposed."[25] Morale fell further when it became clear that the fast, agile Mitsubishi Zero could make mincemeat of the RAF's menagerie of Buffaloes, Wildebeestes and Walruses. Aptly known as "flying coffins," these cumbersome and obsolete aeroplanes quickly ceded control of Malaya's skies to Japan.

So, less than a week after the outbreak of war in the East, the British were reduced to defending the peninsula with a single service. Their army was ill trained and poorly equipped for the purpose. Unlike Yamashita's three divisions, which had acquired the art of swift manoeuvre when fighting the Chinese, it had little experience of combat. Many of the green Indian troops had never seen a tank until they encountered those of Nippon, which were arrayed against Rolls-Royce armoured cars of Great War vintage, real "museum pieces."[26] In fact the British had plenty of other motor transport, but this kept them glued to the roads that ran through the rubber estates, banana plantations and palm groves beside Malaya's jungle-clad mountain spine. The Japanese travelled light, riding bicycles (on the rims when the tyres punctured) and wearing canvas shoes (which did not harden like English boots when drenched by the monsoon). Thus they constantly outflanked their scattered foes, who fell back in disarray. As one officer supervising the retreat quipped, his business was a running concern. Apart from the 2nd Argyll and Sutherland Highlanders, who had done bush exercises, British and imperial units simply could not stem the advance. Compared to the Japanese veterans, said one Australian gunner, "we were babies."[27]

The contrast between their leaders was equally marked. The brutal Yamashita enforced "discipline as rigorous as the autumn frost"[28] and earned his title, the "Tiger of Malaya." The British commanding officer, General Arthur Percival, never got a proper grip on his subordinates, who knew him as the "Rabbit" of Singapore.[29] Actually his buck teeth, his receding chin, his apologetic little moustache and his high, nervous laugh belied his character, for Percival was both clever and brave. But unlike the tough, bulky Yamashita, who believed that Japanese who traced their descent from gods must defeat Europeans who traced their descent from monkeys, he was also painfully shy and woefully irresolute. His calls for popular resistance were more of an embarrassment than an inspiration. Lacking personality, conviction and dynamism himself, he failed to galvanise Singapore. He could not control refractory generals under him such as the Australian Gordon Bennett, who was said to have a chip on each shoulder. He did nothing about bundles of pamphlets on anti-tank defence that were found lying unopened in a cupboard at his headquarters, Fort Canning, nicknamed "Confusion Castle." He opposed the training of Malays and Chinese for guerrilla operations because "a scheme which admitted the possibility of enemy penetration would have a disastrous psychological effect on the Oriental mind."[30] Indeed, he shared the standard British view that Malays possessed no "martial qualities"[31] and Tamils did not "make soldiers."[32] As the Japanese seized Penang and Kuala Lumpur, he did not impose an efficient scorched-earth policy to deny them supplies—communicating by telephone, he even suffered the indignity of being cut off by the operator when his three minutes were up. At first Percival refused to establish fixed defences on the north shore of Singapore island because it would be bad for civilian morale. Then he announced that it would be done, revealing his secrets, in Churchill's angry opinion, like a convert at a Buchmanite revival.

Still horrified by the discovery that Singapore was not the fortress that he had imagined, the Prime Minister urged Percival to mobilise its population and fight to the finish. But, as Yamashita prepared his final assault, the island remained in a state of fantasy and apathy. Cinemas were crowded, bands played on club lawns and dancing continued at Raffles Hotel. Censors forbade journalists to use the word "siege." When a colonel arrived at the Base Ordnance Depot to collect barbed wire he found that it had shut for a half-holiday. When a major tried to turn the Singapore Golf Club into a strong point its secretary said that a special committee meeting would have to be convened. When an architect in the Public Works Department used bricks from a colleague's patio to construct an air-raid shelter, he "caused a most acrimonious altercation."[33] When the civil defence authority began to dig slit trenches as protection against the heavy bombing, the government objected that they would become breeding grounds for mosquitoes. Some Australian troops refused to dig trenches themselves because "it was too bloody hot."[34]

It was decreed that labourers going to work in danger areas could receive no extra payment because this would lead to inflation. So Tamils needed to build coastal redoubts went on scything grass verges inland. British units crying out for detailed maps of Singapore island at last received them, only to find that they were maps of the Isle of Wight. There were real concerns about a local fifth column. Some doubted the loyalty of the Sultan of Johore, who had been banned from entering Singapore where he caused trouble over his favourite hostess, a Filipino called Anita, in the dance hall at the "Happy World" fairground. One serviceman "definitely saw lights at night from the Sultan's property . . . which could have guided enemy aircraft."[35] Equally sinister in the eyes of the authorities was the fact that the Sultan had given Lady Diana Cooper a parrot that spoke only Japanese. All told, Sir Charles Vyner Brooke, last hereditary white Rajah of Sarawak, was surely right to stigmatise Singapore officials as "lah-di-dah old-school-tie incompetents."[36] Still more striking was the comment of a schoolboy at Raffles College when the Johore causeway, connecting the island to the mainland, was loudly (but not completely) demolished. When the headmaster asked what the explosion was, Lee Kuan Yew, the future Prime Minister of Singapore, replied: "That is the end of the British Empire."[37]

As it happened, Percival so bungled his dispositions that he handed victory to the Japanese on a plate. Having dispersed his troops round the shore, he placed the weakest formations in the north-west, where the Johore Strait narrowed to a thousand yards and the landings duly took place. He kept no central reserve to counter-attack. He deployed no military police to round up deserters, stragglers and looters—when the Singapore Club's whisky was poured away to deny it to the enemy, Australian soldiers were seen "with their faces deep down in the open monsoon drain scooping up as much Scotch as they could."[38] Percival also instructed his artillery to fire only twenty shells a day in order to conserve supplies for a long struggle. It turned out to be a brief encounter. As demolition teams set fire to the naval base, filling the sky with a pall of oily smoke, the Japanese used terror to create panic. They mounted a murderous attack on a military hospital, even bayoneting a patient on the operating table, and cut the city from its reservoirs. Europeans made frantic efforts to escape from the shattered harbour, often shoving Asians off the boats. Echoing Churchill, who exhorted officers to die with their troops for the honour of the British Empire, Percival declared: "It will be a lasting disgrace if we are defeated by an army of clever gangsters many times inferior in numbers to our men."[39] Had he employed all the resources of Singapore, Percival might have lived up to these sentiments, for the Japanese were dangerously short of ammunition. But on 15 February 1942 he surrendered. George Washington caught 7,200 combatants in his mousetrap at Yorktown; Yamashita's juggernaut secured more than 130,000 in Singapore. Churchill, who had given his reluctant consent, famously wrote that this was "the worst disaster and largest capitulation in British history."[40] He regarded it as particularly disgraceful when contrasted with the sustained American resistance to Japanese forces at Bataan in the Philippines (though here, too, defenders outnumbered attackers). Subhas Chandra Bose, who would recruit prisoners taken during the Malayan debacle into the Indian National Army, described Singapore as "the grave-yard of the British Empire."[41]

In military terms, as Churchill had always said, the acquisition of America as an ally more than compensated for the depredations of Nippon as an enemy. Moreover, so barbarous was its occupation of Malaya that Britain's imperial system seemed refined by comparison. The first major crime that the Japanese committed was "Operation Clean-up," the "purification by elimination" (sook ching) of some 25,000 Chinese. Their treatment of white captives was also notoriously cruel and they made special efforts to humiliate Britons before their former subjects. They forced emaciated men to sweep the streets in front of newsreel cameras and displayed naked women in shop windows. Such indignities did more to discredit their authors than their victims. Furthermore, Japan's ruthless exploitation of Malaya's resources undermined all propaganda about the Greater East-Asia Co-Prosperity Sphere. Characteristically, the Emperor Hirohito's New Order paid for rubber and tin in worthless scrip, known from its central motif as "banana money." In Syonan ("Light of the South"), as the Japanese rechristened Singapore, they also threatened to behead anyone who misspelled the Emperor's name. For these and other reasons, people in Malaya (especially the Chinese) welcomed back the old colonial order in 1945 with "whole-hearted and unstinted joy."[42]

Yet nothing could be the same again. After the loss of Z Force, the British had tried to hold the Singapore naval base largely for reasons of imperial pride. So its loss was primarily a loss of face, a terrible blow to their prestige. White superiority had been the basis of their rule and Yamashita smashed it in a campaign lasting a mere seventy days. The one Japanese slogan that continued to resonate after the atom bombs fell on Hiroshima and Nagasaki was "Asia for the Asiatics." In the words of Lee Kuan Yew, who became Prime Minister of independent Singapore in 1959, "When the war came to an end in 1945, there was never a chance of the old type of British colonial system ever being re-created. The scales had fallen from our eyes and we saw for ourselves that the local people could run the country."[43] The shock of Singapore's fall was felt well beyond the Orient. It even reverberated in the remote recesses of the North-West Frontier, where Pathans expressed "disdain that so grave a reverse should have been suffered at the hands of such foes."[44]

At home intellectuals now blamed themselves for having "undermined confidence"[45] in the Empire by deriding the principles of force on which it was built, just as the philosophes had sapped the ancien régime before the

French Revolution. In *The Times* Margery Perham called for an urgent adjustment of colonial administrations, especially in the field of race relations: Britons were "earning the reproach, while we blamed Hitler for his policy of *Herrenvolk,* that we were denying full equality within the Empire."[46] Australians felt betrayed by the mother country and, as their Prime Minister John Curtin famously declared, they now looked for protection to the United States "free of any pangs as to our traditional links or kinship with the United Kingdom."[47] Two days after Singapore fell, Henry Luce published his article "The American Century" in *Life* magazine, which stated that the United States must occupy the place once filled by great powers such as the Roman and British Empires. But America would reign benevolently, providing aid, culture, technology, democracy and peace. Critics dismissed this as "Luce Thinking,"[48] messianic froth about a new world order that might well be worse than the old. But whether highminded or woolly-minded, Luce was influential in forming opinion. He helped to define America's future role at the very moment when Britain seemed poised to lose its Empire.

Even American aid, in the shape of General "Vinegar Joe" Stilwell's Chinese armies and General Claire Chennault's "Flying Tigers," could not stem the simultaneous Japanese advance in Burma. Once again the British retreat had all the characteristics of a rout. And as in Malaya, it had a fatal impact on the standing of the colonial power. The Governor, Sir Reginald Dorman-Smith, who had to leave behind his large collection of top hats, said that the British would never be able to hold up their heads in Burma again. For they could neither defend themselves against Japanese infiltration nor protect the civilian population from ground and airborne assault. Early in April 1942, for example, a heavy raid almost obliterated Mandalay. The first strike destroyed the Upper Burma Club, where a luncheon party was taking place. Bombs killed hundreds of people, blowing some of them into the moat of Fort Dufferin. They also sparked off fires that gutted bamboo-and-thatch houses in seconds and smashed most of the more substantial buildings such as the hospital and the railway station. As an Indian official, N. S. Tayabji, observed in his unpublished memoir, such an onslaught "doomed any lingering sense of loyalty or sympathy for the British cause among the Burmese and Chinese elements of the local population." Tayabji helped to organise the evacuation of 400,000 Indians and others from Burma. He catalogued the dreadful circumstances of the overland trek: the monsoonsodden jungle swarming with leeches; the muddy mountain paths choked with panic-stricken humanity; the filthy refugee camps rotten with cholera, dysentery and malaria; the clouds of gaudy butterflies hovering over bloated corpses. He witnessed the effects of Japanese high explosive: "Dismembered limbs and tattered pieces of clothing littered the area, presenting a ghastly sight." He also noted that whites took priority even in flight and complained of "blatant discrimination." By the end of May the Japanese occupied the entire country. They had, in Tayabji's words, "destroyed the myth of western invincibility and with it whatever tenuous links may have survived the 100 odd years of exploitation and mindless domination."[49]

This was fair comment since the Burmese* had always resented, more bitterly than most colonised races, their bondage to Britain. From the first they had felt "very rancorous"[50] towards their conquerors and the annexation of 1885 filled them with "a passion of insurrection, a very fury of rebellion against the usurping foreigners."[51] What fundamentally antagonised them was the sudden attack on a social, political and religious system that had prevailed in Burma for three hundred years. It was hierarchical in structure, supported by a hereditary elite and dominated by the King. Behind the machicolated, red-brown brick walls of his Mandalay palace and under the graceful tiered spire that topped his Hall of Audience, the theocratic monarch reigned and ruled. He alone could display the peacock emblem and wear brocaded silk garments, velvet sandals, precious jewels and twenty-four-strand gold chains. He shaped every aspect of life, lending money, fostering commerce, regimenting monks, patronising the arts and determining etiquette. He also bestowed rank, signified by clothes, ornaments, appropriately hued umbrellas and suitably sized spittoons. The royal writ was supposed to run from the Kra Isthmus to the marches of the Himalayas, from the green Bengal plains to the purple Shan uplands. But the last Burmese king, Thibaw, only exercised a tenuous suzerainty over the Karen, Kachin, Shan, Chin and other clans of the mountains that ringed the arid upper reaches of the Irrawaddy Valley. And even in that valley lawlessness prevailed. The British therefore plumped for deposition and direct rule, and they determined to coerce their three million new subjects.

It took the invaders five years to crush the opposition. Patriots combined with bandits and freedom fighters merged with terrorists to sustain the resistance. Burmese dacoits, armed with razor-sharp *dahs* (long knives) and a burning faith that magic charms and tattoos of reptiles, ogres and monsters made them invulnerable, earned a fearsome reputation for brutality.

---

* The word "Burmese" denotes the predominant race in Burma, whereas all the country's inhabitants are known as Burmans. Similarly Sinhalese and Malay are ethnic terms, while Ceylonese and Malayans signify the total populations of their respective countries.

They were quite capable of pouring kerosene over women and setting fire to them or pounding babies in rice mortars to "a literal jelly."[52] Counter-demonstrations of violence did not necessarily intimidate the Burmese, who had "a great eye for the comic element in the terrible." A unit of the Naval Brigade discovered this when it tried to teach them a lesson by executing twelve dacoits one by one.

> The first man was placed standing with his back to a wall; a conical ball strik-ing him between the eyes, carried off the whole top of his head, which disap-peared in a strange, grotesque, unexpected way. His comrades, standing near, awaiting their turn, screamed with laughter at the sight; they laughed as they went one after the other to be shot in rotation, treating the whole affair as an extraordinary joke.[53]

Even after the British had gained mastery, crime increased to an alarming degree. Doubtless it was often a form of freelance revolt. At any rate Burma remained, in the view of successive Viceroys, not so much a province of India as a nation of rebels. As one of them wrote, his officers attempted to "substitute penal discipline for social order."[54]

The British rule of law was more oppressive than the Burmese yoke of custom, not least because it was so strictly imposed. As late as the 1930s a hundred hangings took place each year, a shockingly high rate in a popula-tion of less than seventeen million—George Orwell classically depicted the horror of such executions. British income tax was more intrusive than the levy on property. The new system of local government destroyed the old sense of community. The traditional gentry gave way to British-appointed village headmen who never commanded the same allegiance, even when they were ceremonially equipped with silver-mounted *dahs* and gilt-flapped red umbrellas. The headmen themselves answered to their new overlords, so much so that boys in the paddy fields chanted: "It is not fit, it is not fit that foreigners should rule the royal Golden Land."[55] The British never won Burmese hearts and minds, their propaganda being often quite inept. Attempts to promote loyalty to King and Empire, for example, ignored the Burmese tradition that popular heroes were those who defied authority.

Even positive British endeavours—railway expansion, public health work, agricultural improvement and so on—gained little favour with the masses. Admittedly, one or two members of the tiny educated elite thought this kind of progress "a historical necessity."[56] But they too hated the abrupt imposition of an administrative system that, while breaking with Burma's past, denied its ablest sons future scope to be more than clerks. As a senior white official wrote, uncongenial reforms had not taken root in Burma or promoted the growth of national life.

> This is why we remain aliens wherever we go. This is why our cut and dry civilisation goes only skin deep. This is why our schemes of self-government find no genuine support among the populations of the East. Our heads are hot and busy, but our hearts are cold as stone.[57]

Sympathy was everywhere lacking—save perhaps in the realm of football, the English version superseding the Burman game and allegedly becoming "the chief item on the credit side"[58] of imperial governance. Yet even football provided an outlet for virulent anti-European feeling, as Orwell himself recalled: "When a nimble Burman tripped me up on the football field and the referee (another Burman) looked the other way, the crowd yelled with hideous laughter."[59]

Other issues provoked greater passions. The British ruthlessly exploited the country's teak forests, oilfields and ruby mines. Their favours to tribal people such as the Karens, who were given a degree of autonomy and recruited into the army as members of a "martial race," infuriated the Burmese. So did the influx of Indians, for it changed the face of the country. Coolies from the subcontinent helped to drive back the snake-infested, insect-ridden jungle in the Irrawaddy delta, planting rice on an industrial scale and creating "a factory without chimneys." Rangoon became a predominantly Indian city, with coolies crowded into foetid barracks or sleeping in the streets, "so tightly packed that there was barely room for a wheelbarrow to pass."[60] Other Indians became money-lenders, fattening on Burman debt and gaining a substantial stake in the land. Still others took plum jobs on railways and steamboats, in gaols, mills and offices. They virtually monopolised communications—before King Thibaw's time the Burmese had set up a telegraph system and adapted Morse code to their own alphabet, whereas afterwards it was impossible to use the telephone without a knowledge of Hindustani. Alien influence also seemed to menace the Burmese religion, symbolised by the Shwedagon Pagoda, its spire reflected in the water of the Royal Lake and piercing the sky above Rangoon like a "shaft of gold."[61] Already English-speaking secular and mission schools were weakening the influence of the Buddhist order of monks (sangha). The British failure to sustain it undermined the central pillar of Burmese civilisation. It was no accident that the Young Men's Buddhist Association (YMBA), founded in 1906, provided the first major nationalist impulse since the fall of Thibaw, last "Defender of the Faith."[62]

The YMBA, an oriental echo of the YMCA, began as a student organisation devoted to spiritual matters but it soon developed cultural interests which promoted patriotism. Efforts to revive Burmese art and literature led to a reassertion of national identity. During the First World War, which dislocated the country's economy, President Wilson aroused desires for self-determination. In 1919 Burmese antipathy towards the British took the form of insisting that they doff their shoes before entering pagodas. The colonial masters made Burmese come into *their* presence barefoot and this was a tit for tat. Refusing to be humiliated, however, the British simply shunned the sacred precincts. They even boycotted the Shwedagon Pagoda, "the shrine of our nation's hopes," as one Burman leader said, "reflecting in its golden beauty, mortal man's tireless striving after the infinite."[63] When Lady Diana Cooper took off her stockings and high heels to visit this temple in 1941, she recorded that her white hosts were horrified by the adventure: "It may, apparently, lose us Burma."[64] Certainly the pagoda issue had prompted Burmese to join the wave of resistance that broke over the British Empire after the Great War. In Rangoon monks turned their gaze from visions of heaven to prospects of earthly salvation. The fiercest political *pongyi* was U Ottama, a saffron-robed revolutionary who preached that souls could not achieve nirvana unless bodies were freed from slavery. He and his ilk were often imprisoned for sedition and the Governor, Sir Reginald Craddock, rebuked them for sacrificing "the veneration of the ages for the nine days' applause of a gaping multitude."[65] In fact, "people thrilled to the marrow of their bones to hear such bold talk from their brave leader."[66] According to a Christian missionary of the time, nationalist agitation "breathes the air of mountain tops and calls to the imagination brilliant pictures of an uncertain but . . . wonderful future."

It became more focused and more secular when the British, having dismissed the possibility of self-rule along Irish lines, denied Burma even the constitutional advances offered to India. The India Office argued that government could not be made responsible to the Burman people because the Burman people did not exist. They were not a homogeneous entity. This assertion caused outrage and led to the establishment of *Wunthanu Athins,* or "Own Race Associations," in many of the country's eleven thousand villages. Members took an oath, vowing to keep it on pain of everlasting torment in Hell: "I will work for Home Rule heart and soul without flinching from duties even if my bones are crushed and my skin torn."[67] The *athins* resisted taxation, opposed the legalised sale of alcohol and opium and freely turned to violence. In 1923 the British banned them and set up a system of dyarchy on the Indian model. The new Legislative Council was a broadly representative body elected by householders, though there were communal and other restrictions on its membership. And despite contributing two ministers to the Governor's Executive Council, it had strictly limited powers. The Governor himself, for example, administered the tribal regions and controlled defence, finance and law and order. This taste of democracy scarcely satisfied the nationwide appetite for freedom. Indeed, its main achievement was evidently to provide a fresh field of corruption. The graft was ubiquitous—like that pervading the cabinet of Abraham Lincoln, whose Secretary of State would reputedly steal anything but a red-hot stove.

Most people shunned the polls in disgust and political agitation continued. During the late 1920s it found expression in bodies such as the *Dobama* Association. Meaning "We Burmans" in imitation of Sinn Féin, it began by boycotting western cigarettes, hairstyles and clothes. Members urged the merits of white Burmese cheroots. They extolled the beauty of agate-sleek locks garlanded with scarlet dak blossoms, orchid sprays or jasmine stars. They hymned the virtues of rose-pink *lungyis* and apple-green *pasohs* (types of skirt) made of Mandalay silk, and of damask *gaung-baungs* (headscarfs) brocaded with amber. The global Depression, which caused a slump in rice prices and a spate of foreclosures that transformed many Burman landowners into tenants, increased communal tension. In May 1930 anti-Indian riots convulsed Rangoon, men being hunted through the streets like vermin and women ripped to pieces. At the end of the year, in which Gandhi marched to the sea for salt, nationalist fervour erupted into rebellion. Its leader was a self-proclaimed saviour-king called Saya San, who took the title of *Galon Raja*. The *galon* was a fabulous bird that would, with the aid of village magicians *(weiksas)* and local spirits *(nats)*, kill the British snake *(naga)*.

Although the *Galon Raja* attracted widespread support, he was crushed in the powerful coils of his adversary. For gongs, spells, amulets and cabalistic signs made little impression on ten thousand imperial troops armed with machine guns. But the courage of Saya San's disciples was contagious and their message was compelling: "Burma is meant only for Burmans, but the heretics took away King Thibaw by force and robbed him of Burma. They have ruined our race and religion and now they have the effrontery to call us rebels."[68] New leaders emerged, notably two ambitious lawyers who defended Saya San (unsuccessfully) in his treason trial. They were the flamboyant, westernised Ba Maw and the uncouth, gangsterish U Saw, both of whom would become Prime Ministers under British rule and seek to end it with Asian help. Old antagonisms grew more venomous. Nationalists railed against foreign arrogance, typified by exclusive enclaves such as the Pegu and Gymkhana Clubs. More exasperating still was the racial bias of the law. When a drunk British officer seriously injured two Burman women in a car crash, his sentence of imprisonment was overturned on appeal and the magistrate who passed it, Maurice Collis, was moved to another job. Collis's account of the episode may well have been the germ of Julian Maclaren-Ross's classic short story, "A Bit of a Smash in Madras," with its reiterated imperial imperative: "Boy, bring Master a large brandy."[69]

As the economic blizzard continued to rage, nationalists also excoriated alien capitalism. Rangoon exemplified its evils, being nearly as bad as Bombay, Calcutta, Singapore and Shanghai, "a garish show on top and a pretty stinking world underneath."[70] The city's centre boasted art deco buildings and neo-classical offices with Corinthian porticoes; but white tycoons went home to the lush suburb of Golden Valley while brown workers dwelt in noisome dockside slums. In the delta region, where the Irrawaddy poured forth more water in a day during the rainy season than the Thames did in a year, dyeing the ocean brick red a hundred miles out to sea, the British had not even managed to construct a proper sewage system. Indeed, matters had worsened since Victorian times, when thousands dwelt in hovels on swamps, with "the most disgusting filth piled up in heaps or fermenting in pools at their very doors."[71] The health of Burmese minds was neglected as much as that of their bodies. The educational system had deteriorated since the reign of Thibaw and Rangoon had only a single public library, which spent £10 a year on books. During the early 1930s, therefore, ardent young radicals of different political persuasions (some Marxist) began the Thakin movement. Thakin meant Sahib and Burmans adopted the title in defiance of their colonial masters, against whom they directed strikes, boycotts and demonstrations. The outstanding Thakins were U Nu (to give the first Premier of free Burma his most familiar name) and Aung San, the father of Aung San Suu Kyi, leader of the opposition to the country's military junta today. Aung San was a tempestuous revolutionary, willing to adopt almost any course to break the imperial bond. Not to be outdone, older politicians such as Ba Maw denounced the "race enslavement" of his countrymen. He declared that "Our first task is to get rid of the ogre riding on our backs."

The ogre clung on tenaciously, changing its grip as circumstances demanded. Ba Maw attended the 1933 Round Table Conference in London, which the India Office organised to quiet the recalcitrant Burmese. He found the atmosphere formal, frigid and even hostile, and thought that his hosts were entirely cynical in devising means to save an Empire which "they knew deep within themselves to be historically doomed." His account of their tactics was characteristically subtle:

The colonial power was faced with the recurrent colonial dilemma of trying to give and yet not to give, of taking with an air of giving, of moving forward and yet remaining in the basic things where it was; and, to solve this dilemma as best it could, it had to resort to its usual devices of dividing to rule and delaying to defeat, of inventing escape clauses and conditions which would make a good deal of whatever it had been forced to give empty when given.

What Britain gave, by the Government of India Act of 1935, was the greatest measure of self-rule inside the Empire (excluding the dominions) as well as separation from India. Burma actually got more than India for, although the two constitutions were similar, the princes prevented the operation of a national assembly in Delhi. By contrast, Rangoon received a two-chamber parliament. And the House of Representatives, to which the cabinet answered, was elected by a quarter of the Burman people. But nationalists voted without enthusiasm. For although Ba Maw became Prime Minister in 1936, the Governor still had the last word. Having Indian forces at his disposal, he retained extensive powers of veto and full control of the tribal areas—40 per cent of Burma's territory. Ba Maw, who combined egalitarian rhetoric with totalitarian pretensions, was known as the "proletarian Pharaoh." But he and venal successors such as U Saw could achieve little, even though they mustered private armies with exotic names such as the Green Army, the Steel Army and the Army of Knives.

With increasing impatience the Thakins called for bolder measures to unseat the British. Aung San, who came from a family of rural gentry in Upper Burma, was only twenty-four in 1939 but he had already established himself as the sea-green incorruptible of this nebulous party. He was austere and upright, lived in a simply furnished suburban house and dressed modestly in a white singlet and a tartan *lungyi*. A slight, lean figure with a close-shorn bullet head, he had a diamond-sharp mind, a chiselled bronze face and a barbed tongue. He was a man of moods, sometimes sullen and menacing, sometimes bubbling with boyish laughter, and in the service of nationalism he veered from Communism to Nazism. He was willing to fly either the hammer and sickle or the swastika provided that he could do so over a free Burma. Thus in September 1939 Aung San joined forces with Ba Maw to create the Freedom Bloc, in imitation of Subhas Chandra Bose's organisation. According to Ba Maw its object was to oppose Burma's participation in the war against Germany and to fight Britain with its own weapons—the ideals of liberty, democracy and fair play. But the Freedom Bloc had a hidden agenda which Ba Maw was not prepared to divulge.

When Sir Stafford Cripps asked him in 1940 what the Burmese would do, he answered: "The Burmese will act in the Burmese way." "What is the Burmese way?" Cripps persisted. Ba Maw replied, "That's a Burmese secret."[72]

The secret was wrapped up in a slogan, "Eastward Ho!"[73] Ba Maw and others looked to Japan, which they expected to enter the conflict, as a means of breaking the imperialist hold. But as the Freedom Bloc's campaign against the British war effort grew more aggressive, its leaders were arrested. A virtuoso of faction fighting, the new Prime Minister U Saw took particular pleasure in imprisoning his old rival Ba Maw. Aung San went underground and was mortified to find that the British had offered a reward for him of only five rupees, "the price of a fair-sized chicken."[74] They should have offered more. In August 1940 Aung San escaped disguised as a coolie and made his way to Japan. The following year the War Office in Tokyo arranged for his clandestine return to Rangoon. Here he recruited a cadre of Thakins and others to undergo a ferocious course of military training under Japanese instructors in China. The Thirty Comrades, as they were called, attained a legendary status—comparable to that of Horatius and his companions on the bridge, who saved Rome from the legions of Lars Porsena. In December 1941 Aung San's Comrades assembled in Bangkok, where they enlisted other expatriates to form the thousand-strong Burma Independence Army (BIA). There they invested themselves with extravagant titles: Aung San was hailed as "Fire General" and Ne Win (Burma's future military dictator) became "Sun of Glory General." Finally, they took an ancient warrior's oath. The Thirty Comrades ritually slit their fingers, poured the blood into a silver bowl from which they drank, and swore to liberate their homeland.

Meanwhile, Prime Minister U Saw proposed to visit Churchill and obtain a promise of independence in return for full Burmese cooperation in the war effort. Before setting off he sought spiritual aid, though not by the usual means of climbing barefoot up one of the four great staircases to the Shwedagon Pagoda. Instead, U Saw uttered "vows and supplications" while flying in his private Tiger Moth around its glittering finial, known as "the jewelled umbrella."[75] Of course, he obtained nothing from the embattled Churchill; and Roosevelt, whom he visited next, was equally noncommittal. So, having witnessed, en route for home, the wreckage of Pearl Harbor the day after it was attacked, U Saw made overtures to the Japanese. But the British intercepted his message and arrested him. What this episode illustrates is the gravitational pull exerted on oriental nationalists in European colonies by the rising sun of Nippon. As the Japanese stormed up the

Irrawaddy Valley, wrote Ba Maw, "Burmese hearts beat wildly." Each Asian victory seemed to be another nail in the coffin of the British Empire. It is true that Burma, at war with Japan by British decree, was utterly ravaged during the conflict. Alexander's forces scorched the earth as they retreated and Stilwell's Chinese armies disintegrated into gangs of bandits. Aung San's BIA, its ranks swelled by dacoits and "political vermin,"[76] pillaged everywhere and provoked a communal war with pro-British Karens in the delta. The Japanese killed, raped, looted, tortured, slapped faces, extorted labour, desecrated pagodas, turned churches into brothels and transformed Rangoon cathedral into a sauce and saki factory. Within months the common saying was that "the British sucked Burman blood but the Japanese went to the marrow of the bone."[77] Yet, unlike the British, the Japanese gave Burmans their hearts' desire—freedom.

Needless to say, it was a mirage. Burma's Declaration of Independence, which Ba Maw promulgated on 1 August 1943, was the political equivalent of the Greater East Asia Co-Prosperity Sphere, an illusion designed to conceal the reality of Japanese domination. Ba Maw himself was merely the false front of Japanese power. He took the Sanscrit title Adipadi ("He Who Stands First") and mouthed the watchwords of fascism: "one blood, one voice, one leader."[78] He even adopted the manners and trappings of royalty. For example, he appeared in

a glossy, black long-sleeved silk shirt under a blood-red silk waistcoat, blood-red silk pyjamas tightened at the waist and ankles with elastic and black velvet Burmese slippers. The strange *tout ensemble* was completed with a black beret and both his cheeks were rouged.[79]

Burmans ridiculed Ba Maw's androgynous looks and regal airs, saying of him: "If you're marvellous, you're marvellous; if you're crazy, you're crazy."[80]

The Japanese were more contemptuous still, not even bothering to consult Ba Maw about ceding border areas of Burma to their ally Thailand. They ritually humiliated the Adipadi, scolded him, kept him waiting, refused to let him occupy Government House, a neo-Gothic monstrosity of red brick and white stone nicknamed St. Pancras Station by the British and said to be the second ugliest building in Rangoon. Yet Ba Maw stubbornly resisted Japanese efforts to make him behave as a puppet. According to his Foreign Minister, U Nu, a quixotic figure who recognised "the 'Made in Japan' stamp"[81] on his own forehead, the Adipadi refused to let his military masters pull the strings. This so enraged them that they tried to have him assassinated. As courageous as he was meretricious, Ba Maw continued to assert the rights of his country. Burmese nationalism was forged on the anvil of the anti-British struggle but tempered in the furnace of Japan's war. For if Ba Maw's 1943 Declaration was spurious, it was also glorious. It stated that Burma had resumed "her rightful place among the free and sovereign nations of the world."[82]

In the vain hope of making these words mean something, Ba Maw refused to desert Nippon, though he did connive at the growth of a secret resistance movement led by Aung San. Curiously enough, the Japanese military had more faith in this volatile young man than in the Prime Minister. They were especially struck, at an early meeting, by Aung San's torn shirt and impassive mask, indications of a samurai spirit. He gave further evidence of that spirit by using his sword to execute a village headman during the war—an act of "real justice," he later claimed, since in "such slave states as Burma it cannot be said that conformity with the law is justice."[83] So although the Japanese shattered Aung San by disbanding his unruly BIA, they made him a major-general and gave him command of a smaller, better disciplined force called the Burmese National Army (BNA). Its soldiers, who wore Japanese uniforms and badges of rank as well as the blue peacock emblem of Burma, adored him. Aung San also became Defence Minister and the Emperor Hirohito presented him with the Order of the Rising Sun (Third Class). None of these stopped him from conspiring with Communists, Karens and other anti-fascist guerrillas as soon as the tide of battle turned against Nippon.

On 27 March 1945 the BNA marched out of Rangoon to music played by Japanese military bands, with the avowed purpose of fighting against the Allies. It then vanished into the jungle and began to kill the soldiers of the sun. Aung San declared: "We are now at war."[84] A week earlier General Sir William Slim's 14th Army had taken Mandalay (destroying the remains of Thibaw's palace in the process) and it now thrust southwards. Regarded by its commander as "the Cinderella of all armies of the Empire," it had fought its way through what he called "the world's worst country" with "the world's worst climate" amid "some of the world's worst diseases."[85] As lines of communication lengthened, Slim's forces learned how to improvise, using jute parachutes, surfacing roads with strips of bitumen-soaked hessian ("Bithess") and making log rafts that looked like Noah's Arks. They even fed themselves by breeding ducks in the Chinese fashion, hatching the eggs in rice husks. So, marginally assisted by the BNA, the 14th Army just managed to beat the monsoon to Rangoon. When Slim met Aung San a couple of weeks later he was impressed by his genuine patriotism, despite his Japanese uniform and sword, and afterwards wrote that he might "have proved a Burmese Smuts." But at the time Slim could not resist twitting Aung San with changing sides only because the Allies were winning. He replied, "It wouldn't be much use coming to you if you weren't, would it?"[86]

Aung San claimed to represent the Burmese Provisional Government, formed by those coordinating resistance to the Japanese. Slim did not recognise this government and told his visitor that he was lucky not to be arrested as a traitor and a war criminal. But it became plain that only Aung San could galvanise popular support for the Allies in Burma. So Mountbatten, the Supreme Commander in South-East Asia, backed him. It was a swift, bold decision. And it set Mountbatten on a collision course with the exiled Governor. Dorman-Smith was planning to "make Burma an Empire gem," as Ernest Bevin urged, and to lead its people, in a process lasting several years, to "the full stature of nationhood."[87] Churchill was suspicious, charging Dorman-Smith with wanting "to give away the Empire."[88] Impatient liberal critics accused Dorman-Smith of having "learned nothing and forgotten nothing."[89] But in May a government White Paper, couched in grim "Whitehallese,"[90] endorsed his policy. Dorman-Smith maintained, therefore, that it was "sheer madness" to build up Aung San. Mountbatten insisted that sustaining him was a military necessity and he threatened to court-martial anyone who tried to sabotage this strategy. So at the Victory Parade held on 15 June 1945, the BNA joined Allied contingents and goosestepped through the ruins of Rangoon. And Mountbatten treated Aung San, still in his Japanese uniform, "as an ex-rebel who has seen the light."

What Aung San actually saw was that Mountbatten had a million men under arms, making full cooperation with him essential. But after Japan's sudden surrender in August, the Allied forces were quickly demobilised, whereas Aung San strengthened his private army. This was, according to one British observer, a cross between the Home Guard and the British Legion. But it enabled Aung San, now also heading a political coalition called the Anti-Fascist People's Freedom League (AFPFL), to exert pressure on Dorman-Smith, who returned to Rangoon in October 1945. "We Burmese are not the Burmese of 1942," Aung San declared, "and if we have to use force and fight we are fully prepared." So while Dorman-Smith tried to implement the White Paper, Aung San tried to make the country ungovernable. Asserting that there was no difference between British and Japanese imperialism, he stirred up violent agitation for immediate independence. The ailing Dorman-Smith dithered, sometimes wanting Aung San on his Council, sometimes wanting him in prison. Mountbatten thought that his "idiotic and vacillating policy was the worst piece of work ever done in Burma." In May 1946 Attlee concluded that the Governor had lost his grip and recalled him. Dorman-Smith quipped, "I depart 'Unhonoured and Aung San.'"

By the time that Mountbatten's protégé, Major-General Sir Hubert Rance, took up residence in Government House, lawlessness had become chronic. As usual, it was hard to distinguish crime from terrorism—miscreant heads were brought in for identification and the British hoped that "the bandits were dead before decapitation."[91] In September the police went on strike, protesting about low pay at a time of rampant inflation. The AFPFL encouraged them and soon civil servants, postal workers, railwaymen, gaolers and others followed suit. The nation was on the brink of chaos. The Governor inveighed against the "evil genius"[92] of Aung San, yet it was clear that he "had the country behind him." So Rance bowed to the inevitable. He reached an accord whereby Aung San ended the strikes (on conditions favourable to the strikers) and the AFPFL received in return a majority of seats on the Executive Council. This revolution in government, said a senior official, marked "the effective passing of power from British to Burmese." True, the British were slow to grasp the fact: in November 1946 they sent twenty probationers to swell the ranks of the Burma Civil Service, only to ship them home again within a few months. But in his new position as Defence Minister, Aung San was able to demand swift progress towards self-determination, hammering home his points with a mailed fist.

Rance could no longer draw on Indian troops. And in Whitehall the Chiefs of Staff warned that British forces, already at full stretch in Palestine, Malaya and elsewhere, could hardly maintain security in Burma, let alone crush a rebellion. In any case, the cost would be prohibitive. Burma, which lacked Malaya's vital dollar-earning capacity, was more trouble than it was worth. Attlee disliked making concessions to the dictatorial AFPFL which, though preferable to the Communists, might oppress non-Burmese minorities. But his only option was to abandon the White Paper and seek accommodation with Aung San. Churchill growled about the haste. And in due course he composed a variation on his famous indictment of Gandhi: "I certainly did not expect to see U Aung San, whose hands were dyed with British blood and loyal Burmese blood, marching up the steps of Buckingham Palace as the plenipotentiary of the Burmese Government."[93]

Other English auguries were unfavourable. At one dinner the Foreign Secretary, Ernest Bevin, said to Aung San with a great belly laugh: "So we are going to give Burma away to you, are we? Well, you know what they say about the British, they gives something with one 'and and they takes it back with the other."[94] Nevertheless, in January 1947 an agreement was signed setting out the procedure by which Burma would become a sovereign state. When Aung San returned home he tolerated no delay. In effect he ran the government, vainly trying to destroy the Frankenstein's monster of violence to which he had given new life—it dominates Myanmar to this day. British officials left Burma in droves. Shan, Kachin and Chin minorities agreed to help form a united Burma, though Karens determined to fight for their own independence. In the April general election for the Constituent Assembly, the AFPFL won 204 out of the 210 seats. But Aung San was not to reap the fruits of his long struggle. On 19 July 1947, in pelting monsoon rain, several men wearing army uniforms drove Jeeps up to the Secretariat Building where he was holding a Council meeting and burst into the chamber firing Sten guns. They killed Aung San together with five of his colleagues and fled.

Shock and grief overwhelmed the nation. Huge crowds gathered to see Aung San's embalmed body lying in a glass-lidded sarcophagus at the Jubilee Hall. Ba Maw and other opposition figures were arrested. In due course U Saw was charged with the murders, found guilty and hanged. Meanwhile, Rance had acted swiftly, inviting U Nu, President of the Consituent Assembly, to form a new Executive Council. It was haunted by a spectral presence. As a visiting British minister observed, "Aung San dead is an even greater influence in Burma than alive."[95] Despite Rance's blandishments, therefore, U Nu fell in with his lost leader's wishes and took the country out of the Commonwealth. At 4:20 a.m. on 4 January 1948 Burma became an independent republic. Rance found the time highly inconvenient but it was prescribed by the stars—the devout U Nu had supposedly consulted every astrologer in Rangoon. The usual ceremonies took place amid widespread rejoicing. Popular dramatic performances represented "a free people dancing in a rain of gold and silver."[96]

15

The Aim of Labour Is to Save the Empire

Ceylon and Malaya

Ceylon won freedom by quite different means though in many ways its colonial history resembled that of Burma. To help secure India, the British had seized Ceylon by force. They overthrew the ancient Kandyan kingdom. They exiled its monarch to the subcontinent, looting his throne, sceptre, sword, footstool and other royal regalia. They turned his Audience Hall first into a church and later into a court. They imposed their own system of rule. They suppressed resistance ferociously, provoking a national abhorrence for the conquerors. They invested their Governors with quasi-regal status, so much so that one of them, Sir Arthur Gordon, came close to imitating Caligula. Unable to attend a ceremony inaugurating a new province, he arranged to be represented by his horse.

> At the function itself, which consisted of a large procession of elephants, tom-tom beaters, chiefs, dancers, and the rag-tag and bobtail of the populace, the pony was led in solemn state, closely followed by the officials. On its back was a saddle, upon which rested a cushion, that in turn carried a silver tray, on which rested Sir Arthur Gordon's message to "The chiefs and people of Sabaragamuwa" . . . expressed in a ponderous mass of verbiage.[1]

The British used forced labour and despoiled virgin forests. They imported Tamils to serve first King Coffee and then the tyrant tea in conditions tantamount to slavery—planters kept them in squalor and thought nothing of "thumping a coolie for nearly half an hour."[2]

The colonial masters held aloof from both Sinhalese and Tamils, seldom learning their language and sometimes regarding them with contempt or even hatred. Samuel Baker described the typical native as "a treacherous villain, who would perpetrate the greatest rascality had he only the pluck."[3] James Bowes, Assistant Superintendent of Police in Jaffna, would trot through the town's palm-fringed streets in a gig cursing the drivers of bullock carts and others who got in his way: "Get out, you ugly stinking fucking son of a black buggered bitch."4 Later Bowes said that his superiors had encouraged "harsh and overbearing conduct towards Orientals." And he admitted to having thought that "dark blood" guaranteed certain disabilities, "including a tendency to megalomania."5 Yet in general the Ceylonese replied softly to racial antagonism. And although during the late nineteenth century a revived Buddhism stimulated nationalism in Ceylon as it did in Burma, the two peoples diverged on the issue of violence. Whereas the Burmese sought independence through conflict, the Ceylonese pursued the same end by means of cooperation.

They had had much longer than the people of Burma to learn the art of accommodating Europeans. As early as 1505 the Portuguese landed on "India's utmost isle" (to use Ovid's phrase), avid for cinnamon. They got a grip on coastal regions and converted many of the inhabitants (notably members of the *karava* fishing caste) to Christianity. They also earned a reputation for hellish cruelty. One famously punned as he slaughtered the children of Galle, "How the young *gallos* (cocks) crow."6 For centuries the Sinhalese represented their first white invaders as devils who ate stones and drank blood. The Dutch, who drove the Portuguese from their last fortress in 1658, were also harsh rulers. They persecuted Catholics and administered the maritime provinces with remorseless efficiency. Suspecting that the Dutch were "dangerous, turbulent or crafty Jacobins,"7 the British expelled them and (in 1802) made Ceylon a crown colony. But the new masters were no less implacable than the old. To crush rebellion in Kandy in 1818 the Governor, Sir Robert Brownrigg, set off in person, his escort of mounted dragoons led by tusked elephants with swinging bells while he himself rode in a "tom-john," a hooded and curtained armchair carried by four bearers. His force killed some ten thousand people. This was more than 1 per cent of the population of an island that the British idealised as "the pearl drop on the brow of India."8

Once the country was secured, Governors conducted a "paternal despotism."9 Their avowed object was to plant the germ of western civilisation while preserving what was sacred to the East. The British rarely intermarried with the Sinhalese, unlike their predecessors, who sired clans of Fernandos, Pereras and de Silvas, and a whole race of Burghers. But in the 1830s the new rulers did set up a Legislative Council and appoint to it natives of Ceylon, who were also given other minor posts. The British abolished slavery and compulsory labour. They established law and order, occasionally resorting to repression. The only uprising worthy of the name, which occurred in 1848, killed not a single European. But two hundred alleged rebels were hanged or shot, and more were flogged or imprisoned, the Governor establishing courts martial as "instruments of terror and vengeance."[10] The colonisers, who could buy land, invested sweat and cash in commerce and agriculture. Planters provided the only opposition to Governors, one of whom, Lord Torrington, said that they would think him an able man while the price of coffee rose, "and if it falls a great fool."[11]

Convinced that "coffee could not prosper without rice,"[12] the authorities began to restore the gigantic irrigation works that had been the wonder of ancient Ceylon. They reclaimed from jungle the huge tanks or reservoirs, some as large as inland seas. And to a lesser extent they restored the vital tracery of canals—the British saw these more as a means of transport than a system of arteries, veins and capillaries for giving life to Ceylon's arid north and east. By the 1850s they had linked all the main towns with good roads, where there had been none under the Dutch. They also built railways, which the planters so favoured that, in order to fund them, they took "the desperate course of proposing to be taxed." Workers on the iron road paid in blood, for "every sleeper was laid at the cost of a human life."[13] As a Scottish merchant acknowledged, the state of the nation was measured by the prosperity of the eight thousand Europeans; "but as regards the welfare and happiness of the Ceylonese all are silent as midnight on Pedrotallagalle."*[14] Nevertheless, the educated elite learned to live with the British, to speak their language, play their games, adopt their habits and benefit from their Empire.

The British found Ceylon exceptionally easy to control. The maritime powers were said to have netted the island like a fish and for 150 years it remained in thrall to the Royal Navy. Ships flying the white ensign found safety in the magnificent haven at Trincomalee and awed the polyglot craft trading round the coast—Arab dhows, Chinese junks, patamars from Malabar, Coromandel dhoneys, Ceylonese catamarans. The pearl banks south of Adam's Bridge in the Gulf of Mannar, which were periodically opened for fishing, drew thirty thousand people from all over Asia. Yet the operation was supervised by two or three British officials with walking sticks. One of them, Leonard Woolf, observed that Ceylon in 1906 was "the exact opposite of a 'police state.'"[15] Ports such as Colombo and Galle also attracted a picturesque mixture of races, umbrella'd Europeans, whiskered Malays, white-capped Moors, earringed Chetties, Parsees in their arched hats of flowered silk as well as Sinhalese wearing their hair in a bun as they did at the time of the Ptolemies. Yet the authorities seldom needed to use force here or in the

---

* This is the highest summit in the mountain core of Ceylon, from which can be seen on a clear day the island's entire coastline, nearly nine hundred miles in circumference.

country at large, where the population was also fragmented. There were not only communal hostilities between Sinhalese and Tamils but rivalries within each community. For example, anglicised lowland Sinhalese were at odds with feudal highlanders, typified by their chiefs' old-fashioned ceremonial dress—protruding muslin skirt, stiff silk brocade jacket and "large four-cornered cocked-hat, richly embroidered with gold-lace"[16] and topped with a little jewelled pagoda. Sophisticated Burghers had nothing in common with cave-dwelling Veddas, thought to be descendants of the country's aboriginal inhabitants. Caste antipathies ran deep. And some people, such as the Rodiyas, who carried out polluting tasks like preparing monkey skins for tom-toms, were treated as pariahs. On one occasion, when ordered to arrest some Rodiyas for murder, policemen refused to lay hands on them "but offered *to shoot them down from a distance.*"[17]

Religious differences were profound. Hindus were ranged against Muslims. Christians, some 10 per cent of the three million population in the late nineteenth century, resented Britain's early pledge to defend the faith of the majority. And one Victorian Governor withdrew the military Guard from the Tooth, revered relic of the Buddha swathed in red silk and swaddled in a nest of gorgeous caskets inside its Chinese-style temple at Kandy, so as not to sanction "idolatrous veneration."[18] Buddhists blamed the British for the decayed state of the sacred Bo-tree at Anuradhapura. Their sensitivities were particularly acute because they looked on Ceylon as the spiritual home of their faith, just as Catholics looked on Rome. Yet whereas Christianity was a proselytising religion, Buddhism was a quietist philosophy, its goal being the extinction of desire in the bliss of enlightenment. So it did not pose a serious challenge to British rule in conservative Ceylon. Rather, the "blessed isle" (to translate the ancient and modern name of Sri Lanka) was to be cherished as a foretaste of nirvana. Christians had their own belief—that this was the site of the garden God had created for Adam and Eve. Muslims said that it was "a new elysium to console them for the loss of paradise."

Certainly the British hymned the delights of Ceylon. Every prospect pleased (and only man was vile) in what Bishop Heber called one of the loveliest spots in the universe. Leaving this "dear colony," Radnadipa ("Island of Gems"), Governor Stewart Mackenzie lamented his transfer to Corfu, "as bare as Ulysses would have found himself in Ithaca."[19] Arriving at Galle, Sir Emerson Tennent, a senior official, rhapsodised over the sapphire-blue water, the golden sands, the shore "gemmed with flowers"[20] and the jade-green jungle draping the flanks of the country's natural shrine, Adam's Peak. Other visitors extolled the unbridled luxuriance of the tropics, the floral garlands enveloping the white, red-tiled houses of Colombo, the crimson carpets of goat's foot convolvulus, and miniature bananas said to be the "figs of paradise."[21] Those who took the train up to Kandy gazed with rapture on the terraced rice fields, the palm and bamboo groves, the forested hills riven by rocky gorges, silvery streams and feathery waterfalls. Equally entrancing were the jewelled creatures of the air: opalescent bee-eaters, crystalline sun-birds, bronze drongos, azure kingfishers red in bill and claw, lambent glow-worms three inches long and "green enamelled dragonflies" darting over pools on "wings that flash like sliced emeralds set in gold."[22] Here, in short, was a "matchless panoply of beauty and romance."[23] But the more aliens lauded the genius of the place, the more natives asserted their title to it. In about 1850 one Kandyan chief lamented its fate: "A country enslaved—a nobility falling into the depths of servility, a religion tottering under the incessant attacks, open and secret, of that patronised by our rulers."[24] He and his ilk did not wish to share their Eden.

Of course it contained mosquitoes as well as serpents—to say nothing of leeches, ticks, scorpions, millipedes, spiders, stinging flies and poison-ous caterpillars. As late as the 1930s malaria killed 100,000 people in a single epidemic and the infection had helped to destroy the medieval Sin-halese kingdom in its golden age. Nevertheless, the historic as well as the natural splendours of Ceylon gave every impetus to national pride. It was impossible to ignore the wreckage of pre-Christian Taprobane, as the Greeks and Romans had called this remote world, which they imbued with mythic purity. The ruined city of its first capital, Anuradhapura, founded a century before Rome subjugated Italy, was an awesome monu-ment to vanished greatness. It covered an area twice the size of Victorian London and on a visit in 1890 Edward Carpenter said that "it is as if Lon-don had again become a wilderness."[25] Vegetable had triumphed over mineral and the stones were split by roots, throttled by lianas and buried by undergrowth. Yet scattered in astonishing profusion were plinths, pavements, cisterns, steps, pavilions, moonstones, inscribed columns, noble statues, and carvings of monkeys, horses, geese, snakes, dragons, demons and other creatures. There were also enormous blocks of granite, some hollowed out to make elephant baths, and the remains of brick dagobas second in size only to the pyramids. British archaeologists did much to unearth these petrified records of a vanished civilisation. They also explored other impressive sites such as the palace-fortress perched on its pillar of gneiss at Sigiriya and the marshy metropolis of Polonnoruwa, where the Prince's Bath had been fed by streams flowing from the mouths of stone crocodiles. Some of the finest artefacts were preserved in the Italianate Colombo Museum,* inaugurated by Governor Sir William Gregory in 1872. Cultural relics excited political aspirations. The old patriot Ponnambalam Arunachalam wrote in his 1903 diary: "Thought much of the unhappy condition of our country and what a glorious thing it would be for Ceylon to emulate and excel her great past."[26] Having visited the lost cities of Ceylon, the young nationalist leader and future Prime Minister S. W. R. D. Bandaranaike said that its people were now like caged animals at a zoo, unaware of their captivity. "It is not right," he declared, "that a servile race should inhabit the same locality which their ancestors inhabited in power and glory."[27]

Significantly, Bandaranaike's forebears had been among the most prominent allies of the British. Sir Emerson Tennent described his loyal grandfather as "a noble specimen of the native race." And S. W. R. D. Bandaranaike's father proudly repeated this patronising encomium. He was Sir Solomon Bandaranaike, a wealthy patrician who became more English than the English. He espoused their Anglican faith, adopted their mode of dress, matched their enthusiasm for horses and dogs and outmatched them in snobbery. He would have sympathised with the member of his clan who refused to entertain Nehru because she did not eat with coolies. And he would have agreed with the critic who said that Ceylon's colonial society was "suburbia at its worst."[28] Sir Solomon trumped the British in devotion to their monarchy. His autobiography, published in 1929 when he was sixty-seven, records in numbing detail a lifetime's acquaintance with royal personages—every invitation sent, every banality exchanged, every bauble bestowed. A high point in this saga of sycophancy is his being presented with a "beautiful scarf-pin" by Edward Prince of Wales,[29] who expressed pleasure that Bandaranaike was already wearing the cuff links which his father, now King George V, had given him twenty years earlier. Sir Solomon received many other honours and titles. As Maha Mudaliyar, or Great Chief, he was a staunch supporter of successive Governors. He even named his son after one of them (West Ridgeway, who became the boy's godfather) and he frequently visited Queen's House, their colonnaded, verandahed residence in the old Dutch fort at Colombo. Other educated Ceylonese understandably deemed the Bandaranaikes (or Bandarlog, as they sometimes called themselves in homage to Kipling) "lackeys of the British, and flunkeys at the governor's 'court.'"[30]

Yet the elite also chose the way of collaboration, if not toadyism. Its chil-

---

* At the behest of a Governor of Fiji, this provided the model for a new Government House at Suva.

dren were educated at schools such as Trinity College, Kandy, where pupils were punished for not speaking English. As one wrote, they were taught to "mimic alien ways, much as the ancient Britons were Romanised under Agricola, a process they thought to be civilisation when it was actually slavery."[31] But westernised Ceylonese also learned the lessons of liberty from such instructors as Locke, Burke and Mill. By 1910 they had gained a single democratic crumb: one Ceylonese was elected to the Legislative Council. Five years later, though, an outbreak of communal violence took place in Kandy and elsewhere. It was anything but an insurrection—one District Judge treated it as a joke and suggested that the police should pepper the rioters' rumps. But the Governor, Sir Robert Chalmers, heeded hysteria about a wartime conspiracy against the Empire masterminded by a European-educated "set of skunks."[32] He succumbed to an acute "attack of treasonitis." So, with the automatic endorsement of Sir Solomon Bandaranaike, the Governor declared martial law. According to a subsequent report, this resulted in the dispatch of a posse of vigilantes "to deal with desperadoes in the manner depicted in kinema shows and dime novels of the Wild West."[33] Dozens of people were shot, some of them in cold blood, most of them entirely innocent. Before one execution a British officer declared, "You, Sinhalese, wanted to fight the Moors [i.e. Muslims] and then to fight us. Now you see what has happened. This man will be shot in ten minutes and your wives will be delivered to be ravished by the Moors."[34] Other punishments included flogging, banishment and collective fines. Hundreds were imprisoned, among them the architect of the country's independence, Don Stephen Senanayake. This "reign of terror"[35] provoked "widespread horror and consternation and a sense of rankling injustice among the Sinhalese people."[36] Chalmers's replacement tried to restore the Empire's moral reputation. He acknowledged both native loyalty and "official brutality."[37] Remarkably, too, at a time when Allied propaganda was spreading lurid stories about German atrocities, he also said that some actions had been "Hunnish in their violence and injustice."[38] However, what might have provoked revolution in Ireland or upheaval in India merely prompted calls for more reform in Ceylon.

In 1919 reform associations that had sprung up in the wake of the repression amalgamated with the new Ceylon National Congress. The CNC was not meant to resemble India's nationalist body. It was not aggressive. It was not a mass movement but the vehicle of the Anglophone elite. Its President urged his countrymen to become "Britishers first and Ceylonese afterwards."[39] The CNC was also hopelessly prone to splits, which were exploited by Governors pursuing a "policy of *divide-et-impera*."[40] Tamils,

Burghers, Kandyans and urban workers set up rival organisations during the 1920s, as did Marxists and Sinhalese chauvinists during the 1930s. Nevertheless, the CNC's members campaigned manfully for progress towards independence within the Empire, drafting addresses, presenting petitions, dispatching deputations. This polite pressure paid dividends and Governors included more Ceylonese representatives in their Councils. But they then found it hard to work with the likes of D. S. Senanayake, who robustly undermined the myth of European superiority. So the system had to change again and in 1927 the President of Congress declared that they had reached the borders of the Promised Land. That year the British appointed a Commission led by Lord Donoughmore to determine means of further constitutional reform. Unlike the Simon Commission in India, it was warmly received. And its Report was correspondingly "revolutionary,"[41] so much so that Lord Donoughmore was compared to Lord Durham. This was not because he recommended a form of dyarchy, whereby the Governor would rule with the aid of a Ceylonese-dominated State Council. It was because this Council would be elected by universal suffrage. Britain itself had only just given all adults the vote and in 1931 Ceylon became the first Asian and colonial nation to do the same. The Ceylon plantocracy was appalled. One Governor called its old-fashioned leaders "Rip van Winkles" for they continued to dismiss brown people as children and they were quite capable of smashing an official's umbrella because "it was impudent for a native to carry one in the face of a European." Ironically, Congress was no less shocked by Donoughmore's new franchise. It was carrying democracy too far. Members opposed it because they believed that self-government was government by themselves.

As it happened a deferential people, nearly 90 per cent living in rural poverty, 60 per cent unable to read and less than 30 per cent casting their vote, duly endorsed its elite at the polls. But the Governor remained in command, with wide powers and control, through three appointed ministers, over justice, finance, defence and foreign policy. However, the State Council elected seven Ceylonese ministers, who were in charge of health, education, agriculture, communications and so on. One said that the country had thus achieved seven-tenths of self-rule and they expected it to advance swiftly to complete independence. The British, though, likened Ceylon to other colonies where constitutional progress had stalled—Jamaica, Malta, Cyprus, British Guiana—and they regarded the Donoughmore constitution as a fixture. Actually it taught Ceylonese ministers to govern and demonstrated that the art was not a European monopoly. No one mastered it more completely than Senanayake, the Minister of Agriculture. A tall, bulky landowner with a bristling moustache, he was neither clever nor well educated. Sir Andrew Caldecott, Governor from 1937 to 1944, wrote that Senanayake's "scope of vision is no less limited than his power of expression" and described him as a "village bully" and a "mud-buffalo."[42] But the British valued intellect less than character, which Senanayake possessed in abundance. Viscount Soulbury said that he resembled "the best type of English country-gentleman, able, shrewd, practical, good-humoured, kindly, modest."[43] Senanayake ruled his department with a rod of iron, tackling drought and famine, expanding cultivation in the dry zone and providing Crown lands for the rural poor at the expense of British interests. The planters, who rejoiced in names such as the Kelani Valley Boys and the Merry Men of Uva, hated him with undisguised passion.

To be sure, Senanayake was an ambitious man. He once said that to succeed in Ceylonese politics one had to be a Buddhist, which meant that he had been obliged to give up his two favourite recreations, hunting and beer. But he was a model of probity compared to his most brilliant rival, S. W. R. D. Bandaranaike, who actually became (in Caldecott's words) "a pervert for political purposes from Christianity to Buddhism."[44] Bandaranaike loved to parade his spiritual emancipation, once suggesting to the Bishop of Colombo that the Christian God should "give up the privileged position of an English gentleman and become a brown and simple Sinhalese villager."[45] In public Bandaranaike also adopted a somewhat spurious national costume, whereas at home he relaxed in trousers and shirts—though he had his riding breeches made of homespun cloth. Sir Solomon condemned his sartorial treachery; an amusing photograph shows the father looking furious in a morning suit complete with spats and grey felt gloves, while the rebellious son wears a white *dhoti,* toga, shawl and sandals. But it was clear that the young Bandaranaike, who had been the star orator of his day at the Oxford Union, dressed, as he spoke, for effect. He had boundless faith in his own greatness and had early adopted the Latin motto *"Primus aut Nullus"* ("First or Nothing"), but he changed his mind as often as he changed his clothes. He first espoused western ideals, then preached the gospel according to Gandhi, next stoked up Sinhalese antagonism towards the Tamils. In 1941 he advocated "bloody revolution" against the British,[46] for which the Governor slapped him down effectively. For all his eloquence, therefore, the imperious and mercurial Bandaranaike was widely distrusted. When the Second World War began it was the solid, unpretentious Senanayake who emerged as the unchallenged leader of Congress. Even though he wore a sarong at home and a suit, often with an orchid in its buttonhole, to work, he could never have been lampooned, in the way that

Bandaranaike was, as a British–Sinhalese hybrid. On the contrary, Senanayake was already being seen as the founder of a new nation.

The war both delayed and secured its foundation. Churchill tried to block progress for the duration and the Colonial Office made a virtue of procrastination. Yet Caldecott himself urged that Ceylon's full-hearted assistance with the war effort should be encouraged and rewarded. In any case, he argued, the country's nationalism could no more be checked than "the waves which wetted Canute." The tidal flow, he noted, came from England. A sentence in Sir Norman Angell's Overseas League pamphlet *What is the British Empire?* seemed to promise the freedom that was denied, thus stirring up passions throughout Ceylon: "We have done our best to unconquer our conquests; disannex our annexations; turn what was originally an empire into a group of sovereign nations; indeed the empire, so far as most of it is concerned, long since came to an end."[47]

There were signs that the Empire was reaching a terminal state in Ceylon. Since 1937 no European had been appointed to the Civil Service and Ceylonese were widely promoted to other professional jobs, an essential part of "nation-building."[48] In 1942 ministers became, in effect, the Governor's cabinet. This reflected the country's vital new strategic and economic role. After the fall of Malaya, Ceylon was in the front line against Japan and it produced nearly two-thirds of the Allies' rubber, slaughter-tapping the trees to meet their needs. Admiral Sir Geoffrey Layton, who became Commander-in-Chief of the island in March 1942, was a crusty old salt with a "rough, tough quarterdeck manner, like one of Nelson's captains."[49] He seemed bound to offend and, indeed, he immediately had a blazing row with Senanayake. But they soon became friends and Layton rapidly endorsed Caldecott's view that Ceylon should receive concessions in return for cooperation. In May 1943, after dragging their feet unconscionably, the British undertook to introduce full internal self-government when hostilities ceased.

A further Commission, led by Lord Soulbury, confirmed this offer in 1945. It naturally failed to satisfy the Ceylonese, who wanted control over defence and foreign policy as well. Senanayake told the Colonial Office that his country was "like a cow tied to a tree with a rope. A longer rope was better than a shorter one, but still the restriction remained."[50] This was a compelling image. But Senanayake used the Vice-Chancellor of Ceylon University, Ivor Jennings, to make a more sophisticated case. Jennings contended that Ceylon, then the most prosperous nation in Asia, was qualified for dominion status as Britain's premier colony. He also drafted a Westminster-style constitution that attempted to protect Ceylon's minorities. "Lack of responsibility encouraged irresponsibility,"[51] Jennings warned, and unless responsible government were granted soon Ceylon would become like India in its hostility to Britain. But instead of demanding, or threatening in the manner of Aung San, Senanayake accepted the Soulbury scheme as a bridge to liberty. Soulbury himself, along with the new Governor, Sir Henry Moore, helped Ceylon to cross it. Moore told the Colonial Office that it had a "golden opportunity, by the exercise of a little courage now, of making a generous and spontaneous gesture to Ceylon." Soulbury said that its people resembled the Irish and that it would be "a tragedy to repeat in Ceylon the colossal mistakes we have made in Ireland." He believed that Ceylon's loyalty to the Crown must be secured and, he pronounced sagely, "giving too much too soon will prove to be wiser than giving too little too late."[52]

The Colonial Office itself was impressed by Senanayake's strength of character, sincerity of purpose and hostility to Communism. Officials had expected a slick politician and they warmed to "a rugged farmer with a sense of humour."[53] But none of this might have sufficed if Aung San had not made the case for him. The argument was quite simple: Britain could hardly grant full independence to Burma, thus rewarding a nation that had fought for Japan, while denying it to Ceylon, thus punishing a nation that had remained loyal to the Allies. The Labour Colonial Secretary, Arthur Creech Jones, accepted this logic but feared accusations that he was "squandering the Empire."[54] So he maintained that Ceylon, politically stable and strategically vital, was a "special case." It was not being lost as a result of ad hoc decision-making, he speciously asserted, it was being added to the Commonwealth in fulfilment of a long-term development plan. More sincerely Creech Jones claimed that Ceylon's membership would demonstrate that dominion status was not restricted to whites. The Colonial Office hoped it would also show that the day of the British Empire was not done, that the Commonwealth was no "mere afterglow following sunset, ending in night."[55] On the contrary, it was a means of retaining a British presence without having to bear the burdens of command. It was a union of hearts, as long ago foreshadowed in the Durham Report. Socialist ministers argued the case aggressively: "If Churchill were in power, he would lose the Empire, just as George III lost the thirteen colonies. The aim of Labour is to save the Empire; this will be achieved by giving the colonies self-government."[56] So, having followed the primrose path of negotiation, Senanayake was able to lead his country to freedom. Early on 4 February 1948, wrote a Ceylonese newspaper, bells pealed and drums sounded to wake its people from their "slumber of servitude."[57]

. . .

In Malaya the people, often deemed by their alien masters to be soft and indolent, had apparently enjoyed that slumber before the Second World War. Here, as in Ceylon, society was held together by deference, but the British adroitly allied themselves to the Malayan upper crust. Colonial officials ruled while local royalty reigned and both fostered "the myth that the Sultans were still independent." Thus they upheld traditions of loyalty among the predominantly rural Malays, while the Chinese (about half the five million population) supported the imperial power that protected them. The largest Malayan nationalist organisation between the wars, the *Sahabat Pena,* or "Friends of the Pen," began as a correspondence column in the children's pages of a newspaper and remained as callow as its origin suggests. Malaya's well-being seemed to depend chiefly on playing an English game. As one journalist wrote, "To stop football would be like destroying the medicine of the people." Nevertheless, pressure for political change was bubbling beneath the surface. Islamic reformers, vernacular teachers and a minuscule English-educated elite all contributed to the growth of "nationalist feeling."[58] So did a new corps of professional pressmen. They drew attention to the advance of the English language and the erosion of Malay culture: "Bedsteads replace mats; and the custom of the people is no longer to sit cross-legged but many rent tables and chairs."[59] Radical influences spread from China and Chinese Communists in Malaya formed a "League against Imperialism." Economic competition between peasant Malays and entrepreneurial Chinese fed communal antagonism. Then Japanese infantry on bicycles conquered Malaya in 1941–2 as swiftly as German panzers had conquered France in 1940, destroying the legend of European supremacy at a stroke. The soldiers of Nippon gave an incomparable stimulus to Asian pride, not only by their boldness and vigour but by their unrivalled capacity for self-sacrifice. One Malay wrote, "The British fought in order to live, the Japanese in order to die."[60]

When contemplating the cosmic impact of Nippon on Britain's Empire, Franklin D. Roosevelt mused: "It almost seems that the Japs were a necessary evil in order to break down the old colonial system."[61] Yet although the Japanese fatally undermined British standing in Asia, they did little to promote Malayan independence apart from briefly patronising Ibrahim Yaacob's Young Malay Union, the rough equivalent to Aung San's Burma Independence Army. Indeed, the main achievement of the invaders, who predictably posed as liberators, was to destroy. They wrecked Malaya's economy, cutting off its export markets and wiping out its currency. They monopolised the rice harvest, causing widespread malnutrition and disease. They behaved so brutally to their forced labourers that nearly a third of them died. They divided the races, treating Malays and Indians less harshly than Chinese, whom they tortured and decapitated freely, decorating bridges over the Singapore River with severed heads. Most members of all races cooperated with their new masters on pain of death, but most members of the resistance were Chinese. Supplied with Allied arms, inspired by Communist beliefs and assisted by aboriginal hill tribes *(Orang Asli)*, the Malayan Peoples' Anti-Japanese Army (MPAJA) fought a savage jungle war. Anticipating subsequent British tactics, the Japanese tried to isolate the guerrillas from those who might help them. They herded Chinese squatters—unemployed workers and urban refugees scratching subsistence from the forest fringe—into "fortress villages."[62] But with astonishing suddenness, on 15 August 1945, the Emperor Hirohito announced his country's capitulation, saying that the war "had developed not necessarily to Japan's advantage."[63] Since Nippon surrendered before Mountbatten's forces could invade, the Communists claimed that theirs was the victory. They often raised the three-starred emblem of the MPAJA next to the hammer and sickle.

In the weeks after the war guerrillas, gaunt and deathly pale from their years in the jungle, emerged to bask in the glory of their triumph and to wreak vengeance on those who had helped their foes. They executed thousands, condemning some in kangaroo courts, lynching others out of hand and killing still more indiscriminately. They butchered men, raped women and bayoneted babies. A "Whispering Terror" convulsed Singapore, where hushed words snuffed out the lives of many supposed traitors, informers and collaborators. Policemen, denounced as the running dogs of fascism, came in for particular brutality—their eyes were gouged out and their bodies mutilated. "It was a world gone mad," said one sergeant, "a world turned upside down."[64] Malays, the main victims of these atrocities, duly retaliated. They carried out village massacres, matching their persecutors in ferocity. Islamic holy warriors in red sashes added to the carnage, cutting up the heathen, pork-eating Chinese with their long knives—the *kris, lembing, pedang* and *tombak*. At a time of shortages amounting to famine in some districts, when plundering and profiteering put further strains on the country's social fabric, ethnic communities also divided against themselves. They were torn by leadership rivalries and ideological feuds, rent by Triad gangsters, millenarian Sufis and labour militants. To contain this anarchy the British at first had to employ Japanese troops, delaying their repatriation—a vast operation, involving six million people throughout South-East Asia, thoughtfully code-named "Nipoff."[65] Nevertheless, the British proposed an imperial restoration. The Singapore debacle had by no means shattered their confidence: fearing that the Japanese would melt down Malaya's coins for their metal during the war, they actually manufactured replacements in London. Ironically, since Malaya was the Royal Mint's source of supply, the fifty million one-cent pieces contained "only the barest trace of tin."[66] During the war, too, the Colonial Office worked out plans for Malaya's future constitution on the inestimable basis of complete ignorance about its current situation.

Their scheme was to establish a Malayan Union with the long-term aim that the united states (plus Malacca and Penang but not Singapore, which would become a crown colony and a free port) should evolve into a South-East Asian dominion. Their immediate purpose was to impose direct rule in order to carry out two—sharply divergent—policies. First, in the spirit of Attlee's Socialist government, they tried to introduce a progressive form of imperialism. By improving education, health and welfare, they hoped to win the allegiance of a unified people and to persuade other countries (especially America) that the Empire was a force for good. Secondly, the British aimed to exploit Malaya during the post-war balance of payments crisis. Malaya was, as Creech Jones said, "by far the most important source of dollars in the Colonial Empire."[67] Its rubber alone earned more hard currency than all Britain's domestic exports to America. The prospect of bankruptcy hardened Britain's resolve to profit from its Empire, especially in view of the impending loss of India, Burma and Ceylon. It is true that, as one historian has written, "Colonialism and capitalism were never married." Yet they sometimes conducted a liaison. This was especially the case during the "second colonial occupation"[68] of Malaya. So Britain's relative economic decline actually postponed its imperial fall in the Orient.

Nevertheless, the contradictions of British policy finally undermined its regime in Malaya. Liberal principles invariably gave way to the imperatives of coercion. For example, trade union militants were tolerated in theory but deported in practice. The post-war British Military Administration (BMA) talked the language of liberation, but it was not only inept and corrupt (nicknamed the Black Market Administration), but so overbearing that Malayans were generally antagonised. The official sent to lay the foundation for the strong central government that would take its place in 1946 was Sir Harold MacMichael, who had become even more arrogant since his days in the Sudan. Like other old imperial hands, he tried to enhance his own standing on the grounds that he could thus better impress the natives. Before his departure he demanded an honour, a resounding title, a warship for transport—"the larger the better"—and a "large size" saloon car to waft him round the country.[69] Once there he intimidated and cajoled the nine sultans into signing away their sovereignty so that their states could be consolidated into the Union. The Sultan of Kedah was particularly stubborn, though MacMichael dismissed him as a "small, shy and retiring 'failed B.A.' type."[70] The envoy used methods that the Sultan himself likened to "the familiar Japanese technique of bullying."[71] A menacing question secured the royal compliance: "Perhaps Your Excellency would prefer to return to your friends in Siam?"[72] Malays, who revered the sultans as quasi-divine beings, protested at their involuntary abdication. They also denounced the grant of citizenship to Chinese, Indians and others. Far from ushering in an enlightened new administration, MacMichael seemed to have entrenched the old imperialism of order and obey. Moreover, he incensed Britain's traditional allies, the sultans' Malay subjects. In May 1946 Dato Onn bin Jafar, chief minister of Johore, founded the United Malays National Organisation (UMNO), the country's first major political movement. Onn was a charismatic but erratic aristocrat, bold, astute, flamboyant and ambitious. No one played a more important role in forcing the British to stifle the Malayan Union at birth.

Dato Onn mobilised Malays, women as well as men, from top to bottom of society. He persuaded sultans to boycott the inauguration of the new Governor, Sir Edward Gent. This was "an unprecedented discourtesy"[73] made still more offensive when the sultans greeted cheering supporters outside their Kuala Lumpur hotel, many of them dressed in ceremonial mourning clothes. Onn exploited fears over the prospect of Chinese domination, fears that mustered tens of thousands of Malays to declare that "this is *our* country."[74] But the struggle over the Malayan Union was only one element in the continuing turmoil. Crime, disease and hunger were still rife—children aged ten looked as if they were six and some adults resembled victims of Belsen. Faction fighting within communities persisted, notably between the followers of Mao Tse-tung and Chiang Kai-shek. Government attempts to control agriculture and preserve the forests produced a violent reaction. In 1946 two million days' work were lost in strikes resulting from official attempts to hold wages down at a time of spiralling prices. Malayans generally kicked against growing state intervention. They protested about restrictions on the use of water and electricity, the regulation of printers and hawkers, new imposts such as income tax, a "tax on amusement, a licence fee for the rearing of dogs." All told, the British were intruding into their lives, one newspaper claimed, "even more comprehensively and minutely than Mayor Odate of the Syonan regime."[75]

Gent soon decided that there was a "serious likelihood of organised and widespread non-cooperation and disorder."[76] The country was evidently becoming ungovernable. So although he was one of the chief begetters of the Malayan Union, the Governor now advocated its demise. It was therefore replaced in 1948 by a Malayan Federation which gave Onn, who had been consulted this time, most of what he wanted. The sultans returned to their thrones. Chinese citizenship was curtailed. Gent was transmogrified from Governor to High Commissioner. His accommodation with UMNO was understandable. It is true that Onn exploited his countrymen's propensity towards xenophobia, embodied in his slogan "Malaya for the Malays," and that he denounced the predatory British, colloquially known as *lintah puteh*, white leeches. Nevertheless, he was a conservative who did not mind working with them. By contrast, many Chinese saw the Federation as flagrant treachery. The Communists were particularly enraged, having fought against Nippon and afterwards followed the path of agitation rather than revolution. In fact their post-war tameness stemmed largely from the fact that the leader of the Malayan Communist Party (MCP), Lai Tek, was a serial traitor who had sold out to the British. The faithful had long worshipped him as "a mysterious 'hero' and a man of superhuman ability"[77] who could fly planes, drive tanks and elude arrest. So his exposure as a double agent (who added insult to injury by absconding with the party's funds) discredited his peaceful policy. In 1948 the MCP, under its Maoist new leader Chin Peng, determined to overthrow the fascist imperialists, "whose outrages are the same as those of the Japanese."[78] Aiming to seize power, they embarked on an armed struggle.

Young and inexperienced, Chin Peng could only mobilise four thousand guerrillas, few of whom knew much about jungle warfare—some set off in clogs rather than boots. So his campaign made a poor start. It began with sporadic attacks on mines and plantations in outlying districts where, ever since the war, "the gun and the knife had held sway."[79] When three white planters were killed in June 1948 Gent declared a state of emergency. This gave the police wide powers of search, arrest, detention, deportation and confiscation. Europeans, especially those in the front line, were not satisfied. Many wanted martial law, some advocated public hanging. Their complaints about Gent were summed up in a famous newspaper headline, "Govern or Get Out."[80] Malcolm MacDonald, son of the first Labour Prime Minister and the Colonial Office's roving Commissioner-General in South-East Asia, clinched the matter. "A natty little man who dressed rather loudly"[81] and sat in his Rolls-Royce like an orchid wrapped in cellophane, he identified the Communist threat and thought it required a more determined opponent. So Gent was summoned home, dying en route in an air crash, to be replaced by the suave and aloof Sir Henry Gurney. He was a diplomat of the old school. But he had supposedly learned new tricks while combating terrorists in the Holy Land, where his unruffled calm in the midst of crisis had infuriated Jewish leaders such as Golda Meir. The new High Commissioner received reinforcements, including policemen from Palestine and fresh troops, many of them raw recruits—virgin soldiers. They helped to turn the military "sweeps" (assisted by futile RAF bombing raids) that had begun before Gurney's arrival into a vicious and self-defeating campaign of counter-terror.

The security forces found it hard to capture or kill the so-called "bandits," who soon became adept at butcher-and-bolt tactics. Their small "Blood and Steel" units were especially elusive. These mobile murder squads committed terrible atrocities such as disembowelling their victims, and then vanished into bamboo and palm-thatch encampments in the jungle. So army patrols vented their fury on Chinese squatter communities suspected of feeding the guerrillas. Many were doing so, sometimes under duress, sometimes voluntarily in response to appeals from ten thousand plain-clothes Communist auxiliaries known as the *Min Yuen* (People's Movement). Policemen who had served in Palestine operated along the lines of the Black and Tans. Empire soldiers interrogated suspects under torture. They shot or lynched those found guilty. They burned villages and uprooted their inhabitants. In December 1948 Scots Guards murdered at least twenty-four Chinese at Batang Kali in Selangor, claiming that they were trying to escape. Gurney hushed up the incident though two decades later it leaked out, described in the press as Britain's own My Lai massacre. But the High Commissioner acknowledged privately that "the police and the army are breaking the law every day." He apparently had no scruples about this, for he reckoned that the Chinese were "inclined to lean towards whichever side frightens them more and at the moment this seems to be the Government." He was mistaken. Many Chinese thought that the British were behaving worse than the Japanese. And this inclined them to support, even to join, their revolutionary compatriots who supposedly preferred "to woo rather than to murder."[82]

By 1950 the Communists seemed to be getting the upper hand, but Malaya found salvation through Korea. Hostilities began there in June. At the same time General Harold Briggs initiated his campaign to deny Chin Peng's guerrillas aid by resettling hundreds of thousands of Chinese squatters in fortified villages—he likened this method of defeating Communism to eradicating malaria by depriving mosquitoes of their breeding grounds. The two Asian conflicts were closely connected. For the Korean War dramatically raised the price of rubber and tin, thus enabling the British to pay for this vast feat of social engineering. It was also possible to evict the Chinese without undue difficulty. They hated being torn from their homes, smallholdings, fishponds, poultry and pigs. They loathed the new settlements which, a few model villages apart, were insalubrious slums situated on wasteland. They detested the barbed wire and searchlights, the curfews and food searches, the continuing insecurity, the inadequate schools and health care. They also resented the petty regulations, over carrying identity cards, for example, that gave ample scope for extortion by corrupt policemen and officials. However, thanks to the boom, amenities gradually improved. More important, the Chinese found compensation in high wages and full employment. They also found it increasingly hard to deliver supplies to the "bandits," who were now renamed "Communist Terrorists."

The term had international resonance. London worried about whether Washington would perceive it as "waging a valiant struggle against Communism or as fighting a dirty little colonial war designed to hang on to sterling balances."[83] Attlee had shocked transatlantic opinion by recognising Red China, but he promised self-government to Malaya and spent enough blood and treasure there to convince America that Britain was a sound ally in the Cold War. As it happened, 1951 was the worst year of the emergency. More than a thousand civilians and members of the security forces were killed. Among the casualties was Gurney himself, shot in an ambush, almost the last British colonial Governor to be killed on duty. Yet the policy of concentrating the squatters was beginning to work. It extended to displacing many of the eighty thousand *Orang Asli*, caught up in a conflict which destroyed some 10 per cent of these "confused and traumatised people,"[84] most of them from disease caused by confinement. The guerrillas faced starvation. They hunted everything from wild boar to monkeys, from rats to elephants. They devoured grassy reeds, bamboo shoots and boiled rubber leaves. They even explored the possibility of making rubber seeds edible, but Peking assured Chin Peng that they contained an ineradicable toxin. He concluded that food was "our Achilles' heel."[85]

Chin Peng retreated the better to advance, hiding deeper in the jungle and focusing more on sabotage and the infiltration of trade unions. But although the British knew of this strategic shift, they failed to realise the precariousness of his position. Determined to avoid another defeat like that of 1942, Winston Churchill, now back in Downing Street, personally appointed General Sir Gerald Templer to succeed Gurney. "You must have power—absolute power—civil and military power," the Prime Minister told him. "And when you've got it grasp it, grasp it firmly. And then never use it. Be cunning—very cunning. That's what you've got to be."[86] Templer is generally reckoned to have obeyed Churchill's exhortation to the letter, defeating the Communists by winning the battle for Malayan "hearts and minds"—an expression attributed to him. In the process, it is said, he built a nation that was fit for self-government within the Commonwealth. This was now the Tory policy, as explained by the new Colonial Secretary, Oliver Lyttelton.

> Fifty million islanders shorn of so much of their economic power can no longer by themselves expect to hold dominion over palm and pine on the nineteenth century model . . . which made us the greatest nation in the world. We may regain our pinnacle of fame and power by the pursuit of this new policy.[87]

Certainly Templer shocked Europeans by treating Malayans with a novel respect. Against official advice, he shook hands with the servants at his official residence in Kuala Lumpur, King's House. He offended the city's Rotarians by saying that Chinese Communists seldom threw cocktail parties or went to the races and "they don't play golf."[88] When the Lake Club barred the Sultan of Selangor from a function Templer forced it to elect a new committee, which admitted Asians as guests, though they could not become members until after independence. Templer even took to eating durians in the garage with his Malay ADC—he had a tigerish passion for this exotic fruit, which his wife banned from the house since it smelt like "rotten melon and onions" or "custard passed through a gas main."[89]

 Yet Templer was essentially conventional though, like his mentor Field-Marshal Montgomery, he made an electrifying impact. He looked like a standard senior officer, spare-framed, stiff-backed and lean-faced, with a late-imperial moustache "so thin as to be barely perceptible"[90]—a contrast to growths still favoured by the sultans, which resembled black buffalo horns "dropped in the manner of the handlebars of a racing bicycle."[91] But Templer was not afraid of his superiors, later literally coming to blows with the Defence Minister Duncan Sandys. And he galvanised his subordinates, not least by his habit of stubbing out his cigarettes in their sherry glasses. In a high-pitched voice Templer discharged staccato sentences pungent with profanity and driven home with prods of his swagger stick. Dynamic and dogmatic, he was also surprisingly lucid—as his police chief said, "somehow one expects a soldier to be dumb."[92] Templer whirled round the country, sacked incompetents, improved intelligence and raised morale. He so ameliorated conditions in the Chinese "resettlement areas," changing their name to "New Villages," that one or two were compared to holiday camps instead of concentration camps.

He gave huge rewards to informers and defectors. He employed more armoured cars to avert ambushes and helicopters to carry out lightning raids. He cranked up the propaganda war, using radio, mobile cinemas and loudspeaker aircraft—the citizens of Kuala Lumpur were startled to hear a silvery female voice from the clouds announcing in Chinese, "World Communism is Doomed."[93] Templer also distributed millions of leaflets, among them ninety thousand coronation pictures of Queen Elizabeth II. And although he encouraged Malayan culture, he seemed to think that the nation could be saved by the spread of Women's Institutes and youth movements—he enthused about jamborees and often wore a Scout uniform himself. He literally tried to drum up loyalty with the band of the Coldstream Guards, though he was told that the Chinese "worship noise rather than harmony."[94] Templer was crass and unsophisticated as well as energetic and ruthless. He despised anything academic. He distrusted men who used hair oil. At King's House, a kind of mock-Tudor cricket pavilion complete with flagstaff, he enjoyed dancing the conga. But every time he led the dancers round a sentry saluted and the whole place was surrounded by barbed wire—so much so that the press quipped, "The High Commissioner has resettled himself."

The barbed wire was an apt symbol of Templer's rule, for his capture of Malayan hearts and minds is something of a myth. It is true that he successfully employed persuasion; but he relied more heavily on coercion. Even admirers acknowledged that he presided over "a police state."[95] Critics claimed that there was "no human activity from the cradle to the grave that the police did not superintend." Templer imposed "totalitarian" restrictions on the New Villages. He berated communities violently and punished them collectively. He conscripted Chinese into the police force, such an affront that it gained more recruits for the MCP than for the police. The state of his prisons was reported to be "WORSE than that experienced by internees under [the] Jap regime."[96] He had few scruples about the tactics adopted in jungle warfare, even employing early chemical weapons such as defoliants. According to Chin Peng, "If anyone employed terrorist measures, he did."[97] Certainly Templer gave free rein to his forces, among them Gurkhas, Dyak head-hunters and Fijians descended from cannibals, some of whom claimed to be Scots "by absorption."[98]

This led, in the spring of 1952, to a scandal. The *Daily Worker* published a series of trophy photographs, the most notorious featuring a smiling Royal

Marine Commando holding up two severed Chinese heads, one of them female. After first denouncing the pictures as fakes, the government acknowledged their authenticity. Whitehall privately admitted, too, that they would have been evidence of war crimes had not the Malayan conflict been a mere emergency—one reason for keeping it so. But Templer was unabashed by the revelations. He said that guerrilla fighting was a nasty business and that decapitation was necessary for identification. The practice ceased but harsh measures continued. In 1956 the Director of Operations said that "in spite of a sullenly hostile population, we are making very good military progress by screwing down the people in the strongest and sternest manner."[99]

By then the Communists were facing defeat. Hundreds had surrendered and the so-called "White Areas," purged of insurgents and freed from restrictions, were expanding. Planters, of whom 7 per cent had lost their lives, could now move freely through most of the country's three thousand rubber estates. Chin Peng had retreated into Thailand and even sued for peace though his terms, notably that the MCP should be legalised, were rejected. But although Malaya witnessed one of the last great imperial struggles undertaken by the British, it was not their strength so much as guerrilla weakness that led to the collapse of the uprising. Chin Peng only drew support from a minority of Chinese, themselves divided into competing communities, some of which, such as long-established, English-speaking immigrants, remained fiercely loyal to the Crown. Almost all Malays were hostile to the Communists, not least because their own *kampongs* languished in poverty while the state spent money on the Chinese New Villages. Malay farmers or fishermen sometimes butchered armed guerrillas who strayed into their territory.

Meanwhile, a political alliance between Malays, Chinese and Indians looked set to bring about peaceful *Merdeka* (Independence) for Malaya, thus making revolution redundant. This inter-racial accord was a surprise. Dato Onn had not only failed to turn UMNO into a national party that could succeed the British but, after resigning as leader, he had also failed to create such a party himself. But his successor as head of UMNO, Tunku Abdul Rahman, the brother of the Sultan of Kedah, possessed more finesse. First insisting that UMNO was a Malay and Muslim organisation, he achieved a rapprochement with the Malayan Chinese Association and the Malayan Indian Congress. The Alliance built on its success in local polls and in 1955 it won a landslide victory in the election for the Federal Legislative Council. This demonstration of national unity was irresistible, though it did not convince everyone. Asked how long Britain would stay in Malaya, a visiting Tory MP, Robert Boothby, replied: "A thousand years."[100]

In fact the British were stampeded into granting *Merdeka* as early as 1957. They had announced their intention of going when the emergency ended (which did not happen until 1960). And they were reluctant to cede command to the Tunku (or Prince), regarding him as a quicksilver combination of western playboy and oriental despot. He was notorious for dancing, horse-racing, driving fast cars and getting into tight corners with loose women. So anglicised as to lack fluency in Malay, he displayed on official business a "general air of mild befuddlement."[101] Yet he also gave the impression of aiming to create an "old-fashioned Muslim dictatorship."[102] The British feared that he would then deal ruthlessly with other members of the Alliance, especially the Chinese, whose leader was "in the unenviable position of the young lady of Riga."[103]

As it happened, the Tunku proved to be a moderate politician who understood the need for communal harmony. In any case the British were bound by their principles to heed the voice of democracy. Moreover, handing over to the Tunku might well serve their interests. They would retain a dominant share in Malaya's economy, itself less crucial because synthetic rubber was being produced at home, where capital might be more profitably invested. They would also keep a military presence in the region. London took responsibility for the defence of Malaya and then of Malaysia—the confederation of former colonies, Malaya, Singapore, Sarawak and North Borneo (Sabah), created in the early 1960s. Even with American help, though, Britain could not afford to sustain this role for long. Its day as an eastern power was done. After quitting India, it had recoiled from Burma under threat of main force. It had left Ceylon when liberal logic dictated. It departed from Malaya sadly, reluctantly and in some disarray, its pace determined by Chin Peng's retreat and Tunku Abdul Rahman's advance. Britain was intent on making a dignified exit not just to contrast with the French defeat at Dien Bien Phu in 1954 but to compensate for the disastrous invasion of Suez in 1956—an event which Americans also saw as a victory for Communism. Britain used the Far East to restore the moral prestige it had lost in the Middle East. As a propaganda ploy it was quite successful, particularly the claim that Templer's counter-insurgency techniques had won hearts and minds, which influenced America in Vietnam. But nothing could disguise the fact that the end of empire was, as Gibbon said, a scene of desolation.

16

A Golden Bowl Full of Scorpions

The Holy Land

As the imperial legions withdrew from India, Burma and Ceylon after the war, Britain tried to shore up its ascendancy in the Middle East. In April 1945 Anthony Eden declared that the defence of the eastern Mediterranean was "a matter of life and death to the British Empire."[1] Labour's Prime Minister Clement Attlee had his doubts about this but Eden's successor as Foreign Secretary, Ernest Bevin, agreed—he was said to have dropped nothing from Eden's policies except the aitches. Bevin saw the region primarily as an oil-rich stronghold protecting African colonies which needy Britain could exploit for many years to come. The Levant, to be kept in the British sphere of influence by fresh treaties, was vital to "our position as a great Power."[2]

By this time, of course, Communism presented the gravest menace to that position, the Red Army having smashed its way to the heart of Europe. The Soviet juggernaut now threatened to roll south, towards Greece, Turkey and Persia. Ironically, the first statesman to rally anti-Communist forces was the new leader of His Majesty's loyal opposition. In 1945 Winston Churchill advocated a "United States of Europe" whereby the Continent would be conjoined "in a manner never known since the fall of the Roman Empire"[3]—a project of which Bevin would memorably remark, "If you open that Pandora's Box you never know what Trojan 'orses will jump out."[4] The following year, in his "iron curtain" speech at Fulton, Missouri, Churchill called for "a special relationship between the British Commonwealth and Empire and the United States."[5] As the Cold War began to heat up, America did indeed provide tacit support to the British Empire, giving it a brief new lease of life. In March 1947 President Truman took over Britain's role in sustaining Greece and Turkey against Stalin's thrust. This historic initiative, formulated as the Truman Doctrine, helped Bevin to exert imperial influence elsewhere in the Mediterranean and the Middle East. But that proved a frustrating endeavour, notably in Palestine, where the conflict between Jew and Arab caused a rift between London and Washington. Britain's subsequent exodus from the Holy Land would mark a further stage, and a particularly inglorious one, in the dissolution of the Empire.

Ever since the Great War, of course, Britain's contradictory pledges had bedevilled the situation in Palestine. The country had been declared the site of a national home for the Jews. But the Arabs had been assured that they would have the right to self-government. The Promised Land had been promised once too often. And it seemed that the British would only honour their word to the Jews. The League of Nations incorporated the Balfour Declaration into Britain's 1923 mandate to rule Palestine. Balfour and Lloyd George privately told Chaim Weizmann that by a national home they had "always meant an eventual Jewish state."[6] At the same time Winston Churchill secretly approved Jewish gun-running whereby an underground army, the Haganah (meaning "Defence"), was equipped: "We won't mind it, but don't speak of it."[7] Even the cosmos seemed to be on the side of the Jews, science apparently combining with religion to ensure the survival of the worthiest. Secular Zionists liked to justify their creed on Darwinian grounds. Arthur Koestler, for example, said that the Palestinian Arabs lived in "a primitive, anachronistic way which carries its own doom. To ask whether this premise is 'right' or 'wrong' is meaningless. History carries a whip in its hand, and in this case the Jews, its traditional victim, were the whip."[8]

The Old Testament also provided sanction for the ending of the second Babylonian exile and the building of a New Jerusalem. Some Christians, indeed, augured the second coming of Jesus from the return of the Chosen People to the Holy Land. Certainly they were moved by the spectacle of Jews arriving with tears of joy, songs of praise and cries of "Zion." A British policeman wrote, "There was a strange glory about this shambling procession of dirty, wan-faced people. A majesty showed in their eyes."[9] For they were marvellously fulfilling the prophecy in Chapter 11 of Isaiah:

> And it shall come to pass in that day, that the Lord shall set his hand again
> the second time to recover the remnant of his people . . . And he shall set up
> an ensign for the nations, and shall assemble the outcasts of Israel, and gather
> together the dispersed of Judah from the four corners of the earth.

No wonder David Ben-Gurion, the socialist Zionist who became first Prime Minister of Israel, declared: "The Mandate is not our Bible; rather, it is the Bible that is our mandate."[10] No wonder, too, that Jews saw the Arabs as Moses had seen the Canaanites—mere instruments in God's plan for the children of Israel.

Arabs interpreted this messianic programme as a challenge to their faith that could only be met by firm resistance, perhaps by *jihad*. They believed that the Jews aimed to establish sole possession of the Holy Land. The Chosen People could only enter into their scriptural inheritance at the expense of Muslim claims. So the Star of David must triumph over both the Crescent and the Cross. Similarly, Arabs thought, the flood of Jewish immigrants would dislodge the native peasantry from its holdings. However legally vague, the Arab title to the soil was of this world rather than the next, resting as it did on long occupation and deep attachment. To quote their ablest advocate, the Christian George Antonius, "there is no room for a second nation in a country that is already inhabited." And the League of Nations had no right to place the burden of alleviating the ills of the Jewish diaspora upon Arab Palestine. "No code of morals can justify the persecution of one people in an attempt to relieve the persecution of another."[11] The Jews amounted to 8 per cent of the population in 1918 and the Arabs maintained that Palestine "by no means consents to its mountains being converted into volcanoes spitting fire, and the waters of its Jordan being turned into blood."[12] Any significant attempt to increase Jewish immigration would spark off "an unpredictable holocaust of Arab, Jewish and British lives."[13]

The first British High Commissioner, Sir Herbert Samuel, soon found that his countrymen had completely underestimated the degree of Arab opposition to the Jewish presence. It had, he wrote, "the irritating effect of an alien body in living flesh."[14] Zionism inflamed Arab nationalism. It threatened "to reproduce in Palestine,"[15] others observed, the conditions of Ireland—"two peoples living in a small country hating each other like hell."[16] Jews from Europe often treated the "natives" with European arrogance, quickly adopting settler attitudes. But the new Zionist dispensation differed from the old colonial order. For whereas the British occupation of Palestine proposed to be temporary, the Jewish expropriation promised to be permanent. Samuel did his best to reconcile the irreconcilable communities. An Oxford-educated Liberal who thought that life was "one Balliol man after another,"[17] he was high-minded to the point of naïveté. Moreover, he had a refined aversion to autocracy, not wanting to govern a land "flowing with licensed milk and registered honey." But the Arabs could only regard him as a Zionist Jew, one whose well-trimmed black moustache "exuded a kind of military vigour and frigid aloofness."[18] In 1921 they shattered his emollient policy with riots and disturbances. Samuel therefore restricted immigration, inaugurating the first in a series of British attempts to dilute the Balfour Declaration without obviously betraying its beneficiaries. In the words of one British officer, also a Jew, their aim was "to hold the balance very evenly so as not to offend Muslim opinion which would endanger the whole Empire, or Jewish opinion either, which would raise difficulties throughout the world."[19] Incensed by what they saw as the High Commissioner's treachery, Jews called Samuel "Judas."

In fact, most British soldiers and officials sympathised with those they saw as the underdogs. The army was supposed to be neutral, said its commander in the Middle East, General Congreve, but Arabs were the "victims of an unjust policy forced upon them by the British Government."[20] The military view was summed up in a chorus sung by his troops in Jerusalem:

> And they sold the Holy City
> To the Zionist Committee.

Senior civilians echoed the sentiments if not the verse, noting that the "ancient dwellers of the land would eventually have to give place to Zionists who were backed by big financial concerns."[21] What lay behind these opinions? The pro-Zionist Colonel Meinertzhagen accused his fellow officers of "hebraphobia"[22] and there is no doubt that many were more or less anti-Semitic, including Meinertzhagen himself. G. K. Chesterton epitomised their aversion with his attack on Orthodox Jews in fur-trimmed hats and "grand but greasy robes of bronze or purple," whose ringlets prompted him to describe Jerusalem as a "fantasia for barbers."[23] But if Catholics were British, the British were catholic, in their prejudices. The Palestinian Arabs, especially townsfolk reviled as the Levantine detritus of the Ottoman Empire, were also subject to discrimination. Racist administrators abused the people in their care as "a tiresome gaggle of yids and wogs."[24] According to Leo Amery, the second-rate official was most objectionable, "the Clerk in the Telegraphs, who stands arms akimbo in the doorway of the Malta Club, just to show he is an English white man with the entrée."[25] However, in the eyes of the authorities, immigrant Jews were the least preferred. They were the *"babus"* or "mission boys" of the Holy Land. Most of them were literate and urbanised—only about 10 per cent worked on kibbutzim. Many had practical or professional skills and spoke two or more languages. They wore western clothes and appreciated European culture. Education made them unamenable to colonial discipline. This was the main charge that Lord Northcliffe levelled against refugees who were recoiling from the bondage of the ghetto. Apparently "obsessed by a nightmare of crooked hands clutching scimitars in defence of the Holy Land,"[26] he condemned "the over-pushfulness of the Zionists."[27]

The Arabs, by contrast, were clearly inured to oppression and unspoilt by civilisation. "When an Arab is dirty he is picturesque," said the wife of a British official, "when a Jew is dirty he is filthy."[28] In their 850 villages Arabs carried on a way of life apparently hallowed by the ages. For all that they worshipped Allah instead of Jehovah, it vividly conjured up scenes from the Old Testament. Their patriarchal form of existence appealed to the imagination of romantic and religious Britons. So did the oriental pageant on display in the old city of Jerusalem. This was a honey-coloured labyrinth smelling of dung and wood smoke. The din of crowing cocks, barking dogs and braying donkeys competed with the blare of commerce and the clamour of piety. Burnoused Bedouin in camel-hair cloaks and turbaned fellaheen wearing sheepskin coats and blue-and-white-striped *gallabeahs* overflowed from narrow lanes, roofed alleys and steep defiles. They rubbed shoulders with Kurdish porters bearing huge packs, effendi in scarlet fezzes and dervishes in high cylindrical hats. Ladies in black muslin veils and copious white draperies bought cucumbers from sable-robed, velvet-jacketed countrywomen with tattooed chins and lips and tinkling silver jewellery. Little Arab boys with baskets strapped to their shoulders darted between booths heaped with silk and kiosks piled with spices. Merchants in *keffiyehs* or *faisaliyehs* (brown service caps) plied their trade amid hawkers, beggars, eaters of sweetmeats, smokers of hubble-bubbles and "coffee-sellers clashing their brazen saucers."[29] This was a world that might have been conjured up by the tongue of Scheherazade. But Britons foresaw its destruction in the Jewish resurrection. If Zionists rebuilt the walls of Jerusalem, they would encompass the ruin of what was still a "Saracen city."[30]

After all, the relics of other creeds and civilisations were buried in the fabric of Jerusalem like fossils embedded in veins of rock. The ancient city, set on its rugged Judean plateau overlooking the deep blue expanse of the Dead Sea, had endured "forty sieges and destructions."[31] In their turn had come Nebuchadnezzar and Alexander the Great, Ptolemy I and Judas Maccabaeus, Pompey and Herod, Caliph Omar and the Hohenstaufen Emperor Frederick II, who indulged in the "profane thought that if Jehovah had seen the kingdom of Naples, he would never have selected Palestine for the inheritance of his chosen people." Much of the past was interred in grottoes, vaults, crypts, ossuaries and catacombs. From Golgotha to Gethsemane, above "the sacred ground of mystery and miracle,"[32] shards of every epoch testified to "the transience of religions and empires."[33] There was Hebraic limestone, Roman marble and Saracen porphyry. There were Greek arches, Persian tiles and Byzantine piers. Each victorious ruler, each triumphant priest, had sought to efface the monuments of his predecessors. Thus Titus ordered the destruction of the Temple of Solomon, a reconstructed wonder in white that the Jewish historian Josephus likened to "a mountain of snow."[34] Hadrian built a new city, raising a shrine to Jupiter on the site of Calvary and a temple to Venus over the tomb of Christ.

In due course, Constantine replaced that with the Church of the Holy Sepulchre, which itself became the focus of rivalry between Greek, Latin, Armenian, Coptic and other branches of Christianity—so much so that each seemed to worship a local deity. And where Jehovah and Jove had been venerated, Saracen caliphs erected Islamic sanctuaries, the great Al Aqsa Mosque and the sublime Dome of the Rock. The Crusaders, riding through the city "in blood up to their knees and bridle reins,"[35] made the mosque a palace and converted Omar's lustrous gem into a chapel. But the Dome was rescued by Saladin (who himself turned the Church of St. Anne into a *madrasseh*) and renovated by Suleiman the Magnificent. They and their ilk set a Muslim mark upon the face of Jerusalem. In Herbert Samuel's time it remained a medieval mosaic of towers, cupolas, minarets, pinnacles and battlements. But the dense geological encrustations, the overlaying of synagogue by temple and church by mosque, told their own story. The city was a parable in stone. Arabs became convinced that Jews aimed to recreate the Temple of Solomon on the rubble of the Dome of the Rock. As the chief Ashkenazi rabbi proclaimed in 1928, "The Holy Sanctum is consecrated to Israel for ever and it should in the end revert to Israel and the Temple be rebuilt with great splendour, as promised by the Prophet Ezekiel."[36] Once restored to its altar, the Ark of the Covenant would obliterate the footprint of Mohammed.

Until the rise of Hitler, Arabs and Jews in the Holy Land generally held their fire. Immigration was only a trickle and during the late 1920s more Jews left the country than arrived. Neither community was united. Many Jews, secular as well as religious, opposed Zionism. Feuding among rural clans and urban factions hindered the development of Arab nationalism. The British treated Palestine as a colony and ruled it with a tiny garrison. Possessing no artillery for a Remembrance Day salute on 11 November 1925, the army borrowed an ancient cannon which the Islamic authorities fired to signal the start of the fast of Ramadan. High Commissioners presided in state, first from a Kaiser-inspired "Wagnerian *schloss*"[37] on the Mount of Olives and later from a square-towered, purpose-built Government House, complete with ballroom and minstrels' gallery, on the Hill of Evil Counsel. As usual the British kept to themselves and followed their own pursuits. They hobnobbed in the exclusive Jerusalem Sports Club. They chased jackals with the pink-coated Ramleh Vale Hunt. They took picnics in Galilee where the air was limpid and the earth was carpeted with wild flowers—anemone, narcissus, cyclamen, asphodel and ranunculus. Beside the Dead Sea, with Moab rising beyond it like a wall of brass, they played on the briny, sandy nine-hole course of the Sodom and Gomorrah Golf Club, competing annually for the prize of a marble statuette known as "Lot's Wife." They kept the peace and suppressed disturbances, the bloodiest of which occurred over a dispute about the Western ("Wailing") Wall in 1929. They attended to matters like justice, health and education. They promoted agriculture, helping Jews to make the desert "blossom as the rose"[38] and assisting Arabs, who still reaped with the sickle and used asses to trample out the corn. Inspired by Lutyens's New Delhi, they even planned to build their own new Jerusalem. But if the British were making Palestine "cleaner, richer and duller," they were not making it happier, said Sir Ronald Storrs, Governor of Jerusalem and Judea. "Thou hast multiplied the harvest but not increased the joy, is my epitaph for the British Empire."[39]

Successive proconsuls failed to achieve political cooperation between Jews and Arabs, who ran parallel administrations. The Jewish Agency consolidated its hold on strategic areas, especially the coastal plain and Galilee where Jews bought land (which absentee owners sold even though thousands of their Arab tenants were evicted). From afar Weizmann guided the Agency with consummate skill, though even he could be provocative. He wrote, for example, that "the only rational answer" to dissension over the Wailing Wall was "to pour Jews into Palestine."[40] The Supreme Muslim Council was led by Haj Amin al-Husseini, whom Samuel had appointed Mufti of Jerusalem, a pre-eminent religious and legal office. Mild-mannered, soft-spoken, red-bearded and black-robed, with a white turban around his scarlet tarbush, the Mufti had the rare gift of immobility. But his impassive and dignified exterior concealed a burning ambition to maintain the Muslim majority in Palestine. Amin believed that the Balfour Declaration had stemmed from a Jewish intrigue with the British and he reminded one High Commissioner that a Jewish intrigue with the Romans had led to the judicial murder of Christ. No mean intriguer himself, the Mufti tried to destroy the Jewish national home first by treating with the British and later by embracing Muslim militants. Initially he shunned any council or congress that might give legitimacy to the Jewish presence. During the early 1930s he temporised, recognising that Arabs would dominate an elected assembly by dint of numbers. This was precisely why Weizmann and his allies rejected proposals to form such a body. All round the world Jews faced hostility from majorities in their adopted countries. It was the prime goal of Zionism that Jews in Palestine should "cease at last to lead a minority life."[41]

. . .

That goal was to be achieved as a result of the most terrible tragedy in Jewish history. As anti-Semitism became more virulent in Germany, Poland and elsewhere in Eastern Europe during the years before the Holocaust, many more of its victims sought to reach the Promised Land. After the riots of 1929, the British had made a further effort to restrict the immigration of Jews and their acquisition of acres. But the effort was not sustained thanks to Zionist protests in London, the Labour Party's sympathy for the Jews and the Foreign Office's view that repudiation of the Balfour Declaration would damage imperial prestige. So between 1933 and 1936 166,000 Jews arrived in Palestine, swelling their share of the population to more than a quarter. Tension increased accordingly. An English archaeologist observed the symptoms during a showing of the film *Ben Hur* at a cinema in Jericho. "For 'Roman' everyone read English of course," he wrote. And when the Roman officer Messala told Ben Hur that he was "a snivelling sneaking Jew" whose race would always be trodden in the dirt, Arabs in the audience shouted and stamped with glee. Jews in turn let out a "splendid seditious cheer" at Ben Hur's reply: "My afflicted nation has shaken off its other persecutors before now, and the day will come, be sure, when it will rise up and shake off the yoke of Rome."[42]

Those who now sat in the seat of Pontius Pilate faced a hideous dilemma. To keep out Jews was to condemn them to persecution, if not extermination—several years before embarking on the Final Solution, Adolf Eichmann himself told a prominent English Jew that Zionism was "the only rational solution of the Jewish question."[43] To let in Jews was to threaten the existence of the Arab community and thus antagonise the entire Muslim world. As George Antonius wrote, for Arabs the matter was "essentially one of self-preservation."[44] So it was for Jews, who were denied asylum in Britain, America and elsewhere. In 1936 their influx into Palestine crystallised Arab resistance. This took the form of attacks on Britons as well as Jews. Arab strikes, boycotts, riots, assassinations and bombings multiplied. They were met by collective punishments and acts of counter-terror, which intensified hatred for the government. The British blew up much of the old city of Jaffa in an effort to dislodge guerrillas, adding insult to injury by claiming that the destruction was part of a town-planning scheme. As unholy strife engulfed the Holy Land, a constitutional agreement became impossible. "We and they both want the same thing," said David Ben-Gurion. "We both want Palestine. And that is the fundamental conflict."[45] As a result, an official observed, there was more hatred to the square mile in Palestine than in any other country on earth. One Arab demagogue, "prying into history's cess-pits,"[46] even demonstrated British barbarity by citing the Tasmanian genocide. Christians compared the atmosphere in Jerusalem to that prevailing at the crucifixion of the Prince of Peace.

The Zionist strategy was to retain favour with the mandatory power. Ben-Gurion had assured the High Commissioner that "the Jews wanted Palestine to become a fraction of the British Empire; there alone safety lay."[47] A tiny man with a huge, craggy head, a mass of curly white hair and penetrating green-brown eyes, Ben-Gurion was a ruthless politician who spoke in "barks and grunts"[48] but knew when to dissimulate—in the first Israeli census he entered his occupation as "agricultural worker."[49] His assurance fulfilled the naïve ambition of British Zionists such as Josiah Wedgwood, who wanted to make Jews "proud to be English . . . the goal should be a 7th Dominion."[50] But what Ben-Gurion meant was that Jews would remain imperial auxiliaries until they could muster the strength to forge their own state. So instead of taking an eye for an eye, he said, they should respond to Arab provocations with restraint (havlagah). Weizmann also conciliated Britain, asserting that the Arab revolt was part of an age-old struggle between civilisation and the desert. Arabs "are a destructive element," he declared. "We build!"[51]

For pragmatic reasons Zionists even accepted the conclusion of the Royal Commission led by Lord Peel, which investigated the causes of the uprising. Among others giving Peel secret advice was that champion of the Balfour Declaration, Leo Amery, who proposed to cut "out of Palestine an 'Ulster,' a completely Arab area which should be set up as a separate Administration or attached to Trans-Jordan."[52] In 1937, deciding that Jews and Arabs were irreconcilable, the Commission duly recommended partition. Weizmann and, even more, Ben-Gurion had grave reservations about it. They were especially dissatisfied by the minuscule size of their prospective state, though Peel allotted Jews a third of Palestine when they only owned about 5 per cent of the land, and allowed for the expulsion of the Arab inhabitants, who comprised 49 per cent of the population. However, at least and at last it would be a state. It might grow from Dan to Beersheba. It might even expand, as "Revisionist" Jews such as Vladimir Jabotinsky and Menachem Begin envisaged, "from the Nile to the Euphrates."[53] The Negev Desert was not going to run away, quipped Weizmann. What mattered was the first step. This was not an end, said Ben-Gurion, but a beginning.

For that very reason the Arabs dismissed partition out of hand. In desperation they concluded that Peel's plan had to be fought. During the autumn of 1937 their rebellion, which had died down during the previous year after costing five hundred lives, once more burst into life. Although encouraged by the Mufti (who fled to Lebanon) and assisted from Iraq and Syria, it flared up from the grass roots. This was essentially a revolt of the villages, where over a fifth of Arabs were now landless and nearly all were denied employment by Jews. Their front-line irregulars, some three thousand of them, attacked buses, trains, bridges, orange groves, telephone exchanges, police posts, government offices, the oil pipeline from Iraq to Haifa, even the new airport at Lydda. They robbed banks and arsenals. Ambushes, explosions and assassinations became everyday events. The violence was unconfined. Arabs killed those deemed traitors on their own side as well as Jews and Britons. Jewish militants, members of what became known as Irgun and the Stern Gang, also murdered those deemed traitors as well as carrying out terrorist atrocities. They consciously acted in the spirit of the Sicarii during the time of Herod, so called because they carried a dagger *(sica)* under their cloaks and stabbed collaborators with Rome. They also let off bombs in the Arab markets in Haifa, the old city of Jerusalem and elsewhere. The young poet Yaacov Cohen summed up their faith: "In blood and fire Judea will be restored."[54] Like an inferno throwing off sparks, the civil war kindled battles and skirmishes throughout Palestine.

The British tried to snuff out each blaze piecemeal. But their intelligence was poor, despite the establishment of "Arab investigation centres" at which police, some recruited from the Black and Tans, tortured suspects. Finding guerrilla tactics hard to counter, they stepped up reprisals. After the bombing of a coffee bar frequented by his colleagues, one policeman wrote: "We then descended into the sook & thrashed every Arab we saw, smashed all shops & cafés, & created havoc and bloodshed . . . running over an Arab is the same as a dog in England except we do not record it."[55] Needless to say, Italian and German propaganda exaggerated the degree of British coercion, which was modest by Fascist and Nazi standards. But when the Anglican Bishop in Jerusalem complained of atrocities carried out by the army in the northern village of Bassa, the general commanding the 8th Division, Bernard Montgomery, shocked him by replying to every question: "I shall shoot them."[56]

The Colonial Secretary, William Ormsby-Gore, was driven to despair by the communal violence and he eventually wished a plague on both houses: "the Arabs are treacherous and untrustworthy, the Jews greedy and, when freed from persecution, aggressive."[57] The new High Commissioner, Sir Harold MacMichael, immaculate in his pale tussore suitings, complete with waistcoat and gold fob watch, did not improve matters. He aimed to mete out justice with an even hand, "never wavering, *never forgiving*"[58]—a concept of law derived from the Romans which was, in his view, incomprehensible both to orientals and to women. Cool and cynical as ever, he held so aloof from the fray that he earned the title "Simon Stylites." By the summer and autumn of 1938 his writ had ceased to run in much of Galilee and Judea and for a time rebels actually controlled major towns, including Bethlehem and Jerusalem. So in October MacMichael surrendered civil power to soldiers, subjecting Palestine, in all but name, to martial law.

The British Army pioneered many of the techniques which the state of Israel later employed against Arabs. These included corralling them with fences and pillboxes, attacking them from the air, raiding their villages and blowing up their houses. Sweeps, searches and arrests led to the detention of many thousands in concentration camps. Over a hundred were hanged. However, small bands of Arabs travelling after dark proved elusive. To quell them the British increased their surreptitious enlistment of volunteers from the illegal Haganah. Many of them served in Special Night Squads commanded by the so-called "Lawrence of Judea."[59] He was Captain Orde Wingate, Sir Reginald's nephew, one of the last in a long line of nonconformist heroes who made such an idiosyncratic contribution to Britain's imperial saga. A slim figure with a slight stammer, pale blue eyes and a beaky nose jutting from a bony face, Wingate converted to Zionism with all the ardour of one brought up among Plymouth Brethren. The new creed was said to devour him like an inner fire. Yet it might easily have been dismissed as a fad for the eccentricities of this violent, caustic and unkempt soldier were legion. He would massage his bare toes with a pencil at dinner and hold interviews while lying naked on a bed and combing his body hair with a toothbrush. For long periods he would eat nothing but onions. He once demanded rams' horn trumpets to blow against the walls of a hostile village, as used by Joshua against Jericho and Gideon against the hosts of Midian. However, Wingate's very peculiarities helped to make him a charismatic leader. As often as not he and his patrols beat the guerrillas at their own homicidal game. Weight of men and metal crushed them. It was clear by 1939, after a death toll of over three thousand, that the Arabs had lost the war. But in May they seemed set to win the peace.

This was because the British government, facing an imminent explosion in Europe, once again changed direction over the Holy Land. It issued a White Paper reversing the policy of partition and imposing strict limits on Jewish immigration and land purchase. It also promised an independent, Arab-dominated Palestine within ten years. Jewish Zionists were incensed, blaming the new Colonial Secretary, Malcolm MacDonald, whom they described as "so anti-Semitic as to be almost demented."[60] Weizmann himself accused MacDonald of betrayal, remarking contemptuously that "you can spit in his face and he'll say it's raining."[61] Gentile Zionists such as Churchill denounced the White Paper as a fatal capitulation to force. The policy of appeasement had spread to the Middle East. By sacrificing another small people to Nazi Germany, Ben-Gurion said, Neville Chamberlain had produced "a new edition of Munich."[62] Moreover, it followed an earlier edition, the "Jewish Munich"[63] at Evian-les-Bains the previous summer, when an international conference had barred nearly all the world's doors against the victims of pogroms. Having inflamed Arabs, the British Empire antagonised Jews. They proved a more implacable foe. The Arab revolt itself had made them "stronger and more determined."[64] The White Paper established "a virtual ghetto" in Palestine, said Ben-Gurion, and the Jews would fight it "even if their blood be shed."[65]

It was now the turn of Jews to assert, as Arabs had asserted in 1936, that their only option was to employ terrorism against the mandatory power. Zealots blasted the Law Courts in Tel Aviv and the offices of the Palestine Broadcasting Service in Jerusalem. Illegal immigration grew apace, sustaining the campaign of violence. The Gestapo initiated the exodus of Jews from Europe while the Haganah smuggled them into Palestine aboard decrepit freighters, leaky tramp steamers and stinking cattle boats, meeting British attempts to stop them with bombs and bullets. In August 1939 the Zionist Congress at Geneva encouraged Jewish belligerence. But when war broke out in Europe there was a lull in the struggle for the Holy Land. Arabs as well as Jews declared against Hitler, though both the Mufti and the Stern Gang came to favour an alliance with the Third Reich against the British Empire. The Mufti, whose assassination Churchill approved in 1940, tried to prevent transfers of Jewish children from Europe to Palestine during the Holocaust as part of the "battle against world Jewry."[66] Abraham Stern wanted Jews to wage war on Britain and "shout 'Heil Hitler' in Jerusalem."[67] Ben-Gurion condemned "Jewish Nazis," among them members of the Irgun, as "bubonic plague."[68] He famously pronounced that Jews would fight the war on Britain's side "as if there were no White Paper and fight the White Paper as if there were no war."

Ben-Gurion's injunction proved as contradictory as Balfour's Declaration. It was, as one of his colleagues said, an epigram not a programme. And it aggravated emotional turmoil among the Jews of Palestine during the war. On the one hand they yearned to strike at Nazi Germany. On the other, they ached to assail Britain for barring from Zion the pathetic few who managed to escape the clutches of Hitler. They also rioted against the so-called "Nuremberg Laws"[69] controlling Jewish land purchase. The Haganah itself was divided. Many of its fighters served with the Allies, some assisted illegal immigrants, a few did both. Occasionally they acted with British connivance, often not. On 25 November 1940, for example, Haganah agents blew up the *Patria* in Haifa Harbour to stop the British deporting 1,800 Jewish refugees to Mauritius. The explosion was apparently intended to cripple the twelve-thousand-ton vessel but it killed some 260 Jews plus about a dozen British policemen. The Jewish Agency explained the incident as a despairing act of mass suicide. This seemed plausible in view of the plight of European Jewry, which sharpened the horns of Britain's own dilemma.

Churchill and others in his government wanted to scrap the White Paper for reasons of common humanity. Duff Cooper said in New York that the Nazi atrocities imposed a moral obligation on Britain to "do more rather than less for the Jews than she ever promised or intended."[70] However, General Wavell, commanding British forces in the Middle East, warned that any concession to the Jews would, by incensing the Arabs, jeopardise his already precarious position. This was an argument that the embattled Churchill could not ignore. It became still more persuasive in 1941, when Wavell had to crush a rising in Iraq. Furthermore, MacMichael, demoralised by official vacillations, told his superiors that the Jewish Agency was exploiting the tragedy in Europe to create a state in Palestine. So the London government hardened its heart. For example, it refused to admit the 769 Romanian Jews crowded in cages on the narrow deck of the *Struma*. After a prolonged diplomatic wrangle this rusting hulk was sunk in the Black Sea on 24 February 1942 with the loss of all but two lives. Soon a poster appeared in Palestine announcing that MacMichael was "Wanted for Murder."

Escaping assassination attempts, Micmac himself finally decided that a Jewish state was desirable. As evidence accumulated about the Nazi genocide, others concluded that Jews could never be safe inside an alien society. In America, where Roosevelt had introduced Jews to high office, a Zionist Conference held at New York's Biltmore Hotel in May 1942 endorsed Ben-Gurion's resolution that "Palestine be established as a Jewish commonwealth."[71] In Britain the case for the assimilation of Jews among Gentiles, made and exemplified by Disraeli, was rebutted by his successors. In 1943 Lloyd George stated, "The revolting treatment of the Jews by the Nazis has made any other solution than a Jewish State in Palestine unthinkable." In December the following year Clement Attlee took the same view. Indeed, the Labour resolution went further, maintaining that a stable settlement required the transfer of population. "Let the Arabs be encouraged to move out," it said, "as the Jews moved in" to a Palestine that might expand across the Jordan.[72] This was too inflammatory for Ben-Gurion himself, since

Attlee seemed to confirm the worst fears of the Arabs. They would have to pay the debt Europeans owed to Jews for their suffering. Muslims would be punished for Christian sins while Jews used their moral capital to acquire *Lebensraum* in Palestine from people they treated as *Untermenschen*. The state of Israel would be atonement for the Holocaust. The Middle East would be sacrificed on the altar of imperialism to assuage the guilty conscience of the West.

Furthermore, it seemed that Attlee was bowing to force. For nearly a year the Irgun, under the leadership of Menachem Begin, had been attacking British installations. At the same time remnants of the Stern Gang were taking British lives. Their most prominent victim was Britain's Resident Minister in the Middle East, Lord Moyne, a close friend of Churchill, who became disillusioned with Zionism as a result of the murder and allowed his scheme for partitioning Palestine to lapse. Abraham Stern himself, known as "the Illuminator," or "Yair," the heroic foe of Roman oppression, had been shot by this time. But his violent spirit lived on in extremists such as Itzhak Shamir, the planner of Moyne's murder and the future Israeli Prime Minister, who saw Germany as the enemy but Britain as the arch-enemy. Nazis killed Jews but the mandatory power, like the Emperor Titus, destroyed Jewish sovereignty. Modern zealots thought that "Britain was playing the role of Titus in our age."[73] Begin glorified the role of insurrectionist: "To stand against today's Rome, the British Empire, that was about as revolutionary as one could get."[74]

The death of Moyne provoked such revulsion in Palestine, however, that the Jewish Agency made a show of cooperating with the British authorities until the end of the war. The Haganah even helped to hunt down Jewish terrorists. A few they abducted, imprisoned and brutalised themselves. Others they turned over to detectives. Begin denounced this policy as fratricide. The Haganah was Cain, subjecting its brothers to "Gestapo-like tortures in orange groves" before delivering them to the "Nazi-British secret police," whose hands were "stained with the blood of millions thrown back from the homeland's shore into the foundries of Majdanek."[75] In fact the Haganah was often settling personal and political scores, and its assistance to the British was equivocal at best. After Germany's defeat it concentrated on organising the illegal immigration of as many as possible of the million Jews remaining in Europe. Most escapees from the gas chambers, often still behind barbed wire in Displaced Persons' camps, regarded that continent as "one vast crematorium."[76] They yearned to reach the Promised Land, despite the harsh words of Ben-Gurion addressed to them. He said that their war was just beginning and that in the struggle for a Jewish state they must operate as a "political factor."[77] They were to be his moral Praetorian Guard.

The Haganah prosecuted the struggle all the more vigorously as the new Labour government at first hesitated over Zionist demands and then reneged on its previous commitments. Ernest Bevin, to whom Attlee often deferred over foreign policy, was chiefly responsible for the volte-face. A burly trade unionist with thick glasses and flashing eyes, he exuded power from every pore. In his ministry he galvanised suave diplomats and generated an "electric atmosphere."[78] Formidable in any mood, he veered between elephantine jollity and tigerish rage. Bevin had broad sympathies but his knowledge hardly extended beyond England. Asked whether he would admit that the Scots had made the Empire, he replied: "I've 'eard they made the 'ippodrome, and that's about it."[79] However, the Foreign Secretary learned from the Foreign Office. He became convinced that a Jewish state would be unjust to the Arabs, whose oil was of vital importance to Britain, and dangerous, perhaps as a Communist bridgehead, to the Middle East. Favouring the federal union of Palestine and Transjordan (itself given nominal independence in 1946), Bevin restricted Jewish immigration. This brought him into conflict with President Harry S. Truman.

Appalled by the Holocaust, the President disregarded the State Department and Roosevelt's pledges to the Arabs. Instead, lacking Arab constituents (as he acknowledged) and heeding voters "anxious for the success of Zionism,"[80] he demanded that 100,000 European Jews should be allowed into Palestine. Bevin was outraged and his gross utterances exposed him to charges of racial prejudice. To conciliate Truman, he agreed to send an Anglo-American Committee of Inquiry to Palestine but his only remark to one of its members, Richard Crossman, was to ask whether he "had been circumcised."[81] When Truman endorsed the Committee's recommendation that the 100,000 refugees should be admitted but ignored its view that Palestine should become a joint Jewish–Arab state, Bevin made his most notorious gaffe. He said that the American immigration demand had been made for "the purest of motives. They do not want too many Jews in New York."[82] Bevin's point was that Zionism often stemmed from anti-Semitism. But no remark was more calculated to reinforce American support for the Haganah, now secretly allied with the Stern Gang and the Irgun, in its assault on the British Empire.

The assault grew more violent in the spring of 1946, when Attlee refused entry to the 100,000 refugees unless the "illegal armies"[83] of Palestine were disbanded. As well as smuggling in Jews, Zionist forces had promoted strikes, riots, demonstrations and attacks. They now stepped up the offensive against the mandatory power's ships, trains, barracks, offices and officers. With one soldier to every five Jews, the British conducted extensive operations to track down arms and round up terrorists. Several thousand suspects were arbitrarily arrested through emergency regulations so draconian that observers deemed Palestine "a police state."[84] Jews made manifest their anger. They taught their children to spit at British Tommies and to scream "Nazis" and "Gestapo." Cries of "Anemone" greeted men of the 6th Airborne Division, an allusion to their distinctive red berets and their putative black hearts. The troops duly retaliated, sometimes shouting "Heil Hitler" and daubing swastikas on the walls of Jewish houses. The cycle of provocation and reprisal became more vicious. Arthur Koestler said that Britain was creating "a second Ireland in the Levant."[85]

The worst atrocity occurred on 22 July 1946 when members of the Irgun blew up Jerusalem's King David Hotel, a caravanserai so luxurious that one tourist thought it was the renovated Temple of Solomon. Such was the force of the blast that an entire corner of the building collapsed and Gerald Kennedy, the Postmaster General, was hurled across Julian's Way into the YMCA—his body had to be scraped off the wall of the recreation hall. Among the dead were forty-one Arabs, twenty-eight Britons and seventeen Jews. Then and later members of the Irgun asserted that they were "freedom fighters, of the highest moral standards."[86] But the Haganah publicly condemned the bombing which it had privately approved. Having broken the Jewish Agency's codes, the British knew that it was implicated in terrorism despite the denials of Weizmann, Ben-Gurion and others. Yet the Haganah remained ambivalent. Sometimes it helped the security forces and denounced terrorist organisations for sustaining themselves by "gangsterism, smuggling, large-scale drug traffic, armed robbery, organising the black market and thefts."[87] Anyway, the King David bombing should have won global sympathy for Britain. Instead it became a propaganda disaster, especially in America, thanks to an outburst from the army commander. General Sir Evelyn Barker ordered his troops to shun Jews and to punish them "in a way the race dislikes as much as any, by striking at their pockets and showing our contempt for them."[88]

As the mandatory power entered the last phase of its struggle to square the circle in Palestine, it was outmanoeuvred and demoralised. When the army flogged Jews the Irgun kidnapped soldiers and repaid them in kind, thus preventing further recourse to that degrading punishment. When the British barricaded their own people inside barbed-wire enclosures known as "Bevingrads," they were mocked for having rounded themselves up. Faced with electrically detonated roadside mines and booby traps disguised as steel helmets, they evacuated civilians early in 1947, only to be accused of cowardice. Even by turning Jerusalem into a fortress the British could not stop bombings. In March 1947 Begin's men smashed a lorry filled with explosives into their Officers' Club, causing twenty deaths. Despite cordons, curfews, passes, searches and collective punishments, General Barker found it impossible to paralyse the "cells of evil."[89] All tactics, indeed, from planned military crackdowns to spontaneous acts of vigilantism by exasperated troops, prompted charges of tyranny. They were also used to justify widespread sabotage and bloody revenge.

When the authorities executed terrorists, the Irgun hanged two British sergeants and booby-trapped their bodies, an action that outraged the Jewish Agency almost as much as the public in Britain, where swastikas were painted on synagogues. When the Royal Navy intercepted ships carrying illegal immigrants, most of whom were sent to Cyprus, Ben-Gurion stated that terrorism was "nourished by despair." Making an accusation echoed in the United States, he said that Britain had "proclaimed war against Zionism" and that its policy was "to liquidate the Jews as a people."[90] Nothing seemed to dramatise imperial cruelty better than the long-running saga of the *Exodus 1947*. This was the name given to a converted river steamer arrested that summer with its 4,500 Jewish passengers, who were then shipped to Hamburg. The British convoy was said to be a "floating Auschwitz,"[91] a charge on which Zionists played variations in their propaganda. When a baby died at sea they issued a statement saying "The dirty Nazi-British assassins suffocated this innocent victim with gas." As they acknowledged *sotto voce,* this "satanic lie"[92] (as one British officer called it) was aimed not at their captors but at the world's press. Such poisoned barbs weakened the resolve of the mandatory power. Ben-Gurion had rightly judged that his strongest allies were the "refugees from hell."[93]

So whereas the British had used main force to crush the Arab revolt during the late 1930s, they now had no stomach for a full-scale colonial conflict against the Jews. Other constraints hampered Bevin and his colleagues. Their own country was *in extremis.* It was afflicted by financial crises, bread rationing and fuel shortages. Power cuts had even blacked out Anglo-Jewish talks during the arctic early months of 1947, prompting one of Bevin's ponderous jokes—"there was no need for candles as they had the Israe*lites.*"[94] Yet Britain was paying £40 million a year to keep 100,000 men in Palestine. Writing to Attlee, the Chancellor of the Exchequer, Hugh Dalton, persuasively called for the nation to cut its losses:

I am quite sure that the time has almost come when we must bring our troops out of Palestine altogether. The present state of affairs is not only costly to us in man-power and money but is, as you and I agree, of no real value from the strategic point of view—you cannot in any case have a secure base on top of a wasps' nest—and it is exposing our young men, for no good purpose, to abominable experiences, and is breeding anti-Semites at a most shocking speed.[95]

The arguments for quitting India and Burma equally supported a British withdrawal from Palestine.

Disengagement there was even more desirable since Palestine divided Britain from America when they needed unity against Russia at the start of the Cold War. Moreover, after interminable plans and negotiations, Bevin concluded that he could not solve the Palestine problem despite having wagered his political future on doing so. The Arabs were weak, divided and poorly led (the Mufti having been internationally discredited by seeking support from the Axis) but they refused to give ground. The Jews were likewise intransigent, especially as Weizmann's power waned while Ben-Gurion's waxed. There were also sinister indications, among them the attempted bombing of the Colonial Office and the discovery of an Irgun explosives factory in London, that Jewish terrorists would bring the war home to their foes. In America Jews even assailed their best friend, President Truman, who exclaimed to his cabinet: "Jesus Christ couldn't please them when he was here on earth, so how could anyone expect that I would have any luck?"[96]

Throughout 1947 Britain's own fortunes faded. At the start of the year Bevin had lamented that his compatriots had lost the will and the skill to live up to their imperial responsibilities. Without the resources of the Middle East, he saw "no hope of our being able to achieve the standard of life at which we are aiming in Great Britain."[97] But having failed to find agreement with Jews or Arabs, he had referred the Palestine question to the United Nations, which succeeded to the League's authority over mandated territories. "Bevin throws in the towel," wrote Dean Acheson, the American Under-Secretary of State.[98] Actually Bevin reckoned that the UN would create a single state in Palestine with Britain as the arbitrating power. But he had certainly surrendered the initiative and the outcome took him by surprise. It seems that Stalin wanted to break a "weak link"[99] in Britain's chain of imperial defences, for Russia, unexpectedly siding with America, voted for the partition of Palestine. So did a number of smaller countries, responding to intense Jewish and American pressure. On 29 November 1947, therefore, despite Arab opposition and British abstention, the General Assembly passed by a comfortable majority the resolution dividing the Holy Land into two states. The Jews got eastern Galilee, most of the fertile coastal plain and the Negev Desert, with a Red Sea port. The Arabs were allotted Judea, Samaria, most of Galilee, Gaza and the region around Acre. Jerusalem was to be at the centre of a UN enclave. Bevin thought that the split was grossly unfair to the Arabs and refused to impose it. On 11 December Britain confirmed its decision, announced earlier but almost universally disbelieved, to quit Palestine. Moreover, at the insistence of Attlee, who had the Indian model in mind, a firm date was set for the withdrawal. Come chaos or bloodshed, the British would surrender the mandate on 15 May 1948. When Bevin heard that the RAF wished to remain and keep the peace he responded brusquely, "if they want to stay, they'll 'ave to stay up in 'elicopters."[100]

This exodus marked a fresh stage in the disintegration of the British Empire. The Chief Justice of Palestine lamented,

> it is surely a new technique in our imperial mission to walk out and leave the pot we placed on the fire to boil over . . . India, Burma, and now Palestine! Can the lesson be doubted? Socialist sentimentalism in England has caused more deaths and misery among the common people than all the exponents of our so called imperialistic expansion were ever responsible for, since the ancient Briton first launched his skin canoe on the waters of the English Channel.[101]

The final six months of the mandate were especially damaging to Britain's morale and prestige. As Jewish–Arab hostilities intensified, the last High Commissioner, Sir Alan Cunningham, washed his hands of the conflict. Although secretly a Zionist, he had to remain neutral. His duty was "to allow both sides to defend themselves"[102] and to resort to force only when British lives were at risk. Cunningham also had to govern Palestine until the end without handing over to any other authority—UN representatives were barred because the British would have to protect them and would thus be acting as midwife to partition, which the Arabs aimed to abort. The Chief Secretary, Sir Henry Gurney, likened the task to cutting off the branch on which one was sitting. Cunningham himself asked Creech Jones plaintively, "Is the last soldier to see the last locomotive into the engine shed, lock the door and keep the key?"[103] The High Commissioner and his staff tried to sustain an illusion of continuity, now opening a British sports clubhouse in

Jerusalem, now prohibiting the establishment of dance floors near the Sea of Galilee. But as everything came under attack—railways, courts, newspapers, hospitals, reservoirs, abattoirs—it was clear that the British had responsibility without power. As both Americans and Jews also observed, in the hands of Attlee's socialists the Empire was visibly losing its grip.

This state of affairs was especially repugnant to the army and the police. They handed over the control of Tel Aviv and Jaffa to Jews and Arabs respectively. Elsewhere they intervened less and less except in self-defence. When Arabs burned down the Jewish Commercial Centre in Jerusalem, for example, British troops stood around their green armoured cars smoking cigarettes and taking photographs. Often, though, they were caught in the crossfire and sometimes they were deliberately attacked for their weapons. Usually their riposte was muted. Soldiers sang "Baa, baa, black sheep" to the tune of the Jewish national anthem "Hatikva" ("the Hope"). Underneath a Jewish graffito saying "TOMMY GO HOME" one soldier wrote, "I WISH I FUCKING WELL COULD."[104] But rogue elements in the army, as a senior official noted, "openly approve of the policy of Hitler."[105] They carried out vicious acts of counter-terrorism, the worst being the detonation of a lorry bomb in Jerusalem's Ben Yehuda Street, which killed more than fifty people. Equally repulsive was the Arab habit of mutilating Jewish corpses, exhibiting handfuls of severed fingers, parading heads round the Holy City. Yet Jews, Cunningham observed, in their mood of "mixed hysteria and braggadocio" conveyed through radio broadcasts "remarkably like those of Nazi Germany," inflicted "many more casualties on the Arabs than the reverse."[106] The most frightful atrocity, starkly demonstrating the collapse of the mandatory regime, occurred near Jerusalem. At the village of Dir Yassin, on 9 April 1948, the Irgun and the Stern Gang murdered more than 250 Arabs, many of them women and children. According to a recent Israeli historian, this and other massacres were "aimed at securing all Palestine for the Jews."[107] Certainly Ben-Gurion talked of an ethnic "clean out"[108] as organised resistance to the Haganah crumbled. All told, some 750,000 Arabs fled or were expelled from the new state of Israel—proclaimed on 14 May and at once recognised by Truman.

Meanwhile, the British departed amid humiliation and confusion. At home that old member of Milner's kindergarten, Leo Amery, who had read Gibbon at the age of fifteen, lamented this new sign of imperial decline.

> What I cannot respect is our simply throwing over the work of 30 years to destruction and washing our hands of all responsibility for either Jews or Arabs . . . It looks as if our whole moral, as well as material position in the

Middle East has been disastrously weakened. We shall not win any favour from the Arabs over this. After all, their passionate resentment against the Jews is only part of their more general xenophobia, and we shall find them more difficult in Egypt and Iraq than ever.[109]

In Palestine, during the last days of the mandate, the army got into a muddle, simultaneously evacuating troops and calling for reinforcements. Living in and leaving behind a vacuum, the administration could do nothing and had nothing to do. Towards the end Gurney played a lot of tennis and dwelt on the contrast between natural glories and man-made horrors in the Holy City. He was struck by the coruscating brilliance of the "sunlight in which every stone and tree becomes a jewel—urbs Sion aurea, Jerusalem the golden; or, as Josephus put it, a golden bowl full scorpions." At sunset the towers of the city and "the deep obscurities of the valleys had the colours of a Japanese print."[110] But red tracers streaked across the pale blue sky. Most civilians kept their heads down and had their cars stolen. The High Commissioner was an exception. After inspecting a guard of honour drawn from the Highland Light Infantry, Cunningham drove through the Damascus Gate and out of the city in an armour-plated Daimler with one-inch-thick glass loaned to him by King George VI, for whom it had been built during the Blitz. Even so Cunningham was stopped at both Jewish and Arab checkpoints. The majesty of his vehicle scarcely compensated for the ignominy of his exit.

17

The Destruction of National Will

Suez Invasion and Aden Evacuation

No sooner had the British left Palestine than its Arab neighbours entered, eager to strangle the state of Israel at birth. Egypt, Jordan, Syria, Lebanon and Iraq expected an easy victory. King Farouk, who had inherited the crown of Egypt from his father Fuad in April 1936, staked it on the outcome of the war in May 1948—he sent his forces into battle without even consulting his Prime Minister. This proved to be one of the rashest gambles in his rakish career. The Haganah, with guns, tanks and even Messerschmitt fighter planes purchased from Czechoslovakia, routed all but Jordan's Arab Legion. Commanded by John Glubb, known as Glubb Pasha, together with a cadre of British officers, it captured the Old City of Jerusalem. King Abdullah was able to incorporate the West Bank of the Jordan River into his realm, an appropriation that Israel preferred to the creation of a Palestinian state. The triumph of "Mr Bevin's Little King"[1] emphasised the disaster that overtook his royal rival for the leadership of the Arab world. Farouk exposed not only his own ineptitude but the failings of his army.

No one observed them with a sharper eye than Captain Gamal Abdel Nasser, a fiery young patriot who was wounded during the fighting. He noted that the high command tried to hide its incompetence by fostering fantastic myths about the enemy, who were said to have electrically operated towers that rose from the ground and fired in all directions. Yet on his own side, wrote Nasser, there was "no concentration of forces, no accumulation of ammunition and equipment. There was no reconnaissance, no intelligence, no plans."[2] Nor was there military secrecy: Cairo newspapers published Nasser's marching orders before he had time to obey them. So in the end Israel secured the Negev, which was likened to a dagger blade dividing the Arab world, splitting the Muslims of Asia from those of Africa. And until restrained by Truman, the Haganah menaced the land of the Nile itself. Nasser attributed the spoiling of the Egyptians less to Jewish invaders than to British occupiers. During a truce he even quizzed an Israeli counterpart about how the Zionists had succeeded in their "struggle with the English." Nasser concluded that Egypt, so long demoralised by colonial oppression, had become prey to a corrupt and decadent ruling order. It had been "left to the mercy of monsters."[3]

The most profane of these monsters was King Farouk himself, who typified the impotence of Egyptian government under British tutelage. In theory, of course, the treaty of 1936 had confirmed Egypt's independence, withdrawing foreign privileges and confining the British garrison of ten thousand troops to the zone around the Suez Canal. In practice, the imperial force always exceeded that limit and it swelled to vast proportions during the Second World War. Similarly, Sir Miles Lampson was demoted from High Commissioner to ambassador in 1936 but he was urged by the Foreign Secretary, Anthony Eden, to make his new role "in fact, though not in appearance,"[4] as effective as his old one. Nothing loath, Lampson continued to dominate the land of the Nile in the spirit of Lord Cromer. He kept the Union Jack flying at the Residency, travelled the country by special train and rode through Cairo in a Rolls-Royce preceded by two motorcyclists blowing whistles. Too grand to carry money, he maintained "an exceptionally grandiose establishment." It even included a clerk to look after his game book. Mad about blood sports, Lampson shot kites on the golf course as well as ducks in the Delta. He amused his hard-worked staff by saying, "I like coot; they kill so well."[5] A huge man with a bulbous nose and a blistering manner, the ambassador bullied Egyptian politicians and lectured the King. Farouk nicknamed him "Professor" and "Gamoose"—water buffalo. Lampson called Farouk "the boy" and said that he was "becoming a fair pickle."[6]

He meant that the monarch was a grotesque voluptuary who, like Heliogabalus, "abandoned himself to the grossest pleasures with ungoverned fury."[7] Gourmand, libertine, kleptomaniac, drug-trafficker and buffoon, Farouk surrounded himself with a camarilla of Nubian flunkeys, Italian toadies and Levantine pimps. He played cruel practical jokes. He sold fine titles and bought smart cars, which he drove at breakneck speed. He was an insatiable collector, hoarding everything from paperweights to pornography, from Fabergé eggs to match-box tops, from cuckoo clocks to pictures of copulating elephants. Farouk also liked to accumulate the latch keys of nubile young women. His sexual antics caused scandal even in a city with an international reputation for vice—during the war one Cairo brothel displayed a sign saying "Esperanto spoken here."[8] A slave to caprice, Farouk resisted all other forms of control. In February 1942 he tried to defy Lampson himself, just as German panzers were sweeping across the western desert and Cairo mobs were shouting, "Forward Rommel; Long Live Rommel."[9]

The only thing that could hold up Rommel, wits suggested, was the slow service in Shepheard's Hotel. The ambassador demanded that the King should invite the pro-British Mustafa Nahas, leader of the Wafd, to form a government. When Farouk procrastinated, Lampson ringed the Abdin Palace with troops, tanks and armoured cars, and burst in with a letter of abdication for him to sign. According to Lampson's gloating account, Farouk "asked almost pathetically and with none of his previous bravado if I would not give him one more chance."[10]

The ambassador reluctantly agreed, convinced that "we have a rotter on the Throne" who would seize any opportunity to "stab us in the back."[11] It was a shrewd summation. Farouk fantasised about shooting Lampson and evicting the British. The bitterness of the humiliation poisoned his life and apparently induced persecution mania. Despite strict censorship, the palace coup could not be kept secret for long. News of it particularly outraged Egyptian soldiers. General Mohammed Neguib offered to resign because he was ashamed to wear his uniform. Nasser thought that the army was disgraced by its failure to intervene: "If it had dared the English would have retreated like pansies (khawalates)."[12] He and other young officers began to plot revenge. So did politicians, writers, students, workers and nationalists of all sorts when wartime restrictions were lifted. Inspired by creeds ranging from Islam to Marxism, they agitated for radical programmes. Militants held mass demonstrations that led to bloody clashes with police and troops. Terrorists assassinated Egyptian collaborators and threw bombs into British barracks and clubs. Behind the disturbances was a common demand for the complete evacuation of all foreign servicemen, without which independence was a sham.

Bevin wanted an equal alliance and hoped to lease the Suez Canal base. Early in 1946, as an earnest of his good intentions, he recalled Lampson (now ennobled as Lord Killearn). The ambassador's parting shot was to assure the Foreign Office, in an echo of Cromer, that Egyptians were much like children and needed "a fair and helpful hand to guide them." The removal of Killearn's hand delighted many in Egypt, no one more than its sovereign. But others thought that the new ambassador merely implemented the old "colonialist policy with silken gloves."[13] This was not entirely fair. In May 1946 Attlee announced that all British forces would quit Egypt. And when Churchill damned the decision, Bevin, his mouth so swollen after the extraction of three teeth that he looked just like a bloodhound, decried his "Poona mentality."[14] Yet no agreement was reached. This was because Bevin rejected Egypt's claim to the Sudan, which should also, he insisted, enjoy eventual self-government. Farouk won some fleeting popularity by wearing the crown of both countries and claiming to embody in his increasingly corpulent person the unity of the Nile Valley. But when it came to resolving the Anglo-Egyptian stalemate, the King was a pawn. Moreover, he discredited himself hopelessly in 1948, divorcing his popular wife Farida ("the only one") and appearing at casinos during the war against Israel dressed in the uniform of a field-marshal. After the defeat he presided over a victory parade. Like England's Prince Regent, who sometimes claimed to have fought heroically at Waterloo, Farouk afterwards boasted that he had personally led his troops into battle.

Such extravagances encouraged the revival of Nasser's dormant conspiracy. Many of those who joined the ranks of his Free Officers had, like Nasser himself, humble origins. They deplored the abject plight of the fellaheen and Nasser quoted Mustapha Kemal: "To live in despair is not to live at all."[15] They contrasted the grinding poverty of the many with the flaunted opulence of the few. This was a familiar refrain. Winston Churchill himself had urged Farouk to promote social welfare since "nowhere in the world were the conditions of extreme wealth and poverty so glaring."[16] But coming from him it was an audacious criticism. For during the war Churchill's own government had squeezed Egypt more fiercely than ever, incurring a debt of over £350 million. The Free Officers blamed Britain not only for gross exploitation but also for inadequate military training and deficient weaponry, which put them at the mercy of the Haganah in 1948. The arms scandal also reflected corruption in high places of the Egyptian government. The wife of Mustafa Nahas, who himself led the Wafd to victory in the election of 1950, was heavily implicated. Moreover, the Prime Minister, primped, powdered and perfumed, with a gleaming Cabochon emerald ring worn outside his grey silk gloves, seemed a model of decadence to rival the King himself. The Free Officers were not impressed that Nahas now became more politically radical, championing social reform and repudiating the treaty of alliance with Britain that he himself had signed in 1936. And the Egyptian masses, their struggle for survival aggravated by a slump in cotton prices, were not appeased by the fact that British forces had (in 1947) withdrawn into the Canal Zone. For this was a mortifying symbol of Egyptian subservience, "a state within the state."[17]

Eclipsing Singapore, as well as the spreading archipelago of American bases in Arab states (Morocco, Libya, Saudi Arabia and Bahrein), it was the most elaborate overseas military installation in the world. The Canal Zone consisted of 750 square miles of desert between Suez and the Nile delta, equipped with ports and seaplane docks, ten airfields, a railway system for nine hundred carriages and a road network for thousands of vehicles. It contained barracks, hospitals, factories, bakeries, power stations, coal bunkers, oil tanks, supply depots, ammunition dumps, sewage farms, water filtration plants and recreation facilities. But by the end of 1951 the garrison, intended to protect the jugular vein of the Empire, faced the task of protecting itself. The 38,000 troops (their number soon doubling) were beset by Egyptian strikers, saboteurs and so-called "liberation commandos," or *fedayeen*. These were mainly peasants, workers, students and members of the Muslim Brotherhood, acting with the tacit support of the government. Back in power and fuelled by whisky, Churchill responded like the cavalry subaltern of Omdurman. Advancing towards Eden with clenched fists, he growled: "Tell them that if we have any more of their cheek we will set the Jews on them and drive them into the gutter from which they should never have emerged."[18] Guerrilla raids prompted regular retaliation. On 25 January 1952 British soldiers used tanks and artillery to demolish the police barracks at Ismailiya, with the loss of over fifty lives. The following day, *The Times* indignantly reported, "frenzied crowds" subjected Cairo to "anarchy, destruction, incendiarism and pillage," leaving the streets looking "as though they had been attacked by a fleet of bombers."[19]

The prime targets on this "Black Saturday" were British bastions such as Thomas Cook's travel agency, Barclays Bank, Shepheard's Hotel and the Turf Club. But the mob also burned edifices patronised by pashas and beys—smart department stores, luxury cinemas and fashionable nightclubs such as Madame Badia's, haunt of Farouk's favourite belly dancer, Tahia Carioca, known to the British as "Gippy Tummy." They even menaced the Abdin Palace where the King was holding a vast, gold-plated banquet to celebrate the birth of a crown prince. The authorities were slow to restore order, the Minister of the Interior being preoccupied with the purchase of a house and the Prime Minister, Nahas, being "busy having his corns cut."[20] In fact the riots signalled the start of a revolution against an *ancien régime* in the last stages of decrepitude. What ultimately brought it down was its failure to get rid of the British. In July 1952 the Free Officers completed the work of the mob. They mounted a putsch and forced the King to abdicate. Dressed in an admiral's uniform and given a twenty-one-gun salute, Farouk sailed away from Alexandria on board the *Mahroussa*. It was the same royal yacht, once again freighted with gold ingots, that had taken his grandfather, Khedive Ismail, into exile in 1879. The Free Officers, led by General Neguib but dominated by Colonel Nasser, had resisted the temptation to execute the King. "History will sentence him to death," said Nasser.[21] He himself was intent on liquidating the twin evils of colonialism and feudalism.

Despite a power struggle lasting two years, he made progress on both counts. First the new regime crushed external opponents, including the Wafd and the Muslim Brotherhood. Then Nasser purged rivals within the junta, notably the pipe-puffing Neguib, who had put forward liberal-democratic policies known as "the ideas of March."[22] The new dictator was initially awkward and unpopular, the son of a postal clerk who had usurped the purple. He admitted to remaining a revolutionary conspirator at heart, "suspicious of everyone."[23] But Nasser was a model of probity beside Farouk. He lived modestly with his family in the suburb of Heliopolis, building extra rooms on to his house as they became necessary. The CIA merely demonstrated its ineptitude by offering him a $3 million bribe—though he did use part of a huge sum given to Neguib by Kermit Roosevelt, a ubiquitous CIA operative, to build the Cairo Tower, the granite landmark that Nasser called "Roosevelt's erection."[24] Nasser's worst vice was chain-smoking Craven A cigarettes. Unlike the King, he radiated energy. Tall and muscular, he moved like a panther. His olive-skinned countenance, white teeth gleaming between aquiline nose and prognathous jaw, was spellbind-ingly expressive. Whether plotting, raging, joking, gossiping or orating, he behaved like the embodiment of the national will.

Without delay he assaulted the old order, abolishing Ottoman pashadom, founding a republic and initiating agrarian reform at a time when landless labourers were earning ten piastres (ten pence) a day. He also set about restoring the dignity of Egypt, fatally impaired by the alien incubus. A vital step was to abandon Egyptian claims to the Sudan, on the grounds that its people too had the right to decide their own destiny. At a stroke the Nile Valley, though itself divided, united against the imperial power. Britain felt bound to honour its pledge granting Sudanese independence, which came into effect in 1956. Anthony Eden was responsible for this course of action, designed to secure a settlement in Egypt. Ironically, in view of his subsequent gunboat diplomacy, the Foreign Secretary told the cabinet that it was impossible "to maintain our position in the Middle East by the methods of the last century."[25] Eden further succeeded in reaching an agreement whereby British forces would leave the Canal Zone within twenty months, by June 1956, though they would have the right to return if Egypt were attacked. Under pressure from President Eisenhower's ponder-ous Secretary of State, John Foster Dulles, Churchill was reluctantly per-suaded to accept this. The Prime Minister inveighed against "Dull, Duller, Dulles."[26] And he harped on a perennial theme, the eclipse of British power by the United States. His doctor, Lord Moran, said that "it was a canker in his mind, he grieves that England in her fallen state can no longer address America as an equal, but must come, cap in hand, to do her bidding."[27]

Churchill would have grieved more had he known that Nasser referred to the Americans and the British respectively as the "coming" and the "going"—"*el gayin wa el rayin.*"[28]

Yet Churchill remained furiously ambivalent about the "scuttle"[29] from Egypt. With his head he recognised that the Canal Zone was only held at crippling cost—over £50 million a year. The bill was harder to bear since Britain, which had produced more than a quarter (in value) of the world's manufactured exports in 1950, was now being swiftly overtaken by European rivals recovering from the devastation of the world war. Moreover, there would be additional demands, for blood as well as money, if the Egyptians mounted another guerrilla campaign. Although a third of the ships passing through Suez were still British, the Canal was no longer the vital imperial artery it had been in the days of the Indian Raj. Its importance was further diminished by the advent of the hydrogen bomb, which meant that Britain's global strategy might rest on a scattering of Gibraltars. Coming to terms with Nasser could win Egypt for the West in the Cold War and help to improve the lot of a people whose average expectation of life was about half that of Britons. Yet in his heart Churchill detested any surrender of British power. He had condemned Attlee's refusal to confront Mohammed Mossadeq ("Mussy Duck," in Churchill's parlance), the pyjama-wearing Prime Minister who nationalised Iran's oil, including the largest refinery in the world at Abadan. And Churchill supported the secret American coup to change the regime in 1953, which put the Shah on the peacock throne and left Dulles "purring like a giant cat."[30]

Now Churchill kept grumbling about the "appeasement" of military dictators in Egypt. He wanted to kick "Neg-wib" and said that "he never knew before that Munich was situated on the Nile."[31] Capitulation there would lead to the collapse of Britain's colonial position from the Niger to the Limpopo. Churchill's gut feelings were best expressed by the "Suez Group" of right-wing Conservatives, devotees of the evanescent cult of Empire. They believed that it was shameful for a nation which had won "the biggest war in history" to retreat in the face of Egyptian "terrorism." The evacuation of the Canal Zone, wrote Leo Amery's die-hard son Julian, "would mean the end of the Commonwealth as an independent force in the world." If pushed too far, Churchill should take vigorous action, ignoring opposition from aspirant arbiters of international conduct in the United States and the United Nations. Britain should "occupy Cairo and install a new and friendlier Egyptian government."[32] Invited to a meeting of Conservative backbenchers to discuss the government's policy, Churchill said: "I'm not sure I'm on our side!"[33]

Churchill was also uncertain about Anthony Eden's capacity to lead the country. Keen to remain Prime Minister himself, he did not hide his doubts that the Tory crown prince (or, as he wickedly called him, "my Princess Elizabeth") might turn out to be a dud. In particular Churchill suspected that the sleek, buck-toothed Eden lacked the moral fibre to defend Britain's interests overseas. "I'm worried about this myxomatosis," Churchill told the Minister of Agriculture in cabinet. "You don't think there's any chance of Anthony catching it?"[34] Certainly Eden was prone to ill health and he was plagued by inflammation of the bile duct resulting from a botched operation on his gall bladder. He was also subject to tantrums and nerve storms. When they subsided he would apologise effusively, confessing to being "a bloody prima donna."[35] The son of a half-mad baronet and an exceedingly beautiful woman, Eden was said to be a bit of both. He veered between consuming vanity and crippling self-doubt. Eden usually advocated sensible colonial policies and always had the courage of his clichés—Bevin was famously quoted as saying that he uttered "clitch after clitch after clitch."[36] But Eden had been equivocal over Munich and, despite his progressive instincts, he was fearful of adopting any course that could be branded as appeasement. After succeeding the octogenarian Churchill in April 1955, he writhed at charges that he was inclined to dither and scuttle, that he was incapable of administering the smack of firm government. One journalist wrote that when he made the emphatic gesture of punching his fist into the palm of his hand, no sound was heard. Another said that his words of command had all the dynamism of a radio "talk on the place of the potato in English folklore."[37] Psychologically Eden became a prisoner of the Suez Group, which itself reflected public anxiety about British decline and "advancing American imperialism."[38] The Group's members were not immune to the dazzling charm that made Eden, it was said, "the best hostess in London."[39] But they generally disliked his effete ways, his addiction to double-breasted waistcoats and his habit of calling men "my dear." Especially offensive was the manner in which his "moustache curled inside out."[40] One young Tory MP said, "Eden had to prove he had a real moustache."[41] Clarissa Eden did her best to help. Moments before her husband's eve-of-invasion broadcast on 3 November 1956, she saw on a television monitor that his moustache was almost invisible and quickly blackened the bristles with her mascara.

The symbol of Eden's determination to maintain British paramountcy in the Middle East, despite the withdrawal from Egypt, was the Baghdad Pact. This was a security agreement signed in 1955 by Turkey, Iraq, Britain, Pakistan and Iran. Its avowed aim was to defend the region from any Soviet threat. But the Pact was also a form of diplomatic imperialism. Although apt to confuse nationalists with Communists, Eisenhower would not sign it for that reason, though he did support it. And over the air waves Nasser vehemently denounced it for splitting the Arab world, which he aspired to lead. Eden found him adamant, even bitter, on the subject during their only personal encounter, which took place at the British embassy in Cairo on 20 February 1955. Immaculate in a dinner jacket, Eden upstaged the khaki-uniformed Nasser by addressing him in Arabic, which he had learned at Oxford (where the oriental syllabus ended in the Middle Ages). When Nasser said that he was interested to see inside the building from which Egypt had been governed, Eden, who had instructed Lampson to ape Cromer, silkily corrected him. "Not governed perhaps," he said, "advised, rather."[42] According to one of several differing accounts of the evening, Nasser felt patronised by Eden, who behaved like "a prince dealing with vagabonds."[43] He had acted in a similar manner towards Mussolini, giving the impression that he thought "Wogs begin at Calais."[44]

Nasser became more bellicose a few days after meeting Eden, when Egypt's smouldering conflict with Israel once more burst into flame. On Ben-Gurion's orders a young officer called Ariel Sharon led a ferocious attack on three Egyptian camps in Gaza. Nasser's forces were too weak to retaliate in kind so he at once embarked on a quest for arms. Frustrated by months of fruitless negotiation with the West, he struck a weapons-for-cotton deal with the Soviet Union. All the old fears about the advance of the Russian Bear, now metamorphosed by Bolshevism and slavering for Suez, returned to haunt the British. One senior official at the Foreign Office concluded that "we must first try to frighten Nasser, then to bribe him, and if neither works, get rid of him."[45] Nasser, influenced towards non-alignment by Nehru among others, could not be intimidated. So Eden and Dulles attempted to outbid the USSR by proffering aid to build the Aswan Dam. Intended to harness the Nile, transform Egypt's economy through hydro-electricity and feed its rapidly increasing population by means of irrigation, this was the biggest civil engineering project in the world, one that would raise a structure seventeen times larger than the Great Pyramid. Indeed the "Red Pharaoh,"[46] as Americans called Nasser, referred to it as his pyramid. But he remained intransigent over Israel and he continued to attack the Baghdad Pact. Eden blamed him for Jordan's refusal to join, comparing him to Mussolini and saying that "his object was to be a Caesar from the Gulf to the Atlantic, and to kick us out of it all."[47]

Then, on 1 March 1956, the young King Hussein, determined to be master in his own house, summarily dismissed Glubb Pasha from command of the Arab Legion. Vilified as "an imperialist scorpion"[48] by Egyptian propaganda, Glubb had been the personification of British sway in the Middle East. For Eden his sacking was an unbearable "blow to Britain's waning prestige as an imperial power."[49] The Prime Minister was further tormented by the reaction of the Suez Group. Julian Amery told *The Times* that Glubb's expulsion, which followed the retreats from Palestine, Abadan, the Sudan and the Suez Canal, attested to the complete "bankruptcy of the policy of appeasement."[50] The Prime Minister was harried in the Commons and took out his fury on Nasser. Over an open telephone line he told the junior minister at the Foreign Office, Anthony Nutting, "I want him murdered."[51]

Doubtless at the Prime Minister's behest, the Secret Intelligence Service did hatch plots to assassinate Nasser and to topple his government. Its agents, who proposed to pour nerve gas into Nasser's office through the ventilation system, were by no means discreet. They spoke to CIA officers without employing euphemisms such as "liquidation" and they collaborated with the Israelis, referred to as "snipcocks."[52] British ministers and diplomats were shocked by their schemes, which never came to fruition. But later in the year President Eisenhower, who authorised covert action of this sort himself on occasion though he would not sanction American involvement in killing Nasser, took a more robust view of imperial prerogatives. "I just can't understand why the British did not bump off Nasser. They have been doing it for years and then when faced with it they fumble."[53] Dulles also fumbled. At first he agreed with the British to let the Aswan loan "wither on the vine"[54] in order to punish Nasser for his continuing links with Communism—in May 1956 Egypt recognised "Red China." But in the face of mounting American opposition to the offer, Dulles abruptly cancelled it and the British followed suit.

Nasser was expecting the rebuff but he was enraged by the insulting manner in which it was delivered. He thought that Dulles's slur on Egypt's economy was a deliberate "slap in the face."[55] Nasser, newly elected President and the first native Egyptian to rule his country for 2,600 years, had no intention of turning the other cheek. He laid his plans carefully. On 26 July 1956, the fourth anniversary of Farouk's abdication, he addressed 250,000 people from a balcony overlooking Alexandria's Liberation Square. The speech, broadcast throughout the Arab world, showed that he had finally mastered the demagogue's black art. It vilified the West for attempting to return Egypt to financial bondage, an enterprise that he called "imperialism without soldiers." It contained a code name—Ferdinand de Lesseps—

which sent Nasser's occupation squads into action. And it announced, in a peroration greeted with wild enthusiasm, that "some of your Egyptian brethren . . . are taking over the Canal Company at this very moment."[56] The Canal would pay for the Dam and its control would restore the nation's pride.

Britain was correspondingly humiliated. So was Eden, who became quite unbalanced by Nasser's affront to his *amour propre*. As the crisis developed the Prime Minister raged more furiously than ever at his aides, as if to sharpen the jibe of Churchill's private secretary, who had told them: "I work for a great historical figure, and you work for a great hysterical one."[57] Eden resorted to a pharmacopoeia of drugs, taking morphine to calm himself down and Benzedrine to pep himself up. He blamed the glare of the lights in a television studio on Communists at the BBC. He became erratic and apocalyptic, saying that, rather than have the Empire nibbled away, he would prefer to see it "fall in one crash."[58] But Eden's reaction was not just a matter of wounded vanity and impaired ability. He genuinely lamented the collapse of imperial power, agreeing with Harold Macmillan, his initially pugnacious Chancellor of the Exchequer, that unless they met Nasser's challenge "Britain would become another Netherlands."[59] Like many others, he saw Nasser as heir to the European dictators of the 1930s. Eden compared Nasser's mildly idealistic book *The Philosophy of Revolution* to *Mein Kampf* and thought his expropriation of the Canal Company resembled Hitler's invasion of the Rhineland. He warned that Nasser's appetite would grow with feeding and that he would commit further acts of aggression, perhaps stopping the flow of oil from the Gulf.

On 2 August 1956 the British cabinet approved military preparations to overthrow Nasser and seize the Canal. This was the antithesis of appeasement, itself condemned by most British newspapers. None wrote with more vim than *The Times*, eager to compensate for its pusillanimity towards Nazi Germany:

> Nations live by vigorous defence of their own interests . . . Doubtless it is good to have a flourishing tourist trade, to win Test matches, and to be regaled by pictures of Miss Diana Dors being pushed into a swimming pool. But nations do not live by circuses alone. The people, in their silent way, know this better than the critics. They still want Britain great.[60]

Eden flattered himself that he "had one outstanding quality and that was his capacity to gauge public opinion."[61] Yet only a third of the population supported the use of force (though that figure rose to just over a half after the conflict ceased). And some people in the know, such as Sir Dermot Boyle, Chief of the Air Staff, quickly concluded that "Eden has gone bananas."[62]

Eden's mental state was not improved over the next three months by having to deal with Dulles, whom he compared unfavourably to Ribbentrop. The Secretary of State's leaden manner was tiresome enough: his speech was slow, Macmillan memorably observed, but it easily kept pace with his thought. Still more exasperating, though, were Dulles's tortuous opinions. His message, delivered at Eisenhower's behest, was that Britain should not try to "break Nasser" by force; but it contained enough ambivalence to foster Eden's illusion that he might secure American acquiescence, if not support. Dulles's initial response was that Nasser must be made to "disgorge his theft"[63] so that the Canal could be internationalised and oil supplies secured. After his first meeting with Eden at the start of the crisis, Dulles concluded that Britain and France (intent on ending Egypt's aid to Algerian rebels) would invade the Canal area. He told Eisenhower, "I am not (repeat not) sure from their standpoint they can be blamed." But he added, with characteristic contrariness, "I believe I have persuaded them that it would be reckless to take this step."[64]

Eisenhower himself was addicted to "zigging and zagging"[65] and averse to making categorical statements. The President later claimed that he had told Eden of "our bitter opposition to using force."[66] But he expressed no bitterness. Eisenhower said that force was justifiable as a last resort and, the soul of Rotarian affability, he never threatened a hostile American response to British aggression in Egypt. Furthermore, after seeing him in September, Macmillan confirmed the President's soft line. They had been comrades in the Mediterranean theatre of war, where Macmillan learned the "strange language of his own"[67] that Eisenhower spoke. Macmillan had also learned a more crucial lesson after narrowly surviving a plane crash in Algiers—he emerged from the wreckage with his moustache "burning with a bright blue flame."[68] In hospital he read Gibbon's *Decline and Fall*, concluding from it that Britons were the Greeks in America's new Roman Empire and that they must surreptitiously direct their brash masters just "as the Greek slaves ran the operations of the Emperor Claudius."[69] So Macmillan wilfully misinterpreted the President's words. He reported, "Ike is really determined, somehow or other, to bring Nasser down."[70]

Thus encouraged, Eden cooperated with Dulles's various attempts to find a peaceful solution. There were conferences of interested parties and appeals to the United Nations. A Canal Users' Association was formed and the Australian Prime Minister Sir Robert Menzies was sent as an envoy to

Cairo, where he decided that "These Gypos are a dangerous lot of backward adolescents."[71] Nothing came of these efforts. Nasser stood firm, encouraged by the fact that, contrary to western prognostications, Egyptian pilots proved quite capable of running the Canal on their own. So Anglo-French military preparations continued, plagued by predictable snags. The invasion was at first code-named "Hamilcar" but only after British soldiers had painted large capital aitches on their vehicles for aircraft recognition did they realise that the French spelled it "Amilcar." Although equipped to fight guerrillas in Cyprus, Malaya and Kenya (to which Cairo Radio beamed pro–Mau Mau propaganda in Swahili), British forces were ill prepared to mount a major seaborne invasion. The army had to hire civilian lorries, Coca-Cola trucks and Pickford's furniture vans to help transport munitions. Moreover, its old breech-loading rifles were inferior to the semi-automatic Czech weapons of the Egyptians. The RAF was beset by technical problems and an acute shortage of transport aircraft; and beside those of the French its planes looked "almost Victorian."[72] The navy was obliged to requisition freighters and passenger ships and to bring back into service Second World War landing craft that had been pensioned off as ferries and pleasure boats. An American admiral thought the British capacity for amphibious lift "nothing short of pitiful."[73] In the days of the Raj London would have expected India to make good some of its military deficiencies. Shrewd observers reckoned that it might recruit Israelis to fill the role of sepoys.

An emissary of the French Prime Minister, Guy Mollet, suggested the idea of a clandestine Anglo-French pact with Ben-Gurion during a meeting with Eden on 14 October 1956. The proposal attracted him. It offered an end to Dulles's interminable negotiations and an instant pretext for Britain and France to intervene in Egypt. While Israel thrust across the Sinai Desert, its main object being to smash Nasser's blockade of the Gulf of Aqaba and gain permanent access to the Red Sea, the two European powers would have a justification for "protecting" the Suez Canal, separating the combatants and ousting Nasser. Eden thus embarked on his fatal course. Goaded by the Suez Group, desperate to assert his political virility, convinced that the Empire would rot away unless it took a firm stand, he brushed aside all obstacles. He dismissed political and military reservations. He got an obliging Lord Chancellor to rule that Nasser's confiscation of the Canal Company was illegal and that the "infringement of an international possession is the equivalent of an attack on national property giving one the right to self-defence."[74] The Prime Minister also overcame the few scruples of his Foreign Secretary, Selwyn Lloyd, who was described by an English diplomat as Eden's "bell-hop"[75] and by an American diplomat as a "crooked

Welsh lawyer."[76] In tribute to his glossy pliability, Churchill called him "Mr. Celluloid."[77]

Lloyd was secretly dispatched to a villa at Sèvres, near Paris, with orders to take matters forward with Mollet and Ben-Gurion. The Foreign Secretary disliked foreigners—a positive advantage in such a job, Churchill allegedly told him. Furthermore, Lloyd later wrote, France and Israel were "the two nations in the world I most mistrust."[78] He made his feelings plain after opening the conclave with a joke that fell flat, to the effect that he should have worn a false moustache. According to General Moshe Dayan, Lloyd gave the impression that he was "bargaining with extortionate merchants" and showed a distaste for "the place, the company, and the topic."[79] Nevertheless, progress was made and the negotiations were ratified at a subsequent meeting. To the cynical amusement of the French and the angry scorn of the Israelis, the Foreign Office's main concern was that Albion's perfidy should never be divulged. Clearly this was Eden's chief anxiety, as evidenced by his efforts to purge the written record. He revealed little or nothing to officials. He informed few ministers about the Sèvres protocols, merely getting the cabinet to accept that "in the event of an Israeli attack"[80] Britain would join France to separate the belligerents. He misled parliament and the press, though he did confide in the gentlemen of *The Times,* rightly thinking that they regarded discretion as the better part of journalism. He kept Eisenhower in the dark. Eden did not even take the high command into his confidence. General Sir Hugh Stockwell, the land task force commander, only gathered from the French three days before the event that Israel would assail Egypt. The British invasion fleet itself could not set off from Malta until the expiry of the Anglo-French ultimatum demanding Nasser's withdrawal from the Canal. In short, the whole enterprise was vitiated by hypocrisy.

So Britain's military operation, unlike that of its allies, was initially hamstrung and ultimately doomed by the need to conceal its true purposes. The Israelis stormed into the Sinai on 29 October and, after some fierce battles, soon had the Egyptians retreating to guard the Canal. France did not wait for the expiry of the ultimatum demanding the withdrawal of both sides and hardly bothered to hide the fact that it was fighting on behalf of Israel—to Eden's acute embarrassment. But from its congested base at Akrotiri in Cyprus the RAF was hesitant about unleashing its squadrons of Canberras and Valiants on Egyptian military targets, which prompted Ben-Gurion to impugn Britannia's virtue: "The old whore!"[81] Moreover, the British armada of 130 warships, sailing from their deep harbour at Valletta in

Malta at the pace of the slowest landing craft, could not reach Port Said until 6 November. During that week the military were hampered by contradictory and unpremeditated orders from their political masters, who wanted them to win the war while pretending to keep the peace. Meanwhile, there was ample time for opposition to coalesce at home and abroad.

It began in the Tories' own ranks. Anthony Nutting resigned, unwilling to reveal his motives at the time but unable to stomach what he later called "this squalid piece of collusion."[82] Others followed suit. Foreign Office mandarins protested about a conspiracy that one junior minister called "the most disastrous combination of the unworkable and the unbelievable."[83] Eden's press secretary quit, evidently thinking that the gods wished to destroy his beleaguered boss, who was now "mad, literally mad."[84] There was also disaffection in the services, Mountbatten begging Eden to "turn back the assault convoy before it is too late."[85] The Labour Party, led by Hugh Gaitskell, made a cogent case against the so-called "police action," which was really an undeclared war in breach of the United Nations charter and other covenants. Moreover, the ultimatum was self-evidently absurd, since if each side moved ten miles from the Canal Nasser's forces would have to retreat while Ben-Gurion's advanced into Egyptian territory. Bombing Egypt, the victim of aggression, rather than Israel, its perpetrator, indicated that Britain's peace-keeping role was a sham. Using its veto to defeat the motion for a cease-fire in the UN Security Council showed that Britain's true object was to seize the Canal. Grey-faced, red-eyed and hoarse-voiced, Eden was pushed on to the defensive in parliament. And Selwyn Lloyd was obliged to assure the Commons that there had been "no prior agreement"[86] with Israel—a lie that did not prevent him from later becoming Speaker of that honourable House.

Professed patriots of all classes and political persuasions rallied behind the embattled government, regarding the Gaitskellite assault as treason. Lord Home, an appeaser at Munich but an aggressor at Suez, assured Eden: "If our country rediscovers its soul and inspiration, your calm courage will have achieved this miracle."[87] The Suez Group cheered the affirmation of imperial power, one of its members asserting that the area around the Canal was "in some essential sense part of the United Kingdom."[88] The Beefeater press was equally staunch. Lord Beaverbrook's *Daily Express* declared that Eden was acting to "safeguard the life of the British Empire."[89] It was aptly said, though, that no cause was truly lost until it won the backing of the *Express*. Even more telling than its support was the defection of *The Times*, whose recent history, Beaverbrook wrote, "was also a history of the decline of the British Empire."⁹⁰ The Thunderer rumbled about the damage done to Anglo-American relations by deceiving Eisenhower. Britain was "not a satellite" of the United States but an ally, it stoutly maintained, and what that alliance "cannot stand is a lack of candour."⁹¹

Eisenhower too reckoned that "nothing justifies double-crossing us."⁹² Actually both he and Dulles would have accepted even the duplicity if Britain and France had presented them with a swift *fait accompli*. As it was, the President had to face a fraught hiatus during which Russia crushed the uprising in Hungary (2 November), Dulles went into hospital for a cancer operation (3 November) and he himself was fighting for re-election (6 November). During that critical week he quelled his rage and excelled himself as a global statesman. Freezing out Eden politically, "Ike" affirmed that their personal friendship remained warm. He even professed to understand why the Prime Minister had responded to Nasser's affront "in the mid-Victorian style," while wondering if "the hand of Churchill might not be behind this."⁹³ The President opposed Russian intervention in the Middle East and rejected Moscow's proposal that the Soviet Union and the United States should make common cause against Britain and France. To enforce his will he deployed America's overwhelming economic might, instantly transforming Harold Macmillan from hawk to dove. "We must stop, we must stop," the Chancellor exclaimed, "or we will have no dollars left by the end of the week."⁹⁴

Eisenhower not only refused to buoy up sterling but insisted that "the purposes of peace and stability would be served by not being too quick in attempting to render extraordinary assistance" to Britain over oil supplies.⁹⁵ He took advantage of the hostility to the Suez operation in Commonwealth countries such as Canada, India and Pakistan. And he mobilised support in the United Nations, not only the forum of world opinion but a body capable of imposing sanctions on pariah states. In the face of this pressure Eden crumbled. He held a cabinet meeting on 6 November at which Macmillan's warning about a run on the pound proved decisive. Eden therefore telephoned Mollet and told him that he could not continue. A French official recorded this frantic outburst of despair:

> I'm finished. I can't hold on. The whole world reviles me . . . I can't even rely on all Conservatives. The Archbishop of Canterbury, the Church, the oil-men, everyone is against me. The Commonwealth is tearing itself apart. Nehru wants to smash its bonds. Canada and Australia no longer follow our lead. I can't dig the Crown's grave . . . I can't make England the only champion.⁹⁶

So a cease-fire was announced on the very day when the seaborne invasion took place at Port Said. Eden had deemed the Egyptians yellow but they resisted strongly and the Allied forces could only occupy the northern tip of the Canal, itself now blocked with ships sunk by Nasser. So abruptly did hostilities cease that the first British troops were being withdrawn as later units were landing. General Stockwell wryly informed the War Office, "We've now achieved the impossible. We're going both ways at once."[97]

Eisenhower single-mindedly pursued his own course, determined to restore the status quo. He bullied and cajoled the Israelis until they withdrew from Sinai. He refused to supply a financial "fig leaf"[98] to hide Anglo-French nakedness until Suez was handed over to a UN force. This was agreed within a month. The British government did its best to present retreat as victory, even claiming that the intervention had saved the situation in the Middle East by bringing in the United Nations—a conceit punctured by the future Labour Chancellor, Denis Healey, who said that it was "like Al Capone taking credit for improving the efficiency of the Chicago police."[99] In fact, Nasser only let in the UN peacekeepers on sufferance. His prestige waxed as Eden's waned. The Prime Minister had conducted, as a Labour MP said, the most spectacular retreat from Suez since the time of Moses. The Suez Group had nothing but contempt for his weakness. Churchill's verdict was widely quoted: "I doubt whether I would have dared to start; I would never have dared to stop."[100] To mount the invasion and then call it off almost at once, said the Minister of Defence, was "like going through all the preliminaries without having an orgasm."[101] Eden further demonstrated his impotence by flying off to recuperate in Jamaica, despite a friend's warning that "all the doctors were black."[102]

On his return Conservative daggers were out for him, the sharpest wielded by Macmillan. Enough time had elapsed, in the prophetic words of that radical firebrand Aneurin Bevan, "to permit the amenities of political assassination. Even a minor Caesar is entitled to be despatched with due decorum."[103] Ill health provided a genuine excuse for Eden's resignation. Conservatives preferred Macmillan to R. A. Butler as his successor. So did Eisenhower, who extolled Macmillan's straightness but failed to recognise his Janus face. But on the very day when Queen Elizabeth asked Macmillan to form a government, 10 January 1957, the President had second thoughts. He said that Butler would have been easier to work with because "Macmillan and Eden were somewhat alike in the fact that both could not bear to see the dying of Britain as a colonial power."[104] Although the French, incensed by the desertion of their ally, had other ideas, Eisenhower himself reckoned that Britain's post-imperial destiny lay in Europe. A possible "blessing" might emerge from Suez, he said, "in the form of impelling them to accept the Common Market."[105] The corollary of this, he considered, was that America would have to fill the vacuum left by Britain (and France) between the Mediterranean and the Gulf "before it is filled by Russia."[106] So early in 1957 he enunciated the so-called "Eisenhower Doctrine." In the name of the global struggle against Communism, it stipulated that America would give economic aid and, if requested, military assistance to Middle Eastern countries. Few welcomed this neo-colonial overture. Nasser condemned it as an informal version of the Baghdad Pact. The Arab world in general feared, and had some reason to fear, the imposition of a new overlord, Uncle Sam instead of John Bull.

Britain's retreat from Suez was a "disgraceful and calamitous event" comparable to the expulsion of Byzantium from Alexandria in AD 640, when the Saracens planted the standard of Mohammed on "the walls of the capital of Egypt."[107] Many of Eden's critics at the time thought that the fiasco spelled the end of the Empire. Anthony Nutting described Suez as the "dying convulsion of British imperialism."[108] The Deputy Cabinet Secretary, appropriately named Burke Trend, judged that the crisis of 1956 was "the psychological watershed, the moment when it became apparent that Britain was no longer capable of being a great imperial power."[109] Even right-wing Tories were downcast. Julian Amery considered that the "destruction of national will power [was] the greatest casualty" of Suez. He further wrote that it marked the end of the Commonwealth as "a military or economic bloc," dashing hopes that this voluntary association might be an informal substitute for the Empire. Suez also gave a fresh impetus to "our enemies" in Aden, Cyprus, Malta and the "African dependencies."[110] Nasser reached the same verdict, saying that it helped African countries to "insist about their independence" and adding hopefully that it ruled out the future use of the colonial "methods of the nineteenth century."[111] King Hussein of Jordan, who now looked to Washington, exclaimed: "What a tragedy: the day Britain finally fell off its pedestal, particularly around here."[112]

Americans also sensed that the tectonic plates of history had shifted at Suez. Reading the fashionable Arnold Toynbee rather than the old-fashioned Edward Gibbon, they reckoned that British civilisation was palpably giving way to their own. And Nasser was evidently a virile new Asian Caesar responding to the challenge of the superpowers. Such conclusions were too catastrophic for some. Duncan Sandys, who became Defence Minister in Macmillan's government, went so far as to say that fundamentally "the Suez crisis has altered nothing." For the time being, no doubt, it had "sadly impaired Britain's prestige." But Britain had not suddenly become a "second class power" and he anticipated a swift "revulsion of world opinion in our favour."[113] At the beginning of 1957 *The Economist* issued a more moderate warning against those who envisioned an apocalypse now.

> There are few left who doubt that Britain has been trying to play a bigger role than can be sustained by the resources, political, military or financial, that it can bring to bear. Indeed, there are some signs that the reaction has gone too far: there are people who seem to think that there are no intermediate steps between the Empire On Which the Sun Never Sets and the fate of Nineveh or Byzantium.[114]

That the British did not at once share their fate was largely due to America. Because Eden had suspected that the United States was out "to replace the British Empire" he had made the cardinal mistake over Suez, as Churchill intimated, of not "consulting the Americans."[115] His successors, recognising their country's satellite status, did not make the same mistake—quite the opposite. For his part Eisenhower aimed to employ the British Lion, injured though it was, in his struggle with the Russian Bear. This meant rebuilding the damaged alliance and shoring up Britain's position in the Middle East.

Contrary to myth, therefore, the imperial legions did not march home in 1956. Of course, London's freedom of action was circumscribed by Washington. And severe economic constraints did cause a reduction in the size of the Royal Navy (which lost its last four battleships) and the phasing out of conscription for military service. But in 1957 Macmillan's government also provided for a strong airborne task force. Although Suez brought the Commonwealth to "the verge of dissolution,"[116] according to the Canadian Foreign Minister Lester Pearson, it remained a global body. And Britain, possessing other allies as well as nuclear weapons, still aspired to be a great power. After Suez and with American help, it kept the weakened Baghdad Pact in being under another name, the Central Treaty Organisation. It sustained friends such as the King of Jordan and the Sultan of Muscat. It retained influence in Iraq and Libya until their nationalist coups in 1958 and 1969 respectively. When Kuwait became independent in 1961 its ruler signed a treaty of friendship with Britain to guard against an irredentist Iraq. As late as 1967 there were more than ten thousand British troops in the Persian Gulf. Until financial and anti-imperial pressures combined between 1968 and 1971, Britain dominated feudal sheikhdoms on the fringe of the Arabian peninsula, themselves once gatekeepers to the Indian jewel, now guardians of the Gulf's black gold.

Moreover, successive governments in London engaged in a bloody contest to preserve the base at Aden. This was one of the most bitter and confused of all independence struggles and it showed that Britain still possessed the resolve and the capacity to remain in the Middle East. On the other hand, Suez had been a clear notice to quit. The debacle had galvanised Arab nationalism. It had inspired a popular loathing and contempt for Britain best expressed by "The Voice of the Arabs" on Cairo Radio. Even members of the Middle East's Anglophile intelligentsia were alienated by the crass ineptitude of Eden's adventure. As an Egyptian lawyer said to an English friend in Aden: "You gave us Shakespeare, Oscar Wilde, Dickens . . . And all this spoilt, spat upon by Suez, by alliance with the Israelis. How, how could you do it?"[117]

An equally pertinent question was why, why did the British stay in Aden until 1967 when the base had lost its former *raison d'être*? The tiny colony had always been an outpost of India, valued for its fine natural harbour enclosed by two reddish volcanic peninsulas sticking "into the sea like the claws of a lobster buried in the sand."[118] Aden was seized as a coaling station and a bastion in 1839, and for almost a century thereafter it was governed from Bombay. Admittedly, Calcutta, Delhi and London had also intervened. For a time, between the wars, the RAF was in charge of Aden's defence. And when the Colonial Office took control in 1937 (the year of Britain's last campaign of imperial conquest, in the Hadramaut region of South Yemen) it consigned the crown colony to its Central African Department. Yet the town, which had grown from a decaying cluster of hovels into a thriving free port, still seemed a suburb of the Indian subcontinent. Many of its buildings, notably in the white enclave at Steamer Point, resembled the Indo-Saracenic edifices of Bombay. The dusty cantonments built on cinders and clinker inspired Kipling's famous simile: Aden was "like a barrick-stove/That no one's lit for years."[119] The lush public gardens boasted a two-ton bronze statue of Queen Victoria on a white marble throne surveying her first colonial acquisition. Parsee merchant houses flourished. *Dhotis* were almost as common as *futas* (Yemeni kilts) in the cosmopolitan old city of Crater. Here the gutters were stacked with *charpoys* (wooden rope beds, for outdoor sleeping) because "no breath of wind disturbs the sweltering air, and the barren circle of morose grey rock stops the view and traps the sun, turning it into a bake-oven."[120] The mud-brick bazaars, browsed by cows and goats, reeked of curry and spice. The khaki-clad police wore scarlet Punjabi turbans.

Furthermore, apart from restoring its ancient fortifications and the water tanks that had supported a city of 350 mosques in the time of Marco Polo, the Bombay Presidency subjected Aden to the hallowed process of salutary neglect. It remained a lava-strewn purgatory for adulterous officers and disgraced Indian regiments. But in 1947 Aden lost its vital strategic role as a link to India. By the time of Suez it had become a stagnant colonial backwater, sustained by past flummery more than present purpose. Under a sun that struck like a scimitar, the senior British dignitaries still paraded in full-bottomed wigs or helmets crested with red and white cocks' feathers. Even ordinary civil servants had to turn out in white drill tunic with gilt buttons, high collar with oak-leaf gorgets of gold lace, medals, kid gloves, buckskin shoes and tasselled sword. It was garb reminiscent, one complained, of "the stirring days of Omdurman or the annexation of Scinde."[121] The new Governor, Sir William Luce, thought the antique fustiness "as depressing as stale tobacco smoke."[122] He tried to liven up Government House, dominated by another image of Queen Victoria, with games of bicycle polo played on its colonnaded terrace. But imperial Aden was moribund. After the liquidation of the Raj, as an ambassador wrote to Selwyn Lloyd in December 1956, British bases around the Arabian peninsula had become "stations on the route to nowhere."[123]

Inside Aden, moreover, hostility to the British presence was crystallising. This was partly because few efforts had been made to improve social conditions. The Colonial Development and Welfare Act (1940) had offered meagre help since, as one minister acknowledged, it was "little but a gesture."[124] Local people also benefited little from the half-million pounds raised annually from a tax on imported *qat,* a narcotic leaf that plunged those who chewed it into an "ecstatic torpor"[125] and turned the faces of addicts green. The state of public welfare could be measured by conditions in Crater's gaol, which as late as 1967 contained both criminals and lunatics. A visiting English lawyer was horrified by the way in which sane Christian men treated mad Muslim women: "Like animals they were fed, their food being pushed to them between the bars; and like animals they were occasionally hosed down, together with their cells. The whole scene had, shut away under the brilliant blue sky, the quality of a nightmare."[126] Labour relations were equally backward and, with British approval, an Aden Trade Union Congress was formed in 1956. It began by organising strikes and, as political progress was limited, soon became a focus for opposition to imperial rule.

The Suez crisis showed that Britain was vulnerable. And the blocking of the Canal exacerbated animosity since it impaired the prosperity of one of the busiest oil bunkering ports in the world. Cairo Radio poured streams of molten propaganda into Crater. The British could produce nothing to compete with its "appeals to Arab brotherhood and denunciations of colonialism."[127] Pictures of Nasser smiled from every wall and urchins taunted Europeans by shouting his name. The nationalist animus was summed up in a letter sent to one of the most sympathetic (if old-fashioned) British officials. He was a future High Commissioner of Aden, Sir Kennedy Trevaskis, who had long striven to eradicate the race prejudice which he regarded as a "cancer rampant throughout our imperial government." The letter addressed Trevaskis as "the infidel master of slaves."[128]

Aden's situation had worsened after the Second World War because its hinterland became a siege platform instead of a rampart. From time immemorial, as Gibbon wrote, "Arabia Felix" had been almost immune from landward conquest. The centre of the incense trade in ancient days, it was a natural fortress rising in jagged steps from russet shore to amber massif. Protected by wilderness and desert, the fierce sons of Ishmael had not only kept Pompey and Trajan at bay, they had also denied the Turkish Sultan more than "a shadow of jurisdiction."[129] True, Ottoman forces did reach the outskirts of Aden, known as the Eye of Yemen, during the Great War. According to legend their mortar fire interrupted golf on the Khormaksar links, causing the Committee of the Union Club, "the most powerful body in Aden," to impel the military "to mount a long overdue counter-offensive."[130] The scattered sheikhdoms in the arid wastes stretching from the Red Sea to the Empty Quarter took note of British weakness. But they could not exploit it since they lived by a "system of anarchy."[131] Their fiefs might consist of little more than an oasis, a pass, a shrine or a hill-top fort set amid stunted acacia and parched tamarisk. Wider suzerainty was limited by intrigue, betrayal and blood feud, just as local authority had always been restricted by "the domestic licence of rapine, murder and revenge."[132]

Britain took advantage of this Hobbesian condition to secure its Aden base. It signed dozens of treaties with disruptive neighbours, offering subventions and protection in return for collaboration. Otherwise it adopted a policy of "masterly inactivity in Arabian politics."[133] Between the wars the spread of modern rifles and the claims of the brutal Imam of Yemen to extend his medieval theocracy to the Gulf of Aden aggravated tribal turbulence. RAF bombers quelled it for a time and the British reached an accord with the Imam. This proved ambiguous, giving him ample scope to stir up trouble in the southern protectorates. By the 1950s armed incursions from the Yemen had become more frequent. At the same time, from the other end of the political spectrum a triumphant Nasser fomented revolution in what Cairo Radio provocatively called "Occupied South Yemen." In 1956 the British Commander-in-Chief failed to recognise that a guerrilla war was in the making and dismissed the clashes as "military tiddlywinks."[134]

So the British kept Aden because they could and because they were conditioned by the past. Indeed, neither the death of the Raj nor the disaster of Suez prompted a fundamental readjustment of Britain's imperial policy. According to official opinion, the United Kingdom remained "much too important a part of the free world"[135] to let itself sink into a passive role like that of Sweden or Switzerland. No one in Westminster or Whitehall heeded Lord Curzon's prophecy, made half a century earlier, that once India and the great colonies had gone, the smaller dependencies would follow.

> Your ports and coaling stations, your fortresses and dockyards, your Crown Colonies and protectorates will go too. For either they will be unnecessary as the toll-gates and barbicans of an empire that has vanished, or they will be taken by an enemy more powerful than yourselves.

Labour's former War Minister John Strachey did call for a revision of Britain's global strategy, which meant ceasing to "behave as if we were still the leading world empire."[136] But comprehensive plans gave way to piecemeal expedients. It was almost as though, having acquired the Empire in a fit of absence of mind and afterwards taken little interest in it, Britain refused to face its loss. Yet fears were expressed that abandoning imperial commitments would have a catastrophic domino effect. Handing over territory would reduce Britain's military reach, threaten its control of raw materials, damage its anti-Communist alliance with America, impair its prestige, weaken sterling, harm trade (especially invisible exports) and undermine the domestic standard of living. British politicians and civil servants therefore had reasons, persuasive in the short term but reflecting a long-term reluctance to acknowledge their country's diminished international position, for denying Aden independence.

At a time when Cyprus threatened to become "a second Palestine,"[137] Aden was hailed as a vital link in a chain of strongholds stretching from Gibraltar to Hong Kong. With Washington's approval, it guarded and serviced the Gulf. It gave Britain an enduring stake in the Middle East. Aden's hinterland might even contain oil and, as Harold Macmillan cynically observed, this possibility meant that Britain should continue to divide and rule. He thought that it would be better to leave the local Sheikhs and Rulers in a state of simple rivalry and separateness, in which they are glad of our protection and can, where necessary, be played off one against the other rather than to mould them into a single unit which is most likely (and indeed expressly designed) to create a demand for independence and "self-determination."[138]

However, in 1958 a state of emergency was declared after more Yemeni-inspired strife. London reluctantly concluded that Aden would best be secured by further modest advances towards democracy and by amalgamating the protected Arab states to form a *cordon sanitaire*—though, as one official wrote, it "proved more like a chastity belt: uncomfortable but not proof against impregnation."[139] The merger was celebrated in 1959 by the lofty Colonial Secretary, Alan Lennox-Boyd, who survived a welcoming salute of rifle fire that came perilously close to his head and "dispensed charm like largesse."[140] In 1963, after much haggling and a promise of self-government qualified by Britain's avowed determination to retain troops in Aden "permanently," the colony itself joined the union. Its Governor would now be called the High Commissioner for Aden and the Protectorate of South Arabia. This was, he observed mournfully, like replacing "a classical Roman title, brief, lapidary and to the point, with a late Byzantine one, long, honorific and utterly ambiguous."[141] As his plaint suggests, the South Arabian Federation was doomed. Like the federations in Malaya, the West Indies and central Africa, it was form without substance, the worthless legacy of a senile Empire.

The South Arabian Federation was unable to unite its disparate elements. But its downfall was ensured by Colonel Abdullah Sallal, who in 1962 led a military coup in the Yemen which triggered a bitter civil war that crossed its southern border. Cairo and Moscow supported Sallal, whereas London and Riyadh backed his monarchist foes. Once again, therefore, the British Empire sided with feudal reactionaries against nationalist revolutionaries. Although riven by tribal and personal vendettas, Aden's own nationalist revolutionaries retaliated. In particular a militant new group called the National Liberation Front (NLF) belied the persistent British belief that the "people of Aden Colony are, like most Arabs in other countries, coffee house politicians whose views change with the mood of the hour."[142] The NLF were responsible for a growing number of strikes, riots and assassinations in the city, which now contained nearly 250,000 inhabitants, many of them migrant workers from the Yemen. High Commissioner Trevaskis himself was wounded by a grenade, which killed his assistant. In October 1963 the NLF launched a full-scale rebellion in the wilds of Radfan, a mountainous region close to the Yemeni frontier. Its impoverished people had a long tradition of brigandage and they were skilled guerrilla fighters. Owing allegiance to no overlord, they called themselves the "Wolves of Radfan."[143] Against them the British deployed some of their most sophisticated armaments, including Centurion tanks, Wessex helicopters and Hunter ground-attack aircraft. Duncan Sandys, now Colonial Secretary and kitted out in an emerald-green shirt, slacks and a straw hat, witnessed their assaults on a flying visit. The RAF not only fire-bombed villages but sprayed crops with poison "in the hope of terrorising the rebels into submission." Sandys's secretary later recalled, "it was a pretty nasty policy, a real throwback to colonial times, and it didn't work."[144]

Nothing worked, least of all the bounty of two rifles which the army gave for each mine handed in by tribesmen, who could obtain a mine in the Yemen for one rifle. It proved impossible to eradicate resistance in Radfan, where at least eight thousand people were made homeless. Meanwhile, repressive emergency measures in Aden were ineffective against snipers, let alone bombs, bazookas and booby traps. In this campaign of sabotage and slaughter, the NLF's favourite targets were the oil pipeline leading to the British Petroleum refinery and the local "running dogs of imperialism," especially broadcasters and intelligence agents. Eventually they murdered the entire Arab Special Branch. In 1965 the British suspended the constitution and imposed direct rule. To counter terror and obtain information, the army sent suspects to the Interrogation Centre set up in Fort Morbut at Steamer Point. Here the standard forms of brutality were employed but, as an official investigation later revealed, more scientific methods of torture were also secretly developed. Used in Kenya, Cyprus, Brunei, the British Cameroons, the Persian Gulf, Northern Ireland and elsewhere, these techniques included disorientation, electric shocks, "wall-standing, hooding, noise, bread and water diet and deprivation of sleep." The screams of Aden's victims could be heard in the nearby Corporals' Club, where they prompted jokes and comments such as, "That's another cunt getting fucking done in."[145]

In response to pressure from President Lyndon Johnson, who was becoming embroiled in the Vietnam war, Harold Wilson's Labour government expressed its determination to hang on to Aden. Washington wanted its transatlantic ally to remain East of Suez in order to allay fears that the United States was intent on "dominating the world by trying to become 'another Rome.'"[146] Wilson himself had some feeling for the romance of the Empire. As a schoolboy he had hero-worshipped Baden-Powell and as a flag-wagging politician he was largely immune to Duncan Sandys's clandestine attempt to identify him with "the best hated man in Britain," Colonel Nasser.[147] Wilson also valued American help in propping up the pound. But he and senior colleagues increasingly came to believe that sterling could only be saved by a drastic reduction in commitments. They dissembled, none more so than the Defence Minister, Denis Healey, who had privately wanted to get out of Aden "from the word go."[148] On 2 February 1966 Healey said that Britain had "no intention of ratting" on its imperial obligations in the Middle East and fully intended "to remain in a military sense a world power."[149] Three weeks later Healey's Defence White Paper announced severe cuts in British forces east of Suez. All South Arabia would be abandoned including the base at Aden. The decision was confirmed by another financial crisis, which caused a general drawing in of horns. In future, for example, no bases would be held in the face of local opposition—though this proviso was met in the case of the Indian Ocean island of Diego Garcia by deporting the entire population, to Britain's continuing shame and disgrace.

Furthermore, Wilson hoped to reorientate British foreign policy by joining the European Common Market. Finally, it had become clear that the Aden base was less of a shield than a target. This was certainly true once the White Paper appeared. Now friends of the Federation had nothing more to gain from the alien power, while its foes were encouraged by the assurance of victory. Unable to drum up local support, the British garrison in Aden felt betrayed. In the words of the last High Commissioner, Sir Humphrey Trevelyan, "When a Colonial Power turns its back, it presents its bottom to be kicked."[150] The NLF duly mounted more assaults on the British Army, which suffered 369 casualties in 1967, 44 of them fatal.[151] It also struck at its main rival, the Nasserite Front for the Liberation of South Yemen (FLOSY), founded in January 1966. A visiting trio of UN representatives, described by the *Sunday Telegraph* as "three stormy petulants,"[152] did nothing to keep the peace but much to discredit Britain's role in a colonial conflict growing more vicious by the minute. Race hatred charged the atmosphere of Aden like thunder. It was almost tactile, "a palpable thing, seeping into one's skin, seeking to . . . take possession of one's senses."[153]

Israel's victory over Egypt in the Six Day War of June 1967 further inflamed the antagonism. Aden's Arabs chanted the slogan "A bullet against Britain is a bullet against Israel." The security forces were assailed by rockets, mortars, grenades and bombs as well as small arms fire. One private had a narrow escape when a bullet entered the barrel of his rifle, "peeling it back like a banana skin and knocking him across the room."[154] Outside a wire-fenced picket post the Lancashire Fusiliers put up a sign saying "Please do not fire rockets at this structure, which is unsafe."[155] The injunction was ignored. Later in June, the Federation disintegrated and its forces mutinied. NLF fighters seized Crater, looting, burning and murdering at will. The Argyll and Sutherland Highlanders under the command of Colonel Colin Mitchell, an imperial throwback nicknamed "Mad Mitch," reoccupied it. He and his men went in to the sound of a pipe band playing "The Barren Rocks of Aden," putting on "a bloody marvellous show."[156] But they advanced only to cover Britain's retreat. Everywhere the NLF gained ground. It was dedicated to winning power through the barrel of a gun. So while negotiations took place in Geneva, firefights still raged in the streets of Aden. Leaders of the Federation fled to Saudi Arabia and elsewhere, sending their limousines by sea.

The British left with as much dignity as they could muster. On the dark, overcast evening of 14 November 1967 two hundred expatriates attended the final cocktail party at Government House presided over by Trevelyan, a tough little man with enormous ears which wiggled when he talked. All clutched their drinks and chattered with "that especial, glassy frenzy found only on such occasions."[157] The frenetic mood was tempered by nostalgia, best expressed in an official's pastiche of Gray's *Elegy:*

> Now fades the glimmering heat haze from our view,
> The Union Jack descends its downward track,
> Far off explodes a hand grenade or two
> And still is heard the sharp bazooka's crack . . .
> The Flag is down, another flag is raised,
> Gone is the symbol of the heir to Rome.
> The Bedou stop and stare, amazed,
> And, empty-handed, wander slowly home.[158]

Two weeks later Trevelyan inspected a guard of honour drawn from all the services. Disdaining "Auld Lang Syne," the band of the Royal Marines from HMS *Eagle* struck up "Fings Ain't Wot They Used To Be." The High Commissioner's Security Adviser was the last man to board the RAF *Britannia,* which stood with its engines idling on the tarmac at Khormaksar airfield. He climbed the steps backwards, holding a Walther PPK pistol in his hand.

Trevelyan was unhappy about transferring power to Marxist revolutionaries. But at least, he said, the British had not been forced to fight their way out of Aden leaving anarchy behind, as in Palestine. Some of his colleagues were equally sanguine. A future Foreign Secretary, David Owen, went so far as to extol "our glorious decolonisation record." But an old imperial hand,

Sir Brian Crowe, sharply reminded Owen that "there was the small matter of Aden, South Arabia, which we handed over to an unknown gang of violent thugs whose only credential was that they beat another gang of thugs in a civil war."[159] Others who served in Aden saw Britain's involvement in the region as morally defective from start to finish. In his unpublished memoir Reginald Hickling, the High Commissioner's Legal Adviser, deplored the unprincipled dominion that Britons had exercised over Arabs for whom they had no sympathy. He speculated about what a

> distant historian will make of Britain's last days of colonialism in the Arabian peninsula. I think he will see our whole exercise, from 1799 to 1968, as one of selfish power politics, overtaken in its decline by a casual interest in self-government. If he is something of a philosopher, he will also conclude that a nation cannot successfully govern a people it dislikes.[160]

Towards the end, Trevelyan's predecessor complained, the colonial power had conducted its activities in Aden with an air of guilt. As Hickling's comments suggest, it lingered on in Britain after the evacuation, adding to the climate of anti-imperial feeling.

The abandonment of Aden took place at a time of acute anxiety about Britain's decline. During the fortnight between Trevelyan's valedictory cocktail party and his flight from Khormaksar, the pound was devalued by 14.3 per cent. Harold Wilson did his best to present this as a patriotic triumph, particularly when speaking to the bevy of tame journalists known as the "White Commonwealth."[161] "We're on our own now," he told the nation, in a vain attempt to conjure up the Dunkirk spirit. "It means Britain first."[162] It also meant an end to the Prime Minister's inflated rhetoric about being a world power or nothing. Admittedly he did try to safeguard the country's prestige by clinging to nuclear weapons. But aircraft carriers would be sacrificed to keep Polaris submarines. And there was no more talk about the frontiers of the United Kingdom being situated in the Himalayas. The change of heart was not just a matter of cutting Britain's commitments to fit its capacities. Saudi Arabia and the Gulf States offered to subsidise a continuing British presence east of Suez. Wilson was now convinced that, despite the French veto, his country's future lay in Europe, which involved sloughing off imperial entanglements. In January 1968 he made the momentous announcement that Britain would withdraw from the Far East (except Hong Kong) and the Gulf region within three years.

Wilson was widely reckoned to have signed the death warrant of the British Empire. And he caused shock and upset from Amman to Bahrain, from Singapore to Canberra, from Wellington to Washington. When George Brown, the British Foreign Secretary, crossed the Atlantic with prior news of his country's retreat, the American Secretary of State, Dean Rusk, was "bloody unpleasant." The soft-spoken Rusk much resented "the acrid aroma of the fait accompli" but said that he would leave it to Brown, who was vociferous as well as bibulous, "to add several decibels" when reporting his comments to London. Rusk "could not believe that free aspirins and false teeth were more important than Britain's role in the world." He deplored its withdrawal into a "little England" isolationism and urged, "for God's sake be Britain." It was ironic that the United States, which had once repulsed and often reviled the British Empire, should officially regard its current contraction as "a catastrophic loss to human society."[163] Rusk feared that the United States would have to face the cost of taking over as the global policeman, since it would be impossible for Britain to play an effective part from its European base. He was right. Britain's power vanished with its eagles. Yet America had long regarded the process as inevitable and quickly resigned itself to filling the vacuum. Lyndon Johnson was not above mocking Harold Wilson musically, once ensuring that his mendicant guest was serenaded with "Buddy, Can You Spare a Dime?" But Wilson was happy that the only reference to Britain's withdrawal from east of Suez on his visit to the White House in February 1968 was baritone Robert Merrill's after-dinner rendition of "The Road to Mandalay."

18

Renascent Africa

The Gold Coast and Nigeria

The British anticipated turmoil in Asia after the Second World War but they were optimistic about the stability of their African possessions. Indeed, they discerned in Africa the lineaments of a new Raj, with its axes on the Volta, the Nile and the Limpopo. It would be another barrack in an alien sea, a vast tropical plantation, a bottomless pit of mineral wealth. After all, Africa had provided a million men to fight on the side of the Allies, many of them conscripted from such remote areas that they stared "with astonishment at cars and lorries."[1] Compensating for the losses caused by Japanese conquests, Britain's seventeen African dependencies had supplied the sinews of war in huge quantities—cotton, sisal, tea, cocoa, palm oil, bauxite, tin, copper, rubber and much else. Moreover, the colonial authorities were able to harness inconceivable amounts of muscle power. Often they employed forced labour, notoriously in the open cast tin mines of the Jos Plateau in northern Nigeria, where 200,000 peasants were treated as serfs. Such exploitation rested on a continuing assumption that Africans were among the most primitive races in the Empire, perhaps even a "sub-human species."[2] As such, they would obey their superiors with canine fidelity. Wondering about his next proconsular billet, Sir Ronald Storrs wrote in 1930: "More than 26 years' service with the ancient, frequently hostile, always corrupt but never uninteresting civilisation of the Near and Middle East have wholly unfitted me for the dog-like loyalty of devoted blacks."[3]

Between the wars even quite an enlightened District Commissioner such as Charles Arden-Clarke expected abject submission from the Nigerian "savages" to whom he was "something like judge, emperor and pope rolled into one." He recorded,

> Every native one meets kicks off his sandals, if he happens to be wearing any, gets off the path, gets down on his haunches and touches the ground with his right hand or both hands, at the same time murmuring "Zaiki" or "O Lion." If he is feeling very respectful he says "O Lion King of the World." Some-

times we passed through a village market place. Immediately everyone gets down and a great sigh of "Zaiki" goes up to the heavens.[4]

Such genuflexions were understandable in view of Arden-Clarke's propensity to enforce order by means of the whip, the torch and the noose. As he acknowledged, they also magnified Englishmen's ideas of their own importance in the scheme of creation. Thus it was generally thought in London that Africans were so backward that *"many generations"*[5] or "centuries"[6] or "an infinity of time"[7] must pass before they could rule themselves. Herbert Morrison said that granting them self-government would be like giving a child of ten "a latch-key, a bank account and a shot gun."[8]

On the other hand, it was clear even from a distance that the second global conflict was stirring Africa much more than had the first. True, little fighting took place south of the Sahara. But one campaign actually signalled the turn of the colonial tide just after it had reached full flood. When the Italians surrendered in Ethiopia in 1941, the Emperor Haile Selassie was restored to his throne, though with British strings attached. Elsewhere the impact of the war was less direct but more profound. The Atlantic Charter inspired the educated elite from the Atlas Mountains to the Drakensberg. Talk of Indian independence galvanised African nationalists. The war widened the horizons, developed the skills and enhanced the confidence of many who took part in it. The fact that "civilised" Europeans were killing each other (and being killed by Asiatics) helped to shatter "the crumbling edifice of white superiority."[9] So did the appearance of many working-class European and American soldiers, who did manual work and mingled with Africans in dance halls, bars and brothels.

Incoming troops were instructed:

> In all contact with the natives, let your first thought be the preservation of your own dignity. The natives are accustomed to dealing with very few white people and those they meet hold positions of authority. The British are looked up to, put on a very high level. Don't bring that level down by undue familiarity.[10]

The authorities also tried to promote African loyalty, though their efforts sometimes backfired. One poster depicted black soldiers in smart khaki uniforms but insultingly gave them "the bright scarlet lips of a Nigger minstrel on Brighton beach."[11] Another contrasted Mussolini's regimented, rifle-bearing youth with cheerful, ragged British Boy Scouts—Africans admired the former, as readers of Evelyn Waugh's *Black Mischief*, which had satirised a similar propaganda campaign, might have anticipated. What really altered the African worldview was the economic revolution sparked off by the conflict. Business boomed. New factories rose to fill import gaps (beer and cigarettes, for example) and to process raw materials such as cotton, fish and palm oil. Towns filled with wage-labourers, who were susceptible to radical ideas. However, state controls caused serious grievances, Africans being systematically exploited because of their political impotence. Inflation raised the cost of imported goods while the price of their exports was fixed to enable colonial governments to sell them profitably on the world market, thus helping Britain to pay for the war and to shore up the pound. In Accra, Lagos, Nairobi and Salisbury intellectuals dreamed of the "*risorgimento* of the African."[12]

Although hopeful that Africa could become Britain's third empire, greater than those of America or India, the Colonial Office did worry about the awakening colossus. As early as 1942 it recognised that exhausted little post-war Britain would have to find a new approach towards its African possessions.

> Nineteenth century concepts of empire are dead. Forces released by the war are gathering great velocity . . . populations in Africa will seek . . . a wider measure of control over their own affairs. To surmount this danger will require statesmanship, or we shall lose the African continent as we did the American in the eighteenth century.[13]

Progressive officials thus began to think less in terms of trusteeship, with its antique connotations, and more of partnership with Africans. They aimed to replace Lugard's system of indirect rule through tribal chiefs with a form of local democracy. In due course they revived the idea that the Empire was a self-liquidating entity and asserted that decolonisation was the "culmination of an evolutionary process which can be traced back to the end of the 18th century"[14]—a claim justifiable in itself but specious when used to suggest that the whole undertaking was the result of a grand design. They looked for a steady access of influence through an orderly transfer of power. In places such as Kenya and Rhodesia the presence of white settler communities made that impossible. But for most countries, and all those in West Africa, the key question was not whether, but when, self-government should be granted. The pace of change was crucial, since any miscalculation might provoke Communist insurgency or nationalist insurrection. The Colonial Office was confident that it could retain the initiative, despite the fundamental contradiction of its position. Critics pointed out that since the British interpreted the white man's burden as training their "wards in the exercise of freedom and democracy" they were invoking forces that would compel them "to lay down the burden prematurely."[15]

The fifth Pan-African Congress, held at Chorlton Town Hall in Manchester in 1945, warned that the future could hold bullets as well as ballots. It declared that Africans might "have to appeal to force in an effort to achieve freedom."[16] Future leaders such as Kwame Nkrumah and Jomo Kenyatta attended the Congress. Prominent, too, were ideologues such as W. E. B. Du Bois and George Padmore, who said that, whereas Rome had failed to save itself by abandoning its colonies, Britain could succeed—by making its own liberated colonies "the foundations of a new Commonwealth."[17] But for the first time trade unionists and other representatives of working people were also present. By demanding freedom now, said Nkrumah, they "shot into limbo the gradualist aspirations of our African middle classes and intellectuals."[18] They also sharpened the Colonial Office's dilemma. How fast should Britain's African colonies become independent members of the Commonwealth?

The Gold Coast, now Ghana, provided the first answer to that question. It was seen as a "model colony,"[19] well suited to pioneer the process of imperial mutation in Africa. After centuries of trading with Europe, the Gold Coast had reached a sophisticated state of development. It had prospered thanks to gold, then slaves, then palm oil and finally cocoa, a wholly indigenous enterprise. By the outbreak of the Second World War the Gold Coast's glossy beans made half the world's chocolate. Affluence afforded education. During the nineteenth century missions had multiplied and by 1881 five thousand children were being taught in 139 primary schools, all in the south. An African professional class emerged even as the tenuous control of British merchants turned into a colonial administration, which subjugated the war-like Ashanti and defined the national frontiers.

By 1901 the country had three components, a fourth in the shape of the west Togoland mandate being added after 1918. First there was the Coastal Colony, a low-lying belt of arid scrub pierced by towering silk cotton trees and coconut palms. Secondly, there was the Ashanti hinterland of thick tropical rainforest whose King was called the Asanthene. Third came the Northern Territories, burnt savannah drained by the Black and White Volta rivers and scourged by the *harmattan*. This was the chill, dusty "wind of the white horsemen,"[20] which had hidden desert raiders and which turned the land dull grey or lurid ochre. Its inhabitants, illiterate, acephalous and mostly pagan, often bore elaborate facial scars. The Ashanti called them *odonkos* (slaves) and the British, noting their taste for mashed (but not evis-cerated) dogs and rats, complained of "sights fit to turn one's stomach."[21] The southern part of the Gold Coast was by far the most advanced, thanks partly to improved communications. By 1903 the railway reached as far north as Kumasi, in the steamy heart of the West African jungle. Simultane-ously the first roads began to push inland. A few even had experimental tarred surfaces—when these gave carriers sore feet an attempt was made to tar the soles of the black folk. Governors welcomed other signs of progress. The head chief of Srah had formed a drum and fife band, indicating a wholesome "disposition on the part of the natives to abandon the hideous performances on tom-toms, gong-gongs and native horns in favour of music of a more civilised character." King Mate Kole discarded his tradi-tional dress and asked permission to wear a European outfit. The Colonial Office approved, but it added superciliously that "if the King is to wear this uniform, which seems to be something between that of a Turkish general officer and a superior kind of postman, he certainly ought to have brass spurs on his patent leather boots."[22]

Whitehall might condescend but at the turn of the century the newly formed Aborigines' Rights Protection Society, the seed of a nationalist movement, thwarted a British attempt to assign unoccupied land in the Gold Coast to the Crown. Its people were developing a West African con-sciousness and a tendency, as Mary Kingsley had put it, to think black. Moreover, Africans continued to hold senior posts in government service as they had long done—in 1850 there had even been a half-African Lieutenant-Governor. To be sure, white officials increasingly replaced black as medical advances made West Africa safer, if by no means safe. If the Grim Reaper was so busy in 1898 that the Lagos *Standard* asked for relief for overworked grave diggers, a member of the Accra Club could complain as late as 1939 that his only exercise was "walking as a pall-bearer behind the funerals of my friends. People die out here for no reason at all."[23] Yet by then there were enough African lawyers, doctors, clergymen, journalists and teachers to pre-sent a growing challenge both to the British and to the traditional chiefly order. Between the wars, though, society was still relatively homogeneous.

Unlike Nigeria, the Gold Coast seemed to be a nation in the making. The different ethnic groups had cultural similarities. The main languages spoken by the country's four million people were related and English was becoming a lingua franca. Whether in the expanding coastal towns of the Fanti, in the old kingdom of Ashanti, or in the scattered northern settle-ments of the Frafra, there was a common respect for ancestors, customs and kinship obligations. There was a general reverence for the throne or stool, especially for the Golden Stool of Ashanti with its paraphernalia of "gold finger rings, silver neck-plates, talisman sandals, umbrella crest, elephant tail, palanquin cushions, and so forth."[24] Brought down from heaven in a black cloud, according to myth, this Stool enshrined the soul of the Ashanti people. But chiefs never quite became gods. Indeed, they could be deposed, or "de-stooled," by popular demand—through an incipient process of democracy.

The British, who had first weakened native rulers, now upheld them; and none did so more ardently than the most popular inter-war Governor, Sir Gordon Guggisberg. Tall, gaunt and handsome, he was a mixture of patriarch, engineer and Scoutmaster. He aimed to conduct the people of the Gold Coast along the broad "Highway of Progress." Under his guidance they would advance "by gentle gradients over the Ridges of Difficulty and by easy curves around the Swamps of Doubt and Superstition, to those far-off Cities of Promise—the Cities of Final Development, Wealth and Happiness."[25] Drawing more inspiration from Baden-Powell than from Bunyan, Guggisberg fostered vocational training and made practical improvements. He built a deep-water harbour at Takoradi, a boon to a country that had relied on surf boats. He founded Achimota teacher training college. He completed Korle Bu hospital. He expanded the road and rail network. Guggisberg, a Jew whom his white enemies denounced as "the Niggers' friend,"[26] believed in promoting Africans to responsible positions. But he followed Lugard in preferring grizzled old chiefs to bright young men or so-called "verandah boys," impoverished youths who slept on the verandahs of the urban rich. Guggisberg admitted to the charge of running a "grand-motherly administration" and said that its purpose was to prevent "a child running before it can walk."[27]

The cliché incensed educated Africans, more and more of whom regarded colonial rule as a façade of benevolence barely concealing a sink of oppression. It was typified by Accra, where "vast, vulgarly ostentatious Government buildings," replete with balustrades, gables and "stone gingerbread icing,"[28] overshadowed a warren of concrete boxes with corrugated-iron roofs, thatched cabins and mud huts standing in a slough of their own detritus. For all the European architectural grandeur, there was no modern sewage system. The black slums around Ussher Fort had open drains, scavenged by pigs and dogs. The white bungalows of Victoriaborg had septic tanks, which polluted the sandy ground; and town council men *(tankas)* collected night soil for the trains that transported it to the sea. To the dismay of Sir Alan Burns, who became Governor in 1941, his own headquarters, Christiansborg Castle, contained only "thunder-boxes."

He quickly installed water closets, one of many modifications to the fortified trading post built by the Danes in the seventeenth century with stone brought from home as ballast in slave ships. Often changing hands and occasionally battered by earthquakes, Christiansborg had even served briefly as a lunatic asylum. Now it consisted of a cluster of white wooden buildings perched on massive cliff-top ramparts dotted with rusty cannons in which kingfishers made their nests. Supposed to be haunted, the whole place was permanently damp from the spray of huge Atlantic rollers. Apart from constructing an aviary, the portly, efficient Burns made few improvements. As a former secretary to both Lugard and Sir Hugh Clifford, he was by no means an unequivocal champion of progress. For example, he deplored the unfortunate African addiction to European dancing, especially to "a kind of jitterbugging" known as the "High Life."[29] But Burns had to cope with much labour unrest during the war and he detected the nationalist spirit abroad. He responded to it while trying to maintain the initiative. "The secret of good administration is always to be one jump ahead of the people," he said. "Give them what they want before they know they want it."[30] So Burns persuaded a gingerly Colonial Office, still "sure that we have unlimited time in which to work" in Africa,[31] to advance natives of the Gold Coast in local and central government. And in 1946 he secured a new constitution providing for the election of eighteen members of his thirty-strong Legislative Council. In fact most of these new members were not directly elected but nominated by chiefs and the Governor himself retained ample reserve powers. Nevertheless Africans were now in the majority and they had taken a significant step towards self-government. Burns thus hoped to forestall trouble from the educated elite who were, he acknowledged, "less amenable to our suggestions, less friendly, and less willing to accept us as supermen."[32]

"The people are really happy," Burns boasted, "and really satisfied with the new Constitution."[33] He regarded it as the fulfilment of his labours. Of course, the Colonial Office would continue with the "the slow work of nation-building."[34] Africans would gradually be trained to fill government posts. White administrators would more and more play an advisory, rather than an executive, role. But it was a substantial and enduring one. Quoting Gibbon, Burns compared the British to the Roman official, whose probity was guaranteed by his exclusion from provinces where "his interest was concerned, or his affections were engaged." The Gold Coast could not lightly dispense with such magisterial virtue. In 1947, back in London, Burns rejected suggestions that "our Empire is coming to an end, that our Colonies are now ready and anxious to stand by themselves."[35] But he was given the lie by mounting turbulence in the Gold Coast. It had many causes, notably inflation, high food prices, the compulsory felling of cocoa trees to control swollen-shoot disease, and unemployment among the seventy thousand demobilised servicemen. Furthermore, the intelligentsia feared that the new constitution would be a bar instead of a bridge to independence.

Led by a liberal lawyer called Joseph Danquah, they formed the United Gold Coast Convention (UGCC), a movement demanding "self-Government in the shortest possible time."[36] This was hardly a call to the barricades. But a new secretary galvanised the UGCC, a man whose recreation was work and whose ambition was (said Elspeth Huxley) to found "a great African empire, with himself as Caesar."[37] His name was Kwame Nkrumah. The son of a goldsmith from the Ivory Coast, he had attended Achimota College and told friends that, if he failed to free his country, "bury me alive."[38] Nkrumah had gone on to Lincoln University in Pennsylvania, paying his way by working as a dish-washer, bell-hop, soap-maker and fish-peddler. For want of a bed, he sometimes slept on subway trains shuttling between Harlem and Brooklyn. Among other subjects, he studied theology. He also preached in Negro churches, improving his diction by having his gappy front teeth replaced with false ones—when his mother saw him again she did not recognise him. In 1945, aged thirty-six, Nkrumah left the United States for the United Kingdom to crusade against imperialism in the heart of the Empire. He was a grey-suited, mild-mannered revolutionary. The novelist Richard Wright described him as "slightly built, a smooth jet black in colour; he had a largish face, a pair of brooding, almost frightened eyes, a set of full soft lips. His head held a thick growth of crinkly hair and his hands moved with a slow restlessness, betraying a contained tension." But when he returned to the Gold Coast in 1947 nothing could hide the fact that he was a man with a mission—"to throw the Europeans out of Africa."[39]

His zeal alarmed the middle-class lawyers and prosperous businessmen of the UGCC, particularly when he addressed them as "Comrade." They wanted an agent who would promote their claim to be the natural rulers of the Gold Coast, whereas Nkrumah seemed intent on becoming another Lenin. The British thought he rather resembled Stalin, organising a dictatorship of the secretariat, though they also accused him of "aping Hitler."[40] Undoubtedly he was a Marxist. Nkrumah believed that imperialism was the last stage of capitalism, a vicious form of economic exploitation against which colonies must rebel. And he hoped to use the UGCC intelligentsia as the "vanguard in the struggle against alien rule."[41] But he was a Christian Marxist—at meetings his supporters sang "Onward Christian

Soldiers" and "Lead Kindly Light." Nkrumah had also been influenced by Gandhi and he eschewed violent revolution. Instead he pursued a policy of political education, organisation and, in due course, peaceful non-cooperation. Using the UGCC as his base, he appealed to a broad constituency of clerks, cocoa farmers, elementary school teachers, market traders, artisans, ex-soldiers, young men and women. But even as he sought to mobilise these disaffected classes, touring the country in a wheezing jalopy, they gave vent to their grievances in a boycott of overpriced European goods that culminated in spontaneous riots. On 28 February 1948 a two-thousand-strong march, including former servicemen who wished to present a petition to the Governor at Christiansborg Castle, clashed with police. When Superintendent Imray's order to fire into the stone-throwing crowd was ignored, he himself grabbed a rifle, killing two and wounding several more—the Commissioner later congratulated him on a "Bloody good show." However, the shots stampeded the demonstrators. Some of them actually ran across the Oval cricket ground during a European match, the Superintendent recorded, to the "horror and disgust of players, umpires and supporters."[42]

Meanwhile, unruliness in the centre of Accra spiralled into "the wildest excesses of mob violence, bloodshed, looting and arson." Tens of thousands of people rampaged through the streets. Getting drunk on liquor pillaged from the Kingsway Stores, they attacked Europeans, overturned cars and set them alight, smashed down the gates of Ussher Fort Prison and released some of the inmates. As the violence spread to other towns and the death toll rose to twenty-nine, the Governor panicked, fearing a Communist coup. He imposed a state of emergency, called for reinforcements and arrested the UGCC leaders, among them Danquah and Nkrumah. They were soon released to give evidence to a commission of inquiry led by a barrister named Aiken Watson. This reported that Nkrumah's aim was to establish a Union of West African Soviet Socialist Republics. The charge was false but it confirmed Nkrumah's position as the most radical nationalist leader in the Gold Coast. Furthermore the Watson Commission said that the Burns constitution, conceived as the acme of enlightenment two years earlier, was "outmoded at birth."[43] It should be revised to give capable Africans a proper role in running the country, which had not been well served by a colonial government relying on feudal chiefs. The Colonial Office was stung by the criticisms and shocked by the proposals for such headlong change. But the riots had conjured up febrile anxieties that the Gold Coast might become another Burma or Palestine. In 1949 the Colonial Secretary, Creech Jones, appointed a new Governor, Sir Charles Arden-Clarke. He was evidently well qualified for the post, having begun his service in West Africa and just returned from the wilds of Sarawak where he had needed "a strong head, an asbestos stomach and a cast-iron sit-upon." Creech Jones warned him that the Gold Coast "is on the edge of revolution. We are in danger of losing it."[44]

Nkrumah seemed set to play Robespierre to Danquah's Mirabeau. The idealistic secretary of the UGCC had become ever more aggressive. He had published incendiary newspapers and conducted rallies where his magnetic personality and theatrical delivery impressed even those who could not understand what he was saying. He had embroidered on Danquah's myth of an idyllic state of Ghana, stretching from Timbuktu to the Atlantic in medieval times and now enslaved by European imperialists. He had urged the youth to demand "Self-government Now," or "SG,"[45] initials they shouted at police officers in Accra and District Officers in the bush. In June 1949 the UGCC dismissed Nkrumah from his post and he retaliated by setting up a rival organisation, the Convention People's Party (CPP). This condemned the "spinelessness" of the UGCC's policies and denounced its members as "stooges." Chunky, arrogant and articulate, Danquah reviled Nkrumah as an upstart, a renegade and a petty tyrant. The British were equally hostile, regarding Nkrumah as a "cold, humourless, intense individualist, offensively cynical and repeatedly guilty of double-crossing his benefactors and associates."[46] But the CPP became a magnet for militants, whether elementary-schooled sans-culottes in revolt against the tribal *ancien régime* or English-speaking plebeians rebelling against the new patrician class represented by Danquah.

Such respectable leaders were precisely those whom Arden-Clarke tried to back on his arrival. He also attempted to quell the rabble-rousing of the CPP. But Nkrumah reacted sharply when an African commission including Danquah proposed a new constitution that would have put more blacks in office while keeping whites in power. Dismissing the scheme as "bogus and fraudulent,"[47] he urged civil disobedience. "Mark my words, my good man," a British official warned him, "within three days the people here will let you down."[48] Africans would never support Nkrumah, the official said, as Indians had supported Gandhi. But in January 1950 a general strike, sustained by intimidation as well as exhortation, stopped trains, shut stores, paralysed business and brought government service to a halt. With the help of a curfew and other emergency regulations, Arden-Clarke soon suppressed the subsequent disturbances. Moreover, the police obeyed his order that there should be "batons but no bullets" and "bloody coxcombs but no bodies."[49] They also arrested most of the CPP leaders, including Nkrumah himself. Quickly convicted, they were imprisoned in Accra's James Fort. Here they were treated as common criminals and fed on maize porridge, corn meal and boiled cassava—yet Nkrumah kept up his habit of fasting for two days a week. He and ten companions shared a cell containing only cockroaches, sleeping mats and a stinking bucket. The black Jacobin kept control of his organisation by smuggling out messages pencilled on lavatory paper.

The CPP's many branches were active throughout the country, dashing Arden-Clarke's hope that a moderate party might "keep these buggers out."[50] Nkrumah's candidates won handsomely in the 1950 municipal elections and some Britons discerned a "Red Shadow over the Gold Coast." This was the title of a celebrated article in the London *Daily Telegraph,* which portrayed Nkrumah's party as the spawn of a sinister alliance between the Politbureau and "the Ju-Ju of darkest Africa."[51] But the CPP, as it campaigned in the general election held under the new constitution, was actually more like a congregation of evangelists. It held "harvest festivals"[52] to raise cash, prayed that the party would sanctify members through its truth and repeated Nkrumah's maxim, "Seek ye first the political kingdom and all things shall be added unto you."[53] Supporters chanted "Ci Pi Pi" and "Free-Dom." They saluted with raised arms and open palms. They displayed the party's red, white and green colours on flags and on the silk *kente* cloth of their robes. They participated in elaborate rituals, some wearing "PG" caps to proclaim that they were Prison Graduates. Spokesmen promised heaven on earth: free schools, cheap kerosene, more hospitals, smooth roads, mechanised agriculture, abundant yams and plantains, a welfare state, self-government now. If the people voted wisely, they said, God would save Ghana from the imperialists. In February 1951 the CPP gained thirty-five of thirty-eight seats in the popular ballot, and Nkrumah won overwhelmingly in Accra Central. Arden-Clarke quickly released him, fearing that otherwise "the Gold Coast would be plunged into disorders, violence and bloodshed."[54]

The new Prison Graduate described being carried like a ship on a sea of upturned faces to perform the customary expiation ceremony. He stepped seven times into the blood of a sacrificed sheep in order to cleanse himself from "the contamination of prison."[55] In Christiansborg Castle he met Arden-Clarke for the first time and, bearing no malice for his incarceration, accepted the post of Leader of Government Business—a title changed in 1952 to Prime Minister. The two men established an immediate rapport, the pragmatic official warming to the idealism of the mercurial politician. In fact, though, Nkrumah's dramatic election victory had worked a revolution in the mind of the Governor. He recognised that the CPP's leader was, as he put it, the only dog in his kennel. Nkrumah had visibly transformed his compatriots: "They carried themselves differently, stood up straighter, held their heads higher and looked like proud independent people."[56] So Arden-Clarke had to adapt to Nkrumah's pace, even though his masters in London thought he was "going too far and too fast."[57] Yet they themselves had few other options. Arden-Clarke was regarded as "one of the aces in the Colonial Office pack." And he claimed that, far from being hasty, the operation to make Ghana independent should be called "Cunctator"[58] after the Roman General Fabius Maximus, who earned the nickname because of his delaying tactics against Hannibal. It turned out that the determined man on the spot could play as crucial a role in ending as he had in extending the Empire. Between 1951 and 1957 Arden-Clarke became the foremost proconsular champion of "creative abdication."[59] The *Ghana Evening News* hailed him as "the man who came, who saw and who compromised."[60]

The creative assumption of power, as Nkrumah found, proved equally difficult and delicate. The CPP had fought for immediate independence and its leader now had to achieve it through negotiations requiring tact as much as tactics. He feared imperialist wiles and tried to ban fraternisation lest supporters who had resisted British "strong-arm methods" should be seduced by "cocktail parties."[61] He was obliged to rely on white civil servants, some disaffected, others seeking early retirement, all owing their first loyalty to the Crown. Accustomed to the culture of *dashee*—bribery and extortion—his own party succumbed to rampant graft. As MI5 discovered, Nkrumah himself raised money through "diamond smuggling."[62] The economy was still largely in European hands, none more grasping than those of General Sir Edward Spears, Chairman of Ashanti Goldfields. He professed to like and admire Nkrumah, describing him as imaginative, energetic, "receptive and intelligent."[63] But whenever he called on the Prime Minister, the general brought him presents of clockwork toys, "a monkey that clashed cymbals, a clown that blew bubbles from detergent, a lion that flashed its eyes and roared."[64] Apparently Nkrumah laughed at these novelties to humour Spears, who revealed his true colours in this tribute to West Africans who had suddenly been propelled into the modern world.

> After the first sense of wonder and amazement has passed, the manifestations of civilisation will become commonplace. Indeed, wonder is already being replaced by the desire to work wonders, even if for the moment and for some

time to come that desire is like that of a child demanding to be given a startling piece of machinery, unconscious of the dangers and uncomprehending
of its mechanism.[65]

A fractious reactionary and an old friend of Winston Churchill, Spears was
especially keen that no African should get near the levers of power in the
Ashanti gold mines. And so determined was he that as little as possible of
their vast profits should go to the Gold Coast that he tried to divide and rule
in the traditional fashion. Nothing daunted, Nkrumah struggled to forge a
modern state. He worked as if possessed by the Furies.

In a land where tropical disease was endemic he built nine new hospitals
before 1957, though he enraged people in Kumasi by attempting to name
theirs after himself. In a land where 80 per cent of the population was illiterate, he doubled the number of primary school pupils. In a land where
agriculture was crippled by debt, he lent farmers over £1 million at low rates
of interest. In a land plagued by what a British District Commissioner called
"witchcraft as foul as the slime of the mangrove swamps,"[66] Nkrumah even
tried to root out superstition. It was an equivocal effort. For he himself,
once an aspirant Jesuit, studied the occult, consulted oracles and heeded the
spirits of his ancestors. Still, the old Colonial Film Unit did expose the
activities of a fetish priest, obtaining remarkable footage with the paid assistance of the priest's son, who no longer believed in mumbo-jumbo because
he had become a Roman Catholic and needed the money to take his sick
wife to Lourdes. Meanwhile, Nkrumah permitted his own personality cult
to assume the character of a national faith. He was hailed as "Sun of
Ghana," "Star of Africa," "Man of Destiny" and "Wonder Boy," though his
usual title was *Osagyefo,* which meant "Victor" or "Redeemer."[67] Alighting
from Cadillac or Jaguar, he was paraded in a white palanquin under a state
umbrella of red, white and green velvet. He presented himself, said Danquah, as "the nation's holy angel and saint of self-government."[68] He seemed
to act the part of martyr-saviour, as Elspeth Huxley observed, noting his
"sultry, sensual expression and a trace of petulance, of *prima donna* touchi-
ness."[69]

Perhaps Nkrumah began to believe his own propaganda. In private he
compared himself to Christ and talked of the "inevitability of deification."[70]
And on his gramophone he played nothing but the "Hallelujah Chorus"
from Handel's *Messiah.* But Nkrumah also invested himself with spiritual
power in order to challenge the chiefs. He thus won votes and made it
harder for Britain to resist the drive towards independence. This impetus

was best expressed in his "Motion of Destiny," proposed to the Legislative Assembly on 10 July 1953:

> The old concepts of Empire, of conquest, domination and exploitation are fast dying in an awakening world. Among the colonial peoples, there is a vast untapped reservoir of peace and goodwill towards Britain, would she but divest herself of the outmoded, moth-eaten trappings of two centuries ago, and present herself to her colonial peoples in a new and shining vestment . . . and give us a guiding hand in working our own destinies.[71]

That hand was already extended. The Colonial Office had no intention of risking a major clash with Nkrumah. It was reconciled to an all-African cabinet if the CPP won the 1954 general election—as it did. In a curious metaphor which officials seemed to relish, the Colonial Office had approved of throwing almost everything "to the wolves before they overtake the political sledge carrying full self-Government."[72]

It was not so much British reluctance as Ashanti truculence that postponed this dénouement. After the CPP's red cockerel proved the most potent symbol at the polls, a reaction took place in the tropical heartland of the Gold Coast. Chiefs protesting against the villainous dictatorship of Accra joined farmers, still denied a fair price for their cocoa, to form the National Liberation Movement (NLM). Aiming to assert the power of Ashanti, it was inaugurated on 19 September 1954. Some forty thousand people assembled at Prince of Wales Park in the lush garden city of Kumasi, pleasantly shaded by okum trees. They banged drums, fired muskets and chanted battle cries. The Ashanti flag (green for its forests, gold for its minerals and black for its thrones) was decorated with a cocoa pod and a porcupine *(kotoko),* emblem of the nation's war machine. The porcupine's quills were young men keen to shed CPP blood. Flamboyant as well as aggressive, chewing kola nuts instead of betel or gum, they liked to dress in "the movie version of American cowboy costumes, black satin with a white fringe, and they wore high-heeled black Texas boots brilliantly studded with the letters NLM and the words 'King Force.'"[73]

Shooting opponents, burning their cars and blowing up their houses, these new Ashanti warriors fomented serious civil conflict. They even stoned the Governor, rightly seen as Nkrumah's ally, when he came to Kumasi. But they apparently first held up a placard saying "We have no quarrel with the Queen, God Bless Her."[74] Perhaps Arden-Clarke embellished this story for his sovereign's benefit, for he revered the British throne much as the Ashantis did the Golden Stool. Certainly Nkrumah made light of the disturbances even though they were more akin to a national uprising than to tribal ferment or party strife. His newspapers dismissed the violence as Chicago gangsterism and derided the NLM leaders as feudal reactionaries and infantile cocoa politicians. The *Osagyefo* himself called on the young men "to make the Gold Coast a paradise" so that when St. Peter opened the pearly gates "we shall sit in heaven and see our children driving their aeroplanes, commanding their own armies."[75]

By contrast, the Colonial Secretary, Alan Lennox-Boyd, was perturbed by the NLM's campaign and alert to its plea for a federal constitution that would stunt the growth of Nkrumah's autocracy. A lifelong right-wing Tory, described by the left-wing Michael Foot as "a Junior Imp who never grew up, a Primrose League Peter Pan,"[76] Lennox-Boyd was instinctively inclined to delay imperial withdrawal. Despite an equal and opposite inclination to back the Governor, he subscribed to the conventional Whitehall wisdom that the Gold Coast was no more "ready" for independence than "one's teen-age daughter is 'ready' for the proverbial latch-key."[77] So he took the Ashanti troubles as an opportunity to insist on a further election, in 1956. Nkrumah, who had sought a compromise with the intransigent NLM, angrily submitted. He feared the outcome. But the NLM could not extend its influence much beyond the Ashanti region and even here the CPP did surprisingly well, winning altogether 71 of 104 seats in the Legislative Assembly. Lennox-Boyd had to accept Arden-Clarke's recommendation that he should fix a date for ending British rule—or face carnage.

The Colonial Secretary did manage to achieve a feeble measure of regional autonomy and this had to satisfy the Ashanti people, who had looked to him to save them from Nkrumah. It was with mixed feelings of pride and shame that, on a visit to Kumasi where 100,000 mourning people greeted him, Lennox-Boyd read their banners proclaiming "British don't go" and "We don't want independence."[78] At midnight on 5 March 1957 they got independence. Accra led the celebrations. Arden-Clarke said that, thanks to the splendour of the decorations and the appearance of Princess Alexandra in their midst, the city had assumed "the magic qualities of a fairy tale."[79] Among the international dignitaries present were two Americans of very different persuasions, Martin Luther King Jr. and Vice-President Richard M. Nixon. King, Nkrumah's personal guest, made an eloquent speech condemning the racial violence in the USA's Deep South. Echoing the euphoria of his Ghanaian hosts, Nixon slapped one man on the shoulder and asked him how it felt to be free. "I wouldn't know, Sir," came the memorable reply. "I'm from Alabama."[80]

The Gold Coast gained its freedom because a forceful leader commanded a party which evidently expressed the national will. Once in power, though, Nkrumah fully exercised that freedom which (as he often said) resulted from independence, the freedom to make mistakes. He swiftly abandoned democratic practices and eroded civil liberties. He passed repressive measures, crushed opposition, controlled the press and radio, subverted the rule of law, and eventually turned Ghana into a corrupt despotism. In the process the country reached "the verge of bankruptcy," wrote General Spears, "largely due to the inexcusable extravagances and personal prestige schemes embarked upon by Dr. Nkrumah."[81] This was fair comment. The *Osagyefo's* megalomania waxed, Ghanaians observed, as his charisma waned. He founded his own ideology, Nkrumaism. His statue graced the front of parliament and his name went up in neon lights. His profile adorned stamps and banknotes. Coins bore his head haloed with the Latin inscription, *"Kwame Nkrumah, civitatis Ghaniensis conditor"*—founder of the state of Ghana.

In due course other self-proclaimed founders of new African states matched or out-matched Nkrumah in dictatorship, thus providing Spears and others with retrospective vindications of imperial rule. Yet from the slave trade to apartheid that rule was always authoritarian and often brutal. Under King Leopold of the Belgians, to cite the worst example, the Congo lost perhaps ten million people, "half of its population"—eclipsing anything essayed by Joseph Mobutu, the so-called "Zairian Caligula."[82] Furthermore, empire-builders had carved artificial boundaries on the face of a continent already ravaged by drought, famine, isolation, ignorance, poverty and disease. They had imposed white geometrical patterns on amorphous black landscapes, drawing frontiers that cut through tribal communities, ethnic units and linguistic entities. By introducing alien authority, religion, education and commerce, they had also undermined old cultural and social structures. Of course, Africans did not become helpless prisoners of their colonial past. They were masters of their own fate. But by the mid-twentieth century their states were primed for internal strife. Once European control was relinquished, they veered between anarchy and tyranny, seldom finding a democratic equilibrium. Even in Ghana, the Ashanti region and the Northern Territories agitated for secession; the Ewe people wanted their own homeland; and further groupings, such as Muslim immigrants *(Zongos)*, resisted integration. Other nations created by the imperial powers were much less compact and far more divided. They also lacked many of Ghana's additional advantages. Yet the Gold Coast had set such a rapid pace towards independence that Britain was hard pressed to moderate it elsewhere on the continent.

· · ·

West Africa, free of white settlers, moved most rapidly and within three years Nigeria followed in Ghana's footsteps, despite being little more than a geographical expression. The largest country in tropical Africa possessed no intrinsic unity. Like Gaul—and Ghana—it was divided into three parts. And its thirty million inhabitants, who by the early 1950s comprised a third of the Empire's remaining subjects, were unevenly split into a familiar trinity of major groupings. On the vast undulating plain of the Muslim north dwelt the pastoral Fulani, bronze-skinned, hawk-featured invaders from the Sahara now intermingled with the vanquished Hausa. In the swamps and forests of the south-east, where the tsetse fly killed cattle and horses, lived the Ibo, atomised into innumerable village communities. Finally, the south-west was the domain of the Yoruba, where towns such as Ibadan, Oyo and Benin bore witness to the former might of kingdoms shattered by collision with slave-hungry Europe. Yet a simple, tripartite description gives no idea of the country's baffling diversity. The northern territories were as alien to the southern as China was to Europe. According to Julian Huxley, the cultures ranged from "the neolithic level to something roughly equivalent to our medieval."[83]

In fact, Nigeria was the most heterogeneous country in Africa. It was an ethnic mosaic, a cultural patchwork and a "linguistic crossroads."[84] Wars and migrations had thoroughly mixed up the populations of the north, where Kanuri, Nupe, Tiv and a plethora of other tribes coexisted. Many of them were pagan—when a District Officer, trying to administer an oath, asked a witness what he believed in, he answered, "It all depends where I am."[85] The south was more Christian but scarcely more uniform, churches competing with ju-ju stalls packed with the fetishes that shocked white visitors—sheep gizzards, snake fangs, bat wings, dog paws, parrot intestines, dried monkey penises. Elspeth Huxley found a characteristic image to express her horror at the prolific exuberance of Lagos: its "sheer naked human life, mere human existence, bubbles and pullulates with the frightening fecundity of bacteria."[86] But the best measure of Nigeria's fissiparous condition was the Babel of 250 tongues, some spoken by fewer than a thousand people. When the Governor gave a speech in one town he was surprised to find that his three interpreters were between them translating it into six languages.

In theory, British rule harmonised Nigerian discord. It established law and order, inaugurated free trade, created a network of roads and railways, introduced a common currency instead of gin or iron bars or cowrie shells or Maria Theresa dollars. According to Margery Perham, empire-builders imposed a superstructure like a "great steel grid over the amorphous cellular tissue of tribal Africa and the hundreds of independent and often hostile communities were held within its interstices in peace."[87] In fact they had acquired Nigeria by force, making up its frontiers as they went along and sustaining it as a whole by dividing the sum of its parts. Britain seized Lagos after heavy fighting in 1851 and instituted a protectorate in the delta in 1885 before, fifteen years later, taking over the Royal Niger Company's claims to the vast hinterland. Despite the efforts of Lugard, colonial government took many forms and the British never imposed constitutional coherence. Indeed, they undermined existing structures of authority. Traders assisted in this process, demoralising the population with raw spirits that provided half the state's tax revenue. Missionaries also assisted in the process, attacking polygyny (which united families), ancestor worship (which cemented communities), initiation ceremonies (which educated youths) and other creative conventions. Dancing was especially condemned, "a mixture of Breughel and Bedlam."[88] Chinua Achebe's best-known novel was a lament on the disintegration of his hero's clan: white men "put a knife on things that held us together and we have fallen apart."[89] Reflecting the mutual antagonism of their regions, colonial officials were even at odds with each other. It was said that if all the Nigerians were expelled from the country, British administrators in the north would go to war with those in the south.

So nationalism was slow to germinate and people's loyalties were essentially local, directed towards family, clan and region. Millions lived and died without knowing that they were Nigerians, let alone subjects of the British Empire. They seldom, if ever, saw a white face, even when Europeans took to travelling by bicycle and Ford instead of hammock and canoe. Where District Officers did appear they found it hard to establish a rapport with such linguistically diverse people: one man only did so by playing on his portable gramophone a record called "The Laughing Policeman."[90] Nigerians spent their lives scratching subsistence from the earth and wrestling with a land that seemed to spawn biblical plagues—there were 750,000 lepers. As late as 1952 less than 10 per cent of the population was literate and the figure fell to 2 per cent in the north.

Here the colonial authorities kept their feudal raj in a "fossilised" condition, "hermetically sealed"[91] from the rest of the country. Southerners, mostly Ibo migrants doing skilled work as clerks, storekeepers, railwaymen and so on, were segregated in strangers' quarters outside the red walls of cities such as Kano and Sokoto. Christian missionaries were excluded. Islamic customs were respected, among them purdah so strict that there were no female teachers or nurses, and only prostitutes could aspire to adult education. Until the 1930s British officials even veiled their own wives on public occasions. The emirs, jewelled and scented potentates in embroidered white robes and capacious indigo turbans beaten clean so that they shone with a metallic glint, repaid social deference with political allegiance. Like Indian princes, they obeyed advice. In return the British prevented the assassinations that had formerly tempered their despotism. However badly these rulers treated their own people, they could usually count on the backing of local officials. "What!" exclaimed one Chief Commissioner to a subordinate who wanted to remove a petty tyrant in Niger Province. "Depose a Second Class Chief? Heav'n forfend!"[92] Having united Nigeria, the British divided it to cement their rule and they found the ossified north most compliant and congenial. They felt a natural affinity for polo-playing Fulani aristocrats, with their "predominant characteristics of Moslem dignity, courtesy and courage."[93]

Yet hardly less amenable, between the wars, were the ambitious Ibos and the proud Yorubas of the south. It is true that occasional disturbances did mar the tranquillity, notably millenarian convulsions and women's riots over taxation which cost more than thirty lives in 1929. But Nigerians had no grievances like those that blighted African colonies containing European settlers. There was no overt conflict between white capital and black labour, as would surely have occurred if the soap magnate Lord Leverhulme, who favoured treating Africans like children, had been allowed to acquire palm oil plantations. There was no organised resistance to British rule, which did little to impair the dignity of Nigerians. Visitors from Nairobi or Cape Town were surprised to find that a "proud, assertive people, with their blacker skins and more Negroid faces, walked the streets in their bright flowing robes as if Lagos and its suburbs, its markets and its official buildings was entirely *their* city and subject to no suzerain power."[94] This was not a complete misapprehension: whites had to stop playing polo on the race course, which they had built and maintained on public land, because "it interfered with the black boys' football."[95] It was even possible for an intelligent British official, who himself called Europeanised Africans "Wogs," to boast that in Nigeria there was "virtually no racial prejudice."[96]

He would have been right to say that little institutionalised discrimination existed—the government outlawed it completely in 1948. However, there was also little informal fraternisation. As one District Officer recorded, "You could sleep with black women provided you did it very discreetly, but you couldn't drink with black men."[97] Furthermore, nothing could hide the familiar contrast between European palaces and African shantytowns. Beside the paved, well-lit Marina rose the imposing monuments to British political and commercial dominance. Notable among them was Government House, a white, three-storey Victorian palace with arcaded verandahs, green jalousies and a huge *porte cochère* under a canopy of thumbergia, "whose white orchid-like flowers swayed gently on their stems."[98] Equally elegant was the segregated suburb on Ikoyi island, which contained luxurious villas with garages and parquet floors and verdant lawns set amid bamboo, banana and palm groves descending to the lagoon. Behind this bright façade Africans were packed into "festering catacombs of filth"[99] close to Carter Bridge. John Gunther thought this the worst slum in Africa outside Johannesburg. By day, he said, it was even shunned by flies. At night it was "as dark as Erebus."[100]

Such glaring disparities fostered bitterness. As one official ironically remarked, the citizens of Lagos did not display that "dog-like devotion to the Government and its officers which is expected of all nice black people."[101] Yet, as it happened, the longest-serving Governor, Sir Bernard Bourdillon (1935–43), was also the most popular. Sympathetic and understanding, he recognised that the future of the country lay in the hands of educated young nationalists, whom he refused to regard as "mere mischief-makers."[102] They in turn hailed him as "a sportsman and a gentleman."[103] They even went so far as to adopt the pork pie hat he habitually wore, an item of fashion marketed in Lagos as the "Bourdillon." The Governor also tried to erode the isolationism of the north, saying that it "must step down from behind the plate-glass windows through which it surveys disdainfully the antics of its plebeian neighbour, tuck up its long sleeves and join in the mêlée." Bourdillon was not, though, an especially dynamic or progressive proconsul. Tall, handsome and vain, he had a penchant for practical jokes, a roving eye for the pretty wives of his subordinates and (to quote his sympathetic biographer) "formidable powers of relaxation." Finding the climate of Lagos decidedly better than that of Colombo, he enjoyed riding, hunting, "good tennis, indifferent golf, indifferent (but cheap and amusing) polo" as well as "exceptionally good tarpon-fishing." For further recreation he established a hill station on the Jos Plateau.

Bourdillon travelled widely, viewing the country from a seat fixed in front of the engine pulling his train and from his comfortable stern-wheeler, the *Valiant,* which had a skittles alley on the upper deck. He also drove his Railton sports car around Lagos so fast that he once killed a young Nigerian. Yet on official occasions the Governor was the soul of dignity. He imposed such rigid protocol at Government House, where the oven heat was somewhat reduced by a six-leaf punkah pulled by two "boys," that he was nicknamed "the Mikado." When Bourdillon returned home the Colonial Secretary thought he was suffering from *"maladie de grandeur."* Nigerians criticised his "swanky"[104] stewardship, which emphasised the great gulf fixed between white rulers and black subjects. No one resented this more than Herbert Macaulay, the self-styled "Gandhi of Nigeria." An angry old man in a white suit and a white moustache that stuck out like cat's whiskers, he was the grandson of the first African to become an Anglican bishop. And he ran the inflammatory *Lagos Daily News,* which was "ultra-radical, intensely nationalistic, virulently and implacably anti-white."[105] It agitated against economic ills, such as the control by the "Cocoa Pool" of 90 per cent of the trade. Its political line was still more potent: "The African has now reached the age of puberty and demands the right to assume . . . the *toga virilis* [garb of manhood]."[106]

However, this was an expression of racial rather than territorial nationalism. Macaulay and his followers, who were almost entirely confined to Lagos, espoused the unity of West Africa not Nigeria. One Governor, Sir Hugh Clifford, dismissed their goal as manifestly absurd, comparable to the quest for a European nation. But between the wars they believed that local loyalties were impeding the development of a wider, pan-African solidarity. This was certainly the view of Macaulay's political heir, Nnamdi Azikiwe, who in 1937 returned from the United States after an educational odyssey that served as an inspiration to Nkrumah. Always known as Zik, he had changed his first name from Benjamin in 1934 when a South African objection prevented him from competing for his country in the British Empire Games—he was "as powerful as an ox"[107] and reckoned that he could run a mile in four and a half minutes. At about the same time he vowed to dedicate his life to "the emancipation of the continent of Africa from the shackles of imperialism." Loftily idealistic and unscrupulously self-serving, he came home in order "to infuse into the indigenous African a spirit of constitutional resistance to foreign rule."[108] That was the burden of his book *Renascent Africa* (1937), described as "the Bible of West African youth."[109]

It was also the message of the newspaper chain he set up, modelled on the yellow press of America—*Time* magazine dubbed him "the Bertie McCormick of the Niger Delta" as well as "the jungle George Washington."[110] Like McCormick's Chicago *Tribune,* Zik's *West African Pilot* was printed demagogy. Not content with directing scurrilous invective at the few thousand Europeans in Nigeria, it pilloried African rivals as "imperialist stooges" and "Uncle Toms." Readers were "elec-zik-fied."[111] But the war, with all its dislocations, opportunities, hardships and hopes, changed Zik's political direction. It translated continental patriotism into Nigerian nationalism. Aiming to draw its sting, the British increased its venom. In 1942 they appointed the first Nigerians to the Executive Council, holding out the prospect of further constitutional progress. But this merely provoked nationalists to rally their ranks. In 1944 Macaulay and Zik founded the National Council of Nigeria and the Cameroons* (NCNC) in order to "weld the heterogeneous masses of Nigeria into one solid block."[112]

This proved impossible, partly because the NCNC was itself vitiated by tribalism. Aspiring to create a national movement that would sweep Nigeria to freedom, Zik could not resist favouring his own people, the Ibos. He would even assert that they had a divine mission to redeem Africa. So while Ibos hailed Zik as a New Messiah, Yorubas christened him the Arch Devil. Northern leaders, fearing post-colonial domination by a southern "gang of agitators,"[113] threatened to continue the Fulani march to the sea. Nevertheless, the NCNC was the first party to attract widespread support in Nigeria. Zik skilfully exploited labour disputes (including a general strike) and other troubles caused by the high cost of living at the end of the war. The new socialist government in Westminster unwittingly assisted him. Espousing the welfare state abroad as well as at home, it dispatched fresh cohorts of officials to implement a variety of authoritarian measures in Africa, particularly in the fields of agriculture and public works. According to one historian, this "amounted to a second colonial invasion."[114]

The claim is scarcely exaggerated. Between 1945 and 1947 the number entering the Colonial Service was equal to that of eleven years' normal recruitment and in the following decade its intake increased by 50 per cent. And there is no denying African umbrage at an influx of Europeans bent on introducing, say, anti-erosion terracing, cattle inoculation and modern methods of cultivation. Writing about the training of such administrators, Sir Ralph Furse wondered whether the Colonial Service had not "too closely followed the Roman model." It had perhaps concentrated too much on achieving material prosperity and should find room for "the Greek spirit," he suggested, teaching recruits "more about the artistic and spiritual background of the people among whom they come to live."[115] This was cant. Moreover, it failed to reflect the stern imperatives of the post-war world. Socialism, like Caesarism, elevated the power of the state for thoroughly practical purposes.

* The British Cameroons was a mandated territory administered as part of Nigeria.

When the state was foreign, its intervention was all the more likely to offend. An especially provocative instance occurred in 1945 when the colonial authorities vested Nigerian minerals and common lands in the British Crown by means of what Zik called the "obnoxious ordinances."[116] They were intended to achieve a form of protective nationalisation. But the more these measures were said to be for their own good, the more Nigerians protested. They feared the British bearing gifts almost as much as they loathed them extorting profits. Reaping was, indeed, the corollary of imperial sowing. Faced with its own financial crises, Attlee's government matched Churchill's in exploiting overseas dependencies, which were kept inside their "economic cage."[117] It bought colonial goods cheaply and withheld the dollars they earned, lodging Nigerian balances in London at very low rates of interest. Having contributed to the war effort with a "forced loan,"[118] Africans now helped Britain to finance the Beveridge Plan for peace-time social welfare. It was, Zik declared, something his compatriots needed more themselves.

To be sure Britain did grant its colonies some £40 million between 1946 and 1951, but this was investment rather than charity. The cash was designed to promote the supply of raw materials such as cotton, cocoa, coffee, palm oil and (notoriously) groundnuts for the home market and as dollar-earning commodities. It was also intended to stimulate orders for British manufactured goods, cement, steel, motor vehicles, railway equipment and the like. Moreover, while Labour was in power colonial sterling balances in London rose to well over a billion pounds and Britain extracted about £140 million from its overseas territories. Still, as a British official observed, Nigeria's economic woes hardly counted beside its political grievances. What mattered was "not poverty but passion, passion about the colonial relationship."[119] Educated Nigerians revolted against their humiliating state of tutelage. They conjured with "Negritude." They celebrated "the African personality."[120] They invoked a glorious past. Those who had "built the pyramids, fought with Caesar's battalions . . . and dominated the Pyrenees" knew that they could "be great again and be slaves no more."[121] Unable to live a full life without freedom, said Zik, they were united in their blazing indignation against alien rule.

Of course they were far from being united, as the Colonial Office well knew, but it wanted to mollify the NCNC by making cautious progress towards independence. However, the regime had changed in Lagos. Zik had enjoyed quite good relations with Bourdillon, playing tennis at Government House and hailing him as a far-sighted statesman. When Bourdillon's wife asked why his newspapers nevertheless attacked the Governor, Zik replied laconically: "Politics, Ma."*[122] Bourdillon's successor, Sir Arthur Richards, was less affable and more conservative. His aim was not to conciliate but to dominate the NCNC. Moreover, his Whitehall masters had to chivvy him into devising a new constitution to match that of Burns in the Gold Coast. Admittedly his task was more difficult, for Richards had to balance national unity against greater regional diversity as well as giving Nigerians more say in government. But he introduced his flawed scheme with scant consultation, which drew criticism even from the retired Bourdillon and inspired a vitriolic campaign in the Zik press. Richards banned two of his papers and ridiculed his claim that the British plotted to murder him. Zik had nothing to fear, said the Governor, except "the dark shadows of his own imagination."[123] The London *Times* dismissed the allegation as another hysterical publicity stunt and said that although Zik presented himself as the spokesman of exploited Africa, he was "anti-imperialistic and at times anti-British and anti-white."[124]

Still, Zik brought politics to life during the first whistle-stop tour made by a Nigerian. He travelled by train, car, lorry and horse, speaking in compounds, schools, cinemas and churches to the accompaniment of flute, cow horn and brass bands. Clever, articulate and urbane, though ultimately unfathomable, Zik galvanised his countrymen. The NCNC grew with "electrical rapidity."[125] Zik's more militant young acolytes began to call for revolution, doubtless heeding his reminder that the tree of liberty was "watered with the blood of tyrants."[126] Inter-regional tensions grew and there were even stirrings in the holy north. Meanwhile, the Richards constitution, endorsed after a debate at Westminster lasting just twenty-nine minutes, was dying at birth. Nothing could save it, not even large transfusions of British cash to build schools, hospitals, reservoirs and other amenities. Richards, like Burns in the Gold Coast, had failed to meet the aspirations of educated Africans. In 1948 he was replaced with a less old-fashioned Governor, Sir John Macpherson. The *Nigerian Eastern Mail* welcomed him as "the harbinger of a new political era." His advent was a sign that the Colonial Office had "revolted against the old ways of leopards and wolves, of the strong devouring the weak."[127]

Actually the danger was that strong Nigerians would devour their own weak. This might occur through the emergence of an educated oligarchy or a regional tyranny, one probably compounding the other. The Colonial Office still respected Lugard's principle that power should not fall into the

---

* "Ma" was not short for madam, or even for mother. It was a term of respect in the Efik language for a woman whose word is final.

hands of a minority of "Europeanised natives."[128] Yet they were the most vociferous in demanding it and the best equipped to exercise it. Since the "mission boys" of today would be the statesmen of tomorrow, the British authorities thought they should be trained for the role—between 1947 and 1951 the number of Nigerians holding senior service posts rose from 182 to 628. However, nearly all the new officials were Yorubas and Ibos, who seemed poised to take the place of British administrators in the north. One of these administrators spoke for many in deploring the prospect that "our likeable, lazy northerners will be handed over to the tender mercies of the southern 'trousered apes' within a few years."[129] And the leader of the northern resistance, Abubakar Tafawa Balewa, warned that Nigerian independence "would mean handing over one region to the others."[130] Macpherson's task was to devise a constitution that would prevent such indigenous empire-building. He had to ensure that the traditional rulers and their people checked the westernised elite and that the north balanced the south. Keen to avoid the mistake of his predecessor, Macpherson spent several years consulting all parties and regularly had Zik to drinks and dinner. But the discussion process encouraged all three main groupings to flex their muscles and sharpen their weapons.

Zik's more extreme adherents, whom he disowned as "viviparous lieutenants and cantankerous followers," dabbled in sedition. These "Zikists" called on people not to pay their taxes. They told "the British to go to hell with their Empire Day when they celebrate our enslavement."[131] They fomented trouble in the Enugu collieries, to which panicky police reacted by shooting twenty-one miners. This provoked disturbances elsewhere and "a great political awakening."[132] Then, in 1950, a militant attempted to assassinate the Chief Secretary, Sir Hugh Foot, for which the Zikists were duly suppressed. Meanwhile, a radical lawyer, Obafemi Awolowo, was creating the Action Group as an expression of Yoruba political aspirations. Its prime purpose was to cast off the British yoke, which Awolowo deemed "immeasurably baneful."[133] But the Action Group also demanded unity through federation, perhaps with as many as thirty or forty provincial houses of assembly. Awolowo hoped thus to prevent Zik from becoming a dictator at the head of a master race. To protect his own region from fascist or, still worse, Christian incursions, Abubakar formed the Northern People's Party (NPC). Southerners derided its representatives as the "mindless mouthpieces of senior white officials."[134]

Macpherson's constitution, a cumbersome compromise between British power and Nigerian devolution, could not meld together the divergent elements. In 1953 their communal and political rivalries came to a head at

Kano. Thousands of Ibos and Yorubas lived in the strangers' quarter *(Sabon Gari)* just outside the walled city, itself a squalid labyrinth of rufous mud hovels, stinking goatskin tanneries and ancient markets selling almost everything: morocco leather, dyed cloth, ivory, hippopotamus teeth, spears, knives, cartridges, red peppers, peanuts stacked in green pyramids and blue antimony to beautify the eyes. The southerners often used their bureaucratic positions to patronise and exploit illiterate Hausa–Fulani people; and when the Action Group and the NCNC threatened to crusade for freedom in the north, Kano erupted. During the riots dozens of people lost their lives, some being castrated and otherwise mutilated. Macpherson's constitution was also damaged beyond repair. It seemed to one chief that Nigeria would reach independence "not in peace, but in pieces."[135]

Decentralisation was the only way to avert disintegration. So in 1954 Nigeria received its third constitution in seven years, this one being named after the Colonial Secretary, Oliver Lyttelton. It gave the regions a large measure of autonomy, leaving the federal parliament in Lagos responsible only for such matters as customs, currency, immigration, policing, defence and foreign affairs. The separation of powers provided a basis for nationhood and Zik rejoiced that Lyttelton had offered Nigeria "self-government on a platter of gold." There was a delay of six years before it was served to the nation. More splintering took place within regions and parties, which struggled to consolidate their position. Torn between local and national loyalty, the NCNC was especially prone to mutiny and Zik complained that it was his "misfortune to lead an undisciplined army."[136] But his own generalship came under attack when he was accused of funnelling public money into the party's coffers through a bank which he had founded. Lyttelton's successor, Alan Lennox-Boyd, condemned what he called corruption and what Nigerians called "paytriotism." Yet he could do little more than give Zik a severe "talking to," fearing that any form of sanction might turn Nigeria into another Malaya or Kenya. Contrary to the Colonial Office's racist view that "Black man like strong word," Zik resented Lennox-Boyd's "insulting high-handedness." He hit back, turning the episode into an indictment of "the devilish colonial system," which sustained a European banking monopoly as well as subjecting Africans to proconsuls who behaved "worse than Nero."[137]

Zik charged the Colonial Secretary with wanting to "appoint a Spanish Inquisition on my biography even when I was in the womb of my mother."[138] Moreover, he said, Lennox-Boyd himself had business interests in Nigeria: his family firm, Guinness, was shortly to build a brewery in Lagos, the stout being esteemed in West Africa as an aphrodisiac. This whole affair seemed to epitomise the Colonial Office's problem. "The fact must be faced," wrote one senior official, "the West African negro is not capable of honest democratic self-government in this generation; and probably won't be in the next." To grant independence would be to invite crookery and chaos, to justify South Africa's apartheid system, and to discredit British colonial policy. "All we can do now is to play for as much time as we can get."[139] Lennox-Boyd agreed. The dispute with Zik confirmed his mistrust of radical southern politicians and his preference for feudal northern aristocrats, such as the Sardauna of Sokoto. That title meant "Captain of the Bodyguard" (effectively Prime Minister) and its holder reminded Harold Macmillan (he told the Queen) of Trollope's Duke of Omnium. For the sake of such congenial figures Lennox-Boyd attempted to postpone the ending of imperial rule.

Whether exalting the Empire or easing its transition into Commonwealth, the attractive young Queen Elizabeth II was a trump card in the British pack; and nothing was better calculated to inspire Nigerian loyalty to the Crown than a royal tour. So in 1956 elaborate preparations were made to present the monarch to her Nigerian subjects and vice versa. Government Houses were expensively refurbished, new carpets alone costing the country £1,500. The northern durbar arena was turned from dust bowl into green field. Lagos was disguised by "a gigantic camouflage operation."[140] The dilapidated market was hidden behind metal fences and the municipal rubbish dump was covered with black slag to masquerade as a coal tip. The Queen and the Duke of Edinburgh, said to be "manly" in his crisp naval uniform, received an ecstatic welcome. On the dozen-mile journey from the airport to Lagos, a British journalist wrote, "The black face of Nigeria was all one white grin."[141] The crowds were so thick in the island city that policemen walked on their shoulders. And the spectators expressed their pent-up feelings for Her Majesty with "a long-drawn A-a-a-ah."[142] Such was the enthusiasm at Kaduna that the sovereign's daïs, shaded under a portable canopy designed by Norman Hartnell, almost succumbed to a mock cavalry charge.

This was the climax of a sumptuous pageant at which, to quote another visiting reporter, "emirs and great chieftains . . . spearsmen and archers, clowns and tumblers and half-naked pagans gathered in all their barbarous magnificence to salute their ruler."[143] Some had doubted whether the Queen could cut "a sufficiently regal figure" to satisfy Nigerians, who were accustomed to see their own "petty kings and chiefs moving around in medieval sartorial splendour, like figures from the Field of the Cloth of Gold."[144] However, throughout the searing round of ceremonies, inspections, assemblies, banquets and garden parties, the sovereign graciously met official requests to don her most glittering finery. Having inherited a Golconda of imperial gems, she was not to be eclipsed. At the House of Representatives in Lagos she appeared "in an ivory satin gown encrusted with gold and pearls and wearing the dazzling tiara that once belonged to Queen Mary."[145] At Lugard Hall in Kaduna, wrote the Sardauna of Sokoto, the Queen's "diamonds and jewels flashed in the glare of lamps like lightning across a rippled lake; her beautiful dress spread about her like a brilliant waterfall."[146]

Such was royalist euphoria that crime as well as party conflict virtually ceased; yet the mood, which the British authorities hoped to exploit, was neither all-pervading nor long-lasting. This was partly due to the Queen's own demeanour. Throughout the tour, as one chief complained, she made not a single extemporary gesture in public. If only she had been able to respond to the throbbing dancers of Itsekiri, for example, not just "as a monarch but as a woman and a mother." Instead she always behaved like a royal automaton, with "complete predictability . . . [when] we prefer warm spontaneity."[147] Doubtless the sovereign was inhibited as well as unsophisticated. In 1948 she had accompanied her father to South Africa where, at a "native" investiture, he passed medals to an official "so that the King's pure white hands at no time came in contact with a black man."[148] And she later acknowledged that among her favourite television programmes was *The Black and White Minstrel Show*. Anyway, strict protocol prevailed in Nigeria.

Furthermore, British officials tended to monopolise the Queen and her thirty-strong entourage. One Nigerian protested in verse:

> They cannot see the real north
> Nor meet the common people,
> For now the edict has gone forth:
> "The Government must keep all
> Those gracious smiles, those greeting hands,
> Receptions, feasts, parades and bands,
> In pleasure's proper habitat,
> Which is the Secretariat."[149]

The exclusiveness was justified by a concern for the Queen's safety amidst people who were said to be "notoriously excitable."[150] Zik claimed that the police cowed citizens and at times security was so tight that the royal procession went down "avenues almost entirely empty of spectators."[151] However, white civil servants craved the prestige magically conferred by propinquity to the Queen. From the centre of the hive they also restricted the flow of royal jelly—a number of them received decorations whereas only one African was awarded a medal for his services. This offended a few prominent Nigerians, but many more objected to the crude stereotypes depicting them in the British press. Black journalists denounced Fleet Street for "spitting on Nigeria's African race" during the tour and called for punitive measures to halt the "ghastly tirade of venom."[152] If such misrepresentation continued, they added, Nigeria might opt to become a republic. So indeed it did, in 1963, three years after independence. Three years later still, one of the few Africans to have seen the monarch at close quarters while she was in the country, her ADC Major Ironsi, became Nigeria's first military dictator.

All told, then, the Queen's visit had little positive impact and Lennox-Boyd could not sustain imperial rule for long despite the deep divisions within Nigeria which gave him ample excuse for procrastination. The Colonial Office still had some room for manoeuvre. It held conferences. It dispatched commissions. It devised compromises. It also supported the modest, eloquent and malleable Abubakar, who became the country's first Prime Minister in 1957. He was preferred to Awolowo, deemed a dangerous "hothead," and to Zik, a cowardly "twister" surrounded by "hyaena lieutenants."[153] But there is no evidence, as has been alleged, that the last Governor, Sir James Robertson, who retained ultimate control, employed dirty tricks or used his senior staff to organise "election rigging."[154] Nor does it seem likely that Zik's communications were intercepted, though he certainly blamed the devilish colonial system for exploiting tribal antipathies. Zik, who became the country's first President, later wrote: "Nigerian leaders were manoeuvred by imperial interests into dissipating their energies and turning against their own people."[155]

However, the emergence of free Ghana in 1957 sent a "shock wave"[156] of emotion through nationalist circles in Nigeria, beginning a domino effect which freed one West African dependency after another. Abubakar himself, representing the conservative north, added to the momentum and it became irresistible. Britain's position was weakened by the exodus of colonial officials, who could see the writing on the wall. It was further eroded by the advent of General de Gaulle, who in 1958 gave France's West African territories, which entirely surrounded Nigeria, the right to decide their own fate. So Robertson recommended that the Colonial Office should abandon arguments about waiting to see if the regions could govern themselves and set a firm date for national independence. It should be bestowed voluntarily, he argued, rather than being wrested from Britain after a campaign of anti-imperial agitation such as Zik and Awolowo would delight to spearhead.

Lennox-Boyd reluctantly concurred, keen to secure British interests, military as much as commercial, with a friendly new member of the Commonwealth. The cabinet decided that Nigeria should raise its own flag on 1 October 1960. Perturbed by the hazards of schism and graft, Lennox-Boyd doubted whether "self-government will in Nigeria be good government."[157] Gibbon might have riposted that independence is the first of earthly blessings and that corruption is "the most infallible symptom of constitutional liberty."[158]

Neighbouring dominoes tumbled with still greater rapidity. In 1959 Iain Macleod, who had transformed himself from playboy into politician, succeeded Lennox-Boyd as Colonial Secretary with an overriding determination to move fast in Africa. That was dangerous, he acknowledged, appraising the odds with a gambler's eye. But it was far less dangerous than trying to hold back the current of nationalism. This was especially true in the settler colonies, where Macleod became "the white hope of the Blacks and the *bête noire* of the Whites."[159] He therefore instituted "a deliberate speeding-up of the movement towards independence."[160] In West Africa, accordingly, Sierra Leone got its freedom in 1961 and tiny Gambia, which was scarcely self-supporting, followed in 1965. So Britain's entire position in the region collapsed within the space of eight years. Yet the process was less straightforward than the domino image suggests.

The fall was precipitated not only by nationalist pressures but by international impulses and domestic stresses. Zik and his ilk might be expected to say that imperialism was "a crime against humanity."[161] In the wake of the Suez crisis, though, that sentiment became a global mantra. It was heard in the United States. It was repeated in Canada, where the discovery of Britain's imperial guilt was said to be like "finding a beloved uncle arrested for rape."[162] It reverberated throughout Asia. It echoed around Africa, as de Gaulle extricated France from the bloody civil war in Algeria, and Belgium, fearing a similar catastrophe in the Congo, also cut and ran. "Empire" became a dirty word in many languages and "colonialism," as Margery Perham said, was a universal term of "abuse."[163] The combined animus was reflected in the United Nations, which in December 1960 passed its momentous Resolution (No. 1514) demanding "a speedy and unconditional end to colonialism." Shortly afterwards the Soviet leader, Nikita Khrushchev, declared that if the imperialist powers ignored this resolution their subjugated peoples would have to sweep away all obstacles to independence. With more than a hint of menace, he promised that "they will not be alone in that struggle."[164]

This was the culmination of a change in the climate of world opinion which seriously eroded British self-confidence. One response to the change, during the late 1950s, was a campaign of linguistic cleansing. Of course, propaganda is integral to politics and the Emperor Augustus was not alone in recognising that "mankind is governed by names."[165] Over the years British imperialists had carried out many exercises in euphemism. Using the term "Commonwealth" for "Empire" in conversation with Senator Arthur Vandenburg during the war, Churchill had leeringly remarked that "we keep trade labels to suit all tastes."[166] In the Gold Coast Arden-Clarke had discovered "how effective the device of changing names could be." When he transmogrified "Chief Commissioner" into "Regional Officer" and "District Commissioner" into "Government Agent," they all seemed "to smell much sweeter in the public nose."[167] Now other appellations were purged and new aliases were invented. The British Colonial Service became Her Majesty's Overseas Civil Service. In 1958 Empire Day, deemed by the Minister of Education "dead beat and a non-starter,"[168] was rechristened Commonwealth Day. *United Empire* appeared as the *Journal of the Royal Commonwealth Society.* There was talk of subsuming the Colonial Office, its name thought to be "a serious handicap,"[169] into the Commonwealth Relations Office—the two departments did merge in 1966, only to be incorporated into the Foreign and Commonwealth Office two years later. Traditionalists resisted verbal appeasement and the Australian Prime Minister, Sir Robert Menzies, deprecated "the idea that we ought to apologise for the word 'Empire.'"[170] It denoted Victorian glories, Elizabethan valour and a mission that was "Roman in its nobility."[171] The British Empire, said one loyalist, was "a bridge over which civilisation had marched." It was, according to another, "the finest organisation the world had ever seen or ever would see."[172] In comparison the term "Commonwealth" savoured of republicanism and retreat. It was also a reminder of Sir Thomas More's famous remark, cited by J. A. Hobson: "Everywhere do I perceive a certain conspiracy of rich men seeking their own advantage under the name and pretext of commonwealth."[173]

Britons had other reasons for disparaging their own Commonwealth. It was increasingly ramshackle and riddled with anomalies. Its only unifying element, the Crown, was snubbed by republics and seen by some constituent states as "a symbol of colonial repression."[174] The Commonwealth was largely defined by negatives. It had no racial or cultural identity. It had, by 1962, no common citizenship. It possessed no religious or linguistic coherence. It was not a military coalition, or a diplomatic alliance, or a customs union. It looked to the United States for defence and even for leadership. In 1960, at a time of acute crisis in the balance of payments which Harold Macmillan hoped to resolve by joining the European Community, people "scoffed openly at the inadequacy of the Commonwealth as an association which could confer economic or political benefits on Britain."[175] Certainly trade with Commonwealth countries was shrinking rapidly: British exports to them fell from nearly half the total in 1950 to just under a quarter in 1970 and imports declined proportionately. And as the almighty dollar became the world's reserve currency, the sterling area, which consisted mainly of Commonwealth countries bound to the pound, crumbled and (in 1972) collapsed. Furthermore, many people in Britain disliked the Commonwealth's racial mixture, among them the Prime Minister himself. With characteristic condescension Macmillan said that Afro-Asian entry meant that becoming a member of the Commonwealth was no longer like gaining admission to Brooks's or Boodles but like joining the RAC. Despite all this backbiting, though, British governments earnestly promoted what Macmillan called "our Commonwealth Club."[176] All former colonies should belong, thus becoming part of a multi-racial fraternity from which benefits must flow like milk and honey.

However, in Westminster and Whitehall self-interest counted for more than altruism as far as the Commonwealth was concerned. The fundamental motive behind official attempts to "sell"[177] this nebulous body was to sustain British prestige by concealing the decay of British power. Like the Papacy—Hobbes's ghost of the Roman Empire sitting crowned upon its grave—the Commonwealth was a phantom of former glory. It was also a shade of imperial immortality, a portent of the vital influence Britain could wield on earth despite the extinction of its global sway. Like Winston Churchill in his first political speech, Harold Macmillan publicly condemned "the croakers, the moaners, the faint-hearted and the cynical" for descrying "the decline and fall of the British Empire." What they were really witnessing, he insisted, was "a rebirth, an empire transforming itself into a free Commonwealth family."[178] The Commonwealth might even become, as Leo Amery had hoped, the nucleus around which "the ultimate world order would coalesce."[179] Other Tories were more realistic. Enoch Powell opposed the Commonwealth "as a sticking plaster for the wound left by the amputation of empire."[180] Macmillan himself privately acknowledged that once "the Commonwealth begins to disintegrate I feel it is really finished" and he was anxious not "to play the role of Lord North." He thought that Gaitskell was more suited to it, "both by temperament and appearance."[181] Macmillan's theatrical skills were devoted to preserving the illusion of British greatness. At times he evidently saw himself as a latter-day Caesar, disguising artfulness under a cloak of "calm dignity"[182] and keeping the barbarians at bay for just long enough to hold a final triumph. "This is the age of Diocletian," he said, "the end of Empire."[183]

Harold Macmillan had trodden a dogged but tortuous path to 10 Downing Street. A shy, introspective publisher, he had been crushed by a dominant American mother and humiliated by an adulterous English wife—Lady Dorothy, a daughter of the Duke of Devonshire, conducted a long and barely concealed liaison with one of her husband's fellow Conservative MPs, the raffish, bisexual Robert Boothby. Macmillan was once seen banging his head against the window of a railway compartment from sheer despair. During the 1930s he was too left-wing to gain preferment and even his old nanny declared, "Mr Harold is a dangerous Pink."[184] With his fussy manner and his clammy handshake, he struck others as a bore and a prig. However, he made a bold stand against appeasement and in 1938 he burned Neville Chamberlain in effigy on his Guy Fawkes bonfire. Churchill promoted Macmillan during the war, when he shed his radical sympathies and began to conjure with "the glories of the future empire."[185] It was Macmillan's aggressiveness in this cause at the beginning of the Suez crisis that won him support among his colleagues. He also managed to hide his subsequent panic, to say nothing of his brains, manifest cleverness being a notorious handicap in the Tory party. So in January 1957, aged sixty-two, Macmillan succeeded Eden. He was the last British Prime Minister to sport a moustache,* relic of his gallant service during the Great War and earnest of imperial orthodoxy. Actually, like much else about Macmillan, it was a form of camouflage. The Prime Minister concealed his wounded psyche behind a façade of Edwardian insouciance. The very private man wore flamboyant hats in the manner of Churchill. The intellectual bourgeois pretended to be an antique grandee, extolling the merits of overripe grouse when he really preferred cold chicken. The old entertainer, who consulted the comedian Bud Flanagan about his delivery and employed a speech writer called Christ, was often physically sick before addressing the Commons. Above all, the Conservative did not scruple to retreat from empire.

Macmillan was a pragmatist who recognised as early as 1955 that the tide of the world had set in the direction of national "autonomy and identity."[186] On becoming Prime Minister, he wondered whether he was destined to liquidate or to remodel the Empire. In public he naturally took the Churchillian line, denying any "intention of presiding over the liquidation

---

* Dorothy Macmillan also had a faint moustache. Seeing it in a photograph, a family member remarked: "At last I know what it was that Bob [Boothby] saw in her."

of the British Empire."[187] Behind the scenes he initiated a series of reviews to weigh up its advantages, which concluded that the costs and benefits were about equal. Such audits were bound to be speculative because they contained so many imponderable factors. For example, it was not possible to calculate whether preserving colonies would weaken the pound by depleting British resources or strengthen it by augmenting British prestige. That question was intimately connected with the Anglo-American "special relationship," which one U.S. ambassador in London dismissed as "little more than sentimental terminology."[188] Macmillan tried to reinvigorate that relationship after Suez in order to uphold sterling and otherwise to buttress Britain, particularly in the fields of intelligence and nuclear weapons. He affected an aristocratic disdain for Americans, asserting that they all looked the same, like Japanese or Chinese, or dentists. But he continued to think that they were the new Romans, "great big, vulgar, bustling people, more vigorous than we are and also more idle."[189] And he still believed that the British should play the part of Greeks, guiding America with the sophisticated counsel of a more mature civilisation. Despite his friendship with Eisenhower and John F. Kennedy, Macmillan carried little real weight in Washington. On the contrary, Britain's weakness meant that it was more susceptible to American influence, especially in the colonial sphere.

Responding to transatlantic, nationalistic and other pressures, Macmillan hesitantly acquiesced in the Empire's "progressive dissolution."[190] He rejected "the vulgar and false jibe that the British people by a series of gestures unique in history abandoned their Empire in a fit of frivolity or impatience."[191] Rather, he put forward the familiar argument that they had long been preparing to bestow freedom on their colonies inside the Commonwealth. He even cited Macaulay's celebrated demolition of the adage that no people ought to be free until they were fit to use their freedom—it was worthy of the fool in the old story who resolved not to go into the water until he had learned to swim. Macmillan had a fair case as regards West Africa. Actually he thought that Nigeria and neighbouring dependencies were quite unready for self-government; but he believed that it should be granted because Britain had nothing to lose and influence to gain, while the alternative might be rebellion and repression. However, by the end of the 1950s, when French and Belgian withdrawal left Britain's settler colonies exposed, Macmillan faced an acute dilemma in East and central Africa. He was reluctant to sacrifice even decadent kith and kin in Kenya, Rhodesia and elsewhere to native "barbarians."[192] Indeed, he privately denounced the treachery of European intellectuals who "attacked the whites of Africa and championed the blacks."[193]

Yet in the famous speech Macmillan made to the South African Parliament in Cape Town on 3 February 1960, he asserted that a "wind of change" was blowing through the continent. "Ever since the break-up of the Roman Empire," he said, "one of the constant facts of political life in Europe has been the emergence of independent nations."[194] They had come into existence in Asia fifteen years earlier and now national consciousness was awakening in Africa. Macmillan shocked an audience steeped in the principles of apartheid and Prime Minister Verwoerd's face "clouded with anger."[195] The rhetoric suggested that Macmillan was ready to ride the storm. In reality he hoped to trim and tack in a zephyr. Unlike Macleod, he preferred conservative equivocations to radical solutions. Macmillan's stated aim was to find means by which each racially mixed community "can become more of a community, and fellowship can be fostered between its various parts."[196] Yet even as he uttered this anodyne formula, the Prime Minister must surely have been aware that it would not solve the problem of Britain's own white outposts in Africa.

19

Uhuru—Freedom

Kenya and the Mau Mau

African opposition to colonial rule in Kenya had been smouldering ever since the advent of European settlers, but it came to a blaze after the Second World War. The burning issue had always been the invaders' expropriation of the land. "When someone steals your ox," a Kikuyu elder told the Labour MP Fenner Brockway, "it is killed and roasted and eaten. One can forget. When someone steals your land, especially if nearby, one can never forget. It is always there, its trees which were dear friends, its little streams. It is a bitter presence."[1] Or, to quote a less literate African, "no other thing is good than soil, land, all good things belonged to soil, milk, fat, meat, fruits, gold jewery, diamond, silver coins, petrol, oil, breads."[2] Land was life to the Kikuyu, Brockway observed, and its seizure was a "classic example of the injustice of colonialism."[3] What made its loss more galling was the gross discrepancy between white and black holdings. Some three thousand European farmers owned twelve thousand square miles of cultivable land whereas over a million Kikuyu were allotted only two thousand square miles. The authorities even whittled away this area by constructing missions, roads, sports grounds and other public works.

As the African population multiplied between the wars, land hunger caused hunger—90 per cent of Kikuyu recruits to the army were rejected because they suffered from malnutrition. Pressure on the soil intensified, sapping its fertility and causing erosion so drastic that the red earth of the Kikuyu hills, carried away by the Tana River, stained the Indian Ocean twenty-five miles out to sea. Settlers accused the 200,000 squatters on their farms of eating *"the heart out of the land."*[4] With government connivance they imposed increasingly harsh conditions on the squatters, adding to their work load, eliminating their livestock and transforming them from tenants into serfs. In the name of conservation the Nairobi administration also resorted to coercion on the "native reserves." In 1938, for example, it tried to reduce overgrazing in the Machakos district, south of the capital, by the

forced sale of 22,500 Kamba cattle. Many of them were bought by white settlers at knockdown prices, which provoked fierce protests. So the battle lines
were drawn for internal strife before the outbreak of the global conflict,
which itself aggravated ethnic discord in Kenya.

This was because the settlers became much stronger during the war. The
Depression had hurt them, many relying on state subsidies to keep in the
business of growing export crops such as coffee, tea and sisal. By contrast
African peasants and squatters had done well, using modern ploughs and
hoes to till more ground and supply low-cost commodities such as maize for
the domestic market. The war transformed this situation. Settlers could sell
at a profit everything they produced. So they paid off their mortgages and
sought to improve and mechanise their estates, often at further cost to the
squatters. True, the settlers were by no means a homogeneous community.
They were a congeries of individualists, not to say eccentrics, liable to breakfast on pink gin or to serve guests a lunch of scrambled eggs and puff adder.
As one official wrote, they comprised "a number of European tribes"[5] as distinct from each other as those of the Africans. They belonged to different
clubs and hunted with rival packs. They also pursued competing ends: for
example, arable farmers relied on squatters while cattle ranchers wanted to
be rid of them. What united the settlers, though, was their visceral determination to control the "raw savages" who could turn Kenya into a "second
Liberia."[6]

They managed this through district councils (which gained power over
squatters in 1937) and by filling administrative posts left vacant by the
wartime manpower shortage. So the Nairobi government, which had previously maintained a façade of impartiality, became much more closely identified with the interests of the settlers. It appointed "native chiefs" who
would readily cooperate with them, dividing Africans from their nominal
leaders so sharply as to foment civil war. It ensured that the system of taxation and trade regulation favoured the whites. It bore down more heavily on
black farmers, telling them what to plant, how to grow and where to sell.
According to the Chief Native Commissioner, Kenya's maize marketing
organisation was "the most barefaced and thorough-going attempt at
exploitation the people of Africa have ever known since Joseph cornered all
the corn in Egypt."[7] The government also supported evictions. Various
schemes were initiated during the war, notably the removal of eleven thousand squatters who had been expelled from the Rift Valley to a bleak area of
the Mau escarpment adjoining a bamboo forest, known as Olenguruone.
They at once claimed ownership of the place. They rejected the dictation of

officialdom and engaged in a long, bitter, doomed struggle to establish their claim. In 1944 they took the first bloody oaths of solidarity.

At about the same time, an agricultural field officer named George Nightingale supervised a less well-known but equally abortive scheme at Kilifi, just north of Mombasa. It proposed to give ex-squatters twelve-acre plots on which to grow coconuts, cashew nuts, oil palms, bananas, oranges, lemons, grapefruit and cassava. According to Nightingale's typed memoir, the Governor personally assured them that after three years they would receive a

> certificate of ownership of their plots if they had carried out the Department's instructions and proved otherwise suitable. As I was the only official they dealt with, it was to me they looked for the government part of the bargain to be carried out. Well it never was and that fact, and the government turning the whole settlement on to cotton production after the war, was the reason I resigned from the Agricultural Department. Of course there was a long history of promises to Africans broken by the government.[8]

State direction might have been more tolerable had it been less fickle. But during the war Africans were pressed to use every bit of ground as intensively as possible, abandoning fallow periods and ignoring the dangers of soil erosion or exhaustion. At the end of the war the fat little Governor, Sir Philip Mitchell, warned that "the native reserves are just frankly going to the devil."[9]

He therefore approved a programme to raise fertility and ward off a "really shocking disaster."[10] It involved an enormous amount of backbreaking unpaid work, imposed by white men and largely carried out by black women, to terrace, mulch and otherwise conserve the land. Not only was tillage limited and the cultivation of profitable crops such as coffee, tea, sisal and pyrethrum prohibited on the African reserves, but herds were reduced. Compulsion was disguised as welfare provision. Meanwhile the Europeans, their numbers swelled by another post-war influx of soldier-settlers, increased the pace of eviction from their own farms. Between 1946 and 1952 a hundred thousand squatters were deprived of their livestock without compensation (on the excuse that moving it might spread disease) and forcibly "repatriated"[11] to so-called homelands that few of them had ever seen. Here they placed an additional burden on the earth. Such contradictory and repressive policies sowed the seeds of revolution, especially among the poorer Kikuyu. Demands for "land and freedom" were accompanied by more ferocious oathing ceremonies, which aimed to unify resistance to what was seen as a white tyranny. One woman said, "I took the oath so that my children would not be enslaved in the way I had been."[12]

The subjugation of Africans was also apparent in urban jungles such as Nairobi, especially to the 97,000 African servicemen who returned after the war. Having fought for liberty beside white troops overseas, they faced repression at home because they were black. Colour prejudice was enshrined in law: white men who had sexual intercourse with black women faced no penalty, for example, whereas black men who had sexual intercourse with white women were liable to be hanged. Unlike Tanganyika, a mandated territory where the races mixed freely, Kenya imposed a colour bar. Post offices, hospitals, schools, churches, cinemas, railways and lavatories were segregated. Africans and Asians were excluded from hotels, bars, restaurants and other amenities, including polling booths. Clubs, of course, "were strictly Europeans only and not all Europeans at that."[13] The Jockey Club even refused one Governor's request to make the Aga Khan a temporary member. Nairobi, a bursting city of nearly 150,000 people by 1950, was a monument to development "along racial lines."[14] Sir Herbert Baker's hilltop Government House, a Palladian mansion boasting an arboretum and ample wine cellars, overlooked the luxuriant western suburbs sprouting tennis courts and swimming pools at every turn, the official quarter with its pillared and porched bungalows set amid dahlias and gladioli, and the commercial centre, a late flowering of concrete and glass. Asian districts were squalid by comparison, the Eastlands bazaar consisting of rickety, flyblown shops *(dukas)* reeking of sweat, smoke, dung and offal. Finally, African "locations" such as Pumwani were among the most noisome of what Margery Perham called "tropical East Ends."[15]

On his visit to Nairobi in 1950, when he outraged settlers by staying with Africans, Fenner Brockway reported to the Colonial Secretary on the clear demarcation of areas between the three races.

> I was driven through the residential district of Muthaiga, a wooded valley with entrancing glimpses of deep descents to a winding river. It is lined with beautiful houses, enclosed in large gardens bright with flowering trees . . . No African is allowed to have a house amidst the loveliness of Muthaiga. The next day I went to the residential quarters of Nairobi which are reserved for Africans . . . The land is treeless, bare and flat, covered by coarse, brown grass . . . Visiting this dreary expanse, I could understand the bitterness of the Africans who accompanied me when, pointing to the wooded hills where

the Europeans lived, they asked why they should be condemned to the wilderness.[16]

Brockway anticipated Frantz Fanon, who noted in his classic indictment of colonialism *The Wretched of the Earth* (1961) that the look "the native turns on the settler's town is a look of lust, a look of envy; it expresses his dreams of possession."[17] Such dreams reflected the nightmare of the African shanty-towns.

In Nairobi's dark agglomerations of stone, bamboo, wood, tin, cardboard, tarred sacking and corrugated iron, men might sleep fourteen to a room, with verandahs, packing cases and derelict buses serving as overflow dormitories. The water supply was inadequate, long queues forming at standpipes hours before dawn. Sanitation was minimal and disgusting, with perhaps one public lavatory for a thousand persons. Disease was rife. Few could struggle out of the morass of poverty, though most citizens were Kikuyu, enterprising people whom whites called "the Jews of Kenya"—a description not intended to flatter either race. Unemployment was endemic. Wages were the lowest in the Empire and Africans doing the same job as Europeans received a fifth of their salary. Child labour was ubiquitous since schooling was not compulsory for Africans and young mouths had to be filled as the cost of living spiralled. Between 1939 and 1953 the price of maize flour rose by some 700 per cent and by 1948 few Africans in Nairobi ate "more than one meal a day, very few indeed."[18] Only a minority could afford decent clothes, most wearing blankets or ragged European garb.

Often terrorised by criminals, who roamed the streets in armed gangs, Africans were also harried by the forces of law. Policemen checked passes, inspected tax receipts, executed removal orders and enforced petty regulations, notably over the sale of spirits, which was prohibited to Africans. Bribes were frequently extorted in lieu of fines or beatings. Women were treated as prostitutes and men as vagrants—those suspected of having venereal disease were publicly mustered on Bahati Road. Whites seldom strayed into the "Black Zoo,"[19] which they sometimes explained away by remarking that "Rome was not built in a day."[20] In fact Africans were generally invisible to Europeans, though they were noticed to be humiliated, to have their laughter hushed, their hats doffed and their heads bowed. Sometimes, wrote the Luo trade union leader Tom Mboya, white missionaries even insisted that black church-goers should ruffle their hair and bare their feet. Africans responded to racial discrimination on such a scale by intoning "the one word *uhuru*—freedom."[21]

It soon became apparent that the Kenya African Union (KAU), founded as the party of moderate nationalists in 1944 to take the place of Harry Thuku's banned Kikuyu Central Association, could not win *uhuru*. That goal was opposed from the top. Sir Philip Mitchell, Governor from 1944 to 1952, believed that Britain should not attempt to give the immature African "an excessive degree of freedom from control before he is ready for that freedom."[22] Mitchell was a conservative with a liberal reputation, gained by advocating the creation of a multi-racial society in East Africa. Yet even this was a reactionary concept as he envisaged it, for Mitchell maintained that the different ethnic groups should "have a share and vital interest according to their several needs and capacities."[23] So only the European settlers could improve the land and guide Kenya's native people from their state of "primitive ignorance and indolence."[24] In this task they should be assisted by the British-appointed chiefs on the reserves, Mitchell thought, rather than by urban politicians, whom he regarded as agitators and troublemakers. Clever, articulate and acerbic, the Governor was also fiercely competitive—he longed to crown his career with a peerage and he apparently married his wife because she was the first woman to beat him at golf. Claiming that progress was being made with agricultural and other welfare measures, Mitchell largely managed to impose an old-fashioned colonial policy on Kenya. He tightened restrictions on KAU meetings. He impeded the collection of party funds. He limited press freedom and trade union activity. He played down the sporadic disturbances, responding to protests, strikes, riots, cattle maimings and arson attacks with more white repression instead of more black representation. He excluded Africans from his Executive Council (until 1952) and refused to appoint the new leader of the KAU to his Legislative Council. This was Jomo Kenyatta, whom Mitchell regarded as a dangerous firebrand.

In fact Kenyatta was a man of moderation, as Mitchell himself had recognised when they first met in 1931. By then Kenyatta, born into a peasant family and educated by Scottish missionaries, had become Secretary of the Kikuyu Central Association and editor of its journal *Muigwithania,* which means "The Reconciler." His own contributions were notably emollient: he praised the British Empire for preserving freedom and justice. Less a radical than a rake, Kenyatta sported plus-fours, drank literally inflammatory Nubian gin and so indulged his sexual appetites that he was suspended from church membership. He lived an equally bohemian existence in England, which became his base after 1931. Ostensibly he was there to plead the African cause with the British government. But his mission grew more hazy over the years, though absence inflated his reputation at home. Travelling and conferring widely, Kenyatta adopted a variety of expedients to survive. He sponged off sympathisers, bilked his landlady and took money from Moscow during a flirtation with Communism. He did odd jobs, even acting as an extra in Alexander Korda's film (starring Paul Robeson) of Edgar Wallace's drum-beating, empire-building novel *Sanders of the River*—a role that he did his best to forget. Kenyatta assisted with academic research into Kikuyu phonology, though he would not allow his voice to be recorded "for fear of evil consequences."[25] He contributed to Nancy Cunard's avant-garde tribute to the *Negro* (1934), declaring that the confiscation of ancestral lands in Kenya had stricken the African soul "nigh unto death" and denouncing Britain's "imperialist system of slavery, tax-paying, pass-carrying and forced labour."[26] Still worse was Mussolini's rape of Ethiopia. Kenyatta not only condemned it in print but, to honour the Emperor Haile Selassie, grew his famous beard. Elspeth Huxley thought it "gave him a Mephistophelian look."[27]

Kenyatta also studied anthropology under Malinowski, which led to the production of an important book entitled *Facing Mount Kenya* (1938). This was a vindication of the organic Kikuyu traditions that were being undermined by colonialism; but it left him facing in two directions at once. Whereas Kenyatta the social conservative looked back to a tribal golden age, Kenyatta the political progressive looked forward to a modern democratic state. However, he believed that "full self-government" should be achieved through reform rather than revolution. Going against the grain of the fifth Pan-African Congress, he declared that it would be impossible to force the British from his homeland and he abjured "a bloody insurrection."[28] By now Kenyatta had matured from prodigal son to exiled father of his people. He had become a benign combination of statesman and showman, dignified and eloquent but jovial and flamboyant. When he returned to Kenya in 1946, leaving an English wife and child behind, he alone could aspire to transcend tribal differences and become the national patriarch. A British journalist described him the following year:

> A big, paunchy man, bearded, with slightly bloodshot eyes, a theatrically monstrous ebony elephant-headed walking stick, a gold-rimmed carnelian signet ring about the size of a napkin-ring, an outsize gold wrist-watch fastened to his hefty arm with a gold strap, dressed in European tweed jacket and flannel slacks—with as pleasant, ingratiating and wary a manner as you have ever met.

Later, after his arrest, Kenyatta's stick and ring were confiscated, and he wondered sardonically whether the British thought they had taken his ju-ju.

At the time, too cautious to give anything away to a white stranger, the black leader conversed in a series of equivocal grunts, *"Unh-hunh!"*[29]

Over the next few years Kenyatta was obliged to master several types of ambiguity. Hailed as Saviour by the Kikuyu, he had to appeal over their heads to the other two-thirds of Kenya's non-white population. He had to rally indifferent Masai and hostile Luo, to reconcile distant Somalis and hesitant Indians. But while trying to drive forward the KAU as the vehicle of national liberation, he had to steer clear of sedition. He did crusade against obvious ills such as the colour bar, the forced labour of women on terracing and the tyranny of the *kipande*. Like Zik in Nigeria, he said that the tree of liberty must be watered with blood. He even promised to hold open the lion's mouth if his people could "bear its claws."[30] However, aware of the constant presence of the Special Branch, he generally spoke in Delphic language. He preached patriotism and moral uplift. He recommended education and self-help. He repeated the Kikuyu proverb: "That which bites you is within your own clothes."[31] Yet his words were imbued with the power of his "burning personality."[32] It was this incandescent force that made Kenyatta, despite his inordinate greed, ambition and vanity, a natural leader. Transmitted through eyes like red-hot coals, it seemed messianic to Africans, satanic to Europeans. And it caused all to study his utterances like oracles. On hearing Kenyatta's tame explanation of the KAU flag, one supporter wrote: "What he said must mean that our fertile lands (green) could only be regained by the blood (red) of the African (black). That was it!"[33] When Kenyatta agreed to condemn African militants known as the Mau Mau in 1952, Britons interpreted his solemn curse as a blessing in disguise. In fact the ascent of these dispossessed extremists within the bourgeois ranks of the KAU took Kenyatta by surprise. While he had been slowly building a national coalition they had been secretly administering mass oaths, collecting weapons and preparing to fight for land and freedom. Revere Kenyatta though they might, the young men of violence, who had already assassinated Kikuyu chiefs loyal to the government, threatened to kill him if he continued to oppose the Mau Mau. Speaking more softly, he compared himself to "a tongue between the molars and the lower teeth."[34]

The name Mau Mau was as obscure in its origin as the movement was nebulous in its structure and vague in its strategy. Evidently a loose amalgam of evicted squatters, deprived farmers and urban poor, it seemed to be part Kikuyu conspiracy, part peasant revolt and part criminal gang. According to one African, Mau Mau was nothing but "a hunger of land in Kenya."[35] A white official described it as "a form of Spartacus uprising of the unemployed and landless Kikuyu."[36] Anyway, bound together by dark rituals, it espoused revolutionary terror. As such it was banned in 1950. But Sir Philip Mitchell, who wanted to end his governorship in an aura of multi-racial harmony, refused to dignify the Mau Mau by taking stronger action. He assured his successor, Sir Evelyn Baring, that although Nairobi contained "riff-raff" and the rural peasantry were easily misled, "The Africans in the mass have no politics." Mitchell seemed more interested in domestic matters. He gave Baring much advice about managing "native servants" and divorced whites. The latter should be excluded from luncheons and dinners at Government House but might be invited to "Garden Parties and large Cocktail Parties, unless, of course, there is an open scandal."[37] However, as Mau Mau attacks on white farms and black collaborators increased during 1952, while a few militants joined ex-soldiers such as Warahui Itote ("General China") in the forest, the new Governor came under acute pressure from Europeans to crack down on Africans. The son of Lord Cromer, Baring kept a portrait of his father in his office and would stop ministers in front of it and ask what they thought *he* would have done under the circumstances.

As this suggests, Baring was weak where his own countrymen were concerned. Indeed, the "tall, lean, greying, immaculate"[38] and clean-shaven Governor seemed positively effete to the settlers, many of whom were still "moustached heavily, in the guardee fashion, with the hairs upcurling into their nostrils."[39] Baring was devoted to theology and the classics, fond of playing charades and sardines in Government House, keen on exotic birds and wild flowers—the bourgeois aspidistra he (and a coterie of equally refined Oxford contemporaries, including the future Prime Minister Lord Home) had vowed to destroy whenever he saw it. The Governor allowed himself to be convinced that Kenyatta was the master spirit behind a diabolical plot, a view confirmed by his solitary sight of the KAU's President, across the grave of a murdered chief, when he felt "the demoniac force of Kenyatta's personality." Writing to the Colonial Secretary, Oliver Lyttelton, Baring denied being "carried away by panic on the part of excitable Europeans." But he recommended the arrest of Kenyatta and his henchmen, and the declaration of a state of emergency. All this was accomplished on 20 October 1952. The operation and its aftermath showed that Baring had more than a streak of the paternal ruthlessness when confronting "lesser breeds." In the words of his sympathetic biographer, he was not "very fastidious about the exercise of imperial power."[40] In the opinion of a recent critic, he was laying the foundations of one of the most brutal and "restrictive police states in the history of the empire."[41]

Ironically the state of emergency created the emergency, for it turned the Mau Mau from a scattered jacquerie into a guerrilla army. Baring acted harshly from the start, hoping to destroy the "hydra" at a stroke.[42] As well as decapitating the KAU and rounding up scores of the best-educated nationalists, he paraded Lancashire Fusiliers through the slums of Nairobi, where they were greeted with looks of sullen animosity. (The Royal Navy staged a more Pavlovian but less pertinent show of force by sending a cruiser to Mombasa.) In a hundred-mile arc north of the capital stretching from the cedar-clad flanks of the Aberdare Range to snow-capped Mount Kenya, the authorities detained and interrogated tens of thousands of Kikuyu. They also herded thousands of squatters from the White Highlands back to the reserves, many via squalid transit camps, depriving them of homes, possessions and livestock. This vast piece of social engineering swelled the ranks of the Mau Mau, within a year driving some fifteen thousand, mostly Kikuyu but many Meru and Embu, and some Kamba and Masai, into the forests. There they began to organise and to retaliate, killing the first white settler in October 1952. Hundreds of horrifying murders followed, mostly of Kikuyu "Judases."[43] Ordinary Africans had to pay for these hit-and-run attacks in doubled taxation, collective punishments such as the confiscation of cattle and the closure of schools, as well as sporadic reprisals, official and unofficial. European settlers had often taken the law into their own hands and now, whether acting as freelance vigilantes or as members of the Kenya Regiment or the Police Reserve, aptly compared to the Black and Tans, they took the emergency as a licence to kill. They hunted down "Kikuyu troublemakers"[44] like wild animals. They tortured them at will, sometimes castrating men and raping women. They exterminated them without mercy. In the words of one farmer, "We just take out our sten guns and, vee-vee-vee, vee-vee-vee, we let the bloody vermin have it."[45]

Settlers in the security forces were more systematic. They formed "strike squads"[46] to carry out assassinations, shot civilians in cold blood and massacred the innocent with the guilty. Called "little Hitlers of the Highlands," "Kenya cowboys" or the "white Mau Mau,"[47] they often boasted about their exploits. Their hackneyed motto was, "The only good Kikuyu is a dead one."[48] Some advocated genocide, suggesting that the atomic bomb should be used on Kikuyu or recalling how Americans "used to poison the wells of their Red Indians and infect the blankets with smallpox."[49] All this alienated liberal opinion in Britain and the United States, while providing ammunition to anti-imperialists like Nasser and Nehru. Pointing this out, one white woman said that the harm caused by the brutality "can't be computed—it could be the down-fall of this country."[50] Moreover, as intelligent and sensitive District Officers like Thomas Cashmore said, perpetrators of atrocities were the best recruiting agents for the Mau Mau. Upset by the sight of a colleague bringing in dead bodies, Cashmore asked whether there were many prisoners:

> He laughed and asked me what did I expect, or was I yellow? When I responded that taking no prisoners meant more desperate terrorists, he merely commented that he had probably set back my "education" by several months, but the realities of the situation would eventually register . . . Of course, I hated to be thought a coward, yet I also believed such action was not only morally wrong but plain stupid.[51]

It was certainly foolish, from the colonial standpoint, to sustain the view that the Mau Mau had genuine grievances. For the British maintained that, far from being a national liberation movement, it was an obscene reversion to savagery. Kenyatta was its evil genius. Its witch doctors practised perverted forms of black magic. Its warriors were, in the words of a leading settler, Michael Blundell, "debased creatures of the forest."[52] According to Elspeth Huxley, Mau Mau was "the yell from the swamp."[53]

The most sinister evidence for this verdict lay in Mau Mau ceremonies which, in the words of a police report, were "driving the Kikuyu to become primitive [sic] beasts who will ultimately massacre all Europeans in Kenya."[54] On pain of death, militants forced most Kikuyu and many others to swear allegiance to their cause. Before taking the oath, initiates stripped naked and passed through a banana stalk arch seven times. They also took seven bites from the heart and lungs of a goat and drank a concoction containing its blood. Men and women making homicidal vows would, respectively, place their penises inside goat meat or insert goat meat into their vaginas. There were more revolting variations and, exceptionally, forest fighters swore "advanced oaths involving human blood and flesh."[55] The use of such taboo substances, apparently a desperate measure in the face of defeat, shocked Africans themselves. But the usual oaths were merely adaptations of traditional Kikuyu rites. Educated Africans likened them to "the oaths of Freemasons" and described an experience akin to Evangelical conversion. "I felt exalted with a new spirit of power and strength," wrote J. M. Kariuki. "I had been born again."[56]

Europeans, by contrast, depicted a Saturnalia of horrors. By their account crazed fanatics drank semen and menstrual blood, ate human faeces and babies torn from their mothers' wombs, and indulged in bestial orgies. Some whites explained this behaviour as a pathological reaction caused by the exposure of barbarism to civilisation. Others, including the now-conservative Harry Thuku, saw it as a manifestation of pure evil. From retirement Sir Philip Mitchell denounced the Mau Mau as "carrion-eating reptiles" who, in the spirit of Belsen, perpetrated "monstrous, nauseating wickedness."[57] In a famous commination Oliver Lyttelton waxed still more hysterical about the hellish character of Mau Mau, identifying Kenyatta as its Lucifer. Lyttelton said that, while penning memoranda about Kenya, "I would suddenly see a shadow fall across the page—the horned shadow of the Devil himself."[58] Of course, there was authentic evidence of Mau Mau viciousness: 1,800 African civilians murdered, captives tortured to death, black families incinerated in their huts, white settlers butchered with heavy-bladed knives (pangas). But by demonising the movement the British authorities attempted to vindicate a counter-attack more ferocious than anything contemplated in the forest.

The settlers demonstrated the kind of measures they wanted when the Mau Mau campaign against their farms began in earnest during 1953. On 25 January, after trusted servants had hacked to death a popular young family, hundreds of white men and women marched on Government House. Clad in their Sunday best, light suits, hats and ties, or print dresses, they assembled on the grass in front of its white Palladian portico, screaming obscenities and baying for lynch law. Some waved pistols. Others frothed at the mouth. Still others, in what Michael Blundell called the settlers' invariable preface to "some desperate action to demonstrate their contempt of Colonial Office rule," sang "God Save the Queen."[59] Furious at being held back by a cordon of African police, they shouted "dirty niggers"[60] and stubbed out their cigarettes on the bare, linked arms of the askaris. Then they tried to storm Baring's barricaded ten-foot front doors, which bent and shook under the assault but did not give. Eventually, Blundell persuaded the mob to disperse. It had achieved its aim for, despite the Governor's refusal to appear, he had understood its message. Baring quickly brought in General W. R. N. ("Loony") Hinde to reorganise the security forces and regain the initiative from the forest bands. Meanwhile, they were made to pay heavily for each attack. On 26 March, for example, insurgents massacred nearly a hundred loyalist Kikuyu in the village of Lari. Government units, including the African "Home Guard," at once took a hideous but hidden revenge. They killed at least twice as many Mau Mau sympathisers and blamed all the deaths on "terrorists insatiable for blood."[61]

This intensified hostilities between so-called "Black Europeans," those prosperous, privileged Kikuyu who were collaborating with the British, and the indigent and usually illiterate militants. Baring relentlessly supported the loyalist side in this developing civil war. He turned the Home Guard into an armed militia, 25,000 strong, manning a chain of entrenched strongholds reminiscent of "the days of Caesar and the fortified camps of the Gallic Wars."[62] He pursued a clandestine policy of counter-terror. He imposed the death penalty for offences that ranged from taking Mau Mau oaths to possessing a single bullet. The Colonial Office feared that this would lead to "expeditious injustice,"[63] and summary executions did follow. Between 1952 and 1958 1,090 Africans were hanged, some on a travelling gallows built at the Governor's behest. In fact, Baring sacrificed justice to expediency. The most notorious instance was the rigged trial of Kenyatta and five colleagues. Baring was determined to eliminate the KAU leadership even though the security services doubted whether Kenyatta could control the Mau Mau and said that he had "advised against violence."[64] Accordingly witnesses were bribed, defence lawyers were harassed and the judge was paid £20,000. This was enough to secure a guilty verdict and to remove Kenyatta from active politics until 1961. Ironically, the champion of constitutional progress, who had himself been menaced by the Mau Mau, was imprisoned for being its architect. Kenyatta's martyrdom ensured that he would one day rule Kenya; more immediately it consigned the country to further violence.

Britain demonstrated its resolve to smash the Mau Mau by superseding "Loony" Hinde, who had been instructed simply "to jolly things along."[65] His replacement was General Sir George ("Bobbie") Erskine, a tetchy, portly, untidy figure who came armed with a warrant from his friend Winston Churchill authorising him, if necessary, to proclaim martial law and take over the government. He kept this paper in his spectacles case which, to emphasise his points, he opened and loudly snapped shut. Erskine tried "gingering up" the Governor, who was "terribly wobbly."[66] He scarcely bothered to conceal his disdain for the settlers. They were "middle-class sluts" and Kenya was, to repeat his oft-quoted but unoriginal remark, "a sunny place for shady people."[67] Erskine blamed them and their rotten administration for the rebellion. And he proposed to eradicate it with military might such as only the imperial power could marshal, thus ensuring that Kenya's fate would be decided in London rather than Nairobi. By the autumn of 1953 Erskine had deployed twelve British battalions, supported by armoured cars, artillery and two RAF squadrons consisting of obsolete Harvard and Lincoln bombers, later supplemented by Vampire jets. Along with local contingents, these forces carried out patrols, raids and ambushes in an effort to root out and break up the forest bands. At first the "bag" remained small though, until Erskine put a stop to it, cash prizes were awarded for "kills." Despite their overwhelming advantage in weaponry, his troops had much to learn about guerrilla warfare. They transported super-fluous comforts into the bush by mule, among them iron bedsteads. They gave themselves away by disturbing wild animals and exuding the smell of soap, cigarettes and brilliantine. They inflicted many, perhaps most, of their casualties on themselves—one battalion even managed to kill its own colonel. By calling in air strikes, which were terrifying but ineffective, they indicated areas temporarily safe from ground attack. No wonder African commanders taunted them. One informed Erskine that the Mau Mau were building a canning factory so that they could eat tinned white flesh.

This was a joke but it suggested the most serious weakness of the self-styled Land Freedom Army. Like other guerrilla forces, it relied on the sur-rounding population for food, clothes, munitions, information and other aid. From the first Erskine had tried to cut its sources of supply. He sealed off African locations in Nairobi. He created a *cordon sanitaire,* clearing banana and sugar cane plantations between the forests and the Kikuyu reserves. He constructed a barrier worthy of Hadrian, a fosse extending a hundred miles along the forest fringe. Those who still managed to help the combatants faced further collective punishments and systematic violence from the Home Guard. More effective still was the incarceration of sus-pected Mau Mau adherents. In April 1954 Erskine delivered his *coup de grâce,* Operation Anvil, the complete blockade of Nairobi with twenty thousand troops. They seized most black people for questioning or "screen-ing" and sent some 24,000 men and women, nearly half the city's Kikuyu population, to hastily established detention camps. The British pulled no punches in this huge round-up, which destroyed much of the central Mau Mau organisation and dealt a crushing blow to the revolt.

As Kenya's captives multiplied more than fifty camps were built to accom-modate them. By the end of 1954 about seventy thousand Africans were detained or imprisoned, about half the total number held in camps during the course of the emergency. Yet Erskine was already embarking on a still more ambitious exercise in confinement, one that would place almost the whole Kikuyu nation under restraint. Following Templer's example in Malaya rather than Kitchener's in South Africa, he masterminded the evic-tion of more than a million people from their scattered homesteads, many of which were then looted and burned by the Home Guard, and their reset-tlement in 850 gaol-villages. Here, surrounded by barbed wire and over-looked by watchtowers, loyalists were protected and subversives were punished—subjected to a regime of searches, curfews, contagions, restric-tions, shortages and forced labour. So the forest Mau Mau were starved as well as hunted. They became increasingly desperate, reduced to wearing monkey skins and fighting with bows and arrows. And they took the disastrous course of preying on their own supporters. "Henceforth," wrote one, "freedom-fighters were treated like wild animals by everybody."[68]

As the Mau Mau reeled from Erskine's hammer blows, many guerrillas defecting, others hiding deeper in the jungle, Baring tried to win African hearts and minds. His efforts, though encouraged by Churchill, were feeble. For anything that smacked of conciliation enraged the white settlers, who "still believed themselves to be the sole and natural heirs of colonial rule." Thus when the Governor proposed a negotiated settlement in 1954 they accused him of shaking hands with murder. Blundell even charged Baring with having taken the Mau Mau oath, though he quickly apologised. Meanwhile, as Thomas Cashmore cynically wrote, the state tried to give its rule "a touch of strength through joy."[69] It sponsored welfare programmes. It fostered adult education and vocational training. It encouraged Boy Scouts, sports clubs and dance troupes. It promoted football, though some feared that the game "had become the successor to tribal warfare."[70] Cashmore, who noted that "a majority of single white officers probably did, on a casual basis, sleep with African women," found to his embarrassment that one of the "ladies involved, an ex-Chief's daughter," was several times his co-judge in local needlework competitions. Officials also recruited soothsayers, known as "Her Majesty's Witchdoctors" or the "Wizards of Oz," to "cleanse"[71] involuntary oath-takers.

Much more important were endeavours to improve African living standards. Permitted to develop, trade unions negotiated wage rises in new industries such as brewing and oil refining. An agricultural revolution was in train, as land holdings were consolidated and Africans were allowed to cultivate cash crops such as coffee. There remained a strong dash of paternalism. It annoyed George Nightingale, now a District Officer, that the government tried to teach the Kikuyu how to grow coffee when, as they laughingly said, "we planted the coffee trees in Kenya for the Europeans, and have always done the pruning, spraying and harvesting."[72] British soldiers were also encouraged to be friendly, though this led to the spread of venereal disease and to the dissemination of a colloquial expression with which African children greeted a startled Oliver Lyttelton, "Fuck off."[73] The Colonial Secretary continued to demand more political progress in Kenya. In fact he made it clear that unless whites agreed to the election of more black representatives on the Legislative Council, he would disown them. Like other Colonial Secretaries, he disliked these "parasites in paradise."[74] Lyttelton especially deplored their eagerness to mete out semi-official murder and he once rebuked Blundell for suggesting that the government should "line up 50 people and shoot them."[75]

Throughout their imperial history the British always paid lip service to legality, but by the mid-1950s it was an open secret that Kenya had become a police state that dispensed racist terror. After all Dr. Malan, the Nationalist Prime Minister of South Africa, took it as a model for his apartheid regime. Frequent reports of institutional cruelty reached the outside world, some of them reminiscent of worse regimes. When Kenya's interrogators "screened" suspects, they generally began by softening them up with "a series of hard blows across the face"—the standard shock tactic used on prisoners in Stalin's Lubianka. In most cases further beatings followed, some of them fatal. This treatment was variously justified on the grounds that the Mau Mau were subhuman and that it would purge them of political sickness or sin. But those who administered the violence displayed "a strong streak of sadism . . . under the red heat of action."[76] This was still more evident in further torments to which "screeners" subjected men and women, mostly Kikuyu. These included electric shocks, burnings, near-drownings, mutilations and sexual abuse.

The Special Branch, known as "Kenya's SS," were particularly expert at inflicting pain but freelance interrogators could be even more vicious. According to a recent historian, one settler in the Rift Valley was christened the "Doctor Mengele of Kenya" for exploits that included "burning the skin off live Mau Mau suspects and forcing them to eat their own testicles."[77] Everyone in the security services knew that such atrocities occurred; many units were involved, some notoriously so; but there was a concerted effort to hush everything up in the interests of imperial solidarity. Michael Seward, a humane community development officer in Meru much upset by his countrymen's activities, "was told to be a good chap and get on with your job . . . and keep your mouth shut."[78] When protests were made, Lyttelton himself turned a deaf ear and a blind eye. With "soapy smoothness," as that outspoken parliamentary critic Barbara Castle put it, Baring conducted "complacent cover-ups."[79] Soldiers looked after their own. Cashmore recounted how a private in the Kenya Regiment was court-martialled because, when questioning a young Kikuyu woman, he "had forced a beer bottle into her and caused her not only pain but bodily harm." The private was acquitted and "the judgement was thought to be good for morale and welcomed by many in the regiment." Even Cashmore felt it right to suppress his squeamishness about such matters, "for it is not possible to impose the civilities of Cheltenham in the foothills of Chuka."[80] Needless to say, episodes of this kind stiffened opposition, global as well as local, to the colonial order.

Yet the "screening" process was a mere prologue to the immense volume of suffering inflicted on Africans in what has exaggeratedly been called Britain's "gulag."[81] The avowed purpose of the camp complex was rehabilitation. Hardcore Mau Mau suspects (significantly categorised as "black," whereas the doubtful were "grey" and the innocent were "white") had to be cured of their "disease." This Europeans continued to diagnose in different ways, some maintaining that the forest fighters were suffering from a "communal psychosis," others insisting that they were infected by atavism and had become "primitive beasts."[82] But there was wide agreement about the remedy. The Mau Mau ruled by fear so, according to one alleged expert, "we had to create a greater fear of our camp."[83] This meant that punishment, designed to extort confession and enforce submission, became almost an end in itself. There were humane commandants but in most cases torture was used to break the spirit of the detainees. Thus on arrival at camps such as Manyani they had to run the gauntlet of baton-wielding guards—the very same routine practised at Dachau. Forced labour was illegally exacted, often by means of violence and starvation. An inscription over the gate at Aguthi recalled the Nazi motto, *Arbeit Macht Frei:* "He who helps himself will be helped."[84]

Beatings were savage enough to leave Kenya with hundreds of "crippled beggars."[85] Evenings and nights at South Yatta Camp were "a holiday from pain," wrote J. M. Kariuki, but each day was one "long agony."[86] Elsewhere inmates were so habituated to whip and club that they flinched and jerked from the guards like marionettes. The violence took many forms and sexual atrocities were commonplace. Prisoners were often killed, some by being released in lion country. One guard later confessed that he and others in the Kenya Regiment regularly liquidated "hard-core scum": "Never knew a Kuke had so many brains until we cracked open a few heads."[87] More than twenty thousand Mau Mau fighters lost their lives during the emergency but how many died in the camps is not known, though it far exceeded the figure, a mere thirty-two, for white civilian deaths. Clearly, however, the Kenyan archipelago was one of the worst blots on Britain's imperial escutcheon. The assistant police commissioner, Duncan McPherson, told Barbara Castle, still leading the assault on abuses, that conditions in some camps "were worse than anything I experienced in my four and a half years as a prisoner of the Japanese."[88]

By 1956, though, Baring could feel more confident about the situation in Kenya. With steely resolve he had managed to obscure the worst excesses of the colonial regime. He had effectively legalised torture by approving his Attorney General's spurious distinction between "punitive force," officially banned, and "compelling force," which was permitted. He had designated the emergency a civil disturbance, thus depriving detainees of rights as prisoners of war. He had made efforts to square the Red Cross, to squash the churches and to mislead hostile MPs such as Barbara Castle—"that Castellated Bitch."[89] The Governor had received stalwart support from Alan Lennox-Boyd, nicknamed "Bwana Kilimanjaro" in East Africa and described by Barbara Castle as a "Guardsman type"[90] imbued with the conviction that the British ruling class could do no wrong. Under his aegis the Colonial Office continued to use every technique to defend Baring. It denied the more serious charges against his administration. It suppressed evidence, discredited witnesses and spun a web of deception worthy of Albion at its most perfidious. While burying bad news, Lennox-Boyd advertised the real progress being made in Kenya. Improved counter-insurgency measures had virtually eradicated the Mau Mau. The detention camps were being phased out, all but "black" inmates gradually gaining their freedom. Rehabilitation officers such as Major and Mrs. Breckenridge had achieved genuine success in killing sedition by kindness. If the mass of unpublished letters they received from detainees are to be believed, the Breckenridges persuaded many Kikuyu to condemn "the evils brought about by the Mau Mau" and to "come to the side of good citizenship." A pupil-teacher named Cyrus Karuga praised the Major for his work in "reforming the hardest of hard-cores, of whom I was one . . . I thank you very much for the battle you fight behind the scenes so that I may be accepted back home."[91]

Loyalist Kikuyu were prospering. In 1957 the first Africans were elected to the Legislative Council, among them Tom Mboya and his inveterate rival Oginga Odinga. The latter outraged white members by appearing at the Assembly "with a skin round my waist, a coat of long tails, beaded stockings, sea-shell sandals, a beaded collar and cap, and carrying a whisk of a cow's tail."[92] Odinga dismissed Mboya, a dynamic pragmatist who himself sometimes wore Luo robes and goatskin sashes, as "a rabid black dog that barked furiously and bit all in his path."[93] Baring was equally hostile, describing Mboya as a "rabble rouser"[94] and a "lapsed Roman Catholic with the morals of a monkey."[95] Nevertheless, for a time Lennox-Boyd hoped to persuade such anti–Mau Mau, non-Kikuyu nationalists to support a constitution based on multi-racial power sharing. A moderate minority of settlers led by Blundell, who actually thought Mboya a "ruthless and ambitious thug,"[96] was becoming reconciled to such a compromise. By 1959 black people gained the right to acquire land in the White Highlands and some districts were seeing a rapprochement between the races. Social relations became "much more relaxed," wrote Cashmore, because "young settlers had fought alongside African loyalists and grown to trust and like them." Despite engrained "suspicions and prejudices," he himself was "completely taken by Mboya's very real charm." However, he also noted that the old attitudes died hard. When a few members proposed to invite Africans and Indians to the Meru Club they were "bitterly opposed by a majority of white officials, seemingly out of fear that the guests might dance with the officials' wives." Moreover, as the emergency neared its end, nothing was done to reconcile the "black" detainees. On the contrary, they were "threatened, flogged, shaved," and warders sent them on their way with "additional heavy blows and kicks." Cashmore thought this valedictory violence was "crazy and that it was bound to backfire in the end as a result of some incident taken to excess."[97] On 3 March 1959 his prophecy was realised at Hola Camp, where eleven prisoners were beaten to death.

Hola, situated in a torrid, mosquito-ridden wilderness near the coast, was the chosen repository of the last "black" detainees. Baring called them "political thugs."[98] Reporting that they were the "inner core of the hard core of the Mau Mau," the London *Times* described them as "degraded and fanatical ruffians, detained and put to labour in the hope of redemption by means of stern discipline."[99] What precipitated the massacre was the sudden introduction of a scheme to force the toughest of them to work. The scheme, afterwards deemed unlawful, was designed by the senior prison superintendent, John Cowan, who reckoned that coercion in the camps was "all just like a good clean rugger scrum."[100] But while trying to make prisoners dig an irrigation ditch at Hola the guards, commanded by an inexperienced ex-naval officer called G. M. Sullivan, got out of hand. Sullivan claimed that the deaths were caused by contaminated drinking water and, after a cursory investigation, Baring endorsed this account. However, the inquest soon exposed its falsity, also revealing that many other prisoners had suffered serious injuries. The whole episode, as a Labour leader said, "shocked and dismayed civilised opinion all over the world."[101] Outrage grew as it emerged that no one would be prosecuted for any offence—indeed, Cowan was awarded the MBE. The British Empire was best sustained, Lennox-Boyd concluded, by declaring that it would not surrender power in Kenya for the foreseeable future, by issuing an amnesty to wrongdoers on both sides, and by changing Hola's name. Critics remained vociferous. The most eloquent of them was Enoch Powell, a fervid Tory radical whom Macmillan would move from the seat opposite him at the cabinet table because he could not bear the look of his wild, staring eyes.

In a speech which electrified the Commons, Powell described Hola as "a great administrative disaster." Failure to take responsibility for it, he argued, undermined Britain's endeavour to plant responsible government in its dependencies.

> All government, all influence of man upon man, rests upon opinion. What we can still do in Africa . . . depends on the opinion which is entertained of the way in which this country and we Englishmen act. We cannot, we dare not, and in Africa of all places, fall below the highest standards in the acceptance of responsibility.[102]

Powell specifically exonerated Lennox-Boyd, which did not please all who congratulated him on having spoken for "everything that is finest in the British tradition—things that will last longer than any empire."[103] For example, Lady Violet Bonham Carter, Asquith's daughter and Churchill's friend, protested that Lennox-Boyd had again and again refused public inquiries into conditions in the camps when "the fact that their inmates were rotting with scurvy *alone* warranted some enquiry." The chain of responsibility, she told Powell, "goes right up to the top."[104]

Lennox-Boyd did, in fact, offer to resign. But on the eve of a general election, and at a time when the Devlin Report charged that Britain had turned Nyasaland into a police state, Macmillan was determined to keep his ministry intact. So the Colonial Secretary expressed complete confidence in Baring and dismissed as fanciful Labour's accusations of an official whitewash. To his successor, though, Lennox-Boyd justified the iron-fisted tactics employed in Kenya. It was impossible, he told Iain Macleod, who was appointed after the Tory victory in October 1959, to "apply the canons of a cloister to a battle in tribal Africa."[105] Macleod was horrified, as he was by the Hola murders. He cross-questioned Blundell about them minutely. He observed the acute pangs of conscience they provoked in his compatriots, a significant number of whom were now convinced that imperialism necessarily involved the violation of human rights and thought it "better to accelerate the grant of independence to colonial peoples than to become responsible for such appalling events as the Hola Camp incident."[106] He heeded the words of Enoch Powell. Macleod later said that "this was the decisive moment when it became clear to me that we could no longer continue with the old methods of government in Africa and that meant inexorably a move towards African independence."[107]

Almost at once Macleod decided to end the emergency and to release nearly all the remaining Mau Mau detainees. He acted quickly because internal tensions were rising in Kenya, there was a resurgence of terrorism and he feared "terrible bloodshed."[108] More generally he was responding to the pressures that produced Macmillan's "wind of change" speech. Macleod was especially susceptible to international opinion, as expressed in the United Nations and the United States. Tom Mboya's plea for "undiluted democracy"[109] won a sympathetic audience in America, where he was seen as a black George Washington intent on making the British, who had scrambled for Africa, "scram out of Africa."[110] Many Americans, too, thought that western interests in the Cold War would now best be served by the swift dismantling of reactionary European empires. Macleod was particularly concerned that France and Belgium would win the race to decolonise in Africa and that Britain would be left behind with Portugal, still ruled by the quasi-fascist dictator Antônio Salazar. The £60 million cost of the emergency also perturbed Macleod, as did the ending of National Service. In more senses than one, he concluded, Kenya was becoming impossible to defend. So in January 1960 he convened a meeting of the country's white and black leaders (excluding Kenyatta) in London.

It took place at Lancaster House, a massive square edifice of honey-coloured Bath stone built between Green Park and St. James's Park in 1825 for the Duke of York. Queen Victoria, crossing the road to visit this mansion, said that she had left her house for a palace. Now refurbished to recall for new Elizabethans the majesty of the Victorian era, it was the stage on which many colonial conferences were set. And it was intended to awe representatives from the far corners of the shrinking Empire, as the Septizonium had awed barbarians approaching Rome along the Appian Way. As Alan Lennox-Boyd wrote, throughout his negotiations with colonial leaders "the dignity and splendour of the building" exerted "a potent and helpful influence."[111] What met their gaze was the Corinthian portico, the Baroque atrium, the black caryatids, the rococo fireplaces, the crystal chandeliers, the Italianate pictures, the gigantic marble staircase embellished by Charles Barry, and the Great Gallery with its painted ceiling supported by gilded columns in the shape of Palmyra palms. Critics, though, deplored a showy eclecticism extending from Augustus to Louis XV and dismissed Lancaster House as casino architecture. And Blundell was struck by a theatrical contrast between the blue tables and the red velvet plush of the conference chamber and the linoleum floors, cage lifts and plywood partitions behind the scenes. Here most of the work was done and here was revealed the threadbareness of Britain's imperial panoply. This also emerged in Macleod's opening speech. It acknowledged the inevitability of majority rule in Kenya and, in the words of the popular press, "promised independence."[112]

This was a momentous concession, leading as it soon did to a Legislative Council dominated by Africans. But although the democratic principle had triumphed and the shift of power was irreversible, the transition to self-government was anything but straightforward. The various parties, all divided among themselves, remained at odds. Personal animosities rankled. For example, Blundell had found it particularly difficult to deal with Macleod.

> He is an aggressive, tough and ruthless character; very ambitious, with a first-class brain; and very close indeed to the Prime Minister. Not a likeable personality and not a straightforward one. We caught him in falsehoods on several occasions during the negotiations . . . I would not trust him an inch.[113]

The timing of change was problematic. Macleod envisaged that the hand-over of sovereignty would take about a decade and his constitutional checks and balances (for example, the Governor retained the right to choose his own ministers) aimed to retard the process. Moreover, the Colonial Secretary reluctantly supported Baring's successor, Sir Patrick Renison, when he declared that the courts had established Kenyatta's guilt as "the African leader of darkness and death."[114]

Renison was endeavouring to pacify hard-line settlers, who fumed that Blundell's moderates had handed victory to the Mau Mau at Lancaster House. Blundell himself acknowledged that the promise of independence came as "a tremendous shock to European opinion in Kenya." But he argued that in a country of six million increasingly militant Africans, "60,000 Europeans aren't really a firm base for self-government."[115] The *enragés* continued to insist on white supremacy, maintaining that, but for this, Kenya's prospective black leaders would still be "racing through the bush, spear in hand, dressed as the Heavenly Tailor had turned them out."[116] When Blundell returned to Nairobi one of these settlers threw a bag of thirty silver sixpences at his feet, shouting "Judas."[117] Renison, an unimaginative civil servant influenced by his own community, could not grasp that Kenyatta, designated President of the new Kenya African National Union (KANU, the successor of KAU), was the inescapable man. As late as 1961 the Governor gave District Commissioners a forty-minute lecture on the political situation without once mentioning Kenyatta's name. Asked why this was, Renison replied: "He is a busted flush."[118]

In August that year the Governor was obliged to release Kenyatta, who alone could secure the cooperation of KANU, the majority party. His return delighted Africans as much as it disgusted Europeans, who feared that a race war was about to engulf the continent. There were troubles in Algeria, Angola, the Congo, Kenya itself and, especially, in South Africa, which left the Commonwealth a year after police massacred sixty-seven black people at

Sharpeville and three months before Kenyatta was freed. The Colonial Secretary pressed for an understanding with him precisely because Britain sought to distance itself from the apartheid state and to avert such bloody confrontations in Kenya. Despite his long and harsh imprisonment, Kenyatta remained a reconciler. Apparently bearing no malice, he reassured whites that they would be secure in a black man's country. But many whites lambasted the likes of Blundell for "fawning at the feet of this evil thing."[119] One was moved to denounce such race Quislings in verse:

> We are the renegade whites, praying "Forgive us our skin!"
> False to our own flesh and blood, wronging our own kith and kin . . .
> We are the renegade whites, drumming up black, yellow, brown,
> Laying the burden aside, bringing the jungle to town.[120]

Whites of this persuasion could not bear the fact that "life in Paradise was changing."[121]

Six thousand of them, a tenth of the European population, left in 1961 and the British government (assisted with dollars provided by the World Bank) gave grants to buy out Europeans and to pay for African resettlement. This took some of the "steam out of the land kettle."[122] It also accelerated the march towards Kenyan independence since the Treasury wished to minimise further claims. Meanwhile, Kenyatta reiterated his new watchword *"Harambee"*[123]— "Pull Together"—in an attempt to unite rival African constituencies during the scramble for land and freedom. He was by no means successful. Tribal and other minorities feared domination by a Kikuyu-controlled KANU and pressed for a federal constitution. When Reginald Maudling, Macleod's successor as Colonial Secretary, visited Kenya the Kalenjin people greeted him with banners urging "Reggie for regions."[124] Despite Tory objections at home, Maudling pressed forward—Macmillan said that he was *"plus noir que les nègres."*[125] Leading the KANU delegation to a second Lancaster House conference in 1962, Kenyatta conceded many of the devolutionary demands. He was rightly confident that he could transform Kenya into a strong unitary state when he gained the power that would stem from compromise. In June 1963, after a KANU victory at the polls, Kenyatta duly became Prime Minister. Six months later he led his country to *uhuru.*

During the independence ceremony, staged in a floodlit stadium on the outskirts of Nairobi, Kenyatta took the cockerel badge from his lapel and pinned it on to the white uniform of the Duke of Edinburgh, who was representing the Queen. The cockerel was also incorporated into Kenya's national crest. It symbolised Kenyatta's determination to turn a multi-racial country into a one-party state. He himself was to be its avatar, as appeared from his developing personality cult. Soon every shop had to display his picture. His face was engraved on stamps and cash. He dominated the air waves and the newsreels, a film crew accompanying him everywhere. As well as monopolising power, Kenyatta engaged in what a critic called the "senseless accumulation of property."[126] Insofar as avarice and misgovernment had characterised the imperial order, Kenyatta represented continuity—like white settlers, he even spoke of England as "home."[127] However, the rampant corruption of his regime was a novelty and it provided yet another retrospective justification of the Empire.

Even as the Union Jack was being lowered in Nairobi, Margery Perham affirmed the merits of the colonial inheritance:

> A large part of this inheritance is the patient, quiet construction of hundreds of British officials; of missionaries who brought western education and opened the door to Christendom; of Asians who contributed their commercial enterprise and manual skills. To the disinherited and abused settlers Kenya owes a wealth of agricultural and economic achievement won by long and costly experiment.[128]

Other old imperial hands elaborated the argument. They stressed the benefits of British rule: the elimination of slavery and tribal warfare, the control of famine and disease, the growth of prosperity and population, the drive "to lead Africans towards civilisation."[129] Of course, for the sake of their own *amour propre,* many officials who served in Kenya felt bound to believe that they had contributed to a progressive venture. One appraised the British achievement in Kenya thus: "I wouldn't wish any of it undone. It was absolutely vital to advance."[130] For their own reasons Labour politicians and conservative historians echo this view today, urging their compatriots, as Gordon Brown did in 2004, to "be proud . . . of the empire."[131] But thoughtful liberals such as Thomas Cashmore, looking back on his experience of Kenya, were doubtful. He hoped that the British record was not without virtue, and certainly it was better than that of all other European countries in Africa. Contemplating the many mistakes and injustices, though, he feared that future generations would "judge us more harshly for failing in our trust; because we did not prepare our successors adequately for the perils of independence, and left too soon." Alternatively, they would "curse us for not going sooner, or for even coming at all."[132] If the final verdict was fair to Kenya, it was equally so to central Africa, the scene of Britain's last and most protracted colonial struggle on the continent.

20

Kith and Kin

Rhodesia and the Central African Federation

Rhodesia may or may not have been far from God but it was certainly close to South Africa, the prime source of its troubles for almost a century. The pioneers who trekked north in 1890, sustained by the resources of the British South Africa Company (BSAC), spread racial poison over the rugged plateau between the Limpopo and the Zambesi. Having routed Lobengula in 1893, Cecil Rhodes's invaders behaved with harshness worthy of the Boers. Dr. Jameson distributed vast tracts of land, favouring especially "Lord this and the Honble that." Their holdings often ended up in the hands of speculators while the former occupiers were consigned to barren reserves which they regarded "as *cemeteries* not homes."[1] Under the menace of the Maxim gun, Africans were reduced to the status of helots. They were subjected to a hut tax. They were forced to provide cheap labour, which they found a "galling interference with personal liberty."[2] A "Loot Committee"[3] seized most of their cattle, cutting at the root of their communal life and threatening their very existence. Minions of law and order were liable to rape their women on the veldt, while the Chief Native Commissioner got so furious at the sight of "a raw native wearing boots"[4] that he had the man flogged. As Milner himself acknowledged, the usage of the blacks was a scandal and "cannot be defended."[5]

Like Bengal after Plassey, Rhodesia had become the prey of white harpies. They were encouraged by Jameson, who puffed the "highly payable" land he administered as "a happy combination of Canaan, Ophir and the Black Country."[6] They soon suspected that this promise was illusory, finding little wealth and much expense—whisky, costing half-a-crown a bottle in London, sold for ten shillings a tot in Salisbury, where kittens needed to control a plague of rats fetched five pounds apiece. Still dreaming of "marble palaces and steam yachts," if not "the roc's egg of Sinbad or the golden valley of Rasselas,"[7] the pioneers did not hide their voraciousness from the Colossus himself. "I would have ye know, Mr. Rhodes," said a dour Scottish trader, "that we didna come here for posterity."[8] Rhodes duly responded by conjuring up golden visions of Great Zimbabwe, awesome African ruins near Fort Victoria which he identified, by reference to Holy Writ, as an "old Phoenician residence." He wrote, in his usual slapdash style, that "the word 'peacocks' in the bible may be read as parrots and amongst the stone ornaments from Zimbabye are green parrots the common kind of that district for the rest you have gold and ivory also the fact that Zimbabye is built of hewn stone without mortar."[9] Rhodes turned antiquarianism to profit, setting up a company, Rhodesia African Ruins Ltd., with exclusive rights to work such sites for treasure.

Although his pioneers might condemn German and Belgian methods, they had no scruples about exploiting the continent for all it was worth. Moreover, they adopted Afrikaner ideas about dealing with Africans. They asserted that colour prejudice was a "wise provision of nature to preserve the superior race."[10] They imposed Roman-Dutch law and tried blacks with white juries. Such was their self-confidence that they even raised, armed and trained an African police force. Many of its recruits deserted in March 1896 when, driven to near-suicidal desperation, the Matabele, and afterwards the Mashona, raised the standard of revolt. The chief administrator, Lord Grey, who rode to work on a solid-tyred red bicycle with a gold coronet engraved on its back mudguard, admired their pluck. He also blamed the Company for employing them in their own districts. "The right principle is that followed by Caesar when he kept England quiet with a legion raised on the Danube and the Danube quiet with a British legion."[11]

Fired by a spontaneous explosion of wrath, the rising was ill coordinated. But it did take place at an opportune moment, when the British were weakened and distracted by the Jameson Raid. Moreover, the Iron Age warriors of Lobengula's spear kingdom had learned lessons from their defeat in 1893. Then their impis, embodiments of the offensive spirit, had charged across open country and put their trust in cold steel—much as Haig's battalions would do on the Somme. The Matabele had also failed to grasp the use of firepower, raising their rifle sights to give the bullets added force and sometimes shooting at shell-bursts. Now their Martini-Henrys (Rhodes's gift to Lobengula) were better aimed and their tactics were more adroit. They attacked in small bodies over broken ground, slaughtering nearly 150 people in two months and driving the rest into fortified laagers at Bulawayo, Gwelo and elsewhere. Relief columns from Salisbury and Mafeking were slow to arrive, thanks in part to a devastating outbreak of rinderpest, which killed trek oxen as well as thinning still further the Matabele herds. And the victory of imperial troops was by no means assured once they did engage in what Baden-Powell called "a tussle with the niggers."[12]

The Matabele took advantage of the terrain, especially the Matopos Hills south of Bulawayo. These were range upon range of granite kopjes piled with gigantic boulders tilting at crazy angles. Some of the rocks, veined with quartz and sacred to the Matabele, looked like "the ruins of old castles perched on crags unassailable to aught but time."[13] Others resembled fantastic animals or monumental obelisks, and one was eerily reminiscent of Queen Victoria. All were guarded by dense, thorny bush and honeycombed with crevices, caverns and canyons. As a natural stronghold the Matopos were said to be more formidable than the Himalayas. Here British Tommies were mortified to find that, despite their high explosive, machine guns and long-range Lee-Metford rifles, they could only "exact life for life when pitted against a horde of naked savages."[14] However, the Matabele failed to stop the advent of more men and metal. By June 1896 they were on the defensive. One lieutenant complained that his patrol was

always on the point of a fight, but the niggers [were] always disappearing when we got close to them. It was trek, trek, day after day, through bush with no road to go by . . . We had a few skirmishes with small bodies of the enemy, killing a few and taking some prisoners (who were always shot immediately). We burnt dozens of kraals and captured a lot of cattle and women.[15]

Then, before the Matabele had been crushed in the south, the Mashona rose in the north, terrorising an enormous area around Salisbury which had been largely denuded of its garrison. Altogether Africans slew more than 370 Europeans, about 10 per cent of the white population—a decimation not achieved by the Indian mutineers let alone by the Mau Mau. But the second phase of the rebellion *(chimurenga)* was all the more shocking because settlers had protected the supposedly tame Mashona from the martial Matabele. One pioneer, who came from the United States, said that the Mashona tribesman was worse than the "cruel and treacherous American Indian, while massacring the hated Paleface."[16]

The mood of mortal dread and homicidal rage that flared up among whites was similar to that provoked by the Indian Mutiny. The merciless butchery of women and children, wrote the famous hunter F. C. Selous, "seems to the colonist not merely a crime, but a sacrilege, and calls forth all the latent ferocity of the more civilised race." It awoke the "slumbering fiend"[17] in the soul of the empire-builder. As one volunteer told his mother, "after those cold-blooded murders you may be sure there will be no quarter and everything black will have to die, for our men's blood is fairly up."[18] Lord Grey himself, hailed as "a Paladin of Empire," blazed away with the best of them. "He rides through the veldt seeking whom he may shoot," wrote his private secretary, "and has to be restrained from committing most inexcusable murders."[19] Even missionaries called for retribution. One Roman Catholic priest thought that the only chance for the future of the diabolical Mashona was "to exterminate the whole people, both male and female, over the age of 14."[20] The most notorious symbol of vengeance and the prime instrument of lynch law was Bulawayo's hanging tree. Here African suspects were dispatched after summary judicial process, being forced from its branches with ropes tied around their necks. One young tradesman remarked that "it is grand fun potting niggers off, and seeing them fall like nine-pins." The dead fruit of this fun he considered "quite a nice sight."[21] However, Olive Schreiner printed a photograph of the spectacle, dangling black corpses being viewed by a group of whites, as the frontispiece to her celebrated attack on Rhodes, *Trooper Peter Halket of Mashonaland* (1897). This assisted Henry Labouchere's crusade against the rapacity of the BSAC. His journal *Truth* was bitterly denounced in Rhodesia, not least by Baden-Powell, who justified the "blind fury" of pioneers conducting reprisals and derided the softness of "dear, drowsy, after-lunch Old England." Fascinated by executions, he even held one of his own, illegally court-martialling and shooting a "fine old savage"[22] called Uwini. Baden-Powell also acquired a copy of Olive Schreiner's photograph to stick in his campaign scrapbook, entitling it "The Christmas Tree."[23]

In those parts of the countryside affected by the insurrection, which was far from being universal, British regulars and Company volunteers carried out a scorched-earth policy. They burned kraals and dynamited caves. They scourged the veldt, sometimes exterminating "friendlies" as well as enemies and occasionally collecting trophy ears or patches of black skin for making tobacco pouches. They shot "non-combatant women and had no qualms about killing children."[24] They destroyed crops and grain stores. They commandeered livestock and prevented harvesting. In fact, the BSAC created famine. By August 1896 the rebels were reduced to eating monkeys, roots, berries, the pith of palm trees and the pounded-up hides of plague-dead cattle. Over the next few months a large number died of starvation and disease. The survivors fought each other for food and surrendered in droves. Bulawayo, linked to South Africa by rail in 1897, filled with skeletal black refugees. "Look at my body, my arms, my legs," said one. "I am just like a rugged koppie, am all corners."[25] Rhodes organised and financed a dole of mealies, though for many it came too late. Anxious about the heavy drain on the BSAC's exchequer caused by a prolongation of guerrilla warfare, he also squared the Matabele.

Bulky, breathless and prematurely old, his voice increasingly falsetto and his handshake ever more limp, Rhodes showed impressive sang-froid. Perhaps he thought, as a friend surmised, that he was not fated "to be killed by a damned nigger."[26] At any rate he faced the Matabele *indunas* (officers of state) with only a few companions, to whom he issued a characteristic rebuke for coming armed to the *indaba* (conference): "You're all stuffed full of revolvers like partridges." Rhodes held many informal meetings, riding through the Matopos and discovering the massive granite dome of Malindudzimu, "one of the world's views," which he chose as his mausoleum. He also promised to right African wrongs, to abolish the overbearing Native Police, to give the *indunas* authority, salaries and horses, to provide Matabele with more living space. "You will give us land in our own country!" exclaimed a young chief. "That's good of you."[27] Rhodes was conciliatory. He induced the hungry warriors to lay down arms and take up ploughshares. He earned the title *Umlamulanmkunzi,* "the bull who separates the two fighting bulls."[28]

Yet Rhodes had no intention of permitting Africa's first colonial "war of independence"[29] to end in a draw, much less in a black victory. In fact, when accused of being "too soft on the Kaffirs,"[30] he assured settlers that it was their destiny to govern Rhodesia. His vision was realised between 1898, when the so-called "Chartered libertines"[31] of the BSAC dominated the new Legislative Council, and 1923, when the white inhabitants gained virtual self-rule. During that quarter of a century the Britons of Rhodesia twice took up arms for the Empire, during the Boer War and the Great War. They also acted as a bastion against Afrikaner expansion. General Smuts, who became Prime Minister of South Africa in 1919 and tried unsuccessfully to extend the Union to the Zambesi and beyond, called them "little Jingoes."[32] Unquestionably white Rhodesians rejected political assimilation, so much so that King George V (among others) described their country as "the Ulster of South Africa."[33] But they still relied heavily on their powerful southern neighbour, which exercised a considerable influence over their culture. This was dominated by traumatic memories of the 1896 revolt, by heroic myths about pioneer resistance to "hordes of unreasoning barbarians," and by persistent fears that a future black tidal wave might drown the tiny islands of white.

During the conflict, after all, Africans had proved their capacity; and later, in Lord Grey's view, they showed their educability by learning to sing "God Save the Queen." So the Boer mantra was constantly repeated north of the Limpopo, that the natives must be kept in their place. They must be cherished and chastised like "grown-up children." They must be taught habits of industry, perhaps by serving "an apprenticeship in bondage."[34] Certainly they must not be spoilt. "The way boys are treated now, what with monkey nuts and lard, is enough to break the heart and pocket of an employer," wrote one white citizen. "They will be wanting feather beds next."[35] There was just no liberal way of dealing with the "dirty, greasy, woolly-headed, naked, flat-footed and thick-lipped, raw Mashona." En masse Africans were a menace. Whites must adopt a steadfast policy of "divide et impera."[36]

In truth, the Mashona and the Matabele had already been hounded and starved into submission. Their patriarchal system had disintegrated, *indunas* becoming junior officials who could be dismissed at will. Their people were reduced to an abject state under the shadow of the sjambok—to win prompt compliance from black workers, accompanied by "a sickly grin," whites had only to mention the standard number of lashes : "Twenty-five."[37] African miners endured especially brutal conditions, suffering mortality rates similar to those of an army in time of war. African farmers, who had sustained the country during the decade after the rising, were crushed by a battery of rents, dues, fees and other imposts. There was even a five-shilling Dog Tax, which impaired their efforts to keep down vermin. It prompted complaints that landowners "will be taking money from the flies in our kraals next; better be dead than pay such demands." Worse still was the white erosion of increasingly congested black reserves, which were not only reduced in size but in quality. Europeans laid hold of "rich red chocolate soil," consigning its occupiers to inhospitable regions infested by baboons, mosquitoes and tsetse flies. The settlers aspired to pursue a "white agricultural policy" that would, while retaining migrant black labour, entirely banish from their own areas what they called "Kaffir farming."[38]

Africans were so dispirited that some lost faith in their own spirits, adopting the creed of the conquerors. The early missionaries had made little impression, their endeavours hardly being assisted by the first Bishop of Mashonaland, a habitual absentee who regarded Africans as a "repulsive degradation of humanity."[39] Lobengula's warriors had used pages of the gospel, recently translated, to embellish their ostrich-feather headdresses. But after 1896 the seed fell on less stony ground. Indeed, churchmen often found it easier to proselytise black heathens than white Christians. The latter, when not making a fetish of sport—bicycling, shooting, horse-racing, hunting jackals, playing billiards, cricket, rugby and so forth—tended to worship Bacchus. Lucky prospectors bathed in champagne and after one race meeting, when all its citizens got dead drunk, Umtali resembled a morgue. By the 1920s, though, nearly a tenth of Rhodesia's million Africans had been converted to Christianity. Some had attended mission schools, the only form of education open to them until 1920. As usual, the proliferation of "mission boys" exacerbated ethnic tensions. A typical settler complained that missionaries

> laid too much emphasis on the "man-and-brother" theory, and overlooked the necessity for starting at the bottom and gradually inculcating ideas of discipline, hygiene and thrift, with the result that the black man was led to regard himself as the equal of the white and became uppish and troublesome.[40]

Such settlers particularly objected to language teaching. They themselves addressed Africans in Kitchen Kaffir or Fanagolo, a profane mixture of Afrikaans, Zulu and English expressed in the imperative voice. And they considered it "a sign of disrespect for Kaffirs to speak to them in English."[41] Alarmed by the advent of the "educated native,"[42] who knew about his own civilisation and complained of living under "a veiled form of slavery,"[43] Rhodesia's rulers sought to entrench white supremacy through racial segregation.

In theory, after the introduction of internal self-rule in 1923, the imperial government remained the guardian of Rhodesia's black majority. It paid lip service to Britain's special responsibility for African interests, as directly exercised in the protected territories of Basutoland, Bechuanaland and Swaziland. Indeed, the Colonial Office would probably have agreed with the BSAC's last chief administrator, who said that "the local whites were no more fit to govern the natives than the Bolsheviks were fit to rule Russians."[44] So London restricted the powers of Salisbury's new legislative assembly in order to protect African rights. In practice, though, the British government never intervened positively and seldom invoked its veto. The Dominions Office took charge of Rhodesia and treated it as a dominion. Few Africans had the vote and settlers ran the country in their own interest, later buying out the BSAC's remaining stake in minerals and railways. White rule included control of the armed forces as well as the civil service, which put Rhodesia's settlers in a "quite different position"[45] from those of Kenya. But while they were stronger they were also poorer—the only true Rhodesian was allegedly one who could not afford to leave. Efforts were made to attract wealthy immigrants and the long-serving Prime Minister, Godfrey Huggins, said that what the country needed was young men who had "fagged at school and had been flogged at school."[46] What the country mostly got was settlers mortgaged to the hilt, accompanied by a distressing number of "bar-loungers and general 'slackers.'"[47] During the 1920s most white farmers were in dire straits. They lived, as the novelist Doris Lessing said, with "karosses as blankets, furniture of petrol boxes, flour sack curtains."[48] Many put their faith in tobacco, only to find that overproduction devalued the "leaf of gold." The Great Depression pushed them further into debt while encouraging skilled African workers to undercut European artisans. As whites felt the draught, they ensured that blacks bore the brunt of the economic blizzard. "The Native," as the Chief Native Commissioner wrote, "has always been the shock-absorber—the 'snubber'—in the State motor car."[49]

The most notorious measure, long contemplated and passed in 1930, was the Land Apportionment Act, which became the white *"Magna Carta."*[50] It divided the country into colour cantons, restricting the million Africans to twenty-eight million acres (including reserves) and assigning forty-eight million acres (including municipalities) to the fifty thousand Europeans. The Act was presented as a way of securing native rights to land that might have been purchased by richer immigrants, a means of protection via segregation. As such it gained wide acceptance in Britain as well as Rhodesia. Yet it was plainly designed to entrench white supremacy on the South African model of separate but unequal development. It put intolerable pressure on the soil in black rural areas, to which some 425,000 people were eventually removed. By denying Africans permanent residence, it encircled towns and cities with a fringe of squalid locations and turned peasants into proletarians. The territorial carve-up was a prelude to further repression. In 1931 a Maize Control Act imposed a complicated marketing system which favoured struggling white farmers at the expense of blacks. In the same year the Public Service Act excluded Africans from all but menial posts in the civil service—the "native clerk" was designated a "messenger interpreter."[51] In 1934 an Industrial Conciliation Act stopped them from competing with Europeans for skilled jobs elsewhere. Two years later a Native Registration Act tightened up the pass laws, placing particular "restrictions on African women's mobility."[52] Some took advantage of new opportunities but many had little alternative to prostitution. Salisbury's so-called "tea parties" became notorious: long queues formed for prostitutes and "intercourse apparently took place within sight of the next on the line." A few of these women became shebeen queens. They profited hugely from the ban on black consumption of white liquor by selling an illegal brew called *skokiaan,* which consisted of yeast, sugar and maize meal fortified with such ingredients as tobacco, methylated spirits and boot polish.

Finally, a Sedition Act (1936) tried to prevent the spread of subversive literature, much of it attacking racial discrimination. The colour bar operated in schools, hospitals, pubs and so on but there were further galling regulations—for example, Africans were long prohibited from walking on city pavements. Meanwhile, the black urban ghettoes, built of grass, tin, sacking and *dagga* (mud and cow dung mixed with ox blood), were incubators of disease. Rates of tuberculosis, pneumonia, bilharzia, hookworm and malnutrition increased especially fast in the stinking, smoke-blackened shanty-town outside Bulawayo's industrial area, which was terrorised by gangs in short coats and wide trousers and had some claim to be "the worst slum in the world."[53] Yet whites asserted that they kept Africans at bay for the sake of health and hygiene. The Prime Minister expressed the common view: "You cannot expect the European to form up in a queue with dirty people, possible an old umfazi [African woman] with an infant on her back mewling and puking."[54] Huggins was a convinced segregationist who once advocated sending all "advanced natives"[55] across the Zambesi, an idea quashed in London. Africans would later describe their Prime Minister as the "Rhodesian Doctor Malan."[56] The maverick Labour MP Tom Driberg said that talking to Huggins about blacks was like talking to Streicher about Jews.

This was an outrageous slur. Huggins was an Edwardian medical man whose prescriptions were out of date. He advocated a partnership between black and white, the kind of partnership that existed between horse and rider. Although literally as well as metaphorically deaf to the African voice, he was an old-fashioned paternalist. He even set up free health clinics for blacks (justified as prophylactics for whites) whereas one British Governor apparently dismissed proposals for an African hospital on the grounds that "there are too many natives in the country already."[57] Nevertheless Huggins did try to abort the birth of a nation, to stifle what a leading missionary had called "the dawning of Bantu race consciousness." This "profound psychological revolution,"[58] inspired by memories of the 1896 uprising, was a reaction against white dominion. Huggins's policies provoked fresh African hostility towards the colonial state. Sometimes it took millenarian forms, with prophecies that American aeroplanes flown by Negroes would smash "European control" or that Armageddon would blast "the works of Caesar."[59] Often black resistance was local and individual, ranging from violence to non-cooperation. As a female legislator remarked, Africans evolved ways of boycotting a bad employer, "who soon finds that the privilege of walloping his own nigger is too expensive."[60]

Frequently, too, there were general protests. Several hundred people in one reserve challenged Huggins's agricultural decrees: "Even the white farmers' dogs can ride in motor cars and are better treated by the Government than we are."[61] As well as holding mass meetings, Africans organised petitions, sent delegations, issued propaganda and chanted slogans, such as "Africa for Africans."[62] They also formed trade unions, notably the militant Industrial and Commercial Union (ICU), which had nearly five thousand members by 1932. The Sedition Act suppressed the ICU but it revived as unions proliferated after the war. By that time the high hopes stemming from the Atlantic Charter had been dashed by horrid consequences of the conflict. Among them were forced labour, cramped locations, exhausted land in the reserves, and stronger links with South Africa—Huggins and Smuts were close imperial allies. In October 1945 black railwaymen went on strike in Rhodesia, sparking off a series of labour troubles. The railwaymen won a partial victory, prompting a journalist to proclaim the end of white exploitation and black tribalism. "The railway strike has proved that Africans have been born."[63]

The claim was premature. African leadership, smashed after the *chimurenga* of 1896, remained fragmented. In fact, it had to follow its more militant rank and file. Ordinary Africans were bitterly disappointed to receive no reward for their wartime sacrifices other than rude remarks about "Kaffirs" in uniform. They were incensed by stricter controls on the population of their bursting urban ghettoes, which reached 100,000 in 1946 and doubled over the next decade. They resented the post-war influx of white immigrants, particularly unskilled workers from Britain who adopted Rhodesia's master-race doctrine, "simply wallowing in its full intoxicating glory, indeed almost to the point of open hatred of the African."[64] They suffered from sharp increases in the cost of living: wages stayed pitifully low but between July and December 1947 food prices rose by more than 20 per cent. Moreover, they were inspired by moves towards colonial independence from India to the Gold Coast. Thus pressure from below forced hesitant trade union bosses to endorse a general strike in 1948, the climax of the current labour unrest. But their trumpet gave an uncertain sound. They were divided by tribal rivalry, personal ambition and mutual jealousy. Acutely conscious of the limitations of black power, they sought to work "within the existing system."[65] Joshua Nkomo, secretary of the railwaymen's union and aspirant nationalist leader, was typical in hankering for compromise. Fat, genial and self-indulgent, he tried to be all things to all men. More, he endeavoured to appease God as well as mammon, successively embracing Congregationalism, Methodism and Roman Catholicism, while continuing to worship the deity of his ancestors under the sacred trees of the shrine at Dula. Nkomo means bull, but he had the horns of a snail. So, even though

Rhodesia's only general strike was supported by black domestic servants who jeered at their employers as they emptied their own dustbins, it fizzled out like a damp squib. White troops suppressed violence and Huggins talked peace. Finally he threw a sop to his demoralised adversaries, changing the hated name of Salisbury's "Native Location" to the "Harare African Township."

Northern Rhodesia offered Huggins a more substantial means of shoring up white supremacy in Southern Rhodesia.* Stretching from the Zambesi to Lake Tanganyika, this butterfly-shaped protectorate, where the Colonial Office supposedly ensured that African interests were paramount, contained rich deposits of copper and a thin sprinkling of Europeans. Huggins, who aimed to exploit its mineral wealth and to repel black nationalism, had long been in favour of amalgamating the two Rhodesias. So had Roy Welensky, though the settlers' leader in Lusaka, that "Koh-i-Noor of rough diamonds,"[66] could hardly have differed more starkly from the polished Prime Minister in Salisbury. The thirteenth child of an Afrikaner woman and a drunken Polish-Jewish doss-house keeper, Welensky went barefoot to primary school, never slept between sheets before he was sixteen and, as he famously said, swam "bare-arsed in the Makabusi with many picannins." Subsequently he became a heavyweight boxing champion, an engine driver and an outstanding trade unionist. Describing himself as "a socialist conservative,"[67] he wanted to create a broad British dominion in the heart of Africa where for the next century or so the black man would play his "part as a junior partner." Such schemes had long been resisted in London. For the Colonial Office reckoned that the segregationist policies of Southern Rhodesia would spread to the north, where even progressive whites favoured a certain amount of "slave-driving."[68] But after Dr. Malan's victory in 1948 Attlee's government feared that Huggins might form a union with South Africa's apartheid regime. At a time when Britain was harassed by other colonial problems, this would give the lie to its liberal professions, which were transmitted throughout the region by a vernacular radio service in Lusaka and picked up on cheap receivers known as "Saucepan Specials." A Huggins–Malan marriage would subject millions of Africans to oppression, a cabinet paper noted. "Terrible wars might even be fought between a white-ruled Eastern Africa and a black-ruled Western Africa."[69]

In 1953, therefore, after protracted negotiations and five full-dress conferences, the two Rhodesias and (at British insistence) Nyasaland formed

---

*Southern Rhodesia, now Zimbabwe, was normally called Rhodesia, unless being distinguished from Northern Rhodesia, now Zambia.

the Central African Federation (CAF). It was fatally flawed from the start. Variously intended to safeguard minority white privileges and majority black interests, the CAF was an administrative shambles. It divided power between no fewer than five governments—two in Salisbury (federal and territorial) and the others in Lusaka, Zomba and Westminster. Huggins himself, wrote a British official, "never had the faintest intention whatsoever of making the federation a success,"[70] regarding it simply as a means of absorbing Northern Rhodesia. Worse still, Africans had barely been consulted. Having warned that blacks who refused to cooperate would "meet the fate of the Red Indians in the USA," Welensky said that they could not understand the issues involved. In fact they understood all too well, assisted by a European civil servant who checked out of his Victoria Falls hotel when black delegates arrived, saying that "it did not suit his ideas to live with Africans."[71] They declared that the CAF would be a "garden of flowers for the European settlers and a deep grave for the natives."[72] They condemned Joshua Nkomo for not opposing the scheme root and branch. They also accused Britain of "cold, calculated, callous and cynical betrayal."[73] It had, in Huggins's words, handed over "6,000,000 primitive people to a Parliament dominated by local Europeans."[74] In front of a large crowd in Lusaka the President of the new Northern Rhodesian National Congress solemnly burned the British White Papers on federation. The struggle against it, at a time when Nkrumah was leading the Gold Coast towards independence, inspired mass nationalism in all three territories. Before long Africans, who noted that the first federal budget took half-a-crown off a bottle of whisky and put five shillings on a bag of maize, were once again singing the patriotic songs of the *chimurenga*.

Yet at first the CAF's prospects looked bright, as though it would live up to the motto on its coat of arms: *"Magnum Esse Mereamur"* (Let us deserve to be great). Copper boomed and Rhodesia's Virginia tobacco rivalled that of America. Investment poured in, financing metalled roads and ambitious projects such as the Kariba Dam, which provided not only cheap electricity but what Welensky called the concrete wedding band uniting the two Rhodesias. (Actually the "biggest man-made lake in the world" displaced thirty thousand Africans on the north bank of the Zambesi, while the power station was built on the south bank, "symbolising the predominance of Southern Rhodesian interests.")[75] There was also a flood of white settlers, among them expatriates from independent India—the "Bengal Chancers" supposedly transformed Umtali into "Poonafontein." Garden suburbs sprouted around the office blocks of Salisbury, the federal capital which Africans from the north nicknamed *Bamba Zonke*—Take All. Skyscrapers

sprang up along the geometric, switchback boulevards of Bulawayo, which
had been made wide enough to turn an ox wagon. Africans gained a modest
share in the rising prosperity, though they still got less than a tenth of white
incomes. In the hope of creating a tame black middle class, Garfield Todd,
the charismatic missionary who had followed Huggins as Southern Rhodesia's Prime Minister, even began to relax the colour bar. Africans, after
protesting, obtained entry to some Salisbury hotels. After picketing, they
got equal treatment in Lusaka's shops, notably butchers, where white customers had unashamedly rejected meat for their dogs as "it was fit for Kaffirs only."[76] They were permitted to drink European beer and wine (but not
spirits). They were officially called "Mr." instead of being habitually
"described as 'It.'"[77] There seemed to be a real hope of what Welensky called
"partnership between the African and his European master."[78] In fact, the
first few years of the CAF were a "golden age of participation."[79]

The gold turned to dross after 1956, when the bottom dropped out of
the copper market. Many Africans lost their jobs and with them their
houses. As real wages fell and living costs rose, strikes and disturbances multiplied, the authorities taking emergency powers and carrying out mass
arrests. At a time when African workers spent a third of their incomes on
transport, higher bus fares in Salisbury provoked boycott and violence—
young women who defied the boycott were raped. Grievances were still
more acute in the countryside, where compulsory conservation measures
such as cattle culling caused "a significant number of richer peasants . . . to
embrace nationalist politics."[80] Simultaneously urban Africans were embittered when changes in land tenure deprived them of communal rights in the
reserves. Garfield Todd never shrank from coercion. He had not only put
down labour troubles by force but, in his preaching and teaching days,
when he recommended Christianity to blacks both for its own sake and
"because it made people more amenable to being ruled,"[81] he had caned
refractory girl pupils on the buttocks. Nevertheless he now tried to take the
sting out of African resentment by a slight widening of the franchise. Britain
approved this and other liberal initiatives, such as improving black education. But they were mistrusted by white Rhodesians, who ousted Todd in
1958, preferring Sir Edgar Whitehead, a lonely, boozy eccentric, clever but
almost blind and nearly deaf, who was rumoured (wrongly) to invite his
prize bull into his parlour. However, Welensky, the federal Prime Minister,
tried to induce the Tory government in London to grant the CAF dominion
status on the basis of its increased black representation, though the Labour
opposition was now committed to NIBMAR, "No Independence before
Majority Rule."[82]

North and south of the Zambesi, nationalist opposition crystallised around that democratic principle. It was led by Joshua Nkomo in Salisbury, Kenneth Kaunda in Lusaka and Hastings Banda in Nyasaland, who returned home in 1958 after having practised as a doctor in England for so long that he had almost forgotten his native tongue. But he was greeted as "our Mahatma, our Messiah, our Saviour."[83] And his translated speeches, extravagant displays of mob oratory directed against the "stupid and hellish Federation,"[84] which he delivered wearing a Homburg hat and a three-piece suit, aroused wild enthusiasm. Disorder spread like a veldt fire. Resistance to the CAF had always been fiercer in the two northern territories and now Nyasaland, in particular, seemed on the brink of revolt. There were rumours, moreover, that Banda planned to poison the country's eight thousand whites with forty tons of arsenic, while Kaunda's organisation was said to resemble the Chicago gang known as "Murder Incorporated." Early in 1959 all three territories declared states of emergency. Black leaders were arrested, including Kaunda and Banda (who was hustled off to Southern Rhodesia in his pyjamas) but not Nkomo (who was, as usual, abroad), along with hundreds of their supporters. Nationalist parties were banned. Troops helped to quell the subsequent riots—fifty demonstrators were killed after the detention of Banda and his lieutenants, which was code-named "Operation Sunrise" as a riposte to his promised dawn *(kwacha)* of freedom. As whites in the south threatened to "go it alone,"[85] Whitehead passed a battery of measures giving his government dictatorial powers and drastically curtailing freedom of expression and association. Eventually Sir Robert Tredgold, the Federal Chief Justice, resigned in protest, asserting that despite his good brain Whitehead suffered from "mental myopia." His legislation had "scrubbed out" the clauses in the Declaration of Human Rights one by one and created "a police state."[86] At least one white newspaper agreed, saying that the new laws signified "Totalitarian Rhodesia."[87] An Anglican archbishop detected in them an "echo of the Hitler regime."

Although Whitehead could thus hold down black nationalists in the south, resistance to white rule stiffened in the northern territories. When the Governor of Nyasaland, Sir Robert Armitage, hoped that Banda's incarceration in Gwelo would provide a two-year political lull, the *Guardian* retorted, "One might as well ask for a two-year lull in the flow of the Zambesi."[88] There was also turmoil in London, where Lennox-Boyd maintained that the crackdown in Nyasaland had foiled a conspiracy to massacre whites. In a vain attempt to calm the storm, the British government appointed a commission of inquiry into the emergency led by Lord Devlin. Macmillan later questioned the choice of this high court judge, asking whether he was not "Irish, lapsed Catholic and deformed?"[89] Certainly Devlin produced a report that, while approving action instead of abdication in Nyasaland, made unpleasant reading for the Prime Minister. It dismissed the "murder plot" as the convenient "frontispiece" of a story designed to justify repression. It confirmed that the security services had habitually bullied, beaten and otherwise maltreated Africans. It dismissed house burnings and other collective punishments, imposed for good administrative reasons according to the colonial government, as straightforward breaches of the law. And it came to the devastating conclusion that "Nyasaland is—no doubt temporarily—a police state where it is not safe for anyone to express approval of the policies of the Congress Party."[90]

During the summer of 1959 British ministers held urgent discussions about how "events in Nyasaland might be likened to Mau Mau or—astonishingly—to the Indian Mutiny."[91] In the end they rejected Devlin's report, Macmillan congratulating his "manly cabinet"[92] while Aneurin Bevan derided the "squalid" parliament. Welensky also rejected Devlin, accusing him of profound hostility to the Central African Federation. One journalist compared Welensky to the Roman Governor Paulinus Suetonius, who refused to accept the verdict of Nero's commission of inquiry which found that Britain had suffered enough punishment after Boadicea's rebellion. Doubtless Devlin summoned up Welensky's fighting spirit but, more important, he inclined Macmillan to appeasement in Africa. Macmillan appreciated the weight of black hostility towards the CAF. He feared that the northern territories could become a bloody British Algeria. And he recognised that the southern settlers were contemplating a Salisbury Tea Party involving separation rather than copulation.

To compound his difficulties, Macmillan was committed both to sustaining the CAF as a multi-racial partnership and to moving "towards self-government in Northern Rhodesia and Nyasaland as soon as possible."[93] There were also external complications, such as the Hola scandal. To escape from this labyrinth, the Prime Minister conjured up another commission. It was led by the suave courtier Lord Monckton, known as "the Oilcan," and its task was to advise about the future of the Federation. Deeply suspicious, Welensky fought the Commission tooth and nail. So did the settlers, who christened it the "Monkey Commission" and told it to "go to Hell."[94] They were anxious about Macmillan's "wind of change" speech and angry about Iain Macleod's resolve to achieve "constitutional advance" in Nyasaland. His resolve was strengthened when he opened a Commonwealth Exhibition in Leeds where demonstrators waved placards saying "Stand up to Welensky," "No prison without trial" and "Keep faith with Africa."[95] Progress in Nyasaland could only occur, the Colonial Secretary decided, after the release of Banda, whom he called "the White hope of the Blacks and the *bête noire* of the Whites."[96] In the face of Welensky's opposition and Macmillan's hesitation, Macleod had to threaten resignation to get his way. So on 1 April 1960, ten days after the Sharpeville bloodbath, Banda was freed. Saying that he was not embittered by his imprisonment since Nkrumah, de Valera, Gandhi and Nehru had suffered the same fate, Banda flew home determined to bring independence to his country. Zomba greeted him calmly, confounding critics who had forecast a riotous assembly. But at Government House the jubilant Colonial Secretary, down there on a visit, did go on the rampage. He hurled "cushions across the room, in the style of a rugby scrum-half, while the hapless Governor retrieved them."[97]

By the middle of that traumatic year, which saw civil strife in Algeria and white refugees from the shattered Congo arriving in Salisbury as well as increasingly violent protests in Southern Rhodesia, a new constitution was devised for Nyasaland. It provided for an African majority and pointed the way to self-rule. The Monckton Commission, which published its conclusions in October 1960, permitted Northern Rhodesia to follow the same course. The Report, as Welensky had feared, was "a terrible piece of high explosive" calculated to blow the Federation to smithereens. It sanctioned national secession and recommended democratic reform. Wafted hither and thither by winds of change, Macmillan's government first proposed majority rule. Then it gave way to Welensky. Finally, it submitted to Kaunda, who had told Macleod that if he (Kaunda) adopted non-violence "he might well be committing political suicide."[98] Now out of gaol, Kaunda organised a campaign of civil disobedience, extending to sabotage, arson and murder. It would soon, he warned, make the Mau Mau insurgency look like "a child's picnic."[99] Under a revised constitution, therefore, Kaunda won an election in 1962 and two years later, sustained by another poll, based on universal suffrage, he led Northern Rhodesia to full independence as Zambia. Well before Kaunda's first victory, though, it had become clear that Britain would abandon the Federation. The Marquess of Salisbury, reactionary grandson of the Prime Minister who had given his name to the Rhodesian capital, deplored the cynical handover of power to Africans who could only be described as "irresponsible, malicious children."[100] He thought Macleod "a complacent defeatist."[101] In parliament Salisbury famously stigmatised him as "too clever by half," adding that he used his bridge-playing skills to outwit his white "opponents" on behalf of his black "partners." If this was "gutter oratory," as one Labour peer charged, it was not confined to Westminster.[102]

Welensky said that an attack by Macleod was "like being bitten by a sheep."[103] He identified Duncan Sandys as the "white man in the woodpile (one mustn't use the term nigger now)."[104] He refused to shake hands with R. A. Butler, a gutless, spineless "feather pillow."[105] He declined an invitation to have lunch with Macmillan, whose disastrous policy was "to liquidate what is left of the British Empire as quickly as possible,"[106] saying that the food would choke him. The old prizefighter was on the ropes but he did not pull his punches. He raged against feckless and perfidious Albion. It was abandoning the Commonwealth for the European Community. It was selling out, rotting from within, heading for "a hellfire dust-up."[107] It had lost the "will to govern,"[108] which Welensky attributed to American pressure and blamed for giving him a bad migraine.

> The British Government have ratted on us. They have gone back on the most solemn understandings and intentions. They have wrecked the foundations upon which they themselves built the Federation . . . Britain is utterly reckless of the fate of the inhabitants, including those of our own kith and kin.[109]

Embittered by what they saw as the mother country's treachery, the kith and kin did wish to govern.

Whitehead made liberal overtures, such as desegregating post offices and promising land reform, in order to conciliate middle-class Africans and to convince London that Rhodesia was becoming a multi-racial state fit for autonomy. The ploy nearly worked. Britain granted a new constitution, relinquishing its right to veto discriminatory laws in return for an extension of the franchise which fell far short of majority rule. Furthermore, Nkomo at first accepted the deal, only to disavow it when assailed by more militant nationalists. Among them was his incipient rival Robert Mugabe, the Lenin of Rhodesia, who shared Kaunda's contempt for such "chicken-in-the-basket warriors."[110] Meanwhile, a new party emerged in Salisbury, the Rhodesian Front. In 1962 it comprehensively defeated Whitehead, who had by now, Welensky observed, "as much chance of being elected as a snowball in Beira."[111] Implacable for white supremacy, the Front was backed by tobacco magnates and beef barons such as "Boss" Lilford, a hatchet-faced millionaire who liked to "take his house guests hunting for African game poachers with Land Rovers, searchlights and shotguns."[112] Huggins had once hoped that Rhodesia would not have to use its defence force as "the North American colonies had to use theirs, because we are dealing with a stupid government in the United Kingdom."[113] Now the Rhodesian Front was prepared to risk internal violence and external hostility in order to achieve the goal of independence.

It was gall and wormwood to the Front, which consistently retained the support of most whites, that Rhodesia was still tied to Britain while black countries were gaining their freedom. Thus in 1961 the Colonial Office, fearing a Congo-style insurrection, handed power in Tanganyika to its pre-eminent nationalist, Julius Nyerere. The following year the British pulled out of Uganda, harassed by local difficulties ranging from King "Freddie" Mutesa's penchant for one "blonde popsy"[114] after another to the unruliness of what a Governor called "these bumptious, beer-swilling, bible-punching, bullying, braggart Baganda."[115] After the formal dissolution of the CAF in 1964 Nyasaland, now Malawi, became self-governing along with Zambia. Less viable states would also be groomed for independence, Basutoland (Lesotho, 1966), Bechuanaland (Botswana, 1966) and Swaziland (1968). More irksome still for the Rhodesian Front was the fact that the growing number of black countries in the Commonwealth, from which South Africa withdrew in 1961, pressed London to take a hard line with Salisbury. In fact they acted rather like the United Nations. And that body increasingly regarded the British as being friends with Welensky, Salazar and Verwoerd, and "accomplices in a policy of repression in Southern Rhodesia." Indeed Sir Hugh Foot, a British envoy to the UN, resigned in 1962 because he thought his country was taking the "wrong side in a losing battle" between black "nationalism and white domination in Africa."[116] In this climate of opinion Britain could not simply hand over Rhodesia to a white minority. But ministers intimated that they would connive with the Rhodesian Front if they could do so without incurring international opprobrium. Lord Home, who as Sir Alec Douglas-Home succeeded Macmillan at 10 Downing Street in 1963 though he lacked a chin as well as a moustache, suggested that the status quo could be maintained if it were disguised by an electoral façade. R. A. Butler "implied that it would be embarrassing for Britain to give Rhodesia independence, but if Rhodesia took it herself, it might get Britain off the hook."[117] Ian Smith, who became leader of the Rhodesian Front and the country in 1964, took the hint. As he later wrote, "the time for shilly-shallying had come to an end."[118]

Few saw in Smith the makings of a white knight. Home dismissed him as a peasant. Huggins (now Lord Malvern) said that he was "a farm boy from Selukwe, devious, parochial and suspicious."[119] Welensky reckoned that he could talk about nothing but cattle and daylight saving—"He's no more a strong man than I'm King of Siam."[120] At the age of forty-five, Smith seemed about as prosaic as his name. His personality was dull and subfusc, like his baggy, grey double-breasted suits. He was an indifferent speaker with a nasal twang and a precise but inaccurate vocabulary—he would say, for example, "the factual situation" when he meant "the actual situation."[121] Smith had a callow sense of humour and few interests apart from sport. He had little political experience and less technical aptitude. As the Front's Finance Minister he was once seen looking blankly at columns of official figures, as though they would have made as much sense "if he had held the pages upside down."[122] Nevertheless, Ian Douglas Smith, the son of a Scottish butcher and the first Prime Minister of Rhodesia to be born in the country, proved to be a canny, dogged and popular leader. He had a fine war record as a fighter pilot and bore the stamp of valour on his face. After being badly injured in a crash Smith had had a skin graft on his right cheek, which left his eye drooping and his nose crooked and gave an apt but disconcerting rigidity to his appearance. He was adamant about nothing so much as the impossibility of black rule in his lifetime, or that of his children. Moreover, he quickly gave an earnest of his intentions, detaining African leaders such as Mugabe and smashing their organisations. With his "cowboy cabinet,"[123] Smith invoked the spirit of 1896. The embodiment of the laager mentality, he entrenched white privilege. He drew inspiration as well as aid and comfort from South Africa. As a black nationalist said, "Smith is a racist. He is an apartheid man. He is no better than Verwoerd."[124] At one political meeting, where he was heckled by African students, Smith sang an Afrikaans song: *"Bobbejaan, klim die berg"* ("Baboon, climb the hill").[125]

During the eighteen months before he issued the Unilateral Declaration of Independence (UDI) Smith pursued a dual strategy of preparation and negotiation. He consolidated support in the judiciary, police, armed forces and civil service, promoting his own men where necessary. He tried to mould public opinion, holding rallies, censoring newspapers, controlling radio and television, and issuing what his own intelligence chief called "Goebbels-type propaganda."[126] He bribed, threatened, gaoled and expelled recalcitrant journalists, employing as his press officer an avowed fascist who had once supported Sir Oswald Mosley. Smith intimidated other opponents, white liberals as well as black militants. One settler told Duncan Sandys, "The opposition to Smith is very considerable but this is a small place and every so-called intelligent person is scared stiff of honestly pronouncing themselves against him for fear of restriction or business reprisals."[127] Smith also campaigned hard at the polls, claiming to stand for national unity but really promoting the cause of UDI. When Welensky fought against this proposal at a by-election he was not only trounced but reviled as "a bloody Jew, a Communist, a traitor and a coward."[128] Meanwhile Smith tried to persuade a sympathetic but sceptical Douglas-Home that Rhodesians of all hues would support independence in order to preserve civilisation in a primitive country. To prove this contention he canvassed the opinions of tribal chiefs, who were supposed to speak for their people. But since the *indaba* was held under conditions of strict secrecy and sealed off by troops, it was no surprise that the headmen, in reality bucolic stooges of the government, gave Smith the answer that he wanted. Lord Malvern rightly dismissed the whole exercise as "a swindle."[129]

Harold Wilson, who became Prime Minister after narrowly defeating Douglas-Home in the general election of October 1964, was not duped. He at once warned Smith of the disastrous economic and political consequences that would flow from illegally cutting Rhodesia's ties with Britain. But in power Wilson gave ground. Abandoning NIBMAR for a time, he sanctioned independence with guarantees of "unimpeded progress to majority rule" provided that this was "acceptable to the people of Rhodesia as a whole." Sustained by his own voters, Smith rejected these terms. Further negotiations proved fruitless, especially during Wilson's eleventh-hour descent on Salisbury, which one member of his cabinet, Richard Crossman, compared to Chamberlain's flight to Munich. Wilson was so incensed by the casual maltreatment of Nkomo and other detained black leaders, who were held in a stifling police van without food or water for hours before meeting him, that he literally saw "red flashes before my eyes." At Smith's house, moreover, Wilson showed his disgust when one Rhodesian minister, the Duke of Montrose, mimicked the obscene antics of an American dancer "trained in the art of displaying her charms"[130] by cavorting around the dinner table with a coin clenched between his buttocks. Wilson did not allow these manifestations of colonial culture to goad him into conflict. On the contrary, anxious to avert a Tory attack in Westminster, he renounced the use of force against Rhodesia. There would be no "thunderbolt hurtling through the sky," he said, "in the shape of the Royal Air Force."[131]

Wilson thus disappointed not only the UN and the Commonwealth but the many British enemies of racism. Among them were the left-wing firebrand Barbara Castle and the shaggy, saintly figure of Dr. Michael Ramsey, Archbishop of Canterbury, who shocked white Rhodesians by his belligerence—they threatened to send him the ashes of their burned Bibles and proposed that the Anglican Church should sing a new hymn, "Onward Christian Soldiers, shoot your kith and kin."[132] However, Wilson's public refusal to fight gave Smith the final confidence to take emergency powers and implement his plans. Back in London, Wilson pleaded with him in vain over the telephone, finding him evasive but "astonishingly calm—almost friendly—the calm of a madman."[133] So, on the eleventh day of the eleventh month of 1965, Smith read the proclamation, wreathed in red, green and gold scrolls, announcing that Rhodesia was independent. The date was heavy with irrelevant symbolism and the language echoed that of the last rebellious British colonists to issue a Declaration of Independence. Unlike Thomas Jefferson, though, Ian Smith continued to profess atavistic loyalty to the Crown. He concluded his broadcast with a ringing "God save the Queen."[134] As the national anthem played, white Rhodesians in shops, offices and workplaces stood stiffly to attention.

In fact, the Queen's representative in Salisbury, Sir Humphrey Gibbs, had already dismissed Smith. When the Prime Minister called at Government House, an attractive bungalow mansion with white Dutch gables and long pillared stoep, set in secluded gardens containing an aviary and fishponds, the Governor said that the declaration deprived him and his ministers of all legal authority. But the rogue regime possessed what mattered more, power. Smith isolated Gibbs, cutting off his telephone and his salary, taking away his official car and his police guard. The Governor became a virtual prisoner, a mere simulacrum of royal supremacy. He was a stuffed dress shirt, a bemedalled, white-uniformed dummy, a feathered and topeed totem of Britain's lost imperial might. Meanwhile, Harold Wilson faced a division of opinion at home best summed up by rival car stickers, "Support Rhodesia" and "Rhodesia: One Man, One Vote." Under pressure, he turned out to be the antithesis of Lord Palmerston. He took all actions against Smith short of those that would have any effect, aggravating complaints from the Front's opponents that they had received not "even the smallest crumb of assistance from London."[135] Wilson imposed economic sanctions on Rhodesia, freezing its reserves, interdicting its trade and eventually banning its importation of oil. But just as Smith had wrongly forecast that UDI would be "a three-day wonder,"[136] Wilson erroneously predicted that his measures might end the rebellion within "weeks rather than months."[137] Actually Rhodesia flourished for at least seven years, attracting tourists and thousands more white immigrants. The worst hardship they had to endure was a shortage of Scotch whisky. Also, for the first time since its foundation in 1893, the Salisbury Club ran out of port.

Although not a single country recognised Smith's government, it got help from Portuguese Mozambique and the Republic of South Africa. They constituted two gaping holes in the blockade, which Wilson was unable and unwilling to fill. South Africa was especially problematic. It was the West's anti-Communist ally in the Cold War, a source of gold and uranium, and a vital trading partner. Barbara Castle herself acknowledged that a suspension of British exports to the Cape, worth £265 million in 1965 (nearly eight times more than those to Rhodesia), "would almost certainly wreck sterling."[138] Smith thus tried to keep his uneasy friendship with Verwoerd and his successor, John Vorster, in good repair. He strengthened social and commercial bonds between Salisbury and Pretoria. He tightened sporting relations—it was said that for cricket and rugby "Rhodesia and South Africa become one and the same."[139] In 1967 he accepted military aid from Vorster. Many liberal Rhodesians disliked "the politics of our neighbour to the south" as much as they disliked the "repressive legislation" that had turned their own country into a "fascist state."[140] But even they opposed the speedy advent of African rule, and Smith retained the backing of about 80 per cent of whites. His supporters believed that the alternative to the Rhodesian Front was a black dictatorship. They dwelt obsessively on the murders and rapes that would follow the enfranchisement of "the African . . . No matter what education he has, what degree he rises to, he will always remain a savage and a barbarian."[141] In fact the nationalist movement was hopelessly divided and demoralised, and Rhodesian forces easily contained the small-scale guerrilla activity. But the menace remained real enough, particularly to an illegal regime. As the eighty-two-year-old Lord Malvern said after UDI, even Smith's totalitarian government should realise that "what a revolting minority can do, a revolting majority can do so much better."[142] Thus white Rhodesians closed ranks in response to internal terrors and external threats. As the trade embargo faltered, Britain proved increasingly impotent.

Wilson therefore reneged on his pledge not to negotiate with treason. In 1966 he met Smith aboard the warship *Tiger,* off Gibraltar. Appropriately enough, Smith and others were seasick while the cruiser went round in circles. Wilson himself back-pedalled. In return for an extension of African rights he agreed that majority rule could be postponed until the next millennium. On returning home Smith decided that he could afford to decline the offer. Rhodesia was enjoying a boom. The economy was becoming more diverse and self-sufficient. Despite UN endorsement, sanctions were evaded on an international scale. Rhodesia received assistance from Greece and Japan, from the Vatican and the Kremlin, from German printing firms and from British oil companies—with the complicity of Wilson's own government. Zambia, landlocked and impoverished, could hardly avoid trading with (and through) Rhodesia. De Gaulle's France served its own interests. So did embattled Israel. Others contravened sanctions for racist motives. The virulently segregationist Senator for Mississippi, Jim Eastland, visited Salisbury with businessmen from the Deep South who wanted to help

Smith "put the niggers right back where they belonged."[143] Later, embroiled
in Vietnam, the United States openly flouted the embargo by lifting its ban
on imports of Rhodesian chrome, nickel and other strategic materials.
Meanwhile, Wilson insisted that sanctions were biting—to which Kaunda
retorted that "even a flea bites."[144] Accordingly, Wilson initiated a further
round of talks in 1968. They were again held in the Mediterranean, this time
on board HMS *Fearless,* and they were equally futile. Wilson was, as a
Labour minister wrote, "absolutely determined to settle with Ian Smith."[145]
But Smith remained stubborn, despite Britain's definitive abandonment of
NIBMAR. Indeed, the following year he introduced a new constitution for
Rhodesia, approved by a referendum, which established a white republic for
the foreseeable future. Sir Humphrey Gibbs, the apparition of majesty, was
glad to fade away.

Although by 1970 Britain was preoccupied by fresh troubles in Northern
Ireland, another blood-stained legacy of empire, Alec Douglas-Home, Foreign Minister in Edward Heath's new Conservative government, made a
final effort to cut the Rhodesian knot. He admitted that Britain had "very
little influence and no power."[146] But he himself was popular with Rhodesian leaders. A charming, if somewhat effete, Old Etonian, Douglas-Home
had seemed at school "honourably ineligible for the struggle of life."[147] He
had remained engagingly amateurish, facetiously admitting that he worked
out financial problems with matchsticks. He enjoyed rural pursuits, keeping
Ruff's *Guide to the Turf* on his desk at the Foreign Office and sending
Welensky presents of salmon he had caught. He was an authentic Scottish
aristocrat, the owner of broad acres who plainly saw Rhodesia as a country
estate managed by white factors and worked by black crofters. Surely their
differences could be reconciled. Having been an ardent appeaser during the
late 1930s, so much so that he destroyed the more incriminating evidence
when Winston Churchill came to power, Douglas-Home had tried to persuade Iain Macleod that Southern Rhodesia was "the essential nucleus of a
nation devoted to the ultimate co-operation between the races."[148] Now he
sought a Munichite solution. After long discussions Douglas-Home reached
an agreement with Smith that was "little more than a smoke screen"[149] to
conceal British capitulation.

Many of the terms were ambiguous, as if to confirm the Rhodesian view
that Douglas-Home was "honestly dishonest."[150] But the settlement evidently guaranteed white rule for generations. What Douglas-Home felt
bound to stipulate, though, was that a majority of all Rhodesians must find
it acceptable. Both he and Smith were confident that the commission of
inquiry into African opinion, which was led by a retired judge, Lord Pearce,

would get the affirmative answer it was encouraged to seek. Smith, indeed, uttered his notorious boast that Rhodesia had "the happiest Africans in the world."[151] But they were altogether unhappy about the Home–Smith compact, deeming it "a vicious and subtle device" to enable Britain to accept UDI. It would set the seal on another apartheid state. A Methodist bishop named Abel Muzorewa led the opposition, requesting and receiving from black Rhodesians "an *emphatic 'No.'*" Pearce's report on their verdict, said Muzorewa, resembled a "flash of lightning and crash of thunder at the finale of a violent summer storm."[152] Britain had shot its imperial bolt. Henceforth others would have to solve what America's Central Intelligence Agency called its "thorniest decolonisation problem."[153]

What eventually forced Smith to negotiate was an irresistible combination of military subversion and political dictation. From 1972 the guerrilla war intensified, becoming a *chimurenga* more vicious than anything seen in 1896. Admittedly, the insurgents were hampered by murderous infighting between the nationalist factions. And cities such as Salisbury and Bulawayo, where most Europeans lived, were hardly affected by the bloodshed. But guerrillas, some backed by China and others by Russia, crossed the frontier from Mozambique and Zambia to attack remote farmsteads, railways and roads. Rural whites turned their houses into fortresses, protected by sandbags, searchlights, barbed wire and guard dogs. The guerrillas tried to enlist the native population, using terror tactics against anyone who resisted. Chiefs were regularly tortured and murdered. Schoolteachers were raped. Villages were looted and burned. Counter-insurgency measures were no less savage. They included collective punishments, the closure of schools and clinics, the establishment of free-fire zones and protected villages similar to concentration camps. African cattle were seized or deliberately infected with anthrax. Captured combatants were given electric shocks, dragged through the bush by Land Rovers or "hung upside down from a tree and beaten." One District Commissioner engaged in "stamping on them" said that he had "never had so much fun in my life."[154] The Selous Scouts committed the worst atrocities, especially during cross-border raids and hot pursuits. Sometimes in the guise of guerrillas, they poached ivory and smuggled guns as well as brutalising and slaughtering civilians. Such violence and trickery envenomed race relations. But Smith, who extended segregation, had more faith in coercion than conciliation. Doubtless he subscribed to the white cliché: "Why bother about [winning] the munt's heart or mind? If you've got him by the balls, his heart and mind will follow."[155]

By 1974, though, more insurgents were being recruited than killed and Smith's position was becoming precarious. During the spring an officers' coup in Lisbon hastened the end of the Portuguese empire and produced an independent Mozambique. Within a matter of months Rhodesia's eastern border, 764 miles long, was dominated by a hostile state. Moreover its leader, Samora Machel, who felt honour-bound to help his fellow Marxist revolutionary Robert Mugabe, controlled the ports through which 80 per cent of Rhodesia's exports flowed. Smith was left with only a single friendly neighbour. But South Africa, formerly Rhodesia's evil genius, now became its nemesis. For the politicians in Pretoria preferred a stable black regime on their northern flank to an unstable white one. So Vorster squeezed Smith, who responded by declaring a cease-fire. He also released Nkomo, Mugabe and other detainees. And he prepared to discuss a compromise constitution. Britain's role in the Rhodesian imbroglio was typified by the fruitless visit paid to the region by Foreign Secretary James Callaghan in January 1975. One journalist described his remarks as "the winds of flatulence."[156] Callaghan certainly had no influence on Smith, who withdrew after one day from talks with feuding nationalist leaders held in railway carriages on the bridge over the Victoria Falls, an "engineering wonder"[157] that spectacularly symbolised the imperial conquest of nature. As the American Secretary of State Henry Kissinger observed, Rhodesia had power without legitimacy whereas Britain had legitimacy without power. In fact, Kissinger wrote, the failure of successive London governments to quell the rebel regime was a painful reminder of their country's decline. So Britain ceded to the United States its "traditional role of leadership in Southern Africa."[158] The Secretary of State was not renowned for his modesty. But in 1976 he did bring American influence to bear on both Vorster and Smith. At last, it was said, Kissinger "had discovered Africa."[159]

The discovery occurred as a result of growing fears that the continent was about to become the new battleground in the Cold War. Previously Kissinger had assumed that whites were there to stay and that blacks could not "gain the political rights they seek through violence."[160] Now, as the old empires collapsed, Russian and Chinese Communists were helping national liberation movements to change the political complexion of Africa. Even more sinister, in Angola Cuban forces with Soviet T-54 tanks and MIG fighters routed the faction backed by South Africa and the United States. The Secretary of State read the writing on the wall. As one of his biographers said, Kissinger was an exponent of Talleyrand's maxim that "The art of statesmanship is to foresee the inevitable and to expedite its occurrence."[161] He therefore reversed his previous policy and tried to win over black countries by opposing minority white regimes. Shuttling to and fro, he met the leaders of the so-called "front-line states," those directly confronting Rhodesia. Kissinger was impressed. Machel, who had just closed Mozambique to the passage of Rhodesian goods, was bouncy and resilient. Slim, graceful and elegant, despite his Hitlerian moustache, Nyerere was formidably intelligent and displayed an awesome command of English—he had translated Shakespeare's *Julius Caesar* into Swahili. With his white hair, flashing eyes and ready smile, Kaunda "exuded authority."[162] Not all the African leaders were equally impressed by Kissinger. Nkomo compared him to a businessman doing a quick deal and felt that he was talking to a robot. Yet in Lusaka, at the end of April 1976, Kissinger made a speech that sounded the death knell of Britain's last African colony.

He pledged American support for majority rule, equal rights and human dignity for all the peoples of southern Africa. He also promised that Rhodesia would "face our total and unrelenting opposition until a negotiated settlement is achieved."[163] Kissinger followed this up by inducing Vorster to tighten the screw on Smith. South Africa withdrew more of its forces, starved Rhodesia of munitions and strangled its trade. On 19 September, in Pretoria, Kissinger finally met Smith face-to-face. The Secretary of State blew cool and warm. He opened with this admonition: "Your reputation as a devious lying twister is even worse than mine. But let me warn you not to try any funny stuff with me because this time you will have met your match." Kissinger went on to point out the hopelessness of Rhodesia's military and economic position. Its only viable option was to accept a settlement, mostly devised by the British, which would provide for majority rule within two years in return for the lifting of sanctions and the ending of the guerrilla war. Smith said, "You want me to sign my own suicide note."[164] Kissinger remained stonily silent. But he mellowed as Smith, after haggling over white safeguards and obliging the Secretary of State to fudge or, as he put it, to engage in "constructive ambiguity,"[165] accepted his proposals. In a show of sympathy at their parting, Kissinger shed crocodile tears. When Smith announced the terms of the deal, it seemed as though the Secretary of State had worked another diplomatic miracle. America had apparently lowered the curtain on the final act of Britain's imperial drama on the African stage. Some Westminster politicians even resented the fact that this was a transatlantic triumph, that their own government had been "inert and supine" over Rhodesia, merely providing a Whitehall official as part of Kissinger's "baggage train." White citizens of Salisbury, where the Jacaranda Festival was in full swing, lamented Smith's surrender. In Cecil Square, on the spot where Rhodes's pioneers had raised the Union Jack in 1890, they flew a white flag at half-mast.

Actually Smith had by no means exhausted his Gladstonian capacity for prevarication. As he said in a quasi-Churchillian broadcast, this was not the end, or even the beginning of the end, but it was, "perhaps, the end of the beginning."[166] Kissinger's much-vaunted breakthrough had left Smith ample room for manoeuvre and he emphasised his commitment to *responsible* majority rule. There was a further bar to progress. The nationalist leaders had not endorsed the deal. Indeed, Mugabe and Nkomo, who formed a troubled alliance called the Patriotic Front in October 1976, refused to order a cease-fire until they gained control of the interim government. Thus the conference held under British auspices in Geneva, which aimed to implement Kissinger's proposals, ran into the sand. So did further efforts by the new Foreign Secretary, David Owen, who apparently saw himself as ringmaster of a bizarre diplomatic menagerie. He characterised Smith as the jackal, Vorster as the hippopotamus, Nkomo as the elephant and Mugabe as the panther. To complicate the metaphor, the American eagle was circling overhead and Owen was not sure whether the British lion would roar. Mugabe, who believed that nothing could be settled without "a bitter and bloody war," provided an answer. He told reporters, "Dr Owen has failed to convince us that Britain is in a position to effect the transfer of power to the people of Zimbabwe."[167]

Smith was equally dismissive about Britain's "travelling circus." He concentrated on dividing the African opposition, reaching agreement with its most pliable representative, Bishop Muzorewa, and creating a black puppet regime. This required some concession and much persuasion. During 1977 Smith's task became more urgent thanks to the "spread of terrorism throughout the country."[168] Guerrillas in their thousands ravaged the provinces, harassed the cities and even menaced the skies—they eventually shot down two Viscount airliners with SAM-7 missiles. The war was costing £500,000 a day, a quarter of all government spending, and the economy was in ruins. Despite strict emigration and exchange controls, 1,500 whites a month took the "yellow route" or the "chicken run." So Smith was relieved when, in March 1978, Muzorewa signed the so-called Salisbury Agreement. In theory it ushered in majority rule, opening Rhodesia to what Gibbon had called "the inconveniences of a wild democracy."[169] In practice the whites retained clandestine control. Smith had retreated in order to stay in the same place.

The deception became increasingly obvious during the course of the year. Smith did little to alleviate racial discrimination. As the guerrilla war intensified, he exacerbated mistrust between black leaders by trying (and failing) to detach Nkomo from Mugabe. Finally, Smith approved a new constitution which gave Africans a majority in parliament (though one black got one vote while one white got two) but maintained European power over the judiciary, the police, the civil service and the armed forces. Muzorewa, who fancied himself as an African George Washington, was condemned by his own side for accepting these arrangements. Mugabe called the Bishop "Baa Baa Black Sheep" because he always followed his white master. Yet in a hard-fought general election Muzorewa won two-thirds of the popular vote and fifty-one out of ninety-two parliamentary seats. So, on 1 June 1979, he became Prime Minister of the new state of Zimbabwe-Rhodesia—the Afro-English name was almost universally vilified. When he arrived at his official residence, Smith wrote in his diary, Muzorewa looked

> like a colourful rooster, and a bantam at that, sitting on a replica of the ox-wagons used by the Pioneer Column when they occupied the country in 1890. I cringed and closed my eyes. Muzorewa and his ancestors had not even invented the wheel by the time the white man arrived.[170]

The new British Prime Minister, Margaret Thatcher, was a right-wing Tory who instinctively favoured white Rhodesia and might well have sympathised with these sentiments. Certainly she mistrusted black nationalists and their demanding Commonwealth acolytes. In fact, she liked to say that the acronym CHOGM (Commonwealth Heads of Government Meeting) stood for "Compulsory Hand-outs for Greedy Mendicants."[171]

However, Mrs. Thatcher was reluctantly converted by her patrician Foreign Secretary, Lord Carrington, who aimed to withhold recognition from Muzorewa's government. It was spurious as well as illegal, he argued, and it guaranteed the continuation of a civil war that had already cost twenty thousand lives. Britain should keep in line with the United States, whose President, Jimmy Carter, was dedicated to achieving racial justice. Yet Carrington offered his Prime Minister a chance of decolonising without American help, of finding her own way out of Africa. Having been branded a racist by the Zambian press, she arrived for the August Commonwealth Conference in Lusaka wearing dark glasses, convinced that acid would be thrown in her face. In fact she was greeted with cheers and her change of front was a triumph. Mrs. Thatcher announced that she was "wholly committed to genuine black majority rule in Rhodesia."[172] She danced with Kaunda, calling him "a dear sweet man."[173] He declared that "the Iron Lady has brought a ray of hope on the dark horizon." Zambians had witnessed the "apotheosis of the Blessed Margaret," according to the *Daily Telegraph's* reporter. They would not have been surprised, he said, to see her home-bound plane "drawn skywards by cherubim."[174]

So, during the autumn of 1979, a final gathering of all interested parties took place at Lancaster House. Mugabe only participated because Machel threatened to shut down his guerrilla bases in Mozambique. But he proved a dominant presence, highly educated, ruthlessly clever and unpleasantly abrasive. "It is we who have liberated Rhodesia," he told Lord Carrington. "You are simply intervening now to take advantage of our victory."[175] This barb was painfully close to the mark. But Mugabe concluded that he could secure lasting power through the ballot box. Braving placards saying "Hang Carrington," brandished by Tory loyalists backing a rebel regime, as he ironically observed, the Foreign Secretary devoted many weeks to securing an agreement. He isolated Smith, who felt betrayed by compromisers in his own delegation—he reflected bitterly (but without irony) on Cicero's maxim that a nation "cannot survive treason from within."[176] Carrington extorted a cease-fire from Nkomo and Mugabe, though it was never wholly respected despite the arrival of British troops. He forced Muzorewa, weakened by a diet of carrots and vichyssoise, the only food he found palatable at his hotel, to give way to a British Governor. "Really?" asked Nkomo. "Will he have plumes and a horse?"[177]

Actually Lord Soames, Winston Churchill's son-in-law, who agreed to take up the post, brought to it a rich combination of diplomatic urbanity and military bluffness. His task was to supervise the elections which would decide the fate of Zimbabwe. He acknowledged, in his inimitable manner, that they would hardly occur without violence. Africans, he said, did not behave like the natives of Little Puddleton-on-the-Marsh. "They think nothing of sticking poles up each other's whatnot, and doing filthy, beastly things to each other."[178] As Smith and Nkomo complained, there was ample evidence of intimidation, even terror. But Soames refused to cancel the elections and Mugabe won so handsomely, with 63 per cent of the national vote, as to put the result beyond doubt. On 17 April 1980, therefore, Africans celebrated what their new leader called the "birthday of great Zimbabwe." Britain, now out of Africa for good and with less discredit than Portugal in Angola let alone France in Algeria, was palpably relieved.

After ninety years Rhodes's colonial dream, long a nightmare, had vanished into thin air. For good or ill—and Rhodesia's whites had hardly set a good democratic example—Rhodesia's blacks were now masters of their own destiny. South Africa was exposed as the last bastion of apartheid. The world hadn't got, as the London *Times* put it (echoing Richard Nixon's famous valediction), "imperial and racist Britain to kick around any more."[179] Yet many Britons cherished a poignant nostalgia for the fallen Empire and some yearned to restore its glory as Charlemagne had revived the majesty of Rome. A mood of melancholy resentment permeated the Prime Minister's room in the House of Commons as she and Conservative colleagues gathered around the television to watch the Union Jack come down at Government House in Salisbury and to hear the dying strains of the Last Post. "The poor Queen," exclaimed Mrs. Thatcher. "Do you realise the number of colonies that have been handed over from the British Empire since she came to the Throne?"[180] The Iron Lady wept.

21

Rocks and Islands

The West Indies and Cyprus

The wheel of fortune turned slowly in the case of Rome but, as Gibbon said, its awful revolution took the city and the Empire from the height of greatness and buried them "in a common grave."[1] By contrast, Britain survived but its Empire, though not obliterated utterly, disappeared with astonishing speed. Between 1945 and 1965 the number of people under British colonial rule shrank from seven hundred million to five million. Within a generation some twenty-six countries, comprising the vast bulk of the British Empire, became independent. A number of factors, already mentioned, helped to precipitate this collapse: loss of prestige in Asia accompanied by post-war military weakness, emergent nationalism in the colonies, global opposition to imperialism and its retreat on nearly all fronts, fiascos such as Suez and scandals such as Hola, Britain's recurrent economic crises and its move towards Europe, the democratic preference for welfare at home rather than ascendancy abroad. Whatever the causes, though, many patriotic Britons deplored the swift removal of such huge swathes of red from the map. They lamented it as a grievous national humiliation. They denounced it as a foul slur on the virility of their race. They damned it as an inglorious betrayal of Albion's manifest destiny. Ministers and officials did their utmost to brand the croakers as anachronistic and reactionary. Those who complained that "we are 'selling the Empire,' abdicating our responsibilities, indulging in a policy of 'scuttle,'" said ex-head of the Colonial Office Sir John Macpherson in 1960, were "mostly elderly gentlemen with bristling white moustaches sitting in comfortable armchairs in clubs."[2]

It was a shrewd crack since the moustache was vanishing as fast as the Empire. True, it had ceased to be compulsory in the army as early as 1916, when King's Regulations had permitted shaving the upper lip. Allegedly that change took place to accommodate the Prince of Wales, who was ill equipped with the "manly growth."[3] But according to his secretary, General Sir Nevil Macready made the order because he intensely disliked his own moustache, "a bristly affair resembling the small brushes with which kitchen maids and others clean saucepans." Be this as it may, the moustache was plainly outmoded by the 1950s. It had become a joke thanks to Charlie Chaplin and Groucho Marx. It had become an international symbol of "villainy"[4] thanks to Hitler's toothbrush and "the huge laughing cockroaches"[5] under Stalin's nose. In Britain it was seen primarily as the badge of Colonel Blimp, the mark of the Poona mentality. The plot of a P. G. Wodehouse novel written in 1954, for example, turned on the "delicate wisp of vegetation" cultivated by Bertie Wooster to give himself an air of diablerie but stigmatised by Jeeves, infallible arbiter of fashion, as a "dark stain like mulligatawny soup."[6] More seriously, Sir John Macpherson reiterated the established defence of the "evolution of Empire into Commonwealth."[7] Britain was merely completing, at a somewhat quickened pace, the deliberate process of trusteeship whereby its colonies progressed from tutelage to liberty. If Macpherson rightly depicted Greater Britain as a self-liquidating entity, he put an exceedingly favourable gloss on what has been called "the stampede . . . from empire."[8] During his time as its leading mandarin in the late 1950s, the Colonial Office had privately expressed dismay at the imminent prospect of becoming a department of "rocks and islands."[9]

The United Kingdom seemed destined to retain a scattering of some two hundred minuscule dependent territories. At home and abroad hostile observers regarded these as the fragments of a discredited world order, the nebulae of an exploded system. They were, particularly in American eyes, the sea-girt tokens of four centuries of acquisitiveness. Franklin D. Roosevelt had chided Churchill about this in 1944, saying that the Prime Minister would have to adjust himself to the new period that had opened in the planet's history. Meanwhile, the President warned his Secretary of State, the "British would take land anywhere in the world even if it were only a rock or a sand bar."[10] Some Britons did value strategically situated and otherwise attractive remnants of imperial sway. After all, the atomic particles of former glory could become the granular foundations of future might. Soon after his "wind of change" speech Harold Macmillan decided that "we only need our 'Gibraltars.'"[11] A chain of strongholds, linked by air and ocean, was the modern way to sustain Britain's influence around the globe. They would be easy to defend. They would be cheap to administer. They would involve few complications with the native inhabitants. Ideally, indeed, they would contain no native inhabitants. Referring to the forced removal of the people of Diego Garcia, an atoll (soon leased to the United States) in the Chagos archipelago, the head of the Foreign Office wrote in 1966: "The object of the exercise is to get some rocks which will remain *ours*. There will be no indigenous population except seagulls." A senior official commented, "Unfortunately, along with the Birds go some few Tarzans or Men Fridays whose origins are obscure, and who are being hopefully wished on to Mauritius etc."[12] Such islands, deserted or not, would afford power without responsibility, the prerogative of the imperialist throughout the ages.

In providing this boon, they resembled the string of Caribbean bases which Britain had granted to the United States in 1940 in exchange for fifty old destroyers. The arrangement was a wartime expedient by which Churchill hoped to tighten transatlantic bonds, not a Rooseveltian ploy to supersede Britain in the eastern approaches to the Panama Canal and the American mainland. However, it was another step towards U.S. hegemony in this region and elsewhere. It was an acknowledgement that Britain had a diminishing need for a strategic stake in what had increasingly become an American sphere of interest. Furthermore, the deal, which was reached without any local consultation, reflected Britain's long-standing disregard for poor, costly and superfluous islands. When sugar was still king the West Indies had been among "the richest jewels in the crown of Great Britain."[13] Once sugar had been dethroned, they became, in Joseph Chamberlain's phrase, the "Empire's darkest slum."[14]

The story of the British West Indies during the Victorian era was one of stagnation punctuated by misfortune. After the abolition of slavery in 1833 the old plantation system fell into decay. In lieu of free labour, the owners got free trade. First they suffered the destruction of protective tariffs, then they had to bear competition from foreign slave-grown sugar and from sugar beet. Between 1805 and 1850 sugar prices fell by 75 per cent. Some proprietors kept solvent. On Barbados, virtually monopolised by great estates and "as thickly populated as an anthill,"[15] former slaves had little alternative to becoming wage labourers. But in most places, Jamaica especially, a "stupendous" decline took place, with scenes of "wreck and ruin, destitution and negligence."[16] Kingston appeared derelict, steeped in "neglect and apathy." Anthony Trollope likened it to a city of the dead. In the countryside roads and bridges had fallen into a chronic state of disrepair. Cane fields had reverted to bush. The jungle choked mansions and sugar factories as remorselessly as the parasitic fig strangled the enormous silk cotton tree—a phenomenon known as "The Scotchman hugging the Creole." Fauna seemed as monstrous as flora to those plagued by gallinippers and marabuntas. Visitors to the Caribbean dilated on "mosquitoes as big as turkey-cocks,"[17] "fireflies as large as cockchafers" and butterflies "the size of English bats."[18] Nature's malignity was apparently confirmed by disasters such as droughts, earthquakes, epidemics and hurricanes.

Between 1848 and 1910 the number of plantations in Jamaica shrank from 513 to 77, many being sold for less than the price of their sugar boilers. They were broken up into smallholdings and worked by ex-slaves, now peasants. A similar situation prevailed in St. Lucia, St. Vincent, Grenada, Tobago and elsewhere. The white population waned while American influence waxed. During the 1860s Barbados was said to be full of Yankee clocks, Yankee buggies and Yankee dollars—preferred to a chaotic coinage that included escudos, pistoles and doubloons. The black population, while developing a distinctive Creole culture, remained poor and heavily taxed. Britain did virtually nothing for it in the way of investment or amelioration. During his 1859 Caribbean tour Trollope said that the British should "without a stain on our patriotism . . . take off our hats and bid farewell to the West Indies."[19] Nearly thirty years later J. A. Froude wrote that "a silent revolution"[20] had taken place whereby his countrymen had loosened their hold on the region. England, he said, would soon be no more than a name in the Antilles.

Actually, far from relinquishing its Caribbean possessions, Britain managed to combine indifference with interference. Even those enjoying representative institutions had been made crown colonies by the end of Queen Victoria's reign. They were subjected to dictation from Whitehall in order to safeguard them from white oligarchies, "little groups of local Pooh-Bahs."[21] The exception was Barbados. It retained an elected assembly, dating from 1639, which met in a chamber illuminated by Gothic stained-glass windows portraying British sovereigns (including Cromwell) and their coats of arms, and presided over by a periwigged Speaker enthroned under a heraldic Lion and Unicorn. Whatever the form of government, though, whites continued to dominate the West Indies. The Governor usually sided with his own kind—in British Guiana it was said that once he attended the smart Georgetown Club he had "sold out to the local gentry."[22] So racial discrimination caused frequent tremors of unrest and occasional explosions of violence. Sometimes an enlightened Governor could effect improvement. Public life in St. Lucia, for example, had traditionally been "a medley of farce, scandal and tragedy."[23] Its 35,000 people, nearly all black, spoke a French patois, conformed to Quebec law and endured the corvée. In 1869 William Des Voeux became Governor and used his autocratic powers— "extremely dangerous"[24] in the wrong hands—to make his rule popular. Among other things, he impeached the Chief Justice for corruption, debt and drunkenness—having convicted a man of burglary the Chief Justice "addressed him as though his offence had been rape."[25] Des Voeux abolished forced labour. He set up the first central factory for processing sugar in the

West Indies. He even conducted a successful campaign against the deadly fer-de-lance, first by paying sixpence for each snake killed (1,200 in seven months) and then by introducing mongooses.

Modest advances also took place elsewhere, notably in health and education. But disease, squalor and malnutrition were still rife. A majority of West Indians remained illiterate and as late as the 1930s Caribbean primary schooling was the most backward in the Empire. Territories, each one an intricate and contrasting racial and social mosaic, struggled to survive in different ways. Some encouraged emigration, the Panama Canal providing abundant employment. Others promoted tourism, the Bahamas offering Americans, as Winston Churchill said, "soft breezes and hard liquor."[26] Bootlegging and drug-smuggling were a common recourse. Most countries cultivated alternative crops such as coffee, cotton, rice, tobacco, indigo and coconuts. Jamaica grew bananas and bred beef cattle. St. Vincent produced arrowroot, Grenada nutmeg and Montserrat limes. The Cayman Islands harvested sponges, turtles and conch shells. Before the traffic was stopped in 1917, Trinidad and British Guiana had recruited almost 400,000 indentured labourers from the Indian subcontinent to work the sugar plantations, adding to ethnic tensions. These territories also exploited mineral resources such as oil, asphalt and bauxite. During the 1890s they trapped, stuffed and exported tens of thousands of hummingbirds to the hatters and dressmakers of Europe. Such expedients scarcely relieved the plight of the West Indies, which the Royal Commission of 1897 described as "usually deplorable and sometimes desperate." Joseph Chamberlain wanted Britain to provide grants so that its dependencies did not "fall into anarchy and ruin."[27]

Even in decline, sugar sustained the Caribbean. Prices rose during the Great War and despite later falls the industry employed 175,000 West Indians by the end of the 1920s, approaching a tenth of the population. They were ruthlessly exploited. Trade unions were prohibited, pay was exiguous and slavery cast a long shadow. Most white employers believed that "coloured workers are animals or worse than animals"[28] and treated them accordingly. Some planters cut down breadfruit trees "to try to force work out of the lazy nigger."[29] It is true that a small black middle class was emerging, lighter shades of skin often conferring social advantage—in the mating game most people longed, as they said, to add a bit of cream to their coffee. However, the British made few concessions to democracy. The Caribbean basin remained a backwater. Its territories were even cut off from one another. There were no direct links from British Honduras to Antigua, Grenada or Tobago; or between islands within sight of each other, such as St. Vincent and St. Lucia. Letters sent from Jamaica to Barbados had to go via Halifax, New York or London. Senior local officials were granted leave passages home instead of to the region. Most Britons "thought the West Indies had to do with India"[30] and only became interested in them because of Learie Constantine's prowess at cricket. When the Great Depression caused widespread unemployment and acute hardship, no constitutional channels existed to give vent to popular anger. So, as the price of sugar reached an all-time low of £5 a ton and wages in some islands fell to 1s 3d a day, a level hardly above that of the 1830s, the Caribbean was shaken by a series of more or less bloody disturbances. In 1933 jobless workers protested in Trinidad. The following year riots convulsed British Honduras. St. Kitts, where absentee whites owned most of the land, erupted in 1935. Subsequently Trinidad became the scene of further carnage. Strikes paralysed the Jamaica docks and the coaling station at St. Lucia. Trouble occurred in British Guiana, Barbados, St. Vincent and elsewhere. The common man, said a future Prime Minister of Jamaica, Norman Manley, would no longer endure inhuman conditions and was prepared "to raise hell in his own way to call attention to his wrong."[31]

West Indian nationalism was born out of this civil strife. There had been signs of its gestation earlier, especially during the Great War, when the West Indies Regiment had become a source of Caribbean pride. Advances towards self-rule had followed, notably in Jamaica, British Guiana and Trinidad. But it was the long economic crisis that spawned trade unions, co-operative societies, reform leagues and other bodies, which often developed into political parties. Nationalist leaders also emerged, such as Robert Bradshaw in St. Kitts and Albert Gomes in Trinidad. Many were influenced by socialism. Cheddi Jagan espoused Marxist ideas in Guiana. And even the conservative Grantley Adams sang "The Red Flag," waved the Hammer and Sickle, and prosecuted a "social revolution"[32] that ended white dominance and imperial rule in Barbados. Others, such as Norman Manley, a brilliant lawyer, and the influential historian Eric Williams, were an intellectual match for the brightest colonial officials. At Oxford Williams had humbled a white classmate, who expressed surprise that a Trinidadian could speak English, by excelling in classics and explaining: "You see, we speak Latin in Trinidad."[33] Some leaders, though, were crooked, erratic and power-hungry. Vere Bird of Antigua was involved in small-scale financial scandals. So was the rumbustious, lubricious and superstitious Eric Gairy, leader of Grenada's Labour Party, who was fined for obscenity and disenfranchised for conducting a steel band through a rival's meeting. William Bramble, founder of the Montserrat Trades and Labour Union, was guilty of corruption, "megalomania and inefficiency."[34]

No future West Indian Prime Minister was more volatile or flamboyant than Alexander Bustamante, often hailed as the "Uncrowned King" of Jamaica. A pistol-packing condottiere, he shrouded his origins in mystery but claimed, "I come from the gutter of poverty."35 A bold figure who combined guile with charm, he was likened to a Jamaican folk hero, the crafty spider-man Anansi. A raucous demagogue, "Busta" specialised in earthy wit and vitriolic invective, boasting that his followers "'would vote for a dog' if he so directed."36 In fact, he was less radical than his rival and brother-in-law, Norman Manley. But Bustamante championed "the middle course with a positively incendiary violence."37 He became "the Messiah of the unenfranchised, the unemployed, the underemployed and the underpaid." And he united them by promising "a better life, here and now, in a country of which they formed a majority, but from whose society they had hitherto been actively excluded."38 The British themselves recognised that present troubles had been caused by past neglect and a Royal Commission under the chairmanship of Lord Moyne, a plutocratic paternalist, recommended more subsidies to improve social conditions. But by 1939 prominent West Indians with mass support were seeking to dismantle the colonial order itself.

During and after the war Britain tried to fulfil its obligations and to meet the nationalist challenge by means of welfare and development grants. The payments were also an acknowledgement of the West Indies' new strategic and economic value as well as their moral support. Specks on the map proudly rallied behind the British Empire, one telegram to London reading: "Don't worry; Barbados is with you."39 Furthermore, the Colonial Office approved broad extensions of the franchise, starting with Barbados, Jamaica and Trinidad. From 1943, however, it maintained that the development of self-governing institutions, within the framework of the British Empire, "should be linked up with the question of West Indian federation."40 The idea of a "closer union" between Britain's Caribbean possessions had been long mooted and occasionally essayed.41 Many radical West Indians advocated federation as an alternative to disintegration. They saw it as a means of acquiring independence and dominion status en bloc, something that individual units were too small and too weak to accomplish on their own. But others rejected such proposals. Bustamante, so inconstant that he would vote against the motions of his own ministry, said that in order to keep the colonies in bondage Britain planned to create a "federation of paupers."42 Actually, as other West Indian leaders charged, Britain's purpose was to strengthen the Caribbean economy and to streamline the administration. It wanted to shed a financial liability and to form a body that was easier to manage in the short term and capable eventually of standing on its own feet. As a Colonial Office civil servant later wrote, the United Kingdom's "fundamental aim in the area since 1945 has been political disengagement."[43]

Negotiations between Britain and the West Indies and among the Caribbean territories themselves over the proposed union lasted for more than a decade. This "shilly-shallying and hemming and hawing," as Eric Williams called it, might have suggested to the Colonial Office that the Federation would speedily fall to pieces. But Whitehall persevered. It was intent on producing another of the "tidy packages that would be acceptable to Westminster or in the United Nations."[44] Britain's two mainland Caribbean territories, distant British Honduras (later Belize) and British Guiana (later Guyana), which hoped to prosper as a South American state, refused to be part of the parcel. But in 1958 ten islands (Jamaica, St. Kitts, Antigua, Montserrat, Dominica, St. Lucia, Barbados, St. Vincent, Grenada and Trinidad), some with attendant islets, merged to form the West Indies Federation. It was the futile exhalation of a dying Empire. From the start, the Federation frustrated what West Indians regarded as its main purpose—to give them independence. This was partly because Britain retained control of foreign affairs and its Governor-General, Lord Hailes, a former Tory Chief Whip, possessed wide discretionary powers—he could both disallow bills and dissolve parliament. And it was partly because local autonomy proved stronger than federal authority. Islands retained their own currency and tariff barriers. The two giants, Jamaica and Trinidad, which achieved internal self-government in 1959 and together contained 83 per cent of the land, 77 per cent of the population and 75 per cent of the wealth, refused submission to Grantley Adams, the Federal Prime Minister. He carried little weight and could not even raise taxes, but he seemed to favour the Lilliputians at the expense of the Brobdingnagians. Personal rivalries, constitutional disputes, religious differences and insular prejudices further weakened his position. Eventually Bustamante coined a slogan for separation: "Jamaica must lead—or secede."

A divorce on grounds of incompatibility seemed inevitable. But the Colonial Office struggled to save the marriage. It tried "to ensure that as many as possible of the federated territories remain in some way grouped with either Jamaica or Trinidad who alone have the resources and sophistication of governmental apparatus to 'carry' pensioner territories as satellites."[45] However, Britain could count on little goodwill, particularly from Jamaica and Trinidad. Nationalist leaders such as Eric Williams bitterly repudiated colonialism in all its forms. "Massa Day Done," he declared, adding that "the West Indian Massa constituted the most backward ruling class in history."[46] Black pride sashayed along Kingston's tawdry Paradise Street. Racial segregation came under attack in Bridgetown, where bars, restaurants and dance halls kept out Negroes by masquerading as clubs. Among Port of Spain's squalid barrack dwellings calypso singers hailed the revolution:

> Well, the way how things shaping up,
> All this nigger business going to stop.
> And soon in the West Indies
> It will be, "Please, Mr Nigger, please."[47]

As Britain proposed to join the European Common Market and to limit Commonwealth immigration, West Indians understandably assumed that it had selfish motives for trying to perpetuate what Bustamante called "the farcical Federation." In 1961, therefore, Jamaica held a referendum, amid rumours that a Federal ship loaded with chains had arrived to reimpose slavery, and voted to quit. Vain attempts were made to keep the mutilated body alive. But in 1962 the Federation was formally liquidated. Eric Williams explained the political arithmetic: "One from ten left nothing, not nine."[48] Jamaica and Trinidad at once became sovereign states, as did Barbados four years later. The smaller islands, which the Colonial Office itself considered "museum pieces,"[49] could barely survive on their own. They were made internally self-governing "Associated States" until they could be set adrift, to become imperial flotsam in the doldrums.

British Guiana posed a more awkward problem, not only to the United Kingdom but to the United States. The "Colossus of the North" had long treated the Caribbean as its backyard, an underdeveloped zone subject to economic penetration, political intervention and military coercion. The much-decorated Major-General Smedley D. Butler gave a vivid indication of American policy, whether carried out with a big stick or as a good neighbour. He boasted between the wars,

> I helped make Mexico, and especially Tampico, safe for American oil interests. I helped make Haiti and Cuba a decent place for the National City Bank to collect revenue. I helped pacify Nicaragua for the international banking house of Brown Brothers. I brought light to the Dominican Republic for American sugar interests. I helped make Honduras "right" for American fruit companies.[50]

However, now that Fidel Castro had succeeded, at the height of the Cold War, in bringing Communism so close to home, Americans were even more anxious to impose their will on the region. In 1962 Dean Rusk, President Kennedy's Secretary of State, told the British Foreign Secretary, Lord Home, that "the United States were really terrified of another Cuba on their continent."[51] After sustained vacillation, Kennedy's government decided that the Premier of British Guiana, the American-educated dentist Cheddi Jagan, was a serious menace. He was not an anti-colonialist radical like Thomas Jefferson, as an English minister suggested, but a Red dictator "cast from the same mould as Premier Fidel Castro."[52]

Rusk told Home that "it is not possible for us to put up with an independent British Guiana under Jagan," who "should not accede to power again." Observing that the United States was pursuing the very same policies for which it attacked Britain in the United Nations, Macmillan deplored Rusk's "cynicism," which he found particularly surprising in one who was "not an Irishman, nor a politician, nor a millionaire." Replying to Rusk, Home descanted on America's historic role in being "the first crusader and the prime mover in urging colonial emancipation." It was not possible, he said, to stop British Guiana from gaining its freedom. Britain could hardly introduce direct rule here while refusing to intervene in Rhodesia, nor could it prevent Jagan from being elected without subverting democracy. This was clap-trap. After more high-level discussions, during which the British claimed that Guiana was now primarily an American responsibility, London yielded to Washington. The Colonial Office delayed independence and imposed a new electoral system designed to produce what Kennedy called "a good result."[53] Meanwhile, the CIA helped to undermine Jagan by fomenting "riots, arson and strikes (including the longest general strike in history—ten weeks)."[54] In the election of 1964 Jagan was defeated by a coalition which led Guiana to independence and set up a repressive regime. Not until the Cold War was over did the White House permit him to return to office.

The evolution of the West Indies illustrates the way in which the United States not only superseded the British Empire but, as many contemporaries observed, took on the mantle of Rome. "America's decision to adopt Rome's role has been deliberate," said Arnold Toynbee. In an influential series of lectures delivered during 1960, he drew ancient and modern parallels, large and small. The United States, like Rome, was "leader of a world-wide anti-revolutionary movement in defence of vested interests." Similarly the "American Empire" established bases on alien territory but handed some of them back in the West Indies, a "gracious gesture" comparable to Rome's evacuation of three Macedonian fortresses known as the "fetters of Greece."[55] Toynbee was rightly criticised for drawing facile analogies between diverse civilisations and for giving an over-schematic account of their rise and fall—one American scholar said that his twelve-volume *Study of History* contained "anything but history."[56] But Toynbee did recognise the uniqueness of America's unacknowledged empire. He remarked, for instance, that it was the first ever to pay, through voluntary aid, for its dominant position—a technique Adlai Stevenson described as shackling allies with "golden chains."[57] Toynbee also noted that, at a time of Soviet expansionism, the United States abhorred the void caused by the implosion of the British Empire. This was especially true with regard to the West Indies. Although painfully ambivalent about colonialism, Washington had valued the stability afforded by the British presence in the Caribbean after 1945. Successive American governments welcomed the Federation and deplored its fission into precarious miniature states—Grenada became independent in 1974, Dominica in 1978, St. Lucia and St. Vincent in 1979, Antigua in 1981 and St. Kitts in 1983. Washington feared that the British "might pull out of the area altogether leaving a dangerous vacuum behind them."[58]

Like John F. Kennedy, President Ronald Reagan regarded "the great American archipelago"[59] of banana republics and client countries as his chief area of concern. In particular he feared that one Caribbean domino after another might fall victim to the unholy alliance between Castro and the Kremlin. Some Americans regarded this as a primitive superstition. "There is a kind of voodoo about American foreign policy," wrote Senator William Fulbright. "Certain drums have to be beaten regularly to ward off evil spirits."[60] But Reagan stuck to his drums. He was especially keen to exorcise Communism from Grenada, a sovereign state with just over 100,000 inhabitants, after its 1979 revolution. This had been masterminded by a fiery lawyer, Maurice Bishop, founder of the radical New Jewel Movement. He offended America by his independence as much as his socialism, declaring, "We are not in anybody's back-yard, and we are definitely not for sale."[61] So when a vicious Leninist faction murdered Bishop and his lieutenants in October 1983 Reagan unleashed Operation Urgent Fury. This was the invasion of the island by a naval armada together with five thousand paratroopers, dozens of helicopter gunships and an arsenal of sophisticated equipment and heavy weaponry. The Americans soon crushed the lightly armed opposition, though the campaign was marred by the usual accompaniments of colonial (and other) conquest. During a news blackout official spokesmen stated that the offensive was carried out with surgical precision, yet American forces killed thirty mental patients during a mistaken attack on a lunatic asylum. Reagan asserted that Grenada housed a huge Soviet-Cuban war machine ready to export terror and destroy democracy, but few modern munitions were found. Although conducted, and initially welcomed, in the name of liberty, the invasion became an occupation.

A puppet regime was established. Suspected Communists were imprisoned and tortured. The United States made a sustained effort to expand and exploit Grenada's economy in the interests of capitalism, a process described as "dollar-colonialism or coca-colanisation."[62] Thus copious aid was given to private enterprise while public services were curtailed and free trade unions suffered emasculation. It is understandable that, after early protests in Congress about "gunboat diplomacy" and introducing "democracy at the point of a bayonet,"[63] Americans should have rejoiced at Reagan's easy Caribbean triumph. The global outcry was also predictable, though the Soviet Union's denunciations lost some of their force because its television service initially assumed that Grenada was a province in southern Spain.

Quite surprising, though, was Britain's feeble acceptance of the coup. Margaret Thatcher, Reagan's personal friend and ideological soulmate, heard of it only hours in advance and telephoned him on the "hot line" to protest. "You have invaded the Queen's territory and you didn't even say a word to me."[64] But the President, determined to assert himself in the aftermath of a terrorist atrocity in Lebanon that had killed 241 American Marines, politely brushed aside her objections. She fumed privately and later showed her annoyance—before becoming reconciled to Reagan's action. Yet at the time her government did not publicly condemn the assault on a Commonwealth state. Nor did it support the United Nations resolution stating that the attack was a flagrant violation of international law and demanding American withdrawal. The Labour opposition made hay. Denis Healey said that Reagan's aggression in the West Indies represented "an unpardonable humiliation of an ally" and that it was "time that the Prime Minister got off her knees" to the United States.[65] The Iron Lady's uncharacteristic attitude was a tacit acknowledgement of Britain's auxiliary status, which became still more humiliatingly evident during the Premiership of Tony Blair. British compliance reflected America's increasing confidence as well as dominance. A colossus had arisen which eclipsed the power of Greater Britain and matched the pretensions of Rome. As a leading Caribbean historian suggests, Gibbon would have interpreted Reagan's invasion of Grenada as "what takes place between the empire and the barbarian provinces."[66]

.   .   .

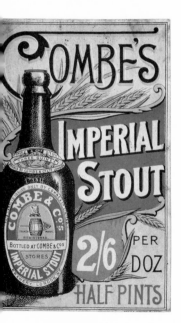

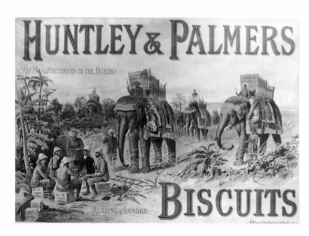

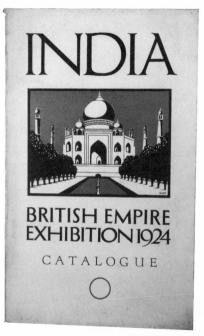

33. The Imperial Appeal

Well-known but unknown, the Empire had a romantic as well as
a patriotic appeal. Lady Curzon said that India seemed to most
British people more remote than the moon.

34. GANDHI'S SALT MARCH, 1930

The march began a huge civil disobedience campaign. Believing himself guided by "God's hand," Gandhi mobilised moral force against a Raj that thought "might is right."

35. NEHRU AND JINNAH, 1946

Tragically, the brilliant, opulent and inspiring leaders of rival political movements could find no means of uniting an independent India.

36. THE LAST VICEROY AND VICEREINE OF INDIA

Mountbatten professed democratic sentiments but no Viceroy
gloried more in the trappings of majesty.

37. THE VICTIMS OF PARTITION, 1947

The British Raj ended in widespread bloodshed and the mass
migration of refugees between India and Pakistan. Some of the
worst massacres occurred on the railways.

38. Jewish Refugees Arrive in the Promised Land, 1946

Survivors of the Holocaust dock at Haifa on board the *Dov Hoz* (named after a founder of Haganah) thanks to American intervention and in spite of British opposition.

39. The Exodus of Palestinian Refugees to Gaza

A Jewish-Arab conflict followed the end of British rule in the Holy Land. As a result hundreds of thousands of Palestinians fled, many to the tiny Gaza strip.

40. British Soldiers Confront Cypriots, Nicosia, 1955

In the vicious struggle to hold Cyprus for the Empire, British troops faced hostility from civilians, especially school-children, as well as from terrorists.

41. The Troopship *Empire Ken* at Port Said, November 1956

Even as British troops landed in Egypt, their compatriots at home were bitterly divided over the invasion, which was soon aborted. Many saw the Suez fiasco as the end of the Empire.

42. DETAINING MAU MAU SUSPECTS IN KENYA, 1952

The suppression of the Mau Mau rebellion during the 1950s,
which involved atrocities on both sides, was one of the most
horrific episodes in imperial history.

43. JOMO KENYATTA IS HAILED AS PRIME MINISTER, 1963

Like other nationalist leaders, Kenyatta was first demonised
and martyred by the British and afterwards canonised and
venerated by his own people.

44. THE AFRICAN QUEEN

Queen Elizabeth II stuck rigidly to white official protocol during her 1956 tour of Nigeria, where black people greeted her with spontaneous warmth and affection.

45. KWAME NKRUMAH LEADS GHANA TO FREEDOM, 1957

Nkrumah rose to prominence by his uncompromising demand for "self-government NOW." Ghana became Britain's first sub-Saharan African colony to win independence.

46. END OF AN ERA, 1997

The Union Jack descends in Hong Kong and the sun sets
on the greatest empire in history—though it vanished far
more swiftly than that of Rome.

Cyprus also fell victim to successive empires. Among those who occupied it were Egyptians, Mycenaeans, Phoenicians, Assyrians and Persians. The island, which mined copper *(kupros)* for the Pharaoh Akhenaton and sent ships to the siege of Troy, fell under the sway of Xerxes and Alexander the Great. It became an important crossroads between East and West. A source of corn, wine, oil and salt, it was also an entrepôt for gold, silver, ivory, silk, scarabs and other precious goods. The name of Cyprus, said Gibbon, "excites the ideas of elegance and pleasure."[67] It also excited contention. Rome made it a province, given to Cleopatra by Mark Antony as a token of love but taken back by Augustus. Evangelised by St. Paul, it was assailed by Jewish rebels who destroyed the rich city of Salamis. During the seven-hundred-year rule of the Byzantine Emperors, Saracens attacked and over-ran the island. In 1191 it was seized by the English Crusaders of Richard the Lion Heart, who sold it to the Knights Templars. Franks, Genoese and Venetians, whose massive stone ramparts still dominate Nicosia and Fama-gusta, kept the Cross (albeit Latin) in the ascendant. But the Crescent waxed again in the sixteenth century, when the Turks won sovereignty and turned Gothic cathedrals into mosques. Despite squeezing sweat and blood from their subjects, the Muslim sultans tolerated Orthodox Christianity and Hellenic culture. So while Cyprus, with its stunted olive groves and its scorched plains, belonged geographically to Asia Minor, it retained a spiri-tual attachment to distant Greece. The highest peak in the island's pine-cloaked Troodos Mountains was called Olympus. Most Cypriots spoke the language of Homer and revered the civilisation of Plato. After the Greek war of independence in 1821, they insisted that their forebears had been Greeks before Socrates.

In an island riven by millennia of imperial conflict, the gulf widened between those in skullcaps who identified with the Acropolis and those in turbans who paid obeisance to the Sublime Porte. This was the situation when the Ottoman Empire ceded control of Cyprus to the British Empire in 1878. The island was a gratuity acquired by Disraeli for supporting Sultan Abdul Hamid "the Damned" against Tsar Alexander II, whose forces had come so close to Constantinople that they could see the minarets of Hagia Sophia and the silhouettes of British ironclads on the Golden Horn. The Premier made much of his prize, diadem of the wine-dark sea and "rosy realm of Venus."[68] From the Congress of Berlin he also brought home "peace with honour"—a phrase Neville Chamberlain rashly repeated sixty years later, from the same window in Downing Street, on his return from Munich. Disraeli's compatriots greeted him, an ailing figure in a long white overcoat, with pomp and joy. Prominent among the manifestations was a triumphal arch topped by a "Union Jack entwined with bay leaves as a sign of bloodless victory." Now Earl of Beaconsfield, Disraeli was hailed "Duke of Cyprus."[69] Writing to Queen Victoria, he described the island as the key to Asia.

The image better fitted Suez, which opened the way to India and the Orient. When Britain secured the Canal by conquering Egypt in 1882, Cyprus became a spare key at best and at worst a rusty padlock to a Mediterranean dead end. Possessing Gibraltar, Malta and Alexandria, the British did not even bother to deepen the silt-clogged harbour at Famagusta, which fatally precluded its naval use in 1956. The glow of "imperial optimism"[70] stirred up by Disraeli soon faded, therefore, and Cyprus was widely seen as "the whitest of white elephants."[71] Its new masters adopted the old principle of salutary neglect. They inaugurated a Legislative Council, but it was so impotent that one Cypriot deputy called it "the pumpkin."[72] They permitted Hellenic education because it was partly funded by Greece. They granted religious freedom but did not recognise the temporal power of the Church. Its autocephalic character and theocratic pretensions stemmed from Zeno, the first Emperor to reign alone in the East after the extinction of the Roman Empire in the West, who had endowed the Archbishop of Cyprus with the shadow of his omnipotence. According to Gibbon, Zeno was at his "least contemptible"[73] in ecclesiastical matters. And he authorised the island's priestly ruler, or Ethnarch, to wield a sceptre (instead of a pastoral staff), to don the purple and to sign his name in imperial vermilion. The British dismissed all this as hocus-pocus. But they did acknowledge the devotion most Cypriots felt for the Greek "Motherland." As early as 1907 Winston Churchill said that, while Muslim rights must be respected, it was only natural for Orthodox Cypriots to cherish the ideal of union *(enosis)* with Greece "earnestly, devoutly and feverishly."[74] The Great War almost triggered that consummation. Britain formally annexed the island when Turkey sided with the Central Powers, but in 1915 Asquith's government offered it to Greece as an inducement to join the Allies. The offer was rejected and not renewed. But it seemed to legitimise the goal of *enosis*. It also raised hopes that the British would act in the spirit of Byron and live up to their Greek-Cypriot sobriquet, *phileleftheri*—freedom lovers.

As part of the peace settlement, Turkey recognised Britain's sovereignty over the island. In 1925 Cyprus, which was civilised (patriots liked to say) when the British were still "jumping from tree to tree,"[75] became a crown colony. The following year, as if to soften the blow, it received a Governor who was a philhellene to the last sleek strand of his red-gold moustache. He was Sir Ronald Storrs, late of Cairo and Jerusalem. Suave and sophisticated, he could produce a classical tag for all occasions—the Governor was said to wear his learning lightly but ostentatiously. However, Storrs and his wife were taken aback by the primitive conditions on Cyprus, which lacked even a telephone system. Arriving at their official residence in Nicosia, Lady Storrs approached a long, low, barn-like building and commented: "Anyhow, the stables are good."[76] She was looking at Government House itself. The prefabricated wooden hutment, originally destined by the War Office for the Commander-in-Chief in Ceylon (who promptly found himself a stone palace), had been diverted to Cyprus, carried from Larnaca in pieces on the backs of camels and fitted together by the Royal Engineers like a child's box of bricks. Whitehall's promise of a more appropriate, permanent dwelling proved "as unrealisable as a further appearance of Aphrodite from the adjacent sea."[77] So, after nearly half a century, the floors of Government House were rotten, its roof leaked and its white plank walls let in the winter cold. Despite these inadequacies, Storrs concluded wanly, the edifice was "not without charm."[78] That he was able to impose himself on the local population despite such domestic disadvantages, the new Governor attributed to unexpected powers of hypnotism.

In fact Storrs sought to woo, not to mesmerise, the people of Cyprus. He mingled freely with them and tried to induce his compatriots to do the same, though the mixed tea parties at Government House were as stiff and awkward as adolescent dances. He appointed Cypriots to official posts, particularly when he found that British civil servants were "misfits and incompetents." This was because Cyprus could only afford to pay officials relatively low salaries (between £500 and £1,500 annually) and the Colonial Office tended to treat the island as "a 'sanatorium' for tropical invalids."[79] Thinking the inhabitants "most damnably wronged"[80] by a mean and indifferent Britain, Storrs tried to alleviate their grinding poverty—the average income was ten pounds a year. He promoted agriculture and public works. He improved roads, schools and health—malaria was eventually eradicated. He and his wife took an interest in social problems, the condition of the blind, the treatment of lepers. Yet Storrs was soon "hated." In spite of (or because of) his charm, wit and brilliance, he conveyed an air of insincerity. Cypriots of every hue despised his unctuous gesture of wearing, on appropriate occasions, a sprig of Muslim green in his buttonhole or a blue and white tie, the colours of Greece. The Governor's pronouncements were arrogant and his quips were patronising.

When the Depression struck he opposed cuts in official pay and enforced tax increases. Predictably, economic grievance sparked off political resistance. Taxation without proper representation prompted Cypriots to damn alien rule as "the worst of evils." They aspired to win national liberation through *enosis,* essential even if the island "were swimming in seas of gold." In an open letter to Storrs, Bishop Nicodemos of Kition wrote: "You are proud that Liberty and Right reign in England, but you wish that tyranny and injustice should continue to reign in Cyprus." The Bishop and others resigned from the Legislative Council, which provoked turmoil. In the late evening of 21 October 1931 several thousand demonstrators marched on Government House. Armed with banners, torches, sticks and stones they surged forward, the priests tucking up their long skirts. Shouting *"Enosis"* and singing the Greek national anthem, the crowd occupied a circular terrace around the front door. The Governor sent a message saying that he would see one or two ringleaders if the rest withdrew "to a respectful distance."[81] Instead they broke windows, overwhelmed the police and set fire to the house. Shafts of flame pierced the darkness and the wooden structure was quickly reduced to ashes.

Although this and other disturbances were soon quelled, colonial rule in Cyprus was never the same again. For, as usual, the British over-reacted. They treated a spontaneous combustion, in which no more than six people (all Cypriots) died, as a premeditated revolution. At home the Dominions Secretary waxed apocalyptic. Cypriots had joined the international "enemies of the British Empire," he said, and if Britain "goes down the world will go down too."[82] So troops garrisoned the island, the Royal Navy showed the flag and RAF Vickers Victorias patrolled the sky. In Nicosia the Governor waxed autocratic. He told the King that "any wavering at this juncture would be hopeless and that the thing was to strike and strike hard."[83] Storrs suspended the constitution and abolished the Legislative Council and municipal councils, appointing his own local headmen *(mukhtars).* He deported Bishop Nicodemos, said to be the Cypriot Gandhi, and other prominent "agitators." He prohibited the carrying of arms and the holding of assemblies. He restricted the flying of Greek flags and the ringing of church bells. Storrs imposed a collective fine of nearly £35,000 and personally claimed about twice the true value of his incinerated pictures, books, stamps, jade, Greek sculptures, Bokkara embroideries and other *objets d'art.* Their loss put him in mind of the destruction of "the Alexandrine Library, the sacks of Byzantium and Rome, and such setbacks to civilisation's progress."[84]

After the disorder there were several thousand arrests, trials and convictions. According to many inhabitants, the island itself became a penitentiary. By the time Storrs left in 1932, professing himself heartily sick of the place and the people, they could only beat against the bars. The regime suppressed all opposition, banning the Communist Party and shackling the Church. Most Cypriots, anyway, were preoccupied with surviving the Depression. "Together with the illiberal measures put in force and the imposed silence, lasting more than eight years," wrote a nationalist, "drought and unemployment ravage the island."[85] Rulers and ruled were temporarily reconciled during the Second World War, when a quixotic Churchill came to the aid of Greece. But local hostilities resumed in the wake of global peace. As Britain's grip on Palestine and Egypt slackened, Cyprus was once more deemed strategically vital. So although Attlee's government initiated reforms, it refused demands for "Enosis and only Enosis." This clarion call was also a warning that Greek-Cypriots should shun the British—senior figures who collaborated were called "Sir Traitors."[86] To assert imperial authority, Sir Andrew Wright was made Governor in 1949. Once Storrs's lieutenant, he was described as "a fine Victorian type now almost extinct in the British Colonial Service." Wright "looked upon Cypriots somewhat as children who needed a firm hand [and] . . . an occasional spanking."[87]

Almost at once they seemed to invite chastisement. In 1950 the Church held a plebiscite in which some 215,108 Greek-Cypriots, 96 per cent of the adult Greek-Cypriot population, voted for *enosis*—many of them genuflecting to the document enshrining it as though to an icon. Announcing that the issue of sovereignty was closed, Wright asked for extra powers to lock up subversives. Inside and outside Whitehall doubters wondered whether Britain had any right, purely for its own military convenience, to maintain colonial rule over "a civilised and educated population."[88] But the Colonial Office was clear that the Governor already had enough powers. He could not be allowed "to embark on a policy of repression in the hope that no-one will notice."[89] So Wright could only strike at sedition where it appeared. He tried to erase its most obvious manifestations, the graffiti which blossomed on every available surface. A typical slogan read: "Greeks, liberty is won with blood—*Enosis.*"[90] Less visible but more sinister was the new alliance hatched between ethnarchy and terror.

In 1950 Makarios III was elected Archbishop of Cyprus. The son of a goatherd, he had been an ardent believer in *enosis* since serving as a novice in Kykko monastery. On the monks' kitchen wall he had even scrawled the legend "Long Live Union," later describing it as "my first political statement."[91] Having studied in Greece and America, Makarios rose swiftly in the ecclesiastical hierarchy. Now, aged thirty-seven, he aimed to use his position as Ethnarch to rid Cyprus of the alien yoke. "I shall not let my eyes close in sleep," he declared on assuming the throne of St. Barnabas, "until the golden wings of the sun arise to announce the longed-for day of national liberation."[92] An impressive figure with black beard, stove-pipe hat and long robes, Makarios preached the gospel of *enosis* with evangelical fervour. His sermons, political and religious, were a blend of music and poetry, the mellow voice intoning the cadences like free verse. Yet Makarios, veiled in cigarette smoke inside his dilapidated palace, was deliberately Delphic. He was outspoken but equivocal, dynamic but enigmatic, inspiring but devious. He managed to transmit benevolence through slightly hooded eyes, to smile yet to remain impassive. This "pious-looking replica of Jesus Christ" was, in the opinion of a close American observer, "just the craftiest of Greeks."[93]

By contrast Colonel George Grivas was an unvarnished fanatic, direct, brutal and ruthless. An old-fashioned disciplinarian with a bristling moustache, he had been committed from his schooldays in Nicosia to "the crusade for a greater Greece."[94] During the war he had founded a pro-royalist resistance movement on the mainland, though it devoted more time to killing Communists than to fighting Germans. Afterwards he decided, in the spirit of the IRA and Irgun, that the British could only be removed by force. The colonel met the Ethnarch and they agreed on the aim of *enosis,* taking a sacred oath to accomplish it. But they disagreed over methods. Makarios hoped to restrict violence to sabotage whereas Grivas, with the connivance of the Greek government, prepared for a vicious guerrilla war. Whatever the tactics, Cypriots knew by 1954 that an insurrection was imminent. The Ethnarch remained ambiguous about bloodshed. But he announced that "we shall accept assistance even from unclean hands."[95]

Despite the ominous signs, though, few Britons perceived that Cyprus was on the brink of revolt. This was partly because they distanced themselves from the local community. The Governor was a remote being. During the hot weather he moved to his Troodos mountain retreat, a rambling grey stone building which had been constructed in 1880 under the supervision of Arthur Rimbaud and resembled "a Scottish shooting-lodge."[96] Otherwise he was insulated in the new Government House, an imposing affair designed to echo local French Gothic and Greek Orthodox architecture. It had a cupola, a portico, a tower and a circular staircase. It had sandstone gargoyles and limestone fireplaces. It had wrought-iron balustrades and timbered galleries, with imperial wood such as Burmese teak, Canadian maple and Columbia pine supplementing local eucalyptus, juniper, carob, casuarina and cypress. It had curtains hand-embroidered with heraldic devices and a stone-carved coat of arms. In private Governors lived quite modestly— their heavy furniture was "arranged as though it were being stored" and their bedroom contained "two ugly standard Public Works beds and awful little bedside tables which stand very high and have place for potty."⁹⁷ Soon they would become prisoners in their own house, surrounded by guards, searchlights and barbed wire.

British officials were almost equally inaccessible. They had improved since the days recalled by one visitor: "I shall never forget the horror of the English club, and the knobbly knees of middle-aged civil servants in shorts and their ghastly talk about the natives." But they remained a caste apart. Few of them spoke modern Greek. Fewer still met Cypriots, "except in the course of their duties."⁹⁸ British civilian expatriates, many from imperial outposts that had achieved independence, also kept to themselves. Their existence was one of "blameless monotony" conducted in an atmosphere of "suffocating inertia." They dwelt in hideous villas reminiscent of Wimbledon or, when they became very old, in the Dome Hotel—"it was as if every forgotten *pension* between Folkestone and Scarborough had sent a representative to attend a world conference on longevity." They sailed and played games. They drove to church in Morris Minors. They drank at the Yacht Club. On Sunday afternoons they listened to a military band playing selections from *Oklahoma* at the English Club, where pride of place was given to Annigoni's portrait of the Queen. They "suffered agonies of apprehension at the thought of not being invited to Government House" on the sovereign's birthday.

The novelist Lawrence Durrell, author of these sneers, was understandably sour about his compatriots' way of calling the islanders a "'bunch of Cyps'—as one might say 'Chimps.'" Attitudes had not changed since 1878, he said, when a British observer had described Cypriots as

> an indolent, careless and mimetic people, but without a spark of Turkish fire, without a touch of Grecian taste . . . they live on in a limpid state, like creatures of the lower types, clinging to life for life's own sake; voluptuaries of the sun and sea; holding on by simple animal tenacity through tempests which have wrecked the nobler races of mankind.

Durrell, himself a practising voluptuary, was a late addition to that band of romantic exiles inspired by the Mediterranean passion. From the age of Byron to the time of Norman Douglas, many had been writers. And they were drawn southwards by the classical culture, or by the cheap or simple life, or by the opportunities for sensual pleasure—some Britons were said to have left home under a cloud no bigger than a boy's hand. Few of these literary *émigrés* were more pretentious than Lawrence Durrell. Yet while despising his Philistine compatriots, Durrell shared some of their opinions.

He patronised *"babu"* Cypriots, cherished unspoilt peasants and basked in the illusion that they all loved England. Nothing, he thought, could induce them to fight. On the issue of *enosis* the Foreign Office "will set a time-limit after a brisk haggle and we'll all subside into sun-bemused tranquillity."[99] This was also the official view. As the cliché had it, Cypriots made very good waiters. Their "tribal temperament," according to a member of the Colonial Office Information Department, was compounded of "niceness, lethargy or plain lack of guts."[100]

Thus the British had every confidence that they could retain Cyprus as their stronghold in the Near East. Anthony Eden brusquely told the Greek Prime Minister, Field-Marshal Papagos, that the question of the island's sovereignty was closed. Papagos, as vain and prickly as Eden himself, expostulated afterwards: "He told me *never*—not even *we shall see!* "[101] On 28 July 1954 a Colonial Office minister, Henry Hopkinson, confirmed that the government was thinking in terms of the Greek kalends. He informed the House of Commons that some colonial territories could "never" expect to be fully independent. Among them, he implied, was Cyprus, which might hope for self-government under British aegis but not for self-determination leading to fusion with Greece. The word "never" infuriated the Labour opposition. Aneurin Bevan urged Tories to accept that "peoples could only be governed by consent." Britain was "starting trouble in Cyprus on the same day that had seen scuttle in Egypt," said Richard Crossman. "People were learning that British imperialism gave them nothing until they were in a position to take it by force." Others predicted that Hopkinson's statement "would inflame the spirit of nationalism in Cyprus."[102] Protests did occur and the indecisive new Governor, Sir Robert Armitage, cracked down on them in the spirit of his predecessor.

His Whitehall masters worried less about disquiet in Nicosia than disquiet in the United Nations, where Greece lodged an appeal that Cyprus should be allowed to decide its own fate. Eisenhower was unsympathetic to Britain because Eden had taken a dim view of his neo-imperialist coup in Guatemala, rightly described as "one of the most sordid and inane 'security' operations in American history."[103] To win the backing of the President and his Secretary of State required rare diplomatic sleight of hand. Eden proved willing to compromise over Guatemala and he also managed to transform Cyprus from a colonial into an international problem. A British defeat here, he maintained, would be a victory for Communism in the Cold War. His case was simple. *Enosis* would precipitate a conflict between Greece and Turkey, two old enemies that were, bizarrely, both members of the North Atlantic Treaty Organisation (NATO). Turkey occupied an important strategic position on the flank of Soviet Russia and its role as a western ally would be undermined if it became embroiled in a struggle to protect the Muslims of Cyprus.

As it happened, Istanbul was lukewarm over the matter and perfidious Albion, for its own local purposes, had to encourage a more heated response. Similarly, ministers such as Harold Macmillan urged agents in Cyprus "to stir up the Turks in order to neutralise the Greek agitation."[104] The British increased their reliance on that impoverished fifth of the population. They recruited most policemen from this source. They built up the Turkish-Cypriot leader, Rauf Denktash, and fostered loyalty to the status quo. All this polarised the two communities. Of course, there was a deep-seated hostility between them and their relationship was punctuated by bouts of violence. Yet since 1878 they had generally lived together in peace. So here, in short, was a classic British exercise in divide and rule. It was comparable to that carried out on a larger scale in India and ran the same risks of civil war and partition.

At the end of 1954, as the United Nations postponed discussion of Cyprus, there were riots in Athens and Nicosia. Anticipating Macmillan's metaphor, Makarios declared: "The wind of freedom is blowing everywhere, tearing down the colonial regimes."[105] Grivas collected arms and men. The capture of one consignment of weapons did not deter him any more than it alerted Armitage, for whom the whole problem of *enosis* resembled "the velvety blackness of a nightmare."[106] On April Fool's Day 1955 the revolt began. Bombs exploded at government buildings, which were unguarded, in Nicosia, Limassol and Larnaca. Little damage was done here or elsewhere, though the transmitters of the Cyprus Broadcasting Service were demolished. But Grivas, who adopted the *nom de guerre* Dighenis, the Greek god of legend, had signalled the advent of EOKA, the National Organisation of Cypriot Fighters. In due course it prompted the formation of TMT, the Turkish Defence Force. Far from being neutral arbiters, the "British consciously permitted TMT to operate as a counter-foil to EOKA."[107]

Grivas's campaign stuttered into life. His fighters were ill armed and ill disciplined, so he concentrated on seizing weapons from police stations. EOKA's initial amateurishness was matched only by that of the police themselves, a force that had changed little since British rule began. Not only was it ill paid and ill trained, it possessed minimal equipment—no radios, no torches and almost no transport. Overwhelmed by hit-and-run raids and stone-throwing protests in which schoolchildren played the role of young Spartans, the constabulary was quickly reinforced with Turkish auxiliaries and British soldiers. Grivas knew that he could not overthrow the colonial regime, but he aimed to pin down an army, to inflame patriotic sentiment and to win the propaganda war. Eden, who had just succeeded Churchill as Prime Minister, involuntarily assisted with the last part of this strategy by rejecting any solution that smacked of appeasement. So when the Colonial Secretary visited Cyprus, where he was greeted with bombs, he could not discuss the question of self-determination. Equally fruitless was the conference held between Britain, Greece and Turkey in August 1955. Its purpose was to give all three countries a stake in Cyprus through a partnership known as a tridominium—one official called it a "Pan-demonium."[108] Greece predictably repudiated the scheme and the Turkish government connived at destructive anti-Greek riots in Istanbul—not condemned by Britain because advantageous to its position in Cyprus. Then Nicosia erupted. Angry demonstrations took place in Metaxas Square, usually the scene of neon-lit evening promenades, where a Greek-Cypriot mob burned down the British Institute. Sporadic violence spread through the island, confirming Eden's decision to replace Armitage with a tough, unimaginative field-marshal, Sir John Harding. His arrival, said Grivas, signified that "the mailed fist would rule in Cyprus."[109]

Certainly Grivas had every reason to hope that the new Governor would provide the coercion that EOKA aimed to provoke. But Harding first tried to negotiate with Makarios. The Field-Marshal had little room to manoeuvre and the Archbishop changed his ground with beatific composure. Professing himself an unworldly priest, Makarios incensed Harding, who claimed to be a simple soldier. As their talks petered out, EOKA stepped up its bombings and shootings. Clashes occurred in many places and preparations were made for a general strike. Harding was determined that Cyprus should not go the way of Ireland or Palestine. On 25 November 1955 he declared a state of emergency. This gave him a further arsenal to use against terrorists: arrest without warrant, detention without trial, life imprisonment for sabotage and the death penalty for carrying arms. Other weapons included censorship, deportation, flogging, curfews, collective fines and the banning of assemblies and strikes. Harding reorganised and augmented his forces. By 1956 he had mustered twelve thousand troops and two thousand police to deal with a thousand EOKA fighters. He demanded vigorous action.

His men patrolled, set up road blocks, invaded monasteries, gathered intelligence and eradicated graffiti, sometimes substituting their own— "GREEKS ARE SNEAKS" and "PLATO IS A POTATO." They locked recalcitrant pupils out of schools, where blue pencils as well as blue and white flags were prohibited. They also carried out rough and often brutal searches. Soldiers would surround a village and use bayonets and rifle butts to force males into hastily erected barbed-wire cages. While their houses were ransacked or vandalised or looted, the "bloody wogs" (as Tommies called them) had to stand in the hot sun for hours with their hands in the air. After being questioned, they were scrutinised by hooded informers, known to the security forces as "chained toads."[110] Those identified as members of EOKA were taken away in lorries. While trying to crush Grivas, though, Harding continued to court Makarios. He made concessions, recognising that Hopkinson's "never" meant "sometime." And at the end of February 1956 the Colonial Secretary again visited Nicosia to meet the Archbishop, whom he found elegant and amiable. Lennox-Boyd was particularly fascinated by his hands, which were "quite beautiful" and "spotlessly clean."[111] The Colonial Secretary wished to give the Archbishop "a little sugar-coating."[112] But he was restrained by Eden, who still regarded Cyprus as a test of his political virility. No agreement was reached and as he left the room Lennox-Boyd said to Makarios, "God save your people."[113]

It proved a timely supplication. Within days Harding exiled Makarios to the Seychelles. Damned by the British as a latter-day Rasputin, the Archbishop was hailed by the Greeks as a modern Sebastian, one who had the inestimable advantage of not being dead. Within months the nasty little colonial conflict reached its climax—the year 1956 witnessed 2,500 acts of violence resulting in 210 deaths. The struggle was embittered by the hanging of the first convicted terrorists, followed by Grivas's execution of two captured British NCOs. But homicide was ubiquitous—it was even "respectable,"[114] according to Harold Macmillan, who said that while the British amended the Decalogue to sanction adultery, the Cypriots did so to permit murder. Grivas exterminated Greek "traitors" without mercy. Communal strife exploded: when EOKA killed a Muslim policeman in May 1956, Grivas recorded, "Turkish hordes poured into the Greek quarter of Nicosia, raiding, burning, looting, murdering and behaving more like wild beasts than human beings." By now Harding had twenty thousand troops, who conducted sweeps through the Troodos and Kyrenia mountains. Assisted by helicopters and tracker dogs, they scored victories against the guerrillas, who were bombarded with messages from loudspeaker aircraft announcing, "The game is up."[115]

Harding also benefited from better intelligence, some of it obtained through torture. This was standard practice during the interrogation of suspects, who were beaten on the stomach with flat boards, hit in the testicles, half-suffocated with wet cloths and otherwise abused. At least six men died under questioning and others were shot "while trying to escape."[116] Yet some officers privately justified torture as a way of "defeating terrorism and saving human lives." Furthermore, it was "tolerated and covered up by higher authority." So too were instances of brutality in the gaols and internment camps which held many hundreds of Cypriots. Despite elaborate official denials, though, there was sufficient evidence to sustain serious accusations against the British imperialists. Fortunately for them, the Greeks just mounted a "smear campaign." For example, they said that Kyrenia Castle was "a second Dachau" staffed by "a new Gestapo" under the supreme command of "Butcher Harding." The British easily refuted such allegations, which were as absurd as their own propagandist claim that the notoriously puritanical EOKA prostituted twelve-year-old girls. Indeed, Harding might well have been astonished at his own moderation. But his measures were "too strong for the weak and too weak for the strong."[117] In other words, they antagonised the Greek population without eradicating EOKA. Counter-terrorism was counter-productive. It crystallised popular support for Grivas. Now, declared the Mayor of Nicosia, "We are all EOKA!"[118]

Later Grivas said that Greeks should erect a statue of Harding since he had done more than anyone to keep alive the spirit of Hellenic resistance in Cyprus. Yet the truth was that the Field-Marshal came close to defeating the colonel. Grivas had to declare a cease-fire in August 1956 and, while spurning Harding's crass appeal to surrender, he only regained the initiative as a result of the Suez crisis. But after "Black November," which saw the worst bloodshed of the conflict, British forces once more got the upper hand. In March 1957 Grivas announced a truce. This brought his sustained campaign to an end, though outbursts of violence continued for another twenty-one months. Indeed, Grivas became, if anything, more pugnacious. He contemplated a pogrom against the entire Turkish community but was restrained by Makarios, who thought "we should throw a grenade or two among them from a roof-top, so they will be taught a lesson and will not dare to congregate in mobs in future."[119] Grivas also wanted to put arsenic in selected aqueducts and he tried to obtain typhus germs for use against the British—subordinates refused to obey him because such tactics would "ruin the liberation struggle."[120] On the other hand, meanwhile, Cyprus's annual prison report noted: "The scaffold, which is rather antiquated, should be modernised."[121]

Harding's tragedy was that he could never transmute military repression into political reconciliation. After the humiliating withdrawal from Suez, the Tory government had to stand firm in Cyprus, especially as the security forces seemed to be on the point of victory. Similarly, Lord Radcliffe, who was commissioned to design a constitution for Cyprus, had to build into it a measure of British sovereignty. On the other hand Macmillan was anxious to escape from the Cypriot labyrinth, not least because there was so much sniping at British imperialism in the United Nations and the United States. Even more embarrassing were Greek moves to arraign Britain before the European Court in Strasbourg for violations of human rights. Shocked by totalitarian atrocities, the Foreign Office had promoted the European Convention, which came into force in 1953. But it had wrongly assumed that "human rights were for foreigners." Instead the Convention boomeranged on its champions, causing anger at Government House in Nicosia and anxiety in Whitehall. The Foreign Secretary, Selwyn Lloyd, was especially perturbed. When European commissioners were about to be sent to investigate the situation in Cyprus, he expressed "dismay and incredulity that the Convention could have got us into this fix, and even more incredulity that it applies to so many colonies."[122]

Meanwhile, in April 1957, Macmillan made a pacific gesture. He authorised the release of Makarios from the Seychelles, where he had been living at the Governor's summer residence, Sans Souci—moved there when Lennox-Boyd found that the Archbishop was to be accommodated in a house called La Bastille. The Colonial Office remained nervous about names. It stopped Makarios from embarking on a vessel called *World Harmony* (though its replacement, *Olympic Thunderer,* was not much better) and it worried that a BBC interviewer might address him as "Your Beatitude."[123] The Archbishop was prohibited from returning to Cyprus and had to languish in Athens, staying at the Hotel Grand Bretagne. Harding, who distrusted him more than ever owing to revelations of his involvement with EOKA contained in Grivas's captured diaries, tried to discredit this turbulent priest with a pamphlet entitled *The Church and Terrorism*—it was originally called *The Flaming Cassock.* Clearly the Field-Marshal was not the man to treat with the Archbishop. So, frustrated more by British politicians than by Greek terrorists, he departed. Macmillan chose as his successor a liberal-minded idealist, Sir Hugh Foot. Arriving in Cyprus on 3 December 1957, the new Governor was soon known as "Pussyfoot."

This was because Foot radiated benevolence and advocated a democratic denouement. He asked for a honeymoon period and denounced violence as "the servant of tyranny."[124] He walked down Ledra Street ("Murder Mile") in Nicosia and toured the island on horseback, shaking hands with all and sundry. He released detainees, lifted restrictions and tried to calm rioting schoolchildren in person. Later, on his own initiative, Foot even sought to arrange a clandestine meeting with Grivas, who ignored the overture of this "cunning and dangerous diplomat."[125] Grivas was right in one respect: Foot could offer nothing new but a show of conciliation. The civilian Governor had less freedom of action than his military predecessor. When Lennox-Boyd learned of his approach to Grivas, which horrified British commanders on the island, he told the Governor not to do it again. The Prime Minister was equally stern. Vulnerable to attack from champions of reaction like Lord Salisbury, who had resigned from the cabinet over the release of Makarios, Macmillan was as keen as Eden to avoid a Middle Eastern Munich. So all Foot could do was to press ahead with a revised partnership scheme, a second tridominium. Yet it could hardly work in the face of Greek opposition and the Governor saw no way out of the maze of conflicting interests. Indeed, he liked to repeat that "anyone who understood the situation in Cyprus had been misinformed."[126] It grew still more tortuous in the spring of 1958. Then terrorist campaigns, spearheaded by a revived EOKA still pursuing the grail of *enosis* and a TMT now committed to "PARTITION OR DEATH,"[127] looked set to spiral into civil war.

As Grivas began boycotting British goods, bombing British targets and killing British servicemen, Foot discreetly and unhappily took the side of the Turks. Yet they were responsible for much of the communal violence. In a bloody effort to purge their enclaves of Greeks, they resorted to riot, arson, pillage and murder. EOKA retaliated in kind. But, as usual, Grivas was fighting on several fronts—not only against Turks but against Britons, Communists, defectors and others. Soon Foot had become responsible, against all his magnanimous instincts, for a campaign of repression worthy of Harding. In July 1958, when the ethnic struggle reached its climax, some thirty thousand troops arrested almost two thousand EOKA suspects in an operation resembling a "lucky dip."[128] This doubled the population of the camps. After a lull in August, the security forces reacted ever more severely to EOKA attacks. Soldiers bulldozed houses and blew up buildings such as sports halls and cinemas if they could be connected to terrorism. They bayoneted villagers and set priests' beards on fire. They made Greek-Cypriot hostages ride in their vehicles to prevent the detonation of roadside bombs. When one British woman was shot and another badly wounded in Famagusta on 3 October, exasperated troops went on the rampage, rounding up a thousand Greek-Cypriots and beating them so ferociously that two died and hundreds were injured. "Black October" 1958, which saw forty-five people killed and brought Cyprus to the top of the political agenda in Britain, was the worst month since "Black November" two years earlier.

Yet a note of new hope crept into the struggle being simultaneously conducted in the diplomatic arena. The Athens government, while making its case once again in the United Nations, prevailed on Grivas to cease fire. And conciliatory signs from Istanbul at Christmas prompted Foot to reprieve two EOKA murderers minutes before they were due to be executed. He then visited the prison to give them the tidings himself, taking his son Paul who wrote an account of this midnight adventure. An Oxford undergraduate at the time, Paul noted the incongruousness of their dinner jackets in the cold, gloomy passages of the prison. He heard the lamentation of male inmates, a grim chorus augmented by the thin wailing of women. "Most of them are operatic sopranos out of a job," said a fat English warder. Paul penned staccato impressions of the scene:

> A sudden light; the two hangmen standing straight and blue, their work for the evening cancelled; a hysterical priest; the two recently condemned killers receiving the news with a quiet doubtful smile, cool and handsome in their simple clothes; the grateful authorities; the inevitable soldiers saluting; a final devastating roar of applause from the "politicals" (news travels fast, apparently, in a prison).

Driving back to Government House in the silence of his father's bullet-proof Humber, Paul was struck by the idea that "a murderer can be patriotic."[129] For Sir Hugh Foot, the reprieve represented a dramatic change of heart in those concerned with the fate of Cyprus. It indicated a prospect of peace for an island shaken by the colliding tectonic plates of three empires—Byzantine, Ottoman and British—all more or less defunct save in pride and prejudice.

What caused Greece to show the olive branch was its failure to make progress in the United Nations. Constantine Karamanlis's government feared that Macmillan would press ahead with his plan for a partnership, which would end in partition. To prevent this, Makarios himself was willing to sacrifice *enosis* on the altar of independence. What caused Turkey to restrain its janissaries was the nationalist revolt in Iraq, which deprived the Baghdad Pact of Baghdad. Turkey was now exposed on its southern as well as its northern flank. So Adnan Menderes's government sought to strengthen the NATO alliance. It aimed to secure rapprochement with Britain and to achieve détente with Greece by removing the Cypriot apple of discord from their common table. In February 1959, therefore, Karamanlis and Menderes met in Zurich. In secret conclave at the homely Hotel Dolder, they agreed on a constitution which would provide protection for the minority in the new sovereign state of Cyprus. This agreement was ratified in London. Makarios signed with a painful show of reluctance. Grivas, despite "moments of agony," accepted the *fait accompli*. He could not now rely on Greek or even Cypriot support and if he battled on alone the result would be "a national split . . . [in which] WE SHALL LOSE EVERY-THING."[130] The colonel secured an amnesty for most EOKA fighters and left Cyprus in March 1959, still packing his pistol. The British Army was determined to do him no honour. Detailed to supervise his departure was a tall, aristocratic officer who had lost his right arm and therefore could not salute Grivas.

The British Empire ended as haphazardly as it began, with different territories gaining independence in different ways. Some fought for freedom; others combined minimal force with hard bargaining; still others cooperated with colonial authorities to achieve an orderly transfer of power. The diversity was especially apparent in the Mediterranean. Britain retained (and retains) Gibraltar, an anachronism and an anomaly. Malta got self-rule in 1964, but only after the collapse of a scheme for its political union with the United Kingdom—a scheme not so much British (since imperial federation had always been a fantasy) as French or Roman "in its vision of a single *respublica* and a common citizenship."[131] The case of Cyprus, which became a republic led by President Makarios in August 1960, was strangest of all. Britain had encouraged Turkish aspirations in order to protect its imperial position. From Paphos to Famagusta it had thus sowed dragons' teeth, reaping a harvest of strife until December 1959. Yet as early as March 1957 Macmillan had concluded that Britain did not "need more than an air-field" on the island. However the Prime Minister was so fearful of the Tory response to his "selling out in Cyprus"[132] that he continued to insist on a military victory. At the very least he wanted to have some "symbol of our success."[133] In other words, British forces on the island had been fighting for prestige. Foot had to save face. Ultimately it was Karamanlis and Menderes, not Macmillan, who cut through "the Cyprus tangle."[134] The British were excluded from the Greco-Turkish negotiations in Switzerland. Macmillan was able to acquire sovereign bases ample enough to satisfy national *amour propre* and to present the London settlement as a triumph. Otherwise, having shaped the island's past for ill, Britain was denied the chance to shape its future for good. In Cyprus, as elsewhere, conflict would be the legacy of empire.

22

All Our Pomp of Yesterday

The Falklands and Hong Kong

Another island conflict provided a curious epilogue to the British Empire. It was caused, paradoxically, by the continuing desire of governments in London to shed burdensome dependencies. That process was usually made easier because colonies yearned to be born again as nations. But the inhabitants of the Falkland Islands, 1,800 people of British stock, wished to stay securely in the imperial womb. Above all, they were determined not to be absorbed into the body politic of Argentina. Only three hundred miles away, this South American country had long claimed sovereignty over islands whose Spanish name was Las Malvinas, along with their icy, empty satellites such as South Georgia and South Thule, the Shag Rocks and the Clerke Rocks. Who discovered and who owned the Falklands had been a matter of dispute since Tudor times. In fact Britain nearly went to war with Spain over the issue in 1770, when the Admiralty maintained that the islands were "the key to the whole Pacifick Ocean"[1]—another key, but a world away from its putative holder. Dr. Johnson denounced the folly of such a conflict in lapidary prose that was still relevant two centuries later. "The Rubicon was ennobled by the passage of Caesar," he wrote, "and the time is now come when the Falkland's Islands demand their historian."

Alas, there was nothing to say since nothing had happened there save the occasional advent of "wandering navigators, who passed them by in search of better habitations." Here, in the freezing ocean adjacent to Tierra del Fuego, was a

> bleak and gloomy solitude . . . thrown aside from human use, stormy in winter and barren in summer . . . which not [even] the southern savages have dignified with habitation; where a garrison must be kept in a state that contemplates with envy the exiles of Siberia; of which the expence will be perpetual, and the use only occasional.[2]

Johnson exaggerated. The climate of the Falklands was temperate. Permanently occupied by the British in 1833, the islands would provide employment for a small colony of shepherds and "kelpers"—seaweed gatherers. Port Stanley proved its worth as a coaling station before Admiral Sturdee's victorious naval battle in December 1914. Yet the Great Cham's remonstrance rang down the ages, resonating along the corridors of Whitehall and echoing through the lobbies of Westminster. There was no point in fighting to become the undisputed lords of a tempest-torn wilderness.

Certainly by the 1960s London had become disenchanted with this South Atlantic relic of empire. It had no strategic value. It was a political liability. It had few economic prospects. It was sadly impoverished. The Falklands' largest source of income, after the half-million sheep ranging over the treeless, tussocky peat, came from stamps. And the Government Printing Office was "a working museum." Other amenities were notable by their absence. As one Governor despairingly exclaimed, there was "no banker, no solicitor, no accountant, no estate agent, no cobbler, no greengrocer, no dry-cleaner, no hairdresser, no garage mechanic, no mason, no builder, no undertaker. How did the islands work?"[3] The answer is that they barely worked at all. Lacking the resources to become independent, as Johnson had said, they required constant support from the mother country. But the mother country was slow to invest and reluctant to subsidise. Communications presented a particularly expensive challenge—the islands had a toy airfield and only seven miles of road. Britons had little faith in the commercial enterprise or pioneering spirit of the kelpers. Most of them, in any case, worked for the Falkland Islands Company, which owned half the land and conducted most of the business. And "with frighteningly few exceptions," wrote an English visitor who actually liked the islanders, the labour force was "a drunken, decadent, immoral and indolent collection of dropouts."[4] The Falklands, said another visitor, might conjure up a "vision of romantic solitude." But the reality was "an unending diet of mutton, beer and rum, with entertainment restricted to drunkenness and adultery, spiced with occasional incest."

Whatever the truth of this, the population, already smaller than that of an average English parish, was undoubtedly ageing and shrinking. Yet after the United Nations resolved in 1965 that Britain and Argentina should reach a peaceful settlement over what most countries seemed to regard as a colonial issue, Labour and Tory ministers proclaimed that the islanders' wishes must be paramount. The British insisted on the principle that people should be free to decide their own political fate, the very principle that had cut at the root of the Empire. To their chagrin they now found that this principle saddled them with responsibility for a territory which they would gladly have ceded to its powerful neighbour, who claimed it with such avidity. Throughout the 1970s, therefore, Britain counselled its colonists to enter into some kind of association with Argentina. It urged the virtues of joint sovereignty. It proposed transferring ownership of the islands but retaining them on a long lease. It stressed the benefits that would flow from cooperation with Argentina. Lord Shackleton, son of the Antarctic explorer, said that the Falklands were "islands entirely surrounded by advice." The Foreign Office grew increasingly exasperated by their refusal to take it. The British ambassador in Buenos Aires even offered to go to Port Stanley and make Councillors' "flesh creep with expert advice on potential Argentine frightfulness."[5] Meanwhile he and his ilk exhorted governments of Argentina, which became notorious by the end of the decade for violating the rights of their own people, to court the islanders with kindness. As the diplomat in charge of Britain's dependent territories liked to say: "Rape of the Falklands, no; seduction, by all means."[6]

In fact, the military junta in Buenos Aires became ever more impassioned. Crowds chanted with growing fervour, *Las Malvinas son argentinas.* As Britain played for time, Argentina dealt out provocations. Its aircraft flew over the Falklands. Its navy harassed foreign vessels around the islands. Its transport services to Port Stanley became erratic. Its soldiery landed on South Thule. In 1977 James Callaghan's government grew so concerned about the prospect of Argentine aggression that it covertly sent a small force to the South Atlantic. This was a temporary "insurance policy,"[7] for it was deemed too expensive to secure the islands on a permanent basis, to create a Fortress Falklands. Other options were equally unacceptable. London ruled out Lord Shackleton's proposals for major investment, including the further modernisation of Stanley airport and an extension of the runway. Resettling white Falkland islanders would have been politically impossible—unlike resettling brown Chagos islanders. So Margaret Thatcher's ministers continued negotiations in the hope of somehow reconciling the islanders' right to self-determination and the continentals' right to territorial integrity. A clandestine understanding to promote the leaseback arrangement was reached between the Argentine Foreign Minister and Nicholas Ridley, a singularly abrasive Thatcherite, who told the Falklanders to accept it or "take the consequences."[8] Instead they became even more obdurate, fearful that they were being sold up the River Plate. The British could only keep talking to the Argentinians, even though they had nothing to say. In the words of their Buenos Aires ambassador, they had "no strategy at all beyond a general Micawberism."[9]

Meanwhile, Mrs. Thatcher was struggling with a major recession at home. Three million people were unemployed. Bankruptcies reached record levels. Inflation stood at 15 per cent. Riots occurred in London, Liverpool and Manchester. Of the shambles in Toxteth, the grocer's daughter famously exclaimed: "Oh, those poor shopkeepers!" The Labour opposition was in a harsher mood, charging that the century's worst outbreak of civil unrest stemmed from the ruthless implementation of Tory monetarist policies. The Prime Minister blamed the disturbances on human wickedness and sank to unprecedented depths in public opinion polls. Preoccupied with the domestic crisis, she overcame her reluctance to sacrifice the sovereignty of the Falkland Islands. Furthermore, she made economies which appeared to encourage an Argentine invasion and to confirm the end of the British Empire. Most important was the plan to reduce defence expenditure, "a bombshell"[10] which struck the Royal Navy far harder than the other services. The Defence Minister John Nott argued persuasively that proponents of a navy with global reach were victims of "nostalgia for the days of Empire."[11] But he forgot that vestiges of the Empire remained—when Argentine aggression was imminent he had to hunt for the Falklands on a large globe in his office.

The diminution of the fleet was bound to affect Britain's defensive capacity and Admiral Sir Henry Leach, the First Sea Lord, said that Nott's attempt to pretend otherwise was "the con trick of the century."[12] As Leach asserted, the proposed cuts would have "emasculated"[13] the senior service. They included the scrapping of two assault ships and the loss of two aircraft carriers—Americans scoffed that they were broken up for "razor blades."[14] There would also be a halving of the sixty-strong complement of frigates and destroyers, "the backbone of the fleet."[15] Yet the Prime Minister vehemently supported the savings. She even briefed against Nott for being too timid. And she plucked "the Red Plum" of Antarctica. This was the ruddy-coloured ice-patrol vessel HMS *Endurance,* commanded by the redoubtable Captain Nick Barker, which cost £3 million a year. Mrs. Thatcher, who retained the royal yacht *Britannia* for reasons of prestige, said that *Endurance* was "a military irrelevance."[16] In fact, the survey ship was "a key intelligence asset."[17] It was also a potent symbol of Britain's commitment to the Falklands. News of its impending withdrawal was "greeted with unalloyed joy in the Argentine press."[18]

Other signals reached General Leopoldo Galtieri, who became leader of the Argentine junta in 1981, suggesting that Mrs. Thatcher had washed her hands of the Falklands. None seemed clearer than her government's Nationality Act. This was designed to deny any right of abode in Britain to Hong

Kong Chinese by excluding all but those descended from a parent or grand-parent born in the United Kingdom. It also excluded eight hundred Falk-landers—though Gibraltarians were given a special dispensation. In the South Atlantic the Act was seen as a flagrant abdication of imperial respon-sibility, comparable to Mrs. Thatcher's desertion of the whites in Southern Rhodesia. Galtieri, who sought to divert attention from an internal crisis far worse than Britain's, concluded that he could seize Las Malvinas with impunity. After all, the British had pursued a policy of appeasement with-out deterrence—little was done even when, late in the day, Mrs. Thatcher called for contingency planning to meet hostilities. Her ministers were not interested in the islands—Ridley quipped that the only alien territory that he wanted to claim was Bordeaux. The British had tried to disburden them-selves of the islanders. It seemed inconceivable that they would shed blood to reverse an Argentine *fait accompli*. So, after much preparation and a pre-liminary sortie to South Georgia, which caused alarm in London where ear-lier journalistic and diplomatic warnings had been ignored, the junta launched the invasion. Signals intelligence picked up in Britain, where cryp-tographers had cracked Argentine codes, indicated that enemy forces would land in the Falklands on 2 April 1982. The Foreign Office sent its diminutive Governor, Rex Hunt, a helpful telegram saying: "You will wish to make your dispositions accordingly." Hunt could only deploy his few dozen Marines, shred his secret papers and issue a general caveat via the Falkland Islands Broadcasting Service (FIBS). Reflecting bitterly that soft answers had failed to turn away Argentine wrath, he said: "It looks as if the buggers really mean it this time."[19]

Margaret Thatcher reached the same conclusion and she determined to get the islands back—if necessary, by force. She had emulated Chamberlain in attempting to negotiate a settlement with a dictator from a position of weakness. Now she donned the mantle of Churchill and set out to defend "our honour as a nation."[20] Such rhetoric disguised the incongruity of fight-ing to preserve a micro-colony which successive governments had tried to liquidate; and fighting, moreover, against a regime equipped with weaponry often purchased from Britain. But the Iron Lady was resolute and fortune favoured the bold. The popular press raged not at 10 Downing Street but at the Foreign Office, "rotten to the core, rotten with appeasement, rotten with real scorn for British interests."[21] The defence cuts had not yet bitten and within seventy-two hours Admiral Leach was able to dispatch a power-ful "Task Force." The Prime Minister's military ignorance proved a positive advantage. It was surprisingly comprehensive, perhaps the product of a "television view of war."[22] When Leach said that the armada would take three weeks to reach the Falklands, Mrs. Thatcher riposted: "Three weeks, you mean three days?"[23] The admiral pointed out that the distance was eight thousand nautical miles. However, she listened to men in uniform with a grace seldom seen by ministers and civil servants. These she hectored fiercely, earning her nickname "Attila the Hen."

Yet they frequently deserved better. Lord Carrington resigned as Foreign Secretary, taking the blame for having "miscalculated that the Argentines would invade."[24] Although "rattled and blubbery," obsessed by the Suez fiasco and haunted by the spirit of an ancestor who had been caught up in the debacle of the First Afghan War, John Nott remained willing to bear "responsibility without power."[25] Britain's ambassador to the United Nations, Sir Anthony Parsons, deftly obtained a resolution in the Security Council demanding an Argentine withdrawal. Just as necessary was help from the United States. It included permission to use the American-built runway on the vital staging post of Ascension Island, itself a British possession—though today security agencies deny its native people the "right of abode"[26] enjoyed by sooty terns and masked boobies. Ronald Reagan's Defence Secretary, Caspar Weinberger, provided unstinting aid, despite the diplomatic and linguistic tergiversations of his Secretary of State, General Alexander Haig. Eventually the President decided that his South American ally, despite its staunch anti-Communism, was less important than his European ally. But he could not really understand why Mrs. Thatcher was so keen to regain the "little ice-cold bunch of land down there."[27]

She told Haig that "it was essentially an issue of dictatorship versus democracy."[28] And the Falklands conflict was presented as a struggle for freedom. Fortunately for the Prime Minister, most Britons shared that view. The press and public opinion favoured retaliation, on the assumption that it would not result in a big butcher's bill. The left-wing leader of the Labour opposition, Michael Foot, opposed fascist aggression as "a moral duty, a political duty and every other kind of duty."[29] Liberals extolled the rule of law and denounced the evils of the junta (though Tory ministers played these down because they feared countercharges about abuses of human rights in Ulster). Thoughtful officers going south reckoned that, despite the absurdity of sending 28,000 men to fight for islands that Britain did not want, the "*ideal* is most praiseworthy."[30] But ideals were muted in the crescendo of neo-colonial chauvinism. As ships sailed, bands played "Rule, Britannia!" and "Land of Hope and Glory." People waved Union Jacks and sported T-shirts saying "Don't cry for me Argentina, we're going to knock the **** out of you."[31] There was talk of reversing the nation's shameful decline and putting the Great back into Britain. As the radical historian

E. P. Thompson wrote, this was "a moment of imperial atavism, drenched in the nostalgias of those now in their late middle-age."[32]

None was more atavistic than Rupert Murdoch, whose tabloid newspaper, the *Sun,* dismissed peace proposals with headlines such as "STICK IT UP YOUR JUNTA." It also celebrated the sinking of the Argentine cruiser *General Belgrano* with the infamous illiteracy, "GOTCHA." The satirical magazine *Private Eye* mocked the *Sun's* squalid antics with a competition entitled "KILL AN ARGIE AND WIN A METRO." And as Murdoch's biographer acknowledged, men aboard the expeditionary force were offended by the paper's "trivial, ghoulish jingoism."[33] Yet their own senior officers maintained that victory was the due of the "bulldog breed."[34] The commanding admiral, Sandy Woodward, expressed contempt for "a job lot of spics flying ageing Canberras" and after Marines recaptured South Georgia he forecast "a walkover."[35] In the words of Lieutenant David Tinker, who was killed during the campaign, "the Navy felt that we were British and they were wogs, and that would make all the difference."[36] As for the army's special forces, they were sometimes regarded as supermen. The commanding general, Jeremy Moore, suspected that "fatuous expectations" of what they could achieve stemmed from "avid reading of Boy's Own or Beano."[37]

In fact, British self-confidence took some hard knocks during the few weeks of war. Intelligence proved inadequate. Lieutenant Tinker said that it consisted of an Education Officer "who knew where the Falklands were because he had an atlas and *Jane's Fighting Ships* to tell us what the Argentinians had in their navy."[38] There were farcical cases of mistaken identity: ships depth-charged whales and troops machine-gunned elephant seals. Despite heavy losses, the Argentine air force fought with courage and skill. Equipped with modern Mirages and Super-Etendards carrying sea-skimming Exocet missiles, it inflicted severe injuries on the British fleet. Altogether fifteen ships were damaged and seven sunk, including the supply vessel *Atlantic Conveyor* with its vital cargo of Chinook helicopters and the auxiliary *Sir Galahad,* which was slow to disembark soldiers and suffered forty-eight fatalities. Admiral Woodward had to keep his carriers so far east of the Falklands that he was known as "the South African."[39] This meant that the Harrier jump jets, armed with deadly American Sidewinder missiles, could only spend a few minutes over the islands. So the main amphibious landing, at San Carlos Water on 21 May 1982, went ahead without the promised air cover. The British were lucky with the weather and the lack of opposition. But they soon found that their own missiles (Sea Dart, Sea Wolf, Rapier and Blowpipe) did not provide a proper shield against low-level air attacks. These would have been even more devastating had not many of the Argentine bombs failed to explode. The Argentine pilots were also deterred by a fusillade of old-fashioned weaponry, Bren guns and Bofors guns, as well as small-arms fire. It was, said a witness, "real cowboy stuff."[40]

Political pressure forced a costly attack on Goose Green. Advance news of this leaked, allegedly as the result of a briefing by John Nott himself—the worst security lapse of the war. Nott also maintained that the *Belgrano* was "closing in on"[41] the Task Force when it was torpedoed whereas it was actually moving away, a line repeated by Mrs. Thatcher which generated corrosive conspiracy theories. In its approach to public relations the Ministry of Defence resembled the Kremlin. It appointed "brain police"[42] who imposed a capricious censorship on reporters. And its own spokesman, a civil servant called Ian MacDonald who made announcements like an animated speak-your-weight machine, became a national joke. Argentine snipers had better rifles and night-vision glasses than British troops and some of their units put up fierce resistance. But many consisted of raw conscripts, ill led, ill fed and ill clad, who soon capitulated. General Menéndez, who had done little but sit behind fixed defences, surrendered on 14 June 1982. The journalist Max Hastings, who accompanied the relief force into Stanley, wrote that it was "like liberating an English suburban golf club."[43] Yet some of the liberators were down to their last few rounds of ammunition. It had been a close-run thing. Sandy Woodward said that "if the Args could only breathe on us, we'd fall over!"[44]

Most of the doubts and deprecations vanished in the euphoria of victory. "We won," Nott wrote to the Prime Minister, "and that is good enough for the overwhelming proportion of the British people." What mattered was the heroism of servicemen who had overcome fearful odds. Fascist aggression had got its just deserts. National pride, which had suffered such a crippling blow at Suez, was miraculously restored. The cost was certainly exorbitant: 253 Britons killed and over 750 wounded; nearly £2 billion for the relief expedition and billions more to secure the Falklands against any future attack. But few were prepared to say that the blood had been shed in vain. And when the Jewish Chief Secretary to the Treasury, Leon Brittan, tried to squeeze payment for the campaign out of the existing defence budget, Nott accused him of behaving like "a Pakistani accountant."[45] The cabinet worried that it might be criticised by the committee set up under Lord Franks to assess how well governments since 1965 had dealt with the Falkland Islands. But like many such chairmen Franks had been selected because he was a pillar of orthodoxy and a quintessential member of the Establishment—the economist Roy Harrod unkindly called him a "bum-faced purveyor of last year's platitudes."[46] The worst his report did was to state that announcing the withdrawal of *Endurance* had been "inadvisable."[47] Otherwise Franks produced a classic whitewash, which said in essence that everyone was responsible and no one was culpable.

Mrs. Thatcher needed no such official vindication for she had been swept back into popular favour on the wave of nationalist sentiment. In a state of personal exaltation bordering on self-intoxication, she did much to foster the triumphalist mood. She played Boadicea at a victory parade in the City of London, inviting no members of the royal family and taking the salute herself. She declared that a glorious new chapter had been written in the history of liberty. She invoked "the spirit of the South Atlantic—the real spirit of Britain." She proclaimed that the war had dissolved the "secret fears" of her compatriots that "Britain was no longer the nation that had built an Empire and ruled a quarter of the world."[48] The response was Pavlovian. Illusion outlived reality and the past governed the present. The Empire had gone but the emotions associated with it survived, like phantom feelings after an amputation. This boded ill for Britain's future since subsequent leaders would face the temptation to exploit imperial longings—to promote general nostalgia while encouraging selective amnesia—in order to justify overseas interventions. Of course, Britain could only participate in substantial conflicts as a junior partner of the United States. But, as the historian Linda Colley put it, there has been "a persistent inclination to pursue empire vicariously by clambering like a mouse on the American eagle's head."[49] Ministers such as Douglas Hurd tried to disguise Britain's subordinate role, claiming that it was "punching above its weight in the world."[50] And despite having led Britain through what was evidently its last colonial war (though in 2006 Argentina made "a renewed push for the islands"),[51] Mrs. Thatcher herself became increasingly belligerent. This was all too evident on her trip to the Far East three months after the victory. In China she ignored emollient Foreign Office counsel. Instead she expressed her wish to retain control of Britain's last major colony, Hong Kong, whose loyal Executive Council voted to contribute £10 million to the cost of the Falklands War.

The final episode in the history of the British Empire was in some ways the strangest. For Hong Kong did not mature, in the standard fashion, from colonial tutelage to self-government. It regressed from the relative freedom afforded by *laissez-faire* capitalism to subordination under the shadow of a Communist colossus. Unlike other British possessions, it did not nurture a nationalist movement committed to smashing the imperialist yoke. Nor, since Red China insisted that Hong Kong was an internal matter, did it become the focus of international anti-colonialist pressure. It could never hope to become an independent sovereign state, let alone a member of the Commonwealth. Instead it would revert to China as a Special Administrative Region. The transfer of power might be postponed but it could not be avoided, especially when Britain's ninety-nine-year lease on the New Territories surrounding the crown colony expired in 1997. Margaret Thatcher's "heart kept cherishing the alternative," recalled her Foreign Secretary Geoffrey Howe, "dreaming of a way in which we could have something more permanent."[52] But it was just a dream, a neo-imperialist pipe dream. Hong Kong was, in Richard Hughes's well-worn adaptation of Han Suyin's phrase, a "borrowed place, living on borrowed time."[53] In this "most brilliant and bullish of the world's entrepôts,"[54] as Jan Morris noticed, every deed of estate ran out before the end of the millennium. The glittering emporium of Asia was, as travel brochures liked to repeat, "the pearl in the dragon's mouth." It could have been swallowed at a gulp. Why did China take so long to consume it? And how was its ingestion accomplished when the time came?

Of course, the decaying Manchu Empire could not have seized Hong Kong. On the contrary, by the late nineteenth century Britain and other imperial powers dominated the Orient. And they had begun (in Lenin's words) "to rob China as ghouls rob corpses."[55] But even if Victorian Hong Kong had been liable to attack from the mainland, it was scarcely much of a prize. To be sure, Hong Kong was strategically valuable to Britain as terminus in the line of naval stations running from Plymouth via Gibraltar, Valletta, Alexandria, Aden, Trincomalee and Singapore. It was also a deliciously picturesque possession, extolled by Victorian travellers such as Isabella Bird. As she observed, every oriental costume, often "emphasised by the glitter of 'barbaric gold,'" seemed to float through the island's streets:

> Parsees in spotless white, Jews and Arabs in dark rich silks; Klings in Turkey red and white; Bombay merchants in red and white turbans, full trousers, and draperies, all white with crimson silk girdles; Malays in red *sarongs;* Sikhs in pure white Madras muslin . . . ; and Chinamen of all classes from the coolie in his blue or brown cotton, to the wealthy merchant in his frothy silk crêpe and rich brocade, make up an irresistibly fascinating medley.[56]

More than a generation later another visiting writer, Stella Benson, was equally excited by the "extraordinary exoticness and variation of the Hong Kong crowd." Watching passengers as they flooded with "dramatic-cinematic" intensity from the ferry at Kowloon, she admired "the gentle, coarse young kilted soldiers; Indian police with their dyed scarlet beards"; yellow parchment-skinned old men and "lovely slim young Chinese girls in . . . [their] neat and graceful half-foreign dresses."[57] Local colour apart, though, Hong Kong was a drab backwater.

It was commercially quiescent, politically insignificant and socially stagnant. After 1860 the vast bulk of British mercantile interests were concentrated in the treaty port of Shanghai, at the mouth of the Yangtse. Hong Kong was never more than a pawn in the great game of Sino-British relations. Parochial but pretentious, whites created what one colonel called a "serviette civilisation."[58] The state of the colony was most clearly illustrated in the person of its Governor. Although an autocrat "next to the Almighty,"[59] he had little to do and sometimes, like Sir Arthur Kennedy in the 1870s, did "as little as possible."[60] Sir William Des Voeux found that his work was far lighter than it had been in tiny St. Lucia and said that Hong Kong was "a paradise to a man inclined to be idle." Most Governors had leisure for playing golf and tennis, or sailing aboard their sumptuous yacht, or taking the steam-driven Peak Tram (the first funicular railway in Asia) up to their summer retreat, Mountain Lodge, with its Pompeian red-and-yellow tiled floors. What occupied them most were the ceremonial duties attached to their role as petty viceroys, bonsai Grand Ornamentals. At Government House, a square, granite, neo-classical edifice overlooking the Botanical Gardens that was smoothly run by pig-tailed Chinese in long blue gowns, they gave magnificent balls and entertainments. They travelled in state, bearers of the Governor's sedan chair clad in "bright-red liveries, white gaiters, and 'mutton-pie' hats with red tassels."[61] They welcomed visiting dignitaries, spending vast sums on multi-gun salutes which shook the floating slums of Victoria Harbour. They presided over public occasions such as jubilees, regattas, horse races, parades and banquets. Sir Frederick Lugard grumbled about having to attend incessant functions, standing "first upon one leg and then upon another, or bowing like a Chinese image on a mantelpiece whose head wags for an hour if you touch him under the chin."[62] Everywhere Governors imposed a strict regard for protocol—Sir Matthew Nathan complained that Hong Kong wives were "pushful persons who would like to 'get into society.'"[63] And they set high standards of formality in an already artificial community. It was said to be social death for a man to forget "to put a flower in his coat, or to curl the ends of his moustache."[64]

Controversial matters certainly arose, which prompted interference from London, such as licensed gambling, prostitution and drug-smuggling. Governors tried to suppress crime, piracy, slavery, infanticide, spitting and foot-binding—Isabella Bird said that Chinese women had hooves. They also had to respond to the demands of the few thousand Europeans, led by opulent and rapacious taipans. Whites insisted on their supremacy. They used pidgin English because it was "easier to a Chinaman's intellect."[65] They said that the "heathen Chinee" was morally defective because of his "carnal conscience."[66] *The Hong Kong Guide* of 1893 noted that the Chinese pony "resembles his human compatriot for treachery."[67] In the streets Europeans habitually struck Chinese with their canes and umbrellas. And they demanded that Governors should be equally stern. "The cry was for a Caesar."[68] Thus over the years the Chinese were subjected to a host of discriminatory ordinances, including segregation, a night-time curfew and pass laws. Three hundred thousand of them (by Lugard's time) huddled together in noisome tenements on the coastal rim, often shared with pigs and fowls, overlooked by a European Surbiton rising towards the social eminence of Victoria Peak. The Chinese also received harsh punishments, among them public flogging and hanging. Any Governor who spared the rod, such as Sir John Pope Hennessy, was accused of "mollycoddling."[69] Pope Hennessy, who introduced the treadmill, was more eccentric than progressive. Preferring the good earth, he had a morbid aversion to water closets and denounced the "evils of sewage flushing."[70] He therefore delayed sanitary reform, which advanced cholera. The delay may also have helped the spread of bubonic plague, which was hardly checked by the Medical Officer of Health who thought it "more probable that rats caught the plague from man rather than that men were infected through rats."[71] So noxious was this island, where health was regularly sacrificed to wealth, that the first body with an elected element to be set up in Hong Kong (in 1888) was the Sanitary Board. Virtually no further progress was made towards democracy for almost a century. At least, though, as the historian John Darwin wittily remarks, "Hong Kong recognised the principle of no sanitation without representation."[72]

As appeared during the 1898 uprising of the Boxers ("Righteous Harmonious Fists"), the Chinese repaid British xenophobia with interest. They never overcame their aversion to "foreign devils." They resented western interference in oriental customs. They distrusted European medicines, suspecting that British doctors used the eyes of Chinese babies to treat plague victims and favouring herbal and other remedies, including decoctions of snake and hedgehog skin, dried lizard and cockchafer. They kicked against colonial discipline—every year some 10 per cent of Hong Kong's population were hauled before an English magistrate. In the streets of Victoria township Chinese men often jostled, cursed and spat at whites. Hatred of the alien dispensation sharpened after the First World War. Hong Kong workers struck against starvation wages, spiralling inflation and abysmal living standards. The Hong Kong Club was reduced to providing "tiffins on cafeteria lines."[73] The labour troubles led to violence which worsened in 1925 when protests spread to Shanghai and Canton, where British-commanded police and troops shot down dozens of demonstrators.

In Hong Kong hostility towards the imperialists reached fever pitch. A general strike paralysed the island and 250,000 strikers decamped to Canton where sympathisers gave them food and shelter. Canton also imposed a damaging boycott on Hong Kong's trade. Rather than responding with force, as the Governor Sir Cecil Clementi wanted, Britain "preferred to endure the almost untenable conditions."[74] For a time it seemed that the ruthless, bullet-headed leader of the nationalist Kuomintang, General Chiang Kai-shek, might abrogate the unequal treaties and eliminate all foreign settlements. Instead, identifying Bolshevism with "Red imperialism,"[75] he turned against his Communist allies. In 1926 he embarked on a civil war, later complicated by Japanese aggression, which lasted until Mao Tse-tung's victory in 1949. Chiang quickly lifted the boycott and the British restored order in Hong Kong. It was subsequently an important station on the "Red Underground Communication Line"[76] and when the Communists took power they continued to regard Hong Kong as a nexus of subversion. It also became a key conduit for arms and other supplies vital to the Kuomintang. In 1930 Chiang did get agreement in principle to abolish the anachronistic treaty ports. But Hong Kong faced no threat until the rising of the blood-red sun, with its sixteen fiery rays, of imperial Nippon.

Meanwhile, despite the Depression, Hong Kong made sufficient progress to ensure the collaboration of its Chinese population, who numbered nearly a million by 1937. They gave passive assent to a colonial government that was detached, paternalistic and wedded to the rule of law. It had long since abandoned grosser forms of discrimination, repealing pass regulations, for example, as early as 1897. In 1922 it introduced the colony's first labour legislation, prohibiting the industrial employment of children under the age of ten. Subsequent reformers made further attempts, some of them inept, to improve social conditions. Shocked by the government's toleration of a system that *"makes the enslavement of the girls more rigid,"*[77] they got brothels outlawed in 1932. But this increased the incidence of venereal disease, especially among British troops. Tommies had little to comfort them except prostitutes, who "were outcasts from their society," one soldier wrote, just as "we were outcasts from ours." And no decree could eradicate the oldest profession, which remained active in Hong Kong.

> Slant-eyed Chinese maidens all around I see
> Calling out "Artillery man, abide with me!"[78]

Even in one of its periodic fits of morality, though, the British Empire was preferable to the decadent and oppressive Manchu regime. Indeed, the father of the Chinese republic, Sun Yat-sen, had been impressed by its good governance. He said that his "ideas for the revolution had come entirely from Hong Kong."[79]

The British were also far less brutal and authoritarian than Chiang Kai-shek. His quasi-fascist New Life Movement prohibited spitting, smoking, drinking, guzzling, using lipstick and letting off firecrackers. Chiang also claimed to have suppressed the opium trade. In fact he tried to monopolise this vital source of Kuomintang funds, disguising his operation behind Orwellian terminology. Thus the "Opium Suppression Bureau" ran the business and "de-toxification clinics" sold drugs under the label "anti-opium medicine." In Hong Kong the British were less cynical but more hypocritical. Since late Victorian times there had been increasing opposition at home to Hong Kong's role as an opium entrepôt. One MP said that for "every soul our missionaries send to Heaven from China, the British Government was sending ten to hell by this traffic."[80] Such sentiments were echoed abroad and America, especially, put pressure on Britain. In 1913, therefore, India officially ceased to sell opium to China and Hong Kong imposed restrictions on drug use. But Governors wanted to postpone prohibition. This was because "the finances of the Hong Kong government had become as dependent on opium as any addict on his drug."[81] Half the revenue of the colony derived from the poppy in 1918. So between the wars successive Governors, abetted by the Colonial Office, engaged in an elaborate (and sometimes clandestine) rearguard action to defend the commodity that had been Hong Kong's *raison d'être*. Yet they also tried to live up to high-minded professions about social welfare. They therefore found other sources of income, opium providing only 5 per cent by the beginning of the Second World War and finally being outlawed at its end.

Before its outbreak, as China was ravaged by civil strife and foreign invasion, with the forces of Hirohito advancing faster than those of Genghis Khan, life seemed sweet under the Union Jack. Of course, it was much sweeter for Hong Kong's Europeans and the contrast between white and yellow existence was stark. Stella Benson might snipe at the narrowness, Philistinism and games-mindedness of her compatriots—"In Hong Kong it really isn't what you are but what you play that matters." But she herself indulged in an interminable round of entertainments. There were beach parties, boat picnics and ladies' tiffins with afternoon bridge. There were fencing displays at the Yacht Club, dances at the Peak Club and teas at the Fanling Golf Club, itself "spotted with rules . . . [and] hedged about with verbotens." There were cocktails at the Jockey Club, sundowners at the Repulse Bay Hotel and dinners at the Peninsula. There were outings to the cinema, where Europeans wore evening dress in the dress circle, while Chinese occupied the stalls. There were glittering receptions at Government House—"The Governor himself has a very *gentlemanly* face."[82] A few prominent Chinese were invited to selected functions, though even when they met their colonial masters they did not mix. Yet despite social constraint and racial prejudice, as well as the uneven distribution of wealth and privilege, oriental attitudes towards Britons were by no means entirely "belligerent and one-sided."[83] Some Chinese admired western achievements, imitated western fashions, even adopted western sexual tastes, preferring women with broad hips and big breasts. Above all, the Chinese benefited from a free enterprise system of which, in an increasingly protectionist world, Hong Kong was the brazen epitome. Through skill and diligence, they developed many industries, the largest being textiles, which together with trade and financial services were to make Hong Kong a dragon economy in the "East Asian Miracle."[84]

Prior to that, of course, the colony became an involuntary part of Nippon's Greater East Asia Co-Prosperity Sphere. Hong Kong was scarcely better prepared for war than Fiji, which received two 4.7-inch guns from New Zealand in September 1939 only to find that they were dummies. Churchill had long assumed that if Japan declared war all Britain's interests in the Yellow Sea would be "temporarily effaced."[85] Unlike Singapore, Hong Kong could not be held, he said, adding in January 1941 that its garrison should be "reduced to a symbolical scale."[86] Actually it was reinforced with two illtrained and largely French-speaking battalions of Canadian infantry. These were supplemented by a contingent of elderly volunteers called, after their founder, the "Hughesiliers"—or "Methuseliers."[87] But there were still not enough men to defend the aptly named Gin Drinkers' Line, which snaked for a dozen miles through the New Territories. And the authorities' refusal to arm the Chinese caused "a disastrous disaffection"[88] among the local population. The Chief Information Officer went so far as to say that "the ultimate cause" of Hong Kong's fall was the failure to tap "the vast reservoir of manpower within our own gates."

In Hong Kong there were about 300,000 able-bodied men. Making all possible allowance for fifth columnists, expatriates and jelly-fish who ooze quietly to the winning side, there cannot have been less than 75,000 Chinese who would willingly have borne arms and fought, not particularly for the British Empire, but against the hated monkey men from Japan.[89]

But colonial society in Hong Kong had succumbed to the kind of racist torpor that infected Singapore. "It was not so much fatuous complacency," said one officer, "as a determined unwillingness to have the pleasant routine of their lives disturbed by those 'short-arsed yellow bastards' who were overrunning China."[90]

The Japanese, who controlled the air and the sea, quickly drove their foes from the mainland. On 18 December 1941 their hardened troops mounted an amphibious assault on Hong Kong island and, despite being heavily outnumbered, achieved an immediate breakthrough. In the hope that this "forlorn outpost"[91] could survive for weeks or even months, Churchill cabled: "We expect you to resist to the end. The honour of the Empire is in your hands."[92] The Japanese swept aside all opposition with ruthless force, shooting prisoners, bayoneting hospital patients, raping nurses and committing other atrocities against civilians. On Christmas Day Sir Mark Young surrendered, something no British colonial Governor had ever done before. Meanwhile, his ADC, Captain Battye-Smith, went round telling the fugitives congregated at Government House not to drop cigarette ash on the Governor's carpet. The loss of Hong Kong in seventeen days was the first major blow to the prestige of white imperialists in Asia. It was compounded by the humiliation of captive Europeans, who were subjected to malnutrition, forced labour and hideous cruelties. A doctor who treated survivors found it heartbreaking "to learn that the elderly emaciated gentleman before your eyes was a boy in his twenties."[93] Some were so skeletal as to be unrecognisable, prompting one British police superintendent to incoherent fury: "What insufferable swine these yellow dogs are."[94] However, the conquerors inflicted worse horrors on the Chinese, face-slapping, looting, exiling, torturing, starving and executing on an unimaginable scale. The Japanese said that the Chinese could eat grass, of which there was plenty growing in the streets. Some were driven to cannibalism, buying human flesh in night markets. The vicious and corrupt Co-Prosperity Sphere was an excellent advertisement for the British Empire.

As the war continued, though, it seemed as if the Empire might relinquish its rights to Hong Kong. In 1943 Britain and the United States signed agreements with China abolishing all extra-territorial concessions and handing over treaty ports such as Shanghai (after the expulsion of Nippon). Encouraged by President Roosevelt, Chiang Kai-shek also expected the return of Hong Kong. The Foreign Office leant towards conciliation. When the Chinese pressed Anthony Eden over the lease of the New Territories, he accepted that Britain should "discuss its surrender after the war."[95] But the acting head of the Far Eastern Department, Sir Maurice Peterson, took a tougher line. He said that "in view of the ignominious circumstances in which we were bundled out of Hong Kong, we owe it to ourselves to return there and I personally do not believe that we will ever regain the respect of the East until we do."[96] Needless to say, Churchill shared this opinion. He was scathing about "people who got up each morning asking themselves how much more of the empire they could give away."[97] And in March 1945 he confronted Roosevelt's ambassador to China, Patrick Hurley, a bluff Irish-American who echoed the President's hostility to British colonialism in the Far East. Churchill "'took him up with violence' about Hong Kong and said that he would never yield an inch of territory that was under the British flag."[98] President Truman was not prepared to make an issue of this pimple on China's backside, especially when Bevin turned out to be as stubborn as Churchill. Equally intransigent was the senior British official in Hong Kong, Franklin Gimson. Released from prison camp after Japan's capitulation on 14 August 1945, he took charge of the colony in the name of His Majesty's Government. By sheer force of will Gimson made the Japanese obey him until the arrival of the Royal Navy at the end of the month. Admiral Sir Cecil Harcourt accepted the Japanese surrender on behalf of China and Britain. Invested with emergency powers, he also began to impose order on chaos. Harcourt stopped revenge killings, provided food relief, restored public services and breathed new life into the economy. In lieu of a police force, he employed seven hundred Chinese gangsters.

Hong Kong's position was still precarious when Sir Mark Young returned as Governor in 1946. So in addition to carrying out physical reconstruction he proposed political reform. Young advocated a kind of dyarchy, which would devolve control of local affairs to elected representatives of the people. This would, he hoped, meet the general desire of Hong Kong's "inhabitants to remain under British rule and to resist absorption by China."[99] Here was a real opportunity, in the turbulent aftermath of the war, to inject a democratic element into the constitution. But mandarins at the Colonial Office failed to grasp it, a fundamental "mistake."[100] Their reason, according to Young's successor Sir Alexander Grantham (Governor from 1947 to 1957), was that Hong Kong would inevitably be reabsorbed by China, almost certainly when the lease of the New Territories expired. The Kuomintang's Governor of Kwangtung Province, T. V. Soong, told Grantham personally that in due course China would "ask for Hong Kong back and we shall expect to get it."[101] There was no point in planting a democratic seed since it could not engender independence, as happened in other colonies. In fact, of course, Hong Kong might have enjoyed a measure of self-rule for half a century, good in itself and better than the last-minute token it received. But the British had another reason for maintaining the status quo. Any change might antagonise China's dictators, first Chiang Kai-shek and, after 1949, Mao Tse-tung. To be sure, voters in the United Kingdom "didn't care a brass farthing about Hong Kong."[102] But they would certainly have cared if it had been seized by China. While being reluctant to appease, therefore, London could not afford to provoke Peking. It did, indeed, send heavy reinforcements to deter the victorious Communist People's Liberation Army from crossing the border. To American delight, Grantham even talked of making Hong Kong "the Berlin of the East." But, as China-watchers repeated over the next twenty-five years, Mao could take city-state with a telephone call.

Under Grantham's auspices the colony experienced political and social stasis. He remained a benevolent despot, convinced that the Chinese were "politically apathetic." So long as they got law and order and low taxes, they were "content to leave the business of government to the professionals."[103] Actually, the Chinese had little scope for action and their Reform Association, which pressed for popular suffrage, "was kept under police surveillance."[104] Meanwhile, the Governor was much preoccupied with his decorative functions. He maintained in an interview that Hong Kong now "lacked the pomposity of the Taipan era," when "we juniors . . . always had to walk out backwards" from the presence of seniors.[105] Yet, as emerges from Grantham's smug memoir, published in 1965, he and his wife spent an unconscionable time fussing over the minutiae of their pygmy court.

> Fortunately we had a very good domestic staff, presided over by Ah Yau, the number 1 boy, a most admirable and kindly man. Even so, constant supervision was necessary . . . The cooks—three of them—had to be kept up to the mark. In the same way, the table boys, if not watched, might appear in grubby uniforms, or during lunch or dinner, stand around daydreaming, failing to notice that the water or wine glasses needed replenishing . . . It took eternal vigilance to maintain a high standard.

Grantham was especially exercised about correct seating plans and suitable arrangements for entertaining royalty. Having invited the Crown Prince of Iraq, who turned out to be aggressively anti-Semitic, the Governor felt obliged to tell another dinner guest, the Jewish film producer Michael

Todd, that for the evening he must "be a Scot or anything but a Jew."[106] Paying such nice attention to the proprieties, Grantham preserved Hong Kong society in aspic. A new civil servant, Austin Coates, who had been told to equip himself with a white, gold-braided, brass-buttoned uniform, aiguillettes, pith helmet and sword, concluded that Grantham's government was "still living in the Victorian era."

Yet when Coates arrived, in 1949, he was as much struck by the furious human energy inside the Hong Kong hive as by its ossified colonial carapace. Refugees from Communism thronged into its narrow confines, joining those who had fled from the Kuomintang and quickly increasing the population from two to three million. Coates recorded:

> All over the rocky hillsides near the urban area, tens of thousands of ramshackle little huts were sprouting day and night, built of packing cases, sacks, kerosene tins, linoleum, worn-out rubber tyres, anything anyone could lay their hands on, tied together with bits of wire, or even with rice straw.[107]

In the farming valleys of Kowloon entire shantytowns sprang up like mushrooms. Peasants, workers, beggars and wounded soldiers hobbled across the border, which was closed in May 1950. Simultaneously Rolls-Royces and Cadillacs arrived, their springs groaning under the weight of evacuated gold. Since 1945 Hong Kong had become, in effect, the last treaty port. And Shanghai, with all its professional skill, industrial drive and entrepreneurial flair, "transferred itself bodily there."[108] Labour and capital would combine to make Hong Kong's economy astoundingly progressive at a time when its colonial regime was increasingly obsolete. The contrast between new dynamism and old fogyism appalled some visitors and appealed to others. Amid the indigenous boom of the 1950s, Jan Morris noted, Britons habitually bullied Chinese—so abused them, indeed, that their English sometimes consisted entirely of such phrases as "'Fuck you,' 'bastard,' 'son of a bitch.'"[109] Ian Fleming, the creator of James Bond, exulted that Hong Kong was "the last stronghold of feudal luxury in the world."[110]

The Cold War was the making of Hong Kong. Nothing promoted its prosperity more than the trade embargo which the United Nations imposed on China as a result of its intervention in the Korean conflict in November 1950. It is true that the colony's role as an entrepôt, which had been boosted during the first months of the war, was damaged by the prohibitions. But contraband had always been the lifeblood of Hong Kong and significant supplies of strategic materials were smuggled into China, which earned nearly half its foreign revenue from sending exports through the free port. These were reduced to a trickle by the United States' total ban on commerce with China, imposed in order to stem what *Time* magazine called "the red tide that threatens to engulf the world."[111] American hysteria, aggravated by Senator Joseph McCarthy, manifested itself in Hong Kong in a frenetic investigation into exports to the United States (such as ducks, prawns and timber) which might have had Communist origins. However, such curbs had the inestimable benefit of stimulating diversification. Industry took the place of commerce as the engine of economic progress in Hong Kong. Textiles remained the staple. But now backroom factories produced toys, plastic goods, basic electronic equipment and other items. Growth was phenomenal: within fifteen years Hong Kong went from making a tenth to making three-quarters of its exports.

Rising profits depended on continuing stability and Hong Kong was fortunate that every interested party accepted that its status should not change for the moment. China, preoccupied with letting a hundred flowers bloom (1956), with taking the great leap forward (1958) and with unleashing the Cultural Revolution (1966), found it convenient to wait. The view of the Hong Kong Chinese was well expressed by one of their number on the Legislative Council: "Hong Kong is a lifeboat; China is the sea. Those who have climbed into the lifeboat naturally don't want to rock it."[112] The United States, which treated Hong Kong as part of its own informal empire, came to appreciate its worth as a centre for diplomacy, propaganda, journalism, espionage, rest and recreation, and duty-free shopping. For Britain Hong Kong was a political and strategic liability without being much of a financial asset. But the territory (as Hong Kong was now called, though the word "colony" remained on banknotes until 1985) was valuable in terms of prestige. Declining in the West, Britain relished its oriental eminence. Westminster and Whitehall preferred to keep Hong Kong than to lose face.

Despite its constitutional inertia, the territory became a showplace in which the colonial masters could take pride. Of course, it was embarrassing that the Chinese were excluded from top jobs in the civil service as well as from government and that they played little or no part in the direction of princely hongs such as Jardine, Matheson. It was also unpleasant to hear the charge that Hong Kong was the sweatshop of the world. Yet its authoritarian regime eventually managed to graft an embryonic welfare state on to a Victorian system of unbridled free enterprise. During the early 1950s, after fires at squatter camps left tens of thousands homeless, Grantham initiated an ambitious building programme. The first dwellings were "barrack-like hutments,"[113] with no amenities except communal kitchens and bathrooms—some tenants preferred to return to their cardboard boxes. But standards slowly improved and in forty years three million people were housed. Grantham's successor, Sir Robert Black, extolled the "wonderful partnership" between the British administrators and the local inhabitants. It was "a creative experience as far as I was concerned, and, without doubt an inspiration for the people of Hong Kong."[114]

Subsequent Governors could afford large investment in health, education, transport and other services. There was even legislation to improve working conditions in factories. In fact, the state did not hesitate to intervene. It arbitrarily detained or deported "trouble-makers." It banned films and prosecuted newspapers deemed to be seditious. It quelled disturbances that spilled over the border from China. It even tackled police corruption, though this was so endemic that the Governor concerned, Sir Murray Maclehose, issued an amnesty, confirming Chinese suspicions that he would "swat the flies, not catch the tigers."[115] After the rapprochement with China that followed President Richard Nixon's historic visit in 1972 and the American recognition of the People's Republic, the British even cooperated with Peking to stop the flow of illegal immigrants ("eye-eyes") into Hong Kong—though "snakeheads" (people smugglers) remained active. Earlier the Communists had portrayed the white imperialists as pigs and their Chinese collaborators as "yellow running dogs."[116] Now, when the British Foreign Secretary Sir Alec Douglas-Home followed in Nixon's footsteps, a military band in the Great Hall of the People played the Eton Boating Song.

Good relations partly stemmed from Peking's recognition, especially after the death of Mao in 1976, of how much China benefited from the stupendous money-making machine on its doorstep. Where the colonial economy was concerned, the British had allowed a virtual free-for-all. Regulation was conspicuous by its absence. Taxation and public expenditure were kept to a minimum. Wages found their own level and profits soared. In the two decades after 1960 Hong Kong's gross national product increased at nearly 10 per cent a year in real terms. By the 1980s Hong Kong was China's biggest trading partner and provided 70 per cent of its foreign investment. It exported more than China and four times as much as India. But it also moved many factories to Kwangtung province, where labour was cheap, transforming the local economy. Meanwhile, it developed a financial and services sector to rival those in the West. Oriental tycoons multiplied, threatening the dominance of occidental taipans. For example, the shipping magnate Sir Y. K. Pao, who started as a trader in duck feathers and bean curd, took over those quintessential colonial institutions, the Peak Tram, the Lane Crawford department store ("the Harrods of the East"), and Star Ferries, whose snub-nosed, green-and-white vessels linked the island to the mainland. The growing opulence of Hong Kong was reflected in its tumescent architecture, which glowed in the city's "neon orgasm."[117] With incontinent speed towers of glass and concrete thrust themselves heavenwards, only to be superseded by yet more virile erections. Even the Hong Kong Club became upwardly mobile, sacrificing its Mughal palace to a high-rise monolith. That size did matter was illustrated by the Bank of China's steely, angular skyscraper, which was designed not only to direct emanations of bad feng shui towards Government House but to overshadow the Hongkong and Shanghai Bank. The British lions in front of the "Honkers and Shaggers" were reclining; the white stone lions flanking the Bank of China, modelled on those in the Forbidden City, were rampant.

No one could mistake the symbolism. China was in the ascendant. It could beat the capitalists at their own game. Hong Kong, if properly handled, would suit Chinese economic purposes just as well, if not better, under the control of Peking. Politically, the restoration of sovereignty was essential to the self-respect of the motherland. Arguing from analogy, Whitehall officials had long recognised this. If Chinese invaders had turned the Isle of Wight into a pagoda-covered "heaven on earth," they said, Britain would still "want it back."[118] For China itself the recovery of Hong Kong was a "sacred mission."[119] Nothing else could purge the unbearable hurt and shame that the nation had suffered at the hands of the barbarous imperialists. Nothing else could allay what pro-Chinese demonstrators in Hong Kong called "the agony of our ancestors."[120] One experienced journalist even perceived a "thinly disguised desire on the part of the Chinese leaders to humiliate Britain in some way in order to wipe clean the sheet of the 19th century."[121] It would surely be poetic justice for renascent China to impose on Britain, at its last gasp as a colonial power, an unequal treaty.

This was hardly what Margaret Thatcher had in mind when she visited Peking in September 1982 to decide the future of Hong Kong. Buoyed up with the afflatus of victory over Argentinians, she was in no mood to be dictated to by "Chinamen"—a term she was eventually persuaded to drop. Indeed, she saw distinct similarities between the Falkland Islands and Hong Kong. Both were distant colonies threatened by neighbouring totalitarian states. Britain's claim to both was sound yet in both cases the Foreign Office canvassed "ideas for pre-emptive surrender." The Prime Minister bitterly attacked defeatism over Hong Kong. Against appeasing diplomats such as Sir Percy Cradock, the British ambassador in Peking, she conducted "a species of guerrilla warfare." She even hankered to hold Hong Kong by force, until convinced that China was not Argentina and that the island was "militarily indefensible."[122] Without the New Territories, which comprised 92 per cent of the colony, it was also untenable. So the Iron Lady confronted Chinese leaders with this proposal: parliament would give up sovereignty over Hong Kong in return for a continuing British administration that would preserve its prosperity. "The Quite Honourable Margaret Thatcher," as the interpreter called her, was repelled by the evident cruelty of Deng Xiaoping. Deaf, squat and having the glazed look of a Chinese figurine, he smoked, hawked and made copious use of a white enamel spittoon. But she held her ground, even insisting on the validity of the Victorian treaties. Deng was so outraged that what he said could not be translated, his most printable remark being that he couldn't talk to this "stinking woman." Suffering from a head cold and having failed to budge Deng, the Prime Minister tripped on the steps as she left the Great Hall of the People and fell on her hands and knees. Unkind Chinese journalists said that at last she had decided to kowtow.

They were wrong. Although Mrs. Thatcher had insisted on secret covenants secretly arrived at, she herself resorted to megaphone diplomacy. At a press conference in Hong Kong she repeated her faith in the sanctity of the "unequal treaties," remarking pointedly that a country which would not stand by one treaty might not stand by another. Peking reacted fiercely, excoriating aggressive British imperialism. Fears of a clash sent the Hang Sen stock market index down by 25 per cent inside a week. Property prices tumbled and the Hong Kong dollar began a slide in value that only stopped when it was pegged to the American greenback in 1983. *The Times*'s correspondent, David Bonavia, declared: "Seldom in British colonial history was so much damage done to the interests of so many people, in such a short space of time by a single person."[123] But all Margaret Thatcher had really done was to make negotiations over the inevitable handover of Hong Kong more difficult and protracted. She continued to chafe, suggesting the creation of democratic structures in Hong Kong and the holding of a UN-supervised referendum with a view to granting the colony independence. Soon, though, as Sir Geoffrey Howe observed, logic overcame emotion. Despite further wobbles, she now "contended that a deal *had* to be sought because the Chinese would get everything they wanted anyway in 1997."[124]

Sir Percy Cradock, the champion of this analysis, was detailed to reach a settlement. He made no progress. Indeed, he likened his discussions with the "tough and unyielding" Chinese to trudging through mud "on the Western Front"—scarcely an apt analogy. More apt was the showing of a new film in Peking entitled *The Burning of the Summer Palace*, which focused less on the barbarity of the Europeans than on the humiliation of the Chinese. Eventually the ambassador, who found his experiences in China comparable to those of Lord Macartney in the eighteenth century, had to give way on the key questions of continuing British sovereignty and administration. Being such a skilled diplomat, Cradock disguised each retreat as a "finesse."[125] He saved face but he could not save his case. As one Hong Kong politician put it, British negotiators could only "rearrange the cards in the Chinese hand: for they hold them all."[126] Nevertheless, the agreement that Howe clinched in 1984 was surprisingly favourable. Once inside the belly of the Communist dragon, Hong Kong would not be digested. For at least fifty years after 1997 it would retain its capitalist identity. Except in matters of defence and foreign policy, it would have a high degree of autonomy. It would have an elected legislature to which the executive would be responsible, though there was ambiguity about how this machinery would work. Hong Kong would keep its way of life, its educational system, its laws, its own currency and rate of taxation. There would be no interference with freedom of speech or assembly. There would be no censorship of the press. The new Special Administrative Region would even have its own flag. In short, it would embody Deng's long-standing formula: "one country, two systems." That concept, Margaret Thatcher told him when she returned to Peking in December 1984 to sign the Joint Declaration, was a "stroke of genius."[127]

The people of Hong Kong, in whose interest Mrs. Thatcher professed to act, were not informed, let alone consulted, about the Sino-British accord. Opinion polls revealed that they would have preferred to retain the status quo. But, accepting that the handover was inescapable, they welcomed its terms. Stability and prosperity seemed assured. There was not even much resentment about that consummate piece of parliamentary humbug, the British Dependent Territories passport. This identified Hong Kong citizens as overseas British Nationals without giving them the right to live in the United Kingdom *or* in Hong Kong. The optimistic mood was sustained in 1986, when Queen Elizabeth became the first British sovereign to make a state visit to mainland China. The Duke of Edinburgh punctuated the tour with characteristic gaffes. Not only did he harrumph about the pollution caused by Chinese factories but he remarked, when meeting an English student on a protracted visit: "Good heavens, if you stay here much longer you'll develop slitty eyes."[128] But when Howe formally apologised the Chinese made nothing of the insult, which anticipated a more considered royal contribution to Sino-British relations. This was Prince Charles's unhappy valediction to Hong Kong. Distributed to friends and inevitably leaked to the press, his account described the Chinese leaders as "appalling old wax-works."[129]

However, in the later 1980s there were already underlying tensions between London and Peking. Deng regarded Margaret Thatcher's claim to feel a moral responsibility for the people of Hong Kong as both impertinent and disingenuous. In his view the imperialists had always been intent on exploitation and he feared that before 1997 they would suck Hong Kong dry. "Watch those British," he said, "lest they abscond with the capital."[130] Britain in turn distrusted China, which posed in an insoluble form the most acute problem of decolonisation: how to prevent the imperialist hegemony from lapsing into a nationalist autocracy. Before they left other colonies the British tried to lay the foundations of democracy. In Hong Kong they had barely begun and could scarcely proceed without obstruction from the Red Empire. The first election to the Legislative Council only took place in 1985 and a mere seventy thousand citizens (out of a population of nearly six million) had the vote. When liberals in the territory campaigned for wider, speedier and more direct suffrage, they provoked opposition from nervous capitalists in Hong Kong as well as hard-line Communists in Peking. Deng stated flatly, "We cannot accept people who want to use democracy to turn Hong Kong into an anti-communist base."[131] Anxious to ride towards the "convergence" of their systems aboard a "through train," the British capitulated and dissimulated. They secretly agreed to postpone further constitutional changes and conducted a fraudulent opinion survey to confirm that this was what the Hong Kong Chinese wanted. In fact, they wanted the opposite. One million of them proved this point when they took to the streets in the spring of 1989 to protest at the massacre of hundreds of pro-democracy demonstrators in Peking's Tiananmen Square.

No one was more appalled by this atrocity than Margaret Thatcher. According to her friend Woodrow Wyatt, what she was "most excited about is how we can hand over Hong Kong at all to these dreadful people who do these awful things to their own subjects."[132] Her response was to force through legislation permitting fifty thousand of the colony's top administrators and businessmen to settle in the United Kingdom. Right-wing Tories opposed the measure. But the new Foreign Secretary, Douglas Hurd, asserted convincingly that "the last main chapter in the story of this country's empire . . . should not end in a shabby way."[133] Of course, there were limits to British generosity. And the Prime Minister accepted that the only way to protect most Hong Kong people was through cooperation with China. Thus Britain did not repudiate the Joint Declaration. Indeed, Hurd exchanged confidential letters with the Chinese, enabling them to codify it into a Basic Law, promulgated in 1990. In particular, he agreed that Hong Kong should receive only gradual accretions of democracy; there would be eighteen directly elected members of the Legislative Council in 1991, twenty in 1997 and thirty (half the total) in 2003. By a disastrous oversight the last Governor was not told of this accord. Appointed by the new Prime Minister, his friend John Major, Chris Patten was a successful ex-minister and Chairman of the Conservative Party who had lost his seat in the 1992 general election he did much to win. Patten was dynamic, forthright, charming, humorous and magnanimous. He felt a generous compulsion to shield the inhabitants of Hong Kong from the so-called "butchers of Beijing." He would calm the colony's fears and meet its hopes by a swifter extension of the franchise and a deeper entrenchment of human rights. Backed by Major and Hurd (who had changed course in deference to the Prime Minister), Patten announced his plans without consulting the Chinese leaders. Yet he himself correctly predicted their reaction. "I think some of them suspect that, having come to democracy rather late in Hong Kong, we're trying to construct some democratic time bomb to blow their system to smithereens." They retaliated in the Maoist manner, denouncing Patten as a "serpent," "assassin," "clown," "dirty trickster," "tango dancer," "strutting prostitute" and "Triple Violator."[134]

British critics, especially Old China Hands, were equally insulting in their way. Sir Percy Cradock, who condemned his "dangerous and reckless policy,"[135] said that Patten was "on an ego trip." He was striking "a heroic pose"[136] and salving his conscience at the expense of the inhabitants of Hong Kong. Doubtless the last Governor had purer motives for attempting to make his mark. An ardent champion of the Westminster system, he was attempting to compensate for Britain's past constitutional failure and to satisfy the aspirations of people facing engorgement by a tyranny red in tooth and claw. But Patten, who had no experience of China, misjudged the situation. He did not comprehend how the collapse of Communism in Europe had exacerbated paranoia in Peking. Nor did he appreciate Chinese bitterness over what appeared to be the ultimate piece of imperialist chicanery. The Deputy Prime Minister, Michael Heseltine, who drummed up trade in China, was not alone among Patten's colleagues in recognising this.

> How could one expect the Chinese to accept such a unilateral approach so shortly before 1997? We had governed Hong Kong for long enough to introduce a democratic constitution if we had believed it necessary or desirable. Perhaps it was to our discredit that we did not, but deathbed repentance,

however genuine, looked very different when viewed from Beijing . . . [The reason for this last-minute change of heart] could only be that we wished to create restraints for the mainland government which we had not suffered under ourselves.[137]

Chinese suspicions were understandable since British hypocrisy over Hong Kong dated back to the Opium Wars. Now Patten seemed to be making a parade of liberalism in order to embarrass, or even to subvert, Communism. He would thus assuage his country's guilt for the sins of colonialism and contrive an honourable exit.

The Chinese had real grounds for doubting Patten's sincerity. Although eschewing the ceremonial uniform and "chicken feathers"[138] of previous Governors, he proved to be no less masterful. He ruthlessly overruled his Legislative Council. And in a belated effort to conciliate Peking he not only banned anti-Communist dissidents from Hong Kong but opposed the establishment of a Human Rights Commission. Moreover, his propaganda was accomplished and his policy was chimerical. Patten conjured up a glittering illusion of democracy that could not be realised. After seventeen futile rounds of negotiation, he introduced new representative structures in 1994 and just three years later the Chinese fulfilled their promise to dismantle them. During this time Patten did achieve agreement over important matters such as the construction of a new airport. But the political sterility of his governorship became ever more apparent as the seconds ticked away on the electronic signboard in Tiananmen Square indicating that China's sovereignty was just a matter of time. The hard-headed Cradock had been right in saying that Britain's only chance (and it *was* only a chance) of safeguarding the people of Hong Kong was to cooperate with China over implementing the Joint Declaration. The high-minded Patten chose confrontation. But the Chinese had no reason to give ground. The British Empire—weak even in its prime, though more than a match for the decadent Manchus—was now moribund. It might persuade but it could not compel. In 1997, therefore, China subordinated Hong Kong to the political control of Peking while encouraging it to forge its own identity as an economic unit. It was almost as though the new Chinese leader, Jiang Zemin, had devised a fresh formula: one system, two countries.

So the curtain was rung down and the lights were extinguished in the great theatre of the British Empire. The grand finale took place on 30 June 1997. The ceremony was staged at the new Convention and Exhibition Centre, nicknamed "the Flying Cockroach."[139] According to *The Times*, it was "lifted unchanged from every retreat-from-empire textbook."[140] Others saw it as a carnival of kitsch. There were choirs and orchestras, parades and masquerades, orations, gyrations and pyrotechnics. The spectacular did not dispel the atmosphere of apprehension in Hong Kong, especially among demonstrators for democracy, though even its doom provided a marketing opportunity—hawkers sold a "Handover Beer" called Red Dawn Lager, T-shirts proclaiming "The Great Chinese Takeaway," and spray cans of "colonial air" said to be "The Last Gasp of Empire." The British mood, already lachrymose, was further dampened by the monsoon—loyalists said that the heavens wept. Patten certainly did, biting his lip and wiping away his tears with a handkerchief. He tried, though, to strike a positive note in his farewell address. Britain had provided, he claimed, "the scaffolding that enabled the people of Hong Kong to ascend; the rule of law, clean and light-handed government, the values of a free society."[141] He shook hands stiffly with Jiang Zemin. But it was plain that the Chinese, who had boycotted the earlier banquet, still considered him "the last colonial aggressor." Faced with massed ranks of Communists, Margaret Thatcher looked "fierce and unforgiving."[142] Bored by a drama ending in anti-climax, her husband stifled yawns. The white-uniformed Prince of Wales, who made an anodyne speech on behalf of his mother, privately deplored the "ridiculous rigmarole" and "awful Soviet-style display" of goose-stepping Chinese troops. He also disliked Jiang Zemin's "'propaganda' speech which was loudly cheered by the bussed-in party faithful."[143] At the stroke of midnight, as the Union Jack was lowered and the yellow-star flag was raised, the Hong Kong police ripped the royal insignia from their uniforms and replaced them with the badges of Communism. The Governor's party embarked on *Britannia,* where a band of the Royal Marines played "Rule, Britannia" and "Land of Hope and Glory." The royal yacht, now looking old and frail, set off on its final voyage. To most Britons it was the "symbol of a vanished age."[144] But to Prince Charles it was a beloved emblem of British prestige. Its demise, which compounded the loss of "the last jewel in the British Crown"[145] and the dissolution of the imperial monarchy, filled him with "a kind of exasperated sadness."[146]

Britannia faded into the gloom a hundred years to the week after Queen Victoria's Diamond Jubilee. At that imperial apogee, as many deemed it, Kipling had warned of Britain's faltering dominion over palm and pine while urging Americans to take up the white man's burden. Reflecting on the fact that the British Empire had now passed away (except for a sprinkling of rocks and islands containing fewer than 200,000 people), whereas the United States had become the heir to Rome, the *New York Times* quoted Kipling's famous lines:

> Lo, all our pomp of yesterday
> Is one with Nineveh and Tyre!

Epitaphs and obituaries multiplied. For some commentators the handover of Hong Kong, with £37 billion in reserves and inhabitants who were richer per capita than those of the United Kingdom, was a crowning vindication of Britain's colonial stewardship. Others thought that no end to the Empire could be more fitting than the sanctimonious consignment of six million people to the mercies of the most monstrous despotism on earth. Immediate historical judgements varied in their emphasis, as did later ones. Some were coloured by nostalgia for imperial glories; others were infused with indignation about imperial crimes. Still others reflected the impact of the Empire on post-war British society. Opinions clashed, for example, about Commonwealth immigration. Liberals such as Ralph Dahrendorf believed that modern Britain, "like ancient Rome," was enriched by transfusions of new blood. But many opposed the alien influx and quite a few shared Enoch Powell's vision of the "Tiber foaming with much blood."[147]

Some instant historians ascribed much to the credit of the British Empire: roads, railways, culture, language, free speech, good governance, democratic institutions, the rule of law, sport and the ideal of fair play, faith in progress, liberalism and Christianity. Its relatively bloodless end amounted to "a triumph for all that was best in British life."[148] According to one pundit, the British Empire had been "a force for good unrivalled in the modern world."[149] Western Europe lived on the legacy of Rome, he said, and "our Empire leaves at least as rich a legacy to the whole world." Critics reckoned that the balance sheet of Empire was deeply in the red. On the debit side were arrogance, violence, exploitation, jingoism, racism and authoritarianism. At its heart was a betrayal of the civilised values which the British claimed to espouse. They had professed *libertas* but practised *imperium,* subjugating alien lands in the name of freedom. In the words of a disapproving journalist, "much of the world, including Hong Kong, will remember us as perfidious Albion, an inheritance of Empire that will outlive all of us."[150] No doubt hypocrisy was integral to the British Empire, which deployed fine words to hide its ultimate reliance on coercion. Whereas a "torrent of Barbarians might pass over the earth," as Gibbon said, "an extensive empire must be supported by a refined system of policy and oppression." At any rate, one thing was sure. The British system, after more than two centuries, was defunct.

It had been the product of temporary circumstances that occurred after the loss of the American colonies—the supremacy of the Royal Navy, the establishment of the workshop of the world and the relative weakness of rival states. When these circumstances changed, the Empire, which anyway had within it the germ of its own destruction in the shape of Burke's libertarian commitment to trusteeship, was doomed. Its passing was good for the newly independent nations since, to repeat Gibbon's essential argument, there is nothing "more adverse to nature and reason than to hold in obedience remote countries and foreign nations, in opposition to their inclination and interest."[151] It was also good for Britain, which lacked the strength to carry out its overseas responsibilities after 1945 and needed to adapt to its reduced global position. Yet in Britain and elsewhere round the earth, empire is more than just a romantic memory. It is the embodiment of real ambitions. Nations ache for territorial aggrandisement. The craving for power and wealth is an atavistic instinct. The lust for conquest is part of the human condition. The spirit of imperialism is not dead: it haunts the modern world and its manifestations are legion.

ABBREVIATIONS USED IN THE NOTES

AA	*African Affairs*
AfHS	*African Historical Studies*
AHR	*American Historical Review*
AHS	*Australian Historical Studies*
BDEEP	*British Documents on the End of Empire Project*
BIHR	*Bulletin of the Institute of Historical Research*
CBH	*Contemporary British History*
CHA	*The Cambridge History of Africa* 8 vols. (Cambridge, 1975–86), edited by J. D. Fage and R. Oliver
CHBE	*The Cambridge History of the British Empire* 8 vols. (Cambridge, 1925–59), edited by J. Holland Rose, A. P. Newton and E. A. Benians
CHI	*The Cambridge History of India* 6 vols. (Cambridge, 1922–32), edited by E. J. Rapson et al.
CHJ	*Ceylon Historical Journal*
CJHSS	*Ceylon Journal of Historical and Social Studies*
CQ	*China Quarterly*
CSJ	*Commonwealth Society Journal*
CSSH	*Comparative Studies in Society and History*
DNB	*Dictionary of National Biography*
EAH	*East Asian History*
EconHR	*Economic History Review*
EEH	*Explorations in Economic History*
EHR	*English Historical Review*
HJ	*Historical Journal*
HMC	Historical Manuscripts Commission
HRNSW	*Historical Records of New South Wales*
HSANZ	*Historical Studies Australia and New Zealand*
HT	*History Today*
IA	*International Affairs*
IndHR	*Indian Historical Review*
IJAHS	*International Journal of African Historical Studies*
IHS	*Irish Historical Studies*
JAH	*Journal of African History*
JBS	*Journal of British Studies*
JCH	*Journal of Contemporary History*
JEH	*Journal of Economic History*
JHSN	*Journal of the Historical Society of Nigeria*
JICH	*Journal of Imperial and Commonwealth History*
JMAS	*Journal of Modern African Studies*
JMH	*Journal of Modern History*
JPS	*Journal of Palestine Studies*
JRAS	*Journal of the Royal African Society*
JSeAS	*Journal of Southeast Asian Studies*
JSAS	*Journal of Southern African Studies*
LRB	*London Review of Books*

MAS	*Modern Asian Studies*
MES	*Middle Eastern Studies*
NZJH	*The New Zealand Journal of History*
ODNB	*Oxford Dictionary of National Biography*
OHBE	*The Oxford History of the British Empire* 5 vols. (Oxford 1998–9), edited by W. R. Louis
PA	*Pacific Affairs*
PP	*Past and Present*
SA	*South Asia*
SAHJ	*South African Historical Journal*
SWJN	*Selected Works of Jawaharlal Nehru* 15 vols. (Delhi, 1972–82), edited by S. Gopal
TOPI	*The Transfer of Power 1942–7* 12 vols. (1970–83), edited by N. Mansergh et al.

NOTES

Introduction

The place of publication is London unless otherwise stated.

1. J. W. Burrow, *Gibbon* (Oxford, 1985), 3.
2. G. A. Bonnard (ed.), *Edward Gibbon: Memoirs of My Life* (1960), 3.
3. F. M. Turner, *Contrasting Cultural History* (1993), 248.
4. E. Gibbon, *The History of the Decline and Fall of the Roman Empire*, III, ed. D. Womersley (Harmondsworth, 1994 edn), 139. I cite this edition throughout because of its excellence and availability.
5. L. S. Amery, *The Forward View* (1935), 434.
6. S. Freud, "Civilisation and Its Discontents," in J. Strachey (ed.), *The Complete Psychological Works of Sigmund Freud*, XXI (1981 edn), 70.
7. C. Edwards, *Roman Presences: Receptions of Rome in European Cultures, 1789–1945* (Cambridge, 1999), 224.
8. A. Quiller-Couch, *On the Art of Writing* (Fowey, 1995 edn), 25. Appointed Professor of English at Cambridge University in 1912, "Q" made this assertion in his inaugural lecture.
9. J. A. Froude, *Caesar* (1879), 1.
10. J. Bryce, *The Ancient Roman Empire and the British Empire in India* (1914), 54.
11. C. Lucas, *Greater Rome and Greater Britain* (1912), 154.
12. Gibbon, *Decline and Fall*, II, 186.
13. Lord Cromer, *Ancient and Modern Imperialism* (1910), 74.
14. R. Symonds, *Oxford and Empire* (1986), 33.
15. *Edinburgh Review*, 135 (1872), 307.
16. J. West, *History of Tasmania*, II (1852), 347.
17. A. Sampson, *Macmillan: A Study in Ambiguity* (1967), 137.
18. *ODNB*.
19. Gibbon, *Decline and Fall*, III, 652.
20. N. Mansergh, *The Commonwealth Experience* (1969), 158.
21. *The Times*, 21 November 1942.
22. S. Walpole, *A History of England*, V (1886), 146.
23. P. Craddock (ed.), *Gibbon's English Essays* (Oxford, 1972), 507.
24. R. Porter, *Gibbon Making History* (1995 edn), 124. Jacob Burckhardt also described a philosophy of history as a centaur.
25. R. McKitterick and R. Quinault (eds), *Edward Gibbon and Empire* (Cambridge, 1997), 296.
26. Gibbon, *Decline and Fall*, II, 666.
27. J. Morris, *The Spectacle of Empire* (1982), 95.

1. The World Turned Upside Down

1. H. P. Johnston, *The Yorktown Campaign and the Surrender of Cornwallis, 1781* (1881), 167.
2. D. Jackson (ed.), *The Diaries of George Washington*, III (Charlottesville, VA, 1978), 432.
3. J. Bowle, *The Imperial Achievement* (1974 edn), 158.
4. E. Wright (ed.), *The Fire of Liberty* (1984), 236.
5. D. S. Freeman, *George Washington*, V (1952), 388. The story is suspiciously apt but it does seem likely that this popular contemporary tune was among those played.
6. J. C. Fitzpatrick (ed.), *The Writings of George Washington*, 6 (Washington, DC, 1931–44), 111.

7. B. Mitchell, *The Price of Independence* (New York, 1974), 118.

8. R. Harvey, *A Few Bloody Noses* (2001), 306.

9. R. W. Clark, *Benjamin Franklin* (1983), 270. The phrase was Emerson's.

10. Harvey, *Bloody Noses,* 156.

11. *CHBE,* I, 704.

12. PRO 30/11/68/11-13, Cornwallis Papers, Clinton to Cornwallis, 2 March 1781.

13. P. Toynbee (ed.), *The Letters of Horace Walpole,* XII (Oxford, 1904), 176.

14. Wright (ed.), *Fire of Liberty,* 178.

15. Fitzpatrick (ed.), *Writings of George Washington,* 21, 439.

16. T. J. Fleming, *Beat the Last Drum* (New York, 1963), 138.

17. M. Cunliffe, *George Washington* (1959), 99.

18. H. S. Commager and R. B. Morris (eds), *The Spirit of 'Seventy-Six* (1967 edn), 1219.

19. Johnston, *Yorktown Campaign,* 95.

20. J. C. Dann (ed.), *The Revolution Remembered* (Chicago, 1980), 240.

21. PRO 30/11/68/11-13, Clinton to Cornwallis, 30 September 1781.

22. N. A. M. Rodger, *The Insatiable Earl* (1993), 164. Rodger's scholarly defence of Sandwich is not altogether convincing.

23. *CHBE,* I, 742.

24. Toynbee (ed.), *Letters of Walpole,* X, 240.

25. N. W. Wraxall, *Historical Memoirs of My Own Time* (1904 edn), 398.

26. P. J. Marshall, "Burke and Empire," in S. Taylor et al. (eds), *Hanoverian Britain and Empire* (Woodbridge, 1998), 290.

27. V. T. Harlow, *The Founding of the Second British Empire 1763–1793,* I (1952), 227.

28. Lord Fitzmaurice, *Life of William, Earl of Shelburne,* II (1912), 83.

29. A. Calder, *Revolutionary Empire: The Rise of the English-Speaking Empire from the Fifteenth Century to the 1780s* (1981), 172.

30. Harlow, *Second British Empire,* I, 158.

31. J. C. Miller, *Origins of the American Revolution* (Boston, 1943), 33.

32. *CHBE,* I, 625.

33. R. Hofstadter, *Great Issues in American History* (New York, 1959), 61.

34. L. H. Gipson, *The British Empire Before the American Revolution,* XIII (New York, 1967), 204.

35. *CHBE,* I, 763.

36. R. R. Palmer, *The Age of Democratic Revolution,* I (Princeton, NJ, 1959), 190.

37. A. Pagden, "The Struggle for Legitimacy and the Image of the Empire in the Atlantic to c. 1700," in *OHBE,* I, 54.

38. P. Burke, "Tradition and Experience: The Idea of Decline from Bruno to Gibbon," in G. W. Bowerstock, J. Clive and S. R. Grauberd (eds), *Edward Gibbon and the Decline and Fall of the Roman Empire* (1977), 95.

39. F. Bacon, "Of Plantations," in *Essays* (1903 edn), 139. T. Hobbes, *Leviathan* (Oxford, 1960 edn), 161.

40. A. A. Luce and T. E. Jessop (eds), *The Works of George Berkeley Bishop of Cloyne,* VI (1955), 373. Cf. R. Koebner, *Empire* (Cambridge, 1961), 96, where Berkeley's line is said to be utopian rather than predictive, and a counter to Matthew Prior's complacent view that Britannia was fulfilling the prophecy that "Arts and Empire learn to travel West." Whatever Berkeley's intention, he seemed to validate the classic pattern of empire's occidental movement.

41. R. Dixon, *The Course of Empire* (Melbourne, 1986), 104.

42. L. Baritz, "The Idea of the West," *AHR* 66 (April 1961), 640.

43. B. Bailyn, *Voyagers to the West* (New York, 1987), 41.

44. Toynbee (ed.), *Letters of Walpole*, IX, 100–101.

45. Gibbon justified Sixtus V's use of the stones of the Septizonium in "the glorious edifice of St. Peter's," though what he thought of the Pope's crowning Trajan's Column with a statue of the saint is not recorded. (P. B. Craddock, "Edward Gibbon and the 'Ruins of the Capitol,'" in A. Patterson [ed.], *Roman Images* [Baltimore, 1984], passim.)

46. Gibbon, *Decline and Fall*, III, 1063. This is the phrase of the Renaissance scholar Poggio but on his Grand Tour in 1765 Boswell was shocked to find that parts of the Colosseum were "full of dung," though so inspired by the grandeur of the Roman remains that he "began to speak in Latin." (F. Brady and F. A. Pottle, *Boswell on Grand Tour: Italy, Corsica, France, 1765–1766* [1955], 61–2.)

47. Gibbon, *Decline and Fall*, III, 1073.

48. A. J. Toynbee, *A Study in History*, IX (1954), 426. Toynbee's animus doubtless stemmed from the fact that he perceived rhythms in history whereas, as Gibbon showed, human beings and all their works were subject to "the vicissitudes of fortune." (*Decline and Fall*, III, 1062.)

49. Gibbon, *Decline and Fall*, II, 512.

50. Ibid., 356.

51. E. H. Gould, "American Independence and Britain's Counter-Revolution," *PP*, 154 (February 1997), 114.

52. Toynbee (ed.), *Letters of Walpole*, XII, 73.

53. P. B. Craddock, *Edward Gibbon, Luminous Historian 1772–1794* (1989), 97.

54. Koebner, *Empire*, 111.

55. Wraxall, *Memoirs*, 388.

56. J. Fortescue (ed.), *The Correspondence of King George the Third*, IV (1928), 351.

57. B. W. Tuchman, *The March of Folly* (1984), 219.

58. R. Coupland, *The American Revolution and the British Empire* (1930), 149.

59. T. Pocock, *Horatio Nelson* (1987), 72.

60. H. T. Manning, *British Colonial Government After the American Revolution 1782–1820* (1933), 290. Fox seems to say that the phrase was "emphatically stiled" by Henry Dundas (*Parliamentary History*, XXII, col. 1285). William Cowper applied the same image to the thirteen colonies and William Beckford applied it to Jamaica.

61. C. C. O'Brien, *The Great Melody: A Thematic Biography and Commented Anthology of Edmund Burke* (1992), 329.

62. R. E. Prothero (ed.), *Private Letters of Edward Gibbon*, II (1896), 251.

63. *Edinburgh Review*, II (1803), 32–3.

64. Bonnard (ed.), *Gibbon: Memoirs*, 192.

65. A. Smith, *An Inquiry Into the Nature and Causes of the Wealth of Nations* (Chicago, 1952 edn), 256, 266 and 270.

66. J. Ross (ed.), *Contemporary Responses to Adam Smith* (Bristol, 1998), xiii.

67. *DNB*. Cf. C. Hobhouse, *Fox* (1964 edn), 227 and 168, where it is said that Fox did read Smith but despised political economy as "abracadabra."

68. J. Bowring (ed.), *The Works of Jeremy Bentham*, IV (1843), 417. Bentham wrote these words in 1793, urging the French to make "the declaration of rights your guide." He added a curious postscript in 1829, saying that as a British citizen he stuck by his opinions but that as a citizen of the British Empire he had reversed them. In part this seems to have been because he expected that the Australian settlements would emancipate themselves from the Crown before the end of the century and become "a representative democracy."

69. H. M. Scott, *British Foreign Policy in the Age of the American Revolution* (Oxford, 1990), 339.

70. D. B. Davis, *The Problem of Slavery in the Age of Revolution 1770–1823* (1975), 175.

71. B. Bailyn, *The Ideological Origins of the American Revolution* (Cambridge, MA, 1971), 240.

72. Smith, *Wealth of Nations*, 254.

73. Harvey, *Bloody Noses,* 184.
74. T. Clarkson, *The History . . . of the Abolition of the African Slave Trade,* I (1968 edn), 95.
75. Gould in *Past and Present* (February 1997), 137.
76. Koebner, *Empire,* 225.
77. W. E. H. Lecky, *A History of England in the Eighteenth Century,* VII (1892), 362.
78. S. Mintz, *Sweetness and Power* (1985), 120, quoting E. Ayrton, *The Cookery of England* (1974), 429–30.
79. G. F. Dow, *Slave Ships and Slaving* (New York, 1970 edn), 92.
80. M. Daunton, "Britain's Imperial Economy," *JEH,* 61, no. 2 (June 2001), 479.
81. J. Newton, *Thoughts upon the African Slave Trade* (1788), 1.
82. Mortality rates on the Middle Passage fell to about 10 per cent during the eighteenth century, similar to those of convict ships, which improved their own record dramatically (to under 1 per cent) by the 1820s. For a recent statistical analysis see H. S. Klein, *The African Slave Trade* (Cambridge, 1999), 136ff.
83. J. H. Parry, P. M. Sherlock and A. P. Maingot, *A Short History of the West Indies* (1987), 88.
84. Baron Dupin, *The Commercial Power of Great Britain,* II (1825), 271.
85. J. W. Krutch, *Samuel Johnson* (New York, 1963 edn), 243.
86. Klein, *Slave Trade,* 214.
87. R. Anstey, *The Atlantic Slave Trade and British Abolition, 1760–1810* (1975), 31. Anstey says that contemporaries accepted the necessity of what would "certainly now be, and possibly then was, regarded as brutal." But while guarding against anachronistic judgements about the ethics of the slave trade, he surely discounts the moral sensibilities of what was an age of faith as well as an age of reason.
88. Dow, *Slave Ships,* 156.
89. J. Conrad, *Heart of Darkness* (1995 edn), 69.
90. M. Park, *Travels in the Interior of Africa* (1984 edn), xv.
91. R. Law, "Human Sacrifice in Pre-Colonial West Africa," *AA,* 84 (January 1985), 55, 67 and passim.
92. R. Law, "'My Head belongs to the King': On the Political and Ritual Significance of Decapitation in Pre-Colonial Dahomey," *JAH,* 30 (1989), 406. Contemplating the blood shed to propitiate the gods of Egypt, Rome and Carthage, Gibbon wrote: "The life of a man is the most precious oblation to deprecate a public calamity." (Gibbon, *Decline and Fall,* III, 169.)
93. A. W. Lawrence, *Fortified Trade-Posts* (1963), 166.
94. H. Thomas, *The Slave Trade* (1998 edn), 354.
95. M. Perham, *Lugard: The Years of Adventure 1858–1898* (1956), 497.
96. J. Matthews, *A Voyage to the River Sierra-Leone* (1791), 4.
97. Dow, *Slave Ships,* 251.
98. *Abstract of Evidence delivered before a select committee of the House of Commons . . . for the Abolition of the Slave Trade* (1791), 52.
99. F. Cundall (ed.), *Lady Nugent's Journal* (1934), 132.
100. Edwards, *West Indies,* IV, 312.
101. E. Long, *The History of Jamaica,* II (1970 edn), 354, 352 and 365. The identification of Africans with orang-utans, proposed by Jefferson among others, was refuted in *The European Magazine & London Review,* XIII (1788), 75ff.
102. Dow, *Slave Ships,* 61.
103. A. Benezet, *Some Historical Account of Guinea* (1788), 9 and 101.
104. Matthews, *Sierra-Leone,* 152.
105. Edwards, *West Indies,* II, 150.
106. P. D. Curtin, *Africa Remembered* (1967), 92.
107. *Abstract . . . of the Slave Trade,* 35.

108. A. Falconbridge, *An Account of the Slave Trade* (1788), 29 and 46.
109. Newton, *Slave Trade,* 11 and 20.
110. Dow, *Slave Ships,* 241.
111. R. Gray (ed.), *CHA,* IV, 606.
112. Falconbridge, *Slave Trade,* 23.
113. *Abstract . . . of the Slave Trade,* 41.
114. O. Cugoano, *Thoughts and Sentiments on the Evil of Slavery* (1787), 29.
115. Falconbridge, *Slave Trade,* 32.
116. Edwards, *West Indies,* I, 27.
117. J. M. Cohen (ed.), *The Four Voyages of Christopher Columbus* (1969 edn), 171.
118. W. Beckford, *A Descriptive Account of . . . Jamaica,* I (1790), 32.
119. T. Roughley, *The Jamaica's Planter's Guide* (1823), 220.
120. M. Scott, *Tom Cringle's Log* (1895), 50.
121. Long, *Jamaica,* II, 286.
122. Scott, *Cringle's Log,* 44.
123. T. Clarkson, *An Essay on the Impolicy of the Slave Trade* (1788), 57.
124. J. Walvin, *Black Ivory* (1993 edn), 69.
125. Long, *Jamaica,* I, 363.
126. L. G. Ragatz, *The Fall of the Planter Class in the British Caribbean 1763–1833* (1928), 71ff.
127. R. B. Sheridan, *Doctors and Slaves* (Cambridge, 1985), 164.
128. Cundall (ed.), *Nugent's Journal,* 108.
129. D. Hall, *In Miserable Slavery: Thomas Thistlewood in Jamaica, 1750–86* (1989), 309.
130. Long, *Jamaica,* II, 328 and 288–9.
131. N. A. M. Rodger, *The Command of the Ocean* (2004), 493–4. Rodger says that surgeons would usually stop such punishments "after a hundred lashes or so."
132. Anstey, *Slave Trade,* 289.
133. Hall, *Miserable Slavery,* 72–3.
134. Edwards, *West Indies,* II, 74.
135. T. F. Buxton, *The African Slave Trade and Its Remedy* (1967 edn), 189.
136. Gibbon, *Decline and Fall,* I, 68.
137. *Supplement to Mr. Cooper's Letters on the Slave Trade* (Warrington, 1788), 24.
138. Hall, *Miserable Slavery,* 204.
139. Anstey, *Slave Trade,* 36–7 and 310.
140. B. Edwards, *The History . . . of the West Indies,* III (1819 edn), 340.
141. J. R. Ward, *British West Indian Slavery, 1750–1834* (Oxford, 1988), 2.
142. Edwards, *West Indies,* II, 168.
143. Beckford, *Jamaica,* II, 281.
144. B. Martin and M. Spurrell (eds), *The Journal of a Slave Trader* (1962), xii.
145. Newton, *Slave Trade,* 1.
146. *Edinburgh Review,* XI (1808), 342.
147. G. Smith, *History of Wesleyan Methodism,* I (1862 edn), 683.
148. Clarkson, *Abolition of the African Slave Trade,* I, 54.
149. W. Doyle, *The Oxford History of the French Revolution* (Oxford, 1989), 412.
150. R. Reilly, *Josiah Wedgwood 1730–1795* (1992), 286.
151. Cup in the author's possession.
152. A. Bell, *Sydney Smith* (Oxford, 1980), 72.
153. I. Bradley, *The Call to Seriousness* (1976), 136.
154. T. Paulin, *The Day-Star of Liberty* (1998), 246.
155. F. K. Brown, *Fathers of the Victorians* (Cambridge, 1961), 3.
156. C. Lawson, *The Private Life of Warren Hastings* (1905), 121.

157. W. S. Hathaway (ed.), *The Speeches of . . . William Pitt,* II (1806), 70 and 51.

158. J. Ehrman, *The Younger Pitt,* I (1984 edn), 400.

159. Hathaway (ed.), *Speeches of . . . Pitt,* II, 80 and 82–3.

160. B. Spiller (ed.), *Cowper: Poetry and Prose* (1968), 987.

161. C. L. R. James, *The Black Jacobins* (1963 edn), 55.

162. Davis, *Slavery in the Age of Revolution,* 194.

163. J. Keane, *Tom Paine* (1995), 341.

164. R. I. and S. Wilberforce, *The Life of William Wilberforce,* I (1838), 344.

165. R. Coupland, *Wilberforce* (1945), 144.

166. R. I. and S. Wilberforce, *Wilberforce,* I, 343.

167. R. Hyam, "The Primacy of Geopolitics: The Dynamics of British Imperial Policy, 1763–1963," *JICH,* XXVII (May 1999), 31.

168. S. Schama, *Citizens* (1989), 173.

169. L. Colley, *Britons* (1994 edn), 169–70.

170. *The Poetical Works of William Cowper* (Edinburgh, 1864), 400.

171. L. Colley, *Captives: Britain, Empire and the World 1600–1850* (2002), 10.

172. G. F. Leckie, *An Historical Survey of the Foreign Affairs of Great Britain* (1808), 143.

173. H. Brogan, *Longman History of the United States of America* (1985), 201.

174. J. T. Flexner, *George Washington,* III (1970), 149.

175. L. Hönninghausen and A. Falke, *Washington, D.C.* (Tübingen, 1993), 196. The phrase was attributed to Jefferson.

176. J. W. Reps, *Monumental Washington* (Princeton, NJ, 1967), 9.

177. G. R. Mellor, *British Imperial Trusteeship 1783–1850* (1951), 22.

178. R. A. Austin and W. D. Smith, "Images of Africa and British Slave-Trade Abolition: The Transition of an Imperialist Ideology, 1787–1807," *AfHS,* II (1969), 83.

2. An English Barrack in the Oriental Seas

1. *Calcutta Gazette,* 26 April 1792.

2. Bryce, *Ancient Roman Empire,* 12.

3. S. Wolpert, *A New History of India* (New York, 1977), 134.

4. *Lord Macaulay's Essays* (1886), 502.

5. *CHI,* V, 151.

6. P. J. Marshall, *East Indian Fortunes* (Oxford, 1976), 15.

7. J. W. Kaye, *Lives of Indian Officers,* I (1889), 94.

8. P. J. Cain and A. G. Hopkins, *British Imperialism: Innovation and Expansion 1688–1914* (1993), 92.

9. *Macaulay's Essays,* 527.

10. B. Russell, *Freedom and Organisation 1814–1914* (1934), 415.

11. P. J. Marshall, *Problems of Empire: Britain and India 1757–1813* (1968), 30–31.

12. R. K. Ray, "Colonial Penetration and the Initial Resistance: The Mughal Ruling Class, the English East India Company and the Struggle for Bengal 1756–1800," *IndHR,* XII (1986), 2.

13. P. Spear, *Master of Bengal* (1975), 34.

14. Marshall, *East Indian Fortunes,* 206.

15. Pemberton Papers, 7/5/1–6, 31 October 1770.

16. K. Feiling, *Warren Hastings* (1954), 236.

17. J. L. Brockington, "Warren Hastings and Orientalism," in G. Carnall and C. Nicholson (eds), *The Impeachment of Warren Hastings* (Edinburgh, 1989), 97.

18. G. R. Gleig, *Memoirs of the Life of the Right Hon. Warren Hastings,* II (1844), 149–50.

19. Feiling, *Hastings,* 248–9.

20. E. Fay, *Original Letters from India* (1927), 196.

21. A. Spencer (ed.), *Memoirs of William Hickey,* III (1918), 359.

22. S. C. Grier (ed.), *The Letters of Warren Hastings to his Wife* (1905), 32.

23. P. J. Marshall, "The Personal Fortune of Warren Hastings, *EconHR,* XVII (1964), 285.

24. Prothero (ed.), *Letters of Edward Gibbon,* II, 172. The story that Sheridan really said "voluminous" is apocryphal, for Gibbon "much admired" the compliment.

25. Lawson, *Hastings* (1905), 108, 110 and 115.

26. *Calcutta Gazette,* 9 August 1792.

27. Spencer (ed.), *Hickey,* III, 155.

28. *CHI,* V, 195.

29. T. R. Metcalf, *The New Cambridge History of India,* III.4 (Cambridge, 1995), 13. With rather more justice, Sir William Jones aspired to the title. Cf. *DNB.*

30. G. Cannon (ed.), *The Letters of Sir William Jones,* II (Oxford, 1970), 712–13.

31. P. Marshall, *The New Cambridge History of India,* II.2 (1987), 134.

32. *Calcutta Gazette,* 4 October 1792.

33. F. and M. Wickwire, *Cornwallis: The Imperial Years* (Chapel Hill, NC, 1980), 72.

34. PRO 30/11/172, Cornwallis to Charles Stuart, 2 December 1791.

35. C. Ross (ed.), *Correspondence of Charles, First Marquess of Cornwallis,* I (1859), 280, 383 and 233.

36. Kaye, *Lives of Indian Officers,* I, 128.

37. *Calcutta Gazette,* 21 August 1788.

38. W. S. Seton-Karr, *Cornwallis* (Oxford, 1890), 102.

39. G. Forrest, *Lord Cornwallis* (1926), 27.

40. A. Embree, *Charles Grant and British Rule in India* (1962), 52, 274 and 78.

41. H. E. Busteed, *Echoes from Old Calcutta* (1908), 177.

42. P. Quennell (ed.), *Memoirs of William Hickey* (1975 edn), 272.

43. Kaye, *Lives of Indian Officers,* I, 79 and 87.

44. Spencer (ed.), *Hickey,* II, 322.

45. PRO, 30/11/172, Cornwallis to Charles Stuart, 17 April 1792.

46. PRO 30/11/182, Cornwallis to Robert Adair, 10 August 1789.

47. Ross (ed.), *Cornwallis,* I, 401 and 292.

48. PRO 30/11/151, Cornwallis to Dundas, 9 August 1790.

49. Pemberton Papers, 7/5/76, 22 May 1792.

50. K. Ballhatchet, *Race, Sex and Class under the Raj* (1980), 2.

51. Ross, *Cornwallis,* II, 20 and 87.

52. G. Forrest (ed.), *Selections of the State Papers of the Governors-General of India: Lord Cornwallis,* I (1926), 178.

53. 1 PRO 30/11/172, Cornwallis to Charles Stuart, 11 June 1792.

54. *Calcutta Gazette,* 5 July 1792.

55. A. Dirom, *A Narrative of the Campaign in India . . .* (1793), 229.

56. D. Forrest, *Tiger of Mysore* (1970), 187.

57. PRO 30/11/152, Cornwallis to Grenville, 4 March 1792.

58. P. J. Marshall, "'Cornwallis Triumphant': War in India and the British Public in the Late Eighteenth Century," in Marshall, *Trade and Conquest* (Aldershot, 1993), XIV, 71.

59. R. Holmes, *Shelley the Pursuit* (1974), 346.

60. OIOC H/436, John Taylor Papers, 132.

61. I. Butler, *The Eldest Brother: The Marquess Wellesley, the Duke of Wellington's Eldest Brother* (1973), 352.

62. Embree, *Grant,* 226.

63. K. Brittlebank, *Tipu Sultan's Search for Legitimacy* (Delhi, 1997), 27.

64. PRO 30/11/208/2, Abstract of the State of political Affairs in India . . .
65. M. Martin (ed.), *The Despatches . . . of the Marquess Wellesley,* I (1836), 460.
66. A. Chatterjee, *Representations of India 1740–1840* (1998), 177 and 179.
67. M. Wilks, *Historical Sketches of South India,* III (1810), 269.
68. OIOC, H/436, 134.
69. OIOC, MSS Eur C10, Munshi Qasim, "Tippoo Sooltan's Court," 204.
70. A. Beatson, *A View of the Origins and Conduct of the War with Tippoo Sultan* (1800), 153–4.
71. OIOC, MSS Eur F206, Macnabb Papers, James Munro Macnabb to his grandmother, 30 July 1800.
72. OIOC, H/436, 141 and 144.
73. OIOC, MSS Eur C10, 205 and 204.
74. PRO 30/11/209, Narrative of operations during the siege and capture of Seringapatam . . . by Lord Mornington, 7 June 1799.
75. Dirom, *Narrative,* 188.
76. Brittlebank, *Tipu,* 136.
77. Wilks, *Sketches of South India,* III, 20.
78. Martin (ed.), *Despatches,* I, 369; IV, 155.
79. PRO 30/11/209, Narrative . . . by Lord Mornington, 7 June 1799.
80. W. Trousdale (ed.), *War in Afghanistan 1878–9: The Personal Diary of Major-General Sir Charles Metcalfe MacGregor* (Detroit, 1985), 156.
81. P. Magnus, *Kitchener* (1968 edn), 183.
82. PRO 30/11/209, Narrative . . . by Lord Mornington, 7 June 1799.
83. H. Dodwell, *The Nabobs of Madras* (1926), 65.
84. E. Longford, *Wellington: The Years of the Sword* (1969), 82.
85. Butler, *Eldest Brother,* 229, 225 and 193.
86. M. S. Renick, *Lord Wellesley and the Indian States* (Agra, 1987), 220.
87. Lord Valentia, *Voyages and Travels,* I (1809), 253.
88. J. W. Kaye, *The Life and Correspondence of Major-General Sir John Malcolm,* I (1856), 305.
89. Martin (ed.), *Despatches,* V, 326; III, 382.
90. Spencer (ed.), *Hickey,* IV, 278.
91. Martin (ed.), *Despatches,* V, 156 and 154.
92. *Edinburgh Review,* XII (1805), 469–70.
93. E. Ingram (ed.), *Two Views of British India* (1970), 166.
94. Martin (ed.), *Despatches,* V, 314 and 317.
95. W. M. Torrens, *Marquess Wellesley* (1880), 218.
96. P. E. Roberts, *India under Wellesley* (1929), 299.
97. Embree, *Grant,* 209 and 216.
98. Spencer (ed.), *Hickey,* IV, 236.
99. Lord Curzon, *British Government in India,* II (1925), 8.
100. M. Graham, *Journal of a Residence in India* (1813), 137.
101. Curzon, *India,* I, 80.
102. Butler, *Eldest Brother,* 386 and 245.
103. Valentia, *Voyages,* 235–6.
104. H. Morris, *The Life of Charles Grant* (1904), 254.
105. Lord Lindsay, *The Lives of the Lindsays,* III (1849), 406.
106. Butler, *Eldest Brother,* 272.
107. Kaye, *Lives of Indian Officers,* I, 551.
108. E. Roberts, *Scenes and Characteristics of Hindostan,* III (1835), 70.
109. OIOC, MSS Eur F206, 1 September 1806.

110. HMC, *Report on the Manuscripts of J. B. Fortescue, Esq., preserved at Dropmore*, IV (1905), 474 and 383.
111. C. C. Coffin, *Our New Way Round the World* (1883 edn), 222.
112. OIOC, MSS Eur C97, Sir Henry Thoby Prinsep, "Three Generations in India, 1771–1904," 2–3.
113. Valentia, *Voyages*, 236.
114. Graham, *Journal*, 132.
115. J. P. Losty, *Calcutta: City of Palaces* (1990), 49.
116. M. Archer, *Early Views of India* (1980), 3.
117. T. Williamson, *The East Indian Vade-Mecum*, II (1810), 4.
118. Lord Roberts, *Forty-one Years in India*, I (1897), 5.
119. M. Fowler, *Below the Peacock Fan: First Ladies of the Raj* (1987), 120 and 183.
120. Roberts, *Hindostan*, I, 3.
121. J. D. Collet, *The Life and Letters of Raja Rammohun Roy* (Calcutta, 1962 edn), 170–71.
122. OIOC, MSS Eur C97, 3.
123. Martin (ed.), *Despatches*, IV, 672.
124. C. A. Bayly, *Imperial Meridian: The British Empire and the World 1780–1830* (1989), 148.
125. Spencer (ed.), *Hickey*, III, 213–14.
126. Roberts, *Hindostan*, III, 82.
127. OIOC, MSS Eur D1160, William Prinsep, "Memoir," II (1870), 16.
128. OIOC, MSS Eur C97, 263.
129. CUL, SPCK Papers, Letter from Secretary of Mission at Tinnivally, 18 September 1818.
130. R. G. Collingwood, *Roman Britain* (1932), 8.
131. Valentia, *Voyages*, 241.
132. J. Malcolm, *The Political History of India*, II (New Delhi, 1970 edn), 143.
133. Roberts, *Hindostan*, III, 75.
134. V. Jacquemont, *Voyage dans l'Inde . . .* (Paris, 1841), 459.
135. M. A. Laird (ed.), *Bishop Heber in Northern India: Selections from Heber's Journal* (Cambridge, 1971), 45.
136. BL, Add 29178, J. Palmer to Hastings, 10 October 1802.
137. Roberts, *Hindostan*, I, 187.
138. Spencer (ed.), *Hickey*, IV, 318.
139. Ross (ed.), *Cornwallis*, III, 542, 548 and 546.
140. OIOC, H/MISC/507, Vellore Mutiny Correspondence, 235.
141. M. Gupta, *Lord William Bentinck in Madras and the Vellore Mutiny, 1803–7* (New Delhi, 1986), 192.
142. Kaye, *Lives of Indian Officers*, I, 240.
143. OIOC, H/MISC/507, 238.
144. Ibid., 149, Cradock to Bentinck, 4 July 1806.
145. BL, Add 29181, S. Toone to Hastings, 20 January 1808.
146. E. D. Potts, *British Baptist Missionaries in India, 1793–1837* (Cambridge, 1967), 220.
147. OIOC, H/MISC/507, 532.
148. *DNB*.
149. OIOC, H/MISC/507, 406.
150. Ibid., 532.
151. P. Spear, *The Nabobs* (1932), 59.
152. G. Moorhouse, *India Britannica* (1986 edn), 63.
153. Embree, *Grant*, 246.
154. Bryce, *Ancient Roman Empire*, 57.

155. Kaye, *Lives of Indian Officers*, I, 623–4.
156. Butler, *Eldest Brother*, 237.
157. *OHBE*, III, 404.
158. R. Robinson and J. Gallagher, *Africa and the Victorians* (1965), 12.
159. Bayly, *Imperial Meridian*, 126.
160. H. Martineau, *British Rule in India* (1857), 161.
161. Collet, *Roy*, 336.
162. T. H. Beaglehole, *Thomas Munro and the Development of Administrative Policy in Madras 1792–1818* (Cambridge, 1966), 121–2.
163. Jacquemont, *Letters from India 1829–1832* (1936), xxv.
164. Collet, *Roy*, 387–8.
165. Bayly, *Imperial Meridian*, 163.
166. An Indian Officer, *How I Spent My Two Years' Leave* (1875), 97–8.
167. Kaye, *Lives of Indian Officers*, I, 366.
168. D. Gilmour, *The Ruling Caste: Imperial Lives in the Victorian Raj* (2005), 42.
169. Harlow, *Second British Empire*, II (1964), 140.
170. A. Roberts, *Salisbury: Victorian Titan* (1999), 532.
171. A. Frost, *Convicts and Empire* (Melbourne, 1980), 65.
172. Leckie, *Foreign Affairs of Great Britain*, 121.
173. Pocock, *Nelson*, 293.
174. J. Rosselli, *Lord William Bentinck* (1974), 147.
175. J. E. Tennent, *Ceylon*, II (1860 edn), 486.
176. R. Coupland, *Raffles* (1934), 7.
177. S. Raffles, *Memoir of the Life and Public Services of Sir Thomas Stamford Raffles* (Singapore, 1991 edn), 399 and 422–8.
178. Ibid., 462 and 460.
179. D. C. Boulger, *Life of Sir Stamford Raffles* (1973 edn), 162.
180. J. C. Beaglehole, *The Exploration of the Pacific* (1947), 343.
181. G. Martin (ed.), *The Founding of Australia* (Sydney, 1978), 230 and 263.
182. G. Blainey, *The Tyranny of Distance* (Melbourne, 1966), 72.
183. R. Hyam, *Britain's Imperial Century* (1993 edn), 68.
184. A. G. Stapleton, *George Canning and His Times* (1859), 411.
185. B. Smith, *European Vision and the South Pacific 1786–1850* (Oxford, 1969), 133.

3. Exempt from the Disaster of Caste

1. *The Works of the Rev. Sydney Smith*, I (1839), 49 and 50. On 2 October 1807 *The Times* went further than Smith, saying that Australia, like Rome, might be destined to become "mistress of the world."
2. *HRNSW*, I, ii (Sydney, 1892), 53.
3. D. Collins, *An Account of the English Colony in New South Wales* (1798), 74.
4. Martin (ed.), *Founding of Australia*, 176.
5. *CHBE*, VII, 63.
6. T. Delamothe and C. Bridge, *Interpreting Australia* (1988), 41.
7. *HRNSW*, II, 666.
8. *HRNSW*, II, 758.
9. Collins, *New South Wales*, 5.
10. T. Kenneally, *The Commonwealth of Thieves* (2006), 240 and 76.
11. *HRNSW*, II, 392–3.
12. W. Tench, *1788* (Melbourne, 1996), 47.

13. ML, Microfilm CY Reel 1301, 12 July 1788.
14. Collins, *New South Wales,* 72.
15. R. Southey, *Life and Works of William Cowper,* VII (1835–7), 85.
16. *CHBE,* VII, 68.
17. *St James's Chronicle,* 16–18 January 1787.
18. G. Williams and A. Frost (eds), Terra Australis *to Australia* (Melbourne, 1988), 192.
19. *HRNSW,* I, ii, 212.
20. Williams and Frost, *Australia,* 202–3.
21. Tench, *1788,* 75.
22. Smith, *European Vision,* 170.
23. Collins, *New South Wales,* 3.
24. *CHBE,* VII, 89.
25. Tench, *1788,* 264, 71, 142, 91, 122 and 119.
26. C. Bateson, *The Convict Ships* (1959), 112.
27. Collins, *New South Wales,* 123.
28. *HRNSW,* II, 791.
29. Bateson, *Convict Ships,* 113.
30. *HRNSW,* II, 768. None of the captains was brought to justice though the system of payment was altered to reward the safe delivery of convicts, which improved matters but did not altogether prevent future atrocities.
31. T. Watling, *Letters from an Exile at Botany-Bay* (Penrith n.d., c. 1794), 8.
32. *HRNSW,* III, 65.
33. L. Macquarie, *A Letter to the Right Honourable Viscount Sidmouth . . .* (1821), 12.
34. L. L. Robson, *The Convict Settlers of Australia* (Melbourne, 1965), 128.
35. J. Clay, *Maconochie's Experiment* (2001), 35–6.
36. Baron C. von Hügel, *New Holland Journal,* ed. D. Clark (Melbourne, 1994), 222.
37. T. C. Croker, *Memoirs of Joseph Holt,* II (1838), 219 and 270.
38. C. M. H. Clark (ed.), *Select Documents in Australian History 1788–1850* (Sydney, 1950), 133.
39. C. M. H. Clark, *A History of Australia* (1962), 224.
40. J. Damousi, *Depraved and Disorderly: Female Convicts, Sexuality and Gender in Colonial Australia* (Cambridge, 1997), 46.
41. *A Confidential Despatch from Sir John Franklin on Female Convicts in Van Diemen's Land* (Sullivan's Cove, 1996), 55 and 36.
42. R. Hughes, *The Fatal Shore* (1996 edn), 487 and 383.
43. Clark (ed.), *Select Documents,* 123 and 140.
44. CUL, RCMS 278/40, H. M. Hull, The Aborigines of Tasmania 1873. Probably Tasmanian Aborigines numbered around four thousand before the European invasion.
45. P. H. Barrett and R. B. Freeman (eds), *The Works of Charles Darwin,* III, *Journal of Researches,* Pt II (1986), 417.
46. A. McGrath, *Contested Ground* (Sydney, 1995), 332.
47. Hughes, *Fatal Shore,* 120.
48. J. Frost, *A Letter . . . on Transportation* (n.d.), 17.
49. *Historical Records of Australia,* I (Sydney, 1914), 272.
50. Hughes, *Fatal Shore,* 293. This view has recently been much contested.
51. M. H. Ellis, *Lachlan Macquarie: His Life, Adventures and Times* (Sydney, 1952 edn), 176 and 492.
52. *Works of Smith,* II, 171.
53. J. Ritchie, *The Evidence of the Bigge Reports,* I (Melbourne, 1971), 199.
54. *Sydney Gazette,* 18 August 1821.
55. P. Cunningham, *Two Years in New South Wales* (1966 edn), 215, 186 and xxxvi.

56. *Blackwood's Edinburgh Magazine,* 22 (November 1827), 603.

57. Quoted by R. White, *Inventing Australia* (1981), 68.

58. Ellis, *Macquarie,* 316 and 318.

59. V. A. C. Gatrell, *The Hanging Tree* (Oxford, 1994), 578.

60. White, *Inventing Australia,* 24, 50 and 53.

61. Dixon, *Course of Empire,* 105 and 164.

62. L. Woodward, *The Age of Reform 1815–1870* (Oxford, 1987 edn), 387.

63. P. Fitzgerald (ed.), *The Works of Charles Lamb,* III (1895), 300.

64. W. J. Lines, *Taming the Great South Land* (Berkeley, CA, 1991), 49.

65. D. Pike, *Paradise of Dissent: South Australia 1829–1857* (1957), 7.

66. J. Morris, *Heaven's Command* (1973), 146. Actually Australians were not free of class distinction; but the common European opinion, as expressed by Thackeray, was that after the emigrant woman's last curtsy on English soil "her back won't bend except to her labour." Cf. M. Forster (ed.), *Drawn from Life: The Journalism of William Makepeace Thackeray* (1984), 29.

67. C. A. Bayly, *The Birth of the Modern World 1780–1914* (Oxford, 2004), 101.

68. A. J. P. Taylor, *From Napoleon to the Second International* (1993), 374.

69. C. A. Bodelsen, *Studies in Mid-Victorian Imperialism* (1960), 44.

70. CUL, Add 7888, Sir James Stephen's Journal II/119, 4 March 1846.

71. *The Autobiography of Henry Taylor,* II (1885), 34.

72. H. L. Hall, *The Colonial Office* (1937), 49.

73. E. T. Williams, "The Colonial Office in the Thirties," *HSANZ,* II (1942–3), 144.

74. W. A. Baillie Hamilton, "Forty-four Years at the Colonial Office," *The Nineteenth Century and After,* LXV (1909), 603.

75. R. C. Snelling and T. J. Barron, "The Colonial Office and Its Permanent Officials 1801–1914," in G. Sutherland (ed.), *Studies in the Growth of Nineteenth-century Government* (1972), 153.

76. Hall, *Colonial Office,* 112 and 17–18.

77. W. L. Burn, *Emancipation and Apprenticeship in the British West Indies* (1937), 128.

78. CUL, Add 7888, II/119, 19 January 1846.

79. L. Stephen, *The Life of Sir James Fitzjames Stephen* (1895), 63.

80. CUL, Add 7888, II/119, 4 March 1846.

81. Stephen, *Life of Fitzjames Stephen,* 64.

82. *The Autobiography of Henry Taylor,* II (1885), 304.

83. CUL, Add 7888, II/119, 31 March and 13 January 1846.

84. Stephen, *Life of Fitzjames Stephen,* 50.

85. CUL, Add 7888, II/119, 4 March 1846.

86. G. E. Marindin (ed.), *Letters of Frederic Lord Blachford* (1896), 299.

87. *OHBE,* III, 104.

88. D. Read, *Cobden and Bright* (1967), 238.

89. J. R. McCulloch, *A Statistical Account of the British Empire* (1837), 597.

90. P. Colquhoun, *Treatise on the Wealth, Power, and Resources of the British Empire* (1815), 314.

91. G. Martin, *Britain and the Origins of Canadian Confederation, 1837–67* (1995), 63.

92. Colquhoun, *Treatise,* 311.

93. W. Cobbett, *The Emigrant's Guide . . .* (1829), 41.

94. D. G. Creighton, *Dominion of the North* (1958), 239.

95. J. Pickering, *Emigration or No Emigration* (1830), 69.

96. E. W. Watkin, *A Trip to the United States and Canada* (1852), 28 and 32.

97. *The Report of the Earl of Durham* (1902 edn), 132.

98. J. Morley, *Life of Richard Cobden,* I (1881), 31.

99. A. Greer, *The Patriots and the People* (Toronto, 1993), 123, quoting *Quebec Mercury*, 27 October 1806.

100. CUL, Add 9556, Richard Cornwallis Neville, "Diary of Military Life in Canada 1838–40," 14 November 1838.

101. *Report of the Earl of Durham,* 56.

102. P. A. Buckner, *The Transition to Responsible Government* (Westport, CT, 1985), 222.

103. *CBHE,* VI, 243.

104. F. Ouellet, *Lower Canada 1791–1842* (Toronto, 1980), 216.

105. Greer, *Patriots,* 191.

106. F. Bradshaw, *Self-Government in Canada* (1903), 80.

107. S. J. Reid, *Life and Letters of the First Earl of Durham 1792–1840,* II (1906), 179.

108. CUL, Add 9556, 9 and 12 November 1838.

109. Goldwin Smith, *Canada and the Canadian Question* (Toronto, 1971 edn), 81.

110. C. Lindsey, *William Lyon Mackenzie* (Toronto, 1938), 263 and 346–7.

111. J. Marlow, *The Tolpuddle Martyrs* (1974 edn), 253.

112. L. F. Gates, *After the Rebellion* (Toronto, 1988), 338.

113. *HSANZ,* II, 152.

114. Reid, *Durham,* II, 137–8.

115. E. M. Wrong, *Charles Buller and Responsible Government* (Oxford, 1926), 26.

116. M. Francis, *Governors and Settlers: Images of Authority in the British Colonies 1820–60* (1992), 85.

117. Reid, *Durham,* I, 319.

118. Morris, *Heaven's Command,* 132.

119. H. Reeve (ed.), *The Greville Memoirs,* III (1888), 232.

120. Reid, *Durham,* II, 165.

121. Bradshaw, *Self-Government,* 23.

122. Reid, *Durham,* II, 277.

123. J. Richardson, *Eight Years in Canada* (1967 edn), 53.

124. Reid, *Durham,* II, 320 and 339.

125. *Report of the Earl of Durham,* xxvi.

126. [J. S. Mill], "Lord Durham's Return," *Westminster Review,* XXXII (1838–9), 260.

127. Bradshaw, *Self-Government,* 23.

128. J. A. Roebuck, *The Colonies of England* (1849), 188.

129. E. W. Watkin, *Canada and the States: Recollections* (1887), 16.

130. Creighton, *Dominion,* 313.

131. R. S. Thompson, *Empires on the Pacific* (2001), 45.

132. *The Times,* 23 March 1849.

133. *The Economist,* 8 March 1851.

134. J. Pope (ed.), *Memoirs of . . . Sir John Alexander Macdonald . . . ,* I (1894), 313.

135. Martin, *Canadian Confederation,* 171.

136. Smith, *Canada,* 125.

137. *Annual Register 1839* (1840), 177.

138. G. Martin, *Edward Gibbon Wakefield* (Edinburgh, 1997), 12.

139. C. Woodham Smith, *Florence Nightingale* (1964 edn), 375.

140. H. T. Manning, "Lord Durham and the New Zealand Company," *NZJH,* 6 (April 1972), 5.

141. T. Carlyle, "Chartism," in *English and Other Essays* (Everyman edn, n.d.), 235, 238 and 211.

142. W. Gisborne, *New Zealand Rulers and Statesmen 1840–1897* (1897), 63.

143. P. Adams, *Fatal Necessity: British Intervention in New Zealand 1830–1847* (Auckland, 1977), 96, 101 and 110.

144. F. E. Maning, *Old New Zealand* (1956 edn), 109, 176 and 8.

145. W. P. Reeve, *The Long White Cloud* (1950 edn), 108.

146. C. Hursthouse, *New Zealand or Zealandia, The Britain of the South,* I (1857), 32.

147. A. S. Thomson, *The Story of New Zealand,* I (1859), 303.

148. Ellis, *Macquarie,* 318.

149. R. McNab (ed.), *Historical Records of New Zealand,* I (Wellington, 1908), 321.

150. *CHBE,* VII, ii, 35.

151. A. T. Yarwood, *Samuel Marsden* (Melbourne, 1977), 173.

152. A. Lycett, *Rudyard Kipling* (1999), 483.

153. J. Belich, *Making Peoples: A History of New Zealanders from Polynesian Settlement to the End of the Nineteenth Century* (1996), 136.

154. J. R. Elder (ed.), *The Letters and Journals of Samuel Marsden, 1765–1838* (Dunedin, 1932), 415, 403 and 219.

155. *The Works of the Rev. Sydney Smith,* I (1839), 173. Macaulay waxed still more eloquent on the religious impulses to which tinkers succumbed. *Lord Macaulay's Essays* (1886), 556.

156. N. Gunson, *Messengers of Grace* (Melbourne, 1978), 31.

157. British and Foreign Bible Society Annual Report (1835), lxxiv.

158. E. Dieffenbach, *Travels in New Zealand,* II (1843), 41.

159. E. T. Williams, "The Treaty of Waitangi," *History,* 25 (1940–41), 242.

160. A. Earle, *Narrative of a Residence in New Zealand* (Oxford, 1966 edn), 57–9.

161. Dieffenbach, *Travels,* II, 20 and 128–30.

162. Barrett and Freeman (eds), *Works of Charles Darwin,* III, 397 and 398.

163. F. Darwin (ed.), *The Life and Letters of Charles Darwin,* I (1887), 264.

164. CUL, British and Foreign Bible Society Foreign Correspondence, 10 May 1842.

165. Adams, *Fatal Necessity,* 140.

166. E. J. Wakefield, *Adventure in New Zealand* (Christchurch, 1908 edn), 62 and 148.

167. Belich, *Making Peoples,* 338.

168. J. C. Beaglehole, *Captain Hobson and the New Zealand Company* (Northampton, MA, 1927), 108.

169. Thomson, *Story of New Zealand,* II, 22.

170. CUL, RCMS 278/55, Letters to Colonists by G. F. Young, Young to Arthur Wakefield, 13 November 1842.

171. CUL, Add 7888, II/119, 18–19 March 1846.

172. Adams, *Fatal Necessity,* 240.

173. Reeves, *White Cloud,* 142. When this book was published in 1898 Maori numbers had reached their nadir at just over forty thousand; but they subsequently began to rise, belying the common notion that the race was doomed.

174. Mansergh, *Commonwealth Experience,* 103.

175. Hursthouse, *New Zealand,* I, 97 and 11.

176. B. Porter, *The Lion's Share: A Short History of Imperialism 1850–1983* (1984 edn), 22.

177. J. Belich, *The New Zealand Wars* (Auckland, 1986), 23.

178. A. Trollope, *Australia and New Zealand,* II (1873), 457.

179. E. G. Wakefield, *A View of the Art of Colonization* (1849), 221.

180. Hursthouse, *New Zealand,* II, 640.

181. T. Cholmondeley, *Ultima Thule* (1854), 324.

182. CUL, RCMS 304, Thornhill Family Letters, George to Minnie Thornhill, 1 January 1890.

183. *OHBE,* III, 582.

184. R. Taylor, *New Zealand and Its Inhabitants* (1853), 269.

185. S. Butler, *A First Year in Canterbury Settlement* (1964 edn), 33.

186. Reeves, *White Cloud,* 179.

187. Thomson, *Story of New Zealand*, II, 213.
188. Hursthouse, *New Zealand*, II, 631.
189. Thomson, *Story of New Zealand*, II, 307.
190. P. Raby, *Samuel Butler* (1991), 66.
191. *HSANZ*, II, 158.
192. Quoted by Belich, *Making Peoples*, 302.
193. *Macaulay's Essays*, 542.
194. G. O. Trevelyan, *The Life and Letters of Lord Macaulay* (1895), 359.
195. *Review of Reviews*, II (September 1890), 252.
196. P. Knaplund, *James Stephen and the British Colonial System 1813–1847* (Madison, WI, 1953), 278.

4. To Stop Is Dangerous, To Recede, Ruin

1. E. T. Williams, "James Stephen and British Intervention in New Zealand, 1838–40," *JMH*, 13 (1941), 33.
2. *Asiatic Journal*, IV, 3rd series (1845), 489.
3. Hyam, *Imperial Century*, 7.
4. Hall, *Colonial Office*, 177 and 145.
5. Sutherland (ed.), *Studies in . . . Government*, 195 and 164.
6. D. K. Fieldhouse, *Economics and Empire 1830–1914* (1973), 81.
7. N. Mostert, *Frontiers* (1992), 932.
8. B. Gardner, *The East India Company* (1971), 203.
9. *OHBE*, III, 191.
10. Bayly, *Imperial Meridian*, 104.
11. S. Lane Poole, *The Life of Lord Stratford de Redcliffe* (1890), 180 and 190.
12. Morris, *Pax Britannica*, 28.
13. For an early criticism of the concept see D. C. M. Platt, "'Imperialism of Free Trade': some reservations," *EconHR*, 21 (1968), 300.
14. S. Winchester, *Outposts* (1985), 115.
15. Kaye, *Metcalfe*, I, 320.
16. *Blackwood's Edinburgh Magazine*, LIII (January 1843), 1–2.
17. Hall, *Colonial Office*, 195.
18. R. Hyam and G. Martin, *Reappraisals in British Imperial History* (1975), 115.
19. E. Stokes, *The English Utilitarians and India* (Oxford, 1959), 44.
20. E. Ashley, *Life of Viscount Palmerston*, I (1879), 346.
21. D. Cecil, *Melbourne* (1954 edn), 346.
22. Woodward, *Age of Reform*, 300.
23. J. Ridley, *Lord Palmerston* (1972 edn), 676.
24. *Punch*, 26 September 1857.
25. Ridley, *Palmerston*, 526.
26. W. Baring Pemberton, *Lord Palmerston* (1954), 181 and 213.
27. Ridley, *Palmerston*, 524.
28. Trevelyan, *Macaulay*, 391.
29. J. Morley, *The Life of William Ewart Gladstone*, I (1908 edn), 168.
30. Ridley, *Palmerston*, 350.
31. J. K. Fairbank, *Trade and Diplomacy on the China Coast*, I (Cambridge, MA, 1953), 19.
32. A. Peyrefitte, *The Collision of Two Civilisations* (1993), 538.
33. *Annual Register, 1840*, 83.
34. W. C. Hunter, *Bits of Old China* (1911), 19.

35. Quennell (ed.), *Hickey*, 121.
36. H. B. Morse, *The International Relations of the Chinese Empire* (1910), 545.
37. P. W. Fay, *The Opium War 1840–1842* (Chapel Hill, NC, 1975), 49.
38. J. Spence, *Opium Smoking in Ch'ing China* (2000 edn), 162.
39. F. Wakeman, *Strangers at the Gate* (Berkeley, CA, 1997 edn), 25.
40. J. Heria, *Cherishing Men from Afar* (1995), 68.
41. S. Warren, *The Opium Question* (1840), 125.
42. T. De Quincey, *Confessions of an English Opium Eater*, ed. A. Hayter (1971 edn), 71.
43. Warren, *Opium*, 75.
44. G. O. Trevelyan, *The Competition Wallah* (1864), 65.
45. F. G. Whelan, *Edmund Burke and India* (Pittsburgh, PA, 1996), 96.
46. A. P. Stanley, *The Life and Correspondence of Thomas Arnold* (1846 edn), 515.
47. Fay, *Opium War*, 117.
48. De Quincey, *Confessions*, 114.
49. A. Waley, *The Opium War Through Chinese Eyes* (1953), 29–30.
50. CUL, JMP, C5/4, James Matheson to William Jardine, 30 May 1839.
51. G. Graham, *The China Station: War and Diplomacy 1830–1860* (Oxford, 1978), 105.
52. CUL, JMP, B1/10, 35, W. Crawford to R. Crawford, 8 August 1839.
53. Ibid., 41, W. Jardine to J. Jeejeebhoy, 5 October 1839.
54. M. Greenberg, *British Trade and the Opening of China 1800–42* (2000 edn), 104.
55. D. R. Headrick, *The Tools of Empire* (New York, 1981), 50 and 52.
56. Graham, *China Station*, 234.
57. S. Hoe, *The Private Life of Old Hong Kong* (Hong Kong, 1991), 77.
58. A. Cunynghame, *An Aide-de-Camp's Recollections of Service in China* . . . (1844), 96.
59. CUL, JMP, C6/3, Alexander Matheson to J. Adam Smith, 13 February 1843.
60. F. Welsh, *A History of Hong Kong* (1993), 122 and 197.
61. CUL, JMP, C6/3, 10 September 1843.
62. Ibid., Matheson to John Purvis, 21 April 1843.
63. E. J. Eitel, *Europe in China* (Hong Kong, 1983 edn), 290 and 246.
64. Morris, *Heaven's Command*, 90.
65. Ashley, *Palmerston*, I, 361.
66. Fairbank, *Trade and Diplomacy*, I, 380.
67. CUL, Parkes Papers, H1, Harry Parkes to E. Hammond, 14 November 1856.
68. Pemberton, *Palmerston*, 249.
69. D. Hurd, *The Arrow War* (1967), 228.
70. G. R. Barmé, "The Garden of Perfect Brightness, a Life in Ruins," *EAH,* 11 (June 1996), 113.
71. Peyrefitte, *Two Civilisations*, 529.
72. J. Lehmann, *All Sir Garnet* (1964), 106–7.
73. Gibbon, *Decline and Fall*, III, 966.
74. Graham, *China Station*, 182.
75. CUL, JMP, C 6/4, A. Matheson to J. Abel Smith, 31 December 1845.
76. Hurd, *Arrow War*, 237.
77. Ashley, *Palmerston*, II, 32.
78. Welsh, *Hong Kong*, 158.
79. CUL, JMP, C 6/4, A. Matheson to J. Abel Smith, 31 December 1845.
80. Fairbank, *Trade and Diplomacy*, I, 160–61.
81. L. Oliphant, *Elgin's Mission to China and Japan,* II (Hong Kong, 1970 edn), 268.
82. R. Bickers, "Shanghailanders: The Formation and Identity of the British Settler Community in Shanghai 1843–1947," *PP,* 159 (May 1998), 193.
83. P. D. Coates, *The China Consuls* (Hong Kong, 1988), 265.

84. A. Moorehead, *The Blue Nile* (1974 edn), 237.

85. CUL, Crewe Papers, C/19–24, Crewe to Hardinge, 5 September 1912.

86. Fairbank, *Trade and Diplomacy,* I, 462.

87. N. R. Clifford, *Spoilt Children of Empire* (Hanover, NH, 1991), 34.

88. R. Pares, "The Economic Factors in the History of Empire," *EconHR,* 7, no. 2 (May 1937), 144.

89. H. W. C. Davis, *The Great Game in Asia* (1926), 4 and passim.

90. E. O'Ballance, *Afghan Wars 1839–1992* (1993), 7.

91. J. A. Norris, *The First Afghan War 1838–1842* (Cambridge, 1987), 30.

92. K. Bourne, *The Foreign Policy of Victorian England* (Oxford, 1970), 36.

93. OIOC, MSS Eur, D634, Hutchinson Family Papers, Journal of Lt. Christopher Codrington, 8 February 1841.

94. Trousdale (ed.), *War in Afghanistan,* 78.

95. P. Macrory, *Signal Catastrophe* (1966), 159.

96. *Blackwood's Magazine,* LIII (January, 1843), 258.

97. *The Times,* 5 April 1842.

98. Macrory, *Signal Catastrophe,* 86.

99. "Account of Mrs. Waller's Experiences in the Afghan War of 1842 and as a Prisoner," typescript in possession of C. and G. Woolley.

100. OIOC, MSS Eur C703, Journal of Captain William Anderson, 8 January 1842.

101. J. W. Kaye, *History of the War in Afghanistan,* II (1857), 371.

102. OIOC, MSS Eur C703, 12 January 1842.

103. Lady Sale, *The First Afghan War,* ed. P. Macrory (1969), 162.

104. Kaye, *War in Afghanistan,* II, 359.

105. *The Times,* 20 April 1842.

106. H. Lushington, *A Great Country's Little Wars* (1844), 144.

107. *Blackwood's Magazine,* LIII (1843), 144.

108. Stanley, *Thomas Arnold,* 601.

109. *Blackwood's Magazine,* LIII, 540.

110. Norris, *First Afghan War,* 396–7 and 451.

111. G. W. Forrest, *Life of Field-Marshal Sir Neville Chamberlain* (1909), 146.

112. C. Allen, *Soldier Sahibs* (2000), 52.

113. Curzon, *British Government in India,* 199.

114. *DNB.*

115. Kaye, *War in Afghanistan,* III, 381.

116. P. Hopkirk, *The Great Game* (1990), 282.

117. A. Law (ed.), *India under Lord Ellenborough* (1926), 53.

118. R. Lawrence, *Charles Napier* (1952), 179 (the expression is Thackeray's) and 170.

119. BL, Add 49140, Sir Charles Napier's India Journal, 1 and 21 January 1846.

120. S. G. Baird (ed.), *Private Letters of the Marquess of Dalhousie* (Shannon, Ireland, 1972), vii.

121. T. R. E. Holmes, *Four Famous Soldiers* (1889), 46.

122. BL, Add 49115, Napier to Captain Porteous, 9 October 1842. The letter is marked "Not sent. I do not know Capt. Porteous sufficiently."

123. Lawrence, *Napier,* 201.

124. See W. Doniger, "'I Have Scinde': Flogging a Dead (White Male Orientalist) Horse," *JAS* 58 (November 1999), 940ff.

125. Holmes, *Famous Soldiers,* 67.

126. *Edinburgh Review,* LXXIX (1844), 559.

5. Sacred Wrath

1. R. Dudley Edwards, *The Pursuit of Reason:* The Economist *1843–1993* (1993), 53 and 52.
2. J. Mokyr and C. Ò Gràda, "Height and Health in the United Kingdom, 1815–1860: Evidence from the East India Company Army," *EEH*, 33 (1996), 152.
3. Mr. and Mrs. S. C. Hall, *Ireland*, I (1841), 7.
4. W. H. Dunn, *James Anthony Froude*, I (Oxford, 1961), 68.
5. L. Perry Curtis, *Apes and Angels* (Newton Abbot, 1971), 1.
6. Dunn, *Froude*, I, 69.
7. *Charles Kingsley: His Letters and Memories of His Life*, edited by his wife (1888), 236.
8. C. Hall, *Cultures of Empire* (Manchester, 2000), 209.
9. C. Ò Gràda, *Black '47 and Beyond* (Princeton, NJ, 1999), 160.
10. J. Prunty, *Dublin Slums, 1800–1925* (Dublin, 1999), 69.
11. P. Brendon, *Head of Guinness* (1979), ix.
12. D. Knight (ed.), *Cobbett in Ireland* (1984), 44.
13. D. Thomson and M. McGusty (eds), *The Irish Journals of Elizabeth Smith 1840–1850* (Oxford, 1980), 308.
14. C. E. Trevelyan, *The Irish Crisis* (1848), 184.
15. *The Times*, 22 September 1846, quoted by P. Gray, *Famine, Land and Politics* (Dublin, 1999), 227.
16. Ò Gràda, *Black '47*, 41.
17. C. Woodham-Smith, *The Great Hunger* (1964 edn), 149.
18. Ò Gràda, *Black '47*, 203.
19. P. Bishop, *The Irish Empire* (1999), 90.
20. S. Kierse, *The Famine Years in the Parish of Killaloe 1845–1851* (Killaloe, 1984), 59.
21. NAM, 2000-12-632, Journal of Captain Frederick Charles Aylmer, 15 May 1849.
22. A. Trollope, *The Irish Famine*, ed. L. O. Tingay (1967), 13.
23. R. F. Foster, *Modern Ireland 1600–1972* (1988), 363.
24. T. Coleman, *Passage to America* (1972), 130.
25. E. Laxton, *The Famine Ships* (1997 edn), 35.
26. P. Gray, *The Irish Famine* (1995), 178–9.
27. C. C. O'Brien, *The Siege* (1986), 330.
28. Lord Macaulay, *The History of England*, I (1889), 390. The Roman poet was presumably Horace, *Odes*, 2, I, 7–8.
29. M. Davis, *Late Victorian Holocausts* (2001), 37.
30. Trevelyan, *Irish Crisis*, 201.
31. L. Cazamian, *The Social Novel in England* (1973 edn), 88.
32. Gray, *Famine, Land and Politics*, 315.
33. J. O'Rourke, *The Great Irish Famine* (1969 edn), 266.
34. A. Nicholson, *The Bible in Ireland*, ed. A. T. Shepherd (1926), 16.
35. Woodham-Smith, *Great Hunger*, 357.
36. J. Mitchel, *The Last Conquest of Ireland (Perhaps)* (New York, 1873), 266, 243, 322, 313 and 325.
37. G. F. Lewis (ed.), *Letters of Sir George Cornewall Lewis* (1870), 190.
38. Rosselli, *Bentinck*, 108.
39. P. Brendon, *Thomas Cook: 150 Years of Popular Tourism* (1991), 147.
40. R. Singha, "'Providential Circumstances': The Thuggee Campaign of the 1830s and Legal Innovation," *MAS*, 27, 1 (1993), 107.
41. C. A. Bayly, *Empire and Information* (Cambridge, 1996), 218.
42. M. E. Chamberlain, *Britain and India* (Newton Abbot, 1974), 105.
43. Rosselli, *Bentinck*, 129.

44. Gupta, *Bentinck,* 1.

45. Rosselli, *Bentinck,* 105–6.

46. H. R. Puckridge, *A Short History of the Bengal Club* (Calcutta, 1927), 13.

47. *Voyage dans l'Inde par Victor Jacquemont . . .* , I (1841), 212.

48. Morris, *Heaven's Command,* 179.

49. P. Stanley, *White Mutiny: British Military Culture in India, 1825–1875* (1998), 93.

50. E. M. Collingham, *Imperial Bodies* (2001), 106.

51. J. and R. Godden, *Two Under the Indian Sun* (1968), 13.

52. J. Lawrence and A. Woodiwiss (eds), *The Journals of Honoria Lawrence* (1980), 149.

53. J. K. Fairbank et al. (eds), *Entering China's Service: Robert Hart's Journals, 1854–1863* (1986), 61.

54. *Notes & Queries,* 127 (3 April 1853), 331.

55. Schama, *Citizens,* 776.

56. F. Parkes, *Wanderings of a Pilgrim in Search of the Picturesque* (1975 edn), 22 and 320.

57. Davis, *Great Game,* 30. Victor Jacquemont noted that his own "long mustachios" had "a very imposing effect on the scarcely-bearded people of the Himalaya." (Jacquemont, *Letters,* I, 213.)

58. *Blackwood's Magazine,* 53 (February 1843), 234.

59. Baird (ed.), *Dalhousie,* 43.

60. *The Times,* 18 April 1959.

61. N. Mansergh, *The Irish Question* (1975 edn), 126.

62. R. Reynolds, *Beards* (1950), 270.

63. *Royal Automobile Club Journal* (28 March 1907), 391.

64. Jacquemont, *Letters,* 23 and 92.

65. Trevelyan, *Competition Wallah,* 447.

66. C. C. Coffin, *Our New Way Round the World* (1883), 186.

67. R. S. S. Baden-Powell, *Indian Memories* (1915), 17.

68. Lawrence and Woodiwiss (eds), *Journals of Honoria Lawrence,* 67 and 97.

69. Allen, *Soldier Sahibs,* 107.

70. V. Dickinson (ed.), *Miss Eden's Letters* (1919), 281–2.

71. Bell, *Smith,* 96.

72. T. Pinney (ed.), *The Letters of Thomas Babington Macaulay,* III (Cambridge, 1976), 64, 35 and 37.

73. J. Clive, *Thomas Babington Macaulay* (1973), 295.

74. *LRB* (11 May 2006), 30.

75. Trevelyan, *Macaulay,* 553, 304, 305 and 323.

76. C. Allen, *The Buddha and the Sahibs: The Men Who Discovered India's Lost Religion* (2002), 165.

77. Trevelyan, *Macaulay,* 291.

78. *The Works of Lord Macaulay,* XI (1898), 586.

79. Lawrence, *Napier,* 136.

80. S. Wolpert, *A New History of India* (New York, 1977), 228.

81. C. Hibbert, *The Great Mutiny India 1857* (1980 edn), 51.

82. T. R. Metcalf, *The Aftermath of the Revolt: India 1857–1870* (Princeton, NJ, 1965), 40.

83. Baird (ed.), *Dalhousie,* 62, 225 and 283.

84. S. David, *The Indian Mutiny 1857* (2002), 62 and 77.

85. CSAS, Sampson Papers, 18 June 1857.

86. W. G. Broehl Jr., *Crisis of the Raj* (Hanover, NH, 1986), 49.

87. S. Gopal, *British Policy in India 1858–1905* (Cambridge, 1965), 1.

88. CSAS, Mill Papers, 12, 48, 23 and 7.

89. Broehl Jr., *Crisis,* 154.

90. R. M. Martin, *The Indian Empire,* II (n.d., c. 1860), 394.

91. J. W. Kaye, *A History of the Sepoy War in India,* II (1876), 677.

92. Allen, *Soldier Sahibs,* 293.

93. W. H. Russell, *My Indian Mutiny Diary,* ed. M. Edwardes (1957), 45.

94. CSAS, Campbell/Metcalfe Papers, Box IV, Captain Edward to Georgina Campbell, 26 and 13 July 1857.

95. A. N. Wilson, *The Victorians* (2002), 223.

96. OIOC, MSS Eur C910, Cracklow Papers, George Cracklow to his mother, 28 October 1857.

97. Hibbert, *Great Mutiny,* 212 and 317.

98. V. D. Majendie, *Up Among the Pandies* (1859), 223.

99. A. Taylor, *Laurence Oliphant* (Oxford, 1982), 50.

100. A. Ward, *Our Bones are Scattered* (1996), 447.

101. R. Mukherjee, "'Satan Let Loose upon Earth': The Kanpur Massacres in India in the Revolt of 1857," *PP,* 128 (August 1990), 92.

102. Metcalf, *Aftermath,* 306.

103. Kaye, *Sepoy War,* II, 491.

104. OIOC, MSS Eur C860, Talbot Letters, J. R. Block to Gerald Talbot (Canning's secretary).

105. Martin, *Indian Empire,* II, 409.

106. *Punch,* 22 August 1857.

107. Trevelyan, *Macaulay,* 656.

108. H. H. Greathed, *Letters Written during the Siege of Delhi* (1858), 31.

109. Broehl Jr., *Crisis,* 97.

110. Greathed, *Letters,* 176.

111. OIOC, MSS Eur C910, George Cracklow to his mother, 22 September 1857.

112. Roberts, *Forty-one Years in India,* I, 258–9.

113. CSAS, Campbell/Metcalfe Papers, Box IV, Georgina to Captain Edward Campbell, 1 October 1857.

114. Allen, *Soldier Sahibs,* 335.

115. Pemberton Papers, 7/18/28, Francis Pemberton Campbell to his mother, 18 January [1859?].

116. Russell, *Mutiny Diary,* 114. Russell was quoting from Thomas Campbell's poem "Pleasures of Hope" (1899), I, l. 376. I am grateful to Dr. Richard Duncan-Jones for tracking down this elusive line.

117. Gopal, *British Policy in India,* 57. Disraeli himself thought that the habit of referring to Indians as "niggers" was disgusting, ignorant, brutal and mischievous (M. Bentley, *Lord Salisbury's World* [Cambridge, 2001], 223–4). Despite his ugly reputation, the explorer Henry Morton Stanley also condemned the term. As late as 1933 a character in Bernard Shaw's political play *On the Rocks* says, "That one word nigger will cost us India." Not until the Second World War, under pressure from the West Indian George Padmore, described by MI5 as one of the country's "most prominent left wing negros" [sic], did the BBC cease to use the word "nigger."

118. Metcalf, *Aftermath,* 154.

119. I. Klein, "Materialism, Mutiny and Modernization in British India," *MAS,* 34, 3 (2000), 561.

120. *The Times,* 4 January 1878.

121. *Rudyard Kipling's Verse* (New York, 1938), 233.

122. C. Trevelyan, *On the Education of the People of India* (1838), 190. Trevelyan not only wrote in the spirit of Macaulay but also of Gibbon, who had deplored the fact that Muslims deprived themselves of classical learning which might have "unlocked the fetters of eastern despo-

tism, diffused a liberal spirit of enquiry and toleration, and encouraged the Arabian sages to suspect that their caliph was a tyrant, and their prophet an impostor." (Ibid, 45.)

123. *Daily Telegraph,* 3 September 1897. The offensive adjective was frequently attached to the noun, on this occasion by young Winston Churchill.
124. C. Hibbert, *Queen Victoria* (2000), 251.
125. *Englishman,* 5 November 1858.
126. G. Ritchie, *The Ritchies in India* (1920), 204.
127. Majendie, *Pandies,* 358.

6. Spread the Peaceful Gospel—with the Maxim Gun

1. J. Lord, *The Maharajahs* (1972), 56.
2. Hibbert, *Queen Victoria,* 365.
3. M. Alexander and S. Anand, *Queen Victoria's Maharajah* (1980), 45 and 49.
4. E. Longford, *Queen Victoria* (1964), 427.
5. *Annual Register* (1876), 12.
6. N. Vance, *The Victorians and Ancient Rome* (Oxford, 1997), 225.
7. R. Blake, *Disraeli* (1974 edn), 563.
8. B. S. Cohn, "Representing Authority in Victorian India," in E. Hobsbawm and T. Ranger (eds), *The Invention of Tradition* (1983), 200.
9. N. Parsons, *King Khama, Emperor Joe and the Great White Queen* (1998), 221.
10. Morris, *Pax Britannica,* 44.
11. D. R. Morris, *The Washing of the Spears* (1994 edn), 296.
12. J. E. Flint, *Sir George Goldie and the Making of Nigeria* (1960), 209.
13. D. Gilmour, *Curzon* (1994), 234.
14. Morris, *Spectacle of Empire,* 185.
15. A. Draper, *The Amritsar Massacre* (1985), 64.
16. S. Bolt, *Pseudo Sahib* (Aylesbeare, 2007), 208.
17. P. Gillingham, *At the Peak: Hong Kong between the Wars* (Hong Kong, 1983), 25. In India there was little iconoclasm after independence. Some statues of Queen Victoria were consigned to an imperial necropolis of the kind created outside Delhi and Lucknow. Others were sold to the West Indies. I found one at the end of a corridor in the Udaipur public library. Even in Allahabad, citadel of the Congress Party, the Queen was revered. There, Sydney Bolt records, the "removal of her statue was effected surreptitiously by night, with an armed force standing by in case of riot." (*Pseudo Sahib,* 209.)
18. G. Lamming, *In the Castle of My Skin* (1970 edn), 56.
19. C. Dunn, *Central African Witness* (1959), 100.
20. D. Cannadine, *Ornamentalism: How the British Saw Their Empire* (2001), 105.
21. O. Anderson, "The Growth of Christian Militarism," *HRE,* 86 (1971), 49.
22. J. Ellis, *The Social History of the Machine Gun* (1975), 99.
23. *The Times,* 6 October 1873.
24. A. Allfrey, *Man of Arms: The Life and Legend of Sir Basil Zaharoff* (1989), 67.
25. J. A. Hobson, *Imperialism* (1948 edn), 126.
26. R. Baden-Powell, *The Matabele Campaign 1896* (1897), 398, 64 and 155.
27. *OHBE,* III, 248.
28. D. C. M. Platt, *Latin America and British Trade 1806–1914* (1972), 222.
29. R. Burton, *Wanderings in West Africa,* II (1863), 213.
30. H. T. Bernstein, *Steamboats on the Ganges* (1987 edn), 74.
31. J. H. Clapham, *An Economic History of Modern Britain,* II (Cambridge, 1926), 5.

32. Coffin, *Round the World,* 507.

33. Busteed, *Calcutta,* 66.

34. R. E. B. Duff, *100 Years of the Suez Canal* (1969), 55.

35. *Punch,* 18 May 1861.

36. A. Moorehead, *The White Nile* (1976), 147.

37. Blake, *Disraeli,* 584.

38. D. A. Farnie, *East and West of Suez: The Suez Canal in History, 1854–1956* (Oxford, 1969), 235.

39. W. Hepworth Dixon, *British Cyprus* (1879), 10.

40. Farnie, *Suez,* 233.

41. The title of J. R. Jefferies' book (1876), subtitled *Or, How Miss Britannia Bought a Dirty Puddle and Lost Her Sugar-Plums.*

42. Gibbon, *Decline and Fall,* I, 77.

43. Bryce, *Ancient Roman Empire,* 13.

44. *Quarterly Review,* 125 (1868), 55 and 65.

45. C. O. Burge, *The Adventures of a Civil Engineer* (1909), 120.

46. R. MacLeod and D. Kumar (eds), *Technology and the Raj* (1995), 178.

47. J. Richards and J. M. McKenzie, *The Railway Station: A Social History* (Oxford, 1986), 68.

48. I. J. Kerr, *Building the Railways of the Raj 1850–1900* (Delhi, 1995), 141.

49. D. Arnold, *The New Cambridge History of India,* III.5: *Science, Technology and Medicine in Colonial India* (Cambridge, 2000), 122.

50. H. Perkin, *The Railway Age* (1970), 119.

51. Davis, *Late Victorian Holocausts,* 26.

52. T. Pinney (ed.), *Kipling's India: Uncollected Sketches 1884–8* (1986), 33.

53. Mansergh, *Commonwealth Experience,* 50.

54. *Quarterly Review,* 125, 77.

55. Seeley, *Expansion,* 61.

56. CSAS, Macpherson Papers, Reel 9, Section 74, Dr. William Dick to William Macpherson, 25 November 1801. This prophylactic had probably been known to the Incas but Europeans were slow to adopt it.

57. J. R. Ryan, *Picturing the Empire: Photography and the Visualization of the British Empire* (1997), 72.

58. G. Geary, *Burma, After the Conquest* (1886), 241.

59. Eldridge, *England's Mission,* 45.

60. M. Kingsley, *West African Studies* (1899), 386.

61. M. Adas, *Machines as the Measure of Men: Science, Technology, and Ideologies of Western Dominance* (Ithaca, NY, 1989), 300.

62. J. Hunt, *On the Negro's Place in Nature* (1863), 27, 45, 18, 21, 20 and 46.

63. J. A. B. Horton, *West African Countries and Peoples . . . a Vindication of the African Race* (1868), 34 and 30. Horton's book echoed sentiments and phrases from W. Armistead's notable *Tribute for the Negro* (Manchester, 1848).

64. J. C. Nott, "The Negro Race," *Popular Magazine of Anthropology,* III (July 1866), 117.

65. J. C. Greene, *The Death of Adam* (Ames, IA, 1959), 318.

66. H. Spencer, *An Autobiography,* I (1904), 363.

67. P. Knaplund (ed.), "Gordon–Gladstone Correspondence, 1851–1896," *Transactions of the American Philosophical Society,* 51 (1961), 89.

68. Dilke, *Greater Britain,* 85.

69. W. Reade, *The Martyrdom of Man* (1968 edn), 412.

70. W. Reade, *Savage Africa* (1863), 587.

71. *Popular Magazine of Anthropology,* I (January 1866), 10.

72. G. Himmelfarb, *Darwin and the Darwinian Revolution* (1959), 213.

73. P. Appleman (ed.), *Darwin* (New York, 1970), 646.

74. Reade, *Savage Africa,* 509.

75. *The Times,* 18 November 1865.

76. L. Huxley, *Life and Letters of Thomas Henry Huxley,* I (1900), 280–81.

77. B. Porter, *The Absent-Minded Imperialists* (2004), 48.

78. J. A. Froude, *Carlyle's Life in London,* II (1891), 351 and 390.

79. T. Carlyle, "The Nigger Question," in *English and Other Critical Essays* (Everyman, n.d.), 310.

80. *The Autobiography of John Stuart Mill* (1958 edn), 254.

81. *Westminster Review,* 84 (1865), 489.

82. Wilson, *Victorians,* 272.

83. P. A. Brunt, "Reflections on British and Roman Imperialism," *CSSH,* VII (1965), 282.

84. *Contemporary Review,* XXXIV (December 1878), 6.

85. S. W. Baker, *Albert N'Yanza,* I (1866), 63.

86. F. Driver, *Geography Militant: Cultures of Exploration* (2001), 45.

87. H. M. Stanley, *How I Found Livingstone* (1872), 112.

88. R. I. Rotberg (ed.), *Africa and Its Explorers* (Cambridge, MA, 1970), 301.

89. T. Pocock, *Rider Haggard and the Lost Empire* (1993), 6 and 110.

90. Conrad, *Heart of Darkness,* 52, 51 and 69.

91. Baker, *Albert N'Yanza,* I, 67; and II, 94, 25–6.

92. S. W. Baker, *Eight Years in Ceylon* (1874), 62.

93. Baker, *Albert N'Yanza,* II, 51.

94. Baker, *Ceylon,* 316.

95. Baker, *Albert N'Yanza,* I, xxii.

96. Baker, *Ceylon,* 313.

97. Burton, *Wanderings,* II, 58.

98. T. Jeal, *Livingstone* (1973), 131.

99. D. Livingstone, *Missionary Travels* (1857), 551.

100. W. S. Blunt, *My Diaries,* I, *1888–1900* (1919), 94.

101. E. Huxley, *White Man's Country: Lord Delamere and the Making of Kenya,* I (1935), 83.

102. R. Burton, *The Lake Regions of Central Africa,* I (1860), 389.

103. Burton, *Wanderings,* II, 93, 86 and 72.

104. *Blackwood's Magazine,* 82 (March 1858), 282.

105. W. S. Blunt, *My Diaries,* II, *1900–1914* (1920), 134.

106. E. W. Said, *Orientalism* (Harmondsworth, 1978), 195. Having condemned the West's misapprehensions about the Orient, themselves the product of imperial hegemony, Said characteristically condemns Burton's knowledge as a means of domination.

107. R. Burton, *The Sotadic Zone* (New York, n.d.), 18.

108. Burton, *Wanderings,* I, 65–6 and 51.

109. F. McLynn, *Burton: Snow upon the Desert* (1990), 118.

110. R. Coupland, *The Exploitation of East Africa 1856–1890* (1939), 327.

111. T. Jeal, *Stanley* (2007), 178.

112. Stanley, *Livingstone,* 140.

113. H. M. Stanley, *In Darkest Africa,* I (1890), 301.

114. *Saturday Review,* 42, 2 September and 26 August 1876.

115. F. McLynn, *Stanley: The Making of an African Explorer* (1989), 215.

116. Hall, *Stanley,* 228.

117. B. Bond (ed.), *Victorian Military Campaigns* (1967), 10–11.

118. F. Harcourt, "Disraeli's Imperialism, 1866–1868: A Question of Timing," *HJ,* 31, 1 (1980), 99.

119. Gibbon, *Decline and Fall*, II, 999.
120. D. Cumming, *The Gentleman Savage: The Life of Mansfield Parkyns 1823–1894* (1987), 156.
121. BECM, 1999/054, Diary of Godfrey Twiss, 1 March 1868.
122. H. M. Stanley, *Coomassie and Magdala* (1874), 338.
123. BECM, 1999/054, 29 February and 5 March 1868.
124. Stanley, *Coomassie and Magdala,* 419 and 457–9.
125. BECM, 1999/054, 17 May 1868.
126. P. D. Curtin, *Disease and Empire* (Cambridge, 1988), 30.
127. H. A. C. Cairns, *Prelude to Imperialism* (1965), 27. This was Lugard's opinion.
128. *Blackwood's Magazine,* 83 (February–May, 1858), 203. This was Burton's description.
129. D. Stanley (ed.), *The Autobiography of Sir Henry Morton Stanley* (1909), 296.
130. Stanley, *Livingstone,* 411. Tim Jeal (*Stanley,* 117) subjects the famous greeting to close analysis and has doubts about its authenticity.
131. Stanley (ed.), *Autobiography of Stanley,* 272.
132. Stanley, *Livingstone,* 434–5.
133. CUL RCMS, Col. Luke Norman's Diary, 27 December 1868.
134. D. O. Helly, *Livingstone's Legacy* (Athens, OH, 1987), 234.
135. Jeal, *Livingstone,* 206 and 208.
136. J. P. R. Wallis (ed.), *The Zambesi Journal of James Stewart 1863–1863* (1952), 190.
137. Coupland, *Exploitation of East Africa,* 131.
138. I. Schapera (ed.), *Livingstone's African Journal 1853–56,* I (1963), 32.
139. J. Thomson, "The Results of European Intercourse with the African," *Contemporary Review,* LVII (March 1890), 343.
140. C. Dickens, *Bleak House* (New York, 1962 edn), 49.
141. C. Bolt, *Victorian Attitudes to Race* (1971), 8.
142. Helly, *Livingstone's Legacy,* 215.
143. *British Quarterly Review,* 61 (1875), 397.
144. Symonds, *Oxford and Empire,* 221.
145. F. Jackson, *Early Days in East Africa* (1930 edn), 77.
146. Jeal, *Livingstone,* 356.
147. Hall, *Stanley,* 199.
148. Stanley (ed.), *Autobiography of Stanley,* 328, 324 and 327.
149. R. Stanley and A. Neame (eds), *The Exploration Diaries of H. M. Stanley* (1961), 163 and 165.
150. F. Driver, "Henry Morton Stanley and His Critics: Geography, Exploration and Empire," *PP,* 133 (November 1991), 135.
151. Stanley (ed.), *Autobiography of Stanley,* 352.
152. V. Kiernan, *The Lords of Human Kind* (1995 edn), 244.
153. T. Youngs, *Travellers in Africa* (Manchester, 1994), 194.
154. Jeal, *Livingstone,* 382.
155. *Edinburgh Review,* 159 (1884), 591.
156. *CHBE,* III, 61.
157. Eldridge, *England's Mission,* 152.
158. W. D. Rubinstein, *Capitalism, Culture, and Decline in Britain 1750–1990* (1993), 136.
159. M. J. Wiener, *English Culture and the Decline of the Industrial Spirit 1850–1980* (Cambridge, 1985 edn), 18 and 22.
160. *The Times,* 30 August 1944.
161. E. J. Hobsbawm, *Industry and Empire* (1969 edn), 186.
162. E. C. Mack, *Public Schools and British Opinion since 1860* (New York, 1941), 242.
163. T. Hughes, *Tom Brown at Oxford* (1889 edn), 48.
164. D. Landes, *The Unbound Prometheus* (Cambridge, 1969), 285.

165. Cain and Hopkins, *British Imperialism,* 172–3. The Chancellor was George Goschen.
166. L. Edel (ed.), *Henry James Letters,* II (1975), 145.
167. P. Magnus, *Gladstone* (1970 edn), 262.
168. R. T. Harrison, *Gladstone's Imperialism in Egypt* (Westport, CT, 1995), 160.
169. W. E. Gladstone, "Aggression on Egypt and Freedom in the East," *Nineteenth Century,* II (August 1877), 158–9.
170. E. Dicey, "Mr. Gladstone and Our Empire," *Nineteenth Century,* II (September 1877), 307.
171. P. Gifford and W. R. Louis, *France and Britain in Africa* (1971), 73.
172. Magnus, *Gladstone,* 261.
173. E. Stokes, "Milnerism," *HJ,* VI (1962), 47.
174. J. Morley, *The Life of William Ewart Gladstone,* II (1903), 595.
175. W. E. Gladstone, *Midlothian Speeches 1879* (Leicester, 1971), 128.
176. PRO, 30/40/9, Ardagh Papers.
177. Robinson and Gallagher, *Africa,* 96–7.
178. A. G. Hopkins, "The Victorians and Africa: A Reconsideration of the Occupation of Egypt, 1882," *JAH,* 27 (1986), 384.
179. *DNB.*
180. Dilke, *Greater Britain,* 560.
181. H. W. Wilson, *Ironclads in Action,* I (1897), 353.
182. W. S. Blunt, *A Secret History of the British Occupation of Egypt* (1907), 14.
183. Lehmann, *All Sir Garnet,* 312.
184. G. Arthur (ed.), *The Letters of Lord and Lady Wolseley 1870–1911* (1922), 74 and 72.
185. A. Preston, "Wolseley, the Khartoum Relief Expedition and the Defence of India, 1885–1900," *JICH,* VI (May 1978), 257.
186. W. Butler, *An Autobiography* (1913), 240.
187. R. Churchill, *The Rise and Fall of Sir Anthony Eden* (1959), 298.
188. Blunt, *Secret History,* 428.
189. CUL RCMS 113/11, Gordon Letters, Gordon to Baker, 21 July 1882.
190. Butler, *Autobiography,* 248–9.
191. W. E. H. Lecky, *Democracy and Liberty,* I (1899), xxviii and xxvi.
192. *Edinburgh Review,* 154 (1881), 549.
193. A. Moore-Harell, *Gordon and the Sudan* (2001), 51.
194. CAC, ESHR 13/7, December 1880.
195. C. Chenevix Trench, *Charley Gordon: An Eminent Victorian Reassessed* (1978), 157.
196. Butler, *Autobiography,* 191.
197. PRO, 30/40/9.
198. Magnus, *Gladstone,* 309.
199. R. L. Schults, *Crusader in Babylon* (Lincoln, NB, 1972), 66.
200. R. Jenkins, *Sir Charles Dilke* (1968 edn), 181.
201. J. Pollock, *Gordon: The Man Behind the Legend* (1993), 303.
202. Earl of Cromer, *Modern Egypt,* I (1908), 448.
203. Lord Elton (ed.), *General Gordon's Khartoum Journal* (1961), 56.
204. O. Woods and J. Bishop, *The Story of the Times* (1983), 130.
205. Lehmann, *All Sir Garnet,* 341.
206. [Edwarda Gibbon], *The History of the Decline and Fall of the British Empire* (1884), 12, 4 and 32.
207. Elton (ed.), *Khartoum Journal,* 49 and 73.
208. W. F. Butler, *The Campaign of the Cataracts* (1887), 119.
209. C. Knox, *It Might Have Been You* (1938), 223.
210. R. Kipling, *Selected Verse* (1983 edn), 163.

211. Cromer, *Modern Egypt*, II, 11.
212. A. Preston (ed.), *In Relief of Gordon: Lord Wolseley's Campaign of the Khartoum Relief Expedition 1884–1885* (1967), 136.
213. Cromer, *Modern Egypt*, II, 364 and 128.
214. J. Marlowe, *Cromer in Egypt* (1970), 109 and 142.
215. P. Mansfield, *The British in Egypt* (1971), 58.
216. R. Kipling, *Letters of Travel (1892–1913)* (n.d.), 232.
217. [M. Bell], *Khedives and Pashas* (1884), 245.
218. Earl of Cromer, *Modern Egypt*, I (1908), 7.
219. CAC, OCON, 2 April 1892.
220. Lord d'Abernon, *Portraits and Appreciations* (1931), 14.
221. A. Lutfi al-Sayyid, *Egypt and Cromer* (1968), 78.
222. Hobson, *Imperialism*, 207–11.
223. L. Strachey, *Eminent Victorians* (1934 edn), 301.
224. R. Kipling, *Letters of Travel* (1920), 254.
225. al-Sayyid, *Egypt and Cromer*, 63.
226. Cromer, *Modern Egypt*, II, 476.
227. *Review of Reviews*, XXI (April 1900), 324.
228. R. Owen, *Lord Cromer* (2004), 306.
229. G. W. Steevens, *From Capetown to Ladysmith and Egypt in 1898* (1900), 240 and 233.
230. D. Sladen, *Egypt and the English* (1908), 73.
231. Blunt, *Diaries*, II, 198.
232. Brendon, *Cook*, 231, 201, 232 and 223.
233. W. M. Fullerton, *In Cairo* (1891), 6–7.
234. Cumming, *Gentleman Savage*, 17.
235. D. Landes, *Bankers and Pashas* (1958), 318.
236. M. Rodenbeck, *Cairo: The City Victorious* (1998), xi.
237. Fullerton, *Cairo*, 16.
238. A. Edwards, *A Thousand Miles up the Nile* (1982 edn), 151.
239. F. Nightingale, *Letters from Egypt*, ed. A. Sattin (1987), 63 and 74.
240. Cromer, *Modern Egypt*, II, 571.
241. M. E. Chamberlain, "Lord Cromer's 'Ancient and Modern Imperialism,'" *JBS*, XII (November 1972), 66.
242. Cromer, *Ancient and Modern Imperialism*, 118.

7. A Magnificent Empire Under the British Flag

1. Mostert, *Frontiers*, 174 and 781.
2. R. W. F. Drooglever, *The Road to Isandhlwana* (1992), 153.
3. Morris, *Spears*, 148.
4. *Edinburgh Review*, 145 (April 1877), 469.
5. T. Keegan, *Colonial South Africa and the Origins of the Racial Order* (Leicester, 1996), 288.
6. Froude, *Short Studies*, III, 493 and 499.
7. P. Lewsen (ed.), *Selections from the Correspondence of J. X. Merriman 1879–1890* (Cape Town, 1960), 24.
8. Pocock, *Haggard*, 21.
9. B. Worsfold, *Sir Bartle Frere* (1923), 225.
10. *DNB*.
11. *Edinburgh Review*, 182 (July 1895), 163.

12. A. Preston (ed.), *The South African Journal of Sir Garnet Wolseley 1879–1880* (Cape Town, 1973), 39.
13. Worsfold, *Frere*, 137.
14. R. L. Cope, "Written in Characters of Blood? The Reign of King Cetshwayo Ka Mpande 1872–9," *JAH*, 36 (1995), 247.
15. W. R. Haggard, *Cetywayo and His White Neighbours* (1888), 215.
16. C. W. De Kiewiet, *The Imperial Factor in South Africa* (1965 edn), 230.
17. Morris, *Spears*, 400.
18. I. Knight, *The Anatomy of the Zulu Army from Shaka to Cetshwayo* (1993), 219.
19. Morris, *Spears*, 387.
20. Pakenham, *Scramble*, 70.
21. S. Taylor, *Shaka's Children* (1994), 249.
22. R. B. Edgerton, *Like Lions They Fought* (1988), 14.
23. J. Meintjes, *President Paul Kruger* (1974), 93.
24. D. M. Schreuder, *Gladstone and Kruger* (1969), 63 and 88.
25. *CHBE*, VIII (1963), 494.
26. Schreuder, *Gladstone and Kruger*, 123.
27. W. F. Butler, *The Life of Sir George Pomeroy-Colley* (1899), 400.
28. O. Ransford, *The Battle of Majuba Hill* (1967), 114.
29. B. Bond, "The Disaster at Majuba Hill 1881," *HT* (July 1985), 493.
30. H. C. G. Matthew (ed.), *The Gladstone Diaries*, X (1990), 25.
31. Schreuder, *Gladstone and Kruger*, 207 and 97.
32. L. Woolf, *Empire and Commonwealth in Africa* (1920), 34.
33. P. Gifford and W. R. Louis, *Britain and Germany in Africa* (1967), 4 and 340.
34. Robinson and Gallagher, *Africa*, 204.
35. Schreuder, *Gladstone and Kruger*, 440.
36. Robinson and Gallagher, *Africa*, 178.
37. Lewsen (ed.), *Merriman*, 266 and 245.
38. *Review of Reviews*, XX (July 1899), 35.
39. W. T. Stead, *The Last Will and Testament of Cecil John Rhodes* (1902), 58–9 and 73.
40. H. Kingsmill, *After Puritanism* (1929), 200.
41. D. M. Reid, "Cromer and the Classics: Imperialism, Nationalism and the Greco-Roman Past in Modern Egypt," *MES*, 32 (January 1996), 7.
42. R. I. Rotberg, *The Founder: Cecil Rhodes and the Pursuit of Power* (Oxford, 1988), 8.
43. O. Spengler, *The Decline of the West* (1926 edn), 37.
44. E. Rosenthal, *Gold! Gold! Gold!* (New York, 1970), 34.
45. A. Trollope, *South Africa* (Cape Town, 1973 edn), 362.
46. Rotberg, *Rhodes*, 190.
47. A. Nutting, *Scramble for Africa* (1970), 121.
48. M. Tamarkin, *Cecil Rhodes and the Afrikaners* (1996), 139.
49. Hobson, *Imperialism*, 59.
50. S. D. Chapman, "Rhodes and the City of London: Another View of Imperialism," *HJ*, 28, 3 (1985), 657 and 653.
51. Rotberg, *Rhodes*, 233.
52. W. A. Wills and L. T. Collingridge, *The Downfall of Lobengula* (Bulawayo, 1971 edn), 32.
53. I. Colvin, *Life of Jameson*, I (1922), 140.
54. F. Welsh, *A History of South Africa* (1998), 315.
55. *The Memoirs of Paul Kruger*, I (1902), 216.
56. T. L. Makhura, "Another Road to the Raid: The Neglected Role of the Boer–Bagananwa War as a Factor in the Coming of the Jameson Raid, 1894–1895," *JSAS*, 21, 2 (June 1995), 264.

57. Chapman, *HJ*, 28, 660.
58. J. L. Garvin, *The Life of Joseph Chamberlain*, III (1934), 42.
59. J. van der Poel, *The Jameson Raid* (Cape Town, 1951), 56 and 71.
60. *Westminster Budget*, 17 November 1893.
61. H. M. Hole, *Old Rhodesian Days* (1928), 33.
62. NAM, 1999–07–20, Lieutenant Edward Leary's Diary, July 1897.
63. Poel, *Jameson Raid*, 75, 85 and 104.
64. Blunt, *Diaries*, I, 262.
65. Gilmour, *Recessional*, 134.
66. W. O. Baylen, "W. T. Stead's *History of the Mystery* of the Jameson Raid," *JBS*, 4 (November 1964), 108.
67. M. Friedmann's introduction to O. Schreiner, *Trooper Peter Halket of Mashonaland* (Johannesburg, 2001 edn), 10.
68. CAC, ESHR 5/6, Chamberlain to R. Brett, 3 January 1896.
69. V. Harlow, "Sir Frederic Hamilton's Narrative of Events Relative to the Jameson Raid," *EHR*, 72 (April 1957), 301.
70. CAC, STED 5/1, B. F. Hawksley to Rhodes, 9 April 1897.
71. E. Longford, *Jameson's Raid* (1982 edn), 264. The phrase was apparently coined by W. T. Stead.
72. W. S. Churchill, *The World Crisis* (1938 edn), 14.
73. Robinson and Gallagher, *Africa*, 335.
74. R. Coupland, *East Africa and Its Invaders* (1939), 457.
75. *CHA*, VI, 107.
76. Pakenham, *Scramble*, 13.
77. L. H. Gann and P. Duignan, *Rulers of British Africa 1870–1914* (1978), 22.
78. *Fortnightly Review*, 37 (January 1885), 193.
79. Gifford and Louis, *Britain and Germany*, 341.
80. G. M. Tuckwell, *The Life of Sir Charles Dilke*, II (1917), 256.
81. P. French, *Younghusband* (1994), 95.
82. Woolf, *Empire and Commerce*, 45.
83. K. Rose, *The Later Cecils* (1975), 34.
84. P. Smith (ed.), *Lord Salisbury on Politics* (Cambridge, 1972), 48.
85. Roberts, *Salisbury*, 43 and 169.
86. P. A. Baran, *The Political Economy of Growth* (1957), 145.
87. Roberts, *Salisbury*, 722.
88. Rose, *Later Cecils*, 23.
89. [Lord Salisbury], "Disintegration," *Quarterly Review*, 156 (1883), 562.
90. Roberts, *Salisbury*, 43.
91. D. Kimble, *A Political History of Ghana* (Oxford, 1967), 13.
92. R. Oliver, *Sir Harry Johnston and the Scramble for Africa* (1957), 121–2 and 175.
93. H. H. Johnston, *British Central Africa* (1897), 183–4.
94. D. Wellesley, *Sir George Goldie* (1934), 80, 94 and 91.
95. M. Perham and M. Bull, *The Diaries of Lord Lugard*, IV (1963), 82.
96. B. Porter, *Critics of Empire* (1968), 62.
97. Wellesley, *Goldie*, 62.
98. J. S. Galbraith, *Mackinnon and East Africa 1878–1895: A Study in the "New Imperialism"* (Cambridge, 1972), 228.
99. *Review of Reviews*, II (July 1890), 8.
100. Robinson and Gallagher, *Africa*, 301.

101. W. R. Louis, "Sir Percy Anderson's Grand African Strategy 1883–1896," *EHR*, 81 (April 1966), 305.

102. Lady G. Cecil, *Life of Robert, Marquis of Salisbury*, IV (1933), 323.

103. M. Perham, *Lugard: The Years of Adventure 1858–1898* (1956), 513 and 499.

104. Flint, *Goldie*, 263.

105. Wellesley, *Goldie*, 70.

106. T. Falola, *The History of Nigeria* (Westport, CT, 1999), 70.

107. Lord Lugard, *The Dual Mandate in Tropical Africa*, ed. M. Perham (1965), 618–19, xlvii and 80–81.

108. M. Perham, *Lugard: The Years of Authority 1898–1945* (1960), 199 and 201.

109. P. J. Crozier, *Five Years Hard* (1932), 161–3 and 149–50.

110. R. Hyam, *Elgin and Churchill at the Colonial Office* (1968), 208.

111. B. Semmel, *Imperialism and Social Reform 1895–1914* (1960), 16.

112. Gann and Duignan, *Rulers of British Africa*, 36.

113. P. Fraser, *Joseph Chamberlain* (1966), 206.

114. Blunt, *Diaries*, I, 346.

115. F. Balfour, *Ne Obliviscaris*, II (1930), 332.

116. J. Mordaunt Crook, *The Rise of the Nouveaux Riches* (1999), 30.

117. K. Muggeridge and R. Adam, *Beatrice Webb: A Life 1858–1943* (1967), 89.

118. J. Amery, *The Life of Joseph Chamberlain*, V (1969), 69.

119. J. L. Garvin, *The Life of Joseph Chamberlain*, III (1934), 16.

120. Balfour, *Ne Obliviscaris*, II, 270.

121. Blunt, *Diaries*, I, 262.

122. Jackson, *East Africa*, 321.

123. Oliver, *Johnston*, 293.

124. G. W. Steevens, *With Kitchener to Khartoum* (1990 edn), 4.

125. W. Churchill, *The River War*, I (1899 edn), 276.

126. W. Storrs, *Orientations* (1945 edn), 105.

127. PRO, 30/57/10, Kitchener Papers, Kitchener to Sir Edward Barrington, 21 May 1896.

128. Ibid., Wolseley to Kitchener, 14 April 1898.

129. P. Warner, *Kitchener* (1985), 13.

130. P. Magnus, *Kitchener: Portrait of an Imperialist* (1968 edn), 175.

131. J. Pollock, *Kitchener* (2001), 101.

132. French, *Younghusband*, 152.

133. Storrs, *Orientations*, 105.

134. J. Lees-Milne, *The Enigmatic Edwardian* (1986), 215.

135. Lycett, *Kipling*, 426.

136. P. Brendon, *Winston Churchill: A Brief Life* (2001 edn), 26.

137. Magnus, *Kitchener*, 158.

138. Steevens, *Kitchener*, 266.

139. R. S. Churchill, *Winston S. Churchill*, I (1966), 425.

140. L. James, *The Savage Wars* (1985), 4.

141. H. and M. Cecil, *Imperial Marriage* (2002), 90.

142. M. W. Daly, *Empire on the Nile* (Cambridge, 1986), 6.

143. D. Scott (ed.), *Douglas Haig: The Preparatory Prologue 1861–1914* (Barnsley, 2006), 102–3.

144. Private information: Colonel Maurice Willoughby.

145. D. L. Lewis, *The Race to Fashoda* (1988), 220.

146. Blunt, *Diaries*, I, 367.

147. E. N. Bennett, "After Omdurman," *Contemporary Review*, LXXV (January 1899), 23.

148. Churchill, *River War*, II, 196.

149. R. Wallace, "The Seamy Side of Imperialism," *Contemporary Review*, LXXV (June 1899), 783.

150. W. Churchill, *The Story of the Malakand Field Force* (1974 edn), 95.

151. W. Churchill, *Savrola* (1990 edn), 78. Churchill maintained (78–9) that the British had moral ascendancy as well as might on their side whereas the Romans "had only their swords . . . and when they became effete they could no longer wield them."

152. CAC, CHAR 8/2/7.

153. R. Kipling, *Stalky and Co.* (1982 edn), 214.

154. W. S. Churchill (ed.), *Never Give In!* (2003), 4.

155. R. Hyam, *Empire and Sexuality: The British Experience* (Manchester, 1990), 78.

156. P. Brendon, *Eminent Edwardians* (2003 edn), 215.

157. T. Hodgkin, "The Fall of the Roman Empire and Its Lessons for Us," *Fortnightly Review*, LXXIII (January 1898), 70.

158. A. Lyall, *The Rise and Expansion of the British Dominion in India* (1907 edn), 346.

159. M. G. Jessett, *The Bond of Empire* (1902), xi.

160. *Review of Reviews*, XVI (July 1897), 83–4.

161. M. Twain, *Europe and Elsewhere* (1923), 206 and 207.

162. *Illustrated London News*, 12 June 1897.

163. Gibbon, *Decline and Fall*, I, 211.

164. Garvin, *Chamberlain*, III, 195.

165. F. Driver and D. Gilbert, *Imperial Cities: Landscape, Display and Identity* (Manchester, 1999), 96.

166. *Illustrated London News*, 12 June 1897.

167. C. Hibbert, *Queen Victoria in her Letters and Journals* (1984), 335.

168. G. W. Steevens, *Things Seen* (1900), 193–4.

169. Twain, *Europe*, 209.

170. Hibbert, *Letters and Journals*, 335.

171. *Review of Reviews*, XVI (July 1897), 85.

172. R. Shannon, *Gladstone: Heroic Minister 1865–1898* (1999), 588.

173. C. Hibbert, *Queen Victoria* (2000), 458.

174. Roberts, *Salisbury*, 663.

175. F. Harrison, "The Monarchy," *Fortnightly Review*, LXVI (June 1872), 624.

176. J. A. S. Grenville, *Lord Salisbury and Foreign Policy: The Close of the Nineteenth Century* (1970 edn), 4.

177. A. Wilson, *The Strange Ride of Rudyard Kipling* (1977), 202.

178. Kipling, *Verse*, 130.

179. W. Clarke, "The Social Future of England," *Contemporary Review*, 78 (December 1900), 860.

180. Ritortus, "The Imperialism of British Trade," *Contemporary Review*, 67 (August 1899), 296.

181. Steevens, *Things Seen*, 23, 28, 30 and 36.

182. A. M. Gollin, *Proconsul in Politics* (1964), 17. The phrase was Rosebery's.

183. J. Springhall, *Youth, Empire and Society* (1977), 42.

184. D. Judd, *Balfour and the British Empire* (1968), 44.

185. *Review of Reviews*, XVI (August 1897), 153.

186. Thompson, *Empires on the Pacific*, 45. (I have improved the punctuation.)

187. H. Brogan, *Longman History of the United States of America* (1985), 453.

188. Garvin, *Chamberlain*, III, 302.

189. C. S. Campbell, *Anglo-American Understanding 1898–1903* (Baltimore, 1957), 45–6.

190. J. Keay, *Last Post: The End of Empire in the Far East* (1997), 117, 104 and 115–16.

191. Goldwin Smith, *Commonwealth or Empire: A Bystander's View of the Question* (1902), 48, 60, 31 and 52.

8. Barbarians Thundering at the Frontiers

1. W. K. Hancock, *Smuts,* I (Cambridge, 1962), 109.
2. F. Wheen, *Karl Marx* (1999), 370.
3. D. Judd and K. Surridge, *The Boer War* (2002), 241 and 243.
4. D. Steele, "Salisbury and the Soldiers," in J. Gooch (ed.), *The Boer War* (2000), 14.
5. J. Wilson, *CB: A Life of Sir Henry Campbell-Bannerman* (1973), 349.
6. C. Headlam (ed.), *The Milner Papers,* I (1931), 234.
7. Garvin, *Chamberlain,* III, 405.
8. A. Porter, "The South Africa War (1899–1902): Context and Motive Reconsidered," *JAH,* 31 (1990), 46.
9. R. Hyam and P. Henshaw, *The Lion and the Springbok* (Cambridge, 2003), 44.
10. J. S. Marais, *The Fall of Kruger's Republic* (Oxford, 1961), 172.
11. *DNB.*
12. T. Pakenham, *The Boer War* (1979), 79.
13. *Review of Reviews,* XX (July 1899), 19.
14. A. G. Gardiner, *Pillars of Society* (1913), 326.
15. According to Blunt (*Diaries,* I, 412–13), Milner had told Lady Cowper before setting off: "If I come back without having made war I shall consider my mission has failed."
16. J. Benyon, "'Intermediate' imperialism and the test of Empire: Milner's 'excentric' High Commission in South Africa," in D. Lowry (ed.), *The South African War Reappraised* (Manchester, 2000), 94.
17. *Review of Reviews,* XX (September 1899), 277.
18. Hyam and Henshaw, *Lion and Springbok,* 45.
19. Headlam (ed.), *Milner Papers,* I, 58.
20. Butler, *Autobiography,* 403.
21. Pakenham, *Boer War,* 65.
22. E. Drus, "Select Documents from the Chamberlain Papers concerning Anglo-Transvaal relations 1896–1899," *BIHR,* 27 (1954), 189.
23. Roberts, *Salisbury,* 725.
24. Marais, *Kruger's Republic,* 318.
25. B. Farwell, *The Great Boer War* (1977), 126.
26. Biddesden MSS, Walter Guinness, 8 September 1900.
27. L. S. Amery, *The Times History of the War in South Africa* (1900–1906), II, 26.
28. J. B. Atkins, *The Relief of Ladysmith* (1900), 131.
29. Pakenham, *Boer War,* 204.
30. Amery, *The Times History,* II, 350.
31. H. Kochanski, "Wolseley and the South African War," in Gooch (ed.), *Boer War,* 68.
32. E. R. and J. Pennell, *The Life of James McNeill Whistler* (1908), 395. Apparently the joke was not original to Whistler. See J. and E. Pennell (eds), *The Whistler Journal* (1921), 240, where it is attributed to Harrison Morris.
33. *Fortnightly Review,* LXVII (January 1900), 8.
34. *Review of Reviews,* XXI (January 1900), 3.
35. Amery, *The Times History,* II, 460.
36. Royal Commission on Militia and Volunteers (1904), Cd. 2061, 28, and Butler, *Autobiography,* 207. It seems clear that Butler was referring to Buller, though he does not mention him by name.

37. Farwell, *Great Boer War*, 151.
38. Quoted by J. Montgomery, *1900: The End of an Era* (1968), 68. For the original quatrain see L. S. Amery, *My Political Life*, I (1953), 135.
39. Stead, *Last Will*, 180.
40. Biddesden MSS, Walter Guinness, 2 August 1900.
41. H. W. Nevinson, *Ladysmith: The Diary of a Siege* (1900), 267.
42. Lycett, *Kipling*, 324.
43. F. Saunders, *Mafeking Memories*, ed. P. T. Smith (1996), 10.
44. P. M. Krebs, *Gender, Race, and the Writing of Empire* (Cambridge, 1999), 13.
45. Viscountess Milner, *My Picture Gallery* (1951), 122.
46. R. Price, *An Imperial War and the British Working Class* (1972), 175. This was Halévy's charge.
47. Biddesden MSS, Walter Guinness, 15 June 1900.
48. Pollock, *Kitchener*, 181 and 176.
49. S. B. Spies, *Methods of Barbarism?* (Cape Town, 1977), 44.
50. *The Times*, 25 February 1902.
51. E. Hobhouse, *The Brunt of War* (1902), 255.
52. *Review of Reviews*, XXII (July 1901), 9.
53. Pakenham, *Boer War*, 508–9.
54. R. van Reenen (ed.), *Emily Hobhouse: Boer War Letters* (Cape Town, 1984), 101.
55. CAC, JACB 957, Treherne Journal, 167.
56. *Daily News*, 31 January 1902.
57. K. Jeffery, "The Irish Soldier in the Boer War," in Gooch (ed.), *Boer War*, 141.
58. Elveden MSS, R. Guinness, "Boer War Diary," 21 September 1900.
59. To quote the title of J. F. C. Fuller's book (1937).
60. C. Carrington, *Rudyard Kipling: His Life and Work* (1955), 327.
61. Spies, *Methods of Barbarism?*, 126, 80 and 299.
62. Stead, *Last Will*, 184.
63. I. R. Smith, *The Origins of the South African War, 1899–1902* (1996), 10.
64. Pakenham, *Boer War*, 563 and 119.
65. R. Hyam, "British Imperial Policy and South Africa 1901–10," in P. Warwick (ed.), *The South African War* (1980), 376.
66. G. H. L. Le May, *British Supremacy in South Africa 1899–1907* (Oxford, 1965), 29.
67. R. Kruger, *Good-bye Dolly Gray* (1959), 371.
68. W. N. Tilchin, "The United States and the Boer War," in *The International Impact of the Boer War*, ed. K. Wilson (Chesham, 2001), 110.
69. *National Review*, 203 (January 1900), 670.
70. *Review of Reviews*, XXI (January 1900), 11.
71. J. A. Smith, *John Buchan* (1965), 110.
72. G. B. Pyrah, *Imperial Policy and South Africa 1902–1910* (Oxford, 1955), 249.
73. I. Hexham, "Afrikaner Nationalism 1902–14," in Warwick (ed.), *South African War*, 391.
74. Porter, *Critics of Empire*, 293.
75. A. P. Thornton, *The Imperial Idea and its Enemies* (1959), 108–9.
76. D. Lowry, "'The Boers were the beginning of the end?': The wider impact of the South African War," in Lowry (ed.), *South African War*, 224.
77. P. M. Kennedy, *The Rise and Fall of British Naval Mastery* (1983 edn), 217.
78. G. Searle, "'National Efficiency' and the 'Lessons' of the War," in D. Omissi and A. S. Thompson (eds), *The Impact of the South African War* (Basingstoke, 2002), 199.
79. Kennedy, *British Naval Mastery*, 205.
80. Quoted by A. L. Friedberg, *The Weary Titan* (Princeton, NJ, 1988), 21.

81. J. Amery, *Chamberlain*, VI, 461.

82. M. Gilbert, *Churchill* (1991), 146.

83. R. S. S. Baden-Powell, *Scouting for Boys* (1908), 337.

84. G. R. Searle, *The Quest for National Efficiency* (Oxford, 1971), 60.

85. Montgomery, *1900*, 78.

86. N. Mackenzie (ed.), *The Letters of Sidney and Beatrice Webb*, II (1978), 72.

87. *The Decline and Fall of the British Empire* (1905), 50. The true author is unknown.

88. F. G. Hutchins, *The Illusion of Permanence: British Imperialism in India* (Princeton, NJ, 1967), 145.

89. D. Omissi, "India: Some Perceptions of Race and Empire," in Omissi and Thompson (eds), *South African War*, 224.

90. M. K. Gandhi, *An Autobiography* (Ahmedabad, 1958 edn), 78.

91. J. M. Brown, "Gandhi—A Victorian Gentleman: An Essay in Imperial Encounter," *JICH*, XXVII (May 1999), 69ff.

92. Chaudhuri, *Thy Hand*, 436.

93. D. G. Tendulkar, *Mahatma*, II (Delhi, 1951), 113.

94. C. Tsuzuki, *Edward Carpenter 1844–1929: Prophet of Human Fellowship* (Cambridge, 1980), 115 and 64.

95. Y. Chadha, *Rediscovering Gandhi* (1997), 189, 82 and 87.

96. Hancock, *Smuts*, I, 328.

97. W. Denison, *Varieties of Vice-Regal Life*, II (1870), 83.

98. Bence-Jones, *Viceroys*, 44.

99. Gopal, *British Policy in India*, 59.

100. CUL, Add 7490, Mayo Papers, File 149, Mayo to Argyll, 19 April 1869.

101. A. Seal, *The Emergence of Indian Nationalism* (Cambridge, 1968), 152.

102. P. Mason, *The Men Who Ruled India* (1985), 207.

103. G. Pottinger, *Mayo* (1990), 132.

104. Woodham Smith, *Nightingale*, 370.

105. CUL, Add 7490, File 149, Mayo to Disraeli, 2 May 1869.

106. Ibid., File 153, Mayo to Argyll, 6 April 1870.

107. Ibid., Mayo to Lord Napier, 15 May 1870.

108. Ibid., Mayo to Argyll, 26 August 1870.

109. Ibid., Mayo to Napier, 6 August 1870.

110. Ibid., File 149, Mayo to Argyll, 17 October 1869.

111. Ibid., 30 November 1869.

112. Ibid., File 153, Mayo to Argyll, 9 November 1870.

113. L. Stephen, *The Life of Sir James Fitzjames Stephen* (1895), 293.

114. CUL, Add 7490, File 153, 15 May 1870.

115. B. Balfour, *Lord Lytton's Indian Administration* (1899), 108 and 110.

116. N. Gradia, *Lord Curzon* (Delhi, 1993), 135. The phrase was Mary Curzon's.

117. Seal, *Indian Nationalism*, 247.

118. Balfour, *Lytton's Indian Administration*, 110.

119. V. Prinsep, *Imperial India* (n.d.), 36.

120. Gibbon, *Decline and Fall*, I, 389.

121. W. W. Hunter, *The India of the Queen* (1903), 150.

122. W. S. Blunt, *India under Ripon* (1909), 237.

123. Davis, *Late Victorian Holocausts*, 31.

124. P. Moon, *The British Conquest and Dominion of India* (1989), 843.

125. M. Lutyens, *The Lyttons in India* (1979), 61.

126. Davis, *Late Victorian Holocausts,* 54.

127. M. Cowling, "Lytton, the Cabinet and the Russians, August to November 1878," *EHR,* 76 (January 1961), 70.

128. CUL, Add 7349, Sir James Fitzjames Stephen Papers, Box 2, Lytton to Stephen, 28 January 1878.

129. Gopal, *British Policy in India,* 86.

130. Blunt, *Secret History,* 60.

131. Trousdale, *War in Afghanistan,* 101 and 124.

132. CUL, Add 7349, Box 2, Lytton to Stephen, 20 January 1880.

133. S. Gopal, *The Viceroyalty of Lord Ripon 1880–1884* (Oxford, 1953), 84.

134. R. R. Choudhury, *Calcutta A Hundred Years Ago* (Calcutta, n.d.), 159.

135. Blunt, *India under Ripon,* 18.

136. Pinney (ed.), *Kipling's India,* 83–4.

137. Gopal, *Ripon,* 143.

138. A. Pollen, *John Hungerford Pollen* (1912), 342.

139. Seal, *Indian Nationalism,* 291.

140. B. Martin, *New India, 1885* (Berkeley, CA, 1969), 56.

141. M. Cumpston, "Some Early Indian Nationalists and Their Allies in the British Parliament, 1851–1906," *EHR,* 76 (April 1961), 290.

142. Thant Myint-U, *The Making of Modern Burma* (Cambridge, 2001), 191.

143. H. T. White, *A Civil Servant in Burma* (1913), 105.

144. Thant Mint-U, *Modern Burma,* 53.

145. A. T. Q. Stewart, *The Pagoda War* (1972), 105.

146. Geary, *Burma,* 244–5.

147. Seal, *Indian Nationalism,* 190.

148. R. Guha, *A Corner of a Foreign Field* (2002), 51 and 35.

149. R. N. Cust, *Pictures of Indian Life* (1881), 272.

150. W. S. Churchill, *India* (1931), 136.

151. B. M. Bhatia, *Famines in India* (Delhi, 1967 edn), 271.

152. Seal, *Indian Nationalism,* 196.

153. N. C. Chaudhuri, *The Autobiography of an Unknown Indian* (1951), 223.

154. S. A. Wolpert, *Tilak and Gokhale* (Berkeley, CA, 1962), 253.

155. R. J. Moore, "Curzon and Indian Reform," *MAS,* 27, 4 (1993), 722.

156. Gilmour, *Curzon,* 30, 104, 102.

157. H. Nicolson, *Curzon: The Last Phase* (New York, 1974 edn), 12.

158. D'Abernon, *Portraits,* 25 and 28.

159. Gibbon, *Decline and Fall,* III, 836.

160. D. Dilks, *Curzon in India,* I (1969), 95 and 237.

161. Earl of Ronaldshay, *The Life of Lord Curzon,* II (1928), 143.

162. *The Times,* 31 January 1921.

163. D. Dilks, *Curzon in India,* II (1970), 39.

164. Ronaldshay, *Curzon,* II, 229.

165. D. Cannadine, "Lord Curzon as Ceremonial Impressario," in Cannadine, *Aspects of Aristocracy* (1994), 85.

166. Omissi, "India: Some Perceptions of Race and Empire," in Omissi and Thompson (eds), *South African War,* 221.

167. Curzon, *British Government in India,* II, 123.

168. CSAS, Iris Portal, Unpublished Memoir, 33.

169. P. Kanwar, *Imperial Simla: The Political Culture of the Raj* (New Delhi, 2003 edn), 69.

170. P. H. Hansen, "Vertical Boundaries, National Identities: British Mountaineering on the Frontiers of Europe and the Empire, 1868–1914," *JICH*, XXIV (January 1996), 63.

171. Bence-Jones, *Viceroys*, 93.

172. CSAS, Campbell/Metcalfe Papers, Box IX, Emily (Annie) Metcalfe to Georgiana, 22 July 1849.

173. French, *Younghusband*, 193.

174. Dilks, *Curzon*, II, 24.

175. C. Allen, *Raj* (1979 edn), 19.

176. S. A. Wolpert, *Morley and India 1906–1910* (Berkeley, CA, 1967), 47.

177. A. M. Zaidi et al. (eds), *The Encyclopaedia of India National Congress*, V (Delhi, 1978), 211.

178. S. E. Koss, *John Morley at the India Office 1905–1910* (1969), 184.

179. Zaidi et al. (eds), *India National Congress*, V, 215.

180. *National Review*, 203 (February 1900), 842.

181. M. Gilbert, *Servant of India* (1966), 119.

182. J. W. Robertson Scott, *The Life and Death of a Newspaper* (1952), 42.

183. V. Chirol, *Indian Unrest* (1910), 55.

184. Wolpert, *Morley and India*, 127.

185. Hyam, *Britain's Imperial Century* (1976 edn), 241.

186. R. Coupland, *The Empire in These Days* (1935), 122.

187. J. Morley, *Recollections*, I (1917), 181.

188. CUL, Crewe Papers, C/19-24, Crewe to Hardinge, 18 July 1912.

189. CAC, BGGF, 1/64, Sir B. Godfrey-Faussett's Journal, 12 December 1911.

190. P. Greenhalgh, *Ephemeral Vistas* (Manchester, 1988), 58.

191. CAC, BGGF, 1/62, 5 January 1912.

192. CUL, Crewe Papers, C/19-24, Crewe to Hardinge, 2 and 24 February 1911.

193. CAC, BGGF, 1/62, 15 December 1911.

194. B. C. Busch, *Hardinge of Penshurst* (Hamden, CT, 1980), 207.

195. CUL, Crewe Papers, C/19-24, Crewe to Hardinge, 14 May 1914.

196. CUL, Hardinge Papers, File 82, Hardinge to Carmichael, 2 August 1912.

197. CUL, Crewe Papers, C/19-24, Crewe to Hardinge, 6 December 1912.

198. *The Letters of Gertrude Bell* (1987 edn), 301.

199. Busch, *Hardinge*, 213.

200. A. Davidson, *Edward Lear* (1950 edn), 210.

201. W. Dalrymple, *City of Djinns* (1993), 84.

202. CAC, PJGG 6, Lady Grigg to Dorothy Hammond, 21 October 1934.

203. R. G. Irving, *Indian Summer: Lutyens, Baker and Imperial Delhi* (1981), 340.

204. CSAS, Portal, Memoir, 25.

205. Irving, *Indian Summer*, 355 and 350.

9. The Empire, Right or Wrong

1. A. G. S. Butler, *The Architecture of Sir Edwin Lutyens*, III (1950), 37. The phrase was Lloyd George's.

2. M. H. Port, *Imperial London* (1995), 21.

3. *East London Observer* (6 January 1906), quoted by J. A. Garrard, *The English and Immigration 1880–1910* (1971), 49.

4. M. Trevelyan, *Britain's Greatness Foretold* (1900), xi.

5. D. Olsen, *The Growth of Victorian London* (1979 edn), 335 and 333.

6. H. G. Wells, *Tono-Bungay* (1972 edn), 73.

7. Port, *Imperial London,* 205 and 209.
8. I. Toplis, *The Foreign Office: An Architectural History* (1987), 164.
9. S. Goetze, *Mural Decorations at the Foreign Office* (1936), 5.
10. Driver and Gilbert (eds), *Imperial Cities,* 42 and 35.
11. *The Times,* 17 May 1911.
12. R. J. B. Bosworth, *Mussolini's Italy* (2005), 12 and 13.
13. *Illustrated London News,* 20 May 1911.
14. *The Times,* 5 May 1911.
15. *Standard of Empire,* 26 March 1911.
16. R. Rhodes James (ed.), *Winston S. Churchill: His Complete Speeches,* VII (1974), 6920.
17. *United Empire,* I (1910), 119. The author was Arthur Bennett.
18. Driver and Gilbert (eds), *Imperial Cities,* 127.
19. A. B. Keith (ed.), *Selected Speeches and Documents on British Colonial Policy 1763–1917,* II (1933 edn), 358. Laurier was repeating what he had said in 1910.
20. J. Buchan, *A History of the Great War,* I (1921), 113.
21. Gilbert, *Churchill,* IV, 158.
22. N. Ferguson, *The Pity of War* (1998), 294.
23. W. Hughes, *The Splendid Adventure* (1929), 271.
24. M. Howard, *Continental Commitment* (1972), 60.
25. T. E. Lawrence, *Seven Pillars of Wisdom* (1976 edn), 4.
26. J. M. Brown, *Gandhi's Rise to Power* (Cambridge, 1972), 126.
27. *OHBE,* IV, 121.
28. *United Empire,* VI (1915), 56.
29. D. Oliver, "A Canadian Armistice," in H. Cecil and P. H. Liddle (eds), *At the Eleventh Hour* (1998), 186.
30. Gibbon, *Decline and Fall,* I, 624.
31. Hobson, *Imperialism,* 223.
32. Gibbon, *Decline and Fall,* II, 509.
33. Hardinge of Penshurst, *My Indian Years 1910–1916* (1948), 34.
34. D. C. Ellinwood and S. D. Prahan (eds), *India and World War,* I (Manchester, 1978), 199.
35. Mulk Raj Anand, *Across the Black Water* (1940), 142.
36. OIOC, L/MIL/5/825, ff. 112, 270 and 242.
37. J. W. B. Merewether and F. Smith, *The Indian Corps in France* (1919), 8.
38. L. Macdonald, *1915: The Death of Innocence* (1993), 96.
39. OIOC, L/MIL/5/825, f. 236.
40. Ibid., f. 250.
41. R. Grimshaw, *Indian Cavalry Officer 1914–15* (1986), 39.
42. J. Willcocks, *With the Indians in France* (1920), 301.
43. OIOC, L/MIL/5/825, f. 245.
44. J. Keegan, *The First World War* (1998), 213.
45. S. Cowasjee, *So May Freedom* (Delhi, 1977), 111.
46. C. Chenevix Trench, *The Indian Army and the King's Enemies 1900–1947* (1988), 42.
47. OIOC, L/MIL/5/825, f. 233.
48. J. Collins, *Dr. Brighton's Indian Patients* (Brighton, 1997), 23.
49. D. Omissi, *The Sepoy and the Raj* (1994), 161.
50. J. Greenhut, "The Imperial Reserve: The Indian Corps on the Western Front, 1914–15," *JICH,* XII (October 1983), 56.
51. Brown, *Gandhi's Rise to Power,* 150.
52. B. Farwell, *Armies of the Raj* (1989), 253.
53. Chenevix Trench, *Indian Army,* 82.

54. E. Candler, *The Long Road to Baghdad* (1919), 231.

55. A. J. Barker, *The Neglected War: Mesopotamia 1916–1918* (1967), 18.

56. D. L. Neave, *Remembering Kut* (1937), 158.

57. S. Bhattacharya, "Anxious Celebrations: British India and the Armistice," in Cecil and Liddle (eds), *Eleventh Hour,* 195.

58. J. M. Brown, "War and the Colonial Relationship: Britain, India and the War of 1914–18," in Ellinwood and Prahan (eds), *India and World War,* I, 22.

59. *DNB.*

60. S. A. Wolpert, "Congress Leadership in Transition: Jinnah to Gandhi, 1914–20," in Ellinwood and Prahan (eds), *India and World War,* I, 132.

61. R. von Albertini, "The Impact of Two World Wars on the Decline of Colonialism," *JCH,* 4.1 (January 1969), 21.

62. M. O'Dwyer, *India as I Knew It 1885–1925* (1925), 369. The pedant was Lionel Curtis, a member of Milner's Kindergarten.

63. R. J. Moore, "Curzon and Indian Reform," *MAS,* 27.4 (1993), 738.

64. E. S. Montagu, *An Indian Diary* (1930), 58 and 185.

65. S. Wolpert, *Jinnah of Pakistan* (New York, 1984), 67 and 62.

66. Brown, *Gandhi's Rise to Power,* 161 and 174.

67. 'Amritsar," *Blackwood's Magazine,* CCVII (April 1920), 445.

68. O'Dwyer, *India,* 274.

69. CSAS, Darling Papers, Malcolm Darling to his sister Irene, 30 April 1919.

70. *Daily Mail,* 4 May 1920.

71. D. Sayer, "British Reaction to the Amritsar Massacre," *PP,* 131 (May 1991), 140.

72. CSAS, Darling Papers, Darling to his sister Irene, 30 April 1919. Darling lost all ambition after the episode and devoted himself to writing books about the peasantry, "a professional cul-de-sac which left his principles intact." (C. Dewey, *Anglo-Indian Attitudes* [1993], 163.)

73. P. N. Furbank, *E. M. Forster: A Life,* II (1978), 61.

74. Gilbert, *Churchill,* 422.

75. A. Rumbold, *Watershed in India 1914–1922* (1979), 202.

76. *The Times,* 9 July 1920.

77. A. Fitzroy, *Memoirs,* II (n.d.), 734.

78. Draper, *Amritsar,* 178.

79. J. Adams and P. Whitehead, *The Dynasty: The Nehru–Gandhi Story* (New York, 1997), 48.

80. R. Tagore, *Letters to a Friend* (1928), 88.

81. Zaidi et al. (eds), *India National Congress,* VII, 457 and 475.

82. J. Nehru, *A Bunch of Old Letters* (1960), 16.

83. S. M. Rai, "The Jallianwala Bagh Tragedy: Its Impact on Political Awakening and Thinking in India," in V. N. Datta and S. Setta (eds), *Jallianwala Bagh Massacre* (Delhi, 2000), 32.

84. S. R. Bakshi, *Indian National Movement and the Raj,* III (Delhi, 1989), 71.

85. S. D. Waley, *Edwin Montagu* (Bombay, 1964), 262.

86. Duke of Windsor, *A King's Story* (1998 edn), 178.

87. G. Souter, *Lion and Kangaroo* (1976), 21.

88. R. Jebb, *Studies in Colonial Nationalism* (1905), 192 and 199.

89. Clark, *History of Australia,* V (1981), 5.

90. E. M. Andrews, *The Anzac Illusion* (Cambridge, 1993), 38.

91. *United Empire,* I (1910), 283.

92. Lawson's lines are quoted by R. Ward, *The Australian Legend* (Melbourne, 1958), 228.

93. J. Masefield, *Gallipoli* (1916), 19.

94. C. E. W. Bean, *Official History of Australia in the War of 1914–1918,* I (Sydney, 1933), 6 and 605.

95. Bean, *Official History,* VI (1942), 1095.
96. A. Thomson, "'Steadfast until Death?' C. E. W. Bean and the Representation of Australian Military Manhood," *AHS,* 23 (October 1989), 477.
97. J. Ross, *The Myth of the Digger* (Sydney, 1985), 110.
98. J. Barrett, "No Straw Man: C. E. W. Bean and Some Critics," *AHS,* 23 (April 1988), 111.
99. Souter, *Lion and Kangaroo,* 118, 64 and 164.
100. Gibbon, *Decline and Fall,* I, 595.
101. T. Higgins, *Winston Churchill and the Dardanelles* (1963), 106 and 134.
102. J. Winter and B. Baggett, *The Great War and the Shaping of the Twentieth Century* (1996), 110.
103. I. Hamilton, *Gallipoli Diary,* I (1920), 122.
104. C. Pugsley, *Gallipoli: The New Zealand Story* (2001 edn), 75.
105. Clark, *History of Australia,* V, 394.
106. J. Robertson, *Anzac and Empire* (1990), 44.
107. A. Herbert, *Mons, Anzac & Kut* (1930), 115.
108. D. Craven, *Peninsula of Death* (n.d.), 27.
109. Robertson, *Anzac,* 68 and 76.
110. L. A. Carlyon, *Gallipoli* (2002), 45.
111. J. H. Morrow, *The Great War in Imperial History* (2004), 73.
112. C. F. Aspinall-Oglander, *Gallipoli,* I (1992 edn), 197.
113. A. Thomson, "'The Vilest Libel of the War?': Imperial Politics and the Official Histories of Gallipoli," *AHS,* 25 (October 1993), 629.
114. Aspinall-Oglander, *Gallipoli,* I, 268.
115. Masefield, *Gallipoli,* 52.
116. B. Carman and J. McPherson (eds), *Bimbashi McPherson* (1983), 144.
117. E. Ashmead-Bartlett, *The Uncensored Dardanelles* (n.d.), 57.
118. J. Murray, *Gallipoli as I Saw It* (1965), 76.
119. C. Mackenzie, *Gallipoli Memories* (1929), 82.
120. K. Fewster (ed.), *Gallipoli Correspondent: The Frontline Diary of C. E. W. Bean* (Sydney, 1983), 157 and 39.
121. IWM, 01/121, Diary of Brigadier-General G. Napier Johnston, 24 August and 4 September 1915, 12 January 1916 and 14 October 1915. Johnston was commanding New Zealander artillery men and as these extracts suggest, his diaries, which were not revised, reflect feelings which varied from day to day under the stress of battle. I have emended his punctuation.
122. Bean, *Official History,* I, 547–8.
123. B. Gammage, *The Broken Years: Australian Soldiers in the Great War* (Canberra, 1974), 89.
124. Andrews, *Anzac Illusion,* 154.
125. Ashmead-Bartlett, *Dardanelles,* 107.
126. R. Rhodes James, *Gallipoli* (1965), 154.
127. K. Sinclair, *A Destiny Apart* (Wellington, NZ, 1986), 144.
128. Hamilton, *Gallipoli Diary,* I, 184–5.
129. Rhodes James, *Gallipoli,* 142.
130. Mackenzie, *Gallipoli,* 152.
131. A. B. Facey, *A Fortunate Life* (1986 edn), 262.
132. Andrews, *Anzac Illusion,* 54.
133. M. B. Tyquin, *Gallipoli: The Medical War* (Kensington, NSW, 1993), 180.
134. S. Roskill, *Hankey: Man of Secrets,* I (1970), 220.
135. Fewster (ed.), *Gallipoli Correspondent,* 163.
136. B. Page, *The Murdoch Archipelago* (2003), 41.
137. R. Owen, *Lord Cromer* (Oxford, 2004), 387.

138. N. Steel and P. Hart, *Defeat at Gallipoli* (1995 edn), 420.

139. Bean, *Official History*, III (Sydney, 1934), 600.

140. C. E. W. Bean, *Letters from France* (1917), 108.

141. Souter, *Lion and Kangaroo*, 238.

142. Gammage, *Broken Years*, 165.

143. Andrews, *Anzac Illusion*, 98.

144. J. Thompson, *On Lips of Living Men* (1962), 124.

145. L. F. Fitzhardinge, *The Little Digger*, II (1979), 48.

146. N. Cowper, "Sir Galahad, the Dauntless Imp and Others," *Australian Quarterly*, XXIII (June 1951), 51.

147. Clark, *History of Australia*, VI, 112.

148. M. MacMillan, *Peacemakers* (2003 edn), 56.

149. W. M. Hughes, *Policies and Potentates* (Sydney, 1950), 242.

150. Fitzhardinge, *Little Digger*, II, 318 and 392.

151. Clark, *History of Australia*, VI, 17.

152. P. White, *Flaws in the Glass* (1981), 232.

153. K. S. Inglis, "World War One Memorials in Australia," *Guerres Mondiales et Conflits Contemporains*, 167 (July 1992), 58.

154. J. Phillips, "Was the Great War New Zealand's War?" in C. Wilcox (ed.), *The Great War* (Canberra, 1995), 67.

155. Robertson, *Anzac and Empire*, 247.

156. Sinclair, *Destiny Apart*, 172.

157. Souter, *Lion and Kangaroo*, 205.

158. Bean, *Official History*, VI, 1086.

159. Hughes, *Splendid Adventure*, 437–8.

160. C. P. Stacey, *Canada and the Age of Conflict*, I (Toronto, 1977), 49–50.

161. Gibbon, *Decline and Fall*, I, 232.

162. W. F. Butler, *The Great Lone Land* (1872), 331.

163. P. Berton, *The National Dream* (Toronto, 1972), 10.

164. S. Zeller, *Inventing Canada: Early Victorian Science and the Idea of a Transcontinental Nation* (Toronto, 1987), 73.

165. W. K. Lamb, *History of the Canadian Pacific Railway* (New York, 1977), 14.

166. J. McNaughton, *Lord Strathcona* (Toronto, 1926), 294.

167. O. Lavallée, *Van Horne's Road* (Don Mills, Ont., 1974), 204.

168. P. Berton, *The Last Spike* (Toronto, 1973), 111.

169. W. Vaughan, *Sir William Van Horne* (Toronto, 1926), 109 and 91.

170. Butler, *Lone Land*, 276.

171. Lavallée, *Van Horne's Road*, 220.

172. Lamb, *Canadian Pacific*, 1.

173. J. A. Eagle, *The Canadian Pacific Railway and the Development of Western Canada* (Kingston, Ont., 1989), 150.

174. Berton, *National Dream*, 295.

175. Elveden MSS, Gwendolen Guinness Diary (1910), 70.

176. Berton, *Last Spike*, 118.

177. Elveden MSS, G. Guinness Diary, 81 and 77.

178. D. Creighton, *John A. Macdonald: The Old Chieftain* (Toronto, 1955), 254.

179. H. Dempsey (ed.), *The CPR West: The Iron Road and the Making of a Nation* (Vancouver, 1984), 151 and 273.

180. K. McNaught, *The History of Canada* (1970), 193.

181. G. Woodcock, *A Social History of Canada* (New York, 1988), 281.

182. L. G. Reynolds, *The British Immigrant* (Toronto, 1935), 269.

183. W. Booth, *In Darkest England and the Way Out* (1970 edn), 93.

184. Zeller, *Inventing Canada,* 260.

185. C. Berger, *The Sense of Power: Studies in the Ideas of Canadian Imperialism 1867–1914* (Toronto, 1970), 132.

186. Gibbon, *Decline and Fall,* I, 233.

187. G. Smith, *The Political Destiny of Canada* (1878), 24 and 36.

188. H. B. Neatby, "Laurier and Imperialism," in C. Berger (ed.), *Imperial Relations in the Age of Laurier* (Toronto, 1969), 1.

189. J. Schull, *Laurier: The First Canadian* (Toronto, 1965), 410.

190. Carrington, *Kipling,* 398.

191. C. Brown, "Goldwin Smith and Anti-Imperialism," in Berger (ed.), *Imperial Relations,* 22.

192. C. Murrow, *Henri Bourassa and French-Canadian Nationalism* (Montreal, 1968), 35.

193. Schull, *Laurier,* 531.

194. Stacey, *Canada,* 176.

195. M. G. McGowan, *The Waning of the Green* (Montreal, 1999), 278 and 253.

196. Elveden MSS, G. Guinness to H. Onslow, 27 June 1916.

197. M. Wade, *The French Canadians,* II (Toronto, 1968), 658.

198. H. P. Grundy, "Sir Wilfrid Laurier and Lord Minto," in Berger (ed.), *Imperial Relations,* 31.

199. W. S. Churchill, *The World Crisis 1911–1918,* II (1938 edn), 1155.

200. IWM, 65/55/1, Major Edison F. Lynn Diary, 1 January 1916.

201. IWM, 01/51/1, Letters of Brigadier J. M. Prower, 13 July 1915.

202. D. Morton, *Canada and War* (Toronto, 1981), 65.

203. P. J. Haythornthwaite, *The World War One Source Book* (1997 edn), 267.

204. D. Morton and J. L. Granatstein, *Marching to Armageddon: Canadians and the Great War 1914–1919* (Toronto, 1989), 114.

205. T. Travers, *The Killing Ground: The British Army of the Western Front and the Emergence of Modern Warfare* (1987), 20.

206. A. McKee, *Vimy Ridge* (1966), 65.

207. B. Rawling, *Surviving Trench Warfare: Technology and the Canadian Corps 1914–1918* (Toronto, 1992), 89.

208. G. W. L. Nicholson, *Canadian Expeditionary Force 1914–1919* (Ottawa, 1962), 244.

209. IWM, 65/55/1, 25 April and 5 May 1917.

210. D. Morton, *When Your Number's Up* (Toronto, 1993), 168.

211. McKee, *Vimy Ridge,* 91.

212. IWM, 65/55/1, 9 April 1917.

213. McKee, *Vimy Ridge,* 126.

214. K. Macksey, *The Shadow of Vimy Ridge* (1965), 77.

215. *War Memoirs of David Lloyd George,* II (1938 edn), 2007.

216. Morton and Granatstein, *Marching to Armageddon,* 197.

217. Stacey, *Canada,* 211 and 239.

218. J. F. Vance, *Death So Noble: Memory, Meaning and the First World War* (Vancouver, 1997), 228.

219. Wade, *French Canadians,* II, 712.

220. Elveden MSS, G. Guinness to H. Onslow, 7 June 1916.

221. R. Craig Brown and R. Cook, *Canada 1896–1921* (Toronto, 1976), 305.

222. D. G. Dancocks, *Spearhead to Victory: Canada and the Great War* (Edmonton, 1987), 237.

223. E. J. Leed, *No Man's Land* (Cambridge, 1979), 193.

10. Aflame with the Hope of Liberation

1. K. Jeffery, "Irish Culture and the Great War," *Bullán,* I, 2 (1994), 89.
2. J. Leonard, "Lest We Forget," in D. Fitzpatrick (ed.), *Ireland and the First World War* (Westmeath, 1988), 67.
3. P. Berton, *Vimy* (Toronto, 1986), 301. Not until the end of the twentieth century, after the Irish peace process, was comparable recognition given to the thirty thousand men from the south who fell in the Great War—in the shape of a one-hundred-foot Celtic round tower at Messines, built with stones from all the thirty-two counties.
4. K. B. Nowlan (ed.), *The Making of 1916* (Dublin, 1969), viii.
5. D. H. Akenson, *The Irish in Ontario* (Montreal, 1984), 41.
6. Magnus, *Gladstone,* 300.
7. Quoted by T. P. O'Connor, *The Parnell Movement* (1886), 202.
8. Foster, *Modern Ireland,* 375.
9. F. S. L. Lyons, *Ireland since the Famine* (1967 edn), 130.
10. F. S. L. Lyons, *Charles Stewart Parnell* (1977), 92.
11. D. G. Boyce, "'The Portrait of the King Is the King': The Biographers of Charles Stewart Parnell," in D. G. Boyce and A. O'Day (eds), *Parnell in Perspective* (1991), 294.
12. R. B. O'Brien, *The Life of Charles Stewart Parnell,* I (1899 edn), 73 and 146.
13. *Magdalene College Magazine & Record,* 36 (October 1992), 37.
14. C. C. O'Brien, *Parnell and His Party 1880–1890* (1959), 10.
15. R. F. Foster, *Charles Stewart Parnell* (Hassocks, Suffolk, 1976), 290. The term was used by Parnell's brother John.
16. T. M. Healy, *Letters and Leaders of My Day,* I (1928), 89.
17. R. B. O'Brien, *Parnell,* I, 145.
18. Healy, *Letters,* I, 83.
19. C. Townshend, *Political Violence in Ireland* (Oxford, 1983), 7 and 106.
20. R. V. Comerford, *The Fenians in Context* (Dublin, 1985), 226.
21. W. O'Brien and D. Ryan (eds), *Devoy's Postbag, 1871–1928,* I (Dublin, 1948), 16.
22. K. O'Shea, *Charles Stewart Parnell,* I (1914), 172.
23. W. S. Blunt, *The Land War in Ireland* (1912), 400.
24. G. Moore, *Parnell and His Island* (1887), 250.
25. Brendon, *Eminent Edwardians,* 91.
26. J. L. Hammond, *Gladstone and the Irish Nation* (1938), 284.
27. S. Gwynn and G. M. Tuckwell, *Life of Sir Charles Dilke,* I (1917), 441.
28. E. D. Steele, "Gladstone and Ireland," *IHS,* XVII, 65 (March 1970), 74.
29. Hammond, *Gladstone,* 710.
30. R. B. O'Brien, *Parnell,* II, 42.
31. Mansergh, *Irish Question,* 213.
32. S. B. Cook, *Imperial Affinities* (New Delhi, 1993), 30.
33. L. P. Curtis, *Coercion and Conciliation in Ireland 1880–1892* (1963), 33.
34. Rose, *Superior Person,* 134.
35. *Edinburgh Review,* 165 (1887), 585.
36. S. H. Zebel, *Balfour* (1973), 67.
37. Curtis, *Coercion and Conciliation,* 223.
38. B. Alderson, *Arthur James Balfour* (1903), 72.
39. Moore, *Parnell,* 252.
40. R. Ellmann, *Yeats* (Oxford, 1979 edn), 100.
41. J. Joyce, *Dubliners* (1996 edn), 151.
42. M. Brown, *The Politics of Irish Literature* (1972), 324.
43. V. S. Pritchett, *Dublin* (1991 edn), 36.

44. S. O'Grady, *The Story of Ireland* (1894), 211.
45. E. Norman, *A History of Modern Ireland* (1971), 224.
46. Gibbon, *Decline and Fall,* I, 999.
47. A. Bairner, "Ireland, sport and empire," in K. Jeffery (ed.), *"An Irish Empire?"* (Manchester, 1996), 68.
48. T. Fishlock, *Conquerors of Time* (2004), 410.
49. G. Moore, *Hail and Farewell* (Gerrards Cross, 1976 edn), 290, 26 and 238.
50. D. McCartney, "Hyde, D. P. Moran and Irish Ireland," in F. X. Martin (ed.), *Leaders and Men of the Easter Rising: Dublin 1916* (1967), 46.
51. S. O'Casey, *Autobiographies,* I (1963 edn), 428 and 456.
52. J. Lee, *The Modernisation of Irish Society 1848–1918* (Dublin, 1973), 138.
53. Moore, *Hail and Farewell,* 223.
54. D. McCartney, "Gaelic Ideological Origins of 1916," in O. Dudley Edwards and F. Pyle (eds), *1916: The Easter Rising* (1968), 46.
55. Brown, *Politics of Irish Literature,* 355.
56. L. MacNeice, *Selected Poems* (1958), 62.
57. T. Jones, *Whitehall Diary,* III (Oxford, 1969), xxiii.
58. R. Blake, *The Unknown Prime Minister* (1955), 129.
59. Brendon, *Churchill,* 66.
60. P. H. Pearse, *Three Lectures on Gaelic Topics* (Dublin, 1898), 49.
61. R. Dudley Edwards, *Patrick Pearse: The Triumph of Failure* (1977), 179, 335 and 245.
62. D. Ryan, *The Rising* (Dublin, 1957 edn), 16.
63. Townshend, *Political Violence,* 283.
64. O'Casey, *Autobiographies,* I, 626.
65. F. Shaw, "The Canon of Irish History—A Challenge," *Studies* (1972), 126.
66. Lyons, *Ireland since the Famine,* 360.
67. Edwards, *Pearse,* 277.
68. Ryan, *Rising,* 128.
69. J. Good, *Enchanted by Dreams* (Dublin, 1996), 32.
70. Ryan, *Rising,* 130.
71. R. Dudley Edwards, *James Connolly* (Dublin, 1981), 139.
72. S. O'Casey, *Three Plays* (1980 edn), 194.
73. G. Githens-Mazer, *Myths and Memories of the Easter Rising* (Dublin, 2006), 126.
74. O'Casey, *Autobiographies,* I, 660.
75. M. Foy and B. Barton, *The Easter Rising* (Guildford, 1999), 140.
76. K. O'Brien, *My Ireland* (1962), 114.
77. Good, *Enchanted,* 77.
78. J. Stephens, *The Insurrection in Dublin* (Dublin, 1916), 73.
79. K. Jeffery, *The GPO and the Easter Rising* (Dublin, 2006), 174.
80. E. O'Halpin, *The Decline of the Union* (Dublin, 1987), 120.
81. C. Townshend, "The Suppression of the Easter Rising," *Bullán,* I, 1 (Spring 1994), 30.
82. Dudley Edwards and Pyle (eds), *1916,* 67.
83. BL, Add 49740, Balfour Papers, Sir C. Spring-Rice to Balfour, 5 December 1916.
84. G. B. Shaw, *The Complete Prefaces,* I, ed. D. H. Laurence and D. J. Leary (1993), 239.
85. Porter, *Critics of Empire,* 267.
86. D. Ryan, *The Man Called Pearse* (Dublin, 1919), 1–2.
87. *The Collected Poems of W. B. Yeats* (1950), 205.
88. Dudley Edwards, *Connolly,* 120.
89. Dudley Edwards and Pyle (eds), *1916,* 194.
90. D. Kiberd, *Inventing Ireland* (1995), 259.

91. Townshend, *Political Violence*, 323.
92. J. Augusteijn, *From Public Defiance to Guerrilla Warfare* (Dublin, 1996), 57.
93. G. Dangerfield, *The Damnable Question* (1977), 259.
94. T. Ryle Dwyer, *De Valera: The Man & the Myths* (Swords, Co. Dublin, 1991), 40.
95. R. Kee, *The Green Flag*, III (1972 edn), 30.
96. M. Laffan, *The Resurrection of Ireland* (Cambridge, 1999), 53.
97. A. T. Q. Stewart, *Michael Collins: The Secret File* (Belfast, 1997), 29.
98. D. Ryan, *Remembering Sion* (1934), 235 and 251.
99. T. P. Coogan, *De Valera: Long Fellow, Long Shadow* (1993), 121 and 122.
100. S. Milne, "Britain: Imperial Nostalgia," *Global Policy Forum* (May 2005).
101. A. J. Ward, *Ireland and Anglo-American Relations* (1969), 229 and 166.
102. Rhodes James (ed.), *Churchill: His Complete Speeches*, III, 3022.
103. J. Campbell, *F. E. Smith First Earl of Birkenhead* (1983), 552.
104. Stewart, *Collins*, 6.
105. Kee, *Green Flag*, III, 112.
106. D. Duff, *Sword for Hire* (1934), 64.
107. F. S. L. Lyons, *John Dillon* (1968), 467.
108. F. Pakenham, *Peace by Ordeal* (1992 edn), 49.
109. F. Owen, *Tempestuous Journey* (1954), 572.
110. D. Macardle, *The Irish Republic* (Dublin, 1951 edn), 416.
111. *Irish Times,* 14 March 1921.
112. H. Martin, *Ireland in Insurrection* (1921), 11.
113. Jones, *Whitehall Diary,* III, 65.
114. P. S. O'Hegarty, *A History of Ireland under the Union* (1952), 781.
115. Hancock, *Smuts,* II, 61.
116. Lyons, *Ireland since the Famine,* 444.
117. N. C. Johnson, *Ireland, the Great War and the Geography of Remembrance* (Cambridge, 2003), 149.
118. Dwyer, *De Valera,* 285.
119. Lawrence, *Seven Pillars,* 42.
120. P. Knightley and C. Simpson, *The Secret Lives of Lawrence of Arabia* (1969), 215.
121. J. Buchan, *Memory Hold-the-Door* (1945 edn), 226.
122. M. FitzHerbert, *The Man Who Was Greenmantle* (1983), 144.
123. Lawrence, *Seven Pillars,* 368, 272 and 450.
124. R. Meinertzhagen, *Middle East Diary* (1959), 30 and 32.
125. J. E. Mack, *A Prince of Our Disorder* (1976), 501. The author was Malcolm Muggeridge, writing in the *New York Times Book Review,* 10 May 1964.
126. E. Kedouri, *Islam and the Modern World* (1980), 273 and 270.
127. J. Wilson, *Lawrence of Arabia* (1979), 339.
128. Lawrence, *Seven Pillars,* 450.
129. Gibbon, *Decline and Fall,* III, 189.
130. G. de S. Barrow, *The Fire of Life* (n.d.), 207.
131. Wilson, *Lawrence,* 349.
132. L. James, *The Golden Warrior: The Life and Legend of Lawrence of Arabia* (1990), 163.
133. C. M. Andrew, "France, Britain and the Peace Settlement: A Reconsideration," in U. Dann (ed.), *The Great Powers and the Middle East 1919–1939* (1988), 164.
134. R. Sanders, *The High Walls of Jerusalem* (1983), 243, quoting Gibbon, *Decline and Fall,* III, 608.
135. E. Kedourie, *The Chatham House Version and Other Middle Eastern Studies* (1984), 17.
136. James, *Golden Warrior,* 170.

137. Wilson, *Lawrence*, 414.

138. R. A. Adelson, *Mark Sykes* (1975), 226.

139. C. Weizmann, *Trial and Error* (1950), 223.

140. Storrs, *Orientations*, 415.

141. L. Stein, *The Balfour Declaration* (1961), 154 and 163.

142. M. Egremont, *The Cousins* (1977), 270. The term used by Solzhenitsyn was current in Edwardian England.

143. J. C. Hurewitz, *Diplomacy in the Near and Middle East: A Documentary Record*, II (Princeton, NJ, 1956), 26.

144. Zebel, *Balfour*, 247–8.

145. W. Laqueur, *A History of Zionism* (1972), 187.

146. Cocker, *Meinertzhagen*, 129.

147. H. S. Gullett, *The Australian Imperial Force in Sinai and Palestine* (Sydney, 1923), 755 and 708.

148. D. Garnett (ed.), *The Letters of T. E. Lawrence* (1938), 196.

149. W. T. Massey, *Allenby's Final Triumph* (1920), 234.

150. H. M. Sachar, *The Emergence of the Middle East* (New York, 1969), 240.

151. J. C. Hill, *Chauvel of the Light Horse* (Melbourne, 1978), 178.

152. Gullett, *Australian Imperial Force*, 755.

153. Quoted by M. Glenny, *The Balkans, 1804–1999: Nationalism, War and the Great Powers* (2000 edn), 363.

154. E. Monroe, *Britain's Moment in the Middle East 1914–1971* (1981 edn), 46.

155. *OHBE*, IV, 11.

156. J. Morris, *Farewell the Trumpets: An Imperial Retreat* (1978), 208.

157. J. Darwin, *Britain, Egypt and the Middle East* (1981), 155.

158. H. Mejcher, *Imperial Quest for Oil: Iraq 1910–1928* (1976), 177.

159. *Letters of Gertrude Bell*, 404.

160. J. Vincent (ed.), *The Crawford Papers* (1984), 397.

161. J. Kimche, *The Unromantics* (1968), 74.

162. T. Dodge, *Inventing Iraq* (2003), 74.

163. Candler, *Baghdad*, I, 232.

164. Darwin, *Middle East*, 194.

165. H. St. J. B. Philby, *Arabian Days* (1948), 184.

166. *Letters of Gertrude Bell*, 397.

167. A. T. Wilson, *Mesopotamia, 1917–1920* (1931), 319.

168. A. L. Haldane, *The Insurrection in Mesopotamia, 1920* (1922), 261 and 256.

169. W. Thesiger, *A Life of My Choice* (1987), 171.

170. P. Graves, *The Life of Sir Percy Cox* (1941), 19.

171. *Letters of Gertrude Bell*, 428.

172. C. Catherwood, *Winston's Folly: Imperialism and the Creation of Modern Iraq* (2004), 165.

173. Fitzherbert, *Greenmantle*, 239.

174. R. Lansing, *The Big Four and Others of the Peace Conference* (1922), 169.

175. E. Burgoyne, *Gertrude Bell 1914–1926* (1961), 279.

176. P. Sluglett, *Britain in Iraq 1914–1932* (1976), 77.

177. Graves, *Cox*, 231.

178. Sluglett, *Britain in Iraq*, 281–2.

179. T. Royle, *Glubb Pasha* (1992), 98.

180. D. Omissi, *Air Power and Colonial Control* (Manchester, 1990), 160.

181. *The Times*, 29 November 1998. The RAF's Director of Research said that if mustard gas

could be accepted for "savage warfare, it should prove more efficient than any other known form of frightfulness." (D. Killingray, "'A Swift Agent of Government': Air Power in British Colonial Africa, 1916–1939," *JAH*, 25 [1984], 432.)

182. C. Townshend, "Civilization and 'Frightfulness': Air Control in the Middle East Between the Wars," in C. Wrigley (ed.), *Warfare, Diplomacy and Politics* (1986), 150.
183. Sluglett, *Britain in Iraq*, 264, quoting George Lansbury.
184. Darwin, *Middle East*, 87.
185. Carman and McPherson (eds), *Bimbashi McPherson*, 222.
186. Gibbon, *Decline and Fall*, I, 53.
187. Sanders, *High Walls*, 221.
188. Storrs, *Orientations*, 79.
189. Lord Lloyd, *Egypt since Cromer*, I (1933), 283.
190. J. J. Terry, *The Wafd 1919–1952* (1982), 95.
191. J. Berque, *Egypt: Imperialism and Revolution* (1972), 270.
192. R. Seth, *Russell Pasha* (1966), 144.
193. A. L. al-Sayyid-Marsot, *Egypt's Liberal Experiment: 1922–1936* (Los Angeles, 1977), 21.
194. Kedourie, *Chatham House*, 113.
195. Gollin, *Proconsul*, 593.
196. Darwin, *Middle East*, 123.
197. Kedourie, *Chatham House*, 121.
198. Darwin, *Middle East*, 267.
199. Marsot, *Egypt's Liberal Experiment*, 69.
200. L. Grafftey-Smith, *Bright Levant* (1970), 102.
201. J. Charmley, *Lord Lloyd and the Decline of the British Empire* (1987), 95, 194 and 152.
202. Lloyd, *Egypt since Cromer*, II (1934), 359.
203. P. Ziegler (ed.), *The Diaries of Lord Louis Mountbatten 1920–1922* (1987), 306.
204. C. Petrie, *Life and Letters of Sir Austen Chamberlain*, II (1940), 341.
205. Marsot, *Egypt's Liberal Experiment*, 75 and 152.
206. Charmley, *Lloyd*, 118.
207. G. Waterfield, *Professional Diplomat* (1973), 167.
208. Darwin, *Middle East*, 269.
209. R. A. C. Parker, "Great Britain, France and the Ethiopian Crisis 1935–1936," *EHR*, 89 (1974), 310.
210. J. Bowle, *Viscount Samuel* (1957), 195.
211. *The Times*, 7 October 1922.
212. Lord D'Abernon, *An Ambassador of Peace*, I (1929), 20.

11. Englishmen Like Posing as Gods

1. *OHBE*, IV, 48.
2. W. R. Louis, *In the Name of God, Go!* (1992), 86.
3. A. J. P. Taylor, *English History 1914–1945* (1967 edn), 253.
4. J. McLaren, *Gentlemen of the Empire* (1940), 9.
5. *Spectator*, 8 May 1924.
6. Amery, *Forward View*, 187.
7. J. R. M. Butler, *Lord Lothian* (1960), 52.
8. S. Gopal, "All Souls and India, 1921–47," *JICH*, XXVII (May 1999), 87.
9. Lord Northcliffe, *My Journey Round the World 1921–22* (1923), 159.
10. Quoted by James, *British Empire*, 451.

11. Goetze, *Mural Decorations*, 5ff. N. Ferguson (*Empire*, 312) reproduces portions of the painting, though his interpretation of it differs significantly from that of the artist.

12. G. S. Viereck, *Spreading Germs of Hate* (New York, 1930), 277.

13. M. Grant, *Propaganda and the Role of the State in Inter-War Britain* (Oxford, 1994), 11.

14. V. Cunningham, *British Writers of the Thirties* (Oxford, 1988), 93. C. Day-Lewis used the phrase as a book title.

15. J. M. MacKenzie, *Propaganda and Empire* (Manchester, 1984), 82.

16. P. Brendon and P. Whitehead, *The Windsors* (2000 edn), 52.

17. R. Baden-Powell, *Scouting for Boys* (2004 edn), 278.

18. S. Orwell and I. Angus (eds), *The Collected Essays, Journalism and Letters of George Orwell*, I (Harmondsworth, 1971), 530 and 518.

19. CAC, PJGG 6, Lady Grigg to Dorothy Hammond, 30 August 1934.

20. MacKenzie, *Propaganda*, 253.

21. W. Albig, *Public Opinion* (1939), 290.

22. *Daily Mail*, 24 April 1924.

23. *Spectator*, 26 April 1924.

24. A. N. Wilson, *After the Victorians* (2005), 274–5.

25. *United Empire*, XV (1924), 581.

26. P. M. Taylor, *The Projection of Britain* (Cambridge, 1981), 104.

27. *The Times*, 20 September and 23 April 1924.

28. M. Kennedy, *Portrait of Elgar* (1982), 300.

29. K. Walthew, "The British Empire Exhibition of 1924," *HT*, 31 (August 1981), 39.

30. *The Times*, 30 September 1924.

31. D. Marquand, *Ramsay MacDonald* (1977), 65.

32. S. White, *Britain and the Bolshevik Revolution* (1979), 121. The expression was Radek's.

33. *Daily Herald*, 1 July 1924.

34. *United Empire*, XIV (1923), 544.

35. *The Times*, 23 April 1924.

36. N. and J. MacKenzie (eds), *The Diary of Beatrice Webb* (1985), 198.

37. A. Kirk-Greene, *On Crown Service* (1999), 36.

38. Orwell and Angus (eds), *Orwell*, I, 269.

39. A. Clayton, *The British Empire as a Superpower, 1919–39* (1986), 12.

40. W. Somerset Maugham, "The Outstation," in *Collected Short Stories*, IV (Harmondsworth, 1967 edn), 340. This formality was gradually relaxed before the Second World War, to the dismay of those who thought prestige should come before comfort.

41. E. M. Forster, *A Passage to India* (Harmondsworth, 1959 edn), 29 and 49.

42. Mack, *Public Schools*, 238.

43. Dewey, *Anglo-Saxon Attitudes*, 120. The phrase was Malcolm Darling's.

44. R. Furse, *Aucuparius* (1962), 241.

45. Kirk-Greene, *Crown Service*, 194.

46. R. Heussler, *Yesterday's Rulers* (1963), 116.

47. J. G. Butcher, *The British in Malaya 1880–1941* (Kuala Lumpur, 1979), 41.

48. E. D. Morel, *Nigeria* (1912 edn), 7.

49. I am grateful to the author, Manus Nunan, for sending me his typescript.

50. J. Callaghan, *Time and Chance* (1983), 120.

51. C. Ondaatje, *Woolf in Ceylon* (2005), 39.

52. M. Perham, *West African Passage* (1983), 54.

53. J. Nehru, *An Autobiography* (1936), 442.

54. Mack, *Public Schools*, 267.

55. A. J. Greenberger, *The British Image of India* (1969), 89.

56. D. and S. Howarth, *The Story of P & O* (1986), 59. The opulent new liners of the 1930s were white with buff funnels.

57. R. Kipling, *From Sea to Sea*, I (1924), 261.

58. G. Biliankin, *Hail, Penang* (1932), 1.

59. Morris, *Pax Britannica*, 54.

60. J. H. Harris, *Dawn in Darkest Africa* (1982), 96.

61. Steevens, *Capetown to Ladysmith*, 167.

62. Maugham, "P. & O.," in *Short Stories*, IV, 88.

63. 'Youth," in *The Complete Short Stories of Joseph Conrad* (n.d.), 89.

64. G. Bowker, *George Orwell* (2003), 77. It has been suggested that this episode was a parable "almost too neatly realised" (D. J. Taylor, *Orwell* [2003], 64). In fact, such incidents were commonplace. Witness Jack Moore's prewar memory: "the half-naked brown body of a native lying in the gutter outside the shop [of Cowasgee Dinshaw in Aden] and a white sailor kicking violently at the body—and, as far as I recollect, nobody had the humanity or courage to intervene." (CUL RCMS 57, Jack Moore, "From Aden to . . . Quetta," 15.) Similarly, on arrival at Calcutta in 1945, the future film star Dirk Bogarde saw a porter being thrashed by a "ginger-haired, moustached, red-faced stocky little major from Transport." (Quoted by C. Bayly and T. Harper, *Forgotten Wars: The End of Britain's Asian Empire* [2007], 138.)

65. G. Orwell, *Burmese Days* (2001 edn), 70.

66. M. Muggeridge, *Chronicles of Wasted Time*, I, *The Green Stick* (1972), 96. Muggeridge supposed that this view was held "almost universally" on P&O boats during the 1920s.

67. *New Statesman*, 27 September 1924.

68. K. Tidrick, *Empire and the English Character* (1990), 90.

69. J. van der Poel (ed.), *Selections from the Smuts Papers*, V (Cambridge, 1973), 194.

70. R. Craddock, "Should Englishmen enter the Indian Services?" *Nineteenth Century and After*, 97 (February 1925), 260.

71. A. Grimble, *A Pattern of Islands* (1952), 174.

72. P. Balfour, *Grand Tour* (n.d.), 217.

73. Butcher, *British in Malaya*, 22.

74. CAC, AMEL 2/4/15 (File 5) Malaya, Sir L. Guillemard to L. Amery, 20 November 1924.

75. V. Purcell, *The Memoirs of a Malayan Official* (1965), 268.

76. Hyam, *Empire and Sexuality*, 109.

77. T. N. Harper, *The End of Empire and the Making of Malaya* (Cambridge, 1999), 130, quoting *The Planter* (9 September 1947), 235.

78. J. de V. Allen, "Malayan Civil Service, 1874–1941: Colonial Bureaucracy/Malayan Elite," *CSSH*, 12 (1970), 149.

79. R. H. Bruce Lockhart, *Return to Malaya* (1936), 413 and 333.

80. Harper, *End of Empire*, 23.

81. C. Allen (ed.), *Tales from the South Seas* (1983), 64.

82. Lockhart, *Malaya*, 113.

83. H. Callaway, *Gender, Culture and Empire: European Women in Colonial Nigeria* (1987), 237.

84. J. Cary, *Mister Johnson* (Harmondsworth, 1983 edn), 103.

85. B. Thomson, *The Scene Changes* (1939), 74.

86. J. R. Ackerley, *Hindoo Holiday* (1952), 79.

87. CSAS, Portal Memoir, 58.

88. CAC, PJGG6, Lady Grigg to Dorothy Hammond, 17 July 1934.

89. Quoted from *Malaysia Messenger* (June 1911) by J. N. Brownfoot, "Sisters under the skin: Imperialism and the emancipation of woman in Malaya, *c.* 1891–1941," in J. A. Mangan (ed.), *Making Imperial Mentalities* (Manchester, 1990), 51.

90. Chaudhuri, *Thy Hand*, 61.
91. C. Knapman, *White Women in Fiji 1835–1930* (1986), 9, quoting from Geoffrey Dawson's novel *Queen Emma of the South Seas*.
92. Ondaatje, *Woolf in Ceylon*, 41.
93. S. Leith-Ross, *Stepping-Stones: Memoirs of Colonial Nigeria 1907–1960* (1983), 84.
94. Allen, *CSSH*, 12, 169.
95. Northcliffe, *Journey*, 244.
96. L. Woolf, *Growing* (1967), 135.
97. G. Byng, *Reap the Whirlwind* (1968), 55.
98. D. Foster, *Landscape with Arabs* (Brighton, 1969), 166.
99. Private information: Sydney Bolt.
100. CSAS, Shaw Stewart Papers, Box 1, H. D. Love, "Short History of the Madras Club" (1902), 10.
101. CUL, Add 6799–6801, Stella Benson Diaries, 5 November 1930.
102. H. Sharp, *Good-bye India* (1946), 138, quoted by M. Sinha, "Britishness, Clubbability, and the Colonial Public Sphere: The Genealogy of an Imperial Institution in India," *JBS*, 40 (October 2001), 502.
103. Hill Club Complaints Book, 25 May 1913, 23 April 1901 and 4 May 1900.
104. CUL RCMS, Bombay Club Records, "Complaints and Suggestions," 19 February and 15 November 1882.
105. J. Wyett, *Staff Wallah* (St. Leonards, NSW, 1996), 19.
106. Love, "Madras Club," 11.
107. BECM, 2001/299, Kendall Papers, C. H. B. Kendall's Indian letters, 15 February 1903.
108. P. J. Rich, *Chains of Empire* (1991), 166.
109. Kipling, *From Sea to Sea*, 288.
110. D. J. M. Tate, *The Lake Club 1890–1990* (Singapore, 1990), 111.
111. Clifford, *Children of Empire*, 75.
112. V. Gatrell, *City of Laughter* (2006), 110.
113. Moore, *Parnell*, 31.
114. Gilmour, *Ruling Caste*, 79.
115. E. Wakefield, *Past Imperative* (1966), 4.
116. R. Hunt and J. Harrison, *The District Officer in India 1930–1947* (1980), 34.
117. J. D. N. Banks, *The History of the Hill Club* (Nuwara Eliya, 1988), 34.
118. H. Kuklick, *The Imperial Bureaucrat* (Stanford, CA, 1979), 125.
119. Orwell, *Burmese Days*, 29.
120. CUL RCMS 78, "Minutes Book 1867–1876," 19 October 1870.
121. A. Burns, *Colonial Civil Servant* (1949), 57.
122. T. Kuruvilla, *Fairy Dell: Story of the High Range Club 1909–1993* (Calcutta, 1993), 53.
123. N. Ferguson, *The War of the World* (2006), 523.
124. Russell, *Freedom and Organisation*, 415.
125. R. A. Bickers and J. N. Wasserton, "Shanghai's 'Dogs and Chinese Not Admitted' Sign: Legend, History and Contemporary Symbol," *CQ*, 142 (June 1995), 447. Dogs and Chinese were both refused admission but they were never bracketed in any official sign.
126. Clifford, *Children of Empire*, 75.
127. F. Wakeman, *Policing Shanghai 1927–1937* (1995), 214.
128. *North-China Herald*, 19 January 1932.
129. R. Bickers, *Empire Made Me: An Englishman Adrift in Shanghai* (2003), 122, 126 and 291.
130. I. Nish (ed.), *Anglo-Japanese Alienation 1919–1952* (Cambridge, 1982), 39–40.
131. Orwell, *Burmese Days*, 69.
132. G. Orwell, *The Road to Wigan Pier* (Harmondsworth, 1962 edn), 127.

133. Taylor, *Orwell,* 76.

134. Orwell, *Burmese Days,* 68.

135. R. Pearce, *Once a Happy Valley: Memoirs of an ICS Officer in Sindh, 1938–1948* (Oxford, 2001), 17.

136. Woolf, *Growing,* 158–9.

137. S. Maugham, "The Gentleman in the Parlour" [1930], in *The Travel Books of W. Somerset Maugham* (1955), 10–11.

12. White Mates Black in a Very Few Moves

1. W. M. Ross, *Kenya from Within* (1927), 47, and C. Eliot, *The East Africa Protectorate* (1905), 302.

2. Huxley, *Delamere,* 81.

3. R. Meinertzhagen, *Kenya Diary 1902–1906* (1957), 59.

4. Eliot, *East Africa,* 310.

5. G. Bennett, *Kenya: A Political History* (1963), 14.

6. J. Iliffe, *The African Poor* (Cambridge, 1987), 156.

7. Lord Hindlip, *British East Africa* (1905), 48.

8. G. H. Mungeam, *British Rule in Kenya 1895–1912* (Oxford, 1966), 177.

9. Cocker, *Meinertzhagen,* 48.

10. B. Berman and J. Lonsdale, *Unhappy Valley* (1992), 19.

11. V. Harlow and E. M. Chilver (eds), *History of East Africa* (Oxford, 1965), 32 and 55.

12. R. Hardy, *The Iron Snake* (1965), 242–3 and 247.

13. C. Chenevix Trench, *Men Who Ruled Kenya* (1993), 17.

14. Lord Altrincham, *Kenya's Opportunity* (1955), 224.

15. CUL, RCMS 113/44, George Nightingale Memoirs, Chapter 5, 5.

16. Meinertzhagen, *Kenya Diary,* 78 and 60.

17. Harlow and Chilver, *East Africa,* 268.

18. Mungeam, *British Rule in Kenya,* 195.

19. "The Case of the Masai," *Empire Review,* 35 (October 1921), 389.

20. Meinertzhagen, *Kenya Diary,* 153.

21. Hyam, *Empire and Sexuality,* 160 and 168.

22. C. S. Nicholls, *Red Strangers* (2005), 72.

23. *OHBE,* IV, 267.

24. E. Bradlow, "The Evolution of 'Trusteeship,' in Kenya," *SAHJ,* IV (1972), 60.

25. Eliot, *East Africa,* 143.

26. K. Blixen, *Out of Africa* (Harmondsworth, 1954 edn), 124.

27. Lord Cranworth, *A Colony in the Making or Sport and Profit in East Africa* (1912), 11.

28. D. Kennedy, *Islands of White* (Durham, NC, 1987), 48.

29. Ross, *Kenya,* 103. Lugard's own view was that "The requirements of the settlers, to put it bluntly, are incompatible with the interests and advancement of agricultural tribes, nor could they be otherwise than impatient of native development as a rival in the growing of coffee, flax, and sisal . . . British immigrants should be fully warned of the deficiency of native labour, and discouraged from coming to the country unless they are prepared to dispense with it." (*Dual Mandate,* 397.)

30. W. Rodney, *How Europe Underdeveloped Africa* (Washington, DC, 1982), 165.

31. CUL, RCMS 178, Arnold Paice Letters, Box 1, 3 July 1907, 29 May 1910 and 15 December 1907.

32. Ross, *Kenya,* 95 and 94.

33. CUL, RCMS 178, Box 1, 26 August 1911.

34. B. Berman, *Control & Crisis in Colonial Kenya* (1990), 62.
35. CUL, RCMS 178, Box 1, 9 September 1907.
36. Berman, *Control & Crisis,* 184.
37. Hyam, *Elgin and Churchill,* 215.
38. W. S. Churchill, *My African Journey* (1968 edn), 25.
39. E. Huxley, *Red Strangers* (1999 edn), 268.
40. E. Paice, *Tip & Run: The Untold Tragedy of the Great War in Africa* (2007), 288.
41. Kennedy, *Islands of White,* 78.
42. J. W. Cell, *By Kenya Possessed* (Chicago, 1976), 92.
43. CUL, RCMS 113/44, Chapter on Kiltanon, 2.
44. *Harry Thuku: An Autobiography* (Nairobi, 1970), 18.
45. Ross, *Kenya,* 226 and 228.
46. Huxley, *Delamere,* II, 67, 113 and 138.
47. N. Best, *Happy Valley* (1970), 109.
48. J. G. Kamoche, *Imperial Trusteeship and Political Evolution in Kenya, 1923–1963* (Washington, DC, 1981), 51.
49. S. Ball, *The Guardsmen* (2004), 96.
50. A. Buxton, *Kenya Days* (1927), 15.
51. CUL, RCMS 178, Box 1, 9 October 1907.
52. E. Bache, *The Youngest Lion* (1934), 14.
53. M. Perham, *East African Journey* (1976), 25.
54. M. S. Lovell, *Straight on Till Morning* (1987), 129.
55. E. Huxley, *The Flame Trees of Thika* (1959), 14.
56. L. Powys, *Ebony and Ivory* (New York, 1923), 19.
57. N. Leys, *Kenya* (1973 edn), 182.
58. R. L. Tignor, *The Colonial Transformation of Kenya* (Princeton, NJ, 976), 156.
59. "The 'Black Peril' in British East Africa," *Empire Review,* 35 (June 1921), 199 and 197.
60. J. Fox, *White Mischief* (1982), 46.
61. Kennedy, *Islands of White,* 87.
62. Mungeam, *British Rule in Kenya,* 279.
63. Cell (ed.), *Kenya Possessed,* 114.
64. Harlow and Chilver (eds), *East Africa,* 331.
65. A. H. M. Kirk-Greene, "The Sudan Political Service: A Profile in the Sociology of Imperialism," *IJAHS,* 15 (1982), 22.
66. J. A. Mangan, *The Games Ethic and Imperialism* (1986), 87.
67. O. Keun, *A Foreigner Looks at the Sudan* (1930), 5, 52–3 and 13.
68. *Sudan Notes & Records,* XIV (1931), Pt I, 99.
69. D. C. Smith, *H. G. Wells, Desperately Mortal* (1986), 408.
70. BECM 2001/299, Brian Kendall, "Memories of Sudan Service."
71. Daly, *Empire on the Nile,* 95.
72. *United Empire,* I (1910), 191.
73. Kipling, *Letters of Travel,* 284.
74. Lycett, *Kipling,* 381.
75. DUL, 578/4/1–76, MacMichael Papers, MacMichael to his parents, 14 October 1905.
76. BECM, 2001/299, 1943.
77. K. D. D. Henderson, *The Making of the Modern Sudan* (1953), 109.
78. DUL, MacMichael Papers 585/4/1–383, Diary, 30 November 1906.
79. Daly, *Empire on the Nile,* 366.
80. M. W. Daly, *Imperial Sudan* (Cambridge, 1991), 67 and 152.
81. BECM, 2001/299, 1946 and 1947.

82. Rameses [C. S. Jarvis], *Oriental Spotlight* (1937), 120.

83. Daly, *Empire on the Nile*, 399–400.

84. H. C. Jackson, *Sudan Days and Ways* (1954), 161.

85. C. Allen, *Tales from the Dark Continent* (1986 edn), 107.

86. Daly, *Empire of the Nile*, 400 and 142.

87. R. O. Collins, *Shadows in the Grass* (New Haven, CT, 1983), 138.

88. Daly, *Empire of the Nile*, 415.

89. R. O. Collins and F. M. Deng (eds), *The British in the Sudan, 1898–1956* (1984), 52.

90. BECM, 2001/299, 1946.

91. D. H. Johnson (ed.), *The Upper Nile Province Handbook 1931* (1995), 28.

92. D. Cameron, *My Tanganyika Service and Some Nigeria* (1939), 103.

93. P. Mitchell, *African Afterthoughts* (1954), 129.

94. Collins and Deng (eds), *British in the Sudan*, 107 and 169.

95. Thesiger, *Life of My Choice*, 202.

96. C. A. E. Lea, *On Trek in Kordofan*, ed. M. W. Daly (Oxford, 1994), 43.

97. Henderson, *Modern Sudan*, 11–12.

98. P. Woodward, *Condominium and Sudanese Nationalism* (1979), 32.

99. Daly, *Imperial Sudan*, 42.

100. F. M. Deng, *Africans of Two Worlds* (1978), 156.

101. Collins and Deng (eds), *British in the Sudan*, 85.

102. F. M. Deng and M. W. Daly, *Bonds of Silk* (East Lansing, MI, 1989), 75.

103. C. H. Johnston, *The View from Steamer Point* (1964), 192.

104. Henderson, *Modern Sudan*, 172, 542, 555 and 558.

105. *The Times*, 17 May 1944.

106. Deng and Daly, *Bonds of Silk*, 97.

107. R. I. Rotberg, *The Rise of Nationalism in Central Africa* (Cambridge, MA, 1966), 111.

108. G. Padmore, *How Britain Rules Africa* (1936), 4.

109. I. Henderson, "The Origins of Nationalism in East and Central Africa: The Zambian Case," *JAH*, XI, 4 (1970), 598.

110. A. Roberts, *A History of Zambia* (1976), 193.

111. Porter, *Lion's Share*, 282.

112. J. Cary, *The Case for Africa and Other Writings on Africa* (Austin, TX, 1962), 17.

113. R. I. Rotberg, *Black Heart: Gore-Browne and the Politics of Multiracial Zambia* (Berkeley, CA, 1977), 300.

114. *CHA*, VII, 64.

115. Mitchell, *Afterthoughts*, 18.

116. M. Crowder, *West Africa under Colonial Rule* (1968), 460–61.

117. Harris, *Darkest Africa*, 107.

118. Lord Hailey, "Nationalism in Africa," *JRAS*, 36 (April 1937), 138.

119. R. Robinson, "The Moral Disarmament of the African Empire 1919–1947," *JICH*, VIII (October 1979), 99.

120. G. Shepperson, "Notes on Negro American Influences on the Emergence of African Nationalism," *JAH*, I, 2 (1960), 300.

121. Cary, *Case for Africa*, 20–21.

122. R. G. Gregory, *India and East Africa* (Oxford, 1971), 417.

13. Spinning the Destiny of India

1. Nehru, *Autobiography*, 129–30.

2. Chadha, *Gandhi*, 425.

3. Nehru, *Autobiography*, 254.

4. Nehru, *Old Letters*, 59.

5. S. P. and P. Chablani (eds), *Motilal Nehru* (Delhi, 1961), 205.

6. *SWJN*, I, 4 and 76–7.

7. S. Gandhi (ed.), *Freedom's Daughter* (1989), 77.

8. *SWJN*, I, 167.

9. S. P. and P. Chablani (eds), *Motilal Nehru*, 32.

10. Nehru, *Autobiography*, 230 and 52.

11. *SWJN*, I, 257.

12. S. C. Bose, *The Indian Struggle 1920–1942* (Delhi, 1997 edn), 110.

13. Chadha, *Gandhi*, 272.

14. Nehru, *Autobiography*, 95. Nehru doubtless read J. B. Bury's seven-volume edition of the *Decline and Fall* (1st edn, 1896). So did Gandhi.

15. H. Pollitt (ed.), *Lenin on Britain* (1934), 52.

16. S. Gopal, *Jawaharlal Nehru*, I (1975), 103.

17. Nehru, *Autobiography*, 506.

18. J. Campbell, *F. E. Smith First Earl of Birkenhead* (1983), 756 and 733.

19. J. Barnes and D. Nicholson (eds), *The Empire at Bay: The Leo Amery Diaries 1929–1945* (1988), 48.

20. S. Wolpert, *Nehru* (New York, 1996), 76.

21. S. Gopal, *The Viceroyalty of Lord Irwin 1926–1931* (Oxford, 1957), 23.

22. Nehru, *Autobiography*, 180.

23. J. N. Sahni, *Fifty Years of Indian Politics 1921–1971* (Delhi, 1971), 52.

24. K. Harris, *Attlee* (1982), 78.

25. Nehru, *Autobiography*, 204 and 207.

26. K. N. Hutheesing with A. Hatch, *We Nehrus* (New York, 1967), 126.

27. *SWJN*, I, 311. From *Marino Faliero*, Act II, Scene 2.

28. Tendulkar, *Mahatma*, II, 372.

29. *The Times*, 15 April 1930.

30. A. Roberts, *The Holy Fox* (1991), 31.

31. Bakshi, *Indian Nation Movement*, III, 44.

32. Chaudhuri, *Thy Hand*, 292.

33. D. Keer, *Mahatma Gandhi* (Bombay, 1973), 519.

34. T. Weber, *On the Salt March* (Delhi, 1997), 133.

35. *The Collected Works of Mahatma Gandhi*, XLII (Ahmedabad, 1970), 500.

36. *The Times*, 11 April 1930.

37. *New York Times*, 6 April 1930.

38. Keer, *Gandhi*, 524.

39. *The Times*, 10, 14, 12 and 10 April 1930.

40. Private Information, Mrs. Morvyth Seely.

41. CUL RCMS 52, G. E. Wheeler, "The Pathography of a Cuckoo," 68.

42. S. M. Burke and S. A. Quraishi, *The British Raj in India* (Karachi, 1995), 280.

43. B. R. Nanda, *In Gandhi's Footsteps* (Delhi, 1990), 187.

44. Lord Birkenhead, *Halifax* (1965), 284 and 248.

45. Campbell, *Smith*, 734.

46. P. Addison, *The Road to 1945* (1975), 84.

47. Nehru, *Autobiography*, 543.

48. F. Younghusband, *Dawn in India* (1930), 151 and 29.

49. Vijaya Lakshmi Pandit, *The Scope of Happiness* (1979), 39.

50. Wolpert, *Nehru*, 122.

51. P. Murphy, *Alan Lennox-Boyd* (1999), 30.
52. Birkenhead, *Halifax*, 247.
53. Tendulkar, *Mahatma*, III, 56.
54. L. Fischer, *The Life of Mahatma Gandhi* (1982 edn), 348.
55. Louis, *In the Name of God*, 110.
56. S. Gopal, "Churchill and India," in R. Blake and W. R. Louis (eds), *Churchill* (Oxford, 1992), 460.
57. Gilbert, *Churchill*, V, 467.
58. W. S. Churchill, *The Second World War*, I (6 vols, 1948–54), 26.
59. Gilbert, *Churchill*, V, 376.
60. *Answers*, 21 July 1934.
61. CAC, CHAR 2/169/60, Sir Abe Bailey to Churchill, 17 September 1930.
62. R. A. Callahan, *Churchill: Retreat from Empire* (1984), 35.
63. H. Pelling, *Winston Churchill* (1974), 352.
64. Barnes and Nicholson (eds), *Empire at Bay*, 326.
65. G. Best, *Churchill: A Study in Greatness* (2001), 135.
66. C. Bridge, *Holding India to the Empire* (1986), 73.
67. B. R. Tomlinson, *The Political Economy of the Raj 1914–1947* (1979), 141.
68. S. P. Cohen, *The Indian Army* (Berkeley, CA, 1971), 122.
69. Sahni, *Fifty Years*, 102–3.
70. Gopal, *Nehru*, I, 170.
71. Bence-Jones, *Viceroys*, 272.
72. Sahni, *Fifty Years*, 95.
73. J. Darwin, "Imperialism in Decline? Tendencies in British Imperial Policy between the Wars," *HJ*, 23, 3 (1980), 677.
74. A. Read and D. Fisher, *The Proudest Day* (1998 edn), 255.
75. Mansergh, *Commonwealth Experience*, 267. Churchill made it clear that he said "sham" not (as is often quoted) "shame."
76. CAC, CHAR 9/113.
77. CAC, PJGG 6, Lady Grigg to Tom Jones, 13 April 1935.
78. J. Glendevon, *The Viceroy at Bay: Lord Linlithgow in India, 1936–1943* (1971), 119.
79. Gopal, *Nehru*, I, 231.
80. J. Nehru, *The Unity of India* (1948 edn), 65, 181 and 196.
81. Bose, *Indian Struggle*, 368.
82. J. M. Brown, *Modern India: The Origins of an Asian Democracy* (Oxford, 1994 edn), 300.
83. CSAS, Darling Papers, Box 27, April to Irene Darling, 7 March 1939.
84. Nehru, *Unity of India*, 36.
85. G. Rizvi, *Linlithgow and India* (1978), 135.
86. Nehru, *Old Letters*, 178.
87. D. A. Low, *Britain and Indian Nationalism* (Cambridge, 1997), 300.
88. R. J. Moore, *Endgames of Empire* (Delhi, 1988), 83.
89. J. Nehru, *The Discovery of India* (1946), 374.
90. CAC, PJGG 2, Grigg to Sir Philip Chetwode, 18 July 1936.
91. *SWJN*, X, 191.
92. A. S. Ahmed, *Jinnah, Pakistan and Islamic Identity* (1997), 81.
93. Nehru, *Old Letters*, 427.
94. S. S. Pirzada, *Foundations of Pakistan* (Karachi, 1970), 337.
95. Gilbert, *Churchill*, V, 886.
96. *News of the World*, 22 May 1938.
97. Clarke, *Cripps*, 111.

98. M. Gilbert, *Churchill* (1991), 646.

99. Barnes and Nicholson (eds), *Empire at Bay*, 637.

100. Louis, *Name of God*, 20.

101. Nehru, *Unity of India*, 418.

102. Rizvi, *Linlithgow*, 166.

103. S. Gandhi, *Two Alone, Two Together: Letters between Indira Gandhi and Jawaharlal Nehru 1940–1961* (1992), 101 and 9.

104. E. Roosevelt, *As He Saw It* (1946), 37.

105. R. Hyam, "Churchill and the British Empire," in Blake and Louis (eds), *Churchill*, 180.

106. Gilbert, *Churchill*, VI, 1163.

107. Churchill, *Second World War*, II, 386. Actually the text was prepared for Churchill by Sir Alexander Cadogan, head of the Foreign Office.

108. N. Angell, "A Re-Interpretation of Empire," *United Empire*, 43 (September-October 1952), 255.

109. Gopal, *Nehru*, I, 260.

110. W. F. Kimball, *The Juggler: Franklin Roosevelt as Wartime Statesman* (Princeton, NJ, 1991), 133.

111. M. and S. Harries, *Soldiers of the Sun* (1991), 93.

112. Low, *Britain and Indian Nationalism*, 335.

113. Barnes and Nicholson (eds), *Empire at Bay*, 783.

114. Rizvi, *Linlithgow*, 183.

115. *TOPI*, I, 440.

116. R. Rhodes James (ed.), *Chips: The Diaries of Sir Henry Channon* (1967), 423 and 446.

117. Clarke, *Cripps*, 355.

118. A. M. Browne, *Long Sunset* (1995), 76. Linlithgow also used this nickname, so perhaps Churchill did not coin it. Cf. P. French, *Liberty or Death* (1997), 142.

119. P. Moon (ed.), *Wavell: The Viceroy's Journal* (1973), 33.

120. Moore, *Endgames*, 92.

121. Clarke, *Cripps*, 305.

122. *TOPI*, I, 634.

123. W. F. Kimball, *Forged in War: Churchill, Roosevelt and the Second World War* (1997), 140.

124. W. F. Kimball (ed.), *Churchill & Roosevelt: The Complete Correspondence*, I (1984), 446–7.

125. Private information: Mae Berger.

126. *TOPI*, I, 665.

127. French, *Liberty or Death*, 159.

128. Barnes and Nicholson (eds), *Empire at Bay*, 842.

129. *Churchill by His Contemporaries—An Observer Appreciation* (1965), 97.

130. Quoted by S. Wolton, *Lord Hailey, the Colonial Office and the Politics of Race and Empire in the Second World War* (Basingstoke, 2000), 101.

131. E. Sevareid, *Not so Wild a Dream* (1946), 239 and 241.

132. W. R. Louis, *Imperialism at Bay: The United States and the Decolonization of the British Empire 1941–1945* (Oxford, 1977), 433.

133. CAC, CHAR 9/191A/3–12.

134. Gibbon, *Decline and Fall*, I, 37–8.

135. *TOPI*, III, 35.

136. Nehru, *Discovery of India*, 426.

137. Mason, *Men who Ruled India*, 333.

138. Bhatia, *Famines*, 324.

139. P. S. Gupta (ed.), *Towards Freedom: Documents on the Movement for Independence in India*, Pt II (Delhi, 1997), 1890.

140. J. Connell, *Auchinleck* (1959), 736.

141. Bhatia, *Famines*, 339.

142. CAC, CHAR 9/191/33 ff.

143. Moon (ed.), *Wavell*, 78.

144. Wolpert, *Nehru*, 335.

145. CAC, CHAR 9/191/33 ff.

146. Barnes and Nicholson (eds), *Empire at Bay*, 943.

147. Louis, *Name of God*, 173.

148. Lord Casey, *Personal Experience 1939–1946* (1962), 210.

149. J. Colville, *The Fringes of Power* (1985), 563.

150. Moon (ed.), *Wavell*, 89.

151. *The Times*, 3 November 1921.

152. K. Young (ed.), *The Diaries of Sir Robert Bruce Lockhart*, II (1980), 390.

153. Moon (ed.), *Wavell*, 165.

154. *Daily Mail*, 6 September 1932.

155. *Answers*, 21 July 1934.

156. Young (ed.), *Lockhart*, II, 243.

157. *TOPI*, V, 765.

158. Read and Fisher, *Proudest Day*, 354.

159. W. Wyatt, *Confessions of an Optimist* (1985), 154.

160. Moon (ed.), *Wavell*, 168.

161. Wolpert, *Nehru*, 333.

162. *The Times*, 12 January 1942.

163. S. Howe, *Anticolonialism in British Politics* (Oxford, 1993), 139.

164. A. Bullock, *Ernest Bevin: Foreign Secretary 1945–1951* (1983), 234.

165. Taylor, *English History*, 599.

166. Moon (ed.), *Wavell*, 165 and 387.

167. A. Jalal, *The Sole Spokesman* (Cambridge, 1985), 137.

168. R. J. Moore, *Escape from Empire* (1984), 76.

169. Moon (ed.), *Wavell*, 295, 314 and 341.

170. S. Bose and A. Jalal, *Modern South Asia* (1998), 179.

171. S. Ghosh, *Gandhi's Emissary* (1967), 105.

172. P. Moon, *Divide and Quit* (Delhi, 1998 edn), 81.

173. F. Tuker, *While Memory Serves* (1950), 160.

174. Gopal, *Nehru*, I, 337.

175. Moon (ed.), *Wavell*, 402.

176. H. V. Brasted and C. Bridge, "The Transfer of Power in South Asia: An Historiographical Review," *SA*, XVII, 1 (1994), 108.

177. B. Fergusson, *The Trumpet in the Hall 1930–1958* (1970), 176.

178. A. Roberts, *Eminent Churchillians* (1994), 60.

179. Ahmed, *Jinnah*, 168.

180. H. V. Hodson, *The Great Divide* (Karachi, 1997 edn), 531.

181. B. Loring Vila, *Unauthorized Action: Mountbatten and the Dieppe Raid 1942* (Oxford, 1990), 256.

182. P. Ziegler (ed.), *Personal Diary of Admiral the Lord Louis Mountbatten 1943–1946* (1988), 204.

183. *TOPI*, IX, 453.

184. J. Morgan, *Edwina Mountbatten: A Life of Her Own* (1991), 298.

185. P. Ziegler, *Mountbatten* (1986 edn), 475 and 368.

186. S. Qureshi, *Jinnah* (Karachi, 1999), 37.

187. G. D. Khosla, *Stern Reckoning* (1989 edn), 102.

188. M. N. Das, *End of the British-Indian Empire,* I (Cuttack, 1983), 290.

189. I. Copland, *India 1885–1947* (2001), 74.

190. *TOPI,* XI, 826 and 39.

191. *United Empire,* XXXIX (July-August 1948), 195.

192. *The Memoirs of General the Lord Ismay* (1960), 416.

193. *The Times,* 27 August 1947.

194. L. Mosley, *The Last Days of the Raj* (1961), 57.

195. *Times of India,* 30 May 1947.

196. R. Hudson (ed.), *The Raj: An Eyewitness History of the British in India* (1999), 580.

197. *TOPI,* XI, 131.

198. Gibbon, *Decline and Fall,* II, 120.

199. Quoted from the Calcutta *Statesman* by Tuker, *While Memory Serves,* 588.

200. *TOPI,* XII, 444.

201. A. K. Azad, *India Wins Freedom* (1960), 190.

202. L. A. Sherwani, *The Partition of India and Mountbatten* (Karachi, 1986), 183.

203. CSAS, Patrick Brendon, "Disaster in Gurgaon," 60.

204. Hodson, *Great Divide,* 534.

205. I. Copland, *The Princes of India in the Endgame of Empire 1917–1947* (Cambridge, 1997), 269.

206. Moon, *Divide and Quit,* 107.

207. *The Times,* 15 August 1947.

208. L. Collins and D. Lapierre, *Freedom at Midnight* (1982 edn), 125.

209. *TOPI,* XII, 770–71.

210. V. P. Menon, *The Transfer of Power in India* (1957), 413.

211. Azad, *India Wins Freedom,* 209.

212. *The Times,* 16 August 1947.

213. Collins and Lapierre, *Freedom at Midnight,* 309.

214. *TOPI,* XII, 773.

215. A. Campbell-Johnson, *Mission with Mountbatten* (1951), 161.

216. *The Times,* 15 August 1947.

217. *New York Times,* 24 August 1947.

218. S. Heffer, *Like the Roman* (1998), 98.

219. P. Hennessy, *Never Again: Britain 1945–51* (1992), 235.

220. Azad, *India Wins Freedom,* 190. Azad had warned Mountbatten of this and said that "the British would be responsible for the carnage."

221. *New York Times,* 15, 20 and 21 August 1947.

222. S. S. Hamid, *Disastrous Twilight* (1986 edn), 225.

223. Khosla, *Stern Reckoning,* 123.

224. *The Times,* 25 August 1947.

225. Read and Fisher, *Proudest Day,* 498.

226. P. Singh, *Of Dreams and Demons* (1994), 26.

227. Chaudhuri, *Thy Hand,* 837.

228. R. Symonds, *In the Margins of Independence* (Oxford, 2001), 3.

229. Menon, *Transfer of Power,* 434.

230. Ziegler, *Mountbatten,* 437.

231. T. Royle, *The Last Days of the Raj* (1997 edn), 218, 213 and 214.

232. Angell in *United Empire,* XLIII (September-October 1952), 255.

233. Khosla, *Stern Reckoning,* 296.

234. Hamid, *Disastrous Twilight,* 238.

14. That Is the End of the British Empire

1. Brown, *India*, 320.
2. Gopal, *JICH*, XXVII (May 1999), 107.
3. J. Gallagher, *The Decline, Revival and Fall of the British Empire* (Cambridge, 1982), 145.
4. R. C. H. McKie, *This Was Singapore* (n.d.), 19 and 101.
5. O. D. Gallagher, *Retreat in the East* (1942), 68.
6. *Sydney Morning Herald,* 14 February 1938, quoted by C. M. Turnbull, *A History of Singapore* (Kuala Lumpur, 1977), 163.
7. S. Roskill, *Hankey,* II (1973), 544.
8. R. Douglas, *Liquidation of Empire* (2002), 37.
9. W. R. Louis, *Ends of British Imperialism* (2006), 308.
10. R. Callahan, *The Worst Disaster: The Fall of Singapore* (Newark, NJ, 1977), 31.
11. A. Warren, *Singapore 1942* (2002), 26.
12. P. S. Chapman, *The Jungle Is Neutral* (1949), 17.
13. K. Attiwill, *The Singapore Story* (1959), 19.
14. *The Times,* 8 December 1941.
15. Turnbull, *Singapore,* 141.
16. Attiwill, *Singapore,* 66.
17. Kipling, *Sea to Sea,* I, 258.
18. Wyett, *Staff Wallah,* 87.
19. Warren, *Singapore,* 43.
20. B. Bond (ed.), *Chief of Staff,* II (1974), 67.
21. P. Elphick, *Singapore: The Pregnable Fortress* (1995), 153.
22. I. Morrison, *Malayan Postscript* (1942), 157.
23. D. Cooper, *Old Men Forget* (1953), 305.
24. Chapman, *Jungle,* 18.
25. CUL, RCMS, BAM Addenda, Mic. 8239, K. A. Brundle, "Escape from Singapore 1942," 3, in "An Architect's Memoirs of Malaya."
26. Gallagher, *Retreat,* 65.
27. Elphick, *Singapore,* 257.
28. M. Tsuji, *Singapore 1941–1942: The Japanese Version of the Malayan Campaign of World War,* II (Oxford, 1988), 68.
29. H. P. Willmott, *Empires in the Balance* (1982), 241 and 247.
30. Chapman, *Jungle,* 15.
31. L. Allen, *Singapore 1941–1942* (1977), 255.
32. W. D. McIntyre, *The Rise and Fall of the Singapore Naval Base, 1919–1942* (1979), 226.
33. CUL, RCMS, BAM Addenda, Mic. 8239, 6.
34. Elphick, *Singapore,* 285.
35. CUL, RCMS, BAM Addenda, Mic. 8239, 3.
36. E. M. Glover, *In 70 Days* (1946), 122.
37. C. Bayly and T. Harper, *Forgotten Armies: The Fall of British Asia 1941–1945* (2005), 130.
38. CUL, RCMS, BAM Addenda, Mic. 8239, 10.
39. Warren, *Singapore,* 278.
40. Churchill, *Second World War,* IV, 81.
41. Turnbull, *Singapore,* 215.
42. Glover, *70 Days,* 239.
43. E. C. T. Chew and E. Lee (eds), *A History of Singapore* (Singapore, 1991), 117.
44. James, *Rise and Fall,* 453.
45. H. Nicolson, *Diaries and Letters 1939–1945* (1967), 214.
46. *The Times,* 14 March 1942.

47. *Melbourne Herald,* 27 December 1941.
48. R. E. Herzstein, *Henry R. Luce* (1994), 177.
49. CSAS, Tayabji Papers, "The Burma Story," 20, 36, 21 and 3.
50. Thant Myint-U, *Modern Burma,* 102.
51. H. F. Hall, *The Soul of the People* (1905), 53.
52. D. M. Smeaton, *The Loyal Karens of Burma* (1887), 26.
53. Geary, *Burma,* 245.
54. J. S. Furnivall, *An Introduction to the Political Economy of Burma* (Rangoon, 1931), xii.
55. J. S. Furnivall, *Colonial Policy and Practice* (New York, 1956), 162.
56. Ba Maw, *Breakthrough in Burma* (1968), xxii.
57. Smeaton, *Loyal Karens,* 26 and 216–17.
58. Furnivall, *Colonial Policy,* 108.
59. Orwell and Calder (eds), *Collected Orwell,* I, 265.
60. Furnivall, *Colonial Policy,* 90 and 150.
61. White, *Civil Servant,* 11.
62. Smeaton, *Loyal Karens,* 4.
63. H. Tinker (ed.), *Burma: The Struggle for Independence 1944–1948,* I (1983), 608.
64. Cooper, *Old Men Forget,* 295.
65. J. F. Cady, *A History of Modern Burma* (Ithaca, NY, 1958), 231.
66. J. Silverstein (ed.), *The Political Legacy of Aung San* (Ithaca, NY, 1993), 81.
67. Cady, *Modern Burma,* 218 and 252.
68. M. Collis, *Trials in Burma* (1945), 213.
69. C. Connolly (ed.), *Horizon Stories* (1953), 93.
70. R. Slater, *Guns Through Arcady: Burma and the Burma Road* (Sydney, 1941), 12.
71. Furnivall, *Colonial Policy,* 175 and 149.
72. Ba Maw, *Breakthrough,* 24, 21, 20 and 89.
73. Cady, *Modern Burma,* 418.
74. Ba Maw, *Breakthrough,* 65.
75. M. Collis, *Last and First in Burma* (1946), 32–3.
76. Ba Maw, *Breakthrough,* 174 and 206.
77. Cady, *Modern Burma,* 442.
78. R. Butwell, *U Nu of Burma* (Stanford, CA, 1969), 42.
79. C. Bayly, "Rangoon (Yangon) 1939–49: The death of a colonial metropolis," CSAS, Occasional Paper No. 3 (2003), 16.
80. Tinker (ed.), *Burma,* I, 65.
81. Thakin Nu, *Burma under the Japanese* (1954), 77.
82. F. N. Trager (ed.), *Burma: Japanese Military Administration, Selected Documents, 1941–1945* (Philadelphia, 1971), 164.
83. Tinker (ed.), *Burma,* I, 727.
84. H. Tinker, *The Union of Burma* (1967), 14.
85. *United Empire,* XXXVII (March 1946), 81 and 84.
86. Viscount Slim, *Defeat into Victory* (1956), 520 and 518.
87. N. Tarling, *The Fourth Anglo-Burmese War* (Gaya, Bihar, 1987), 42 and 47.
88. Collis, *First in Burma,* 210.
89. J. S. Furnivall, "Twilight in Burma: Reconquest and Crisis," *PA,* XXII (1949), 9.
90. N. Tarling, *The Fall of Imperial Britain in South-East Asia* (New York, 1993), 161.
91. Tinker, *Burma,* I, 284, 1018, 1034, 934, 938 and 910.
92. Tinker, *Burma,* II, 13.
93. Tarling, *Anglo-Burmese War,* 342, 244 and 338.

94. Tinker, *Burma,* II, 877.
95. Tarling, *Anglo-Burmese War,* 329.
96. Bayly and Harper, *Forgotten Wars,* 374.

15. The Aim of Labour Is to Save the Empire

1. F. Lewis, *Sixty-Four Years in Ceylon* (Colombo, 1926), 217–18.
2. R. Moxham, *Tea: Addiction, Exploitation and Empire* (2003), 180.
3. Baker, *Ceylon,* 47.
4. Woolf, *Growing,* 48.
5. C. S. Blackton, "The Europeans of the Ceylon Civil Service in the Nineteen Twenties: The View from the Kachcheri," *CJHSS,* NS, VIII (1978), 38.
6. C. M. Enriquez, *Ceylon Past and Present* (1927), 35 and 116.
7. Sri Lanka National Archives, 7/39, Governor's Secret Diary (1798), 2.
8. W. Knighton, *Forest Life in Ceylon,* I (1854), 97.
9. Tennent, *Ceylon,* II, 167.
10. R. W. Kostal, "A Jurisprudence of Power: Martial Law and the Ceylon Controversy of 1848–51," *JICH,* 28 (January 2000), 6.
11. K. M. de Silva (ed.), *Letters on Ceylon 1846–50* (Colombo, 1965), 137.
12. A. C. M. Ameer Ali, "Rice and Irrigation in 19th Century Sri Lanka," *CHJ,* XXV (October 1978), 259.
13. G. F. Perera, *The Ceylon Railway* (1925), 44 and 86.
14. H. A. J. Hulugalle, *British Governors of Ceylon* (Colombo, 1963), 85.
15. Woolf, *Growing,* 92.
16. R. K. de Silva (ed.), *19th-Century Newspaper Engravings of Ceylon-Sri Lanka* (1998), 159.
17. Tennent, *Ceylon,* II, 189.
18. Hulugalle, *British Governors,* 73.
19. Sri Lanka National Archives, 25/5, Stuart Mackenzie Collection, Mackenzie to James Stephen, 14 March 1841.
20. Tennent, *Ceylon,* I, 3, and II, 99.
21. E. Haeckel, "A Visit to Ceylon," *CHJ,* 23 (1975), 59.
22. Tennent, *Ceylon,* II, 255.
23. H. Williams, *Ceylon: Pearl of the East* (1950), 17.
24. Knighton, *Forest Life,* I, 150.
25. Tsuzuki, *Carpenter,* 105.
26. M. Roberts, "Stimulants and Ingredients in the Awakening of Latter-Day Nationalism," in M. Roberts (ed.), *Collective Identities: Nationalism and Protest in Modern Sri Lanka* (Colombo, 1979), 226.
27. J. Manor, *The Expedient Utopian: Bandaranaike and Ceylon* (Cambridge, 1989), 63.
28. S. A. Pakeman, *Ceylon* (1964), 108.
29. S. Bandaranaike, *Remembered Yesterdays* (1929), 16, 273 and 224.
30. K. M. de Silva and H. Wriggins, *J. R. Jayewardene,* I (1988), 17.
31. C. T. Blackton, "The Empire at Bay: British Attitudes and the Growth of Nationalism in the Early Twentieth Century," in Roberts (ed.), *Collective Identities,* 381.
32. H. A. J. Hulugalle, *The Life and Times of Don Stephen Senanayake* (Colombo, 1975), 25.
33. Hulugalle, *British Governors,* 159 and 164.
34. Sri Lanka National Archives, 25/7/1, S. C. Fernando/Woolf Papers, E. W. Perera and D. E. Jayatitaka to Colonial Secretary, 18 September 1917. The authors said that the Attorney-General withheld this remark from the commission of inquiry because foreign critics

"might make capital out of it, and because it was a shameful thing." Perera also accused the Attorney, in a letter to Leonard Woolf (26 October 1917), of trying "to blacken the character of the men shot."

35. *Manchester Guardian,* 28 August 1917.

36. Sri Lanka National Archives, 25/7/1, Perera and Jayatitaka, 18 September 1917.

37. C. S. Blackton, "The 1915 Riots in Ceylon," *CJHSS,* X (1967), 62.

38. M. Vythilingam, *The Life of Sir Ponnambalam Ramathan,* II (Chunnakam, 1977), 234.

39. K. M. de Silva, "The Formation and Character of the Ceylon National Congress 1917–1919," *CJHSS,* X (1967), 100.

40. K. M. de Silva, "The Ceylon National Congress in Disarray II: The Triumph of Sir William Manning," *CJHSS,* NS, III (1973), 17.

41. C. Jeffries, *Ceylon—The Path to Independence* (1962), 51.

42. K. M. de Silva (ed.), *BDEEP,* Series E, Vol. II, *Sri Lanka,* Pt I (1997), 107, 156, 11 and 44.

43. Viscount Soulbury, "D. S. Senanayake the Man," *CHJ,* V (1955–6), 64.

44. De Silva (ed.), *Sri Lanka,* Pt I, 132.

45. Blackton, "Empire at Bay," in Roberts (ed.), *Collective Identities,* 381.

46. Manor, *Expedient Utopian,* 152.

47. De Silva (ed.), *Sri Lanka,* Pt I, 133 and 135.

48. K. M. de Silva (ed.), *University of Ceylon History of Ceylon,* III (Colombo, 1973), 419.

49. Hullugalle, *Senanayake,* 136.

50. De Silva (ed.), *Sri Lanka,* Pt II, 92.

51. ICS, JENN/125, Papers of Sir Ivor Jennings, C/14/1, "Road to Peradeniya," 131.

52. De Silva (ed.), *Sri Lanka,* Pt II, 96, 113 and 112.

53. ICS, JENN/125, C/14/1, 139.

54. De Silva (ed.), *Sri Lanka,* Pt II, 284.

55. K. M. de Silva, "The Transfer of Power in Sri Lanka—A Review of British Perspectives," *CJHSS,* NS, IV (1974), 19.

56. H. Grimal, *Decolonization* (1978 edn), 135. The speaker was Patrick Gordon Walker, a junior minister in the Commonwealth Relations Office.

57. Ludowyk, *Ceylon,* 204.

58. W. R. Roff, *The Origins of Malay Nationalism* (Kuala Lumpur, 1994 edn), 235, 183 and 232.

59. A. Milner, *The Invention of Politics in Colonial Malaya* (Cambridge, 1995), 264.

60. P. H. Kratoska, *The Japanese Occupation of Malaya* (Cambridge, 1998), 349.

61. Thorne, *Allies,* 728.

62. Chin Peng, *My Side of History* (Singapore, 2003), 267.

63. *The Times,* 16 August 1945.

64. Cheah Boon Kheng, *Red Star over Malaya* (Singapore, 1983), 138 and 133.

65. Bayly and Harper, *Forgotten Wars,* 270.

66. D. Mackay, *The Malayan Emergency, 1948–60* (1997), 157.

67. A. J. Stockwell (ed.), *BDEEP,* Series B, Vol. 3, *Malaya,* Pt II (1995), 37.

68. N. J. White, *Business, Government and the End of Empire* (Kuala Lumpur, 1996), 275 and 8.

69. A. Lau, *The Malayan Union Controversy 1942–1948* (Singapore, 1991), 101.

70. S. C. Smith, "The Rise, Decline and Survival of the Malay Rulers during the Colonial Period, 1874–1957," *JICH,* 22 (January 1994), 97.

71. A. J. Stockwell, *British Policy and Malay Politics during the Malayan Union Experiment, 1942–1948* (Kuala Lumpur, 1979), 57.

72. Kheng, *Red Star,* 277.

73. R. Heussler, *Completing a Stewardship: The Malayan Civil Service 1942–1957* (Westport, CT, 1983), 97.

74. M. Shennan, *Out in the Midday Sun: The British in Malaya 1880–1960* (2000), 304.

75. T. Harper, "The Politics of Disease and Disorder in Post-War Malaya," *JSeAS*, 21 (March 1990), 99.

76. R. B. Smith, "Some Contrasts between Burma and Malaya in British Policy towards South-East Asia, 1942–1946," in R. B. Smith and A. J. Stockwell (eds), *British Policy and the Transfer of Power in Asia: Documentary Perspectives* (1988), 63.

77. R. Stubbs, *Hearts and Minds in Guerrilla Warfare* (Singapore, 1989), 55.

78. A. Short, *The Communist Insurrection in Malaya 1948–1960* (1975), 61.

79. Stockwell (ed.), *Malaya*, Pt II, 21.

80. *Straits Times,* 17 June 1948.

81. Shennan, *Midday Sun,* 318.

82. Stubbs, *Hearts and Minds,* 75 and 90.

83. P. Deery, "The Terminology of Terrorism: Malaya, 1948–52," *JSeAS*, 34 (2003), 241.

84. J. D. Leary, *Violence and the Dream People* (Athens, OH, 1995), 42.

85. Chin Peng, *History,* 270.

86. J. Cloake, *Templer, Tiger of Malaya* (1985), 204.

87. Stockwell (ed.), *Malaya*, Pt II, 330.

88. Cloake, *Templer,* 263.

89. M. R. Henderson, *Malayan Journal* (1987), 13.

90. Muggeridge, *Chronicles of Wasted Time*, II, 116.

91. Purcell, *Malayan Official,* 272.

92. K. Ramakrishna, "'Transmogrifying' Malaya: The Impact of Sir Gerald Templer," *JSeAS*, 32 (February 2001), 84.

93. Cloake, *Templer,* 220 and 239.

94. Harper, *End of Empire,* 281.

95. Cloake, *Templer,* 214 and 230.

96. Short, *Communist Insurrection,* 380, 292 and 193.

97. Chin Peng, *History,* 301.

98. M. C. A. Henniker, *Red Shadow over Malaya* (1955), 112.

99. K. Hack, "'Iron Claws on Malaya': The Historiography of the Malayan Emergency," *JSeAS*, 30 (March 1999), 118.

100. A. Burgess, *Little Wilson and Big God* (1978), 395.

101. K. Ramakrishna, *Emergency Propaganda* (Richmond, 2002), 165.

102. Harper, *End of Empire,* 355.

103. Stockwell (ed.), *Malaya*, Pt II, 455.

16. A Golden Bowl Full of Scorpions

1. D. Reynolds, *Britannia Overruled: British Policy and World Power in the Twentieth Century* (1991), 167.

2. W. R. Louis, *The British Empire in the Middle East* (Oxford, 1984), 31.

3. Gilbert, *Churchill,* VIII, 171.

4. Bullock, *Bevin: Foreign Secretary,* 659.

5. D. Reynolds, *In Command of History* (2005), 43.

6. B. Wasserstein, *The British in Palestine* (1978), 111.

7. C. Sykes, *Cross Roads to Israel* (1965), 88.

8. A. Koestler, *Promise and Fulfilment: Palestine 1917–1949* (1949), 33.

9. D. Duff, *Bailing with a Teaspoon* (1953), 76.

10. A. Shapira, "Ben-Gurion and the Bible: The Forging of an Historical Narrative," *MES*, 33 (October 1997), 651.

11. G. Antonius, *The Arab Awakening* (2000 edn), 409 and 411.

12. Wasserstein, *British in Palestine,* 60.
13. Antonius, *Arab Awakening,* 411.
14. Wasserstein, *British in Palestine,* 79.
15. D. Ingrams (ed.), *Palestine Papers 1917–1922* (New York, 1973), 171.
16. T. Segev, *One Palestine, Complete* (2000), 147.
17. N. Rose, *Harold Nicolson* (2005), 20.
18. Segev, *One Palestine,* 160 and 155.
19. Sherman, *Mandate Days,* 45.
20. Wasserstein, *British in Palestine,* 107.
21. J. M. N. Jeffries, *Palestine: The Reality* (1939), 279 and 333.
22. Meinertzhagen, *Middle East Diary,* 48.
23. G. K. Chesterton, *The New Jerusalem* (1920), 93–4.
24. Sykes, *Cross Roads,* 39.
25. CAC, AMEL 1/5/46, "Secret and Confidential: Josiah Wedgwood's Recollections After a Dinner 26-7-1928."
26. Pembroke College, Cambridge, Storrs Papers, Reel 8, Storrs to unnamed recipient, 9 February 1922. Storrs said that Northcliffe "arrived in Palestine still a Zionist by reputation but far other at heart and soon in speech."
27. Pound and Harmsworth, *Northcliffe,* 845.
28. B. Pimlott (ed.), *The Political Diary of Hugh Dalton* (1986), 207.
29. E. Keith-Roach, *Pasha in Jerusalem* (1994), 56.
30. P. Loti, *Jerusalem and the Holy Land* (2002 edn), 58.
31. Storrs, *Orientations,* 439.
32. Gibbon, *Decline and Fall,* III, 648 and 564.
33. Loti, *Jerusalem,* 62.
34. H. C. Luke (ed.), *The Traveller's Guide for Palestine and Syria* (1924), 145.
35. R. Andrews, *Blood on the Mountain* (1999), 198.
36. Keith-Roach, *Pasha,* 119.
37. S. Perowne, *The One Remains* (1954), 82.
38. G. A. Smith, *The Historical Geography of the Holy Land* (1966 edn), 212.
39. Pembroke College, Cambridge, Storrs Papers, Reel 8, Storrs to George Lloyd, 1 September 1922.
40. P. Mattar, *The Mufti of Jerusalem* (New York, 1988), 38.
41. J. C. Hurewitz, *The Struggle for Palestine* (New York, 1976 edn), 74.
42. E. C. Hodgkin (ed.), *Thomas Hodgkin: Letters from Palestine 1932–1936* (1986), 22.
43. N. Bentwich, *My 77 Years* (1962), 163.
44. Antonius, *Arab Awakening,* 408.
45. S. Teveth, *Ben-Gurion and the Palestinian Arabs* (New York, 1985), 166.
46. D. Duff, *Palestine Picture* (1936), 68.
47. A. M. Kayyali, *Palestine: A Modern History* (1978), 175.
48. A. Eban, *An Autobiography* (1977), 43.
49. S. Teveth, *Ben-Gurion: The Burning Ground 1886–1948* (Boston, 1987), 437.
50. CAC, AMEL 1/5/46, "Wedgwood's Recollections After a Dinner 26-7-1928."
51. B. Litvinoff (ed.), *The Letters and Papers of Chaim Weizmann,* XVII, Series A (Jerusalem, 1979), 268.
52. CAC, AMEL 1/5/46, "Secret Note of Conversation on 23 Feb. 1937."
53. Segev, *One Palestine,* 456.
54. A. Perlmutter, *The Life and Times of Menachem Begin* (New York, 1987), 67.
55. Sherman, *Mandate Days,* 109.

56. Keith-Roach, *Pasha,* 194.
57. M. J. Cohen, *Palestine: Retreat from the Mandate* (1978), 49.
58. SAC, GB 165–0196, MacMichael Papers, File 6, Notes for speech 16 June 1944.
59. C. Sykes, *Orde Wingate* (1959), 133.
60. Cohen, *Retreat,* 85.
61. C. Sanger, *Malcolm MacDonald: Bringing an End to Empire* (Liverpool, 1995), 171.
62. Teveth, *Ben-Gurion,* 194.
63. L. Baker, *Days of Sorrow and Pain: Leo Baeck and the Berlin Jews* (New York, 1978), 227.
64. A. M. Lesch, *Arab Politics in Palestine, 1917–1939* (1979), 227.
65. A. J. Toynbee (ed.), *Survey of International Affairs 1938,* I (1941), 468.
66. Mattar, *Mufti,* 105.
67. J. Heller, *The Stern Gang* (1995), 46.
68. Segev, *One Palestine,* 471–2.
69. N. Bethell, *The Palestine Triangle* (1979), 74 and 83.
70. G. Kirk, *The Middle East in the War* (1952), 231.
71. *New York Times,* 12 May 1942.
72. Kirk, *Middle East,* 317.
73. Bethell, *Palestine Triangle,* 145 and 126.
74. Perlmutter, *Begin,* 71.
75. Bethell, *Palestine Triangle,* 190.
76. R. Crossman, *Palestine Mission* (1947), 90.
77. Teveth, *Burning Ground,* 872.
78. C. Mayhew, "British Foreign Policy since 1945," *IA,* 26 (1950), 484.
79. M. Jebb (ed.), *The Diaries of Cynthia Gladwyn* (1995), 24.
80. R. Ovendale, "The Palestine Policy of the British Labour Government 1945–1946," *IA,* 55 (July 1979), 413.
81. A. Howard, *Crossman* (1990), 116.
82. Louis, *British Empire in the Middle East,* 428.
83. *New Statesman,* 11 May 1946.
84. Crossman, *Palestine Mission,* 138.
85. Koestler, *Promise and Fulfilment,* 117.
86. *The Jewish War,* BBC 2, 26 November 2004. Yet at the time members of the Stern Gang did describe themselves as terrorists.
87. G. Kirk, *The Middle East 1945–1950* (1954), 229.
88. Louis, *British Empire in the Middle East,* 446.
89. *The Times,* 3 March 1947.
90. *Zionist Review* (11 April 1947), 3.
91. Bethell, *Palestine Triangle,* 336. The phrase was coined by the French Communist newspaper *L'Humanité.*
92. R. D. Wilson, *Cordon and Search* (1949), 110.
93. A. Gill, *The Journey Back from Hell* (1988), 269.
94. J. and D. Kimche, *Both Sides of the Hill* (1960), 22.
95. M. J. Cohen, *Palestine and the Great Powers, 1945–1948* (Princeton, NJ, 1982), 268.
96. Louis, *British Empire in the Middle East,* 435.
97. Bullock, *Bevin: Foreign Secretary,* 359.
98. D. Acheson, *Present at the Creation* (1969), 180.
99. W. R. Louis and R. W. Stookey (eds), *The End of the Palestine Mandate* (1982), 66.
100. Pimlott (ed.), *Diary of Hugh Dalton,* 414.
101. SAC, GB 165-0196, File 4, W. I. Fitzgerald to MacMichael, 8 November 1947.

102. N. Shepherd, *Ploughing Sand: British Rule in Palestine 1917–1948* (1999), 232.
103. P. Gifford and W. R. Louis (eds), *Decolonization and African Independence: The Transfer of Power, 1960–1980* (New Haven, CT, 1988), x.
104. T. Clarke, *By Blood and Fire* (1981), 165.
105. R. M. Graves, *Experiment in Anarchy* (1949), 147.
106. W. R. Louis, "Sir Alan Cunningham and the End of British Rule in Palestine," *JICH,* XVI (May 1988), 134 and 142.
107. S. Flapan, *The Birth of Israel* (1987), 95.
108. Segev, *One Palestine,* 509.
109. CAC, AMEL 1/5/47, Amery to Lord Salisbury, 21 May 1948.
110. SAC, GB 165–0128, Sir Henry Gurney Collection, File 2, Diary 20 March and 6 April 1948.

17. The Destruction of National Will

1. Louis, *British Empire in the Middle East,* 378.
2. W. Khalidi, "Nasser's Memoirs of the First Palestine War," *JPS,* II (Winter 1973), 10.
3. J. Lacouture, *Nasser* (1973), 265 and 65.
4. H. G. A. Nasser, *Britain and the Egyptian Nationalist Movement* (Reading, 1994), 100.
5. E. Shuckburgh, *Descent to Suez* (1986), 4 and 6.
6. T. E. Evans (ed.), *The Killearn Diaries 1934–1946* (1972), 101.
7. Gibbon, *Decline and Fall,* I, 167.
8. A. Cooper, *Cairo in the War 1939–1945* (1989), 115.
9. P. J. Vatikiotis, *The Modern History of Egypt* (1969), 348.
10. Evans (ed.), *Killearn Diaries,* 214.
11. W. Stadien, *Too Rich* (1992), 205.
12. Lacouture, *Nasser,* 48.
13. Nasser, *Egyptian Nationalist Movement,* 296 and 132.
14. Louis, *British Empire in the Middle East,* 241.
15. Lacouture, *Nasser,* 32.
16. Evans (ed.), *Killearn Diaries,* 329.
17. Farnie, *Suez,* 632.
18. Shuckburgh, *Descent to Suez,* 29.
19. *The Times,* 28 and 29 January 1952.
20. R. Stephens, *Nasser* (1971), 101.
21. A. Nutting, *Nasser* (1972), 41.
22. Lacouture, *Nasser,* 135.
23. H. Trevelyan, *The Middle East in Revolution* (1970), 86.
24. J. Ranelagh, *The Agency: The Rise and Decline of the CIA* (1986), 301. Much folklore surrounds this edifice: the Americans allegedly retaliated by calling the Tower "Nasser's Prick."
25. W. R. Louis and R. Owen (eds), *Suez 1956* (Oxford, 1989), 53.
26. Brendon, *Churchill,* 213.
27. Lord Moran, *Churchill: The Struggle for Survival 1940–1965* (1966), 357.
28. M. H. Heikal, *Cutting the Lion's Tail* (1986), 41.
29. Gilbert, *Churchill,* VIII, 897.
30. K. Roosevelt, *Countercoup: The Struggle for the Control of Iran* (1979), 210.
31. Blake and Louis (eds), *Churchill,* 479.
32. CAC, AMEJ 679, Memoranda of 20 July 1954 and March 1953.
33. CAC, AMEJ 483/2, Handwritten Memorandum on the Middle East, 9.
34. D. R. Thorpe, *Selwyn Lloyd* (1989), 173.
35. R. Rhodes James, *Anthony Eden* (1986), 334.

36. D. Carlton, *Anthony Eden* (1986 edn), 292.
37. W. Scott Lucas, *Divided We Stand* (1991), 98.
38. The phrase was Enoch Powell's. CAC, POLL 3/1/12.
39. W. Clark, *From Three Worlds* (1986), 146.
40. Ball, *Guardsmen*, 144.
41. H. Thomas, *The Suez Affair* (1986 edn), 46.
42. Heikal, *Lion's Tail*, 62.
43. M. Heikal, *Nasser: The Cairo Documents* (1972), 81.
44. V. Mussolini, *Vita con mio padre* (Rome, 1957), 62.
45. Shuckburgh, *Descent to Suez*, 281.
46. Lacouture, *Nasser*, 163.
47. Schuckburgh, *Descent to Suez*, 327.
48. Royle, *Glubb*, 439.
49. A. Nutting, *No end of a lesson* (1967), 17.
50. R. S. Churchill, *The Rise and Fall of Sir Anthony Eden* (1959), 225.
51. B. Lapping, *End of Empire* (1985), 262.
52. Andrew, *Secret Service*, 495.
53. EL, Bernard Shanley Diaries, 2239, 4 September 1956.
54. P. L. Hahn, "Discord or Partnership? British and American policy toward Egypt, 1942–1956," in M. J. Cohen and M. Kolinsky (eds), *Demise of the British Empire in the Middle East* (1998), 175.
55. K. Love, *Suez: The Twice-Fought War* (1969), 333.
56. N. Frankland (ed.), *Documents on International Affairs 1956* (1959), 88, 109 and 113.
57. Browne, *Long Sunset*, 132.
58. H. Finer, *Dulles over Suez* (1964), 192.
59. A. Horne, *Macmillan 1894–1956* (1988), 397.
60. I. McDonald, *The History of the Times*, V (1984), 266.
61. CAC, SELO 6/71, Record of conversation between Selwyn Lloyd and Lord Avon, 30 May 1958.
62. K. Kyle, *Suez* (1991), 137.
63. EL, AWF, Eisenhower Diary Series, Box 15, 30 July 1956. Cf. A. Eden, *Full Circle* (1960), 437.
64. EL, AWF, Dulles-Herter Series, Box 5, 2 August 1956.
65. P. Brendon, *Ike: The Life and Times of Dwight D. Eisenhower* (1987), 233.
66. P. G. Boyle (ed.), *The Eden–Eisenhower Correspondence 1955–1957* (Chapel Hill, NC, 2005), 203.
67. H. Macmillan, *War Diaries 1943–1945* (1984), 285.
68. Lord Egremont, *Wyndham and Children First* (1968), 84.
69. R. Davenport-Hines, *The Macmillans* (1992), 223.
70. Horne, *Macmillan 1894–1956*, 422.
71. R. Ovendale, *The English-Speaking Alliance: Britain, the United States, the Dominions and the Cold War 1945–1951* (1985), 124.
72. Lucas, *Divided We Stand*, 270.
73. Brendon, *Ike*, 328.
74. CAC, KLMR 6/9, Notes on Suez.
75. Ball, *Guardsmen*, 319.
76. Thorpe, *Lloyd*, 2.
77. C. Foley, *Island in Revolt* (1962), 64.
78. CAC, SELO 6/65, Correspondence.
79. M. Dayan, *Story of My Life* (1976), 231.

80. Rhodes James, *Eden*, 536.
81. Kyle, *Suez*, 370.
82. Nutting, *No end of a lesson*, 107.
83. D. Dodds-Parker, *Political Eunuch* (1986), 105.
84. Clark, *Three Worlds*, 209. Clark also said Eden was "a criminal lunatic." Tony Benn, who recorded this in his diary, added: "And knowing what a moderate, middle-of-the-road, wishy-washy man Clark is, I was quite surprised to hear such strong language used." (E. Pearce, *Denis Healey* [2002], 180.)
85. Ziegler, *Mountbatten*, 545.
86. G. Warner, "'Collusion' and the Suez Crisis of 1956," *IA*, 55 (April 1979), 229.
87. D. R. Thorpe, *Alec Douglas-Home* (1996), 181.
88. Farnie, *Suez*, 707.
89. *Daily Express*, 1 November 1956.
90. A. Chisholm and M. Davie, *Lord Beaverbrook: A Life* (New York, 1993), 495.
91. *The Times*, 2 November 1956.
92. EL, AWF, Eisenhower Diary Series, 29 October 1956.
93. Ibid., 30 October 1956.
94. Dodds-Parker, *Eunuch*, 112.
95. EL, AWF, Eisenhower Diary Series, 5 November 1956.
96. J. B. Tournoux, *Secrets d'Etat* (Paris, 1960), 169.
97. Love, *Suez*, 630.
98. EL, AWF, Eisenhower Diary Series, 20 November 1956.
99. T. Hoopes, *The Devil and John Foster Dulles* (1974), 405.
100. CAC, AMEJ 483/2, 21.
101. Horne, *Macmillan 1894–1956*, 441.
102. M. Amory (ed.), *The Letters of Ann Fleming* (1985), 188.
103. M. Foot, *Aneurin Bevan*, II, *1945–69* (1973), 521.
104. EL, AWF, Eisenhower Diary Series, Box 8, 10 January 1957.
105. Ibid., Box 20, 20 November 1956.
106. D. D. Eisenhower, *Waging Peace* (1965), 178.
107. Gibbon, *Decline and Fall*, III, 283.
108. Nutting, *No end of a lesson*, 12.
109. P. Hennessy, *Whitehall* (1989), 214.
110. CAC, AMEJ 483/2, 21 and 18.
111. Stephens, *Nasser*, 247.
112. Clark, *Three Worlds*, 214.
113. CAC, DSND 6/29, Suez Operation Reports 1956–7, undated and unsigned paper.
114. *The Economist*, 19 January 1957, quoted by G. Parmentier, "The British Press in the Suez Crisis," *HJ*, 23 (1980), 446.
115. D. Reynolds, "Eden the Diplomatist, 1931–56: The Suezide of a Statesman?" *History*, 74 (February 1989), 71 and 84.
116. J. Eayrs (ed.), *The Commonwealth and Suez: A Documentary Survey* (Oxford, 1964), 194. According to two authoritative Canadian historians, Louis St. Laurent's alignment of his country with the United Nations rather than the United Kingdom "marked the de facto end of the British Empire in Canada." (N. Hillmer and J. L. Granatstein, *Empire to Umpire* [Toronto, 1994], 226.)
117. CAC, HICK 2, Personal Memoir of R. H. Hickling, 138.
118. Johnston, *Steamer Point*, 26.
119. J. Cochrane (ed.), *Kipling* (1983 edn), 209.
120. Tom Stacey in *Sunday Times*, 17 May 1964.

121. Foster, *Landscape with Arabs*, 164.

122. G. Balfour-Paul, *The End of Empire in the Middle East* (Cambridge, 1991), 69.

123. R. Ovendale, *Britain, the United States and the transfer of power in the Middle East, 1945–1962* (1996), 178.

124. S. R. Ashton and S. E. Stockwell (eds), *BDEEP*, Series A, Vol. I, *Imperial Policy and Colonial Practice 1925–1945*, Pt II (1996), 204.

125. F. Halliday, *Arabia Without Sultans* (Harmondsworth, 1974), 89.

126. CAC, HICK 2, 95.

127. R. J. Gavin, *Aden under British Rule 1839–1967* (1975), 333.

128. K. Trevaskis, *Shades of Amber* (1968), xii and 80.

129. Gibbon, *Decline and Fall*, III, 159.

130. D. Ledger, *Shifting Sands* (1983), 200.

131. Trevaskis, *Amber*, 9.

132. Gibbon, *Decline and Fall*, III, 162.

133. Balfour-Paul, *End of Empire*, 56.

134. D. Holden, *Farewell to Arabia* (1966), 49.

135. F. Heinlein, *British Government Policy and Decolonisation 1945–1963* (2002), 172.

136. P. Darby, *British Defence Policy East of Suez 1947–1968* (1973), 1 and 49.

137. R. Hyam and W. R. Louis (eds), *BDEEP*, Series A, Vol. 4, *The Conservative Government and the End of Empire 1957–1964*, Pt I, *High Policy, Political and Constitutional Change* (2000), xlix.

138. Murphy, *Lennox-Boyd*, 192.

139. S. R. Ashton and W. R. Louis (eds), *BDEEP*, Series A, Vol. 5, *East of Suez and the Commonwealth 1964–1971*, Pt I, *East of Suez* (2004), 277.

140. Trevaskis, *Amber*, 143.

141. Johnston, *Steamer Point*, 194 and 117.

142. Hyam and Louis (eds), *Conservative Government*, 619.

143. J. Paget, *Last Post: Aden 1964–1967* (1969), 39.

144. CAC, BDOHP, Denis Doble, 9.

145. Halliday, *Arabia*, 206 and 204. According to Reginald Hickling (CAC, HICK 2, 119 and 279), there was "a substantial body of evidence" that detainees were also tortured in al-Mansoura Gaol. Yet, he concluded, "without being unctuously dishonest, I think no other armed forces, faced with the intense bitterness and fury of South Arabia, could have behaved with such restraint."

146. M. Jones, "A Decision delayed: Britain's withdrawal from South-East Asia reconsidered 1961–8," *EHR*, CXVII (June 2002), 582–3. George Ball, American Under-Secretary of State, made this remark to Harold Wilson on 8 September 1965. Two days later the Chancellor of the Exchequer, James Callaghan, announced that Britain had acquired a short-term stabilisation loan of one billion dollars.

147. CAC, DSND, 8/16, Julian Amery to Sandys, 7 May 1964.

148. K. Pieragostini, *Britain, Aden and South Arabia: Abandoning Empire* (1991), 114.

149. *The Times*, 3 February 1966.

150. Ashton and Louis (eds), *East of Suez*, 248.

151. But according to an undated sheet of figures in Duncan Sandys's papers (CAC, DSND 14/1, File 1), British casualties from terrorism in Aden numbered 111 per month during 1967.

152. Paget, *Last Post*, 194.

153. CAC, HICK 2, 282.

154. Paget, *Last Post*, 202 and 205.

155. Ledger, *Shifting Sands*, 180.

156. BCEM 2003/208, De Heveningham Baekeland Papers, 20.

157. CAC, HICK 2, 276

158. M. Crouch, *An Element of Luck: To South Arabia and Beyond* (1993), 5–6.

159. CAC, BDOHP, Sir Brian Crowe, 17.

160. CAC, HICK 2, Introduction—which Hickling wrote in haste after leaving Aden "while I felt strongly upon many of the issues" but subsequently deleted.

161. B. Pimlott, *Harold Wilson* (1997), 482.

162. BBC TV (audiotape), 19 November 1967.

163. S. R. Ashton and W. R. Louis (eds), *East of Suez,* 132 and 131.

18. Renascent Africa

1. D. Killingray, "Soldiers, Ex-Servicemen, and Politics in the Gold Coast, 1939–50," *JMAS,* 21 (1983), 525.

2. A. E. Ekoko, "Conscript Labour and Tin Mining in Nigeria during the Second World War, *JHSN,* XI (December 1982), 76.

3. Pembroke College, Cambridge, Storrs Papers, Reel 11, Storrs to E. Marsh, 17 December 1930.

4. D. Rooney, *Sir Charles Arden-Clarke* (1982), 5.

5. Gallagher, *Decline, Revival and Fall,* 142.

6. Albertini, *JCH* (January 1969), 33.

7. D. Fieldhouse, "Decolonization, Development and Dependence: A Survey of Changing Attitudes," in P. Gifford and W. R. Louis (eds), *The Transfer of Power in Africa: Decolonization 1940–1960* (New Haven, CT, 1982), 489.

8. Hyam, *Labour Government,* I, xxxv.

9. Leith-Ross, *Stepping-Stones,* 117.

10. J. S. Coleman, *Nigeria: Background to Nationalism* (Berkeley, CA, 1971), 152.

11. Leith-Ross, *Stepping-Stones,* 114.

12. N. Azikiwe, *My Odyssey* (1970), 254.

13. R. Robinson, "Andrew Cohen and the Transfer of Power in Tropical Africa, 1940–1957," in W. H. Morris-Jones and G. Fischer (eds), *Decolonisation and After* (1980), 54.

14. A. H. M. Kirk-Greene, *Africa in the Colonial Period,* III, *The Transfer of Power* (Oxford, 1979), 15. The words were those of Sir Hilton Poynton, who added later that he disliked the word "decolonisation" because it was "flavoured with the garlic of guilt." (Ibid., 65.)

15. A. Creech Jones, "British Colonial Policy with Particular Reference to Africa," *IA,* 27 (April 1951), 177.

16. Grimal, *Decolonization,* 121.

17. J. R. Hooker, *Black Revolutionary* (1967), 66.

18. J. A. Langley, *Pan-Africanism and Nationalism in West Africa* (Oxford, 1973), 353.

19. R. Rathbone (ed.), *BDEEP,* Series B, Vol. 1, *Ghana,* Pt I, *1945–1952* (1992), xxxv.

20. Perham, *West African Passage,* 62.

21. A. W. Cardinall, *The Natives of the Northern Territories of the Gold Coast* (1921), 82.

22. Kimble, *Ghana,* 132 and 134.

23. N. Farson, *Behind God's Back* (1940), 447.

24. D. Austin, *Politics in Ghana 1946–1960* (Oxford, 1970), 97. In 1874, General Wolseley had plundered many other items of the sacred regalia, including "the largest gold work known from Ashanti." (R. Chamberlain, *Loot: The Heritage of Plunder* [1983], 93.)

25. R. E. Wraith, *Guggisberg* (1967), 100.

26. Kimble, *Ghana,* 548.

27. Wraith, *Guggisberg,* 216.

28. Farson, *God's Back,* 443.

29. Burns, *Civil Servant*, 216.
30. K. Bradley, *Once a District Officer* (1966), 146.
31. M. Perham, *The Colonial Reckoning: The End of Imperial Rule in Africa in the Light of Experience* (1961), 114.
32. Burns, *Civil Servant*, 322.
33. Bing, *Whirlwind*, 48.
34. J. D. Hargreaves, *The End of Colonial Rule in West Africa* (1979), 43.
35. Burns, *Civil Servant*, 298 and 318.
36. Rathbone (ed.), *Ghana*, Pt I, xlii.
37. E. Huxley, *Four Guineas* (1954), 85.
38. J. Gunther, *Inside Africa* (1955), 784.
39. B. Davidson, *Black Star* (1973), 46 and 39.
40. Rooney, *Arden-Clarke*, 91.
41. *Ghana: The Autobiography of Kwame Nkrumah* (1957), 91.
42. C. Imray, *Policeman in Africa* (1997), 129 and 130.
43. Rathbone (ed.), *Ghana*, Pt I, 385 and xliv.
44. Rooney, *Arden-Clarke*, 67 and 88.
45. P. Dennis, *Goodbye to Pith Helmets* (Bishop Auckland, 2000), 133.
46. Rathbone (ed.), *Ghana*, Pt I, 391, 121 and 122.
47. Austin, *Ghana*, 87.
48. Nkrumah, *Autobiography*, 116.
49. Rathbone (ed.), *Ghana*, Pt I, 403.
50. Rooney, *Arden-Clarke*, 212.
51. *Daily Telegraph*, 17 October 1950. The article accused the CPP of carrying out violent intimidation and concluded: "We should make it quite plain to the Gold Coast and to the world that the British mission is not yet finished and that in no circumstances will we allow the country to relapse into chaos or to become a Russian outpost on the equator."
52. *CHA*, 8, 52.
53. Austin, *Ghana*, 126.
54. *AA*, 57 (January 1958), 33.
55. Nkrumah, *Autobiography*, 136.
56. *Scotsman*, 15 October 1999. Julius Nyerere observed this phenomenon among Ghanaian students abroad.
57. Lapping, *End of Empire*, 382.
58. Rathbone (ed.), *Ghana*, Pt I, 373, and Pt II, 4.
59. Gunther, *Inside Africa*, 801.
60. *Ghana Evening News*, 1 May 1957.
61. Nkrumah, *Autobiography*, 142.
62. C. Walton, "British intelligence and threats to national security, c. 1941–1951" (Cambridge Ph.D. thesis, 2006), 694.
63. CAC, SPRS, 1048, Box 1, R, 31 January 1953.
64. E. Powell, *Private Secretary (Female)/Gold Coast* (1984), 74.
65. CAC, SPRS, 1048, Box 1, R, 17 January 1953.
66. Bradley, *District Officer*, 145.
67. Austin, *Ghana*, 219.
68. H. K. Akyeampong (ed.), *Journey to Independence and After*, II (Accra, 1971), 96.
69. Huxley, *Four Guineas*, 81.
70. T. P. Omari, *Kwame Nkrumah* (1970), 144.
71. Nkrumah, *Autobiography*, 197.
72. Rathbone (ed.), *Ghana*, Pt I, 35.

73. J-M. Allman, "The Youngmen and the Porcupine: Class, Nationalism and Asante's Struggle for Self-Determination," *JAH*, 31 (1990), 275.

74. Rooney, *Arden-Clarke*, 175.

75. Austin, *Ghana*, 334.

76. Murphy, *Lennox-Boyd*, viii.

77. D. Goldsworthy (ed.), *BDEEP*, Series A, Vol. 3, *The Conservative Government and the End of Empire 1951–1957*, Pt I (1994), liv.

78. Lapping, *End of Empire*, 387.

79. SOAS, MS 380596, Papers of Sir Charles Arden-Clarke, File 1, speech made at midnight on 5 March 1957.

80. Purcell, *Private Secretary*, 106.

81. CAC, SPRS, BOX 1, T, 9 March 1966.

82. M. Meredith, *The State of Africa* (2005), 96 and 307.

83. *The Times*, 10 June 1944.

84. Coleman, *Nigeria*, 15.

85. J. Morley, *Colonial Postscript: Diary of a District Officer 1935–56* (1992), 75.

86. Huxley, *Four Guineas*, 167.

87. J. Wheare, *The Nigerian Legislative Council* (1950), x.

88. G. Gorer, *Africa Dances* (1935), opposite 129.

89. C. Achebe, *Things Fall Apart* (1965 edn), 160.

90. J. Smith, *Colonial Cadet in Nigeria* (Durham, NC, 1968), 22.

91. O. Awolowo, *The People's Republic* (Ibadan, 1968), 65.

92. B. Sharwood Smith, *"But Always As Friends"* (1970), 150.

93. H. Foot, *A Start in Freedom* (1964), 108.

94. Perham, *West African Passage*, 25.

95. H. L. Ward Price, *Dark Subjects* (1939), 199.

96. W. R. Crocker, *Nigeria: A Critique of British Administration* (1936), 206–7.

97. I. Brook, *The One-Eyed Man Is King* (1966), 90.

98. A. Grantham, *Via Ports* (Hong Kong, 1965), 50.

99. Gunther, *Inside Africa*, 740.

100. Coleman, *Nigeria*, 151.

101. Ward Price, *Dark Subjects*, 230.

102. M. Lynn (ed.), *BDEEP*, Series B, Vol. 7, *Nigeria: Managing Political Reform 1943–1953*, Pt I (2001), xlvi.

103. J. E. Flint, "Managing Nationalism: The Colonial Office and Nnamde Azikiwe, 1932–43," in R. D. King and R. W. Wilson (eds), *The Statecraft of British Imperialism* (1999), 148.

104. R. D. Pearce, *Sir Bernard Bourdillon* (Oxford, 1987), 338, 309, 198, 313, 351 and 345.

105. O. Awolowo, *Awo* (Cambridge, 1960), 69.

106. Gorer, *Africa Dances*, 274.

107. R. L. Sklar, *Nigerian Political Parties* (Princeton, NJ, 1963), 50.

108. Azikiwe, *Odyssey*, 174 and 252.

109. P. S. Zachernuk, *Colonial Subjects: An African Intelligentsia and Atlantic Ideas* (Charlottesville, VA, 2000), 110.

110. W. R. Crocker, *Self-Government for the Colonies* (1949), 47.

111. Awolowo, *Awo*, 141 and 137.

112. Coleman, *Nigeria*, 264.

113. T. Clark, *A Right Honourable Gentleman: Abubakar From the Black Rock* (1991), 97.

114. A. Low, "The End of the British Empire in Africa," in Gifford and Louis (eds), *Decolonization and African Independence*, 45–6.

115. *The Times*, 30 May 1946.

116. M. Crowder, *The Story of Nigeria* (1973 edn), 275.

117. D. K. Fieldhouse, *Black Africa 1945–80* (1986), 7.

118. A. G. Hopkins, *An Economic History of West Africa* (1973), 266.

119. Crocker, *Self-Government*, vi.

120. T. Falola, "British Imperialism: Roger Louis and the West African Case," in King and Wilson (eds), *Statecraft*, 135.

121. Gunther, *Inside Africa*, 736.

122. Pearce, *Bourdillon*, 274.

123. Coleman, *Nigeria*, 286.

124. *The Times*, 20 August 1946.

125. C. U. Uwanaka, *Zik & Awo in Political Storm* (Lagos, 1982), 8.

126. N. Azikiwe, *Zik: A Selection of the Speeches of Nnamde Azikiwe* (Cambridge, 1961), 165.

127. Zachernuk, *Colonial Subjects*, 156.

128. Crowder, *Story of Nigeria*, 268.

129. R. Pearce (ed.), *Then the Wind Changed: Nigerian Letters of Robert Hepburn Wright, 1936–49* (1992), 124.

130. Clark, *Abubakar*, 182.

131. M. S. O. Olisa and O. M. Ikejiani-Clark (eds), *Azikiwe and the African Revolution* (Onitsha, 1989), 224.

132. S. O. Jaja, "The Enugu Colliery Massacre in Retrospect: An Episode in British Administration of Nigeria," *JHSN*, XI (December 1982), 88.

133. Awolowo, *People's Republic*, 62.

134. Sharwood Smith, *But Always*, 276.

135. Zachernuk, *Colonial Subjects*, 164.

136. Sklar, *Nigerian Political Parties*, 144 and 195.

137. Lynn (ed.), *Nigeria*, Pt II, 259, 184, 333 and 334.

138. Sklar, *Nigerian Political Parties*, 173.

139. Lynn, *Nigeria*, Pt II, 183.

140. CUL, RCMS 133/1, A. Kirk-Greene, "Scrapbooks of News Cuttings of Royal Visit to Nigeria 1956."

141. Ibid., 133/2.

142. *United Empire*, XLVII (May-June 1956), 78.

143. CUL, RCMS 133/2.

144. Ibid.

145. *United Empire*, XLVII (May-June 1956), 78.

146. A. Bello, *My Life* (1960), 182.

147. A. Enahoro, *Fugitive Offender* (1965), 152.

148. C. Douglas-Home, *Evelyn Baring: The Last Proconsul* (1978), 153.

149. CUL, RCMS 133/1. I have standardised the punctuation and capitalisation.

150. Sharwood Smith, *But Always*, 317.

151. Bello, *My Life*, 180.

152. CUL, RCMS 133/3.

153. Lynn, *Nigeria*, Pt II, 80, 184 and 3.

154. CUL, RCMS 113/23, H. Smith, "A Squalid End to Empire," *Ruskin Record* (August 1992), 2. I am grateful to John Smith, David Angus and Manus Nunan for exposing the untrustworthiness of this source. For an authoritative account, see K. Post, *The Nigerian Federal Election of 1959: Politics and Administration in a Developing Political System* (1963).

155. CUL, RCMS 136/31, B. Azikiwe, "Military Revolution in Nigeria" (Chapter 30), 32.

156. Sharwood Smith, *But Always*, 362.

157. Lynn (ed.), *Nigeria*, Pt II, 567.

158. Gibbon, *Decline and Fall*, I, 805.
159. R. Blake, *A History of Rhodesia* (1977), 328.
160. R. Shepherd, *Iain Macleod* (1995 edn), 162.
161. Azikiwe, *Speeches*, 158.
162. Mansergh, *Commonwealth Experience*, 347.
163. Perham, *Colonial Reckoning*, 9.
164. *The Times*, 28 December 1960.
165. Gibbon, *Decline and Fall*, I, 96.
166. Lord Halifax, *Fulness of Days* (1957), 273.
167. *United Empire*, XLIX (March-April 1958), 65.
168. J. English, "Empire Day in Britain 1904–1958," *HJ*, 49 (March 2006), 274.
169. Heinlein, *British Government Policy*, 107.
170. *United Empire*, XLVII (July-August 1956), 119.
171. N. Annan, *Our Age* (1990 edn), 43.
172. *United Empire*, XLVIII (July-August 1956), 179.
173. Hobson, *Imperialism*, 46. P. E. Hallett (ed.), *Utopia* (1937 edn), 224–5—the translation is slightly different.
174. P. Brendon, *Our Own Dear Queen* (1986), 230.
175. J. Darwin, *The End of the British Empire: The Historical Debate* (Oxford, 1991), 80–81.
176. H. Macmillan, *Riding the Storm 1956–1959* (1971), 383.
177. *United Empire*, XLVIII (July-August 1956), 179.
178. *The Times*, 27 February 1961.
179. Heinlein, *British Government Policy*, 144.
180. *ODNB*.
181. A. Horne, *Harold Macmillan 1957–1986*, II (1989), 204.
182. Gibbon, *Decline and Fall*, I, 376.
183. Davenport-Hines, *Macmillans*, 277.
184. Horne, *Macmillan*, I, 109.
185. P. Brendon, "An Anachronism in His Own Time," *New York Times Book Review* (26 November 1989), 11.
186. Hyam and Louis (eds), *Conservative Government*, Pt I, xxvii.
187. Clarke and Trebilcock (eds), *Understanding Decline*, 238.
188. C. Ponting, *Breach of Promise: Labour in Power 1964–1970* (1989), 43.
189. Horne, *Macmillan 1894–1956*, 160.
190. Macmillan, *Storm*, 378.
191. H. Macmillan, *Pointing the Way 1959–1961* (1972), 116.
192. Ball, *Guardsmen*, 345.
193. S. J. Ball, "Macmillan, the Second World War and the Empire," in R. Aldous and S. Lee (eds), *Harold Macmillan: Aspects of a Political Life* (1999), 172.
194. Macmillan, *Pointing*, 475.
195. *Daily Herald*, 4 February 1960.
196. Macmillan, *Pointing*, 477.

19. *Uhuru*—Freedom

1. F. Brockway, *African Journeys* (1955), 87–8.
2. RH, MSS Afr.s.746, Blundell Papers, Box 12, File 1, I. W. Idakho to Blundell, 24 January 1953.
3. CAC, FEBR 22/9, Brockway quoted by the Nairobi *Daily Chronicle*, 9 September 1950.
4. T. Kanogo, *Squatters and the Roots of Mau Mau 1905–63* (1987), 59.

5. CUL RCMS 318/1/3, Memoirs of Thomas and Florence Edgar, 24.

6. Bache, *Young Lion,* 66 and 279.

7. J. Iliffe, *Africans: The History of a Continent* (Cambridge, 1995), 217.

8. CUL RCMS 113/44, Chapter XIII, 1.

9. Berman, *Control & Crisis,* 274.

10. Throup, *Origins of Mau Mau,* 68.

11. D. Anderson, *Histories of the Hanged* (2005), 26.

12. Kanogo, *Squatters,* 127.

13. CUL RCMS 113/44, Chapter XI, 1. However, the multi-racial United Kenya Club was founded in 1946.

14. A. Hake, *African Metropolis* (1977), 57.

15. J. Lewis, *Empire State-Building: War & Welfare in Kenya 1925–52* (Oxford, 2000), 99.

16. CAC, FEBR 3/48k, Brockway's "Report to the Secretary of State for Colonial Affairs."

17. F. Fanon, *The Wretched of the Earth* (Harmondsworth, 1967 edn), 30.

18. H. H. Werlin, *Governing an African City: A Study of Nairobi* (New York, 1974), 61.

19. M. Gicaru, *Land of Sunshine* (1958), 133.

20. R. M. Gatheru, *Child of Two Worlds* (1964), 75.

21. B. A. Ogot and W. R. Ochieng', *Decolonization & Independence in Kenya 1940–1993* (1995), 33.

22. R. Frost, *Enigmatic Proconsul: Sir Philip Mitchell and the Twilight of Empire* (1992), 181.

23. P. Mitchell, *African Afterthoughts* (1954), 273.

24. Lewis, *Empire State-Building,* 272.

25. J. Murray-Brown, *Kenyatta* (1972), 190.

26. N. Cunard (ed.), *Negro* (1970 edn), 454.

27. E. Huxley, *The Sorcerer's Apprentice* (1948), 60.

28. B. Berman and J. M. Lonsdale, "The Labours of *Muigwithania:* Jomo Kenyatta as Author, 1928–45," *Research in African Literatures,* 29 (Spring 1998), 38 and 37.

29. N. Farson, *Last Chance in Africa* (1953), 113.

30. D. L. Barnett and K. Njama, *Mau Mau from Within* (1966), 75.

31. H. Muoria, *I, The Gikuyu and the White Fury* (Nairobi, 1994), 17.

32. J. M. Kariuki, *"Mau Mau" Detainee* (1963), 12.

33. Barnett and Njama, *Mau Mau,* 75.

34. Lapping, *End of Empire,* 411.

35. RH, MSS Afr.s.746, Box 12, File 1, I. W. Idakho to Blundell, 24 January 1953.

36. T. Askwith, *From Mau Mau to Harambee* (Cambridge, 1995), 112.

37. DUL, Baring Papers, GRE/1/18/1 and 29, Mitchell to Baring, 25 March and 16 June 1952.

38. *East African Standard,* 10 April 1952.

39. R. Ruark, *Something of Value* (1955), 177.

40. Douglas-Home, *Baring,* 231, 229 and 230.

41. C. Elkins, *Britain's Gulag: The Brutal End of Empire in Kenya* (2005), 61.

42. DUL, Baring Papers, GRE 1/19/150, Baring to Lyttelton, 9 October 1952.

43. Gicaru, *Land of Sunshine,* 17.

44. CUL RCMS 175, T. H. R. Cashmore, "Kenya Days," 35.

45. R. B. Edgerton, *Mau Mau* (1990), 152.

46. Anderson, *Histories of the Hanged,* 85.

47. Gicaru, *Land of Sunshine,* 115. Graham Greene also thought the settlers "a kind of white Mau Mau." (N. Sherry, *The Life of Graham Greene,* II [1994], 462.)

48. Barnett and Njama, *Mau Mau,* 208.

49. Ruark, *Something of Value,* 406.

50. RH, MSS Afr.s.746, Box 12, File 1, Nini Langmead to Blundell, 4 March 1953.

51. CUL, RCMS 175, 26.
52. M. Blundell, *So Rough a Wind* (1964), 145.
53. Anderson, *Histories of the Hanged*, 1.
54. BECM, 2001/299, Undated Police Report on "Mau Mau Ceremonies as Described by Participants."
55. M. S. Clough, *Mau Mau Memoirs* (Boulder, CO, 1998), 120.
56. Kariuki, *Detainee*, 18 and 27.
57. Mitchell, *African Afterthoughts*, xvii–xviii and 220.
58. O. Lyttelton, *The Memoirs of Lord Chandos* (1962), 394–5.
59. M. Blundell, *A Love Affair with the Sun* (Nairobi, 1994), 139.
60. Douglas-Home, *Baring*, 237.
61. Edgerton, *Mau Mau*, 80.
62. Blundell, *Rough a Wind*, 133.
63. Anderson, *Histories of the Hanged*, 152.
64. H. Cuss, "British Intelligence and the Leaders of Colonial Independence Movements: The Cases of Kwame Nkrumah and Jomo Kenyatta" (Cambridge M.Phil., 2006), 54.
65. A. Clayton, *Counter-Insurgency in Kenya 1952–60* (Yuma, KA, 1984), 5.
66. Douglas-Home, *Baring*, 243 and 256.
67. Clayton, *Counter-Insurgency*, 11.
68. R. Buijtenhuijs, *Mau Mau: Twenty Years After* (The Hague, 1973), 107.
69. CUL RCMS 175, 11 and 16.
70. L. White, *The Comforts of Home: Prostitution in Colonial Nairobi* (Chicago, 1990), 185.
71. CUL RCMS 175, 68–9 and 26.
72. CUL RCMS 113/44, Chapter XXI, 3.
73. Lyttelton, *Memoirs*, 405.
74. Anderson, *Histories of the Hanged*, 79. The phrase was coined by Ngūgī wa Thiong'o.
75. Edgerton, *Mau Mau*, 143.
76. CUL RCMS 175, 28.
77. Elkins, *Britain's Gulag*, 67.
78. CUL RCMS 175, Appendix, 5.
79. B. Castle, *Fighting All the Way* (1993), 271 and 273.
80. CUL RCMS 175, 33 and 26.
81. Caroline Elkins takes this expression as the title for her book and David Anderson describes the comparison with the Soviet archipelago made by M. Clough (*Mau Mau*, 205) as "tellingly accurate" (*Histories of the Hanged*, 315). But Ronald Hyam rightly criticises this "abuse of language," saying that we must have words left "to denounce the worst evils of all." (*Britain's Declining Empire: The Road to Decolonisation, 1918–1968* [Cambridge, 2007], 192.)
82. C. G. Rosberg and J. Nottingham, *The Myth of "Mau Mau": Nationalism in Kenya* (New York, 1966), 334, 346 and 378.
83. Blundell, *Rough a Wind*, 198.
84. W. Itote, *"Mau Mau" General* (Nairobi, 1974 edn), 125.
85. Barnett and Njama, *Mau Mau*, 209.
86. Kariuki, *Detainee*, 89.
87. Elkins, *Britain's Gulag*, 193.
88. *The Times*, 16 June 1959.
89. Elkins, *Britain's Gulag*, 283. The phrase was coined by Baring's compliant Attorney General, Eric Griffith-Jones.
90. Castle, *Fighting*, 262.
91. BECM 2002/218, Breckenridge Papers, Bernard Mwai Gathua, 24 March 1956, J. W.

Mwathi, 22 October 1954, Cyrus Gakuo Karuga, 18 February 1957—all writing to Mrs. Breckenridge.

92. O. Odinga, *Not Yet Uhuru* (1968 edn), 141.

93. D. Goldsworthy, *Tom Mboya* (New York, 1982), 74.

94. DUL, Baring Papers GRE/1/98/1–29, Kenya Notebook 1959.

95. Douglas-Home, *Baring*, 279.

96. RH, Welensky Papers, 592/2, Blundell to Welensky, 3 January 1960.

97. CUL RCMS 175, 71, 34, 68, 71 and 62.

98. DUL, Baring Papers GRE/1/98/1–29, Kenya Notebook 1959.

99. *The Times,* 7 May 1959.

100. Edgerton, *Mau Mau,* 194.

101. *The Times,* 16 June 1959.

102. *The Times,* 28 July 1959.

103. CAC, POLL 3/1/18, J. Mcleod to Powell, n.d.

104. Ibid., V. Bonham Carter to Powell, 31 July 1959.

105. Heinlein, *British Government Policy,* 195.

106. A. W. B. Simpson, *Human Rights and the End of Empire* (Oxford, 2001), 1057.

107. Shepherd, *Macleod,* 159.

108. *Spectator,* 31 January 1964.

109. *New York Times,* 17 July 1959.

110. Murray-Brown, *Kenyatta,* 298.

111. J. Yorke, *Lancaster House* (2001), 171.

112. *Daily Herald* and *Daily Mail,* 21 January 1960.

113. RH, Welensky Papers 592/2, Blundell to Welensky, 29 February 1960.

114. Bennett, *Kenya,* 153.

115. RH, Welensky Papers, 592/2, Blundell to Welensky, 29 February 1960.

116. Edgerton, *Mau Mau,* 208.

117. Blundell, *Rough a Wind,* 283.

118. CUL RCMS 175, 95.

119. RH, Welensky Papers, 592/8, Welensky to Lord Salisbury, 18 August 1961.

120. Nicholls, *Red Strangers,* 273.

121. BCEM, 2003/208, 16.

122. G. Wasserman, *Politics of Decolonisation: Kenya Europeans and the Land Issue 1960–1965* (Cambridge, 1976), 162.

123. Murray-Brown, *Kenyatta,* 309.

124. Sanger, *MacDonald,* 390.

125. Heinlein, *British Government Policy,* 257.

126. N. wa Thiong'o, *Writers in Politics* (Oxford, 1997), 106.

127. Murray-Brown, *Kenyatta,* 320.

128. *The Times,* 12 December 1963.

129. Askwith, *Mau Mau to Harambee,* 101.

130. CUL, RCMS 175, 103.

131. Milne, *Global Policy Forum* (May 2005). The press did not quote Brown's qualifying remarks.

132. CUL, RCMS 175, 103.

20. Kith and Kin

1. T. O. Ranger, *Revolt in Southern Rhodesia 1896–7* (1967), 104 and 319.
2. W. H. Brown, *On the South African Frontier* (1899), 322.
3. N. Jones, *Rhodesian Genesis* (Bulawayo, 1953), 113.
4. A. Keppel-Jones, *Rhodes and Rhodesia* (Kingston, Ont., 1983), 401.
5. Headlam (ed.), *Milner Papers*, I, 141.
6. *The Times*, 29 January 1895.
7. I. Phimister, *An Economic and Social History of Zimbabwe, 1890–1948* (1988), 8 and 7.
8. Colvin, *Jameson*, I, 214.
9. M. Hall, "The Legend of the Lost City: Or, the Man with Golden Balls," *JSAS*, 21 (June 1995), 188. This bird, symbolising the link which Rhodes tried to construct between North and South Africa, features in the décor of Rhodes House.
10. Brown, *South African Frontier*, 400. Rhodes himself endorsed this book.
11. Ranger, *Revolt*, 119.
12. Baden-Powell, *Matabele Campaign*, 329.
13. T. Ranger, *Voices from the Rocks* (Bloomington, IN, 1999), 14.
14. F. W. Sykes, *With Plumer in Matabeleland* (1897), 168.
15. NAM, 1999-07-20, 5 June 1897 ff.
16. Brown, *South African Frontier*, 369.
17. F. C. Selous, *Sunshine and Storm in Rhodesia* (1896), 30 and 193.
18. Ranger, *Revolt*, 131.
19. G. Sims, *Paladin of Empire: Earl Grey and Rhodesia* (Salisbury, 1970), 3 and 45.
20. Ranger, *Revolt*, 14.
21. Selous, *Sunshine and Storm*, 137.
22. Baden-Powell, *Matabele Campaign*, 131–2 and 290.
23. T. Jeal, *Baden-Powell* (1989), 175.
24. C. Summers, *From Civilization to Segregation* (Athens, OH, 1994), 52.
25. J. Iliffe, *Famine in Zimbabwe 1890–1960* (Gweru, 1990), 26.
26. Rotberg, *Rhodes*, 561.
27. Keppel-Jones, *Rhodes and Rhodesia*, 503–4.
28. Rotberg, *Rhodes*, 568.
29. Pakenham, *Scramble for Africa*, 500.
30. Blake, *Rhodesia*, 145.
31. L. H. Gann, *A History of Southern Rhodesia* (1965), 209.
32. Hancock, *Smuts*, II, 154.
33. E. Tawse Jollie, *The Real Rhodesia* (1924), 85.
34. Brown, *South African Frontier*, 384, 394 and 391.
35. I. Henderson, "White Populism in Southern Rhodesia," *CSSH*, 14 (September 1972), 390.
36. Ranger, *Revolt*, 323 and 376.
37. P. Mason, *The Birth of a Dilemma* (1958), 204.
38. R. Palmer, *Land and Racial Domination in Rhodesia* (1977), 97, 118, 71 and 89.
39. T. Burke, *Lifebuoy Men, Lux Women* (1996), 19.
40. Hole, *Rhodesian Days*, 98.
41. Kennedy, *Islands of White*, 158–9.
42. Summers, *Civilization to Segregation*, 139.
43. Palmer, *Land and Racial Domination*, 152.
44. Gann, *Southern Rhodesia*, 229.
45. K. Good, "Settler Colonialism in Rhodesia," *AA* (1974), 11.
46. L. H. Gann and M. Gelfand, *Huggins of Rhodesia* (1964), 70.
47. *Southern Rhodesia: Information for Settlers* (1905), 35.

48. D. Lessing, *Under My Skin* (1994), 160.
49. Phimister, *Zimbabwe,* 183.
50. Palmer, *Land and Racial Domination,* 178.
51. R. Gray, *The Two Nations* (1960), 103.
52. E. Schmidt, "Negotiated Spaces and Contest Terrain: Men, Women and the Law in Colonial Zimbabwe, 1890–1939," *JSAS,* 16, 4 (1990), 646.
53. Gray, *Two Nations,* 261 and 255.
54. A. DeRoche, *Black, White and Chrome: The United States and Zimbabwe 1953–1998* (Trenton, NJ, 2001), 16.
55. Phimister, *Zimbabwe,* 196.
56. Gann and Gelfand, *Huggins,* 266.
57. L. Vambe, *From Rhodesia to Zimbabwe* (1976), 73.
58. T. O. Ranger, *The African Voice in Southern Rhodesia 1898–1930* (1970), 224.
59. Phimister, *Zimbabwe,* 156 and 198.
60. Tawse Jollie, *Real Rhodesia,* 243.
61. Phimister, *Zimbabwe,* 187.
62. Gann, *Southern Rhodesia,* 314.
63. Gray, *Two Nations,* 319.
64. Vambe, *Rhodesia to Zimbabwe,* 159.
65. J. Parker, *Rhodesia: Little White Island* (1972), 62.
66. Dunn, *Central African Witness,* 177.
67. *ODNB.*
68. Rotberg, *Black Heart,* 260 and 188.
69. R. Hyam, "Africa and the Labour Government, 1945–1951," *JICS,* 16 (May 1988), 168.
70. P. Murphy (ed.), *BDEEP,* Series B, Vol. 9, *Central Africa,* Pt I (2005), 331.
71. A. Cousins, "State Ideology and Power in Rhodesia, 1958–1972," *IJAHS,* 24, 1 (1991), 39.
72. H. Franklin, *Unholy Wedlock* (1963), 49 and 87.
73. Rotberg, *Nationalism in Central Africa,* 248. The phrase was Banda's.
74. L. W. Bowman, *Politics in Rhodesia* (Cambridge, MA, 1973), 19–20.
75. Roberts, *History of Zambia,* 213.
76. Rotberg, *Nationalism in Central Africa,* 265.
77. N. M. Shamuyarira, *Crisis in Rhodesia* (New York, 1966), 33.
78. Franklin, *Unholy Wedlock,* 82.
79. T. O. Ranger (ed.), *Aspects of Central African History* (1968), 238.
80. I. Phimister, "Rethinking the Reserves: Southern Rhodesia's Land Husbandry Act Reviewed," *JSAS,* 19 (June 1993), 239.
81. *Nkomo: The Story of My Life* (1984), 53.
82. J. R. T. Wood, *The Welensky Papers* (Durban, 1983), 535.
83. R. Welensky, *Welensky's 4000 Days* (1964), 98.
84. P. Short, *Banda* (1974), 104.
85. Wood, *Welensky Papers,* 663.
86. R. C. Tredgold, *The Rhodesia That Was My Life* (1968), 227, 229 and 230.
87. *Rhodesia Herald,* 27 October 1960.
88. C. Sanger, *Central African Emergency* (1960), 262 and 286.
89. Lapping, *End of Empire,* 482.
90. *The Times,* 24 July 1959.
91. J. Darwin, "The Central African Emergency, 1959," *JICH,* 21 (September 1993), 230.
92. Horne, *Macmillan,* II, 182.
93. *The Times,* 29 and 22 July 1959.
94. Franklin, *Unholy Wedlock,* 155.

95. *The Times,* 8 January 1960.
96. Blake, *Rhodesia,* 327.
97. Shepherd, *Macleod,* 203.
98. Murphy (ed.), *Central Africa,* Pt II, 141.
99. Welensky, *4000 Days,* 270 and 299.
100. RH, Welensky Papers, 665/5, Lord Salisbury to Welensky, 7 August 1963.
101. Ibid., 592/8, Lord Salisbury to Welensky, 5 February 1961.
102. *The Times,* 8 March 1961.
103. R. Maudling, *Memoirs* (1978), 96.
104. RH, Welensky Papers, 770/3, Welensky to Lord Salisbury, 3 March 1964.
105. Ibid., 665/5, Welensky to Lord Salisbury, 25 January 1963.
106. Ibid., 592/8, Welensky to Lord Salisbury, 7 October 1961.
107. Ibid., 25 May 1961.
108. L. J. Butler, "Britain, the United States, and the Demise of the Central African Federation, 1959–63," *JICH,* 28 (September 2000), 132.
109. Bowman, *Politics in Rhodesia,* 28.
110. Parker, *Rhodesia,* 94.
111. Lord Butler, *The Art of the Possible* (1971), 220.
112. Parker, *Rhodesia,* 100.
113. D. Lowry, "'Shame upon "Little England" while "Greater England" Stands!' Southern Rhodesia and the Imperial Idea," in A. Bosco and A. May (eds), *The Round Table and British Foreign Policy* (1997), 306.
114. P. Allen, *Interesting Things: Uganda Diaries 1955–1986* (Lewes, 2000), 29.
115. Hyam and Louis (eds), *Conservative Government and the End of Empire,* xlviii.
116. Foot, *Start in Freedom,* 219–20.
117. A. Megahey, *Humphrey Gibbs: Beleaguered Governor* (1998), 88.
118. I. D. Smith, *Bitter Harvest* (2001), 67.
119. Blake, *Rhodesia,* 361.
120. RH, Welensky Papers, 770/3, Welensky to Lord Salisbury, 4 May 1964.
121. D. Caute, *Under the Skin* (1983), 89.
122. Megahey, *Gibbs,* 81.
123. Shamuyarira, *Crisis in Rhodesia,* 210.
124. K. Young, *Rhodesia and Independence* (1969), 109.
125. M. Meredith, *The Past Is Another Country* (1979), 64–5.
126. K. Flower, *Serving Secretly* (1987), 36.
127. CAC, DSND 14/25/1, A. F. Hopkinson to Sandys, 13 July 1966.
128. Bowman, *Politics in Rhodesia,* 71.
129. Young, *Rhodesia and Independence,* 174.
130. H. Wilson, *The Labour Government 1964–1970: A Personal Record* (1971), 143, 159 and 163.
131. Pimlott, *Wilson,* 371.
132. Smith, *Bitter Harvest,* 96.
133. B. Castle, *The Castle Diaries* (1984), 67.
134. Smith, *Bitter Harvest,* 105.
135. CAC, DSND 14/25/1, Vera Bromley to Sandys, 14 October 1965.
136. Bowman, *Politics in Rhodesia,* 89.
137. Young, *Rhodesia and Independence,* 370.
138. Castle, *Castle Diaries,* 162.
139. Hyam, *South African Expansion,* 185.
140. CAC, DSND 14/25/1, Vera Bromley to Sandys, 14 October 1965.

141. CAC, DSND 14/25/1, I. Collyer to Sandys, 12 July 1966.

142. *The Times*, 15 November 1965.

143. Flower, *Serving Secretly*, 73.

144. R. Hall, *My Life with Tiny: A Biography of Tiny Rowland* (1987), 116.

145. T. Benn, *Office without Power: Diaries 1968–72* (1988), 115.

146. H. R. Strack, *Sanctions: The Case of Rhodesia* (Syracuse, 1978), 29.

147. *ODNB*. The author of the article on Home, Douglas Hurd, is quoting from Cyril Connolly's *Enemies of Promise*.

148. RH, Welensky Papers, 624/10, A. Douglas-Home to Welensky, 29 February 1960.

149. Bowman, *Politics in Rhodesia*, 123.

150. RH, Welensky Papers, 770/3, Welensky to Lord Salisbury, 3 March 1964. Winston Field, the Rhodesian Prime Minister, coined this phrase.

151. Meredith, *Past Is Another Country*, 79.

152. A. T. Muzorewa, *Rise up and Walk* (1978), 95 and 117.

153. DeRoche, *Black, White & Chrome*, 99.

154. J. Alexander, J. McGregor and T. Ranger, *Violence & Memory* (Oxford, 2000), 122–3.

155. Flower, *Serving Secretly*, 134.

156. Meredith, *Past Is Another Country*, 171.

157. J. McGregor, "The Victoria Falls 1900–1940: Landscape, Tourism and the Geographical Imagination," *JSAS*, 29 (September 2003), 728.

158. H. Kissinger, *Years of Renewal* (1999), 917.

159. K. O. Morgan, *Callaghan: A Life* (Oxford, 1997), 595.

160. *The Kissinger Study on Southern Africa* (Nottingham, 1975), 11.

161. W. Isaacson, *Kissinger* (1992), 686.

162. Kissinger, *Years of Renewal*, 937.

163. *The Times*, 28 April 1976.

164. Meredith, *Past Is Another Country*, 52 and 254.

165. G. R. Berridge and A. James, *A Dictionary of Diplomacy* (Basingstoke, 2001).

166. *The Times*, 18 and 24 September 1976.

167. D. Owen, *Time to Declare* (1992), 301.

168. Flower, *Serving Secretly*, 185 and 194.

169. Gibbon, *Decline and Fall*, I, 92.

170. Smith, *Bitter Harvest*, 309.

171. Brendon and Whitehead, *The Windsors*, 208.

172. M. Thatcher, *Downing Street Years* (1993), 75.

173. M. Charlton, *The Last Colony in Africa* (1990), 58.

174. H. Young, *One of Us* (1989), 179.

175. M. Meredith, *Our Votes, Our Guns* (New York, 2002), 8.

176. Smith, *Bitter Harvest*, 320.

177. Lord Carrington, *Reflect on Things Past* (1988), 298 and 302.

178. Meredith, *Our Votes*, 9.

179. *The Times*, 18 April 1980.

180. J. Campbell, *Margaret Thatcher*, II (2003), 74–5.

21. Rocks and Islands

1. Gibbon, *Decline and Fall*, III, 1062.

2. *CSJ*, 3 (1960), 125.

3. Reynolds, *Beards*, 282.

4. *The Times,* 10 April 1950 and 25 August 1947.
5. O. Mandelstam, *Selected Poems,* trans. C. Brown and W. S. Merwin (Harmondsworth, 1977), 98.
6. P. G. Wodehouse, *Jeeves and the Feudal Spirit* (1963 edn), 12. By 1963 *Private Eye* was not only giving a mock-Gibbonian account of "the twilight of the British Empire" but mercilessly tweaking Macmillan's "ludicrous moustache." (D. Sandbrook, *Never Had It So Good* [2005], 667.) The moustache would return, of course, as a sign of male homosexual virility.
7. *CSJ,* 3 (1960), 126.
8. F. Madden (ed.), *The End of Empire: Dependencies since 1948 Select Documents . . . ,* VIII (Westport, CT, 2000), xiv.
9. Hyam and Louis (eds), *Conservative Government and the End of Empire,* xxxii.
10. T. M. Campbell and G. C. Herring (eds), *The Diaries of Edward R. Stettinius, Jr., 1943–1946,* I (New York, 1975), 40.
11. *OHBE,* IV, 344.
12. *Guardian,* 29 May 2006.
13. Beckford, *Jamaica,* I, xiii.
14. S. R. Ashton and D. Killingray (eds), *BDEEP,* Series A, Vol. 6, *The West Indies* (1999), xl.
15. J. A. Froude, *The English in the West Indies* (1888), 37.
16. G. Sewell, *The Ordeal of Free Labour in the British West Indies* (1862), 174 and 172.
17. A. Trollope, *The West Indies and the Spanish Main* (1860), 31 and 169.
18. Froude, *West Indies,* 247 and 70.
19. Trollope, *West Indies,* 84.
20. Froude, *West Indies,* 121.
21. Parry et al., *West Indies,* 132.
22. G. K. Lewis, *The Growth of the Modern West Indies* (1968), 105.
23. Burn, *Emancipation and Apprenticeship,* 69.
24. J. Brown, "William Des Voeux: A portrait of a Crown Colony Governor," *Chronicle of the West India Committee,* LXXXIX (January 1964), 23.
25. G. W. Des Voeux, *My Colonial Service,* I (1903), 157.
26. C. Cross, *The Fall of the British Empire* (1968), 126.
27. E. Wallace, *The British Caribbean: From the Decline of Colonialism to the End of Federation* (Toronto, 1977), 17.
28. A. Calder-Marshall, *Glory Dead* (1939), 117.
29. W. M. Macmillan, *Warning from the West Indies* (1936), 136.
30. C. L. R. James, *Beyond a Boundary* (1983 edn), 120.
31. Wallace, *British Caribbean,* 32.
32. F. A. Hoyos, *Grantley Adams and the Social Revolution* (1974), 245.
33. E. Williams, *Inward Hunger: The Education of a Prime Minister* (1969), 35.
34. Ashton and Killingray (eds), *West Indies,* 367 and 522.
35. *ODNB.*
36. W. Bell, *Jamaican Leaders* (Berkeley, CA, 1964), 17.
37. P. Leigh Fermor, *The Traveller's Tree* (1950), 347.
38. Bell, *Jamaican Leaders,* 17.
39. A. Jackson, *The British Empire and the Second World War* (2006), 1.
40. Ashton and Killingray (eds), *West Indies,* xliv.
41. J. Mordecai, *The West Indies: The Federal Negotiations* (1968), 28.
42. Wallace, *British Caribbean,* 99.
43. Ashton and Killingray (eds), *West Indies,* 400.
44. W. P. Kirkman, *Unscrambling the Empire* (1966), 203.
45. Ashton and Killingray (eds), *West Indies,* lxiv and 400.

46. S. R. Cudjoe (ed.), *Eric E. Williams Speaks* (Wellesley, MA, 1993), 238 and 245.

47. V. S. Naipaul, *The Middle Passage* (1962), 78.

48. Wallace, *British Caribbean*, 169 and 198.

49. Madden (ed.), *End of Empire*, 134.

50. J. Gerassi, "The United States and Revolution in Latin America," in N. D. Houghton (ed.), *Struggle Against History* (New York, 1968), 166.

51. Ashton and Killingray (eds), *West Indies*, 489.

52. C. Fraser, *Ambivalent Anti-Colonialism: The United States and the Genesis of West Indian Independence, 1940–1964* (Westport, CT, 1994), 192.

53. Ashton and Killingray (eds), *West Indies*, 487, 488 and 597.

54. Ranelagh, *The Agency*, 390.

55. A. Toynbee, *America and the World Revolution* (1962), 17, 32 and 31.

56. D. W. White, *The American Century* (1996), 121. The art critic Bernard Berenson called Toynbee's work "romance, philosophical, theological, anything you like but not history." (R. Davenport-Hines [ed.], *Letters from Oxford* [2006], 36.)

57. Julien, *America's Empire*, 369.

58. Ashton and Killingray (eds), *West Indies*, 718.

59. G. K. Lewis, *Grenada: The Jewel Despoiled* (1987), 115.

60. J. W. Fulbright, *The Arrogance of Power* (1967), 32.

61. A. Payne et al., *Grenada: Revolution and Invasion* (1984), 49.

62. Thornton, *File on Empire*, 324.

63. Payne, *Grenada*, 165 and 164.

64. Campbell, *Thatcher*, II, 274.

65. Payne, *Grenada*, 170.

66. Lewis, *Grenada*, 1.

67. Gibbon, *Decline and Fall*, III, 663.

68. Lehmann, *All Sir Garnet*, 241.

69. *The Times*, 17 July 1878.

70. M. Roussou-Sinclair, *Victorian Travellers in Cyprus: A Garden of Their Own* (Nicosia, 2002), 82.

71. J. Reddaway, *Burdened with Cyprus* (1986), 10. The phrase was Sir Charles Dilke's.

72. G. S. Georghallides, *Cyprus and the Governorship of Sir Ronald Storrs: The Causes of the 1931 Crisis* (Nicosia, 1985), 676.

73. Gibbon, *Decline and Fall*, II, 964.

74. N. Crawshaw, *The Cyprus Revolt* (1978), 23.

75. I. D. Stefanides, *Isle of Discord* (1999), 292.

76. Storrs, *Orientations*, 457.

77. H. Foot, *History of Government House* (Nicosia, 1958), 8.

78. Storrs, *Orientations*, 457.

79. Georghallides, *Cyprus*, 143.

80. Pembroke College, Cambridge, Storrs Papers, Reel 11, Storrs to E. Marsh, n.d., 1927.

81. Georghallides, *Cyprus*, 700, 612, 614, 689 and 698.

82. *The Times*, 26 October 1931.

83. Pembroke College, Cambridge, Storrs Papers, Reel 11, Storrs to George V, 17 November 1931.

84. Ibid., Reel 13, Storrs to W. D. Cane, 25 October 1931.

85. A. Azinas, *50 Years of Silence*, Vol. A (Nicosia, 2002), 28.

86. Reddaway, *Burdened with Cyprus*, 40 and 41.

87. R. Holland, *Britain and the Revolt in Cyprus 1954–1959* (Oxford, 1998), 16.

88. Stefanides, *Isle of Discord*, 116.

89. R. Holland, "Never, Never Land: British Colonial Policy and the Roots of Violence in Cyprus, 1950–54," *JICH*, XXI (September 1993), 151.

90. Holland, *Revolt in Cyprus*, 27.

91. S. Mayes, *Makarios* (1981), 18.

92. Azinas, *50 Years*, Vol. A, 146.

93. A. James, *Keeping the Peace in the Cyprus Crisis of 1963–64* (Basingstoke, 2002), 8. The American observer was George Ball.

94. C. Foley (ed.), *The Memoirs of General Grivas* (1964), 3.

95. Azinas, *50 Years*, Vol. A, 257.

96. C. Thubron, *Journey into Cyprus* (1975), 110.

97. S. Foot, *Emergency Exit* (1960), 20.

98. P. Balfour, *The Orphaned Realm* (1951), 198–9.

99. L. Durrell, *Bitter Lemons* (1957), 35, 136, 36, 168 and 118.

100. Stefanides, *Isle of Discord*, 156.

101. C. Hitchens, *Hostage to History* (1997 edn), 37.

102. *The Times*, 29 July 1954.

103. S. Schlesinger, "How Dulles Worked the Coup d'Etat," *Nation* (28 October 1978), 439.

104. C. M. Woodhouse, *Something Ventured* (1982), 134.

105. Holland, *Revolt in Cyprus*, 52.

106. C. Baker, *Retreat from Empire: Sir Robert Armitage in Africa and Cyprus* (1998), 109.

107. D. M. Anderson, "Policing and Communal Conflict: The Cyprus Emergency, 1954–60," *JICH*, XXI (September 1993), 192.

108. Holland, *Revolt in Cyprus*, 64.

109. Foley (ed.), *Memoirs of Grivas*, 46.

110. Foley, *Island in Revolt*, 158 and 186.

111. Murphy, *Lennox-Boyd*, 117.

112. Holland, *Revolt in Cyprus*, 112–13.

113. D. W. Markides, "Britain's 'New Look' Policy for Cyprus and the Makarios–Harding Talks, January 1955–March 1956," *JICH*, XXIII (September 1995), 497.

114. S. L. Carruthers, *Winning Hearts and Minds* (1995), 196.

115. Foley (ed.), *Memoirs of Grivas*, 73 and 82.

116. Foley, *Island in Revolt*, 119.

117. F. Crouzet, *Le Conflit de Chypre*, II (Brussels, 1973), 620, 602, 561 and 626.

118. J. B. Bell, *On Revolt* (Cambridge, MA, 1976), 124.

119. Mayes, *Makarios*, 114.

120. Azinas, *Fifty Years*, Vol. B, 658.

121. Foley, *Island in Revolt*, 85.

122. Simpson, *Human Rights and the End of Empire*, 347 and 982.

123. Carruthers, *Winning Hearts*, 227.

124. Crawshaw, *Cyprus Revolt*, 264.

125. Foley (ed.), *Memoirs of Grivas*, 131.

126. Foot, *Start in Freedom*, 167.

127. Crawshaw, *Cyprus Revolt*, 287.

128. Holland, *Revolt in Cyprus*, 266.

129. *Oxford Opinion*, 31 January 1959.

130. Azinas, *Fifty Years*, Vol. B, 761 and 764.

131. D. Austin, *Malta and the End of Empire* (1971), 106.

132. Macmillan, *Riding the Storm*, 226 and 657.

133. Holland, *Revolt in Cyprus*, 302.

134. Macmillan, *Riding the Storm*, 657.

22. All Our Pomp of Yesterday

1. L. Freedman, *The Official History of the Falklands Campaign,* I (2005), 5.
2. D. J. Greene (ed.), *The Yale Edition of the Works of Samuel Johnson,* X (1977), 350 and 369.
3. R. Hunt, *My Falkland Days* (1992), 53 and 31.
4. M. Hastings and S. Jenkins, *The Battle for the Falklands* (1992 edn), 24.
5. Freedman, *Falklands Campaign,* I, 47, 46 and 134.
6. Hastings and Jenkins, *Falklands,* 23.
7. N. West, *The Secret War for the Falklands* (1997), 220.
8. Freedman, *Falklands Campaign,* I, 127.
9. *The Franks Report* (1983), 37.
10. A. Dorman, "John Nott and the Royal Navy: The 1981 Defence Review Revisited," *CBH,* 15 (Spring 2001), 103.
11. CAC, NOTT, 1/2/5.
12. Young, *One of Us,* 239 and 275.
13. *The Times,* 13 November 1986.
14. *The Economist,* 3 March 1984.
15. H. Leach, *Endure No Makeshifts* (1993), 198.
16. Thatcher, *Downing Street Years,* 177.
17. West, *Secret War,* 57.
18. D. K. Gilbran, *The Falklands War* (Jefferson, NC, 1998), 34.
19. Hunt, *Falkland Days,* 202–3.
20. Thatcher, *Downing Street Years,* 173.
21. *Daily Mail,* 5 April 1982.
22. Campbell, *Thatcher,* II, 139.
23. Leach, *Makeshifts,* 221.
24. Lord Carrington, *Reflect on Things Past* (1988), 370.
25. J. Nott, *Here Today, Gone Tomorrow* (2003), 269 and 246.
26. *Guardian,* 18 January 2006.
27. *The Economist,* 3 March 1984.
28. Thatcher, *Downing Street Years,* 196.
29. A. Barnett, *Iron Britannia* (1982), 31.
30. D. Tinker, *A Message from the Falklands* (Harmondsworth, 1983), 169.
31. R. Fox, *Eyewitness Falklands* (1982), 1.
32. *The Times,* 29 April 1982.
33. W. Shawcross, *Rupert Murdoch* (1992), 257–9.
34. Fox, *Eyewitness,* 58.
35. Freedman, *Falklands Campaign,* II, 302 and 403.
36. Tinker, *Message,* 187.
37. Freedman, *Falklands Campaign,* II, 729.
38. Tinker, *Message,* 172.
39. West, *Secret War,* 2.
40. M. Middlebrook, *The Falklands War, 1982* (2001 edn), 225.
41. *The Times,* 5 May 1982.
42. Fox, *Eyewitness,* 9.
43. Hastings and Jenkins, *Falklands,* 309.
44. S. Woodward, *One Hundred Days: The Memoirs of the Falklands Battle Group* (1992), 331.
45. Nott, *Here Today,* 319 and 242.
46. Davenport-Hines (ed.), *Letters from Oxford,* 290.
47. *Franks Report,* 86.
48. Margaret Thatcher Foundation website: speech at Cheltenham, 3 July 1982.

49. Colley, *Captives*, 376.
50. *The Times*, 15 January 1993.
51. *Guardian*, 1 July 2006.
52. J. Dimbleby, *The Last Governor* (1997), 48.
53. R. Hughes, *Hong Kong* (1968), 9.
54. J. Morris, *Among the Cities* (Harmondsworth, 1987 edn), 151.
55. V. I. Lenin, *Collected Works*, IV (Moscow, 1960), 374.
56. I. Bird, *The Golden Chersonese* (1883), 114.
57. CUL, Add 6799–6801, Stella Benson Diary, 12 November 1930.
58. J. Grant, *Stella Benson* (1987), 275.
59. Grantham, *Via Ports*, 107.
60. Eitel, *Europe in China*, 573.
61. Des Voeux, *Colonial Service*, II, 244 and 205.
62. Perham, *Lugard*, II, 290.
63. A. P. Haydon, *Sir Matthew Nathan* (St Lucia, Queensland, 1976), 110.
64. Welsh, *Hong Kong*, 326.
65. J. Pope Hennessy, *Half-Crown Colony* (1969), 69.
66. C. Mun, "The Criminal Trial under Early Colonial Rule," in Tak-Wing Ngo (ed.), *Hong Kong's History* (1999), 53.
67. *The Hong Kong Guide 1893* (Hong Kong, 1982 edn), 92.
68. Eitel, *Europe in China*, 411.
69. J. Pope Hennessy, *Verandah* (1964), 194.
70. Welsh, *Hong Kong*, 257.
71. G. B. Endacott, *A History of Hong Kong* (Hong Kong, 1973 edn), 278.
72. J. Darwin, "Hong Kong in British Decolonisation," in J. M. Brown and R. Foot (eds), *Hong Kong's Transitions, 1842–1997* (Basingstoke, 1997), 20.
73. Gillingham, *At the Peak*, 31.
74. Chan Lau Kit-ching, *China, Britain and Hong Kong 1895–1945* (Hong Kong, 1990), 226.
75. K. Furuya, *Chiang Kai-shek: His Life and Times* (New York, 1981), 196.
76. Chan Lau Kit-ching, *From Nothing to Nothing: The Chinese Communist Movement and Hong Kong, 1921–1936* (1999), 200.
77. CUL, Add 6799–6801, 4 March 1931.
78. Gillingham, *At the Peak*, 114.
79. S. Tang, "Government and Politics in Hong Kong: A Colonial Paradox," in Brown and Foot (eds), *Hong Kong's Transition*, 64.
80. Perham, *Lugard*, II, 320.
81. N. Miners, *Hong Kong under Imperial Rule 1912–1941* (Hong Kong, 1987), 256 and 240.
82. CUL, Add 6799–6801, 17 August 1931, 19 August 1930 and 3 November 1931.
83. Virgil Kit-yin Ho, "The Limits of Hatred: Popular Attitudes towards the West in Republican Canton," *EAH*, II (December 1991), 104.
84. Tak-Wing Ngo, "Industrial History and the Artifice of *laissez-faire* Colonialism," in Tak-Wing Ngo (ed.), *Hong Kong's History*, 120.
85. Reynolds, *Command of History*, 115.
86. Churchill, *Second World War*, III, 157.
87. Jackson, *British Empire and the Second World War*, 455.
88. A. Birch, *Hong Kong: The Colony that Never Was* (Hong Kong, 1991), 63.
89. RH, MSS Ind Oc. s.300, D. MacDougall Papers, Notebook describing the days after 8 December 1941.
90. O. Lindsay, *The Lasting Honour* (1978), 20.
91. M. Gilbert, *Road to Victory* (1986), 19.

92. Welsh, *Hong Kong*, 415.
93. Lindsay, *Lasting Honour*, 197.
94. RH, MSS Ind Oc. s.73, L. A. Searle Diary, 17 May 1942.
95. Barnes and Nicholson (eds), *Empire at Bay*, 851.
96. Chan Lau Kit-ching, *China, Britain and Hong Kong*, 303.
97. D. Irving, *Churchill's War*, II (2001), 564.
98. L. Woodward, *British Foreign Policy in the Second World War*, IV (1975), 539–40.
99. S. Tang, "Government and Politics in Hong Kong: A Colonial Paradox," in Brown and Foot (eds), *Hong Kong's Transitions*, 72.
100. S. Yui-San Tsang, *Democracy Shelved: Great Britain, China, and Attempts at Constitutional Reform in Hong Kong, 1945–1952* (Hong Kong, 1988), 74.
101. Grantham, *Via Ports*, 138.
102. RH, MSS Brit Emp. s.288, Interview with Sir Alexander Grantham (1968), 12.
103. Grantham, *Via Ports*, 171 and 112.
104. RH, MSS Ind Oc. s.348, Interview with Sir Robert Black (1987), 13.
105. RH, MSS Brit Emp. s.288, 9 and 6.
106. Grantham, *Via Ports*, 122 and 124.
107. A. Coates, *Myself a Mandarin* (1968), 2 and 5–6.
108. R. A. Bickers, "The Colony's Shifting Position in the British Informal Empire in China," in Brown and Foot (eds), *Hong Kong's Transitions*, 53.
109. *Independent*, 30 June 1997.
110. I. Fleming, *Thrilling Cities* (1963), 19.
111. *Time*, 20 June 1949.
112. N. Miners, *The Government and Politics of Hong Kong* (Hong Kong, 1998 edn), 22.
113. RH, MSS. Brit Emp. s.288, 17.
114. RH, MSS. Ind Oc. s.348, 123.
115. S. Tang in Brown and Foot (eds), *Hong Kong's Transitions*, 75.
116. D. Bonavia, *Hong Kong 1997* (Bromley, 1984), 56.
117. Hughes, *Hong Kong*, 73.
118. Louis, *Ends of British Imperialism*, 341.
119. Bonavia, *Hong Kong*, 119.
120. M. Roberti, *The Fall of Hong Kong* (New York, 1996), 51.
121. Bonavia, *Hong Kong*, 107–8.
122. P. Cradock, *Experiences in China* (1999 edn), 175, 176 and 177.
123. R. Cottrell, *The End of Hong Kong: The Secret Diplomacy of Imperial Retreat* (1993), 92, 90 and 94.
124. S. Howe, *Conflict of Interest* (1994), 368.
125. Cradock, *Experiences*, 231, 184 and 188.
126. Howe, *Conflict*, 373.
127. Thatcher, *Downing Street Years*, 493.
128. Howe, *Conflict*, 381.
129. *Independent*, 18 November 2005.
130. M. Yahuda, *Hong Kong: China's Challenge* (1996), 14.
131. Roberti, *Hong Kong*, 192.
132. S. Curtis (ed.), *The Journals of Woodrow Wyatt*, II (1999), 104.
133. M. Stuart, *Douglas Hurd: The Public Servant* (1998), 351.
134. Dimbleby, *Last Governor*, 96 and 156.
135. Stuart, *Hurd*, 361.
136. *The Times*, 1 July 1997 and 1 December 1992.
137. M. Heseltine, *Life in the Jungle* (2000), 459.

138. *Daily Telegraph,* 1 July 1997.

139. *Daily Mail,* 1 July 1997.

140. *The Times,* 1 July 1997.

141. *New York Times,* 1 July 1997.

142. *Daily Mail,* 1 July 1997.

143. *Guardian,* 19 November 2005.

144. *Daily Telegraph,* 1 July 1997.

145. *Daily Mail,* 1 July 1997.

146. *Guardian,* 19 November 2005.

147. R. Winder, *Bloody Foreigners: The Story of Immigration to Britain* (2004), 295 and 291.

148. K. O. Morgan, "Imperialists at Bay: British Labour and Decolonization," in R. D. King and R. K. Wilson (eds), *The Statecraft of British Imperialism* (1999), 253.

149. *Daily Mail,* 1 July 1997. The writer was Allan Massie.

150. *Independent,* 30 June 1997. The journalist was Andrew Marshall.

151. Gibbon, *Decline and Fall,* III, 142.

SOURCES

Manuscripts

Biddesden MS
Papers of Walter Guinness

British Empire and Commonwealth Museum (BECM)
Breckenridge Papers, 2002/218
De Heveningham Baekeland Papers, 2003/208
Kendall Papers, 2001/299
Diary of Godfrey Twiss, 1999/054

British Library (BL)
Balfour Papers, Add 49740
Warren Hastings Papers, Add 29176 and 29181
Sir Charles Napier's India Journal, Add 49140
Sir Charles Napier's Letters, Add 49115

Cambridge University Library (CUL)
British and Foreign Bible Society Foreign Correspondence
Stella Benson Papers, Add 6799–6801
Crewe Papers
Hardinge Papers
Jardine, Matheson Papers (JMP)
Mayo Papers, Add 7490
Richard Cornwallis Neville, "Diary of Military Life in Canada," Add 9556
Parkes Papers
Society for the Propagation of Christian Knowledge (SPCK) Papers
Sir James Stephen's Journal, Add 7888
Sir James Fitzjames Stephen Papers, Add 7349

Cambridge University Library, Royal Commonwealth Society Manuscripts (CUL RCMS)
B. Azikiwe, "Military Revolution in Nigeria," 136/31
Bombay Club Records, 78
British Association of Malaya (BAM) Addenda, Mic. 8239
Thomas Cashmore, "Kenya Days," 175
Memoirs of Thomas and Florence Edgar, 318/1/3
Gordon Letters, 113/11
H. M. Hull, "The Aborigines of Tasmania 1873," 278/40
A. Kirk-Greene, "Scrapbooks of News Cuttings of Royal Visit to Nigeria 1956,"
    133/1–3
Jack Moore, "From Aden to . . . Quetta," 57
George Nightingale Memoirs, 113/44
Col. Luke Norman Diary, 25
Arnold Paice Letters, 178
Harold Smith, "A Squalid End to Empire," 113/23
Thornhill Family Letters, 304

G. E. Wheeler, "The Pathography of a Cuckoo," 52
G. F. Young, "Letters to Colonists," 278/55

Centre for South Asian Studies, Cambridge (CSAS)
Brendon Papers
Campbell/Metcalfe Papers
Darling Papers
Macpherson Papers
Mill Papers
Portal Papers
Sampson Papers
Shaw Stewart Papers
Tayabji Papers

Churchill Archives Centre (CAC)
Julian Amery Papers, AMEJ
Leo Amery Papers, AMEL
British Diplomatic Oral History Programme (BDOHP), Denis Doble, Sir Brian Crowe
Fenner Brockway Papers, FEBR
Churchill Papers, CHAR
Esher Papers, ESHR
Journal of Sir Godfrey-Faussett, BGGF
Grigg Papers, PJGG
Hickling Papers, HICK
Jacob Papers, JACB, Treherne Journal
Kilmuir Papers, KLMR
Nott Papers, NOTT
O'Conor Papers, OCON
Enoch Powell Papers, POLL
Duncan Sandys Papers, DSND
Selwyn Lloyd Papers, SELO
Stead Papers, STED
Spears Papers, SPRS

Durham University Library (DUL)
Baring Papers, GRE
MacMichael Papers, Sudan Archive

Eisenhower Library, Abilene, Kansas (EL)
Anne Whitman File (AWF), Eisenhower Diary Series
Anne Whitman File (AWF), Dulles–Herter Series
Bernard Shanley Diaries

Elveden MSS
Gwendolen Guinness Diary and Correspondence
Rupert Guinness, "Boer War Diary"

The Hill Club, Nuwara Eliya
Complaints Book

Imperial War Museum (IWM)
Diary of Brigadier-General G. Napier Johnston, 01/12/1
Diary of Major Edison F. Lynn, 65/55/1
Letters of Brigadier J. M. Prower, 01/51/1

Institute of Commonwealth Studies, London (ICS)
Papers of Sir Ivor Jennings, JENN/125

Mitchell Library, State Library of New South Wales (ML)
Letters of David Blackburn, CY Reel 1301

National Army Museum (NAM)
Military Journal of Captain Frederick Aylmer, 2000–12–632
Diary of Lieutenant Edward Leary, 1999–07–20

Oriental and India Office Collections (OIOC)
Journal of William Anderson, MSS Eur C703
Cracklow Papers, MSS Eur C910
Hutchinson Papers, Journal of Lt. Christopher Codrington,
      MSS Eur D634
Indian Letters from the Western Front, L/MIL/5/825
Macnabb Papers, MSS Eur F206
Sir Henry Thoby Prinsep, "Three Generations in India," MSS Eur C97
William Prinsep, "Memoir" (1870), MSS Eur D1160
Munshi Qasim, "Tippoo Sooltan's Court," MSS Eur C10
Talbot Letters, MSS Eur C860
John Taylor Papers, H/436
Vellore Mutiny Correspondence, H/MISC/507

Pemberton Papers
F. W. Pemberton Papers, 7/5/1–109
F. Pemberton Campbell Papers, 7/18/28

Pembroke College, Cambridge
Papers of Sir Ronald Storrs

Private Papers
"Account of Mrs. Waller's Experiences in the Afghan war of 1842 and as a Prisoner" (G. Woolley,
      née Waller)

Public Record Office (PRO)
Ardagh Papers, 30/40/9
Cornwallis Papers, 30/11
Kitchener Papers, 30/57

Rhodes House, Oxford (RH)
Blundell Papers, MSS Afr. s.746
Interview with Sir Robert Brown Black, MSS Ind Oc. s.348
Papers of D. M. MacDougall, MSS Ind Oc. s.300
Interview with Sir Alexander Grantham, MSS Brit Emp. s.288

Diary of L. A. Searle, MSS Ind Oc. s.73
Welensky Papers, Parts 6 and 7

School of Oriental and African Studies, London (SOAS)
Papers of Sir Charles Arden-Clarke, MS 380596

Sri Lanka National Archives
Governor's Secret Diary, 7/39–45
S. C. Fernando/Woolf Papers, 25/7/1
Stewart Mackenzie Collection, 25/5

St Antony's College, Oxford (SAC)
Sir Henry Gurney Collection, GB 165–0128
MacMichael Papers, GB 165–0196

Published Works

The Notes constitute a detailed running bibliography. They indicate the literature on which this book is based and suggest lines of further reading and research. What follows here is a brief selection of the most useful general books on the subject. Again, the place of publication is London unless otherwise stated.

Allen C. *Plain Tales from the Raj* (1976 edn)
Allen C. *Tales from the Dark Continent* (1986 edn)
Anderson D. *Histories of the Hanged* (2005)
Anstey R. *The Atlantic Slave Trade and British Abolition, 1760–1810* (1975)
Antonius G. *The Arab Awakening* (2000 edn)
Ashton S. R. and Killingray D. (eds) *BDEEP,* Series A, Vol. 6, *The West Indies* (1999)
Ashton S. R. and Louis W. R. (eds) *BDEEP,* Series A, Vol. 5, *East of Suez and the Commonwealth 1964–1971,* Pt I, *East of Suez* (2004)
Ashton S. R. and Stockwell S. E. (eds) *BDEEP,* Series A, Vol. I, *Imperial Policy and Colonial Practice 1925–1945* Pt II (1996)
Austin D. *Malta and the End of Empire* (1971)
Austin D. *Politics in Ghana 1946–1960* (Oxford, 1970)
Ba Maw, *Breakthrough in Burma* (1968)
Balfour-Paul G. *The End of Empire in the Middle East* (Cambridge, 1991)
Ballhatchet K. *Race, Sex and Class under the Raj* (1980)
Barnes J. and Nicholson D. (eds) *The Empire at Bay: The Leo Amery Diaries 1929–1945* (1988)
Barnett D. L. and Njama K. *Mau Mau from Within* (1966)
Bayly C. A. *The Birth of the Modern World 1780–1914* (Oxford, 2004)
Bayly C. A. *Imperial Meridian: The British Empire and the World 1780–1830* (1989)
Bayly C. and Harper T. *Forgotten Armies: The Fall of British Asia 1941–1945* (2005)
Bayly C. and Harper T. *Forgotten Wars: The End of Britain's Asian Empire* (2007)
Belich J. *Making Peoples: A History of the New Zealanders from the Polynesian Settlement to the End of the Nineteenth Century* (1996)
Belich J. *Paradise Reforged: A History of the New Zealanders from the 1880s to the Year 2000* (2001)
Berman B. *Control & Crisis in Colonial Kenya* (1990)
Bethell N. *The Palestine Triangle* (1979)
Blake R. *A History of Rhodesia* (1977)

Bodelsen C. A. *Studies in Mid-Victorian Imperialism* (1960)

Bourne K. *The Foreign Policy of Victorian England* (Oxford, 1970)

Bowle J. *The Imperial Achievement* (1974)

Brogan H. *Longman History of the United States of America* (1985)

Brown J. M. *Gandhi's Rise to Power* (Cambridge, 1972)

Brown J. M. *Modern India: The Origins of an Asian Democracy* (Oxford, 1994 edn)

Burn W. L. *Emancipation and Apprenticeship in the British West Indies* (1937)

Cady J. F. *A History of Modern Burma* (Ithaca, NY, 1958)

Cain P. J. and Hopkins A. G. *British Imperialism* 2 vols (1993)

Cairns H. A. C. *Prelude to Imperialism* (1965)

Calder A. *Revolutionary Empire: The Rise of the English-Speaking Empire from the Fifteenth Century to the 1780s* (1981)

Callahan R. *The Worst Disaster: The Fall of Singapore* (Newark, NJ, 1977)

Cannadine D. *Ornamentalism: How the British Saw Their Empire* (2001)

Clark C. M. H. *A History of Australia,* 6 vols (1962–87)

Clayton A. *The British Empire as a Superpower, 1919–39* (1986)

Clifford N. R. *Spoilt Children of Empire* (Hanover, NH, 1991)

Collingham E. M. *Imperial Bodies* (2001)

Cottrell R. *The End of Hong Kong: The Secret Diplomacy of Imperial Retreat* (1993)

Coupland R. *The American Revolution and the British Empire* (1930)

Crocker W. R. *Nigeria: A Critique of British Administration* (1936)

Crouzet F. *Le Conflit de Chypre,* 2 vols (Brussels, 1973)

Crowder M. *The Story of Nigeria* (1973 edn)

Crowder M. *West Africa under Colonial Rule* (1968)

Curtin P. D. *Africa Remembered* (1967)

Curtin P. D. *Disease and Empire* (Cambridge, 1988)

Daly M. W. *Empire on the Nile* (Cambridge, 1986)

Daly M. W. *Imperial Sudan* (Cambridge, 1991)

Darwin J. *The End of the British Empire: The Historical Debate* (Oxford, 1991)

Davis M. *Late Victorian Holocausts* (2001)

De Kiewiet C. W. *The Imperial Factor in South Africa* (1965 edn)

de Silva K. M. (ed.) *BDEEP,* Series E, Vol. II, *Sri Lanka,* Pts I and II (1997)

Driver F. and Gilbert D. *Imperial Cities: Landscape, Display and Identity* (Manchester, 1999)

Durrell L. *Bitter Lemons* (1957)

Edwards C. *Roman Presences: Receptions of Rome in European Cultures, 1789–1945* (Cambridge, 1999)

Elkins C. *Britain's Gulag: The Brutal End of Empire in Kenya* (2005)

Fage J. D. and Oliver R. (eds) *The Cambridge History of Africa,* 8 vols (Cambridge, 1975–86)

Farnie D. A. *East and West of Suez: The Suez Canal in History, 1854–1956* (Oxford, 1969)

Fay P. W. *The Opium War 1840–1842* (Chapel Hill, NC, 1975)

Ferguson N. *Empire* (2003)

Fieldhouse D. K. *Economics and Empire 1830–1914* (1973)

Foley C. (ed.) *The Memoirs of General Grivas* (1964)

Foster R. F. *Modern Ireland 1600–1972* (1988)

Fraser C. *Ambivalent Anti-Colonialism: The United States and the Genesis of West Indian Independence, 1940–1964* (Westport, CT, 1994)

Freedman L. *The Official History of the Falklands Campaign,* 2 vols (2005)

Furnivall J. S. *Colonial Policy and Practice* (New York, 1956)

Furse R. *Aucuparius* (1962)

Gallagher J. *The Decline, Revival and Fall of the British Empire* (Cambridge, 1982)

Gibbon E. *The History of the Decline and Fall of the Roman Empire,* 3 vols, edited by D. Womersley (Harmondsworth, 1994 edn)

Gifford P. and Louis W. R. (eds) *Decolonization and African Independence: The Transfer of Power, 1960–1980* (New Haven, CT, 1988)

Gifford P. and Louis W. R. (eds) *The Transfer of Power in Africa: Decolonization 1940–1960* (New Haven, CT, 1982)

Gilmour D. *Curzon* (1994)

Gilmour D. *The Ruling Caste: Imperial Lives in the Victorian Raj* (2005)

Goldsworthy D. (ed.) *BDEEP,* Series A, Vol. 3, *The Conservative Government and the End of Empire 1951–1957,* Pt I (1994)

Gollin A. M. *Proconsul in Politics* (1964)

Gopal S. *British Policy in India 1858–1905* (Cambridge, 1965)

Gregory R. G. *India and East Africa* (Oxford, 1971)

Grimal H. *Decolonization* (1978 edn)

Hamid S. S. *Disastrous Twilight* (1986 edn)

Hancock W. K. *Smuts,* 2 vols (Cambridge, 1962–8)

Hargreaves J. D. *The End of Colonial Rule in West Africa* (1979)

Harlow V. and Chilver E. M. (eds) *History of East Africa,* II (Oxford, 1965)

Harlow V. T. *The Founding of the Second British Empire 1763–1793,* 2 vols (1952–64)

Harper T. N. *The End of Empire and the Making of Malaya* (Cambridge, 1999)

Headrick D. R. *The Tools of Empire* (New York, 1981)

Heinlein F. *British Government Policy and Decolonisation 1945–1963* (2002)

Heussler R. *Completing a Stewardship: The Malayan Civil Service 1942–1957* (Westport, CT, 1983)

Hibbert C. *The Great Mutiny India 1857* (1980 edn)

Hillmer N. and Granatstein J. L. *Empire to Umpire: Canada and the World to the 1990s* (Toronto, 1994)

Hobsbawm E. J. *Industry and Empire* (1969 edn)

Hobson J. A. *Imperialism* (1948 edn)

Holland R. *Britain and the Revolt in Cyprus 1954–1959* (Oxford, 1998)

Holland R. *European Decolonization 1918–1981: An Introductory Survey* (Basingstoke, 1985)

Holland Rose J., Newton A. P. and Benians E. A. (eds) *The Cambridge History of the British Empire,* 8 vols (Cambridge, 1925–59)

Hopkirk P. *The Great Game* (1990)

Howe S. *Anticolonialism in British Politics* (Oxford, 1993)

Hoyos F. A. *Grantley Adams and the Social Revolution* (1974)

Hughes R. *The Fatal Shore* (1996 edn)

Huxley E. *White Man's Country: Lord Delamere and the Making of Kenya,* 2 vols (1935)

Hyam R. and Henshaw P. *The Lion and the Springbok* (Cambridge, 2003)

Hyam R. and Louis W. R. (eds) *BDEEP,* Series A, Vol. 4, *The Conservative Government and the End of Empire 1957–1964,* Pt I, *High Policy, Political and Constitutional Change* (2000)

Hyam R. *Britain's Declining Empire: The Road to Decolonisation, 1918–1968* (Cambridge, 2006)

Hyam R. *Britain's Imperial Century* (1993 edn)

Hyam R. *Empire and Sexuality: The British Experience* (Manchester, 1990)

Iliffe J. *Africans: The History of a Continent* (Cambridge, 1995)

Irving R. G. *Indian Summer: Lutyens, Baker and Imperial Delhi* (1981)

James, L. *The Rise and Fall of the British Empire* (1994)

Judd D. *Balfour and the British Empire* (1968)

Judd D. and Surridge K. *The Boer War* (2002)

Keay J. *Last Post: The End of Empire in the Far East* (1997)

Kennedy D. *Islands of White* (Durham, NC, 1987)

Kennedy P. M. *The Rise and Fall of British Naval Mastery* (1983 edn)

Kiernan V. *The Lords of Human Kind* (1995 edn)

Kirk-Greene A. *On Crown Service* (1999)

Kirk-Greene A. H. M. *Africa in the Colonial Period, III: The Transfer of Power* (Oxford, 1979)

Kirkman W. P. *Unscrambling the Empire* (1966)

Koebner, K. *Empire* (Cambridge, 1961)

Krebs P. M. *Gender, Race, and the Writing of Empire* (Cambridge, 1999)

Kyle K. *Suez* (1991)

Landes D. *The Unbound Prometheus* (Cambridge, 1969)

Lapping B. *End of Empire* (1985)

Longford E. *Queen Victoria* (1964)

Louis W. R. *Ends of British Imperialism* (2006)

Louis W. R. *Imperialism at Bay: The United States and the Decolonization of the British Empire 1941–1945* (Oxford, 1977)

Louis W. R. *In The Name of God, Go!* (1992)

Louis W. R. (general editor) *The Oxford History of the British Empire*, 5 vols (Oxford 1998–9)

Low D. A. *Britain and Indian Nationalism* (Cambridge, 1997)

Lycett, A. *Rudyard Kipling* (1999)

Lynn M. (ed.) *BDEEP*, Series B, Vol. 7, *Nigeria: Managing Political Reform 1943–1953,* Pt I (2001)

MacKenzie J. M. *Propaganda and Empire* (Manchester, 1984)

Madden F. (ed.) *The End of Empire: Dependencies since 1948 Select Documents . . .* VIII (Westport, CT, 2000)

Magnus P. *Kitchener: Portrait of an Imperialist* (1968 edn)

Mangan J. A. *The Games Ethic and Imperialism* (1986)

Manning H. T. *British Colonial Government after the American Revolution 1782–1820* (1933)

Mansergh N. *The Commonwealth Experience* (1969)

Mansergh N. et al. (eds) *The Transfer of Power 1942–7* 12 vols (1970–83)

Marais J. S. *The Fall of Kruger's Republic* (Oxford, 1961)

Martin G. *Britain and the Origins of Canadian Confederation, 1837–67* (1995)

Mason P. *The Men Who Ruled India* (1985)

Mayes S. *Makarios* (1981)

McNaught K. *The History of Canada* (1970)

Moon P. *Divide and Quit* (Delhi, 1998 edn)

Moon P. (ed.) *Wavell: The Viceroy's Journal* (1973)

Moore R. J. *Endgames of Empire* (Delhi, 1988)

Moore R. J. *Escape from Empire* (1984)

Moorehead A. *The Blue Nile* (1974 edn)

Moorhouse G. *India Britannica* (1986 edn)

Morgan K. O. *Callaghan: A Life* (Oxford, 1997)

Morris J. *Farewell the Trumpets: An Imperial Retreat* (1978)

Morris J. *Heaven's Command: An Imperial Progress* (1973)

Morris J. *Pax Britannica: The Climax of Empire* (1975)

Morrow J. H. *The Great War in Imperial History* (2004)

Mungeam G. H. *British Rule in Kenya 1895–1912* (Oxford, 1966)

Murphy P. *Alan Lennox-Boyd* (1999)

Murphy P. (ed.), *BDEEP*, Series B, Vol. 9, *Central Africa*, Pt I, *1945–1958*, and Pt II, *1959–1965* (2005)

Murray-Brown J. *Kenyatta* (1972)

Nehru J. *The Discovery of India* (1946)

Nkomo J. *Nkomo: The Story of My Life* (1984)

Nkrumah K. *Ghana: The Autobiography of Kwame Nkrumah* (1957)

Oliver R. *Sir Harry Johnston and the Scramble for Africa* (1957)

Ovendale R. *Britain, the United States and the Transfer of Power in the Middle East, 1945–1962* (1996)

Pakenham T. *The Scramble for Africa* (1991)

Parry J. H., Sherlock P. M. and Maingot A. P. *A Short History of the West Indies* (1987)

Perham M. *The Colonial Reckoning: The End of Imperial Rule in Africa in the Light of Experience* (1961)

Pieragostini K. *Britain, Aden and South Arabia: Abandoning Empire* (1991)

Platt D. C. M. *Latin America and British Trade 1806–1914* (1972)

Port M. H. *Imperial London* (1995)

Porter B. *Critics of Empire* (1968)

Porter B. *The Lion's Share: A Short History of Imperialism 1850–1983* (1984 edn)

Qureshi S. *Jinnah* (Karachi, 1999)

Ranger T. O. *Revolt in Southern Rhodesia 1896–7* (1967)

Rapson E. J. et al. (eds) *The Cambridge History of India*, 6 vols (Cambridge, 1922–32)

Rathbone R. (ed.), *BDEEP,* Series B, Vol. 1, *Ghana,* Pt I, *1945–1952* (1992)

Reeve W. P. *The Long White Cloud* (1950 edn)

Reynolds D. *Britannia Overruled: British Policy and World Power in the Twentieth Century* (1991)

Roberti M. *The Fall of Hong Kong* (New York, 1996)

Roberts A. *A History of Zambia* (1976)

Robertson J. *Anzac and Empire* (1990)

Robinson R. and Gallagher, J. *Africa and the Victorians* (1965)

Rodney W. *How Europe Underdeveloped Africa* (Washington, DC, 1982)

Rosberg C. G. and Nottingham J. *The Myth of "Mau Mau": Nationalism in Kenya* (New York, 1966)

Rotberg R. I. *The Founder: Cecil Rhodes and the Pursuit of Power* (Oxford, 1988)

Rotberg R. I. *The Rise of Nationalism in Central Africa* (Cambridge, MA, 1966)

Ryan J. R. *Picturing the Empire: Photography and the Visualization of the British Empire* (1997)

Said E. W. *Orientalism* (Harmondsworth, 1978)

Sanger C. *Malcolm MacDonald: Bringing an End to Empire* (Liverpool, 1995)

Seal A. *The Emergence of Indian Nationalism* (Cambridge, 1968)

Searle G. R. *The Quest for National Efficiency* (Oxford, 1971)

Short P. *Banda* (1974)

Semmel B. *Imperialism and Social Reform 1895–1914* (1960)

Sewell G. *The Ordeal of Free Labour in the British West Indies* (1862)

Shuckburgh E. *Descent to Suez* (1986)

Simpson A. W. B. *Human Rights and the End of Empire* (Oxford, 2001)

Souter G. *Lion and Kangaroo* (1976)

Springhall J. *Youth, Empire and Society* (1977)

Stephens R. *Nasser* (1971)

Stockwell A. J. (ed) *BDEEP,* Series B, Vol. 3, *Malaya,* Pt II (1995)

Tarling N. *The Fall of Imperial Britain in South-East Asia* (New York, 1993)

Taylor S. et al. (eds) *Hanoverian Britain and Empire* (Woodbridge, 1998)

Teveth S. *Ben-Gurion: The Burning Ground 1886–1948* (Boston, 1987)

Thornton A. P. *The Imperial Idea and its Enemies* (1959)

Tidrick K. *Empire and the English Character* (1990)

Tinker H. (ed) *Burma: The Struggle for Independence 1944–1948*, I (1983)

Vance N. *The Victorians and Ancient Rome* (Oxford, 1997)

Vatikiotis P. J. *The Modern History of Egypt* (1969)

Wallace E. *The British Caribbean: From the Decline of Colonialism to the End of Federation* (Toronto, 1977)

Wasserstein B. *The British in Palestine* (1978)

Welensky R. *Welensky's 4000 Days* (1964)

Welsh F. *A History of Hong Kong* (1993)

Whelan F. G. *Edmund Burke and India* (Pittsburgh, PA, 1996)

White D. W. *The American Century* (1996)

Williams E. *Inward Hunger: The Education of a Prime Minister* (1969)

Wolpert S. *Jinnah of Pakistan* (New York, 1984)

Wolpert S. *A New History of India* (New York, 1977)

Wood J. R. T. *The Welensky Papers* (Durban, 1983)

Woodcock G. *A Social History of Canada* (New York, 1988)

Woodham-Smith C. *The Great Hunger* (1964 edn)

Ziegler P. *Mountbatten* (1986 edn)

Piers Brendon is the author of more than a dozen books, including biographies of Churchill and Eisenhower, the best-selling *Eminent Edwardians* and *The Dark Valley*, a highly praised history of the 1930s. He also writes for television and contributes frequently to the press. Formerly Keeper of the Churchill Archives Centre, he is a Fellow of Churchill College, Cambridge. He lives in Cambridge, England.

A NOTE ON THE TYPE

This book was set in Adobe Garamond. Designed for the Adobe Corporation by Robert Slimbach, the fonts are based on types first cut by Claude Garamond (c. 1480–1561). Garamond was a pupil of Geoffroy Tory and is believed to have followed the Venetian models, although he introduced a number of important differences, and it is to him that we owe the letter we now know as "old style." He gave to his letters a certain elegance and feeling of movement that won their creator an immediate reputation and the patronage of Francis I of France.

Composed by Creative Graphics,
Allentown, Pennsylvania
Printed and bound by R.R. Donnelley,
Crawfordsville, Indiana

NO MAP has or ever will be drawn giving a true picture of the world. For maps are flat and the world is round, and the surface of the globe can no more be accurately reproduced on a sheet of paper than a circle can be squared. On the most familiar maps, Mercator's, the lines of longitude (running from North to South) are drawn parallel; there is the same distance between them at the poles as at the Equator. But on the globe these lines get nearer and nearer until they meet at the poles. The result is that places like Greenland, which are relatively quite small on the globe, are expanded by Mercator until they appear quite impressively big.

HIGHWAYS OF EMPIRE tackles the insoluble problem in a new way. It shows the world as it would appear from an aeroplane so high above London that the pilot saw the continents stretched out beneath him. He would thus be given a vivid idea of how the British Empire is scattered in relation to the home country. He could also (if he had a strong enough telescope) watch the shipping and notice how the outward bound steamers, with cargoes of steel or coal or boots or cotton goods, and those homeward bound, with wheat or wool or mutton or fruit, cluster most thickly where they are sketched in on the map. Some of the details, such as the position of Canada and the United States, will look odd at first to eyes accustomed to Mercator. It is only by remembering where the North Pole and the Equator are

that the grouping will be made plain.

STRANGE sea monsters and talking beasts ornament the continents or the oceans, but nobody to-day will be misled by them. Yet even the wisest man alive a few centuries ago would have taken Mr. Macdonald Gill's menagerie not merely as a jolly decoration but as sober truth. To us these beasts are jokes, but to the Englishmen, who blazed the first trails along the high-ways of Empire, they would have seemed as real as a cow in a Devonshire meadow. The world, according to the old writers and atlas-makers, teemed with the oddest inhabitants.

ANTS as big as mastiffs; serpents that devoured elephants; fish a hundred yards long (but very timid); dolphins that leapt over the mainsails of ships; sea horses exactly like those on land except only that their manes reach to their feet; hyenas whose shadows robbed dogs of their bark; a creature like a mule but with so long an upper lip that he could not feed except walking backwards; birds that shone fiercely in the dark be the night never so close and cloudy; men who lived on the smell of fruit; men with feet so large that they used them as shade from the sun; the Bird Pegasus with horse's ears and wolves that would strike a man dumb if they saw him without themselves being seen —— all these and many other curiosities were gravely recorded in travel books and on maps.

NOR need we be two or three years to wonder anything was believed agree that the world has with what remarkable swift us. We have lived in the la that brought about by the happened may be found of an old man still alive to

WHEN such a man London now is from takes to get to Australia wool clippers that wou over a good passage. India h desert sand, and there wa of Panama. Sailormen, ra

ISSUED BY THE EMPIRE MARKETING BOARD (It may be found convenient to cut off the wording below the map before framing)